THE 1992 ELIAS BASEBALL ANALYST

SEYMOUR SIWOFF, STEVE HIRDT,
TOM HIRDT & PETER HIRDT

A FIRESIDE BOOK • Published by Simon & Schuster

New York   London   Toronto   Sydney   Tokyo   Singapore

FIRESIDE
Simon & Schuster Building
Rockefeller Center
1230 Avenue of the Americas
New York, New York 10020

Designed by Bonni Leon
Manufactured in the United States of America

10   9   8   7   6   5   4   3   2   1

ISBN: 0-671-73326-5

CONTENTS

ACKNOWLEDGMENTS

In recognition of the invaluable assistance provided by so many of our colleagues, the authors would like to thank the following:

The rest of the Elias Sports Bureau staff: Rocky Avakian, John Carson, Jay Chesler, John Chymczuk, Keung Hui, Frank Labombarda, John Labombarda, Santo Labombarda, Christopher Lasch, Jeff McGowan, Bob Rosen, Alex Stern, Christopher Thorn, Gil Traub, Bob Waterman, and Jon Wynne;

Eliot Cohen, former editor of *Major League Monthly* and coauthor of *The 1990 Baseball Annual,* who contributed several of the team essays in this book;

Our agent, Nat Sobel, and the rest of his staff, particularly Craig Holden;

Our publicists, Steve Brener and Toby Zwikel;

At Americomp, Jim Bristol and Wendy James;

At Simon & Schuster, Dan Farley, Emi Battaglia, Caroline Cunningham, Gypsy da Silva, Suzanne Donahue, Sue Fleming, Stuart Gottesman, Tim McGuire, Jay Schweitzer, George Turianski, and especially our editor, Jeff Neuman, whose insight and care help to shape this book every bit as much as we ourselves do.

And special thanks to our families and to those of the people listed here who made individual sacrifices as we rode this book hard to the finish line. Without their support, we wouldn't have made it through the stretch.

INTRODUCTION

Back in the spring of 1975, Gary Carter, Dennis Eckersley, Jim Rice, and Fred Lynn were gearing up for their rookie seasons. And the Elias Sports Bureau was about to undertake a new project of its own—the start of the first baseball database ever compiled to analyze play-by-play data. It seemed to us at the time that there might be an interest among baseball executives in statistics that could identify the strengths and weaknesses of their own players and their opponents to a greater and more meaningful degree than the basic traditional figures did. Until the mid-1970s, there simply was no source for the breakdowns that we now see thrown around on every baseball broadcast, and in every newspaper or periodical that covers baseball—who hits best with runners in scoring position, which pitchers are truly tougher on left-handed batters than on right-handers, and so on.

We had no idea 17 years ago that what we envisioned as a special service to subscribers within the baseball industry would be valued as greatly by fans as by managers, and would become an integral part of a successful annual publication, *The Elias Baseball Analyst*.

This is our eighth edition of the *Analyst*. And true to its roots, it remains a valuable source of information for those in the industry. General managers, managers, players, broadcasters, and writers rely on the accuracy of its statistics. We take great pride in the fact that so many of the statistics cited on the air or written in newspapers and magazines are taken directly from the *Analyst*. This is one case where fans truly have access to the same information the insiders use.

This year's book is different in several ways from past editions. First, you may have already noticed that our cover price has been lowered. (The recession has created problems for everyone. Enough said.) For that reason, the book has been scaled down with several of the purely statistical sections eliminated; we have incorporated the most important information from those sections into the player comments. Finally, we've added a new section—*Rookies and Prospects*. Its content is explained in detail in the section introduction; here we'll just say that this material will be invaluable to any baseball fans looking to put some of the game's bright young stars into historical perspective, and indispensable to those looking for an edge in their fantasy-league drafts.

The other features remain unchanged—team essays, statistics on all players, and the expanded player comments that were so well received last season. We hope you enjoy our eighth edition, and will take the time to let us know what you'd like to see in the ninth.

THE 1992
ELIAS
BASEBALL
ANALYST

TEAM SECTION

The Team Section consists of comments and statistics for each of the twenty-six major league teams.

The first of three tables that follow the essay for each team is the Won-Lost Record by Starting Position chart. This chart lists, for each player on a team, the team's won-lost record in games started by that player at each position, and in the leadoff and cleanup spots in the batting order. In addition, the number of games started by each player against left-handed and right-handed pitchers is listed. The players are listed alphabetically.

WON-LOST RECORD BY STARTING POSITION

Baltimore Orioles	C	1B	2B	3B	SS	LF	CF	RF	DH	P	Leadoff	Cleanup	Starts vs. LH	Starts vs. RH	Total Starts
Brady Anderson	-	-	-	-	-	15-18	7-17	3-0	-	-	6-16	-	6	54	25-35
Jeff Ballard	-	-	-	-	-	-	-	-	-	6-16	-	-	7	15	6-16
Jose Bautista	-	-	-	-	-	-	-	-	-	-	-	-	-	-	-
Juan Bell	-	-	22-32	-	-	-	-	-	-	-	-	-	8	46	22-32
Glenn Davis	-	18-18	-	-	-	-	-	-	1-9	-	-	16-23	15	31	19-27
Francisco De La Rosa	-	-	-	-	-	-	-	-	-	-	-	-	-	-	-
Mike Devereaux	-	-	-	-	-	-	60-78	-	-	-	53-73	-	41	97	60-78
Dwight Evans	-	-	-	-	-	-	-	23-36	1-8	-	-	3-16	34	34	24-44
Mike Flanagan	-	-	-	-	-	-	-	-	-	0-1	-	-	-	1	0-1
Todd Frohwirth	-	-	-	-	-	-	-	-	-	-	-	-	-	-	-
Leo Gomez	-	1-0	-	44-58	-	-	-	-	3-3	-	-	-	32	77	48-61
Kevin Hickey	-	-	-	-	-	-	-	-	-	-	-	-	-	-	-
Chris Hoiles	37-43	0-1	-	-	-	-	-	-	5-5	-	-	-	27	64	42-49
Sam Horn	-	-	-	-	-	-	-	-	42-50	-	-	28-34	-	92	42-50
Tim Hulett	-	-	4-6	12-18	-	-	-	-	1-7	-	-	-	16	32	17-31
Dave W. Johnson	-	-	-	-	-	-	-	-	-	4-10	-	-	2	12	4-10
Stacy Jones	-	-	-	-	-	-	-	-	-	1-0	-	-	-	1	1-0
Paul Kilgus	-	-	-	-	-	-	-	-	-	-	-	-	-	-	-
Chito Martinez	-	-	-	-	-	-	-	22-31	2-2	-	-	-	3	54	24-33
Ben McDonald	-	-	-	-	-	-	-	-	-	9-12	-	-	4	17	9-12
Jeff McKnight	-	0-2	-	-	-	1-4	-	0-1	1-1	-	-	-	4	6	2-8
Bob Melvin	23-44	-	-	-	-	-	-	1-0	-	-	-	-	25	43	24-44
Luis Mercedes	-	-	-	-	-	7-5	-	1-1	-	-	8-6	-	10	4	8-6
Jose Mesa	-	-	-	-	-	-	-	-	-	11-12	-	-	8	15	11-12
Bob Milacki	-	-	-	-	-	-	-	-	-	13-13	-	-	9	17	13-13
Randy Milligan	-	41-62	-	-	-	4-5	-	-	10-10	-	-	8-10	40	92	55-77
Mike Mussina	-	-	-	-	-	-	-	-	-	5-7	-	-	2	10	5-7
Gregg Olson	-	-	-	-	-	-	-	-	-	-	-	-	-	-	-
Joe Orsulak	-	-	-	-	-	29-49	-	17-23	-	-	-	12-12	8	110	46-72
Jim Ri. Poole	-	-	-	-	-	-	-	-	-	-	-	-	-	-	-
Arthur Rhodes	-	-	-	-	-	-	-	-	-	4-4	-	-	1	7	4-4
Cal Ripken	-	-	-	-	67-95	-	-	-	-	-	-	-	42	120	67-95
Billy Ripken	-	-	41-57	-	-	-	-	-	-	-	-	-	34	64	41-57
Jeff M. Robinson	-	-	-	-	-	-	-	-	-	6-13	-	-	6	13	6-13
David Segui	-	7-12	-	-	-	11-14	-	1-3	-	-	-	-	24	24	19-29
Roy Smith	-	-	-	-	-	-	-	-	-	7-7	-	-	2	12	7-7
Jeff Tackett	2-1	-	-	-	-	-	-	-	-	-	-	-	1	2	2-1
Anthony Telford	-	-	-	-	-	-	-	-	-	1-0	-	-	1	-	1-0
Shane Turner	-	-	-	-	-	-	-	-	-	-	-	-	-	-	-
Ernie Whitt	5-7	-	-	-	-	-	-	-	-	-	-	-	-	12	5-7
Mark Williamson	-	-	-	-	-	-	-	-	-	-	-	-	-	-	-
Craig Worthington	-	-	-	11-19	-	-	-	-	-	-	-	-	8	22	11-19

Below this chart are the team's batting and pitching totals in a variety of categories and breakdowns. These breakdowns are explained in the introductory text to the Batter Section (see page 81) and the Pitcher Section (see page 235). To see how each team stacks up against the overall totals for its league, compare its totals to the league stat summaries on the next page.

American League

	AB	H	2B	3B	HR	RBI	BB	SO	BA	SA	OBA
Season	77603	20195	3680	453	1953	9610	7730	12944	.260	.395	.329
vs. Left-Handers	22460	5956	1070	121	612	2782	2303	3574	.265	.405	.334
vs. Right-Handers	55143	14239	2610	332	1341	6828	5427	9370	.258	.391	.327
vs. Ground-Ballers	36275	9526	1706	196	830	4446	3480	5747	.263	.389	.329
vs. Fly-Ballers	41328	10669	1974	257	1123	5164	4250	7197	.258	.400	.329
Home Games	37862	9962	1848	252	965	4796	4021	6138	.263	.402	.336
Road Games	39741	10233	1832	201	988	4814	3709	6806	.257	.388	.322
Grass Fields	55263	14334	2556	277	1444	6915	5603	9218	.259	.394	.329
Artificial Turf	22340	5861	1124	176	509	2695	2127	3726	.262	.397	.329
April	8792	2223	398	52	204	1036	932	1467	.253	.380	.327
May	13079	3415	591	80	329	1631	1399	2130	.261	.394	.333
June	13230	3410	604	66	343	1639	1292	2150	.258	.391	.326
July	12877	3436	629	76	362	1646	1178	2091	.267	.412	.330
August	14076	3720	710	94	371	1770	1332	2370	.264	.407	.329
Sept./Oct.	15549	3991	748	85	344	1888	1597	2736	.257	.382	.327
Leading Off Inn.	18668	4754	898	101	488	488	1644	2980	.255	.392	.319
Runners On	33692	9028	1615	210	885	8542	3775	5498	.268	.407	.340
Bases Empty	43911	11167	2065	243	1068	1068	3955	7446	.254	.385	.320
Runners/Scor. Pos.	19208	5093	914	139	478	7374	2721	3392	.265	.402	.350
Runners On/2 Out	14336	3615	642	99	377	3428	1853	2447	.252	.390	.342
Scor. Pos./2 Out	9237	2277	407	66	231	2974	1447	1660	.247	.380	.353
Late-Inn. Pressure	11471	2826	447	46	268	1241	1176	2180	.246	.363	.319
Leading Off	2881	679	119	15	59	59	254	544	.236	.349	.301
Runners On	4794	1182	188	16	113	1086	611	911	.247	.363	.332
Runners/Scor. Pos.	2711	654	117	10	58	942	448	560	.241	.356	.346

RUNS BATTED IN	From 1B	From 2B	From 3B	Scoring Position
Percentage	5.4%	18.7%	42.2%	27.1%

Miscellaneous statistics: Ground outs-to-air outs ratio: 1.13. Leaders in batter comments based on 250 plate appearances. . . . Grounded into 1823 double plays in 16,433 opportunities (one per 9.0). Leaders based on 40 opportunities. . . . Drove in 2473 of 4323 runners from third base with less than two outs (57%). Leaders based on 15 opportunities. . . . Base running: Advanced from first base to third on 1410 of 4035 outfield singles (35%); scored from second on 1653 of 2265 (73%). Leaders based on 10 opportunities. . . . Assists per nine innings: first basemen, 0.72; second basemen, 3.08; shortstops, 3.06; third basemen, 2.06. Putouts per nine innings: left fielders, 2.11; center fielders, 2.70; right fielders, 2.11. Leaders based on 500 innings. . . . Opposing base stealers: 1469-for-2227 (66%). Leaders based on 50 attempts.

National League

	AB	H	2B	3B	HR	RBI	BB	SO	BA	SA	OBA
Season	65365	16363	2819	441	1430	7438	6254	11446	.250	.373	.317
vs. Left-Handers	23162	5855	1041	143	504	2670	2190	3990	.253	.375	.318
vs. Right-Handers	42203	10508	1778	298	926	4768	4064	7456	.249	.371	.316
vs. Ground-Ballers	29544	7471	1252	207	563	3314	2703	4852	.253	.366	.317
vs. Fly-Ballers	35821	8892	1567	234	867	4124	3551	6594	.248	.378	.317
Home Games	31952	8124	1425	215	744	3778	3168	5456	.254	.382	.323
Road Games	33413	8239	1394	226	686	3660	3086	5990	.247	.363	.311
Grass Fields	33090	8334	1316	191	807	3835	3025	5734	.252	.376	.315
Artificial Turf	32275	8029	1503	250	623	3603	3229	5712	.249	.369	.318
April	7994	1938	327	59	155	882	803	1329	.242	.356	.312
May	10801	2732	451	79	252	1244	1041	1854	.253	.379	.320
June	11259	2876	509	77	224	1284	1134	1898	.255	.374	.325
July	10208	2595	435	62	254	1222	960	1732	.254	.384	.319
August	11888	2973	525	81	263	1338	1090	2202	.250	.374	.314
Sept./Oct.	13215	3249	572	83	282	1468	1226	2431	.246	.366	.311
Leading Off Inn.	15992	4009	705	98	374	374	1359	2634	.251	.377	.313
Runners On	27608	7190	1224	224	608	6616	3018	4778	.260	.387	.331
Bases Empty	37757	9173	1595	217	822	822	3236	6668	.243	.362	.306
Runners/Scor. Pos.	16212	4185	721	143	341	5789	2240	3013	.258	.383	.342
Runners On/2 Out	11896	2847	501	103	251	2600	1498	2179	.239	.362	.328
Scor. Pos./2 Out	7841	1840	319	74	160	2291	1198	1504	.235	.355	.339
Late-Inn. Pressure	10247	2546	395	60	190	1101	1140	1935	.248	.354	.325
Leading Off	2568	632	113	8	51	51	277	464	.246	.356	.323
Runners On	4401	1123	163	37	80	991	568	837	.255	.364	.340
Runners/Scor. Pos.	2578	651	91	21	48	883	424	510	.253	.360	.353

RUNS BATTED IN	From 1B	From 2B	From 3B	Scoring Position
Percentage	4.9%	17.2%	41.1%	25.7%

Miscellaneous statistics: Ground outs-to-air outs ratio: 1.16. Leaders in batter comments based on 250 plate appearances. . . . Grounded into 1198 double plays in 13,166 opportunities (one per 11.0). Leaders based on 40 opportunities. . . . Drove in 2056 of 3623 runners from third base with less than two outs (57%). Leaders based on 15 opportunities. . . . Base running: Advanced from first base to third on 1083 of 3167 outfield singles (34%); scored from second on 1274 of 1838 (69%). Leaders based on 10 opportunities. . . . Assists per nine innings: first basemen, 0.75; second basemen, 2.99; shortstops, 3.00; third basemen, 2.00. Putouts per nine innings: left fielders, 2.13; center fielders, 2.53; right fielders, 1.98. Leaders based on 500 innings. . . . Opposing base stealers: 1651-for-2460 (67%). Leaders based on 50 attempts.

American League

	W-L	ERA	AB	H	HR	BB	SO	BA	SA	OBA
Season	1134-1134	4.09	77603	20195	1953	7730	12944	.260	.395	.329
vs. Left-Handers			32030	8444	689	3289	4847	.264	.389	.332
vs. Right-Handers			45573	11751	1264	4441	8097	.258	.399	.326
vs. Ground-Ballers			36418	9617	621	3201	5354	.264	.374	.325
vs. Fly-Ballers			41185	10578	1332	4529	7590	.257	.413	.332
Home Games	598-536	3.99	39741	10233	988	3709	6806	.257	.388	.322
Road Games	536-598	4.21	37862	9962	965	4021	6138	.263	.402	.336
Grass Fields	810-810	4.10	55263	14334	1444	5603	9218	.259	.394	.329
Artificial Turf	324-324	4.08	22340	5861	509	2127	3726	.262	.397	.329
April	131-131	3.85	8792	2223	204	932	1467	.253	.380	.327
May	190-190	4.15	13079	3415	329	1399	2130	.261	.394	.333
June	193-193	4.09	13230	3410	343	1292	2150	.258	.391	.326
July	186-186	4.22	12877	3436	362	1178	2091	.267	.412	.330
August	206-206	4.21	14076	3720	371	1332	2370	.264	.407	.329
Sept./Oct.	228-228	3.99	15549	3991	344	1597	2736	.257	.382	.327
Leading Off Inn.			18668	4754	488	1644	2980	.255	.392	.319
Bases Empty			43911	11167	1068	3955	7446	.254	.385	.320
Runners On			33692	9028	885	3775	5498	.268	.407	.340
Runners/Scor. Pos.			19208	5093	478	2721	3392	.265	.402	.350
Runners On/2 Out			14336	3615	377	1853	2447	.252	.390	.342
Scor. Pos./2 Out			9237	2277	231	1447	1660	.247	.380	.353
Late-Inn. Pressure			11471	2826	268	1176	2180	.246	.363	.319
Leading Off			2881	679	59	254	544	.236	.349	.301
Runners On			4794	1182	113	611	911	.247	.363	.332
Runners/Scor. Pos.			2711	654	58	448	560	.241	.356	.346
First 9 Batters			40158	10144	940	4218	7305	.253	.379	.326
Second 9 Batters			20211	5382	521	1859	3134	.266	.406	.329
All Batters Thereafter			17234	4669	492	1653	2505	.271	.419	.336

Miscellaneous statistics: Ground outs-to-air outs ratio: 1.13. Leaders in pitcher comments based on 500 batters faced. . . . Induced 1823 double-play ground outs in 16,433 opportunities (one per 9.0). Leaders based on 100 innings pitched. . . . Allowed 1268 first-inning runs in 2268 starts (4.62 ERA). . . . Batting support: 4.49 runs per start. . . . Stranded 2338 inherited runners, allowed 1233 to score (65%). Leaders based on 25 inherited runners. . . . Opposing base stealers: 1469-for-2227 (66%). Leaders based on 10 attempts.

National League

	W-L	ERA	AB	H	HR	BB	SO	BA	SA	OBA
Season	970-970	3.68	65365	16363	1430	6254	11446	.250	.373	.317
vs. Left-Handers			28590	7301	573	3145	4882	.255	.375	.329
vs. Right-Handers			36775	9062	857	3109	6564	.246	.370	.307
vs. Ground-Ballers			29180	7091	407	2664	5349	.243	.338	.308
vs. Fly-Ballers			36185	9272	1023	3590	6097	.256	.401	.324
Home Games	533-437	3.51	33413	8239	686	3086	5990	.247	.363	.311
Road Games	437-533	3.87	31952	8124	744	3168	5456	.254	.382	.323
Grass Fields	489-489	3.76	33090	8334	807	3025	5734	.252	.376	.315
Artificial Turf	481-481	3.61	32275	8029	623	3229	5712	.249	.369	.318
April	120-120	3.57	7994	1938	155	803	1329	.242	.356	.312
May	159-159	3.78	10801	2732	252	1041	1854	.253	.379	.320
June	167-167	3.65	11259	2876	224	1134	1898	.255	.374	.325
July	152-152	3.81	10208	2595	254	960	1732	.254	.384	.319
August	175-175	3.68	11888	2973	263	1090	2202	.250	.374	.314
Sept./Oct.	197-197	3.61	13215	3249	282	1226	2431	.246	.366	.311
Leading Off Inn.			15992	4009	374	1359	2634	.251	.377	.313
Bases Empty			37757	9173	822	3236	6668	.243	.362	.306
Runners On			27608	7190	608	3018	4778	.260	.387	.331
Runners/Scor. Pos.			16212	4185	341	2240	3013	.258	.383	.342
Runners On/2 Out			11896	2847	251	1498	2179	.239	.362	.328
Scor. Pos./2 Out			7841	1840	160	1198	1504	.235	.355	.339
Late-Inn. Pressure			10247	2546	190	1140	1935	.248	.354	.325
Leading Off			2568	632	51	277	464	.246	.356	.323
Runners On			4401	1123	80	568	837	.255	.364	.340
Runners/Scor. Pos.			2578	651	48	424	510	.253	.360	.353
First 9 Batters			34681	8485	708	3546	6699	.245	.361	.316
Second 9 Batters			16411	4120	366	1442	2726	.251	.377	.313
All Batters Thereafter			14273	3758	356	1266	2021	.263	.396	.324

Miscellaneous statistics: Ground outs-to-air outs ratio: 1.16. Leaders in pitcher comments based on 500 batters faced. . . . Induced 1198 double-play ground outs in 13,166 opportunities (one per 11.0). Leaders based on 100 innings pitched. . . . Allowed 1091 first-inning runs in 1944 starts (4.65 ERA). . . . Batting support: 4.10 runs per start. . . . Stranded 1601 inherited runners, allowed 816 to score (66%). Leaders based on 25 inherited runners. . . . Opposing base stealers: 1651-for-2460 (67%). Leaders based on 10 attempts.

BALTIMORE ORIOLES

Twenty years ago, Dave McNally came to the Orioles' training camp following a 21–5 season, equaling the highest winning percentage in the now 91-year history of the franchise. McNally's 21 wins ranked fourth in the American League in 1971, and his 2.89 ERA ranked seventh. All right, now suppose you were a clairvoyant baseball fan who somehow knew in that spring of '72 that in the upcoming season McNally would post a nearly identical ERA to his mark in the preceding season. Given his 21–5 mark a year earlier, what record would you have expected for him in 1972?

In fact, McNally's ERA in 1972 was 2.95, or 0.06 higher than in 1971; that difference is the equivalent of two earned runs higher over the course of an entire season. But despite pitching for the same team and compiling in effect the same ERA in each season, McNally's record fell from 21–5 to 13–17. That difference in the records of these consecutive seasons is perhaps the most outstanding example in major league history of the effect of batting support on a pitcher's won-lost record. McNally's teammates scored only half as many runs per game behind him in 1972 as they had a year earlier. In the following table (as in the Pitcher Section), batting support is defined as runs scored by the pitcher's team in games he started:

Year	GS	W	L	ERA	Support
1971	30	21	5	2.89	5.73
1972	36	13	17	2.95	2.89

Frankly, there's nothing unusual about any of these figures. Why shouldn't a pitcher who allows only half as many runs as his team scores compile a 21–5 record? And a pitcher who allows about as many runs as his team scores should post a .500 record or thereabouts—a 17–13 mark with a little luck, a 13–17 mark if he's unlucky. But the wide swing from one season to the next in the batting support McNally received shows vividly how a factor over which the pitcher has virtually no control (absolutely none in the American League) can drastically affect his won-lost record. It makes you wonder whether a pitcher's record should be the most often cited measure of his individual performance.

From 1982 through 1990, about three-quarters of all regular starting pitchers (that is, those who made 30 or more starts) received normal batting support from their teams—within a half-run per game of the team's overall scoring average. For the rest, the difference between the support they received and what their staffmates got had an enormous impact on their won-lost records. Those who received support above and beyond the call had a combined winning percentage 149 points higher—about five wins per season—than their poorly-supported peers, despite the fact that the two groups had virtually identical ERAs:

	ERA	Won	Lost	Pct.
Oversupported Pitchers	3.63	1816	1116	.619
Undersupported Pitchers	3.70	1096	1234	.470

That's compelling widespread evidence of the importance of batting support—a statistic that has

only recently become available (and, to the best of our knowledge, available only in the *Analyst*), and whose effect has been vastly underestimated. For years, baseball fans ranging from general managers (real and wannabes) to bleacherites have been frustrated or perhaps confused by the year-to-year fluctuation of pitchers' won-lost records. You can never have enough pitching, they'd say, since pitchers are so inconsistent.

Well, even when they're consistent they're inconsistent—if your measure of effectiveness is won-lost records. We looked at all the pitchers from 1900 through 1990 who, like McNally in 1971–72, did the following: (1) made at least 30 starts in each of two consecutive seasons; (2) pitched for only one team during those two years; (3) compiled ERAs in those seasons that varied by no more than 0.10—one-tenth of a run per nine innings. There were 182 such cases over the 90 years under study and if ever any pitchers should have compiled similar won-lost records from one season to the next, this was the group—regular starters with nearly identical ERAs for the same team. But even *their* winning percentages varied by an average of .099 from one season to the next—or by three wins over 30 starts. A quarter of them had percentages that varied enough to account for a difference of five wins from one season to the next. Four, McNally included, had remarkable differences of more than 300 percentage points—attributable mostly, perhaps wholly, to batting support:

Pitcher	Year	ERA	Supp.	W–L
Hooks Dauss	1919	3.55	5.97	21–9
	1920	3.57	4.13	13–21
Charlie Root	1928	3.57	3.40	14–18
	1929	3.47	6.26	19–6
Tex Hughson	1942	2.59	5.40	22–6
	1943	2.64	3.28	12–15
Dave McNally	1971	2.89	5.73	21–5
	1972	2.95	2.89	13–17

Because batting support data wasn't always compiled on a systematic, league-wide basis, we can't tell you how much of the year-to-year variation for the entire group of 182 pitchers was attributable to batting support. But for the 24 instances during the 1980s, as with the four most extreme historical examples listed above, batting support played a major role. In all but five of those 24 cases, when the support increased so did the winning percentage, and the same was true for a decrease. The average support for the recent pitchers in their "better" years was more than a half-run per game higher than in their "worse" years (by a margin of 4.7 to 4.1).

The best high-profile example over the last 10 years of how an increase in a pitcher's support can produce an apparent individual breakthrough occurred in 1990. That season, three pitchers met the three criteria outlined above: 30-plus starts with nearly identical ERAs for the same teams for a second consecutive season. One was Ed Whitson; the other two won Cy Young Awards:

Pitcher	Year	ERA	Supp.	W–L
Doug Drabek	1989	2.80	2.91	14–12
	1990	2.76	5.36	22–6
Bob Welch	1989	3.00	4.58	17–8
	1990	2.95	5.03	27–6
Ed Whitson	1989	2.66	3.94	16–11
	1990	2.60	4.44	19–9

Pittsburgh scored nearly twice as much for Drabek in 1990 as it had in 1989, turning a solid but ordinary starter into a nearly unbeatable 20-game winner. Oakland boosted its scoring for Welch by a half-run per game and, thanks to the kind of luck that accompanies such seasons, one of baseball's perennial winningest pitchers became the first to win as many as 27 games since Steve Carlton in 1972.

Last season, Orioles pitcher Jeff Robinson provided a less visible but equally powerful indication of what happens when a pitcher's support is drastically reduced. During his four years with Detroit, only two pitchers in baseball received better support than Robinson. The best-supported starting pitchers from 1987 through 1990 (minimum: 50 starts):

Pitcher	GS	Runs	Avg.	ERA	W–L
Mike Smithson	57	315	5.53	5.58	20–27
Roy Smith	54	297	5.50	4.20	19–16
Jeff Robinson	87	461	5.30	4.65	36–26
Dwight Gooden	110	577	5.25	3.34	61–27
Ron Robinson	76	392	5.16	3.54	29–22

Only one pitcher in major league history has had a higher winning percentage with an ERA above 4.50 than Jeff Robinson (minimum: 50 decisions): Erv Brame, who compiled a 52–37 record for the Pittsburgh Pirates from 1928 through 1932 despite a 4.77 ERA. In 1930 alone, Brame went 17–8 with an ERA of 4.70 that was actually below the league ERA (4.97). The Pirates scored 6.5 runs per start for Brame that season.

But let's get back to Robinson. Last season, the Orioles scored an average of 3.58 runs in his 19 starts, the sixth-lowest average in the American League among pitchers with at least 15 starts. Combined with his 5.18 ERA—which wasn't *that* much higher than his four-year mark with Detroit—Robinson posted a 4–9 mark, prompting his first-ever demotion to the minors on July 30. Were it not for the tremendous batting support he received from the Tigers, might such a move have come years earlier? Would the Orioles have traded Mickey Tettleton for him if they'd realized how much of his "success" was not of his own making? And in a less analytical age, wouldn't Robinson have been labelled "one of those pitchers who just know how to win"? Now we know better.

Without a doubt, a pitcher's batting support must be considered by anyone interested in determining whether a pitcher is likely to maintain or improve his won-lost record from one season to the next—be it Roland Hemond running the Baltimore Orioles or any one of our readers playing big-league G.M. for their fantasy-league squads. Knowledge is power, and knowing which pitchers are most likely to improve or decline can pay some pretty heavy dividends. Here are three ways to exploit the batting-support data found for each starter in the Pitcher Section of this book:

(1) Use 3.50 and 5.50 as your flashpoints. Any pitcher receiving more than five-and-a-half runs per start last season can be expected to decline by three wins this year. Those whose teams provided less than three-and-a-half runs per start can be expected to improve by three wins. The following table summarizes the change from one season to the next for pitchers who fell outside those boundaries from 1981 through 1989; "Up" indicates the number of pitchers whose winning percentages increased, "Down" those whose percentage decreased. And remember, a shift of .100 in winning percentage means roughly three wins:

Batting Support	No.	Up	Down	Avg. Change
More than 5.50	29	7	22	−.107
Less than 3.50	54	37	17	+.080

(2) For even more exaggerated results, further restrict the group described above by eliminating well-supported pitchers who compiled losing records, and poorly-supported starters with winning records. An example: In 1989, the Cardinals scored 3.33 runs per start for Jose DeLeon. He qualifies initially because his average support was less than 3.5 runs. But since he managed a winning record (16–12) anyway—thereby standing to gain less than if he had posted a losing record—he would be excluded. (This restriction may run against intuition, but as the numbers below show, it works.) With those limitations, pitchers stand to gain or lose an average of five wins:

Batting Support	No.	Up	Down	Avg. Change
More than 5.50	24	4	20	−.146
Less than 3.50	34	29	5	+.146

(3) Best and simplest of all: Consider only the pitchers who ranked among their league's top or bottom 10 in run support last season among those who made at least 20 starts. (Those ranks are indicated, where applicable, in the Pitcher Section.) Isolate on well-supported pitchers with winning records and poorly-supported pitchers with losing records. During the period from 1981 through 1989, pitchers who qualified according to those rules showed the greatest change of all—on average, plus or minus five wins, respectively. And what's more, this method also identified the largest group of qualifiers:

Batting Support	No.	Up	Down	Avg. Change
Top 10/Winning Record	100	16	84	−.151
Bottom 10/Losing Record	70	61	9	+.150

According to that system, the pitchers most likely to improve their won-lost record in 1992 are: Allan Anderson, Jeff Ballard, Brian Barnes, Jim Deshaies, Alex Fernandez, Mark Gardner, Greg A. Harris, Brian Holman, Jimmy Jones, Kirk McCaskill, Charles Nagy, Dennis Rasmussen, Greg Swindell, and Frank Viola. Those most likely to decline: Don August, Steve Avery, Mike Bielecki, Chris Bosio, Scott Erickson, Dwight Gooden, Bill Gullickson, Jose Guzman, Orel Hershiser, Jack McDowell, Jose Rijo, Bryn Smith, Randy Tomlin, and Bob Walk.

WON-LOST RECORD BY STARTING POSITION

Baltimore Orioles	C	1B	2B	3B	SS	LF	CF	RF	DH	P	Leadoff	Cleanup	Starts vs. LH	Starts vs. RH	Total Starts
Brady Anderson	-	-	-	-	-	15-18	7-17	3-0	-	-	6-16	-	6	54	25-35
Jeff Ballard	-	-	-	-	-	-	-	-	-	6-16	-	-	7	15	6-16
Jose Bautista	-	-	-	-	-	-	-	-	-	-	-	-	-	-	-
Juan Bell	-	-	22-32	-	-	-	-	-	-	-	-	-	8	46	22-32
Glenn Davis	-	18-18	-	-	-	-	-	-	1-9	-	-	16-23	15	31	19-27
Francisco De La Rosa	-	-	-	-	-	-	-	-	-	-	-	-	-	-	-
Mike Devereaux	-	-	-	-	-	-	60-78	-	-	-	53-73	-	41	97	60-78
Dwight Evans	-	-	-	-	-	-	23-36	-	1-8	-	-	3-16	34	34	24-44
Mike Flanagan	-	-	-	-	-	-	-	-	-	0-1	-	-	-	1	0-1
Todd Frohwirth	-	-	-	-	-	-	-	-	-	-	-	-	-	-	-
Leo Gomez	-	1-0	-	44-58	-	-	-	-	3-3	-	-	-	32	77	48-61
Kevin Hickey	-	-	-	-	-	-	-	-	-	-	-	-	-	-	-
Chris Hoiles	37-43	0-1	-	-	-	-	-	-	5-5	-	-	-	27	64	42-49
Sam Horn	-	-	-	-	-	-	-	-	42-50	-	-	28-34	-	92	42-50
Tim Hulett	-	-	4-6	12-18	-	-	-	-	1-7	-	-	-	16	32	17-31
Dave Johnson	-	-	-	-	-	-	-	-	-	4-10	-	-	2	12	4-10
Stacy Jones	-	-	-	-	-	-	-	-	-	1-0	-	-	-	1	1-0
Paul Kilgus	-	-	-	-	-	-	-	-	-	-	-	-	-	-	-
Chito Martinez	-	-	-	-	-	-	-	22-31	2-2	-	-	-	3	54	24-33
Ben McDonald	-	-	-	-	-	-	-	-	-	9-12	-	-	4	17	9-12
Jeff McKnight	-	0-2	-	-	-	1-4	-	0-1	1-1	-	-	-	4	6	2-8
Bob Melvin	23-44	-	-	-	-	-	-	1-0	-	-	-	-	25	43	24-44
Luis Mercedes	-	-	-	-	-	7-5	-	1-1	-	-	-	8-6	10	4	8-6
Jose Mesa	-	-	-	-	-	-	-	-	-	11-12	-	-	8	15	11-12
Bob Milacki	-	-	-	-	-	-	-	-	-	13-13	-	-	9	17	13-13
Randy Milligan	-	41-62	-	-	-	4-5	-	-	10-10	-	-	8-10	40	92	55-77
Mike Mussina	-	-	-	-	-	-	-	-	-	5-7	-	-	2	10	5-7
Gregg Olson	-	-	-	-	-	-	-	-	-	-	-	-	-	-	-
Joe Orsulak	-	-	-	-	-	29-49	-	17-23	-	-	-	12-12	8	110	46-72
Jim Poole	-	-	-	-	-	-	-	-	-	-	-	-	-	-	-
Arthur Rhodes	-	-	-	-	-	-	-	-	-	4-4	-	-	1	7	4-4
Cal Ripken	-	-	-	-	67-95	-	-	-	-	-	-	-	42	120	67-95
Billy Ripken	-	-	41-57	-	-	-	-	-	-	-	-	-	34	64	41-57
Jeff M. Robinson	-	-	-	-	-	-	-	-	-	6-13	-	-	6	13	6-13
David Segui	-	7-12	-	-	-	11-14	-	1-3	-	-	-	-	24	24	19-29
Roy Smith	-	-	-	-	-	-	-	-	-	7-7	-	-	2	12	7-7
Jeff Tackett	2-1	-	-	-	-	-	-	-	-	-	-	-	1	2	2-1
Anthony Telford	-	-	-	-	-	-	-	-	-	1-0	-	-	1	-	1-0
Shane Turner	-	-	-	-	-	-	-	-	-	-	-	-	-	-	-
Ernie Whitt	5-7	-	-	-	-	-	-	-	-	-	-	-	-	12	5-7
Mark Williamson	-	-	-	-	-	-	-	-	-	-	-	-	-	-	-
Craig Worthington	-	-	-	11-19	-	-	-	-	-	-	-	-	8	22	11-19

TEAM TOTALS: BATTING

	AB	H	2B	3B	HR	RBI	BB	SO	BA	SA	OBA
Season	5604	1421	256	29	170	660	528	974	.254	.401	.319
vs. Left-Handers	1487	381	62	10	47	157	167	254	.256	.406	.331
vs. Right-Handers	4117	1040	194	19	123	503	361	720	.253	.399	.315
vs. Ground-Ballers	2437	633	103	14	74	301	222	376	.260	.405	.324
vs. Fly-Ballers	3167	788	153	15	96	359	306	598	.249	.398	.316
Home Games	2701	659	121	12	80	318	258	463	.244	.387	.311
Road Games	2903	762	135	17	90	342	270	511	.262	.414	.327
Grass Fields	4704	1178	207	24	147	549	440	817	.250	.398	.316
Artificial Turf	900	243	49	5	23	111	88	157	.270	.412	.337
April	589	136	21	2	18	66	67	128	.231	.365	.315
May	917	231	39	1	28	100	104	164	.252	.388	.327
June	1001	267	50	6	29	129	100	154	.267	.416	.337
July	942	238	43	3	28	105	84	152	.253	.394	.314
August	1007	259	57	8	25	127	80	171	.257	.404	.311
Sept./Oct.	1148	290	46	9	42	133	93	205	.253	.418	.311
Leading Off Inn.	1348	328	59	5	44	44	119	225	.243	.392	.308
Runners On	2378	595	109	13	68	558	245	416	.250	.393	.319
Bases Empty	3226	826	147	16	102	102	283	558	.256	.406	.319
Runners/Scor. Pos.	1266	319	62	9	32	462	175	251	.252	.391	.338
Runners On/2 Out	1034	238	46	3	25	224	128	197	.230	.353	.321
Scor. Pos./2 Out	618	143	27	3	15	193	101	130	.231	.358	.347
Late-Inning Pressure	862	206	26	2	22	75	80	159	.239	.350	.305
Leading Off	218	50	6	0	5	5	17	41	.229	.326	.288
Runners On	347	77	6	1	7	60	41	62	.222	.305	.305
Runners/Scor. Pos.	178	41	3	0	5	53	28	31	.230	.331	.329

RUNS BATTED IN	From 1B	From 2B	From 3B	Scoring Position
Totals	99/1802	171/998	220/532	391/1530
Percentage	5.5%	17.1%	41.4%	25.6%

TEAM TOTALS: PITCHING

	W-L	ERA	AB	H	HR	BB	SO	BA	SA	OBA
Season	67-95	4.59	5626	1534	147	504	868	.273	.412	.333
vs. Left-Handers			2511	664	58	240	400	.264	.389	.328
vs. Right-Handers			3115	870	89	264	468	.279	.431	.337
vs. Ground-Ballers			2729	734	51	219	388	.269	.385	.324
vs. Fly-Ballers			2897	800	96	285	480	.276	.437	.341
Home Games	33-48	4.33	2871	775	72	245	478	.270	.398	.328
Road Games	34-47	4.86	2755	759	75	259	390	.275	.427	.338
Grass Fields	58-80	4.45	4757	1284	120	428	732	.270	.402	.331
Artificial Turf	9-15	5.37	869	250	27	76	136	.288	.471	.345
April	6-12	4.85	616	170	17	61	76	.276	.424	.346
May	10-17	4.69	925	250	23	92	131	.270	.404	.338
June	14-14	5.01	1005	284	26	96	148	.283	.435	.346
July	10-17	4.77	942	252	28	66	135	.268	.413	.315
August	13-16	4.29	1003	269	25	86	165	.268	.401	.327
Sept./Oct.	14-19	4.11	1135	309	28	103	213	.272	.402	.330
Leading Off Inn.			1353	345	46	99	190	.255	.410	.310
Bases Empty			3201	818	84	263	513	.256	.387	.316
Runners On			2425	716	63	241	355	.295	.446	.355
Runners/Scor. Pos.			1340	406	37	186	222	.303	.460	.379
Runners On/2 Out			1018	282	24	116	153	.277	.413	.354
Scor. Pos./2 Out			621	168	14	88	101	.271	.409	.364
Late-Inning Pressure			785	198	15	80	134	.252	.371	.322
Leading Off			210	47	4	17	27	.224	.348	.282
Runners On			312	89	5	32	52	.285	.394	.349
Runners/Scor. Pos.			183	49	1	27	37	.268	.350	.353
First 9 Batters			3025	794	73	299	514	.262	.394	.329
Second 9 Batters			1540	429	37	117	236	.279	.410	.330
All Batters Thereafter			1061	311	37	88	118	.293	.467	.348

WON-LOST RECORD BY STARTING POSITION

Boston Red Sox	C	1B	2B	3B	SS	LF	CF	RF	DH	P	Leadoff	Cleanup	Starts vs. LH	Starts vs. RH	Total Starts
Wade Boggs	-	-	-	76-64	-	-	-	-	-	-	63-45	-	36	104	76-64
Tom Bolton	-	-	-	-	-	-	-	-	-	9-10	-	-	3	16	9-10
Mike Brumley	-	-	3-1	2-4	7-11	-	2-1	-	-	-	-	-	15	16	14-17
Tom Brunansky	-	-	-	-	-	-	-	63-59	-	-	-	7-9	43	79	63-59
Ellis Burks	-	-	-	-	-	63-60	-	1-0	-	-	5-7	-	37	87	64-60
Jack Clark	-	-	-	-	-	-	-	-	68-66	-	-	63-60	38	96	68-66
Roger Clemens	-	-	-	-	-	-	-	-	-	23-12	-	-	12	23	23-12
Scott Cooper	-	-	-	4-4	-	-	-	-	-	-	-	-	3	5	4-4
Danny Darwin	-	-	-	-	-	-	-	-	-	4-8	-	-	4	8	4-8
John Dopson	-	-	-	-	-	-	-	-	-	-	-	-	-	-	-
Tony Fossas	-	-	-	-	-	-	-	-	-	-	-	-	-	-	-
Mike Gardiner	-	-	-	-	-	-	-	-	-	11-11	-	-	6	16	11-11
Jeff Gray	-	-	-	-	-	-	-	-	-	-	-	-	-	-	-
Mike Greenwell	-	-	-	-	-	75-66	-	-	0-1	-	-	10-3	35	107	75-67
Greg A. Harris	-	-	-	-	-	-	-	-	-	8-13	-	-	5	16	8-13
Joe Hesketh	-	-	-	-	-	-	-	-	-	11-6	-	-	7	10	11-6
Wayne Housie	-	-	-	-	-	-	0-1	-	-	-	-	-	-	1	0-1
Daryl Irvine	-	-	-	-	-	-	-	-	-	-	-	-	-	-	-
Dana Kiecker	-	-	-	-	-	-	-	-	-	4-1	-	-	1	4	4-1
Dennis Lamp	-	-	-	-	-	-	-	-	-	-	-	-	-	-	-
Steve Lyons	-	-	3-5	2-5	-	0-1	15-14	1-2	-	-	2-4	-	-	48	21-27
Josias Manzanillo	-	-	-	-	-	-	-	-	-	-	-	-	-	-	-
Mike Marshall	-	4-1	-	-	-	0-1	-	1-1	4-2	-	-	3-1	2	12	9-5
John Marzano	15-15	-	-	-	-	-	-	-	-	-	-	-	11	19	15-15
Mike Miller	-	-	-	-	-	-	-	-	-	-	-	-	-	-	-
Kevin Morton	-	-	-	-	-	-	-	-	-	8-7	-	-	2	13	8-7
Tim Naehring	-	-	-	0-1	9-6	-	-	-	-	-	-	-	5	11	9-7
Dave Owen	-	-	-	-	-	-	-	-	-	-	-	-	-	-	-
Tony Pena	69-63	-	-	-	-	-	-	-	-	-	-	-	33	99	69-63
Dan Petry	-	-	-	-	-	-	-	-	-	-	-	-	-	-	-
Phil Plantier	-	-	-	-	-	6-6	-	14-10	3-1	-	-	-	4	36	23-17
Jeff Plympton	-	-	-	-	-	-	-	-	-	-	-	-	-	-	-
Carlos Quintana	-	58-52	-	-	-	1-0	-	5-5	-	-	-	-	43	78	64-57
Jeff Reardon	-	-	-	-	-	-	-	-	-	-	-	-	-	-	-
Jody Reed	-	-	78-72	-	0-1	-	-	-	-	-	14-22	-	41	110	78-73
Luis Rivera	-	-	-	-	68-60	-	-	-	-	-	-	-	35	93	68-60
Kevin Romine	-	-	-	-	-	2-3	2-1	0-1	-	-	-	-	8	1	4-5
Mo Vaughn	-	22-25	-	-	-	-	-	-	8-8	-	-	-	3	60	30-33
Eric Wedge	-	-	-	-	-	-	-	-	-	-	-	1-5	-	-	-
Matt Young	-	-	-	-	-	-	-	-	-	6-10	-	-	4	12	6-10
Bob Zupcic	-	-	-	-	-	0-1	2-1	-	-	-	-	-	4	-	2-2

TEAM TOTALS: BATTING

	AB	H	2B	3B	HR	RBI	BB	SO	BA	SA	OBA
Season	5530	1486	305	25	126	691	593	820	.269	.401	.340
vs. Left-Handers	1481	426	81	9	39	212	159	197	.288	.433	.355
vs. Right-Handers	4049	1060	224	16	87	479	434	623	.262	.389	.335
vs. Ground-Ballers	2525	648	123	7	49	292	250	376	.257	.369	.326
vs. Fly-Ballers	3005	838	182	18	77	399	343	444	.279	.428	.352
Home Games	2749	762	183	12	69	359	316	389	.277	.428	.352
Road Games	2781	724	122	13	57	332	277	431	.260	.375	.328
Grass Fields	4646	1242	261	18	105	580	512	686	.267	.399	.340
Artificial Turf	884	244	44	7	21	111	81	134	.276	.413	.339
April	607	145	28	2	16	58	62	93	.239	.371	.315
May	968	273	52	5	21	132	114	123	.282	.411	.357
June	879	220	49	2	20	107	94	144	.250	.379	.322
July	961	252	49	5	27	113	99	139	.262	.408	.330
August	996	281	57	8	18	123	97	138	.282	.410	.346
Sept./Oct.	1119	315	70	3	24	158	127	183	.282	.414	.357
Leading Off Inn.	1316	362	81	6	28	28	117	177	.275	.410	.337
Runners On	2529	687	150	11	56	621	305	375	.272	.406	.346
Bases Empty	3001	799	155	14	70	70	288	445	.266	.397	.335
Runners/Scor. Pos.	1438	379	80	7	34	553	231	222	.264	.400	.356
Runners On/2 Out	1092	289	66	5	20	252	152	155	.265	.389	.356
Scor. Pos./2 Out	704	174	38	3	15	227	125	104	.247	.374	.361
Late-Inning Pressure	648	148	32	1	8	63	68	127	.228	.318	.306
Leading Off	163	39	12	1	2	2	15	27	.239	.362	.311
Runners On	284	65	9	0	4	59	36	58	.229	.303	.312
Runners/Scor. Pos.	166	40	7	0	1	53	23	43	.241	.301	.326

RUNS BATTED IN

	From 1B	From 2B	From 3B	Scoring Position
Totals	73/1882	218/1166	274/630	492/1796
Percentage	3.9%	18.7%	43.5%	27.4%

TEAM TOTALS: PITCHING

	W-L	ERA	AB	H	HR	BB	SO	BA	SA	OBA
Season	84-78	4.01	5477	1405	147	530	999	.257	.402	.323
vs. Left-Handers			2093	517	36	205	370	.247	.364	.315
vs. Right-Handers			3384	888	111	325	629	.262	.425	.328
vs. Ground-Ballers			2514	624	44	242	411	.248	.359	.314
vs. Fly-Ballers			2963	781	103	288	588	.264	.438	.331
Home Games	43-38	3.91	2865	757	76	285	523	.264	.406	.331
Road Games	41-40	4.13	2612	648	71	245	476	.248	.397	.314
Grass Fields	70-67	4.04	4677	1200	128	454	863	.257	.400	.324
Artificial Turf	14-11	3.87	800	205	19	76	136	.256	.409	.321
April	11-7	2.76	584	125	8	70	115	.214	.322	.302
May	15-13	4.91	943	249	31	99	180	.264	.415	.334
June	11-16	3.66	904	229	26	80	157	.253	.405	.316
July	11-16	4.39	966	266	31	83	166	.275	.443	.333
August	18-11	3.72	957	239	25	87	190	.250	.397	.314
Sept./Oct.	18-15	4.18	1123	297	26	111	191	.264	.398	.330
Leading Off Inn.			1318	342	37	116	236	.259	.412	.323
Bases Empty			3131	799	81	256	593	.255	.397	.315
Runners On			2346	606	66	274	406	.258	.408	.334
Runners/Scor. Pos.			1357	344	33	206	234	.254	.396	.346
Runners On/2 Out			970	230	25	139	181	.237	.378	.336
Scor. Pos./2 Out			639	151	16	120	112	.236	.383	.360
Late-Inning Pressure			744	176	19	71	140	.237	.379	.308
Leading Off			191	35	3	12	32	.183	.298	.243
Runners On			276	70	6	44	61	.254	.391	.361
Runners/Scor. Pos.			165	40	5	34	35	.242	.406	.376
First 9 Batters			2851	694	73	270	536	.243	.380	.312
Second 9 Batters			1455	384	38	127	275	.264	.409	.321
All Batters Thereafter			1171	327	36	133	188	.279	.447	.352

BOSTON RED SOX

When Dwight Gooden won 24 games and struck out 268 batters with a 1.53 ERA as a 20-year-old sophomore in 1985, he became an instant legend—a player who was capable on any given day, or in any given season, of matching the achievements of the most dominant pitchers ever. Unlike anyone since Willie Mays, Gooden inspired hope among fans, right from the start of his career, that he could be perfect. It was as though contemporary baseball fans had found a way to travel back in time, and watch the development of a new Walter Johnson or Christy Mathewson. When Bob Gibson and Tim McCarver dissented, they were treated as heretics—scoffed at for warning that we'd better enjoy Gooden's run while it lasted; that it was possible (just *possible*, mind you) that he might never be better than he was at age 20.

It appears that most of us were wrong to tar Gibson and McCarver, but right about witnessing the development of a pitcher destined to become one of the all-time greats—perhaps the best in the entire history of baseball. It's just that we were wrong about his identity; it wasn't Gooden, but Roger Clemens.

Clemens made his major league debut on May 15, 1984, five weeks after Gooden (who was two years younger than Clemens) debuted. Clemens was bombed in his first outing—five runs on 11 hits in 5⅔ innings. That game came four days after Doc pitched the first complete-game shutout of his career, a four-hit 11-strikeout gem at Chavez Ravine over the Dodgers' own still-reigning king of the hill, Fernando Valenzuela.

Gooden's superiority at the time was such that over the next few years, every Clemens achievement seemed a hollow echo of something Gooden had done weeks or months earlier. By the time Clemens announced his arrival as a superstar, with 20 strikeouts in a three-hit victory over Seattle in April 1986, Gooden had already buried his own 16-K performance among a series of outstanding games on his way to that 24–4 record the previous season. In fact, Clemens matched Gooden with a 24–4 record and a Cy Young Award of his own in 1986, but by that time Doc had already been annointed the Chosen Phenom.

It wasn't until 1987, when Clemens embarked on a second consecutive Cy Young season as Gooden spent time in rehabilitation for a substance abuse problem, that the Rocket began to earn the respect that Doc was slowly losing. Five years later, it's a measure of the degree to which Gooden outperformed Clemens in their first two seasons that not until September 20, 1991, did Clemens pass Gooden in career victories (with the exception of a single day in mid-June). Of course, while Gooden was establishing his reputation in 1985, Clemens missed nearly three months of his sophomore season with a shoulder injury that eventually required surgery. Ironically, Gooden himself was disabled following shoulder surgery last season when Clemens moved past him. By then, that passing of the crown was merely symbolic; we may have come late to the party, but most of us had realized long before that it was Clemens who could eventually accomplish what was dreamt of for Gooden.

Last year, we published the results of a study that measured a pitcher's value by comparing his career winning percentage against that of his teammates. The results were used to show that Nolan Ryan was much more than the greatest strikeout pitcher in baseball history—that he was, in fact, one of the most valuable pitchers of all time. Current figures show that Ryan's .530 career winning percentage is 40 points higher than that of his teammates. By assuming that a typical replacement pitcher would have a winning percentage of .400 on a .500 team, we estimated that Ryan's total of 314 career victories was 83 more than his teams would have won had Ryan not been available and they were forced to use someone else. That total, incidentally, is the 14th highest in major league history.

We've updated the study to include the 1991 season, because as Clemens approaches the 200th decision of his career, the 188-point margin between his winning percentage and that of his teammates is the largest in major league history by far, dwarfing the 157-point gap of his nearest competitor—ironically, the fading Gooden. The top 10 follows for the period since 1893, to coincide with the placement of the pitching rubber 60 feet, six inches from the plate. Pitchers needed at least 100 decisions to qualify:

Pitcher	W	L	Pct.	Team	Diff.
Roger Clemens	134	61	.687	.499	.188
Dwight Gooden	132	53	.714	.556	.157
Russ Ford	98	71	.580	.432	.148
Ted Higuera	92	56	.622	.476	.146
Grover Alexander	373	208	.642	.498	.144
Walter Johnson	416	279	.599	.460	.138
Bert Cunningham	81	79	.506	.370	.137
Gene Packard	86	67	.562	.426	.136
Al Maul	62	55	.530	.399	.130
J.R. Richard	107	71	.601	.474	.127

That list raises a red flag. If eight of the top 10 had between 100 and 199 decisions, the minimum of 100 decisions must be unrealistically low; pitchers with substantially fewer than 200 decisions obviously can't be compared on the same basis to those with more than 200 decisions. But that doesn't mean the table has no value. The fact that Clemens has distanced himself from the pack to such an extent is significant. Note that the gap between Clemens and Gooden is greater than that between Gooden and J.R. Richard in 10th place. And that raises an intriguing question: Does this mean that Clemens is on track to be the best ever? Have others done as well through the 200-decision mark, but faded in their later years?

We estimate that, had Clemens not been available, replacements would have won 78 of his 195 decisions, or 56 fewer than Clemens has actually won. (That assumes a typical replacement would have a .400 winning percentage for an average team. Yes, it's arbitrary, but the relative value of one pitcher to another would be the same if we chose .450 or .350 as a basis.) Has any other pitcher been worth as many victories *above replacement level* at the same point in his career? The answer: Only one—and Clemens can surpass his mark simply by winning three of his first five decisions in 1992. The following table shows the pitchers with the most value (that is, wins above replacement level) after their first 200 decisions:

Pitcher	Wins	Replacement Level	Value
Grover Alexander	135	77.9	57.1
Bob Feller	134	80.6	53.4
Tom Seaver	129	76.5	52.5
Walter Johnson	110	58.2	51.8
Dazzy Vance	121	69.4	51.6
Wes Ferrell	126	77.9	48.1
Juan Marichal	138	90.0	48.0
Eddie Rommel	109	62.7	46.3
Ron Guidry	135	88.8	46.2
Urban Shocker	124	79.5	44.5

Incidentally, Gooden already has a value of 48 wins above replacement level over only 185 decisions. He could move past Feller by winning 12 of his first 15 this season.

It is also interesting to note that many pitchers had many more wins in their first 200 decisions than Johnson and Rommel. But both played for teams so poor that our "typical replacement pitcher" would have managed only about a .300 mark. Hence the low replacement levels.

Now this doesn't mean that Clemens is already the greatest pitcher of all time. Longevity is an issue as well, and certainly he has experienced arm problems over the past few years serious enough to raise the question of how much longer he will be able to pitch at his peak. But no pitcher in this century has been as valuable as Clemens over the same period of his career. If that makes him a contender to become the greatest pitcher in the history of baseball, well, three Cy Young awards by age 29 already suggested that.

There were lots of ways to slice up the 1991 season and conclude that for most of the season Boston was a better team than the ultimate division winners, the Toronto Blue Jays. The Red Sox led the A.L. East as late as June 22. Their 34–21 mark from August 8 to the end of the season was four games better than Toronto's record during that stretch. But Boston's 14–27 mark in between was Toronto's ticket to the A.L.C.S.

There was also the matter of Boston's record against the league's stronger teams. The Red Sox posted a 60–51 mark against teams that finished the season above the .500 mark, including nine wins in 13 games against the Jays themselves. It was the best such mark in the division. But Boston won only 24 of 51 games

against the four teams at or below the .500 mark: Baltimore (5–8), California (4–8), Cleveland (9–4), and New York (6–7). And while this may have been the most frustrating of the team's weaknesses, there is at least a glimmer of hope that it may eventually prove to be the most auspicious.

Boston became only the tenth team in the past 50 years to compile a winning record against teams above the .500 mark and a losing record against the weaker teams. But included among those nine others are three that established minidynasties or close to it immediately thereafter:

Year	Team	Vs. Winners W–L	Vs. Winners Pct.	Vs. Losers W–L	Vs. Losers Pct.
1971	Cincinnati Reds	52–50	.510	27–33	.450
1986	Toronto Blue Jays	44–32	.579	42–44	.488
1987	Oakland Athletics	38–36	.514	43–45	.489

The Reds won five division titles over the next eight years, never finishing lower than second in the N.L. West. The Blue Jays have a pair of A.L. East titles and were runners-up twice in five seasons since then. Oakland, of course, made three consecutive World Series appearances starting in 1988.

The bad news is that the sample is too small to matter. And frankly, nothing in the records of the other six teams suggests that this is anything other than a statistical fluke. For the record, those teams are:

Year	Team	What Happened After That
1983	Los Angeles Dodgers	Below .500 three of next four.
1973	Detroit Tigers	Consecutive last-place finishes.
1973	Minnesota Twins	Not higher than 3d until 1984.
1973	Houston Astros	Not higher than 3d until 1979.
1967	Washington Senators	Last place two of next three.
1959	Chicago Cubs	Three straight 90 + losses.

Now ask yourself this question: Is there any reason to believe that such a pattern—a good record against good teams, but a bad record against bad teams—should precede a championship period? If you can think of one, then you probably won't be surprised if Boston dominates the A.L. East for the next few years. And if that happens, we'll invite you to write the Red Sox essay for the 1996 *Analyst*.

CALIFORNIA ANGELS

The 1991 Angels compiled the best record ever by a last-place team—an 81–81 mark in a division in which every other team compiled a winning record. Of course, prior to divisional play it was mathematically impossible for a team to finish in sole possession of last place without losing more games than it won. But don't think for a minute that a last-place .500 team, or anything close to it, has been commonplace since the leagues split themselves into divisions in 1969. Prior to 1991, the best record by a last-place team in the divisional era—sole possession or not—was 78–84, by the Cleveland Indians and the Toronto Blue Jays in 1982 (.481). The best by a team that finished alone in its division's cellar was 76–85 (.472), by the 1987 Chicago Cubs. The best by a team from the predivision era was substantially lower: a 69–83 mark by the 1915 New York Giants (.454). The following table summarizes the records of outright last-place teams since 1900; we have excluded 1981, as is our wont:

	Below .300	.300–.349	.350–.399	.400–.449	.450–.499	.500–up
1900–68	19 (14%)	54 (40%)	45 (33%)	16 (12%)	1 (1%)	0 (0%)
1969–91	0 (0%)	9 (11%)	34 (40%)	34 (40%)	7 (8%)	1 (1%)

California's last-place .500 season was also a telling sign of the dominance of the A.L. West, considered for much of the past 20 years to be the weakest of baseball's four divisions. If ever a team was in the right place at the wrong time, it was last season's Angels. There were a pair of seasons during the 1980s when a .500 record would have placed a team smack in the middle of the A.L. West pennant race. The standings for 1984 and 1987:

Team	W–L	Pct.	GB	Team	W–L	Pct.	GB
Kansas City	84–78	.519	—	Minnesota	85–77	.525	—
California	81–81	.500	3	Kansas City	83–79	.512	2
Minnesota	81–81	.500	3	Oakland	81–81	.500	4
Oakland	77–85	.475	7	Seattle	78–84	.481	7
Chicago	74–88	.457	10	Chicago	77–85	.475	8
Seattle	74–88	.457	10	California	75–87	.463	10
Texas	69–92	.429	14½	Texas	75–87	.463	10

But that was before Canseco, McGwire, Welch, Stewart, and Eckersley led Oakland to three consecutive American League titles; before Chicago became a contender on the strength of four straight first-round draft choices who reached the majors by age 22 (Ventura, McDowell, Thomas, and Fernandez); before Texas sprouted a pair of potential superstars, Ruben Sierra and Juan Gonzalez; and before the Twins and Mariners made noteworthy breakthroughs—Minnesota from a last-place finish in 1990 to the world championship last year, and Seattle through the .500 barrier for the first time in their 15 years. Those developments, along with the deterioration of two perennial powers in the A.L. East, Detroit and New York, have produced three straight seasons in which the A.L. West has won its series against the East—one more than it won over the first 20 years of divisional play:

	American League				National League		
Year	Winner	W	L	Pct.	Winner	W	L	Pct.
---	---	---	---	---	---	---	---	---
1969	East	245	187	.567	West	220	212	.509
1970	East	243	189	.563	West	223	208	.517
1971	**West**	215	214	.501	East	221	210	.513
1972	East	217	215	.502	East	217	215	.502
1973	East	226	206	.523	West	231	201	.534
1974	East	219	213	.507	West	231	201	.534
1975	East	221	206	.518	East	222	209	.515
1976	East	223	209	.516	West	221	211	.512
1977	**West**	257	247	.510	East	230	202	.532
1978	East	281	220	.561	West	233	198	.541
1979	East	327	259	.558	East	236	194	.549
1980	East	329	255	.563	West	233	199	.539
1981	East	209	180	.537	West	142	123	.536
1982	East	323	265	.549	East	219	213	.507
1983	East	332	256	.565	West	228	204	.528
1984	East	320	267	.545	East	235	197	.544
1985	East	304	283	.518	East	223	208	.517
1986	East	320	268	.544	East	217	214	.503
1987	East	307	281	.522	East	244	187	.566
1988	East	295	291	.503	East	214	213	.501
1989	**West**	314	273	.535	East	218	214	.505
1990	**West**	313	274	.533	East	225	207	.521
1991	**West**	324	264	.551	East	217	215	.502

There were seasons other than 1991 in which one division dominated another to a greater degree. But it's worth noting that last season no team in the A.L. West had a losing record against the East—a nearly unprecedented occurrence. (Texas had the division's worst mark at 42–42.) That happened only once before: in 1987, when every team in the N.L. East had a winning mark versus teams from the N.L. West.

Other than moving from Orange County to South Orange, N.J., we're not sure what the Angels can do about this untimely turn of events. Well, maybe if they move to *West* Orange, N.J. . . . .

The Angels ranked second in the American League last season with a 3.69 ERA, but scored an average of 4.0 runs per game, the second-lowest mark in the league. California's pitchers weren't only more effective than its position players, they were younger as well by a margin of more than three years. Angels pitchers averaged 28.2 years of age, a half-year younger than the major league average; their position players averaged 31.3 years of age, giving them the oldest lineup in the majors.

With an aging and unproductive lineup, it's clear that Whitey Herzog, the team's new director of player personnel, will have to reconstruct his roster around that pitching staff. And what a foundation it is: three left-handed starters, all coming off seasons of at least 18 wins. Mark Langston, Jim Abbott, and Chuck Finley are unique in major league history in this sense: Only four other teams had three southpaws with as many as 15 wins each; the 1991 Angels are the only team on which all three won at least 18 games:

Year	Team	Left-Handers with 15 or More Wins
1917	Giants	Schupp (21–7), Sallee (18–7), Benton (15–9)
1974	Orioles	Cuellar (22–10), Grimsley (18–13), McNally (16–10)
1980	Yankees	John (22–9), Guidry (17–10), May (15–5)
1991	Braves	Glavine (20–11), Avery (18–8), Leibrandt (15–13)
1991	Angels	Langston (19–8), Finley (18–9), Abbott (18–11)

We explain in the Mariners essay how difficult it is to maintain a strong and stable starting rotation for more than a year or two, no matter how young and accomplished it may be. So we won't wax overly optimistic over the possibility that Langston, Finley, and Abbott will remain the nucleus of California's rotation into the latter part of the decade. For one reason or another, that's just not likely to happen. But there is another noteworthy reason for Angels fans to relish the presence of those three pitchers in their rotation—namely, the enormous and inexplicable success of teams with an abundance of left-handed pitching.

Over the past 30 years, teams with a preponderance of left-handed pitching—which we will define as those with at least 55 percent of their innings pitched by southpaws—have compiled a remarkable record that almost defies logic: 10 of 23 won division or league titles, including three World Series champions (the 1965 Dodgers and the Athletics in both 1973 and 1974), and both of last season's National League division champs (Pittsburgh and Atlanta). Compare their accomplishments to those of all teams during the expansion era (since 1961 in the American League, 1962 in the National League) with fewer innings by left-handed pitchers. The category headed "Titles" includes league championships prior to 1969, division titles since then:

	Pct.	Teams	Titles	90+ Wins	.500 or Better	Below .500
Left-Handed Teams	.546	23	10 (43%)	12 (52%)	19	4
All Other Teams	.499	709	97 (14%)	150 (21%)	375	334

Division or league titles were more than three times as likely by predominantly left-handed staffs as by other teams. Losing records were nearly three times as likely for teams in the control group (47%) as they were among the southpaw staffs (17%).

Why this is so remains a mystery. But we can tell you that just as teams loaded with left-handers perform significantly better than other teams, those with a paucity of southpaws tend to underperform. To choose a group of teams similar in size to the left-handed group, it was necessary to drop the percentage of innings pitched by lefties all the way down below 10 percent. The results for these "right-handed" teams:

	Pct.	Teams	Titles	90+ Wins	.500 or Better	Below .500
Right-Handed Teams	.494	28	2 (7%)	3 (11%)	11	17
All Other Teams	.500	704	105 (15%)	159 (23%)	383	321

Teams with almost no left-handed pitching (that is, less than 10 percent of their team total of innings) finished below the .500 mark more than 60 percent of the time. And their chance of winning a title was less than half that of a team with more pitching from the port side. By the way, the only team to qualify as a predominantly right-handed team over the past seven seasons has been the Kansas City Royals, who did so in each of the last two, suggesting that this most inexplicable trend is nevertheless respected by the 26 major league teams. For nearly a decade, few have been willing to compose an entirely right-handed staff, or anything close to it.

This would seem to account for the presumed longevity of mediocre left-handers who keep pitching at an age when comparable right-handers are out of baseball. But while there once may have been such a trend, there is no longer. Southpaws now account for roughly the same percentage of innings as they did 10 years ago, but the contribution of left-handers has dropped among pitchers 35 and older. The percentage of innings pitched by left-handers in each of the last 10 seasons:

Left-Handed Pct.	1982	1983	1984	1985	1986	1987	1988	1989	1990	1991
All Pitchers	30.1	31.2	30.9	31.3	31.3	32.3	30.7	31.8	33.9	31.9
Age 35 or Older	35.7	35.0	40.7	24.0	18.9	24.5	21.5	33.9	23.2	16.6

Actually, it wasn't too long ago that teams did subscribe to the theory that any left-hander, washed up or not, was worth putting on the mound. As recently as 1978, left-handers over the age of 35 pitched more innings than right-handers in that bracket (52 percent, to be exact). But last season, right-handers 35 or older out-pitched lefties by a margin of five innings to one, the largest disparity since 1969. The days of a 45-year-old Tommy John facing a 43-year old Steve Carlton (no, it never happened, but it could have) are over. At least for the time being.

WON-LOST RECORD BY STARTING POSITION

California Angels	C	1B	2B	3B	SS	LF	CF	RF	DH	P	Leadoff	Cleanup	Starts vs. LH	Starts vs. RH	Total Starts
Jim Abbott	-	-	-	-	-	-	-	-	-	20-14	-	-	8	26	20-14
Kyle Abbott	-	-	-	-	-	-	-	-	-	1-2	-	-	-	3	1-2
Shawn Abner	-	-	-	-	-	-	16-10	0-1	-	-	0-1	-	16	11	16-11
Ruben Amaro	-	-	2-0	-	-	1-2	-	-	-	-	1-0	-	1	4	3-2
Scott Bailes	-	-	-	-	-	-	-	-	-	-	-	-	-	-	-
Floyd Bannister	-	-	-	-	-	-	-	-	-	-	-	-	-	-	-
Chris Beasley	-	-	-	-	-	-	-	-	-	-	-	-	-	-	-
Chris Cron	-	3-2	-	-	-	-	-	-	-	-	-	-	3	2	3-2
Mark A. Davis	-	-	-	-	-	-	-	-	-	-	-	-	-	-	-
Gary Disarcina	-	-	2-5	1-0	7-3	-	-	-	-	-	-	-	5	13	10-8
Mark Eichhorn	-	-	-	-	-	-	-	-	-	-	-	-	-	-	-
Junior Felix	-	-	-	-	-	-	32-30	2-0	-	-	-	-	14	50	34-30
Mike Fetters	-	-	-	-	-	-	-	-	-	0-4	-	-	1	3	0-4
Chuck Finley	-	-	-	-	-	-	-	-	-	22-12	-	-	6	28	22-12
Kevin Flora	-	-	1-2	-	-	-	-	-	-	-	-	-	-	3	1-2
Gary Gaetti	-	-	-	76-75	-	-	-	-	-	-	-	7-6	42	109	76-75
Dave Gallagher	-	-	-	-	-	3-3	21-29	10-7	-	-	2-8	3-2	33	40	34-39
Joe Grahe	-	-	-	-	-	-	-	-	-	2-8	-	-	3	7	2-8
Bryan Harvey	-	-	-	-	-	-	-	-	-	-	-	-	-	-	-
Donnie Hill	-	0-2	13-16	-	17-6	-	-	-	-	-	-	-	5	49	30-24
Jack Howell	-	1-0	7-3	4-3	-	0-1	-	2-1	-	-	-	-	1	21	14-8
Wally Joyner	-	72-68	-	-	-	-	-	-	-	-	-	-	34	106	72-68
Mark Langston	-	-	-	-	-	-	-	-	-	21-13	-	-	7	27	21-13
Scott Lewis	-	-	-	-	-	-	-	-	-	5-6	-	-	4	7	5-6
Barry Lyons	-	0-1	-	-	-	-	-	-	-	-	-	-	-	1	0-1
Mike Marshall	-	0-1	-	-	-	-	-	-	-	-	-	0-1	1	-	0-1
Kirk McCaskill	-	-	-	-	-	-	-	-	-	10-20	-	-	12	18	10-20
Bob McClure	-	-	-	-	-	-	-	-	-	-	-	-	-	-	-
John Orton	12-10	-	-	-	-	-	-	-	-	-	-	-	7	15	12-10
Dave Parker	-	-	-	-	-	-	-	-	59-60	-	-	32-26	23	96	59-60
Lance Parrish	53-49	0-1	-	-	-	-	-	-	2-3	-	-	1-0	32	76	55-53
Luis Polonia	-	-	-	-	-	71-69	0-1	2-2	-	-	73-72	-	28	117	73-72
Jeff D. Robinson	-	-	-	-	-	-	-	-	-	-	-	-	-	-	-
Bob Rose	-	0-2	6-2	0-2	-	2-3	-	-	-	-	-	-	11	6	8-9
Dick Schofield	-	-	-	-	56-72	-	-	-	-	-	1-5	-	37	91	56-72
Luis Sojo	-	-	50-53	0-1	1-0	0-1	-	-	-	-	2-1	-	37	69	51-55
Lee Stevens	-	5-4	-	-	-	1-0	-	5-3	-	-	-	-	4	14	11-7
Ron Tingley	16-22	-	-	-	-	-	-	-	-	-	-	-	9	29	16-22
Fernando Valenzuela	-	-	-	-	-	-	-	-	-	0-2	-	-	2	-	0-2
Max Venable	-	-	-	-	-	3-2	12-11	6-10	-	-	-	1-0	2	42	21-23
Dave Winfield	-	-	-	-	-	-	-	56-59	18-16	-	-	41-48	42	107	74-75
Cliff Young	-	-	-	-	-	-	-	-	-	-	-	-	-	-	-

TEAM TOTALS: BATTING

	AB	H	2B	3B	HR	RBI	BB	SO	BA	SA	OBA
Season	5470	1396	245	29	115	607	448	928	.255	.374	.314
vs. Left-Handers	1561	397	77	8	32	182	120	254	.254	.375	.309
vs. Right-Handers	3909	999	168	21	83	425	328	674	.256	.373	.316
vs. Ground-Ballers	2537	660	118	13	54	291	191	417	.260	.381	.315
vs. Fly-Ballers	2933	736	127	16	61	316	257	511	.251	.368	.314
Home Games	2650	645	94	13	59	266	235	438	.243	.355	.307
Road Games	2820	751	151	16	56	341	213	490	.266	.391	.321
Grass Fields	4514	1131	188	23	90	475	371	749	.251	.362	.310
Artificial Turf	956	265	57	6	25	132	77	179	.277	.428	.333
April	679	183	27	6	12	78	62	112	.270	.380	.336
May	919	238	43	8	22	118	71	152	.259	.395	.316
June	941	254	43	6	19	117	68	152	.270	.389	.323
July	871	221	35	2	18	97	68	148	.254	.361	.308
August	960	223	41	3	32	93	79	173	.232	.381	.293
Sept./Oct.	1100	277	56	4	12	104	100	191	.252	.343	.315
Leading Off Inn.	1314	317	54	7	27	27	118	207	.241	.355	.310
Runners On	2346	636	105	11	42	534	204	373	.271	.379	.330
Bases Empty	3124	760	140	18	73	73	244	555	.243	.370	.302
Runners/Scor. Pos.	1356	372	66	7	24	480	150	211	.274	.386	.343
Runners On/2 Out	969	248	46	6	25	240	110	146	.256	.393	.335
Scor. Pos./2 Out	621	162	31	5	14	208	87	94	.261	.395	.354
Late-Inning Pressure	681	152	16	2	13	51	57	134	.223	.310	.286
Leading Off	170	39	6	0	3	3	17	28	.229	.318	.303
Runners On	274	58	5	0	2	40	24	53	.212	.252	.281
Runners/Scor. Pos.	144	29	2	0	1	37	17	25	.201	.236	.291

RUNS BATTED IN	From 1B	From 2B	From 3B	Scoring Position
Totals	67/1673	203/1019	222/574	425/1593
Percentage	4.0%	19.9%	38.7%	26.7%

TEAM TOTALS: PITCHING

	W-L	ERA	AB	H	HR	BB	SO	BA	SA	OBA
Season	81-81	3.69	5399	1351	141	543	990	.250	.383	.321
vs. Left-Handers			1669	454	42	140	275	.272	.407	.329
vs. Right-Handers			3730	897	99	403	715	.240	.372	.318
vs. Ground-Ballers			2521	626	41	212	422	.248	.346	.309
vs. Fly-Ballers			2878	725	100	331	568	.252	.415	.331
Home Games	40-41	3.30	2744	649	74	251	520	.237	.366	.303
Road Games	41-40	4.11	2655	702	67	292	470	.264	.400	.340
Grass Fields	64-71	3.70	4506	1125	125	449	830	.250	.383	.320
Artificial Turf	17-10	3.63	893	226	16	94	160	.253	.381	.327
April	10-10	3.35	658	158	14	64	117	.240	.363	.311
May	16-11	3.62	906	229	25	81	165	.253	.376	.317
June	15-12	4.53	924	251	31	104	195	.272	.431	.347
July	11-15	3.95	867	220	26	73	154	.254	.403	.313
August	11-18	3.49	945	240	19	92	147	.254	.388	.322
Sept./Oct.	18-15	3.23	1099	253	26	129	212	.230	.338	.314
Leading Off Inn.			1305	325	31	132	211	.249	.369	.321
Bases Empty			3105	771	75	307	535	.248	.373	.319
Runners On			2294	580	66	236	455	.253	.395	.324
Runners/Scor. Pos.			1269	321	38	167	273	.253	.405	.335
Runners On/2 Out			988	246	34	116	208	.249	.410	.334
Scor. Pos./2 Out			617	146	22	90	132	.237	.402	.338
Late-Inning Pressure			792	184	21	73	194	.232	.346	.298
Leading Off			197	43	4	18	44	.218	.320	.284
Runners On			316	70	9	35	81	.222	.348	.301
Runners/Scor. Pos.			171	40	7	23	44	.234	.404	.323
First 9 Batters			2648	616	63	263	524	.233	.357	.306
Second 9 Batters			1365	364	36	142	237	.267	.407	.336
All Batters Thereafter			1386	371	42	138	229	.268	.408	.336

WON-LOST RECORD BY STARTING POSITION

Chicago White Sox	C	1B	2B	3B	SS	LF	CF	RF	DH	P	Leadoff	Cleanup	Starts vs. LH	Starts vs. RH	Total Starts
Wilson Alvarez	-	-	-	-	-	-	-	-	-	4-5	-	-	3	6	4-5
Esteban Beltre	-	-	-	-	1-0	-	-	-	-	-	-	-		1	1-0
Jeff Carter	-	-	-	-	-	-	-	-	-	1-1	-	-		2	1-1
Joey Cora	-	-	36-27	-	1-1	-	-	-	-	-	0-1	-	12	53	37-28
Brian Drahman	-	-	-	-	-	-	-	-	-	-	-	-			-
Tom Drees	-	-	-	-	-	-	-	-	-	-	-	-			-
Wayne Edwards	-	-	-	-	-	-	-	-	-	-	-	-			-
Alex Fernandez	-	-	-	-	-	-	-	-	-	16-16	-	-	14	18	16-16
Carlton Fisk	43-48	7-5	-	-	-	-	-	-	6-6	-	-	26-23	41	74	56-59
Scott Fletcher	-	-	35-33	-	-	-	-	-	-	-	-	-	30	38	35-33
Ramon Garcia	-	-	-	-	-	-	-	-	-	10-5	-	-	3	12	10-5
Craig Grebeck	-	-	16-15	11-5	5-10	-	-	-	-	-	-	-	31	31	32-30
Ozzie Guillen	-	-	-	-	80-64	-	-	-	-	-	-	-	34	110	80-64
Brian Harrison	-	-	-	-	-	-	-	-	-	-	-	-			-
Roberto Hernandez	-	-	-	-	-	-	-	-	-	2-1	-	-	1	2	2-1
Greg Hibbard	-	-	-	-	-	-	-	-	-	13-16	-	-	5	24	13-16
Charlie Hough	-	-	-	-	-	-	-	-	-	18-11	-	-	10	19	18-11
Mike Huff	-	-	-	-	-	0-4	4-3	8-4	-	-	1-4	-	17	6	12-11
Bo Jackson	-	-	-	-	-	-	-	-	12-9	-	-	2-5	8	13	12-9
Lance Johnson	-	-	-	-	-	-	77-69	-	-	-	1-2	-	34	112	77-69
Ron Karkovice	28-21	-	-	-	-	-	-	-	-	-	-	-	19	30	28-21
Ron Kittle	-	10-4	-	-	-	-	-	-	-	-	-	2-1	5	9	10-4
Rod McCray	-	-	-	-	-	-	-	-	-	-	-	-			-
Jack McDowell	-	-	-	-	-	-	-	-	-	20-15	-	-	8	27	20-15
Matt Merullo	8-5	5-5	-	-	-	-	-	-	2-1	-	-	7-2		26	15-11
Warren Newson	-	-	-	-	-	3-8	-	14-11	-	-	2-0	-		36	17-19
Donn Pall	-	-	-	-	-	-	-	-	-	-	-	-			-
Dan Pasqua	-	33-21	-	-	-	4-4	-	23-23	4-2	-	-	40-31	5	109	64-50
Ken Patterson	-	-	-	-	-	-	-	-	-	-	-	-			-
Melido Perez	-	-	-	-	-	-	-	-	-	3-5	-	-	4	4	3-5
Scott Radinsky	-	-	-	-	-	-	-	-	-	-	-	-			-
Tim Raines	-	-	-	-	-	77-54	-	-	5-14	-	82-68	-	43	107	82-68
Cory Snyder	-	2-7	-	-	-	3-5	-	7-5	-	-	-	0-1	26	3	12-17
Sammy Sosa	-	-	-	-	-	-	6-3	35-32	-	-	1-0	-	35	41	41-35
Bobby Thigpen	-	-	-	-	-	-	-	-	-	-	-	-			-
Frank Thomas	-	25-31	-	-	-	-	-	-	58-43	-	-	10-11	48	109	83-74
Robin Ventura	-	5-2	-	76-70	-	-	-	-	-	-	-	0-1	40	113	81-72
Don Wakamatsu	8-1	-	-	-	-	-	-	-	-	-	-	-	4	5	8-1
Steve Wapnick	-	-	-	-	-	-	-	-	-	-	-	-			-

TEAM TOTALS: BATTING

	AB	H	2B	3B	HR	RBI	BB	SO	BA	SA	OBA
Season	5594	1464	226	39	139	722	610	896	.262	.391	.336
vs. Left-Handers	1782	459	63	6	47	194	186	305	.258	.379	.330
vs. Right-Handers	3812	1005	163	33	92	528	424	591	.264	.396	.339
vs. Ground-Ballers	2591	674	95	13	54	306	269	386	.260	.369	.332
vs. Fly-Ballers	3003	790	131	26	85	416	341	510	.263	.409	.340
Home Games	2713	735	108	20	74	361	305	426	.271	.407	.346
Road Games	2881	729	118	19	65	361	305	470	.253	.375	.326
Grass Fields	4765	1271	195	33	119	622	526	756	.267	.396	.342
Artificial Turf	829	193	31	6	20	100	84	140	.233	.357	.303
April	601	163	26	3	13	75	57	83	.271	.389	.337
May	963	242	26	3	16	95	95	177	.251	.334	.319
June	996	257	38	9	21	121	94	151	.258	.378	.324
July	944	247	43	6	33	143	113	133	.262	.425	.345
August	1016	279	46	8	31	150	107	153	.275	.427	.344
Sept./Oct.	1074	276	47	10	25	138	144	199	.257	.389	.346
Leading Off Inn.	1353	327	61	7	27	27	114	227	.242	.357	.306
Runners On	2387	643	97	21	71	654	312	370	.269	.417	.352
Bases Empty	3207	821	129	18	68	68	298	526	.256	.371	.323
Runners/Scor. Pos.	1409	382	64	12	35	557	224	240	.271	.408	.367
Runners On/2 Out	1034	257	38	9	26	255	160	175	.249	.378	.353
Scor. Pos./2 Out	689	169	27	4	17	227	117	130	.245	.370	.360
Late-Inning Pressure	1002	274	37	6	27	120	104	154	.273	.403	.343
Leading Off	264	79	9	2	7	7	16	41	.299	.428	.342
Runners On	431	108	20	2	12	105	55	64	.251	.390	.335
Runners/Scor. Pos.	229	58	14	0	5	87	44	31	.253	.380	.371

RUNS BATTED IN	From 1B	From 2B	From 3B	Scoring Position
Totals	105/1719	218/1102	260/628	478/1730
Percentage	6.1%	19.8%	41.4%	27.6%

TEAM TOTALS: PITCHING

	W-L	ERA	AB	H	HR	BB	SO	BA	SA	OBA
Season	87-75	3.79	5448	1302	154	601	923	.239	.374	.315
vs. Left-Handers			2163	507	51	237	365	.234	.361	.310
vs. Right-Handers			3285	795	103	364	558	.242	.383	.319
vs. Ground-Ballers			2521	620	53	243	373	.246	.361	.313
vs. Fly-Ballers			2927	682	101	358	550	.233	.386	.317
Home Games	46-35	3.70	2767	668	79	281	452	.241	.378	.312
Road Games	41-40	3.88	2681	634	75	320	471	.236	.370	.319
Grass Fields	74-64	3.73	4659	1104	129	521	807	.237	.371	.314
Artificial Turf	13-11	4.15	789	198	25	80	116	.251	.392	.324
April	11-6	4.30	588	139	17	84	125	.236	.371	.333
May	10-17	4.04	957	236	28	126	161	.247	.388	.335
June	17-12	3.34	951	214	28	84	153	.225	.352	.290
July	19-8	3.48	915	220	30	80	124	.240	.378	.304
August	12-18	4.23	983	245	22	101	175	.249	.387	.320
Sept./Oct.	18-14	3.57	1054	248	29	126	185	.235	.369	.316
Leading Off Inn.			1330	314	39	142	205	.236	.380	.314
Bases Empty			3178	728	88	328	542	.229	.360	.305
Runners On			2270	574	66	273	381	.253	.394	.329
Runners/Scor. Pos.			1251	321	37	181	224	.257	.396	.342
Runners On/2 Out			946	219	32	140	162	.232	.381	.334
Scor. Pos./2 Out			593	144	20	100	110	.243	.390	.355
Late-Inning Pressure			880	210	26	108	153	.239	.366	.325
Leading Off			217	48	5	29	36	.221	.323	.319
Runners On			368	84	10	54	68	.228	.361	.327
Runners/Scor. Pos.			202	47	4	39	41	.233	.347	.353
First 9 Batters			2731	624	74	319	491	.228	.355	.311
Second 9 Batters			1398	361	41	145	235	.258	.413	.327
All Batters Thereafter			1319	317	39	137	197	.240	.373	.313

CHICAGO WHITE SOX

Psychologists tell us that daydreaming is a perfectly normal activity—in fact, they say it's beneficial. All normal people at least occasionally play "What If . . . ?", and so do sports fans like ourselves. What if Bobby Orr's knees had been sound? What if Ruffian hadn't broken down in her match race against Foolish Pleasure? What if the Red Sox had traded Williams for DiMaggio? What if Mike Tyson had a clue?

But as with Orr and Ruffian, the most popular version of "What If . . . ?" concerns players whose careers were compromised or terminated by injury or otherwise—a game played all across the country last spring when Bo Jackson was released by the Royals. Some doctors speculated that Jackson would never play baseball or football again, raising the question of "what might have been" to the level of a national mantra—at least until the White Sox gambled several million dollars on the possibility that Bo would return.

As regular readers of the *Analyst* know, one of our favorite gadgets is a forecasting model that projects the most likely paths a player's career will take by identifying statistical clones from the past. That model is the cornerstone of our new Rookies and Prospects Section. But it can also be placed anywhere in a player's career and pointed in either direction, allowing us to play an elaborate high-tech version of "What If . . . ?"

For example: What if Bo Jackson had eluded Bengals linebacker Kevin Walker and had never taken the shot that caused his hip injury? The forecasting model found dozens of players who, at roughly the same age and to varying degrees, had career statistics resembling Jackson's, and who were coming off seasons comparable to Bo's in 1990. The bottom line: Few developed into superstars. Some examples:

Year	Player	—Most Recent Season—					—Career-to-Date Totals—				
		BA	2B	3B	HR	RBI	BA	2B	3B	HR	RBI
1990	Bo Jackson	.272	16	1	28	78	.250	66	14	109	313
1963	Frank Howard	.273	16	1	28	64	.280	67	12	99	313
1968	Ken Harrelson	.275	17	4	35	109	.246	77	10	95	314
1979	Butch Hobson	.261	26	7	28	93	.256	92	19	83	319

Of course, the players are matched on a much broader spectrum of categories than those shown above, and the eventual projections are based, in many cases, on groups of more than 100 similar players. When that analysis was performed, the model estimated that Bo Jackson—minus his hip injury—would have compiled these career statistics:

	G	AB	R	H	2B	3B	HR	RBI	BB	SO	SB	BA
1986–90	511	1837	278	460	66	14	109	313	145	638	81	.250
1991–	649	2004	281	482	67	9	110	319	172	729	51	.241
Totals	1160	3841	559	942	133	23	219	632	317	1367	132	.245

The figures above would fit nicely with those of Gus Zernial, Wally Post, and Dick Stuart, but would leave Bo far short of superstar status—even when you consider that none of those leaden-legged sluggers had anywhere near Jackson's preinjury speed. (Although it's not apparent from the comparisons cited, stolen bases *is* one of the categories used to determine similarity.) But the model not only projects the most likely middle track; it also evaluates a player's chances of reaching various statistical milestones. That's where Jackson's potential is illustrated: Bo had roughly one

chance in three of reaching the 400-home-run mark, and one in seven of reaching 500 homers. Even the best-case assumption conceded Jackson a batting average only in the .260s.

That was hardly the case for another Jackson who played for the White Sox nearly 75 years ago, and whose career ended with a .356 batting average and a lifetime suspension. Shoeless Joe was only 31 years old when suspended for life by Commissioner Landis in 1921, and he was coming off the best season of his career: a .382 batting average (3d highest in the A.L.), with 42 doubles (3d) and 20 triples (led the league). What if there were no Black Sox Scandal, or if Landis had ruled more leniently? The model does not, in its present form, take into account the fact that the years Jackson lost saw the blossoming of the "live-ball" era, which helped boost the production of such contemporaries as Ty Cobb and Tris Speaker. Nonetheless, it still suggests he had more than 1000 hits left in his bat. Projected totals:

	G	AB	R	H	2B	3B	HR	RBI	BB	SO	SB	BA
1908–20	1330	4981	873	1774	307	168	54	785	519	158	202	.356
1921–	857	3369	495	1116	193	75	23	486	444	104	69	.331
Totals	2187	8350	1368	2890	500	243	77	1271	963	262	271	.346

Getting the hang of it? Then let's look at two others whose careers were compromised by injuries: Pete Reiser and Bob Horner. Reiser was a promising center fielder for the Brooklyn Dodgers before his habit of running into brick walls took its toll. In 1941, his first season as an everyday player, Reiser led the National League in runs (117), doubles (39), triples (17), batting average (.343), and slugging average (.558). Over the 50 years since then, no player as young as Reiser has led the National League in runs; only one has led the league in extra-base hits (Frank Robinson). But he missed nearly 30 games the next season, then spent three years in military service, and never again played even 125 games. By 1950, his career was all but over. But here's what might have been:

	G	AB	R	H	2B	3B	HR	RBI	BB	SO	SB	BA
1940–1941	195	761	151	250	50	21	17	96	61	104	6	.329
1942–Beyond	1577	5914	1017	1790	324	101	132	794	597	530	52	.303
Totals	1772	6675	1168	2040	374	122	149	890	658	634	58	.306

Based on those best-guess projections, Reiser was not a Hall-of-Fame candidate. But our forecasting indicates that he had the potential to develop into a legitimate power hitter as well, rating his chances for 300 career home runs at slightly more than 30 percent. Given his batting average, speed, and fielding ability, 300 home runs would have greatly enhanced his resume for the Cooperstown voters.

Bob Horner, on the other hand, was clearly destined for the Hall before a series of injuries in the early 1980s ruined his career. Horner joined the Atlanta Braves in 1978 straight from Arizona State, hit the ground running with 23 home runs in 89 games, and kept right on going: He hit more home runs in his first 300 games than any other player in major league history (84). But like Reiser, Horner never played an injury-free season; he missed an average of nearly 50 starts per season over his first six full years with Atlanta, and played in only 32 games before breaking his wrist in 1984, an injury that would plague him throughout the rest of his career. But without those injuries, Horner's first three seasons suggest his career total might have looked like this:

	G	AB	R	H	2B	3B	HR	RBI	BB	SO	SB	BA
1978–80	334	1273	197	363	46	3	91	250	73	166	3	.285
1981–	1640	5353	820	1498	170	7	363	1086	407	699	10	.280
Totals	1974	6626	1017	1861	216	10	454	1336	480	865	13	.281

Like Bo Jackson's projections, Horner's are even more impressive when we take the optimistic scenarios. The figures above represent a best guess; but we estimate, based on his first three seasons, that Horner had an 18-percent chance of passing Babe Ruth's career total of 714 home runs, and a 15-percent chance of passing Hank Aaron as the all-time leader. Whew!

Here's a question we can look at now: What if some of the great Negro League players had reached the majors sooner? (Unfortunately, we can't use the forecasting model to evaluate Hall of Famers like Josh Gibson and Cool Papa Bell, who never played in the majors.)

Jackie Robinson was 28 years old when he made his major league debut for the Brooklyn Dodgers in 1947. He batted .297, the highest mark among National League rookies, led the league in stolen bases (29), and ranked second in runs (125). Players simply don't have seasons like that at age 28 unless they were ready to play in the majors long before—and at an All-Star level. Bill Madlock had the most comparable season at age 28 in major league history. That was in 1979, his sixth season in the majors. Ben Chapman had the next-most similar season as a 28-year-old—in 1937, his 10th in the bigs. What if the prejudices of the era hadn't prevented Robinson from making his major league debut years earlier? His projected totals:

	G	AB	R	H	2B	3B	HR	RBI	BB	SO	SB	BA
1941–46	821	3123	615	905	150	27	66	242	370	233	187	.290
1947–56	1382	4877	947	1518	273	54	137	734	740	291	197	.311
Totals	2203	8000	1562	2423	423	81	203	976	1110	524	384	.303

As substantial as Robinson's losses were, they were slim compared to those of Luke Easter, a teammate of Satchel Paige and Larry Doby on the Homestead Grays before he joined the Cleveland Indians in August 1949. Easter, a 35-year-old "rookie" in 1950, had at least 25 home runs and 100 RBIs in each of his first two full seasons in the majors. Only four other players that old ever reached those levels in consecutive seasons: Babe Ruth, Stan Musial, Hank Aaron, and Mike Schmidt. So what if Easter had been permitted to join the Indians (or any other big-league team) years earlier? Our projection puts him in a class with Dave Winfield, Billy Williams, and Willie Stargell:

	G	AB	R	H	2B	3B	HR	RBI	BB	SO	SB	BA
1937–49	1777	6661	1147	2006	367	89	344	1222	1059	769	12	.301
1949–54	491	1725	256	472	54	12	93	340	174	293	1	.274
Totals	2268	8386	1403	2478	421	101	437	1562	1233	1062	13	.295

While Robinson, Easter, and others were being denied equal opportunity, military service in World War II was costing others some prime seasons in the bigs. The focus of such a discussion is usually on superstars like Ted Williams, Joe DiMaggio, and Hank Green-

berg, all of whom lost at least three seasons. (We'll get to them shortly.) Seldom mentioned, however, are many less familiar players whose burgeoning careers were sidetracked by military hiatus and sputtered thereafter. As a result, you may have never heard of Pat Mullin, a Tigers outfielder whose .345 batting average in 1941 has been exceeded by only three rookies in 50 years since then (minimum: 250 BA); or Ray Lamanno, a strong-armed catcher whose rapid development at age 22 prompted the Reds to sell Hall of Famer-to-be Ernie Lombardi to the Braves. Lamanno led N.L. rookies with 12 home runs in 1942, one more than Willard Marshall, two more than Stan Musial.

The following projections represent best-case scenarios. (The introduction to the Rookies and Prospects Section discusses this concept.) It's unlikely that both Lamanno and Mullin would have reached these totals; it's also unlikely that neither would have:

Player	G	AB	R	H	2B	3B	HR	RBI	BB	SO	SB	BA
Lamanno	1732	6137	757	1721	230	37	334	891	748	479	6	.280
Mullin	1431	4621	856	1509	224	81	210	511	515	175	186	.327

Which current players might Lamanno and Mullin have resembled most closely under ideal circumstances? Lance Parrish and Pedro Guerrero are a pretty close fit.

Among the three superstars mentioned earlier who served in the war, DiMaggio suffered least—at least according to our model. Restore the three seasons he missed and DiMaggio easily surpasses the 400-home-run plateau; his actual total was 361, and our model adds 63 more. His career batting average actually dropped slightly.

But Greenberg spent most of five seasons in the military during WWII. Williams missed a total of five as well, serving during both the Big One and Korea. Our model estimates that Greenberg lost an average of 36 home runs per year from 1941 through 1945, enough to have vaulted him from his actual standing of 53d in major league history to a tie for 12th (and 3d at the time he retired) with a projected total of 512 HRs. And by our estimation, had Williams not taken those military detours, it's possible that in 1974, Hank Aaron would have been chasing Ted Williams's record, not Babe Ruth's. Note in the projections below that Williams's totals in runs, RBIs, extra-base hits, and bases on balls would be all-time major league records:

Player	G	AB	R	H	2B	3B	HR	RBI	BB	SO	BA
DiMaggio	2146	8373	1701	2706	469	151	424	1846	934	436	.323
Greenberg	2022	7577	1583	2403	551	98	512	1943	1252	1097	.317
Williams	2947	10296	2457	3573	695	102	686	2476	2818	893	.347

Here's a big "What If . . . ?": What if, in 1960, a 42-year-old Williams, coming off a 29-homer season, was within striking distance of the 700-HR mark? Could even the Splendid Splinter have resisted the temptation to remain in uniform long enough to pass 714?

At least Williams had a great career—albeit one that could have been even greater. But the actual accomplishments of Luke Easter, even putting aside his potential ones, have been almost completely overlooked. And the two biggest "What Ifs", in our estimation, involved careers that only hinted at what might have been. One started too late, the other ended tragically early. Their stories are told in the Chicago Cubs essay, on page 49.

CLEVELAND INDIANS

History, it's been said, is the endless story of man repeating his mistakes. But rarely have circumstances been so familiar as those leading to the collapse of the Indians last season, a mirror image of another Cleveland decline nearly a quarter-century earlier.

Following the 1967 season, their first losing season in three years, the Indians sought several National League home-run hitters, including Willie Stargell and Johnny Callison, to fill the vacuum left in the middle of their order by the decline of Rocky Colavito. Unable to acquire a legitimate long-ball threat, Cleveland elected to trade its remaining power, unloading Fred Whitfield and Chuck Hinton in separate deals for a pair of base stealers, Tommy Harper and Jose Cardenal. To exploit their shift from power to speed, the Indians pushed back the Cleveland Stadium fences, daring their opponents to hit fly balls in the direction of an outfield comprised of three of the swiftest runners in the league—Harper, Cardenal, and Vic Davalillo.

But as we pointed out in last year's *Analyst*, the concept of accentuating speed and de-emphasizing power isn't new, and it rarely works. That trade-off has a track record as long and dubious as a five-thousand-dollar claiming horse's, and it took the 1968 Indians only a few months to realize their mistake. But at midseason, Cleveland compounded its losses with an ill-advised desperation deal for a washed-up former home-run phenom named Jimmie Hall.

As Yogi would say, for the 1991 Indians, it was *déjà vu* all over again. You'll recall that the Indians announced after the 1990 season that they would forsake power for speed, and moved back the fences at Cleveland Stadium. Sound familiar? Cleveland chose not to retain its home-run leader, free agent Candy Maldonado, and then traded runner-up Cory Snyder. Base-stealer Alex Cole was to be the focus of the team's offense, at least on the off-season blueprint. But by June, with the team playing below .400, the experiment was deemed a failure.

Had the Indians anticipated the resurrection of Albert Belle's career, the fences probably would have remained where they were, or maybe even been moved closer to home plate. But Belle's development, as pleasant a surprise as it might have been, was also somewhat frustrating, since the reconfiguration of Cleveland Stadium appears to have cost him about 10 home runs. Consider this: Prior to the changes, Cleveland Stadium had only a slight effect on home runs; in the 1991 *Analyst*, we calculated its impact as a 4 percent decline. But last season, no stadium in baseball had a greater negative impact on home runs than Cleveland Stadium did—a 51 percent decline. Since Belle hit eight home runs at home, you can roughly double that to account for the stadium's 50 percent share. That jibes with the 20 homers that Belle hit on the road.

Of course, the team's collapse wasn't due entirely to its shift in offensive philosophy. Nearly half of Cleveland's 1990 starting lineup had hugely disappointing seasons in 1991, including Sandy Alomar, Jerry Browne, Brook Jacoby, and Chris James. Those four combined for nearly 600 hits and more than 250 RBIs in 1990; they barely reached 250 hits and 100 RBIs for Cleveland last season. The figures below do not include Jacoby's time with Oakland after the Indians traded him in late July:

Player	—1990 Statistics—						—1991 Statistics—					
	AB	R	H	HR	RBI	BA	AB	R	H	HR	RBI	BA
Alomar	445	60	129	9	66	.290	184	10	40	0	7	.217
Browne	513	92	137	6	50	.267	290	28	66	1	29	.228
Jacoby	553	77	162	14	75	.293	231	14	54	4	24	.234
James	528	62	158	12	70	.299	437	31	104	5	41	.238
Totals	2039	291	586	41	261	.287	1142	83	264	10	101	.231

Perhaps in the case of Alomar our expectations were too high, given the brevity of his major-league resume—although having won the 1990 American League Rookie of the Year Award, he had the pedigree to suggest stardom. And had Alomar not spent more than half the season sidelined with injuries, his sophomore-season totals might have approached the 134 hits, 10 home runs, and 62 RBIs that our projection system computed as a best-guess estimate. But even without Alomar's decline, the fallout from the other three players alone would have constituted a huge obstacle to Cleveland's chances for improvement last season.

Elsewhere in this book (the Atlanta Braves essay, page 45), we introduce the concept of a "breakthrough season," one in which a player exceeds a previously established level of ability to a significant degree—Terry Pendleton in 1991, for example. But in the case of the 1991 Indians, the opposite was true: three veteran players experienced what might be called "break*down* seasons," in which they failed even to approach the levels they established earlier in their careers. In fact, Browne, Jacoby, and James all fell so far short of those expected levels that the odds on even one of them performing that poorly would have been 84-to-1.

As you might expect, it's uncommon for a team to endure three such extreme breakdown seasons in one year; in fact, there have been only seven instances over the past 20 years. Naturally, it's extremely rare for one of those teams to withstand the collapse of three established players and actually improve its record. The last team to do so was the 1968 Yankees, who raised their record from 72–90 to 83–79 despite breakdowns by Horace Clarke, Mickey Mantle, and Tom Tresh. (Then again, the major leagues as a whole experienced an offensive breakdown that year.) Those seven recent teams accounted for an average decline of 86 percentage points, or 14 wins over a 162-game schedule:

Year	Team	From	To	Breakdown Players
1972	Orioles	101–57	80–74	Belanger, Buford, Rettenmund
1976	Orioles	90–69	88–74	Blair, Muser, Robinson
1985	Pirates	75–87	57–104	Hendrick, LeMaster, Wynne
1988	Braves	69–92	54–106	Morrison, Murphy, Royster
1989	Mets	100–60	87–75	Carter, Hernandez, Wilson
1991	Indians	77–85	57–105	Browne, Jacoby, James
1991	White Sox	94–68	87–75	Fletcher, Raines, Snyder

The 1991 Indians reacted as quickly to last season's ominous start as did their predecessors a generation earlier. But if history taught the Indians anything—and this seems an appropriate time to point out that

Hank Peters, who called the shots in 1991, was an assistant to Indians general manager Gabe Paul in 1968—it was to write off the rest of the season in progress and build for the long term. So when the Indians began to aggressively retool their roster early last summer, they avoided the quick-fix temptation of a trade similar to Paul's Vic Davalillo-for-Hall deal. Instead, the cornerstone of Cleveland's reconfiguration was a deal that shipped Tom Candiotti—eligible for free agency at the end of the season—to Toronto for Mark Whiten, Glenallen Hill, and Denis Boucher.

But that wasn't all. Late-season scorecard sales must have soared at Cleveland Stadium, as the Indians changed their roster over a few months more than most teams do over several years. The following table shows the midseason change in each American League team's lineup between May and August:

Cleveland	50%	Texas	21%	Seattle	15%
Kansas City	38%	Chicago	21%	Detroit	14%
Baltimore	28%	Toronto	20%	California	10%
Oakland	26%	Milwaukee	18%	Minnesota	10%
New York	22%	Boston	16%		

By the end of the season, Cleveland had by far the youngest team in the American League. The average age of Indians' batters during September was 25 years, 2 months—more than two years younger than any other team in the league. Their season-long average of 26 years, 1 month gave the Indians the youngest lineup in the American League since the 1982 Minnesota Twins. That was the rookie season for Kent Hrbek, Tom Brunansky, Gary Gaetti, and Tim Laudner (as well as pitcher Frank Viola).

The Indians also had the youngest pitching staff in their league in 1991, with an average age of 27 years, 2 months. It was Cleveland's youngest staff since 1971, when their rotation included five pitchers all under the age of 30: Sam McDowell, Steve Dunning, Ray Lamb, Alan Foster, and Steve Hargan.

But most noteworthy of all was Cleveland's regular starting infield for the last month of the 1991 season: Reggie Jefferson at first base, Carlos Baerga at second, Mark Lewis at shortstop, and Jim Thome at third. Baerga is the oldest of that group; he will be just 23 years, 5 months on opening day. If Cleveland leaves Arizona with those four penciled in as its everyday infield for 1992, take note: No team in major league history has survived a season with four regular infielders all under the age of 24. But two teams that came close in terms of age were among the most unexpected champions in major league history—the 1967 Boston Red Sox, with George Scott (23), Mike Andrews (23), Rico Petrocelli (23), and Joe Foy (24); and the 1969 New York Mets, with Ed Kranepool (24), Ken Boswell (23), Bud Harrelson (24), and Wayne Garrett (21).

With a potential starting outfield of Glenallen Hill, Alex Cole, and Mark Whiten, and with Sandy Alomar apparently set behind the plate for years to come, it's possible this season's Indians lineup could be the youngest in American League history. But ironically, there's another chance here for Cleveland to repeat an earlier mistake.

The league's youngest lineup to date was that of the 1973 Indians, whose regular starters included Chris Chambliss (24 on opening day), Buddy Bell (21), George Hendrick (23), and Oscar Gamble (23). Those four players accounted for a total of 3283 runs from 1974 through the ends of their careers (a half-run for each run scored, and a half for each run driven in). But only 662 of those runs—just 20 percent—were scored while playing for Cleveland. And only in the case of Bell, swapped even-up for Toby Harrah after the 1978 season, did the Indians acquire players even remotely as valuable when they traded away these young stars.

Chambliss was the first to go, sent to the Yankees early in the 1974 season for New York's pitching overstock—Fritz Peterson, Tom Buskey, Steve Kline, and Fred Beene won a total of 43 games during their careers with the Indians. Gamble brought Pat Dobson from New York to Cleveland, but with only one good season left. Hendrick was traded to San Diego for Hector Torres, Fred Kendall, and Johnny Grubb; Grubb might have justified that deal, had the Indians not parlayed him less than two years later into a pair of prospects who never made it. Had the Indians kept all four—Bell, Chambliss, Gamble, and Hendrick—or even traded them for players of equivalent value, it's reasonable to assume that Cleveland wouldn't have compiled the most dismal record in the majors during the divisional era.

And don't underestimate how extraordinarily futile the Indians have been over more than two decades. The last time Cleveland finished a season with more teams below them in the standings than above was in 1968, when the Tribe finished a distant third to the Tigers. During 23 years of divisional play, the Indians' "good years" have been four fourth-place finishes, only one of which has come since 1976. Cleveland's streak of 23 consecutive seasons without a first-division placing—that is, in the top half of their division; fourth among seven doesn't count—is the longest in major league history. In fact, only nine other teams compiled streaks even half that long:

Team	Yrs	(From–To)
Cleveland Indians	23	(1969–1991)
Chicago Cubs	20	(1947–1966)
Phil./K.C./Oak. Athletics	16	(1953–1968)
Boston Red Sox	15	(1919–1933)
Wash. Senators/Minn. Twins	15	(1947–1961)
San Diego Padres	15	(1969–1983)
Seattle Mariners	15	(1977–1991)
Philadelphia Phillies	14	(1918–1931)
St.L. Browns/Balt. Orioles	14	(1946–1959)
Wash. Senators/Texas Rangers	13	(1961–1973)

Although no other team has ever compiled a streak as long as Cleveland's, a closer look at that table reveals that one *district* did. The original Senators failed to finish in the American League's first division in their last 14 years in Washington, a municipal streak extended by the expansion Senators for another 11 years before they headed for Texas. Maybe that 25-year span in the nation's capital can serve as something for the Indians to strive to avoid as their own streak approaches the quarter-century mark.

WON-LOST RECORD BY STARTING POSITION

Cleveland Indians	C	1B	2B	3B	SS	LF	CF	RF	DH	P	Leadoff	Cleanup	Starts vs. LH	Starts vs. RH	Total Starts
Mike Aldrete	-	12-21	-	-	-	5-9	-	-	0-6	-	-	-	-	53	17-36
Beau Allred	-	-	-	-	-	6-7	-	9-16	-	-	-	-	1	37	15-23
Sandy Alomar	15-30	-	-	-	-	-	-	-	0-4	-	-	0-5	9	40	15-34
Carlos Baerga	-	-	27-46	27-50	0-1	-	-	-	-	-	0-1	4-6	37	114	54-97
Eric Bell	-	-	-	-	-	-	-	-	-	-	-	-	-	-	-
Albert Belle	-	-	-	-	-	33-54	-	0-1	10-21	-	-	36-65	34	85	43-76
Willie Blair	-	-	-	-	-	-	-	-	-	2-3	-	-	3	2	2-3
Denis Boucher	-	-	-	-	-	-	-	-	-	1-4	-	-	1	4	1-4
Jerry Browne	-	-	12-24	6-8	-	4-10	-	-	1-3	-	0-5	-	21	47	23-45
Tom Candiotti	-	-	-	-	-	-	-	-	-	8-7	-	-	4	11	8-7
Alex Cole	-	-	-	-	-	2-3	32-58	-	1-3	-	34-64	-	13	86	35-64
Bruce Egloff	-	-	-	-	-	-	-	-	-	-	-	-	-	-	-
Jose Escobar	-	-	1-1	-	0-2	-	-	-	-	-	-	-	2	2	1-3
Felix Fermin	-	-	-	-	47-80	-	-	-	-	-	-	-	36	91	47-80
Jose Gonzalez	-	-	-	-	-	1-1	0-5	3-9	-	-	-	-	9	10	4-15
Mauro Gozzo	-	-	-	-	-	-	-	-	-	0-2	-	-	2	-	0-2
Glenallen Hill	-	-	-	-	-	1-3	11-15	-	0-1	-	10-14	-	11	20	12-19
Shawn Hillegas	-	-	-	-	-	-	-	-	-	3-0	-	-	1	2	3-0
Mike Huff	-	-	1-1	-	-	-	12-20	0-1	-	-	13-20	-	18	17	13-22
Brook Jacoby	-	20-27	-	3-11	-	-	-	-	-	-	-	1-0	17	44	23-38
Chris James	-	3-10	-	-	-	5-15	-	4-13	25-33	-	-	2-4	34	74	37-71
Reggie Jefferson	-	10-16	-	-	-	-	-	-	-	-	-	1-4	3	23	10-16
Doug Jones	-	-	-	-	-	-	-	-	-	3-1	-	-	-	4	3-1
Eric King	-	-	-	-	-	-	-	-	-	10-14	-	-	7	17	10-14
Wayne Kirby	-	-	-	-	-	-	-	8-5	-	-	-	-	1	12	8-5
Garland Kiser	-	-	-	-	-	-	-	-	-	-	-	-	-	-	-
Tom Kramer	-	-	-	-	-	-	-	-	-	-	-	-	-	-	-
Mark Lewis	-	-	16-32	-	10-20	-	-	-	-	-	-	-	20	58	26-52
Luis Lopez	2-4	2-6	-	-	-	-	-	1-4	-	-	-	-	14	5	5-14
Ever Magallanes	-	-	-	-	-	-	-	-	-	-	-	-	-	-	-
Jeff Manto	0-1	1-6	-	9-21	-	-	-	-	-	-	-	-	15	23	10-28
Carlos Martinez	-	9-19	-	-	-	-	-	16-25	-	-	-	10-16	25	44	25-44
Luis Medina	-	-	-	-	-	-	-	1-4	-	-	-	0-3	4	1	1-4
Jeff Mutis	-	-	-	-	-	-	-	-	-	0-3	-	-	1	2	0-3
Charles Nagy	-	-	-	-	-	-	-	-	-	12-21	-	-	10	23	12-21
Rod Nichols	-	-	-	-	-	-	-	-	-	2-14	-	-	2	14	2-14
Steven Olin	-	-	-	-	-	-	-	-	-	-	-	-	-	-	-
Jesse Orosco	-	-	-	-	-	-	-	-	-	-	-	-	-	-	-
Dave Otto	-	-	-	-	-	-	-	-	-	4-10	-	-	2	12	4-10
Tony Perezchica	-	-	0-1	-	0-2	-	-	-	-	-	-	-	2	1	0-3
Rudy Seanez	-	-	-	-	-	-	-	-	-	-	-	-	-	-	-
Jeff Shaw	-	-	-	-	-	-	-	-	-	0-1	-	-	-	1	0-1
Joel Skinner	33-57	-	-	-	-	-	-	-	-	-	-	-	30	60	33-57
Greg Swindell	-	-	-	-	-	-	-	-	-	11-22	-	-	11	22	11-22
Eddie Taubensee	7-13	-	-	-	-	-	-	-	-	-	-	-	2	18	7-13
Jim Thome	-	-	-	12-15	-	-	-	-	-	-	-	-	5	22	12-15
Efrain Valdez	-	-	-	-	-	-	-	-	-	-	-	-	-	-	-
Sergio Valdez	-	-	-	-	-	-	-	-	-	-	-	-	-	-	-
Mike Walker	-	-	-	-	-	-	-	-	-	-	-	-	-	-	-
Turner Ward	-	-	-	-	-	-	0-2	10-17	-	-	-	0-1	8	21	10-19
Mitch Webster	-	-	-	-	-	0-3	1-0	2-3	-	-	-	-	6	3	3-6
Mark Whiten	-	-	-	-	-	1-5	21-40	2-1	-	-	-	3-2	19	51	24-46
Mike York	-	-	-	-	-	-	-	-	-	1-3	-	-	-	4	1-3

TEAM TOTALS: BATTING

	AB	H	2B	3B	HR	RBI	BB	SO	BA	SA	OBA
Season	5470	1390	236	26	79	546	449	888	.254	.350	.313
vs. Left-Handers	1504	394	66	9	22	160	127	233	.262	.362	.321
vs. Right-Handers	3966	996	170	17	57	386	322	655	.251	.346	.310
vs. Ground-Ballers	2510	612	98	12	31	208	189	383	.244	.329	.300
vs. Fly-Ballers	2960	778	138	14	48	338	260	505	.263	.368	.324
Home Games	2693	705	122	15	22	253	221	393	.262	.343	.321
Road Games	2777	685	114	11	57	293	228	495	.247	.357	.306
Grass Fields	4670	1209	201	25	72	490	395	729	.259	.359	.319
Artificial Turf	800	181	35	1	7	56	54	159	.226	.299	.278
April	583	137	21	3	9	44	48	99	.235	.328	.300
May	912	247	40	6	17	118	83	146	.271	.384	.335
June	933	215	32	2	8	65	82	125	.230	.295	.294
July	911	236	36	4	18	91	71	150	.259	.367	.315
August	1028	267	49	4	18	114	78	185	.260	.368	.316
Sept./Oct.	1103	288	58	7	9	114	87	183	.261	.351	.315
Leading Off Inn.	1323	336	57	8	21	21	130	209	.254	.357	.326
Runners On	2344	610	106	13	32	499	190	360	.260	.358	.315
Bases Empty	3126	780	130	13	47	47	259	528	.250	.345	.312
Runners/Scor. Pos.	1276	325	54	8	16	443	135	222	.255	.347	.322
Runners On/2 Out	1016	256	39	7	18	214	96	163	.252	.357	.320
Scor. Pos./2 Out	633	154	21	4	9	184	72	109	.243	.332	.325
Late-Inning Pressure	970	224	25	5	13	76	71	183	.231	.307	.288
Leading Off	243	55	8	2	2	2	19	45	.226	.300	.285
Runners On	396	89	6	2	5	68	35	72	.225	.288	.291
Runners/Scor. Pos.	217	47	3	1	1	57	27	42	.217	.253	.306

RUNS BATTED IN	From 1B	From 2B	From 3B	Scoring Position
Totals	69/1717	164/979	234/557	398/1536
Percentage	4.0%	16.8%	42.0%	25.9%

TEAM TOTALS: PITCHING

	W-L	ERA	AB	H	HR	BB	SO	BA	SA	OBA
Season	57-105	4.23	5623	1551	110	441	862	.276	.398	.329
vs. Left-Handers			2306	669	32	201	311	.290	.399	.346
vs. Right-Handers			3317	882	78	240	551	.266	.397	.317
vs. Ground-Ballers			2589	733	36	180	342	.283	.388	.328
vs. Fly-Ballers			3034	818	74	261	520	.270	.406	.330
Home Games	30-52	4.08	2900	788	41	207	447	.272	.373	.321
Road Games	27-53	4.39	2723	763	69	234	415	.280	.423	.337
Grass Fields	53-85	4.14	4837	1323	92	369	746	.274	.390	.326
Artificial Turf	4-20	4.81	786	228	18	72	116	.290	.443	.347
April	7-10	2.61	586	136	6	37	104	.232	.307	.278
May	10-17	4.64	943	256	22	72	162	.271	.401	.324
June	7-21	3.99	966	260	19	83	155	.269	.394	.331
July	9-18	4.17	934	266	20	80	142	.285	.419	.338
August	10-20	4.71	1034	299	21	81	151	.289	.424	.342
Sept./Oct.	14-19	4.59	1160	334	22	88	148	.288	.403	.337
Leading Off Inn.			1357	356	28	80	221	.262	.392	.309
Bases Empty			3118	844	50	205	492	.271	.382	.320
Runners On			2505	707	60	236	370	.282	.417	.340
Runners/Scor. Pos.			1425	389	31	177	224	.273	.403	.343
Runners On/2 Out			1040	257	20	94	163	.247	.365	.314
Scor. Pos./2 Out			645	151	12	81	109	.234	.355	.325
Late-Inning Pressure			749	212	11	78	122	.283	.387	.350
Leading Off			188	47	3	18	35	.250	.346	.322
Runners On			333	94	5	44	57	.282	.399	.360
Runners/Scor. Pos.			186	54	3	37	34	.290	.430	.394
First 9 Batters			2671	732	50	255	469	.274	.390	.338
Second 9 Batters			1522	414	31	91	210	.272	.399	.314
All Batters Thereafter			1430	405	29	95	183	.283	.409	.329

WON-LOST RECORD BY STARTING POSITION

Detroit Tigers	C	1B	2B	3B	SS	LF	CF	RF	DH	P	Leadoff	Cleanup	Starts vs. LH	Starts vs. RH	Total Starts
Scott Aldred	-	-	-	-	-	-	-	-	-	5-6	-	-	1	10	5-6
Andy Allanson	24-20	-	-	-	-	-	-	-	-	-	-	-	22	22	24-20
Skeeter Barnes	-	-	2-2	5-4	-	8-4	2-2	4-2	1-0	-	-	-	24	12	22-14
Dave Bergman	-	23-19	-	-	-	-	-	-	3-6	-	-	-	-	51	26-25
Tony Bernazard	-	-	-	-	-	-	-	-	0-1	-	-	-	-	1	0-1
John Cerutti	-	-	-	-	-	-	-	-	-	2-6	-	-	4	4	2-6
Milt Cuyler	-	-	-	-	-	-	67-69	-	-	-	22-14	-	34	102	67-69
Mike Dalton	-	-	-	-	-	-	-	-	-	-	-	-	-	-	-
Rob Deer	-	-	-	-	-	-	-	66-63	-	-	-	-	43	86	66-63
Luis de los Santos	-	-	-	-	-	1-1	-	-	2-4	-	-	-	7	1	3-5
Cecil Fielder	-	61-59	-	-	-	-	-	-	23-19	-	-	84-78	44	118	84-78
Travis Fryman	-	-	-	44-40	34-29	-	-	-	-	-	-	-	43	104	78-69
Dan Gakeler	-	-	-	-	-	-	-	-	-	2-5	-	-	2	5	2-5
Paul Gibson	-	-	-	-	-	-	-	-	-	-	-	-	-	-	-
Jerry Don Gleaton	-	-	-	-	-	-	-	-	-	-	-	-	-	-	-
Bill Gullickson	-	-	-	-	-	-	-	-	-	24-11	-	-	12	23	24-11
David Haas	-	-	-	-	-	-	-	-	-	-	-	-	-	-	-
Shawn Hare	-	-	-	-	-	2-2	-	-	0-1	-	-	-	-	5	2-3
Mike Henneman	-	-	-	-	-	-	-	-	-	-	-	-	-	-	-
Pete Incaviglia	-	-	-	-	-	20-28	-	2-2	22-18	-	-	-	30	62	44-48
Jeff Kaiser	-	-	-	-	-	-	-	-	-	-	-	-	-	-	-
John Kiely	-	-	-	-	-	-	-	-	-	-	-	-	-	-	-
Mark Leiter	-	-	-	-	-	-	-	-	-	8-7	-	-	3	12	8-7
Scott Livingstone	-	-	-	18-18	-	-	-	-	-	-	-	-	1	35	18-18
Rusty Meacham	-	-	-	-	-	-	-	-	-	3-1	-	-	-	4	3-1
Lloyd Moseby	-	-	-	-	-	33-26	-	2-2	-	-	1-4	-	4	59	35-28
John Moses	-	-	-	-	-	-	2-2	-	-	-	-	-	-	4	2-2
Mike Munoz	-	-	-	-	-	-	-	-	-	-	-	-	-	-	-
Johnny Paredes	-	-	3-1	-	-	-	-	-	-	-	-	-	4	-	3-1
Dan Petry	-	-	-	-	-	-	-	-	-	2-4	-	-	2	4	2-4
Tony Phillips	-	-	14-21	17-16	5-5	12-8	3-3	10-7	11-6	-	61-60	-	39	99	72-66
Kevin Ritz	-	-	-	-	-	-	-	-	-	1-4	-	-	2	3	1-4
Rich Rowland	-	-	-	-	-	-	-	-	0-1	-	-	-	1	-	0-1
Mark Salas	1-1	-	-	-	-	-	-	-	4-4	-	-	-	-	10	5-5
Steve Searcy	-	-	-	-	-	-	-	-	-	3-2	-	-	2	3	3-2
John Shelby	-	-	-	-	-	8-9	12-4	0-2	0-1	-	-	-	16	20	20-16
Frank Tanana	-	-	-	-	-	-	-	-	-	19-14	-	-	7	26	19-14
Walt Terrell	-	-	-	-	-	-	-	-	-	15-18	-	-	9	24	15-18
Mickey Tettleton	59-57	-	-	-	-	-	-	-	13-10	-	-	-	22	117	72-67
Alan Trammell	-	-	-	-	45-44	-	-	-	2-3	-	-	-	30	64	47-47
Lou Whitaker	-	-	65-54	-	-	-	-	-	1-2	-	-	-	11	111	66-56

TEAM TOTALS: BATTING

	AB	H	2B	3B	HR	RBI	BB	SO	BA	SA	OBA
Season	5547	1372	259	26	209	778	699	1185	.247	.416	.333
vs. Left-Handers	1529	390	79	7	60	206	181	307	.255	.434	.336
vs. Right-Handers	4018	982	180	19	149	572	518	878	.244	.410	.331
vs. Ground-Ballers	2757	714	135	10	95	405	330	524	.259	.419	.340
vs. Fly-Ballers	2790	658	124	16	114	373	369	661	.236	.414	.326
Home Games	2680	673	110	14	109	416	399	554	.251	.425	.349
Road Games	2867	699	149	12	100	362	300	631	.244	.409	.316
Grass Fields	4683	1168	218	22	174	666	615	995	.249	.417	.337
Artificial Turf	864	204	41	4	35	112	84	190	.236	.414	.306
April	637	146	32	4	22	90	80	132	.229	.396	.318
May	920	226	41	4	33	142	139	186	.246	.407	.344
June	926	217	27	6	38	119	111	194	.234	.400	.318
July	915	247	56	3	41	131	85	199	.270	.472	.333
August	1033	243	52	4	42	153	160	263	.235	.415	.339
Sept./Oct.	1116	293	51	5	33	143	124	211	.263	.406	.337
Leading Off Inn.	1301	295	52	8	40	40	151	269	.227	.371	.309
Runners On	2393	612	112	12	103	672	334	505	.256	.442	.345
Bases Empty	3154	760	147	14	106	106	365	680	.241	.397	.323
Runners/Scor. Pos.	1349	345	65	7	48	538	216	309	.256	.421	.351
Runners On/2 Out	1009	217	38	6	38	238	167	223	.215	.378	.332
Scor. Pos./2 Out	632	132	21	3	22	195	116	147	.209	.356	.335
Late-Inning Pressure	838	183	34	0	24	91	98	200	.218	.345	.303
Leading Off	207	36	9	0	4	4	30	53	.174	.275	.278
Runners On	337	73	16	0	4	76	46	79	.217	.344	.313
Runners/Scor. Pos.	173	43	10	0	4	64	31	42	.249	.376	.359

RUNS BATTED IN

	From 1B	From 2B	From 3B	Scoring Position
Totals	130/1777	202/1095	237/567	439/1662
Percentage	7.3%	18.4%	41.8%	26.4%

TEAM TOTALS: PITCHING

	W-L	ERA	AB	H	HR	BB	SO	BA	SA	OBA
Season	84-78	4.51	5596	1570	148	593	739	.281	.422	.348
vs. Left-Handers			2126	597	61	229	220	.281	.434	.349
vs. Right-Handers			3470	973	87	364	519	.280	.415	.348
vs. Ground-Ballers			2683	774	55	294	288	.288	.413	.348
vs. Fly-Ballers			2913	796	93	340	445	.273	.430	.349
Home Games	49-32	4.56	2860	784	89	295	405	.274	.421	.340
Road Games	35-46	4.45	2736	786	59	298	334	.287	.423	.357
Grass Fields	74-63	4.51	4756	1321	134	503	642	.278	.420	.345
Artificial Turf	10-15	4.48	840	249	14	90	97	.296	.431	.365
April	10-9	3.43	642	174	10	67	85	.271	.377	.337
May	13-14	5.27	975	303	32	110	111	.311	.480	.380
June	14-14	4.45	954	253	24	108	125	.265	.391	.339
July	14-12	5.87	918	284	28	100	110	.309	.464	.377
August	18-12	4.23	1042	288	33	106	148	.276	.423	.341
Sept./Oct.	15-17	3.73	1065	268	21	102	160	.252	.386	.318
Leading Off Inn.			1347	373	38	102	163	.277	.421	.329
Bases Empty			3130	854	86	271	429	.273	.419	.333
Runners On			2466	716	62	322	310	.290	.426	.367
Runners/Scor. Pos.			1414	407	31	239	192	.288	.417	.379
Runners On/2 Out			1082	306	27	169	157	.283	.420	.382
Scor. Pos./2 Out			709	195	12	133	103	.275	.385	.392
Late-Inning Pressure			738	205	18	89	112	.278	.396	.353
Leading Off			175	47	3	18	26	.269	.371	.337
Runners On			360	97	11	46	52	.269	.386	.346
Runners/Scor. Pos.			207	54	4	32	35	.261	.353	.347
First 9 Batters			2883	789	79	340	440	.274	.416	.350
Second 9 Batters			1438	393	34	139	171	.273	.398	.336
All Batters Thereafter			1275	388	35	114	128	.304	.461	.359

DETROIT TIGERS

The ancient Greek lyric poet Archilochus wrote: *The fox knows many tricks, the hedgehog just one—one good one.*

Epigraphists believe Archilochus was a Detroit Tigers fan.

The Tigers' one trick echoes ancient Greece, the legendary land of Homer. Last season, the Tigers hit a major league high 209 home runs and ranked second in runs scored. They pushed those runs across the plate despite ranking dead last in batting average in the American League and leaving the league's second-highest total of runners on base.

Along with their homeric exploits, the Tigers struck out impressively. Four of the American League's top six strikeout victims were Tigers. Overall, Detroit fanned 1185 times, breaking the junior-circuit record of 1148 established by the 1986 Seattle Mariners, a 67–95 last-place team. The Tigers barely missed the 1968 New York Mets' major league mark of 1203. The Mets may have been just 12 months away from a miracle, but when they set the strikeout record they scored just 2.9 runs per game and finished ninth in a 10-team league.

Obviously strikeouts are no way to get runs across the plate. When the Mariners said bye-bye to homer-hitting strikeout specialist Steve Balboni a couple years ago, then-Seattle manager Jim Lefebvre said "the game stops" when a Balboni-style batter steps into the box. Certainly the one time in 20 or so when that slugger hits one out is inspiring and useful, but are the rest of his at-bats merely a waste of time?

In the Cardinals essay of the 1987 *Analyst,* we showed that teams that advance more than a fair share of base runners on outs tend to score more runs than otherwise similar teams that don't. We've continued to notice that runners rarely advance on strikeouts. So if only the Tigers would put the ball in play a little more often, they'd score more runs, right?

We went back into history to examine that supposition, seeking teams with the same offensive characteristics as the 1991 Tigers, but with lower strikeout totals. Although the '91 Tigers seem to be a team out of the 1930s (their still-classic period uniforms further enhancing that image), 16 of the 17 most-similar teams played after 1960. The most similar team we found should warm the hearts of those who believe that ballparks shape ballclubs; it was the 1962 Tigers:

	G	AB	H	2B	3B	HR	BB	SO	SB	BA	SLG
1991	162	5547	1372	259	26	209	699	1185	109	.247	.416
1962	161	5456	1352	191	36	209	651	894	69	.248	.411

That's a close match as far as the condiments go. Now here's the beef: One of those Tigers teams scored 758 runs (or 4.7 per game); the other scored 817 runs (5.0 per game), or 7 percent more. And, ladies and gentlemen, the team that scored more runs was last season's strikeout kings.

O.K., maybe that's a fluke. But the odds of such an aberration get longer the further you progress down the list of statistical clones. You'd be unlikely to mistake any of the following teams for last season's Tigers in a dark alley. Compare the rest of the 10 most-similar teams, and note that all were outscored by the 1991 Tigers:

	G	R	R/G	AB	H	2B	3B	HR	BB	SO	BA	SLG
1991 Tigers	162	817	5.04	5547	1372	259	26	209	699	1185	.247	.416
1969 Red Sox	162	743	4.59	5494	1381	234	37	197	658	923	.251	.415
1956 Dodgers	154	720	4.68	5098	1315	212	36	179	649	738	.258	.419
1961 Angels	162	744	4.59	5424	1331	218	22	189	681	1068	.245	.398
1979 Orioles	159	757	4.76	5371	1401	258	24	181	608	847	.261	.419
1985 Tigers	161	729	4.53	5575	1413	254	45	202	526	926	.253	.424
1987 Yankees	162	788	4.86	5511	1445	239	16	196	604	949	.262	.418
1987 Athletics	162	806	4.98	5511	1432	263	33	199	593	1056	.260	.428
1970 Red Sox	162	786	4.85	5535	1450	252	28	203	594	855	.262	.428
1987 Orioles	162	729	4.50	5576	1437	219	20	211	524	939	.258	.418

The fact is that despite—or perhaps on account of?—their ponderous strikeout total, the 1991 Detroit club outscored nearly every comparable team (strikeouts notwithstanding) in recent major league history. In fact, last season's Tigers outscored every one of the similar teams until we reach number 15 on the hit list: the 1985 Baltimore Orioles, who scored one more run in one fewer game. We don't insist you take these figures as an endorsement for strikeouts, or even as a comeback plea for Dave Kingman. But they make it awfully difficult to claim that strikeouts are a bigger drag on a team's offense than other outs; they suggest that an out is an out. A hitter may look pitiful when striking out, but very few look too impressive popping out either. If a major league hitter wants to avoid strikeouts, it's likely he can do just that—and tap out to short every time up. But in the modern game, players swing for the fences, and unless they're Joe DiMaggio that means more strikeouts—but not necessarily fewer runs.

In previous eras, strikeouts were stigmatized, perhaps rightfully so. A half-century ago, smaller gloves, generally less-skillful fielders, and more-poorly-maintained fields (without carpets, no less) turned many more batted balls into adventures. It made sense to emphasize putting the ball in play, since almost anything could happen. But this Tigers case study shows that such an approach may not be important any more, if you have a lineup of sluggers doing the striking out. Besides, when batters strike out, they're not hitting into double plays and they're increasing pitch counts, thereby (according to the current statistical vogue) wearing down pitchers and giving base runners more opportunities to steal.

It's been known for years that home runs help teams win games and players win bigger salaries. Ralph Kiner said he gripped his bat at the bottom because "that's where the Cadillacs are." (Ol' Ralph was pretty darn proud of his Cadillac, wasn't he?) Arbitration has institutionalized the connection between statistics and salary, and homers rank among the numbers that pay best. Today's Tigers seem to be leading the major leagues' charge toward the one-trick hedgehog, er, pony—or better still, ballplayer. Blame the usual suspects—expansion, the designated hitter, competition for top athletes from other major sports—as more players than ever before stay in the majors on the strength of a single skill.

Football turned the similar narrowing of its players' skills into a positive by declaring them "specialists." Well, last year there were nine specialists in major league baseball as well—defined as players with at least 20 home runs and less than five steals, or 20 steals and less than five home runs, while batting at least 10 points below the league average. And 1991 was a *slow* year for that sort of thing. Over the last decade, there have been an average of 11 one-tool wonders per season, with more qualifying on the home-run end than the stolen-base end. That 11-specialist average for the past decade is higher than every season during the 1970s except one; more than any two years during the 1950s combined (or any *three* during the 1960s); and more than for the entire decades of the 1940s, 1930s, or 1920s.

Rob Deer typifies the trend; he's been on the list for the last three seasons. Surprisingly, he's the only Tiger in this thicket. Pete Incaviglia is a two-time specialist, but he didn't homer enough to make the list in 1991; with no tricks left in his bag, Big Pete wasn't good enough even to remain on the Tigers roster for 1992. But striking out a lot and hitting home runs doesn't necessarily make a player a hedgehog.

Deer fanned 175 times to lead the A.L. last season, en route to his 25 homers and .179 batting average. He didn't hit his weight, but Deer is a better (and heavier) than average right fielder, and he walked 89 times, for a .314 on-base average. That's better than Lance Johnson's, whose batting average was 90 points higher than Deer's. Deer scored as many runs as Don Mattingly and knocked in just four less in 100 fewer plate appearances. This Deer may be a hedgehog, but he ain't a worthless one by any stretch of the imagination.

Cecil Fielder is a big burly bruiser (a.k.a. lummox) who hit 44 homers and struck out 151 times in 1991, with no triples, no steals, and just 25 doubles. More home runs than doubles often indicates a lumbering slugger, the single-tool stereotype; Harmon Killebrew did it 18 times, the most in major league history. But Fielder isn't on the specialist list either, because he batted .261, a point above the league average. That's also one point better than Mo Vaughn, the much ballyhooed young slugger, and Robin Yount, the vaunted all-around performer; it's five points better than John Olerud, the purported natural (actually, we've done some of that purporting ourselves) whose spot Fielder could well be filling in Toronto if the Blue Jays had wanted it that way. Fielder also walked 78 times, giving him a .347 on-base percentage. That's five points better than Devon White, the reborn leadoff hitter who saved the Blue Jays, and 21 points better than aging but still athletic Dave Winfield. Of course, none of those other players approached Fielder's power numbers, and baseball history suggests they never will. Sure, some of them bring other skills to the table; but Fielder does a lot more than homer and fan, too.

Then there's Mickey Tettleton, who struck out 131 times last season—the sixth-highest total in the A.L. and his third consecutive season of 117 or more. He has now struck out 674 times in 2816 plate appearances—roughly one for every four PAs, almost exactly equal to Lew Burdette's career rate. But Tettleton also drew 101 walks last year, his second straight season with 100-plus free passes—a nice complement to his 31 homers, wouldn't you say? All that from a switch hitter and pretty fair defensive catcher, to boot. Until Sandy Alomar Jr. reproduces his rookie-season numbers, Tettleton could be the best receiver in the American League, if not all of baseball.

Here's the point: The Tigers picked Tettleton, Fielder, and Deer off the discard pile. Toronto gave up on Fielder, perhaps understandably, because they fell in love with long, lean Fred McGriff's left-handed power stroke. The Milwaukee Brewers let Deer leave as a free agent, replacing the devil they knew with Franklin Stubbs. And when Tettleton became a free agent after a disappointing 1990 season, the Baltimore Orioles offered arbitration simply to ensure they'd get a draft choice when he signed elsewhere. Tettleton hit just 15 homers in 1990, down from 26 the year before, although still third most among A.L. catchers. But he also fanned 160 times (a major league record for switch-hitters, if you follow that kind of stuff). The O's couldn't have been too delighted when Tettleton took them up on the arbitration offer; faced with the prospect of paying an unwanted player more than a million bucks, Baltimore traded Tettleton to the Tigers for pitcher Jeff M. Robinson. This past winter, Detroit signed Tettleton to a three-year deal, while the Orioles released Robinson.

The Orioles can say they needed to make room for minor league slugger Chris Hoiles, who may yet develop into the kind of threat Tettleton already is. Or they can say they had to cut their payroll in order to accomodate Glenn Davis, a more accomplished slugger. But you have to wonder how much of Baltimore's decision to let Tettleton go for so small a price was simply a reflection of the disdain with which most teams regard players who strike out often—no matter what their other skills.

The Tigers are clearly the majors' most enlightened team on this count, not letting strikeouts cloud their judgments about players, particularly those well suited to their own unique ballyard. Of course, other factors contributed to the team's willingness to go bottom fishing. For years, the Tigers seldom chased big-ticket free agents, allowing much of their 1984 runaway championship team to trickle away, one at a time, uncontested: Ruppert Jones in 1984, followed by Aurelio Lopez (1985), Lance Parrish (1986), Kirk Gibson (1987), Darrell Evans (1988), and ultimately Jack Morris (1990). And the organization's farm system, perhaps the most productive of the 1970s when it spawned the foundation for that 1984 title, went dry in the late 1980s. Last season, Milt Cuyler became the first Tigers rookie since Trammell and Whitaker in 1977 to accumulate as many as 400 plate appearances. Nonetheless, Detroit's trawling has yielded several big ones like Fielder, Tettleton, and 20-game winner Bill Gullickson to more than compensate for the flops (like Tony Bernazard and Andy Allanson, who also opened the 1991 season on Detroit's roster).

Detroit has found its niche for the time being pulling frequent fanners from the bottom of the barrel. But as other teams realize how they've helped restore respectability to the recently helpless Tigers, it could be that the availability of such players will dwindle. To paraphrase Dick Stuart, the Tigers are showing the rest of baseball how to stop worrying about the strikeout and learn to love it. Once those rivals wise up, there might not be any more Fielders or Tettletons to snap up so cheaply; and unless the Detroit farm system regains its lost touch, the big club may be forced to field a lineup of Bernazards and Allansons. A team of apparent hedgehogs on the field has made the front office look pretty foxy, but they won't survive in the woods much longer on that one trick alone.

KANSAS CITY ROYALS

Anyone out there think the Royals can contend for a division title within the next, say, 30 years? So do we, of course. But there is a team that hasn't finished within 10 games of first place in more than three decades (that is, if you overlook the second half of the split 1981 season, which didn't give them enough time to fall that far behind). The last time the Cleveland Indians were even near contenders was 1959, when Rocky Colavito led the team in home runs and RBIs, and Cal McLish led in wins and ERA (minimum: 25 starts). Following the season, both were traded—Colavito to the Tigers for Harvey Kuenn; McLish with Billy Martin and Gordy Coleman to the Reds for Johnny Temple.

Right about now you may find yourself asking, What's that got to do with Kansas City? Funny you should ask. Last season, Danny Tartabull led the Royals in home runs and RBIs; Bret Saberhagen led the team in wins (tying Kevin Appier) and ERA. That will make the 1992 Royals the first team since the 1960 Indians to take the field on opening day with both an incumbent HR/RBI leader and a wins/ERA leader playing elsewhere. Of course, it took a lot more than the loss of Colavito and McLish to pull the Tribe into such a prolonged slide. (Some of those other blunders are discussed in the Blue Jays essay on page 43.) And the Royals are hardly without suitable replacements; they signed free agent Wally Joyner in anticipation of losing Tartabull, and acquired Kevin McReynolds and Gregg Jefferies from the Mets for Saberhagen. But the fact that no team in 30 years had to endure the departure of two such integral players (at least as we have defined them) illustrates the degree to which the character of the Royals' roster changed during the past off-season.

The loss of Tartabull alone constitutes an unusual turn. Only two other players in the history of major league baseball started a season with a new club after batting at least .300 with 30 home runs and 100 RBIs; both were part of the austerity program of the Philadelphia Athletics during and after the Great Depression. Right after the 1932 season ended, the A's sold Al Simmons (with Jimmy Dykes and Mule Haas) to the White Sox for one hundred fifty thousand dollars, after he had batted .322 with 35 home runs and 151 RBIs. Three years later, they sold Jimmie Foxx (with Johnny Marcum) to the Red Sox for the same amount after Double-X had led the league in home runs. (In other deals during that era, Philadelphia also auctioned Lefty Grove, Mickey Cochrane, Max Bishop, George Earnshaw, and Bing Miller. Where was Bowie Kuhn when we needed him?)

From 1920 to 1990, 954 players earned at least a share of their team lead in both home runs and RBIs in the same season. Sixty-two started the next season with different teams—roughly one a year. Those totals don't include last season, which was typical: 21 of the 26 teams had a player who led the club in both categories, and as of January 1, the only one to have changed teams during the off-season was Tartabull.

While the advent of free agency has increased the rate of these combined leaders' changing teams, it's not by as much as you might think. During the 16 off-seasons since the abolition of the reserve clause, that rate climbed by about one-third: 43 of 709 (6.1%) from 1920 through 1975; 21 of 266 (7.9%) since then. And since 1976, of the 21 players who joined new teams after leading their old clubs in both categories, nine did so via free agency. (Actually, the trend might be growing: Of those nine who changed over 16 years, seven did so since 1986.) Besides Tartabull, that group of nine included: Larry Hisle (from Minnesota to Milwaukee after 1977); Dave Winfield (San Diego to the Yankees, 1980); Andre Dawson (Montreal to the Cubs, 1986); Jack Clark (St. Louis to the Yankees, 1987); and Nick Esasky (Boston to Atlanta, 1989), Darryl Strawberry (Mets to Los Angeles, 1990), Candy Maldonado (Cleveland to Milwaukee, 1990), and Franklin Stubbs (Houston to Milwaukee, 1990). For the record, only two of the eight teams that lost those players showed an improvement the next season: the 1987 Expos and the 1990 Red Sox.

The hurdle of having to replace Tartabull prompted the team to trade Saberhagen, a player who contributed nearly as much to the team's pitching as Tartabull did to its offense. Even in what qualified as an "off year," Saberhagen tied Kevin Appier for the team lead in wins and compiled the staff's lowest ERA. Pitchers who lead their teams in both wins and ERA switch clubs about as often as HR/RBI leaders; only 17 of 266 have done so since 1976 (6.4%). What differs is their mode of transportation: Only one of those 17 who joined new teams to start the next season did so as a free agent (Jack Morris, who left Detroit for Minnesota in 1991). It's also worth noting that Saberhagen is a far more accomplished pitcher than most of the wins/ERA leaders who were traded, the most recent of whom include Kevin Gross, Floyd Bannister, Ted Power, and Rick Rhoden.

The following table shows the eight teams in this century that lost a HR/RBI leader and a wins/ERA leader to other teams in the same off-season (including the early years, when RBIs and ERA were not compiled on an official basis), and the team's change in wins the following season:

Year	Team	Batter (HR/RBI)	Pitcher (Wins/ERA)	Next Year
1908	Cardinals	Red Murray (7/62)	Bugs Raymond (15/2.03)	+5
1917	Athletics	Ping Bodie (7/74)	Joe Bush (11/2.47)	−3
1927	Giants	Rogers Hornsby (26/125)	Burleigh Grimes (19/3.53)	+1
1932	Browns	Goose Goslin (17/104)	Lefty Stewart (14/4.61)	−8
1935	Athletics	Jimmie Foxx (36/115)	Johnny Marcum (17/4.07)	−5
1947	White Sox	Rudy York (15/64)	Ed Lopat (16/2.81)	−19
1959	Indians	Rocky Colavito (42/111)	Cal McLish (19/3.64)	−13
1991	Royals	Danny Tartabull (31/100)	Bret Saberhagen (13/3.07)	—

One byproduct of the losses of Tartabull and Saberhagen will be a Royals roster more dependent on players from other organizations than at any time since the franchise's infancy. It's quite possible that Wally Joyner, Gregg Jefferies, Kevin McReynolds, Kirk Gibson, Jim Eisenreich, Keith Miller, Bob Melvin, and Chris Gwynn—none of whom came up in the Kansas City system—could account for more than 3000 plate appearances, or roughly half of what an entire team gathers over the course of a season. Barring injuries, Mike Boddicker, Mark Davis, Luis Aquino, and Jeff Montgomery (all from other organizations) should face at least 2750 batters combined; if Davis and Aquino both win spots in Kansas City's rotation, that total would easily exceed 3000.

Those totals are in line with the current major league averages. Last season, fewer than half of all plate appearances were made by players on the same teams for which they made their big-league debuts; slightly more than half were made against pitchers still working for their first major league clubs. Those averages have flirted with the 50-50 mark ever since the Messersmith-McNally ruling pulled them down to that level. The following table shows how the percentage of plate appearances and batters faced (for batters and pitchers, respectively) by home-grown players has varied from decade to decade, with the 1970s split to reflect the dawn of free agency:

Years	PA	BFP	Years	PA	BFP
1900–09	34.7	51.8	1960–69	56.7	59.4
1910–19	49.5	59.2	1970–76	56.0	53.7
1920–29	50.8	50.3	1977–79	45.9	51.1
1930–39	58.7	56.4	1980–89	50.1	51.4
1940–49	60.7	62.7	1990–91	48.5	48.9
1950–59	60.8	61.3			

With the exception of its start-up period, the Royals franchise has almost always exceeded the major league average for self-sufficiency. Since Kansas City won its first division title in 1976, the Royals have fallen below the major league standard only four times in 16 years, and even then only slightly below. A comparison of Kansas City's rate compared to the major league average for the past 15 years; the MLB mark is the average of plate appearances and batters faced:

Year	—Kansas City— PAs	BFPs	Avg.	MLB Avg.	Year	—Kansas City— PAs	BFPs	Avg.	MLB Avg.
1976	49.6	70.9	60.2	54.0	1984	66.6	53.7	60.1	51.7
1977	43.0	51.3	47.1	48.6	1985	54.5	56.9	55.7	52.2
1978	50.2	63.1	56.7	49.0	1986	49.3	66.9	58.1	52.5
1979	51.7	64.0	57.9	47.9	1987	58.9	57.5	58.2	53.9
1980	57.4	72.2	64.8	49.7	1988	62.0	42.5	52.3	53.7
1981	58.0	76.3	67.5	47.2	1989	54.1	49.4	51.7	46.7
1982	56.0	36.0	46.0	47.7	1990	59.4	49.4	54.4	47.8
1983	65.0	36.2	50.6	51.4	1991	58.0	53.7	55.9	49.6

We wrote in the 1990 *Analyst* about how the Dodgers had been the most self-sufficient organization in baseball for most of the past 50 years, but that under current general manager Fred Claire the team has become increasingly dependent on expatriates. In only one year on the job, Royals G.M. Herk Robinson has instituted a similar policy, and for the same combination of reasons. Like the Dodgers' system, the Royals' organization recently suffered through an unproductive period. Combined with the availability of star players that free agency has provided, the Royals and Dodgers have done what they had to do in order to compete in what have become the stronger divisions in their respective leagues.

The addition of Joyner, Jefferies, and McReynolds gives Kansas City the potential for its strongest lineup from top to bottom since 1979, when Brian McRae was the 12-year-old son of the Royals' designated hitter, and Willie Wilson, Amos Otis, and Darrell Porter were the complements to Hal the D.H. and George Brett. Of

course, it could be that Kansas City's three new starters will merely offset the loss of Tartabull and the possible decline of Brett (who turns 39 on May 15) and Gibson (35 on May 28). But if those aging players stay healthy, the only thing lacking in the Royals lineup could be a Tartabull-like presence in the middle. And there's a very good chance that one of the newest Royals could fill that void as well.

As we explain elsewhere in this book, our projection model uses statistical clones from the past to derive for any player not only a best-guess estimate for the coming season, but also an optimistic scenario which the player has roughly a 20 percent chance of achieving. Simple mathematics indicates that among any group of three players, there's a 50-50 chance that at least one will attain that 20 percent level. The following table shows both levels of estimates; there's a good chance that one of the players will hit the high notes:

Jefferies	G	AB	R	H	2B	3B	HR	RBI	BB	SO	SB	BA
Best Guess	141	510	74	141	29	2	11	64	40	38	12	.277
Optimistic	152	587	101	178	41	5	25	89	65	30	36	.303

Joyner	G	AB	R	H	2B	3B	HR	RBI	BB	SO	SB	BA
Best Guess	145	517	70	143	25	1	16	80	49	53	3	.276
Optimistic	154	589	91	176	35	3	25	109	78	44	7	.298

McReynolds	G	AB	R	H	2B	3B	HR	RBI	BB	SO	SB	BA
Best Guess	139	473	63	127	23	3	19	77	40	62	4	.268
Optimistic	153	568	88	168	33	6	32	106	69	53	12	.296

Joyner's best-case projection is reminiscent of his "Wally World" years with the Angels, particularly his sophomore season of 1987 (.285, 34 HR, 117 RBI). And that's not really too far a stretch, especially when you consider that the one player in baseball history who most closely matched Joyner's statistical profile—both for career totals to date and the most recent season—is Bobby Bonilla. First their career statistics, then their figures for 1991:

Career	G	AB	R	H	2B	3B	HR	RBI	BB	SO	BA	SLG	OBA
Joyner	846	3208	455	925	170	11	114	518	323	331	.288	.455	.353
Bonilla	918	3294	510	931	201	37	116	526	397	497	.283	.472	.357

1991	G	AB	R	H	2B	3B	HR	RBI	BB	SO	BA	SLG	OBA
Joyner	143	551	79	166	34	3	21	96	52	66	.301	.488	.360
Bonilla	157	577	102	174	44	6	18	100	90	67	.302	.492	.391

The most startling projection is Jefferies's; let's not discount the possibility that he has the potential to approach 30/30 status—and bat .300 to boot! Except for significantly lower walk and strikeout totals, his offensive statistics to date are quite similar to those compiled by Joe Morgan, Dave Winfield, and Keith Hernandez early in their own careers. In the interest of balanced reporting, we'll also point out that on the downside, Jefferies has a 20 percent chance at a .255 season of roughly 400 at-bats, with just three home runs and three stolen bases. Sound strange? Maybe so, but the fact is that we still have an awful lot to learn about 24-year-olds. But for those who wondered what kind of dreams might prompt a general manager to trade a pitcher like Saberhagen, the answer can be found in Jefferies's upside potential.

WON-LOST RECORD BY STARTING POSITION

Kansas City Royals	C	1B	2B	3B	SS	LF	CF	RF	DH	P	Leadoff	Cleanup	Starts vs. LH	Starts vs. RH	Total Starts
Kevin Appier	-	-	-	-	-	-	-	-	-	18-13	-	-	12	19	18-13
Luis Aquino	-	-	-	-	-	-	-	-	-	9-9	-	-	6	12	9-9
Todd Benzinger	-	39-31	-	-	-	-	-	-	1-0	-	-	7-1	21	50	40-31
Sean Berry	-	-	-	11-8	-	-	-	-	-	-	-	-	9	10	11-8
Mike Boddicker	-	-	-	-	-	-	-	-	-	13-16	-	-	3	26	13-16
George Brett	-	4-6	-	-	-	-	-	-	63-55	-	-	1-1	31	97	67-61
Dave Clark	-	-	-	-	-	-	-	-	-	-	-	-	-	-	-
Stu Cole	-	-	-	-	0-1	-	-	-	-	-	-	-	1	-	0-1
Archie Corbin	-	-	-	-	-	-	-	-	-	-	-	-	-	-	-
Steve Crawford	-	-	-	-	-	-	-	-	-	-	-	-	-	-	-
Warren Cromartie	-	15-11	-	-	-	0-1	-	-	-	-	0-3	-	-	27	15-12
Storm Davis	-	-	-	-	-	-	-	-	-	3-6	-	-	4	5	3-6
Mark W. Davis	-	-	-	-	-	-	-	-	-	4-1	-	-	2	3	4-1
Jim Eisenreich	-	6-8	-	-	-	20-19	4-5	12-8	0-1	-	4-7	10-7	11	72	42-41
Wes Gardner	-	-	-	-	-	-	-	-	-	-	-	-	-	-	-
Kirk Gibson	-	-	-	-	-	51-38	-	1-1	12-17	-	13-10	4-7	24	96	64-56
Tom Gordon	-	-	-	-	-	-	-	-	-	5-9	-	-	4	10	5-9
Mark Gubicza	-	-	-	-	-	-	-	-	-	11-15	-	-	10	16	11-15
Dave Howard	-	-	10-11	-	32-28	-	-	-	-	-	-	-	20	61	42-39
Joel Johnston	-	-	-	-	-	-	-	-	-	-	-	-	-	-	-
Nelson Liriano	-	-	3-3	-	-	-	-	-	-	-	-	-	-	6	3-3
Mike Macfarlane	31-35	-	-	-	-	-	-	-	1-3	-	-	0-4	31	39	32-38
Mike Magnante	-	-	-	-	-	-	-	-	-	-	-	-	-	-	-
Carlos Maldonado	-	-	-	-	-	-	-	-	-	-	-	-	-	-	-
Carmelo Martinez	-	16-18	-	-	-	-	-	-	0-1	-	-	-	19	16	16-19
Brent Mayne	36-27	-	-	-	-	-	-	-	-	-	-	-	-	63	36-27
Andy McGaffigan	-	-	-	-	-	-	-	-	-	-	-	-	-	-	-
Brian McRae	-	-	-	-	-	-	74-68	-	-	-	56-38	-	42	100	74-68
Jeff Montgomery	-	-	-	-	-	-	-	-	-	-	-	-	-	-	-
Bobby Moore	-	-	-	-	-	1-0	0-2	-	-	-	1-2	-	3	-	1-2
Russ Morman	-	1-3	-	-	-	1-1	-	-	-	-	-	-	6	-	2-4
Bill Pecota	-	1-2	5-5	43-45	1-2	0-1	-	-	-	-	-	-	36	69	50-55
Jorge Pedre	3-3	0-1	-	-	-	-	-	-	-	-	-	-	5	2	3-4
Terry Puhl	-	-	-	-	-	-	-	1-1	-	-	-	-	-	2	1-1
Harvey Pulliam	-	-	-	-	-	2-3	3-2	-	-	-	-	-	10	-	5-5
Bret Saberhagen	-	-	-	-	-	-	-	-	-	18-10	-	-	7	21	18-10
Dan Schatzeder	-	-	-	-	-	-	-	-	-	-	-	-	-	-	-
Kevin Seitzer	-	-	-	28-27	-	-	-	-	-	-	-	-	13	42	28-27
Terry Shumpert	-	-	64-61	-	-	-	-	-	-	-	-	0-1	42	83	64-61
Tim Spehr	12-15	-	-	-	-	-	-	-	-	-	-	-	18	9	12-15
Kurt Stillwell	-	-	-	-	49-49	-	-	-	-	-	-	-	29	69	49-49
Danny Tartabull	-	-	-	-	-	-	-	60-64	4-2	-	-	60-60	38	92	64-66
Gary Thurman	-	-	-	-	-	7-17	4-5	6-5	-	-	-	8-19	32	12	17-27
Hector Wagner	-	-	-	-	-	-	-	-	-	1-1	-	-	1	1	1-1
Paul Zuvella	-	-	-	-	-	-	-	-	-	-	-	-	-	-	-

TEAM TOTALS: BATTING

	AB	H	2B	3B	HR	RBI	BB	SO	BA	SA	OBA
Season	5584	1475	290	41	117	689	523	969	.264	.394	.328
vs. Left-Handers	1820	481	95	11	36	211	171	297	.264	.388	.330
vs. Right-Handers	3764	994	195	30	81	478	352	672	.264	.396	.328
vs. Ground-Ballers	2566	684	139	18	44	305	238	439	.267	.386	.331
vs. Fly-Ballers	3018	791	151	23	73	384	285	530	.262	.400	.327
Home Games	2767	732	143	29	47	328	273	437	.265	.388	.333
Road Games	2817	743	147	12	70	361	250	532	.264	.399	.324
Grass Fields	2154	572	115	7	59	284	182	412	.266	.408	.322
Artificial Turf	3430	903	175	34	58	405	341	557	.263	.385	.332
April	637	159	34	5	9	68	45	126	.250	.361	.299
May	897	222	37	5	20	98	82	148	.247	.367	.313
June	982	267	51	5	30	145	93	157	.272	.426	.333
July	945	286	55	7	24	148	93	143	.303	.452	.368
August	972	256	56	13	15	101	91	174	.263	.394	.328
Sept./Oct.	1151	285	57	6	19	129	119	221	.248	.357	.321
Leading Off Inn.	1364	368	88	14	37	37	95	252	.270	.436	.322
Runners On	2410	656	114	19	52	624	270	394	.272	.400	.343
Bases Empty	3174	819	176	22	65	65	253	575	.258	.389	.317
Runners/Scor. Pos.	1414	408	73	12	30	554	208	258	.289	.421	.373
Runners On/2 Out	1002	252	35	9	19	124	127	251	.251	.361	.336
Scor. Pos./2 Out	664	165	28	6	9	193	101	130	.248	.349	.351
Late-Inning Pressure	846	198	34	7	15	69	97	167	.234	.344	.314
Leading Off	218	58	12	5	7	7	16	47	.266	.463	.322
Runners On	347	71	9	2	6	60	53	68	.205	.294	.309
Runners/Scor. Pos.	207	39	5	2	3	53	44	48	.188	.275	.325

RUNS BATTED IN	From 1B	From 2B	From 3B	Scoring Position
Totals	84/1670	223/1100	265/611	488/1711
Percentage	5.0%	20.3%	43.4%	28.5%

TEAM TOTALS: PITCHING

	W-L	ERA	AB	H	HR	BB	SO	BA	SA	OBA
Season	82-80	3.92	5640	1473	105	529	1004	.261	.380	.327
vs. Left-Handers			2699	753	46	267	434	.279	.403	.344
vs. Right-Handers			2941	720	59	262	570	.245	.358	.311
vs. Ground-Ballers			2776	747	28	217	436	.269	.356	.325
vs. Fly-Ballers			2864	726	77	312	568	.253	.403	.329
Home Games	40-41	3.92	2927	746	40	257	513	.255	.367	.319
Road Games	42-39	3.93	2713	727	65	272	491	.268	.394	.336
Grass Fields	31-31	3.96	2075	557	55	211	371	.268	.400	.337
Artificial Turf	51-49	3.90	3565	916	50	318	633	.257	.368	.321
April	8-11	3.66	641	166	15	53	104	.259	.382	.320
May	13-14	3.74	896	228	12	79	145	.254	.357	.316
June	12-15	4.47	1020	282	20	95	164	.276	.405	.340
July	16-10	4.40	962	263	20	92	180	.273	.403	.339
August	18-11	2.64	980	234	13	83	192	.239	.340	.302
Sept./Oct.	15-19	4.50	1141	300	25	127	219	.263	.389	.339
Leading Off Inn.			1347	340	20	111	219	.252	.365	.314
Bases Empty			3142	798	54	272	562	.261	.372	.317
Runners On			2498	675	51	257	442	.270	.390	.339
Runners/Scor. Pos.			1475	385	27	178	285	.261	.379	.339
Runners On/2 Out			1083	280	22	140	188	.259	.367	.349
Scor. Pos./2 Out			719	178	14	106	134	.248	.346	.349
Late-Inning Pressure			801	207	11	73	148	.258	.338	.324
Leading Off			199	52	2	11	35	.261	.332	.307
Runners On			351	90	5	44	68	.256	.336	.342
Runners/Scor. Pos.			214	52	3	32	44	.243	.336	.341
First 9 Batters			2841	728	35	309	547	.256	.356	.331
Second 9 Batters			1528	415	38	119	244	.272	.414	.325
All Batters Thereafter			1271	330	32	101	213	.260	.394	.320

WON-LOST RECORD BY STARTING POSITION

Milwaukee Brewers	C	1B	2B	3B	SS	LF	CF	RF	DH	P	Leadoff	Cleanup	Starts vs. LH	Starts vs. RH	Total Starts
Don August	-	-	-	-	-	-	-	-	-	11-12	-	-	5	18	11-12
James Austin	-	-	-	-	-	-	-	-	-	-	-	-	-	-	-
Dante Bichette	-	-	-	-	-	-	1-3	54-51	-	-	-	0-1	45	64	55-54
Chris Bosio	-	-	-	-	-	-	-	-	-	19-13	-	-	7	25	19-13
Greg Brock	-	8-8	-	-	-	-	-	-	-	-	-	1-1	2	14	8-8
Kevin D. Brown	-	-	-	-	-	-	-	-	-	5-5	-	-	1	9	5-5
George Canale	-	9-3	-	-	-	-	-	-	-	-	-	-	-	12	9-3
Matias Carrillo	-	-	-	-	-	-	-	-	-	-	-	-	-	-	-
Chuck Crim	-	-	-	-	-	-	-	-	-	-	-	-	-	-	-
Rick Dempsey	16-28	-	-	-	-	-	-	-	-	-	-	-	37	7	16-28
Cal Eldred	-	-	-	-	-	-	-	-	-	3-0	-	-	1	2	3-0
Jim Gantner	-	-	23-30	49-34	-	-	-	-	-	-	-	-	24	112	72-64
Chris George	-	-	-	-	-	-	-	-	-	0-1	-	-	1	-	0-1
Darryl Hamilton	-	-	-	-	-	7-7	23-19	27-20	-	-	2-5	-	16	87	57-46
Doug Henry	-	-	-	-	-	-	-	-	-	-	-	-	-	-	-
Ted Higuera	-	-	-	-	-	-	-	-	-	3-3	-	-	4	2	3-3
Darren Holmes	-	-	-	-	-	-	-	-	-	-	-	-	-	-	-
Jim Hunter	-	-	-	-	-	-	-	-	-	0-6	-	-	-	6	0-6
Mike Ignasiak	-	-	-	-	-	-	-	-	-	0-1	-	-	1	-	0-1
Mark Knudson	-	-	-	-	-	-	-	-	-	4-3	-	-	3	4	4-3
Mark O. Lee	-	-	-	-	-	-	-	-	-	-	-	-	-	-	-
Julio Machado	-	-	-	-	-	-	-	-	-	-	-	-	-	-	-
Candy Maldonado	-	-	-	-	-	6-7	-	2-7	1-6	-	-	3-11	8	21	9-20
Tim McIntosh	-	-	-	-	-	-	1-1	-	-	-	-	-	2	-	1-1
Paul Molitor	-	21-25	-	-	-	-	-	-	60-52	-	81-74	-	46	112	81-77
Jaime Navarro	-	-	-	-	-	-	-	-	-	15-19	-	-	8	26	15-19
Edwin Nunez	-	-	-	-	-	-	-	-	-	-	-	-	-	-	-
Jim Olander	-	-	-	-	-	1-0	0-1	-	-	-	-	-	2	-	1-1
Dan Plesac	-	-	-	-	-	-	-	-	-	5-5	-	-	4	6	5-5
Willie Randolph	-	-	60-48	-	-	-	-	-	1-1	-	-	-	46	64	61-49
Ron Robinson	-	-	-	-	-	-	-	-	-	0-1	-	-	1	-	0-1
Gary Sheffield	-	-	-	16-27	-	-	-	-	2-3	-	-	-	12	36	18-30
Bill Spiers	-	-	-	-	67-58	-	-	-	-	-	-	-	24	101	67-58
Franklin Stubbs	-	45-43	-	-	-	2-2	-	-	2-1	-	-	13-16	16	79	49-46
B.J. Surhoff	67-51	-	-	0-2	-	-	-	-	0-5	-	-	-	14	111	67-58
Dale Sveum	-	-	0-1	18-16	16-21	-	-	-	1-2	-	-	-	37	38	35-40
Greg Vaughn	-	-	-	-	-	67-63	-	-	5-5	-	-	16-15	44	96	72-68
Bill Wegman	-	-	-	-	-	-	-	-	-	18-10	-	-	10	18	18-10
Robin Yount	-	-	-	-	-	-	59-57	-	10-3	-	-	50-35	39	90	69-60

TEAM TOTALS: BATTING

	AB	H	2B	3B	HR	RBI	BB	SO	BA	SA	OBA
Season	5611	1523	247	53	116	750	556	802	.271	.396	.336
vs. Left-Handers	1614	420	59	11	29	196	189	240	.260	.364	.337
vs. Right-Handers	3997	1103	188	42	87	554	367	562	.276	.409	.336
vs. Ground-Ballers	2675	738	115	27	52	370	268	350	.276	.397	.341
vs. Fly-Ballers	2936	785	132	26	64	380	288	452	.267	.395	.331
Home Games	2698	729	136	27	62	376	299	394	.270	.410	.343
Road Games	2913	794	111	26	54	374	257	408	.273	.384	.330
Grass Fields	4729	1303	208	46	102	654	496	660	.276	.404	.343
Artificial Turf	882	220	39	7	14	96	60	142	.249	.357	.296
April	650	164	36	2	19	86	60	93	.252	.402	.316
May	971	259	44	10	22	116	94	141	.267	.401	.330
June	897	227	34	7	20	129	94	159	.253	.373	.326
July	907	237	40	10	15	109	80	134	.261	.377	.320
August	1045	319	51	10	20	152	104	125	.305	.431	.364
Sept./Oct.	1141	317	42	14	20	158	124	150	.278	.392	.347
Leading Off Inn.	1363	357	57	10	38	38	98	170	.262	.402	.315
Runners On	2490	721	107	28	52	686	287	361	.290	.418	.357
Bases Empty	3121	802	140	25	64	64	269	441	.257	.379	.319
Runners/Scor. Pos.	1449	410	64	23	38	636	209	231	.283	.438	.362
Runners On/2 Out	1038	292	43	11	26	287	136	169	.281	.419	.367
Scor. Pos./2 Out	697	196	33	11	21	269	110	115	.281	.451	.381
Late-Inning Pressure	861	234	32	5	20	115	86	134	.272	.390	.340
Leading Off	211	45	5	0	7	7	14	31	.213	.336	.265
Runners On	376	109	20	3	8	103	49	59	.290	.423	.369
Runners/Scor. Pos.	231	60	12	3	6	95	32	39	.260	.416	.346

RUNS BATTED IN	From 1B	From 2B	From 3B	Scoring Position
Totals	83/1819	235/1113	316/663	551/1776
Percentage	4.6%	21.1%	47.7%	31.0%

TEAM TOTALS: PITCHING

	W-L	ERA	AB	H	HR	BB	SO	BA	SA	OBA
Season	83-79	4.14	5623	1498	147	527	859	.266	.398	.332
vs. Left-Handers			2674	712	69	257	346	.266	.393	.332
vs. Right-Handers			2949	786	78	270	513	.267	.402	.332
vs. Ground-Ballers			2611	710	50	222	346	.272	.380	.332
vs. Fly-Ballers			3012	788	97	305	513	.262	.413	.331
Home Games	43-37	4.20	2866	762	73	275	468	.266	.390	.332
Road Games	40-42	4.09	2757	736	74	252	391	.267	.406	.332
Grass Fields	75-62	4.03	4774	1257	122	450	742	.263	.392	.329
Artificial Turf	8-17	4.81	849	241	25	77	117	.284	.432	.349
April	10-9	4.34	664	179	19	61	118	.270	.416	.336
May	12-15	3.74	962	243	27	86	150	.253	.380	.315
June	12-15	4.30	916	237	23	88	142	.259	.376	.326
July	9-18	5.18	932	286	22	102	115	.307	.440	.381
August	19-10	4.30	1030	281	34	97	145	.273	.437	.336
Sept./Oct.	21-12	3.29	1119	272	22	93	189	.243	.349	.302
Leading Off Inn.			1338	353	40	124	223	.264	.407	.330
Bases Empty			3129	829	84	278	481	.265	.399	.330
Runners On			2494	669	63	249	378	.268	.396	.334
Runners/Scor. Pos.			1409	394	40	168	228	.280	.421	.352
Runners On/2 Out			1061	264	29	105	179	.249	.392	.321
Scor. Pos./2 Out			677	175	23	75	126	.258	.425	.339
Late-Inning Pressure			858	217	33	81	135	.253	.403	.318
Leading Off			215	55	13	19	34	.256	.470	.316
Runners On			372	91	12	36	65	.245	.376	.308
Runners/Scor. Pos.			187	51	7	23	36	.273	.439	.344
First 9 Batters			2937	753	76	306	528	.256	.381	.329
Second 9 Batters			1473	395	36	123	198	.268	.396	.328
All Batters Thereafter			1213	350	35	98	133	.289	.440	.343

MILWAUKEE BREWERS

Phil Garner will be one of five managers to open the 1992 season with no previous experience in the majors. Amid the perception that teams routinely select new managers from a stagnant pool composed of those who failed elsewhere, this is only the second time in the past 60 years that as many as five first timers will be in the dugouts on opening day. That group, all in the American League, includes Garner, Butch Hobson (Red Sox), Gene Lamont (White Sox), Bill Plummer (Mariners), and Buck Showalter (Yankees). The only managers hired during the offseason who previously worked in the majors were Jim Lefebvre (Cubs) and Jeff Torborg (Mets).

Actually, the trend toward a new breed of managers—if 10 hirings in less than a year does indeed constitute a trend—didn't start during the past off-season. Of the seven managers hired during the 1991 season, only two had previous experience in the majors: Jim Fregosi (Phillies) and Buck Rodgers (Angels). The other five were first-time major league managers: Jim Essian (Cubs), Mike Hargrove (Indians), Hal McRae (Royals), Johnny Oates (Orioles), and Tom Runnels (Expos).

The practice of choosing managers from a pool of retreads is almost universally criticized by fans and the media as proof of a baseball buddy network that effectively blocks qualified new applicants, including minority candidates, from gaining employment at the major league level. It's natural for fans to feel betrayed when their teams hire managers who failed in other cities (e.g., Don Zimmer by the Cubs in 1988 and John McNamara by the Indians in 1990). But think about it: What other job exists in which experience is considered a negative factor? Only in a profession where amateurs honestly believe they know as much as a professional could something like that happen. As a result, few fans place a tangible value on previous managerial experience—and that's a mistake.

From 1900 through 1991, nearly 400 managers were hired between seasons. Roughly half had managed previously in the majors, and they outperformed the first-time managers to a slight but statistically significant degree. The following table contrasts the performance of the two groups. Each manager was rated according to the difference between the number of games his team won and the number they were expected to win. (See the Atlanta Braves essay for more on this technique.) The column headed "Wins" indicates the average margin for each group, expressed in wins over a 162-game schedule. The columns headed by plus and minus signs show the number of managers who exceeded or fell short of their expected victory totals:

	Mgrs.	Wins	+	−
First Time in Majors	188	+0.02	89	99
Previous Experience	185	+0.92	105	80

On average, first timers had a negligible effect on their teams' records; those who had previously managed in the majors added an average of roughly one win per 162 games. The experienced managers were more likely to have had a positive effect; a majority of first timers had a negative effect. Roughly 60 percent of each group came within five wins of their expected totals. The table doesn't show that among those who *didn't* fall within five wins, experienced managers were far more likely to have had a positive effect (69%) than were the others (52%). Those margins might not seem substantial enough to draw any conclusions, but keep in mind that the effect of a manager on a team's record is usually small to begin with. And considering the number of managers included in the survey, you'd have only one chance in 67 of producing a margin that large if you divided them into two groups simply at random.

The next table classifies the performance of each manager hired during any off-season in this century according to how many times he had previously been hired. It's noteworthy that even for managers with prior experience at the major league level, the more experience the better:

Prev. Hired	Mgrs.	Wins	+	−
0	188	+0.02	89	99
1	101	+0.71	54	47
2	45	+1.08	27	18
3+	39	+1.27	24	15

Of course, Brewers fans aren't as concerned with their new manager's ability to add a few wins in 1992 as they are with the chance that he could eventually lead them to a division title or better. On that count as well, experienced managers have outperformed first timers by a small but significant margin: 43 of 185 with previous experience eventually won a title for that team (23%), compared to 30 of 188 with none (16%).

The surprising fact is that recycled managers have consistently outperformed inexperienced managers. Frank White, who is currently learning the trade in the Red Sox system, said prior to the season that taking a managerial position with a minor league team would allow him to see whether or not he would make a good manager. Exactly. So with a cadre of experienced professionals available, why would a general manager entrust his team—and with it, perhaps, his own job—to someone untrained and possibly unskilled in such a demanding position?

Although such a decision would seem to require quite an act of confidence (or loyalty), five GMs chose that route during the past off-season. In light of this sobering research, here's a list to cheer them up—the 16 managers who won titles in their first seasons in the majors: Clark Griffith (1901 White Sox), Hughie Jennings (1907 Tigers), Pat Moran (1915 Phillies), Kid Gleason (1919 White Sox—okay, bad example), Bucky Harris (1924 Senators), Joe Cronin (1933 Senators), Mickey Cochrane (1934 Tigers), Eddie Dyer (1946 Cardinals), Ralph Houk (1961 Yankees), Yogi Berra (1964 Yankees), Dick Williams (1967 Red Sox), Billy Martin (1969 Twins), Sparky Anderson (1970 Reds), Bill Virdon (1972 Pirates), Jimmy Frey (1980 Royals), and Hal Lanier (1986 Astros). And even though hiring a first-time manager is risky, what general manager wouldn't want credit as being the first to hire a Dick Williams or a Sparky Anderson?

* * *

We won't know for a while whether Garner will put bigger numbers under the "W" column than did his predecessor, Tom Trebelhorn. But it's almost certain that he'll put bigger ones under the columns headed "PH," "PR," and "DR," representing the team's totals for pinch hitters, pinch runners, and defensive replacements used. Last season, only one team made fewer in-game player changes than the Brewers (not including pitching changes). Oakland may have ended Milwaukee's streak of four consecutive seasons leading the American League in stolen bases. But the Brewers extended another streak to twice that length: For the eighth consecutive season, Milwaukee used fewer pinch hitters than any other team in the majors.

Team	PH	PR	DR	Total
Texas	239	54	160	453
Chicago	200	77	139	416
Kansas City	216	53	139	408
Minnesota	189	70	145	404
Seattle	207	51	133	391
Baltimore	209	57	107	373
Oakland	166	45	143	354
Toronto	150	42	103	295
Boston	114	42	117	273
Detroit	152	38	76	266
Cleveland	141	28	93	262
New York	139	24	84	247
Milwaukee	78	31	73	182
California	83	22	63	168

This seems like as good an opportunity as we'll get to put the topic of pinch-hitting under the microscope. Some of the numbers will merely confirm what you suspected; others may surprise you.

Let's start with one that we think will fall into the latter category. Did you know that pinch hitters were more common in the American League last season than they were 50 years ago, when the designated hitter was just a gleam in Joe Cronin's eye? Despite the inception of the DH rule nearly 20 years ago, pinch hitters still account for one of every 40 at-bats in the A.L., compared to one per 50 in 1941. That rate jumped to one per 43 ABs immediately after World War II, and increased steadily until the DH rule was adopted in 1973. The designated hitter caused an immediate reduction of 62 percent in the American League, from one pinch AB per 28 overall to one per 73 ABs, the lowest mark in either league since 1918. The number of players with at least 25 at-bats as a pinch hitter fell from 19 in 1972 to just one in 1973 (Winston Llenas). By the next season, more than one quarter of that reduction was restored, and the rate of A.L. pinch hitters resumed its increase until the mid-1980s. But the use of pinch hitters remains substantially lower in the A.L. than in the N.L. (43 percent lower in 1991), where they have accounted for a greater slice of the total pie in *every* season since 1946 than in *any* season prior to that.

On average, pinch hitters are older than other batters, a trend that cuts across both leagues, and one that has existed throughout most of this century:

	1900	1920	1940	1960	1970	1980	1990	1991
League Average	28.6	28.7	28.3	28.6	28.0	28.7	28.9	28.9
Pinch Hitters	27.4	27.7	29.2	29.9	28.3	29.3	29.3	29.5
Difference	−1.2	−1.0	+0.9	+1.3	+0.3	+0.6	+0.4	+0.6

Despite the apparent consistency of the figures for the past decade, the average age of "full-time" pinch hitters has fallen dramatically over the past few seasons. Players with 20 or more pinch ABs had an average age of 32.4 years in 1985, 31.6 in 1988, and 29.9 last season. Economics could be responsible, with teams reluctant to pay veteran players a million dollars or more for a couple dozen at-bats when younger players are available at considerably lower salaries. If so, a breakdown of pinch-hitting by age suggests this is a reasonable attitude: from 1987 to '91, pinch hitters below age 30 batted .225, while those above 30 hit .223.

Naturally, pinch hitters are much more likely to bat in key situations than are other players. With so many pinch-ABs coming in the late innings, it's not surprising that 57 percent occur in Late-Inning Pressure Situations, more than four times the rate of other at-bats (14%). They are also a little more likely to bat with the tying or lead run on base or at the plate than others (by a margin of 45.4% to 44.1%). And with managers able to spot their pinch hitters according to who's on the mound (that is, a left- or right-hander), PHs are far more likely to be batting with the platoon advantage (85%) than are other hitters (59%).

Even so, the major league batting average for pinch hitters last season was just .227—and that was the *highest* mark since 1987. It's obvious that such a low figure is attributable to the difficulties of batting as a pinch hitter: coming off the bench cold, often to bat against a team's top relief pitcher. Over the past four years, those same hitters who compiled a .222 pinch-batting average batted .255 in other at-bats. Still, it's worth noting that prior to 1988, a higher quality of pinch hitter was commonplace; from 1980 through 1987, pinch hitters batted .232 in that role, .263 in other at-bats. So while it's not true that veteran players who lost their jobs due to economic considerations outhit younger players in the role of pinch hitter, the roster spots they vacated may have forced some of the better younger players off the bench and into the starting lineup. The expanding waistlines of those veteran pinch hitters of the past (remember Smoky Burgess?) leads us to suggest that today's owners are being penny-wise and pound-foolish.

MINNESOTA TWINS

Prior to 1987, there had never been a World Series in which the home team won every game. But it's happened twice since then, and in both instances it was the Minnesota Twins who won the series by sweeping their four games at the Metrodome, with the result that Minnesota's accomplishments have been unfairly discredited or dismissed as the product of a freakish ballpark. The fact is that over the past two decades the home-field advantage has grown from negligible to nearly insurmountable in baseball's postseason—not only at the Metrodome, but everywhere.

From the inception of the World Series in 1903 through 1968, there were nearly 400 postseason games played. Home teams won only 11 more games than road teams—a margin of 196 to 185, which represents a difference of 29 percentage points. That was far lower than the regular-season spread for the same period (88 points). Although the margin has shrunk for regular-season games since 1969, it's grown enormously in postseason play:

Years	Regular-Season Games			Postseason Games		
	Home	Road	Diff.	Home	Road	Diff.
1900–68	.544	.456	.088	.514	.486	.029
1969–91	.540	.460	.079	.586	.414	.172

The increase since 1969 is even larger if only World Series games are considered. The home-field advantage for playoff games during that time (including the division championship series in 1981) was 111 points, higher than the regular-season rate but low compared to the 265-point margin in World Series play. Some of the increase can be explained by the rule adopted in 1986 that set up "house rules" on the DH; home teams have won 24 of 34 Series games since then. But they also had a 216-point advantage from 1969 through 1985.

It's not surprising that the single most successful home team in postseason play, the Minnesota Twins, has the greatest home-field advantage during the regular season as well. Minnesota has a .557 regular-season winning percentage (the seventh highest in the league) at the Metrodome in the 10 years since the stadium opened, but ranks next-to-last in the American League with a .410 mark on the road during the same period. That margin of 147 points is the largest in either league since 1982:

American	Home	Road	Diff.	National	Home	Road	Diff.
Minnesota	.557	.410	.147	Houston	.557	.437	.120
Kansas City	.580	.453	.127	Philadelphia	.540	.434	.106
Texas	.523	.411	.112	San Francisco	.547	.443	.104
Detroit	.581	.479	.102	New York	.587	.496	.091
New York	.566	.460	.106	Chicago	.528	.447	.081
Boston	.575	.476	.100	Los Angeles	.562	.488	.075
Oakland	.568	.473	.095	San Diego	.536	.461	.075
Cleveland	.485	.396	.089	St. Louis	.556	.489	.067
Milwaukee	.546	.460	.086	Pittsburgh	.517	.467	.050
Chicago	.546	.461	.085	Atlanta	.481	.436	.044
Seattle	.488	.413	.075	Montreal	.528	.484	.043
Toronto	.581	.519	.062	Cincinnati	.504	.473	.031
Baltimore	.513	.457	.056	League Avg.	.537	.463	.074
California	.532	.491	.041				
League Avg.	.546	.454	.092				

(The fact that Houston had the largest margin in the National League suggested that domed stadiums might produce a greater home-field advantage than outdoor fields do. But the Blue Jays have had little advantage since moving into the Skydome (.032), and Seattle ranks near the bottom of the American League playing in the Kingdome. Minnesota and Houston leading their leagues appears to be a coincidence—but an odd one, in that the Oilers (.316) and Vikings (.211) rank first and eighth among 28 NFL teams in home-field advantage over the past 10 years. But here, too, the full list of NFL teams also fails to support the "Dome Advantage Theory," despite the fact that the Seahawks rank seventh. The Colts and Saints rank among the bottom nine teams, and the Lions in the middle of the pack.)

But the home-field advantage in postseason has grown since 1969, nine points higher than the regular-season advantage for the period even excluding the 14–0 home record in the last two World Series involving the Twins. And frankly, a plausible explanation escapes us. The best we've come up with—and it hardly explains the *extent* to which the postseason home-field advantage has grown—is this: Throughout this century, the home-field advantage in a particular game is related to how closely the teams are matched. That makes sense intuitively: Whatever it is that causes a home-field advantage is more likely to affect the outcome of a one-run game than a 10-run laugher. Notice in the following table that home teams had a higher winning percentage in games between teams separated by fewer than five games in the standings than in games between less closely matched teams. At each level, the closer the teams are matched, the greater the home-field advantage:

Margin in Wins	0–5	5–10	10–15	15–Up
Home-Team Winning Pct.	.545	.542	.538	.537
Road-Team Winning Pct.	.455	.458	.462	.463
Home-Field Advantage	.089	.084	.076	.073

Postseason games presumably involve teams that, on the whole, are more evenly matched than a cross section of regular-season games would be. As a result, it's normal that the home-field advantage should be greater in postseason as well. And since the gap between the best teams and the rest of the pack is narrower now than at any other time in baseball history, the advantage should even have peaked in recent years. But even the figures above do little to explain the single most outstanding characteristic of the home-field advantage in postseason play: its enormity over the past 23 years.

Whatever its causes, the trend has certainly produced some bizarre trivia. Minnesota's predecessors, the Washington Senators, played in three World Series (1924, 1925, and 1933) and weren't much better on the road than the Twins. They lost both games played at the Polo Grounds in 1933, and lost the last three games played at Forbes Field in 1925. Combined with Minnesota's nine straight road losses (three apiece at Los Angeles in 1965, St. Louis in 1987, and Atlanta in 1991), the Senators/Twins franchise has a 14-game losing streak on the road in World Series play, nearly double the length of the second-longest such streak (8, by Brooklyn from 1916 to 1941). Although the Twins have won a pair of World Series titles, the last pitcher to earn the franchise a World Series victory on the road was Walter Johnson, who defeated the Pirates in Pittsburgh on October 7, 1925. But while compiling the longest road-game losing streak in Series history, Minnesota has equaled the longest home-game winning streak: 8, done only once before, by Lou Gehrig's Yankees from 1927 through 1936.

After more than a century of play, there isn't much that happens in baseball that's absolutely without precedent. Last season, the Twins and the Braves came close, as each rebounded from last-place finishes in 1990 to win league titles. But throughout September, it was widely reported that if either team won a division title, it would mark the first time *ever* that a team advanced from last place to first in one season. In fact, to say it was reported widely is a gross understatement—Minnesota's and Atlanta's twin achievements were almost universally reported as "first evers." That was also dead wrong. And as so often happens, the reason for all those journalistic errors had to do with the cavalier manner in which 19th-century baseball is portrayed in the media, and how the hard-earned deeds of its players and teams are often discounted, minimized, or—as in this case—flat-out ignored.

Here's a simple trivia question for you: How many games did Cy Young win? If your answer is 511 and not 246, you're acknowledging that the 19th century counts. Like it or not, major league baseball dates its origin from the year 1876, not 1900. Now it's true that in the early days some things were a little different. The number of balls and strikes that it took to earn a walk or a strikeout varied for a while, with the current combination of four and three not arrived at until 1889. Walks counted as at-bats in 1876 and as hits in 1887, and a foul ball didn't count as a strike until 1901 in the National League and 1903 in the American. And get this: Before 1887, batters were allowed to ask for a high or a low pitch.

But despite those differences, the game was called baseball, there were three outs to an inning, and nine innings to a game. There was one winning team and one loser in each game, and the teams were ranked in the standings from best record to worst. And even though the game is now different in some ways than it was in the 1800s, that's no disqualifier; it's also significantly different than it was in 1941. Or haven't you heard of free agency, artificial turf, the designated hitter, and African-American players? Despite those changes over the past half-century, most of the media spent nearly as much energy last season, it seemed, reporting the day-to-day facts of Joe DiMaggio's half-century-old 56-game hitting streak as they did on the 1991 season itself. History in that case wasn't ignored, it was glorified—disproportionately so, perhaps. Apparently, for some writers and editors whose job it is to maintain perspective and inform others, the statute of

limitations dates back no further than their own childhood baseball memories. *Cogito ergo baseball.*

Now about this last-to-first business. The National League began in 1876 and the American League was first recognized as a major league in 1901, but prior to 1900 there were also three other leagues that are recognized as major. One was the American Association, which operated from 1882 to 1891. And it was in the American Association that the Louisville team, known as the Colonels, finished last in 1889 and first in 1890.

The 1889 Louisville team wasn't just your ordinary last-place team; it was horrible—as in 27–111, for a .196 won-lost percentage. (Is there a Mendoza Line for teams?) But after the season, a third league was begun when the players in the National League and the American Association, at war with management (some things never change), started their own league, inventively called the Players League. There were defections from every team in the existing leagues, but Louisville wasn't hit as hard as many others, and the frogs of 1889 became the princes of 1890. The team was led, of course, by the redoubtable Chicken Wolf, who led the league in batting, and by pitcher Scott Stratton, who went from 3–13 to 34–14 in a year's time (and would have had one hell of an arbitration case in '91).

All of this was documented in *The Complete Baseball Record Book,* published by *The Sporting News,* right there on page 111. Not the 1891 edition, but the 1991 volume. You'd think that anyone looking in the book to find out the largest gain in a team's position from the previous season would have had to run across the entry for Louisville in 1890. But no, today's saturation coverage of baseball demands that every current performance be cited as a "first" or a "best" of some sort—even if that means sweeping under the rug an extraordinary but inconvenient piece of baseball history.

Was Minnesota's accomplishment diminished by the fact that the Twins were the second team to advance from last to first? Or that Atlanta was the third? Hardly; they still accomplished something that hadn't been done in 101 years—a pretty impressive little milestone. But the pursuit of "firsts" that so dominates today's sports reporting—whether it's finding a way to twist some mundane achievement into a unique one (no matter how pointless) or being the first with an exclusive revelation of some hot trade rumor that never comes to be—blinds us to those feats that are worth celebrating. It also destroys credibility. H. L. Mencken defined newspaper editing as the process of separating the wheat from the chaff and publishing the chaff. He'd feel right at home with much of today's sports reporting. Maybe it's time for us to put aside that obsession with what's first, and get back to pondering what's interesting—or at least true. And if the result is that Chicken Wolf's name comes to the attention of a new generation of fans, so much the better—even if there is no film of him to run at eleven (make that eleven-thirty).

WON-LOST RECORD BY STARTING POSITION

Minnesota Twins	C	1B	2B	3B	SS	LF	CF	RF	DH	P	Leadoff	Cleanup	Starts vs. LH	Starts vs. RH	Total Starts
Paul Abbott	-	-	-	-	-	-	-	-	-	1-2	-	-	1	2	1-2
Rick Aguilera	-	-	-	-	-	-	-	-	-	-	-	-	-	-	-
Allan Anderson	-	-	-	-	-	-	-	-	-	9-13	-	-	4	18	9-13
Willie Banks	-	-	-	-	-	-	-	-	-	2-1	-	-	2	1	2-1
Steve Bedrosian	-	-	-	-	-	-	-	-	-	-	-	-	-	-	-
Jarvis Brown	-	-	-	-	-	0-1	1-2	-	-	-	1-2	-	1	3	1-3
Randy Bush	-	2-2	-	-	-	1-3	-	11-13	4-2	-	2-3	-	-	38	18-20
Larry Casian	-	-	-	-	-	-	-	-	-	-	-	-	-	-	-
Carmen Castillo	-	-	-	-	-	-	-	1-0	0-1	-	-	-	2	-	1-1
Chili Davis	-	-	-	-	-	-	-	-	88-61	-	-	33-24	39	110	88-61
Tom Edens	-	-	-	-	-	-	-	-	-	3-3	-	-	-	6	3-3
Scott Erickson	-	-	-	-	-	-	-	-	-	23-9	-	-	8	24	23-9
Greg Gagne	-	-	-	80-47	-	-	-	-	-	-	6-5	-	37	90	80-47
Dan Gladden	-	-	-	-	68-42	-	-	-	-	-	67-40	-	30	80	68-42
Mark Guthrie	-	-	-	-	-	-	-	-	-	8-4	-	-	4	8	8-4
Brian Harper	64-50	-	-	-	-	-	-	1-0	-	-	-	0-1	30	85	65-50
Kent Hrbek	-	75-51	-	-	-	-	-	-	-	-	-	59-39	25	101	75-51
Chuck Knoblauch	-	-	84-57	-	-	-	-	-	-	-	7-14	-	37	104	84-57
Gene Larkin	-	16-8	-	-	-	-	-	25-15	1-1	-	3-1	-	23	43	42-24
Terry Leach	-	-	-	-	-	-	-	-	-	-	-	-	-	-	-
Scott Leius	-	-	-	27-19	2-4	-	-	-	-	-	4-1	-	42	10	29-23
Shane Mack	-	-	-	-	-	21-17	7-9	40-21	-	-	3-1	1-1	36	79	68-47
Jack Morris	-	-	-	-	-	-	-	-	-	20-15	-	-	9	26	20-15
Pedro Munoz	-	-	-	-	4-4	-	15-12	1-0	-	-	-	-	9	27	20-16
Denny Neagle	-	-	-	-	-	-	-	-	-	2-1	-	-	-	3	2-1
Al Newman	-	1-0	11-10	2-2	13-16	1-0	-	-	-	-	2-0	-	12	44	28-28
Junior Ortiz	26-15	-	-	-	-	-	-	-	-	-	-	-	11	30	26-15
Mike Pagliarulo	-	-	66-46	-	-	-	-	-	-	-	-	-	-	112	66-46
Kirby Puckett	-	-	-	-	-	87-56	3-6	-	-	-	-	1-1	41	111	90-62
Paul Sorrento	-	1-6	-	-	-	-	-	0-2	-	-	-	1-1	2	7	1-8
Kevin Tapani	-	-	-	-	-	-	-	-	-	20-14	-	-	9	25	20-14
Gary Wayne	-	-	-	-	-	-	-	-	-	-	-	-	-	-	-
Lenny Webster	5-2	-	-	-	-	-	-	-	-	-	-	-	1	6	5-2
David West	-	-	-	-	-	-	-	-	-	7-5	-	-	5	7	7-5
Carl Willis	-	-	-	-	-	-	-	-	-	-	-	-	-	-	-

TEAM TOTALS: BATTING

	AB	H	2B	3B	HR	RBI	BB	SO	BA	SA	OBA
Season	5556	1557	270	42	140	733	526	747	.280	.420	.344
vs. Left-Handers	1511	440	82	21	46	214	163	191	.291	.465	.359
vs. Right-Handers	4045	1117	188	21	94	519	363	556	.276	.403	.338
vs. Ground-Ballers	2498	701	113	22	67	332	226	334	.281	.424	.341
vs. Fly-Ballers	3058	856	157	20	73	401	300	413	.280	.416	.346
Home Games	2764	834	139	29	62	383	276	354	.302	.440	.366
Road Games	2792	723	131	13	78	350	250	393	.259	.399	.322
Grass Fields	2159	572	106	8	67	289	198	293	.265	.415	.329
Artificial Turf	3397	985	164	34	73	444	328	454	.290	.423	.354
April	656	172	25	7	16	77	71	93	.262	.395	.336
May	965	267	51	7	21	108	92	115	.277	.409	.340
June	962	268	45	5	31	137	83	120	.279	.432	.340
July	914	274	45	10	23	131	93	117	.300	.446	.363
August	1006	291	54	10	23	134	84	139	.289	.431	.347
Sept./Oct.	1053	285	50	3	26	146	103	163	.271	.398	.337
Leading Off Inn.	1316	355	56	8	30	30	110	156	.270	.393	.331
Runners On	2490	699	115	18	72	665	266	347	.281	.428	.348
Bases Empty	3066	858	155	24	68	68	260	400	.280	.413	.341
Runners/Scor. Pos.	1433	376	66	10	37	556	191	230	.262	.400	.343
Runners On/2 Out	1038	277	49	8	33	259	119	154	.267	.425	.345
Scor. Pos./2 Out	693	170	37	3	19	216	96	108	.245	.390	.340
Late-Inning Pressure	725	205	36	3	19	95	69	111	.283	.419	.349
Leading Off	176	48	10	0	4	4	16	29	.273	.398	.340
Runners On	322	97	13	2	9	85	33	44	.301	.438	.368
Runners/Scor. Pos.	189	57	9	1	6	75	26	32	.302	.455	.384

RUNS BATTED IN	From 1B	From 2B	From 3B	Scoring Position
Totals	121/1800	205/1095	267/628	472/1723
Percentage	6.7%	18.7%	42.5%	27.4%

TEAM TOTALS: PITCHING

	W-L	ERA	AB	H	HR	BB	SO	BA	SA	OBA
Season	95-67	3.69	5491	1402	139	488	876	.255	.392	.317
vs. Left-Handers			2360	630	44	219	322	.267	.386	.327
vs. Right-Handers			3131	772	95	269	554	.247	.397	.308
vs. Ground-Ballers			2454	639	45	182	340	.260	.374	.313
vs. Fly-Ballers			3037	763	94	306	536	.251	.407	.319
Home Games	51-30	3.90	2821	725	75	224	469	.257	.402	.313
Road Games	44-37	3.48	2670	677	64	264	407	.254	.382	.320
Grass Fields	35-27	3.50	2046	518	50	204	316	.253	.382	.320
Artificial Turf	60-40	3.81	3445	884	89	284	560	.257	.399	.314
April	9-11	3.98	676	184	14	73	99	.272	.399	.348
May	14-14	3.82	954	240	23	97	152	.252	.391	.319
June	22-6	2.81	949	237	21	64	133	.250	.365	.297
July	16-10	3.71	885	237	25	68	142	.268	.431	.321
August	17-12	4.52	987	245	34	89	154	.248	.397	.311
Sept./Oct.	17-14	3.42	1040	259	22	97	196	.249	.377	.313
Leading Off Inn.			1348	364	45	98	197	.270	.436	.323
Bases Empty			3184	837	81	257	527	.263	.403	.321
Runners On			2307	565	58	231	349	.245	.378	.310
Runners/Scor. Pos.			1319	310	30	172	233	.235	.357	.316
Runners On/2 Out			1011	238	26	115	172	.235	.365	.315
Scor. Pos./2 Out			664	154	15	93	120	.232	.346	.328
Late-Inning Pressure			807	194	17	76	139	.240	.359	.309
Leading Off			205	48	4	18	28	.234	.351	.302
Runners On			322	77	8	39	52	.239	.366	.318
Runners/Scor. Pos.			175	44	4	29	31	.251	.377	.351
First 9 Batters			2743	675	63	254	473	.246	.369	.310
Second 9 Batters			1475	398	42	122	205	.270	.422	.327
All Batters Thereafter			1273	329	34	112	198	.258	.408	.319

WON-LOST RECORD BY STARTING POSITION

New York Yankees	C	1B	2B	3B	SS	LF	CF	RF	DH	P	Leadoff	Cleanup	Starts vs. LH	Starts vs. RH	Total Starts
Jesse Barfield	-	-	-	-	-	-	-	40-36	-	-	-	6-2	28	48	40-36
Mike Blowers	-	-	-	3-7	-	-	-	-	-	-	-	-	4	6	3-7
Greg Cadaret	-	-	-	-	-	-	-	-	-	3-2	-	-	2	3	3-2
Chuck Cary	-	-	-	-	-	-	-	-	-	3-6	-	-	1	8	3-6
Darrin Chapin	-	-	-	-	-	-	-	-	-	-	-	-	-	-	-
Dave Eiland	-	-	-	-	-	-	-	-	-	4-9	-	-	3	10	4-9
Alvaro Espinoza	-	-	-	0-2	59-77	-	-	-	-	-	-	-	47	91	59-79
Steve Farr	-	-	-	-	-	-	-	-	-	-	-	-	-	-	-
Bob Geren	21-21	-	-	-	-	-	-	-	-	-	-	-	40	2	21-21
Lee Guetterman	-	-	-	-	-	-	-	-	-	-	-	-	-	-	-
John Habyan	-	-	-	-	-	-	-	-	-	-	-	-	-	-	-
Mel Hall	-	-	-	-	-	30-26	-	19-38	5-5	-	-	26-45	27	96	54-69
Andy Hawkins	-	-	-	-	-	-	-	-	-	0-3	-	-	2	1	0-3
Steve Howe	-	-	-	-	-	-	-	-	-	-	-	-	-	-	-
Mike Humphreys	-	-	0-4	-	-	1-1	-	1-1	2-0	-	-	-	8	2	4-6
Jeff Johnson	-	-	-	-	-	-	-	-	-	10-13	-	-	9	14	10-13
Scott Kamieniecki	-	-	-	-	-	-	-	-	-	5-4	-	-	6	3	5-4
Pat Kelly	-	-	6-8	37-40	-	-	-	-	-	-	-	-	33	58	43-48
Roberto Kelly	-	-	-	-	-	20-32	36-36	-	-	-	19-21	9-7	42	82	56-68
Tim Leary	-	-	-	-	-	-	-	-	-	9-9	-	-	5	13	9-9
Jim Leyritz	2-1	-	-	9-7	-	-	-	-	-	0-1	-	-	8	12	11-9
Torey Lovullo	-	-	6-9	-	-	-	-	-	-	-	-	-	2	13	6-9
Scott Lusader	-	-	-	-	-	0-1	-	-	-	-	0-1	-	-	1	0-1
Kevin Maas	-	14-21	-	-	-	-	-	-	43-60	-	-	26-31	33	105	57-81
Don Mattingly	-	55-69	-	-	-	-	-	-	9-13	-	-	-	47	99	64-82
Hensley Meulens	-	2-1	-	-	-	20-31	-	5-6	7-6	-	-	2-1	55	23	34-44
Alan Mills	-	-	-	-	-	-	-	-	-	0-2	-	-	-	2	0-2
Rich Monteleone	-	-	-	-	-	-	-	-	-	-	-	-	-	-	-
Matt Nokes	45-67	-	-	-	-	-	-	-	1-2	-	-	2-5	9	106	46-69
Pascual Perez	-	-	-	-	-	-	-	-	-	9-5	-	-	6	8	9-5
Eric Plunk	-	-	-	-	-	-	-	-	-	1-7	-	-	3	5	1-7
John Ramos	3-2	-	-	-	-	-	-	-	3-0	-	-	-	6	2	6-2
Carlos Rodriguez	-	-	-	5-4	-	-	-	-	-	-	-	-	1	8	5-4
Scott Sanderson	-	-	-	-	-	-	-	-	-	19-15	-	-	9	25	19-15
Steve Sax	-	-	65-83	3-2	-	-	-	-	1-3	-	33-34	-	55	102	69-88
Pat Sheridan	-	-	-	-	-	0-1	2-2	6-10	0-1	-	0-1	-	-	22	8-14
Wade Taylor	-	-	-	-	-	-	-	-	-	7-15	-	-	8	14	7-15
Randy Velarde	-	-	13-20	7-10	-	-	-	-	-	-	-	-	20	30	20-30
Bernie Williams	-	-	-	-	-	-	33-52	-	-	-	19-34	-	30	55	33-52
Mike Witt	-	-	-	-	-	-	-	-	-	1-1	-	-	1	1	1-1

TEAM TOTALS: BATTING

	AB	H	2B	3B	HR	RBI	BB	SO	BA	SA	OBA
Season	5541	1418	249	19	147	630	473	861	.256	.387	.316
vs. Left-Handers	2002	542	89	3	61	257	189	289	.271	.410	.336
vs. Right-Handers	3539	876	160	16	86	373	284	572	.248	.375	.305
vs. Ground-Ballers	2579	631	110	9	52	274	224	381	.245	.355	.308
vs. Fly-Ballers	2962	787	139	10	95	356	249	480	.266	.416	.324
Home Games	2685	692	129	7	82	333	242	394	.258	.403	.320
Road Games	2856	726	120	12	65	297	231	467	.254	.373	.313
Grass Fields	4687	1193	211	13	128	548	414	715	.255	.387	.317
Artificial Turf	854	225	38	6	19	82	59	146	.263	.389	.314
April	574	146	21	3	13	75	79	96	.254	.369	.342
May	927	222	46	1	35	102	80	169	.239	.405	.304
June	967	264	38	2	30	119	55	143	.273	.410	.314
July	868	221	44	2	26	101	79	138	.255	.400	.320
August	1044	275	44	7	20	126	88	154	.263	.376	.323
Sept./Oct.	1161	290	56	4	23	107	92	159	.250	.364	.305
Leading Off Inn.	1363	360	57	3	37	37	94	191	.264	.392	.313
Runners On	2326	600	115	5	60	543	230	362	.258	.389	.324
Bases Empty	3215	818	134	14	87	87	243	499	.254	.386	.310
Runners/Scor. Pos.	1296	333	66	3	33	470	159	211	.257	.389	.334
Runners On/2 Out	995	247	59	3	32	236	112	168	.248	.410	.332
Scor. Pos./2 Out	644	152	36	3	18	199	82	114	.236	.385	.330
Late-Inning Pressure	826	198	29	1	26	95	80	150	.240	.372	.310
Leading Off	204	49	4	0	6	6	20	34	.240	.348	.308
Runners On	334	82	14	0	10	79	39	66	.246	.377	.327
Runners/Scor. Pos.	182	46	11	0	6	69	29	40	.253	.412	.356

RUNS BATTED IN	From 1B	From 2B	From 3B	Scoring Position
Totals	84/1696	177/1017	222/559	399/1576
Percentage	5.0%	17.4%	39.7%	25.3%

TEAM TOTALS: PITCHING

	W-L	ERA	AB	H	HR	BB	SO	BA	SA	OBA
Season	71-91	4.42	5574	1510	152	506	936	.271	.421	.334
vs. Left-Handers			2300	625	65	220	363	.272	.427	.337
vs. Right-Handers			3274	885	87	286	573	.270	.417	.332
vs. Ground-Ballers			2574	683	38	198	386	.265	.381	.321
vs. Fly-Ballers			3000	827	114	308	550	.276	.455	.345
Home Games	39-42	4.31	2831	761	84	243	466	.269	.415	.329
Road Games	32-49	4.53	2743	749	68	263	470	.273	.427	.339
Grass Fields	64-74	4.36	4749	1271	133	442	797	.268	.417	.332
Artificial Turf	7-17	4.80	825	239	19	64	139	.290	.445	.344
April	6-11	5.13	585	162	16	62	102	.277	.424	.348
May	14-13	3.49	920	227	20	102	139	.247	.383	.323
June	13-14	4.25	937	255	22	65	153	.272	.403	.320
July	13-13	4.36	890	250	24	63	142	.281	.419	.333
August	12-19	5.50	1077	300	42	102	215	.279	.481	.346
Sept./Oct.	13-21	4.01	1165	316	28	112	185	.271	.409	.337
Leading Off Inn.			1325	350	35	111	211	.264	.415	.326
Bases Empty			3141	841	76	248	520	.268	.409	.326
Runners On			2433	669	76	258	416	.275	.436	.344
Runners/Scor. Pos.			1414	396	41	179	262	.280	.442	.357
Runners On/2 Out			1010	263	25	133	174	.260	.401	.350
Scor. Pos./2 Out			661	177	15	103	118	.268	.408	.371
Late-Inning Pressure			724	182	13	63	142	.251	.347	.316
Leading Off			182	45	2	12	38	.247	.335	.301
Runners On			298	69	5	34	62	.232	.315	.313
Runners/Scor. Pos.			160	35	3	21	40	.219	.313	.310
First 9 Batters			3107	816	67	280	576	.263	.392	.326
Second 9 Batters			1510	423	46	134	231	.280	.434	.341
All Batters Thereafter			957	271	39	92	129	.283	.492	.349

NEW YORK YANKEES

The New York Yankees and Baltimore Orioles provided a graphic illustration last season that even in an era when relief pitching seems more important than ever before, the quality of a team's bullpen is still far less important than that of its starting rotation.

For most of the 1991 season, New York's bullpen was one of the team's bright spots. Steve Farr was unhittable during the middle months of the season, pitching 27 consecutive scoreless innings from May 29 through August 4 (the longest streak in the majors by a relief pitcher last season). Steve Howe was equally tough in his set-up role, holding his ERA below 1.00 through the end of June and compiling a 1.68 mark for the season—the third lowest in team history among pitchers with at least Howe's number of appearances (37). Left-handers Greg Cadaret and Lee Guetterman filled the middle relief roles, complementing John Habyan and Eric Plunk.

At its height, New York had the best bullpen in baseball, allowing only 38 earned runs over a 48-game period from May 26 through July 21 for a 2.12 ERA, and winning 10 of 12 decisions during that time. Although the success of New York's pen might have surprised even the Yankees themselves, it shouldn't have. Many of the Yankees' relievers had career-long patterns of success pitching in relief, despite reputations as journeyman earned by their failures as starters:

Pitcher	As a Starter			In Relief		
	W	L	ERA	W	L	ERA
Greg Cadaret	8	9	4.87	21	10	3.41
Steve Farr	10	11	3.77	32	29	3.06
Lee Guetterman	10	8	4.86	21	18	3.77
John Habyan	3	10	5.68	10	2	2.70
Eric Plunk	9	16	4.99	22	13	3.54
Totals	40	54	4.78	106	72	3.34

Now, contrast the success of New York's bullpen with the failure of its starting rotation. From May 4 through the All-Star break, the Yankees set an all-time record with 59 consecutive incomplete games. Following the complete game by Scott Sanderson on July 11 that broke the streak, New York began a new streak of 83 games without a CG to finish the season and break their own mark. The Yankees' total of three complete games for the season was, of course, an all-time low. The ultimate pathetic statement of the failure of New York's rotation: Yankees starters earned victories in the first two games after the All-Star break, and never won two in a row again.

Four different Yankees pitchers compiled ERAs above 5.00 but still started at least 10 games: Dave Eiland (5.33), Jeff Johnson (5.95), Tim Leary (6.49), and Wade Taylor (6.27). When Johnson's ERA improved to that final mark in his last start, the Yankees avoided becoming the only team in American League history with three pitchers at 6.00 or higher (minimum: 15 GS). But Leary, Taylor, and Johnson did manage to compile the three highest ERAs in franchise history among pitchers with at least 15 starts—*all in the same year.* The top 10:

Year	Pitcher	ERA	Year	Pitcher	ERA
1991	Tim Leary	6.49	1921	Rip Collins	5.45
1991	Wade Taylor	6.27	1990	Andy Hawkins	5.37
1991	Jeff Johnson	5.95	1979	Catfish Hunter	5.31
1989	Dave LaPoint	5.62	1937	Bump Hadley	5.31
1962	Rollie Sheldon	5.49	1930	Roy Sherid	5.23

From mid-June until mid-August, the Yankees' bullpen maintained an ERA more than two runs better than their rotation. It wasn't until the final day of August that the margin closed to below 1.77 runs per nine innings—which had been the largest gap in major league history prior to last season, established by the 1987 Cincinnati Reds. (By that time, the margin between Baltimore's relievers and starters had grown to 1.84, a level the Orioles maintained to the end of the season to establish a new all-time high.) But a look at the records of teams whose bullpens far outshone their rotations proves the point that a good bullpen won't help much without a foundation of a solid starting rotation. Among the teams with a spread of at least a run and a half per nine innings since 1900, only one had a winning record; the composite winning percentage was .454, representing a record of 74–88:

Year	Team	SP	RP	Diff.	W	L	Pct.
1991	Baltimore Orioles	5.29	3.45	1.84	67	95	.414
1987	Cincinnati Reds	4.87	3.10	1.77	84	78	.519
1983	New York Mets	4.25	2.50	1.75	68	94	.420
1990	Detroit Tigers	5.00	3.26	1.74	79	83	.488
1991	New York Yankees	5.07	3.41	1.66	71	91	.438
1984	Cleveland Indians	4.84	3.21	1.62	75	87	.463
1960	Cincinnati Reds	4.48	2.94	1.53	67	87	.435

Incidentally, teams whose starters had ERAs at least 1.50 lower than their relievers, although more successful than the teams listed above, fared poorly as well. The composite winning percentage of 32 such teams in this century was just .470. And it's noteworthy that only one of those teams played in the last 30 years: the 1980 Oakland Athletics (83–79). Apparently, few teams are willing to let their bullpens deteriorate to a degree that was somewhat common prior to 1950. And with so many capable pitchers being rerouted from the rotation to the bullpen even at the minor league level, it's getting harder and harder for those teams to find five able-armed starters. Ironically, it appears the cure may be worse than the disease.

For many years during the great Yankees dynasty, nothing characterized the team's power more than the strength of its lineup from the left side of the plate. From Ruth and Gehrig to Mantle and Maris (and beyond), the Yankees offense has traditionally been fueled by left-handed home-run hitters. In fact, only two of the top 13 home-run hitters in franchise history batted from the right side only: Joe DiMaggio and Dave Winfield. Of the other 11, 10 were left-handers; Mantle was the sole switch-hitter. (Time out for trivia: When Torey Lovullo was sent to the minors during the opening week of the 1991 season, it left the Yankees without a switch-hitter for the first time since Mantle joined the team 40 years earlier.)

An amazing streak: Left-handed hitters have produced at least 50 home runs for the Yankees in every season since Babe Ruth joined the team in 1920, with the exception of 1944—when they fell just one homer short despite the loss of Charlie Keller and Tommy Henrich to military service. If that streak doesn't astound you, it should; only two other teams—Detroit and Pittsburgh—have current streaks *even five years long.* And neither of those streaks is as long as 10 years. But the Yankees have hit at least 50 left-handed home runs in each of the past 47 years; for want of a single home run in 1944, the streak would be 72 years.

Of course, no one will mistake last season's Yankees for the 1927 edition. But even in 1991, New York's lineup continued to reflect an emphasis on left-handed power. Last season, four of its top five in RBIs batted left-handed: Mel Hall, Matt Nokes, Don Mattingly, and Maas. Roberto Kelly was the lone right-handed hitter in that group. That fact not only underlines the team's cultivation of a lineup dominated by left-side power, but also reflects the effect of its home ballpark.

Yankee Stadium was long considered among the best home-run parks in baseball for lefties, although that reputation has faded since the field was reconstructed in the mid-1970s. But as we pointed out in last year's *Analyst*, the "new" stadium is actually far more conducive to home runs for left-handers than the old place was. Data from the 1961 season indicated that Yankee Stadium's reputation as a great left-handed hitters' park was based more on its detrimental effect on right-handers than on its benefits to lefties. We estimated that the stadium's effect on home runs by left-handers was negligible.

But since its reconfiguration, the Stadium has become the home-run haven for left-handers that the old Stadium was incorrectly perceived to have been. Over the past three seasons, Yankee Stadium has increased home runs for left-handed hitters by approximately 48 percent, compared to a 5 percent decrease for right-handers.

But the question remains as to whether or not the team's home-field advantage, even in its strongly skewed ballpark, is significantly affected by filling the lineup with left-handed hitters. Last season marked the tenth time in 16 years since the reconstruction of the Stadium that left-handed hitters drove in more runs than right-handers for the Yankees. We decided to take a look at these differing seasons to see if a left-handed imbalance led to an offensive edge at home. The following table contrasts the team's home- and road-game scoring averages depending on whether left-handed or right-handed hitters had a majority of the team's RBIs. Per-game scoring averages:

	Home	Road	Diff.
Left-Handed Seasons	4.66	4.79	−2.8%
Right-Handed Seasons	4.50	4.35	+3.4%

The surprising fact is that Yankees lineups skewed toward right-handed hitters have produced a greater home-field advantage than teams dominated by left-handed hitters—at least since 1976, when the reconfiguration of Yankee Stadium actually increased the edge it provided for left-handed hitters. But from 1923, when the Stadium opened, through 1974, when it was closed for renovation, the ballpark's general bias against scoring was lessened when the team had a predominantly left-handed lineup:

	Home	Road	Diff.
Left-Handed Seasons	5.02	5.20	−3.5%
Right-Handed Seasons	4.79	5.19	−7.8%

A confusing issue, for sure: The original configuration apparently penalized right-handed hitters to such an extent that it provided even more reason for the Yankees to load their lineup with left-handers than the new shape provides with its enticing right-field seats. But the fact is that neither period demonstrates a *pronounced* advantage for teams with greater left-side strength. Amazing as it may seem in our statistics-obsessed age, it appears that even a home ballpark that boosts home runs by nearly 50 percent for left-handed batters may not justify lineup decisions made on that basis alone.

OAKLAND ATHLETICS

There is no shortage of cover boys for spring speculation about the Oakland Athletics' chances of regaining the top spot in the American League West.

There's Mark McGwire: Can he stop his transformation into Dave Kingman?

There's Jose Canseco: Can he ignore abusive fans, angry card-show promoters, and jealous music performance artists to keep tormenting American League pitchers?

There's Rickey Henderson: Has the green kryptonite of salary envy robbed the man of steal's superhuman powers?

There's Carney Lansford: Was the man who wasn't there, famed for his "Contentment Stinks/Stay Focused" T-shirts, the difference between a division champ and an also-ran?

Forget them all. Those are nice stories, especially for writers who need to file every day throughout spring training, but none will determine the fate of the A's in 1992. The one question that really matters for the A's this season is whether Dave Stewart can rebound to the 20-win form of his previous four seasons after last year's 11–11, 5.18 debacle. The A's front office has, by all indications, already cast its vote: They're banking on Stewart's comeback.

Starting pitchers of all stripes changed teams last winter, from Bret Saberhagen, Jack Morris, and Frank Viola to Ken Hill and the A's old buddy Storm Davis. But the Athletics watched from the sidelines as if they didn't need the help. They couldn't have missed their staff's 13th-place finish in the league ERA rankings, with a 4.57 mark just 0.02 better than the last-place Orioles. Moreover, since the A's play their home games in the best pitcher's park in baseball, the staff was even worse than the raw numbers show. In road games only, Oakland had by far the highest ERA in the majors (5.13).

The A's had only one starter with a winning record last season, Mike Moore at 17–8 with a 2.96 ERA. He was 13–15, 4.65 in 1990, and has never put together back-to-back winning seasons at any level of professional baseball. The next-best ERA among Oakland starters last year belonged to latecomer Ron Darling at 4.08. He went 3–7 in 12 starts, and has been resigned for 1992 to fill the fourth spot in the rotation. Bob Welch and a mystery guest (Reggie Harris? Joe Slusarski? Kirk Dressendorfer? Blue Moon Odom?) will round out the rotation. Clearly, Stewart is the choice for ace of this group.

But rather than supplement the rotation with some reliable veteran help for 1992, when the A.L. West again figures to be a strong, closely-contested division, the A's have chosen to rely on Stewart, who had the highest ERA among 162-inning qualifiers in 1991. That's bold, even for a team on which such a designation might be seen as encouragement, considering that Dennis Eckersley posted a major league high ERA of 5.61 in 1983. The off-season line, about Stewart in particular and the A's in general, is they were embarrassed in 1991, and that last season's kick in the pride will spur them to recapture their championship form in 1992.

The reality is that Stewart will be 35 years old when the 1992 season begins. Since 1969, only four other pitchers 33 or older had ERAs over 5.00 in 30-plus starts:

| Year | Age | Pitcher | W–L | ERA | —Next Season— | | | After | |
					GS	W–L	ERA	Yrs	Wins
1980	34	Mike Torrez	9–16	5.09	22	10–3	3.69	3	20
1982	36	Mike Torrez	9–9	5.23	34	10–17	4.37	1	1
1986	41	Steve Carlton	9–14	5.10	21	6–14	5.74	1	0
1987	33	Bob Knepper	8–17	5.27	27	14–5	3.14	2	10
1988	37	Bert Blyleven	10–17	5.43	33	17–5	2.73	1	8

Those numbers are somewhat encouraging for Stewart in 1992, although short of the victory total the A's are hoping for. Stewart managed a better won-lost record than most of those listed above, but his other statistics made him one of the boys. These guys' mothers couldn't tell 'em apart:

Year	Pitcher	GS	CG	SHO	IP	H	HR	BB	SO
1991	Dave Stewart	35	2	1	226.0	245	24	105	144
1980	Mike Torrez	32	6	1	207.1	256	18	75	97
1982	Mike Torrez	31	1	0	175.2	196	20	74	84
1986	Steve Carlton	32	0	0	176.1	196	25	86	120
1987	Bob Knepper	31	1	0	177.2	226	26	54	76
1988	Bert Blyleven	33	7	0	207.1	240	21	51	145

Of course, the fact that three of the pitchers bounced back for strong seasons immediately following their breakdowns avoids the obvious and most troublesome aspect of Stewart's inclusion in this group—namely, the unmistakable suggestion that 1992 will be the best of the very few seasons remaining in his career. (Even a strong Blyleven comeback in 1992, however unlikely, wouldn't upset the trend.) Notice in the first of the two tables above that none of the pitchers won more than 20 games over the rest of their careers beyond that first comeback season. No matter how much optimism the A's have about their arms on the farm, it can't be comforting to see the clock nearing the two-minute warning on Stew.

A total of 411 pitchers earned their 100th victories in this century; Stewart is one of 169 not to reach that plateau until after their 32d birthdays. Among those late bloomers, only 18 had a 20-win season thereafter. Stewart, who notched number 100 in 1989 and won 22 games in 1990, is among that elite group that includes only four who had more than one 20-win season past that point: Ron Guidry, Jerry Koosman, Phil Niekro, and Luis Tiant. Guidry and Tiant had their last 20-win seasons at 35, Koosman at 36, and Niekro at 40.

That would be wonderfully impressive company for Stewart to join. However, neither Guidry, Koosman, or Tiant ever had a season at any point in their careers as bad as Stewart's 1991 season (Kooz went 3–15 in 1978, but with a 3.75 ERA), let alone one that's supposed to be a prelude to a strong comeback. Niekro's only horrid year was his last, when he went 7–13 with an ERA above six at the age of 48.

Moreover, none of the other 168 late bloomers had more than four 20-win seasons in their careers, and Stewart has already reached that total. The others with four were Mike Cuellar, Johnny Sain, Urban Shocker, and Tiant. Cuellar's career offers some hope for Stewart in that he won 22 games at age 37 in 1974;

of all the pitchers cited here, Cuellar is perhaps the one whose career most closely parallels Stewart's. But it's also true that throughout his prime, Cuellar never had an off year; after joining the dominant Orioles in 1969, he won at least 18 games every season until 1975, when he went 14–12. The next season he collapsed to 4–13, and for practical purposes that was it.

So all things considered, the odds are against Stewart recording another 20-win season. That doesn't mean he won't give the A's another respectable year and can't be part of another division-winning pitching staff, but expecting more, as the A's clearly are, is probably wishful thinking.

But Stewart supporters can offer a host of reasons why their man will defy the odds. For one thing, he had his left knee arthroscopically repaired over the winter. But most of the confidence that Stewart inspires among his teammates and fans stems from his personality.

From inauspicious beginnings, Stewart grew into an almost ideal athletic hero during the late 1980s. His success grew from a combination of extraordinary talent and exceptional competitiveness. Stewart was notably ingracious after the A's improbable 1990 World Series loss at the hands of the Reds. Holistic baseball believers might contend Stewart's 1991 season was punishment for his impertinence, and for his complaints about being passed over for the Cy Young Award during that string of four 20-win seasons. However, those statements simply reflected the competitive drive that makes Stewart a winner. He is Mr. Death Stare and once threw a karate kick at an opposing manager charging the mound in a brawl. Stay out of his office while he's working.

That competitive fire and his spectacular performance between the lines are leavened with good works off the field, especially in his hometown of Oakland. In an era when professional athletic contracts (and even the college athletic contracts known as scholarships) are seemingly issued with licenses for petulance and selfishness, Stewart offers a refreshing contrast.

It may strain credulity to think that major decisions in the multibillion dollar baseball industry are made on the basis of personality rather than performance, but it's true. Just ask dour Danny Tartabull, who watched from the free-agent sidelines as bubbly Bobby Bonilla collected the first installments of his 29-million-dollar contract. (Or ask Al Rosen.) The bottom-line suits who run the business end of the game understand that players like Stewart and Bonilla gain added value from a positive image, even if that leads baseball people to make decisions with their hearts, not their heads.

Still, it is curious that a team with one last shot at maintaining its dynasty would fail to hedge its bets on Stewart, especially with the leading contenders adding significant newcomers (Kevin Mitchell in Seattle, Kirk McCaskill in Chicago). In the amorphous concept of team chemistry, a player like Stewart is considered a master chemist. Considering his 1991 performance, the A's better hope he's an alchemist as well.

Who's the active player most likely to reach 500 home runs? It's a tough question; no one under the age of 35 at the end of the 1991 season had reached even the 300 mark, directing most of our attention to the younger players. Although he'll be only 22 on opening day 1992, Ken Griffey, Jr., already has more home runs

(60) than any other player under the age of 26. Ruben Sierra leads the 26-year-olds (139), and 27-year-old Jose Canseco leads all players 30 and under with a total of 209.

But odds are that if we'd asked that question a few years ago, Mark McGwire would have been among the favorites—quite possibly the leading vote getter based on the publicity generated in 1987 when he hit 49, breaking Wally Berger's 57-year-old mark for homers by a rookie (which Frank Robinson tied in 1956). But as we suggested earlier, McGwire's career has taken an unexpected southbound turn onto the Dave Kingman Memorial Off-Ramp. Compare his 1991 and career statistics to those of Kingman in 1977 and through that point (Kingman was 10 months older then than McGwire was last season):

| Player | Most Recent Season | | | | | | Career-to-Date Totals | | | | | |
	BA	2B	3B	HR	RBI	SO	BA	2B	3B	HR	RBI	SO
McGwire	.201	22	0	22	75	116	.244	106	5	178	504	592
Kingman	.221	20	0	26	78	143	.227	111	11	176	469	853

We used our projection model to evaluate the chance of each active player to reach the 500-HR mark, and the answer was loud and clear. By a wide margin, the most likely player to do so is Jose Canseco; he's the only active player odds-on to reach that plateau. And a look back at comparable figures over the past few years indicates that even though Canseco had hit 37 and 42 home runs in his two previous full seasons, his 44 home runs in 1991 was a watershed event, nearly doubling the estimate of his shot at 500 homers. In fact, the following graph shows that until last season, Canseco and McGwire had run neck-and-neck, with nearly identical chances for reaching the 500 level:

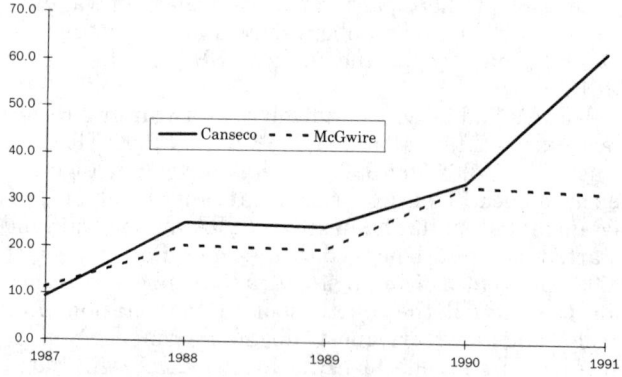

Despite a tapering off of his career trajectory, McGwire still ranks among the players most likely to reach the 500 mark. The only player other than Canseco with a better shot is Darryl Strawberry (38%). The others with at least a 10 percent chance are Howard Johnson (20%), Eddie Murray (17%), Fred McGriff (15%), Barry Bonds (14%), Ken Griffey, Jr. (13%), and Juan Gonzalez (13%).

Where are Cecil Fielder, David Justice, Matt Williams, Danny Tartabull, Ron Gant, and Kevin Mitchell? They are the next-most likely group to reach 500, but their chances aren't all that good. Think of them as "the field;" all together, for better or worse, we estimate the chance to be less than 40 percent that even one of them will overinflate his rookie card's value by hitting 500 homers.

WON-LOST RECORD BY STARTING POSITION

Oakland Athletics	C	1B	2B	3B	SS	LF	CF	RF	DH	P	Leadoff	Cleanup	Starts vs. LH	Starts vs. RH	Total Starts
Troy Afenir	1-2	-	-	-	-	-	-	-	-	-	-	-	-	3	1-2
Dana Allison	-	-	-	-	-	-	-	-	-	-	-	-	-	-	-
Harold Baines	-	-	-	-	-	1-0	-	4-3	61-61	-	-	59-60	13	117	66-64
Lance Blankenship	-	-	13-15	5-4	-	2-5	-	1-1	0-1	-	3-4	-	17	30	21-26
Mike Bordick	-	-	0-1	-	42-40	-	-	-	-	-	-	-	22	61	42-41
John Briscoe	-	-	-	-	-	-	-	-	-	-	-	-	-	-	-
Scott Brosius	-	-	-	2-5	-	2-0	-	6-2	0-1	-	2-0	-	7	11	10-8
Todd Burns	-	-	-	-	-	-	-	-	-	-	-	-	-	-	-
Kevin Campbell	-	-	-	-	-	-	-	-	-	-	-	-	-	-	-
Jose Canseco	-	-	-	-	-	-	-	62-63	15-8	-	-	-	41	107	77-71
Steve Chitren	-	-	-	-	-	-	-	-	-	-	-	-	-	-	-
Ron Darling	-	-	-	-	-	-	-	-	-	4-8	-	-	5	7	4-8
Kirk Dressendorfer	-	-	-	-	-	-	-	-	-	4-3	-	-	1	6	4-3
Dennis Eckersley	-	-	-	-	-	-	-	-	-	-	-	-	-	-	-
Mike Gallego	-	-	69-57	-	11-15	-	-	-	-	-	1-2	-	41	111	80-72
Johnny Guzman	-	-	-	-	-	-	-	-	-	-	-	-	-	-	-
Reggie Harris	-	-	-	-	-	-	-	-	-	-	-	-	-	-	-
Andy Hawkins	-	-	-	-	-	-	-	-	-	8-6	-	-	4	10	8-6
Scott Hemond	1-1	-	2-1	0-1	-	-	-	-	-	-	-	-	3	3	3-3
Dave Henderson	-	-	-	-	-	1-2	71-64	-	2-2	-	-	11-6	42	100	74-68
Rickey Henderson	-	-	-	-	-	59-59	-	-	5-3	-	64-62	-	33	93	64-62
Rick Honeycutt	-	-	-	-	-	-	-	-	-	-	-	-	-	-	-
Dann Howitt	-	0-1	-	-	-	1-1	2-0	1-2	-	-	-	-	-	8	4-4
Brook Jacoby	-	1-1	-	27-20	-	-	-	-	-	-	-	-	16	33	28-21
Doug Jennings	-	-	-	-	-	0-1	-	-	-	-	-	-	-	1	0-1
Joe Klink	-	-	-	-	-	-	-	-	-	-	-	-	-	-	-
Brad Komminsk	-	-	-	-	-	1-1	1-1	2-1	-	-	-	-	5	2	4-3
Carney Lansford	-	-	2-1	-	-	-	-	-	0-1	-	-	-	2	2	2-2
Vance Law	-	-	-	15-21	0-1	-	-	-	-	-	-	-	17	20	15-22
Fred Manrique	-	-	0-1	-	4-2	-	-	-	-	-	1-0	-	4	3	4-3
Mark McGwire	-	74-68	-	-	-	-	-	-	-	-	-	2-5	42	100	74-68
Mike Moore	-	-	-	-	-	-	-	-	-	19-14	-	-	7	26	19-14
Gene Nelson	-	-	-	-	-	-	-	-	-	-	-	-	-	-	-
Jamie Quirk	27-22	3-2	-	-	-	-	-	-	-	-	-	0-1	2	52	30-24
Ernest Riles	-	1-2	0-3	33-26	3-7	-	-	-	-	-	0-1	-	3	72	37-38
Eric Show	-	-	-	-	-	-	-	-	-	3-2	-	-	2	3	3-2
Joe Slusarski	-	-	-	-	-	-	-	-	-	9-10	-	-	8	11	9-10
Terry Steinbach	55-53	4-2	-	-	-	-	-	-	1-0	-	-	12-6	41	74	60-55
Dave Stewart	-	-	-	-	-	-	-	-	-	18-17	-	-	5	30	18-17
Todd Van Poppel	-	-	-	-	-	-	-	-	-	1-0	-	-	1	-	1-0
Bruce Walton	-	-	-	-	-	-	-	-	-	-	-	-	-	-	-
Walter Weiss	-	-	-	-	24-13	-	-	-	-	-	3-0	-	6	31	24-13
Bob Welch	-	-	-	-	-	-	-	-	-	18-17	-	-	9	26	18-17
Willie Wilson	-	-	-	-	-	17-9	10-13	8-6	0-1	-	10-9	-	21	43	35-29
Ron Witmeyer	-	1-2	-	-	-	-	-	-	-	-	-	-	-	3	1-2
Curt Young	-	-	-	-	-	-	-	-	-	0-1	-	-	-	1	0-1

TEAM TOTALS: BATTING

	AB	H	2B	3B	HR	RBI	BB	SO	BA	SA	OBA
Season	5410	1342	246	19	159	716	642	981	.248	.389	.331
vs. Left-Handers	1336	349	71	1	42	167	154	218	.261	.410	.338
vs. Right-Handers	4074	993	175	18	117	549	488	763	.244	.382	.328
vs. Ground-Ballers	2629	661	124	11	63	343	316	448	.251	.379	.326
vs. Fly-Ballers	2781	681	122	8	96	373	326	533	.245	.398	.326
Home Games	2627	633	121	7	76	342	336	473	.241	.379	.328
Road Games	2783	709	125	12	83	374	306	508	.255	.398	.333
Grass Fields	4531	1126	211	15	133	599	538	810	.249	.390	.330
Artificial Turf	879	216	35	4	26	117	104	171	.246	.383	.332
April	646	164	34	5	13	84	89	125	.254	.382	.349
May	923	243	42	4	28	142	137	150	.263	.408	.358
June	906	231	42	2	35	114	119	158	.255	.422	.344
July	952	234	47	2	25	139	100	161	.246	.378	.323
August	950	224	40	3	33	105	86	167	.236	.388	.303
Sept./Oct.	1033	246	41	3	25	132	111	220	.238	.356	.314
Leading Off Inn.	1292	311	59	2	42	42	145	216	.241	.387	.322
Runners On	2363	614	104	13	75	632	304	436	.260	.410	.343
Bases Empty	3047	728	142	6	84	84	338	545	.239	.372	.321
Runners/Scor. Pos.	1359	352	52	11	47	555	217	263	.259	.417	.355
Runners On/2 Out	1006	258	47	7	35	267	141	176	.256	.421	.352
Scor. Pos./2 Out	637	164	26	7	23	234	114	110	.257	.429	.375
Late-Inning Pressure	754	174	32	2	22	104	92	163	.231	.366	.317
Leading Off	189	38	8	1	1	1	18	42	.201	.270	.278
Runners On	308	77	14	1	15	97	51	76	.250	.448	.355
Runners/Scor. Pos.	179	45	8	1	9	84	41	49	.251	.458	.388

RUNS BATTED IN	From 1B	From 2B	From 3B	Scoring Position
Totals	110/1712	195/1051	252/593	447/1644
Percentage	6.4%	18.6%	42.5%	27.2%

TEAM TOTALS: PITCHING

	W-L	ERA	AB	H	HR	BB	SO	BA	SA	OBA
Season	84-78	4.57	5481	1425	155	655	892	.260	.405	.342
vs. Left-Handers			2687	709	55	331	378	.264	.386	.344
vs. Right-Handers			2794	716	100	324	514	.256	.423	.340
vs. Ground-Ballers			2607	709	48	277	348	.272	.393	.343
vs. Fly-Ballers			2874	716	107	378	544	.249	.415	.341
Home Games	47-34	4.05	2772	678	67	306	474	.245	.373	.323
Road Games	37-44	5.13	2709	747	88	349	418	.276	.437	.361
Grass Fields	76-60	4.21	4593	1149	124	552	758	.250	.388	.333
Artificial Turf	8-18	6.60	888	276	31	103	134	.311	.493	.385
April	13-7	3.73	656	165	14	80	88	.252	.354	.338
May	15-12	5.41	945	260	30	115	143	.275	.436	.353
June	13-15	4.91	907	226	21	118	147	.249	.383	.339
July	15-12	4.30	946	239	34	93	150	.253	.413	.326
August	15-14	4.44	971	262	25	107	146	.270	.420	.343
Sept./Oct.	13-18	4.47	1056	273	31	142	218	.259	.406	.350
Leading Off Inn.			1295	321	39	143	202	.248	.398	.326
Bases Empty			3043	758	87	339	493	.249	.391	.330
Runners On			2438	667	68	316	399	.274	.422	.356
Runners/Scor. Pos.			1412	394	39	219	258	.279	.437	.370
Runners On/2 Out			1027	255	32	153	183	.248	.404	.351
Scor. Pos./2 Out			673	173	22	113	128	.257	.423	.369
Late-Inning Pressure			866	218	27	92	188	.252	.402	.331
Leading Off			211	62	7	23	47	.294	.464	.366
Runners On			390	87	12	48	81	.223	.367	.317
Runners/Scor. Pos.			227	50	7	35	53	.220	.357	.333
First 9 Batters			2901	755	79	330	524	.260	.403	.339
Second 9 Batters			1355	339	29	164	201	.250	.373	.334
All Batters Thereafter			1225	331	47	161	167	.270	.445	.357

WON-LOST RECORD BY STARTING POSITION

Seattle Mariners	C	1B	2B	3B	SS	LF	CF	RF	DH	P	Leadoff	Cleanup	Starts vs. LH	Starts vs. RH	Total Starts
Rich Amaral	-	-	0-1	-	0-2	-	-	-	-	-	0-1	-	1	2	0-3
Scott Bankhead	-	-	-	-	-	-	-	-	-	4-5	-	-	2	7	4-5
Scott Bradley	25-22	-	-	2-0	-	-	-	-	-	-	-	-	-	49	27-22
Greg Briley	-	-	-	-	-	24-25	2-0	25-15	-	-	14-7	-	1	90	51-40
Jay Buhner	-	-	-	-	-	-	-	53-57	-	-	-	7-20	42	68	53-57
Dave Burba	-	-	-	-	-	-	-	-	-	1-1	-	-	-	2	1-1
Dave Cochrane	1-5	0-3	-	6-6	-	11-6	-	0-1	0-1	-	-	-	6	34	18-22
Keith Comstock	-	-	-	-	-	-	-	-	-	-	-	-	-	-	-
Henry Cotto	-	-	-	-	-	12-8	6-6	2-4	0-1	-	14-9	-	24	15	20-19
Alvin Davis	-	7-6	-	-	-	-	-	-	60-54	-	-	5-15	12	115	67-60
Rich Delucia	-	-	-	-	-	-	-	-	-	15-16	-	-	8	23	15-16
Dave Fleming	-	-	-	-	-	-	-	-	-	3-0	-	-	-	3	3-0
Ken Griffey Sr.	-	-	-	-	-	14-11	-	-	-	-	-	8-3	-	25	14-11
Ken Griffey Jr.	-	-	-	-	-	-	74-71	-	1-0	-	0-2	2-3	32	114	75-71
Erik Hanson	-	-	-	-	-	-	-	-	-	12-15	-	-	9	18	12-15
Gene Harris	-	-	-	-	-	-	-	-	-	-	-	-	-	-	-
Brian Holman	-	-	-	-	-	-	-	-	-	16-14	-	-	8	22	16-14
Chris Howard	0-1	-	-	-	-	-	-	-	-	-	-	-	1	-	0-1
Mike Jackson	-	-	-	-	-	-	-	-	-	-	-	-	-	-	-
Randy Johnson	-	-	-	-	-	-	-	-	-	17-16	-	-	8	25	17-16
Calvin Jones	-	-	-	-	-	-	-	-	-	-	-	-	-	-	-
Tracy Jones	-	-	-	-	-	10-12	-	1-0	11-8	-	-	10-3	32	10	22-20
Bill Krueger	-	-	-	-	-	-	-	-	-	14-11	-	-	7	18	14-11
Pat Lennon	-	-	-	-	-	-	-	-	0-2	-	-	-	2	-	0-2
Tino Martinez	-	12-14	-	-	-	-	-	-	1-2	-	-	-	7	22	13-16
Edgar Martinez	-	-	-	73-70	-	-	-	-	1-1	-	34-33	11-9	40	105	74-71
Rob Murphy	-	-	-	-	-	-	-	-	-	-	-	-	-	-	-
Pete O'Brien	-	62-56	-	-	-	7-5	-	-	9-8	-	-	40-26	34	113	78-69
Alonzo Powell	-	2-0	-	-	-	5-12	1-2	2-2	0-1	-	-	-	18	9	10-17
Harold Reynolds	-	-	82-76	-	-	-	-	-	0-1	-	21-27	-	39	120	82-77
Pat Rice	-	-	-	-	-	-	-	-	-	1-1	-	-	-	2	1-1
Jeff Schaefer	-	-	1-2	2-3	19-18	-	-	-	-	-	-	-	36	9	22-23
Mike Schooler	-	-	-	-	-	-	-	-	-	-	-	-	-	-	-
Matt Sinatro	2-0	-	-	-	-	-	-	-	-	-	-	-	1	1	2-0
Russ Swan	-	-	-	-	-	-	-	-	-	-	-	-	-	-	-
Bill Swift	-	-	-	-	-	-	-	-	-	-	-	-	-	-	-
Dave Valle	55-51	-	-	-	-	-	-	-	-	-	-	-	38	68	55-51
Omar Vizquel	-	-	-	-	64-59	-	-	-	-	-	-	-	12	111	64-59

TEAM TOTALS: BATTING

	AB	H	2B	3B	HR	RBI	BB	SO	BA	SA	OBA
Season	5494	1400	268	29	126	665	588	811	.255	.383	.328
vs. Left-Handers	1651	432	80	4	41	211	175	233	.262	.389	.334
vs. Right-Handers	3843	968	188	25	85	454	413	578	.252	.380	.325
vs. Ground-Ballers	2458	666	137	13	57	328	250	359	.271	.407	.340
vs. Fly-Ballers	3036	734	131	16	69	337	338	452	.242	.364	.318
Home Games	2706	701	137	19	69	353	314	411	.259	.400	.337
Road Games	2788	699	131	10	57	312	274	400	.251	.366	.319
Grass Fields	2127	544	93	7	47	248	211	308	.256	.372	.323
Artificial Turf	3367	856	175	22	79	417	377	503	.254	.390	.331
April	708	182	28	2	17	81	85	96	.257	.374	.340
May	913	224	34	6	21	107	99	133	.245	.365	.318
June	894	212	45	2	14	100	98	131	.237	.339	.316
July	924	254	48	9	26	122	69	124	.275	.431	.326
August	927	238	54	3	25	107	108	139	.257	.402	.333
Sept./Oct.	1128	290	59	7	23	148	129	188	.257	.383	.333
Leading Off Inn.	1337	329	60	9	28	28	120	194	.246	.367	.312
Runners On	2368	627	123	12	63	602	282	325	.265	.407	.339
Bases Empty	3126	773	145	17	63	63	306	486	.247	.365	.318
Runners/Scor. Pos.	1338	355	62	9	28	505	201	200	.265	.388	.352
Runners On/2 Out	1027	255	45	9	25	251	138	152	.248	.383	.341
Scor. Pos./2 Out	643	178	26	6	17	220	108	94	.277	.415	.384
Late-Inning Pressure	815	203	47	4	19	95	77	146	.249	.387	.314
Leading Off	209	42	8	2	3	3	11	34	.201	.301	.244
Runners On	325	89	22	0	9	85	45	63	.274	.425	.358
Runners/Scor. Pos.	200	58	15	0	4	71	30	43	.290	.425	.374

RUNS BATTED IN	From 1B	From 2B	From 3B	Scoring Position
Totals	92/1701	188/1053	259/593	447/1646
Percentage	5.4%	17.9%	43.7%	27.2%

TEAM TOTALS: PITCHING

	W-L	ERA	AB	H	HR	BB	SO	BA	SA	OBA
Season	83-79	3.79	5486	1387	136	628	1003	.253	.386	.332
vs. Left-Handers			2089	536	42	230	320	.257	.379	.331
vs. Right-Handers			3397	851	94	398	683	.251	.390	.332
vs. Ground-Ballers			2566	645	45	249	428	.251	.362	.319
vs. Fly-Ballers			2920	742	91	379	575	.254	.407	.343
Home Games	45-36	3.46	2833	697	69	273	534	.246	.376	.334
Road Games	38-43	4.14	2653	690	67	355	469	.260	.396	.351
Grass Fields	32-30	3.92	2020	510	55	273	370	.252	.389	.344
Artificial Turf	51-49	3.71	3466	877	81	355	633	.253	.384	.325
April	10-11	3.89	687	185	16	90	116	.269	.408	.355
May	15-12	3.50	919	235	23	108	176	.256	.387	.339
June	14-13	4.04	858	198	30	114	166	.231	.379	.324
July	15-12	2.80	919	224	17	87	166	.244	.358	.309
August	13-15	3.84	972	255	27	95	175	.262	.403	.331
Sept./Oct.	16-16	4.51	1131	290	23	134	204	.256	.385	.338
Leading Off Inn.			1325	320	38	132	227	.242	.382	.315
Bases Empty			3103	772	86	311	563	.249	.388	.322
Runners On			2383	615	50	317	440	.258	.384	.345
Runners/Scor. Pos.			1341	330	25	229	267	.246	.360	.351
Runners On/2 Out			996	240	21	156	179	.241	.368	.348
Scor. Pos./2 Out			664	141	11	124	139	.212	.318	.341
Late-Inning Pressure			875	203	14	93	173	.232	.330	.308
Leading Off			216	45	1	20	45	.208	.278	.275
Runners On			375	91	9	46	79	.243	.320	.327
Runners/Scor. Pos.			222	46	2	36	48	.207	.275	.318
First 9 Batters			2963	725	69	321	535	.245	.369	.322
Second 9 Batters			1337	345	38	167	246	.258	.408	.341
All Batters Thereafter			1186	317	29	140	222	.267	.402	.346

SEATTLE MARINERS

In their fifteenth year of operation, the Mariners finally reached the .500 mark. But it wasn't as easy as it looked. After starting the season with a six-game losing streak, Seattle raised its record to eight games above sea level by mid-May with separate winning streaks of eight games, six games, and six games during a five-week period. Then, over the next three months the Mariners failed to string together more than three consecutive wins, and on September 8 they fell below .500 for the first time since April 21 (except for a single day in mid-July). But they rallied to win 15 of their last 25 games, and finished the season with an 83–79 record, snapping the fourth-longest streak of losing seasons in major league history.

Of course, teams don't usually embark on 15-year plans; it's not very good for season ticket sales. And it takes only a wee dose of cynicism to wonder whether finishing four games over .500 is an accomplishment worth celebrating. For a team like the M's, yes—crossing the line between winning and losing suggests a brighter future for a perennial loser than it does for a team coming off just a few poor years.

Teams that attain the .500 level after a losing season seldom improve again the next year; in fact, only about one team in three moves up further without first taking a step back. But teams that broke through the .500 barrier off streaks of seven or more losing years—a group that currently includes not only the Mariners but the Atlanta Braves as well—have been far more likely to improve a year later than teams that had shorter streaks of losing seasons:

Previous Record	Up	Down	
One losing season	43	73	(37 percent improved)
2 to 6 losing seasons	27	71	(28 percent improved)
7 or more losing seasons	15	18	(45 percent improved)

An unusual sidelight to Seattle's breakthrough was the postseason firing of manager Jim Lefebvre. Only two other managers in this century snapped their teams' streaks of at least five losing seasons but didn't come back the next season, while 44 accepted return invitations. The first was Bucky Harris, who chose to leave the Red Sox after one season to rejoin the Washington Senators; in his one year with Boston, Harris snapped a streak of 15 straight losing seasons. The other deposed manager was Bob Kennedy, dumped immediately after the final game of the 1968 season, in which he led the Athletics to their first winning record since 1952—just Charles O. Finley's way of saying thanks.

Lefebvre's firing was all the more unusual in that it was the second consecutive season in which he won more games with Seattle than the Mariners were expected to win according to the projection model we use to evaluate managers. (The model pegged the Mariners at only 79–83 last season; somehow, we think general manager Woody Woodward, as well as many Mariners fans, were expecting quite a bit more.) In fact, Lefebvre and Red Sox manager Joe Morgan both lost their jobs after posting records in two consecutive seasons that exceeded our projections by at least two wins. No manager had been fired under those condi-

tions in nearly 20 years, since Boston axed Eddie Kasko following the 1973 season. Two years later, the Red Sox were in the World Series.

Seattle's break through the .500 level coincided with the development of several starting pitchers still in their 20s. Randy Johnson, Brian Holman, and rookie Rich Delucia all won at least 12 games last season; Johnson, who turned 28 shortly before the end of the season, is the oldest. And don't forget, that doesn't include 26-year-old Erik Hanson, who won eight games despite an elbow injury that limited his effectiveness, cost him six starts, and eventually required surgery.

The simultaneous rise of several young starting pitchers is usually considered a harbinger of a team's long-term success. And the good folks of Atlanta, smitten by Tom Glavine, Steve Avery, and John Smoltz, are undoubtedly as optimistic on that basis as Seattle's rooters. But a study of past teams with similar young, successful rotations indicates that such a pattern is an encouraging short-term indicator at best. More often than not, by the time a team's starting staff is labeled "young and promising," it's already peaked.

The 1987 New York Mets provide a typical example. Games won by their three qualifying pitchers year by year since then:

Pitcher	Age in 1987	Wins 1987	1988	1989	1990	1991
Ron Darling	26	12	17	14	7	8
Sid Fernandez	24	12	12	14	9	1
Dwight Gooden	22	15	18	9	19	13
Totals		39	47	37	35	22

Darling, Fernandez, and Gooden won a total of 39 games in 1987, and reached that total only once thereafter. But the Mets are only one recent example of a young rotation that failed to fulfill its promise. During a 10-year period from 1978 through 1987, 18 teams qualified according to the criteria outlined above (three pitchers, all under the age of 28 at midseason, who won at least 12 games apiece). Only four of those 18 teams got as many wins from their three pitchers in *any* subsequent season as they did in their qualifying seasons. And in all four of those cases, they did so exactly once—in the season immediately following.

The 1982 Montreal Expos provide a more extreme example of how a team's young rotation can deteriorate. Charlie Lea, Scott Sanderson, and Bill Gullickson won a total of 36 games that season. The next season, they accumulated 39 wins for the Expos. But Lea suffered a torn rotator cuff in 1983, Sanderson was traded a year later, and Gullickson was gone as well not long after that. And the 1979 White Sox are the most extreme case of all: Ken Kravec, Rich Wortham, and Ross Baumgarten won a total of 42 games. Three years later, Kravec's victory—for the Chicago Cubs, no less—was the only game won by any of them. And a decade later, the White Sox, who had *four* young pitchers with at least 12 wins in 1990, are again finding that such a distinction can be more a frustration than a guarantee of success: Only Jack McDowell won more games last season than he did a year earlier. Greg Hibbard spent part of 1991 in the minors; Melido Perez spent much of the season in the bullpen; and Eric King was exchanged for Cory Snyder, who was dumped for a pair of minor leaguers in July. To further complicate matters, the ERA of Alex Fernandez—who didn't win enough games after a mid-1990 recall to qualify—ballooned to 4.51 last season, and Fernandez won only nine of 22 decisions.

It's important to note that this isn't only a recent trend. All told, we found 150 qualifying teams from 1900 through 1988. Only 30 times did the pitchers involved ever again win as many games for the same team as they won in their qualifying seasons. And in half of those 30 cases, they exceeded the total in the season immediately following and never again. In fact, only three teams in the entire group of 150 provided their teams with anything approaching the kind of long-term success that many now predict for the Mariners and Braves: the 1906 Giants (Christy Mathewson, Hooks Wiltse, and Red Ames); the 1916 Cleveland Indians (Stan Coveleski, Jim Bagby, and Guy Morton); and the 1965 Tigers (Denny McLain, Mickey Lolich, and Joe Sparma).

Mariners fans and Braves fans can point optimistically to the fact that the Indians won the World Series in 1920 with their trio still intact, and that the Tigers did likewise in 1968. But the facts above are sobering. Sure, both teams have young rotations. And sure, they're talented. And we can think of 15 or 20 teams that would trade rotations with the Mariners in a minute. But history indicates how tough a task it can be to keep a young and talented starting rotation together and healthy. Last season's injury to Erik Hanson might have been more than an annoying setback on the road to an eventual division title; it might have been the first indication of the kinds of problems faced by the 1985 California Angels (Mike Witt, Kirk McCaskill, and Ron Romanick) or the 1983 Blue Jays (Dave Stieb, Jim Clancy, and Luis Leal)—to cite only two examples. Rather than trading one of their four young starters from a perceived position of strength, the Mariners might be better served to remember the age-old baseball wisdom: you can *never* have too much pitching.

Three years ago, Major League Baseball ended a nine-year experiment by eradicating the game-winning RBI from its statistical record. Fans constantly criticized the rule because so many game winners occurred early in a game, reflecting little if any degree of clutch ability. That criticism was valid; the following table shows the number of game-winning RBIs in each league last season, inning by inning:

	1	2	3	4	5	6	7	8	9	10+
American League	225	125	117	96	87	95	66	80	73	107
National League	200	77	79	83	76	72	75	80	65	94

But even though the "winning run" is likely to be scored before the fourth inning is over, go-ahead runs scored from the seventh inning on are almost twice as likely to stand up as eventual game winners as are those scored in the first four innings.

Last season Mariners batters drove in 27 go-ahead runs in Late-Inning Pressure Situations; all but three of them proved to be game winners (89%). That undoubtedly had a lot to do with their league-high total of 14 wins in games in which they trailed after six innings. And although Seattle's percentage was nearly the highest in the American League, it wasn't out of line with the league-wide average: 317 of 406 go-ahead RBIs in LIPS became game winners (78%). The following table shows the percentage of go-ahead RBIs that held up as game winners in each inning. Obviously, as the game progresses, the likelihood grows that any lead change will be the game's last:

	1	2	3	4	5	6	7	8	9	10+
American League	39%	41%	43%	47%	51%	73%	59%	78%	86%	88%
National League	41%	36%	45%	49%	58%	53%	63%	87%	86%	85%

Think what you will about the dearly departed game-winning RBI. But don't jump to the conclusion that other measures of clutch performance are equally spurious. With a little tinkering, even that rule could have provided a simple and informative measure of each player's performance under pressure. For example, the following table shows last season's major league leaders in go-ahead RBIs from the seventh inning on. For reference, we've included the number that stood up as game winners:

American League	GA	GW	National League	GA	GW
Jose Canseco, Oak.	8	6	George Bell, Chi.	8	4
Robin Ventura, Chi.	7	6	Ron Gant, Atl.	8	7
Dan Gladden, Minn.	6	4	Barry Bonds, Pitt.	7	6
Lance Johnson, Chi.	6	3	Doug Dascenzo, Chi.	7	4
			Kevin McReynolds, N.Y.	7	7
			Dale Murphy, Phil.	7	7

For our money, the late-game go-ahead RBI (why penalize the hitter if the reliever couldn't hold the lead?) would have provided a good measure of a player's clutch hitting—just the kind that everyone sought in the late 1970s when the rules for awarding game-winning RBIs were written to fill that void. The eventual eradication of the game-winning RBI was a case of throwing out the baby with the bath water.

TEXAS RANGERS

Consistency and stability in management are generally considered hallmarks of winning baseball teams. Sure it helps to have Jose Canseco and Mark McGwire in the middle of the order, but the Oakland Athletics have been successful over the last decade because they've taken a consistent approach from the top down, from season to season. The New York Yankees have not, with disastrous results.

But there are exceptions, most notably in Texas, where baseball's longest-standing management team presides over the oldest franchise never to appear in postseason play. The Texas Rangers hired general manager Tom Grieve in September 1984, and eight months later Grieve hired Bobby Valentine, his former teammate on the 1978 Mets, to manage the team. We would have predicted that if Grieve and Valentine were unable to lead the franchise to its first-ever division title within, say, five years, at least one would be gone, or possibly both; that's the way of professional sports. (Ask Sal Bando and Phil Garner how many seasons they expect to survive if they're unable to lead the Brewers to an A.L. East title—a reasonable over/under would be three.) But despite its failure to break a 31-season, two-city title drought, the Grieve-Valentine team was recently given a contract extension through the end of the 1993 season. But is the Rangers' brain-trust just a couple more New Englanders who've stayed at their desks too long, doing a bad job for a boss named George Bush?

Grieve inherited a team that (excepting 1981) hadn't finished above .500 since 1979, and that finished dead last in 1984. Valentine replaced Doug Rader on May 16, 1985 with the team at 9–23 (equaling the worst record to that point in franchise history), and compiled a 53–76 mark for the remainder of the season—better, but not good enough to avoid a second straight last-place finish. The Rangers began changing faces that season, breaking in Oddibe McDowell and Steve Buechele, as well as Don Slaught, whom Grieve had acquired in a four-way deal the previous winter.

The Rangers made a huge advance in 1986, finishing second at 87–75, thanks largely to a pair of sharp deals. The Montreal Expos had drafted Pete Incaviglia but were unwilling to guarantee him a major league spot. The Rangers pounced on the opportunity to acquire the all-time NCAA home-run champ; once the Expos got Incaviglia's name on a contract, they moved him to the Rangers for two minor leaguers, skirting the rules against trading the rights to draft choices so closely that the rule was rewritten imposing a trade blackout for the period of a full year.

Even better, Grieve acquired two other key players from White Sox general manager Hawk Harrelson. Grieve and Harrelson represented opposite ends of the major leaguer-cum-G.M. spectrum—the former moderate in speech and dress, the latter flamboyant and often outrageous. Before he got around to firing Tony LaRussa, the Hawk had suggested that a right-handed middle reliever might be the key to the White Sox' fortunes. Grieve happily obliged him with Dave Schmidt, and threw in Wayne Tolleson, one of several players not filling the hole at short for the Rangers. Texas received shortstop Scott Fletcher, who won the job, and right-hander Edwin Correa, who won a dozen games for the Rangers at age 20.

But more important than those initial deals, the Rangers under Grieve and Valentine became very aggressive in promoting players developed within their own organization. In 1986, their starting rotation featured aging but still-winning knuckleballer Charlie Hough and three pitchers age 23 or younger behind him: Correa, Juan Guzman, and Bobby Witt. Incaviglia became a starter without spending a day in the minors, and 20-year-old Ruben Sierra joined him in the outfield. Everything worked splendidly, and the Rangers had their first winning season since 1981.

Grieve and company proudly took an enlightened approach to baseball. From the hiring of pitching coach Tom House to the design of their new spring home in Port Charlotte, they tried to bring modern training ideas to baseball, based on the principle that their players were world-class athletes. For open-minded managers and G.M.s, Texas proved in 1985 and 1986 that good, healthy minor leaguers could move smoothly into major league roles—now a seemingly obvious truth that nevertheless passed for *avant garde* to some older baseball people as recently as 10 years ago. A corollary was that the cream of the college crop projected into competent big leaguers. Since the Rangers had every reason to expect their fine young players to continue to improve, things looked bright going into 1987.

But that faith in young talent may have contributed to the team's unexpected decline to sixth-place finishes in 1987 and 1988. Management believed it could afford to trade Don Slaught because either Chad Kreuter or Mike Stanley was bound to emerge as a bookend for left-handed hitting catcher Geno Petralli. They believed Witt and Kevin Brown would quickly contribute to the starting rotation; that faith became more costly as Correa and Guzman experienced career-threatening arm problems. When McDowell, Incaviglia, and later addition Jerry Browne stagnated, they had no better alternatives, a consequence of the bare cupboard Grieve had inherited rather than anything he might have done himself.

Cynics would note Grieve and company had taken a last-place club and turned it into a sixth-place club in three seasons, and it seemed to even the most optimistic observers that things were headed in the wrong direction. Complicating matters, owner Eddie Chiles was trying to peddle the team, and his bid to sell to partner Edward Gaylord had already been denied. In the midst of what could have easily become a desperate situation, the Rangers brass shone at the 1988 winter meetings.

First, they made a nine-player deal with the Chicago Cubs that indicated how closely Grieve and Valentine worked together. Ignoring the periphery, the Rangers sent Mitch Williams, a left-handed closer with wicked stuff, to the Cubs for Rafael Palmeiro, a first baseman/left fielder who didn't hit with sufficient power to play either position at Wrigley Field. Valentine may have believed Jeff Russell was ready to assume closing duties, but mostly he just wanted to get Williams out of his bullpen (and his hair). Whether the Rangers guessed from Palmeiro's collegiate background that he'd eventually hit for distance or they just got lucky, it's certain the Cubs now wish they'd kept Palmeiro and traded Mark Grace. Our projection model estimates that Palmeiro is six times as likely as Grace to reach the 1000-RBI mark, and 10 times as likely to accumulate 2500 hits.

The next day, the Rangers made another deal that the other guys would now like to undo, taking advantage of a familiarity-breeds-contempt situation to acquire Julio Franco from the Cleveland Indians. To get him, Texas gave up three members of its 1988 opening-day lineup—McDowell, Browne, and Pete O'Brien. Browne and McDowell couldn't hold starting spots on the Indians and O'Brien is now in Seattle, but Franco has flourished in Texas. He's a key element in their attack, giving them significant offense in what's primarily a defensive position. Compare his 1991 performance to the same number of plate appearances by a typical American League second baseman:

Player	AB	R	H	2B	3B	HR	RBI	BB	SO	SB	BA	SLG	OBA
Franco	589	108	201	27	3	15	78	65	78	36	.341	.474	.408
A.L. Avg.	581	77	156	27	4	7	57	59	69	17	.268	.365	.338

A lineup of guys that far ahead of the curve at their positions will do serious damage, so Franco was a natural building block. He and Palmeiro now form the best right side of an infield in the majors. Texas's right side batted .321 last season, 27 points higher than the runner-up Yankees (sic). Rangers first and second basemen scored and drove in a total of 415 runs, second only (and by a mere six runs) to Cecil Fielder, Lou Whitaker, and friends.

After replacing their first and second basemen, the Rangers hit the jackpot. The Astros were giving soon-to-be 42-year-old Nolan Ryan a hard time about a new contract. In jumped the Rangers.

Two no-hitters later, signing Ryan seems much more obvious than it did in December 1988, when he was not yet a consensus Hall of Famer, let alone a living legend. He'd won two straight National League strikeout titles plus an ERA crown in 1987, but he'd yet to log his 300th win or 5000th strikeout, and his elbow was creaking loudly. But Charlie Hough's success as he neared age 40 (albeit with a knuckler) may have made it easier for the Rangers to believe in Ryan than any other teams that might otherwise have courted him. Additionally, the Rangers probably found the opportunity to sign Ryan irresistible under any circumstances from a business standpoint. As a Ranger, Ryan has helped establish the former Washington Senators as the genuine Texas team; these days, it's the Astros that are up for sale and subject to relocation rumors.

The Rangers got a new ownership group in the spring of 1989. In April they broke out of the gate at 10–1, which suddenly made that elusive division title seem within reach. Still in the race in July but panting to keep up with the mighty A's, Texas made a future-for-now deal, acquiring Harold Baines, the best designated hitter in the league, and Fred Manrique for Fletcher, 20-year-old outfielder Sammy Sosa, and 19-year-old lefthanded pitcher Wilson Alvarez. The deal brought the Rangers a quality player who could help them immediately, but at the cost of two prospects they knew might eventually burn them. (It also shaved Fletcher's salary off the payroll. He'd been resigned after filing for free agency, and Fletcher wasn't a million a year better than Jeff Kunkel—particularly with a new owner watching.)

The Baines deal was immediately questionable for the same reason that the acquisition of Franco was so good: It was designed to improve production from the DH spot, an offensive position where the spread between the best and average performer isn't all that large. Regardless, Baines injured his hamstring within three weeks of his arrival and failed to hit with the same authority he had earlier in the season. It became a worse deal 13 months later, when the Rangers sent him to Oakland (still the team to beat in the division) for a pair of minor league pitchers. The trade looked worse still last season when Alvarez no-hit the Baltimore Orioles while the pitchers Texas got for Baines (Scott Chiamparino and Joe Bitker) weren't helping a team desperate for arms to support the league's highest-scoring attack.

Worth noting in all those negatives is the continuing sound talent judgments the Rangers made about their own players. A few years ago, they had five promising outfielders, each considered a potential All-Star: Sosa, McDowell, Incaviglia, Sierra, and Juan Gonzalez. They kept the right pair. Dumping Incaviglia last year may have been personal and shortsighted; they should have been able to engineer some kind of deal. (Failing that, would starting the season with Incaviglia have been such a disaster?) But it wasn't a mistake as far as talent judgment goes. The team didn't panic over its shortcomings behind the plate when Kreuter and Mike Stanley proved incapable of everyday status because they knew Ivan Rodriguez could play, and soon. Last winter's signing of Dickie Thon filled a spot that was weak even with Fletcher. They need to be proven right about Dean Palmer at third, but let's face it—the difference between Steve Buechele and Palmer isn't three million anythings.

Last season, Grieve tried to shore up his ailing pitching staff by bringing in Oil Can Boyd, on a "best available arm" basis. The Can lost seven of nine decisions for Texas with an ERA that looked like a winning Lotto number (six-six-eight). Then during the off-season, Grieve and friends did nothing more about that staff that allowed the most runs in the majors. An oversight? Uh-uh. The 1991 Rangers also led the majors in disabling injuries to their pitchers. The brass hopes Bobby Witt's rotator cuff and elbow heal sufficiently for him to become at least the fourth starter behind Ryan, Kevin Brown, and Jose Guzman. There's always the chance that Chiamparino or 1987 top draft choice Brian Bohanon (both also injured in 1991) or Hector Fajardo (part of the ransom for Buechele) can fill the five spot. Gerald Alexander pitched best as a starter, and he may also get a shot. The Rangers can be confident they've got an ace, and lots of depth behind him, given a better break on the injury front.

Texas has now put together three straight winning seasons in a tough division, and should have another one in 1992 thanks to a management team that has cleverly assembled talent and has worked effectively within a budget. Above all, they've shown it's easier to make a lousy team better than it is to make a good team a winner. Their attempts to fill specific holes in-season with Baines and Boyd bombed; smarts don't help much when you're drawing to an inside straight. But Grieve and Valentine have proven that the most important decisions are knowing which cards to hold.

WON-LOST RECORD BY STARTING POSITION

Texas Rangers	C	1B	2B	3B	SS	LF	CF	RF	DH	P	Leadoff	Cleanup	Starts vs. LH	Starts vs. RH	Total Starts
Gerald Alexander	-	-	-	-	-	-	-	-	-	5-4	-	-	2	7	5-4
Brad Arnsberg	-	-	-	-	-	-	-	-	-	-	-	-	-	-	-
John Barfield	-	-	-	-	-	-	-	-	-	5-4	-	-	3	6	5-4
Joseph Bitker	-	-	-	-	-	-	-	-	-	-	-	-	-	-	-
Brian Bohanon	-	-	-	-	-	-	-	-	-	7-4	-	-	2	9	7-4
Oil Can Boyd	-	-	-	-	-	-	-	-	-	2-10	-	-	5	7	2-10
J. Kevin Brown	-	-	-	-	-	-	-	-	-	17-16	-	-	8	25	17-16
Steve Buechele	-	-	6-6	54-47	-	-	-	-	-	-	-	-	30	83	60-53
Nick Capra	-	-	-	-	-	-	-	-	-	-	-	-	-	-	-
Scott Chiamparino	-	-	-	-	-	-	-	-	-	3-2	-	-	2	3	3-2
Jack Daugherty	-	1-4	-	-	-	11-14	-	-	-	-	5-10	-	5	25	12-18
Mario Diaz	-	-	2-2	2-0	17-19	-	-	-	-	-	-	-	23	19	21-21
Brian Downing	-	-	-	-	-	-	-	-	53-45	-	50-39	-	41	57	53-45
Hector Fajardo	-	-	-	-	-	-	-	-	-	1-2	-	-	-	3	1-2
Monty Fariss	-	-	1-1	-	-	5-3	-	-	0-1	-	0-1	-	10	1	6-5
Julio Franco	-	-	76-68	-	-	-	-	-	-	-	2-8	26-23	38	106	76-68
Juan Gonzalez	-	-	-	-	-	25-19	44-43	2-0	2-2	-	-	9-11	39	98	73-64
Goose Gossage	-	-	-	-	-	-	-	-	-	-	-	-	-	-	-
Gary Green	-	-	-	4-2	-	-	-	-	-	-	-	-	6	-	4-2
Jose Guzman	-	-	-	-	-	-	-	-	-	15-10	-	-	8	17	15-10
Donald Harris	-	-	-	-	-	1-0	-	-	-	-	-	-	1	-	1-0
Jose Hernandez	-	-	-	18-17	-	-	-	-	-	-	-	-	13	22	18-17
Jeff Huson	-	-	-	46-39	-	-	-	-	-	-	3-1	-	2	83	46-39
Mike Jeffcoat	-	-	-	-	-	-	-	-	-	-	-	-	-	-	-
Chad Kreuter	-	-	-	-	-	-	-	-	-	-	-	-	-	-	-
Barry Manuel	-	-	-	-	-	-	-	-	-	-	-	-	-	-	-
Terry Mathews	-	-	-	-	-	-	-	-	-	2-0	-	-	1	1	2-0
Rob Maurer	-	-	-	-	-	-	-	-	1-1	-	-	-	-	2	1-1
Eric Nolte	-	-	-	-	-	-	-	-	-	-	-	-	-	-	-
Rafael Palmeiro	-	82-70	-	-	-	-	-	-	0-2	-	6-3	4-5	37	117	82-72
Dean Palmer	-	-	-	21-24	-	13-11	-	-	2-2	-	5-5	-	25	48	36-37
Mark Parent	-	-	-	-	-	-	-	-	-	-	-	-	-	-	-
Mark Petkovsek	-	-	-	-	-	-	-	-	-	-	0-1	-	-	1	0-1
Geno Petralli	23-22	-	-	1-2	-	-	-	-	1-1	-	0-1	-	-	50	25-25
Gary Pettis	-	-	-	-	-	-	40-33	-	-	-	13-9	-	22	51	40-33
Jim Poole	-	-	-	-	-	-	-	-	-	-	-	-	-	-	-
Kevin Reimer	-	-	-	-	-	29-27	-	-	25-23	-	-	6-8	-	104	54-50
Ivan Rodriguez	40-41	-	-	-	-	-	-	-	-	-	-	-	22	59	40-41
Kenny Rogers	-	-	-	-	-	-	-	-	-	4-5	-	-	2	7	4-5
Wayne Rosenthal	-	-	-	-	-	-	-	-	-	-	-	-	-	-	-
Jeff Russell	-	-	-	-	-	-	-	-	-	-	-	-	-	-	-
John Russell	2-0	-	-	-	-	2-1	-	-	-	-	-	-	3	2	4-1
Nolan Ryan	-	-	-	-	-	-	-	-	-	16-11	-	-	7	20	16-11
Calvin Schiraldi	-	-	-	-	-	-	-	-	-	-	-	-	-	-	-
Tony Scruggs	-	-	-	-	-	-	0-1	-	-	-	-	-	1	-	0-1
Ruben Sierra	-	-	-	-	-	-	-	83-77	-	-	-	40-30	42	118	83-77
Mike Stanley	20-14	-	2-3	3-1	-	-	-	-	1-0	-	1-0	-	27	17	26-18
Denny Walling	-	-	-	4-3	0-2	-	-	-	-	-	-	-	-	9	4-5
Bobby Witt	-	-	-	-	-	-	-	-	-	8-8	-	-	3	13	8-8

TEAM TOTALS: BATTING

	AB	H	2B	3B	HR	RBI	BB	SO	BA	SA	OBA
Season	5703	1539	288	31	177	774	596	1039	.270	.424	.341
vs. Left-Handers	1516	417	76	11	63	219	180	268	.275	.464	.353
vs. Right-Handers	4187	1122	212	20	114	555	416	771	.268	.410	.337
vs. Ground-Ballers	2714	766	140	12	81	381	265	471	.282	.432	.348
vs. Fly-Ballers	2989	773	148	19	96	393	331	568	.259	.417	.335
Home Games	2734	738	143	21	79	368	292	508	.270	.424	.344
Road Games	2969	801	145	10	98	406	304	531	.270	.424	.339
Grass Fields	4757	1299	239	27	153	663	512	869	.273	.431	.346
Artificial Turf	946	240	49	4	24	111	84	170	.254	.390	.316
April	532	135	25	2	13	63	51	81	.254	.382	.323
May	992	304	54	7	29	152	117	148	.306	.463	.379
June	987	253	47	5	25	130	118	183	.256	.390	.336
July	920	247	44	6	35	122	80	178	.268	.443	.332
August	1115	318	56	7	39	164	96	213	.285	.453	.344
Sept./Oct.	1157	282	62	4	36	143	134	236	.244	.398	.325
Leading Off Inn.	1333	341	67	3	42	42	136	244	.256	.405	.329
Runners On	2559	729	130	16	91	688	287	444	.285	.455	.357
Bases Empty	3144	810	158	15	86	86	309	595	.258	.399	.328
Runners/Scor. Pos.	1456	399	66	12	49	575	202	275	.274	.437	.359
Runners On/2 Out	1098	312	49	8	40	299	147	197	.284	.453	.375
Scor. Pos./2 Out	720	188	30	6	22	248	120	140	.261	.411	.374
Late-Inning Pressure	870	235	34	2	24	111	103	164	.270	.397	.350
Leading Off	212	50	10	0	3	3	26	42	.236	.325	.319
Runners On	388	109	15	1	14	101	56	74	.281	.433	.373
Runners/Scor. Pos.	224	52	8	1	5	81	37	45	.232	.344	.342

RUNS BATTED IN	From 1B	From 2B	From 3B	Scoring Position
Totals	123/1847	236/1167	238/581	474/1748
Percentage	6.7%	20.2%	41.0%	27.1%

TEAM TOTALS: PITCHING

	W-L	ERA	AB	H	HR	BB	SO	BA	SA	OBA
Season	85-77	4.47	5669	1486	151	662	1022	.262	.402	.341
vs. Left-Handers			2313	576	47	283	403	.249	.369	.331
vs. Right-Handers			3356	910	104	379	619	.271	.425	.348
vs. Ground-Ballers			2755	742	55	290	437	.269	.391	.339
vs. Fly-Ballers			2914	744	96	372	585	.255	.412	.343
Home Games	46-35	4.30	2857	741	77	312	553	.259	.399	.333
Road Games	39-42	4.64	2812	745	74	350	469	.265	.405	.349
Grass Fields	71-66	4.58	4780	1252	136	542	877	.262	.406	.339
Artificial Turf	14-11	3.88	889	234	15	120	145	.263	.381	.353
April	8-8	4.00	516	117	15	60	106	.227	.362	.309
May	18-9	4.26	956	257	19	138	156	.269	.392	.360
June	13-14	4.26	997	265	32	117	153	.266	.422	.346
July	13-14	4.34	907	224	40	110	196	.247	.428	.332
August	15-16	4.91	1091	305	22	111	187	.280	.404	.347
Sept./Oct.	18-16	4.72	1202	318	23	126	224	.265	.389	.336
Leading Off Inn.			1349	351	32	130	240	.260	.389	.328
Bases Empty			3116	797	82	341	599	.256	.394	.333
Runners On			2553	689	69	321	423	.270	.412	.350
Runners/Scor. Pos.			1508	382	35	233	275	.253	.377	.349
Runners On/2 Out			1082	270	33	142	183	.250	.401	.344
Scor. Pos./2 Out			703	167	18	108	125	.238	.366	.347
Late-Inning Pressure			936	216	27	113	191	.231	.362	.316
Leading Off			235	48	4	26	51	.204	.315	.286
Runners On			374	89	12	64	67	.238	.369	.348
Runners/Scor. Pos.			220	41	3	47	47	.186	.255	.326
First 9 Batters			3023	774	76	372	586	.256	.388	.339
Second 9 Batters			1421	397	40	155	231	.279	.435	.351
All Batters Thereafter			1225	315	35	135	205	.257	.399	.333

WON-LOST RECORD BY STARTING POSITION

Toronto Blue Jays	C	1B	2B	3B	SS	LF	CF	RF	DH	P	Leadoff	Cleanup	Starts vs. LH	Starts vs. RH	Total Starts
Jim Acker	-	-	-	-	-	-	-	-	-	1-3	-	-	1	3	1-3
Roberto Alomar	-	-	90-69	-	-	-	-	-	-	-	-	-	45	114	90-69
Derek Bell	-	-	-	-	-	3-3	1-0	-	-	-	1-0	-	7	-	4-3
Pat Borders	40-31	-	-	-	-	-	-	-	-	-	-	-	47	24	40-31
Denis Boucher	-	-	-	-	-	-	-	-	-	2-5	-	-	2	5	2-5
Tom Candiotti	-	-	-	-	-	-	-	-	-	10-9	-	-	5	14	10-9
Joe Carter	-	-	-	-	-	28-23	-	57-43	6-5	-	-	20-22	47	115	91-71
Ken Dayley	-	-	-	-	-	-	-	-	-	-	-	-	-	-	-
Rob Ducey	-	-	-	-	-	9-1	-	1-2	0-1	-	-	-	-	14	10-4
Willie Fraser	-	-	-	-	-	-	-	-	-	0-1	-	-	1	-	0-1
Ray Giannelli	-	-	-	5-3	-	-	-	-	-	-	-	-	-	8	5-3
Rene Gonzales	-	-	1-2	6-4	11-11	-	-	-	-	-	-	-	11	24	18-17
Kelly Gruber	-	-	-	59-50	-	-	-	-	2-0	-	-	15-13	31	80	61-50
Juan Guzman	-	-	-	-	-	-	-	-	-	14-9	-	-	6	17	14-9
Tom Henke	-	-	-	-	-	-	-	-	-	-	-	-	-	-	-
Pat Hentgen	-	-	-	-	-	-	-	-	-	1-0	-	-	-	1	1-0
Glenallen Hill	-	-	-	-	-	6-3	-	1-3	8-8	-	-	-	20	9	15-14
Vince Horsman	-	-	-	-	-	-	-	-	-	-	-	-	-	-	-
Jimmy Key	-	-	-	-	-	-	-	-	-	20-13	-	-	12	21	20-13
Randy Knorr	-	-	-	-	-	-	-	-	-	-	-	-	-	-	-
Manny Lee	-	-	-	-	77-57	-	-	-	-	-	-	-	42	92	77-57
Al Leiter	-	-	-	-	-	-	-	-	-	-	-	-	-	-	-
Bob MacDonald	-	-	-	-	-	-	-	-	-	-	-	-	-	-	-
Candy Maldonado	-	-	-	-	-	29-23	-	-	-	-	-	5-3	15	37	29-23
Rance Mulliniks	-	-	-	2-1	-	-	-	-	40-30	-	-	6-0	-	73	42-31
Greg Myers	51-40	-	-	-	-	-	-	-	-	-	-	-	-	91	51-40
John Olerud	-	69-55	-	-	-	-	-	-	-	-	-	35-27	11	113	69-55
Dave Parker	-	-	-	-	-	-	5-5	-	-	-	-	-	-	10	5-5
Cory Snyder	-	1-0	-	1-0	-	-	-	3-5	-	-	-	-	6	4	5-5
Ed Sprague	-	9-9	-	18-13	-	-	-	-	1-1	-	-	-	32	19	28-23
Dave Stieb	-	-	-	-	-	-	-	-	-	4-5	-	-	2	7	4-5
Todd Stottlemyre	-	-	-	-	-	-	-	-	-	21-13	-	-	7	27	21-13
Pat Tabler	-	12-7	-	-	-	-	-	-	16-13	-	-	10-6	44	4	28-20
Mike Timlin	-	-	-	-	-	-	-	-	-	2-1	-	-	-	3	2-1
Duane Ward	-	-	-	-	-	-	-	-	-	-	-	-	-	-	-
Turner Ward	-	-	-	-	-	-	-	1-0	-	-	-	-	-	1	1-0
Dave Weathers	-	-	-	-	-	-	-	-	-	-	-	-	-	-	-
Dave Wells	-	-	-	-	-	-	-	-	-	16-12	-	-	12	16	16-12
Mickey Weston	-	-	-	-	-	-	-	-	-	-	-	-	-	-	-
Devon White	-	-	-	-	-	-	88-68	-	-	-	88-68	-	45	111	88-68
Mark Whiten	-	-	-	-	-	-	-	24-15	-	-	-	-	8	31	24-15
Ken Williams	-	-	-	-	-	-	-	4-3	-	-	-	-	7	-	4-3
Frank Wills	-	-	-	-	-	-	-	-	-	-	-	-	-	-	-
Mookie Wilson	-	-	-	-	-	16-18	2-3	13-8	-	-	-	2-3	5	55	31-29
Eddie Zosky	-	-	-	-	3-3	-	-	-	-	-	-	-	-	6	3-3

TEAM TOTALS: BATTING

	AB	H	2B	3B	HR	RBI	BB	SO	BA	SA	OBA
Season	5489	1412	295	45	133	649	499	1043	.257	.400	.322
vs. Left-Handers	1666	428	90	10	47	196	142	288	.257	.408	.316
vs. Right-Handers	3823	984	205	35	86	453	357	755	.257	.397	.325
vs. Ground-Ballers	2799	738	156	15	57	310	242	503	.264	.391	.324
vs. Fly-Ballers	2690	674	139	30	76	339	257	540	.251	.409	.320
Home Games	2695	724	162	27	75	340	255	504	.269	.432	.337
Road Games	2794	688	133	18	58	309	244	539	.246	.369	.308
Grass Fields	2137	526	103	9	48	248	193	419	.246	.370	.309
Artificial Turf	3352	886	192	36	85	401	306	624	.264	.419	.331
April	693	191	40	6	14	91	76	110	.276	.411	.347
May	892	217	42	13	16	101	92	178	.243	.373	.318
June	959	258	63	7	23	107	83	177	.269	.421	.331
July	903	242	44	7	23	94	64	175	.268	.409	.322
August	977	247	53	6	30	121	74	176	.253	.411	.307
Sept./Oct.	1065	257	53	6	27	135	110	227	.241	.378	.316
Leading Off Inn.	1345	368	90	11	47	47	97	243	.274	.462	.329
Runners On	2309	599	128	18	48	564	259	430	.259	.393	.333
Bases Empty	3180	813	167	27	85	85	240	613	.256	.405	.314
Runners/Scor. Pos.	1369	338	74	9	27	490	203	269	.247	.373	.337
Runners On/2 Out	978	217	42	8	15	187	123	195	.222	.327	.316
Scor. Pos./2 Out	642	130	26	2	10	161	97	135	.202	.296	.315
Late-Inning Pressure	773	192	33	6	16	81	94	188	.248	.369	.333
Leading Off	197	51	12	2	5	5	19	50	.259	.416	.330
Runners On	325	78	19	2	3	68	48	73	.240	.338	.337
Runners/Scor. Pos.	192	39	10	1	2	63	39	50	.203	.297	.331

RUNS BATTED IN	From 1B	From 2B	From 3B	Scoring Position
Totals	84/1573	180/1085	252/621	432/1706
Percentage	5.3%	16.6%	40.6%	25.3%

TEAM TOTALS: PITCHING

	W-L	ERA	AB	H	HR	BB	SO	BA	SA	OBA
Season	91-71	3.50	5470	1301	121	523	971	.238	.352	.307
vs. Left-Handers			2040	495	41	230	340	.243	.347	.321
vs. Right-Handers			3430	806	80	293	631	.235	.355	.299
vs. Ground-Ballers			2518	631	32	217	403	.251	.340	.312
vs. Fly-Ballers			2952	670	89	306	568	.227	.362	.302
Home Games	46-35	3.83	2827	702	72	255	504	.248	.371	.313
Road Games	45-36	3.16	2643	599	49	268	467	.227	.331	.300
Grass Fields	33-30	3.39	2034	463	41	205	367	.228	.337	.300
Artificial Turf	58-41	3.57	3436	838	80	318	604	.244	.361	.311
April	12-9	3.97	693	163	23	70	112	.235	.391	.309
May	15-12	2.97	878	202	14	94	175	.230	.314	.306
June	16-12	3.27	942	219	20	76	159	.232	.330	.292
July	15-11	3.45	894	205	17	81	169	.229	.351	.297
August	15-14	3.94	1004	258	29	95	180	.257	.387	.321
Sept./Oct.	18-13	3.48	1059	254	18	107	192	.240	.344	.315
Leading Off Inn.			1331	300	20	124	235	.225	.311	.297
Bases Empty			3190	721	54	279	597	.226	.323	.294
Runners On			2280	580	67	244	374	.254	.393	.324
Runners/Scor. Pos.			1274	314	34	187	215	.246	.374	.337
Runners On/2 Out			1022	265	27	135	165	.259	.387	.349
Scor. Pos./2 Out			652	157	17	113	103	.241	.367	.357
Late-Inning Pressure			916	204	16	86	213	.223	.310	.292
Leading Off			240	57	4	13	62	.237	.333	.280
Runners On			347	84	10	45	66	.242	.357	.332
Runners/Scor. Pos.			192	51	5	33	35	.266	.385	.377
First 9 Batters			2834	669	63	300	562	.236	.346	.312
Second 9 Batters			1394	325	35	114	214	.233	.362	.293
All Batters Thereafter			1242	307	23	109	195	.247	.353	.310

TORONTO BLUE JAYS

Baseball general managers are keenly aware of how dangerous it can be to tinker with the makeup of a winning ballclub. After several second- and third-place finishes, most GMs pay lip service to the team's need to make a move or two to put them over the top, but act according to the philosophy, "If it ain't broke, don't fix it."

Do any of you remember the 1959 Cleveland Indians, a young and talented club that finished in second place, 10 games ahead of the Yankees (four-time defending champs) and just five games behind the Go-Go White Sox? That club could serve as a warning to any general manager who gets an itchy trigger finger in the face of a near miss or two. Cleveland's lineup included 25-year-old Rocky Colavito and a pair of 27-year-old infielders, slick-fielding Vic Power at first base, and power-hitting Woodie Held at shortstop. The Indians' rotation included three pitchers under the age of 24, all of whom reached double figures in wins: Gary Bell, Jim Perry, and Mudcat Grant.

Two months after the season ended, the Indians began a series of trades that they hoped would bring them a title. First, Cleveland traded its aging left fielder, Minnie Minoso, and some spare parts to the White Sox for third baseman Bubba Phillips and a pair of promising 24-year-olds, catcher Johnny Romano and first baseman Norm Cash. Not bad. But a week before the start of the 1960 season, Cleveland pulled off two one-for-one trades with the Detroit Tigers that would haunt the team for a decade: Cash was traded for third baseman Steve Demeter, and five days later Colavito, the defending A.L. home-run champion, was traded for Harvey Kuenn, the league's defending batting champ. Demeter played four games for the Indians that season, and never again played in the majors. Kuenn played only one season for the Tribe, after which he was traded to San Francisco for pitcher Johnny Antonelli and outfielder Willie Kirkland, in part to fill the power void left by the trade of Colavito. Cleveland spent the next five seasons below the .500 mark, while Cash and Colavito combined for an average of 64 home runs per season.

The final irony: The Indians reacquired Colavito after the 1964 season in yet another ill-advised deal. To get Rocky, Cleveland had to part with Romano and a pair of unproven prospects who would eventually play key roles on a total of seven division-winning teams: Tommie Agee (1969 Mets) and Tommy John (1974, 1977, and 1978 Dodgers, 1980 and 1981 Yankees, 1982 Angels). Cleveland hasn't come within 10 games of a league or division title in the 32 years since that series of trades began (unless you consider the bastardized 1981 season).

Fearing such a worst-case scenario, big league general managers are understandably reluctant to make major changes on winning ballclubs. So the widespread changes made to the Blue Jays roster before and during the 1991 season were not only bold, considering that Toronto had come within a lost weekend of the 1990 A.L. East title, they were also unusual; few teams with a record as good as the 1990 Jays make such sweeping changes, especially those with lineups so young. (The 1990 Blue Jays had the youngest lineup in the American League—on average, 27 years, three months.)

The table below shows the percentage of change in the composition of each team from one season to the next for the years 1961 through 1990, with teams classified according to their winning percentages. The degree of turnover is measured by the percentage of common plate appearances (for batters) and innings (for pitchers) between Year 1 and Year 2. The figures show that the better the team's record in Year 1, the less change in Year 2:

		——Change in Year 2——		
Year 1 Pct.	Teams	Batters	Pitchers	Average
.200–.299	1	62%	51%	57%
.300–.399	67	46%	53%	49%
.400–.499	263	40%	44%	42%
.500–.599	325	31%	37%	34%
.600–.699	58	23%	32%	28%

The addition of Joe Carter, Roberto Alomar, Devon White, and Pat Tabler prior to the season, along with that of Candy Maldonado, Cory Snyder, and Dave Parker as the season progressed, amounted to a 58 percent change from the previous year—roughly twice the change typical of a team coming off a season as successful as that of the Blue Jays in 1990. But as we pointed out, Toronto's changes were even more unusual considering the team's age: Just as winning teams make fewer personnel changes than losing teams, younger teams tend to change their personnel less than older teams do. The following table contrasts the degree of change in teams with lineups with an average age of less than 27½ years to that of older teams, again classified by winning percentage. Notice that at every level, the turnover is lower on younger teams—not to an outstanding degree, but enough to establish the pattern:

	Younger Teams		Older Teams	
Year 1 Pct.	Teams	Change	Teams	Change
.300–.399	37	43.4%	30	49.0%
.400–.499	87	38.4%	176	40.1%
.500–.599	62	29.1%	263	31.0%
.600–.699	7	22.7%	51	23.4%

During the 30-year period ending in 1991, only 11 other teams coming off winning seasons made changes of at least 50 percent in their lineups. Furthermore, the table below shows that only two of those teams—the 1976 Athletics and the 1988 Yankees—surpassed the degree of change on the Jays. Both had pressing reasons: the A's lost more than half their starters to free agency (Sal Bando, Don Baylor, Bert Campaneris, Joe Rudi, and Gene Tenace); the Yankees had the league's second-oldest lineup in 1988, including Jack Clark, Willie Randolph, Claudell Washington, and Dave Winfield. Those 11 teams:

Years	Team	Change	Year 1	Pct.	Year 2	Pct.	Diff.
1990–91	Blue Jays	58.1%	86–76	.531	91–71	.562	+.031
1988–89	Yankees	67.3%	85–76	.528	74–87	.460	–.068
1988–89	Reds	50.4%	87–74	.540	75–87	.463	–.077
1983–84	Phillies	52.2%	90–72	.556	81–81	.500	–.056
1981–82	Rangers	52.9%	57–48	.543	64–98	.395	–.148
1981–82	Reds	55.6%	66–42	.611	61–101	.377	–.235
1979–80	Indians	50.5%	81–80	.503	79–81	.494	–.009
1978–79	Rangers	56.0%	87–75	.537	83–79	.512	–.025
1977–78	White Sox	53.9%	90–72	.556	71–90	.441	–.115
1976–77	Athletics	92.9%	87–74	.540	63–98	.391	–.149
1975–76	Cardinals	56.4%	82–80	.506	72–90	.444	–.062
1967–68	White Sox	54.0%	89–73	.549	67–95	.414	–.136

Toronto was the only one of those 12 to improve its record in the following season, adding the five wins necessary to capture last season's A.L. East title. The other 11 teams lost an average of 98 percentage points, equivalent to an additional 16 losses over a 162-game schedule.

In retrospect, it's fascinating that so much energy was expended a year ago trying to determine who got the better of the trade that brought Alomar and Carter from San Diego for Fred McGriff and Tony Fernandez. Certainly on a long-term basis, the answer to that question is still unclear. But Earl Weaver, who knows a thing or two about winning, once said that when a trade helps a team win even a single championship, any criticism of that trade based on long-term considerations is invalid. For instance, some Cubs fans with short memories might regret the trade in June 1984 in which Dallas Green sent Joe Carter and Mel Hall to Cleveland for Rick Sutcliffe. The truth is, Sutcliffe won 16 of 17 decisions that season to take the team as close to the World Series as it's been in nearly a half-century.

The same principle applies to the 1991 Blue Jays. There's no question that trading McGriff, Fernandez, Glenallen Hill, Mark Whiten, Denis Boucher, and some other minor leaguers whose names aren't yet familiar entailed considerable risk. But if at some future time, Blue Jays fans or even general manager Pat Gillick himself is inclined to regret the loss of some of those players, they can soothe themselves with a peak at the 1991 A.L. East championship flag.

Here's the irony: For all the attention lavished on the changes to his lineup, had Gillick not cemented his starting rotation with the midseason addition of Tom Candiotti—a move that appeared superfluous when the Jays opened a five-game lead in early September—Toronto might have sweated out another close finish in the A.L. East. And certainly the wisdom of his housecleaning would have been challenged, in light of the fact that the Jays scored only 4.2 runs per game last season, the fourth-lowest mark in the American League, after leading the league in 1990, scoring 4.7 runs per game. In fact, Gillick's moves were designed to improve two areas: the top of the batting order and team defense. And they appear to have worked. If the net effect was to rob the team of some offense (actually, the shortfall was to a large degree unavoidable and unrelated to changes in personnel), the gamble was that the team had enough to spare. That too proved correct.

With Devon White and Roberto Alomar regularly batting in the first and second slots and Joe Carter waiting in the circle, the Blue Jays scored an average of 0.58 runs in innings led off by either their first or second hitters. That average was the third highest in the league, up from seventh in 1990. But with batters from the third through ninth slots leading off—accounting for 70 percent of all innings—the Jays scored a league-low average of 0.42 runs, after leading the A.L. a year earlier (0.53). Toronto solved the problem at the top of its order, but the lower portion suffered.

Of course, in 1990 Kelly Gruber, Fred McGriff, and George Bell made the middle of Toronto's batting order among the best in the league. Last season, McGriff was playing in San Diego (by Gillick's choice) and Bell in Chicago (by his own choice), and Gruber missed nearly 50 games due to injury. The Blue Jays scrambled to compensate for the loss of all that power; they added 37 stolen bases and more than tripled their total of sacrifice bunts. But the net loss of 34 home runs proved to be insurmountable. The table below illustrates how the middle of Toronto's order deteriorated, and the character of its attack changed accordingly. League ranks appear in parentheses:

| Year | 3d/4th/5th Hitters | | | | Team Totals | | |
	HR	RBI	BA	Runs	HR	SH	SB
1990	60(2)	182(6)	.276(4)	767(1)	167(2)	18(14)	111(6)
1991	65(8)	263(13)	.257(11)	684(11)	133(8)	56(5)	148(2)

The loss of power barely affected Toronto's ability to score in any given inning. In fact, the Blue Jays scored exactly one run more often than any other team in the majors, but they put "crooked numbers" on the scoreboard only 163 times, down 20 percent from a year earlier, falling from first in the league to 12th in this category.

The net effect of Toronto's offensive breakdown might have been more damaging were it not for the fact that its pitching staff led the league in ERA after a seventh-place finish in 1990. As with most turnarounds, the improvement in Toronto's pitching staff was teamwide: Jimmy Key had his best season since 1987; Todd Stottlemyre improved from 13–17 in 1990 to 15–8; and David Wells and Duane Ward set career highs in wins (15) and saves (23), respectively. But an equally important factor in Toronto's rise to the top spot in ERA was the development of two rookies, Juan Guzman (10–3) and Dave Timlin (11–6)—the first pair of rookie teammates to win at least 10 games each since 1986.

How much of that improvement was attributable to better defense, in large part due to the addition of White and Alomar up the middle? Of course, that's always a difficult question to answer. But remember this: All three starters mentioned above—Key, Stottlemyre, and Wells—and Candiotti, too, are fly-ball pitchers. They benefit more than most from a fly-catcher like White, whose career average of 2.7 putouts per game ranks among the all-time top 20 (minimum: 750 games). Moreover, the player whom White replaced, Mookie Wilson, was far below the major league average in his ability to track and grab a fly ball.

Is there a lesson to be learned here? Maybe so, but one that those of us who revel in analysis are understandably reluctant to accept—namely, that baseball is a game of checks and balances, and that the margins between champs and runners-up are so narrow that chance often plays a more important role than design. A team can emphasize speed and defense, but in so doing it often sacrifices power. A team can strengthen the top of the order, but it might create a weakness in the middle. A team can trade to reshape its offense—or, as in the case of the 1991 Blue Jays, all of the above—but improved pitching could become the key to its success. A funny game, indeed.

ATLANTA BRAVES

Seven years ago, the St. Louis Cardinals came off a pair of near-.500 seasons to win 101 games and capture the N.L. East division title—surely one of the most surprising 100-game winners in major league history. It was a team with little power, an unproven rotation, and a bullpen trying to recover from the off-season loss of its record-setting closer, Bruce Sutter. The explanation for St. Louis's surprising season prompted a phrase that has become part of the lexicon not only for baseball, but for all sports: the "career year."

Three Cardinals starters—Tommy Herr, Willie McGee, and Ozzie Smith—had seasons at the plate well beyond the range of what their past performances suggested. Herr drove in 110 runs (more than double his previous career high) and batted .302, 26 points above his then-career mark. McGee won the Most Valuable Player Award with a .353 batting average; it wasn't until five years later, when he batted .324, that McGee left Norm Cash as the only player in major league history to bat .350 or higher but never reach .300 in any other season. Ozzie continued to develop as an offensive player, batting .276 (18 points higher than his previous best) with a career-high 54 RBIs.

What exactly is a career year? How rare are they, and how can they be measured? Last summer, we developed a standard for career years—an estimate of how far a player's performance in a given season strayed from his previous career record. The equations are based on standard statistical testing routines, of no general interest and far too complex to elaborate here. But here are the ground rules: (1) Forget the term "career year"; let's call them "breakthrough years." A small point, perhaps, but what seems like a career year at one time is often eclipsed later. Chili Davis's 1984 season seemed like a career year at the time, as did Terry Pendleton's in 1987. Not anymore they don't. (2) Breakthrough years are seasons far better than expected. The opposite is a "breakdown year." (For more on breakdown years, see the Indians essay.) (3) We're only talking about hitters; pitchers' records are far too unpredictable. (4) Breakthroughs and breakdowns are expressed in terms of percentages or odds that reflect the chance that a player's performance in that season could have been drawn randomly from his prior career record. For example, Tommy Herr had a 90-to-1 breakthrough (or a 1 percent breakthrough) in 1985; that is, there was only 1 chance in 91 that you could have randomly selected 696 plate appearances from his previous career and constructed a season as good as his actual one.

Breakthrough seasons, unpredictable by definition, provide us with a new device for explaining the success of teams that suddenly and surprisingly jump up in the standings from one season to the next, like the Braves in 1991. Six of Atlanta's regulars had true breakthrough seasons—performances with a less than one-in-four chance (25 percent). The following table contrasts their 1991 seasons (the top line) with a proportional slice of their career statistics to that point (the second line):

Player	Odds	AB	H	2B	3B	HR	RBI	BB	BA	SLG	OBA
Rafael Belliard	24%	353	88	9	2	0	27	22	.249	.286	.296
Projected		346	75	5	3	0	24	28	.218	.253	.283

Player	Odds	AB	H	2B	3B	HR	RBI	BB	BA	SLG	OBA
Jeff Blauser	22%	352	91	14	3	11	54	54	.259	.409	.358
Projected		372	98	20	3	8	37	32	.264	.400	.328
Ron Gant	15%	561	141	35	3	32	105	71	.251	.496	.338
Projected		587	154	29	6	25	71	46	.262	.456	.318
Jeff Treadway	11%	306	98	17	2	3	32	23	.320	.418	.368
Projected		307	85	14	2	5	29	19	.277	.388	.323
Otis Nixon	1%	401	119	10	1	0	26	47	.297	.327	.371
Projected		408	93	10	3	1	27	44	.228	.277	.303
Terry Pendleton	.003%	586	187	34	8	22	86	43	.319	.517	.363
Projected		591	153	27	4	8	76	43	.259	.356	.310

Two of the six qualified at the 1 percent level (there were only five such seasons in all of baseball last year), and one—Terry Pendleton—had the most outstanding breakthrough in the National League since 33-year-old journeyman Jim Hickman batted .315 with 32 home runs and 115 RBIs for the Cubs in 1970. Based on his previous career record, the odds against Pendleton having the season he had in 1991 were nearly 40,000-to-1. The success of Atlanta's young starting pitchers notwithstanding, those individual batting performances go a long way toward explaining the Braves' rise from last to first in 1991.

Think of the 1991 Braves as a "plus-six": they had six breakthrough players with 300 or more ABs, and no breakdown players to offset them. Over the past 20 seasons, seven other teams were plus six or better. This group, including Atlanta's 29-win increase last season, gained an average of 10 games in the standings, and those teams coming off losing seasons advanced by an average of 19 games:

Year	Team	Margin	From	To	Gain
1991	Atlanta Braves	+6	65–97	94–68	+29
1983	Toronto Blue Jays	+7	78–84	89–73	+11
1983	Atlanta Braves	+6	89–73	88–74	–1
1979	Seattle Mariners	+6	56–104	67–95	+10
1978	Milwaukee Brewers	+6	67–95	93–69	+26
1977	New York Yankees	+6	97–62	100–62	+1½
1977	Philadelphia Phillies	+8	101–61	101–61	0
1977	Pittsburgh Pirates	+7	92–70	96–66	+4

Unlike many of the other statistical indicators we've uncovered, like a team's records in one-run games or in spring training, breakthrough seasons aren't *leading* indicators; they can only be used in retrospect. Even so, they provide us with a new and satisfying explanation to some otherwise difficult puzzles like that of Atlanta's 1991 National League title.

Another ingredient in Atlanta's team breakthrough last season, one that received surprisingly little attention, was the man in the manager's office, Bobby Cox. Several years ago, we published the results of a survey in which we estimated the value of each manager in terms of the number of wins per season he added to his team. At that time, Cox stood among the top 10 managers in this century.

The survey was based on the premise that, over a period of time, a portion of the difference between the number of games a team wins and the number they were expected to win reflects the value of the manager. (The basic explanation of how we estimate the number of wins expected for each team appears on page 76 of the 1988 *Analyst*. The system has been further refined since then.) That may seem overly simplistic, but when you think about it, it's the basis on which each season's manager of the year is selected; we've simply added an objective, mathematical element to evaluate each team's expected level. Certain events—injuries, trades, the development of outstanding young players, and of course breakthrough seasons—can have an effect that the projection ignores. But over the course of time, such events tend to even out; good fortune balances bad. And for those teams for which the luck always seems to run in the same direction, at least a partial explanation can probably be found sitting at a desk behind the door to the manager's office. Sure, six breakthrough seasons help. But note that the last plus-six team, the 1983 Blue Jays, was also managed by Bobby Cox. Coincidence? Maybe, maybe not.

Last season marked the fifth time in Cox's 10 seasons as a manager that his teams won at least 10 more games than projected. Over the course of those 10 years, Cox's winning percentage is barely over .500 (755–740). But more importantly, he has won 36 more games than expected, or an average of 3.9 per 162 games. That average is the fifth highest in this century among managers with at least 500 games in the dugout, behind only Bill Armour, Davey Johnson, Pants Rowland, and Billy Martin.

Four years ago, we published a list of the top 20 managers according to our system. This time around, we've divided the list into three parts, according to the number of games they managed. To include all managers with 500 or more games in one single group would be as unfair as basing the batting title on, say, 250 or more at-bats. The tables below show how difficult it is for managers to maintain a three-win average over a long career: five did so over a career of 500 to 999 games, compared to four with 1000 to 1999 games, and only one with 2000 or more games. Since the projections for any given season are based on that team's performance in the recent past, a manager like Earl Weaver, who spent his entire career with the Baltimore Orioles, is, in a real sense, constantly being compared to himself—a difficult burden even for Earl. The records for the three groups:

Manager (2000+ Games)	Actual Record			Projected Record			
	W	L	Pct.	W	L	Pct.	Diff.
Billy Martin	1258	1018	.553	1195	1081	.525	+ 4.50
Joe McCarthy	2126	1335	.614	2062	1399	.596	+ 2.98
Dick Williams	1571	1451	.520	1518	1504	.502	+ 2.83
John McGraw	2754	1922	.589	2673	2003	.572	+ 2.81
Earl Weaver	1480	1060	.583	1438	1102	.566	+ 2.71
Sparky Anderson	1921	1523	.558	1866	1578	.542	+ 2.59
Bill McKechnie	1898	1724	.524	1843	1779	.509	+ 2.44
Danny Murtaugh	1115	950	.540	1085	980	.525	+ 2.37
Miller Huggins	1413	1134	.555	1382	1165	.543	+ 1.99
Fred Clarke	1422	969	.595	1393	998	.583	+ 1.99

Manager (1000-1999 Games)	Actual Record			Projected Record			
	W	L	Pct.	W	L	Pct.	Diff.
Davey Johnson	595	417	.588	564	448	.557	+ 5.02
Bobby Cox	755	740	.505	719	776	.481	+ 3.88
Billy Southworth	1064	729	.593	1027	766	.573	+ 3.38
Paul Richards	923	901	.506	887	937	.486	+ 3.22
Pat Moran	748	586	.561	727	607	.545	+ 2.57
Tony LaRussa	1038	883	.540	1008	913	.525	+ 2.50
Fielder Jones	685	582	.541	666	601	.526	+ 2.46
Herman Franks	605	521	.537	588	538	.522	+ 2.44
Danny Ozark	618	542	.533	601	559	.518	+ 2.35
Steve O'Neill	1039	819	.559	1014	844	.546	+ 2.19

Manager (500-999 Games)	Actual Record			Projected Record			
	W	L	Pct.	W	L	Pct.	Diff.
Bill Armour	382	347	.524	364	365	.499	+ 3.96
Pants Rowland	339	247	.578	325	261	.555	+ 3.96
Joe Morgan	301	262	.535	290	273	.515	+ 3.27
George Gibson	413	344	.546	398	359	.526	+ 3.23
Jim Leyland	496	474	.511	477	493	.492	+ 3.19
Bob Lemon	432	401	.519	417	416	.501	+ 2.97
Pete Rose	414	374	.525	400	388	.508	+ 2.91
Frank Selee	430	364	.542	417	377	.525	+ 2.72
Joe Kelley	337	321	.512	326	332	.495	+ 2.70
Sam Mele	518	427	.548	502	443	.531	+ 2.67

Cox's estimated value of 36 wins through nearly 1500 games is almost without precedent. Only three managers in this century had higher marks at the same points in their own careers: Billy Martin (47), Paul Richards (40), and Bill McKechnie (38). McCarthy won 33 more games than expected to that point; McGraw won 25 more.

The ultimate test for Cox will be whether or not he can manage a talented team of winners as well as he has handled lesser teams. Joe Cronin, Jimmy Dykes, Clark Griffith, and Pinky Higgins, productive managers for teams expected to compile losing records, were unable to improve the fortunes of their more talented teams. But Cox may have given us a glimpse in 1985 of what's to come when, after leading Toronto out of its infancy, he followed consecutive 89-win seasons with the team's first division title. For Atlanta, the only hurdle left is the world championship.

WON-LOST RECORD BY STARTING POSITION

Atlanta Braves	C	1B	2B	3B	SS	LF	CF	RF	DH	P	Leadoff	Cleanup	Starts vs. LH	Starts vs. RH	Total Starts
Steve Avery	-	-	-	-	-	-	-	-	-	24-11	-	-	9	26	24-11
Mike Bell	-	2-4	-	-	-	-	-	-	-	-	-	-	-	6	2-4
Rafael Belliard	-	-	-	-	63-47	-	-	-	-	-	-	-	27	83	63-47
Juan Berenguer	-	-	-	-	-	-	-	-	-	-	-	-	-	-	-
Damon Berryhill	-	-	-	-	-	-	-	-	-	-	-	-	-	-	-
Mike Bielecki	-	-	-	-	-	-	-	-	-	-	-	-	-	-	-
Jeff Blauser	-	-	18-9	5-7	31-20	-	-	-	-	-	-	-	39	51	54-36
Sid Bream	-	42-30	-	-	-	-	-	-	-	-	-	-	2	70	42-30
Francisco Cabrera	8-3	5-4	-	-	-	-	-	-	-	-	-	-	14	6	13-7
Vinny Castilla	-	-	-	-	0-1	-	-	-	-	-	-	-	-	1	0-1
Tony Castillo	-	-	-	-	-	-	-	-	-	-	-	-	-	-	-
Jim Clancy	-	-	-	-	-	-	-	-	-	-	-	-	-	-	-
Marvin Freeman	-	-	-	-	-	-	-	-	-	-	-	-	-	-	-
Ron Gant	-	-	-	-	-	86-59	-	-	-	-	5-4	34-27	42	103	86-59
Tom Glavine	-	-	-	-	-	-	-	-	-	21-13	-	-	7	27	21-13
Tommy Gregg	-	5-7	-	-	-	3-3	-	0-1	-	-	-	0-1	-	19	8-11
Mike Heath	17-20	-	-	-	-	-	-	-	-	-	-	-	15	22	17-20
Danny Heep	-	-	-	-	-	-	-	-	-	-	-	-	-	-	-
Brian Hunter	-	40-23	-	-	-	0-1	-	-	-	-	-	0-1	33	31	40-24
David Justice	-	-	-	-	-	-	-	63-43	-	-	-	56-35	30	76	63-43
Charlie Leibrandt	-	-	-	-	-	-	-	-	-	18-18	-	-	17	19	18-18
Mark Lemke	-	-	32-18	1-1	-	-	-	-	-	-	-	-	27	25	33-19
Rick Mahler	-	-	-	-	-	-	-	-	-	2-0	-	-	1	1	2-0
Kent Mercker	-	-	-	-	-	-	-	-	-	3-1	-	-	1	3	3-1
Keith Mitchell	-	-	-	-	-	1-0	0-1	6-2	-	-	6-3	-	5	5	7-3
Otis Nixon	-	-	-	-	-	21-12	7-7	25-21	-	-	53-40	-	16	77	53-40
Greg Olson	69-44	-	-	-	-	-	-	-	-	-	-	-	24	89	69-44
Jeff Parrett	-	-	-	-	-	-	-	-	-	-	-	-	-	-	-
Alejandro Pena	-	-	-	-	-	-	-	-	-	-	-	-	-	-	-
Terry Pendleton	-	-	-	88-60	-	-	-	-	-	-	-	1-0	39	109	88-60
Dan Petry	-	-	-	-	-	-	-	-	-	-	-	-	-	-	-
Armando Reynoso	-	-	-	-	-	-	-	-	-	4-1	-	-	1	4	4-1
Rico Rossy	-	-	-	-	-	-	-	-	-	-	-	-	-	-	-
Deion Sanders	-	-	-	-	-	8-15	1-1	0-1	-	-	5-10	-	2	24	9-17
Doug Sisk	-	-	-	-	-	-	-	-	-	-	-	-	-	-	-
Lonnie Smith	-	-	-	-	-	61-37	-	-	-	-	25-11	3-4	37	61	61-37
Pete Smith	-	-	-	-	-	-	-	-	-	4-6	-	-	2	8	4-6
John Smoltz	-	-	-	-	-	-	-	-	-	18-18	-	-	6	30	18-18
Mike Stanton	-	-	-	-	-	-	-	-	-	-	-	-	-	-	-
Randy St. Claire	-	-	-	-	-	-	-	-	-	-	-	-	-	-	-
Jeff Treadway	-	-	44-41	-	-	-	-	-	-	-	-	-	-	85	44-41
Jerry Willard	0-1	-	-	-	-	-	-	-	-	-	-	-	-	1	0-1
Mark Wohlers	-	-	-	-	-	-	-	-	-	-	-	-	-	-	-

TEAM TOTALS: BATTING

	AB	H	2B	3B	HR	RBI	BB	SO	BA	SA	OBA
Season	5456	1407	255	30	141	704	563	906	.258	.393	.328
vs. Left-Handers	1591	425	81	11	36	225	157	241	.267	.400	.332
vs. Right-Handers	3865	982	174	19	105	479	406	665	.254	.390	.327
vs. Ground-Ballers	2234	581	96	13	43	269	213	336	.260	.372	.325
vs. Fly-Ballers	3222	826	159	17	98	435	350	570	.256	.408	.331
Home Games	2709	739	127	12	83	388	275	427	.273	.420	.340
Road Games	2747	668	128	18	58	316	288	479	.243	.366	.317
Grass Fields	4008	1058	189	19	114	529	403	641	.264	.406	.332
Artificial Turf	1448	349	66	11	27	175	160	265	.241	.358	.319
April	603	143	28	5	12	71	61	95	.237	.360	.305
May	882	253	41	6	27	139	98	132	.287	.439	.360
June	987	251	46	7	21	110	83	165	.254	.379	.316
July	866	243	43	4	28	130	86	136	.281	.436	.345
August	1009	257	42	2	28	121	97	177	.255	.384	.320
Sept./Oct.	1109	260	55	6	25	133	138	201	.234	.362	.321
Leading Off Inn.	1324	354	55	9	42	42	112	204	.267	.418	.328
Runners On	2358	635	118	14	60	623	280	379	.269	.408	.345
Bases Empty	3098	772	137	16	81	81	283	527	.249	.382	.315
Runners/Scor. Pos.	1442	412	79	9	36	550	205	234	.286	.428	.368
Runners On/2 Out	997	247	41	8	17	232	146	170	.248	.356	.347
Scor. Pos./2 Out	674	173	26	4	10	204	118	113	.257	.352	.371
Late-Inning Pressure	719	168	29	5	11	80	92	130	.234	.334	.323
Leading Off	179	42	9	1	4	4	20	23	.235	.363	.322
Runners On	317	79	12	3	6	75	42	59	.249	.363	.335
Runners/Scor. Pos.	186	54	7	2	5	69	31	37	.290	.430	.385

RUNS BATTED IN	From 1B	From 2B	From 3B	Scoring Position
Totals	87/1607	232/1112	244/602	476/1714
Percentage	5.4%	20.9%	40.5%	27.8%

TEAM TOTALS: PITCHING

	W-L	ERA	AB	H	HR	BB	SO	BA	SA	OBA
Season	94-68	3.49	5429	1304	118	481	969	.240	.364	.303
vs. Left-Handers			1871	492	35	206	318	.263	.390	.335
vs. Right-Handers			3558	812	83	275	651	.228	.350	.286
vs. Ground-Ballers			2544	626	45	206	460	.246	.357	.303
vs. Fly-Ballers			2885	678	73	275	509	.235	.370	.303
Home Games	48-33	3.81	2801	711	73	227	461	.254	.391	.311
Road Games	46-35	3.16	2628	593	45	254	508	.226	.335	.295
Grass Fields	70-50	3.54	4017	969	96	331	683	.241	.372	.300
Artificial Turf	24-18	3.34	1412	335	22	150	286	.237	.341	.313
April	8-10	2.95	602	141	8	63	114	.234	.327	.312
May	17-9	3.14	898	222	26	60	153	.247	.392	.295
June	12-17	4.12	977	250	21	93	164	.256	.384	.318
July	16-10	4.31	846	205	23	80	138	.242	.371	.311
August	19-11	3.31	1004	242	23	86	196	.241	.372	.303
Sept./Oct.	22-11	3.06	1102	244	17	99	204	.221	.326	.287
Leading Off Inn.			1349	332	36	101	226	.246	.385	.301
Bases Empty			3198	744	66	262	572	.233	.348	.294
Runners On			2231	560	52	219	397	.251	.386	.317
Runners On/2 Out			956	218	22	113	170	.228	.356	.313
Scor. Pos./2 Out			623	142	12	95	119	.228	.353	.333
Late-Inning Pressure			843	185	13	73	149	.219	.308	.285
Leading Off			217	49	5	16	35	.226	.355	.282
Runners On			338	69	4	37	70	.204	.266	.284
Runners/Scor. Pos.			197	41	1	30	41	.208	.234	.314
First 9 Batters			2883	681	62	278	578	.236	.359	.305
Second 9 Batters			1366	311	28	109	238	.228	.347	.286
All Batters Thereafter			1180	312	28	94	153	.264	.395	.319

WON-LOST RECORD BY STARTING POSITION

Chicago Cubs	C	1B	2B	3B	SS	LF	CF	RF	DH	P	Leadoff	Cleanup	Starts vs. LH	Starts vs. RH	Total Starts
Paul Assenmacher	-	-	-	-	-	-	-	-	-	-	-	-	-	-	-
George Bell	-	-	-	-	-	69-76	-	-	-	-	-	33-36	64	81	69-76
Damon Berryhill	16-21	-	-	-	-	-	-	-	-	-	-	-	6	31	16-21
Mike Bielecki	-	-	-	-	-	-	-	-	-	15-10	-	-	8	17	15-10
Shawn Boskie	-	-	-	-	-	-	-	-	-	7-13	-	-	9	11	7-13
Frank Castillo	-	-	-	-	-	-	-	-	-	8-10	-	-	6	12	8-10
Doug Dascenzo	-	-	-	-	-	26-17	2-2	-	-	-	20-12	-	17	30	28-19
Andre Dawson	-	-	-	-	-	-	-	68-69	-	-	-	39-39	60	77	68-69
Shawon Dunston	-	-	-	-	60-71	-	-	-	-	-	-	4-3	60	71	60-71
Joe Girardi	9-5	-	-	-	-	-	-	-	-	-	-	-	12	2	9-5
Mark Grace	-	74-81	-	-	-	-	-	-	-	-	-	-	59	96	74-81
Mike Harkey	-	-	-	-	-	-	-	-	-	1-3	-	-	1	3	1-3
Danny Jackson	-	-	-	-	-	-	-	-	-	4-10	-	-	4	10	4-10
Les Lancaster	-	-	-	-	-	-	-	-	-	6-5	-	-	5	6	6-5
Ced Landrum	-	-	-	-	-	2-4	6-10	-	-	-	2-3	-	-	22	8-14
Greg Maddux	-	-	-	-	-	-	-	-	-	20-17	-	-	19	18	20-17
Derrick May	-	-	-	-	-	3-1	-	-	-	-	-	-	-	4	3-1
Scott May	-	-	-	-	-	-	-	-	-	-	-	-	-	-	-
Chuck McElroy	-	-	-	-	-	-	-	-	-	-	-	-	-	-	-
Erik Pappas	2-2	-	-	-	-	-	-	-	-	-	-	-	3	1	2-2
Dave Pavlas	-	-	-	-	-	-	-	-	-	-	-	-	-	-	-
Yorkis Perez	-	-	-	-	-	-	-	-	-	-	-	-	-	-	-
Laddie Renfroe	-	-	-	-	-	-	-	-	-	-	-	-	-	-	-
Luis Salazar	-	2-2	-	39-39	-	-	-	-	-	-	-	-	47	35	41-41
Rey Sanchez	-	-	0-1	-	3-4	-	-	-	-	-	-	-	2	6	3-5
Ryne Sandberg	-	-	76-78	-	-	-	-	-	-	-	-	4-7	62	92	76-78
Bob Scanlan	-	-	-	-	-	-	-	-	-	7-6	-	-	4	9	7-6
Gary Scott	-	-	-	13-14	-	-	-	-	-	-	-	-	12	15	13-14
Heath Slocumb	-	-	-	-	-	-	-	-	-	-	-	-	-	-	-
Dave Smith	-	-	-	-	-	-	-	-	-	-	-	-	-	-	-
Dwight Smith	-	-	-	-	-	2-1	6-7	7-12	-	-	1-0	-	-	35	15-20
Doug Strange	-	-	1-2	-	-	-	-	-	-	-	-	-	2	1	1-2
Rick Sutcliffe	-	-	-	-	-	-	-	-	-	9-9	-	-	8	10	9-9
Hector Villanueva	23-28	1-0	-	-	-	-	-	-	-	-	-	0-1	35	17	24-28
Jose Vizcaino	-	-	1-2	2-3	14-8	-	-	-	-	-	-	-	5	25	17-13
Chico Walker	-	-	0-2	22-25	-	1-1	14-15	-	-	-	31-35	1-0	23	57	37-43
Jerome Walton	-	-	-	-	-	-	25-34	-	-	-	19-30	-	34	25	25-34
Rick Wilkins	27-27	-	-	-	-	-	-	-	-	-	-	-	9	45	27-27
Steve Wilson	-	-	-	-	-	-	-	-	-	-	-	-	-	-	-

TEAM TOTALS: BATTING

	AB	H	2B	3B	HR	RBI	BB	SO	BA	SA	OBA
Season	5522	1395	232	26	159	654	442	879	.253	.390	.309
vs. Left-Handers	2022	523	82	10	67	246	175	284	.259	.409	.318
vs. Right-Handers	3500	872	150	16	92	408	267	595	.249	.380	.304
vs. Ground-Ballers	2290	596	99	12	64	285	172	343	.260	.398	.311
vs. Fly-Ballers	3232	799	133	14	95	369	270	536	.247	.385	.308
Home Games	2829	731	126	10	93	362	217	425	.258	.409	.313
Road Games	2693	664	106	16	66	292	225	454	.247	.371	.305
Grass Fields	3945	1031	165	16	126	497	301	605	.261	.407	.315
Artificial Turf	1577	364	67	10	33	157	141	274	.231	.349	.296
April	698	161	31	3	19	81	63	99	.231	.365	.298
May	909	241	42	4	35	107	57	147	.265	.436	.311
June	967	261	35	4	25	110	76	160	.270	.392	.325
July	885	219	45	3	25	116	80	145	.247	.390	.311
August	1023	263	38	7	20	117	69	167	.257	.367	.304
Sept./Oct.	1040	250	41	5	35	123	97	161	.240	.390	.305
Leading Off Inn.	1354	332	63	6	44	44	95	208	.245	.398	.300
Runners On	2254	596	99	14	68	563	199	352	.264	.411	.320
Bases Empty	3268	799	133	12	91	91	243	527	.244	.376	.302
Runners/Scor. Pos.	1285	320	51	9	41	482	145	214	.249	.398	.318
Runners On/2 Out	993	237	38	5	25	203	100	165	.239	.363	.313
Scor. Pos./2 Out	637	141	24	5	16	178	75	108	.221	.350	.309
Late-Inning Pressure	978	258	41	6	21	112	92	173	.264	.382	.330
Leading Off	244	64	13	1	6	6	25	46	.262	.398	.338
Runners On	413	112	18	4	11	102	47	78	.271	.414	.345
Runners/Scor. Pos.	240	62	6	2	6	86	32	45	.258	.375	.342

RUNS BATTED IN	From 1B	From 2B	From 3B	Scoring Position
Totals	86/1572	158/990	251/567	409/1557
Percentage	5.5%	16.0%	44.3%	26.3%

TEAM TOTALS: PITCHING

	W-L	ERA	AB	H	HR	BB	SO	BA	SA	OBA
Season	77-83	4.03	5499	1415	117	542	927	.257	.384	.324
vs. Left-Handers			2827	757	64	298	447	.268	.404	.337
vs. Right-Handers			2672	658	53	244	480	.246	.363	.310
vs. Ground-Ballers			2401	595	38	239	418	.248	.352	.317
vs. Fly-Ballers			3098	820	79	303	509	.265	.409	.329
Home Games	46-37	3.99	2931	763	75	257	501	.260	.397	.319
Road Games	31-46	4.08	2568	652	42	285	426	.254	.369	.329
Grass Fields	59-56	4.15	3971	1039	93	377	679	.262	.396	.326
Artificial Turf	18-27	3.75	1528	376	24	165	248	.246	.354	.319
April	10-11	3.68	693	158	15	68	107	.228	.352	.296
May	14-12	3.95	881	220	18	83	141	.250	.370	.314
June	10-18	4.08	958	254	16	117	164	.265	.383	.350
July	14-11	4.78	934	274	22	61	159	.293	.421	.336
August	17-12	3.50	1001	249	22	98	179	.249	.384	.314
Sept./Oct.	12-19	4.19	1032	260	24	115	177	.252	.386	.325
Leading Off Inn.			1311	345	30	142	200	.263	.399	.340
Bases Empty			3111	760	63	273	536	.244	.365	.308
Runners On			2388	655	54	269	391	.274	.408	.343
Runners/Scor. Pos.			1447	399	31	199	241	.276	.400	.354
Runners On/2 Out			997	245	23	131	177	.246	.378	.336
Scor. Pos./2 Out			678	160	16	104	127	.236	.372	.339
Late-Inning Pressure			994	262	22	113	211	.264	.378	.340
Leading Off			246	72	8	25	53	.293	.431	.360
Runners On			438	122	9	63	95	.279	.404	.370
Runners/Scor. Pos.			261	80	8	47	48	.307	.467	.406
First 9 Batters			2930	720	67	322	568	.246	.373	.319
Second 9 Batters			1387	357	21	120	200	.257	.373	.318
All Batters Thereafter			1182	338	29	100	159	.286	.424	.343

CHICAGO CUBS

Who was the greatest right-handed hitter in Chicago Cubs history? Ask 100 Cubs fans and we're pretty sure nearly every one would say it was Ernie Banks. Most of the dissenters, probably all of them under the age of 20, would choose either Ryne Sandberg or Andre Dawson. Maybe there would be a vote or two for Ron Santo, or some support for old-timers like Hack Wilson, Gabby Hartnett, or Cap Anson. But would there be even a single vote cast for Hank Sauer? Probably not.

Based on the record, at least as it appears in *The Baseball Encyclopedia*, that doesn't seem a great injustice. Banks, Santo, Hartnett, and Sandberg all hit more home runs for the Cubs than Sauer hit. Those players and seven other right-handers all drove in more runs for Chicago as well. But a look at what *doesn't* appear in the record books under Sauer's name makes you wonder whether, given a chance, he might have grabbed a few votes away from Banks, Sandberg, and Dawson.

A gifted minor league slugger, Sauer was 31 years old by the time he won a regular starting position in Cincinnati's outfield. His rise to the majors was undoubtedly slowed by military service during World War II, but that doesn't explain why Sauer spent two full seasons in the minors *after* the war. Not ready for prime time? In 1947 he batted .336 at Syracuse, with 50 home runs and 141 RBIs. But for some reason the Reds felt he couldn't hit in the majors. There was some feeling that he was a "Triple-A hitter," a label affixed to many players of the era who established a comfort zone one rung below the major league level and failed to make a successful transition from the minors to the bigs. Sauer eventually proved the Reds wrong in a serious way when he belted 35 home runs, a team record at the time, for Cincinnati in 1948, his first full season in the majors.

Rather than admitting their error and reaping the benefits of Sauer's belated arrival, the Reds compounded it by trading him to the Cubs during the 1949 season. Why? Don't forget that this is the same team that later traded Joe Adcock, Frank Robinson, and Lee May—all of whom, like Sauer, would hit at least 200 home runs after leaving the Reds. Lest you conclude that Cincinnati was after younger players, forget it; the deal brought 32-year-old Harry Walker and 30-year-old Peanuts Lowrey to the Rhineland.

What if the Reds had traded Sauer seven or eight years earlier? From his 31st birthday until his 36th— that is, from 1948 through 1952—Sauer hit 165 home runs. Only seven players have had higher totals in that five-year age bracket: Babe Ruth, Willie Mays, Hank Aaron, Lou Gehrig, Mike Schmidt, Frank Howard, and Harmon Killebrew. And the projections below indicate that Sauer lost close to 200 home runs during two years in service to his country and several others in servitude to an unappreciative employer. Here's what Sauer might have done:

	G	AB	R	H	2B	3B	HR	RBI	BB	SO	SB	BA
1941–47	1015	3641	528	1004	169	31	148	579	320	523	18	.276
1948–59	1399	4796	709	1278	200	19	288	876	561	714	11	.266
Totals	2414	8437	1237	2282	369	50	436	1455	881	1237	29	.270

Hard to imagine Sauer in the 400-HR club? The list of players above indicates that once Sauer was let loose, he competed on equal footing with all but the greatest home run hitters in major league history. So it's perfectly reasonable to conclude that had Sauer spent another five or 10 prime years in Wrigley Field, he might now be placed alongside Banks and a few select others as the greatest right-handed hitters in Cubs history.

In the White Sox essay, we promised you *two* more "What Ifs". Where Sauer's was enigmatic, Tony Conigliaro's is tragic. As a 19-year-old rookie in 1964, Tony C. hit 24 home runs, becoming the only teenager ever to reach the 20-mark. A year later, he became the youngest player in major league history to lead his league in home runs. The only younger player ever to reach 30 homers was Mel Ott. In his third season, Conigliaro ranked among the league's top 10 in both home runs (28) and RBIs (93). The next year, he was again among the A.L. leaders in homers and RBIs, and in batting average as well—a key player in Boston's "Impossible Dream" season—when an improbable nightmare occurred.

On August 18, 1967, Tony C. was beaned, causing injuries that interrupted his career, and eventually ended it after a moderately successful comeback a few years later. Conigliaro suffered a heart attack in 1982, and fell into a coma that caused irreversible brain damage. He passed away in 1990. Twenty-five years later, the magnitude of the tragedy has obscured the fact that Tony Conigliaro had the potential to become one of the greatest hitters in the history of baseball.

Four weeks before his beaning, Conigliaro became the second-youngest player ever to reach the 100-HR mark—a distinction he still holds. Conigliaro was 35 days older at the time than Ott was when he reached the 100 mark, and nearly a year younger than Johnny Bench, the third youngest ever to reach that level. Among the six most comparable players to Tony C. at age 22 are four Hall of Famers—Bench, Mickey Mantle, Eddie Mathews, and Frank Robinson—a near-miss, Orlando Cepeda, and Bob Horner, whose own unfulfilled potential was examined in the White Sox essay. So it's appropriate that the model assigns Conigliaro better than a 50-50 chance to have hit at least 500 home runs, and better than a 20 percent chance of hitting as many as 650. The best-guess projection:

G	AB	R	H	2B	3B	HR	RBI	BB	SO	SB	BA
2384	8040	1325	2184	327	65	513	1363	854	1620	34	.272

Conigliaro and Sauer, Williams and Greenberg, Robinson and Easter, that pair of Jacksons from the South Side, and hundreds of others we didn't mention here: Phil Rizzuto, Monte Irvin, Roger Maris, and Ken Hubbs, to name a few; all saw the natural course of their baseball lives interrupted, aborted, or twisted by forces out of their control. When we talk of the luck that must accompany greatness, we include in that the good fortune that keeps such forces at bay. Our "What Ifs" are an attempt to give them back some of what they lost (on the ballfield at least), on the basis of the abilities they demonstrated at the major league level. (Let us know if you'd like to see "What If . . .?" II in the 1993 *Analyst*.) As random and uncertain as events seem at the time, they tend eventually to harden into historical stone, creating the impression that things couldn't have happened any other way. How seriously should you take this stuff? Just seriously enough to serve as an occasional reminder that "what might have been" is often no less probable than history itself.

Every year, all teams—fantasy league or otherwise—cope to various degrees with the uncertainty posed by players coming off seasons in which they were injured. The most basic questions concern the health of those players in the spring, and the likelihood that the injuries will recur. Last season, the Cubs illustrated to an extreme degree how dangerous it is to rely on starting pitchers who spent time on the disabled list in the previous season, regardless of how they look in March.

Nearly everyone loved Chicago's chances throughout the spring of 1991. The addition of free agent George Bell gave the Cubs the most highly regarded lineup in the N.L. East. Danny Jackson and Dave Smith were viewed as solidifying the team's rotation and bullpen, respectively. But the whole house of cards collapsed when Jackson, Rick Sutcliffe, and Mike Harkey collectively spent two-thirds of the season on the disabled list and accumulated only seven wins among them.

But the physical deterioration of Chicago's rotation last season shouldn't have surprised anyone. All three pitchers had also spent time on the disabled list in 1990: Jackson for two months, Sutcliffe for all but five weeks, and Harkey for two weeks. (He also missed the last month of the season, although he wasn't placed on the D.L.) And it's perfectly normal for pitchers coming off injuries to fall far short of their previous season's performance. The Cubs had the bad fortune to go three-for-three.

Fourteen pitchers won at least 10 games in 1990 despite spending time on the disabled list. Only three of them won as many games in 1991 as they had in 1990—*the season in which they were originally injured.* For the record, half of them also spent time on the D.L. in 1991, but that only serves to underline the point: Pitchers coming off injuries can't be relied on. The roster:

Pitcher	1990	1991	Pitcher	1990	1991
Jack Armstrong	12–9	7–13	Jimmy Key	13–7	16–12
Kevin Brown	12–10	9–12	Eric King	12–4	6–11
Tom Candiotti	15–11	13–13	Jose Rijo	14–8	15–6
Lee Guetterman	11–7	3–4	Don Robinson	10–7	5–9
Mike Harkey	12–6	0–2	Nolan Ryan	13–9	12–6
Ted Higuera	11–10	3–2	Kevin Tapani	12–8	16–9
Dave Johnson	13–9	4–8	John Tudor	12–4	0–0

Those pitchers had a combined record of 172–109 in 1990 for a .612 winning percentage. Last season, their composite mark fell to 109–107 (.505). Their collective ERA rose slightly as well, from 3.56 to 3.71, but their total innings pitched declined by 18 percent.

Only one team had three pitchers who hit double figures in wins despite down time last season—the Oakland A's, with starters Dave Stewart and Mike Moore and middle-reliever Joe Klink. Milwaukee also had two starters (Chris Bosio and Bill Wegman) who

may present a similar risk in 1992. (Kansas City has spread its risk to New York; Mike Boddicker and Bret Saberhagen met the same criteria for the Royals last season.) These teams will need a strong dose of good fortune this year to avoid the obstacles that ruined the Cubs' chances last season.

The addition of George Bell to a lineup that already included Andre Dawson and Ryne Sandberg gave the Cubs three past MVP Award winners. While that distinction made the Cubs unique among all major league teams last season, it was hardly a rare occurrence historically.

The Most Valuable Player Award as we know it was first awarded in 1931. But even if the distinction is limited to MVPs since then who were still regular starting players—eliminating teams like the 1957 New York Yankees (Yogi Berra, Mickey Mantle, and pitcher Bobby Shantz) and the 1948 Cardinals (Marty Marion, Stan Musial, and a washed-up Joe Medwick on the bench)—the Cubs still weren't unique. In fact, there were two fairly recent teams on which *four* regular starters were past MVPs: the 1978 Cincinnati Reds (Johnny Bench, George Foster, Joe Morgan, and Pete Rose) and the 1982 California Angels (Don Baylor, Rod Carew, Reggie Jackson, and Fred Lynn). Teams that had three regular starters with MVP Awards already sitting in their trophy cases:

Year	Team	Players
1961	Yankees	Yogi Berra, Mickey Mantle, Roger Maris
1964–66	Yankees	Elston Howard, Mickey Mantle, Roger Maris
1971	Orioles	Boog Powell, Brooks Robinson, Frank Robinson
1979–80	Red Sox	Fred Lynn, Jim Rice, Carl Yastrzemski
1983	Phillies	Joe Morgan, Pete Rose, Mike Schmidt
1991	Cubs	George Bell, Andre Dawson, Ryne Sandberg

Except for the '61 Yankees, who were fortunate enough to have a future MVP (Howard) ready to replace a past one (Berra), this appears to have been a characteristic of dynasties on the edge of decline. (Or, in the case of the Cubs and Red Sox, pretty good teams in great hitters' parks.) But the free-agent era makes the movement of MVPs much more common; only one of the four '82 Angels had achieved that honor while wearing a halo. This distinction is probably nothing more than the answer to a good trivia question.

Of greater value is a lineup with three *future* MVPs. They have included:

Year	Team	Players
1934	Tigers	Mickey Cochrane, Charlie Gehringer, Hank Greenberg
1941–42	Yankees	Joe DiMaggio, Joe Gordon, Phil Rizzuto
1960–61	Yankees	Elston Howard, Mickey Mantle, Roger Maris
1961–64	Giants	Orlando Cepeda, Willie Mays, Willie McCovey
1971	Reds	Johnny Bench, Joe Morgan, Pete Rose
1972	Reds	George Foster, Joe Morgan, Pete Rose

So as Dawson winds his career down over the next few seasons, followed by Bell and Sandberg not too long thereafter, the Cubs will probably regret the potential MVP that got away—Rafael Palmeiro—more than they've savored the excitement of having three past MVP names on the same lineup card.

CINCINNATI REDS

We all make mistakes, and among ours was the well-reasoned but ultimately humbling observation that the 1991 Cincinnati Reds stood a strong chance to successfully defend their division title. That opinion wasn't a reflex reaction of the kind that often follows a World Series victory, especially one as decisive as Cincinnati's sweep of the seemingly invincible Oakland A's in 1990. Even after that, many considered the Reds nothing more than a run-of-the-mill division winner.

Frankly, we shared that opinion until a closer look revealed that the Reds were an unusually young championship team that managed to win the title without any truly spectacular individual performances. As we pointed out in the 1991 *Analyst,* Chris Sabo hit 25 home runs in 1990, but he drove in only 71 runs. Barry Larkin batted .301 and stole 30 bases, but those hardly seemed levels that he wasn't capable of reaching with regularity. The only other everyday player to hit .300 or better was Mariano Duncan (.306). And the average age of Cincinnati's lineup was 27.8 years, the youngest by a World Series victor since the 1969 New York Mets.

We weren't the only purveyors of this logic; others made the general observation that the '90 Reds were a young team without players who had career years that they were unlikely to duplicate. We merely quantified those thoughts—sort of like the economists who helped George Bush prove that the recession ended last summer. So where did we go wrong?

Actually, the notion that young teams are more likely to repeat than older division champs was absolutely correct. We didn't cite these figures last year, but now it can be told: Of the 14 division winners with an average age below 28, half successfully defended their titles, compared to only three of 19 over the age of 30.

But there were problems with our logic. First, the fact that no Reds player hit more than 25 home runs and none drove in 100 runs (or even 90 runs) might have been unusual, but it didn't imply that no one had a breakthrough season. (Moreover, you'll soon see that breakthrough seasons are a *positive* sign for a team in defense of a division title.) Second, we ignored an indicator more important than either a team's age or the number of breakthrough seasons: the margin by which it won its division. And Cincinnati's five-game victory in 1990 simply wasn't an overwhelming recommendation for a repeat win last season—an understatement considering that the 1991 Reds compiled the lowest winning percentage ever by a defending World Series champ. The 11 who finished below the .500 mark:

Year	Team	W–L	Pct.	Year	Team	W–L	Pct.
1991	Reds	74–88	.457	1919	Red Sox	66–71	.482
1918	White Sox	57–67	.460	1961	Pirates	75–79	.487
1932	Cardinals	72–82	.468	1983	Cardinals	79–83	.488
1986	Royals	76–86	.469	1964	Dodgers	80–82	.494
1967	Orioles	76–85	.472	1965	Cardinals	80–81	.497
1989	Dodgers	77–83	.481				

Now let's look at the connection between a team's margin of victory and the likelihood that it will successfully defend its title. Teams winning divisions by seven games or more were 14-for-31 the next season (45%), compared to 11-for-57 by teams with smaller

margins (19%). That latter figure is remarkable when you consider that in a six-team league you could pull the defending champ's name out of a hat nearly as often. The following table shows that even in the mid-range, where the 1990 Reds fell, the chances of a repeat are only about one in three. The division winners from 1969 through 1990 (not including the 1981 champions):

Margin	No. of Teams	Repeat Wins	Pct.
Less than 3 games	23	3	13.0
3 to 5½ games	23	7	30.4
6 to 9½ games	19	7	36.8
10 games or more	19	8	42.1

Not treating Cincinnati's rather slim five-game margin over the Dodgers as a warning sign was one error. Another was our conclusion that no Reds players had "career years" in 1990. Here's where our concept of the "breakthrough season" sheds new light on the topic—and provides an interesting conclusion.

As we've explained throughout this book, a breakthrough season is one in which a player significantly exceeded his previous performance; it is expressed in terms of percentages or odds that reflect the chance that the performance could have been drawn randomly from his prior career record. Above the 25 percent level, we no longer consider the season a breakthrough. Six Reds players had breakthroughs in 1990, five at extreme levels (that is, below 10 percent). Their performances didn't seem noteworthy at the time because, except for Sabo, the players were nondescript; only Duncan and Sabo were regular starters, and Doran's contribution was infinitesimal. As a result, the breakthroughs didn't produce flashy numbers. Nevertheless, combined with expected solid performances from Paul O'Neill, Barry Larkin, and Billy Hatcher, these seasons helped the Reds to a pennant:

Level	Player	AB	R	H	2B	3B	HR	RBI	BB	SO	BA
0.1%	Duncan	435	67	133	22	11	10	55	24	67	.306
0.7%	Doran	59	10	22	8	0	1	5	8	5	.373
7.1%	Sabo	567	95	153	38	2	25	71	61	58	.270
7.2%	Reed	175	12	44	8	1	3	16	24	26	.251
9.9%	Braggs	201	22	60	9	1	6	28	26	43	.299
16.9%	Winningham	160	20	41	8	5	3	17	14	31	.256

Even putting aside any factors directly related to the pitching staff, whose collapse was the real problem for the Reds, those breakthrough seasons would have given us ample reason to suspect that the Reds would not repeat, with so many players unlikely to perform as well as they did in 1990. The irony is that such a conclusion would have been the right call but for the wrong reason. Here's the kicker: Breakthrough seasons are a *positive* indicator for a division champ to defend its title successfully. We counted up the breakthrough seasons for every division-winning team, counting them double if they were extreme breakthroughs (10 percent or less) or if the player were a regular starter (400 or more plate appearances). The teams with 10 or more were 9-for-19 in defense of their title; those with less than four were 2-for-14.

Let's look at how these three factors combine to predict the likelihood that a division winner will repeat. Start by assigning the team a 25 percent chance. Add 2 percent for every game by which it wins the title; for example, add 20 percent for a 10-game margin. Add another 2 percent for each breakthrough season; remember to count it double if the breakthrough were extreme or if the player were a regular starter. (Of course, anyone who would sit around figuring out breakthrough seasons in such detail needs to get a life. So estimate them; you'll probably come pretty close.) Finally, subtract 5 percent for every year by which the team's average age—that is, the average of batters and pitchers—exceeds 25.

By that measure, the Reds were the division winner most likely to repeat last season (42%), and the Red Sox—an old team that won its division by a narrow margin (two games) with no breakthrough seasons—were the least likely in the history of divisional play (2.2%). Among the 10 teams that were given at least a 50 percent chance to repeat, five did; among the 20 assigned less than a 5 percent chance, only one repeated (the 1989–90 Athletics). Incidentally, among the 1991 division champs, Pittsburgh was assigned the best chance of repeating; "BTs" in the table below represents adjusted breakthrough seasons:

Team	Margin	BTs	Age	Chance
Pittsburgh Pirates	14.0	8	28.7	50%
Toronto Blue Jays	7.0	8	28.2	39%
Minnesota Twins	8.0	8	29.3	35%
Atlanta Braves	1.0	10	28.1	32%

Of course, that excludes the "Bobby Bonilla Factor." (Subtract 10 percent.)

Richie Hebner once said, "I stand at the plate in Philadelphia and I don't honestly know whether I'm in Pittsburgh, Cincinnati, St. Louis, or Philly. They all look alike." That may be true, but despite the widespread acknowledgment in recent years of how various ballparks affect the game, too many baseball writers, broadcasters, and fans are unaware of how different those four ballparks really are.

Busch Stadium in St. Louis opened in 1966 with a grass playing surface; artificial turf was installed prior to the 1970 season. Riverfront Stadium in Cincinnati opened in June 1970, Three Rivers Stadium in Pittsburgh in July of that year. Veterans Stadium in Philadelphia was ready for the start of the 1971 season, thereby making three new fields of nearly identical construction opening within a 12-month period, and a fourth of similar type made even more like the others.

We've written in the past about a pair of stadium effects that are nearly universal on artificial turf: an increase in extra-base hit percentage (the rate of doubles and triples compared to singles) and an increase in stolen-base percentage. Those similarities notwithstanding, Hebner's confusion is mystifying. The following table is distilled from the Ballparks Section (pp. 327–338), showing the effect of each of the so-called cookie-cutter parks on various key statistics. The ranks in parentheses show where each stadium stands among the 26 major league parks over the past five seasons:

Stadium	Home Runs	Batting Avg.	Scoring
Riverfront Stadium	+30% (1)	+3.4% (6)	+9.1% (3)
Three Rivers Stadium	−6% (18)	−3.2% (20)	+4.1% (7)
Busch Stadium	−23% (24)	−0.8% (16)	+0.4% (12)
Veterans Stadium	+2% (14)	−0.1% (12)	−4.6% (19)

Riverfront Stadium is the least known great hitters' park in baseball. Over the past five years, no other stadium has boosted home-run totals to as great a degree, and the only fields to increase scoring more are the Launching Pad and the Friendly Confines.

The following table includes everyone who played for the Reds, but for no other teams, in at least four of the past five seasons. They support the data in the Ballparks Section, with three of the six players hitting at least 50 percent more home runs at Riverfront Stadium than on the road:

Player	Home Games BA	HR	Road Games BA	HR
Eric Davis	.263	64	.279	68
Barry Larkin	.295	36	.295	19
Ron Oester	.262	1	.265	2
Paul O'Neill	.281	57	.243	25
Luis Quinones	.246	8	.225	11
Chris Sabo	.295	41	.261	27
Totals	.279	207	.266	152

A few years ago as a broadcaster for ESPN, Bill Robinson contramanded the prevailing attitude that the cookie-cutter stadiums had no redeeming features. He said that as a player, he valued their symmetrical dimensions and their sameness, which he felt provided a balanced opportunity for both batters and pitchers, with no unusual biases. Yeah, right.

You know, it's a funny thing about Hebner and Robinson, a pair of accomplished ex-big leaguers knowledgeable enough about the game to both have been hitting instructors at the major league level. And yet both were apparently blind to the major differences among these ballparks that are so similar, but only on a "surface" level. Although Hebner played for five different teams and Robinson for four, neither ever played for Cincinnati. If they had, you can be sure they'd have been more aware of how different those four ballparks are.

WON-LOST RECORD BY STARTING POSITION

Cincinnati Reds	C	1B	2B	3B	SS	LF	CF	RF	DH	P	Leadoff	Cleanup	Starts vs. LH	Starts vs. RH	Total Starts
Jack Armstrong	-	-	-	-	-	-	-	-	-	7-17	-	-	7	17	7-17
Freddie Benavides	-	-	0-2	-	9-7	-	-	-	-	-	-	-	6	12	9-9
Todd Benzinger	-	10-6	-	-	-	5-6	-	-	-	-	-	-	13	14	15-12
Glenn Braggs	-	-	-	-	-	23-24	-	9-5	-	-	-	2-2	39	22	32-29
Keith Brown	-	-	-	-	-	-	-	-	-	-	-	-	-	-	-
Tom Browning	-	-	-	-	-	-	-	-	-	20-16	-	-	17	19	20-16
Don Carman	-	-	-	-	-	-	-	-	-	-	-	-	-	-	-
Norm Charlton	-	-	-	-	-	-	-	-	-	4-7	-	-	4	7	4-7
Eric Davis	-	-	-	-	-	2-2	33-42	-	-	-	-	26-29	35	44	35-44
Rob Dibble	-	-	-	-	-	-	-	-	-	-	-	-	-	-	-
Bill Doran	-	0-2	29-49	-	-	1-4	-	-	-	-	16-28	-	16	69	30-55
Mariano Duncan	-	-	35-23	-	6-16	3-1	0-1	-	-	-	3-6	-	41	44	44-41
Steve Foster	-	-	-	-	-	-	-	-	-	-	-	-	-	-	-
Kip Gross	-	-	-	-	-	-	-	-	-	4-5	-	-	1	8	4-5
Chris Hammond	-	-	-	-	-	-	-	-	-	8-10	-	-	4	14	8-10
Billy Hatcher	-	-	-	-	-	27-32	23-23	-	-	-	16-13	-	32	73	50-55
Milt Hill	-	-	-	-	-	-	-	-	-	-	-	-	-	-	-
Reggie Jefferson	-	0-1	-	-	-	-	-	-	-	-	-	-	-	1	0-1
Stan Jefferson	-	-	-	-	-	1-1	0-1	-	-	-	1-1	-	-	3	1-2
Chris Jones	-	-	-	-	-	6-6	-	2-1	-	-	2-2	-	11	4	8-7
Brian Lane	-	-	-	-	-	-	-	-	-	-	-	-	-	-	-
Barry Larkin	-	-	-	-	-	57-63	-	-	-	-	13-12	-	41	79	57-63
Tim Layana	-	-	-	-	-	-	-	-	-	-	-	-	-	-	-
Terry Lee	-	1-1	-	-	-	-	-	-	-	-	-	-	2	-	1-1
Carmelo Martinez	-	10-11	-	-	-	6-10	-	-	-	-	-	5-2	23	14	16-21
Gino Minutelli	-	-	-	-	-	-	-	-	-	1-2	-	-	-	3	1-2
Hal Morris	-	53-67	-	-	-	-	0-1	-	-	-	0-1	2-3	19	102	53-68
Randy Myers	-	-	-	-	-	-	-	-	-	3-9	-	-	4	8	3-9
Joe Oliver	40-38	-	-	-	-	-	-	-	-	-	-	-	51	27	40-38
Paul O'Neill	-	-	-	-	-	-	-	63-82	-	-	-	23-36	38	107	63-82
Ted Power	-	-	-	-	-	-	-	-	-	-	-	-	-	-	-
Luis Quinones	-	-	10-14	3-10	2-2	-	-	-	-	-	-	-	11	30	15-26
Jeff Reed	33-44	-	-	-	-	-	-	-	-	-	-	-	-	77	33-44
Jose Rijo	-	-	-	-	-	-	-	-	-	19-11	-	-	9	21	19-11
Chris Sabo	-	-	-	71-78	-	-	-	-	-	-	17-16	16-16	54	95	71-78
Reggie Sanders	-	-	-	-	-	4-5	-	-	-	-	4-5	-	4	5	4-5
Mo Sanford	-	-	-	-	-	-	-	-	-	2-3	-	-	2	3	2-3
Donnie Scott	0-4	-	-	-	-	-	-	-	-	-	-	-	3	1	0-4
Scott Scudder	-	-	-	-	-	-	-	-	-	6-8	-	-	7	7	6-8
Glenn Sutko	1-2	-	-	-	-	-	-	-	-	-	-	-	1	2	1-2
Herm Winningham	-	-	-	-	-	0-1	14-16	-	-	-	2-4	-	-	31	14-17

TEAM TOTALS: BATTING

	AB	H	2B	3B	HR	RBI	BB	SO	BA	SA	OBA
Season	5501	1419	250	27	164	654	488	1006	.258	.403	.320
vs. Left-Handers	1749	446	86	9	49	213	167	359	.255	.399	.321
vs. Right-Handers	3752	973	164	18	115	441	321	647	.259	.405	.319
vs. Ground-Ballers	2617	687	138	12	61	314	213	446	.263	.394	.319
vs. Fly-Ballers	2884	732	112	15	103	340	275	560	.254	.410	.321
Home Games	2704	737	151	15	104	361	257	476	.273	.455	.336
Road Games	2797	682	99	12	60	293	231	530	.244	.352	.304
Grass Fields	1699	440	56	9	47	197	132	326	.259	.386	.314
Artificial Turf	3802	979	194	18	117	457	356	680	.257	.410	.323
April	634	146	30	2	14	59	60	115	.230	.350	.300
May	884	214	31	8	28	95	75	146	.242	.390	.306
June	955	279	53	6	33	141	118	183	.292	.464	.372
July	849	233	41	1	23	101	64	153	.274	.406	.324
August	1055	264	47	5	30	121	93	203	.250	.390	.312
Sept./Oct.	1124	283	48	5	36	137	78	206	.252	.399	.301
Leading Off Inn.	1331	338	64	3	44	44	107	249	.254	.406	.313
Runners On	2282	596	105	16	65	555	247	398	.261	.407	.331
Bases Empty	3219	823	145	11	99	99	241	608	.256	.400	.311
Runners/Scor. Pos.	1313	334	56	15	32	471	177	247	.254	.393	.337
Runners On/2 Out	1032	260	34	9	34	251	131	189	.252	.401	.340
Scor. Pos./2 Out	662	161	26	9	18	214	102	125	.243	.391	.347
Late-Inning Pressure	875	201	21	5	15	69	74	184	.230	.317	.292
Leading Off	215	50	5	0	2	2	18	41	.233	.284	.295
Runners On	366	73	8	4	7	61	39	80	.199	.301	.275
Runners/Scor. Pos.	198	41	5	3	5	56	29	45	.207	.338	.302

RUNS BATTED IN	From 1B	From 2B	From 3B	Scoring Position
Totals	91/1569	165/1037	234/545	399/1582
Percentage	5.8%	15.9%	42.9%	25.2%

TEAM TOTALS: PITCHING

	W-L	ERA	AB	H	HR	BB	SO	BA	SA	OBA
Season	74-88	3.83	5420	1372	127	560	997	.253	.379	.323
vs. Left-Handers			2279	579	46	284	438	.254	.377	.337
vs. Right-Handers			3141	793	81	276	559	.252	.380	.313
vs. Ground-Ballers			2455	607	29	241	481	.247	.337	.314
vs. Fly-Ballers			2965	765	98	319	516	.258	.413	.331
Home Games	39-42	4.24	2758	696	77	321	482	.252	.389	.329
Road Games	35-46	3.41	2662	676	50	239	515	.254	.368	.317
Grass Fields	22-26	3.33	1609	403	33	141	312	.250	.366	.313
Artificial Turf	52-62	4.04	3811	969	94	419	685	.254	.384	.328
April	11-8	2.95	633	144	12	46	119	.227	.310	.281
May	12-15	4.08	883	227	19	94	159	.257	.366	.328
June	18-10	3.69	929	233	26	113	171	.251	.397	.333
July	8-16	4.57	805	226	23	82	125	.281	.436	.344
August	15-16	3.55	1057	250	30	112	213	.237	.367	.312
Sept./Oct.	10-23	4.02	1113	292	17	113	210	.262	.384	.331
Leading Off Inn.			1315	325	36	120	237	.247	.373	.314
Bases Empty			3152	757	77	284	591	.240	.365	.307
Runners On			2268	615	50	276	406	.271	.398	.345
Runners/Scor. Pos.			1336	360	21	193	275	.269	.379	.351
Runners On/2 Out			993	244	16	130	184	.246	.347	.335
Scor. Pos./2 Out			669	163	10	95	133	.244	.344	.339
Late-Inning Pressure			729	192	11	75	188	.263	.365	.332
Leading Off			181	46	2	19	48	.254	.326	.328
Runners On			303	89	6	39	67	.294	.367	.371
Runners/Scor. Pos.			191	56	3	26	47	.293	.387	.372
First 9 Batters			2924	732	53	322	606	.250	.363	.325
Second 9 Batters			1363	342	41	128	230	.251	.390	.316
All Batters Thereafter			1133	298	33	110	161	.263	.408	.329

WON-LOST RECORD BY STARTING POSITION

Houston Astros	C	1B	2B	3B	SS	LF	CF	RF	DH	P	Leadoff	Cleanup	Starts vs. LH	Starts vs. RH	Total Starts
Eric Anthony	-	-	-	-	-	-	-	15-21	-	-	-	4-2	7	29	15-21
Jeff Bagwell	-	60-91	-	-	-	-	-	-	-	-	-	6-11	61	90	60-91
Craig Biggio	53-78	-	2-1	-	-	-	-	-	-	-	7-7	-	49	85	55-79
Ryan Bowen	-	-	-	-	-	-	-	-	-	6-7	-	-	6	7	6-7
Ken Caminiti	-	-	-	61-89	-	-	-	-	-	-	-	23-44	60	90	61-89
Casey Candaele	-	-	43-52	1-4	-	4-10	1-1	0-2	-	-	-	-	46	72	49-69
Mike Capel	-	-	-	-	-	-	-	-	-	-	-	-	-	-	-
Andujar Cedeno	-	-	-	-	28-38	-	-	-	-	-	-	-	27	39	28-38
Jim Clancy	-	-	-	-	-	-	-	-	-	-	-	-	-	-	-
Gary Cooper	-	-	-	2-1	-	-	-	-	-	-	-	-	1	2	2-1
Jim Corsi	-	-	-	-	-	-	-	-	-	-	-	-	-	-	-
Mark Davidson	-	-	-	-	-	4-8	-	5-10	-	-	-	-	24	3	9-18
Jim Deshaies	-	-	-	-	-	-	-	-	-	10-18	-	-	7	21	10-18
Tony Eusebio	1-6	-	-	-	-	-	-	-	-	-	-	-	3	4	1-6
Steve Finley	-	-	-	-	-	-	52-70	9-14	-	-	37-48	-	45	100	61-84
Chris Gardner	-	-	-	-	-	-	-	-	-	2-2	-	-	2	2	2-2
Luis Gonzalez	-	-	-	-	-	53-71	-	-	-	-	-	31-39	31	93	53-71
Pete Harnisch	-	-	-	-	-	-	-	-	-	16-17	-	-	15	18	16-17
Dwayne Henry	-	-	-	-	-	-	-	-	-	-	-	-	-	-	-
Xavier Hernandez	-	-	-	-	-	-	-	-	-	1-5	-	-	1	5	1-5
Jimmy Jones	-	-	-	-	-	-	-	-	-	7-15	-	-	11	11	7-15
Jeff Juden	-	-	-	-	-	-	-	-	-	0-3	-	-	2	1	0-3
Darryl Kile	-	-	-	-	-	-	-	-	-	8-14	-	-	6	16	8-14
Kenny Lofton	-	-	-	-	-	-	7-11	-	-	-	7-11	-	6	12	7-11
Rob Mallicoat	-	-	-	-	-	-	-	-	-	-	-	-	-	-	-
Mark McLemore	-	-	7-10	-	-	-	-	-	-	-	1-0	-	8	9	7-10
Andy Mota	-	-	8-18	-	-	-	-	-	-	-	-	-	12	14	8-18
Carl Nichols	5-9	-	-	-	-	-	-	-	-	-	-	-	7	7	5-9
Ken Oberkfell	-	3-4	-	1-3	-	-	-	-	-	-	-	-	-	11	4-7
Javier Ortiz	-	-	-	-	-	4-6	-	1-7	-	-	-	-	14	4	5-13
Al Osuna	-	-	-	-	-	-	-	-	-	-	-	-	-	-	-
Mark Portugal	-	-	-	-	-	-	-	-	-	15-12	-	-	11	16	15-12
Rafael Ramirez	-	-	5-13	-	9-18	-	-	-	-	-	-	-	21	24	14-31
Karl Rhodes	-	-	-	-	-	-	-	17-23	-	-	-	-	9	31	17-23
David Rohde	-	-	0-3	-	1-1	-	-	-	-	-	-	-	3	2	1-4
Curt Schilling	-	-	-	-	-	-	-	-	-	-	-	-	-	-	-
Mike Scott	-	-	-	-	-	-	-	-	-	0-2	-	-	1	1	0-2
Scott Servais	6-4	-	-	-	-	-	-	-	-	-	-	-	3	7	6-4
Mike Simms	-	-	-	-	-	-	-	18-20	-	-	-	1-0	17	21	18-20
Jose Tolentino	-	2-2	-	-	-	0-1	-	-	-	-	-	0-1	1	4	2-3
Dean Wilkins	-	-	-	-	-	-	-	-	-	-	-	-	-	-	-
Brian Williams	-	-	-	-	-	-	-	-	-	0-2	-	-	-	2	0-2
Eric Yelding	-	-	-	-	27-40	-	-	-	-	-	11-18	-	21	46	27-40
Gerald Young	-	-	-	-	-	0-1	5-15	-	-	-	2-13	-	20	1	5-16

TEAM TOTALS: BATTING

	AB	H	2B	3B	HR	RBI	BB	SO	BA	SA	OBA
Season	5504	1345	240	43	79	570	502	1027	.244	.347	.309
vs. Left-Handers	1964	480	86	9	25	199	192	372	.244	.336	.313
vs. Right-Handers	3540	865	154	34	54	371	310	655	.244	.353	.307
vs. Ground-Ballers	2510	614	106	21	30	263	221	453	.245	.339	.308
vs. Fly-Ballers	2994	731	134	22	49	307	281	574	.244	.353	.311
Home Games	2725	690	136	29	27	285	255	524	.253	.354	.318
Road Games	2779	655	104	14	52	285	247	503	.236	.339	.300
Grass Fields	1655	396	53	7	34	175	141	301	.239	.341	.301
Artificial Turf	3849	949	187	36	45	395	361	726	.247	.349	.313
April	637	141	24	6	6	46	62	129	.221	.306	.291
May	945	246	44	10	15	102	87	150	.260	.376	.322
June	953	219	39	2	13	76	94	169	.230	.316	.299
July	834	223	41	11	16	111	76	139	.267	.400	.332
August	1013	248	50	8	14	130	104	208	.245	.351	.318
Sept./Oct.	1122	268	42	6	15	105	79	232	.239	.327	.292
Leading Off Inn.	1363	336	64	12	16	16	102	243	.247	.346	.304
Runners On	2341	596	106	19	37	528	249	433	.255	.364	.324
Bases Empty	3163	749	134	24	42	42	253	594	.237	.334	.298
Runners/Scor. Pos.	1350	344	66	11	21	473	188	288	.255	.367	.340
Runners On/2 Out	1004	233	48	9	16	204	130	190	.232	.346	.323
Scor. Pos./2 Out	654	151	31	7	9	179	112	109	.231	.341	.346
Late-Inning Pressure	924	240	41	2	11	99	87	177	.260	.344	.326
Leading Off	223	51	10	1	1	1	20	47	.229	.296	.304
Runners On	404	110	14	1	6	94	48	73	.272	.356	.348
Runners/Scor. Pos.	234	70	11	0	2	84	35	49	.299	.372	.384

RUNS BATTED IN	From 1B	From 2B	From 3B	Scoring Position
Totals	70/1642	194/1088	227/518	421/1606
Percentage	4.3%	17.8%	43.8%	26.2%

TEAM TOTALS: PITCHING

	W-L	ERA	AB	H	HR	BB	SO	BA	SA	OBA
Season	65-97	4.00	5454	1347	129	651	1033	.247	.374	.328
vs. Left-Handers			2793	712	62	379	540	.255	.379	.343
vs. Right-Handers			2661	635	67	272	493	.239	.369	.311
vs. Ground-Ballers			2614	617	37	319	534	.236	.326	.319
vs. Fly-Ballers			2840	730	92	332	499	.257	.419	.335
Home Games	37-44	3.55	2775	648	44	318	551	.234	.339	.313
Road Games	28-53	4.49	2679	699	85	333	482	.261	.411	.343
Grass Fields	18-30	4.26	1560	399	50	205	283	.256	.405	.342
Artificial Turf	47-67	3.90	3894	948	79	446	750	.243	.362	.322
April	8-11	3.96	643	156	12	73	104	.243	.370	.320
May	10-18	4.28	934	235	23	122	169	.252	.387	.337
June	11-17	3.28	932	214	19	109	168	.230	.351	.309
July	12-13	3.94	848	220	20	96	152	.259	.384	.333
August	12-17	4.38	996	256	24	122	221	.257	.393	.341
Sept./Oct.	12-21	4.13	1101	266	31	129	219	.242	.362	.323
Leading Off Inn.			1295	318	32	158	226	.246	.378	.330
Bases Empty			3063	721	72	340	606	.235	.356	.314
Runners On			2391	626	57	311	427	.262	.398	.344
Runners/Scor. Pos.			1438	373	35	246	278	.259	.399	.359
Runners On/2 Out			1010	230	16	145	205	.228	.340	.329
Scor. Pos./2 Out			691	153	12	119	147	.221	.337	.339
Late-Inning Pressure			807	202	16	136	157	.250	.372	.359
Leading Off			198	50	6	40	35	.253	.409	.378
Runners On			372	107	8	63	68	.288	.425	.390
Runners/Scor. Pos.			225	67	7	53	40	.298	.453	.423
First 9 Batters			3007	745	67	358	603	.248	.366	.328
Second 9 Batters			1358	334	33	170	246	.246	.384	.332
All Batters Thereafter			1089	268	29	123	184	.246	.385	.323

HOUSTON ASTROS

This year marks the 30th anniversary of the Houston franchise—a sobering reminder of the passage of time for those who clearly remember the eight-team leagues, and a mark of the frustration of lifelong Astros fans who could have expected Houston at least to have hosted a World Series game by this time, if not won the title.

Thirty years without a league title is not a record to be proud of. And yet, from the mid-1960s through the early 1970s Houston built a foundation for the kind of consistent winner that Kansas City constructed in the mid-1970s and Toronto built in the mid-1980s, at comparable points in the history of those franchises.

Houston's early years were humbling; the team was known as the Colt .45s and played in Colt Stadium, otherwise known as "Mosquito Heaven." Their lineup in 1962 reflected the reluctance of the eight established teams to make available any promising young talent in the expansion draft. Houston's regular starting eight included four players over the age of 30 who were coming off seasons in which they had fewer than 300 at-bats in the majors: first baseman Norm Larker, shortstop Bob Lillis, left fielder Roman Mejias, and catcher Hal Smith. The only N.L. team with an older lineup was Pittsburgh, two years removed from their World Series victory. (The league's other expansion team, the Mets, had a lineup with an average age of 29 years, 10 months—or two weeks younger than Houston's.) The Colts' pitching staff was old, too, with an average of 29 years, 1 month (the seventh oldest in the league).

But just three years later, Houston was playing in a new home—and what a home!—and under a new name, the Astros. More importantly, a lineup of young players with exceptional potential suggested a promising future for the club.

The 1965 Astros lost 97 games, but that lineup included 21-year-old Joe Morgan (.271, 14 HR, 97 BB, and 20 SB); 21-year-old Rusty Staub (.256, 14 HR, 63 RBI); and 23-year-old Jim Wynn (.275, 22 HR, 73 RBI). Among the 'Stros-in-waiting was 22-year-old Jerry Grote, who spent the '65 season in Triple-A after being prematurely rushed to the majors a year earlier. And the Astros' pitching staff featured an 18-year-old named Larry Dierker, who became the youngest since Bob Feller in 1937 to strike out as many as 100 batters. The players on the 1965 Astros produced an average of 425 runs after the 1965 season—not the highest total in the majors that season, but second to the Reds, which had Pete Rose, Tony Perez, Vada Pinson, and Leo Cardenas already in place and had begun assembling a team that three years later would produce the highest total of "future runs" in major league history (659). (The method for calculating average future runs was explained in the Red Sox essay in the 1990 *Analyst*.)

For teams with losing records, a total of 400 or more future runs usually reflects an impending turnaround. Examples include the 1957 Pirates (62–92, with a lineup that included 20-year-old Bill Mazeroski, 22-year-old Roberto Clemente, and 26-year-olds Bill Virdon and Dick Groat—a teamwide average of 415 future runs); the 1959 Reds (74–80, with 20-year-old Vada Pinson and 23-year-old Frank Robinson—438 future runs); and the 1966 Red Sox (72–90, with a roster that included George Scott, Rico Petrocelli, and Tony

Conigliaro, all 23 or younger, and 26-year-old Carl Yastrzemski—420 future runs).

To complement the foundation from their 1965 team, the Astros organization continued to produce outstanding young players: Sonny Jackson in 1966; Doug Rader and Don Wilson in 1967; Nate Colbert and Bob Watson in 1968; Tom Griffin in 1969; Cesar Cedeno and John Mayberry in 1970; Cesar Geronimo, Roger Metzger, and Ken Forsch in 1971. But the team's reluctance to commit to several of those players (in particular, Colbert at first and Mayberry later) and some poor trades prevented Houston from fulfilling its potential. Those trades included: Dave Giusti for Johnny Edwards; Mike Cuellar for Curt Blefary; and Rusty Staub for Donn Clendenon, Jesus Alou, Jack Billingham, and Skip Guinn. (Clendenon refused to join the Astros, and the Expos sweetened the deal only with cash.) Colbert was lost to the Padres in the 1969 expansion draft.

Still, that steady stream of young talent produced another potential powerhouse in 1971, when the Astros' regular lineup included Morgan (then 27) and Wynn (29), joined by Cedeno (20), Rader (26), and Metzger (23). On the bench were Watson (25), Geronimo (23), and Mayberry (21). That team had an even higher total of future runs (448) than the '65 Astros. But four years later—after Morgan and Geronimo had been traded to the Reds, Mayberry went to the Royals for almost nothing, and Wynn was on the Dodgers—Houston compiled a 64–97 mark, and its future was in the past. In the 11 years from 1965 to '75, the Astros topped the .500 mark just twice, and never finished within 10 games of first place. Here's what their potential lineup produced in 1975:

NAME	G	AB	R	H	2B	3B	HR	RBI	BB	SB	BA
Mayberry	156	554	95	161	38	1	34	106	119	5	.291
Morgan	146	498	107	163	27	6	17	94	132	67	.327
Metzger	127	450	54	102	7	9	2	26	41	4	.227
Rader	129	448	41	100	23	2	12	48	42	5	.223
Watson	132	485	67	157	27	1	18	85	40	3	.324
Cedeno	131	500	93	144	31	3	13	63	62	50	.288
Staub	155	574	93	162	30	4	19	105	77	2	.282
Grote	119	386	28	114	14	5	2	39	38	0	.295
Totals	1095	3895	578	1103	197	31	117	566	551	136	.283

Those totals represent only the eight starters; they don't even reflect the value of Wynn as a pinch hitter and part-time starter (he hit 18 home runs for the Dodgers in 1975) or Geronimo as a defensive replacement *par excellence*. Nor do they include the more modest contributions of whoever filled the rest of the team's bench. Combined with the pitching of Dierker and rookie J.R. Richard, Houston might have provided strong competition for the Big Red Machine, which certainly wouldn't have been quite as imposing without Morgan and Geronimo.

As Houston progresses through its current rebuilding phase, the lesson of 20 years ago is that an essential part of rebuilding is patience. Biggio, Bagwell, Gonzalez, Taubensee, and another Cedeno provide the team with a foundation deeper, if not as top-heavy, as that of the '65 team. The first two are already household names, and we think the others are capable of stardom as well. (Check the Prospects Section and you'll probably agree.) Time will tell whether they eventually are the stuff of championships, and whether the current Astros administration can stay the course from which their predecessors strayed.

During the Astrodome's first quarter-century, the most sinister opponents faced by the homeboys had names like Mays, Stargell, Murphy, Schmidt, and Strawberry. That could change this summer when the Republican National Convention hits town, and a guy named Duke—as in David, not Snider—challenges favorite-son George Bush, with serious implications both political and moral.

The baseball ramifications are somewhat less weighty, but noteworthy nonetheless as the Astros will be evicted from their home for nearly a month when the elephants set up shop in July. The Stros will embark on a 26-game, 28-day road trip to eight different National League cities—one that would have been unique in recent annals were it not for an impromptu trip of equal length by the Expos last season, made necessary by structural damage to Olympic Stadium.

Does a team's performance deteriorate over the course of a long road trip? If so, the Astros' long road trip would amount to a competitive disadvantage. Four years ago, we noted that throughout most of this century, the road-field disadvantage was greatest in the *first* game of a road trip, but that the trend had lessened during the 1970s. An updated look at those figures confirms that the first-game penalty has indeed disappeared. But teams have recently demonstrated a tendency to play slightly but significantly better during the first five games of a road trip than they do later in the trip:

Years	Overall	First Game	First 5 Games	Game 6 and Later
1990–91	.462	.485	.470	.447
1980–89	.459	.442	.459	.458
1970–79	.462	.463	.462	.462
1960–69	.459	.459	.464	.453
1950–59	.461	.456	.469	.453
1940–49	.456	.432	.455	.456
1930–39	.447	.441	.444	.450
1920–29	.460	.449	.458	.457
1910–19	.460	.456	.461	.459
1900–09	.446	.463	.461	.437

Actually, the tendency toward declining performance after the fifth game started in the late 1980s. Since 1988, the winning percentage over the first five games of road trips (.466) has been 20 points higher than it was thereafter (.446); in fact, that percentage was .460 or higher in each of the first five games of a trip, below .460 in each game from six through ten (as well as collectively from game 11 on):

Game No.	1	2	3	4	5	6	7	8	9	10	11+
Win. Pct.	.467	.460	.466	.468	.470	.442	.435	.452	.440	.458	.446

Of course, to get a handle on the effects of truly long trips recent figures are useless. The average road trip has shrunk by about two games over the last 40 years, from 8.91 games in 1952, to 7.91 games in 1971, to 6.94 games last season. The Astros themselves haven't played more than 12 straight games on the road since

1985; their longest trip ever was 17 games over 17 days in 1968. (They also played 17 road games, over 14 days, in 1966.) And as we point out in the Expos essay, until Montreal's unscheduled trip last September no team had spent as long as 28 days on the road since 1944, when the Philadelphia A's played 25 games during a 31-day trip.

Road trips of even 10 games have become infrequent, accounting for 29 percent of all trips last season; percentages in the low 40s were common from the mid-1930s through the 1950s. And 20-game trips have become as common as 30-game winners, forfeited games, and unassisted triple plays. From 1965 through 1989, the only 20-game trip was made by San Diego in 1978 (one of the 21 games was a make-up of a game postponed earlier in the season). But during the 1950s, there was an average of five 20-game trips per year; and from 1943 through 1947, the average was 16 per year. Over the course of this century there were more than 700, providing us with an ample amount of data—data showing that long trips do carry an additional disadvantage, but only for trips even longer than Houston's upcoming tour of America.

The following summary of winning percentages at each stage of long road trips (20 or more games) shows remarkably little variation over the first 25 games. (Actually, the first-game mark of .406 is a significant departure, obscured when included with games 2 through 5.) But from that point on, performance deteriorates substantially:

1–5	6–10	11–15	16–20	21–25	26–Up
.441	.443	.442	.448	.445	.406

There will undoubtedly be a lot written this summer about the Astros' 28-day road trip, and rightfully so—no team has been scheduled for a trip that long in nearly 50 years. But a careful examination of similar trips throughout baseball history reveals that Houston faces no greater disadvantage from being on the road for so long a time than they would normally incur by leaving the Astrodome.

Actually, Houston's summer vacation does have a nice little benefit attached: The Astros will start the season with 15 consecutive home games. Only 12 other teams in major league history have opened the season with as many as 10 home games; in recent years, that prize has been reserved primarily for west coast teams, so as to minimize the chance of numerous early-season postponements that plague teams in the northeast. The only team ever to open its season with a home stand as long as Houston's was the 1961 Dodgers.

To the extent that Houston may be penalized by spending such a long time on the road later in the season, the season-opening home stand may provide appropriate compensation. While road teams in recent years have played better over the first five games of their trips than from the sixth game on, there's a corresponding effect at home: Since 1988, home teams have a winning percentage 20 points higher from the sixth game to the end (.554) than over the first five games. If they can use that opening stretch as a springboard for a fast start, the Astros may find some comfort for their homesickness during their midsummer marathon.

LOS ANGELES DODGERS

For most of the 16 years since the Messersmith-McNally ruling, the general perception has been that the Yankees and Angels, fueled by the free-spending policies of George Steinbrenner and Gene Autry, have dominated the free-agent market. Of course, over the years those teams have signed an abundance of free agents, from Baylor and Bostock, Reggie, Catfish, and the Goose to Gaetti, Langston, and Sax. But it was the 1991 Dodgers who may have reaped the greatest single-season harvest ever with their twin signings of Brett Butler and Darryl Strawberry, a pair of established and consistent stars coming off excellent 1990 seasons who fit the Dodgers' needs perfectly. Butler added strong defense to an outfield that a year earlier included Kirk Gibson, Kal Daniels, and Hubie Brooks, and his combination of speed and on-base potential solved the team's problems in the leadoff slot, an Achilles heel in 1990. Strawberry provided support for Eddie Murray in the middle of the Dodgers' batting order, which had been weakened by the off-season departures of Brooks and Gibson. Coming off an 86–76 season in a division without an acknowledged dominant team (the Reds' World Series sweep having been widely discounted as a fluke), Los Angeles was established as a heavy favorite in the race for the 1991 N.L. West title.

But like so many other recent teams whose superstar free-agent signings produced overly optimistic expectations, the Dodgers were unable to win their division title, losing a stretch run to Atlanta for a disappointing second-place finish. The Dodgers did manage to win seven more games than in 1990, but the team's improvement was largely attributable to the resurrection of its pitching staff. Despite the addition of Butler and Strawberry, the Dodgers' offensive production actually dropped, though not by nearly as much as their opponents':

Year	W–L	Dodgers' Runs Avg.	Rank	Opponents' Runs Avg.	Rank
1990	86–76	4.49	3d	4.23	7th
1991	93–69	4.10	5th	3.49	1st
Diff.	+ 7 wins	− 0.39 (−9%)		− 0.74 (−17%)	

Teams acquiring the top talent in the free-agent market are often disappointed by their failure to win a title. Over the first 15 free-agent signing seasons, there were 38 players who came to market having reached one or more of the following statistical milestones in the previous season: 30 home runs, 100 runs, 100 RBIs, 175 hits, 50 stolen bases, or a batting average of .300 over at least 502 plate appearances. (That group, it should be noted, doesn't include a couple of the most sought-after and valuable free agents, Reggie Jackson and Bobby Grich. Still, it does comprise most of the high-end talent to have reached the free-agent market.) Only 17 of those 38 players joined teams that improved their records the next season; even fewer of those teams (16) increased their scoring. And there was no collective improvement over the next two seasons either; their performance remained fairly constant.

For the record, a similar pattern emerged among teams that signed star free-agent pitchers. The statistical thresholds were: 15 wins, 25 saves, or an ERA below 3.00 over at least 25 starts. The results: 16 of the 38 pitchers joined teams that improved their records; 18 joined teams whose ERAs declined.

Strawberry and Butler can hardly be blamed for the decline of the Dodgers' offense last season. Butler drew more than 100 walks, scored more than 100 runs, and batted .296, missing only one game. Strawberry hit 28 home runs and drove in 99 runs despite spending two weeks on the disabled list (June 18–July 3). But it's true nonetheless that few of the quality free agents included in the groups above reached those same statistical thresholds the next year. Among the 38 free-agent batters, only 14 would have qualified based on their first seasons thereafter—including Butler, who once again reached the 100-run mark, but not Strawberry, who fell one RBI and two HRs short. (So sue him.) And the rate of players reaching those milestone levels declined steadily after that: 9 of 34 (26%) in year 2 (no, the group didn't shrink; but we don't yet know how Butler, Strawberry, Vince Coleman, and Willie McGee will fare as second-year reborn free agents); 5 of 32 in year 3 (16%); 2 of 30 in year 4 (7%); and none from year 5 on. The average performance of those 38 players in their final seasons before free agency (year 0), and in each of the three seasons thereafter:

Year	G	AB	H	R	2B	3B	HR	RBI	BB	SO	BA
0	147	549	159	84	27	4	17	79	58	76	.290
1	136	502	138	72	22	3	12	61	56	71	.275
2	127	454	121	63	19	2	13	58	48	61	.266
3	110	366	101	52	17	2	12	53	43	50	.275

The pattern of decline by pitchers is only slightly more encouraging. Fewer pitchers than batters would have qualified based on their first seasons after free agency: 13 of 38 (34%). But the pitchers didn't disintegrate quite as fast: 9 of 34 in year 2 (26%); 8 of 29 in year 3 (28%—nearly double the rate of batters at the same point); 6 of 28 in year 4 (21%); 2 of 27 in year 5 (7%).

Mind you, the fact that two-thirds of all players—batters and pitchers—didn't reach the same lofty levels after free agency as before isn't necessarily an indication that they performed poorly. Few players, free agents or otherwise, should be expected to score 100 runs, bat .300, save 25 games, or so on in any season, even if they did it the year before; to fall short of those totals doesn't necessarily mean they had poor or even disappointing seasons. (Strawberry's 1991 season is a case in point.) But the question arises, do free agents underperform other comparable players? There are lots of reasons why that could be so: playing in a new ballpark, for a new manager, and possibly against a new leagueful of unfamiliar pitchers; the pressure of a big-money contract, or the lack of incentive that the first seasons of a multi-year deal might bring; and so on.

Let's compare the number of breakthrough and breakdown seasons (defined in the Atlanta and Cleveland essays, respectively) by recent free agents to a group of comparable players. During the first two seasons after free agency, breakdowns were nearly three times as likely as breakthroughs:

	Yr.1	Yr.2	Yr.3	Yr.4	Total
Breakthroughs	8	3	8	2	21
Breakdowns	15	15	5	8	43

That's a more extreme contrast than you would find among a group of equally accomplished players that hadn't been free agents. The following figures show that for all other players to reach those same thresholds during the same period of time, the number of break-throughs and breakdowns are more evenly divided; in fact, they were nearly equal in year 1, with the relative incidence of breakdowns increasing each season—an observation consistent with what you'd expect from players presumably near their peaks:

	Yr.1	Yr.2	Yr.3	Yr.4	Total
Breakthroughs	181	152	133	104	570
Breakdowns	192	197	185	181	755

The contrast between the 38 high-profile free agents and other similar players was most striking in the first two years. Breakdowns were roughly three times as likely as breakthroughs for the free agents (by a 30–11 margin); they were just 17 percent more common than breakthroughs for the others (389–333). Those figures don't *prove* that the performance of free agents is compromised by issues that other players don't face, but they are totally consistent with such a conclusion. The odds that such a contrast would have occurred merely by chance are 40-to-1.

Can Butler and Strawberry step up their play a notch and put the Dodgers over the top in the N.L. West? Fewer than half of the 38 free agents—17 to be exact—had breakthrough seasons within the first three years. (Two had a pair: Bruce Bochte for the Mariners in 1979 and 1980, and Steve Sax upon leaving the Dodgers for the Yankees, in 1989 and 1991.) And the table of free-agent breakthroughs and breakdowns indicates that the second season is generally more troublesome than the first.

Age becomes a consideration for Butler, whose strengths are built around his speed. Last season, at age 34, he started 160 games in center field and stole 38 bases. The last player that old to steal as many bases was Davey Lopes, for the Cubs in 1985. Few teams rely on players in their mid-30s to fill a role that requires leadoff, baserunning, and defensive skills; but the Dodgers have done so often and successfully. Pee Wee Reese in the 1940s and Jim Gilliam and Maury Wills in the 1960s all combined on-base potential with base-stealing skills similar to those of Butler, as did Willie Randolph, an All-Star in his only full season with the Dodgers (1989).

As we wrote in the 1991 *Analyst*, Strawberry is among the most consistent players in the majors. He is the only player to hit at least 25 home runs in each of the last nine seasons. In fact, the only other player in major league history to reach the 25 mark in nine straight years starting with his rookie season was Eddie Mathews. And with each passing year, the similarity of Straw's statistical record to that of Reggie Jackson's grows. Our projection model suggests that Strawberry has nearly a 40 percent chance to reach the 40-HR mark, and that Butler has roughly a 30 percent shot at a fifth consecutive season scoring 100 or more runs. (He and Rickey Henderson have the only current four-year streaks.) Best-guess estimates for the 1992 season:

Player	G	AB	R	H	2B	3B	HR	RBI	BB	SO	SB	BA
Butler	143	524	86	145	21	8	6	36	68	58	32	.276
Strawberry	147	525	87	140	25	3	38	103	75	144	13	.266

Of course, even a pair of breakthrough seasons by Butler and Strawberry won't guarantee a division title in 1992. By cutting shortstop Alfredo Griffin loose, the Dodgers created a hole at a key position on the diamond, leaving the left side of their infield light years behind that of the Reds (Sabo and Larkin). That means the Dodgers could be more dependent on rookies this season than at any time since the 1970s—a situation with which they have become increasingly uncomfortable over the last decade. Shortstop Jose Offerman, third baseman Dave Hansen, and first baseman Eric Karros are being touted as *Russell, Cey, and Garvey: The Next Generation;* but no Dodgers rookie has gathered as many as 400 plate appearances since Mariano Duncan in 1985. (The only other team with a gap that long is the Yankees.) Unless those prospects give Tom Lasorda a reason to end that streak in 1992, Butler, Strawberry, and newly-acquired Eric Davis could form the greatest outfield ever to play for a second-division team.

WON-LOST RECORD BY STARTING POSITION

Los Angeles Dodgers	C	1B	2B	3B	SS	LF	CF	RF	DH	P	Leadoff	Cleanup	Starts vs. LH	Starts vs. RH	Total Starts
Tim Belcher	-	-	-	-	-	-	-	-	-	19-14	-	-	19	14	19-14
Brett Butler	-	-	-	-	-	-	91-69	-	-	-	91-69	-	67	93	91-69
John Candelaria	-	-	-	-	-	-	-	-	-	-	-	-	-	-	-
Gary Carter	30-25	4-0	-	-	-	-	-	-	-	-	-	-	43	16	34-25
Mike Christopher	-	-	-	-	-	-	-	-	-	-	-	-	-	-	-
Dennis Cook	-	-	-	-	-	-	-	-	-	-	1-0	-	1	-	1-0
Tim Crews	-	-	-	-	-	-	-	-	-	-	-	-	-	-	-
Kal Daniels	-	-	-	-	-	78-54	-	-	-	-	-	4-1	51	81	78-54
Butch Davis	-	-	-	-	-	-	-	-	-	-	-	-	-	-	-
Jose Gonzalez	-	-	-	-	-	1-0	-	0-2	-	-	-	-	3	-	1-2
Tom Goodwin	-	-	-	-	-	-	-	-	-	-	-	-	-	-	-
Jim Gott	-	-	-	-	-	-	-	-	-	-	-	-	-	-	-
Alfredo Griffin	-	-	-	-	61-46	-	-	-	-	-	-	-	44	63	61-46
Kevin Gross	-	-	-	-	-	-	-	-	-	-	5-5	-	5	5	5-5
Chris Gwynn	-	-	-	-	-	9-4	1-0	7-2	-	-	-	-	2	21	17-6
Jeff Hamilton	-	-	-	11-11	-	-	-	-	-	-	-	-	20	2	11-11
Dave Hansen	-	-	-	5-1	-	-	-	-	-	-	-	-	1	5	5-1
Lenny Harris	-	-	9-1	49-40	7-6	-	-	-	-	-	1-0	-	18	94	65-47
Mike Hartley	-	-	-	-	-	-	-	-	-	-	-	-	-	-	-
Carlos Hernandez	1-1	-	-	-	-	-	-	-	-	-	-	-	2	-	1-1
Orel Hershiser	-	-	-	-	-	-	-	-	-	16-5	-	-	7	14	16-5
Jay Howell	-	-	-	-	-	-	-	-	-	-	-	-	-	-	-
Stan Javier	-	0-2	-	-	-	3-7	1-0	9-5	-	-	1-0	-	18	9	13-14
Eric Karros	-	2-0	-	-	-	-	-	-	-	-	-	1-0	2	-	2-0
Barry Lyons	0-1	-	-	-	-	-	-	-	-	-	-	-	1	-	0-1
Ramon Martinez	-	-	-	-	-	-	-	-	-	19-14	-	-	14	19	19-14
Roger McDowell	-	-	-	-	-	-	-	-	-	-	-	-	-	-	-
Mike Morgan	-	-	-	-	-	-	-	-	-	17-16	-	-	10	23	17-16
Eddie Murray	-	84-64	-	-	-	-	-	-	-	-	-	60-44	60	88	84-64
Jose Offerman	-	-	-	-	22-15	-	-	-	-	-	-	-	15	22	22-15
Bob Ojeda	-	-	-	-	-	-	-	-	-	16-15	-	-	12	19	16-15
Juan Samuel	-	-	83-68	-	-	-	-	-	-	-	-	-	63	88	83-68
Mike Scioscia	62-42	-	-	-	-	-	-	-	-	-	-	-	24	80	62-42
Mike Sharperson	-	3-3	1-0	28-17	3-2	-	-	-	-	-	-	-	47	10	35-22
Greg Smith	-	-	-	-	-	-	-	-	-	-	-	-	-	-	-
Darryl Strawberry	-	-	-	-	-	-	-	76-60	-	-	-	28-24	56	80	76-60
Mitch Webster	-	-	-	-	-	2-4	1-0	-	-	-	-	-	7	-	3-4
John Wetteland	-	-	-	-	-	-	-	-	-	-	-	-	-	-	-
Steve Wilson	-	-	-	-	-	-	-	-	-	-	-	-	-	-	-

TEAM TOTALS: BATTING

	AB	H	2B	3B	HR	RBI	BB	SO	BA	SA	OBA
Season	5408	1366	191	29	108	605	583	957	.253	.359	.326
vs. Left-Handers	2322	565	75	13	41	256	230	444	.243	.340	.313
vs. Right-Handers	3086	801	116	16	67	349	353	513	.260	.373	.336
vs. Ground-Ballers	2292	588	81	13	38	279	239	412	.257	.353	.328
vs. Fly-Ballers	3116	778	110	16	70	326	344	545	.250	.363	.324
Home Games	2625	667	82	8	57	309	315	464	.254	.357	.334
Road Games	2783	699	109	21	51	296	268	493	.251	.360	.318
Grass Fields	3985	1018	138	18	86	461	432	691	.255	.364	.328
Artificial Turf	1423	348	53	11	22	144	151	266	.245	.344	.319
April	661	165	24	3	11	78	54	108	.250	.345	.306
May	881	213	29	3	19	105	118	176	.242	.346	.332
June	932	253	33	5	16	104	89	144	.271	.369	.334
July	857	215	32	6	18	100	89	158	.251	.365	.323
August	963	242	29	5	18	95	124	184	.251	.348	.338
Sept./Oct.	1114	278	44	7	26	123	109	187	.250	.372	.318
Leading Off Inn.	1333	333	39	6	24	24	119	219	.250	.342	.313
Runners On	2294	616	83	17	51	548	283	407	.269	.386	.347
Bases Empty	3114	750	108	12	57	57	300	550	.241	.338	.310
Runners/Scor. Pos.	1323	342	42	11	33	485	212	245	.259	.382	.354
Runners On/2 Out	1003	241	32	9	23	216	127	182	.240	.359	.330
Scor. Pos./2 Out	656	152	17	7	17	191	101	122	.232	.357	.338
Late-Inning Pressure	842	226	31	7	14	107	114	168	.268	.372	.356
Leading Off	209	61	9	1	6	6	30	34	.292	.431	.383
Runners On	396	110	15	4	6	99	59	79	.278	.381	.370
Runners/Scor. Pos.	248	64	8	0	5	89	47	55	.258	.351	.367

RUNS BATTED IN	From 1B	From 2B	From 3B	Scoring Position
Totals	83/1680	172/1043	242/593	414/1636
Percentage	4.9%	16.5%	40.8%	25.3%

TEAM TOTALS: PITCHING

	W-L	ERA	AB	H	HR	BB	SO	BA	SA	OBA
Season	93-69	3.06	5448	1312	96	500	1028	.241	.341	.306
vs. Left-Handers			2641	652	41	274	477	.247	.344	.319
vs. Right-Handers			2807	660	55	226	551	.235	.338	.294
vs. Ground-Ballers			2425	551	27	204	497	.227	.304	.286
vs. Fly-Ballers			3023	761	69	296	531	.252	.371	.321
Home Games	54-27	3.02	2799	671	46	256	566	.240	.328	.303
Road Games	39-42	3.10	2649	641	50	244	462	.242	.355	.309
Grass Fields	75-45	3.04	4115	985	74	366	788	.239	.334	.303
Artificial Turf	18-24	3.14	1333	327	22	134	240	.245	.362	.316
April	10-10	2.97	667	157	16	47	128	.235	.351	.285
May	17-10	3.11	904	230	15	97	166	.254	.356	.327
June	18-9	2.75	922	213	8	90	177	.231	.305	.300
July	13-13	3.45	873	220	14	84	139	.252	.355	.321
August	13-16	3.37	981	234	21	81	186	.239	.352	.297
Sept./Oct.	22-11	2.77	1101	258	22	101	232	.234	.332	.302
Leading Off Inn.			1365	335	28	90	253	.245	.352	.296
Bases Empty			3191	771	63	236	608	.242	.348	.297
Runners On			2257	541	33	264	420	.240	.331	.318
Runners On/2 Out			997	221	14	145	186	.222	.318	.322
Scor. Pos./2 Out			673	137	6	115	139	.204	.287	.322
Late-Inning Pressure			910	212	12	105	183	.233	.323	.314
Leading Off			225	57	4	24	41	.258	.369	.335
Runners On			394	84	2	60	84	.213	.277	.317
Runners/Scor. Pos.			244	52	1	48	57	.213	.291	.337
First 9 Batters			2819	663	46	250	613	.235	.333	.299
Second 9 Batters			1349	330	26	130	229	.245	.351	.312
All Batters Thereafter			1280	319	24	120	186	.249	.348	.315

WON-LOST RECORD BY STARTING POSITION

Montreal Expos	C	1B	2B	3B	SS	LF	CF	RF	DH	P	Leadoff	Cleanup	Starts vs. LH	Starts vs. RH	Total Starts
Bret Barberie	-	-	7-3	6-3	4-11	-	-	-	-	-	0-2	-	8	26	17-17
Brian Barnes	-	-	-	-	-	-	-	-	-	8-19	-	-	8	19	8-19
Oil Can Boyd	-	-	-	-	-	-	-	-	-	9-10	-	-	3	16	9-10
Eric Bullock	-	0-1	-	-	-	3-0	-	0-2	-	-	-	-	-	6	3-3
Tim Burke	-	-	-	-	-	-	-	-	-	-	-	-	-	-	-
Ivan Calderon	-	0-3	-	-	-	50-69	-	-	-	-	-	3-9	43	79	50-72
Ron Darling	-	-	-	-	-	-	-	-	-	0-3	-	-	1	2	0-3
Delino DeShields	-	-	62-83	-	-	-	-	-	-	-	52-67	-	41	104	62-83
Jeff Fassero	-	-	-	-	-	-	-	-	-	-	-	-	-	-	-
Mike Fitzgerald	16-31	1-2	-	-	-	-	-	0-2	-	-	-	-	23	29	17-35
Tom Foley	-	6-7	1-0	1-0	12-14	-	-	-	-	-	-	-	1	40	20-21
Steve Frey	-	-	-	-	-	-	-	-	-	-	-	-	-	-	-
Andres Galarraga	-	46-53	-	-	-	-	-	-	-	-	-	6-4	36	63	46-53
Mark Gardner	-	-	-	-	-	-	-	-	-	14-13	-	-	16	11	14-13
Marquis Grissom	-	-	-	-	-	-	59-68	3-1	-	-	16-19	-	50	81	62-69
Chris Haney	-	-	-	-	-	-	-	-	-	5-11	-	-	3	13	5-11
Ron Hassey	17-17	-	-	-	-	-	-	-	-	-	-	1-2	-	34	17-17
Barry Jones	-	-	-	-	-	-	-	-	-	-	-	-	-	-	-
Bill Long	-	-	-	-	-	-	-	-	-	-	-	-	-	-	-
Rick Mahler	-	-	-	-	-	-	-	-	-	2-4	-	-	2	4	2-4
Dave Martinez	-	-	-	-	-	7-9	11-19	21-27	-	-	-	-	11	83	39-55
Dennis Martinez	-	-	-	-	-	-	-	-	-	16-15	-	-	5	26	16-15
Greg McCarthy	-	-	-	-	-	-	-	-	-	-	-	-	-	-	-
Chris Nabholz	-	-	-	-	-	-	-	-	-	12-12	-	-	10	14	12-12
Junior Noboa	-	-	1-4	1-0	0-1	-	-	2-4	-	-	1-0	-	12	1	4-9
Spike Owen	-	-	-	-	55-64	-	-	-	-	-	1-1	-	51	68	55-64
Doug Piatt	-	-	-	-	-	-	-	-	-	-	-	-	-	-	-
Gilberto Reyes	28-35	-	-	-	-	-	-	-	-	-	-	-	29	34	28-35
Nikco Riesgo	-	-	-	-	-	-	-	0-2	-	-	-	-	2	-	0-2
Mel Rojas	-	-	-	-	-	-	-	-	-	-	-	-	-	-	-
Scott Ruskin	-	-	-	-	-	-	-	-	-	-	-	-	-	-	-
Bill Sampen	-	-	-	-	-	-	-	-	-	5-3	-	-	5	3	5-3
Nelson Santovenia	10-7	1-2	-	-	-	-	-	-	-	-	-	1-0	9	11	11-9
Dave Schmidt	-	-	-	-	-	-	-	-	-	-	-	-	-	-	-
John Vanderwal	-	-	-	-	-	8-9	-	-	-	-	-	3-1	3	14	8-9
Dave Wainhouse	-	-	-	-	-	-	-	-	-	-	-	-	-	-	-
Larry Walker	-	17-22	-	-	-	-	0-2	42-46	-	-	-	1-3	36	93	59-70
Tim Wallach	-	-	-	63-87	-	-	-	-	-	-	-	56-71	53	97	63-87
Ken Williams	-	-	-	-	-	3-3	1-1	3-6	-	-	1-1	-	16	1	7-10

TEAM TOTALS: BATTING

	AB	H	2B	3B	HR	RBI	BB	SO	BA	SA	OBA
Season	5412	1329	236	42	95	536	484	1056	.246	.357	.308
vs. Left-Handers	1875	464	83	10	40	193	170	386	.247	.366	.312
vs. Right-Handers	3537	865	153	32	55	343	314	670	.245	.353	.306
vs. Ground-Ballers	2481	608	117	19	39	244	215	479	.245	.355	.306
vs. Fly-Ballers	2931	721	119	23	56	292	269	577	.246	.360	.310
Home Games	2217	536	95	13	35	193	213	436	.242	.344	.308
Road Games	3195	793	141	29	60	343	271	620	.248	.367	.308
Grass Fields	1611	400	56	17	33	177	137	329	.248	.366	.307
Artificial Turf	3801	929	180	25	62	359	347	727	.244	.354	.309
April	652	159	24	5	8	52	48	120	.244	.333	.296
May	934	224	35	4	23	99	107	181	.240	.360	.318
June	952	239	52	7	13	104	104	192	.251	.361	.326
July	806	184	27	5	12	69	69	150	.228	.319	.288
August	943	233	50	11	21	89	79	180	.247	.390	.310
Sept./Oct.	1125	290	48	10	18	123	77	233	.258	.366	.305
Leading Off Inn.	1350	325	65	13	27	27	111	250	.241	.368	.300
Runners On	2206	554	89	18	36	477	228	427	.251	.357	.319
Bases Empty	3206	775	147	24	59	59	256	629	.242	.358	.301
Runners/Scor. Pos.	1355	330	58	10	19	420	182	292	.244	.343	.328
Runners On/2 Out	938	203	38	5	15	178	125	200	.216	.316	.311
Scor. Pos./2 Out	650	134	27	3	10	159	105	153	.206	.303	.318
Late-Inning Pressure	922	222	33	4	17	87	93	188	.241	.341	.313
Leading Off	234	53	8	2	4	4	23	46	.226	.329	.296
Runners On	377	95	12	2	6	76	46	83	.252	.342	.337
Runners/Scor. Pos.	249	58	9	2	3	70	37	57	.233	.321	.338

RUNS BATTED IN	From 1B	From 2B	From 3B	Scoring Position
Totals	64/1443	150/1024	227/593	377/1617
Percentage	4.4%	14.6%	38.3%	23.3%

TEAM TOTALS: PITCHING

	W-L	ERA	AB	H	HR	BB	SO	BA	SA	OBA
Season	71-90	3.64	5345	1304	111	584	909	.244	.368	.320
vs. Left-Handers			2269	566	44	286	367	.249	.379	.333
vs. Right-Handers			3076	738	67	298	542	.240	.361	.311
vs. Ground-Ballers			2325	561	30	227	397	.241	.341	.312
vs. Fly-Ballers			3020	743	81	357	512	.246	.390	.327
Home Games	33-35	2.86	2318	530	33	238	425	.229	.334	.302
Road Games	38-55	4.27	3027	774	78	346	484	.256	.394	.334
Grass Fields	19-27	4.49	1516	393	47	171	230	.259	.404	.335
Artificial Turf	52-63	3.32	3829	911	64	413	679	.238	.354	.314
April	7-13	3.75	647	160	13	80	82	.247	.383	.332
May	13-14	3.76	909	217	23	87	164	.239	.377	.306
June	13-15	3.70	976	259	20	99	172	.265	.382	.335
July	10-15	3.08	819	194	16	85	142	.237	.349	.311
August	9-19	3.77	926	216	15	106	151	.233	.350	.314
Sept./Oct.	19-14	3.75	1068	258	24	127	198	.242	.370	.324
Leading Off Inn.			1318	330	24	121	220	.250	.367	.316
Bases Empty			3057	731	58	311	514	.239	.353	.312
Runners On			2288	573	53	273	395	.250	.389	.331
Runners/Scor. Pos.			1377	341	33	198	258	.248	.387	.341
Runners On/2 Out			996	252	28	125	185	.253	.403	.340
Scor. Pos./2 Out			661	164	18	101	127	.248	.396	.353
Late-Inning Pressure			884	226	10	100	141	.256	.356	.334
Leading Off			230	61	3	26	31	.265	.370	.340
Runners On			384	111	5	64	64	.289	.406	.368
Runners/Scor. Pos.			230	65	4	37	41	.283	.400	.379
First 9 Batters			2860	674	58	318	527	.236	.354	.314
Second 9 Batters			1333	321	20	136	231	.241	.347	.313
All Batters Thereafter			1152	309	33	130	151	.268	.430	.344

MONTREAL EXPOS

A year ago, Montreal's infield appeared to be the team's strength. Veterans Andres Galarraga at first base and Tim Wallach at third were expected to provide 20 home runs each. Sophomore second baseman Delino DeShields was considered a potential .300 hitter who could steal 50 bases or more. And for shortstop Spike Owen, well, .250 seemed within reach. The Expos had power at the corners, speed and defense up the middle—the classic infield shape that so few teams now embody. The outfield, meanwhile, was filled with question marks. Marquis Grissom and Larry Walker were coming off somewhat disappointing rookie seasons, and Ivan Calderon would be asked to fill the shoes of Montreal's perennial near-superstar, Tim Raines.

Wrong on both counts! The Expos' outfield was one of baseball's best-kept secrets: Calderon batted .300 with 19 home runs; Walker batted .290 with 16 home runs; and Grissom batted .267 with 76 stolen bases. Expos outfielders had a composite batting average of .281, 10 points higher than that of any other National League outfield. And although their total of 43 home runs was slightly below the league average of 48, Montreal's outfielders also led the league in doubles (95) and stolen bases (129). The same can hardly be said of the team's infield. Although Owen raised his average by 21 points from 1990, actually reaching that elusive .250 mark, DeShields, Galarraga, and Wallach fell short of their 1990 figures by an average of 53 points. Galarraga's 37-point decline was the smallest, but taking into account his decline in extra-base hits from 49 to 24, and in home runs from 20 to 9, his breakdown was the third greatest in the National League last season, behind Rich Gedman and Pedro Guerrero. (An explanation of "breakdown seasons" can be found in the Indians and Cardinals essays.) Kal Daniels, Stan Javier, and Eddie Murray of the Dodgers comprised the only other set of three teammates in the majors last season to fall as far short of their 1990 batting averages. So while Montreal's outfielders batted 10 points higher than those of any other N.L. team, its infielders ranked last in the league, well below the 11th-place Mets:

Outfielders	BA	Infielders	BA
Montreal	.281	Cincinnati	.287
Atlanta	.271	Atlanta	.271
Los Angeles	.270	Pittsburgh	.269
Pittsburgh	.268	Chicago	.267
St. Louis	.267	Los Angeles	.262
San Diego	.263	St. Louis	.261
Chicago	.262	Philadelphia	.258
San Francisco	.261	San Francisco	.256
New York	.260	Houston	.255
Houston	.250	San Diego	.253
Philadelphia	.250	New York	.251
Cincinnati	.246	Montreal	.243

The Expos can only be thankful that they weren't saddled with Cincinnati's outfield. (Then again, imagine if Montreal had the Reds' infield!) But the unpredictability of Montreal's lineup last season only serves to underline a point made in last year's *Analyst:* how difficult it is to select from any class of rookies the players who will become stars. In fact, we may have unwittingly proved our own point: In the 1991 *Analyst* we offered the opinion, backed by an assortment of

numbers, that DeShields would be the true gem among Montreal's rookie class of 1990, despite the fact that Grissom and Walker had been more heralded prior to their rookie seasons. For the moment, though, we'll stand by that prediction. Despite DeShields's disappointing sophomore season, and the fine years by both Grissom and Walker, our projections still indicate that DeShields is the one most likely to have the longest career, the highest batting average, the most walks, and the most runs produced (runs plus RBIs). Here's how we projected the "final career statistics" for all three before last season, then after:

DeShields	G	AB	R	H	2B	3B	HR	RBI	BB	SO	SB	BA
Before	1230	4506	656	1315	220	50	56	522	440	408	169	.292
After	1342	4721	667	1249	204	38	57	472	727	965	310	.265

Grissom	G	AB	R	H	2B	3B	HR	RBI	BB	SO	SB	BA
Before	718	2278	290	596	99	22	28	248	207	238	66	.262
After	1123	3857	545	1016	167	39	38	315	329	627	318	.263

Walker	G	AB	R	H	2B	3B	HR	RBI	BB	SO	SB	BA
Before	929	2981	415	774	129	22	112	404	340	587	67	.260
After	1157	3805	472	980	182	15	137	473	403	867	90	.257

Furthermore, our projections indicate that DeShields is likely to hit at least .270 this season, with roughly one chance in four of surpassing even his .289 rookie-season mark. Such a rebound would be a strong first step toward restoring some offense to the Expos' infield.

Montreal's first major move following the 1991 season—trading Galarraga to the Cardinals—could also help to ease the imbalance between the team's potent outfield and its suddenly weak infield. When Galarraga was disabled last season in late May, it was Walker who became the Expos' first baseman, starting 23 of 37 games there before he himself was placed on the D.L. Still, Walker's outstanding play in right field makes him a less likely candidate to fill the hole at first base than Calderon, whose off-season shoulder surgery was fueled by the team's desire to move him to first base.

Do teams gather and lose momentum during the course of a season, putting together winning and losing streaks according to a sort of teamwide biorhythm cycle? You'd certainly think so, reading any sports section or listening to any baseball telecast. Writers, broadcasters, and fans too, routinely and unconsciously reflect their belief that every team's play rises and falls throughout the season in response to something more than a random pattern. How often have you heard someone say or write that it's a good/bad time for the home team to be facing the slumping/streaking so-and-sos? Or that a certain manager doesn't want to face a given opponent that's going badly, fearing the law of averages is about to turn things in their favor? Or even the newspaper handicappers, who tout a certain team because it's "on a roll"?

Well, maybe what we've got to say will help explain why some of those so-called expert handicappers fare no better each season than your five-year-old daughter, your pet chinchilla, or your ouija board. Momentum might be a handy concept for explaining a 10-game streak *in hindsight,* but teams put together wins and losses in a random pattern. Sure, each year a few teams win 10 or 12 straight games. And, inevitably, the manager, players, and fans will note that the ball is "bouncing right," everyone is "focused," and the team's "playing with confidence." All of those phrases mean the same thing: "We don't have a damned clue as to why this team, at this point in time, suddenly started winning. And we have no idea how long it's going to last." But when the bubble does burst, this much is certain: They'll claim the ball's just not bouncing right, and that the team has lost its focus, and its confidence is gone.

The fact is that a team's recent performance says nothing about how likely it is to win the next game. For any team, a win is no more likely following three straight victories than it is after three consecutive losses. The same can be said of streaks of five wins or losses—and probably any other total as well. We happened to choose those two levels when we published the evidence on this subject in the Expos essay in the 1988 *Analyst*. In fact, the data showed that from 1920 through 1987, more teams had better records after three losses (693) than after three wins (580). The margin after streaks of five wins or losses was even greater: 597–317 in favor of teams on losing streaks.

That's not to say that certain teams in given seasons don't put together more substantial streaks than would be possible if momentum weren't a factor. It's just that when 26 teams play more than 150 games every season—and have done so for more than a century—lots of screwy stuff happens. And last season, the Expos demonstrated a degree of streakiness almost unmatched in this century. Montreal had winning streaks of seven games, six games, and five games (twice), and losing streaks of 11 games, seven games (twice), and five games (twice). The Expos also had 15 runs of three or four games (six winning streaks and nine losing streaks). All told, streaks of three or more wins or losses accounted for nearly two-thirds of Montreal's games (110 of 161). There were only 25 times when the Expos won or lost a single game without extending it to a "streak" of two or more.

Statisticians refer to those discrete streaks as "runs." Come to think of it, so do pool players—as in "a 10-ball run," or "running the table." Because the Expos had so many streaks of three or more wins or losses, their season was divided into only 62 "runs." Montreal had a record of 71–90; the chance of selecting 71 wins and 90 losses at random and producing only 62 runs is more than 300-to-1. During the era of the 162-game schedule, only two teams went through an entire season with fewer runs: the 1962 Mets (59) and the 1969 Padres (61), a pair of expansion teams that won too few games to divide their losing streaks into shorter runs.

But among teams with records closer to the .500 mark, only three in this century had won/lost patterns that were less likely to have happened at random. The streakiest teams of the 1900s:

Year Team	W–L	Runs	Winning Streaks						Losing Streaks					
			5	6	7	8	9	10+	5	6	7	8	9	10+
1920 Cubs	75–79	59	0	1	0	0	1	1	3	0	0	0	0	1
1922 Indians	78–76	59	2	0	0	0	0	1	2	2	0	0	0	0
1940 Dodgers	88–65	57	4	1	1	0	1	0	2	1	0	0	0	0
1991 Expos	71–90	62	2	1	1	0	0	0	2	0	2	0	0	1

One factor that wasn't a part of Montreal's streaky season was the team's 26-game, 28-day season-ending road trip, necessitated by structural problems at Olympic Stadium. The Expos had only one streak longer than three games during that period: a four-game losing streak during the final week of the season.

Incidentally, that road trip was the longest in terms of games played since 1961, when the Los Angeles Angels played 27 straight road games during a 20-day period. Montreal's trip was the longest in terms of days since 1944, when the Philadelphia Athletics spent 31 days on the road, playing 25 games. And the trip helped produce the highest total of road games in one season in major league history: Montreal played a total of 93 games on the road; the previous high was 84, set in 1967 by the Baltimore Orioles and New York Mets. But despite a road record just barely over .400 (38–55), the Expos fell 10 short of the mark for road losses in a season. That was set in 1935 by the Boston Braves, who lost 65 of 78 road games.

As unusual as Montreal's 26-game, 28-day trip seemed at the time, it will be matched on both counts this season—weather and Gene Orza permitting—by the Houston Astros, who are scheduled to vacate the Astrodome for the Republican National Convention in July. Check the Astros essay for an analysis of the effects of long road trips.

NEW YORK METS

Ninety games into last season, the Mets stood at 52–38, just four games behind the division-leading Pirates. They were rolling merrily along with 13 wins in their last 17 games, but little did they know what lay around that next bend; like a little red wagon running up against an 18-wheeler, the Mets found themselves splattered all over the National League roadway. They won just four games in four weeks and wound up with a 77–84 record. No team in this century with that good a record through its first 90 games had ever finished so badly, and only the 1941 Indians, the 1970 Tigers, and the 1905 Naps fell from plus-14 or better to below the .500 mark.

Autumn brought changes: Al Harazin moved into the big office upstairs, and Jeff Torborg took over in the manager's office. Bobby Bonilla and Eddie Murray were added to the middle of the lineup, Willie Randolph was added to the middle infield, and Kevin McReynolds, Gregg Jefferies, and Keith Miller were shipped to Kansas City for Bret Saberhagen and Bill Pecota. The 1992 Mets will resemble the '91 team in uniform only.

In signing free agents Murray and Bonilla for a reported $36.5 million, the Mets added two hitters who have demonstrated remarkable durability. Murray has played in 150 or more games in 13 of 14 full seasons in the majors (excluding strike-shortened 1981) while Bonilla has averaged 160 games over the past four years. But most importantly, each is a certified run producer: Bonilla drove in 100 runs last season; Murray had 96 runs batted in. Since baseball began keeping track of RBIs in 1920, only three other teams have added a pair of 90-RBI men in a single off-season:

1932	Reds	Herman, Bkn. 97	Hafey, St.L. 95
1933	White Sox	Simmons, Phil. 151	Dykes, Phil. 90
1983	Yankees	Kemp, Chi. 98	Baylor, Cal. 93
1992	Mets	Bonilla, Pitt. 100	Murray, L.A. 96

But the most intriguing aspect of Bonilla's and Murray's coming to New York is that the Mets' lineup now contains three power-hitting switch-hitters. Going into spring training, it seems that Howard Johnson, Bonilla, and Murray, in some permutation, will bat three-four-five in the lineup. Never before in baseball history have three switchers with their power credentials been assembled in the same batting order. All three stand among the top 10 switch-hitters in major league history in both slugging percentage and home runs per at-bat:

Slugging Percentage Minimum: 2500 At-Bats				Home Run Ratio Minimum: 100 Home Runs			
	Pct.	AB	TB		Rate	AB	HR
Mickey Mantle	.557	8102	4511	Mickey Mantle	15.1	8102	536
Ripper Collins	.492	3784	1861	Howard Johnson	20.1	3959	197
Reggie Smith	.489	7033	3439	Eddie Murray	21.5	8573	398
Eddie Murray	.488	8573	4181	Mickey Tettleton	22.4	2348	105
Ruben Sierra	.474	3543	1680	Reggie Smith	22.4	7033	314
Bobby Bonilla	.472	3294	1554	Ruben Sierra	25.5	3543	139
Howard Johnson	.466	3959	1845	Tom Tresh	27.8	4251	153
Ted Simmons	.437	8680	3793	Ripper Collins	28.0	3784	135
Ken Singleton	.436	7189	3134	Bobby Bonilla	28.4	3294	116
Frank Frisch	.432	9112	3937	Chili Davis	28.4	5254	185

Including Vince Coleman and rookie catcher Todd Hundley, the Mets may have five switch-hitters in their lineup this season. That has been done before; the Cardinals went to the World Series in 1987 with five regular switch-hitters (Coleman, Willie McGee, Ozzie Smith, Terry Pendleton, and Tommy Herr) as well as supersub Jose Oquendo, who started 55 games. But what makes the Mets' current collection so interesting is the component of power. There have been eight pairs of switch-hitting teammates who had 20 home runs apiece in a single season: Mickey Mantle and Tom Tresh on the Yankees in 1962 and '66, Reggie Smith and Ted Simmons on the '74 Cardinals, Murray and Ken Singleton on the Orioles from 1977 through 1980, and Murray (still on the Orioles) with Mike Young in 1985. There have been three cases in which three switch-hitting teammates have each hit 10 or more home runs: the 1968 Yankees (Mantle 18, Roy White 17, Tresh 11), the 1985 Astros (Kevin Bass 16, Bill Doran 14, Mark Bailey 10), and the 1987 Astros (Bass 19, Doran 16, Alan Ashby 14). But the Mets will have a chance to become the first team in major league history with three switch-hitting teammates hitting 20 or more homers each. Three million Mets fans will expect nothing less.

Now, the bad news. The pitching staff, the cornerstone of the Mets' rise to power during the 1980s, fell apart faster than you could say "Sununu." Remember the good old days, way back in 1990, when the Mets owned six capable starting pitchers? In a 10-month period starting in December 1990, Bob Ojeda and Ron Darling were traded, Frank Viola left the team via free agency, and Dwight Gooden and Sid Fernandez both underwent surgery that at least brings into question, if not imperils, their future effectiveness. Only David Cone remained in good health, although after going 48–21 over the three previous years, he finished 14–14 last year.

But even with the off-season acquisition of two-time Cy Young winner Bret Saberhagen, for the first time in years the major questions surrounding the team are directed at the pitching. In particular, how successfully Messrs. Cone, Fernandez, and Gooden can come back will be the key to how the team does in 1992.

Those three pitchers have each averaged at least eight strikeouts per nine innings throughout their major league careers. Among pitchers who have made at least 100 starts, there are only seven other pitchers in major league history who have done that. Here's a list of the 10 highest strikeout rates in big league history:

Pitcher	Career	GS	IP	SO	Rate
Nolan Ryan	1966–91	733	5163⅓	5511	9.61
Sandy Koufax	1955–66	314	2325	2396	9.27
Sam McDowell	1961–75	346	2492	2453	8.86
Herb Score	1955–62	127	858	837	8.78
Bobby Witt	1986–91	157	980	951	8.73
David Cone	1986–91	138	1017⅓	966	8.55
Sid Fernandez	1983–91	201	1256⅓	1184	8.48
Roger Clemens	1984–91	240	1784⅓	1665	8.40
J.R. Richard	1971–80	221	1606	1493	8.37
Dwight Gooden	1984–91	236	1713⅔	1541	8.09

Six of the top 10 pitchers in this category are still active; only two started their careers before the expansion era, and even those two weren't exactly antediluvian: they each broke into the majors in 1955. But what about all of the flame-throwers of grampa's and great-grampa's time? What about Bob Feller, Dizzy Dean, Dazzy Vance, and Walter Johnson? Why don't they make the list?

The major reason is simply that the number of strikeouts in a typical major league game is greater now than it once was. Here's a look at the major league strikeout rates per nine innings broken down by 10-year segments:

Years	Rate	Years	Rate
1900–09	3.56	1950–59	4.43
1910–19	3.73	1960–69	5.73
1920–29	2.84	1970–79	5.16
1930–39	3.36	1980–89	5.39
1940–49	3.57	1990–91	5.76

The strikeout increase really took hold in the 1950s, perhaps in conjunction with Ralph Kiner's oft-quoted observation that "home-run hitters drive Cadillacs; singles hitters drive Fords." (Nowadays, it's "Singles hitters have to drive their own Cadillacs.") Strikeouts jumped to an even greater degree in the sixties; during that decade, the rule-book strike zone was redefined as "top-of-shoulders to bottom-of-knees" from 1963 to 1968, and baseball added eight expansion teams in a nine-year span. The rate declined in the seventies (some but not all of the decline was induced artificially by the American League's introduction of the DH in 1973). Then it grew again in the eighties, reaching the all-time one-season high of 6.01 strikeouts per nine innings in 1987.

Strikeout rates have also varied by leagues. It's no surprise that in each of the 19 seasons since the DH rule came in, the National League has had a higher rate of strikeouts per game than has the American. But the same was true for 27 of the 34 seasons from 1948 to 1971. From 1901 to 1947, the American had the higher rate in 36 of 47 seasons.

But what about Dizzy and Dazzy, Rapid Robert, and The Big Train? Would they rank among the top 10 in baseball history if we judged each relative to his own era? For each pitcher in this century, we calculated his annual strikeouts per nine innings and compared that rate with the average for his league that year. We used these yearly figures to generate an expected career rate of strikeouts for each pitcher, weighted by the number of innings pitched in each season.

The top 10 below shows each pitcher's actual rate of strikeouts per nine innings, along with his "expected rate"—that is, the rate that an average pitcher would have achieved pitching during the years and in the leagues in which a specific pitcher performed. The pitchers are ranked by the difference between the actual and the expected rates.

	Career	GS	Actual Rate	Expected Rate	Difference
Nolan Ryan	1966–91	733	9.61	5.30	+4.31
Herb Score	1955–62	127	8.78	4.74	+4.04
Sandy Koufax	1955–66	314	9.27	5.57	+3.71
Rube Waddell	1897–1910	340	7.04	3.65	+3.39
Dazzy Vance	1915–35	347	6.20	2.91	+3.29
J.R. Richard	1971–80	221	8.37	5.15	+3.22
Sam McDowell	1961–75	346	8.86	5.73	+3.13
Bobby Witt	1986–91	157	8.73	5.67	+3.06
Cy Seymour	1896–1902	123	5.13	2.34	+2.79
Roger Clemens	1984–91	240	8.40	5.63	+2.77

In one sense, this list is the greatest tribute to the dominance of Nolan Ryan. Not only has he maintained his position at the top of the heap despite the high recent strikeout rates; he also has maintained that ranking despite having started more than twice as many games as any other pitcher on the list.

This adjusted list of baseball's all-time top 10 in strikeout rates barely excludes the Mets' young bulls—Cone stands 11th (+2.72), Fernandez 12th (+2.69), and Gooden 15th (+2.31). Dazzy Vance, who threw smoke for the Dodgers during the twenties and thirties, appears on the list. But the other greats of the past whom we expected to see didn't make the cut. Feller (+2.27) ranks 16th, Dean (+1.97) stands 24th, and Johnson (+1.80) stands 32d on the all-time list. Surprised? So were we.

WON-LOST RECORD BY STARTING POSITION

New York Mets	C	1B	2B	3B	SS	LF	CF	RF	DH	P	Leadoff	Cleanup	Starts vs. LH	Starts vs. RH	Total Starts
Blaine Beatty	-	-	-	-	-	-	-	-	-	-	-	-	-	-	-
Daryl Boston	-	-	-	-	-	3-2	20-26	2-4	-	-	14-17	-	-	57	25-32
Hubie Brooks	-	-	-	-	-	-	-	50-47	-	-	-	20-12	40	57	50-47
Terry Bross	-	-	-	-	-	-	-	-	-	-	-	-	-	-	-
Tim Burke	-	-	-	-	-	-	-	-	-	-	-	-	-	-	-
Chuck Carr	-	-	-	-	-	-	0-1	-	-	-	-	-	1	-	0-1
Mark Carreon	-	-	-	-	-	13-20	10-6	2-2	-	-	1-3	1-0	43	10	25-28
Tony Castillo	-	-	-	-	-	-	-	-	-	3-0	-	-	2	1	3-0
Rick Cerone	32-31	-	-	-	-	-	-	-	-	-	-	-	32	31	32-31
Vince Coleman	-	-	-	-	-	34-36	-	-	-	-	34-36	-	24	46	34-36
Dave Cone	-	-	-	-	-	-	-	-	-	15-19	-	-	12	22	15-19
Ron Darling	-	-	-	-	-	-	-	-	-	8-9	-	-	6	11	8-9
Chris Donnels	-	10-4	-	3-5	-	-	-	-	-	-	-	-	7	15	13-9
Kevin Elster	-	-	-	-	45-53	-	-	-	-	-	-	-	52	46	45-53
Sid Fernandez	-	-	-	-	-	-	-	-	-	3-5	-	-	4	4	3-5
John Franco	-	-	-	-	-	-	-	-	-	-	-	-	-	-	-
Jeff Gardner	-	-	0-2	5-3	-	-	-	-	-	-	-	-	-	10	5-5
Dwight Gooden	-	-	-	-	-	-	-	-	-	16-11	-	-	11	16	16-11
Tommy Herr	-	-	26-14	-	-	-	-	-	-	-	-	-	19	21	26-14
Todd Hundley	7-10	-	-	-	-	-	-	-	-	-	-	-	5	12	7-10
Jeff Innis	-	-	-	-	-	-	-	-	-	-	-	-	-	-	-
Gregg Jefferies	-	-	32-42	24-25	-	-	-	-	-	-	0-2	-	45	78	56-67
Howard Johnson	-	-	-	47-52	12-13	-	-	13-17	-	-	0-1	20-22	58	96	72-82
Dave Magadan	-	56-59	-	-	-	-	-	-	-	-	-	-	35	80	56-59
Terry McDaniel	-	-	-	-	-	0-1	2-1	-	-	-	-	-	3	1	2-2
Kevin McReynolds	-	-	-	-	-	52-58	11-14	1-1	-	-	-	36-50	55	82	64-73
Keith Miller	-	-	19-26	0-1	-	4-2	-	5-5	-	-	23-25	-	35	27	28-34
Charlie O'Brien	29-27	-	-	-	-	-	-	-	-	-	-	-	27	29	29-27
Alejandro Pena	-	-	-	-	-	-	-	-	-	-	-	-	-	-	-
Mackey Sasser	9-16	1-8	-	-	-	5-1	-	4-8	-	-	-	-	2	50	19-33
Rich Sauveur	-	-	-	-	-	-	-	-	-	-	-	-	-	-	-
Pete Schourek	-	-	-	-	-	-	-	-	-	5-3	-	-	2	6	5-3
Doug Simons	-	-	-	-	-	-	-	-	-	0-1	-	-	-	1	0-1
Garry Templeton	-	7-11	-	2-0	15-15	-	-	-	-	-	-	5-0	24	26	24-26
Tim Teufel	-	3-2	-	1-1	-	-	-	-	-	-	-	-	5	2	4-3
Kelvin Torve	-	-	-	-	-	-	-	-	-	-	-	-	-	-	-
Julio Valera	-	-	-	-	-	-	-	-	-	-	-	-	-	-	-
Frank Viola	-	-	-	-	-	-	-	-	-	17-18	-	-	15	20	17-18
Wally Whitehurst	-	-	-	-	-	-	-	-	-	8-12	-	-	9	11	8-12
Anthony Young	-	-	-	-	-	-	-	-	-	2-6	-	-	3	5	2-6

TEAM TOTALS: BATTING

	AB	H	2B	3B	HR	RBI	BB	SO	BA	SA	OBA
Season	5359	1305	250	24	117	605	578	789	.244	.365	.317
vs. Left-Handers	2051	510	94	4	34	196	191	291	.249	.348	.313
vs. Right-Handers	3308	795	156	20	83	409	387	498	.240	.375	.320
vs. Ground-Ballers	2330	589	96	13	51	267	246	303	.253	.371	.324
vs. Fly-Ballers	3029	716	154	11	66	338	332	486	.236	.360	.312
Home Games	2670	657	123	12	57	307	300	390	.246	.365	.322
Road Games	2689	648	127	12	60	298	278	399	.241	.364	.313
Grass Fields	3787	925	176	15	78	425	398	558	.244	.360	.316
Artificial Turf	1572	380	74	9	39	180	180	231	.242	.375	.322
April	646	144	34	4	13	74	100	95	.223	.348	.327
May	859	226	41	4	22	110	85	138	.263	.397	.328
June	908	224	49	4	25	123	117	111	.247	.392	.332
July	893	218	41	1	17	103	95	115	.244	.349	.317
August	966	223	31	5	18	82	68	155	.231	.329	.283
Sept./Oct.	1087	270	54	6	22	113	113	175	.248	.370	.321
Leading Off Inn.	1313	332	66	4	36	36	126	172	.253	.391	.320
Runners On	2262	562	108	9	42	530	285	355	.248	.360	.330
Bases Empty	3097	743	142	15	75	75	293	434	.240	.368	.308
Runners/Scor. Pos.	1356	347	68	5	22	472	202	224	.256	.362	.345
Runners On/2 Out	982	231	44	4	19	218	127	162	.235	.346	.327
Scor. Pos./2 Out	661	159	32	2	13	190	96	113	.241	.354	.341
Late-Inning Pressure	824	188	37	3	24	87	114	140	.228	.368	.322
Leading Off	205	42	11	0	3	3	30	38	.205	.302	.306
Runners On	347	78	14	2	11	74	52	60	.225	.372	.323
Runners/Scor. Pos.	193	43	9	0	6	61	38	36	.223	.363	.346

RUNS BATTED IN	From 1B	From 2B	From 3B	Scoring Position
Totals	67/1580	192/1096	229/566	421/1662
Percentage	4.2%	17.5%	40.5%	25.3%

TEAM TOTALS: PITCHING

	W-L	ERA	AB	H	HR	BB	SO	BA	SA	OBA
Season	77-84	3.56	5466	1403	108	410	1028	.257	.374	.309
vs. Left-Handers			2443	628	36	199	461	.257	.363	.312
vs. Right-Handers			3023	775	72	211	567	.256	.383	.307
vs. Ground-Ballers			2591	652	22	183	514	.252	.333	.301
vs. Fly-Ballers			2875	751	86	227	514	.261	.411	.316
Home Games	40-42	3.73	2886	760	55	215	554	.263	.380	.314
Road Games	37-42	3.37	2580	643	53	195	474	.249	.368	.303
Grass Fields	54-61	3.57	3959	1013	85	292	735	.256	.374	.308
Artificial Turf	23-23	3.52	1507	390	23	118	293	.259	.376	.312
April	12-8	2.98	653	164	6	52	120	.251	.326	.307
May	14-11	3.58	875	227	20	64	160	.259	.390	.313
June	13-15	4.22	961	263	20	72	174	.274	.410	.325
July	16-11	2.86	876	200	24	62	189	.228	.347	.282
August	8-21	4.27	1007	284	17	83	189	.282	.390	.334
Sept./Oct.	14-18	3.26	1094	265	21	77	196	.242	.366	.292
Leading Off Inn.			1359	369	29	76	243	.272	.400	.313
Bases Empty			3152	793	56	214	581	.252	.365	.302
Runners On			2314	610	52	196	447	.264	.387	.319
Runners/Scor. Pos.			1368	348	31	159	289	.254	.372	.327
Runners On/2 Out			991	244	21	113	196	.246	.371	.326
Scor. Pos./2 Out			655	158	16	93	132	.241	.371	.339
Late-Inning Pressure			813	219	13	52	150	.269	.376	.313
Leading Off			204	57	3	10	38	.279	.373	.313
Runners On			364	92	5	23	66	.253	.357	.296
Runners/Scor. Pos.			216	51	3	16	46	.236	.356	.285
First 9 Batters			2796	666	49	231	565	.238	.343	.297
Second 9 Batters			1381	372	24	98	264	.269	.387	.319
All Batters Thereafter			1289	365	35	81	199	.283	.428	.326

WON-LOST RECORD BY STARTING POSITION

Philadelphia Phillies	C	1B	2B	3B	SS	LF	CF	RF	DH	P	Leadoff	Cleanup	Starts vs. LH	Starts vs. RH	Total Starts
Darrell Akerfelds	-	-	-	-	-	-	-	-	-	-	-	-			-
Andy Ashby	-	-	-	-	-	-	-	-	-	3-5	-	-	2	6	3-5
Wally Backman	-	-	11-12	7-10	-	-	-	-	-	-	11-13	-	2	38	18-22
Kim Batiste	-	-	-	3-4	-	-	-	-	-	-	2-1	-	2	5	3-4
Joe Boever	-	-	-	-	-	-	-	-	-	-	-	-			-
Rod Booker	-	-	-	1-0	5-6	-	-	-	-	-	-	-		12	6-6
Clifford Brantley	-	-	-	-	-	-	-	-	-	3-2	-	-	1	4	3-2
Sil Campusano	-	-	-	-	-	-	2-6	-	-	-	-	0-2	5	3	2-6
Amalio Carreno	-	-	-	-	-	-	-	-	-	-	-	-			-
Braulio Castillo	-	-	-	-	-	8-6	-	1-0	-	-	-	0-1	8	7	9-6
Wes Chamberlain	-	-	-	-	-	51-44	0-1	-	-	-	-	0-1	40	56	51-45
Pat Combs	-	-	-	-	-	-	-	-	-	5-8	-	-	7	6	5-8
Danny Cox	-	-	-	-	-	-	-	-	-	9-8	-	-	3	14	9-8
Darren Daulton	38-42	-	-	-	-	-	-	-	-	-	-	-	22	58	38-42
Jose DeJesus	-	-	-	-	-	-	-	-	-	13-16	-	-	11	18	13-16
Len Dykstra	-	-	-	-	-	-	36-26	-	-	-	36-25	-	23	39	36-26
Darrin Fletcher	20-16	-	-	-	-	-	-	-	-	-	-	-	3	33	20-16
Tommy Greene	-	-	-	-	-	-	-	-	-	16-11	-	-	15	12	16-11
Jason Grimsley	-	-	-	-	-	-	-	-	-	2-10	-	-	5	7	2-10
Mike Hartley	-	-	-	-	-	-	-	-	-	-	-	-			-
Charlie Hayes	-	-	-	49-60	0-1	-	-	-	-	-	-	-	51	59	49-61
Von Hayes	-	-	-	-	-	8-12	20-28	1-2	-	-	10-10	1-1	21	50	29-42
David Hollins	-	1-4	-	20-13	-	-	-	-	-	-	-	0-1	13	25	21-17
Ron Jones	-	-	-	-	-	-	-	-	-	-	-	-			-
Ricky Jordan	-	29-38	-	-	-	-	-	-	-	-	-	7-12	33	34	29-38
John Kruk	-	48-41	-	-	-	16-20	5-6	2-2	-	-	-	48-38	45	95	71-69
Steve Lake	20-25	-	-	-	-	-	-	-	-	-	-	-	37	8	20-25
Dave LaPoint	-	-	-	-	-	-	-	-	-	1-1	-	-	2		1-1
Jim Lindeman	-	-	-	-	-	2-5	2-1	3-3	-	-	-	-	13	3	7-9
Doug Lindsey	0-1	-	-	-	-	-	-	-	-	-	-	-		1	0-1
Tim Mauser	-	-	-	-	-	-	-	-	-	-	-	-			-
Roger McDowell	-	-	-	-	-	-	-	-	-	-	-	-			-
Mickey Morandini	-	-	39-46	-	-	-	-	-	-	-	10-14	-	9	76	39-46
John Morris	-	-	-	-	-	1-3	5-11	3-3	-	-	-	-		26	9-17
Terry Mulholland	-	-	-	-	-	-	-	-	-	18-16	-	-	13	21	18-16
Dale Murphy	-	-	-	-	-	-	-	68-73	-	-	-	22-31	56	85	68-73
Randy Ready	-	-	28-26	-	-	-	-	-	-	-	-	5-8	51	3	28-26
Wally Ritchie	-	-	-	-	-	-	-	-	-	-	-	-			-
Bruce Ruffin	-	-	-	-	-	-	-	-	-	8-7	-	-	5	10	8-7
Rick Schu	-	0-1	-	1-1	-	-	-	-	-	-	-	-	2	1	1-2
Steve Searcy	-	-	-	-	-	-	-	-	-	-	-	-			-
Dickie Thon	-	-	-	-	70-73	-	-	-	-	-	4-10	-	60	83	70-73
Mitch Williams	-	-	-	-	-	-	-	-	-	-	-	-			-

TEAM TOTALS: BATTING

	AB	H	2B	3B	HR	RBI	BB	SO	BA	SA	OBA
Season	5521	1332	248	33	111	590	490	1026	.241	.358	.303
vs. Left-Handers	2025	529	103	13	36	225	185	366	.261	.378	.324
vs. Right-Handers	3496	803	145	20	75	365	305	660	.230	.347	.291
vs. Ground-Ballers	2651	650	108	14	43	271	241	463	.245	.345	.309
vs. Fly-Ballers	2870	682	140	19	68	319	249	563	.238	.371	.297
Home Games	2782	697	133	16	61	325	261	509	.251	.376	.316
Road Games	2739	635	115	17	50	265	229	517	.232	.341	.290
Grass Fields	1473	350	56	7	35	154	126	276	.238	.356	.296
Artificial Turf	4048	982	192	26	76	436	364	750	.243	.359	.306
April	735	182	34	3	15	90	77	134	.248	.363	.317
May	891	208	37	4	12	84	71	149	.233	.324	.290
June	971	243	39	9	19	110	79	183	.250	.368	.306
July	799	171	30	5	18	74	75	147	.214	.332	.285
August	986	240	49	7	29	125	111	191	.243	.396	.319
Sept./Oct.	1139	288	59	5	18	107	77	222	.253	.361	.301
Leading Off Inn.	1354	344	58	7	33		113	235	.254	.380	.314
Runners On	2358	568	115	15	48	527	224	433	.241	.363	.306
Bases Empty	3163	764	133	18	63	63	266	593	.242	.355	.302
Runners/Scor. Pos.	1318	315	66	6	28	457	160	254	.239	.362	.313
Runners On/2 Out	989	227	55	6	23	218	104	198	.230	.367	.303
Scor. Pos./2 Out	622	145	32	3	16	187	83	136	.233	.371	.323
Late-Inning Pressure	965	238	37	5	18	88	98	191	.247	.351	.317
Leading Off	246	61	8	1	10	10	24	48	.248	.411	.317
Runners On	414	98	22	0	2	72	44	82	.237	.304	.311
Runners/Scor. Pos.	228	50	11	0	1	67	32	43	.219	.281	.310

RUNS BATTED IN	From 1B	From 2B	From 3B	Scoring Position
Totals	84/1719	166/1025	229/542	395/1567
Percentage	4.9%	16.2%	42.3%	25.2%

TEAM TOTALS: PITCHING

	W-L	ERA	AB	H	HR	BB	SO	BA	SA	OBA
Season	78-84	3.86	5480	1346	111	670	988	.246	.367	.329
vs. Left-Handers			2247	556	44	331	382	.247	.368	.344
vs. Right-Handers			3233	790	67	339	606	.244	.367	.318
vs. Ground-Ballers			2381	558	33	281	423	.234	.331	.317
vs. Fly-Ballers			3099	788	78	389	565	.254	.395	.339
Home Games	47-36	3.64	2877	702	53	347	536	.244	.358	.328
Road Games	31-48	4.11	2603	644	58	323	452	.247	.378	.331
Grass Fields	17-25	4.05	1405	342	39	174	243	.243	.379	.329
Artificial Turf	61-59	3.80	4075	1004	72	496	745	.246	.363	.329
April	9-12	4.31	706	161	12	118	113	.228	.341	.341
May	13-13	2.83	878	199	15	95	164	.227	.322	.305
June	10-18	5.02	961	264	22	135	161	.275	.419	.366
July	10-15	3.44	834	212	20	82	144	.254	.388	.322
August	20-9	3.69	1003	254	21	122	190	.253	.372	.335
Sept./Oct.	16-17	3.89	1098	256	21	118	216	.233	.353	.308
Leading Off Inn.			1307	304	21	148	213	.233	.347	.316
Bases Empty			3029	732	64	342	537	.242	.363	.324
Runners On			2451	614	47	328	451	.251	.373	.336
Runners/Scor. Pos.			1457	350	29	232	284	.240	.366	.337
Runners On/2 Out			1097	254	20	153	204	.232	.349	.329
Scor. Pos./2 Out			718	154	13	115	141	.214	.325	.325
Late-Inning Pressure			901	199	18	144	168	.221	.326	.332
Leading Off			222	41	2	35	38	.185	.266	.312
Runners On			401	83	8	73	82	.237	.317	.329
Runners/Scor. Pos.			217	41	6	52	45	.189	.318	.342
First 9 Batters			2833	669	52	397	546	.236	.351	.333
Second 9 Batters			1395	368	36	147	240	.264	.406	.336
All Batters Thereafter			1252	309	23	126	202	.247	.360	.314

PHILADELPHIA PHILLIES

Each season, several teams are virtually eliminated from contention by the All-Star break, even if they stand a mathematical chance to win long after. The 1991 Cleveland Indians are a good example; they weren't theoretically eliminated from the A.L. East race until early September, but the season was barely half over when even the most optimistic Indians fans gave up on 1991, taking their cue from general manager Hank Peters, who himself started retooling his team for the future. But occasionally one of those teams rebounds to keep pace with the division leaders over the second half, raising its record to a respectable level by the end of the season and generating optimism for the season to come.

According to the blueprint, it's supposed to work like this: The 1986 Oakland Athletics hit bottom two days before the All-Star break with a record of 32–56, in last place, 16½ games behind the front-running Angels. But from that point on, Oakland compiled the best record in the league (44–30), finishing the season only 10 games below the .500 mark. The A's then raised their record to .500 in 1987, and won three consecutive titles from 1988 through 1990.

Last season, the Philadelphia Phillies were among three teams that played at least 100 points better during the second halves of their schedules than the first:

Team	First Half W–L	Pct.	Second Half W–L	Pct.	Totals W–L	Pct.
Braves	41–40	.506	53–28	.654	94–68	.580
Phillies	33–48	.407	45–36	.556	78–84	.481
Brewers	37–44	.457	46–35	.568	83–79	.512

Atlanta played well enough in the first half for that second-half rally to carry them to a National League title. Milwaukee raised its record above the .500 mark by the end of the season despite a slow start. The Brewers never came close enough to the division leaders to become legitimate pennant contenders, but their midseason form reversal did provide a satisfying conclusion to the season. But the Phillies never passed the .500 mark, coming within three games in August on the strength of a 13-game winning streak (more on that later) and again in early September. That strong second half seemed to provide their fans with reason to be optimistic for a further rebound in 1992. But the surprising fact is that a second-half rally is of little value as an indicator of a team's direction in the following season.

The Phillies played 148 points better during the second half of the 1991 season than during the first. But among the last 10 teams with a second-half increase that large, only three posted better overall records in the following season:

Year	Team	1st Half W–L	2d Half W–L	Totals W–L	Pct.	Next Season W–L	Pct.	Gain/ Loss
1989	Blue Jays	38–43	51–30	89–73	.549	86–76	.531	–.019
1987	White Sox	32–49	45–36	77–85	.475	71–90	.441	–.034
1986	Athletics	30–51	46–35	76–86	.469	81–81	.500	.031
1984	Yankees	36–45	51–30	87–75	.537	97–64	.602	.065
1984	Pirates	31–50	44–37	75–87	.463	57–104	.354	–.109
1983	White Sox	42–39	57–24	99–63	.611	74–88	.457	–.154
1982	Twins	24–57	36–45	60–102	.370	70–92	.432	.062
1982	Giants	37–44	50–31	87–75	.537	79–83	.488	–.049
1980	Orioles	44–37	56–25	100–62	.617	59–46	.562	–.055
1979	Pirates	43–38	55–26	98–64	.605	83–79	.512	–.093

As counterintuitive as those figures may seem, they are representative of the general trend. Surprisingly, not only does a second-half rally have no positive carryover effect, but an extreme downturn in the second half doesn't imply a tendency to decline in the next season.

That's particularly good news for the New York Mets, who broke quickly from the gate in 1991 only to hit a wall at midseason and finish the race gasping for breath. New York stood 15 games above the .500 mark on July 14, trailing Pittsburgh by only 2½ games at the time. But the Mets lost 27 of their next 35 games and fell below the .500 mark for good on August 16. Only four other teams in this century had first-half records as good, and second-half records as bad, as last season's Mets (47–34 and 30–50, respectively). They are marked with asterisks in the table below, which includes all teams during the 1900s with second-half winning percentages at least 200 points lower than their first half marks. Note that despite their poor second-half performances, half the teams improved their overall records the next season:

Year	Team	1st Half W–L	2d Half W–L	Totals W–L	Pct.	Next Season W–L	Pct.	Gain/ Loss
1901	Giants	34–35	18–50	52–85	.380	48–88	.353	–.027
*1905	Naps	50–28	26–50	76–78	.494	89–64	.582	+.088
1909	Naps	44–34	27–48	71–82	.464	71–81	.467	+.003
1911	Tigers	53–24	36–41	89–65	.578	69–84	.451	–.127
1913	Athletics	57–20	39–37	96–57	.627	99–53	.651	+.024
*1941	Indians	46–31	29–48	75–79	.487	75–79	.487	—
1943	Athletics	34–44	15–61	49–105	.318	72–82	.468	+.149
1949	Senators	34–43	16–61	50–104	.325	67–87	.435	+.110
*1973	Cubs	48–33	29–51	77–84	.478	66–96	.407	–.071
1975	Brewers	43–38	25–56	68–94	.420	66–95	.410	–.010
*1977	Cubs	51–30	30–51	81–81	.500	79–83	.488	–.012
1983	Angels	44–37	26–55	70–92	.432	81–81	.500	+.068

It's crucial to understand that although the tables include only a small number of teams, they accurately represent the general trend: Even in extreme cases, an improvement or decline in a team's play during the second half of any season is of little value in determining its direction a year later. The following table summarizes the results of all teams from 1900 through 1990 with differences of 100 points or more. Each group comprises nearly 200 teams. Plus and minus signs indicate whether a team raised or lowered its overall record the next season; the first pair of figures shows any improvement or decline, the second indicates changes of more than five wins:

	Teams	+	–	+5	–5
Better in First Half	196	94	100	67	65
Better in Second Half	195	97	94	68	66

Finally, for the mathematician in all of us, we used a common statistical technique (common if you're a math professor, that is) to develop an equation that would compute a team's "best-guess" record for the upcoming season based on its first- and second-half records in the previous year. If a team's record in the second half was actually more indicative of its performance in the following season, it would carry greater weight in the formula. In fact, that was the case—but only to a slight degree. The formula:

$$\text{NPct} = (\text{Pct1} \times .280) + (\text{Pct2} \times .334) + .197$$

"NPct" represents the team's percentage in the upcoming season, and "Pct1" and "Pct2" represent its first- and second-half winning percentages the year before. Based on that formula, the best guess for a team that played .400 in the first half and .600 in the second is only two wins better than it would be if those figures were reversed. (A formula based on only the era of divisional play, which might better reflect the current environment, would produce a three-win margin for teams that finished better.) And don't forget, we're talking about extreme cases here; no team has played 200 points better in the second half than the first since the 1950 New York Giants—not even the '51 Giants, the most renowned come-from-behind team in baseball history (who never would have needed such a miraculous comeback had a carry-over effect from their second half in the 1950 season gotten them off to a strong start in '51).

Based on the empirical data, that two-win margin seems generous. And all things considered, the Phillies' prognosis for 1992 will depend not on its strong finish last season, but on what we will call "The Dykstra/Chamberlain Factor."

Philadelphia's second-half rally was fueled by a 13-game winning streak from July 30 through August 12, the longest in the National League last season. More noteworthy, it equaled the longest in this century by a team with a losing record for the season. The only streaks longer than 10 games by losing teams:

Year	Team	Str.	W–L
1942	Cleveland Indians	13	75–79
1991	Philadelphia Phillies	13	78–84
1905	New York Highlanders	12	71–78
1980	Minnesota Twins	12	77–84
1914	Brooklyn Dodgers	11	75–79
1941	Cleveland Indians	11	75–79
1944	Chicago Cubs	11	75–79
1959	Philadelphia Athletics	11	66–88
1970	Atlanta Braves	11	76–86
1982	Cleveland Indians	11	78–84
1987	Baltimore Orioles	11	67–95

Normally, a table like this would provide us with another opportunity for a technical analysis of how these teams fared a year later, in order to determine whether a long winning streak by a poor team is a leading indicator of an upcoming turnaround season. But this time we'll merely mention that the range of follow-up seasons for the teams listed above was enormous, from Baltimore's disastrous 107-loss season in 1988 to breakthrough seasons for the 1906 Highlanders (90–61) and the 1945 Cubs, who won the National League pennant with a 98–56 record.

The reason those results don't concern us has to do with the key factor that contributed to Philadelphia's 13-game streak. You'll recall that center fielder Len Dykstra spent 110 days on the disabled list last season, first with injuries suffered in an automobile accident, then when he rebroke his collarbone. In addition, it wasn't until mid-June that Philadelphia made Wes Chamberlain its everyday left fielder. Their seasons overlapped for only six weeks, from July 15, when Dykstra returned from his first term on the D.L., through August 26, when he suffered his season-ending injury. During that time, they started 37 of Philadelphia's 38 games, and with both Dykstra and Chamberlain in the starting lineup, the Phillies compiled a 25–12 record, including those 13 straight wins during which Chamberlain batted .321 (17-for-53, 3 HR, 13 RBI) and Dykstra only .235 (12-for-51, 1 HR, 3 RBI), but with 10 walks and six stolen bases.

So it appears that Philadelphia's 13-game winning streak was a good stretch by a team that might have posted a winning record had it been able to field its best lineup throughout the season. For six weeks, the Phillies demonstrated that they have enough talent to compete for the N.L. East title. Had that six-week period fallen earlier in the season, it might have been more conspicuous, but buried during the dog days, few fans even noticed the streak, let alone the reasons for it and what they implied. If Dykstra remains healthy this season, and Chamberlain can produce over a full season as he did for four months last year, all the technical indicators at our disposal are insignificant, and we can expect a strong performance from the Phillies in 1992.

PITTSBURGH PIRATES

The sting of a championship series loss is often short in duration, replaced quickly by the anticipation of another crack at a World Series appearance in the upcoming season. But as the National League title slipped away from the Pirates last October, it seemed less a prelude of greater things to come than a failed last-gasp effort to bring a world championship to Pittsburgh. It was a foregone conclusion that before the 1992 season began, the Pirates would cease to exist—at least as their fans had known them during consecutive championship seasons.

The Pirates and their fans had seen an apocalypse coming for several seasons, with Doug Drabek, Andy Van Slyke, Bobby Bonilla, and Barry Bonds all eligible for first-time free agency between the end of the 1991 season and the start of 1993—a challenging situation even for a free-spending team in a large market (a description never applied to Pittsburgh). Arbitration victories over Bonds and Bonilla following the 1990 season helped to hold down the team's payroll in 1991, but did little to increase its chances of holding onto its star players for much longer.

Still, on the eve of the 1991 N.L.C.S., the Pirates appeared likely for several reasons to reach the World Series in pursuit of that last great hurrah. For one thing, Pittsburgh had the best regular-season record among the four division winners, and the team with the better record had won 26 of 44 previous playoffs (59 percent). For another, the Buccos had a tremendous advantage over Atlanta in postseason experience: 19 of their 25 players had appeared in postseason play prior to 1991, compared to only six Braves players. And Pittsburgh's early clinching on September 22 gave them an edge in preparation over the Braves, who didn't nail down the N.L. West until the next-to-last day of the season. There had been five other championship series in which one team clinched its division title at least 10 days earlier than its opponent. Not only did each of those five teams win the playoffs, but all five swept their opponents: Cincinnati over Pittsburgh in 1970 and 1975; Kansas City over the Yankees in 1980; Detroit over Kansas City in 1984; and Oakland over Boston in 1988. And Pittsburgh's trip to the Series seemed all but assured when the Pirates returned home with a 3 games to 2 lead over the Braves. Who could have foreseen a pair of consecutive shutout losses at Three Rivers Stadium, which had happened only twice in the previous 15 years of regular-season play?

Were it not for the possibility that Bonilla and Bonds had played their last games in Pirates uniforms, even a playoff loss that unexpected and deflating might have been overlooked, especially given the extraordinary success of other teams with pairs of players as young and productive as Pittsburgh's Killer B's. From 1920 (when RBIs were first compiled on an official basis) through 1991, 112 teams had two players under the age of 30 with at least 100 RBIs. We tracked their performance over the next three years and found that 30 percent of those seasons produced winning percentages of .600 or better; fully 51 percent of the teams hit the .600 mark at least once during those next three years. Their average winning percentage during that time was .550, or the equivalent of an 89–73 record over 162 games, regardless of the performance or even presence of the qualifying players. The success of those teams

varied little over the three-year period; the average winning percentages for those seasons were .549, .551, and .550, respectively. There was a statistically significant but nevertheless small decline after that, allowing the teams to maintain a mark well above .500 for the next three seasons as well: .534, .537, and .538 for years four through six. (Incidentally, last season marked the first time since 1979 that as many as three teams had two 100-RBI men both under the age of 30. Besides Pittsburgh, the White Sox with Frank Thomas and Robin Ventura and the Rangers with Ruben Sierra and Juan Gonzalez also qualified.)

Bonilla and Bonds could have formed the nucleus of a Pirates pennant contender deep into the decade—a sort of Mantle and Maris for the '90s, complete with championship rings, MVP awards, and even alliterative names. (Barry and Bobby might not have had a ready-made candy endorsement like the M & M boys, but who knows what the bed-and-breakfast industry could have whipped up for them.) But with Bonilla already gone to the enemy, and Bonds threatening not to return to Pittsburgh in 1993, the Pirates will soon confront a George Bailey scenario come to life: What life would be like if there were no Bonilla and Bonds.

It's been a while since a team was totally undermined by free agency. Over the past decade, the loss of free agents has been fairly balanced, with 21 of the 26 teams losing between seven and 13 players, especially compared to the late 1970s, when several teams chose not to compete with the big spenders for the services of even their own players and suffered accordingly. In fact, three A.L. teams lost at least 10 players via free agency from 1976 through 1980, more than double the major league average: Baltimore (10, including Bobby Grich, Reggie Jackson, Wayne Garland, and Don Stanhouse); Minnesota (11, including Bill Campbell, Lyman Bostock, Larry Hisle, and Dave Goltz); and Oakland (13, including Sal Bando, Don Baylor, Bert Campaneris, Rollie Fingers, Joe Rudi, and Gene Tenace.) Their performance in 1976, the season preceding the first class of free agents, and for the 10 years thereafter:

Team	1976	1977	1978	1979	1980	1981	1982	1983	1984	1985	1986
Baltimore	.543	.602	.559	.642	.617	.562	.580	.605	.525	.516	.451
Minnesota	.525	.522	.451	.506	.478	.376	.370	.432	.500	.475	.438
Oakland	.540	.391	.426	.333	.512	.587	.420	.457	.475	.475	.469

The collapse of the Twins and Athletics indicates that a mass exit of free agents poses a major hurdle that can keep a team below the .500 mark for several seasons. But the Orioles' success proves that it needn't necessarily undermine a team's chances for success, either short- or long-term. The Baltimore organization was so deep with talent in the late 1970s, and its manager Earl Weaver was so adept at extracting maximum value from seemingly marginal players, that the Orioles maintained a winning mark for nine seasons following the loss of Jackson, Garland, and Grich in the first free-agent class. They compiled the highest winning percentage in the majors over the five-year period from 1977 through 1981 (.599), and won the A.L. title in 1979 and the World Series in 1983, fueled by players ranging from superstar farm products like Eddie Murray (a rookie in 1977), Cal Ripken (1982), and Mike Boddicker (1983); to the acquisition of inexpensive but productive role players like Gary Roenicke (a throw-in in the Rudy May-for-Don Stanhouse deal), John Lowenstein (a cash purchase), and Benny Ayala (for the one and only Mike Dimmel); to insightful but less publicized free-agent signings such as Steve Stone and Jim Dwyer.

Unfortunately for the Pirates, their organization pales next to that of the Orioles of the late 1970s. We make no pretense to expertise in this area, but we spoke to the experts at *Baseball America*, who gave Pittsburgh's farm system a grade of C– prior to the 1991 season and see little reason to upgrade that mark. Although Buffalo, the team's Triple-A affiliate, won its division and came within one win of the American Association championship last season, its roster was filled with the semifamiliar names of players who failed in numerous shots at the big leagues: Cecil Espy, Joey Meyer, the wrong Keith Miller, Steve Fireovid, Rick Reed, and so on. No player on the team hit as many as 10 home runs, and only shortstop Carlos Garcia appears to be a legitimate major league prospect.

There aren't many blue chippers at other levels of the organization either. By now, the Pirates should have been reaping the benefits of having the first pick overall in the 1986 amateur free-agent draft and the second in 1987. But the team chose Jeff King and Mark Merchant, respectively. The next three picks in '86 were Greg Swindell, Matt Williams, and Kevin Brown; Merchant's selection was immediately followed by those of Willie Banks (a high-schooler selected by the Twins), Mike Harkey, and Jack McDowell. Those misjudgments are compounded by the fact that, according to *Baseball America*, Pittsburgh "mortgaged the farm system [in 1990] to fortify for the [N.L. East] stretch run." That included trading 1989 first-round pick Willie Greene, outfielder Moises Alou, and pitcher Scott Ruskin to Montreal for Zane Smith alone. The Pirates also lost outfielder Wes Chamberlain by unwittingly placing him on irrevocable waivers. And last season, Pittsburgh traded Hector Fajardo and Kurt Miller, two of the organization's top pitching hopefuls, to Texas for Steve Buechele.

Pittsburgh's approach left recently deposed general manager Larry Doughty open to criticism, especially since the Chamberlain fiasco. But Doughty's personnel moves nearly worked. The Pirates became the first N.L. team in more than a decade to win two straight division titles; they missed consecutive World Series appearances by the margin of a key hit or two. With the six-year clock expiring on Bonilla and Bonds, the Pittsburgh organization decided it had to strike. Doughty's alternative would have been to accept a couple of second- and third-place finishes until Barry and Bobby left, and then hope that the organization would produce a few more just like them (who could also leave after six years). Doughty made the moves

that we think most Pirates fans would have chosen as well, moves that reflect the pervasive philosophy of most sports fans: Just win, baby.

Having sung the praises of Bonds and Bonilla, we must at least mention that if anyone should shoulder the blame specifically for Pittsburgh's consecutive N.L.C.S. losses, it's the Killer B's themselves.

Bonds and Bonilla drove in at least 100 runs apiece in each of the past two seasons, producing a total of 450 RBIs in 324 regular-season games; but they drove in only three runs in 13 playoff games. Throughout the history of postseason play, it's been nearly impossible for teams to win when such dependable run producers suddenly slump.

Eighty-one teams have appeared in postseason play with at least two players who drove in 100 runs or more during the regular season. (That counts twice teams like the 1990 Athletics, led by Jose Canseco and Mark McGwire, who won the A.L.C.S. and then played in the World Series.) All but 10 of those teams got at least three RBIs combined from their 100-RBI men in the postseason series. But among the 10 whose leading run producers combined for two or fewer postseason RBIs, there was only one winner. The 10 are listed below; regular- and postseason RBIs are shown for each player:

Year	Team	Regular-Season RBI Leaders	Result
1930	Cardinals	Frisch (114/0), Hafey (107/2)	Lost WS
1954	Indians	Doby (126/0), Rosen (102/0)	Lost WS
1961	Yankees	Maris (142/2), Mantle (128/0)	Won WS
1969	Twins	Killebrew (140/0), Oliva (101/2)	Lost LCS
1969	Orioles	Powell (121/0), F. Robinson (100/1)	Lost WS
1986	Red Sox	Rice (110/0), Buckner (102/1)	Lost WS
1989	Giants	Mitchell (125/2), Clark (111/0)	Lost WS
1990	Pirates	Bonilla (120/1), Bonds (114/1)	Lost LCS
1990	Athletics	McGwire (108/0), Canseco (101/2)	Lost WS
1991	Pirates	Bonds (116/0), Bonilla (100/1)	Lost LCS

There were cases among those 10 in which the players were hardly to blame; their failure to drive in many runs simply reflected a teamwide offensive breakdown. For instance, Harmon Killebrew didn't have a single at-bat with runners in scoring position in the 1969 A.L.C.S.; Tony Oliva had one. A week later, Boog Powell and Frank Robinson had a total of one AB with RISP in their World Series loss to the Mets. But more often than not, and certainly in the case of the Pirates in both 1990 and 1991, their regular-season saviors just failed in the clutch in October. In last year's playoffs, Bonds and Bonilla were a combined 1-for-12 with runners in scoring position, including an 0-for-9 mark with the tying or lead run either on base, at bat, or on deck. They were 1-for-9 with RISP in the 1990 N.L.C.S. Considering that four of Pittsburgh's eight playoff losses were by the margin of a single run (two in each year), Barry's and Bobby's shoulders will have to be pretty broad to shoulder all the blame that's due them.

WON-LOST RECORD BY STARTING POSITION

Pittsburgh Pirates	C	1B	2B	3B	SS	LF	CF	RF	DH	P	Leadoff	Cleanup	Starts vs. LH	Starts vs. RH	Total Starts
Jeff Banister	-	-	-	-	-	-	-	-	-	-	-	-	-	-	-
Stan Belinda	-	-	-	-	-	-	-	-	-	-	-	-	-	-	-
Jay Bell	-	-	-	-	93-60	-	-	-	-	-	-	-	50	103	93-60
Barry Bonds	-	-	-	-	-	91-55	1-0	-	-	-	-	2-2	42	105	92-55
Bobby Bonilla	-	2-1	-	36-24	-	-	-	56-36	-	-	-	94-61	50	105	94-61
Steve Buechele	-	-	-	20-11	-	-	-	-	-	-	-	-	12	19	20-11
Scott Bullett	-	-	-	-	-	0-1	-	-	-	-	0-1	-	-	1	0-1
Doug Drabek	-	-	-	-	-	-	-	-	-	19-16	-	-	12	23	19-16
Cecil Espy	-	-	-	-	-	-	4-7	4-2	-	-	-	1-3	2	15	8-9
Hector Fajardo	-	-	-	-	-	-	-	-	-	1-1	-	-	-	2	1-1
Carlos Garcia	-	-	1-0	1-2	-	-	-	-	-	-	-	-	1	3	2-2
Jose Gonzalez	-	-	-	-	-	1-0	1-1	-	-	-	-	-	3	-	2-1
Neal Heaton	-	-	-	-	-	-	-	-	-	0-1	-	-	1	-	0-1
Mark Huismann	-	-	-	-	-	-	-	-	-	-	-	-	-	-	-
Jeff King	-	-	-	21-11	-	-	-	-	-	-	-	0-1	10	22	21-11
Bob Kipper	-	-	-	-	-	-	-	-	-	-	-	-	-	-	-
Bill Landrum	-	-	-	-	-	-	-	-	-	-	-	-	-	-	-
Mike LaValliere	56-44	-	-	-	-	-	-	-	-	-	-	-	3	97	56-44
Jose Lind	-	-	85-54	-	-	-	-	-	-	-	-	-	49	90	85-54
Carmelo Martinez	-	2-2	-	-	-	-	-	-	-	-	-	-	2	2	2-2
Roger Mason	-	-	-	-	-	-	-	-	-	-	-	-	-	-	-
Lloyd McClendon	1-0	8-7	-	-	-	1-3	-	8-4	-	-	0-1	2-1	30	2	18-14
Orlando Merced	-	56-39	-	-	-	-	-	0-1	-	-	55-36	-	1	95	56-40
Paul Miller	-	-	-	-	-	-	-	-	-	0-1	-	-	1	-	0-1
Vicente Palacios	-	-	-	-	-	-	-	-	-	5-2	-	-	5	2	5-2
Bob Patterson	-	-	-	-	-	-	-	-	-	1-0	-	-	-	1	1-0
Tom Prince	4-4	-	-	-	-	-	-	-	-	-	-	-	4	4	4-4
Joe Redfield	-	-	-	3-2	-	-	-	-	-	-	-	-	4	1	3-2
Gary Redus	-	28-15	-	-	-	3-3	3-4	-	-	-	-	34-20	49	7	34-22
Rick Reed	-	-	-	-	-	-	-	-	-	-	0-1	-	-	1	0-1
Jeff Richardson	-	-	-	-	-	-	-	-	-	-	-	-	-	-	-
Rosario Rodriguez	-	-	-	-	-	-	-	-	-	-	-	-	-	-	-
Jeff Schulz	-	-	-	-	-	-	-	-	-	-	-	-	-	-	-
Don Slaught	37-16	-	-	-	-	-	-	-	-	-	-	-	45	8	37-16
John Smiley	-	-	-	-	-	-	-	-	-	22-10	-	-	12	20	22-10
Zane Smith	-	-	-	-	-	-	-	-	-	20-15	-	-	8	27	20-15
Randy Tomlin	-	-	-	-	-	-	-	-	-	15-12	-	-	6	21	15-12
Andy Van Slyke	-	-	-	-	-	-	83-46	-	-	-	1-0	-	38	91	83-46
Gary Varsho	-	2-0	-	-	-	2-2	2-2	22-14	-	-	-	6-1	-	46	28-18
Bob Walk	-	-	-	-	-	-	-	-	-	15-5	-	-	8	12	15-5
Mitch Webster	-	-	-	-	-	0-1	4-3	8-7	-	-	1-0	-	8	15	12-11
John Wehner	-	-	12-13	-	-	-	-	-	-	-	-	-	13	12	12-13
Curt Wilkerson	-	-	13-10	5-3	4-2	-	-	-	-	-	-	0-1	8	29	22-15

TEAM TOTALS: BATTING

	AB	H	2B	3B	HR	RBI	BB	SO	BA	SA	OBA
Season	5449	1433	259	50	126	725	620	901	.263	.398	.338
vs. Left-Handers	1894	489	89	19	51	255	211	297	.258	.406	.333
vs. Right-Handers	3555	944	170	31	75	470	409	604	.266	.394	.341
vs. Ground-Ballers	2494	676	117	26	43	313	254	364	.271	.391	.339
vs. Fly-Ballers	2955	757	142	24	83	412	366	537	.256	.405	.338
Home Games	2702	697	131	27	61	359	304	445	.258	.394	.334
Road Games	2747	736	128	23	65	366	316	456	.268	.402	.343
Grass Fields	1501	393	60	13	36	183	140	232	.262	.391	.325
Artificial Turf	3948	1040	199	37	90	542	480	669	.263	.401	.344
April	651	164	28	4	14	90	64	88	.252	.372	.321
May	821	214	35	8	22	112	93	132	.261	.403	.336
June	870	198	38	7	15	80	102	153	.228	.339	.310
July	968	291	44	13	33	168	110	143	.301	.475	.371
August	982	255	58	5	21	123	105	189	.260	.393	.328
Sept./Oct.	1157	311	56	13	21	152	146	196	.269	.394	.352
Leading Off Inn.	1301	339	74	13	21	21	131	176	.261	.386	.332
Runners On	2461	672	117	27	67	666	302	415	.273	.424	.349
Bases Empty	2988	761	142	23	59	59	318	486	.255	.377	.330
Runners/Scor. Pos.	1449	391	72	14	36	569	217	259	.270	.413	.355
Runners On/2 Out	1070	267	47	13	28	271	148	188	.250	.396	.344
Scor. Pos./2 Out	699	177	31	7	20	239	112	120	.253	.403	.360
Late-Inning Pressure	711	179	36	5	14	90	92	119	.252	.376	.339
Leading Off	183	45	9	0	1	1	19	26	.246	.311	.320
Runners On	308	80	17	2	8	84	47	53	.260	.406	.359
Runners/Scor. Pos.	179	43	10	1	5	73	34	28	.240	.391	.360

RUNS BATTED IN	From 1B	From 2B	From 3B	Scoring Position
Totals	103/1744	202/1107	294/688	496/1795
Percentage	5.9%	18.2%	42.7%	27.6%

TEAM TOTALS: PITCHING

	W-L	ERA	AB	H	HR	BB	SO	BA	SA	OBA
Season	98-64	3.44	5522	1411	117	401	919	.256	.373	.308
vs. Left-Handers			1968	507	35	155	328	.258	.360	.314
vs. Right-Handers			3554	904	82	246	591	.254	.381	.304
vs. Ground-Ballers			2348	576	37	167	407	.245	.346	.298
vs. Fly-Ballers			3174	835	80	234	512	.263	.394	.315
Home Games	52-32	3.14	2870	721	55	196	508	.251	.366	.302
Road Games	46-32	3.77	2652	690	62	205	411	.260	.382	.314
Grass Fields	20-22	4.27	1433	379	43	121	218	.264	.397	.323
Artificial Turf	78-42	3.15	4089	1032	74	280	701	.252	.365	.302
April	13-7	3.29	672	156	14	53	93	.232	.342	.291
May	17-8	3.28	846	207	12	61	146	.245	.350	.300
June	15-12	3.15	908	243	16	60	152	.268	.368	.315
July	15-12	3.86	915	232	29	91	161	.254	.410	.320
August	17-12	3.14	983	251	19	59	161	.255	.359	.298
Sept./Oct.	21-13	3.80	1198	322	27	77	206	.269	.396	.315
Leading Off Inn.			1363	354	29	91	214	.260	.378	.309
Bases Empty			3240	788	63	226	533	.243	.353	.296
Runners On			2282	623	54	175	386	.273	.402	.324
Runners/Scor. Pos.			1312	352	27	137	221	.268	.389	.334
Runners On/2 Out			949	242	26	84	179	.255	.395	.339
Scor. Pos./2 Out			600	155	14	72	106	.258	.390	.343
Late-Inning Pressure			893	236	23	77	155	.264	.387	.327
Leading Off			225	59	7	18	44	.262	.396	.320
Runners On			374	105	11	38	63	.281	.422	.350
Runners/Scor. Pos.			214	52	5	26	35	.243	.360	.328
First 9 Batters			2965	744	70	235	554	.251	.374	.307
Second 9 Batters			1379	345	22	89	208	.250	.361	.299
All Batters Thereafter			1178	322	25	77	157	.273	.387	.319

WON-LOST RECORD BY STARTING POSITION

St. Louis Cardinals	C	1B	2B	3B	SS	LF	CF	RF	DH	P	Leadoff	Cleanup	Starts vs. LH	Starts vs. RH	Total Starts
Juan Agosto	-	-	-	-	-	-	-	-	-	-	-	-	-	-	-
Luis Alicea		-	3-3											6	3-3
Rod Brewer		0-1	-											1	0-1
Cris Carpenter													-	-	-
Mark Clark	-									0-2			1	1	0-2
Rheal Cormier										4-6			4	6	4-6
Jose DeLeon										13-15			14	14	13-15
Willie Fraser	-												-	-	-
Rich Gedman	16-11												2	25	16-11
Bernard Gilkey						39-32					21-17		43	28	39-32
Mark Grater	-											-	-	-	-
Pedro Guerrero		56-55										56-55	46	65	56-55
Ken Hill										16-14	16-14		10	20	16-14
Rex Hudler		2-1			-	10-10	9-12	2-2				9-9	44	4	23-25
Tim Jones			2-1		1-3								1	6	3-4
Felix Jose								78-74				3-4	70	82	78-74
Ray Lankford							73-62				40-36		50	85	73-62
Bob McClure	-												-	-	-
Jamie Moyer										1-6			3	4	1-6
Omar Olivares										14-10	14-10		10	14	14-10
Jose Oquendo	-		57-57		7-3								57	67	64-60
Tom Pagnozzi	67-66												68	65	67-66
Geronimo Pena	-		22-17			1-1						3-2	23	18	23-18
Mike Perez	-												-	-	-
Gerald Perry		26-20				2-2						9-3	22	28	28-22
Stan Royer	-			2-2								0-1	1	3	2-2
Tim Sherrill	-									-			-	-	-
Bryn Smith	-									18-13	18-13		15	16	18-13
Lee Smith	-									-			-	-	-
Ozzie Smith	-				76-72							3-2	65	83	76-72
Ray Stephens	1-1												2	-	1-1
Scott Terry	-									-			-	-	-
Bob Tewksbury	-									18-12	18-12		15	15	18-12
Milt Thompson	-					32-32	2-4	4-2				8-12	9	67	38-38
Craig Wilson		0-1		2-2	0-1								4	2	2-4
Todd Zeile	-			80-74								16-15	69	85	80-74

TEAM TOTALS: BATTING

	AB	H	2B	3B	HR	RBI	BB	SO	BA	SA	OBA
Season	5362	1366	239	53	68	599	532	857	.255	.357	.322
vs. Left-Handers	2275	573	118	21	23	244	219	382	.252	.353	.318
vs. Right-Handers	3087	793	121	32	45	355	313	475	.257	.361	.325
vs. Ground-Ballers	2385	574	100	24	21	234	228	360	.241	.329	.308
vs. Fly-Ballers	2977	792	139	29	47	365	304	497	.266	.380	.333
Home Games	2707	682	116	34	32	313	290	394	.252	.355	.325
Road Games	2655	684	123	19	36	286	242	463	.258	.359	.319
Grass Fields	1438	360	72	10	14	154	119	263	.250	.344	.307
Artificial Turf	3924	1006	167	43	54	445	413	594	.256	.362	.327
April	691	180	26	9	8	75	88	84	.260	.364	.345
May	873	238	44	7	7	109	88	136	.273	.363	.339
June	928	242	43	14	8	117	94	128	.261	.363	.327
July	856	212	31	7	16	89	84	142	.248	.356	.315
August	924	236	39	10	9	96	76	162	.255	.348	.311
Sept./Oct.	1090	258	56	6	20	113	102	205	.237	.354	.303
Leading Off Inn.	1314	341	60	7	23	23	124	199	.260	.368	.324
Runners On	2310	627	111	34	21	552	263	361	.271	.376	.343
Bases Empty	3052	739	128	19	47	47	269	496	.242	.343	.305
Runners/Scor. Pos.	1425	387	67	26	10	506	215	241	.272	.376	.360
Runners On/2 Out	930	223	41	17	7	190	125	152	.240	.343	.334
Scor. Pos./2 Out	644	144	24	14	5	176	108	104	.224	.328	.339
Late-Inning Pressure	816	209	27	8	12	96	103	139	.256	.353	.339
Leading Off	202	53	13	0	5	5	29	34	.262	.401	.358
Runners On	358	95	7	7	4	88	50	57	.265	.358	.352
Runners/Scor. Pos.	208	57	4	5	1	79	41	35	.274	.356	.381

RUNS BATTED IN	From 1B	From 2B	From 3B	Scoring Position
Totals	65/1529	188/1082	278/689	466/1771
Percentage	4.3%	17.4%	40.3%	26.3%

TEAM TOTALS: PITCHING

	W-L	ERA	AB	H	HR	BB	SO	BA	SA	OBA
Season	84-78	3.69	5368	1367	114	454	822	.255	.381	.315
vs. Left-Handers			2743	697	47	274	380	.254	.370	.323
vs. Right-Handers			2625	670	67	180	442	.255	.392	.307
vs. Ground-Ballers			2217	550	26	183	365	.248	.344	.310
vs. Fly-Ballers			3151	817	88	271	457	.259	.407	.319
Home Games	52-32	3.15	2840	693	41	229	426	.244	.353	.305
Road Games	32-46	4.31	2528	674	73	225	396	.267	.412	.327
Grass Fields	15-27	4.62	1363	372	40	113	210	.273	.412	.329
Artificial Turf	69-51	3.38	4005	995	74	341	612	.248	.370	.311
April	13-8	3.02	690	163	12	65	117	.236	.342	.304
May	11-14	4.99	836	231	21	73	124	.276	.429	.337
June	16-12	3.19	929	233	13	74	136	.251	.347	.306
July	13-13	4.40	876	239	24	83	129	.273	.424	.339
August	16-12	3.37	926	236	21	62	137	.255	.390	.307
Sept./Oct.	15-19	3.28	1111	265	23	97	179	.239	.356	.303
Leading Off Inn.			1332	326	31	96	197	.245	.372	.301
Bases Empty			3172	778	64	235	497	.245	.364	.302
Runners On			2196	589	50	219	325	.268	.405	.333
Runners On/2 Out			1280	341	29	165	208	.266	.407	.342
Scor. Pos./2 Out			946	232	22	102	156	.245	.381	.325
Late-Inning Pressure			791	201	17	78	139	.254	.375	.322
Leading Off			201	50	5	18	31	.249	.378	.314
Runners On			327	90	10	37	57	.275	.413	.348
Runners/Scor. Pos.			187	48	5	28	34	.257	.364	.348
First 9 Batters			2844	721	52	250	477	.254	.370	.317
Second 9 Batters			1355	329	33	98	204	.243	.372	.298
All Batters Thereafter			1169	317	29	106	141	.271	.418	.332

ST. LOUIS CARDINALS

When a player has what we've defined as a breakthrough season (and what others call a career year; see our two Native American essays for details), his career has advanced to a new plateau. The Cardinals are betting that players who've had the opposite—"breakdown seasons"—can recover from the plunge.

The Cards have on their roster the three players who had the most severe breakdown seasons in the National League last year: Pedro Guerrero, Andres Galarraga, and Rich Gedman. The Redbird brass traded for Galarraga and resigned Gedman and Guerrero, despite having seen their career worsts up close and personal. Perhaps they've got plans to bring back J. Edgar Hoover to rally these G-Men.

Each G-Man is at a different stage of his career, with a different place in the Cardinals' plans, and will measure success by a different standard. The performance of other players coming off similar breakdown seasons may help us guess (and let's be honest, guess is all anyone can do) whether these guys will rebound, remain at last season's low levels of performance, or slide even further.

Barring injuries in the Cardinals catching corps, Gedman may not even be worth a guess, and he surely has no further to fall. He's played just 96 games over the last two seasons, and had an even 100 plate appearances in 1991. His numbers—read 'em and weep:

Age	G	AB	R	H	2B	3B	HR	RBI	BB	SO	SB	BA	SLG	OBA
32	46	94	7	10	1	0	3	8	4	15	0	.106	.213	.140

The odds on a breakdown indicate the chance that a particular season's worth of plate appearances that bad could have been drawn randomly from his previous career record. In Gedman's case, the odds against a 94-at-bat performance that bad were a staggering 1652-to-1, the longest in the National League last year. Reviewing the 96 previous breakdown seasons of 100-to-1 or more (once the numbers get that large, it's the difference between your chances of getting struck by lightning on a sunny day outdoors and indoors), six belong to other back-up catchers, and they're also the closest matches to Gedman in terms of at-bats and embarrassingly low batting average.

Year	Age	Player	AB	R	H	2B	3B	HR	RBI	BA	SLG	OBA
1972	27	George Mitterwald	163	12	30	4	1	1	8	.184	.239	.225
1975	28	Ray Fosse	136	14	19	3	2	0	12	.140	.191	.192
1989	35	Gary Carter	153	14	28	8	0	2	15	.183	.275	.241
1989	32	Jody Davis	231	12	39	5	0	4	19	.169	.242	.246
1989	28	John Russell	159	14	29	2	0	2	9	.182	.233	.225
1990	38	Ernie Whitt	180	14	31	8	0	2	10	.172	.250	.265

The Addams family might reject those seasons as too creepy. Yet each of those backup backstops got at least one more major league contract following those dismal performances. Mitterwald played five more years, including a 16-homer, 64-RBI last stand as a regular in 1973. Fosse hit .301 in limited duty in 1976 (with no power and barely one RBI every 10 plate appearances) and still returned to the majors in 1977 and 1979. Note that both were much younger than Gedman. More

senior backups Whitt and Davis didn't last another whole season, but Carter is still plugging away, as is the youthful Russell.

Since his back-to-back All-Star appearances in 1985 and 1986, Gedman has lived at the major league margin. After 1986, he was one of the marquee victims of what an arbitrator labelled collusion; he was ignored as a free agent, was unable to resign with the Red Sox until May 1987, and then suffered back-to-back injuries, effectively robbing him of two prime years from his career. He'll be 33 by the end of the 1992 season, and after failing to hit his weight for three consecutive campaigns, it appears the only way he'll do so in 1992 is Ultra Slim-Fast. He almost certainly has run out of chances to resume a role as a regular.

That's not to say Gedman has no value. He gave his manager and local beat reporters plenty of opportunity to exercise their cliche glands. Repeat after me: "Young pitchers and catchers can profit from Geddy's experience. He's a guy who's been there before, all the way to World Series game seven." (Frighteningly, one can say the same of Junior Ortiz—and Junior's team won!) And the fact is that left-handed-hitting catchers with championship experience can be as tough to exterminate as left-handed middle relievers. (Just ask Cardinals teammate Bob McClure.) If the Cards don't want him, somebody else will step in, and expansion is only a year away. That's all great news for Gedman.

When Gedman was wrapping up his glory days, Andres Galarraga was just getting started. Remember *Sports Illustrated*'s baseball preview issue in 1986? Six promising rookies were highlighted. Three have become superstars, three have not. But at the time, it wasn't as easy to separate Jose Canseco, Will Clark, and Wally Joyner from Pete Incaviglia, Billy Jo Robidoux, and Galarraga as it is now. Galarraga fell just short of Canseco's physique and Will the Thrill's nickname, though mixing Spanish and French is always fun (as in Galarraga, *Les Gros Chat*) and Andres the Giant gets crossover credit.

Galarraga batted .300 in his sophomore and junior seasons, knocking in 90 runs in each. He made history in 1988 with an unprecedented daily double, leading the National League in hits and strikeouts (and doubles, too). His batting average declined to the .250s in 1989 and 1990, but he still had 20-plus homers and 85-plus RBIs before last season's disaster, which represented a 620-to-1 breakdown:

Year	Age	G	AB	R	H	2B	3B	HR	RBI	BB	SO	SB	BA	SLG	OBA
1990	29	155	579	65	148	29	0	20	87	40	169	10	.256	.409	.306
1991	30	107	375	34	82	13	2	9	33	23	86	5	.219	.336	.268

The 10 players with 100-to-1 breakdowns or worse before the age of 30 provide some hope for a rebound by Galarraga. Eight of them had at least one season in the next three with more homers, more RBIs, and higher batting, slugging, and on-base averages.

That rebound group includes Fred Lynn, who had seven consecutive 20-homer seasons following his 1981 breakdown at age 29. Following a 7054-to-1 breakdown in 1971 as a member of the Astros, Jim Wynn averaged 22 homers, 75 RBI, 14 steals, and 108 walks over the next five years, including a 32-HR, 108-RBI, 108-walk, 18-steal season for the 1974 N.L. champion Dodgers. Others on the list include Tommy Helms, Merv Rettenmund, Dave Cash, Mitchell Page, Mike Davis, Dick Green (a member of three Oakland A's championship teams), and Mike Andrews (who got famous thanks in part to Green and the A's dynasty).

Those nine played an average of four-plus years in the majors beyond their breakdown seasons; only three lasted fewer than three more years. However, the guy with the breakdown most similar to Galarraga's is a player who had his 8710-to-1 breakdown in 1990 and is still active. Here are his before, during, and after breakdown figures, which may provide the best hints about Galarraga's future:

Age	Year	G	AB	R	H	2B	3B	HR	RBI	BB	SO	SB	BA	SLG	OBA
28	1989	158	631	79	191	37	2	23	113	51	30	3	.303	.477	.351
29	1990	102	394	40	101	16	0	5	42	28	20	1	.256	.335	.308
30	1991	152	587	64	169	35	0	9	68	46	42	2	.288	.394	.339

Like Galarraga, this first basemen missed time with an injury during his breakdown season. He fell about the same distance as Galarraga, though from higher prebreakdown levels. He shares Galarraga's revulsion for walks, though notably lacks the Big Cat's affinity for strikeouts. A couple of years ago it would have been a major compliment to say Galarraga was turning into Don Mattingly. But of course, even though he rebounded mightily from his own breakdown season, Don Mattingly still has miles to go to be Don Mattingly again.

Pedro Guerrero, 35 at the end of the 1991 season, had the worst breakdown season among National League regulars last year, batting .272 with only 12 doubles and 8 home runs (an 853-to-1 fall). A breakdown season at that age puts Guerrero in some very select company. Since 1970, 41 players that old had 100-to-1 or worse breakdown years. Eight are Hall of Famers, three are drop-dead candidates for enshrinement, and another is Pete Rose. Their breakdown seasons:

Year	Age	Player	AB	R	H	2B	3B	HR	RBI	BA	SLG	OBA
1975	41	Hank Aaron	465	45	109	16	2	12	60	.234	.355	.332
1978	39	Lou Brock	298	31	66	9	0	0	12	.221	.252	.263
1986	38	Carlton Fisk	457	42	101	11	0	14	63	.221	.337	.263
1983	37	Reggie Jackson	397	43	77	14	1	14	49	.194	.340	.290
1974	39	Al Kaline	558	71	146	28	2	13	64	.262	.389	.337
1974	38	Harmon Killebrew	333	28	74	7	0	13	54	.222	.360	.312
1973	42	Willie Mays	209	24	44	10	0	6	25	.211	.344	.303
1972	34	Willie McCovey	263	30	56	8	0	14	35	.213	.403	.316
1975	38	Brooks Robinson	482	50	97	15	1	6	53	.201	.274	.267
1982	41	Pete Rose	634	80	172	25	4	3	54	.271	.338	.345
1988	39	Mike Schmidt	390	52	97	21	2	12	62	.249	.405	.337
1976	38	Billy Williams	351	36	74	12	0	11	41	.211	.339	.320

Also in that group of 41 are at least another half-dozen players for whom reasonable arguments for a Cooperstown plaque can be made (including Gary Carter, Keith Hernandez, Tony Oliva, Vada Pinson, Jim Rice, and Maury Wills), proving that a player has to be darned good to build a pedestal from which to fall so far at an advanced age.

But of those 41 players, 18—nearly half—had at least a 10-to-1 breakdown the next year, and all but five of those took the hint and retired. Grim tidings for Guerrero when more than half of the group suffers what's normally a one-in-ten disaster. Still, among those who kept playing longer, four—Jackson, Fisk, Ted Simmons, and Bob Boone—made quite substantial contributions as full-time players after their breakdowns. Assuming Guerrero is going to play beyond 1992, the odds on a comeback improve—if, that is, he learns to catch or moves to the American League as a designated hitter, his proper position for more than a decade.

The odds improve further when we consider the mitigating circumstances in Guerrero's 1991 breakdown. He was among the league leaders in RBIs until breaking his leg in early July, and he's been a top run producer for years. Guerrero has even shown signs of becoming a better hitter as he ages, walking more and striking out less. His power numbers should get a boost from the shorter fences at Busch Stadium this season. A shrunken outfield will also aid Guerrero if he's forced to play, gulp, left field.

Of course, Guerrero shouldn't even be a Cardinal. He filed for free agency after last season, and the Redbirds made it clear they had no intention of keeping him by dealing Ken Hill from their thin starting rotation to acquire Galarraga as Guerrero's replacement. St. Louis offered Guerrero arbitration as a formality, to get a draft choice for him when he signed with another team. But after finding little interest in the market, Guerrero queered the plan by accepting arbitration.

The Cardinals have let the last two National League batting champions slip away. Wouldn't it be something if Guerrero's forcing himself on them becomes one of those "best deals never made?" Because if general manager Dal Maxvill decides he can only keep one first baseman with a Spanish surname that starts with a *G*, sentiment and statistics favor Guerrero.

Did the Expos call "no backsies" on the Galarraga trade?

SAN DIEGO PADRES

Twenty-five years ago, baseball saw a golden age of third basemen. As the careers of veterans like Ken Boyer and Eddie Mathews wound down, other perennial All-Stars like Brooks Robinson, Ron Santo, and Harmon Killebrew were joined by a new wave of young stars at the hot corner. They included Dick Allen, Jim Ray Hart, Tony Perez, converted outfielder Mike Shannon, Jim Lefebvre (the 1965 N.L. rookie of the year), and impossible dreamer Joe Foy. And let's not forget Clete Boyer, reborn in Atlanta, and Ty Cobb's conqueror, Maury Wills, playing a new position in 1967 for a new team (Pittsburgh).

That must seem like centuries ago to the San Diego Padres and their fans, who suffered last season as their third basemen compiled a .194 batting average, the lowest by any position for any team in the National League (with the exception of pitchers). You've probably heard about the time Lefty O'Doul told a writer that Ty Cobb would have hit only in the low three-hundreds if he'd played in the 1950s—because, after all, he would have been more than 60 years old! You have to wonder whether Padres general manager Joe McIlvaine might have been tempted at times last season to give Mathews or one of his contemporaries a call. After all, even the low *two* hundreds would have been an improvement for the 1991 Padres.

Actually, third base has always been a trouble spot for San Diego. The Padres have used 72 players at that position during their 23-year history; the only teams to use more since 1969 were San Francisco (75) and Oakland (74). The only Padres third baseman to play more than 400 games was Luis Salazar, and it took him three tours of duty with San Diego to reach his team record of 551 games at third. The top 10:

Luis Salazar	551	Doug Rader	188
Graig Nettles	363	Mike Pagliarulo	165
Dave Roberts	330	Barry Evans	144
Ed Spiezio	287	Kurt Bevacqua	133
Tim Flannery	243	Randy Ready	128

The Padres' problems are indicative of a trend: Third base has become a weak offensive position throughout the majors. Sure there's Chris Sabo in Cincinnati, Matt Williams in San Francisco, and Terry Pendleton in Atlanta—a triple whammy for N.L. West rivals like the Padres—not to mention Howard Johnson, Kelly Gruber, Wade Boggs, Edgar Martinez, and Robin Ventura. A few other teams have "name" third basemen past their primes (like Gary Gaetti and Tim Wallach). But those are the exceptions; 14 players with slugging and on-base averages below their league marks played at least 50 games at third base, including Scott Coolbaugh and Jack Howell of the Padres. As recently as 1989, that total of Brand X third basemen was seven.

The current situation began to develop in the mid-1980s, when many of the best third basemen were nearing the ends of their careers. In 1986, for the only time in the past 58 years, third base was the oldest position in the majors, with an average age of 30.02 years—its highest point since 1933, when four third basemen born in the 1800s were still playing regularly (Sparky Adams, Jimmy Dykes, Joe Sewell, and Pie Traynor). Nine starters were 33 or older on the final day of the 1986 season: Ray Knight (33), George Brett (33), Jim Morrison (34), Buddy Bell (35), Bill Madlock (35), Doug DeCinces (36), Mike Schmidt (37), Phil Garner (38), and San Diego's Graig Nettles (42). That season, third basemen batted .266, eight points higher than the major league average, but the margin declined rapidly thereafter. Over the past two seasons, third basemen have exceeded the average of all players by only two points:

	1985	1986	1987	1988	1989	1990	1991
Third Basemen	.264	.266	.270	.260	.258	.258	.259
Major League Avg.	.257	.258	.263	.254	.254	.258	.256
Difference	+7	+8	+7	+6	+4	0	+3

(For purposes of comparison, third basemen exceeded the league average by at least 10 points in every season from 1963 through 1967.)

Like many teams, the Padres tried a little of everything to solve their third-base problem. Last season's motley crew included Scott Coolbaugh, Jim Presley, Tim Teufel, Garry Templeton, Marty Barrett, and Paul Faries; each was either out of time, out of position, or both. The last four were all displaced middle infielders—Teufel, Tempy, and Barrett desperately trying to keep their careers alive, Faries trying to get his started. Transitions from second base or shortstop to third base have become increasingly common throughout the majors as teams have scrambled to compensate for the dearth of talented third basemen, a practice that has further greased the decline in offensive production from the hot corner.

From the 1950s through the 1980s, it was more common for players to move to third base from primarily offensive positions (first base or the outfield). But among the nine regular third basemen in 1990 or 1991 who had played elsewhere in the previous season, seven were former middle infielders: Lenny Harris, Tony Phillips, and Gary Sheffield moved to third in 1990; Jim Gantner, Scott Leius, Bill Pecota, and Ernest Riles did so last season. And neither of the other two were outfielders; they were catcher Todd Zeile and first baseman Jeff King (who had played third base throughout most of his collegiate and professional career). Contrast that breakdown to the positions from which players moved to third base from 1950 through 1989:

Years	C	1B	OF	2B	SS
1950–89	2	22	36	29	24
1990–91	1	1	0	4	3

We've been wondering: Are so few players moving to third base from positions that are easier to play (first base and the outfield) because they have so much control over their careers? Have teams become overly concerned with a player's comfort? A case in point: Hensley Meulens of the Yankees spent the first four years of his pro career at third base. Two years ago, the Yankees decided to try him in left field, where he was no better but probably would do less damage. But when the team was unable to land a capable third baseman prior to the 1991 season—leaving Mike Blowers, Randy

Velarde, and Torey Lovullo (combined career batting average: .213) as the only candidates—you'd have thought the Yankees would overlook Meulens's defensive shortcomings at third base to get a hitter with his pedigree in the lineup, especially when management spent spring training of 1991 and the first month of the season moaning over its inability to get him more playing time. But apparently that possibility was never seriously considered because Meulens "wasn't comfortable there." Oh.

Our colleague Eliot Cohen lends this analogy: You can't race a horse and breed him at the same time, because once he gets a taste of the latter he'll never want to do anything else. Could it be that contemporary players won't work to become good third basemen if they know left field or first base is the alternative? And maybe third base looks attractive only to players coming from the even more demanding middle-infield positions.

The following table perfectly illustrates the point that, on the whole, the current set of third basemen hit more like shortstops. The first line represents the average of all third basemen in the majors last season scaled down to 500 plate appearances. The next four lines are the 1991 figures for the four players whose statistics most resemble the top line. As you can see, all four are shortstops:

	AB	R	H	2B	3B	HR	RBI	BB	SO	SB	BA	SLG
Third Base Avg.	450	56	118	21	2	12	54	42	70	6	.261	.397
Jeff Blauser	352	49	91	14	3	11	54	54	59	5	.259	.409
Shawon Dunston	492	59	128	22	7	12	50	23	64	21	.260	.407
Greg Gagne	408	52	108	23	3	8	42	26	72	11	.265	.395
Luis Rivera	414	64	107	22	3	8	40	35	86	4	.258	.384

Things could get far worse before they get better, because most of the current third base prospects have little or no potential as power hitters. San Diego's own young contender, Paul Faries, is actually a second baseman with a .300 career batting average and 192 stolen bases in five seasons in the minors, but only 14 home runs in more than 2000 at-bats. You may recognize the names of some of these other third base prospects: Bret Barberie (Expos), Scott Cooper (Red Sox), Chris Donnels (Mets), Leo Gomez (Orioles), Dave Hansen (Dodgers), Scott Leius (Twins), Scott Livingstone (Tigers), Dean Palmer (Rangers), Gary Scott (Cubs), Ed Sprague (Blue Jays), Jim Thome (Indians), and John Wehner (Pirates). Only three have hit as many as 20 home runs in a season in the minors: Gomez, Palmer, and Sprague. Our projection model, based on admittedly small fragments of their major league performance to date, gives only Gomez and Palmer an odds-on chance of doing so in the majors.

With Howard Johnson heading to the outfield (because, we are told, he *wants* to), it appears that one more of the remaining third basemen with some pop in his bat will be leaving the fold. And as some of the above prospects win full-time jobs, third base will stray further from the slugger's profile developed by Ken Keltner and Whitey Kurowski in the 1940s, enhanced by Mathews, Killebrew, and others during the glory years of the 1960s, and continued by Schmidt and Brett through the 1980s. But it's worth noting that the current trend is really a return to the fashion of an earlier time. From 1904 through 1941, the slugging average for third basemen fell below the major league mark 27 times in 38 years (though their batting average was above the league mark in a slight majority of those seasons).

Before wrapping up this topic, let's explore one more unusual characteristic of third basemen over the past 20 years. At every other infield position, fielding rates have improved decade by decade throughout the history of baseball. But at third base, error rates bottomed in the mid-1950s and have risen slowly but steadily since then. The following table shows the number of chances per error at each infield position at 10-year intervals starting in 1900. The figures don't always represent straight lines, but the general trend at every position other than third base is a steady decrease in errors:

	1900	1910	1920	1930	1940	1950	1960	1970	1980	1990
First Base	47	61	98	96	98	95	104	122	129	128
Second Base	16	20	27	29	30	40	42	48	52	61
Shortstop	13	14	17	19	20	26	25	30	28	33
Third Base	10	15	19	19	17	22	21	19	20	18

Although the rate of errors by third basemen improved to one per 21.2 chances in 1991 (its lowest level since 1978), it seems incredible that the rate was no better in 1990 than it was in 1925.

Here's another illustration of the same trend: Ryne Sandberg has a career average of one error for every 98 chances at second base, the best in major league history (minimum: 1000 games). The next three spots also belong to players active in 1991: Tommy Herr, Jim Gantner, and Lou Whitaker, respectively. The highest-ranked player whose career ended more than 30 years ago is Bobby Doerr, who ranks 25th and last played in 1951.

At shortstop, Larry Bowa is the all-time leader with an average of one error for every 49 chances; he retired in 1985. The next five best rates belong to players active in 1991; in order: Tony Fernandez, Ozzie Smith, Cal Ripken, Spike Owen, and Alan Trammell. The highest-ranked player whose career ended more than 30 years ago is Lou Boudreau, who ranks 14th and last played in 1952.

Six of the 10 highest-ranked first basemen played within the last 10 years, including one active player (Don Mattingly). Among the all-time top 20, only two retired prior to 1960: Frank McCormick (who ranks sixth and last played in 1948) and Joe Judge (19th, 1934).

But at third base, the all-time leader, Brooks Robinson, retired 15 years ago. Runner-up Ken Reitz retired following the 1982 season. The highest-ranked active player is Carney Lansford in eighth place. The players ranked between Reitz and Lansford (with their final seasons in parentheses): George Kell (1957), Don Money (1983), Don Wert (1971), Willie Kamm (1935), and Heinie Groh (1927). Only two players active in 1991 other than Lansford can be found in the all-time top 20 (Gary Gaetti and Ken Oberkfell).

Which gets us to thinking, maybe McIlvaine shouldn't call Eddie Mathews. Does anyone have Heinie Groh's phone number? (Try 1–900–BOTT–L–BAT.)

WON-LOST RECORD BY STARTING POSITION

San Diego Padres	C	1B	2B	3B	SS	LF	CF	RF	DH	P	Leadoff	Cleanup	Starts vs. LH	Starts vs. RH	Total Starts
Shawn Abner	-	-	-	-	-	-	13-14	-	-	-	-	-	7	20	13-14
Mike Aldrete	-	-	-	0-2	-	-	-	-	-	-	-	-	-	2	0-2
Larry Andersen	-	-	-	-	-	-	-	-	-	-	-	-	-	-	-
Oscar Azocar	-	-	-	-	-	7-1	-	0-1	-	-	-	-	-	9	7-2
Marty Barrett	-	-	2-0	0-2	-	-	-	-	-	-	-	-	1	3	2-2
Andy Benes	-	-	-	-	-	-	-	-	-	17-16	-	-	14	19	17-16
Dann Bilardello	5-1	-	-	-	-	-	-	-	-	-	-	-	1	5	5-1
Ricky Bones	-	-	-	-	-	-	-	-	-	5-6	-	-	5	6	5-6
Jerald Clark	-	6-3	-	-	-	38-46	-	7-4	-	-	-	3-3	39	65	51-53
Pat Clements	-	-	-	-	-	-	-	-	-	-	-	-	-	-	-
Scott Coolbaugh	-	-	-	26-25	-	-	-	-	-	-	-	-	18	33	26-25
John Costello	-	-	-	-	-	-	-	-	-	-	-	-	-	-	-
Brian Dorsett	-	-	-	-	-	-	-	-	-	-	-	-	-	-	-
Paul Faries	-	-	13-15	4-2	2-2	-	-	-	-	-	-	1-2	16	22	19-19
Tony Fernandez	-	-	-	-	75-68	-	-	-	-	-	-	9-4	48	95	75-68
Wes Gardner	-	-	-	-	-	-	-	-	-	-	-	-	-	-	-
Tony Gwynn	-	-	-	-	-	-	-	66-67	-	-	-	-	46	87	66-67
Atlee Hammaker	-	-	-	-	-	-	-	-	-	0-1	-	-	-	1	0-1
Greg W. Harris	-	-	-	-	-	-	-	-	-	13-7	-	-	7	13	13-7
Jeremy Hernandez	-	-	-	-	-	-	-	-	-	-	-	-	-	-	-
Thomas Howard	-	-	-	-	-	12-6	15-22	10-3	-	-	11-12	-	6	62	37-31
Jack Howell	-	-	-	23-16	-	-	-	-	-	-	-	-	1	38	23-16
Bruce Hurst	-	-	-	-	-	-	-	-	-	19-12	-	-	12	19	19-12
Darrin Jackson	-	-	-	-	-	7-6	41-30	-	-	-	9-10	2-0	45	39	48-36
Tom Lampkin	4-4	-	-	-	-	-	-	-	-	-	-	-	-	8	4-4
Craig Lefferts	-	-	-	-	-	-	-	-	-	-	-	-	-	-	-
Jim Lewis	-	-	-	-	-	-	-	-	-	-	-	-	-	-	-
Derek Lilliquist	-	-	-	-	-	-	-	-	-	0-2	-	-	1	1	0-2
Mike Maddux	-	-	-	-	-	-	-	-	-	1-0	-	-	1	-	1-0
Fred McGriff	-	78-75	-	-	-	-	-	-	-	-	-	73-68	53	100	78-75
Jose Melendez	-	-	-	-	-	-	-	-	-	6-3	-	-	3	6	6-3
Jose Mota	-	-	3-7	-	-	-	-	-	-	-	-	-	2	8	3-7
Eric Nolte	-	-	-	-	-	-	-	-	-	4-2	-	-	-	6	4-2
Adam Peterson	-	-	-	-	-	-	-	-	-	5-6	-	-	2	9	5-6
Jim Presley	-	-	-	7-9	-	-	-	-	-	-	-	-	8	8	7-9
Dennis Rasmussen	-	-	-	-	-	-	-	-	-	9-15	-	-	6	18	9-15
Bip Roberts	-	-	30-34	-	-	10-4	15-12	-	-	-	54-50	-	31	74	55-50
Rich Rodriguez	-	-	-	-	-	-	-	-	-	0-1	-	-	1	-	0-1
Steve Rosenberg	-	-	-	-	-	-	-	-	-	-	-	-	-	-	-
Benito Santiago	75-73	-	-	-	-	-	-	-	-	-	-	6-7	56	92	75-73
Tim Scott	-	-	-	-	-	-	-	-	-	-	-	-	-	-	-
Craig Shipley	-	-	6-4	-	7-8	-	-	-	-	-	-	-	16	9	13-12
Phil Stephenson	-	-	-	-	-	-	-	-	-	-	-	-	-	-	-
Garry Templeton	-	-	-	5-3	-	-	-	-	-	-	-	-	2	6	5-3
Tim Teufel	-	-	30-18	19-21	-	-	-	-	-	-	-	-	38	50	49-39
Jim Vatcher	-	-	-	-	-	-	-	1-2	-	-	-	-	2	1	1-2
Kevin Ward	-	-	-	-	-	10-13	-	0-1	-	-	-	-	20	4	10-14
Ed Whitson	-	-	-	-	-	-	-	-	-	5-7	-	-	5	7	5-7

TEAM TOTALS: BATTING

	AB	H	2B	3B	HR	RBI	BB	SO	BA	SA	OBA
Season	5408	1321	204	36	121	591	501	1069	.244	.362	.310
vs. Left-Handers	1797	452	71	13	57	224	167	315	.252	.401	.315
vs. Right-Handers	3611	869	133	23	64	367	334	754	.241	.343	.308
vs. Ground-Ballers	2722	688	105	18	60	298	245	464	.253	.371	.316
vs. Fly-Ballers	2686	633	99	18	61	293	256	605	.236	.354	.304
Home Games	2640	646	97	14	65	293	247	512	.245	.366	.312
Road Games	2768	675	107	22	56	298	254	557	.244	.359	.308
Grass Fields	3983	979	145	25	99	459	360	796	.246	.369	.310
Artificial Turf	1425	342	59	11	22	132	141	273	.240	.343	.309
April	704	178	21	7	10	78	63	140	.253	.345	.315
May	952	225	35	12	21	100	90	193	.236	.364	.305
June	942	251	42	4	18	105	100	157	.266	.377	.338
July	787	171	30	1	15	55	68	157	.217	.315	.281
August	983	238	34	6	31	117	79	212	.242	.384	.300
Sept./Oct.	1040	258	42	6	26	136	101	210	.248	.375	.317
Leading Off Inn.	1327	317	43	6	33	33	115	250	.239	.355	.303
Runners On	2231	593	90	20	53	523	229	447	.266	.395	.333
Bases Empty	3177	728	114	16	68	68	272	622	.229	.339	.293
Runners/Scor. Pos.	1300	348	54	13	36	470	169	282	.268	.412	.347
Runners On/2 Out	970	247	45	10	19	211	115	222	.255	.380	.337
Scor. Pos./2 Out	651	167	32	7	12	190	91	157	.257	.382	.351
Late-Inning Pressure	844	212	26	3	19	90	82	171	.251	.357	.319
Leading Off	214	58	7	0	7	7	19	40	.271	.402	.333
Runners On	358	102	12	3	7	78	39	73	.285	.394	.355
Runners/Scor. Pos.	208	59	8	2	4	69	27	40	.284	.399	.363

RUNS BATTED IN	From 1B	From 2B	From 3B	Scoring Position
Totals	67/1607	189/1028	214/531	403/1559
Percentage	4.2%	18.4%	40.3%	25.8%

TEAM TOTALS: PITCHING

	W-L	ERA	AB	H	HR	BB	SO	BA	SA	OBA
Season	84-78	3.57	5499	1385	139	457	921	.252	.375	.308
vs. Left-Handers			2250	551	59	203	390	.245	.372	.305
vs. Right-Handers			3249	834	80	254	531	.257	.377	.310
vs. Ground-Ballers			2380	570	40	161	427	.239	.329	.287
vs. Fly-Ballers			3119	815	99	296	494	.261	.410	.324
Home Games	42-39	3.47	2808	691	72	232	501	.246	.366	.304
Road Games	42-39	3.68	2691	694	67	225	420	.258	.385	.313
Grass Fields	62-58	3.66	4096	1027	107	336	676	.251	.372	.306
Artificial Turf	22-20	3.34	1403	358	32	121	245	.255	.383	.313
April	11-10	4.25	724	197	23	63	126	.272	.427	.327
May	13-15	4.20	982	263	30	103	152	.268	.400	.336
June	14-14	3.43	925	231	26	71	131	.250	.377	.304
July	10-14	3.45	798	190	18	78	125	.238	.347	.305
August	15-14	3.35	983	235	19	64	186	.239	.355	.284
Sept./Oct.	21-11	2.98	1087	269	23	78	201	.247	.354	.297
Leading Off Inn.			1357	331	43	96	208	.244	.393	.295
Bases Empty			3268	814	87	242	559	.249	.377	.302
Runners On			2231	571	52	215	362	.256	.372	.317
Runners/Scor. Pos.			1206	302	25	153	212	.250	.361	.326
Runners On/2 Out			987	232	20	107	174	.235	.344	.312
Scor. Pos./2 Out			594	134	12	82	112	.226	.337	.322
Late-Inning Pressure			908	213	14	87	164	.235	.318	.300
Leading Off			231	44	2	22	42	.190	.255	.264
Runners On			364	86	6	36	65	.236	.324	.300
Runners/Scor. Pos.			186	46	2	25	41	.247	.323	.326
First 9 Batters			2846	721	64	261	523	.253	.372	.314
Second 9 Batters			1366	322	38	93	217	.236	.365	.285
All Batters Thereafter			1287	342	37	103	181	.266	.393	.319

WON-LOST RECORD BY STARTING POSITION

San Francisco Giants	C	1B	2B	3B	SS	LF	CF	RF	DH	P	Leadoff	Cleanup	Starts vs. LH	Starts vs. RH	Total Starts
Dave Anderson	-	7-2	0-2	0-3	13-19	-	-	-	-	-	-	-	20	26	20-26
Kevin Bass	-	-	-	-	-	8-10	-	36-36	-	-	-	9-7	30	60	44-46
Rod Beck	-	-	-	-	-	-	-	-	-	-	-	-	-	-	-
Mike Benjamin	-	-	-	-	17-17	-	-	-	-	-	-	-	10	24	17-17
Bud Black	-	-	-	-	-	-	-	-	-	15-19	-	-	15	19	15-19
Jeff Brantley	-	-	-	-	-	-	-	-	-	-	-	-	-	-	-
John Burkett	-	-	-	-	-	-	-	-	-	17-17	-	-	12	22	17-17
Will Clark	-	62-81	-	-	-	-	-	-	-	-	-	0-3	38	105	62-81
Royce Clayton	-	-	-	-	1-7	-	-	-	-	-	0-2	-	2	6	1-7
Darnell Coles	-	-	-	-	-	-	-	1-0	-	-	-	-	1	-	1-0
Steve Decker	29-36	-	-	-	-	-	-	-	-	-	-	-	26	39	29-36
Kelly Downs	-	-	-	-	-	-	-	-	-	3-8	-	-	5	6	3-8
Mike Felder	-	-	-	-	-	14-9	10-14	5-18	-	-	27-36	-	18	52	29-41
Scott Garrelts	-	-	-	-	-	-	-	-	-	1-2	-	-	1	2	1-2
Eric Gunderson	-	-	-	-	-	-	-	-	-	-	-	-	-	-	-
Gil Heredia	-	-	-	-	-	-	-	-	-	2-2	-	-	1	3	2-2
Tommy Herr	-	-	7-3	0-1	-	-	-	-	-	-	-	-	4	7	7-4
Bryan Hickerson	-	-	-	-	-	-	-	-	-	3-3	-	-	2	4	3-3
Terry Kennedy	18-22	-	-	-	-	-	-	-	-	-	-	-	-	40	18-22
Mike Kingery	-	1-1	-	-	-	-	-	8-1	-	-	3-0	-	-	11	9-2
Mike LaCoss	-	-	-	-	-	-	-	-	-	3-2	-	-	-	5	3-2
Mark Leonard	-	-	-	-	-	8-12	-	4-5	-	-	-	2-3	1	28	12-17
Darren Lewis	-	-	-	-	-	-	30-24	-	-	-	30-24	-	21	33	30-24
Greg Litton	-	5-3	3-3	3-3	1-3	0-1	-	0-1	-	-	-	-	9	17	12-14
Kirt Manwaring	28-29	-	-	-	-	-	-	-	-	-	-	-	22	35	28-29
Paul McClellan	-	-	-	-	-	-	-	-	-	5-7	-	-	2	10	5-7
Willie McGee	-	-	-	-	-	-	35-49	20-20	-	-	-	7-5	36	88	55-69
Kevin Mitchell	-	-	-	-	-	45-54	-	-	-	-	-	45-54	34	65	45-54
Francisco Oliveras	-	-	-	-	-	-	-	-	-	0-1	-	-	1	-	0-1
Rick Parker	-	-	-	-	-	0-1	-	-	-	-	0-1	-	-	1	0-1
Tony Perezchica	-	-	1-1	4-4	-	-	-	-	-	-	1-0	-	2	8	5-5
Mike Remlinger	-	-	-	-	-	-	-	-	-	5-1	-	-	1	5	5-1
Rick Reuschel	-	-	-	-	-	-	-	-	-	0-1	-	-	-	1	0-1
Dave Righetti	-	-	-	-	-	-	-	-	-	-	-	-	-	-	-
Don Robinson	-	-	-	-	-	-	-	-	-	7-9	-	-	2	14	7-9
Jose Segura	-	-	-	-	-	-	-	-	-	-	-	-	-	-	-
Robby Thompson	-	-	64-78	-	-	-	-	-	-	-	-	7-16	41	101	64-78
Jose Uribe	-	-	-	-	39-36	-	-	-	-	-	-	-	22	53	39-36
Matt Williams	-	-	-	72-80	0-1	-	-	-	-	-	-	19-20	46	107	72-81
Trevor Wilson	-	-	-	-	-	-	-	-	-	14-15	-	-	6	23	14-15
Ted Wood	-	-	-	-	-	-	-	1-6	-	-	0-3	-	1	6	1-6

TEAM TOTALS: BATTING

	AB	H	2B	3B	HR	RBI	BB	SO	BA	SA	OBA
Season	5463	1345	215	48	141	605	471	973	.246	.381	.309
vs. Left-Handers	1597	399	73	11	45	194	126	253	.250	.394	.306
vs. Right-Handers	3866	946	142	37	96	411	345	720	.245	.375	.310
vs. Ground-Ballers	2538	620	89	22	70	277	216	429	.244	.379	.306
vs. Fly-Ballers	2925	725	126	26	71	328	255	544	.248	.382	.311
Home Games	2642	645	108	25	69	283	234	454	.244	.382	.308
Road Games	2821	700	107	23	72	322	237	519	.248	.379	.309
Grass Fields	4005	984	150	35	105	424	336	716	.246	.379	.307
Artificial Turf	1458	361	65	13	36	181	135	257	.248	.384	.315
April	682	175	23	8	25	88	63	122	.257	.424	.320
May	970	230	37	9	21	82	72	174	.237	.359	.291
June	894	216	40	8	18	104	78	153	.242	.365	.307
July	808	215	30	5	33	106	64	147	.266	.438	.324
August	1041	274	58	10	24	122	85	174	.263	.407	.322
Sept./Oct.	1068	235	27	8	20	103	109	203	.220	.316	.296
Leading Off Inn.	1328	318	54	12	31	31	104	229	.239	.368	.302
Runners On	2251	575	83	21	60	524	229	371	.255	.391	.325
Bases Empty	3212	770	132	27	81	81	242	602	.240	.373	.297
Runners/Scor. Pos.	1296	315	42	14	27	434	168	233	.243	.360	.326
Runners On/2 Out	988	231	38	8	25	208	120	161	.234	.364	.323
Scor. Pos./2 Out	631	136	17	6	14	176	95	114	.216	.328	.323
Late-Inning Pressure	827	205	36	7	14	96	99	155	.248	.359	.330
Leading Off	214	52	11	1	2	2	20	41	.243	.332	.308
Runners On	343	91	12	5	6	88	55	60	.265	.382	.366
Runners/Scor. Pos.	207	50	3	4	5	80	41	40	.242	.367	.363

RUNS BATTED IN	From 1B	From 2B	From 3B	Scoring Position
Totals	86/1583	167/999	211/567	378/1566
Percentage	5.4%	16.7%	37.2%	24.1%

TEAM TOTALS: PITCHING

	W-L	ERA	AB	H	HR	BB	SO	BA	SA	OBA
Season	75-87	4.03	5435	1397	143	544	905	.257	.390	.326
vs. Left-Handers			2259	604	60	256	354	.267	.400	.341
vs. Right-Handers			3176	793	83	288	551	.250	.383	.316
vs. Ground-Ballers			2499	628	43	253	426	.251	.354	.322
vs. Fly-Ballers			2936	769	100	291	479	.262	.421	.330
Home Games	43-38	3.41	2750	653	62	250	479	.237	.353	.303
Road Games	32-49	4.69	2685	744	81	294	426	.277	.427	.350
Grass Fields	58-62	3.75	4046	1013	100	398	677	.250	.373	.320
Artificial Turf	17-25	4.86	1389	384	43	146	228	.276	.438	.345
April	8-12	4.63	664	181	12	75	106	.273	.395	.348
May	8-20	4.14	975	254	30	102	156	.261	.408	.332
June	17-10	3.12	881	219	17	101	128	.249	.360	.327
July	15-9	3.53	784	183	21	76	129	.233	.357	.303
August	14-16	4.51	1021	266	31	95	193	.261	.406	.324
Sept./Oct.	13-20	4.26	1110	294	32	95	193	.265	.403	.326
Leading Off Inn.			1321	340	35	120	197	.257	.381	.322
Bases Empty			3124	784	89	271	534	.251	.386	.315
Runners On			2311	613	54	273	371	.265	.395	.341
Runners/Scor. Pos.			1378	376	29	195	236	.273	.401	.357
Runners On/2 Out			977	233	24	150	163	.238	.366	.344
Scor. Pos./2 Out			652	164	14	120	108	.252	.368	.373
Late-Inning Pressure			774	199	21	100	130	.257	.372	.342
Leading Off			188	45	4	24	28	.239	.340	.332
Runners On			342	85	6	53	56	.249	.345	.343
Runners/Scor. Pos.			210	52	3	36	35	.248	.333	.348
First 9 Batters			2974	749	68	324	539	.252	.374	.328
Second 9 Batters			1379	389	44	124	219	.282	.439	.340
All Batters Thereafter			1082	259	31	96	147	.239	.372	.304

SAN FRANCISCO GIANTS

From 1953 through 1989, only one player changed teams immediately following a three-year period in which he led the majors in home runs: Reggie Jackson, whom Oakland traded to Baltimore prior to the 1976 season rather than lose him as a free agent after the season ended. Of course, other than through free agency (or on account of it, in Reggie's case), it would be hard to imagine what would possess a team, no matter how pressing its other needs, to trade a player of that magnitude. Here's the illustrious list for the three-year spans ending from 1970 through 1989:

Year	Player, Team	HR	Year	Player, Team	HR
1970	Frank Howard, Wash.	136	1980	Gorman Thomas, Mil.	115
1971	Hank Aaron, Atl.	129	1981	Mike Schmidt, Phil.	124
1972	Hank Aaron, Atl.	119	1982	Mike Schmidt, Phil.	114
1973	Willie Stargell, Pitt.	125	1983	Mike Schmidt, Phil.	106
1974	Willie Stargell, Pitt.	102	1984	Mike Schmidt, Phil.	111
1975	Reggie Jackson, Oak.	97	1985	Dale Murphy, Atl.	109
1976	Mike Schmidt, Phil.	112	1986	Mike Schmidt, Phil.	106
1977	Mike Schmidt, Phil.	114	1987	Mike Schmidt, Phil.	105
1978	George Foster, Cin.	121	1988	Jose Canseco, Oak.	106
1979	Jim Rice, Bos.	124	1989	Mark McGwire, Oak.	114

But during the off-season following the 1990 season, both of the coleaders for 1988 through 1990 changed teams: Darryl Strawberry joined the Dodgers as a free agent, and Fred McGriff was traded by Toronto to San Diego. Then last December, San Francisco dealt Kevin Mitchell, who led the majors with a total of 109 home runs over the three previous seasons, to Seattle in a trade so apparently one-sided that it stunned many baseball fans.

Now it's true that Toronto won a division title in the wake of the McGriff trade, and that San Francisco's deal was similar in that they were trying to improve their chemistry. But that's where the similarity ends. In trading McGriff and Tony Fernandez to San Diego, the Blue Jays added Roberto Alomar and Joe Carter in a nearly unprecedented swap of All-Stars in their primes. And although the Jays' stated off-season intention was to change the atmosphere in their locker room (and in so doing they won a division title), most baseball fans agree that their championship was attributable more to an improved pitching staff than to any new-found clubhouse karma. On the other hand, the Giants traded the best home-run hitter in baseball plus a left-handed pitching prospect (Mike Remlinger) for a pair of unremarkable relievers (Mike Jackson and Billy Swift) and a right-handed pitching prospect (Dave Burba).

The McGriff trade notwithstanding, power hitters like Mitchell have been traded rarely and usually only out of financial desperation. Prior to Reggie, the only three-year home-run leaders of this century sent packing were Babe Ruth (from the Red Sox to the Yankees in 1920), Jimmie Foxx (A's to Red Sox, 1936), and Ralph Kiner (Pirates to Cubs, 1953). All were primarily cash deals by teams in dire need of same, although the last two were somewhat disguised by the inclusion of other players (including a future host of *Today*). The Mitchell trade may simply represent desperation of another sort.

San Francisco admits it traded Mitchell because he was a bad actor—*such* a rotten guy, it turned out, that

they couldn't get full value. Even so, to Giants fans Michael Jackson and Billy Swift sounds more like a Saturday morning kids show than appropriate compensation for the successor to Schmidt, Canseco, McGwire, Strawberry, and McGriff. (Well, okay, let's leave McGwire out of it.) And with a starting staff that compiled the league's second-highest ERA last season (4.18, to Chicago's 4.35), even a pair of nondescript starters would have seemed a more reasonable stipend for Mitchell than a pair of nondescript relievers to join an already solid bullpen headed by Jeff Brantley and Dave Righetti.

Now if Righetti, freed by Swift and Jackson of his bullpen responsibilities, finally humors all the off-season pundits and wins 20 as a reborn starter, all of this is moot. The same is true if one of the new relievers thrives as a starter in San Francisco (both failed in that role earlier in their careers), or if Dave Burba, a 2d-round draft choice in 1987, proves to be the All-Star starter that Mike Remlinger's first-round '87 pedigree suggested he would become. But the sad truth for Al Rosen and Giants fans isn't that Mitchell became an intolerable presence, but rather that the collapse of the team's rotation forced their hand. And that's a particularly bitter pill to swallow considering that during the 1980s, the team launched three starters who, had they fulfilled the promise of their early years, might now comprise the foundation of a fine starting rotation.

Since 1982, five starters under the age of 26 had their first 10-win seasons while wearing Giants uniforms: Atlee Hammaker and Bill Laskey in 1982, Scott Garrelts in 1986, John Burkett in 1990, and Trevor Wilson last season. By way of comparison, only four other National League teams had five or more such pitchers during the same period:

- Cincinnati—Tom Browning, John Franco, and Jay Tibbs (1985), Ron Robinson (1986), Jose Rijo (1988), Rob Dibble (1989), and Jack Armstrong (1990).
- New York—Ron Darling and Dwight Gooden (1984), Rick Aguilera (1985), Sid Fernandez and Roger McDowell (1986), and David Cone (1988).
- Pittsburgh—Lee Tunnell (1983), Doug Drabek, Mike Dunne, and Brian Fisher (1987), John Smiley (1988).
- St. Louis—Neil Allen and Dave LaPoint (1983), Greg Mathews (1986), Joe Magrane (1989), and Ken Hill and Omar Olivares (1991).

Each team's list includes some hits, some misses. But all things considered, most got more bang for their buck than the Giants did. As San Francisco's front office crosses their fingers hoping that Burkett and Wilson develop into the nucleus of their rotation of the '90s, that wish has to be tempered with the knowledge that Laskey, Hammaker, and Garrelts never fulfilled their own considerable potential. Laskey was a flash-in-the-pan who won 13 games as a rookie in 1982, with seven complete games and a 3.14 ERA. He never again had an ERA below four. But Hammaker could have been the real deal. He won 12 games as a rookie in 1982 and 10 in 1983, when he compiled an ERA of 2.25, completed eight of 23 starts (including three shutouts), and pitched—memorably—for the N.L. All-Stars. But he was injured early in 1984, and never regained the pinpoint control that had made him so effective prior to the injury. Garrelts pitched impressively in relief for the Giants in the mid-1980s, then emerged from the bullpen in 1989 to lead the National League with a 2.28 ERA. But his ERA nearly doubled in 1990, and last season his chance for a rebound evaporated when a torn tendon in his pitching elbow limited him to 19⅔ innings.

Of those three pitchers, only Garrelts ever exceeded the number of games he won in his first season in double figures; he won 14 games in 1989, one more than he earned in 1986 when he pitched only half the season as a starter. Hammaker's highest total after his rookie season was 10; he did that twice (1983 and 1987). Laskey matched his 13 rookie wins as a sophomore, but never again. None ever topped his breakthrough total by more than a single victory. Compare that to the performance of the 57 other pitchers who first won 10 or more games between 1982 and 1986: 24 eventually surpassed that breakthrough total by at least two wins (42 percent); the Giants went 0-for-3.

Will John Burkett eventually go to the head of the class of 1990? It's too early to tell, of course, but last season six classmates surpassed Burkett's total of 12 wins: Kevin Appier (13), Andy Benes (15), Brian Holman (13), Ramon Martinez (17), Jack McDowell (17), and Todd Stottlemyre (15). Another, Pete Harnisch, matched Burkett's win total and compiled the league's fifth-lowest ERA (2.70) for its second-lowest scoring team. But let's not draw any conclusions on Burkett or on Wilson, who reached double figures for the first time in 1991.

There's a tendency here to conclude that disappointments such as those the Giants have endured go with the territory. Conventional baseball wisdom—a term that many self-annointed, nouveau-savvy analysts consider oxymoronic—holds that a pitcher's progress after an initial success is more erratic and far less predictable than that of batters. (Or, in the words of the tobacco juice set, "Them pitchers break down faster 'n a five-dollar watch.") And certainly it's true that a pitcher's career can be wiped out by a single catastrophic arm or shoulder injury more easily than that of a batter. But let's see if the trend is as clear-cut as the theory would suggest. We compared the group of pitchers age 26 or younger who first won 10 or more

games between 1982 and 1986 to comparable batters who first hit 15 or more home runs during that time. The theory would imply that many more of the pitchers than the batters never blossomed. The following table shows how many from each group failed to win as many games or hit as many home runs *over the rest of their careers* as they did in the initial breakthroughs:

	Total	Duds	Pct.
Batters	55	2	4%
Pitchers	60	9	15%

Those numbers trend in the expected direction, with David Green and George Wright as the only batters to disappear without a trace. The nine pitching duds were Dave Beard, Tim Birtsas, Edwin Correa, Ken Dixon, Joe Johnson, Charlie Kerfeld, Craig McMurtry, Lee Tunnell, and Jerry Ujdur. (Incidentally, that group also suggests that injuries aren't the major factor in sudden early endings to pitchers' careers. Many of those guys weren't injured; they were one-year flukes.) But to confirm the figures above, let's examine a larger group. If sudden injuries (or other factors) curtail the promising careers of pitchers at an early stage more often than those of batters, that difference will be more distinct as the size of the group increases. The following figures apply to players who reached 10 wins or 15 home runs for the first time during a 20-year period from 1960 through 1979:

	Total	Duds	Pct.
Batters	170	10	6%
Pitchers	235	25	11%

For more than 25 years, wipeouts have been roughly twice as common among pitchers as batters. For every Danny Walton, there's been a Mark Fidrych, a John Fulgham, and half a Pat Darcy. (If there's only half a Pat Darcy, does Fisk's homer become a double off the wall?) San Francisco has been unlucky in that all three of their promising starters of the 1980s—Hammaker, Garrelts, and Laskey—failed to fulfill their promise, the first two on account of injuries. Had the Giants been luckier, Burkett and Wilson would have been the final pieces to a decade-long puzzle. As it is, they have become the framework for a new one, prompting the team to trade the 1989–91 major league home-run king in a bold but desperate attempt to accelerate that timetable.

BATTER SECTION

The Batter Section is an alphabetical listing of everyplayer who had at least 250 plate appearances last season. Players are listed alphabetically within each league; if he played for both leagues, he is listed in the league where he finished the season.

Column Headings Information

For each player, information is provided in 11 offensive categories.

Sandy Alomar, Jr.

Cleveland Indians	AB	H	2B	3B	HR	RBI	BB	SO	BA	SA	OBA

AB	At-Bats
H	Hits
2B	Doubles
3B	Triples
HR	Home Runs
RBI	Runs Batted In
BB	Bases on Balls
SO	Strikeouts
BA	Batting Average
SA	Slugging Average
OBA	On-Base Average

Season Summary Information

Season											
Season	445	129	26	2	9	66	25	46	.290	.418	.326
vs. Left-Handers	117	44	5	0	2	18	8	13	.376	.470	.403
vs. Right-Handers	328	85	21	2	7	48	17	33	.259	.399	.298
vs. Ground-Ballers	214	59	11	1	4	33	14	16	.276	.393	.323
vs. Fly-Ballers	231	70	15	1	5	33	11	30	.303	.442	.329
Home Games	227	68	12	0	5	30	13	22	.300	.419	.335
Road Games	218	61	14	2	4	36	12	24	.280	.417	.318
Grass Fields	370	112	21	2	7	50	21	34	.303	.427	.337
Artificial Turf	75	17	5	0	2	16	4	12	.227	.373	.275
April	57	16	3	0	1	9	3	6	.281	.386	.323
May	69	21	3	1	2	13	4	13	.304	.464	.338
June	87	25	2	1	0	8	6	11	.287	.333	.330
July	68	18	5	0	2	11	4	3	.265	.426	.306
August	81	21	4	0	2	10	5	6	.259	.383	.299
Sept./Oct.	83	28	9	0	2	15	3	7	.337	.518	.360

Each player's performance for the season is broken down into a variety of special categories. The first line for each player gives his totals for the whole season. This is followed by breakdowns of his performance against left- and right-handed pitchers, against ground-ball and fly-ball pitchers (defined by whether their ground outs-to-air outs ratio is above or below the league average; our research indicates that this is nearly as effective a basis for platooning as "handedness"), in home and road games, on grass fields and artificial turf, and in each month (regular-season October games are grouped with September). For players who played for more than one team, all totals are combined; the "home" totals for Steve Buechele, for example, include games played at Arlington Stadium while with the Rangers, and at Three Rivers while with the Pirates.

Leading Off Inn.	101	31	2	1	3	3	4	12	.307	.436	.346
Bases Empty	250	70	9	2	8	8	10	31	.280	.428	.313
Runners On	195	59	17	0	1	58	15	15	.303	.405	.343
Runners/Scor. Pos.	127	39	12	0	0	54	11	9	.307	.402	.347
Runners On/2 Out	98	29	8	0	0	27	12	9	.296	.378	.373
Scor. Pos./2 Out	68	23	6	0	0	26	8	6	.338	.426	.408

Following these breakdowns, each batter's performance is divided into specific game situations. Totals are given for each batter when he led off an inning, when he batted with bases empty or runners on, with runners in scoring position (on second or third base, or both), with runners on and two out, and with runners in scoring position and two out.

Late-Inning Pressure	84	25	5	1	3	14	6	10	.298	.488	.344
Leading Off	22	8	1	0	2	2	1	2	.364	.682	.391
Runners On	33	11	4	0	0	11	4	4	.333	.455	.405
Runners/Scor. Pos.	26	8	2	0	0	11	4	3	.308	.385	.400

The next group shows the batter's performance in Late-Inning Pressure Situations (LIPS): any plate appearance occurring in the seventh inning or later with the score tied or with the batter's team trailing by one, two, or three runs (or four runs if there are two or more runners on base).

Each player's totals are listed for all late-inning pressure situations, then broken down for his performance leading off the inning, with runners on base, and runners in scoring position.

RUNS BATTED IN	From 1B	From 2B	From 3B	Scoring Position
Totals	7/144	23/104	27/55	50/159
Percentage	4.9%	22.1%	49.1%	31.4%

The next section, labeled "Runs Batted In," is a measure of the player's ability to drive in runners from each base. For every base, two numbers are listed in the "Totals" line: The first is the number of RBIs credited to the batter for bringing home runners from that base; the second is the total number of opportunities he faced for that situation. Plate appearances that result in a base on balls, hit batsman, sacrifice bunt, or an award of first base for catcher's interference are not treated as "opportunities" if they do not result in a run.

If there is more than one runner on base, there is an "opportunity" to drive in each runner. A single with the bases loaded that scores only the runner from third is an opportunity and an RBI in the "From 3B" line, but an unsuccessful opportunity for both "From 2B" and "From 1B." (The exceptions to this are listed above; a bases-loaded walk is an RBI and opportunity under "From 3B," but goes unrecorded for the other two.)

Also given is the percentage of successful opportunities for each base and a combined total of "From 2B" and "From 3B" to represent runners driven in from scoring position.

The tables are followed by comments for each player. The first of these is a listing of pitchers each batter "loves to face" and "hates to face." The statistics listed for each individual match-up are from all regular-season games since 1975 inclusive. Next are miscellaneous statistics given in text form; these include: the batter's ground outs-to-air outs ratio; his total of double-play ground outs and opportunities (plate appearances with a runner on first and less than two outs); the number and percentage of runners driven in from third base with less than two outs; the direction of balls that reach the outfield, either in the air or on the ground (these may total more than 100 percent because they've been rounded to the nearest whole percentage); the number and percentage of times he advanced from first to third or scored from second on outfield singles; and fielding statistics (assists per nine innings for infielders, putouts per nine innings for outfielders, and the success rate of opposing base stealers for catchers).

For purposes of comparison, the league totals in all of these categories are listed in the introduction to the Team Section (see page 2).

Roberto Alomar

Bats Left and Right

Toronto Blue Jays	AB	H	2B	3B	HR	RBI	BB	SO	BA	SA	OBA
Season	637	188	41	11	9	69	57	86	.295	.436	.354
vs. Left-Handers	191	47	12	3	5	27	11	35	.246	.419	.295
vs. Right-Handers	446	141	29	8	4	42	46	51	.316	.444	.379
vs. Ground-Ballers	324	99	18	5	4	33	27	39	.306	.429	.362
vs. Fly-Ballers	313	89	23	6	5	36	30	47	.284	.444	.346
Home Games	313	93	23	8	6	40	35	36	.297	.479	.367
Road Games	324	95	18	3	3	29	22	50	.293	.395	.341
Grass Fields	255	68	14	1	1	22	15	41	.267	.341	.309
Artificial Turf	382	120	27	10	8	47	42	45	.314	.500	.383
April	82	21	9	0	0	6	7	10	.256	.366	.315
May	106	29	6	3	5	19	13	18	.274	.528	.355
June	107	31	9	2	0	9	11	13	.290	.411	.356
July	106	38	7	2	0	11	5	12	.358	.462	.386
August	121	32	4	3	2	12	8	17	.264	.397	.311
Sept./Oct.	115	37	6	1	2	12	13	16	.322	.443	.395
Leading Off Inn.	122	36	8	3	3	3	15	13	.295	.484	.372
Runners On	247	73	20	2	2	62	25	34	.296	.417	.358
Bases Empty	390	115	21	9	7	7	32	52	.295	.449	.351
Runners/Scor. Pos.	157	44	15	2	1	58	17	22	.280	.420	.344
Runners On/2 Out	97	20	6	0	1	19	12	15	.206	.299	.300
Scor. Pos./2 Out	74	15	6	0	0	17	9	10	.203	.284	.298
Late-Inning Pressure	82	26	4	1	3	14	13	14	.317	.500	.404
Leading Off	18	7	1	1	1	2	5	5	.389	.722	.450
Runners On	41	13	3	0	0	11	7	5	.317	.390	.404
Runners/Scor. Pos.	27	7	3	0	0	11	6	3	.259	.370	.378

RUNS BATTED IN	From 1B	From 2B	From 3B	Scoring Position
Totals	9/150	23/130	28/59	51/189
Percentage	6.0%	17.7%	47.5%	27.0%

Loves to face: Brian Holman (.500, 9-for-18)
Tim Leary (.481, 13-for-27)
Jack McDowell (.667, 6-for-9)

Hates to face: Roger Clemens (.154, 2-for-13)
Charlie Hough (0-for-12)
Mike Moore (.154, 2-for-13)

Miscellaneous statistics: Ground outs-to-air outs ratio: 1.04 last season, 1.30 for career.... Grounded into 5 double plays in 109 opportunities (one per 22).... Drove in 24 of 34 runners from third base with less than two outs (71%).... Direction of balls hit to the outfield: 49% to left field, 24% to center, 26% to right batting left-handed; 43% to left field, 29% to center, 29% to right batting right-handed.... Base running: Advanced from first base to third on 8 of 24 outfield singles (33%); scored from second on 14 of 17 (82%).... Made 2.84 assists per nine innings at second base, 3d-lowest rate in A.L.

Comments: Stole the 100th base of his career on May 22, 1991, at the age of 23 years, 3 months. Only 10 players in this century reached that level sooner; from youngest to oldest: Jimmy Sheckard, Rickey Henderson, Ty Cobb, Sherry Magee, Cesar Cedeno, Tim Raines, Donie Bush, Claudell Washington, Johnny Evers, and Eddie Collins.... Stole third base 21 times last season, a major league high, in 22 attempts. He was caught only by the battery of Nolan Ryan and Ivan Rodriguez.... Played 1420⅔ innings at second base last season, the most of any major leaguer.... Led the N.L. in errors at second base in both 1989 and 1990, but has improved his error rate in each of the past two seasons. Chances per error year by year since 1989: one per 30, 42, and 53.... In three seasons with San Diego, he had 39, 35, and 38 extra-base hits, before belting 61 last season.... Has a career average of .301 batting left-handed, .255 batting right-handed, and has batted at least 40 points higher from the left side in each of the last three seasons. Among active switch-hitters with at least 2500 career plate appearances, only Wally Backman and Spike Owen have wider gaps between their averages from either side of the plate.... Starting with his debut season, he has accumulated over 600 plate appearances for four straight years. Only three other active players started their careers that way: Vince Coleman, Wally Joyner, and Eddie Murray.

Brady Anderson

Bats Left

Baltimore Orioles	AB	H	2B	3B	HR	RBI	BB	SO	BA	SA	OBA
Season	256	59	12	3	2	27	38	44	.230	.324	.338
vs. Left-Handers	36	5	0	1	0	5	11	12	.139	.194	.347
vs. Right-Handers	220	54	12	2	2	22	27	32	.245	.345	.336
vs. Ground-Ballers	124	34	5	3	2	13	13	15	.274	.411	.348
vs. Fly-Ballers	132	25	7	0	0	14	25	29	.189	.242	.329
Home Games	111	25	4	1	1	15	16	17	.225	.306	.340
Road Games	145	34	8	2	1	12	22	27	.234	.338	.339
Grass Fields	199	43	9	1	1	21	27	35	.216	.286	.319
Artificial Turf	57	16	3	2	1	6	11	9	.281	.456	.400
April	19	4	1	0	0	2	5	5	.211	.263	.385
May	56	7	3	0	0	7	10	14	.125	.179	.254
June	54	12	4	0	1	5	9	11	.222	.352	.358
July	37	10	1	1	0	1	4	3	.270	.351	.357
August	38	6	0	0	1	4	4	2	.158	.237	.238
Sept./Oct.	52	20	3	2	0	8	6	9	.385	.519	.448
Leading Off Inn.	69	20	4	1	1	1	13	7	.290	.420	.410
Runners On	97	22	4	1	1	26	9	15	.227	.320	.297
Bases Empty	159	37	8	2	1	1	29	29	.233	.327	.361
Runners/Scor. Pos.	50	14	4	1	0	24	7	8	.280	.400	.361
Runners On/2 Out	37	9	3	0	1	12	6	8	.243	.405	.364
Scor. Pos./2 Out	22	7	3	0	0	10	6	5	.318	.455	.464
Late-Inning Pressure	50	12	0	0	0	1	6	11	.240	.240	.333
Leading Off	15	4	0	0	0	0	2	4	.267	.267	.353
Runners On	16	4	0	0	0	1	0	2	.250	.250	.294
Runners/Scor. Pos.	7	1	0	0	0	1	0	0	.143	.143	.143

RUNS BATTED IN	From 1B	From 2B	From 3B	Scoring Position
Totals	5/71	9/46	11/23	20/69
Percentage	7.0%	19.6%	47.8%	29.0%

Loves to face: Mike Boddicker (.438, 7-for-16)
Scott Sanderson (.455, 5-for-11, 3 2B)
Walt Terrell (.700, 7-for-10)

Hates to face: Mike Moore (.059, 1-for-17, 2 BB)
Dave Stieb (0-for-14)
Bob Welch (0-for-13)

Miscellaneous statistics: Ground outs-to-air outs ratio: 1.07 last season, 0.92 for career.... Grounded into 1 double play in 56 opportunities (one per 56), 2d-best rate in A.L.... Drove in 8 of 11 runners from third base with less than two outs (73%).... Direction of balls hit to the outfield: 31% to left field, 33% to center, 36% to right.... Base running: Advanced from first base to third on 6 of 15 outfield singles (40%); scored from second on 5 of 10 (50%).... Made 1.95 putouts per nine innings in left field.

Comments: The first outfielder in major league history to bat .231 or lower in each of his first four seaons in the majors—at least among those who played 60 games in the outfield in each season.... But he's making progress: He has batted .231 with one walk for every 8.6 plate appearances over the past two seasons, compared to .210 and one BB per 10.3 PAs in his first two years.... Has stolen at least 10 bases in each of his four seasons in the bigs, but never more than 16.... He started 60 games last season, but only four in Baltimore's last 25 games.... Only six of his 60 starts came against left-handed pitchers.... His May batting average was 2d lowest in the majors last season.... Has a career average of .236 vs. right-handed pitchers, but his .160 average against left-handers is the 2d lowest of any nonpitcher over the last 17 years (minimum: 250 PA). The only position player with a lower average against southpaws was Tim Flannery (.158).... Some other career batting-average breakdowns: .237 vs. ground-ball pitchers, .204 vs. fly-ballers; .212 on grass fields; .250 on artificial turf; .261 in day games, .203 at night. So the ideal situation for Anderson is this: a day game in a ballpark with artificial turf, against a right-handed, ground-ball pitcher.... And one more thing—put some runners on base for him. Making the most out of his .219 career batting average, Anderson has career marks of .202 with the bases empty, .246 with runners on base, and .253 with runners in scoring position.

Carlos Baerga

Bats Left and Right

Cleveland Indians	AB	H	2B	3B	HR	RBI	BB	SO	BA	SA	OBA
Season	593	171	28	2	11	69	48	74	.288	.398	.346
vs. Left-Handers	161	53	8	0	2	20	8	14	.329	.416	.376
vs. Right-Handers	432	118	20	2	9	49	40	60	.273	.391	.335
vs. Ground-Ballers	275	75	13	2	6	37	20	40	.273	.400	.321
vs. Fly-Ballers	318	96	15	0	5	32	28	34	.302	.396	.367
Home Games	299	87	13	2	2	32	20	31	.291	.368	.337
Road Games	294	84	15	0	9	37	28	43	.286	.429	.355
Grass Fields	508	150	23	2	11	65	40	53	.295	.413	.350
Artificial Turf	85	21	5	0	0	4	8	21	.247	.306	.323
April	55	14	1	0	2	3	5	5	.255	.382	.317
May	105	31	4	1	3	19	10	8	.295	.438	.362
June	86	23	3	0	3	8	12	10	.267	.407	.364
July	103	33	7	0	1	9	9	15	.320	.417	.372
August	120	35	5	0	2	14	4	22	.292	.383	.317
Sept./Oct.	124	35	8	1	0	16	8	14	.282	.363	.338
Leading Off Inn.	126	36	7	0	2	2	11	10	.286	.389	.348
Runners On	250	78	14	1	5	63	26	31	.312	.436	.379
Bases Empty	343	93	14	1	6	6	22	43	.271	.370	.321
Runners/Scor. Pos.	150	42	5	1	5	59	20	22	.280	.427	.369
Runners On/2 Out	100	27	2	0	3	25	12	14	.270	.380	.354
Scor. Pos./2 Out	69	18	1	0	3	24	9	11	.261	.406	.354
Late-Inning Pressure	102	24	4	0	2	10	6	19	.235	.333	.284
Leading Off	24	6	1	0	0	0	5	3	.250	.292	.379
Runners On	34	11	2	0	1	9	1	5	.324	.471	.343
Runners/Scor. Pos.	23	6	1	0	1	8	1	4	.261	.435	.292

RUNS BATTED IN	From 1B	From 2B	From 3B	Scoring Position
Totals	8/178	23/105	27/67	50/172
Percentage	4.5%	21.9%	40.3%	29.1%

Loves to face: Rich DeLucia (.625, 5-for-8)
Chuck Finley (.526, 10-for-19)
Charlie Hough (.667, 2-for-3, 2 HR, 2 BB)

Hates to face: Erik Hanson (0-for-8)
Joe Hesketh (0-for-9)
David Wells (0-for-11)

Miscellaneous statistics: Ground outs-to-air outs ratio: 1.72 last season, 1.57 for career.... Grounded into 12 double plays in 118 opportunities (one per 10).... Drove in 20 of 34 runners from third base with less than two outs (59%).... Direction of balls hit to the outfield: 19% to left field, 41% to center, 39% to right batting left-handed; 38% to left field, 39% to center, 23% to right batting right-handed.... Base running: Advanced from first base to third on 13 of 46 outfield singles (28%); scored from second on 15 of 17 (88%).... Made 2.36 assists per nine innings at third base, 3d-highest rate in A.L.; made 3.38 assists per nine innings at second base, 2d-highest rate in A.L.

Comments: Baerga had the best season among the players acquired by the Indians in the deal that sent Joe Carter to San Diego. Sandy Alomar batted .217 in 51 games, while Chris James batted .238 in 115 games.... Of his 69 RBIs, 26 gave the Indians a lead (38%), the highest percentage in the A.L. (minimum: 15 go-ahead RBIs). In 1990, he led A.L. rookies with 15 go-ahead RBIs, and 10 game-winners.... Became the fifth player to play as many as 75 games at both second base and third base in the same season. The others: Eddie Foster (1913), Jim Gilliam (1962), Phil Garner (1978 and 1979), and Jerry Royster (1979). No Indians player had ever done it, but Odell Hale came close in 1937, playing 90 games at third and 64 games at second.... The Indians allowed an average of 4.39 runs per nine innings with Baerga playing third base, considerably lower than with others at that position: Jerry Browne (4.46), Jim Thome (4.87), Jeff Manto (5.19), Brook Jacoby (5.92).... His total of ground outs was 4th highest in the league.... Career batting average of .238 in Late-Inning Pressure Situations, .287 in other at-bats.... Career average of .294 at Cleveland Stadium, .278 on other grass fields, .230 on artificial turf.... Career average of .343 (12-for-35, 1 HR) as a pinch hitter.... Cleveland's 1992 infield could include Reggie Jefferson, Baerga, Mark Lewis, and Jim Thome. Baerga, the oldest of the four, won't see his 24th birthday until after the season. For more on this, see the Indians essay.

Harold Baines

Bats Left

Oakland A's	AB	H	2B	3B	HR	RBI	BB	SO	BA	SA	OBA
Season	488	144	25	1	20	90	72	67	.295	.473	.383
vs. Left-Handers	83	25	5	0	4	18	5	14	.301	.506	.348
vs. Right-Handers	405	119	20	1	16	72	67	53	.294	.467	.390
vs. Ground-Ballers	251	72	13	1	9	49	39	33	.287	.454	.381
vs. Fly-Ballers	237	72	12	0	11	41	33	34	.304	.494	.386
Home Games	227	60	11	0	11	52	36	38	.264	.498	.358
Road Games	261	84	14	1	9	38	36	29	.322	.487	.406
Grass Fields	405	122	21	0	19	80	62	58	.301	.494	.391
Artificial Turf	83	22	4	1	1	10	10	9	.265	.373	.344
April	67	15	4	1	0	11	4	12	.224	.313	.274
May	78	31	5	0	5	19	17	9	.397	.654	.505
June	88	30	6	0	4	20	13	12	.341	.545	.417
July	86	27	4	0	4	15	11	12	.314	.500	.388
August	79	19	5	0	3	11	8	11	.241	.418	.307
Sept./Oct.	90	22	1	0	4	14	19	11	.244	.389	.376
Leading Off Inn.	109	26	4	0	1	1	6	14	.239	.303	.278
Runners On	226	71	12	1	11	81	41	32	.314	.522	.412
Bases Empty	262	73	13	0	9	9	31	35	.279	.431	.357
Runners/Scor. Pos.	133	37	8	0	6	69	35	20	.278	.474	.416
Runners On/2 Out	101	32	3	0	6	31	25	15	.317	.525	.452
Scor. Pos./2 Out	62	19	3	0	4	27	22	8	.306	.548	.488
Late-Inning Pressure	64	11	1	0	3	10	12	15	.172	.328	.303
Leading Off	19	2	0	0	0	0	1	5	.105	.105	.150
Runners On	24	5	0	0	2	9	7	4	.208	.458	.387
Runners/Scor. Pos.	18	3	0	0	2	9	6	4	.167	.500	.375

RUNS BATTED IN	From 1B	From 2B	From 3B	Scoring Position
Totals	16/168	28/105	26/55	54/160
Percentage	9.5%	26.7%	47.3%	33.8%

Loves to face: Greg Hibbard (.700, 7-for-10, 1 HR)
Edwin Nunez (.615, 8-for-13, 2 2B, 3 HR)
Todd Stottlemyre (.357, 5-for-14, 2 HR)

Hates to face: Mike Flanagan (.143, 5-for-35, 1 HR)
Mark Langston (.139, 5-for-36, 1 HR, 0 BB)
Melido Perez (.130, 3-for-23, 4 BB)

Miscellaneous statistics: Ground outs-to-air outs ratio: 1.58 last season, 1.31 for career.... Grounded into 12 double plays in 106 opportunities (one per 8.8).... Drove in 21 of 33 runners from third base with less than two outs (64%).... Direction of balls hit to the outfield: 36% to left field, 34% to center, 30% to right.... Base running: Advanced from first base to third on 6 of 26 outfield singles (23%); scored from second on 11 of 20 (55%).... Made 1.55 putouts per nine innings in right field.

Comments: Became nearly a full-time designated hitter in 1987. Since then, his ranks among DHs: AB, 1st (2293); HR, 2d (78, behind Brian Downing with 94); RBI, 1st (365); BA, .294 (2d among those with 500+ at-bats to Paul Molitor's .325 mark).... He became the A's seventh different opening-day DH in the last seven years. The last man to do it in consecutive seasons? Ratboy himself, Dave Kingman (1984–85).... For the first time in 12 major league seasons, he had more walks than strikeouts. His average of one strikeout every 8.4 plate appearances was the best of his career, helped in part by his diminishing role against left-handed pitchers. Plate appearances vs. southpaws year by year since 1988: 212, 176, 106, and 89.... Started 117 of 120 games in which the Athletics faced a right-handed starter, but only 13 of 42 games vs. southpaws.... Among A.L. players, only Cecil Fielder, Danny Tartabull, and Jack Clark started more games as a cleanup hitter than Baines last season (119 of his 130 starts).... His three home runs against the Orioles on May 7 made him the 16th player in history to hit three or more homers in a game for two different clubs. Baines had done it twice previously for the White Sox. The only other active players to do it: Gary Carter and Andre Dawson.... Sixty-four players have accumulated at least 1000 RBIs in the American League. Baines, who enters this season with 990, Dave Winfield (976), and Cal Ripken (942) should all join the club this season.

Jesse Barfield

Bats Right

New York Yankees	AB	H	2B	3B	HR	RBI	BB	SO	BA	SA	OBA
Season	284	64	12	0	17	48	36	80	.225	.447	.312
vs. Left-Handers	108	34	4	0	9	24	17	22	.315	.602	.408
vs. Right-Handers	176	30	8	0	8	24	19	58	.170	.352	.250
vs. Ground-Ballers	132	22	5	0	5	21	20	32	.167	.318	.276
vs. Fly-Ballers	152	42	7	0	12	27	16	48	.276	.559	.343
Home Games	130	30	7	0	11	30	20	31	.231	.538	.331
Road Games	154	34	5	0	6	18	16	49	.221	.370	.294
Grass Fields	236	51	10	0	14	39	30	63	.216	.436	.303
Artificial Turf	48	13	2	0	3	9	6	17	.271	.500	.352
April	55	16	2	0	3	9	9	14	.291	.491	.391
May	88	18	5	0	7	15	14	29	.205	.500	.311
June	100	21	4	0	5	20	7	27	.210	.400	.262
July	41	9	1	0	2	4	6	10	.220	.390	.319
August	0	0	0	0	0	0	0	0	—	—	—
Sept./Oct.	0	0	0	0	0	0	0	0	—	—	—
Leading Off Inn.	50	9	0	0	2	2	5	13	.180	.300	.255
Runners On	131	28	8	0	7	38	17	36	.214	.435	.302
Bases Empty	153	36	4	0	10	10	19	44	.235	.458	.320
Runners/Scor. Pos.	75	19	6	0	4	31	9	25	.253	.493	.329
Runners On/2 Out	55	17	5	0	3	20	9	14	.309	.564	.406
Scor. Pos./2 Out	36	13	4	0	2	17	5	10	.361	.639	.439
Late-Inning Pressure	44	9	3	0	2	4	10	16	.205	.409	.352
Leading Off	14	1	0	0	0	0	2	7	.071	.071	.188
Runners On	13	2	2	0	0	2	6	4	.154	.308	.421
Runners/Scor. Pos.	5	2	2	0	0	2	3	3	.400	.800	.625

RUNS BATTED IN	From 1B	From 2B	From 3B	Scoring Position
Totals	7/94	13/58	11/28	24/86
Percentage	7.4%	22.4%	39.3%	27.9%

Loves to face: Rick Honeycutt (.400, 4-for-10, 1 2B, 3 HR)
Jose Mesa (.571, 4-for-7, 1 HR)
Walt Terrell (.389, 14-for-36, 2 HR)

Hates to face: Roger Clemens (.184, 9-for-49)
Mark Knudson (.118, 2-for-17)
Nolan Ryan (0-for-12, 10 SO)

Miscellaneous statistics: Ground outs-to-air outs ratio: 1.41 last season, 1.09 for career.... Grounded into 11 double plays in 67 opportunities (one per 6.1).... Drove in 7 of 13 runners from third base with less than two outs (54%).... Direction of balls hit to the outfield: 54% to left field, 21% to center, 25% to right.... Base running: Advanced from first base to third on 7 of 11 outfield singles (64%); scored from second on 7 of 9 (78%).... Made 2.36 putouts per nine innings in right field.

Comments: The Yankees had a winning record with Barfield in the starting lineup last season (40–36, .526), but were 31–55 without him (.360). They played .596 ball (19–14) with a starting outfield of Mel Hall, Roberto Kelly, and Barfield.... He played the most innings of any right fielder who didn't commit an error last season (677⅔), but finished the season 27 games shy of qualifying for the fielding title.... Batting average with runners on base was 8th lowest in the league.... Enters the season with a career total of 159 outfield assists, four fewer than Dave Winfield, who leads active players with 163. Barfield's average of one assist every 8.5 games is the best among outfielders who began their careers within the last 50 years (minimum: 500 games in OF). Rounding out the top five: Hal Jeffcoat, one per 8.9; Roberto Clemente, 8.9; Willard Marshall, 9.1; Cory Snyder, 9.4.... Barfield's average of one strikeout every 4.0 plate appearances in pinstripes is the worst in franchise history (minimum: 1000 PA). Mickey Mantle ranks only eighth on that list. Between Jesse and The Mick are Lefty, Reggie, Pags, Whitey, Roberto, and Bobby.... Meacham, of course.... Who says you can't get something for nothing? Norm Cash for Steve Demeter; Jerry Grote for Tom Parsons; Pedro Guerrero for Bruce Ellingsen; David Cone for Ed Hearn; Christy Mathewson for washed-up Amos Rusie; Dennis Eckersley for Dave Wilder, Brian Guinn, and Mark Leonette. Jesse Barfield for Al Leiter?

Albert Belle

Bats Right

Cleveland Indians	AB	H	2B	3B	HR	RBI	BB	SO	BA	SA	OBA
Season	461	130	31	2	28	95	25	99	.282	.540	.323
vs. Left-Handers	132	38	11	1	8	34	5	27	.288	.568	.312
vs. Right-Handers	329	92	20	1	20	61	20	72	.280	.529	.327
vs. Ground-Ballers	203	57	10	0	10	31	15	41	.281	.478	.335
vs. Fly-Ballers	258	73	21	2	18	64	10	58	.283	.589	.313
Home Games	236	60	15	0	8	35	11	49	.254	.419	.294
Road Games	225	70	16	2	20	60	14	50	.311	.667	.352
Grass Fields	413	115	26	2	26	85	24	88	.278	.540	.321
Artificial Turf	48	15	5	0	2	10	1	11	.313	.542	.333
April	56	15	2	0	4	9	3	17	.268	.518	.328
May	99	27	8	1	5	18	8	18	.273	.525	.333
June	31	6	2	0	1	5	0	7	.194	.355	.194
July	78	23	2	0	7	17	4	13	.295	.590	.318
August	108	32	6	0	7	21	5	23	.296	.546	.336
Sept./Oct.	89	27	11	1	4	25	5	21	.303	.584	.337
Leading Off Inn.	113	34	9	1	7	7	4	19	.301	.584	.336
Runners On	234	75	18	1	15	82	17	46	.321	.598	.362
Bases Empty	227	55	13	1	13	13	8	53	.242	.480	.280
Runners/Scor. Pos.	126	39	13	0	6	61	12	31	.310	.556	.357
Runners On/2 Out	107	32	5	1	6	28	11	29	.299	.533	.364
Scor. Pos./2 Out	60	17	4	1	3	18	10	20	.283	.450	.368
Late-Inning Pressure	66	15	1	1	4	9	4	19	.227	.455	.288
Leading Off	13	2	0	1	0	0	0	4	.154	.308	.214
Runners On	23	8	0	0	2	7	2	3	.348	.609	.385
Runners/Scor. Pos.	7	2	0	0	0	3	2	1	.286	.286	.400

RUNS BATTED IN	From 1B	From 2B	From 3B	Scoring Position
Totals	19/186	23/87	25/59	48/146
Percentage	10.2%	26.4%	42.4%	32.9%

Loves to face: Jeff Ballard (.571, 4-for-7, 1 2B, 2 HR)
Chuck Finley (.455, 5-for-11, 2 2B, 2 HR)
Mark Langston (.600, 3-for-5, 1 2B, 1 HR)

Hates to face: Andy Hawkins (0-for-10)
Joe Hesketh (0-for-8)
Jaime Navarro (0-for-9, 5 SO)

Miscellaneous statistics: Ground outs-to-air outs ratio: 1.42 last season, 1.28 for career.... Grounded into 24 double plays in 115 opportunities (one per 4.8), 5th-worst rate in A.L.... Drove in 18 of 38 runners from third base with less than two outs (47%).... Direction of balls hit to the outfield: 46% to left field, 27% to center, 27% to right.... Base running: Advanced from first base to third on 6 of 17 outfield singles (35%); scored from second on 10 of 14 (71%).... Made 2.09 putouts per nine innings in left field.

Comments: Batted .324 in spring training, leading the majors with 11 homers, 27 RBIs, and an .878 slugging percentage during preseason.... He was Cleveland's fifth different opening-day left fielder in the last five years, and one of 13 LFs for the Tribe last season.... Committed nine errors as a left fielder, an American League high.... Disciplinary action by both the Indians and the Commissioner's office cost him a 30 HR, 100 RBI season. He served a six-game suspension (July 12–17) for striking a fan with a thrown ball, and was demoted to Colorado Springs for a couple weeks for lack of hustle (June 7–25).... As a result of his childish behavior, Belle's joined an otherwise illustrious group that he hasn't yet proved worthy of. Only four other players in American League history accumulated that many home runs and RBIs in so few games (123): Babe Ruth (1922), Rudy York (1937), Joe DiMaggio (1939), Ted Williams (1950).... Led visiting players with five home runs at Anaheim Stadium last season, only three fewer than he hit at Cleveland Stadium.... Career batting-average breakdown: .224 with the bases empty, .299 with runners on base, .319 with runners in scoring position.... Has driven in 11 of 17 runners from scoring position in Late-Inning Pressure Situations (65%), an admittedly small sample, but nevertheless the highest rate over the last 17 years among players with at least 10 opportunities. The highest mark with 50 or more: 43 percent, by Eric Soderholm (35-for-82).

Todd Benzinger
Bats Left and Right

Reds/Royals	AB	H	2B	3B	HR	RBI	BB	SO	BA	SA	OBA
Season	416	109	18	5	3	51	27	66	.262	.351	.310
vs. Left-Handers	143	36	6	0	1	16	6	13	.252	.315	.280
vs. Right-Handers	273	73	12	5	2	35	21	53	.267	.370	.324
vs. Ground-Ballers	196	54	8	3	0	27	13	35	.276	.347	.326
vs. Fly-Ballers	220	55	10	2	3	24	14	31	.250	.355	.295
Home Games	216	58	13	3	2	30	10	26	.269	.384	.306
Road Games	200	51	5	2	1	21	17	40	.255	.315	.314
Grass Fields	139	40	5	1	1	18	11	27	.288	.360	.340
Artificial Turf	277	69	13	4	2	33	16	39	.249	.347	.294
April	39	9	2	1	0	9	2	6	.231	.333	.256
May	20	0	0	0	0	0	0	2	.000	.000	.000
June	60	13	1	1	1	2	8	11	.217	.317	.309
July	79	27	4	1	2	18	4	12	.342	.494	.381
August	100	26	4	1	0	7	5	15	.260	.320	.295
Sept./Oct.	118	34	7	1	0	15	8	20	.288	.364	.341
Leading Off Inn.	97	28	3	0	0	0	4	15	.289	.320	.317
Runners On	197	48	9	3	1	49	16	27	.244	.335	.300
Bases Empty	219	61	9	2	2	2	11	39	.279	.365	.319
Runners/Scor. Pos.	131	35	5	1	1	46	11	21	.267	.344	.322
Runners On/2 Out	98	22	5	2	0	20	7	16	.224	.316	.276
Scor. Pos./2 Out	76	16	3	1	0	18	5	13	.211	.276	.259
Late-Inning Pressure	78	17	1	2	0	5	6	14	.218	.282	.274
Leading Off	19	4	1	0	0	0	1	6	.211	.263	.250
Runners On	39	7	0	2	0	5	4	4	.179	.282	.256
Runners/Scor. Pos.	27	5	0	1	0	4	3	3	.185	.259	.267

RUNS BATTED IN	From 1B	From 2B	From 3B	Scoring Position
Totals	6/129	22/107	20/53	42/160
Percentage	4.7%	20.6%	37.7%	26.3%

Loves to face: Tim Belcher (.471, 8-for-17)
Tom Glavine (.357, 10-for-28, 2 HR)
Ed Whitson (.385, 5-for-13, 3 2B, 1 HR)
Hates to face: Mike Bielecki (0-for-12)
Jose DeLeon (.067, 1-for-15, 1 2B)
Greg W. Harris (.063, 1-for-16)

Miscellaneous statistics: Ground outs-to-air outs ratio: 0.85 last season, 1.00 for career.... Grounded into 7 double plays in 73 opportunities (one per 10).... Drove in 14 of 21 runners from third base with less than two outs (67%).... Direction of balls hit to the outfield: 30% to left field, 38% to center, 32% to right batting left-handed; 45% to left field, 23% to center, 31% to right batting right-handed.... Base running: Advanced from first base to third on 9 of 30 outfield singles (30%); scored from second on 3 of 8 (38%).... Made 0.58 assists per nine innings at first base, lowest rate in A.L.

Comments: Royals first basemen combined for only four home runs last season (of which Benzinger had half), the fewest of any team in the majors. Other major league clubs got an average of 19 home runs from their first basemen.... Career batting average of .269 (14-for-52, 2 HR) at his new home, Dodger Stadium.... Career average of .164 (9-for-55, 0 HR) as a pinch hitter.... He had an average of one strikeout every 6.8 plate appearances last season, the best rate of his career.... He has four grand-slam home runs in 79 career at-bats with the bases loaded, an average of one every 20 at-bats, compared to a career rate of one HR every 47 ABs otherwise.... Hitless in 20 at-bats with two outs and the bases loaded over the last three seasons.... Home-run rate has declined steadily since he averaged one every 28 at-bats as a Red Sox rookie in 1987; at-bats per HR year by year since then: one per 31, 37, 75, 139.... Career batting averages are essentially the same from both sides of the plate: .253 batting left-handed, .259 as a right-hander. But he has shown little power from the left side, with one extra-base hit per 16 at-bats; his rate as a right-hander is 34 percent higher (one XBH per 12 ABs).... One of three players who's been caught stealing more than he's been safe in each of the past four seasons. The others: Mark Lemke and Tim Wallach. They're halfway to Nellie Fox's record streak of eight years (1957–64).

Dante Bichette
Bats Right

Milwaukee Brewers	AB	H	2B	3B	HR	RBI	BB	SO	BA	SA	OBA
Season	445	106	18	3	15	59	22	107	.238	.393	.272
vs. Left-Handers	154	39	5	2	6	18	11	37	.253	.429	.299
vs. Right-Handers	291	67	13	1	9	41	11	70	.230	.375	.257
vs. Ground-Ballers	216	57	10	1	6	32	7	44	.264	.403	.283
vs. Fly-Ballers	229	49	8	2	9	27	15	63	.214	.384	.262
Home Games	213	53	10	2	6	30	16	46	.249	.399	.296
Road Games	232	53	8	1	9	29	6	61	.228	.388	.249
Grass Fields	372	91	15	3	13	57	18	85	.245	.406	.277
Artificial Turf	73	15	3	0	2	2	4	22	.205	.329	.247
April	72	17	4	0	2	11	2	10	.236	.375	.253
May	91	19	2	1	6	15	6	27	.209	.451	.255
June	68	16	2	0	3	9	7	18	.235	.397	.308
July	75	23	4	0	1	9	3	18	.307	.400	.325
August	53	7	2	0	1	2	3	16	.132	.226	.179
Sept./Oct.	86	24	4	2	2	13	1	18	.279	.442	.287
Leading Off Inn.	90	24	3	1	3	3	3	22	.267	.422	.290
Runners On	206	50	8	2	7	51	11	48	.243	.403	.274
Bases Empty	239	56	10	1	8	8	11	59	.234	.385	.271
Runners/Scor. Pos.	111	24	4	2	5	46	10	29	.216	.423	.268
Runners On/2 Out	105	26	4	1	4	31	4	24	.248	.419	.275
Scor. Pos./2 Out	65	17	3	1	3	29	4	16	.262	.477	.304
Late-Inning Pressure	78	21	3	1	1	10	2	23	.269	.372	.296
Leading Off	15	4	1	0	0	0	0	5	.267	.333	.267
Runners On	39	11	1	1	1	10	1	10	.282	.436	.300
Runners/Scor. Pos.	18	4	0	1	1	10	1	4	.222	.500	.263

RUNS BATTED IN	From 1B	From 2B	From 3B	Scoring Position
Totals	8/166	16/90	20/48	36/138
Percentage	4.8%	17.8%	41.7%	26.1%

Loves to face: Rick Aguilera (.400, 2-for-5, 1 3B, 1 HR)
Paul Gibson (.600, 3-for-5, 1 2B, 1 3B)
Mark Langston (.400, 4-for-10, 2 2B, 1 HR)
Hates to face: Jimmy Key (.077, 1-for-13)
Bob Milacki (.071, 1-for-14, 1 2B)
Mike Moore (0-for-9)

Miscellaneous statistics: Ground outs-to-air outs ratio: 1.05 last season, 1.04 for career.... Grounded into 9 double plays in 87 opportunities (one per 10).... Drove in 9 of 19 runners from third base with less than two outs (47%).... Direction of balls hit to the outfield: 32% to left field, 34% to center, 34% to right.... Base running: Advanced from first base to third on 4 of 15 outfield singles (27%); scored from second on 6 of 9 (67%).... Made 2.29 putouts per nine innings in right field.

Comments: Brewers outfielders combined for 287 RBIs last season, the 3d-highest total in the majors behind the Pirates and Rangers. Oakland's outfield certainly has a higher profile (and payroll), but they combined to drive in eight fewer runs than the Brewers.... Started seven double plays from right field last season; no other right fielder started more than four. His 14 assists ranked third among major league RFs, behind Felix Jose and Jay Buhner (15 apiece).... Started 45 of 46 games in which the Brewers faced left-handed starting pitchers, 64 of 116 against right-handers.... Batting average in night games (.213) was 10th lowest in the league. He hit .290 in day games.... Has a career batting average of .246 on grass fields, .215 on artificial turf.... He has seven hits in 11 career at-bats with two outs and the bases loaded.... His career percentage of runners driven in from scoring position in Late-Inning Pressure Situations (37.5%) is 4th highest among active players, behind Jose Canseco (38.4%), Eddie Murray (38.1%), and Pedro Guerrero (37.9%).... Let's reprise Doug Rader's post-Canseco remark that Bichette could become baseball's first 40/40 player—in home runs and outfield assists. Rader meant for a season, but Bichette is still short of those totals for his 312-game career, with 33 and 34, respectively. Here's the career record to shoot for: the 250/250 club, which still has only its charter member—Mel Ott.

Wade Boggs

Bats Left

Boston Red Sox	AB	H	2B	3B	HR	RBI	BB	SO	BA	SA	OBA
Season	546	181	42	2	8	51	89	32	.332	.460	.421
vs. Left-Handers	166	44	6	2	2	13	17	10	.265	.361	.333
vs. Right-Handers	380	137	36	0	6	38	72	22	.361	.503	.456
vs. Ground-Ballers	249	78	19	0	3	23	33	11	.313	.426	.389
vs. Fly-Ballers	297	103	23	2	5	28	56	21	.347	.488	.447
Home Games	252	98	28	2	6	32	47	12	.389	.587	.482
Road Games	294	83	14	0	2	19	42	20	.282	.350	.368
Grass Fields	445	147	34	2	8	47	72	24	.330	.470	.420
Artificial Turf	101	34	8	0	0	4	17	8	.337	.416	.429
April	69	21	5	0	3	5	15	3	.304	.507	.429
May	99	35	8	0	1	12	21	6	.354	.465	.467
June	96	26	8	0	1	14	11	8	.271	.385	.339
July	82	34	10	1	1	8	15	5	.415	.598	.495
August	106	35	5	1	1	8	13	6	.330	.425	.400
Sept./Oct.	94	30	6	0	1	4	14	4	.319	.415	.404
Leading Off Inn.	211	63	20	0	3	3	20	7	.299	.436	.359
Runners On	188	61	12	1	3	46	49	13	.324	.447	.453
Bases Empty	358	120	30	1	5	5	40	19	.335	.466	.402
Runners/Scor. Pos.	87	27	6	0	1	38	40	6	.310	.414	.504
Runners On/2 Out	60	18	4	0	0	12	27	4	.300	.367	.517
Scor. Pos./2 Out	30	7	1	0	0	10	24	1	.233	.267	.574
Late-Inning Pressure	56	20	5	0	1	6	11	4	.357	.500	.463
Leading Off	17	5	3	0	0	0	2	1	.294	.471	.368
Runners On	21	10	1	0	1	6	7	2	.476	.667	.607
Runners/Scor. Pos.	9	5	1	0	0	4	7	1	.556	.667	.750

RUNS BATTED IN	From 1B	From 2B	From 3B	Scoring Position
Totals	6/145	16/73	21/33	37/106
Percentage	4.1%	21.9%	63.6%	34.9%

Loves to face: Mauro Gozzo (5-for-5, 1 BB)
Jose Mesa (.556, 10-for-18)
Walt Terrell (.404, 23-for-57, 2 HR)

Hates to face: Chris Bosio (.161, 5-for-31)
Scott Sanderson (.118, 2-for-17)
Bob Welch (.037, 1-for-27, 1 2B, 3 BB)

Miscellaneous statistics: Ground outs-to-air outs ratio: 1.54 last season, 1.37 for career.... Grounded into 16 double plays in 105 opportunities (one per 6.6).... Drove in 17 of 22 runners from third base with less than two outs (77%), 4th-highest rate in A.L.... Direction of balls hit to the outfield: 52% to left field, 29% to center, 19% to right.... Base running: Advanced from first base to third on 6 of 50 outfield singles (12%); scored from second on 14 of 30 (47%).... Made 2.08 assists per nine innings at third base.

Comments: He has batted over .300 in each of his first 10 years in the majors. Only three other players have done that (minimum: 300 AB each season): Paul Waner (12 years), Al Simmons (11), and Ted Williams (10).... Has had at least 100 singles and 50 extra-base hits for seven straight seasons. The last A.L. player with a streak that long: Joe DiMaggio (1936–42).... Was the toughest batter in the A.L. to strike out last season, averaging one strikeout every 20.0 plate appearances.... Led the majors in opposite-field hits (87) and in percentage of hits to the opposite field (48%, 87 of 181).... Home-game batting average was the highest in the majors, a distinction he's earned in five of nine years.... He has hit for a higher average in home games than he has in road games in each of his 10 years in the majors. Jim Rice had a 15-year streak in which he posted a higher average at Fenway than he did on the road.... Talk-show manna: Boston had a 62–45 record with Boggs in the leadoff spot (.579), but was 13–19 when he batted in the 3d spot in the order (.406).... More grist for the talk-show mill: Cynics point to his 51 RBIs as evidence that he can't produce runs (the old, flawed "Rod Carew" theory), but the opportunities just weren't there last season. He batted with only 106 runners in scoring position, by far the fewest in any full season of his career, and 64 fewer than in 1990. He drove in 35 percent of those runners, the 8th-highest average in the American League (minimum: 100 runners), and the best on the Red Sox.

Pat Borders

Bats Right

Toronto Blue Jays	AB	H	2B	3B	HR	RBI	BB	SO	BA	SA	OBA
Season	291	71	17	0	5	36	11	45	.244	.354	.271
vs. Left-Handers	147	35	9	0	1	14	7	19	.238	.320	.271
vs. Right-Handers	144	36	8	0	4	22	4	26	.250	.389	.272
vs. Ground-Ballers	157	42	10	0	1	16	5	24	.268	.350	.287
vs. Fly-Ballers	134	29	7	0	4	20	6	21	.216	.358	.254
Home Games	146	36	10	0	2	18	5	17	.247	.356	.268
Road Games	145	35	7	0	3	18	6	28	.241	.352	.275
Grass Fields	122	31	7	0	3	17	5	23	.254	.385	.281
Artificial Turf	169	40	10	0	2	19	6	22	.237	.331	.264
April	28	2	0	0	0	2	0	3	.071	.071	.069
May	40	15	1	0	0	1	1	7	.375	.400	.390
June	46	9	4	0	0	2	1	6	.196	.283	.213
July	42	13	5	0	1	9	2	5	.310	.500	.356
August	68	20	6	0	0	11	3	13	.294	.382	.319
Sept./Oct.	67	12	1	0	4	11	4	11	.179	.373	.222
Leading Off Inn.	72	13	4	0	1	1	1	11	.181	.278	.192
Runners On	125	39	9	0	4	35	7	13	.312	.480	.346
Bases Empty	166	32	8	0	1	1	4	32	.193	.259	.212
Runners/Scor. Pos.	65	19	4	0	3	30	5	7	.292	.492	.338
Runners On/2 Out	57	12	5	0	1	10	6	5	.211	.351	.286
Scor. Pos./2 Out	31	6	1	0	1	7	5	2	.194	.323	.306
Late-Inning Pressure	49	13	2	0	1	7	2	8	.265	.367	.288
Leading Off	11	1	0	0	0	0	0	4	.091	.091	.091
Runners On	21	7	2	0	1	7	1	0	.333	.571	.348
Runners/Scor. Pos.	9	3	1	0	1	7	0	0	.333	.778	.300

RUNS BATTED IN	From 1B	From 2B	From 3B	Scoring Position
Totals	7/92	12/57	12/30	24/87
Percentage	7.6%	21.1%	40.0%	27.6%

Loves to face: Paul Gibson (.400, 4-for-10, 2 2B, 1 HR, 5 BB)
Rick Honeycutt (.800, 4-for-5, 1 SO)
Frank Tanana (.370, 10-for-27)

Hates to face: Mike Boddicker (0-for-8)
Mark Langston (.136, 3-for-22)
David West (.077, 1-for-13, 1 2B)

Miscellaneous statistics: Ground outs-to-air outs ratio: 1.31 last season, 1.20 for career.... Grounded into 8 double plays in 58 opportunities (one per 7.3).... Drove in 11 of 17 runners from third base with less than two outs (65%).... Direction of balls hit to the outfield: 47% to left field, 28% to center, 25% to right.... Base running: Advanced from first base to third on 1 of 7 outfield singles (14%); scored from second on 1 of 4 (25%).... Opposing base stealers: 50-for-78 (64%).

Comments: Started with 21 hitless at-bats; his first hit came on April 24.... Started all 47 games in which the Blue Jays faced left-handed starters, only 24 of 115 games against right-handers. He started every game in which the Blue Jays faced southpaws in 1990 as well.... Maybe they ought to platoon him according to game time. He has a career average of .235 in day games, .280 at night. That 45-point difference is far wider than the gap between his career averages against left-handers (.272) and right-handers (.255).... Has a career average of one walk every 42 plate appearances vs. right-handers, one every 20 times up against lefties.... Has hit six career triples, all against left-handers.... Ranked 10th in the A.L. with 10 home runs against left-handers in 1990. His only homer off a southpaw last season was a game-winner on September 24 against Jim Abbott.... Last season's .179 batting average during September is deceiving. In the heat of the pennant race, he hit four home runs, two of which were game-winners, after hitting only one all season prior to that.... He has a career average of .307 during July, .259 in all other months combined.... Before last season, 17 of his 23 home runs had come before the All-Star break. Last season, all five came after the break.... Hasn't stolen a base in either of the past two seasons; he was caught once during that time, in 1990.

Mike Bordick

Bats Right

Oakland A's	AB	H	2B	3B	HR	RBI	BB	SO	BA	SA	OBA
Season	235	56	5	1	0	21	14	37	.238	.268	.289
vs. Left-Handers	58	13	1	0	0	6	4	6	.224	.241	.274
vs. Right-Handers	177	43	4	1	0	15	10	31	.243	.277	.293
vs. Ground-Ballers	111	29	3	1	0	8	4	13	.261	.306	.305
vs. Fly-Ballers	124	27	2	0	0	13	10	24	.218	.234	.274
Home Games	106	24	2	1	0	7	7	14	.226	.264	.287
Road Games	129	32	3	0	0	14	7	23	.248	.271	.290
Grass Fields	189	42	5	1	0	11	11	29	.222	.259	.271
Artificial Turf	46	14	0	0	0	10	3	8	.304	.304	.360
April	0	0	0	0	0	0	0	0	—	—	—
May	0	0	0	0	0	0	0	0	—	—	—
June	10	2	1	0	0	0	0	1	.200	.300	.200
July	68	15	2	0	0	7	3	11	.221	.250	.254
August	76	19	1	1	0	4	7	11	.250	.289	.329
Sept./Oct.	81	20	1	0	0	10	4	14	.247	.259	.287
Leading Off Inn.	62	13	2	0	0	0	1	13	.210	.242	.222
Runners On	85	25	1	1	0	21	3	13	.294	.329	.330
Bases Empty	150	31	4	0	0	0	11	24	.207	.233	.265
Runners/Scor. Pos.	53	18	0	1	0	20	3	7	.340	.377	.368
Runners On/2 Out	35	15	0	1	0	6	1	0	.429	.486	.459
Scor. Pos./2 Out	24	9	0	1	0	6	1	0	.375	.458	.400
Late-Inning Pressure	11	3	0	0	0	0	2	0	.273	.273	.385
Leading Off	2	0	0	0	0	0	0	0	.000	.000	.000
Runners On	3	1	0	0	0	0	1	0	.333	.333	.500
Runners/Scor. Pos.	0	0	0	0	0	0	1	0	—	—	1.000

RUNS BATTED IN	From 1B	From 2B	From 3B	Scoring Position
Totals	1/55	8/42	12/25	20/67
Percentage	1.8%	19.0%	48.0%	29.9%

Loves to face: Joe Grahe (.500, 3-for-6, 1 2B, 1 3B)
Wade Taylor (3-for-3)
Hates to face: Rich DeLucia (0-for-5)
Todd Frohwirth (0-for-5)
Juan Guzman (0-for-3, 3 SO)

Miscellaneous statistics: Ground outs-to-air outs ratio: 1.77 last season, 1.74 for career.... Grounded into 3 double plays in 48 opportunities (one per 16).... Drove in 9 of 15 runners from third base with less than two outs (60%).... Direction of balls hit to the outfield: 23% to left field, 26% to center, 52% to right.... Base running: Advanced from first base to third on 6 of 14 outfield singles (43%); scored from second on 5 of 5 (100%).... Made 2.75 assists per nine innings at shortstop, 2d-lowest rate in A.L.

Comments: Played 84 games at shortstop, five at second base, and one at third. The Athletics used eight second basemen last season, the most in the majors. They also used the most different shortstops (7) and third basemen (9) in the American League.... He was the only rookie to start at least half his team's games at shortstop.... Batted only once last season with runners in scoring position in Late-Inning Pressure Situations. As Don Drysdale often says, "That's got to tell you something." Over the past 17 years, only three players had as many plate appearances for a season as Bordick (265) but batted only once in RISP/LIPS: Nelson Norman (383 PAs) in 1979 and Al Newman (295) and Joel Skinner (272) in 1988.... Must be well connected. He was on Oakland's 1990 postseason roster, and played in three of the four World Series games against the Reds, despite playing only 25 regular-season games. Then he started the 1991 season in the minors as a nonroster player, but accumulated 265 plate appearances in the majors.... Is Carney Lansford healthy? How about Walt Weiss? Those questions, along with the release of Vance Law, the departure of Mike Gallego, and the club's refusal to offer arbitration to Ernest Riles give Bordick and Lance Blankenship a darn good shot at a spot on the A's this season. Their competition will come from third baseman Scott Brosius and second baseman Scott Hemond, both of whom saw some action with the A's last season. No wonder Sandy Alderson was so upset by the Yankees' signing of Gallego.

George Brett

Bats Left

Kansas City Royals	AB	H	2B	3B	HR	RBI	BB	SO	BA	SA	OBA
Season	505	129	40	2	10	61	58	75	.255	.402	.327
vs. Left-Handers	167	39	12	1	2	18	20	28	.234	.353	.309
vs. Right-Handers	338	90	28	1	8	43	38	47	.266	.426	.337
vs. Ground-Ballers	219	62	18	1	5	25	32	36	.283	.443	.373
vs. Fly-Ballers	286	67	22	1	5	36	26	39	.234	.371	.292
Home Games	243	60	19	2	3	27	30	33	.247	.379	.326
Road Games	262	69	21	0	7	34	28	42	.263	.424	.329
Grass Fields	211	53	18	0	5	26	19	32	.251	.408	.309
Artificial Turf	294	76	22	2	5	35	39	43	.259	.398	.340
April	47	8	0	0	0	0	3	9	.170	.170	.220
May	29	9	2	0	1	4	5	6	.310	.483	.412
June	105	28	12	0	1	19	12	13	.267	.410	.336
July	102	29	10	0	4	17	11	10	.284	.500	.345
August	108	27	10	2	1	10	13	16	.250	.407	.325
Sept./Oct.	114	28	6	0	3	11	14	21	.246	.377	.326
Leading Off Inn.	105	27	10	1	3	3	5	20	.257	.457	.291
Runners On	216	54	14	1	4	55	37	29	.250	.380	.349
Bases Empty	289	75	26	1	6	6	21	46	.260	.419	.310
Runners/Scor. Pos.	110	26	7	1	1	45	30	17	.236	.345	.378
Runners On/2 Out	64	14	1	1	2	15	14	7	.219	.359	.359
Scor. Pos./2 Out	40	8	1	1	0	11	12	6	.200	.275	.385
Late-Inning Pressure	67	13	4	0	1	5	14	9	.194	.299	.329
Leading Off	25	4	1	0	1	1	0	4	.160	.320	.160
Runners On	21	4	2	0	0	4	9	3	.190	.286	.419
Runners/Scor. Pos.	9	2	0	0	0	3	8	2	.222	.222	.556

RUNS BATTED IN	From 1B	From 2B	From 3B	Scoring Position
Totals	10/155	15/83	26/51	41/134
Percentage	6.5%	18.1%	51.0%	30.6%

Loves to face: Jim Abbott (.600, 12-for-20, 3 HR)
Gene Nelson (.400, 10-for-25, 5 HR, 0 SO)
Todd Stottlemyre (.611, 11-for-18)
Hates to face: Kevin Hickey (0-for-15)
Tim Leary (.056, 1-for-18, 2 BB)
Bobby Thigpen (.067, 1-for-15, 2 BB)

Miscellaneous statistics: Ground outs-to-air outs ratio: 1.32 last season, 1.06 for career.... Grounded into 20 double plays in 117 opportunities (one per 5.9).... Drove in 21 of 30 runners from third base with less than two outs (70%).... Direction of balls hit to the outfield: 40% to left field, 35% to center, 25% to right.... Base running: Advanced from first base to third on 13 of 29 outfield singles (45%); scored from second on 16 of 19 (84%).... Made 0.54 assists per nine innings at first base.

Comments: His batting average decreased 74 points from a .329 mark in 1990, the largest drop of any player who qualified for the batting title in both seasons.... Hit eight of his 10 home runs to the opposite field. That surprised us.... Averaged one strikeout every 7.6 plate appearances last season, the worst rate of his career. His strikeout rate has increased in each of the past three seasons; year by year since 1988: one per 13.4 PAs, followed by 11.2, 9.6, and 7.6.... The only active player with 1000 + extra-base hits (1019), 73 more than runner-up Dave Winfield (946).... His career total of 599 doubles ranks fourth in American League history, behind Hall of Famers Tris Speaker (793), Ty Cobb (724), and Carl Yastrzemski (646).... His transition from third base to first base stalled last season. He played only 10 games in the field, none after returning from the disabled list in late May. His career total of games at first base stands now, and possibly forever, at 446. The only players with 500 games at both positions: Dick Allen, Harmon Killebrew, Tony Perez, Enos Cabell, Darrell Evans, Pete Rose, and Joe Torre.... Brett has played 1424 games on artificial turf, and last season passed Frank White (1391) for the most such games by any player in A.L. history. Pete Rose played 1815 games on artificial turf, 391 more than Brett.... Has driven in over 30 percent of runners from scoring position in each of the 17 years of *The Player Analysis.* No other player has reached the 30 percent mark more than 12 times since 1975.

Greg Briley

Bats Left

Seattle Mariners	AB	H	2B	3B	HR	RBI	BB	SO	BA	SA	OBA
Season	381	99	17	3	2	26	27	51	.260	.336	.307
vs. Left-Handers	39	9	2	1	0	9	1	10	.231	.333	.250
vs. Right-Handers	342	90	15	2	2	17	26	41	.263	.336	.313
vs. Ground-Ballers	178	46	9	1	2	13	11	29	.258	.354	.302
vs. Fly-Ballers	203	53	8	2	0	13	16	22	.261	.320	.311
Home Games	185	46	4	1	2	12	17	19	.249	.314	.310
Road Games	196	53	13	2	0	14	10	32	.270	.357	.303
Grass Fields	142	37	8	2	0	11	7	25	.261	.345	.291
Artificial Turf	239	62	9	1	2	15	20	26	.259	.331	.315
April	43	10	1	0	1	5	7	6	.233	.326	.333
May	78	17	1	0	1	4	2	9	.218	.269	.237
June	51	9	1	0	1	3	1	16	.176	.216	.192
July	44	10	2	0	0	1	3	3	.227	.273	.277
August	68	26	8	0	0	5	6	5	.382	.500	.427
Sept./Oct.	97	27	5	2	0	8	8	12	.278	.371	.330
Leading Off Inn.	102	20	3	1	0	0	6	13	.196	.245	.241
Runners On	150	41	6	2	2	26	11	22	.273	.380	.317
Bases Empty	231	58	11	1	0	0	16	29	.251	.307	.300
Runners/Scor. Pos.	70	17	1	2	1	22	5	8	.243	.357	.282
Runners On/2 Out	57	13	3	2	0	9	3	10	.228	.351	.267
Scor. Pos./2 Out	32	7	1	2	0	8	2	5	.219	.375	.265
Late-Inning Pressure	67	17	4	0	1	4	2	12	.254	.358	.271
Leading Off	19	2	0	0	0	0	0	4	.105	.105	.105
Runners On	24	7	1	0	1	4	1	4	.292	.458	.308
Runners/Scor. Pos.	13	4	1	0	1	4	0	2	.308	.615	.286

RUNS BATTED IN	From 1B	From 2B	From 3B	Scoring Position
Totals	4/118	9/59	11/31	20/90
Percentage	3.4%	15.3%	35.5%	22.2%

Loves to face: Mike Boddicker (.458, 11-for-24)
Kirk McCaskill (.444, 8-for-18, 1 HR)
Roy Smith (.500, 7-for-14)

Hates to face: Tim Leary (.056, 1-for-18, 2 BB)
Scott Sanderson (0-for-17)
Kevin Tapani (.083, 1-for-12)

Miscellaneous statistics: Ground outs-to-air outs ratio: 1.72 last season, 1.34 for career.... Grounded into 7 double plays in 81 opportunities (one per 12).... Drove in 8 of 15 runners from third base with less than two outs (53%).... Direction of balls hit to the outfield: 48% to left field, 32% to center, 20% to right.... Base running: Advanced from first base to third on 3 of 15 outfield singles (20%); scored from second on 7 of 12 (58%).... Made 2.10 putouts per nine innings in left field.

Comments: Started 90 games against right-handed pitchers last season, but only one against a left-hander (vs. Jimmy Key on Sept. 11). Of his 1278 career plate appearances, 1135 have been against right-handers (89%), only 143 vs. lefties (11%).... Has nearly identical career batting averages of .256 vs. left-handers, .258 vs. right-handers. But 20 of his 21 home runs have been hit off right-handers.... Career batting average is .230 with 11 home runs at the Kingdome, compared to .288 with 10 HRs on the road.... Entered 26 games as a pinch hitter, seven as a pinch runner, and 15 as a defensive replacement.... All six of his go-ahead RBIs proved to be game-winners.... He ended the season with an eight-game hitting streak, his longest of the year, and a streak of 320 at-bats without a home run. Considering the circumstances of his last home run (May 5), that drought may have been payback to the Devil: Briley's 16th-inning game-winning home run capped Seattle's second extra-inning comeback of the game against New York, and ended the longest home game in Mariners' history, in terms of both innings and time (5 hours, 31 minutes).... Briley hit 13 home runs as a rookie in 1989, but only seven more over two seasons since then.... What rookies in major league history hit the most home runs among those who never again reached double figures? Three hit 20 as rookies: Ken Hunt (25 for the 1961 Angels at the even friendlier confines of Wrigley Field in L.A.), Joe Charboneau (23 in 1980), and Sam Bowens (22 in 1964).

Jerry Browne

Bats Left and Right

Cleveland Indians	AB	H	2B	3B	HR	RBI	BB	SO	BA	SA	OBA
Season	290	66	5	2	1	29	27	29	.228	.269	.292
vs. Left-Handers	78	18	1	0	0	6	8	9	.231	.244	.310
vs. Right-Handers	212	48	4	2	1	23	19	20	.226	.278	.285
vs. Ground-Ballers	124	23	1	0	0	5	11	17	.185	.194	.248
vs. Fly-Ballers	166	43	4	2	1	24	16	12	.259	.325	.324
Home Games	135	35	3	0	1	16	10	12	.259	.304	.313
Road Games	155	31	2	2	0	13	17	17	.200	.239	.274
Grass Fields	241	55	5	2	1	27	23	23	.228	.278	.295
Artificial Turf	49	11	0	0	0	2	4	6	.224	.224	.278
April	56	8	0	0	0	7	6	4	.143	.143	.215
May	32	6	1	2	0	6	2	6	.188	.344	.229
June	73	19	1	0	0	6	6	4	.260	.274	.316
July	34	8	0	0	1	4	1	4	.235	.324	.278
August	61	18	3	0	0	4	5	5	.295	.344	.348
Sept./Oct.	34	7	0	0	0	2	7	6	.206	.206	.341
Leading Off Inn.	62	10	0	1	0	0	7	9	.161	.194	.246
Runners On	123	33	3	1	1	29	10	13	.268	.333	.319
Bases Empty	167	33	2	1	0	0	17	16	.198	.222	.272
Runners/Scor. Pos.	74	20	3	1	0	27	8	9	.270	.338	.333
Runners On/2 Out	53	16	2	0	1	15	7	6	.302	.396	.383
Scor. Pos./2 Out	38	11	2	0	0	13	6	5	.289	.342	.386
Late-Inning Pressure	64	18	1	0	1	9	5	9	.281	.344	.324
Leading Off	23	5	0	0	0	0	1	6	.217	.217	.250
Runners On	24	8	1	0	1	9	2	3	.333	.500	.357
Runners/Scor. Pos.	17	6	1	0	0	7	2	2	.353	.412	.381

RUNS BATTED IN	From 1B	From 2B	From 3B	Scoring Position
Totals	2/84	11/66	15/28	26/94
Percentage	2.4%	16.7%	53.6%	27.7%

Loves to face: Chuck Crim (.600, 6-for-10, 1 HR)
Jimmy Key (.407, 11-for-27, 0 SO)
Bob Milacki (.368, 7-for-19, 1 HR)

Hates to face: Chuck Finley (.050, 1-for-20, 1 2B)
Erik Hanson (.100, 2-for-20, 1 3B)
Kirk McCaskill (.056, 1-for-18, 3 BB)

Miscellaneous statistics: Ground outs-to-air outs ratio: 1.26 last season, 1.29 for career.... Grounded into 5 double plays in 59 opportunities (one per 12).... Drove in 10 of 14 runners from third base with less than two outs (71%).... Direction of balls hit to the outfield: 32% to left field, 39% to center, 28% to right batting left-handed; 26% to left field, 26% to center, 49% to right batting right-handed.... Base running: Advanced from first base to third on 2 of 14 outfield singles (14%); scored from second on 6 of 10 (60%).... Made 3.00 assists per nine innings at second base.

Comments: Seriously—what is it that Jerry Browne does better than any other player in the majors? He has walked 11 times in 44 career plate appearances with the bags full, the highest rate in the 17 years we've compiled such records.... What about when he swings the bat? He's 7-for-27 (.259) with a double and two strikeouts with the bags full.... Opened the 1991 season as Cleveland's regular second baseman. But his batting average was 4th lowest in the league during April, and he lost the job on May 11 with his average at .160.... He started only five games after September 1, and started only three games at second base over the last two months of the season. He had never before played a position other than second base, but he played 15 games at third base and 17 in left field last season.... He committed an average of one error every 7.5 chances at third base, compared to the major league average of one every 21.2 chances at that position.... Was used as a pinch hitter 37 times, the 4th-highest total in the league, behind Randy Bush (47), Matt Merullo (47), and Warren Cromartie (41).... Batting average in road games was 3d lowest in the league.... He's spent parts of six seasons in the majors, but at 26 years of age he's younger than quite a few of his rookie Indians teammates last season, including Ever Magallanes, Beau Allred, Turner Ward, Bruce Egloff, Dave Otto, Mike York, Jeff Manto, Mike Huff, Wayne Kirby, and 31-year-old Jose Escobar, baseball's 2d-oldest rookie in 1991. (The oldest: 32-year-old Angels catcher, Ron Tingley.)

Tom Brunansky
Bats Right

Boston Red Sox	AB	H	2B	3B	HR	RBI	BB	SO	BA	SA	OBA
Season	459	105	24	1	16	70	49	72	.229	.390	.303
vs. Left-Handers	142	36	7	1	5	22	16	12	.254	.423	.321
vs. Right-Handers	317	69	17	0	11	48	33	60	.218	.375	.294
vs. Ground-Ballers	204	51	12	0	4	28	25	34	.250	.368	.325
vs. Fly-Ballers	255	54	12	1	12	42	24	38	.212	.408	.284
Home Games	234	60	16	0	10	39	27	32	.256	.453	.335
Road Games	225	45	8	1	6	31	22	40	.200	.324	.269
Grass Fields	379	82	18	0	14	54	42	56	.216	.375	.295
Artificial Turf	80	23	6	1	2	16	7	16	.287	.463	.337
April	60	15	4	0	3	11	9	8	.250	.467	.343
May	99	22	5	0	6	25	10	12	.222	.455	.286
June	83	14	3	0	2	8	9	16	.169	.277	.263
July	85	17	6	0	1	4	8	14	.200	.306	.266
August	66	19	1	1	2	8	6	10	.288	.424	.356
Sept./Oct.	66	18	5	0	2	14	7	12	.273	.439	.333
Leading Off Inn.	106	23	5	0	2	2	7	19	.217	.321	.272
Runners On	227	55	12	1	10	64	23	34	.242	.436	.305
Bases Empty	232	50	12	0	6	6	26	38	.216	.345	.300
Runners/Scor. Pos.	142	33	4	1	7	56	16	18	.232	.423	.299
Runners On/2 Out	99	20	7	1	1	16	12	16	.202	.323	.288
Scor. Pos./2 Out	68	12	2	1	1	14	11	7	.176	.279	.291
Late-Inning Pressure	52	16	8	0	0	3	6	5	.308	.462	.373
Leading Off	14	4	2	0	0	0	1	3	.286	.429	.333
Runners On	23	6	3	0	0	3	2	2	.261	.391	.308
Runners/Scor. Pos.	14	2	1	0	0	3	1	1	.143	.214	.188

RUNS BATTED IN	From 1B	From 2B	From 3B	Scoring Position
Totals	8/165	17/113	29/69	46/182
Percentage	4.8%	15.0%	42.0%	25.3%

Loves to face: Mark Eichhorn (.444, 8-for-18, 4 2B, 1 HR)
                Alex Fernandez (.400, 6-for-15, 2 HR)
                Wes Gardner (.600, 3-for-5, 3 HR)

Hates to face: Eric Bell (0-for-9)
                Jack Morris (.156, 7-for-45, 6 BB)
                Scott Sanderson (.048, 1-for-21, 1 2B)

Miscellaneous statistics: Ground outs-to-air outs ratio: 0.57 last season, 4th lowest in A.L.; 0.68 for career.... Grounded into 8 double plays in 110 opportunities (one per 14).... Drove in 22 of 33 runners from third base with less than two outs (67%).... Direction of balls hit to the outfield: 41% to left field, 33% to center, 26% to right.... Base running: Advanced from first base to third on 4 of 22 outfield singles (18%); scored from second on 9 of 12 (75%).... Made 2.17 putouts per nine innings in right field.

Comments: Started 43 of 44 games in which the Red Sox faced left-handed starters, 79 of 118 games against right-handers.... His May RBI total ranked 2d in the league.... June batting average was 4th lowest in the league.... Batting average in road games was also 4th lowest in the league.... Hitless in 14 at-bats with the bases loaded over the last two seasons.... He had only five assists last season, his lowest total in any full season, after averaging more than 10 assists per season over the previous nine years.... His career batting averages both in Late-Inning Pressure Situations and with runners in scoring position are lower than his overall average. His combined performance in those situations is horrendous: a .228 career batting average with RISP in LIPS, with marks below .180 in five of the last six seasons.... Homerless in 124 at-bats in Late-Inning Pressure Situations over the last two seasons; he has an average of one home run per 27 at-bats at other times.... Since joining the Red Sox in May 1990, he's batted .299 with 23 home runs at Fenway Park; on the road, he's batted .195 with only eight HRs.... He has driven in at least 70 runs in each of the last nine seasons. Only five players have longer current streaks. Eddie Murray has a 15-year streak; Andre Dawson, Kent Hrbek, Dale Murphy, and Cal Ripken have 10-year streaks.... He has had at least 20 doubles and 15 home runs in every season since 1982.

Jay Buhner
Bats Right

Seattle Mariners	AB	H	2B	3B	HR	RBI	BB	SO	BA	SA	OBA
Season	406	99	14	4	27	77	53	117	.244	.498	.337
vs. Left-Handers	146	35	5	2	9	26	28	28	.240	.486	.371
vs. Right-Handers	260	64	9	2	18	51	25	89	.246	.504	.316
vs. Ground-Ballers	199	54	7	2	14	48	28	57	.271	.538	.368
vs. Fly-Ballers	207	45	7	2	13	29	25	60	.217	.459	.307
Home Games	212	45	9	2	14	41	31	71	.212	.472	.321
Road Games	194	54	5	2	13	36	22	46	.278	.526	.355
Grass Fields	153	46	3	2	12	32	19	35	.301	.582	.377
Artificial Turf	253	53	11	2	15	45	34	82	.209	.447	.313
April	52	12	3	1	4	7	8	20	.231	.558	.333
May	37	10	1	1	2	9	6	12	.270	.514	.372
June	55	10	1	0	3	12	9	15	.182	.364	.318
July	87	22	3	0	8	15	5	26	.253	.563	.298
August	95	27	6	2	7	25	10	27	.284	.611	.358
Sept./Oct.	80	18	0	0	3	9	15	17	.225	.338	.351
Leading Off Inn.	85	26	3	1	7	7	10	21	.306	.612	.385
Runners On	199	46	9	3	12	62	26	50	.231	.487	.320
Bases Empty	207	53	5	1	15	15	27	67	.256	.507	.353
Runners/Scor. Pos.	107	23	3	2	4	42	21	29	.215	.393	.343
Runners On/2 Out	97	22	4	2	5	31	12	28	.227	.464	.318
Scor. Pos./2 Out	62	15	1	1	4	26	11	17	.242	.484	.365
Late-Inning Pressure	63	15	3	0	3	11	9	17	.238	.429	.329
Leading Off	11	2	0	0	1	1	1	1	.182	.455	.250
Runners On	31	9	3	0	1	9	6	5	.290	.484	.395
Runners/Scor. Pos.	17	5	1	0	1	7	5	2	.294	.529	.435

RUNS BATTED IN	From 1B	From 2B	From 3B	Scoring Position
Totals	15/144	16/88	19/47	35/135
Percentage	10.4%	18.2%	40.4%	25.9%

Loves to face: Mike Boddicker (.500, 5-for-10, 3 2B, 1 HR, 3 SO)
                Alex Fernandez (.500, 5-for-10, 1 HR, 3 SO)
                Bob Welch (.500, 4-for-8, 1 2B, 2 HR)

Hates to face: Roger Clemens (0-for-10)
                Mike Flanagan (.071, 1-for-14)
                Ted Higuera (0-for-11, 8 SO)

Miscellaneous statistics: Ground outs-to-air outs ratio: 0.84 last season, 0.96 for career.... Grounded into 10 double plays in 89 opportunities (one per 8.9).... Drove in 10 of 16 runners from third base with less than two outs (63%).... Direction of balls hit to the outfield: 42% to left field, 33% to center, 25% to right.... Base running: Advanced from first base to third on 10 of 20 outfield singles (50%); scored from second on 6 of 9 (67%).... Made 2.16 putouts per nine innings in right field.

Comments: Has hit 53 homers since being traded by the Yankees to the Mariners on July 21, 1988—not bad considering he spent nearly a season's worth of that time on the disabled list. Yankees HR leaders during that time: Barfield, 60; Mattingly, 55; Hall, 48.... Buhner became the Mariners' seventh different opening-day right fielder in the last seven years. The last to play RF on consecutive Mariners opening days was Al Cowens.... Started all 42 games in which the Mariners faced left-handed starting pitchers, 68 of 120 games against right-handers.... His 15 assists from right field tied Felix Jose for the major league lead.... He was one of five A.L. players who had three game-winning RBIs in extra innings last season. The others: Jose Canseco, Rafael Palmeiro, Danny Tartabull, and Robin Ventura.... Among active players with at least 1000 plate appearances, only Bo Jackson, Rob Deer, John Russell, and Pete Incaviglia have higher career strikeout rates.... He has averaged one home run every 18.2 at-bats since joining the Mariners. That's the 2d-best rate in franchise history, behind Ken Phelps (13.3).... Likes to do that Jerry Browne thing; he drew four bases-loaded walks last season. The only other players to do that were Dwight Evans and Jack Clark, the leader and runner-up in career walks among active players.... Career batting averages are .278 in day games, .236 at night.

Ellis Burks

Bats Right

Boston Red Sox	AB	H	2B	3B	HR	RBI	BB	SO	BA	SA	OBA
Season	474	119	33	3	14	56	39	81	.251	.422	.314
vs. Left-Handers	135	35	12	2	5	23	11	21	.259	.489	.313
vs. Right-Handers	339	84	21	1	9	33	28	60	.248	.395	.315
vs. Ground-Ballers	219	52	11	2	7	25	14	35	.237	.402	.294
vs. Fly-Ballers	255	67	22	1	7	31	25	46	.263	.439	.331
Home Games	232	62	18	2	8	25	20	36	.267	.466	.328
Road Games	242	57	15	1	6	31	19	45	.236	.380	.301
Grass Fields	384	95	25	3	10	44	30	65	.247	.406	.305
Artificial Turf	90	24	8	0	4	12	9	16	.267	.489	.353
April	64	15	6	0	1	4	7	15	.234	.375	.338
May	95	28	5	0	2	7	9	11	.295	.411	.356
June	94	18	5	0	6	13	6	14	.191	.436	.238
July	94	26	5	2	4	14	8	18	.277	.500	.346
August	92	23	9	1	1	10	7	16	.250	.402	.303
Sept./Oct.	35	9	3	0	0	8	2	7	.257	.343	.300
Leading Off Inn.	99	23	8	1	4	4	10	8	.232	.455	.309
Runners On	225	57	15	1	4	46	17	49	.253	.382	.308
Bases Empty	249	62	18	2	10	10	22	32	.249	.458	.320
Runners/Scor. Pos.	133	30	6	1	4	45	16	30	.226	.376	.303
Runners On/2 Out	95	29	8	1	2	33	12	17	.305	.474	.383
Scor. Pos./2 Out	73	23	5	1	2	32	11	14	.315	.493	.405
Late-Inning Pressure	56	11	3	1	0	1	3	12	.196	.286	.262
Leading Off	15	4	1	1	0	0	0	1	.267	.467	.313
Runners On	23	1	0	0	0	1	2	9	.043	.043	.120
Runners/Scor. Pos.	13	0	0	0	0	1	2	7	.000	.000	.133

RUNS BATTED IN	From 1B	From 2B	From 3B	Scoring Position
Totals	5/171	21/106	16/58	37/164
Percentage	2.9%	19.8%	27.6%	22.6%

Loves to face: Erik Hanson (.579, 11-for-19, 2 HR)
Jeff Russell (.500, 9-for-18, 2 HR)
Bill Wegman (.615, 8-for-13, 1 HR)

Hates to face: Dennis Eckersley (.067, 1-for-15, 1 2B)
Mike Flanagan (0-for-10)
Jimmy Key (.091, 2-for-22)

Miscellaneous statistics: Ground outs-to-air outs ratio: 1.27 last season, 1.05 for career.... Grounded into 7 double plays in 109 opportunities (one per 16).... Drove in 8 of 27 runners from third base with less than two outs (30%), lowest rate in A.L.... Direction of balls hit to the outfield: 47% to left field, 31% to center, 21% to right.... Base running: Advanced from first base to third on 13 of 28 outfield singles (46%); scored from second on 12 of 13 (92%).... Made 2.37 putouts per nine innings in center field, 3d-lowest rate in A.L.

Comments: Of 119 hits, only 12 were to the opposite field (10%), the 5th-lowest percentage among A.L. players with at least 60 hits last season. Maybe he's too focused on the Olive Ogre; Burks had only one hit to right field at Fenway between May 13 and September 24. Burks had 39 opposite-field hits in 1990.... Set career lows in batting, slugging, and on-base averages, as well as home-run rate, runs, hits, RBIs, and stolen bases. He is one of the players most often rumored to be on the trading block, but the trade-in value on this model is at an all-time low.... His stolen-base total has decreased in every season since his debut in 1987: 27, 25, 21, 9, 6. Over his first three years, he stole 73 bases in 93 attempts (78%); over the last two, he is 15-for-37 (41%).... After the 1988 season, our projection model would have rated his chances to score 1000 runs (a good yardstick for a player with Burks's skills) at 39 percent; his chances are now roughly half that (23%).... His league-low rate of driving in runners from third base with less than two outs in 1991 lowered his career average to 50.3 percent in those situations, 10th lowest among active players (minimum: 150 opportunities).... Drove in only one of 14 runners from scoring position in Late-Inning Pressure Situations last season. He had one RBI in 56 at-bats in LIPS.... Has a career average of .301 with 43 homers at Fenway Park, .267 with 42 homers in road games.

Jose Canseco

Bats Right

Oakland A's	AB	H	2B	3B	HR	RBI	BB	SO	BA	SA	OBA
Season	572	152	32	1	44	122	78	152	.266	.556	.359
vs. Left-Handers	136	34	9	0	8	21	24	41	.250	.493	.370
vs. Right-Handers	436	118	23	1	36	101	54	111	.271	.576	.356
vs. Ground-Ballers	272	78	19	0	20	64	39	64	.287	.577	.382
vs. Fly-Ballers	300	74	13	1	24	58	39	88	.247	.537	.339
Home Games	267	72	15	0	16	46	39	80	.270	.506	.371
Road Games	305	80	17	1	28	76	39	72	.262	.600	.349
Grass Fields	467	120	27	1	33	91	67	124	.257	.531	.356
Artificial Turf	105	32	5	0	11	31	11	28	.305	.667	.376
April	65	18	5	0	4	13	18	19	.277	.538	.440
May	98	19	5	0	4	13	16	32	.194	.367	.299
June	92	25	8	0	10	23	10	17	.272	.685	.362
July	111	35	8	0	10	35	13	19	.315	.658	.389
August	96	22	1	0	8	12	11	35	.229	.490	.318
Sept./Oct.	110	33	5	1	8	26	10	30	.300	.582	.366
Leading Off Inn.	115	38	5	0	14	14	20	25	.330	.739	.438
Runners On	254	68	12	0	20	98	37	65	.268	.551	.362
Bases Empty	318	84	20	1	24	24	41	87	.264	.560	.357
Runners/Scor. Pos.	154	41	9	0	14	85	25	46	.266	.597	.364
Runners On/2 Out	73	24	7	0	9	41	11	15	.329	.795	.424
Scor. Pos./2 Out	49	17	6	0	6	35	11	11	.347	.837	.475
Late-Inning Pressure	83	22	7	0	7	25	6	23	.265	.602	.311
Leading Off	21	4	1	0	1	1	3	8	.190	.381	.292
Runners On	40	11	3	0	4	22	2	11	.275	.650	.302
Runners/Scor. Pos.	28	8	3	0	2	18	1	10	.286	.607	.300

RUNS BATTED IN	From 1B	From 2B	From 3B	Scoring Position
Totals	22/178	25/110	31/74	56/184
Percentage	12.4%	22.7%	41.9%	30.4%

Loves to face: Allan Anderson (.375, 9-for-24, 2 2B, 5 HR)
Dave Johnson (.600, 6-for-10, 2 HR)
Todd Stottlemyre (.444, 8-for-18, 6 HR)

Hates to face: John Habyan (0-for-10)
Erik Hanson (0-for-16, 8 SO)
Greg A. Harris (0-for-14)

Miscellaneous statistics: Ground outs-to-air outs ratio: 0.88 last season, 0.82 for career.... Grounded into 16 double plays in 144 opportunities (one per 9.0).... Drove in 23 of 50 runners from third base with less than two outs (46%).... Direction of balls hit to the outfield: 39% to left field, 31% to center, 31% to right.... Base running: Advanced from first base to third on 8 of 23 outfield singles (35%); scored from second on 20 of 21 (95%), 4th-highest rate in A.L.... Made 2.03 putouts per nine innings in right field.

Comments: Has more trouble with H's than Eliza Doolittle. He hates Holman (1-for-12), Hurst (4-for-23), Higuera (5-for-28), Hibbard (3-for-16), and Hough (9-for-46), too.... The only player with a slugging percentage of .500 or better in each of the last four years. In fact, his mark has been at least .541 in each of those seasons. The last player with a longer streak of slugging percentages that high was Willie Mays (13 years, 1954–66).... On-base percentage leading off innings was highest in the majors.... Stole 26 bases in 32 attempts last season (81%), his highest percentage since before all that 40/40 stuff.... Committed nine errors, the most of any right fielder in the majors last season.... Hit five homers at Skydome last season, the most by any visiting player, giving him a total of nine there in 49 regular-season at-bats. His combined regular- and postseason figures there: .377 (23-for-61), 10 HR.... His average with two outs and runners in scoring position was 5th highest in the league.... Has the highest career batting average among active players in the mother of all *Player Analysis* categories—runners in scoring position in Late-Inning Pressure Situations (.373). Over the last 17 years, only Eric Soderholm had a higher mark (.429).... The only active player rated by our projection model as an odds-on choice to hit 500 home runs. See the A's essay for more.... Needs 103 RBIs in his next 147 games (slightly below his career average) to become the first player since Ted Williams to reach the 1000-game mark with as many as 750 RBIs.

Joe Carter
Bats Right

Toronto Blue Jays	AB	H	2B	3B	HR	RBI	BB	SO	BA	SA	OBA
Season	638	174	42	3	33	108	49	112	.273	.503	.330
vs. Left-Handers	188	63	12	1	10	32	11	28	.335	.569	.366
vs. Right-Handers	450	111	30	2	23	76	38	84	.247	.476	.315
vs. Ground-Ballers	335	98	19	1	16	51	18	62	.293	.499	.335
vs. Fly-Ballers	303	76	23	2	17	57	31	50	.251	.508	.325
Home Games	321	93	23	1	23	64	23	65	.290	.583	.348
Road Games	317	81	19	2	10	44	26	47	.256	.423	.311
Grass Fields	247	65	12	1	10	37	21	35	.263	.441	.322
Artificial Turf	391	109	30	2	23	71	28	77	.279	.542	.335
April	83	28	8	0	3	15	8	13	.337	.542	.391
May	104	25	5	1	3	10	9	14	.240	.394	.310
June	108	38	11	0	11	29	8	23	.352	.759	.405
July	98	25	5	0	6	18	12	20	.255	.490	.348
August	125	31	7	0	6	20	2	14	.248	.448	.262
Sept./Oct.	120	27	6	2	4	16	10	28	.225	.408	.288
Leading Off Inn.	124	36	10	2	9	9	5	16	.290	.621	.323
Runners On	292	80	16	1	14	89	33	58	.274	.479	.348
Bases Empty	346	94	26	2	19	19	16	54	.272	.523	.313
Runners/Scor. Pos.	184	49	8	1	9	76	27	40	.266	.467	.354
Runners On/2 Out	112	31	4	0	2	27	12	25	.277	.366	.357
Scor. Pos./2 Out	78	24	3	0	2	27	11	18	.308	.423	.407
Late-Inning Pressure	82	15	2	1	1	7	14	21	.183	.268	.309
Leading Off	24	7	1	1	0	0	2	5	.292	.417	.346
Runners On	39	6	1	0	0	6	11	12	.154	.179	.340
Runners/Scor. Pos.	28	4	1	0	0	6	10	11	.143	.179	.368

RUNS BATTED IN	From 1B	From 2B	From 3B	Scoring Position
Totals	11/178	29/128	35/91	64/219
Percentage	6.2%	22.7%	38.5%	29.2%

Loves to face: Charlie Hough (.298, 14-for-47, 6 HR)
Mark Knudson (.571, 8-for-14, 4 HR)
Tim Leary (.636, 7-for-11, 3 HR)

Hates to face: Greg Cadaret (0-for-9)
Mark Gubicza (.167, 8-for-48, 1 HR)
Ted Higuera (.143, 5-for-35, 1 HR)

Miscellaneous statistics: Ground outs-to-air outs ratio: 0.77 last season, 0.68 for career.... Grounded into 6 double plays in 125 opportunities (one per 21).... Drove in 23 of 52 runners from third base with less than two outs (44%).... Direction of balls hit to the outfield: 48% to left field, 27% to center, 25% to right.... Base running: Advanced from first base to third on 12 of 24 outfield singles (50%); scored from second on 10 of 15 (67%).... Made 1.97 putouts per nine innings in right field.

Comments: Leads the majors with 653 RBIs over the last six years.... Became the first player in major league history with at least 100 RBIs in three consecutive seasons for three different clubs.... Only 29 players have been traded immediately after 100-RBI seasons; the odd part is that four, including Carter, were traded twice under that circumstance. The others: Rocky Colavito (after 1959 and 1964), Zeke Bonura (1937 and 1938), and Eddie Robinson (1952 and 1953).... Led the American League in go-ahead RBIs (34) and game-winning RBIs (18).... His June home-run and RBI totals were both highest in the majors.... He hit 32 of his home runs to left field, one to center field, and none to the opposite field. Of his 78 extra-base hits, 11 were hit to the opposite field.... Was hit by 10 pitches, most in the A.L. He's been hit at least seven times in each of the past five seasons.... Has slowly but steadily increased his walk rate from Armas-like levels in the mid-1970s. He walked once for every 22.8 plate appearances through 1987; year by year since then: one per 19.1, 18.1, 14.5, 14.4.... Was one of only four major leaguers to appear in every one of his team's games in 1991. Cal Ripken extended his streak to 1573—557 to Gehrig and counting. Carter is the current runner-up; he has played in 505 consecutive games, with Cecil Fielder third at 214 and Mark Grace fourth at 173.

Jack Clark
Bats Right

Boston Red Sox	AB	H	2B	3B	HR	RBI	BB	SO	BA	SA	OBA
Season	481	120	18	1	28	87	96	133	.249	.466	.374
vs. Left-Handers	117	38	6	0	6	20	34	22	.325	.530	.465
vs. Right-Handers	364	82	12	1	22	67	62	111	.225	.445	.342
vs. Ground-Ballers	228	54	7	0	13	40	39	65	.237	.439	.347
vs. Fly-Ballers	253	66	11	1	15	47	57	68	.261	.490	.397
Home Games	253	71	12	0	18	47	40	68	.281	.542	.377
Road Games	228	49	6	1	10	40	56	65	.215	.382	.372
Grass Fields	409	101	16	0	23	65	76	116	.247	.455	.365
Artificial Turf	72	19	2	1	5	22	20	17	.264	.528	.426
April	57	14	1	0	3	10	12	19	.246	.421	.386
May	84	16	2	0	1	5	20	29	.190	.250	.346
June	74	16	1	0	6	14	16	20	.216	.473	.352
July	89	24	2	0	7	23	17	23	.270	.528	.383
August	88	23	6	1	5	22	17	19	.261	.523	.385
Sept./Oct.	89	27	6	0	6	13	14	23	.303	.573	.394
Leading Off Inn.	122	28	4	0	5	5	15	37	.230	.385	.319
Runners On	239	63	12	1	15	74	58	64	.264	.510	.405
Bases Empty	242	57	6	0	13	13	38	69	.236	.421	.342
Runners/Scor. Pos.	132	32	5	0	8	58	46	44	.242	.462	.429
Runners On/2 Out	114	39	6	1	9	40	34	31	.342	.649	.493
Scor. Pos./2 Out	65	18	2	0	5	30	27	22	.277	.538	.489
Late-Inning Pressure	68	11	1	0	4	7	7	26	.162	.353	.240
Leading Off	22	4	1	0	1	1	1	8	.182	.364	.217
Runners On	27	3	0	0	1	4	5	9	.111	.222	.250
Runners/Scor. Pos.	16	2	0	0	1	2	3	8	.125	.125	.263

RUNS BATTED IN	From 1B	From 2B	From 3B	Scoring Position
Totals	14/185	19/106	26/65	45/171
Percentage	7.6%	17.9%	40.0%	26.3%

Loves to face: Dennis Cook (3-for-3, 1 2B, 1 HR, 2 BB)
Rick Honeycutt (.533, 8-for-15, 2 HR, 7 BB)
David Wells (.500, 4-for-8, 2 HR)

Hates to face: Mike Boddicker (0-for-16)
Scott Erickson (0-for-10)
Ted Higuera (.083, 1-for-12, 9 SO)

Miscellaneous statistics: Ground outs-to-air outs ratio: 1.00 last season, 0.92 for career.... Grounded into 17 double plays in 121 opportunities (one per 7.1).... Drove in 16 of 34 runners from third base with less than two outs (47%).... Direction of balls hit to the outfield: 46% to left field, 32% to center, 23% to right.... Base running: Advanced from first base to third on 6 of 33 outfield singles (18%); scored from second on 7 of 14 (50%).

Comments: Hit a grand slam on opening day; Boston was the fourth different team for which he has slammed. Two players have hit bases-loaded home runs for five different teams: Dave Kingman and Walker Cooper.... He and Bobby Bonds are now the only players with 25-homer seasons for five different clubs.... In his other tour of duty in the A.L., Clark played both outfield and first base for the 1988 Yankees; this time around, he hasn't yet played the field for Boston.... Batting average with two outs and runners on base was 4th highest in the league.... Batting average in Late-Inning Pressure Situations was 6th lowest in the league.... Over the last two seasons, he has a batting average of .351 vs. left-handers, .219 vs. right-handers.... Has drawn an average of 116 walks per season since 1987; his average was only 62 per year from 1977 through 1986.... Strikeout average has risen similarly: 69 per year over his first 10 seasons, 130 per year over the last five.... Hasn't executed a sacrifice bunt since 1980.... Does anyone remember Clark as a competent base stealer in the late 1970s? He stole between 10 and 15 bases in three consecutive seasons starting in 1977.... Is Clark a future Hall Of Famer? He'll need a few more top-notch seasons to improve his chances. As it stands now, his career numbers are similar to those of Norm Cash, who received only six votes in his one season on the ballot.... Are you better off then you were four years ago? In 1988, the top of the Yankees' batting order was Henderson, Randolph, Mattingly, Winfield, and Clark?

Alex Cole
Bats Left

Cleveland Indians	AB	H	2B	3B	HR	RBI	BB	SO	BA	SA	OBA
Season	387	114	17	3	0	21	58	47	.295	.354	.386
vs. Left-Handers	62	24	5	1	0	8	14	7	.387	.500	.500
vs. Right-Handers	325	90	12	2	0	13	44	40	.277	.326	.362
vs. Ground-Ballers	186	56	5	1	0	12	24	24	.301	.339	.382
vs. Fly-Ballers	201	58	12	2	0	9	34	23	.289	.368	.390
Home Games	182	53	9	0	0	14	33	27	.291	.341	.399
Road Games	205	61	8	3	0	7	25	20	.298	.366	.374
Grass Fields	330	93	13	2	0	19	48	43	.282	.333	.373
Artificial Turf	57	21	4	1	0	2	10	4	.368	.474	.463
April	53	17	3	1	0	2	4	7	.321	.415	.368
May	20	6	1	0	0	0	3	0	.300	.350	.391
June	72	20	1	0	0	4	12	9	.278	.292	.384
July	56	14	2	0	0	6	16	6	.250	.286	.417
August	59	16	3	2	0	2	8	12	.271	.390	.358
Sept./Oct.	127	41	7	0	0	7	15	13	.323	.378	.392
Leading Off Inn.	154	48	8	2	0	0	33	23	.312	.390	.433
Runners On	130	34	4	1	0	21	15	12	.262	.308	.338
Bases Empty	257	80	13	2	0	0	43	35	.311	.377	.410
Runners/Scor. Pos.	66	17	0	0	0	20	12	7	.258	.258	.370
Runners On/2 Out	39	10	1	0	0	6	8	2	.256	.282	.383
Scor. Pos./2 Out	26	6	0	0	0	6	7	1	.231	.231	.394
Late-Inning Pressure	66	18	0	0	0	4	7	7	.273	.273	.351
Leading Off	16	6	0	0	0	0	1	3	.375	.375	.412
Runners On	32	7	0	0	0	4	2	3	.219	.219	.286
Runners/Scor. Pos.	21	3	0	0	0	4	2	3	.143	.143	.250

RUNS BATTED IN	From 1B	From 2B	From 3B	Scoring Position
Totals	1/97	4/51	16/26	20/77
Percentage	1.0%	7.8%	61.5%	26.0%

Loves to face: Scott Erickson (.636, 7-for-11)
Roy Smith (.600, 3-for-5)
Todd Stottlemyre (.714, 5-for-7)
Hates to face: Jack McDowell (0-for-8)
Anthony Telford (0-for-7)
Bill Wegman (.077, 1-for-13, 2 BB)

Miscellaneous statistics: Ground outs-to-air outs ratio: 1.45 last season, 1.40 for career.... Grounded into 8 double plays in 79 opportunities (one per 10).... Drove in 12 of 18 runners from third base with less than two outs (67%).... Direction of balls hit to the outfield: 47% to left field, 39% to center, 14% to right.... Base running: Advanced from first base to third on 13 of 23 outfield singles (57%); scored from second on 12 of 18 (67%).... Made 2.76 putouts per nine innings in center field.

Comments: His batting average against left-handed pitchers was the highest of any left-handed batter with at least 50 at-bats vs. southpaws last season.... Only Brett Butler and Rickey Henderson drew more walks leading off an inning last season. Cole's on-base average leading off innings was second highest in the majors last year, and his career average (.422) is second highest among active players, behind Wade Boggs (.425). Indians' on-base average leading off innings was .326 last season, fifth among 14 A.L. teams, but they still wound up scoring the fewest runs in the majors for the first time in the team's 91-year history. In fact, it was only the third time that Cleveland has scored the fewest runs in the American League, although that's now happened twice in the past three years.... He has the most career at-bats of any active player who has never homered (614), followed on both this list and this page by Joey Cora (588); then come Orel Hershiser (487), Zane Smith (394), and Jose DeLeon (387). We'll see if that holds up when the fences are moved in at Cleveland Stadium this season. Cole hit six homers in six years in the minors.... Led A.L. center fielders with seven errors last season.... Career breakdown: 61 steals in 81 attempts on grass fields (74%), only six steals in 11 attempts on artificial turf (55%). That's a reversal from what the league-wide figures show each year; in 1991, as usual, the success rate was higher on carpets (70%) than on dirt (64%).

Joey Cora
Bats Left and Right

Chicago White Sox	AB	H	2B	3B	HR	RBI	BB	SO	BA	SA	OBA
Season	228	55	2	3	0	18	20	21	.241	.276	.313
vs. Left-Handers	57	17	0	0	0	1	5	6	.298	.298	.365
vs. Right-Handers	171	38	2	3	0	17	15	15	.222	.269	.295
vs. Ground-Ballers	110	25	0	1	0	9	12	6	.227	.245	.312
vs. Fly-Ballers	118	30	2	2	0	9	8	15	.254	.305	.313
Home Games	113	36	2	2	0	10	10	6	.319	.372	.394
Road Games	115	19	0	1	0	8	10	15	.165	.183	.233
Grass Fields	192	47	2	3	0	14	20	17	.245	.286	.329
Artificial Turf	36	8	0	0	0	4	0	4	.222	.222	.216
April	5	1	0	0	0	0	0	0	.200	.200	.200
May	22	7	0	0	0	0	2	3	.318	.318	.375
June	51	17	0	2	0	5	4	1	.333	.412	.375
July	61	14	1	1	0	5	4	3	.230	.279	.294
August	64	11	0	0	0	7	5	7	.172	.172	.229
Sept./Oct.	25	5	1	0	0	2	8	4	.200	.240	.394
Leading Off Inn.	60	16	0	1	0	0	7	5	.267	.300	.353
Runners On	86	23	1	1	0	18	7	6	.267	.302	.333
Bases Empty	142	32	1	2	0	0	13	15	.225	.261	.299
Runners/Scor. Pos.	56	11	1	0	0	17	5	4	.196	.214	.262
Runners On/2 Out	41	9	0	0	0	4	2	5	.220	.220	.273
Scor. Pos./2 Out	26	4	0	0	0	4	2	4	.154	.154	.214
Late-Inning Pressure	33	10	0	0	0	1	4	1	.303	.303	.395
Leading Off	11	4	0	0	0	0	1	1	.364	.364	.417
Runners On	13	4	0	0	0	1	2	0	.308	.308	.438
Runners/Scor. Pos.	8	1	0	0	0	1	2	0	.125	.125	.364

RUNS BATTED IN	From 1B	From 2B	From 3B	Scoring Position
Totals	1/59	6/47	11/26	17/73
Percentage	1.7%	12.8%	42.3%	23.3%

Loves to face: Mark Davis (.667, 4-for-6)
Mike Mussina (.500, 2-for-4)
Hates to face: Jim Abbott (0-for-6)
Bob Welch (0-for-12)

Miscellaneous statistics: Ground outs-to-air outs ratio: 1.38 last season, 1.27 for career.... Grounded into 1 double play in 40 opportunities (one per 40).... Drove in 10 of 16 runners from third base with less than two outs (63%).... Direction of balls hit to the outfield: 37% to left field, 28% to center, 35% to right batting left-handed; 12% to left field, 42% to center, 46% to right batting right-handed.... Base running: Advanced from first base to third on 11 of 23 outfield singles (48%); scored from second on 11 of 12 (92%).... Made 2.93 assists per nine innings at second base.

Comments: Split second base job with Scott Fletcher and Craig Grebeck last season. Fletch played 44 percent of innings, Cora 38 percent, Grebeck 18 percent. Only twice in the past six years have the White Sox had one player appear in 100 games at second base (Fred Manrique in 1988 and Fletcher in 1990). But that's new second baseman Steve Sax's forte: He has averaged 157.5 games per year over the past six years.... Cora did lead A.L. in one category last season: his 20 appearances as a pinch runner. The top five, er, six: Cora (20), Jarvis Brown (19), Brady Anderson (18), Juan Bell (17), Kevin Romine (16), Gary Thurman (16).... Had 241 at-bats in his debut season with the Padres (1987), still his major league high.... He has a career average of .270 from the right side of the plate, .236 from the left side, but has only three extra-base hits in 185 career right-handed at-bats.... Only 12 percent of his career hits have been extra-base hits. That's the 4th-lowest percentage among active players with at least 500 at-bats, behind Bob Welch, Felix Fermin, and Rafael Belliard.... How about a home-run hitting contest between the guys on this page against the guys on the previous page? They could hold it at Mile High Stadium, and it would still be off the board in Las Vegas.

Milt Cuyler

Detroit Tigers   Bats Left and Right

	AB	H	2B	3B	HR	RBI	BB	SO	BA	SA	OBA
Season	475	122	15	7	3	33	52	92	.257	.337	.335
vs. Left-Handers	122	33	6	1	0	8	13	19	.270	.336	.345
vs. Right-Handers	353	89	9	6	3	25	39	73	.252	.337	.332
vs. Ground-Ballers	229	53	6	3	1	26	26	44	.231	.297	.317
vs. Fly-Ballers	246	69	9	4	2	7	26	48	.280	.374	.353
Home Games	221	54	6	2	1	15	35	31	.244	.303	.355
Road Games	254	68	9	5	2	18	17	61	.268	.366	.316
Grass Fields	387	95	13	5	2	29	49	76	.245	.320	.335
Artificial Turf	88	27	2	2	1	4	3	16	.307	.409	.337
April	40	9	1	0	0	0	2	6	.225	.250	.262
May	68	18	1	1	1	11	14	11	.265	.353	.386
June	80	18	1	2	2	4	3	13	.225	.363	.271
July	80	19	3	0	0	5	12	17	.237	.275	.333
August	107	24	6	2	0	7	14	25	.224	.318	.325
Sept./Oct.	100	34	3	2	0	6	7	20	.340	.410	.389
Leading Off Inn.	132	36	4	3	1	1	16	22	.273	.371	.351
Runners On	191	39	4	3	1	31	16	45	.204	.272	.274
Bases Empty	284	83	11	4	2	2	36	47	.292	.380	.376
Runners/Scor. Pos.	113	21	3	2	1	30	12	30	.186	.274	.266
Runners On/2 Out	100	17	0	1	1	12	11	24	.170	.220	.259
Scor. Pos./2 Out	63	7	0	0	1	11	9	18	.111	.159	.233
Late-Inning Pressure	62	17	2	0	1	3	6	11	.274	.355	.357
Leading Off	13	4	0	0	0	0	2	1	.308	.308	.400
Runners On	25	3	1	0	0	2	2	7	.120	.160	.241
Runners/Scor. Pos.	11	1	1	0	0	2	2	3	.091	.182	.231

RUNS BATTED IN	From 1B	From 2B	From 3B	Scoring Position
Totals	5/135	9/88	16/49	25/137
Percentage	3.7%	10.2%	32.7%	18.2%

Loves to face: Rich DeLucia (.333, 3-for-9, 1 3B, 1 HR)
         Dave Eiland (.500, 3-for-6, 2 2B, 1 3B)
         Jack Morris (2-for-2, 1 HR, 1 BB)
Hates to face: Joe Grahe (0-for-7)
         Tim Leary (0-for-9)
         Ben McDonald (0-for-5, 4 SO)

Miscellaneous statistics: Ground outs-to-air outs ratio: 1.74 last season, 1.57 for career.... Grounded into 4 double plays in 85 opportunities (one per 21).... Drove in 10 of 22 runners from third base with less than two outs (45%).... Direction of balls hit to the outfield: 27% to left field, 37% to center, 35% to right batting left-handed; 57% to left field, 26% to center, 17% to right batting right-handed.... Base running: Advanced from first base to third on 12 of 26 outfield singles (46%); scored from second on 10 of 15 (67%).... Made 3.02 putouts per nine innings in center field, highest rate in majors.

Comments: Led A.L. rookies with 154 games, two fewer than Jeff Bagwell, who led major league rookies. Only three Detroit rookies over the last 60 years have appeared in more games: Jake Wood (162 in 1961), Harvey Kuenn (155 in 1953), and Dick Wakefield (155 in 1943).... His total of 41 steals ranked second among major league rookies to Ray Lankford (44).... His stolen-base percentage was 6th highest in A.L. (80.4%, 41-for-51), but it wasn't tops among A.L. rookies; Chuck Knoblauch had an 83.3 percentage (25-for-30). Highest stolen-base percentage on record for rookies with at least 20 steals is .923 by Don Baylor (24-for-26) of 1972 Orioles.... Batting average with runners on base was 4th lowest in A.L. and his average with runners in scoring position was 7th lowest. Percentage of runners driven in from scoring position was 3d lowest in A.L. (minimum: 100 opportunities), behind Luis Sojo (12.8%) and teammate Pete Incaviglia (17.3%).... Major league–leading putout rate was helped by Tigers' pitching staff, which had 2d-lowest ground outs-to-air outs rate (1.04) and by far the fewest strikeouts (739; next fewest was 859) among A.L. teams last year. That's not to say that Milt can't go get 'em. His 411 putouts were not the most in team history; Bill Tuttle (442) set that record in 1955. And 411 was not the highest total ever by a rookie; Tom Oliver of the Red Sox (477) set that record in 1930. It wasn't even the most by a Detroit rookie; Barney McCosky had 428 putouts in 1939. But 411 *was* the most ever by a Cuyler; Kiki's best: 405 in 1926.

Alvin Davis

Seattle Mariners   Bats Left

	AB	H	2B	3B	HR	RBI	BB	SO	BA	SA	OBA
Season	462	102	15	1	12	69	56	78	.221	.335	.299
vs. Left-Handers	101	24	2	0	4	14	16	19	.238	.376	.339
vs. Right-Handers	361	78	13	1	8	55	40	59	.216	.324	.288
vs. Ground-Ballers	196	44	6	0	7	36	32	34	.224	.362	.323
vs. Fly-Ballers	266	58	9	1	5	33	24	44	.218	.316	.280
Home Games	226	52	10	0	6	35	29	44	.230	.354	.313
Road Games	236	50	5	1	6	34	27	34	.212	.318	.286
Grass Fields	182	38	3	0	4	21	22	29	.209	.291	.287
Artificial Turf	280	64	12	1	8	48	34	49	.229	.364	.307
April	69	14	0	0	2	9	13	13	.203	.290	.325
May	81	18	3	1	2	14	5	15	.222	.358	.261
June	83	21	3	0	4	13	13	13	.253	.434	.351
July	71	18	2	0	1	13	7	8	.254	.324	.309
August	67	7	0	0	2	8	9	12	.104	.194	.205
Sept./Oct.	91	24	7	0	1	12	9	17	.264	.374	.327
Leading Off Inn.	125	23	4	0	0	0	5	17	.184	.216	.215
Runners On	190	49	7	1	10	67	35	27	.258	.463	.357
Bases Empty	272	53	8	0	2	2	21	51	.195	.246	.253
Runners/Scor. Pos.	108	28	3	1	6	46	29	17	.259	.333	.388
Runners On/2 Out	86	23	4	1	3	26	23	11	.267	.442	.422
Scor. Pos./2 Out	56	17	2	1	1	20	20	7	.304	.429	.487
Late-Inning Pressure	69	14	1	0	4	11	6	16	.203	.391	.263
Leading Off	17	3	0	0	0	0	1	2	.176	.176	.222
Runners On	29	6	0	0	3	10	3	7	.207	.517	.273
Runners/Scor. Pos.	17	3	0	0	0	4	2	5	.176	.176	.250

RUNS BATTED IN	From 1B	From 2B	From 3B	Scoring Position
Totals	15/141	14/86	28/54	42/140
Percentage	10.6%	16.3%	51.9%	30.0%

Loves to face: Jim Acker (.700, 7-for-10, 1 HR)
         Mike Boddicker (.391, 18-for-46, 2 HR)
         Dan Petry (.567, 17-for-30, 2 HR)
Hates to face: Frank Tanana (.152, 7-for-46, 1 HR, 6 BB)
         Kevin Tapani (.091, 2-for-22)
         Bill Wegman (.107, 3-for-28)

Miscellaneous statistics: Ground outs-to-air outs ratio: 0.66 last season, 0.86 for career.... Grounded into 8 double plays in 93 opportunities (one per 12).... Drove in 19 of 28 runners from third base with less than two outs (68%).... Direction of balls hit to the outfield: 27% to left field, 33% to center, 40% to right.... Base running: Advanced from first base to third on 2 of 15 outfield singles (13%); scored from second on 5 of 12 (42%), 4th-lowest rate in A.L.... Made 0.55 assists per nine innings at first base.

Comments: Both his home-run rate (one every 38.5 at-bats) and walk rate (one every 9.4 times up) were the worst of his career, as were his slugging average, on-base average, and batting average, which was 50 points lower than his previous low-water mark (.271 in 1986). Oh, yes, and he struck out more frequently than ever: once every 6.8 trips to the plate. His total of 78 strikeouts was identical to his total as a rookie in 1984, but he had 150 more plate appearances that season than he had last season.... All things considered, Davis's season represented a 13,300-to-1 breakdown, the most extreme by a player this young (30 at season's end) in nearly 90 years—that's right, since the great Ossee Schreckengost Breakdown of 1904. (Breakdowns are defined in the Indians essay.).... On-base percentage leading off innings was lowest in the majors.... Went 1-for-11 with bases loaded after hitting .484 (15-for-31) with bags full over three previous years. He has nine grand-slam home runs; among active players only Eddie Murray (15) and Gary Carter (11) have more.... Started 115 of 120 games in which M's faced a right-handed starter, but only 12 of 42 games vs. lefties. Batting average vs. right-handers was 9th lowest in A.L.... Has hit 101 home runs in the Kingdome (one per 20 AB), 59 on the road (one per 35 AB).... Stole five bases as a rookie (1984), but only two more over the last seven years. Among active players with at least 1000 career games, only Rick Cerone (five) and Terry Kennedy (six) have fewer stolen bases than Davis.

Chili Davis
Bats Left and Right

Minnesota Twins	AB	H	2B	3B	HR	RBI	BB	SO	BA	SA	OBA
Season	534	148	34	1	29	93	95	117	.277	.507	.385
vs. Left-Handers	174	47	9	0	11	32	25	36	.270	.511	.358
vs. Right-Handers	360	101	25	1	18	61	70	81	.281	.506	.397
vs. Ground-Ballers	248	70	14	0	13	43	34	48	.282	.496	.369
vs. Fly-Ballers	286	78	20	1	16	50	61	69	.273	.517	.398
Home Games	267	81	19	1	14	45	54	51	.303	.539	.420
Road Games	267	67	15	0	15	48	41	66	.251	.476	.348
Grass Fields	203	55	14	0	12	42	33	49	.271	.517	.371
Artificial Turf	331	93	20	1	17	51	62	68	.281	.502	.393
April	63	19	2	0	4	11	16	18	.302	.524	.450
May	108	32	10	0	5	17	9	20	.296	.528	.350
June	99	25	4	0	10	23	15	22	.253	.596	.345
July	87	21	5	0	4	18	17	18	.241	.437	.358
August	90	26	8	0	3	13	21	19	.289	.478	.423
Sept./Oct.	87	25	5	1	3	11	17	20	.287	.471	.404
Leading Off Inn.	124	38	8	0	9	9	17	20	.306	.589	.390
Runners On	248	75	22	0	14	78	59	59	.302	.560	.433
Bases Empty	286	73	12	1	15	15	36	58	.255	.462	.339
Runners/Scor. Pos.	152	43	16	0	8	64	39	37	.283	.546	.421
Runners On/2 Out	119	36	14	0	8	36	29	30	.303	.622	.439
Scor. Pos./2 Out	79	21	11	0	4	27	21	18	.266	.557	.420
Late-Inning Pressure	67	22	7	0	3	13	13	12	.328	.567	.439
Leading Off	21	9	3	0	1	1	5	2	.429	.714	.538
Runners On	29	11	4	0	2	12	6	6	.379	.724	.486
Runners/Scor. Pos.	17	7	3	0	1	10	5	4	.412	.765	.522

RUNS BATTED IN	From 1B	From 2B	From 3B	Scoring Position
Totals	13/179	24/105	27/67	51/172
Percentage	7.3%	22.9%	40.3%	29.7%

Loves to face: Rick Honeycutt (.423, 11-for-26, 4 HR, 0 SO)
Mark Knudson (.563, 9-for-16, 1 HR)
David Wells (.435, 10-for-23, 3 HR)

Hates to face: Erik Hanson (.100, 2-for-20, 2 BB)
Ted Higuera (.133, 2-for-15)
Nolan Ryan (.169, 12-for-71, 1 HR)

Miscellaneous statistics: Ground outs-to-air outs ratio: 1.10 last season, 1.21 for career.... Grounded into 9 double plays in 123 opportunities (one per 14).... Drove in 18 of 28 runners from third base with less than two outs (64%).... Direction of balls hit to the outfield: 39% to left field, 25% to center, 35% to right batting left-handed; 29% to left field, 32% to center, 39% to right batting right-handed.... Base running: Advanced from first base to third on 12 of 34 outfield singles (35%); scored from second on 4 of 12 (33%), 2d-lowest rate in A.L.

Comments: Of the 11 switch-hitters active in 1991 with at least 5000 plate appearances in the majors, Davis has the widest gap between his batting averages from respective sides of the plate: .275 from left side, .253 from right side. (Obviously, Wally Backman hasn't been up 5000 times yet!)... Davis averaged one walk every 6.7 plate appearances and one home run every 18.4 at-bats, each a career best.... Prior to 1991, Chili had averaged one homer for every 30.3 major league at-bats; to turn numbers into images, that's the equivalent of going from Bill Freehan's home-run rate to Ernie Banks's.... Batting average in Late-Inning Pressure Situations, also a career high, ranked fifth in A.L.... Had the most home runs in 1991 of any of the previous winter's free agents; runners-up: Jack Clark (28), Darryl Strawberry (28), George Bell (25), Rob Deer (25).... His 29 home runs also let him regain the lead in career home runs among active Davises: Chili 185, Eric 177, Glenn 176, Alvin 160. What kind of odds could you have gotten a year ago that Chili would hit more home runs than Eric and Glenn combined?... Collectively, Davises hit 62 homers in 1991 as they continued their pursuit of the all-time "Family Tree" home-run leaders, the Williamses, who hit 38 last year. All-time Family Tree home-run standings: Williams 1918, Davis 1583, Johnson 1533, Robinson 1520, Smith 1221, Jackson 1098, Thomas 879, Evans 850, Jones 839, Bell 795, Aaron 768, White 722, Ruth 714.

Rob Deer
Bats Right

Detroit Tigers	AB	H	2B	3B	HR	RBI	BB	SO	BA	SA	OBA
Season	448	80	14	2	25	64	89	175	.179	.386	.314
vs. Left-Handers	138	27	6	1	9	18	27	46	.196	.449	.327
vs. Right-Handers	310	53	8	1	16	46	62	129	.171	.358	.307
vs. Ground-Ballers	214	43	5	1	13	38	42	70	.201	.444	.329
vs. Fly-Ballers	234	37	9	1	12	26	47	105	.158	.359	.299
Home Games	218	42	5	2	12	31	46	87	.193	.399	.332
Road Games	230	38	9	0	13	33	43	88	.165	.374	.296
Grass Fields	367	67	12	2	20	51	72	140	.183	.390	.316
Artificial Turf	81	13	2	0	5	13	17	35	.160	.370	.303
April	66	13	3	1	5	17	14	29	.197	.500	.338
May	85	15	1	0	7	14	22	32	.176	.435	.346
June	93	18	3	0	3	10	10	35	.194	.323	.269
July	83	15	3	0	6	10	11	29	.181	.434	.277
August	72	8	1	1	2	6	23	32	.111	.236	.323
Sept./Oct.	49	11	3	0	2	7	9	18	.224	.408	.345
Leading Off Inn.	106	13	4	0	3	3	19	40	.123	.245	.256
Runners On	199	39	4	2	14	53	39	77	.196	.447	.325
Bases Empty	249	41	10	0	11	11	50	98	.165	.337	.304
Runners/Scor. Pos.	101	17	2	0	6	35	43	46	.168	.366	.328
Runners On/2 Out	74	12	0	1	6	19	18	28	.162	.432	.326
Scor. Pos./2 Out	46	6	0	0	3	12	12	20	.130	.326	.310
Late-Inning Pressure	69	12	2	0	4	9	11	27	.174	.377	.287
Leading Off	22	2	1	0	1	1	6	10	.091	.273	.286
Runners On	24	6	0	0	2	7	2	8	.250	.500	.308
Runners/Scor. Pos.	13	2	0	0	0	3	1	5	.154	.154	.214

RUNS BATTED IN	From 1B	From 2B	From 3B	Scoring Position
Totals	14/156	10/85	15/44	25/129
Percentage	9.0%	11.8%	34.1%	19.4%

Loves to face: Lee Guetterman (.429, 3-for-7, 1 2B, 2 HR, 4 BB)
Charlie Hough (.429, 6-for-14, 2 HR)
Mike Moore (.371, 13-for-35, 4 HR)

Hates to face: Erik Hanson (0-for-16, 9 SO)
Randy Johnson (.105, 2-for-19, 10 SO)
Nolan Ryan (0-for-14, 10 SO)

Miscellaneous statistics: Ground outs-to-air outs ratio: 0.53 last season, lowest in A.L.; 0.58 for career.... Grounded into 3 double plays in 117 opportunities (one per 39).... Drove in 10 of 22 runners from third base with less than two outs (45%).... Direction of balls hit to the outfield: 56% to left field, 28% to center, 16% to right.... Base running: Advanced from first base to third on 5 of 21 outfield singles (24%); scored from second on 6 of 9 (67%).... Made 2.43 putouts per nine innings in right field, 2d-highest rate in A.L.

Comments: Yearly batting averages since 1989: .210, .209, .179. He became the second player in major league history who didn't reach even the .211 mark in any of three consecutive years of 400 or more at-bats; the other guy, Jim Donnelly, hit .201, .200, .201 from '86 to '88; that's 1886 to 1888, when Grover Cleveland was in his first term.... How about the last guy to bat below .180 in a single 400 at-bat season? You don't have to go back quite so far—just to Benjamin Harrison's administration, when Ben Conroy hit .171 in the old American Association in 1890. The last sub-.200 batting average in a 400 at-bat season: Dick Schofield (.193) in 1984.... Only three other players in major league history hit even 10 home runs in a sub-.180 season: Deron Johnson (.171, 13 HR in 1974), Pat Seerey (.171, 11 HR in 1947), Gorman Thomas (.179, 10 HR in 1975).... Career ratio of ground outs to air outs is 2d lowest of any player since 1975; Howard Johnson has a lower ratio.... He has driven in only 43 percent of runners from third base with less than two outs, lowest career rate of any player since 1975 (minimum: 150 opportunities).... Deer led A.L. with 179 strikeouts, followed by Jose Canseco (152) and then teammates Cecil Fielder (151) and Travis Fryman (149). Tigers just missed a Gold, Silver, and Bronze sweep of the event, but how about 1927, the only time that three teammates finished one-two-three in the majors in striking out? All three wound up in the Hall of Fame: Babe Ruth (89), Lou Gehrig (84), Tony Lazzeri (82). Ruth's total would have ranked *eighth* on Air Detroit.

Mike Devereaux

Bats Right

Baltimore Orioles	AB	H	2B	3B	HR	RBI	BB	SO	BA	SA	OBA
Season	608	158	27	10	19	59	47	115	.260	.431	.313
vs. Left-Handers	167	49	7	6	6	16	14	30	.293	.515	.350
vs. Right-Handers	441	109	20	4	13	43	33	85	.247	.399	.299
vs. Ground-Ballers	251	64	12	4	8	24	23	51	.255	.430	.314
vs. Fly-Ballers	357	94	15	6	11	35	24	64	.263	.431	.313
Home Games	305	77	13	4	10	35	22	58	.252	.420	.302
Road Games	303	81	14	6	9	24	25	57	.267	.442	.324
Grass Fields	505	127	21	9	17	53	41	97	.251	.430	.307
Artificial Turf	103	31	6	1	2	6	6	18	.301	.437	.345
April	53	11	4	1	2	2	6	7	.208	.434	.300
May	92	32	7	0	4	10	9	22	.348	.554	.402
June	123	25	4	3	3	11	10	18	.203	.358	.261
July	102	31	3	1	3	10	10	15	.304	.441	.363
August	122	29	6	3	3	12	5	26	.238	.410	.271
Sept./Oct.	116	30	3	2	4	14	7	27	.259	.422	.301
Leading Off Inn.	229	61	12	3	7	7	17	46	.266	.437	.320
Runners On	194	48	9	3	6	46	16	30	.247	.418	.302
Bases Empty	414	110	18	7	13	13	31	85	.266	.437	.318
Runners/Scor. Pos.	101	26	5	3	3	39	10	18	.257	.455	.319
Runners On/2 Out	90	22	4	1	1	17	8	12	.244	.344	.306
Scor. Pos./2 Out	51	12	2	1	1	16	5	8	.235	.373	.304
Late-Inning Pressure	96	25	3	0	3	9	3	19	.260	.385	.283
Leading Off	23	5	1	0	0	0	0	3	.217	.261	.217
Runners On	34	10	0	0	2	8	1	5	.294	.471	.314
Runners/Scor. Pos.	17	5	0	0	2	8	1	4	.294	.647	.333

RUNS BATTED IN	From 1B	From 2B	From 3B	Scoring Position
Totals	7/143	16/79	17/43	33/122
Percentage	4.9%	20.3%	39.5%	27.0%

Loves to face: Jim Abbott (.462, 6-for-13, 1 HR)
Bill Krueger (.583, 7-for-12, 1 HR)
Kirk McCaskill (.467, 7-for-15, 2 HR)
Hates to face: Chuck Finley (.080, 2-for-25)
Jack Morris (.067, 1-for-15)
Frank Wills (0-for-10)

Miscellaneous statistics: Ground outs-to-air outs ratio: 1.04 last season, 1.02 for career.... Grounded into 13 double plays in 94 opportunities (one per 7.2).... Drove in 11 of 18 runners from third base with less than two outs (61%).... Direction of balls hit to the outfield: 36% to left field, 39% to center, 25% to right.... Base running: Advanced from first base to third on 9 of 23 outfield singles (39%); scored from second on 12 of 17 (71%).... Made 2.85 putouts per nine innings in center field.

Comments: Nineteen home runs ranked fourth among major league center fielders, behind Ron Gant, Dave Henderson, and Junior Griffey. Time was when you could find three 30-home-run guys playing center field in New York; last year there were only three center fielders with 20 home runs in the majors.... Started in the leadoff spot exclusively until early September, when he spent a few games in the two-hole. Hit 16 of his homers from the top spot in the order, 4th most among major league leadoff hitters, behind Rickey Henderson (18), Paul Molitor (17), and Devon White (17).... Started 41 of 42 games in which Birds faced a left-handed starter, but only 97 of 120 games vs. right-handers. He owns a career mark of .259 vs. southpaws, .245 vs. right-handers.... Completed 134 of his 138 starts last season, a rate of 97.1 percent. Yes, sports fans, complete-game percentages for everyday players are here! Who do you think led the Orioles in that department? No, not ironman Cal Ripken, who completed only 146 of 162 starts, but Devereaux.... Has hit for a higher average in road games than he has at home in each of his three seasons with the Orioles.... In Orioles' 38 years at Memorial Stadium, Devereaux was only fifth player to reach double figures in triples in a season. The others were Luis Aparicio (10 in 1965), Paul Blair (12 in 1967), Al Bumbry (11 in 1973), and Phil Bradley (10 in 1989). All together now for one last time: It's easier to hit a triple at Pimlico than at Memorial Stadium.

Brian Downing

Bats Right

Texas Rangers	AB	H	2B	3B	HR	RBI	BB	SO	BA	SA	OBA
Season	407	113	17	2	17	49	58	70	.278	.455	.377
vs. Left-Handers	139	39	5	0	9	17	25	24	.281	.511	.401
vs. Right-Handers	268	74	12	2	8	32	33	46	.276	.425	.364
vs. Ground-Ballers	179	56	10	0	7	25	23	26	.313	.486	.393
vs. Fly-Ballers	228	57	7	2	10	24	35	44	.250	.430	.364
Home Games	204	52	8	2	8	23	32	39	.255	.431	.365
Road Games	203	61	9	0	9	26	26	31	.300	.478	.389
Grass Fields	348	93	15	2	13	41	50	64	.267	.434	.369
Artificial Turf	59	20	2	0	4	8	8	6	.339	.576	.426
April	40	14	3	0	1	5	9	6	.350	.500	.500
May	82	29	2	1	5	11	11	12	.354	.585	.430
June	67	8	2	0	1	7	9	16	.119	.194	.241
July	80	25	2	0	4	10	10	14	.313	.488	.389
August	51	15	3	0	3	8	5	9	.294	.529	.362
Sept./Oct.	87	22	5	1	3	8	14	13	.253	.437	.369
Leading Off Inn.	156	46	9	0	10	10	16	23	.295	.545	.375
Runners On	148	43	5	1	4	36	33	27	.291	.419	.425
Bases Empty	259	70	12	1	13	13	25	43	.270	.475	.346
Runners/Scor. Pos.	89	23	2	1	3	33	24	17	.258	.404	.414
Runners On/2 Out	65	20	2	1	1	17	13	10	.308	.415	.430
Scor. Pos./2 Out	45	13	1	1	1	16	11	4	.289	.422	.429
Late-Inning Pressure	68	20	2	0	2	13	7	10	.294	.412	.364
Leading Off	19	3	1	0	1	1	0	1	.158	.368	.158
Runners On	39	16	1	0	0	11	5	6	.410	.436	.467
Runners/Scor. Pos.	21	10	1	0	0	11	3	3	.476	.524	.520

RUNS BATTED IN	From 1B	From 2B	From 3B	Scoring Position
Totals	5/99	14/72	13/37	27/109
Percentage	5.1%	19.4%	35.1%	24.8%

Loves to face: Jose Bautista (.429, 6-for-14, 2 HR)
Mike Jeffcoat (.474, 9-for-19, 1 HR)
Bill Krueger (.385, 10-for-26, 4 HR)
Hates to face: Mark Knudson (0-for-12)
Mike Moore (.125, 6-for-48, 1 HR)
Melido Perez (.077, 1-for-13, 1 2B, 2 BB)

Miscellaneous statistics: Ground outs-to-air outs ratio: 0.93 last season, 1.08 for career.... Grounded into 7 double plays in 70 opportunities (one per 10).... Drove in 6 of 17 runners from third base with less than two outs (35%), 4th-lowest rate in A.L.... Direction of balls hit to the outfield: 50% to left field, 25% to center, 25% to right.... Base running: Advanced from first base to third on 15 of 31 outfield singles (48%); scored from second on 15 of 19 (79%).

Comments: He was the last of seven players to join the 2000-Hit Club last season, the largest group of inductees into that club in any season in history.... Started 41 of 43 games in which Rangers faced a left-handed starter, but only 57 of 119 vs. right-handers.... April batting average was 3d highest in the A.L., and his average during May ranked seventh, but he had the lowest average in the majors during June.... On-base percentage leading off innings was 9th highest in the league.... Started 89 games in the leadoff spot in the order, the most of any Rangers player last season. Texas had a .240 team batting average from its top-spot hitters, lowest in the league, but 23 homers from that spot led the majors.... Has been hit by a pitch 121 times in 19 seasons, second among active players to Carlton Fisk (141).... He has played 496 games since last appearing in the field in the final game of the 1987 season. Hal McRae ended his playing career with 658 consecutive games without playing the field.... His career total of 2237 games ranks seventh among active players. Each of the top seven players in that category has played a significant number of games as a designated hitter. Gary Carter ranks eighth among active players, but has the most games of any active player who has never DHed.... Among players who made their major league debuts after the World Series came into existence in 1903, only nine have played more regular-season games than Downing without ever appearing in a World Series.

Jim Eisenreich
Bats Left

Kansas City Royals	AB	H	2B	3B	HR	RBI	BB	SO	BA	SA	OBA
Season	375	113	22	3	2	47	20	35	.301	.392	.333
vs. Left-Handers	87	28	2	1	1	16	4	12	.322	.402	.351
vs. Right-Handers	288	85	20	2	1	31	16	23	.295	.389	.328
vs. Ground-Ballers	201	61	10	1	1	27	9	12	.303	.378	.330
vs. Fly-Ballers	174	52	12	2	1	20	11	23	.299	.408	.337
Home Games	193	60	9	2	2	25	9	14	.311	.409	.337
Road Games	182	53	13	1	0	22	11	21	.291	.374	.330
Grass Fields	145	44	12	0	0	16	7	18	.303	.386	.333
Artificial Turf	230	69	10	3	2	31	13	17	.300	.396	.333
April	69	22	7	1	0	7	0	9	.319	.449	.314
May	78	22	2	0	1	8	7	8	.282	.346	.349
June	64	20	5	0	0	5	3	5	.313	.391	.343
July	52	14	1	0	0	7	4	3	.269	.288	.316
August	41	14	3	1	0	6	2	3	.341	.463	.364
Sept./Oct.	71	21	4	1	1	14	4	7	.296	.423	.321
Leading Off Inn.	86	33	11	1	1	1	4	10	.384	.570	.411
Runners On	171	52	7	2	1	46	12	14	.304	.386	.339
Bases Empty	204	61	15	1	1	1	8	21	.299	.397	.329
Runners/Scor. Pos.	102	33	3	2	1	44	8	8	.324	.422	.353
Runners On/2 Out	73	24	2	0	0	11	6	9	.329	.356	.380
Scor. Pos./2 Out	47	12	0	0	0	10	4	7	.255	.255	.314
Late-Inning Pressure	69	19	5	2	1	5	3	13	.275	.449	.301
Leading Off	19	8	3	1	1	1	0	5	.421	.842	.421
Runners On	29	6	2	1	0	4	3	5	.207	.345	.273
Runners/Scor. Pos.	15	2	1	1	0	4	3	4	.133	.333	.263

RUNS BATTED IN	From 1B	From 2B	From 3B	Scoring Position
Totals	5/128	14/70	26/57	40/127
Percentage	3.9%	20.0%	45.6%	31.5%

Loves to face: Rick Aguilera (.556, 5-for-9)
Lee Guetterman (.545, 6-for-11)
Dave Stewart (.400, 10-for-25, 2 HR, 0 SO)

Hates to face: Chris Bosio (.105, 2-for-19)
Andy Hawkins (.071, 1-for-14)
Nolan Ryan (.118, 2-for-17, 2 BB)

Miscellaneous statistics: Ground outs-to-air outs ratio: 1.26 last season, 1.19 for career.... Grounded into 10 double plays in 84 opportunities (one per 8.4).... Drove in 19 of 28 runners from third base with less than two outs (68%).... Direction of balls hit to the outfield: 42% to left field, 35% to center, 23% to right.... Base running: Advanced from first base to third on 10 of 24 outfield singles (42%); scored from second on 11 of 12 (92%).... Made 1.79 putouts per nine innings in left field.

Comments: One of five left-handed batters to hit .300 or better vs. left-handed pitchers last season (minimum: 75 AB); among them, only Mike Greenwell had a higher average (.327). Career mark of .290 vs. lefties ranks seventh among active left-handed batters (minimum: 400 at-bats vs. LHP). You could probably guess the six guys ahead of him: Tony Gwynn, Wade Boggs, Don Mattingly, Greenwell, Will Clark, and Rafael Palmeiro. Eisenreich has only a .275 career average vs. right-handers, but with an increase in power: one extra-base hit every 11 at-bats vs. right-handers, one every 17 at-bats vs. southpaws.... Although his batting average increased 21 points from 1990 to 1991, he took a dip in both his slugging percentage and his on-base percentage.... His 223 innings in right field were the most among all major league right fielders who failed to get a single assist there last season.... He has hit for a higher average in day games than he has at night in each of his last six seasons. His .322 career average in day games stands eighth among active players; he has hit .261 after dark.... Delivered only three of 22 teammates from scoring position in Late-Inning Pressure Situations.... Has a .290 batting average over past three seasons, actually a hair higher than George Brett's average over the corresponding period. That same hair (or maybe one just like it) separates the leaders over the past three years: Tony Gwynn .3210, Wade Boggs .3208.

Alvaro Espinoza
Bats Right

New York Yankees	AB	H	2B	3B	HR	RBI	BB	SO	BA	SA	OBA
Season	480	123	23	2	5	33	16	57	.256	.344	.282
vs. Left-Handers	161	42	10	0	1	15	7	11	.261	.342	.294
vs. Right-Handers	319	81	13	2	4	18	9	46	.254	.345	.276
vs. Ground-Ballers	220	51	8	1	2	16	9	24	.232	.305	.265
vs. Fly-Ballers	260	72	15	1	3	17	7	33	.277	.377	.296
Home Games	254	63	12	1	2	14	8	30	.248	.327	.273
Road Games	226	60	11	1	3	19	8	27	.265	.363	.292
Grass Fields	403	104	20	1	4	26	15	49	.258	.342	.285
Artificial Turf	77	19	3	1	1	7	1	8	.247	.351	.266
April	49	18	6	1	0	7	3	3	.367	.531	.404
May	83	16	5	0	0	2	3	10	.193	.253	.221
June	82	22	2	0	2	6	4	11	.268	.366	.302
July	66	18	2	1	1	4	4	6	.273	.379	.314
August	88	23	3	0	2	8	0	9	.261	.364	.275
Sept./Oct.	112	26	5	0	0	6	2	18	.232	.277	.243
Leading Off Inn.	112	28	5	0	2	2	2	9	.250	.348	.263
Runners On	186	51	11	0	1	29	7	22	.274	.349	.301
Bases Empty	294	72	12	2	4	4	9	35	.245	.340	.270
Runners/Scor. Pos.	100	25	6	0	1	27	4	12	.250	.340	.280
Runners On/2 Out	83	18	6	0	0	10	4	11	.217	.289	.261
Scor. Pos./2 Out	53	9	4	0	0	9	3	8	.170	.245	.228
Late-Inning Pressure	69	15	3	0	0	3	4	8	.217	.261	.260
Leading Off	22	5	0	0	0	0	1	1	.227	.227	.261
Runners On	22	6	2	0	0	3	1	4	.273	.364	.304
Runners/Scor. Pos.	12	3	2	0	0	3	0	2	.250	.417	.250

RUNS BATTED IN	From 1B	From 2B	From 3B	Scoring Position
Totals	4/144	10/78	14/41	24/119
Percentage	2.8%	12.8%	34.1%	20.2%

Loves to face: Ted Higuera (.550, 11-for-20)
Dave Stewart (.400, 8-for-20, 1 HR)
Frank Tanana (.480, 12-for-25)

Hates to face: Kevin Brown (.150, 3-for-20)
Shawn Hillegas (.083, 1-for-12)
Todd Stottlemyre (.179, 5-for-28, 0 BB)

Miscellaneous statistics: Ground outs-to-air outs ratio: 1.33 last season, 1.48 for career.... Grounded into 10 double plays in 97 opportunities (one per 10).... Drove in 11 of 22 runners from third base with less than two outs (50%).... Direction of balls hit to the outfield: 40% to left field, 28% to center, 33% to right.... Base running: Advanced from first base to third on 10 of 23 outfield singles (43%); scored from second on 10 of 15 (67%).... Made 3.29 assists per nine innings at shortstop.

Comments: The first Yankees player to get into 145 games at shortstop in three straight seasons since Frank Crosetti had a five-year streak from 1936–40. That's right: Scooter never did it, and neither did Stick, Bucky, or Tony Kubek. Espy moved into 10th place in Yankees history in games at short (444); the three who have played in 1000 or more: Rizzuto (1647), Crosetti (1515), and Roger Peckinpaugh (1215).... Had the highest double play rate (DPs compared to innings) among major league shortstops last season (one every 10.6 innings).... His career rate of one walk every 34.1 plate appearances is the lowest among active players (minimum: 1000 PA).... The Yankees had a total of only 75 RBIs from the entire left side of the infield, the fewest by any team in the majors last season; 14 clubs had more than that from either their shortstops or third basemen alone.... George Harrison had Maharishi Mahesh Yogi, Espinoza has Frank Howard. Alvaro has a career batting average of .271 with Howard as his batting coach, .232 without him. Howard returned to the Yankees last season, after serving four months in that position under Dallas Green in 1989.... Here's one that will win you a bar bet: Who has the highest career batting average vs. left-handed pitchers among Espinoza, Wade Boggs, and Don Mattingly? Espinoza has a career mark of .308 against southpaws, five points higher than Mattingly (.303), four points higher than Boggs (.304). Warning to bartenders: Keep your *Elias Analyst* handy at all times.

Dwight Evans

Bats Right

Baltimore Orioles	AB	H	2B	3B	HR	RBI	BB	SO	BA	SA	OBA
Season	270	73	9	1	6	38	54	54	.270	.378	.393
vs. Left-Handers	107	33	3	0	1	10	32	15	.308	.364	.468
vs. Right-Handers	163	40	6	1	5	28	22	39	.245	.387	.339
vs. Ground-Ballers	110	29	3	1	1	18	23	24	.264	.336	.390
vs. Fly-Ballers	160	44	6	0	5	20	31	30	.275	.406	.396
Home Games	135	35	3	0	4	20	24	25	.259	.370	.373
Road Games	135	38	6	1	2	18	30	29	.281	.385	.413
Grass Fields	239	62	6	1	4	34	46	48	.259	.343	.381
Artificial Turf	31	11	3	0	2	4	8	6	.355	.645	.487
April	50	15	2	0	1	8	8	14	.300	.400	.390
May	60	14	1	0	1	9	17	16	.233	.300	.397
June	29	9	2	1	1	6	3	0	.310	.552	.375
July	30	8	1	0	1	5	9	8	.267	.400	.450
August	37	10	1	0	1	4	5	7	.270	.378	.357
Sept./Oct.	64	17	2	0	1	6	12	9	.266	.344	.390
Leading Off Inn.	68	12	1	0	1	1	13	12	.176	.235	.309
Runners On	119	38	5	1	3	35	29	23	.319	.454	.450
Bases Empty	151	35	4	0	3	3	25	31	.232	.318	.345
Runners/Scor. Pos.	65	23	3	0	3	32	22	10	.354	.538	.511
Runners On/2 Out	58	18	3	0	2	23	16	11	.310	.466	.459
Scor. Pos./2 Out	38	12	2	0	2	12	13	5	.316	.526	.490
Late-Inning Pressure	59	14	1	0	2	6	10	10	.237	.356	.348
Leading Off	16	2	0	0	0	0	5	4	.125	.125	.333
Runners On	23	5	0	0	1	5	5	5	.217	.348	.357
Runners/Scor. Pos.	12	3	0	0	1	5	4	1	.250	.500	.438

RUNS BATTED IN	From 1B	From 2B	From 3B	Scoring Position
Totals	6/93	11/56	15/28	26/84
Percentage	6.5%	19.6%	53.6%	31.0%

Loves to face: Dennis Eckersley (.269, 7-for-26, 1 2B, 4 HR, 6 BB)
Erik Hanson (.435, 10-for-23, 2 HR, 7 SO)
David Wells (.500, 10-for-20, 2 HR)
Hates to face: Jim Abbott (.091, 2-for-22, 5 BB)
Tom Henke (0-for-9)
Bill Wegman (.067, 1-for-15, 2 BB)

Miscellaneous statistics: Ground outs-to-air outs ratio: 1.04 last season, 1.05 for career.... Grounded into 7 double plays in 59 opportunities (one per 8.4).... Drove in 5 of 7 runners from third base with less than two outs (71%).... Direction of balls hit to the outfield: 33% to left field, 34% to center, 33% to right.... Base running: Advanced from first base to third on 5 of 19 outfield singles (26%); scored from second on 10 of 11 (91%).... Made 1.99 putouts per nine innings in right field.

Comments: He has a career total of 385 home runs, but has never hit more than two in a game. Graig Nettles's career total of 390 homers is the highest among players who never had a three- or four-homer game. His 1991 rate of one homer every 45 at-bats was his worst home-run rate in any season since 1974.... Last season, Evans moved past Luis Aparicio into 8th place on the all-time list of games played in the American League. Evans would need to play 184 more games to move up another notch on that list, ahead of Tris Speaker. In fact, Evans may slip a spot before long: Although he leads active players with 2606 games, Robin Yount starts 1992 only 27 behind him.... Evans leads active players with 1391 walks, 185 more than runner-up Jack Clark, and 20th on the all-time list.... He walked with the bases full four times last season; that's nothing new for him. Since 1985, he has driven in 23 runs by way of the base on balls, the most in the majors over those seven years. Only two others have more than a dozen: Jack Clark (18) and Mickey Tettleton (17).... Needs four at-bats to become the 47th player in major league history to reach 9000 for his career. He passed Darrell Evans in career at-bats last September, but still trails Darrell by 214 walks and 29 homers.... From the Elias time capsule: Evans made his major league debut pinch-hitting for Luis Tiant, he got his first hit pinch-hitting for Gary Peters, and his first home run came off Eddie Watt. All of that happened in September 1972, the month of the Munich Olympics.

Felix Fermin

Bats Right

Cleveland Indians	AB	H	2B	3B	HR	RBI	BB	SO	BA	SA	OBA
Season	424	111	13	2	0	31	26	27	.262	.302	.307
vs. Left-Handers	121	34	4	0	0	8	10	6	.281	.314	.341
vs. Right-Handers	303	77	9	2	0	23	16	21	.254	.297	.293
vs. Ground-Ballers	197	47	6	1	0	11	10	8	.239	.279	.278
vs. Fly-Ballers	227	64	7	1	0	20	16	19	.282	.322	.332
Home Games	210	61	8	2	0	20	16	11	.290	.348	.339
Road Games	214	50	5	0	0	11	10	16	.234	.257	.274
Grass Fields	363	96	11	2	0	29	24	22	.264	.306	.313
Artificial Turf	61	15	2	0	0	2	2	5	.246	.279	.270
April	32	4	0	0	0	0	2	3	.125	.125	.176
May	64	18	3	1	0	7	2	2	.281	.359	.319
June	96	25	3	0	0	4	5	5	.260	.292	.297
July	84	24	3	1	0	7	7	5	.286	.345	.341
August	89	23	2	0	0	10	6	8	.258	.281	.306
Sept./Oct.	59	17	2	0	0	3	4	4	.288	.322	.333
Leading Off Inn.	98	25	1	0	0	0	5	5	.255	.265	.291
Runners On	185	51	5	2	0	31	15	11	.276	.324	.332
Bases Empty	239	60	8	0	0	0	11	16	.251	.285	.287
Runners/Scor. Pos.	97	27	2	2	0	29	9	6	.278	.340	.342
Runners On/2 Out	81	22	3	2	0	14	10	5	.272	.358	.352
Scor. Pos./2 Out	48	12	1	2	0	12	5	3	.250	.354	.321
Late-Inning Pressure	75	16	2	0	0	3	4	4	.213	.240	.253
Leading Off	17	4	0	0	0	0	0	0	.235	.235	.235
Runners On	39	8	0	0	0	3	4	3	.205	.205	.279
Runners/Scor. Pos.	17	2	0	0	0	3	2	2	.118	.118	.211

RUNS BATTED IN	From 1B	From 2B	From 3B	Scoring Position
Totals	3/135	15/80	13/32	28/112
Percentage	2.2%	18.8%	40.6%	25.0%

Loves to face: Mark Guthrie (.900, 9-for-10, 1 SO)
Terry Leach (.600, 6-for-10)
Bobby Witt (.533, 8-for-15)
Hates to face: Greg Hibbard (.056, 1-for-18, 2 BB)
Jaime Navarro (.071, 1-for-14)
Walt Terrell (.077, 1-for-13)

Miscellaneous statistics: Ground outs-to-air outs ratio: 2.07 last season, 4th highest in A.L.; 2.34 for career.... Grounded into 17 double plays in 95 opportunities (one per 5.6).... Drove in 10 of 17 runners from third base with less than two outs (59%).... Direction of balls hit to the outfield: 20% to left field, 37% to center, 43% to right.... Base running: Advanced from first base to third on 7 of 25 outfield singles (28%); scored from second on 5 of 12 (42%), 4th-lowest rate in A.L.... Made 3.06 assists per nine innings at shortstop.

Comments: The first player since Ozzie Smith, five years ago, to string together three straight seasons of fewer than 30 strikeouts with at least 400 at-bats. Felix's career average of one strikeout every 17.5 times to the plate is 4th best among active players, behind Tony Gwynn (20.8), Don Mattingly (18.3), and Ozzie (17.8). His strikeout rate against left-handed pitchers (one every 22.3 trips) is the best among active players.... His career ratio of ground outs to air outs is 4th highest over the last 17 years, behind Milt Thompson, Wally Backman, and Willie McGee.... The only home run of his career was hit in April 1990 off Don Pall. His current streak of 822 homerless at-bats ranks third among active players behind Rafael Belliard and Al Newman.... Of course, home runs are not a critical component for shortstops. There were fewer home runs hit from that position (211) than from any other (pitcher excluded, of course, where the total was 12); second basemen hit 234 and catchers 307.... Career breakdown of situational hitting: .257 with the bases empty, .247 with runners on base, .227 with runners in scoring position, and .186 with two outs and RISP. The good news is that he has improved his scoring-position batting average in each season since he debuted with the Pirates in 1987: .125, .167, .183, .252, .278.... Career fielding rate of one error every 37.6 chances at shortstop is 2d best in Indians franchise history, behind Frank Duffy (one error 47.3 chances).

Cecil Fielder

Bats Right

Detroit Tigers	AB	H	2B	3B	HR	RBI	BB	SO	BA	SA	OBA
Season	624	163	25	0	44	133	78	151	.261	.513	.347
vs. Left-Handers	159	47	9	0	13	31	25	29	.296	.597	.399
vs. Right-Handers	465	116	16	0	31	102	53	122	.249	.484	.328
vs. Ground-Ballers	309	88	12	0	18	52	35	72	.285	.498	.363
vs. Fly-Ballers	315	75	13	0	26	81	43	79	.238	.527	.332
Home Games	305	78	12	0	27	75	41	72	.256	.561	.348
Road Games	319	85	13	0	17	58	37	79	.266	.467	.345
Grass Fields	524	136	20	0	37	111	72	127	.260	.510	.352
Artificial Turf	100	27	5	0	7	22	6	24	.270	.530	.318
April	72	21	3	0	3	18	6	18	.292	.458	.370
May	101	24	4	0	7	18	18	27	.238	.485	.350
June	106	31	6	0	8	24	15	26	.292	.575	.385
July	105	28	3	0	11	25	6	21	.267	.610	.313
August	121	27	8	0	7	26	13	31	.223	.463	.299
Sept./Oct.	119	32	1	0	8	22	20	28	.269	.479	.371
Leading Off Inn.	160	34	3	0	10	10	14	41	.213	.419	.280
Runners On	298	86	15	0	26	115	48	67	.289	.601	.392
Bases Empty	326	77	10	0	18	18	30	84	.236	.433	.303
Runners/Scor. Pos.	175	50	9	0	13	88	34	45	.286	.560	.400
Runners On/2 Out	136	30	3	0	9	40	22	37	.221	.441	.346
Scor. Pos./2 Out	76	17	2	0	4	29	16	25	.224	.408	.366
Late-Inning Pressure	86	20	3	0	3	16	12	20	.233	.372	.327
Leading Off	28	2	0	0	0	0	2	8	.071	.071	.133
Runners On	34	10	3	0	2	15	7	8	.294	.559	.415
Runners/Scor. Pos.	19	7	3	0	1	13	6	4	.368	.684	.520

RUNS BATTED IN	From 1B	From 2B	From 3B	Scoring Position
Totals	25/213	31/134	33/70	64/204
Percentage	11.7%	23.1%	47.1%	31.4%

Loves to face: Jimmy Key (.364, 8-for-22, 1 2B, 4 HR)
Dave Stewart (.385, 5-for-13, 3 HR)
Mike Timlin (4-for-4, 1 HR)

Hates to face: Roger Clemens (.053, 1-for-19, 10 SO)
Erik Hanson (.067, 1-for-15, 1 2B, 3 BB, 8 SO)
Gene Nelson (0-for-14)

Miscellaneous statistics: Ground outs-to-air outs ratio: 0.84 last season, 0.95 for career.... Grounded into 17 double plays in 138 opportunities (one per 8.1).... Drove in 25 of 43 runners from third base with less than two outs (58%).... Direction of balls hit to the outfield: 41% to left field, 29% to center, 30% to right.... Base running: Advanced from first base to third on 10 of 31 outfield singles (32%); scored from second on 9 of 14 (64%).... Made 0.71 assists per nine innings at first base.

Comments: Since baseball began tabulating RBIs in 1920, he's only the third player to lead the majors in homers and RBIs in consecutive seasons; the others: Babe Ruth (1920–21) and Jimmie Foxx (1932–33). No one had even led the majors just in RBIs for two straight years since George Foster (1976–77); last A.L. player to do that: Vern Stephens (1949–50). (Note: Jose Canseco tied Fielder with 44 home runs last year, but in the sports records business, tying for the lead qualifies as leading.)... Among the 462 players with 100 career home runs, only one hit them out with greater frequency: Ruth (one every 11.8 at-bats), Fielder (13.5), Ralph Kiner (14.1), Harmon Killebrew (14.2), Ted Williams (14.8), Mark McGwire (14.9).... His on-base percentage leading off innings was 6th lowest in A.L.; Canseco led the majors in that category (.438).... Career slugging percentage of .551 since returning from Japan is 2d highest in team history, behind Hank Greenberg (.616); Cecil's career home-run rate with Detroit (one every 12.6 AB) is the best in franchise history.... Some other breakdowns of Fielder's home-run rate: He has averaged one homer every 11.6 at-bats vs. left-handers, one every 15.5 at-bats vs. right-handers, one every 11.3 at-bats at Tiger Stadium, but only one every 33.6 at-bats in Late-Inning Pressure Situations. Fielder has seven homers in 235 career at-bats in LIPS, a very pedestrian rate; Rick Bosetti had seven in 241 at-bats, Carmelo Castillo seven in 231, Jerry Narron nine in 175, and Bo Jackson 15 in 273.

Carlton Fisk

Bats Right

Chicago White Sox	AB	H	2B	3B	HR	RBI	BB	SO	BA	SA	OBA
Season	460	111	25	0	18	74	32	86	.241	.413	.299
vs. Left-Handers	157	36	8	0	5	28	9	24	.229	.376	.274
vs. Right-Handers	303	75	17	0	13	46	23	62	.248	.432	.312
vs. Ground-Ballers	206	50	12	0	5	26	16	42	.243	.374	.305
vs. Fly-Ballers	254	61	13	0	13	48	16	44	.240	.445	.295
Home Games	233	55	13	0	9	39	18	41	.236	.408	.295
Road Games	227	56	12	0	9	35	14	45	.247	.419	.304
Grass Fields	396	98	24	0	14	61	27	71	.247	.414	.306
Artificial Turf	64	13	1	0	4	13	5	15	.203	.406	.257
April	60	20	3	0	7	4	7	7	.333	.383	.394
May	80	19	6	0	1	8	9	18	.237	.350	.319
June	84	19	5	0	4	14	6	15	.226	.429	.286
July	62	15	2	0	2	10	5	15	.242	.371	.299
August	87	25	6	0	6	19	3	13	.287	.563	.326
Sept./Oct.	87	13	3	0	5	16	5	18	.149	.356	.202
Leading Off Inn.	105	24	6	0	2	2	4	22	.229	.343	.283
Runners On	235	58	13	0	13	69	18	42	.247	.468	.306
Bases Empty	225	53	12	0	5	5	14	44	.236	.356	.292
Runners/Scor. Pos.	136	34	8	0	6	53	10	26	.250	.441	.311
Runners On/2 Out	122	27	7	0	6	33	8	23	.221	.426	.275
Scor. Pos./2 Out	78	17	4	0	3	26	4	16	.218	.385	.265
Late-Inning Pressure	79	24	4	0	7	17	7	17	.304	.620	.368
Leading Off	22	8	1	0	2	2	0	5	.364	.682	.391
Runners On	43	12	2	0	4	14	5	9	.279	.605	.354
Runners/Scor. Pos.	24	6	1	0	2	10	3	7	.250	.542	.333

RUNS BATTED IN	From 1B	From 2B	From 3B	Scoring Position
Totals	14/185	20/100	22/63	42/163
Percentage	7.6%	20.0%	34.9%	25.8%

Loves to face: Kevin Appier (.500, 6-for-12, 1 HR)
Scott Sanderson (.615, 8-for-13)
Cliff Young (3-for-3, 1 2B, 2 HR)

Hates to face: Kevin Brown (.105, 2-for-19)
Mike Moore (.156, 5-for-32)
Jack Morris (.141, 9-for-64, 2 HR)

Miscellaneous statistics: Ground outs-to-air outs ratio: 1.01 last season, 0.82 for career.... Grounded into 19 double plays in 96 opportunities (one per 5.1).... Drove in 14 of 28 runners from third base with less than two outs (50%).... Direction of balls hit to the outfield: 53% to left field, 30% to center, 17% to right.... Base running: Advanced from first base to third on 2 of 11 outfield singles (18%); scored from second on 8 of 12 (67%).... Opposing base stealers: 54-for-91 (59%), 3d-lowest rate in A.L.

Comments: Has hit more homers after turning The Big Four-Oh than any player in major league history. The real 40/40 Club: Fisk (68), Darrell Evans (60), Carl Yastrzemski (49), Stan Musial (46), Ted Williams (44), Hank Aaron (42), Graig Nettles (40).... Of his 111 hits, only 10 were to the opposite field (9%), the 2d-lowest percentage among A.L. players with at least 60 hits last season.... His batting average from September 1 on was A.L.'s second lowest.... Needs 79 games behind the plate to pass Bob Boone as baseball's all-time leader in that category. Fisk completed his 22d major league season behind the plate, an A.L. record, but three years shy of Deacon McGuire's major league record for backstops. Fisk has led A.L. catchers in fielding percentage only once (1989).... He did not appear as a batterymate with Charlie Hough last season: too much of an age difference.... Even though he has caught more games wearing White Sox (1157) than Red (990), he holds Boston's career record in that regard, but ranks only third for Chicago behind Ray Schalk (1721) and Sherm Lollar (1241).... Among the 16 pre-expansion franchises in major league baseball, the White Sox are the only team whose all-time leading home run hitter (Fisk, 210) is still active with the club. He'll hold that title for a while, since among his current teammates, the next-highest total is 62 by Dan Pasqua. That's unless, of course, the White Sox get Harold Baines (186) back, or unless Fay Vincent reconsiders his ban on Minnie Minoso (135).

Scott Fletcher
Bats Right

Chicago White Sox	AB	H	2B	3B	HR	RBI	BB	SO	BA	SA	OBA
Season	248	51	10	1	1	28	17	26	.206	.266	.262
vs. Left-Handers	101	19	3	0	0	5	6	13	.188	.218	.248
vs. Right-Handers	147	32	7	1	1	23	11	13	.218	.299	.272
vs. Ground-Ballers	106	20	1	0	0	6	8	12	.189	.198	.256
vs. Fly-Ballers	142	31	9	1	1	22	9	14	.218	.317	.266
Home Games	115	23	4	1	0	14	12	10	.200	.252	.285
Road Games	133	28	6	0	1	14	5	16	.211	.278	.241
Grass Fields	228	48	9	1	1	25	17	23	.211	.272	.272
Artificial Turf	20	3	1	0	0	3	0	3	.150	.200	.143
April	54	18	5	1	1	14	7	3	.333	.519	.419
May	79	12	1	0	0	3	6	10	.152	.165	.209
June	33	3	1	0	0	0	4	4	.091	.121	.211
July	16	3	1	0	0	2	0	2	.188	.250	.188
August	31	8	1	0	0	5	0	2	.258	.290	.258
Sept./Oct.	35	7	1	0	0	4	0	5	.200	.229	.211
Leading Off Inn.	64	10	2	0	0	0	3	10	.156	.188	.194
Runners On	92	23	7	1	1	28	9	8	.250	.380	.314
Bases Empty	156	28	3	0	0	0	8	18	.179	.199	.229
Runners/Scor. Pos.	63	16	7	0	0	25	7	7	.254	.365	.324
Runners On/2 Out	37	11	4	0	0	12	7	4	.297	.405	.422
Scor. Pos./2 Out	29	9	4	0	0	12	5	4	.310	.448	.429
Late-Inning Pressure	54	13	1	0	0	4	3	4	.241	.259	.305
Leading Off	15	3	0	0	0	0	1	2	.200	.200	.250
Runners On	19	5	1	0	0	4	0	1	.263	.316	.263
Runners/Scor. Pos.	12	4	1	0	0	4	0	1	.333	.417	.333

RUNS BATTED IN	From 1B	From 2B	From 3B	Scoring Position
Totals	6/51	8/52	13/27	21/79
Percentage	11.8%	15.4%	48.1%	26.6%

Loves to face: Dave Johnson (.545, 6-for-11)
Gene Nelson (.389, 7-for-18, 1 HR)
Scott Sanderson (.583, 7-for-12, 2 HR)
Hates to face: Jim Abbott (.063, 1-for-16)
Kirk McCaskill (.107, 3-for-28)
Todd Stottlemyre (.056, 1-for-18, 2 BB)

Miscellaneous statistics: Ground outs-to-air outs ratio: 0.93 last season, 1.39 for career.... Grounded into 3 double plays in 41 opportunities (one per 14).... Drove in 8 of 13 runners from third base with less than two outs (62%).... Direction of balls hit to the outfield: 38% to left field, 33% to center, 29% to right.... Base running: Advanced from first base to third on 3 of 12 outfield singles (25%); scored from second on 1 of 2 (50%).... Made 2.66 assists per nine innings at second base, 2d-lowest rate in A.L.

Comments: Yearly batting averages since 1986: .300, .287, .276, .253, .242, .206. Only one other player has seen his batting average decrease in each of the last five seasons (minimum: 200 at-bats each year): Mitch Webster. The last player with a six-year streak was Joe Rudi (1975–80).... Batting average vs. left-handed pitchers was 3d lowest in the league.... He started 38 of the team's first 42 games last season, but started only 30 more after that, finishing with fewer than 500 at-bats for first time since 1985.... Career fielding rate of one error every 91 chances at second base is 3d best among active players with at least 200 games there, behind Jose Oquendo (one every 132 chances) and Ryne Sandberg (98). To qualify for the all-time leader list, a player needs 1000 games at his position; Fletcher has played only 391 games at second base.... He is one of 134 players to appear in a game for both the White Sox and the Cubs.... His batting average with runners in scoring position has been higher than his average in other at-bats in eight of his nine full seasons in the majors. Career breakdown: .291 with RISP, .251 in other at-bats.... In addition, his career batting average with the bases loaded puts him among the top 10 active players in that category (minimum: 25 hits): Pat Tabler .488, Terry Steinbach .466, Tony Gwynn .420, Eddie Murray .403, Kevin McReynolds .379, Wade Boggs .374, Willie McGee .370, Alan Trammell .356, Scott Fletcher .356, Terry Pendleton .351.

Julio Franco
Bats Right

Texas Rangers	AB	H	2B	3B	HR	RBI	BB	SO	BA	SA	OBA
Season	589	201	27	3	15	78	65	78	.341	.474	.408
vs. Left-Handers	155	57	10	3	8	29	16	19	.368	.626	.424
vs. Right-Handers	434	144	17	0	7	49	49	59	.332	.419	.402
vs. Ground-Ballers	283	101	16	0	8	38	33	39	.357	.498	.426
vs. Fly-Ballers	306	100	11	3	7	40	32	39	.327	.451	.392
Home Games	294	101	13	3	7	40	33	42	.344	.480	.409
Road Games	295	100	14	0	8	38	32	36	.339	.468	.407
Grass Fields	482	165	22	3	14	68	56	65	.342	.488	.413
Artificial Turf	107	36	5	0	1	10	9	13	.336	.411	.388
April	67	16	2	0	1	6	3	5	.239	.313	.271
May	110	37	6	1	4	16	13	17	.336	.518	.411
June	108	39	6	0	4	18	13	18	.361	.528	.431
July	91	30	4	0	1	10	11	8	.330	.407	.408
August	93	35	1	1	2	15	14	10	.376	.473	.458
Sept./Oct.	120	44	8	1	3	13	11	20	.367	.525	.417
Leading Off Inn.	127	39	5	0	2	2	8	14	.307	.394	.348
Runners On	262	90	13	2	7	70	31	38	.344	.489	.416
Bases Empty	327	111	14	1	8	8	34	40	.339	.462	.402
Runners/Scor. Pos.	149	48	6	1	2	57	24	25	.322	.416	.418
Runners On/2 Out	107	38	4	0	2	27	22	15	.355	.449	.473
Scor. Pos./2 Out	70	22	0	0	1	23	19	13	.314	.357	.467
Late-Inning Pressure	89	31	4	0	1	5	14	14	.348	.427	.437
Leading Off	20	10	1	0	0	0	2	2	.500	.550	.545
Runners On	38	7	2	0	0	4	7	12	.184	.237	.311
Runners/Scor. Pos.	26	3	0	0	0	4	6	9	.115	.115	.281

RUNS BATTED IN	From 1B	From 2B	From 3B	Scoring Position
Totals	10/185	26/113	27/58	53/171
Percentage	5.4%	23.0%	46.6%	31.0%

Loves to face: Scott Sanderson (.500, 6-for-12, 2 HR)
Bobby Thigpen (.636, 7-for-11, 1 HR)
Frank Viola (.425, 17-for-40, 2 HR)
Hates to face: Scott Erickson (.071, 1-for-14, 2 BB)
Tom Henke (.111, 2-for-18)
Gregg Olson (0-for-4, 3 SO)

Miscellaneous statistics: Ground outs-to-air outs ratio: 1.54 last season, 1.55 for career.... Grounded into 13 double plays in 126 opportunities (one per 10).... Drove in 19 of 30 runners from third base with less than two outs (63%).... Direction of balls hit to the outfield: 21% to left field, 34% to center, 45% to right.... Base running: Advanced from first base to third on 15 of 31 outfield singles (48%); scored from second on 20 of 24 (83%).... Made 2.62 assists per nine innings at second base, lowest rate in A.L.

Comments: Batted .283 during first three full seasons in majors, .309 over next three years, .318 over last three years.... His 45-point increase from 1990 to 1991 (.296 to .341) was third largest among players who qualified for the batting title in both seasons.... His .332 average vs. right-handed pitchers was the best by any right-handed batter in majors last year (minimum: 100 AB vs. RHP).... Batting average in Late-Inning Pressure Situations has been higher than overall average in each of last five years. Over that span, he has batted .348 in LIPS (best in the majors), .309 in other at-bats.... Related note: Franco's 10 hits in extra innings tied teammate Juan Gonzalez for 1991 major league lead; Texas played 24 extra-inning games, one shy of Phils' major league–leading total.... Among active players who have never appeared in a postseason game, only Hubie Brooks (1454) has played more regular-season games than Franco (1367).... He has scored at least 80 runs in each of last eight seasons. Only Wade Boggs and Brett Butler have current streaks as long (each has a nine-year streak).... Hit seven of his 15 home runs to the opposite field.... It was widely reported that no player in Texas/Washington franchise history had ever won the league batting title until Franco did it last season. That's not so unusual; since 1961, when the expansion Senators began, six other A.L. clubs have not had a batting champion: Chicago, Cleveland, Milwaukee, Oakland, Seattle, and Toronto. The White Sox haven't had one since Luke Appling in 1943.

Travis Fryman
Bats Right

Detroit Tigers	AB	H	2B	3B	HR	RBI	BB	SO	BA	SA	OBA
Season	557	144	36	3	21	91	40	149	.259	.447	.309
vs. Left-Handers	152	45	9	2	5	23	11	43	.296	.480	.349
vs. Right-Handers	405	99	27	1	16	68	29	106	.244	.435	.293
vs. Ground-Ballers	271	74	21	0	9	47	17	71	.273	.450	.316
vs. Fly-Ballers	286	70	15	3	12	44	23	78	.245	.444	.302
Home Games	261	65	15	3	8	42	20	76	.249	.421	.303
Road Games	296	79	21	0	13	49	20	73	.267	.470	.313
Grass Fields	472	123	31	3	15	71	31	131	.261	.434	.305
Artificial Turf	85	21	5	0	6	20	9	18	.247	.518	.326
April	62	12	1	1	2	10	7	11	.194	.339	.271
May	85	21	5	0	3	19	6	21	.247	.412	.290
June	103	25	6	0	3	11	7	30	.243	.388	.291
July	91	25	9	1	5	15	7	28	.275	.560	.323
August	108	29	6	1	4	17	6	33	.269	.454	.310
Sept./Oct.	108	32	9	0	4	19	7	26	.296	.491	.347
Leading Off Inn.	98	29	8	2	4	4	9	24	.296	.541	.355
Runners On	260	69	22	0	10	80	15	67	.265	.465	.304
Bases Empty	297	75	14	3	11	11	25	82	.253	.431	.313
Runners/Scor. Pos.	155	45	16	0	3	64	9	38	.290	.452	.322
Runners On/2 Out	116	28	9	0	6	38	9	33	.241	.474	.302
Scor. Pos./2 Out	73	19	6	0	3	31	6	17	.260	.466	.325
Late-Inning Pressure	78	19	4	0	2	8	6	21	.244	.372	.298
Leading Off	16	3	1	0	0	0	2	4	.188	.250	.278
Runners On	35	7	2	0	0	6	2	6	.200	.257	.243
Runners/Scor. Pos.	19	6	2	0	0	6	1	1	.316	.421	.350

RUNS BATTED IN	From 1B	From 2B	From 3B	Scoring Position
Totals	14/206	27/124	29/75	56/199
Percentage	6.8%	21.8%	38.7%	28.1%

Loves to face: Allan Anderson (.750, 6-for-8, 2 2B, 2 HR)
Chuck Finley (.467, 7-for-15, 1 HR)
Mark Williamson (3-for-3, 2 2B)

Hates to face: Luis Aquino (0-for-6)
Rich DeLucia (0-for-8)
Bobby Witt (.100, 1-for-10, 1 2B, 5 SO)

Miscellaneous statistics: Ground outs-to-air outs ratio: 0.82 last season, 0.85 for career.... Grounded into 13 double plays in 123 opportunities (one per 9.5).... Drove in 18 of 38 runners from third base with less than two outs (47%).... Direction of balls hit to the outfield: 47% to left field, 31% to center, 22% to right.... Base running: Advanced from first base to third on 9 of 15 outfield singles (60%); scored from second on 11 of 16 (69%).... Made 1.87 assists per nine innings at third base.

Comments: Not yet 22 years old, he was the second-youngest player in the majors to appear in an opening-day starting lineup last season. The youngest was 21-year-old Ken Griffey.... Since Al Kaline set all kinds of records for being the youngest Detroit player to do just about anything, only three players younger than Fryman have accumulated at least 500 at-bats in a season for the Tigers: Bill Freehan (1964), Willie Horton (1965), and Alan Trammell (1980).... Batted with the bases loaded 28 times last season, the most in the majors; he went 8-for-25 (.320) with one walk and six strikeouts.... His 21 home runs came as a pleasant surprise for the Tigers, considering that he played 122 games for Fayetteville (Class A) in 1988 without hitting any. He has averaged one home run every 26.3 at-bats during his major league career, after averaging one every 67 at-bats in the minors.... He came through the Tigers' minor league system as a shortstop, but was moved to third base after his 1990 call-up to the majors. Last season, his first 61 starts all came at third base, but with Trammell injured, he wound up with 63 starts at shortstop.... Somebody better tell him that third base, not shortstop, is considered a power position: Trav hit .224 with eight home runs in 294 at-bats as a third baseman, but .294 with 13 home runs in 262 at-bats as a shortstop. And while you're at it, tell him that Tiger Stadium is supposed to be a hitters' park. He has a career mark of .252 (13 HR) at home, .286 (17 HR) on the road.

Gary Gaetti
Bats Right

California Angels	AB	H	2B	3B	HR	RBI	BB	SO	BA	SA	OBA
Season	586	144	22	1	18	66	33	104	.246	.379	.293
vs. Left-Handers	159	38	7	0	6	26	13	25	.239	.396	.303
vs. Right-Handers	427	106	15	1	12	40	20	79	.248	.372	.289
vs. Ground-Ballers	264	56	6	0	7	27	18	51	.212	.314	.267
vs. Fly-Ballers	322	88	16	1	11	39	15	53	.273	.432	.314
Home Games	280	77	5	1	12	31	20	59	.275	.429	.331
Road Games	306	67	17	0	6	35	13	45	.219	.333	.257
Grass Fields	487	121	16	1	16	51	29	88	.248	.384	.298
Artificial Turf	99	23	6	0	2	15	4	16	.232	.354	.264
April	77	21	4	1	2	9	3	13	.273	.429	.296
May	111	30	4	0	5	19	1	15	.270	.441	.287
June	79	17	0	0	1	6	5	15	.215	.253	.284
July	94	24	3	0	2	11	5	21	.255	.351	.297
August	108	27	5	0	7	12	8	20	.250	.491	.305
Sept./Oct.	117	25	6	0	1	9	11	20	.214	.291	.287
Leading Off Inn.	141	33	5	0	5	5	7	17	.234	.376	.275
Runners On	241	70	11	0	5	53	15	45	.290	.398	.336
Bases Empty	345	74	11	1	13	13	18	59	.214	.365	.262
Runners/Scor. Pos.	132	38	5	0	4	50	11	21	.288	.417	.340
Runners On/2 Out	93	26	4	0	2	22	9	17	.280	.387	.343
Scor. Pos./2 Out	59	15	2	0	1	19	6	9	.254	.339	.323
Late-Inning Pressure	78	14	1	1	2	5	4	14	.179	.295	.220
Leading Off	24	4	0	0	0	0	0	5	.167	.167	.167
Runners On	27	6	1	0	0	3	2	5	.222	.259	.276
Runners/Scor. Pos.	17	3	0	0	0	2	2	4	.176	.176	.263

RUNS BATTED IN	From 1B	From 2B	From 3B	Scoring Position
Totals	5/180	18/94	25/63	43/157
Percentage	2.8%	19.1%	39.7%	27.4%

Loves to face: Greg A. Harris (.500, 10-for-20, 1 HR, 7 SO)
Mark Leiter (.857, 6-for-7, 1 HR)
Gene Nelson (.414, 12-for-29, 2 HR)

Hates to face: Kevin Brown (.050, 1-for-20)
Greg Hibbard (0-for-18)
Tim Leary (.056, 1-for-18)

Miscellaneous statistics: Ground outs-to-air outs ratio: 0.88 last season, 0.98 for career.... Grounded into 13 double plays in 117 opportunities (one per 9.0).... Drove in 17 of 32 runners from third base with less than two outs (53%).... Direction of balls hit to the outfield: 46% to left field, 32% to center, 22% to right.... Base running: Advanced from first base to third on 8 of 18 outfield singles (44%); scored from second on 11 of 14 (79%).... Made 2.38 assists per nine innings at third base, 2d-highest rate in A.L.

Comments: During three-year period, 1986–88, batted .280 with one homer every 17.7 at-bats; over last three years has batted .241 with a homer every 31.4 at-bats. That's like going from three years' worth of Willie Stargell production to three years of Bill Nahorodny.... For sixth year in a row he hit for a higher batting average vs. fly-ball pitchers than he did vs. ground-ballers, the longest current streak of its kind in the majors. During that time, he has batted .274 vs. fly-ballers, .244 vs. ground-ballers.... On-base average leading off innings was 5th lowest in A.L.... Good balance vs. different types of pitching: .257 career batting average (one home run every 23 at-bats) vs. left-handers, .254 (one every 27 at-bats) vs. right-handers.... Played 1339⅔ innings at third base last season to lead majors.... Has played 150 or more games at third base seven times; only four other A.L. third basemen have as many 150-game seasons: Brooks Robinson (14), Graig Nettles (9), Sal Bando (8), and Aurelio Rodriguez (7).... Career fielding rate of one error every 28.4 chances is good enough for 10th place among third basemen in major league history (minimum: 1000 games there); the top 10: Brooks Robinson (one error every 34.8 chances), Ken Reitz (32.9), George Kell (31.9), Don Money (31.5), Don Wert (30.9), Willie Kamm (30.7), Heinie Groh (30.5), Carney Lansford (29.3), Clete Boyer (28.9), Gaetti (28.4). Only two active players are included on the list; see the San Diego essay on page 76 for more on that phenomenon.

Greg Gagne
Bats Right

Minnesota Twins	AB	H	2B	3B	HR	RBI	BB	SO	BA	SA	OBA
Season	408	108	23	3	8	42	26	72	.265	.395	.310
vs. Left-Handers	118	33	8	2	2	12	12	17	.280	.432	.348
vs. Right-Handers	290	75	15	1	6	30	14	55	.259	.379	.294
vs. Ground-Ballers	191	50	11	2	4	21	10	24	.262	.403	.298
vs. Fly-Ballers	217	58	12	1	4	21	16	48	.267	.387	.321
Home Games	194	51	7	3	3	18	15	28	.263	.376	.321
Road Games	214	57	16	0	5	24	11	44	.266	.411	.300
Grass Fields	165	43	13	0	5	17	11	30	.261	.430	.300
Artificial Turf	243	65	10	3	3	25	15	42	.267	.370	.317
April	53	16	4	1	2	6	4	11	.302	.528	.351
May	79	25	6	0	3	10	8	15	.316	.506	.386
June	75	12	2	1	0	3	3	11	.160	.213	.190
July	77	18	3	0	1	9	4	12	.234	.312	.265
August	52	15	3	1	1	5	2	10	.288	.442	.333
Sept./Oct.	72	22	5	0	1	9	5	13	.306	.417	.346
Leading Off Inn.	89	20	4	0	3	3	6	16	.225	.371	.274
Runners On	193	50	9	2	3	37	11	35	.259	.373	.299
Bases Empty	215	58	14	1	5	5	15	37	.270	.414	.320
Runners/Scor. Pos.	111	28	3	1	3	34	8	19	.252	.378	.296
Runners On/2 Out	79	21	3	1	2	17	4	12	.266	.405	.301
Scor. Pos./2 Out	49	14	1	0	2	15	3	6	.286	.429	.327
Late-Inning Pressure	35	6	0	0	1	3	2	7	.171	.257	.256
Leading Off	10	1	0	0	1	1	0	5	.100	.400	.100
Runners On	19	5	0	0	0	2	1	1	.263	.263	.333
Runners/Scor. Pos.	10	2	0	0	0	2	1	1	.200	.200	.273

RUNS BATTED IN	From 1B	From 2B	From 3B	Scoring Position
Totals	4/139	13/91	17/46	30/137
Percentage	2.9%	14.3%	37.0%	21.9%

Loves to face: Storm Davis (.458, 11-for-24, 2 HR)
Bill Krueger (.444, 8-for-18, 1 HR)
Dave Stewart (.359, 14-for-39, 4 HR)
Hates to face: Shawn Hillegas (0-for-9)
Walt Terrell (.111, 4-for-36, 4 BB)
Bobby Witt (.148, 4-for-27, 1 HR)

Miscellaneous statistics: Ground outs-to-air outs ratio: 0.86 last season, 0.96 for career.... Grounded into 15 double plays in 100 opportunities (one per 6.7).... Drove in 14 of 30 runners from third base with less than two outs (47%).... Direction of balls hit to the outfield: 32% to left field, 32% to center, 35% to right.... Base running: Advanced from first base to third on 8 of 16 outfield singles (50%); scored from second on 9 of 10 (90%).... Made 3.17 assists per nine innings at shortstop.

Comments: Twins posted a .630 winning percentage with Gagne in the starting lineup (80–47), but were 15–20 without him (.429).... His 76-game errorless streak was the longest by any major league shortstop last season, and second longest in A.L. history. Gagne finished year with one error every 63 chances, second in A.L. behind Cal Ripken (one every 73 chances). But difference in backups' performance gave Twins' shortstops a better team error rate than the Orioles' (Minnesota 69.6, Baltimore 68.3).... Gagne's error totals, year by year, since 1986: 26, 18, 18, 18, 14, 9.... Has played 971 games at shortstop; only two players have ever played 1000 games there in franchise history: George McBride (1444 games for Washington, 1908–20) and Zoilo Versalles (1106 games for both Senators and Twins, 1959–67).... What's the opposite of a Pat Tabler? A Greg Gagne, of course. Lowest batting averages with bases loaded (minimum: 50 at-bats) since 1975: Gagne .137 (5-for-51), John Mayberry .138, Rick Dempsey .140, Pete Incaviglia .151, Ted Sizemore .154.... His home run in Game One of 1991 World Series was fourth postseason homer of his career; at the time, that gave him the most by any player in team's Minnesota history. But Gagne was supplanted by Kirby Puckett, who hit two homers later in the Series, and now has five for his career. (We doubt Gagne was crying about losing his record while Kirby was circling the bases after his game-winning extra-inning homer in Game Six.)

Dave Gallagher
Bats Right

California Angels	AB	H	2B	3B	HR	RBI	BB	SO	BA	SA	OBA
Season	270	79	17	0	1	30	24	43	.293	.367	.355
vs. Left-Handers	110	33	7	0	0	9	8	14	.300	.364	.353
vs. Right-Handers	160	46	10	0	1	21	16	29	.287	.369	.356
vs. Ground-Ballers	112	33	9	0	1	11	9	17	.295	.402	.352
vs. Fly-Ballers	158	46	8	0	0	19	15	26	.291	.342	.356
Home Games	126	34	8	0	0	10	14	21	.270	.333	.343
Road Games	144	45	9	0	1	20	10	22	.313	.396	.365
Grass Fields	243	71	14	0	1	28	23	40	.292	.362	.356
Artificial Turf	27	8	3	0	0	2	1	3	.296	.407	.345
April	9	5	0	0	0	1	2	0	.556	.556	.636
May	33	10	1	0	0	3	4	5	.303	.333	.378
June	48	13	3	0	0	5	5	8	.271	.333	.340
July	72	21	4	0	1	10	3	11	.292	.389	.329
August	36	9	3	0	0	1	4	6	.250	.333	.341
Sept./Oct.	72	21	6	0	0	10	6	13	.292	.375	.346
Leading Off Inn.	65	21	4	0	0	0	6	8	.323	.385	.380
Runners On	106	29	4	0	0	29	11	17	.274	.311	.347
Bases Empty	164	50	13	0	1	1	13	26	.305	.402	.360
Runners/Scor. Pos.	64	21	4	0	0	28	6	12	.328	.391	.403
Runners On/2 Out	38	15	1	0	0	16	11	4	.395	.421	.540
Scor. Pos./2 Out	27	12	1	0	0	15	8	2	.444	.481	.571
Late-Inning Pressure	39	10	1	0	0	6	4	7	.256	.282	.326
Leading Off	9	3	0	0	0	0	3	1	.333	.333	.500
Runners On	13	5	1	0	0	6	0	0	.385	.462	.385
Runners/Scor. Pos.	7	4	1	0	0	6	0	0	.571	.714	.571

RUNS BATTED IN	From 1B	From 2B	From 3B	Scoring Position
Totals	3/78	15/46	11/30	26/76
Percentage	3.8%	32.6%	36.7%	34.2%

Loves to face:
Hates to face: Willie Fraser (0-for-6)
Dave Schmidt (0-for-6)
Steve Searcy (0-for-5)

Miscellaneous statistics: Ground outs-to-air outs ratio: 0.95 last season, 1.08 for career.... Grounded into 6 double plays in 62 opportunities (one per 10).... Drove in 5 of 13 runners from third base with less than two outs (38%).... Direction of balls hit to the outfield: 39% to left field, 30% to center, 31% to right.... Base running: Advanced from first base to third on 5 of 12 outfield singles (42%); scored from second on 5 of 9 (56%).... Made 2.60 putouts per nine innings in center field.

Comments: Sweet revenge: Batted .395 (15-for-38), highest in A.L., against his former White Sox teammates.... This right-handed batter has a higher career batting average vs. right-handed pitchers (.279) than vs. left-handers (.270). Still, in 1991 he started 33 of 43 games in which Angels faced a left-handed starter, but only 40 of 119 vs. right-handers.... Mets will be his fifth major league club, all of which play their home games on grass fields (Indians, White Sox, Orioles, and Angels). He has a .282 career batting average on grass fields, .240 on artificial turf, but while that appears to heavily favor grass fields, take it with a grain of salt—he has only 233 career at-bats on artificial turf.... Don't expect much from him on the bases. Over the course of his career he has been caught stealing 16 times but has stolen only 15 bases.... Played 87 games in the outfield without committing an error last season, and has an errorless streak of 104 games extending back into 1990. Last season, he played seven games in left field, 61 games in center, and 23 games in right.... Has played more than 101 games only once in his career: in 1989, when he played every game for Jeff Torborg's White Sox. Torborg thought enough of Gallagher to swap Hubie Brooks for him even-up, but remember that Torborg was also at the helm of the Chisox when the club released Gallagher in 1990.... Has seven career home runs: three in 55 at-bats at Arlington Stadium, and four in 1325 at-bats everywhere else. He answers to "Long Ball" in Texas.

Mike Gallego

Bats Right

Oakland A's	AB	H	2B	3B	HR	RBI	BB	SO	BA	SA	OBA
Season	482	119	15	4	12	49	67	84	.247	.369	.343
vs. Left-Handers	122	38	6	1	5	13	20	16	.311	.500	.408
vs. Right-Handers	360	81	9	3	7	36	47	68	.225	.325	.320
vs. Ground-Ballers	238	62	6	4	4	19	25	35	.261	.370	.338
vs. Fly-Ballers	244	57	9	0	8	30	42	49	.234	.369	.347
Home Games	230	62	8	3	6	20	40	34	.270	.409	.378
Road Games	252	57	7	1	6	29	27	50	.226	.333	.310
Grass Fields	403	101	13	3	9	36	58	69	.251	.365	.348
Artificial Turf	79	18	2	1	3	13	9	15	.228	.392	.315
April	54	12	0	1	0	2	14	10	.222	.259	.382
May	77	22	4	0	2	13	8	9	.286	.416	.360
June	83	17	0	0	0	1	10	13	.205	.205	.287
July	94	28	5	1	4	16	10	17	.298	.500	.377
August	86	17	4	1	3	7	6	15	.198	.372	.255
Sept./Oct.	88	23	2	1	3	10	19	20	.261	.409	.394
Leading Off Inn.	141	32	5	1	5	5	18	23	.227	.383	.314
Runners On	182	47	6	3	4	41	26	28	.258	.390	.358
Bases Empty	300	72	9	1	8	8	41	56	.240	.357	.333
Runners/Scor. Pos.	100	25	3	2	2	36	18	15	.250	.380	.366
Runners On/2 Out	85	21	3	0	3	14	10	14	.247	.388	.340
Scor. Pos./2 Out	46	9	0	0	2	12	8	7	.196	.326	.339
Late-Inning Pressure	74	22	2	1	2	7	13	14	.297	.432	.409
Leading Off	25	7	2	0	0	0	3	5	.280	.360	.357
Runners On	20	6	0	1	1	6	5	2	.300	.550	.462
Runners/Scor. Pos.	12	3	0	1	0	4	5	0	.250	.417	.500

RUNS BATTED IN	From 1B	From 2B	From 3B	Scoring Position
Totals	5/130	12/74	20/45	32/119
Percentage	3.8%	16.2%	44.4%	26.9%

Loves to face: Alex Fernandez (.400, 4-for-10, 1 HR)
Jimmy Key (.391, 9-for-23)
Bill Wegman (.462, 6-for-13, 1 HR)

Hates to face: Kevin Brown (.071, 1-for-14)
Erik Hanson (.067, 1-for-15, 2 BB)
David West (0-for-3, 3 SO)

Miscellaneous statistics: Ground outs-to-air outs ratio: 1.05 last season, 1.26 for career.... Grounded into 8 double plays in 88 opportunities (one per 11).... Drove in 14 of 23 runners from third base with less than two outs (61%).... Direction of balls hit to the outfield: 33% to left field, 30% to center, 37% to right.... Base running: Advanced from first base to third on 9 of 25 outfield singles (36%); scored from second on 9 of 13 (69%).... Made 3.10 assists per nine innings at second base.

Comments: His playing time has increased in each of the last five years. Games played year by year since 1986: 20, 72, 129, 133, 140, 159. Looking for a record of that sort? Check Jerry Lumpe's page in the *Encyclopedia*. ... Hit more home runs in 482 at-bats last season than he had in 1261 ABs prior to 1991 (11).... Along with his new-found power came respect—in the form of the first three intentional walks of his career.... The Athletics allowed 4.64 runs per nine innings with Gallego at second base, compared to 5.57 with Lance Blankenship there.... He has a career batting average of .257 vs. left-handers, .219 vs. right-handers.... Has batted .283 in Late-Inning Pressure Situations over the past two seasons after going 11-for-82 prior to that (.134).... He has a career stolen-base percentage of .447 (21 SB, 26 CS).... When the Yankees' brass projected him as an everyday player at any of three infield positions, they were being optimistic. He has played 434 games at second base and 268 at shortstop, but only 84 at third base—and not one there in 1991 despite the near season-long absence of Carney Lansford.... Has never made an error in 122 chances at shortstop on artificial turf during the regular season.... The Athletics' all-time infield according to fielding percentage would place Mark McGwire at first base (one error per 195 chances), Gallego at second (one per 75), Walt Weiss at shortstop (one per 38), and ... Hank Majeski at third base (one per 38)!

Jim Gantner

Bats Left

Milwaukee Brewers	AB	H	2B	3B	HR	RBI	BB	SO	BA	SA	OBA
Season	526	149	27	4	2	47	27	34	.283	.361	.320
vs. Left-Handers	139	37	3	0	0	13	6	8	.266	.288	.304
vs. Right-Handers	387	112	24	4	2	34	21	26	.289	.388	.325
vs. Ground-Ballers	255	76	13	1	1	21	12	15	.298	.369	.331
vs. Fly-Ballers	271	73	14	3	1	26	15	19	.269	.354	.309
Home Games	254	73	14	1	1	20	15	15	.287	.362	.328
Road Games	272	76	13	3	1	27	12	19	.279	.360	.311
Grass Fields	458	132	22	4	2	39	26	31	.288	.367	.329
Artificial Turf	68	17	5	0	0	8	1	3	.250	.324	.254
April	50	13	5	0	0	8	3	9	.260	.360	.296
May	107	32	6	0	0	5	4	2	.299	.355	.327
June	73	18	2	1	0	10	5	5	.247	.301	.304
July	61	19	4	1	0	2	3	3	.311	.410	.344
August	113	32	4	1	0	12	2	7	.283	.336	.291
Sept./Oct.	122	35	6	1	2	10	10	6	.287	.402	.346
Leading Off Inn.	135	45	5	1	1	1	6	7	.333	.407	.366
Runners On	215	54	8	2	0	45	15	14	.251	.307	.298
Bases Empty	311	95	19	2	2	2	12	20	.305	.399	.335
Runners/Scor. Pos.	123	29	5	2	0	44	12	11	.236	.309	.295
Runners On/2 Out	98	24	5	1	0	17	10	7	.245	.316	.321
Scor. Pos./2 Out	67	13	4	1	0	16	7	6	.194	.284	.270
Late-Inning Pressure	86	26	6	0	2	8	3	4	.302	.442	.330
Leading Off	27	9	1	0	1	1	0	0	.333	.481	.333
Runners On	30	8	3	0	0	6	3	2	.267	.367	.324
Runners/Scor. Pos.	17	4	2	0	0	6	3	1	.235	.353	.333

RUNS BATTED IN	From 1B	From 2B	From 3B	Scoring Position
Totals	3/154	15/94	27/61	42/155
Percentage	1.9%	16.0%	44.3%	27.1%

Loves to face: Greg Cadaret (.538, 7-for-13)
Jose Guzman (.444, 8-for-18)
Frank Viola (.375, 15-for-40, 1 HR, 0 BB, 0 SO)

Hates to face: Roger Clemens (.135, 5-for-37)
Frank Tanana (.143, 6-for-42)
Bobby Thigpen (0-for-11)

Miscellaneous statistics: Ground outs-to-air outs ratio: 1.27 last season, 1.39 for career.... Grounded into 13 double plays in 98 opportunities (one per 7.5).... Drove in 19 of 29 runners from third base with less than two outs (66%).... Direction of balls hit to the outfield: 35% to left field, 35% to center, 30% to right.... Base running: Advanced from first base to third on 9 of 27 outfield singles (33%); scored from second on 8 of 9 (89%).... Made 1.83 assists per nine innings at third base, 3d-lowest rate in A.L.

Comments: Started only about half of the games in which the Brewers faced left-handed starters (24 of 46), but almost all of those in which they faced right-handers (112 of 116).... The Brewers allowed an average of 5.11 runs per nine innings with him at second base, but about one run less when he played third base (4.17 per nine innings). Milwaukee's averages with other third basemen: 4.50 with Dale Sveum; 5.49 with Gary Sheffield.... His batting average was his highest since 1982.... Has hit for a higher average against ground-ball pitchers than against fly-ballers in each of the last six seasons. During that time: .294 vs. ground-ballers, .260 vs. fly-ballers.... Through the first 11 years of his career, Gantner hit 44 home runs for an average of four per season, or one for every 94 at-bats. But over the last four years, he has hit only two home runs in 1797 ABs.... His 1700 career games are fifth most among active players who've spent their entire careers with a single club, behind Robin Yount, George Brett, Lou Whitaker, and Alan Trammell. Paul Molitor has played two fewer games than Gantner, giving the Brewers three veteran lifers. There have been only 40 players in major league history to play that many games all for one club. The teams with the most are the Tigers and the Yankees with five each: Detroit—Al Kaline, Charlie Gehringer, Whitaker, Trammell, and Bill Freehan; New York—Mickey Mantle, Lou Gehrig, Roy White, Bill Dickey, and Joe DiMaggio.

Kirk Gibson

Bats Left

Kansas City Royals	AB	H	2B	3B	HR	RBI	BB	SO	BA	SA	OBA
Season	462	109	17	6	16	55	69	103	.236	.403	.341
vs. Left-Handers	132	26	2	3	2	11	16	31	.197	.303	.307
vs. Right-Handers	330	83	15	3	14	44	53	72	.252	.442	.355
vs. Ground-Ballers	213	42	8	2	6	23	32	45	.197	.338	.315
vs. Fly-Ballers	249	67	9	4	10	32	37	58	.269	.458	.365
Home Games	239	53	5	6	4	26	35	46	.222	.343	.327
Road Games	223	56	12	0	12	29	34	57	.251	.466	.356
Grass Fields	165	43	7	0	12	26	27	40	.261	.521	.372
Artificial Turf	297	66	10	6	4	29	42	63	.222	.337	.324
April	70	18	0	1	6	12	9	14	.257	.543	.342
May	83	18	5	0	1	4	12	16	.217	.313	.316
June	98	23	5	1	5	19	13	15	.235	.459	.321
July	59	15	2	1	0	5	5	9	.254	.322	.333
August	85	24	2	3	4	11	16	20	.282	.518	.408
Sept./Oct.	67	11	3	0	0	4	14	29	.164	.209	.321
Leading Off Inn.	104	23	3	2	4	4	11	22	.221	.404	.319
Runners On	179	45	10	3	8	47	32	43	.251	.475	.364
Bases Empty	283	64	7	3	8	8	37	60	.226	.357	.326
Runners/Scor. Pos.	109	25	5	2	4	35	25	22	.229	.422	.372
Runners On/2 Out	68	13	2	0	1	11	13	19	.191	.265	.321
Scor. Pos./2 Out	49	8	1	0	0	8	11	11	.163	.184	.317
Late-Inning Pressure	71	13	0	1	2	8	13	18	.183	.296	.318
Leading Off	16	2	0	1	0	0	2	5	.125	.250	.263
Runners On	33	7	0	0	2	8	4	11	.212	.394	.297
Runners/Scor. Pos.	21	3	0	0	0	4	3	7	.143	.143	.250

RUNS BATTED IN	From 1B	From 2B	From 3B	Scoring Position
Totals	11/117	13/82	15/43	28/125
Percentage	9.4%	15.9%	34.9%	22.4%

Loves to face: Steve Bedrosian (4-for-4, 1 HR, 1 BB)
Kirk McCaskill (.526, 10-for-19, 4 HR)
Bill Wegman (.364, 8-for-22, 4 HR)

Hates to face: Jimmy Key (.083, 2-for-24, 4 BB)
Tim Leary (.071, 1-for-14)
Duane Ward (0-for-5, 3 SO)

Miscellaneous statistics: Ground outs-to-air outs ratio: 1.02 last season, 0.99 for career.... Grounded into 9 double plays in 83 opportunities (one per 9.2).... Drove in 11 of 23 runners from **third base** with less than two outs (48%).... Direction of balls hit to the outfield: 32% to left field, 32% to center, 36% to right.... Base running: Advanced from first base to third on 12 of 25 outfield singles (48%); scored from second on 10 of 14 (71%).... Made 1.86 putouts per nine innings in left field, 2d-lowest rate in A.L.

Comments: Started 96 of 113 games in which the Royals faced right-handed starters, but only 24 of 49 against left-handers.... Started more **games from the leadoff** spot last season (23) than he did over the previous 12 years of his career (22).... Shared the **American League** home-run lead at the end of April, but was outhomered by no fewer than 63 A.L. players from **May 1** to season's end.... Hit three home runs at Cleveland Stadium; only one player hit more there last season *even including the Indians.* Albert Belle led the Indians with eight home runs at home; Carlos Martinez was the runner-up with three.... Gibson was the Royals' seventh different opening-day DH in the last seven seasons. The last to do it in consecutive years was Hal McRae.... Played 86 games on artificial turf last year, more than twice as many as in any previous season. And while it may not have helped, it doesn't appear to have hurt either: He made 28 of his first 32 starts as a DH, but played the field in 87 of 88 after that.... Career batting average of .219 (14-for-64, 0 HR) as a pinch hitter.... He's not as fast as he used to be, but he's a better base stealer, having raised his stolen-base percentage from 69 percent for 1979–84 to 86 percent since then. And his .870 mark over the past four years (87-for-100) is the best in the majors during that time (minimum: 50 SB). The silver and bronze go to Eric Davis (.858) and Henry Cotto (.851).... If NASA can name a space shuttle after the *Enterprise,* can't the Royals make Kirk their captain?

Dan Gladden

Bats Right

Minnesota Twins	AB	H	2B	3B	HR	RBI	BB	SO	BA	SA	OBA
Season	461	114	14	9	6	52	36	60	.247	.356	.306
vs. Left-Handers	118	30	5	4	1	19	16	10	.254	.390	.341
vs. Right-Handers	343	84	9	5	5	33	20	50	.245	.344	.293
vs. Ground-Ballers	208	61	6	6	2	16	17	28	.293	.409	.350
vs. Fly-Ballers	253	53	8	3	4	36	19	32	.209	.312	.271
Home Games	244	65	9	5	3	27	22	33	.266	.381	.333
Road Games	217	49	5	4	3	25	14	27	.226	.327	.275
Grass Fields	180	43	4	2	3	19	9	20	.239	.333	.276
Artificial Turf	281	71	10	7	3	33	27	40	.253	.370	.325
April	69	13	3	0	1	10	7	5	.188	.275	.278
May	91	25	2	3	2	7	7	11	.275	.429	.333
June	79	24	3	1	1	6	8	10	.304	.405	.368
July	32	13	3	0	1	13	3	7	.406	.594	.457
August	103	22	2	4	0	13	5	8	.214	.311	.257
Sept./Oct.	87	17	1	1	1	3	6	19	.195	.264	.247
Leading Off Inn.	184	46	3	1	4	4	13	21	.250	.342	.310
Runners On	171	42	7	7	2	48	13	24	.246	.404	.300
Bases Empty	290	72	7	2	4	4	23	36	.248	.328	.310
Runners/Scor. Pos.	108	24	6	3	1	41	12	18	.222	.361	.302
Runners On/2 Out	81	17	4	5	0	18	6	16	.210	.383	.264
Scor. Pos./2 Out	56	10	4	2	0	15	6	12	.179	.321	.258
Late-Inning Pressure	47	9	2	1	2	13	6	9	.191	.404	.296
Leading Off	9	1	0	0	1	1	1	2	.111	.444	.200
Runners On	25	7	2	1	1	12	5	5	.280	.560	.419
Runners/Scor. Pos.	16	5	2	1	1	12	4	4	.313	.750	.476

RUNS BATTED IN	From 1B	From 2B	From 3B	Scoring Position
Totals	13/124	16/81	17/49	33/130
Percentage	10.5%	19.8%	34.7%	25.4%

Loves to face: Mike Flanagan (.476, 10-for-21, 1 HR)
Mark Gubicza (.387, 12-for-31)
Jose Guzman (.318, 7-for-22, 2 HR)

Hates to face: Lee Guetterman (.077, 1-for-13)
Melido Perez (.115, 3-for-26)
Bobby Witt (.107, 3-for-28, 3 BB)

Miscellaneous statistics: Ground outs-to-air outs ratio: 0.88 last season, 0.98 for career.... Grounded into 13 double plays in 78 opportunities (one per 6.0).... Drove in 13 of 23 runners from third base with less than two outs (57%).... Direction of balls hit to the outfield: 33% to left field, 39% to center, 29% to right.... Base running: Advanced from first base to third on 18 of 26 outfield singles (69%), highest rate in A.L.; scored from second on 13 of 14 (93%).... Made 2.18 putouts per nine innings in left field.

Comments: His postseason hitting streak was snapped at nine games, just over halfway to Hank Bauer's record of 17 straight. He also had a streak of 14 consecutive postseason games in which he had reached base safely that was snapped in the third game of the A.L.C.S.... Gladden did set a World Series record with 25 putouts, the most by any outfielder in a Series of seven games or fewer.... Became only the eighth player ever to end a World Series by crossing home plate. The others: Bill Mazeroski (1960), Hank Bauer (1953), Mickey Cochrane (1935), Al Simmons (1929), Earle Combs (1927), Muddy Ruel (1924), and Steve Yerkes (1912).... He stole fewer bases last season (15) and for a lower percentage (63%) than in any other full season in his career.... In five years with the Twins, he batted .290 at the Metrodome, .246 on the road. He has a career average of .260 on grass fields, .284 on artificial turf.... Has batted below .200 in Late-Inning Pressure Situations four times in the past six years.... Hey, Sparky, Gladden pitched an inning for the Twins in both 1988 and 1989, something no Tigers position player has done since Mark Koenig threw four shutout innings in 1931. Every other A.L. club, with the exception of the Indians, has used a position player in a mop-up role within the last 10 years. (The last Tribesman to do it was Willie Smith, a one-time minor league pitcher, in 1968.)

Leo Gomez
Bats Right

Baltimore Orioles	AB	H	2B	3B	HR	RBI	BB	SO	BA	SA	OBA
Season	391	91	17	2	16	45	40	82	.233	.409	.302
vs. Left-Handers	114	25	4	0	6	16	13	20	.219	.412	.288
vs. Right-Handers	277	66	13	2	10	29	27	62	.238	.408	.308
vs. Ground-Ballers	175	42	10	1	7	23	16	35	.240	.429	.306
vs. Fly-Ballers	216	49	7	1	9	22	24	47	.227	.394	.300
Home Games	203	47	12	2	7	23	22	38	.232	.414	.303
Road Games	188	44	5	0	9	22	18	44	.234	.404	.302
Grass Fields	334	78	17	2	13	37	34	69	.234	.413	.300
Artificial Turf	57	13	0	0	3	8	6	13	.228	.386	.313
April	36	10	2	0	0	0	5	7	.278	.333	.366
May	9	0	0	0	0	0	0	4	.000	.000	.000
June	70	18	2	1	3	12	13	12	.257	.443	.384
July	98	19	7	0	3	11	9	17	.194	.357	.255
August	85	18	2	1	6	13	7	18	.212	.471	.269
Sept./Oct.	93	26	4	0	4	9	6	24	.280	.452	.317
Leading Off Inn.	82	17	3	0	4	4	11	21	.207	.390	.309
Runners On	172	38	4	0	7	36	20	35	.221	.366	.291
Bases Empty	219	53	13	2	9	9	20	47	.242	.443	.311
Runners/Scor. Pos.	80	15	2	0	2	25	11	19	.188	.287	.265
Runners On/2 Out	76	14	1	0	1	6	8	21	.184	.237	.262
Scor. Pos./2 Out	38	5	0	0	0	3	4	12	.132	.132	.214
Late-Inning Pressure	61	11	1	0	2	5	6	18	.180	.295	.250
Leading Off	8	0	0	0	0	0	2	5	.000	.000	.200
Runners On	29	4	0	0	0	3	3	7	.138	.138	.212
Runners/Scor. Pos.	13	2	0	0	0	3	1	4	.154	.154	.200

RUNS BATTED IN	From 1B	From 2B	From 3B	Scoring Position
Totals	8/147	6/68	15/35	21/103
Percentage	5.4%	8.8%	42.9%	20.4%

Loves to face: Wayne Rosenthal (.667, 2-for-3, 2 HR)
Dave Stewart (.800, 4-for-5)
Wade Taylor (.600, 3-for-5, 2 2B)

Hates to face: Joe Hesketh (0-for-5)
Mark Leiter (.111, 1-for-9, 5 SO)
Kirk McCaskill (0-for-6)

Miscellaneous statistics: Ground outs-to-air outs ratio: 0.66 last season, 0.68 for career.... Grounded into 11 double plays in 99 opportunities (one per 9.0).... Drove in 13 of 21 runners from third base with less than two outs (62%).... Direction of balls hit to the outfield: 42% to left field, 30% to center, 29% to right.... Base running: Advanced from first base to third on 2 of 15 outfield singles (13%); scored from second on 5 of 7 (71%).... Made 1.81 assists per nine innings at third base, 2d-lowest rate in A.L.

Comments: He had the highest slugging percentage among A.L. rookies with at least 250 at-bats last season. His teammate Chito Martinez had the highest mark among rookies who batted slightly less often (.514 in 216 ABs).... Gomez led major league rookies in home runs. Along with Martinez, he gave the Orioles a total of 32 homers by rookies, the most of any team in the league. (Astros rookies led the majors with 44.) ... Gomez and Chito Martinez were the first pair of Orioles rookies with at least 10 home runs apiece since 1960, when Jim Gentile and Ron Hansen did it.... His batting average with runners in scoring position was 8th lowest in the league.... Batting average with two outs and runners in scoring position was 4th lowest in the A.L. ... He hit for a higher average in Orioles losses (.238) than in their wins (.226).... He was the only rookie in the majors last season to start 100 or more games at either third base or shortstop.... Made only seven errors in 253 chances (one per 36), the best rate in American League history by a rookie third baseman. Two N.L. rookies had better rates at third: Don Gutteridge (one per 45 in 1937) and Ken Reitz (one per 38 in 1973). Gomez ranked third in the A.L. last season, trailing only Steve Buechele (one per 60) and Bill Pecota (one per 58), both of whom have gone to the N.L., opening the door for Gomez to lead the A.L. in 1992.

Juan Gonzalez
Bats Right

Texas Rangers	AB	H	2B	3B	HR	RBI	BB	SO	BA	SA	OBA
Season	545	144	34	1	27	102	42	118	.264	.479	.321
vs. Left-Handers	147	44	7	0	9	27	16	28	.299	.531	.366
vs. Right-Handers	398	100	27	1	18	75	26	90	.251	.460	.304
vs. Ground-Ballers	263	72	13	0	14	51	19	60	.274	.483	.323
vs. Fly-Ballers	282	72	21	1	13	51	23	58	.255	.475	.319
Home Games	262	70	16	0	7	40	19	62	.267	.408	.328
Road Games	283	74	18	1	20	62	23	56	.261	.544	.315
Grass Fields	444	125	28	0	22	83	34	94	.282	.493	.337
Artificial Turf	101	19	6	1	5	19	8	24	.188	.416	.248
April	14	6	2	0	1	5	1	4	.429	.786	.467
May	104	34	11	0	5	28	13	20	.327	.577	.403
June	102	26	3	0	4	17	13	20	.255	.402	.336
July	90	23	6	0	7	20	7	27	.256	.556	.316
August	125	38	7	1	9	24	3	24	.304	.592	.323
Sept./Oct.	110	17	5	0	1	8	5	23	.155	.227	.205
Leading Off Inn.	112	24	9	0	4	4	5	21	.214	.402	.248
Runners On	267	79	12	1	19	94	27	58	.296	.562	.365
Bases Empty	278	65	22	0	8	8	15	60	.234	.399	.276
Runners/Scor. Pos.	169	45	6	1	7	68	24	36	.266	.438	.362
Runners On/2 Out	113	33	7	0	10	45	13	23	.292	.619	.375
Scor. Pos./2 Out	82	19	5	0	4	32	12	17	.232	.439	.344
Late-Inning Pressure	78	18	3	0	5	15	6	16	.231	.462	.311
Leading Off	16	1	1	0	0	0	2	2	.063	.125	.167
Runners On	34	10	1	0	4	14	4	10	.294	.676	.409
Runners/Scor. Pos.	16	4	1	0	0	6	3	4	.250	.313	.417

RUNS BATTED IN	From 1B	From 2B	From 3B	Scoring Position
Totals	22/197	28/138	25/67	53/205
Percentage	11.2%	20.3%	37.3%	25.9%

Loves to face: Jim Abbott (.600, 6-for-10)
Tom Gordon (.417, 5-for-12, 2 2B, 1 3B, 1 HR)
Steve Olin (3-for-3, 2 2B)

Hates to face: Randy Johnson (0-for-8)
Mike Moore (0-for-9)
Jack Morris (0-for-5)

Miscellaneous statistics: Ground outs-to-air outs ratio: 0.78 last season, 0.81 for career.... Grounded into 10 double plays in 117 opportunities (one per 12).... Drove in 17 of 27 runners from third base with less than two outs (63%).... Direction of balls hit to the outfield: 47% to left field, 36% to center, 18% to right.... Base running: Advanced from first base to third on 5 of 18 outfield singles (28%); scored from second on 12 of 14 (86%).... Made 2.65 putouts per nine innings in center field.

Comments: Gonzalez was born on October 16, 1969, the day the Amazin' Mets won the World Series.... Only 12 players as young as Gonzalez have had 100-RBI seasons. Last season, he and Ken Griffey, Jr., became the first to do so since Al Kaline in 1956. The others: Sam Crawford, Ty Cobb, Jimmie Foxx, Mel Ott, Joe Vosmik, Hal Trosky, Sr., Joe DiMaggio, Ken Keltner, Ted Williams, and Hank Aaron. Near misses: Ruben Sierra was only two weeks older in 1987, when he drove in 109 runs, than Gonzalez was last season. Eddie Mathews was one week older in 1953.... He didn't make his season debut until April 26, and he hit only one home run after August 27 (in the season finale). But in between he batted .296, and ranked third in the majors in home runs (26), second in RBIs (93), and had one fewer extra-base hit (54) than the four major league coleaders.... His batting average from September 1 on was 3d lowest in the league.... He averaged one home run every 14 at-bats on the road, and one every 37 ABs at Arlington Stadium. That's the statistical equivalent of Harmon Killebrew on the road, Barry Foote at home.... Is his future guaranteed? Not yet, according to our projection model. Although he's likely to hit at least 250 home runs, and has one chance in five to reach 400, we offer Chet Ross and Jim Ray Hart, who had similar seasons at a comparable age, as examples of the downside.... Several publications touted Gonzalez as a leading rookie-of-the-year candidate in 1991, even though he had blown his rookie status by batting 150 times over the previous two seasons.

Craig Grebeck   Bats Right

Chicago White Sox	AB	H	2B	3B	HR	RBI	BB	SO	BA	SA	OBA
Season	224	63	16	3	6	31	38	40	.281	.460	.386
vs. Left-Handers	115	35	8	2	5	21	20	22	.304	.539	.404
vs. Right-Handers	109	28	8	1	1	10	18	18	.257	.376	.367
vs. Ground-Ballers	105	33	8	0	4	16	16	15	.314	.505	.410
vs. Fly-Ballers	119	30	8	3	2	15	22	25	.252	.420	.366
Home Games	109	32	8	0	3	12	19	19	.294	.450	.395
Road Games	115	31	8	3	3	19	19	21	.270	.470	.378
Grass Fields	177	53	15	2	5	29	33	31	.299	.492	.410
Artificial Turf	47	10	1	1	1	2	5	9	.213	.340	.288
April	8	3	0	0	1	1	2	0	.375	.750	.500
May	26	7	2	0	0	4	0	5	.269	.346	.269
June	45	10	3	0	2	5	4	8	.222	.422	.286
July	28	9	1	1	2	4	4	4	.321	.643	.394
August	42	14	4	1	0	6	5	8	.333	.476	.404
Sept./Oct.	75	20	6	1	1	11	23	15	.267	.413	.444
Leading Off Inn.	57	18	3	1	2	2	8	13	.316	.509	.400
Runners On	84	23	8	2	2	27	17	15	.274	.488	.398
Bases Empty	140	40	8	1	4	4	21	25	.286	.443	.379
Runners/Scor. Pos.	58	16	5	0	1	21	14	12	.276	.414	.419
Runners On/2 Out	40	7	0	2	0	8	8	10	.175	.275	.313
Scor. Pos./2 Out	31	5	0	0	0	6	6	9	.161	.161	.297
Late-Inning Pressure	34	10	3	1	1	5	6	5	.294	.529	.405
Leading Off	12	5	0	1	0	0	2	2	.417	.583	.500
Runners On	9	3	2	0	1	5	3	0	.333	.889	.500
Runners/Scor. Pos.	4	1	1	0	0	3	1	0	.250	.500	.429

RUNS BATTED IN	From 1B	From 2B	From 3B	Scoring Position
Totals	6/61	9/51	10/22	19/73
Percentage	9.8%	17.6%	45.5%	26.0%

Loves to face: Kenny Rogers (.750, 3-for-4, 1 2B, 2 HR)
Frank Tanana (.462, 6-for-13)
Matt Young (.538, 7-for-13, 4 SO)

Hates to face: Randy Johnson (0-for-13)
Mark Langston (0-for-6)

Miscellaneous statistics: Ground outs-to-air outs ratio: 0.65 last season, 0.62 for career.... Grounded into 3 double plays in 41 opportunities (one per 14).... Drove in 6 of 7 runners from third base with less than two outs (86%).... Direction of balls hit to the outfield: 54% to left field, 25% to center, 21% to right.... Base running: Advanced from first base to third on 4 of 12 outfield singles (33%); scored from second on 7 of 8 (88%).... Made 3.31 assists per nine innings at second base.

Comments: Grebeck is listed in the White Sox media guide at five feet, eight inches. Among the 13 players in the majors last season listed as no taller than Grebeck, six were infielders, six were outfielders, and one, Mike Felder, played both. We should also point out that the shortest pitcher in the majors last season was also among that group—Doug Dascenzo.... Has a career batting average of .128 (5-for-39) against pitchers listed at six-six or taller. Grebeck's revenge: He's drawn seven walks in 47 plate appearances against them.... Started 31 games vs. left-handers, 31 vs. right-handers.... Has raised his career average with two outs and runners in scoring position to .128 after going 1-for-16 in 1990 ... He has hit for a considerably higher average in day games than in night games in each of his two seasons in the majors. Career breakdown: .305 in 95 at-bats in day games, .221 in 248 ABs at night.... His first major league home run was hit off Nolan Ryan in 1990. His only other home run against a right-hander was against Milwaukee's Doug Henry. He homered twice within eight days against Kenny Rogers, and hit a grand slam off Kyle Abbott in September.... Grebeck played 36 games at second base, 49 at third, and 26 at shortstop. That makes him the first White Sox player with 25 games at each in one season since Scott Fletcher in 1985. But frankly, he's no Al Newman. (See page 127.)

Mike Greenwell   Bats Left

Boston Red Sox	AB	H	2B	3B	HR	RBI	BB	SO	BA	SA	OBA
Season	544	163	26	6	9	83	43	35	.300	.419	.350
vs. Left-Handers	168	55	9	2	4	34	8	12	.327	.476	.357
vs. Right-Handers	376	108	17	4	5	49	35	23	.287	.394	.347
vs. Ground-Ballers	240	62	9	2	2	33	18	17	.258	.408	.308
vs. Fly-Ballers	304	101	17	4	7	50	25	18	.332	.484	.383
Home Games	255	77	17	3	5	42	27	13	.302	.451	.365
Road Games	289	86	9	3	4	41	16	22	.298	.391	.337
Grass Fields	442	132	23	3	8	68	41	22	.299	.419	.358
Artificial Turf	102	31	3	3	1	15	2	13	.304	.422	.314
April	70	21	3	2	3	8	8	4	.300	.529	.372
May	103	29	5	1	1	19	9	8	.282	.379	.333
June	99	36	3	0	1	14	6	6	.364	.424	.396
July	94	25	2	1	2	8	5	2	.266	.372	.303
August	101	33	6	1	1	21	8	8	.327	.436	.363
Sept./Oct.	77	19	7	1	1	13	7	7	.247	.403	.333
Leading Off Inn.	116	41	6	2	3	3	3	5	.353	.517	.370
Runners On	267	79	12	2	4	78	23	21	.296	.401	.343
Bases Empty	277	84	14	4	5	5	20	14	.303	.437	.357
Runners/Scor. Pos.	163	50	9	2	2	74	15	12	.307	.423	.351
Runners On/2 Out	141	35	6	1	3	34	16	7	.248	.369	.325
Scor. Pos./2 Out	93	23	5	1	2	32	12	5	.247	.387	.333
Late-Inning Pressure	61	15	5	0	0	6	5	5	.246	.328	.319
Leading Off	15	5	2	0	0	0	0	0	.333	.467	.333
Runners On	23	5	0	0	0	6	4	2	.217	.217	.321
Runners/Scor. Pos.	11	3	0	0	0	6	3	2	.273	.273	.400

RUNS BATTED IN	From 1B	From 2B	From 3B	Scoring Position
Totals	6/216	28/137	40/75	68/212
Percentage	2.8%	20.4%	53.3%	32.1%

Loves to face: Jose Bautista (.500, 9-for-18, 1 2B, 1 3B, 4 HR)
Bill Krueger (.625, 10-for-16)
Mike Moore (.565, 13-for-23, 0 SO)

Hates to face: Scott Erickson (.063, 1-for-16)
Bryan Harvey (0-for-10)
Jose Mesa (.111, 2-for-18)

Miscellaneous statistics: Ground outs-to-air outs ratio: 1.17 last season, 1.03 for career.... Grounded into 11 double plays in 112 opportunities (one per 10).... Drove in 28 of 40 runners from third base with less than two outs (70%).... Direction of balls hit to the outfield: 32% to left field, 32% to center, 37% to right.... Base running: Advanced from first base to third on 2 of 22 outfield singles (9%), 5th-lowest rate in A.L.; scored from second on 12 of 16 (75%).... Made 1.94 putouts per nine innings in left field, 3d-lowest rate in A.L.

Comments: Both his slugging percentage and his home-run rate have declined in every season since his rookie year of 1987. Year-by-year slugging: .570, .531, .443, .434, .419; home-run rate: one every 22 at-bats, followed by 27, 41, 44, 60.... His .379 average against the Blue Jays (22-for-58) was 2d highest in the league to Wade Boggs's (.439, 18-for-41).... His average of one walk every 13.9 plate appearances last season was also the worst of his career.... Stole 15 bases in 20 attempts last season (75%), the best rate of his career.... Career batting average of .321 at Fenway Park, .301 elsewhere.... Has come to the plate with the bases loaded 129 times over the last five years, the most of any player in the majors, followed by Dwight Evans (109), Ellis Burks (88), and Todd Benzinger (86).... Injuries kept him out of the starting lineup for the last eight games of the 1991 season—even before the Sox were eliminated from the pennant race. A pinch-hit ground out in the season finale, his first at-bat in a week, dropped him below .300 (.2996).... Now that Fay Vincent has resolved the no-hitter mess, maybe he ought to state explicitly that a player who hits .2996 isn't a ".300 hitter," and—more significantly, under certain circumstances—that .3996 isn't a ".400 season." Among the bogus career .300 hitters: Enos Slaughter (.29990), Billy Goodman (.29961), Earl Sheely (.29971), Ethan Allen (.29991), and Emmet Heidrick (.29997). And Sammy West, who had eight apparent .300 seasons? Uh-uh—he had six.

Ken Griffey, Jr.
Bats Left

Seattle Mariners	AB	H	2B	3B	HR	RBI	BB	SO	BA	SA	OBA
Season	548	179	42	1	22	100	71	82	.327	.527	.399
vs. Left-Handers	159	50	10	0	5	26	20	30	.314	.472	.386
vs. Right-Handers	389	129	32	1	17	74	51	52	.332	.550	.404
vs. Ground-Ballers	248	85	22	1	7	47	33	34	.343	.524	.418
vs. Fly-Ballers	300	94	20	0	15	53	38	48	.313	.530	.384
Home Games	282	103	23	0	16	59	36	47	.365	.617	.432
Road Games	266	76	19	1	6	41	35	35	.286	.432	.364
Grass Fields	206	57	14	1	4	33	27	29	.277	.413	.356
Artificial Turf	342	122	28	0	18	67	44	53	.357	.596	.425
April	75	22	4	0	2	7	9	12	.293	.427	.365
May	90	27	7	0	4	15	13	14	.300	.511	.381
June	84	19	6	0	1	10	13	16	.226	.333	.323
July	83	36	8	1	5	25	9	11	.434	.735	.489
August	106	40	12	0	6	17	14	13	.377	.660	.447
Sept./Oct.	110	35	5	0	4	26	13	16	.318	.473	.384
Leading Off Inn.	88	27	7	1	4	4	6	15	.307	.545	.351
Runners On	265	91	19	0	11	89	43	43	.343	.540	.425
Bases Empty	283	88	23	1	11	11	28	39	.311	.516	.373
Runners/Scor. Pos.	166	55	12	0	6	76	35	36	.331	.512	.429
Runners On/2 Out	101	33	7	0	3	29	20	17	.327	.485	.438
Scor. Pos./2 Out	69	23	4	0	2	26	18	14	.333	.478	.471
Late-Inning Pressure	72	22	8	0	2	9	14	21	.306	.500	.414
Leading Off	15	4	3	0	0	0	1	3	.267	.467	.313
Runners On	33	11	2	0	1	8	11	15	.333	.485	.489
Runners/Scor. Pos.	25	7	1	0	0	6	8	14	.280	.320	.441

RUNS BATTED IN	From 1B	From 2B	From 3B	Scoring Position
Totals	14/180	27/120	37/75	64/195
Percentage	7.8%	22.5%	49.3%	32.8%

Loves to face: Paul Gibson (.583, 7-for-12, 1 HR)
Tom Gordon (.389, 7-for-18, 3 HR)
Scott Sanderson (.444, 8-for-18, 2 HR)

Hates to face: Mike Boddicker (.143, 3-for-21)
Chuck Finley (.133, 2-for-15, 2 BB)
Greg Hibbard (.091, 1-for-11)

Miscellaneous statistics: Ground outs-to-air outs ratio: 1.03 last season, 1.03 for career.... Grounded into 10 double plays in 122 opportunities (one per 12).... Drove in 27 of 44 runners from third base with less than two outs (61%).... Direction of balls hit to the outfield: 27% to left field, 32% to center, 40% to right.... Base running: Advanced from first base to third on 15 of 28 outfield singles (54%); scored from second on 16 of 17 (94%).... Made 2.55 putouts per nine innings in center field.

Comments: He has a career total of 436 games, although he didn't turn 22 until last November. Over the past 50 years, only three others played 400 games in the majors prior to their 22d birthdays: Al Kaline, Ed Kranepool, and Robin Yount. Yount's total of 556 games prior to turning 22 is the most in major league history. The runner-up: Mel Ott (539).... For the second straight season he was the youngest player in an opening-day starting lineup.... Although young Griffey already has three seasons under his belt, only two younger players played as many as 80 games last season: Ivan Rodriguez (19) and Mark Lewis (21).... Has hit more career home runs (60) than any other active player under the age of 26 (as of opening day 1992).... His July batting average was the highest of any major leaguer in any month of the season.... His home-game batting average was 3d highest in the majors.... Led major league center fielders with 15 assists last season.... He has hit for a higher average with runners in scoring position than in other at-bats in each of his three seasons in the majors. Career breakdown: .314 with RISP, .294 in other at-bats.... Progressing at a rate to warm the hearts of card collectors across the country. Year-by-year batting averages: .264, .300, .327.... He's the first player to increase his batting average by at least 25 points in each of the two seasons following his rookie year since 1974–75, when it was done by George Brett and someone else named Ken Griffey.

Kelly Gruber
Bats Right

Toronto Blue Jays	AB	H	2B	3B	HR	RBI	BB	SO	BA	SA	OBA
Season	429	108	18	2	20	65	31	70	.252	.443	.308
vs. Left-Handers	112	31	4	0	8	18	8	15	.277	.527	.323
vs. Right-Handers	317	77	14	2	12	47	23	55	.243	.413	.303
vs. Ground-Ballers	240	57	12	0	11	34	14	33	.237	.425	.285
vs. Fly-Ballers	189	51	6	2	9	31	17	37	.270	.466	.336
Home Games	221	58	6	0	8	31	18	34	.262	.398	.327
Road Games	208	50	12	2	12	34	13	36	.240	.490	.288
Grass Fields	166	41	11	1	10	29	12	27	.247	.506	.301
Artificial Turf	263	67	7	1	10	36	19	43	.255	.403	.313
April	74	19	1	1	3	11	7	13	.257	.419	.321
May	2	0	0	0	0	0	1	1	.000	.000	.333
June	54	11	2	0	3	5	6	9	.204	.407	.317
July	70	20	2	0	4	13	5	14	.286	.486	.329
August	110	26	8	0	4	13	7	14	.236	.418	.286
Sept./Oct.	119	32	5	1	6	23	5	19	.269	.479	.302
Leading Off Inn.	94	21	2	1	3	3	4	13	.223	.362	.255
Runners On	202	51	10	1	8	53	18	31	.252	.431	.319
Bases Empty	227	57	8	1	12	12	13	39	.251	.454	.298
Runners/Scor. Pos.	130	31	6	1	3	42	15	23	.238	.369	.320
Runners On/2 Out	80	17	2	0	3	14	5	12	.213	.350	.259
Scor. Pos./2 Out	57	9	1	0	2	12	4	11	.158	.281	.213
Late-Inning Pressure	57	14	1	0	4	10	4	18	.246	.474	.295
Leading Off	14	2	0	0	0	0	0	4	.143	.143	.143
Runners On	22	5	0	0	1	7	3	5	.227	.364	.320
Runners/Scor. Pos.	15	3	0	0	0	5	3	4	.200	.200	.333

RUNS BATTED IN	From 1B	From 2B	From 3B	Scoring Position
Totals	7/126	18/112	20/45	38/157
Percentage	5.6%	16.1%	44.4%	24.2%

Loves to face: Charles Nagy (.545, 6-for-11, 3 2B, 2 HR)
Jeff Reardon (.500, 5-for-10, 1 HR)
Kenny Rogers (.400, 2-for-5, 2 HR)

Hates to face: Dana Kiecker (0-for-11)
Mark Langston (.080, 2-for-25)
Nolan Ryan (.091, 2-for-22)

Miscellaneous statistics: Ground outs-to-air outs ratio: 1.25 last season, 1.04 for career.... Grounded into 7 double plays in 89 opportunities (one per 13).... Drove in 15 of 25 runners from third base with less than two outs (60%).... Direction of balls hit to the outfield: 43% to left field, 31% to center, 25% to right.... Base running: Advanced from first base to third on 4 of 12 outfield singles (33%); scored from second on 5 of 9 (56%).... Made 2.14 assists per nine innings at third base.

Comments: Split his time almost equally between the third, fourth, fifth, and sixth slots in the Blue Jays' batting order last season, after starting all 148 games in 1990 from the 3d slot.... His home-run total was 2d highest among A.L. third basemen last season, behind Robin Ventura's 22, despite missing 49 games with hand injuries.... Batting average with two outs and runners in scoring position was 10th lowest in the league.... Has hit for a higher average with runners on base than with the bases empty in each of his eight seasons in the majors. Career breakdown: .287 with runners on; .245 with bases empty.... Career average of .343 with runners in scoring position in Late-Inning Pressure Situations is 5th highest among active players.... Over the past two seasons, Gruber has committed one error every 15 chances in Late-Inning Pressure Situations, compared to an average of one per 26 chances at other times.... *Sports Illustrated*'s 1986 baseball preview issue touted that season's rookie crop as potentially one of the greatest ever. Although they had a few of the names wrong (anyone writing in Billy Jo Robidoux's name on the 1992 All-Star ballot?), *SI* was right—the class of '86 is not only top-heavy, but it's so deep that Gruber doesn't even rank among the top 10 in career runs produced (runs plus RBIs): Canseco, Clark, Sierra, Bonilla, Bonds, Joyner, Tartabull, Mitchell, Galarraga, and Incaviglia. (Sounds like a follow-up essay in the 1993 *Analyst* to the Twins and Rangers essays in the 1990 edition.)

Ozzie Guillen

Chicago White Sox   Bats Left

	AB	H	2B	3B	HR	RBI	BB	SO	BA	SA	OBA
Season	524	143	20	3	3	49	11	38	.273	.340	.284
vs. Left-Handers	161	34	3	0	1	9	1	15	.211	.248	.213
vs. Right-Handers	363	109	17	3	2	40	10	23	.300	.380	.315
vs. Ground-Ballers	241	62	9	1	3	27	5	15	.257	.340	.269
vs. Fly-Ballers	283	81	11	2	0	22	6	23	.286	.339	.297
Home Games	247	71	10	3	1	29	4	21	.287	.364	.291
Road Games	277	72	10	0	2	20	7	17	.260	.318	.278
Grass Fields	449	123	18	3	3	44	11	34	.274	.347	.287
Artificial Turf	75	20	2	0	0	5	0	4	.267	.293	.267
April	60	17	2	0	0	5	3	4	.283	.317	.313
May	97	28	3	0	0	7	1	9	.289	.320	.290
June	96	24	4	2	0	6	2	5	.250	.333	.263
July	91	22	2	0	0	9	0	7	.242	.264	.242
August	94	25	6	1	2	13	3	6	.266	.415	.283
Sept./Oct.	86	27	3	0	1	9	2	7	.314	.384	.326
Leading Off Inn.	108	32	9	0	0	0	3	12	.296	.380	.315
Runners On	217	61	5	2	3	49	4	12	.281	.364	.285
Bases Empty	307	82	15	1	0	0	7	26	.267	.322	.283
Runners/Scor. Pos.	129	32	4	0	3	46	4	6	.248	.349	.257
Runners On/2 Out	102	24	1	1	1	18	3	4	.235	.294	.257
Scor. Pos./2 Out	71	14	0	0	1	16	3	4	.197	.239	.230
Late-Inning Pressure	118	34	6	0	1	13	2	13	.288	.364	.295
Leading Off	25	7	1	0	0	0	1	3	.280	.320	.308
Runners On	54	19	4	0	1	13	1	5	.352	.481	.351
Runners/Scor. Pos.	27	8	3	0	1	12	1	2	.296	.519	.300

RUNS BATTED IN	From 1B	From 2B	From 3B	Scoring Position
Totals	5/148	15/103	26/64	41/167
Percentage	3.4%	14.6%	40.6%	24.6%

Loves to face: Mike Flanagan (.500, 11-for-22, 1 HR)
Tom Gordon (.615, 8-for-13)
Lee Guetterman (.533, 8-for-15)

Hates to face: Kevin Brown (0-for-22)
Erik Hanson (.100, 2-for-20)
Matt Young (0-for-17)

Miscellaneous statistics: Ground outs-to-air outs ratio: 1.16 last season, 1.34 for career.... Grounded into 7 double plays in 98 opportunities (one per 14).... Drove in 19 of 28 runners from third base with less than two outs (68%).... Direction of balls hit to the outfield: 39% to left field, 29% to center, 32% to right.... Base running: Advanced from first base to third on 5 of 14 outfield singles (36%); scored from second on 10 of 13 (77%).... Made 3.07 assists per nine innings at shortstop.

Comments: His career rate of one walk every 33 plate appearances is the worst among active players (minimum: 2000 PAs). He also has the worst rate in White Sox history.... He's played at least 149 games at shortstop in each of his seven seasons in the majors—a streak that probably doesn't get the respect it deserves in the Ripken era. But besides Ozzie and Cal, only one other shortstop in A.L. history has had a streak that long: Washington's George McBride (1908–14).... Guillen's career fielding rate of one error every 39 chances at shortstop is second best in franchise history, behind Bucky Dent's (one per 41).... Started 112 games from the ninth spot in the batting order. Chicago's ninth-place hitters batted .286, the highest of any club in the league. The combined ninth-place batting average for the other 13 clubs was .242.... His batting average with runners in scoring position was a career low, dropping his career mark below .300 for the first time ever (to .293). He has batted .300 or better with RISP four times in seven seasons.... His home run last Sept. 5, a grand slam off Kansas City's Storm Davis, was the first of his career in a day game, breaking an 0-for-1013 day-game schneid.... His .515 stolen-base percentage over the past two seasons is by far the lowest in the majors during that time among players with at least 25 steals. The runner-up: Mike Devereaux (.580, 29-for-50).

Mel Hall

New York Yankees   Bats Left

	AB	H	2B	3B	HR	RBI	BB	SO	BA	SA	OBA
Season	492	140	23	2	19	80	26	40	.285	.455	.321
vs. Left-Handers	162	50	5	1	5	27	9	9	.309	.444	.353
vs. Right-Handers	330	90	18	1	14	53	17	31	.273	.461	.305
vs. Ground-Ballers	227	63	12	1	8	40	13	21	.278	.445	.321
vs. Fly-Ballers	265	77	11	1	11	40	13	19	.291	.464	.320
Home Games	245	67	9	1	13	48	16	17	.273	.478	.317
Road Games	247	73	14	1	6	32	10	23	.296	.433	.324
Grass Fields	424	120	17	2	18	73	21	29	.283	.460	.317
Artificial Turf	68	20	6	0	1	7	5	11	.294	.426	.342
April	34	6	3	0	1	8	0	3	.176	.353	.171
May	74	22	3	0	7	18	2	6	.297	.622	.329
June	84	28	5	0	3	14	7	8	.333	.500	.385
July	85	30	4	0	3	17	4	8	.353	.506	.380
August	120	36	5	2	4	18	8	7	.300	.475	.338
Sept./Oct.	95	18	3	0	1	5	5	8	.189	.253	.230
Leading Off Inn.	108	28	8	0	3	3	3	12	.259	.417	.279
Runners On	258	71	9	1	11	72	19	15	.275	.446	.323
Bases Empty	234	69	14	1	8	8	7	25	.295	.466	.318
Runners/Scor. Pos.	144	36	4	1	5	59	14	10	.250	.396	.305
Runners On/2 Out	118	29	3	1	6	26	9	10	.246	.441	.310
Scor. Pos./2 Out	71	15	1	1	3	20	7	7	.211	.380	.282
Late-Inning Pressure	70	15	2	0	4	10	3	6	.214	.414	.247
Leading Off	12	3	1	0	1	1	0	0	.250	.583	.250
Runners On	36	9	1	0	3	9	3	3	.250	.528	.308
Runners/Scor. Pos.	17	3	1	0	1	5	2	1	.176	.412	.263

RUNS BATTED IN	From 1B	From 2B	From 3B	Scoring Position
Totals	11/186	19/119	31/64	50/183
Percentage	5.9%	16.0%	48.4%	27.3%

Loves to face: Chuck Finley (5-for-5)
Todd Stottlemyre (.563, 18-for-32, 1 HR)
Bobby Thigpen (.462, 6-for-13, 2 HR)

Hates to face: Tom Henke (0-for-14)
Bill Krueger (0-for-12)
Mark Langston (0-for-8)

Miscellaneous statistics: Ground outs-to-air outs ratio: 0.85 last season, 0.90 for career.... Grounded into 6 double plays in 112 opportunities (one per 19).... Drove in 23 of 36 runners from third base with less than two outs (64%).... Direction of balls hit to the outfield: 27% to left field, 31% to center, 42% to right.... Base running: Advanced from first base to third on 9 of 24 outfield singles (38%); scored from second on 7 of 11 (64%).... Made 2.04 putouts per nine innings in left field.

Comments: Started 96 of 107 games in which the Yankees faced right-handed starters, and nearly half of the games in which they faced left-handers (27 of 55).... His five home runs vs. southpaws exceeded his previous career total (4), and earned him more playing time vs. lefties. His 173 plate appearances vs. left-handers far exceeded his total in any two seasons of his career. He'd never before had more than 70 at-bats or 12 hits against them.... Struck out only once in his first 54 plate appearances vs. left-handers last season, compared to a previous career rate of one SO per 4.4 PAs vs. southpaws. He finished the season with the 2d-lowest strikeout rate among left-handed batters against lefty pitchers, wedged between Tony Gwynn and Wade Boggs.... His batting average vs. left-handers ranked 3d in the majors among left-handed hitters, behind Mike Greenwell (.327) and Ken Griffey, Jr. (.309). John Kruk had the highest mark in the National League (.297).... The Yankees had a 30–26 record with Hall starting in left field, but were 19–38 with Hall starting in place of Jesse Barfield in right field.... His July batting average ranked 8th in the league.... Hit safely in all 11 games he played against the Rangers last season.... His batting average in Late-Inning Pressure Situations has gone into free-fall: 1981–88, .295; 1989–90, .252; last season, .214.... Last season's was more a rebound than a breakthrough for Hall. Compare the line above to his averages for the three seasons from 1986 through 1988: .285, 14 HR, 77 RBI.

Darryl Hamilton

Bats Left

Milwaukee Brewers	AB	H	2B	3B	HR	RBI	BB	SO	BA	SA	OBA
Season	405	126	15	6	1	57	33	38	.311	.385	.361
vs. Left-Handers	87	24	2	1	0	11	4	12	.276	.322	.308
vs. Right-Handers	318	102	13	5	1	46	29	26	.321	.403	.374
vs. Ground-Ballers	199	62	6	3	1	31	22	17	.312	.387	.378
vs. Fly-Ballers	206	64	9	3	0	26	11	21	.311	.383	.342
Home Games	195	67	10	4	0	24	21	21	.344	.436	.406
Road Games	210	59	5	2	1	33	12	17	.281	.338	.317
Grass Fields	344	109	14	5	1	52	29	33	.317	.395	.367
Artificial Turf	61	17	1	1	0	5	4	5	.279	.328	.323
April	32	7	1	0	0	1	6	4	.219	.250	.342
May	30	7	0	0	0	3	0	1	.233	.233	.233
June	43	17	4	0	0	6	1	3	.395	.488	.409
July	84	27	3	2	0	11	8	9	.321	.405	.376
August	114	34	4	2	1	18	6	10	.298	.395	.331
Sept./Oct.	102	34	3	2	0	18	12	11	.333	.402	.400
Leading Off Inn.	90	23	4	0	0	0	8	9	.256	.300	.316
Runners On	189	70	8	4	1	57	13	10	.370	.471	.405
Bases Empty	216	56	7	2	0	0	20	28	.259	.310	.322
Runners/Scor. Pos.	106	39	5	3	1	56	5	6	.368	.500	.386
Runners On/2 Out	67	26	4	1	0	23	5	4	.388	.478	.431
Scor. Pos./2 Out	49	18	3	1	0	23	4	4	.367	.469	.415
Late-Inning Pressure	51	18	1	0	0	7	6	6	.353	.373	.421
Leading Off	13	4	0	0	0	0	1	1	.308	.308	.357
Runners On	23	10	1	0	0	7	2	2	.435	.478	.480
Runners/Scor. Pos.	13	4	1	0	0	7	0	2	.308	.385	.308

RUNS BATTED IN	From 1B	From 2B	From 3B	Scoring Position
Totals	2/146	24/79	30/50	54/129
Percentage	1.4%	30.4%	60.0%	41.9%

Loves to face: Kevin Appier (.800, 4-for-5)
Dave Johnson (.417, 5-for-12)
Mike Schooler (3-for-3, 1 2B, 1 3B, 1 BB)

Hates to face: Jose Guzman (.077, 1-for-13)
Jack McDowell (.118, 2-for-17)
Jeff Montgomery (0-for-8)

Miscellaneous statistics: Ground outs-to-air outs ratio: 1.75 last season, 1.55 for career.... Grounded into 10 double plays in 114 opportunities (one per 11).... Drove in 20 of 27 runners from third base with less than two outs (74%), 5th-highest rate in A.L.... Direction of balls hit to the outfield: 38% to left field, 33% to center, 28% to right.... Base running: Advanced from first base to third on 16 of 32 outfield singles (50%); scored from second on 13 of 15 (87%).... Made 2.17 putouts per nine innings in right field.

Comments: Started 87 games vs. right-handed pitchers, only 16 games vs. left-handers.... His batting average vs. right-handers was 7th highest in the league.... One of seven major leaguers to start at least 10 games at each of the three outfield positions.... His .389 (14-for-36) average against the Royals was 2d highest in the league.... He and Barry Bonds were the only everyday players to drive in at least 40 percent of runners from scoring position last season.... The only major leaguer with a higher batting average with runners on base was Willie Randolph. The two of them batted back to back in the lineup 33 times last season.... Got his annual home run on August 8. He has hit exactly one in each of his three seasons in the majors, despite increasing time at the plate. His at-bat totals year by year: 117, 168, 448.... He spent the winter with the longest current hitting streak among active batters, having hit safely in each of his last 15 games in 1991. It might seem like he's got a long way to go to break DiMaggio's record, but 95 years ago Wee Willie Keeler parlayed a winter-long one-game carryover into the longest streak in National League history. He hit safely in the final game of the 1896 season and the first 44 in 1897; that 45-game streak is one game longer than Pete Rose's, which equaled Keeler's as the longest ever within the limits of a single N. L. season.

Brian Harper

Bats Right

Minnesota Twins	AB	H	2B	3B	HR	RBI	BB	SO	BA	SA	OBA
Season	441	137	28	1	10	69	14	22	.311	.447	.336
vs. Left-Handers	114	36	7	1	2	14	5	8	.316	.447	.344
vs. Right-Handers	327	101	21	0	8	55	9	14	.309	.446	.333
vs. Ground-Ballers	198	64	17	1	7	42	6	8	.323	.525	.343
vs. Fly-Ballers	243	73	11	0	3	27	8	14	.300	.383	.331
Home Games	217	74	14	1	4	35	7	12	.341	.470	.364
Road Games	224	63	14	0	6	34	7	10	.281	.424	.309
Grass Fields	167	46	10	0	6	32	7	7	.275	.443	.313
Artificial Turf	274	91	18	1	4	37	7	15	.332	.449	.351
April	49	16	3	0	2	7	3	3	.327	.510	.370
May	78	27	8	0	1	18	3	3	.346	.487	.361
June	79	24	7	0	0	7	1	5	.304	.392	.333
July	73	21	3	0	2	8	2	2	.288	.411	.303
August	82	26	3	1	3	17	2	7	.317	.488	.341
Sept./Oct.	80	23	4	0	2	12	3	2	.287	.412	.318
Leading Off Inn.	93	29	7	0	1	1	2	1	.312	.419	.333
Runners On	210	74	13	1	9	68	8	11	.352	.552	.374
Bases Empty	231	63	15	0	1	1	6	11	.273	.351	.300
Runners/Scor. Pos.	131	41	9	0	4	56	8	6	.313	.473	.351
Runners On/2 Out	92	28	6	0	4	28	5	4	.304	.500	.347
Scor. Pos./2 Out	61	17	5	0	2	23	5	2	.279	.459	.343
Late-Inning Pressure	64	20	3	1	3	14	1	1	.313	.531	.323
Leading Off	13	3	1	0	0	0	0	0	.231	.308	.231
Runners On	31	12	1	1	3	14	1	1	.387	.774	.406
Runners/Scor. Pos.	18	5	1	0	2	11	1	1	.278	.667	.316

RUNS BATTED IN	From 1B	From 2B	From 3B	Scoring Position
Totals	13/156	25/113	21/49	46/162
Percentage	8.3%	22.1%	42.9%	28.4%

Loves to face: Roger Clemens (.545, 6-for-11)
Alex Fernandez (.800, 4-for-5)
Dan Plesac (.600, 6-for-10, 3 HR)

Hates to face: Chuck Crim (0-for-10)
Charlie Hough (0-for-10)
David Wells (.083, 1-for-12)

Miscellaneous statistics: Ground outs-to-air outs ratio: 1.03 last season, 0.95 for career.... Grounded into 14 double plays in 97 opportunities (one per 6.9).... Drove in 17 of 28 runners from third base with less than two outs (61%).... Direction of balls hit to the outfield: 38% to left field, 33% to center, 29% to right.... Base running: Advanced from first base to third on 3 of 22 outfield singles (14%); scored from second on 7 of 12 (58%).... Opposing base stealers: 98-for-126 (78%), highest rate in A.L.

Comments: He has batted .325, .294, and .313 in three seasons since 1989. Over the last 50 years, only three catchers have batted .300 or better in three consecutive seasons: Manny Sanguillen (1969–71), Ted Simmons (1971–73), and Thurman Munson (1975–77). By dropping the qualifying batting average to .290, we include Harper, but no one else.... He puts the ball in play more often than any other active player: 1781 times in 1993 career plate appearances (89.4%), with strikeouts, walks, hit batters, and catchers' interference accounting for the remaining 212 PAs. The rate is slightly higher than runner-up Ozzie Guillen's (89.3%). But no fewer than 36 players who played within the last 50 years had higher rates. The top three: Emil Verban (93.8%), Don Mueller (92.9%), and Lloyd Waner (92.6%).... Harper has a career average of one walk every 30 times to the plate, and has struck out once every 16 plate appearances. He is the only player to rank among the top-10 active players in both of those categories.... Was the Twins' leading hitter last season with runners in scoring position and against right-handed pitchers.... Batting average with runners on base was 4th highest in the league.... Caught nearly 90 percent of the innings pitched by either Jack Morris or Kevin Tapani.... Playing in the "Double-Dome," his average of one double every 14.4 at-bats is 6th highest in A.L. history. (For the top five, see the Jody Reed comments.)

Dave Henderson

Bats Right

Oakland A's	AB	H	2B	3B	HR	RBI	BB	SO	BA	SA	OBA
Season	572	158	33	0	25	85	58	113	.276	.465	.346
vs. Left-Handers	144	51	14	0	8	24	15	23	.354	.618	.416
vs. Right-Handers	428	107	19	0	17	61	43	90	.250	.414	.322
vs. Ground-Ballers	296	71	15	0	8	38	25	57	.240	.372	.300
vs. Fly-Ballers	276	87	18	0	17	47	33	56	.315	.565	.393
Home Games	282	73	9	0	15	39	29	57	.259	.450	.329
Road Games	290	85	24	0	10	46	29	56	.293	.479	.362
Grass Fields	488	140	25	0	23	77	51	99	.287	.480	.357
Artificial Turf	84	18	8	0	2	8	7	14	.214	.381	.283
April	75	29	9	0	6	18	9	12	.387	.747	.453
May	102	30	5	0	6	21	8	15	.294	.520	.345
June	93	25	3	0	6	11	16	20	.269	.495	.376
July	97	20	5	0	1	10	9	20	.206	.289	.280
August	118	35	5	0	5	15	7	21	.297	.466	.346
Sept./Oct.	87	19	6	0	1	10	9	25	.218	.322	.289
Leading Off Inn.	119	34	7	0	6	6	6	17	.286	.496	.325
Runners On	267	78	17	0	10	70	25	63	.292	.468	.353
Bases Empty	305	80	16	0	15	15	33	50	.262	.462	.340
Runners/Scor. Pos.	154	43	10	0	6	58	17	45	.279	.461	.347
Runners On/2 Out	100	28	6	0	5	29	11	25	.280	.490	.351
Scor. Pos./2 Out	65	14	2	0	4	25	10	21	.215	.431	.320
Late-Inning Pressure	80	17	5	0	0	5	5	18	.213	.275	.267
Leading Off	24	6	1	0	0	0	1	2	.250	.292	.308
Runners On	41	9	3	0	0	5	3	13	.220	.293	.273
Runners/Scor. Pos.	22	4	2	0	0	5	3	10	.182	.273	.280

RUNS BATTED IN	From 1B	From 2B	From 3B	Scoring Position
Totals	14/189	25/127	21/55	46/182
Percentage	7.4%	19.7%	38.2%	25.3%

Loves to face: Jim Abbott (.529, 9-for-17, 1 2B, 5 HR)
Mark Langston (.471, 16-for-34, 3 HR)
David West (.714, 5-for-7, 1 2B, 3 HR)
Hates to face: Rick Aguilera (.071, 1-for-14, 8 SO)
Tom Gordon (0-for-12, 9 SO)
Jeff Montgomery (0-for-7, 4 SO)

Miscellaneous statistics: Ground outs-to-air outs ratio: 0.82 last season, 0.76 for career.... Grounded into 9 double plays in 131 opportunities (one per 15).... Drove in 14 of 26 runners from third base with less than two outs (54%).... Direction of balls hit to the outfield: 42% to left field, 28% to center, 30% to right.... Base running: Advanced from first base to third on 14 of 27 outfield singles (52%); scored from second on 12 of 12 (100%), 2d best in A.L.... Made 2.70 putouts per nine innings in center field.

Comments: His April batting average was 2d highest in the majors, and he owned at least a share of the league lead in RBIs as late as June 12 and in home runs through June 18.... Set a career high with 25 home runs, raising his career total to 172. Only eight players in major league history reached the 200-HR mark but never had a season of more than 25: George Hendrick (total—267, career high—25), Vada Pinson (256/24), Al Oliver (219/22), Chet Lemon (215/24), Ron Fairly (215/19), Richie Hebner (203/25), Buddy Bell (201/20), and Bill Freehan (201/20).... Henderson still ranks fourth on the Mariners' home-run list with 79, but Ken Griffey, Jr. (60) and possibly Jay Buhner (53) appear to be less than a season away from passing him.... Had the American League's 12th-highest batting average vs. fly-ball pitchers, but ranked among the bottom 10 against ground-ballers (52d of 61 qualifiers).... Has batted at least 50 points higher on grass fields than on artificial turf in each of the past three seasons. His combined averages during that time: .276 on grass, .203 on turf.... Made only one error last season, after averaging five per season over the previous nine years.... The Athletics, Mariners, and Braves were the only teams whose center fielders combined for at least 20 home runs last season. Where have you gone, Joe DiMaggio?

Rickey Henderson

Bats Right

Oakland A's	AB	H	2B	3B	HR	RBI	BB	SO	BA	SA	OBA
Season	470	126	17	1	18	57	98	73	.268	.423	.400
vs. Left-Handers	114	33	3	0	8	17	21	19	.289	.526	.401
vs. Right-Handers	356	93	14	1	10	40	77	54	.261	.390	.399
vs. Ground-Ballers	249	68	10	1	5	22	43	41	.273	.382	.386
vs. Fly-Ballers	221	58	7	0	13	35	55	32	.262	.471	.413
Home Games	248	69	10	0	8	28	48	36	.278	.415	.401
Road Games	222	57	7	1	10	29	50	37	.257	.432	.399
Grass Fields	415	112	15	1	14	47	81	62	.270	.412	.395
Artificial Turf	55	14	2	0	4	10	17	11	.255	.509	.432
April	22	6	0	0	0	1	2	3	.273	.273	.360
May	95	24	4	0	3	12	26	18	.253	.389	.410
June	81	26	2	1	1	8	24	7	.321	.407	.481
July	101	25	4	0	4	12	16	17	.248	.406	.367
August	84	20	3	0	5	10	16	14	.238	.452	.363
Sept./Oct.	87	25	4	0	5	14	14	14	.287	.506	.388
Leading Off Inn.	185	54	9	0	7	7	35	26	.292	.454	.410
Runners On	159	42	5	1	8	47	47	24	.264	.459	.431
Bases Empty	311	84	12	0	10	10	51	49	.270	.405	.381
Runners/Scor. Pos.	91	21	2	1	6	41	36	12	.231	.473	.447
Runners On/2 Out	72	13	1	1	4	18	22	10	.181	.389	.372
Scor. Pos./2 Out	53	11	1	1	3	16	19	5	.208	.434	.417
Late-Inning Pressure	63	17	4	0	3	15	16	10	.270	.476	.418
Leading Off	11	4	1	0	0	0	2	2	.364	.455	.462
Runners On	31	9	3	0	2	14	12	4	.290	.581	.488
Runners/Scor. Pos.	18	5	1	0	2	13	11	3	.278	.667	.552

RUNS BATTED IN	From 1B	From 2B	From 3B	Scoring Position
Totals	9/117	8/68	22/47	30/115
Percentage	7.7%	11.8%	46.8%	26.1%

Loves to face: Jimmy Key (.377, 26-for-69, 5 HR)
Ben McDonald (.500, 6-for-12, 2 HR)
Frank Tanana (.367, 33-for-90, 9 HR)
Hates to face: Roger Clemens (.167, 8-for-48, 7 BB)
Goose Gossage (0-for-9, 9 SO)
Nolan Ryan (.118, 2-for-17, 5 BB)

Miscellaneous statistics: Ground outs-to-air outs ratio: 1.02 last season, 1.11 for career.... Grounded into 7 double plays in 83 opportunities (one per 12).... Drove in 15 of 23 runners from third base with less than two outs (65%).... Direction of balls hit to the outfield: 46% to left field, 28% to center, 27% to right.... Base running: Advanced from first base to third on 18 of 32 outfield singles (56%); scored from second on 12 of 14 (86%).... Made 2.28 putouts per nine innings in left field, 2d-highest rate in A.L.

Comments: Henderson has stated that his most cherished remaining goal would be to surpass Ty Cobb's all-time record of 2245 runs scored. Some pertinent figures: He currently ranks 63d in major league history with 1395 runs; that's the 5th-highest total among active players, behind Robin Yount (1499), Dwight Evans (1470), and George Brett and Dave Winfield (tied at 1459).... Henderson could reach the 1500-run mark this season by matching his total of 105 in 1991. By scoring at the same rate as he has over the past three seasons (80 runs per 100 games), he would reach that plateau in his career game #1873. Of the 45 players who scored 1500 runs, 14 reached that level in fewer than 1873 games, but only one of them over the past 50 years (Ted Williams). The fastest ever to 1500 was Billy Hamilton, in approximately 1325 games; no one else reached 1500 in fewer than 1600 games. Finally, our projection model, admittedly limited by the fact that there are no Rickey clones in baseball history, estimates that Rickey has one chance in six to score 2000 runs, but the odds against him breaking Cobb's record are 18-to-1. (We'd take those odds.) ... On-base percentage leading off innings was 4th highest in the majors.... His average with two outs and runners on base was 8th lowest in the league.... Has batted .324 in Late-Inning Pressure Situations over the past five years, the 5th-highest mark in the majors (minimum: 200 AB), behind Julio Franco (.348), Alan Trammell (.333), Kent Hrbek (.332), and Kirby Puckett (.332).

Chris Hoiles
Bats Right

Baltimore Orioles	AB	H	2B	3B	HR	RBI	BB	SO	BA	SA	OBA
Season	341	83	15	0	11	31	29	61	.243	.384	.304
vs. Left-Handers	113	29	6	0	6	8	11	16	.257	.469	.320
vs. Right-Handers	228	54	9	0	5	23	18	45	.237	.342	.296
vs. Ground-Ballers	158	44	7	0	9	26	13	25	.278	.494	.331
vs. Fly-Ballers	183	39	8	0	2	5	16	36	.213	.290	.280
Home Games	153	35	7	0	5	12	16	26	.229	.373	.306
Road Games	188	48	8	0	6	19	13	35	.255	.394	.302
Grass Fields	284	65	11	0	10	23	26	51	.229	.373	.295
Artificial Turf	57	18	4	0	1	8	3	10	.316	.439	.350
April	34	5	1	0	0	0	1	8	.147	.176	.194
May	49	13	2	0	2	4	11	8	.265	.429	.393
June	50	12	3	0	1	5	3	6	.240	.360	.283
July	72	23	4	0	3	10	2	12	.319	.500	.338
August	73	19	5	0	2	6	4	15	.260	.411	.299
Sept./Oct.	63	11	0	0	3	6	8	12	.175	.317	.268
Leading Off Inn.	81	18	3	0	5	5	9	14	.222	.444	.300
Runners On	146	33	7	0	1	21	13	28	.226	.295	.292
Bases Empty	195	50	8	0	10	10	16	33	.256	.451	.313
Runners/Scor. Pos.	67	15	2	0	1	19	9	15	.224	.299	.312
Runners On/2 Out	65	14	4	0	0	8	7	12	.215	.277	.292
Scor. Pos./2 Out	34	6	1	0	0	7	4	7	.176	.206	.263
Late-Inning Pressure	58	10	0	0	3	9	6	16	.172	.328	.250
Leading Off	16	2	0	0	1	1	2	5	.125	.313	.222
Runners On	21	5	0	0	1	7	2	5	.238	.381	.304
Runners/Scor. Pos.	8	4	0	0	1	7	0	1	.500	.875	.500

RUNS BATTED IN	From 1B	From 2B	From 3B	Scoring Position
Totals	4/113	9/54	7/27	16/81
Percentage	3.5%	16.7%	25.9%	19.8%

Loves to face: Chuck Finley (.375, 3-for-8, 1 HR)
Erik Hanson (.667, 4-for-6)
Dave Otto (.800, 4-for-5, 2 HR)
Hates to face: Edwin Nunez (0-for-3, 3 SO)
Dave Stewart (0-for-3, 3 SO)

Miscellaneous statistics: Ground outs-to-air outs ratio: 0.73 last season, 0.64 for career.... Grounded into 11 double plays in 66 opportunities (one per 6.0).... Drove in 5 of 13 runners from third base with less than two outs (38%).... Direction of balls hit to the outfield: 38% to left field, 34% to center, 28% to right.... Base running: Advanced from first base to third on 6 of 15 outfield singles (40%); scored from second on 4 of 5 (80%).... Opposing base stealers: 49-for-75 (65%).

Comments: The Orioles' staff ERA was more than a half-run better with Hoiles behind the plate (4.24) than it was with Bob Melvin (4.91) or Ernie Whitt (5.87) there. Of the 13 Baltimore pitchers who pitched at least 60 innings last season, only four (Mike Flanagan, Ben McDonald, Mike Mussina, and Mark Williamson) had a higher ERA with Hoiles than with Melvin.... He led A.L. catchers in fielding percentage, playing 88 games (seven more than the number needed to qualify) and committing only one error in 477 chances. The league average for catchers is one error every 88 chances.... His error rate was the 2d best ever by an Orioles catcher. The team record is held by Elrod Hendricks, who committed one error in 520 chances in 1969.... April batting average was 6th lowest in the league.... Batting average in Late-Inning Pressure Situations was 9th lowest in the league.... Ten of his 11 home runs were solo shots, but the other was a grand slam.... Another player who was once part of the proverbial "package of minor leaguers"; he was one of three prospects acquired by Baltimore in 1988 from the Tigers for Fred Lynn.... Has played 136 major league games without hitting a triple, stealing a base, or executing a sacrifice bunt. He stole 21 in 500 games in the minors, including 10 in his first pro season (1986). For more on this topic, look to your right.

Sam Horn
Bats Left

Baltimore Orioles	AB	H	2B	3B	HR	RBI	BB	SO	BA	SA	OBA
Season	317	74	16	0	23	61	41	99	.233	.502	.326
vs. Left-Handers	18	2	0	0	1	1	1	7	.111	.278	.158
vs. Right-Handers	299	72	16	0	22	60	40	92	.241	.515	.335
vs. Ground-Ballers	127	33	7	0	10	20	23	33	.260	.551	.382
vs. Fly-Ballers	190	41	9	0	13	41	18	66	.216	.468	.286
Home Games	149	37	8	0	12	28	24	40	.248	.544	.356
Road Games	168	37	8	0	11	33	17	59	.220	.464	.298
Grass Fields	270	67	13	0	23	59	34	80	.248	.552	.336
Artificial Turf	47	7	3	0	0	2	7	19	.149	.213	.273
April	42	9	1	0	3	10	7	21	.214	.452	.327
May	46	11	2	0	3	7	6	14	.239	.478	.327
June	73	18	7	0	5	12	12	21	.247	.548	.360
July	59	15	2	0	4	12	9	16	.254	.492	.357
August	39	5	2	0	1	4	4	10	.128	.256	.209
Sept./Oct.	58	16	2	0	7	16	3	17	.276	.672	.323
Leading Off Inn.	77	12	2	0	2	2	8	24	.156	.260	.235
Runners On	136	42	10	0	14	52	21	40	.309	.691	.406
Bases Empty	181	32	6	0	9	9	20	59	.177	.359	.262
Runners/Scor. Pos.	80	22	7	0	7	36	13	29	.275	.625	.379
Runners On/2 Out	63	19	4	0	5	21	11	20	.302	.603	.421
Scor. Pos./2 Out	37	10	3	0	3	16	10	15	.270	.595	.438
Late-Inning Pressure	43	9	6	0	1	5	2	16	.209	.419	.261
Leading Off	9	2	0	0	0	0	0	4	.222	.222	.222
Runners On	20	4	3	0	1	5	1	6	.200	.500	.273
Runners/Scor. Pos.	9	1	1	0	0	1	0	3	.111	.222	.111

RUNS BATTED IN	From 1B	From 2B	From 3B	Scoring Position
Totals	13/98	13/59	12/32	25/91
Percentage	13.3%	22.0%	37.5%	27.5%

Loves to face: Rich DeLucia (.333, 2-for-6, 1 HR, 5 BB)
Pascual Perez (3-for-3, 1 HR)
Bob Welch (.421, 8-for-19, 1 HR)
Hates to face: Erik Hanson (0-for-14)
Jack Morris (.071, 1-for-14, 2 BB, 7 SO)
Bobby Witt (0-for-10, 7 SO)

Miscellaneous statistics: Ground outs-to-air outs ratio: 0.85 last season, 1.04 for career.... Grounded into 10 double plays in 62 opportunities (one per 6.2).... Drove in 8 of 18 runners from third base with less than two outs (44%).... Direction of balls hit to the outfield: 25% to left field, 29% to center, 46% to right.... Base running: Advanced from first base to third on 5 of 18 outfield singles (28%); scored from second on 4 of 6 (67%).

Comments: Has played 303 major league games without hitting a triple, stealing a base, or executing a sacrifice bunt. Now, we know it's Big Sam Horn, and we don't expect him to be Mr. Finesse. But not even one? Of *any* of them? Except for pitchers, the only player with a longer career who never tripled, stole, or sacked was Hawk Taylor (394 games). No other nonpitcher in major league history pitched "finesse shutouts" over the first 300 games of his career.... You might wonder how a player could strike out 99 times in just 362 plate appearances, but two years ago Rolando Roomes struck out more often (100) in fewer times up (334), as did another player in 1987 whose career path Horn would gladly follow: Fred McGriff (104 SOs in 356 PAs).... Started 92 games last season, all against right-handed pitchers. He has started 189 games since his last start against a southpaw (Oct. 2, 1987).... Only three other players with at least 300 at-bats had more extra-base hits than singles last season: Jose Canseco, Rob Deer, and Howard Johnson.... His average of one home run every 13.8 at-bats was 3d highest in the majors, behind those of Jose Canseco and Kevin Mitchell.... His career home-run rate (one every 15.8 at-bats) is fifth highest among active players (minimum: 50 HR), behind Cecil Fielder (13.5), Mark McGwire (14.9), Jose Canseco (15.4), and Darryl Strawberry (15.7).... Batting average on artificial turf was 2d lowest in the majors.

David Howard

Bats Left and Right

Kansas City Royals	AB	H	2B	3B	HR	RBI	BB	SO	BA	SA	OBA
Season	236	51	7	0	1	17	16	45	.216	.258	.267
vs. Left-Handers	80	18	2	0	1	10	6	12	.225	.287	.276
vs. Right-Handers	156	33	5	0	0	7	10	33	.212	.244	.262
vs. Ground-Ballers	99	23	5	0	0	8	6	18	.232	.283	.276
vs. Fly-Ballers	137	28	2	0	1	9	10	27	.204	.241	.260
Home Games	116	24	3	0	0	7	11	22	.207	.233	.271
Road Games	120	27	4	0	1	10	5	23	.225	.283	.262
Grass Fields	97	23	3	0	0	7	3	18	.237	.268	.267
Artificial Turf	139	28	4	0	1	10	13	27	.201	.252	.266
April	11	1	0	0	0	0	0	1	.091	.091	.091
May	5	0	0	0	0	0	2	1	.000	.000	.286
June	21	2	0	0	0	1	2	6	.095	.095	.174
July	55	14	2	0	1	7	3	8	.255	.345	.300
August	87	24	5	0	0	9	3	15	.276	.333	.297
Sept./Oct.	57	10	0	0	0	0	6	14	.175	.175	.254
Leading Off Inn.	54	7	1	0	0	0	4	12	.130	.148	.190
Runners On	102	25	3	0	1	17	5	16	.245	.304	.275
Bases Empty	134	26	4	0	0	0	11	29	.194	.224	.260
Runners/Scor. Pos.	66	16	3	0	1	17	3	7	.242	.333	.268
Runners On/2 Out	49	10	2	0	0	8	2	9	.204	.245	.235
Scor. Pos./2 Out	37	9	2	0	0	8	2	4	.243	.297	.282
Late-Inning Pressure	18	2	0	0	0	0	0	4	.111	.111	.111
Leading Off	6	1	0	0	0	0	0	2	.167	.167	.167
Runners On	7	1	0	0	0	0	0	0	.143	.143	.143
Runners/Scor. Pos.	4	0	0	0	0	0	0	0	.000	.000	.000

RUNS BATTED IN	From 1B	From 2B	From 3B	Scoring Position
Totals	0/68	6/55	10/25	16/80
Percentage	0.0%	10.9%	40.0%	20.0%

Loves to face:

Hates to face: Matt Young (0-for-6)

Miscellaneous statistics: Ground outs-to-air outs ratio: 1.05 last season, 1.05 for career.... Grounded into 1 double play in 50 opportunities (one per 50), 3d-best rate in A.L.... Drove in 6 of 10 runners from third base with less than two outs (60%).... Direction of balls hit to the outfield: 37% to left field, 27% to center, 36% to right batting left-handed; 31% to left field, 29% to center, 40% to right batting right-handed.... Base running: Advanced from first base to third on 5 of 8 outfield singles (63%); scored from second on 5 of 7 (71%).... Made 3.29 assists per nine innings at shortstop.

Comments: David and his father form one of the more obscure father/son pairs to play in the majors. Bruce won 25 games during five years with the White Sox (1963–67), then split his final season between the Orioles and the Senators. He was traded to Baltimore in the deal that sent Don Buford to the O's and brought Luis Aparicio back to Chicago.... Howard split time at shortstop last season with Kurt Stillwell, whose own dad, Ron, was a Washington Senators shortstop so obscure he'd make Bruce Howard look like Madonna. He played 14 games for them (1961–62).... Two other players on the 1991 Royals had big-league dads, too: Brian McRae, whose father ranks fourth in team history in games played (and can control Brian's chances of approaching that level); and Danny Tartabull, whose father Jose played for the Kansas City A's, the Red Sox, and the Oakland A's during a nine-year career that produced only two home runs—150 fewer than his son has totaled to date. Of course, daddy has one more Series ring; he was part of Boston's impossible dream in 1967.... Howard's .258 slugging percentage was 3d lowest in the American League last season (minimum: 200 AB). Only Al Newman (.211) and Juan Bell (.249) had lower figures.... Lowest slugging percentages in Royals' history (minimum: 200 AB): Onix Concepcion, .245 (1985); Angel Salazar, .246 (1987); and Howard.... We know what you're thinking. Yes, Buddy Biancalana had lower marks than that. But he never batted 200 times.

Kent Hrbek

Bats Left

Minnesota Twins	AB	H	2B	3B	HR	RBI	BB	SO	BA	SA	OBA
Season	462	131	20	1	20	89	67	48	.284	.461	.373
vs. Left-Handers	128	36	3	0	6	25	14	19	.281	.445	.352
vs. Right-Handers	334	95	17	1	14	64	53	29	.284	.467	.380
vs. Ground-Ballers	202	52	5	0	11	40	35	24	.257	.446	.366
vs. Fly-Ballers	260	79	15	1	9	49	32	24	.304	.473	.379
Home Games	236	75	11	0	11	52	37	22	.318	.504	.407
Road Games	226	56	9	1	9	37	30	26	.248	.416	.336
Grass Fields	182	47	9	0	8	32	23	24	.258	.440	.341
Artificial Turf	280	84	11	1	12	57	44	24	.300	.475	.393
April	66	12	1	0	2	13	6	8	.182	.288	.250
May	72	21	3	1	2	7	15	4	.292	.444	.414
June	78	28	6	0	3	18	8	6	.359	.551	.414
July	79	22	2	0	4	17	12	8	.278	.456	.370
August	98	31	6	0	4	18	12	14	.316	.500	.391
Sept./Oct.	69	17	2	0	5	16	14	8	.246	.493	.373
Leading Off Inn.	113	22	3	0	0	0	16	13	.195	.221	.295
Runners On	238	75	10	0	15	84	34	23	.315	.546	.398
Bases Empty	224	56	10	1	5	5	33	25	.250	.371	.346
Runners/Scor. Pos.	126	39	5	0	7	64	20	17	.310	.516	.399
Runners On/2 Out	114	43	5	0	11	46	13	12	.377	.711	.441
Scor. Pos./2 Out	62	23	3	0	6	35	7	8	.371	.710	.435
Late-Inning Pressure	57	20	1	0	3	10	6	5	.351	.526	.413
Leading Off	10	4	0	0	0	0	0	0	.400	.400	.400
Runners On	28	11	0	0	2	9	4	2	.393	.607	.469
Runners/Scor. Pos.	13	7	0	0	1	7	2	1	.538	.769	.600

RUNS BATTED IN	From 1B	From 2B	From 3B	Scoring Position
Totals	18/173	23/94	28/48	51/142
Percentage	10.4%	24.5%	58.3%	35.9%

Loves to face: Jose Guzman (.400, 10-for-25, 3 HR)
Dave Johnson (.545, 6-for-11, 3 2B, 2 HR)
Bill Wegman (.406, 13-for-32, 4 HR)

Hates to face: Greg Cadaret (.063, 1-for-16, 2 BB)
Jimmy Key (.167, 3-for-18)
Matt Young (.161, 5-for-31, 5 BB)

Miscellaneous statistics: Ground outs-to-air outs ratio: 1.30 last season, 1.16 for career.... Grounded into 15 double plays in 113 opportunities (one per 7.5).... Drove in 18 of 22 runners from third base with less than two outs (82%), 2d-highest rate in majors.... Direction of balls hit to the outfield: 25% to left field, 38% to center, 38% to right.... Base running: Advanced from first base to third on 6 of 26 outfield singles (23%); scored from second on 8 of 11 (73%).... Made 0.79 assists per nine innings at first base.

Comments: Lowest postseason batting averages in baseball history (minimum: 75 AB): Kent Hrbek, .154 (14-for-91); Dick Green, .155 (13-for-84); Everett Scott, .156 (14-for-90); Gene Tenace, .158 (18-for-114); and Johnny Roseboro, .160 (12-for-75). Eight players with between 50 and 74 at-bats have averages lower than Hrbek's.... Went hitless in his first 11 at-bats with runners on base in the 1991 L.C.S. vs. Toronto. But his last at-bat of the series was a two-out, two-run single giving the Twins an 8–5 lead that stood up.... Hit his first triple since 1987, and like the 16 that went before, it came on artificial turf. He now has a career total of 1944 at-bats on grass fields without a triple. Of his 17 on artificial turf, 15 have been hit at the Metrodome.... Led the majors with a .377 batting average with two outs and runners on base.... June batting average was 5th highest in the league.... Percentage of runners driven in from scoring position was best on team and 5th highest in league.... On-base percentage leading off innings was 9th lowest in the league.... One of three players to hit at least 20 home runs in each of the last eight seasons. The others: Darryl Strawberry and Cal Ripken.... Ranks sixth in the majors with 242 home runs over the past 10 years, and seventh in RBIs (885).... Has batted .348 or better in Late-Inning Pressure Situations three times in the past five years. See the Rickey Henderson comments for the top five since 1987.

Mike Huff — Bats Right

Indians/White Sox	AB	H	2B	3B	HR	RBI	BB	SO	BA	SA	OBA
Season	243	61	10	2	3	25	37	48	.251	.346	.361
vs. Left-Handers	121	28	4	1	3	9	16	21	.231	.355	.333
vs. Right-Handers	122	33	6	1	0	16	21	27	.270	.336	.388
vs. Ground-Ballers	100	23	2	2	0	12	16	15	.230	.290	.358
vs. Fly-Ballers	143	38	8	0	3	13	21	33	.266	.385	.363
Home Games	125	33	7	2	1	10	17	24	.264	.376	.374
Road Games	118	28	3	0	2	15	20	24	.237	.314	.348
Grass Fields	206	53	9	2	2	20	32	41	.257	.350	.369
Artificial Turf	37	8	1	0	1	5	5	7	.216	.324	.318
April	18	4	0	1	0	0	6	2	.222	.333	.417
May	79	21	5	0	0	6	14	21	.266	.329	.398
June	45	10	1	0	2	4	5	6	.222	.378	.300
July	22	3	1	0	0	3	3	6	.136	.182	.231
August	38	13	2	1	1	10	4	5	.342	.526	.419
Sept./Oct.	41	10	1	0	0	2	5	8	.244	.268	.340
Leading Off Inn.	73	20	4	1	2	2	16	12	.274	.438	.411
Runners On	99	26	4	1	0	22	13	19	.263	.323	.353
Bases Empty	144	35	6	1	3	3	24	29	.243	.361	.366
Runners/Scor. Pos.	58	17	2	1	0	22	9	12	.293	.362	.377
Runners On/2 Out	48	14	3	0	0	12	8	8	.292	.354	.393
Scor. Pos./2 Out	34	10	2	0	0	12	6	7	.294	.353	.400
Late-Inning Pressure	41	12	3	1	0	4	5	7	.293	.415	.383
Leading Off	9	2	0	1	0	0	2	1	.222	.444	.364
Runners On	19	5	2	0	0	4	2	4	.263	.368	.333
Runners/Scor. Pos.	9	4	1	0	0	4	1	1	.444	.556	.500

RUNS BATTED IN	From 1B	From 2B	From 3B	Scoring Position
Totals	1/70	10/46	11/29	21/75
Percentage	1.4%	21.7%	37.9%	28.0%

Loves to face: Chuck Finley (.667, 2-for-3, 4 BB, 1 SO)
Mark Guthrie (.750, 3-for-4, 1 HR)
Bill Krueger (.667, 4-for-6)

Hates to face: Jimmy Key (0-for-7)
Frank Tanana (.100, 1-for-10)
David Wells (.100, 1-for-10)

Miscellaneous statistics: Ground outs-to-air outs ratio: 1.06 last season, 1.12 for career. . . . Grounded into 7 double plays in 49 opportunities (one per 7.0). . . . Drove in 5 of 11 runners from third base with less than two outs (45%). . . . Direction of balls hit to the outfield: 31% to left field, 29% to center, 39% to right. . . . Base running: Advanced from first base to third on 8 of 24 outfield singles (33%); scored from second on 13 of 14 (93%). . . . Made 2.67 putouts per nine innings in center field.

Comments: Finished seventh among A.L. rookies in games played (102) last season, but started only 58 of those games and played the entire game only 41 times. . . . Had highest on-base average among A.L. rookies with at least 200 at-bats last year, in large measure due to his walk rate. Huff averaged one walk for every eight plate appearances last season; the average rate of walks in the majors is one every 11.5 times up. A frequent complaint about rookies is that they usually don't *(a)* have the patience or *(b)* get enough respect from umpires to draw a lot of walks. Actually, the difference is small; last season's results: Rookies drew a walk every 12.2 plate appearances, veterans once every 11.4 trips. . . . Played 51 games with the Indians before being placed on waivers; White Sox claimed him and he played in another 51 with them. . . . Huff and Mark Whiten were the only two rookies to accumulate 100 games playing for two teams last season. They wouldn't mind if their career paths (and incomes) follow those of the last three rookies to do that: Felix Jose (1990), Lenny Harris (1989), and Bobby Bonilla (1986). . . . White Sox outfielders hit only 27 home runs last season, lowest total in majors; Indians outfielders had only 182 RBIs, also the lowest total in the majors. Circumstantial evidence ties Huff to the scene of both crimes, although his attorneys, acknowledging his presence, would call for mercy: Huff was responsible for less than 8 percent of the at-bats by Cleveland's outfielders, and for only 5 percent of those by Chicago's.

Jeff Huson — Bats Left

Texas Rangers	AB	H	2B	3B	HR	RBI	BB	SO	BA	SA	OBA
Season	268	57	8	3	2	26	39	32	.213	.287	.312
vs. Left-Handers	27	2	0	0	0	0	4	6	.074	.074	.194
vs. Right-Handers	241	55	8	3	2	26	35	26	.228	.311	.325
vs. Ground-Ballers	136	29	3	2	1	12	21	14	.213	.287	.318
vs. Fly-Ballers	132	28	5	1	1	14	18	18	.212	.288	.305
Home Games	141	25	1	2	1	15	24	18	.177	.234	.297
Road Games	127	32	7	1	1	11	15	14	.252	.346	.329
Grass Fields	232	54	7	3	2	26	35	28	.233	.315	.332
Artificial Turf	36	3	1	0	0	0	4	4	.083	.111	.175
April	41	10	1	1	0	6	4	6	.244	.317	.304
May	53	9	3	1	0	2	12	10	.170	.264	.323
June	55	12	1	1	1	7	6	6	.218	.327	.295
July	45	9	0	0	1	2	5	5	.200	.267	.280
August	26	11	2	0	0	4	4	3	.423	.500	.500
Sept./Oct.	48	6	1	0	0	5	8	2	.125	.146	.250
Leading Off Inn.	63	13	4	0	0	0	12	9	.206	.270	.333
Runners On	116	27	3	2	2	26	13	9	.233	.345	.308
Bases Empty	152	30	5	1	0	0	26	23	.197	.243	.315
Runners/Scor. Pos.	61	16	1	1	1	21	9	6	.262	.361	.352
Runners On/2 Out	47	10	2	1	2	11	6	4	.213	.426	.302
Scor. Pos./2 Out	27	4	1	0	1	7	4	3	.148	.296	.258
Late-Inning Pressure	29	9	0	0	0	0	5	1	.310	.310	.412
Leading Off	11	3	0	0	0	0	1	0	.273	.273	.333
Runners On	8	2	0	0	0	0	1	0	.250	.250	.333
Runners/Scor. Pos.	5	1	0	0	0	0	1	0	.200	.200	.333

RUNS BATTED IN	From 1B	From 2B	From 3B	Scoring Position
Totals	5/95	6/44	13/30	19/74
Percentage	5.3%	13.6%	43.3%	25.7%

Loves to face: Jack McDowell (.444, 4-for-9)
Jaime Navarro (.429, 3-for-7)
Melido Perez (.375, 6-for-16)

Hates to face: Scott Erickson (0-for-11)
Mike Moore (.071, 1-for-14)
Todd Stottlemyre (0-for-9)

Miscellaneous statistics: Ground outs-to-air outs ratio: 1.35 last season, 1.34 for career. . . . Grounded into 6 double plays in 68 opportunities (one per 11). . . . Drove in 9 of 15 runners from third base with less than two outs (60%). . . . Direction of balls hit to the outfield: 38% to left field, 32% to center, 30% to right. . . . Base running: Advanced from first base to third on 8 of 12 outfield singles (67%), 2d-highest rate in A.L.; scored from second on 6 of 7 (86%). . . . Made 3.14 assists per nine innings at shortstop.

Comments: Like Mike Huff, another player whose "games played" column doesn't tell the entire story: Huson appeared in 119 games last year, but that total included only 85 starts, and perhaps more significantly, only 52 complete games. . . . Started 82 games against right-handed pitchers, but only two against left-handers. His two-year totals with Texas: 179 starts vs. righties, nine vs. lefties. His .195 career batting average in 92 at-bats vs. southpaws won't cause Bobby Valentine to change things, either. No Rangers shortstop has played in 150 games in a season since Toby Harrah in 1974. . . . Home-game batting average was 2d lowest in majors. . . . Huson has never had a hit with two outs and the bases loaded; he's 0-for-13 in that situation. . . . However, in Late-Inning Pressure Situations, he has a .313 career average in 99 at-bats. . . . Had nine sacrifice bunts last season including two while pinch-hitting. He and teammate Mike Stanley were the only two A.L. players with two sacrifice bunts as a pinch hitter last season. Just with those two players, the Rangers' total of four sacrifice bunts by pinch hitters led the A.L.; there were only 10 other pinch-sacrifice bunts in the league. . . . Huson's usual position, shortstop, is where the real sacrifice bunting usually takes place; in the American League last season, 25 percent of all sacrifice bunts season were executed by shortstops; there were more sacrifice bunts by shortstops (180) than by all three outfield positions combined (178).

Pete Incaviglia
Bats Right

Detroit Tigers	AB	H	2B	3B	HR	RBI	BB	SO	BA	SA	OBA
Season	337	72	12	1	11	38	36	92	.214	.353	.290
vs. Left-Handers	97	20	3	1	0	5	8	20	.206	.258	.264
vs. Right-Handers	240	52	9	0	11	33	28	72	.217	.392	.300
vs. Ground-Ballers	164	37	4	1	7	24	14	41	.226	.390	.285
vs. Fly-Ballers	173	35	8	0	4	14	22	51	.202	.318	.294
Home Games	171	35	6	1	6	20	18	49	.205	.357	.283
Road Games	166	37	6	0	5	18	18	43	.223	.349	.297
Grass Fields	292	64	11	1	11	35	35	80	.219	.377	.304
Artificial Turf	45	8	1	0	0	3	1	12	.178	.200	.191
April	53	9	2	0	1	4	4	14	.170	.264	.228
May	79	20	6	0	4	14	7	25	.253	.481	.318
June	35	6	0	0	0	2	3	10	.171	.171	.231
July	42	9	0	0	2	5	3	8	.214	.357	.267
August	43	10	2	0	2	5	10	14	.233	.419	.377
Sept./Oct.	85	18	2	1	2	8	9	21	.212	.329	.287
Leading Off Inn.	66	12	2	0	3	3	8	13	.182	.348	.270
Runners On	159	36	7	0	6	33	17	52	.226	.384	.298
Bases Empty	178	36	5	1	5	5	19	40	.202	.326	.283
Runners/Scor. Pos.	89	15	3	0	2	23	12	29	.169	.270	.262
Runners On/2 Out	64	6	1	0	1	4	10	23	.094	.156	.216
Scor. Pos./2 Out	44	2	0	0	1	4	6	13	.045	.114	.160
Late-Inning Pressure	60	11	4	0	1	5	6	16	.183	.300	.258
Leading Off	11	0	0	0	0	0	3	2	.000	.000	.214
Runners On	21	6	4	0	0	4	1	8	.286	.476	.318
Runners/Scor. Pos.	10	2	1	0	0	2	1	3	.200	.300	.273

RUNS BATTED IN	From 1B	From 2B	From 3B	Scoring Position
Totals	9/126	10/70	8/34	18/104
Percentage	7.1%	14.3%	23.5%	17.3%

Loves to face: Bud Black (.444, 8-for-18, 2 2B, 4 HR)
Neal Heaton (.571, 4-for-7, 1 HR)
Bruce Hurst (.379, 11-for-29, 3 HR, 11 SO)

Hates to face: Tom Candiotti (.138, 4-for-29)
Bret Saberhagen (.150, 3-for-20)
Greg Swindell (.038, 1-for-26, 3 BB, 13 SO)

Miscellaneous statistics: Ground outs-to-air outs ratio: 1.07 last season, 1.14 for career.... Grounded into 6 double plays in 82 opportunities (one per 14).... Drove in 8 of 15 runners from third base with less than two outs (53%).... Direction of balls hit to the outfield: 28% to left field, 39% to center, 34% to right.... Base running: Advanced from first base to third on 0 of 12 outfield singles (0%), worst in A.L.; scored from second on 5 of 5 (100%).... Made 2.07 putouts per nine innings in left field.

Comments: Batting average with two outs and runners on base (.094) and with two outs and runners in scoring position (.045) were both the lowest in the majors.... Entered 1991 season with .154 career average with bases loaded and .061 career mark with bases loaded and two outs. Remarkably, both averages *declined* last year, when he went 0-for-8 with the bases loaded (including 0-for-4 with two outs). His overall bases-loaded average is now .151, second lowest among active players (minimum: 50 at-bats with bases full); he's down to .054 (2-for-37) with bases loaded and two outs.... He's one of a group of big-name A.L. batters to make two visits to the disabled list last season. Others include Sandy Alomar, Gary Sheffield, Carney Lansford, and Walt Weiss. (Okay, semi-big names.)... Inky averaged 24.8 homers and 77.6 RBIs in five seasons with Texas; he didn't even get halfway to either figure with the Tigers.... His home-run ratio, one for every 18 at-bats as a rookie in 1986, has grown worse with each succeeding season; last year, he connected once every 30.6 at-bats. His batting average, .250 as a rookie, rose to .271 the next year and has declined every year since. Here's the thing: Inky is only the second player in major league history to have a decline in both batting average and home-run ratio in each of four consecutive seasons of 300 at-bats. The other guy was his former Texas teammate Pete O'Brien, who declined each year for four years following the 1986 season, and finally snapped out of it last year.

Brook Jacoby
Bats Right

Indians/A's	AB	H	2B	3B	HR	RBI	BB	SO	BA	SA	OBA
Season	419	94	21	1	4	44	27	54	.224	.308	.274
vs. Left-Handers	116	29	4	1	1	13	12	14	.250	.328	.326
vs. Right-Handers	303	65	17	0	3	31	15	40	.215	.300	.252
vs. Ground-Ballers	205	44	8	1	2	21	7	20	.215	.293	.244
vs. Fly-Ballers	214	50	13	0	2	23	20	34	.234	.322	.300
Home Games	190	41	10	0	2	27	15	16	.216	.300	.276
Road Games	229	53	11	1	2	17	12	38	.231	.314	.272
Grass Fields	333	79	19	1	4	44	22	35	.237	.336	.287
Artificial Turf	86	15	2	0	0	5	5	19	.174	.198	.220
April	65	13	3	1	1	5	4	10	.200	.323	.246
May	55	15	0	0	3	10	3	9	.273	.436	.310
June	80	16	4	0	0	4	7	9	.200	.250	.264
July	55	18	5	0	0	8	3	7	.327	.418	.383
August	95	21	5	0	0	10	5	9	.221	.274	.265
Sept./Oct.	69	11	4	0	0	7	5	10	.159	.217	.208
Leading Off Inn.	87	18	2	0	1	1	4	14	.207	.264	.242
Runners On	191	44	10	1	1	41	14	27	.230	.309	.284
Bases Empty	228	50	11	0	3	3	13	27	.219	.307	.264
Runners/Scor. Pos.	104	26	5	1	1	39	11	15	.250	.346	.322
Runners On/2 Out	89	22	6	1	1	24	7	8	.247	.371	.309
Scor. Pos./2 Out	53	15	4	1	1	22	5	6	.283	.453	.356
Late-Inning Pressure	76	12	3	0	1	3	14	14	.158	.237	.210
Leading Off	19	3	1	0	0	0	1	0	.158	.211	.200
Runners On	27	1	0	0	0	2	9	9	.037	.037	.133
Runners/Scor. Pos.	10	0	0	0	0	0	1	5	.000	.000	.167

RUNS BATTED IN	From 1B	From 2B	From 3B	Scoring Position
Totals	6/139	18/85	16/43	34/128
Percentage	4.3%	21.2%	37.2%	26.6%

Loves to face: Brad Arnsberg (.571, 4-for-7, 2 2B, 2 HR)
Jose Guzman (.440, 11-for-25, 2 HR)
Bobby Witt (.308, 8-for-26, 2 2B, 1 3B, 2 HR, 9 BB)

Hates to face: Randy Johnson (.067, 1-for-15, 2 BB)
Gene Nelson (.138, 4-for-29)
David Wells (.059, 1-for-17, 2 BB)

Miscellaneous statistics: Ground outs-to-air outs ratio: 0.97 last season, 1.00 for career.... Grounded into 13 double plays in 83 opportunities (one per 6.4).... Drove in 11 of 23 runners from third base with less than two outs (48%).... Direction of balls hit to the outfield: 37% to left field, 36% to center, 28% to right.... Base running: Advanced from first base to third on 3 of 15 outfield singles (20%); scored from second on 8 of 13 (62%).... Made 1.70 assists per nine innings at third base, lowest rate in majors.

Comments: Batted .300 with 32 home runs in 155 games in 1987. Now *that's* a "career year"—or it should hold up as one when we look back in the *Encyclopedia* 10 years hence. As we explain in the Braves essay, what seems like a career year at one time is often eclipsed later; that's why we developed the concept of breakthrough and breakdown seasons, which are used to evaluate a player's performance in a particular season in the context of his career *to that point*. Career years should be determined against the backdrop of his entire career. By that standard, Jacoby's 1987 season represents the 5th most extreme career year among active players, behind George Brett's .400 challenge in 1980; Terry Pendleton's Comeback of the Century in 1991; and the 1987 seasons of Alan Trammell (.343, 28 HR) and Paul Molitor (.353, 16 HR). Historically, the most outstanding career year was by Norm Cash in 1961, when he hit 41 home runs and batted .361—his only season above .300.... Jacoby's batting average from September 1 on was 6th lowest in the league.... He has hit for a higher average in road games than in home games in each of the last eight seasons.... Only three of his 45 RBIs gave his club a lead (7%), the 3d-lowest percentage of go-ahead RBIs by any player in the league last season (minimum: 25 RBI).... Oakland's third basemen combined for only four home runs last season, the fewest by any club in the majors. Other clubs received an average of 16 home runs from their third basemen.

Chris James
Bats Right

Cleveland Indians	AB	H	2B	3B	HR	RBI	BB	SO	BA	SA	OBA
Season	437	104	16	2	5	41	18	61	.238	.318	.273
vs. Left-Handers	131	26	5	1	2	12	7	20	.198	.298	.239
vs. Right-Handers	306	78	11	1	3	29	11	41	.255	.327	.288
vs. Ground-Ballers	195	35	5	0	0	9	12	27	.179	.205	.238
vs. Fly-Ballers	242	69	11	2	5	32	6	34	.285	.409	.303
Home Games	221	64	8	2	1	21	10	20	.290	.357	.328
Road Games	216	40	8	0	4	20	8	41	.185	.278	.217
Grass Fields	354	87	10	2	4	33	15	46	.246	.319	.281
Artificial Turf	83	17	6	0	1	8	3	15	.205	.313	.241
April	67	16	1	0	1	4	7	8	.239	.299	.320
May	99	30	3	1	2	18	4	15	.303	.414	.327
June	103	25	5	1	1	10	5	14	.243	.340	.284
July	72	10	3	0	0	3	0	12	.139	.181	.149
August	79	21	4	0	1	6	2	11	.266	.354	.284
Sept./Oct.	17	2	0	0	0	0	0	1	.118	.118	.167
Leading Off Inn.	94	18	3	0	0	0	4	13	.191	.223	.240
Runners On	182	39	5	1	3	39	9	26	.214	.302	.253
Bases Empty	255	65	11	1	2	2	9	35	.255	.329	.288
Runners/Scor. Pos.	97	23	3	0	2	35	9	15	.237	.330	.296
Runners On/2 Out	79	19	4	0	3	24	6	11	.241	.405	.302
Scor. Pos./2 Out	50	15	3	0	2	22	6	8	.300	.480	.375
Late-Inning Pressure	78	16	4	0	0	1	4	13	.205	.256	.244
Leading Off	22	3	1	0	0	0	1	3	.136	.182	.174
Runners On	30	5	0	0	0	1	3	6	.167	.167	.242
Runners/Scor. Pos.	12	1	0	0	0	1	3	3	.083	.083	.267

RUNS BATTED IN	From 1B	From 2B	From 3B	Scoring Position
Totals	7/134	14/79	15/43	29/122
Percentage	5.2%	17.7%	34.9%	23.8%

Loves to face: Sid Fernandez (.296, 8-for-27, 1 2B, 1 3B, 3 HR)
Neal Heaton (.450, 9-for-20, 2 HR)
Les Lancaster (.538, 7-for-13, 2 HR)
Hates to face: Tom Browning (.167, 4-for-24)
David Cone (0-for-19)
John Costello (0-for-9)

Miscellaneous statistics: Ground outs-to-air outs ratio: 1.14 last season, 1.10 for career.... Grounded into 9 double plays in 81 opportunities (one per 9.0).... Drove in 9 of 22 runners from third base with less than two outs (41%).... Direction of balls hit to the outfield: 28% to left field, 36% to center, 36% to right.... Base running: Advanced from first base to third on 6 of 17 outfield singles (35%); scored from second on 6 of 9 (67%).... Made 2.35 putouts per nine innings in left field.

Comments: Signed by Giants the same week they announced their intention to move to San Jose—just a bit closer to home for this native Texan.... Started 58 games as DH and 50 games in the field last season.... His July batting average was 2d lowest in the majors; so was his .185 average in road games.... Troubles with left-handed pitching last season evened up his career batting average: It's now .262 vs. left-handers, .262 vs. right-handers. Home-run rate is higher vs. lefties (one every 29.7 at-bats) than vs. righties (one every 44 at-bats).... Has not distinguished himself in the clutch: He owns a .230 career batting average in Late-Inning Pressure Situations, and has batted only .149 in 87 LIPS at-bats with runners in scoring position.... Batted .293 in rookie year with Phillies and .299 in his first year with Indians; maybe the first-year magic will kick in again.... At the least, Giants may have gotten themselves a useful pinch hitter: He has one of the top five pinch-hit batting averages among active players with 40+ pinch at-bats: Terry Steinbach, .405 (17-for-42); Pedro Guerrero, .362 (25-for-69); James and Jeff Treadway, both at .350 (14-for-40); Cecil Espy, .341 (14-for-41).... James has hit two pinch homers in 40 at-bats. Last season, Giants were only N.L. team that did not have a single pinch-hit home run (their pinch hitters had 259 at-bats); the year before, they led the majors with 10 pinch homers, two shy of the major league record for a single season.

Lance Johnson
Bats Left

Chicago White Sox	AB	H	2B	3B	HR	RBI	BB	SO	BA	SA	OBA
Season	588	161	14	13	0	49	26	58	.274	.342	.304
vs. Left-Handers	164	40	3	1	0	8	10	21	.244	.274	.291
vs. Right-Handers	424	121	11	12	0	41	16	37	.285	.368	.309
vs. Ground-Ballers	267	74	4	5	0	21	8	24	.277	.330	.296
vs. Fly-Ballers	321	87	10	8	0	28	18	34	.271	.352	.311
Home Games	286	76	5	6	0	22	14	26	.266	.325	.298
Road Games	302	85	9	7	0	27	12	32	.281	.358	.310
Grass Fields	506	140	11	10	0	43	23	48	.277	.338	.308
Artificial Turf	82	21	3	3	0	6	3	10	.256	.366	.282
April	68	15	2	0	0	1	3	10	.221	.250	.254
May	108	28	1	0	0	8	1	12	.259	.269	.273
June	102	29	2	1	0	9	4	6	.284	.324	.308
July	100	25	2	3	0	10	3	12	.250	.330	.269
August	102	27	2	2	0	8	3	7	.265	.324	.286
Sept./Oct.	108	37	5	7	0	13	12	11	.343	.519	.405
Leading Off Inn.	130	34	4	4	0	0	4	11	.262	.354	.284
Runners On	246	62	4	4	0	49	17	21	.252	.301	.300
Bases Empty	342	99	10	9	0	0	9	37	.289	.371	.308
Runners/Scor. Pos.	138	34	3	2	0	47	13	12	.246	.297	.310
Runners On/2 Out	106	26	4	1	0	22	9	12	.245	.302	.304
Scor. Pos./2 Out	73	18	3	0	0	21	6	8	.247	.288	.304
Late-Inning Pressure	101	26	1	2	0	11	4	12	.257	.307	.290
Leading Off	27	8	0	1	0	0	2	4	.296	.370	.345
Runners On	44	9	1	1	0	11	1	4	.205	.273	.234
Runners/Scor. Pos.	23	6	1	0	0	10	1	1	.261	.304	.308

RUNS BATTED IN	From 1B	From 2B	From 3B	Scoring Position
Totals	2/185	19/104	28/63	47/167
Percentage	1.1%	18.3%	44.4%	28.1%

Loves to face: Allan Anderson (.800, 4-for-5)
Luis Aquino (.444, 4-for-9, 2 3B)
Kevin Brown (.526, 10-for-19)
Dave Johnson (.500, 8-for-16)
Hates to face: Roger Clemens (.160, 4-for-25, 0 BB)
Storm Davis (.077, 1-for-13)
Jaime Navarro (.071, 1-for-14, 1 2B)

Miscellaneous statistics: Ground outs-to-air outs ratio: 1.80 last season, 1.97 for career.... Grounded into 14 double plays in 125 opportunities (one per 8.9).... Drove in 18 of 28 runners from third base with less than two outs (64%).... Direction of balls hit to the outfield: 39% to left field, 32% to center, 28% to right.... Base running: Advanced from first base to third on 11 of 20 outfield singles (55%); scored from second on 17 of 19 (89%).... Made 2.87 putouts per nine innings in center field, 2d-highest rate in A.L.

Comments: It's unusual for a player with so many triples to hit so few doubles—especially in a league of predominantly grass fields. The last players with more than 10 three-baggers and fewer than 15 two-baggers were N.L.'ers Craig Reynolds and Gene Richards, in strike-shortened 1981 no less. The only other A.L. players to do so in the last 75 years were Jo-Jo White (1935) and Jackie Tavener (1925).... One of four outfielders to put together an errorless streak of at least 100 games last season. The top four: Brett Butler (161 games), Devon White (132), Johnson (115), and Dave Henderson (111). All of the streaks except Johnson's will carry over into the 1992 season.... Total of 238 ground outs was 2d highest in the league last season.... On-base percentage leading off innings was 7th lowest in the league.... Reached on 59 infield hits over the past two seasons, the third-highest total in the American League, behind Luis Polonia (74) and Steve Sax (65).... White Sox outfielders combined for only 27 home runs last season, the fewest of any team in the majors and roughly half the major league average (52). The last A.L. team with that few: the 1985 World Champion Royals (25). The last team with fewer than 10: the 1952 Washington Senators (5).... Hit the only home run of his career off Andy Hawkins in 1990; he has accumulated 1492 career at-bats. Among players who hit more than one home run in their careers, two took more than 3000 at-bats to reach that "milestone": Al Bridwell and Mike Tresh.

Wally Joyner
Bats Left

California Angels	AB	H	2B	3B	HR	RBI	BB	SO	BA	SA	OBA
Season	551	166	34	3	21	96	52	66	.301	.488	.360
vs. Left-Handers	189	52	15	1	5	28	9	31	.275	.444	.308
vs. Right-Handers	362	114	19	2	16	68	43	35	.315	.511	.384
vs. Ground-Ballers	265	82	18	1	9	42	24	31	.309	.487	.366
vs. Fly-Ballers	286	84	16	2	12	54	28	35	.294	.490	.353
Home Games	268	74	14	1	10	39	29	30	.276	.448	.343
Road Games	283	92	20	2	11	57	23	36	.325	.527	.375
Grass Fields	473	139	29	2	18	77	45	54	.294	.478	.353
Artificial Turf	78	27	5	1	3	19	7	12	.346	.551	.400
April	66	22	4	0	1	11	11	7	.333	.439	.423
May	100	36	5	0	7	23	13	9	.360	.620	.435
June	113	33	8	2	2	17	4	15	.292	.451	.316
July	96	23	4	0	2	13	10	14	.240	.344	.308
August	110	31	8	1	8	22	7	15	.282	.591	.322
Sept./Oct.	66	21	5	0	1	10	7	6	.318	.439	.378
Leading Off Inn.	100	30	7	0	4	4	14	7	.300	.490	.386
Runners On	243	78	12	1	9	84	26	33	.321	.490	.382
Bases Empty	308	88	22	2	12	12	26	33	.286	.487	.341
Runners/Scor. Pos.	140	46	9	1	5	73	21	19	.329	.514	.407
Runners On/2 Out	90	26	7	1	5	40	13	11	.289	.556	.379
Scor. Pos./2 Out	64	21	6	1	2	33	11	9	.328	.547	.427
Late-Inning Pressure	65	19	4	0	3	12	5	8	.292	.492	.343
Leading Off	20	5	2	0	1	1	2	1	.250	.500	.318
Runners On	29	6	0	0	0	9	1	5	.207	.207	.233
Runners/Scor. Pos.	14	5	0	0	0	9	1	1	.357	.357	.400

RUNS BATTED IN	From 1B	From 2B	From 3B	Scoring Position
Totals	16/167	34/107	25/61	59/168
Percentage	9.6%	31.8%	41.0%	35.1%

Loves to face: Eric Plunk (.692, 9-for-13, 3 HR)
Dave Stieb (.368, 14-for-38, 4 HR)
Walt Terrell (.320, 8-for-25, 3 2B, 1 3B, 2 HR)
Hates to face: Mike Gardiner (0-for-8)
Rick Honeycutt (0-for-10)
Mark Langston (.130, 3-for-23, 1 HR)

Miscellaneous statistics: Ground outs-to-air outs ratio: 0.86 last season, 0.88 for career.... Grounded into 11 double plays in 120 opportunities (one per 11).... Drove in 17 of 30 runners from third base with less than two outs (57%).... Direction of balls hit to the outfield: 37% to left field, 28% to center, 35% to right.... Base running: Advanced from first base to third on 12 of 35 outfield singles (34%); scored from second on 18 of 21 (86%).... Made 0.71 assists per nine innings at first base.

Comments: His statistics for 1991 and his career are strikingly similar to those of Bobby Bonilla (see page 22).... His seven home runs during May tied him for the most in the league.... Batting average in road games was 5th highest in the league last season, as was his average on artificial turf.... He batted .345 on artificial turf in 1990 (though in too few at-bats to qualify), ranked second in the league with a .365 mark in 1989, and fourth in 1987 at .366. His career average on artificial turf (.332) is 2d highest among active players, two points lower than Kirby Puckett's.... Career batting average of .380 (38-for-100, 1 HR) at Royals Stadium.... Last season was the third in which he drove in more than 35 percent of runners in scoring position. Only three other players have reached the 35 percent level in three of the past six seasons (minimum: 100 opportunities): George Brett (4), Pedro Guerrero, and Don Mattingly.... One of nine players with 100 RBIs in both their rookie and sophomore seasons. Joyner's 96 last season was the closest he's come since. Of the other eight, two never again drove in 100 runs: Dale Alexander and Ray Jablonski.... For those who remember the press conference at which a teary-eyed Joyner announced he was leaving the Angels: Only two players in franchise history played their entire careers of at least 500 games for the club. They are: current shortstop Dick Schofield (1060) and current manager Buck Rodgers (932).

Pat Kelly
Bats Right

New York Yankees	AB	H	2B	3B	HR	RBI	BB	SO	BA	SA	OBA
Season	298	72	12	4	3	23	15	52	.242	.339	.287
vs. Left-Handers	99	26	5	0	1	7	4	13	.263	.343	.292
vs. Right-Handers	199	46	7	4	2	16	11	39	.231	.337	.285
vs. Ground-Ballers	138	35	5	2	2	9	6	22	.254	.362	.293
vs. Fly-Ballers	160	37	7	2	1	14	9	30	.231	.319	.283
Home Games	150	38	6	2	3	12	10	26	.253	.380	.307
Road Games	148	34	6	2	0	11	5	26	.230	.297	.268
Grass Fields	253	61	12	2	3	21	13	45	.241	.340	.289
Artificial Turf	45	11	0	2	0	2	2	7	.244	.333	.277
April	0	0	0	0	0	0	0	0	—	—	—
May	32	6	4	1	0	6	3	6	.188	.375	.278
June	77	20	1	1	2	4	2	12	.260	.377	.296
July	82	19	6	0	1	8	5	14	.232	.341	.281
August	83	22	0	2	0	5	4	16	.265	.313	.303
Sept./Oct.	24	5	1	0	0	0	1	4	.208	.250	.240
Leading Off Inn.	69	24	6	0	0	0	1	9	.348	.435	.357
Runners On	119	24	4	1	2	22	8	24	.202	.303	.260
Bases Empty	179	48	8	3	1	1	7	28	.268	.363	.307
Runners/Scor. Pos.	64	12	3	0	0	17	7	14	.188	.234	.280
Runners On/2 Out	54	13	2	0	1	13	4	13	.241	.333	.293
Scor. Pos./2 Out	35	8	2	0	0	11	3	10	.229	.286	.289
Late-Inning Pressure	43	12	3	1	1	4	3	3	.279	.465	.326
Leading Off	11	2	1	0	0	0	0	0	.182	.273	.182
Runners On	18	5	1	0	1	4	3	2	.278	.500	.381
Runners/Scor. Pos.	8	2	1	0	0	2	2	1	.250	.375	.400

RUNS BATTED IN	From 1B	From 2B	From 3B	Scoring Position
Totals	4/88	6/50	10/29	16/79
Percentage	4.5%	12.0%	34.5%	20.3%

Loves to face: Mark Williamson (4-for-4)
Hates to face: Jim Abbott (0-for-5)
Roger Clemens (0-for-6)

Miscellaneous statistics: Ground outs-to-air outs ratio: 1.01 last season, 1.01 for career.... Grounded into 5 double plays in 52 opportunities (one per 10).... Drove in 5 of 15 runners from third base with less than two outs (33%), 3d-lowest rate in A.L.... Direction of balls hit to the outfield: 37% to left field, 32% to center, 31% to right.... Base running: Advanced from first base to third on 6 of 12 outfield singles (50%); scored from second on 4 of 5 (80%).... Made 2.14 assists per nine innings at third base.

Comments: Played every inning of each of New York's first 19 games after joining the team on May 20.... Kelly probably moves back to his natural position, second base, this season with Steve Sax headed for Chicago. We say probably because within days of trading Sax—a second baseman who proved he couldn't play third regularly—the Yankees signed Mike Gallego—a second baseman who's played third well but only on occasion.... The Yankees have a long tradition of second basemen who made impacts as regular starters in their rookie seasons, including Tony Lazzeri (1926), Joe Gordon (1938), Jerry Coleman (1949), Bobby Richardson (1957), and Willie Randolph (1976). But only four rookies—none in the past 20 years—played as many as 100 games at third base: Frank LaPorte (1906), Jimmy Austin (1909), Billy Johnson (1943), and Bobby Cox (1968).... Yankees third basemen didn't play more than 11 games in a row without committing an error last season. Every other club had an errorless streak of at least 18 games at third base.... Among the 38 major leaguers who played at least 50 games at third base last season, the three highest error rates belonged to New Yorkers: Gregg Jefferies (one per 11.9 chances), Kelly (13.5), and Howard Johnson (13.7). All three are now elsewhere: Johnson in left field, Kelly at second base, and Jefferies in Kansas City. What's that lyric? "If you can't make it there, they'll move you anywhere..."

Roberto Kelly
Bats Right

New York Yankees	AB	H	2B	3B	HR	RBI	BB	SO	BA	SA	OBA
Season	486	130	22	2	20	69	45	77	.267	.444	.333
vs. Left-Handers	159	47	4	1	9	26	20	18	.296	.500	.372
vs. Right-Handers	327	83	18	1	11	43	25	59	.254	.416	.313
vs. Ground-Ballers	250	63	9	2	9	34	23	39	.252	.412	.323
vs. Fly-Ballers	236	67	13	0	11	35	22	38	.284	.479	.344
Home Games	232	72	11	0	11	30	21	32	.310	.500	.369
Road Games	254	58	11	2	9	39	24	45	.228	.394	.301
Grass Fields	398	113	20	1	17	58	38	63	.284	.467	.350
Artificial Turf	88	17	2	1	3	11	7	14	.193	.341	.255
April	61	17	2	0	2	11	11	9	.279	.410	.378
May	106	26	6	0	3	9	7	19	.245	.387	.298
June	112	27	3	1	4	13	4	23	.241	.393	.277
July	18	8	1	0	1	3	0	2	.444	.667	.444
August	61	12	0	0	3	9	6	10	.197	.344	.275
Sept./Oct.	128	40	10	1	7	24	17	14	.313	.570	.395
Leading Off Inn.	140	34	6	0	4	4	8	25	.243	.371	.284
Runners On	210	62	13	1	7	56	18	33	.295	.467	.354
Bases Empty	276	68	9	1	13	13	27	44	.246	.428	.316
Runners/Scor. Pos.	117	35	6	0	6	52	12	19	.299	.504	.365
Runners On/2 Out	93	23	6	0	3	23	12	16	.247	.409	.352
Scor. Pos./2 Out	59	15	3	0	2	21	10	9	.254	.407	.380
Late-Inning Pressure	71	20	2	0	6	14	6	12	.282	.563	.346
Leading Off	14	4	0	0	2	2	1	1	.286	.714	.333
Runners On	28	10	2	0	1	9	3	4	.357	.536	.438
Runners/Scor. Pos.	18	7	1	0	1	9	2	2	.389	.611	.476

RUNS BATTED IN	From 1B	From 2B	From 3B	Scoring Position
Totals	7/157	19/87	23/50	42/137
Percentage	4.5%	21.8%	46.0%	30.7%

Loves to face: Todd Stottlemyre (.375, 9-for-24, 1 HR)
Frank Viola (.636, 7-for-11)
Curt Young (.600, 6-for-10, 1 HR)
Hates to face: Tom Gordon (0-for-11)
Jack McDowell (0-for-9, 5 SO)
Jack Morris (.158, 3-for-19)

Miscellaneous statistics: Ground outs-to-air outs ratio: 1.16 last season, 1.12 for career.... Grounded into 14 double plays in 102 opportunities (one per 7.3).... Drove in 13 of 23 runners from third base with less than two outs (57%).... Direction of balls hit to the outfield: 35% to left field, 33% to center, 32% to right.... Base running: Advanced from first base to third on 9 of 22 outfield singles (41%); scored from second on 10 of 13 (77%).... Made 2.34 putouts per nine innings in center field, 2d-lowest rate in A.L.

Comments: Returned from six weeks on the disabled list on August 13 (with a bad wrist, no less) and immediately started running with the big boys. From August 16 to the end of the season, he hit 10 home runs; only two A.L. players hit more: Jose Canseco (13) and Phil Plantier (11).... Played only left field after his return, in deference to rookie Bernie Williams, who arrived during Kelly's D.L. stint. Prior to Bernie's arrival, Kelly had played 405 games in center field but only 13 in left.... His on-base percentage leading off innings was 8th lowest in the league.... Has stolen 109 bases over the past three years to rank 10th in the majors. Of those with more steals, only Barry Bonds and Rickey Henderson also hit more home runs than Kelly.... Hit seven of his 20 home runs to the opposite field last season, making him "15-for-35" over the past two seasons—10-for-16 at Yankee Stadium (which swallows long shots to left), 5-for-19 on the road.... Has bounced around the Yankees' batting order for several years, and has batted 78 points higher in the first three slots (.289) than he has from the middle of the order (.211 batting fourth or fifth). But his home-run rate has been nearly twice as high in the middle (one per 17 at-bats) than at the top (one per 30).... A right-handed hitter who adjusts his power stroke for the cavernous left field of Yankee Stadium, and who exploits his various talents according to where he's batting in the order. Sounds like a pretty smart hitter to us.

Chuck Knoblauch
Bats Right

Minnesota Twins	AB	H	2B	3B	HR	RBI	BB	SO	BA	SA	OBA
Season	565	159	24	6	1	50	59	40	.281	.350	.351
vs. Left-Handers	148	38	8	1	0	6	14	10	.257	.324	.325
vs. Right-Handers	417	121	16	5	1	44	45	30	.290	.360	.360
vs. Ground-Ballers	239	69	9	3	0	22	28	13	.289	.351	.367
vs. Fly-Ballers	326	90	15	3	1	28	31	27	.276	.350	.339
Home Games	287	94	12	5	1	26	30	18	.328	.415	.391
Road Games	278	65	12	1	0	24	29	22	.234	.284	.310
Grass Fields	212	51	9	0	0	17	24	14	.241	.283	.321
Artificial Turf	353	108	15	6	1	33	35	26	.306	.391	.369
April	75	25	3	2	0	9	8	8	.333	.427	.393
May	90	21	5	0	0	6	11	7	.233	.289	.314
June	90	26	2	1	0	7	9	2	.289	.333	.360
July	93	22	5	2	0	8	11	10	.237	.333	.314
August	105	28	5	0	1	10	8	10	.267	.343	.325
Sept./Oct.	112	37	4	1	0	10	12	3	.330	.384	.400
Leading Off Inn.	131	40	5	1	0	0	11	11	.305	.359	.368
Runners On	214	62	8	1	0	49	30	13	.290	.336	.372
Bases Empty	351	97	16	5	1	1	29	27	.276	.359	.337
Runners/Scor. Pos.	117	36	4	1	0	46	18	10	.308	.359	.386
Runners On/2 Out	92	27	2	0	0	18	11	7	.293	.315	.369
Scor. Pos./2 Out	66	19	2	0	0	18	8	7	.288	.318	.365
Late-Inning Pressure	68	16	4	0	0	5	5	4	.235	.294	.284
Leading Off	22	6	1	0	0	0	1	2	.273	.318	.304
Runners On	26	6	1	0	0	5	2	1	.231	.269	.276
Runners/Scor. Pos.	15	3	1	0	0	5	2	1	.200	.267	.278

RUNS BATTED IN	From 1B	From 2B	From 3B	Scoring Position
Totals	4/151	18/85	27/56	45/141
Percentage	2.6%	21.2%	48.2%	31.9%

Loves to face: Jack McDowell (.667, 6-for-9)
Dave Stewart (.364, 4-for-11)
Bob Welch (.545, 6-for-11)
Hates to face: Chris Bosio (0-for-8)
Chuck Finley (.143, 2-for-14)
Juan Guzman (0-for-9)

Miscellaneous statistics: Ground outs-to-air outs ratio: 1.39 last season, 1.39 for career.... Grounded into 8 double plays in 120 opportunities (one per 15).... Drove in 19 of 30 runners from third base with less than two outs (63%).... Direction of balls hit to the outfield: 21% to left field, 40% to center, 39% to right.... Base running: Advanced from first base to third on 18 of 40 outfield singles (45%); scored from second on 11 of 12 (92%).... Made 3.33 assists per nine innings at second base, 3d-highest rate in A.L.

Comments: Collected 15 hits in 12 postseason games, setting a record for hits by a rookie in a single postseason. He was the first rookie to get three hits in his first World Series game since Bill Terry in 1924.... Also set a World Series record for rookies with four stolen bases.... Led A.L. rookies in batting average, starts (141), runs (78), hits, doubles, RBIs, and walks.... His 20-game hitting streak in September was the longest by any rookie last season.... Twins rookies (mostly Knoblauch, Scott Leius, and Pedro Munoz) combined to bat .281 last season, the highest average by rookies on any team in the majors. The major league average for rookie batters was .235.... Became only the third second baseman (or was it the second third baseman?) to win the A.L. Rookie of the Year Award, joining Rod Carew (1967) and Lou Whitaker (1978). Six N.L. second basemen have won rookie honors, including four Dodgers, but *not* Jackie Robinson, who won the honor as a first baseman in 1947.... His stolen-base percentage (.833) was 2d highest in the league, behind Henry Cotto (.842).... The last three American League rookies to play as many as 145 games at second base have all played for Minnesota: Knoblauch, Steve Lombardozzi (1986), and Tim Teufel (1984). And what list of great rookie second basemen would be complete without two other Twins: Bob Randall (1976) and Bernie Allen (1962).

Gene Larkin
Bats Left and Right

Minnesota Twins	AB	H	2B	3B	HR	RBI	BB	SO	BA	SA	OBA
Season	255	73	14	1	2	19	30	21	.286	.373	.361
vs. Left-Handers	88	24	8	0	1	6	13	7	.273	.398	.363
vs. Right-Handers	167	49	6	1	1	13	17	14	.293	.359	.360
vs. Ground-Ballers	114	27	8	1	0	5	15	10	.237	.325	.326
vs. Fly-Ballers	141	46	6	0	2	14	15	11	.326	.411	.390
Home Games	131	41	6	0	0	12	16	8	.313	.359	.387
Road Games	124	32	8	1	2	7	14	13	.258	.387	.333
Grass Fields	104	26	6	1	2	7	10	12	.250	.385	.316
Artificial Turf	151	47	8	0	0	12	20	9	.311	.364	.391
April	31	12	2	0	0	2	0	0	.387	.452	.387
May	52	11	0	0	1	3	6	3	.212	.269	.293
June	49	15	2	0	0	3	6	4	.306	.347	.393
July	26	8	1	1	0	2	4	3	.308	.423	.400
August	47	11	2	0	1	3	5	6	.234	.340	.308
Sept./Oct.	50	16	7	0	0	6	9	5	.320	.460	.410
Leading Off Inn.	67	26	5	0	0	0	6	3	.388	.463	.438
Runners On	115	27	4	1	1	18	13	10	.235	.313	.313
Bases Empty	140	46	10	0	1	1	17	11	.329	.421	.401
Runners/Scor. Pos.	58	11	2	1	0	16	12	7	.190	.259	.329
Runners On/2 Out	46	9	1	0	1	6	6	4	.196	.283	.302
Scor. Pos./2 Out	26	4	1	0	0	4	6	3	.154	.192	.333
Late-Inning Pressure	42	10	3	0	0	2	2	5	.238	.310	.273
Leading Off	13	4	2	0	0	0	1	1	.308	.462	.357
Runners On	18	5	0	0	0	2	0	2	.278	.278	.278
Runners/Scor. Pos.	10	2	0	0	0	2	0	2	.200	.200	.200

RUNS BATTED IN	From 1B	From 2B	From 3B	Scoring Position
Totals	2/85	5/43	10/26	15/69
Percentage	2.4%	11.6%	38.5%	21.7%

Loves to face: Mike Boddicker (.300, 6-for-20, 2 HR)
Al Leiter (3-for-3, 1 HP)
Melido Perez (.368, 7-for-19, 2 HR)
Hates to face: Greg A. Harris (.083, 1-for-12)
Mike Henneman (.100, 1-for-10)
Walt Terrell (.125, 2-for-16)

Miscellaneous statistics: Ground outs-to-air outs ratio: 1.13 last season, 1.00 for career.... Grounded into 9 double plays in 58 opportunities (one per 6.4).... Drove in 7 of 13 runners from third base with less than two outs (54%).... Direction of balls hit to the outfield: 21% to left field, 37% to center, 42% to right batting left-handed; 33% to left field, 38% to center, 30% to right batting right-handed.... Base running: Advanced from first base to third on 4 of 14 outfield singles (29%); scored from second on 9 of 13 (69%).... Made 1.67 putouts per nine innings in right field.

Comments: His hit to end the World Series was the first pinch Series-ender and only the second pinch game-winner ever in a final Series game. The other was quite recent—anyone remember Rusty Kuntz's pinch-hit game-winner that clinched the World Series for the Tigers in 1984? That's the difference in drama between a five-game blowout and a seven-game cliff-hanger.... He has a career average of .196 (11-for-56, 0 HR) as a pinch hitter during the regular season.... Didn't have a game-winning RBI during the season. Only four players without a GW had more at-bats: Milt Cuyler (475), Franklin Stubbs (362), Von Hayes (284), Brady Anderson (256).... Larkin may have been baseball's most valuable spot starter last season. The Twins were 16–8 in games in which he spelled (or misspelled?) Hrbek at first base, and they had a 25–15 record when he started in right field. All told, Minnesota posted a better record with Larkin in the starting lineup (42–24) than without him (53–43).... On-base average leading off innings was highest on the team (minimum: 50 PA), and a career high by far. His previous best: .377 in 1988.... Was hit by only one pitch last season after being hit 29 times over the three previous years.... His batting average with runners in scoring position has been lower than his overall batting average in each of his five seasons in the majors. Career breakdown: .241 with RISP, .282 in other at-bats.

Manny Lee
Bats Left and Right

Toronto Blue Jays	AB	H	2B	3B	HR	RBI	BB	SO	BA	SA	OBA
Season	445	104	18	3	0	29	24	107	.234	.288	.274
vs. Left-Handers	144	41	9	0	0	11	10	25	.285	.347	.333
vs. Right-Handers	301	63	9	3	0	18	14	82	.209	.259	.245
vs. Ground-Ballers	238	61	11	2	0	15	14	56	.256	.319	.299
vs. Fly-Ballers	207	43	7	1	0	14	10	51	.208	.251	.244
Home Games	213	53	12	2	0	12	18	50	.249	.324	.306
Road Games	232	51	6	1	0	17	6	57	.220	.254	.242
Grass Fields	176	39	6	1	0	13	6	43	.222	.267	.250
Artificial Turf	269	65	12	2	0	16	18	64	.242	.301	.289
April	65	17	3	1	0	2	12	18	.262	.338	.377
May	60	20	2	1	0	8	3	13	.333	.400	.369
June	107	23	5	0	0	6	2	27	.215	.262	.227
July	81	15	2	0	0	4	3	22	.185	.210	.214
August	82	18	2	1	0	8	2	17	.220	.268	.241
Sept./Oct.	50	11	4	0	0	1	0	10	.220	.300	.250
Leading Off Inn.	108	29	5	1	0	0	8	24	.269	.333	.319
Runners On	177	40	8	1	0	29	8	45	.226	.282	.262
Bases Empty	268	64	10	2	0	0	16	62	.239	.291	.282
Runners/Scor. Pos.	105	23	4	0	0	28	6	26	.219	.257	.259
Runners On/2 Out	81	22	4	0	0	14	5	17	.272	.321	.314
Scor. Pos./2 Out	53	14	3	0	0	14	3	12	.264	.321	.304
Late-Inning Pressure	61	11	3	0	0	4	7	16	.180	.230	.271
Leading Off	17	5	1	0	0	0	5	5	.294	.353	.455
Runners On	20	3	1	0	0	4	0	6	.150	.250	.182
Runners/Scor. Pos.	15	2	1	0	0	4	0	4	.133	.200	.176

RUNS BATTED IN	From 1B	From 2B	From 3B	Scoring Position
Totals	3/121	10/88	16/40	26/128
Percentage	2.5%	11.4%	40.0%	20.3%

Loves to face: Chuck Finley (.467, 7-for-15)
Frank Viola (.455, 5-for-11)
Curt Young (.308, 4-for-13, 2 HR)
Hates to face: Luis Aquino (0-for-12)
Mark Guthrie (.071, 1-for-14)
Charles Nagy (0-for-13)

Miscellaneous statistics: Ground outs-to-air outs ratio: 2.24 last season, 3d highest in A.L.; 1.87 for career.... Grounded into 11 double plays in 82 opportunities (one per 7.5).... Drove in 10 of 23 runners from third base with less than two outs (43%).... Direction of balls hit to the outfield: 38% to left field, 38% to center, 24% to right batting left-handed; 31% to left field, 25% to center, 44% to right batting right-handed.... Base running: Advanced from first base to third on 9 of 22 outfield singles (41%); scored from second on 6 of 8 (75%).... Made 2.79 assists per nine innings at shortstop, 3d-lowest rate in A.L.

Comments: He became the first player ever to accumulate 100 strikeouts in a season in which he didn't hit a home run. The old record holder was Vince Coleman, with 98 strikeouts in 1986. Others with 90 or more: Steve Jeltz (1986), Tim Johnson (1973), and Gary Pettis (1991).... He has a career average of .233 batting left-handed, .283 batting right-handed. Among active switch-hitters with at least 2000 career plate appearances, only Wally Backman and Ken Caminiti have wider gaps between their averages from either side of the plate.... His batting average vs. right-handed pitchers was 4th lowest in the league.... His longest hitting streak was five games in length. Every other major leaguer with 400 or more at-bats last season had a hitting streak of at least six games.... His batting average has decreased and his strikeout rate has increased in each of the past three seasons. In 1988: .291, one SO per 10 plate appearances; in 1991: .234, one SO per 4.5 PAs.... One of the few batters in baseball with a significantly higher batting average against fly-ball pitchers than vs. ground-ballers. Because fly-ball pitchers tend to allow more home runs than their counterparts, they also have relatively lower opponents' batting averages. (If they didn't, they'd be gone.) But Lee has a career batting average of .266 vs. fly-ballers, 31 points higher than his mark against ground-ball pitchers. For a listing of other similar players, see the Luis Polonia comments.

Mark Lewis — Bats Right

Cleveland Indians	AB	H	2B	3B	HR	RBI	BB	SO	BA	SA	OBA
Season	314	83	15	1	0	30	15	45	.264	.318	.293
vs. Left-Handers	87	24	3	0	0	7	5	12	.276	.310	.305
vs. Right-Handers	227	59	12	1	0	23	10	33	.260	.322	.289
vs. Ground-Ballers	142	31	5	1	0	9	5	15	.218	.268	.243
vs. Fly-Ballers	172	52	10	0	0	21	10	30	.302	.360	.333
Home Games	159	44	6	1	0	15	7	19	.277	.327	.302
Road Games	155	39	9	0	0	15	8	26	.252	.310	.285
Grass Fields	277	76	14	1	0	27	15	42	.274	.332	.307
Artificial Turf	37	7	1	0	0	3	0	3	.189	.216	.184
April	14	6	3	0	0	2	1	2	.429	.643	.467
May	110	39	5	0	0	13	6	15	.355	.400	.381
June	90	13	2	0	0	6	4	9	.144	.167	.179
July	40	6	0	1	0	1	1	8	.150	.200	.167
August	0	0	0	0	0	0	0	0	.000	.000	.000
Sept./Oct.	60	19	5	0	0	8	3	11	.317	.400	.344
Leading Off Inn.	43	10	3	1	0	4	4	4	.233	.349	.298
Runners On	152	46	7	0	0	30	7	21	.303	.349	.323
Bases Empty	162	37	8	1	0	0	8	24	.228	.290	.265
Runners/Scor. Pos.	74	24	4	0	0	30	3	10	.324	.378	.329
Runners On/2 Out	63	19	2	0	0	13	2	8	.302	.333	.323
Scor. Pos./2 Out	41	13	1	0	0	13	1	4	.317	.341	.333
Late-Inning Pressure	60	13	2	0	0	6	5	10	.217	.250	.277
Leading Off	13	2	1	0	0	0	3	2	.154	.231	.313
Runners On	27	7	1	0	0	6	2	5	.259	.296	.310
Runners/Scor. Pos.	17	6	1	0	0	6	1	4	.353	.412	.389

RUNS BATTED IN	From 1B	From 2B	From 3B	Scoring Position
Totals	3/117	9/56	18/36	27/92
Percentage	2.6%	16.1%	50.0%	29.3%

Loves to face: Scott Lewis (.714, 5-for-7, 3 2B)

Hates to face: Jimmy Key (0-for-6)
Jaime Navarro (.091, 1-for-11)
Scott Sanderson (0-for-4, 4 SO)

Miscellaneous statistics: Ground outs-to-air outs ratio: 0.97 last season, 0.97 for career.... Grounded into 12 double plays in 75 opportunities (one per 6.3).... Drove in 11 of 15 runners from third base with less than two outs (73%).... Direction of balls hit to the outfield: 38% to left field, 34% to center, 29% to right.... Base running: Advanced from first base to third on 4 of 13 outfield singles (31%); scored from second on 9 of 10 (90%).... Made 2.91 assists per nine innings at second base.

Comments: Played every inning of each of the Indians' first 35 games after joining the club on April 26. And why not? He didn't commit his first error until game 15 and kept his batting average above the .400 mark through 23 games.... His batting average in May, his first full month in the majors, was 6th highest in the league—then the wheels came off.... June average was 2d lowest.... For the season, his .264 mark ranked second among A.L. rookies with at least 200 at-bats.... The Indians allowed an average of 4.18 runs per nine innings with Lewis playing second base, compared to an average of over five runs per nine innings with either Carlos Baerga or Jerry Browne.... The start of a noteworthy trend? Lewis batted 138 points higher in day games (.365) than in night games (.227). Even though he had only 85 day-game ABs, the odds on a spread that wide simply at random are roughly 50-to-1.... Was one of 24 rookies to play for the Indians last season. The only other club to have anywhere near that many was Houston, who used 20. Indians rookies made a total of 400 starts.... He was the 2d youngest of Cleveland's 24 rooks and the youngest player in the majors to accumulate 300 at-bats—but he's only nine days younger than Ken Griffey, Jr., who's already played 436 games over three full seasons and has hit 60 home runs.... The youngest Indian, by the way, was third baseman Jim Thome, who was born August 27, 1970.

Kevin Maas — Bats Left

New York Yankees	AB	H	2B	3B	HR	RBI	BB	SO	BA	SA	OBA
Season	500	110	14	1	23	63	83	128	.220	.390	.333
vs. Left-Handers	181	40	7	0	9	31	30	51	.221	.409	.338
vs. Right-Handers	319	70	7	1	14	32	53	77	.219	.379	.330
vs. Ground-Ballers	229	49	6	0	11	28	39	60	.214	.384	.330
vs. Fly-Ballers	271	61	8	1	12	35	44	68	.225	.395	.335
Home Games	236	42	8	0	8	25	40	55	.178	.314	.301
Road Games	264	68	6	1	15	38	43	73	.258	.458	.361
Grass Fields	415	87	13	0	18	51	71	109	.210	.371	.328
Artificial Turf	85	23	1	1	5	12	12	19	.271	.482	.357
April	52	12	0	1	2	8	23	12	.231	.385	.467
May	100	30	4	0	7	11	18	28	.300	.550	.412
June	100	21	5	0	4	14	11	19	.210	.380	.289
July	86	13	3	0	1	5	10	24	.151	.221	.245
August	76	12	0	0	4	14	11	19	.158	.316	.273
Sept./Oct.	86	22	2	0	5	11	10	26	.256	.453	.327
Leading Off Inn.	114	31	3	1	6	6	15	24	.272	.474	.357
Runners On	215	39	6	0	7	47	45	58	.181	.307	.322
Bases Empty	285	71	8	1	16	16	38	70	.249	.453	.342
Runners/Scor. Pos.	122	22	3	0	4	40	26	30	.180	.303	.318
Runners On/2 Out	94	15	6	0	4	22	19	27	.160	.351	.301
Scor. Pos./2 Out	58	9	3	0	3	19	10	15	.155	.362	.279
Late-Inning Pressure	83	24	4	0	4	15	12	22	.289	.482	.385
Leading Off	16	6	1	0	1	1	3	5	.375	.625	.474
Runners On	42	12	2	0	1	12	7	12	.286	.405	.388
Runners/Scor. Pos.	21	7	2	0	1	12	5	5	.333	.571	.462

RUNS BATTED IN	From 1B	From 2B	From 3B	Scoring Position
Totals	10/162	11/94	19/49	30/143
Percentage	6.2%	11.7%	38.8%	21.0%

Loves to face: Tom Bolton (2-for-2, 1 HR, 1 HP)
Jose Mesa (.700, 7-for-10)
Jack Morris (.444, 4-for-9, 1 HR)

Hates to face: Tom Gordon (0-for-7, 5 SO)
Jimmy Key (0-for-10)
Jaime Navarro (.100, 1-for-10, 5 SO)

Miscellaneous statistics: Ground outs-to-air outs ratio: 0.56 last season, 2d lowest in A.L.; 0.56 for career.... Grounded into 4 double plays in 120 opportunities (one per 30).... Drove in 15 of 28 runners from third base with less than two outs (54%).... Direction of balls hit to the outfield: 21% to left field, 28% to center, 51% to right.... Base running: Advanced from first base to third on 8 of 24 outfield singles (33%); scored from second on 9 of 13 (69%).... Made 0.66 assists per nine innings at first base.

Comments: Want a truly bizarre list? Most home runs in first 500 at-bats with the Yankees: Babe Ruth, 59; Roger Maris, 39, Johnny Mize and Johnny Blanchard, 34; Kevin Maas and Jim Spencer, 33.... Walked 40 times in his first 40 games last season, but only 43 times in 108 games thereafter.... Started 61 games after the All-Star break and was held hitless in nearly half (30). He had more than one hit in only seven of those games. He had three three-hit games last season, none after May 26.... His July batting average was 4th lowest in the league, and his August average was 3d lowest.... Home-game batting average was 3d lowest in the majors.... Of his 110 hits, only 11 were to the opposite field (10%), the 4th-lowest percentage in the American League (minimum: 60 hits).... Yankees DHs batted .222, the lowest of any team last season—in either league.... Because he debuted around the midpoint of the 1990 season, it's difficult to say who the most similar rookies were. But one year to the day of his debut, Maas had a .251 batting average, with 33 HR and 70 RBI. Similar rookie seasons: Jimmie Hall (.260, 33 HR, 80 RBI), Earl Williams (.260, 33 HR, 87 RBI), and Pete Incaviglia (.250, 30 HR, 88 RBI).... Here's a Maas-related fact we think may come in handy. Of the 20 other players who hit 20 or more homers as both rookies and sophomores, the only one who never hit 20 again was Dale Alexander.... Our model gives Maas only a 45 percent chance of hitting 20 or more again, and the odds against his reaching the 30 mark are 5-to-1.

Mike Macfarlane

Bats Right

Kansas City Royals	AB	H	2B	3B	HR	RBI	BB	SO	BA	SA	OBA
Season	267	74	18	2	13	41	17	52	.277	.506	.330
vs. Left-Handers	112	36	10	1	5	14	7	19	.321	.563	.372
vs. Right-Handers	155	38	8	1	8	27	10	33	.245	.465	.301
vs. Ground-Ballers	129	39	13	1	3	18	7	27	.302	.488	.348
vs. Fly-Ballers	138	35	5	1	10	23	10	25	.254	.522	.314
Home Games	126	36	7	2	6	17	9	20	.286	.516	.348
Road Games	141	38	11	0	7	24	8	32	.270	.496	.314
Grass Fields	112	30	9	0	5	20	6	26	.268	.482	.306
Artificial Turf	155	44	9	2	8	21	11	26	.284	.523	.347
April	56	19	7	1	0	6	3	10	.339	.500	.383
May	81	16	5	0	5	10	7	16	.198	.444	.275
June	81	23	2	1	4	11	3	15	.284	.481	.310
July	27	9	2	0	4	12	3	6	.333	.852	.406
August	0	0	0	0	0	0	0	0	.000	.000	.000
Sept./Oct.	22	7	2	0	0	2	1	5	.318	.409	.375
Leading Off Inn.	65	17	5	1	5	5	4	11	.262	.600	.314
Runners On	121	35	9	0	3	31	6	22	.289	.438	.333
Bases Empty	146	39	9	2	10	10	11	30	.267	.562	.327
Runners/Scor. Pos.	72	20	7	0	2	29	6	17	.278	.458	.325
Runners On/2 Out	53	12	1	0	1	10	2	14	.226	.302	.255
Scor. Pos./2 Out	37	8	1	0	1	10	2	13	.216	.324	.256
Late-Inning Pressure	41	7	3	0	0	2	6	12	.171	.244	.292
Leading Off	12	1	1	0	0	0	1	5	.083	.167	.154
Runners On	16	3	1	0	0	2	1	4	.188	.250	.278
Runners/Scor. Pos.	8	1	1	0	0	2	1	3	.125	.250	.222

RUNS BATTED IN	From 1B	From 2B	From 3B	Scoring Position
Totals	3/90	8/54	17/41	25/95
Percentage	3.3%	14.8%	41.5%	26.3%

Loves to face: Jim Abbott (.500, 8-for-16)
Mark Langston (.368, 7-for-19, 1 HR)
Mark Williamson (.700, 7-for-10, 1 HR)
Hates to face: Chuck Finley (.167, 4-for-24)
Mike Moore (.083, 1-for-12, 1 3B)
Dave Stewart (0-for-8)

Miscellaneous statistics: Ground outs-to-air outs ratio: 0.74 last season, 0.86 for career.... Grounded into 4 double plays in 59 opportunities (one per 15).... Drove in 14 of 25 runners from third base with less than two outs (56%).... Direction of balls hit to the outfield: 59% to left field, 24% to center, 17% to right.... Base running: Advanced from first base to third on 3 of 15 outfield singles (20%); scored from second on 6 of 10 (60%).... Opposing base stealers: 21-for-38 (55%).

Comments: Was on a tear, with six home runs and 16 RBIs in his previous 14 games, when an injury on July 15 required knee surgery. He next played on September 14, but didn't catch after his return.... His rate of one home run for every 21 at-bats more than tripled his previous career rate (one HR per 66 ABs).... Has increased his batting average by more than 20 points in each of the past two seasons; year by year since 1989: .223, .255, .277.... April batting average was 6th highest in the league.... Of his 74 hits, only seven were to the opposite field (9.5%), the 3d-lowest percentage in the American League (minimum: 60 hits).... Hit 10 home runs in 138 at-bats against fly-ball pitchers, the 7th-highest rate in the American League (minimum: 100 AB).... Opposing base stealers were successful on only 55 percent of their attempts against Macfarlane, but on 70 percent against teammate Brent Mayne.... Career fielding rate of one error every 145 chances is the best among active catchers (minimum: 200 games).... He has hit for a higher average with runners on base than he has with the bases empty in each of his five years in the majors. Career breakdown: .285 with runners on base, .235 with the bases empty.... Has batted below .200 in Late-Inning Pressure Situations three times in the past four years. His career BA in LIPS: .226.... Career batting average of .214 (9-for-42, 0 HR) as a pinch hitter.

Shane Mack

Bats Right

Minnesota Twins	AB	H	2B	3B	HR	RBI	BB	SO	BA	SA	OBA
Season	442	137	27	8	18	74	34	79	.310	.529	.363
vs. Left-Handers	137	48	13	4	9	29	14	19	.350	.701	.412
vs. Right-Handers	305	89	14	4	9	45	20	60	.292	.452	.341
vs. Ground-Ballers	188	57	9	1	9	31	13	32	.303	.505	.353
vs. Fly-Ballers	254	80	18	7	9	43	21	47	.315	.547	.371
Home Games	213	71	16	7	4	34	15	35	.333	.531	.383
Road Games	229	66	11	1	14	40	19	44	.288	.528	.345
Grass Fields	178	50	9	0	12	33	17	37	.281	.534	.345
Artificial Turf	264	87	18	8	6	41	17	42	.330	.527	.376
April	35	5	2	1	1	3	2	9	.143	.343	.189
May	42	14	2	0	2	9	5	2	.333	.524	.408
June	86	22	4	0	5	17	8	14	.256	.477	.313
July	82	30	6	3	3	12	9	14	.366	.622	.435
August	102	35	7	4	5	20	7	22	.343	.637	.387
Sept./Oct.	95	31	6	0	2	13	3	18	.326	.453	.363
Leading Off Inn.	105	32	5	2	3	3	3	15	.305	.476	.330
Runners On	197	60	11	2	10	66	16	38	.305	.533	.360
Bases Empty	245	77	16	6	8	8	18	41	.314	.527	.366
Runners/Scor. Pos.	113	30	6	1	6	54	8	25	.265	.496	.313
Runners On/2 Out	87	19	5	1	4	24	6	19	.218	.437	.277
Scor. Pos./2 Out	62	12	4	1	3	21	5	14	.194	.435	.256
Late-Inning Pressure	56	12	0	0	1	5	3	15	.214	.268	.250
Leading Off	15	4	0	0	0	0	0	4	.267	.267	.267
Runners On	25	4	0	0	0	4	2	7	.160	.160	.214
Runners/Scor. Pos.	15	3	0	0	0	4	2	4	.200	.200	.278

RUNS BATTED IN	From 1B	From 2B	From 3B	Scoring Position
Totals	16/150	13/81	27/63	40/144
Percentage	10.7%	16.0%	42.9%	27.8%

Loves to face: Chuck Finley (.450, 9-for-20, 1 HR)
Bill Krueger (.556, 5-for-9, 1 HR)
Kevin Morton (4-for-4, 1 BB)
Hates to face: Alex Fernandez (0-for-5, 5 SO)
Greg Hibbard (.100, 1-for-10)
Jack McDowell (.200, 3-for-15)

Miscellaneous statistics: Ground outs-to-air outs ratio: 1.24 last season, 1.58 for career.... Grounded into 11 double plays in 106 opportunities (one per 10).... Drove in 21 of 34 runners from third base with less than two outs (62%).... Direction of balls hit to the outfield: 29% to left field, 33% to center, 38% to right.... Base running: Advanced from first base to third on 8 of 24 outfield singles (33%); scored from second on 12 of 18 (67%).... Made 2.16 putouts per nine innings in right field.

Comments: Batted .364 after the All-Star break, 3d highest in the majors behind a pair of leaguemates, Ken Griffey, Jr. (.372) and Julio Franco (.366). Against left-handed pitchers, he batted .479 (34-for-71) after the break.... Has batted .360 vs. left-handed pitchers over the past two years, the 3d-highest average in the majors during that time (minimum: 250 AB), behind Frank Thomas (.386) and Mariano Duncan (.369).... Only one major leaguer played more innings in left field without any assists last season: Kevin Reimer of the Rangers.... Was the only American League player to start at least 15 games at all three outfield positions last season.... He was also versatile within the batting order. He and Darrin Jackson of San Diego were the only players to start in eight different batting-order positions. Neither batted ninth.... His July batting average was 5th highest in the league.... Led visiting players with four home runs at Yankee Stadium last season; which is to say, he hit as many dingers in 23 at-bats at the Stadium as he did in 213 ABs in his home dome.... Mack, we are told, is currently a hot fantasy-league property. But our projection model suggests he's as likely to accumulate fewer than 100 hits as he is to reach 150; and he's as likely to score fewer than 50 runs as he is to score 75 or more. The odds against him hitting even 15 home runs are more than 4-to-1. If you got 'im, trade 'im.

Candy Maldonado
Bats Right

Brewers/Blue Jays	AB	H	2B	3B	HR	RBI	BB	SO	BA	SA	OBA
Season	288	72	15	0	12	48	36	76	.250	.427	.342
vs. Left-Handers	76	21	5	0	3	12	15	13	.276	.461	.398
vs. Right-Handers	212	51	10	0	9	36	21	63	.241	.415	.321
vs. Ground-Ballers	153	36	6	0	6	26	18	38	.235	.392	.326
vs. Fly-Ballers	135	36	9	0	6	22	18	38	.267	.467	.361
Home Games	127	29	5	0	7	22	20	40	.228	.433	.340
Road Games	161	43	10	0	5	26	16	36	.267	.422	.344
Grass Fields	177	43	12	0	6	28	22	35	.243	.412	.328
Artificial Turf	111	29	3	0	6	20	14	41	.261	.450	.364
April	5	1	1	0	0	2	2	2	.200	.400	.429
May	0	0	0	0	0	0	0	0	—	—	—
June	10	3	0	0	2	6	2	2	.300	.900	.417
July	76	17	5	0	2	10	6	15	.224	.368	.277
August	98	22	3	0	4	11	8	24	.224	.378	.294
Sept./Oct.	99	29	6	0	4	19	18	33	.293	.475	.418
Leading Off Inn.	64	17	3	0	3	3	5	15	.266	.453	.329
Runners On	135	35	9	0	8	44	24	37	.259	.504	.372
Bases Empty	153	37	6	0	4	4	12	39	.242	.359	.314
Runners/Scor. Pos.	80	20	4	0	5	35	19	20	.250	.488	.388
Runners On/2 Out	55	12	2	0	1	15	10	17	.218	.309	.338
Scor. Pos./2 Out	40	11	1	0	1	14	10	14	.275	.375	.420
Late-Inning Pressure	44	5	0	0	2	4	4	14	.114	.250	.188
Leading Off	10	2	0	0	1	1	1	3	.200	.500	.273
Runners On	18	2	0	0	1	3	1	4	.111	.278	.158
Runners/Scor. Pos.	12	0	0	0	0	1	1	4	.000	.000	.077

RUNS BATTED IN	From 1B	From 2B	From 3B	Scoring Position
Totals	8/91	9/53	19/41	28/94
Percentage	8.8%	17.0%	46.3%	29.8%

Loves to face: Chuck Finley (.583, 7-for-12, 2 HR, 3 SO)
Bob Welch (.308, 8-for-26, 2 2B, 3 HR)
Matt Young (.417, 5-for-12, 1 HR)

Hates to face: Tom Edens (0-for-9)
Tim Leary (.087, 2-for-23, 1 HR, 3 BB)
Kevin Tapani (0-for-10)

Miscellaneous statistics: Ground outs-to-air outs ratio: 0.84 last season, 1.01 for career.... Grounded into 8 double plays in 64 opportunities (one per 8.0).... Drove in 13 of 22 runners from third base with less than two outs (59%).... Direction of balls hit to the outfield: 36% to left field, 31% to center, 33% to right.... Base running: Advanced from first base to third on 3 of 15 outfield singles (20%); scored from second on 4 of 6 (67%).... Made 2.07 putouts per nine innings in left field.

Comments: Candy is the pinch-hit home-run champion of the divisional era, with nine pinch-HRs in 160 ABs. Four players have hit eight pinch homers since 1969: Thad Bosley (288 AB), Mark Carreon (93), Jim Dwyer (387), and Ken Phelps (160).... Twenty-two players have hit at least 10 pinch home runs; the record is 20, by Cliff Johnson.... Has played for three different teams in post-season play: the Dodgers (1983 and 1985), the Giants (1987 and 1989), and the Blue Jays (1991). On the basis of that odd-season progression alone, Toronto would be crazy to let him go before the end of next season.... Only four players in history have played for more than three teams in the postseason competition: Don Baylor (Orioles, Angels, Red Sox, Twins, and Athletics); Danny Heep (Astros, Mets, Dodgers, and Red Sox); Doyle Alexander (Orioles, Yankees, Blue Jays, and Tigers); and Lonnie Smith (Phillies, Cardinals, Royals, and Braves). Only Lonnie made it to the Series with all four.... He has hit for a higher average in road games than he has in home games in each of the last eight seasons, matching Brook Jacoby and Ron Darling for the longest current streak of its kind.... Drove in 95 runs in 155 games for Cleveland in 1990, but the Indians decided against resigning him after the season.... His totals of 93 home runs and 422 RBIs over the past six seasons belie his reputation as a pinch hitter and part-time starter. They are comparable to those of Pete O'Brien (96 and 419), Hubie Brooks (98 and 431) and Andres Galarraga (104 and 429).

Carlos Martinez
Bats Right

Cleveland Indians	AB	H	2B	3B	HR	RBI	BB	SO	BA	SA	OBA
Season	257	73	14	0	5	30	10	43	.284	.397	.310
vs. Left-Handers	80	27	5	0	4	13	6	11	.338	.550	.367
vs. Right-Handers	177	46	9	0	1	17	4	32	.260	.328	.283
vs. Ground-Ballers	110	29	4	0	2	9	4	21	.264	.355	.287
vs. Fly-Ballers	147	44	10	0	3	21	6	22	.299	.429	.327
Home Games	139	44	6	0	3	18	5	21	.317	.424	.338
Road Games	118	29	8	0	2	12	5	22	.246	.364	.278
Grass Fields	223	66	12	0	5	28	9	35	.296	.417	.319
Artificial Turf	34	7	2	0	0	2	1	8	.206	.265	.250
April	0	0	0	0	0	0	0	0	—	—	—
May	0	0	0	0	0	0	0	0	—	—	—
June	0	0	0	0	0	0	0	0	—	—	—
July	75	26	3	0	2	8	3	15	.347	.467	.367
August	77	22	5	0	0	11	3	16	.286	.351	.318
Sept./Oct.	105	25	6	0	3	11	4	12	.238	.381	.264
Leading Off Inn.	56	14	3	0	2	2	2	11	.250	.411	.300
Runners On	110	32	5	0	1	26	6	15	.291	.364	.314
Bases Empty	147	41	9	0	4	4	4	28	.279	.422	.307
Runners/Scor. Pos.	50	18	3	0	0	24	3	8	.360	.420	.362
Runners On/2 Out	45	14	2	0	0	8	5	10	.311	.356	.380
Scor. Pos./2 Out	23	8	1	0	0	8	3	5	.348	.391	.423
Late-Inning Pressure	41	11	1	0	1	3	1	9	.268	.366	.286
Leading Off	14	4	1	0	1	1	0	4	.286	.571	.286
Runners On	16	3	0	0	0	2	0	2	.188	.188	.188
Runners/Scor. Pos.	6	2	0	0	0	2	0	2	.333	.333	.333

RUNS BATTED IN	From 1B	From 2B	From 3B	Scoring Position
Totals	2/83	7/41	16/24	23/65
Percentage	2.4%	17.1%	66.7%	35.4%

Loves to face: Brian Holman (.778, 7-for-9, 1 HR)
Jimmy Key (.400, 8-for-20, 1 HR)
Bob Milacki (.500, 9-for-18, 5 2B, 1 HR)

Hates to face: Andy Hawkins (0-for-10)
Mark Langston (.077, 1-for-13)
Mark Williamson (.091, 1-for-11)

Miscellaneous statistics: Ground outs-to-air outs ratio: 0.96 last season, 1.26 for career.... Grounded into 10 double plays in 53 opportunities (one per 5.3).... Drove in 12 of 14 runners from third base with less than two outs (86%).... Direction of balls hit to the outfield: 39% to left field, 39% to center, 22% to right.... Base running: Advanced from first base to third on 3 of 9 outfield singles (33%); scored from second on 2 of 3 (67%).... Made 0.47 assists per nine innings at first base.

Comments: Rogelio, Marty, Hector, Tony, Buck, Jose, Teddy, Tippy, Dennis, Silvio, Fred, Carmelo, Dave, Edgar, Carlos, Ramon, Tino, and Chito. There have been 18 Martinezes in the majors. Rogelio broke the barrier in 1950, and for 12 years until Marty made his big-league debut, "Martinez" was tied with "Schoonmaker," "Schreckengost," and "Steinbrenner"—yes, Steinbrenner; no, not George—with one representative each in major league history. But the Martinezes have been on something of a roll lately. Buck got things pointed in the right direction, playing more than 1000 games over an 18-year career, and Dennis and Tippy were key members of some fine Orioles teams. More recently, Edgar had back-to-back .300 seasons and Ramon established himself as one of the National League's leading pitchers. Last season, Carmelo became the second Martinez to reach the 1000-game mark. Combined with contributions by Dave, Chito, Tino, and Carlos, the name "Martinez" appeared in box scores more often than any other last season—622 times in all. That's 55 times more than "Smith" (a 27-time leader, including 1990) and 102 times more than "Davis" (the leader for seven straight years from 1983 through 1989). This season, with Chito ready to assume a full-time role and Tino a potential starter in Seattle, the extended Martinez family may even take a run at the all-time record of 1050 box-score lines, set by the Davises in 1986—Glenn, Chili, Jody, Mike, Alvin, Eric, Mark, Ron, Storm, Joel, Trench, and Steve.

Edgar Martinez   Bats Right

Seattle Mariners	AB	H	2B	3B	HR	RBI	BB	SO	BA	SA	OBA
Season	544	167	35	1	14	52	84	72	.307	.452	.405
vs. Left-Handers	156	56	13	0	2	12	24	11	.359	.481	.442
vs. Right-Handers	388	111	22	1	12	40	60	61	.286	.441	.390
vs. Ground-Ballers	237	85	19	1	7	28	37	27	.359	.536	.450
vs. Fly-Ballers	307	82	16	0	7	24	47	45	.267	.388	.369
Home Games	250	80	14	1	8	28	45	33	.320	.480	.427
Road Games	294	87	21	0	6	24	39	39	.296	.429	.385
Grass Fields	222	64	13	0	5	17	32	31	.288	.414	.383
Artificial Turf	322	103	22	1	9	35	52	41	.320	.478	.419
April	68	28	5	0	2	10	18	8	.412	.574	.551
May	87	24	2	0	2	9	14	15	.276	.368	.376
June	86	23	3	0	1	5	6	12	.267	.337	.319
July	87	29	6	1	4	11	11	11	.333	.563	.417
August	95	25	7	0	3	7	17	9	.263	.432	.381
Sept./Oct.	121	38	12	0	2	10	18	17	.314	.463	.400
Leading Off Inn.	165	56	15	1	6	6	21	25	.339	.552	.417
Runners On	216	57	11	0	5	43	41	22	.264	.384	.385
Bases Empty	328	110	24	1	9	9	43	50	.335	.497	.419
Runners/Scor. Pos.	105	23	5	0	2	33	30	10	.219	.324	.390
Runners On/2 Out	95	21	3	0	2	16	21	13	.221	.316	.368
Scor. Pos./2 Out	50	8	1	0	1	12	17	7	.160	.240	.373
Late-Inning Pressure	65	22	4	0	0	8	16	12	.338	.400	.476
Leading Off	19	4	0	0	0	0	2	5	.211	.211	.286
Runners On	24	7	2	0	0	8	9	3	.292	.375	.486
Runners/Scor. Pos.	16	6	1	0	0	7	5	2	.375	.438	.522

RUNS BATTED IN	From 1B	From 2B	From 3B	Scoring Position
Totals	9/165	15/84	14/40	29/124
Percentage	5.5%	17.9%	35.0%	23.4%

Loves to face: Roger Clemens (.429, 6-for-14, 1 HR)
               Mark Gubicza (.500, 6-for-12, 1 HR)
               Dave Stewart (.538, 7-for-13, 6 BB)

Hates to face: Charlie Hough (.118, 2-for-17, 2 BB)
               Jose Mesa (0-for-8)
               Nolan Ryan (.059, 1-for-17)

Miscellaneous statistics: Ground outs-to-air outs ratio: 1.29 last season, 0.99 for career.... Grounded into 19 double plays in 109 opportunities (one per 5.7).... Drove in 10 of 19 runners from third base with less than two outs (53%).... Direction of balls hit to the outfield: 33% to left field, 29% to center, 38% to right.... Base running: Advanced from first base to third on 13 of 42 outfield singles (31%); scored from second on 22 of 24 (92%).... Made 2.17 assists per nine innings at third base.

Comments: As noted on the previous page, Martinez has topped the .300 mark in each of the past two seasons. The only other player to bat .300 or better and to hit double figures in home runs in each of the past two seasons: Rafael Palmeiro.... Led the majors with a .359 batting average against ground-ball pitchers, but ranked only 48th among 82 A. L. qualifiers vs. fly-ballers.... Batting average vs. left-handed pitchers was 4th highest in the majors.... Issued 1991's strongest challenge to Ted Williams's 50-year reign as the last .400 hitter, not dropping into the .300s until May 1.... Hit safely in each of Seattle's first 26 victories, the longest streak of its kind in the A.L. last season.... On-base percentage leading off innings was 3d highest in the majors.... His career average of .322 in Late-Inning Pressure Situations is 5th highest among active players, behind the guys you would probably expect: Gwynn, Puckett, Raines, and Boggs.... Mariners batters didn't hit more than three home runs in any game last season. They hit exactly three homers on three occasions—surprisingly, all on the road. Martinez was one of three Mariners players to pop two in a game; the others were Jay Buhner (twice) and Pete O'Brien. All those individual efforts came in the Kingdome.... According to our projection model, the odds against Edgar getting 200 hits this season are 37-to-1.

Don Mattingly   Bats Left

New York Yankees	AB	H	2B	3B	HR	RBI	BB	SO	BA	SA	OBA
Season	587	169	35	0	9	68	46	42	.288	.394	.339
vs. Left-Handers	227	60	12	0	5	29	18	20	.264	.383	.321
vs. Right-Handers	360	109	23	0	4	39	28	22	.303	.400	.350
vs. Ground-Ballers	282	81	15	0	3	28	24	19	.287	.372	.343
vs. Fly-Ballers	305	88	20	0	6	40	22	23	.289	.413	.335
Home Games	266	81	21	0	7	40	22	20	.305	.462	.356
Road Games	321	88	14	0	2	28	24	22	.274	.336	.325
Grass Fields	484	142	31	0	9	63	43	37	.293	.413	.349
Artificial Turf	103	27	4	0	0	5	3	5	.262	.301	.287
April	68	18	1	0	1	4	11	5	.265	.324	.367
May	90	28	5	0	2	13	8	8	.311	.433	.360
June	104	35	4	0	3	13	4	6	.337	.462	.355
July	102	27	9	0	0	10	6	8	.265	.353	.313
August	99	34	10	0	1	17	9	7	.343	.475	.400
Sept./Oct.	124	27	6	0	2	11	8	8	.218	.315	.267
Leading Off Inn.	109	29	4	0	1	1	6	5	.266	.330	.310
Runners On	257	77	15	0	4	63	24	15	.300	.405	.355
Bases Empty	330	92	20	0	5	5	22	27	.279	.385	.326
Runners/Scor. Pos.	138	40	9	0	2	57	23	11	.290	.399	.382
Runners On/2 Out	73	24	6	0	2	18	10	3	.329	.493	.424
Scor. Pos./2 Out	52	15	4	0	1	16	9	3	.288	.423	.413
Late-Inning Pressure	82	24	4	0	4	13	13	8	.293	.488	.385
Leading Off	23	6	0	0	0	0	3	2	.261	.261	.346
Runners On	33	9	1	0	3	12	7	3	.273	.576	.390
Runners/Scor. Pos.	15	5	1	0	2	10	7	3	.333	.800	.522

RUNS BATTED IN	From 1B	From 2B	From 3B	Scoring Position
Totals	6/179	25/109	28/59	53/168
Percentage	3.4%	22.9%	47.5%	31.5%

Loves to face: Tom Henke (.389, 7-for-18, 2 HR)
               Shawn Hillegas (.444, 4-for-9, 2 HR)
               Edwin Nunez (.375, 6-for-16, 3 HR)

Hates to face: Rick Aguilera (.091, 1-for-11)
               Bobby Thigpen (.083, 1-for-12)
               Kevin Tapani (.125, 2-for-16)

Miscellaneous statistics: Ground outs-to-air outs ratio: 0.93 last season, 0.89 for career.... Grounded into 21 double plays in 146 opportunities (one per 7.0).... Drove in 22 of 36 runners from third base with less than two outs (61%).... Direction of balls hit to the outfield: 30% to left field, 35% to center, 35% to right.... Base running: Advanced from first base to third on 6 of 27 outfield singles (22%); scored from second on 6 of 11 (55%).... Made 0.64 assists per nine innings at first base.

Comments: Is he destined to be the next Ernie Banks? Among active players, only Hubie Brooks, Julio Franco, and Pete O'Brien have played more games without ever appearing in postseason play.... Suffered through a demoralizing September during which his season's batting average fell from .308 to .285. Included were these indignities: 14 consecutive plate appearances in which he failed to hit a ball out of the infield (Sept. 6–9); four consecutive starts without a hit (Sept. 17–21) for the first time since June 1990; and a career-high streak of 27 hitless at-bats with runners on base (Sept. 16–Oct. 2).... Started 19 double plays in the field last season, the most of any first baseman in the majors.... His total of air outs was the 3d highest in the American League last season.... Of his 68 RBIs, 24 gave the Yankees a lead (35%), the 6th-highest rate in the majors last season (minimum: 15 go-ahead RBIs).... Batting average with two outs and runners on base was 9th highest in the league.... Hit safely in 19 straight day games, the longest streak of its kind in the majors.... He has driven in 35.5 percent of runners from scoring position in his career, the highest rate of any player in the 17 years of *The Player Analysis*.... Career rate of one strikeout every 18.3 plate appearances is 2d best among active players (minimum: 1000 plate appearances), behind Tony Gwynn (one SO per 20.8 PA).

Brent Mayne
Bats Left

Kansas City Royals	AB	H	2B	3B	HR	RBI	BB	SO	BA	SA	OBA
Season	231	58	8	0	3	31	23	42	.251	.325	.315
vs. Left-Handers	22	2	0	0	0	3	3	8	.091	.091	.179
vs. Right-Handers	209	56	8	0	3	28	20	34	.268	.349	.332
vs. Ground-Ballers	111	29	3	0	2	13	9	22	.261	.342	.314
vs. Fly-Ballers	120	29	5	0	1	18	14	20	.242	.308	.316
Home Games	130	35	4	0	2	19	13	23	.269	.346	.333
Road Games	101	23	4	0	1	12	10	19	.228	.297	.292
Grass Fields	75	17	4	0	1	10	7	12	.227	.320	.286
Artificial Turf	156	41	4	0	2	21	16	30	.263	.327	.329
April	11	3	1	0	0	2	1	3	.273	.364	.333
May	17	6	0	0	0	1	1	3	.353	.353	.389
June	29	7	0	0	0	5	4	6	.241	.241	.333
July	60	17	3	0	0	6	4	8	.283	.333	.328
August	52	10	2	0	2	8	7	10	.192	.346	.283
Sept./Oct.	62	15	2	0	1	9	6	12	.242	.323	.300
Leading Off Inn.	65	12	1	0	0	0	4	12	.185	.200	.232
Runners On	104	33	5	0	3	31	13	22	.317	.452	.383
Bases Empty	127	25	3	0	0	0	10	20	.197	.220	.255
Runners/Scor. Pos.	63	22	4	0	2	29	9	15	.349	.508	.413
Runners On/2 Out	40	9	4	0	0	7	5	10	.225	.325	.311
Scor. Pos./2 Out	27	7	3	0	0	7	5	8	.259	.370	.375
Late-Inning Pressure	39	7	0	0	1	3	5	10	.179	.256	.273
Leading Off	11	3	0	0	0	0	1	2	.273	.273	.333
Runners On	20	4	0	0	1	3	4	6	.200	.350	.333
Runners/Scor. Pos.	14	3	0	0	1	3	2	4	.214	.429	.313

RUNS BATTED IN	From 1B	From 2B	From 3B	Scoring Position
Totals	1/75	12/48	15/25	27/73
Percentage	1.3%	25.0%	60.0%	37.0%

Loves to face: Tim Leary (3-for-3)
Jaime Navarro (.600, 3-for-5)

Hates to face:

Mark McGwire
Bats Right

Oakland A's	AB	H	2B	3B	HR	RBI	BB	SO	BA	SA	OBA
Season	483	97	22	0	22	75	93	116	.201	.383	.330
vs. Left-Handers	130	26	5	0	5	19	23	28	.200	.354	.316
vs. Right-Handers	353	71	17	0	17	56	70	88	.201	.394	.336
vs. Ground-Ballers	231	53	10	0	13	43	55	49	.229	.442	.377
vs. Fly-Ballers	252	44	12	0	9	32	38	67	.175	.329	.285
Home Games	243	45	10	0	15	48	52	55	.185	.412	.329
Road Games	240	52	12	0	7	27	41	61	.217	.354	.332
Grass Fields	400	82	18	0	21	69	80	96	.205	.408	.339
Artificial Turf	83	15	4	0	1	6	13	20	.181	.265	.289
April	67	14	6	0	0	5	15	15	.209	.299	.354
May	79	18	2	0	5	16	28	22	.228	.443	.426
June	85	15	2	0	8	19	14	27	.176	.482	.297
July	81	14	4	0	1	8	13	20	.173	.259	.292
August	94	24	3	0	6	18	11	17	.255	.479	.330
Sept./Oct.	77	12	5	0	2	9	12	15	.156	.299	.275
Leading Off Inn.	96	16	6	0	5	5	14	17	.167	.385	.279
Runners On	239	55	9	0	14	67	49	62	.230	.444	.355
Bases Empty	244	42	13	0	8	8	44	54	.172	.324	.306
Runners/Scor. Pos.	130	31	3	0	9	57	29	32	.238	.469	.366
Runners On/2 Out	102	25	3	0	5	30	22	25	.245	.422	.379
Scor. Pos./2 Out	67	17	1	0	3	26	14	17	.254	.403	.383
Late-Inning Pressure	65	12	2	0	4	14	12	16	.185	.400	.308
Leading Off	16	3	1	0	0	0	1	2	.188	.250	.235
Runners On	25	6	0	0	4	14	7	9	.240	.720	.394
Runners/Scor. Pos.	13	4	0	0	2	10	4	4	.308	.769	.444

RUNS BATTED IN	From 1B	From 2B	From 3B	Scoring Position
Totals	12/180	18/101	23/57	41/158
Percentage	6.7%	17.8%	40.4%	25.9%

Loves to face: Mike Boddicker (.269, 7-for-26, 1 2B, 4 HR, 12 BB)
Brian Bohannon (2-for-2, 2 HR)
Mark Williamson (.444, 8-for-18, 2 2B, 3 HR)

Hates to face: Roger Clemens (.036, 1-for-28, 1 2B, 3 BB)
Tom Henke (.083, 1-for-12, 1 HR, 10 SO)
Greg Hibbard (.063, 1-for-16, 2 BB)

Miscellaneous statistics: Ground outs-to-air outs ratio: 1.73 last season, 1.61 for career.... Grounded into 6 double plays in 58 opportunities (one per 10).... Drove in 14 of 18 runners from third base with less than two outs (78%), 3d-highest rate in A.L.... Direction of balls hit to the outfield: 40% to left field, 35% to center, 25% to right.... Base running: Advanced from first base to third on 3 of 8 outfield singles (38%); scored from second on 3 of 7 (43%).... Opposing base stealers: 53-for-76 (70%).

Comments: Started 63 games in 1991, and has started 67 in his career, all vs. right-handed pitchers.... Some statistics are just weird: Mayne batted .276 in Royals' losses as opposed to .233 in games that they won, the largest such difference among A.L. batters (minimum: 250 plate appearances).... Caught team-high 41.4 percent of Royals' innings last year; Mike Macfarlane caught 39.5 percent, Tim Spehr 15.7 percent, and Jorge Pedre 3.4 percent. All except Macfarlane (who started 66 games, three more than Mayne) are rookies.... Including David Howard and Terry Shumpert, Royals had three rookies with 250 or more plate appearances, equaling Yankees and Astros for most in the majors.... Left-handed hitting catchers are always a commodity sought by managers; there were 14 lefties or switch-hitters in majors last year who caught at least 50 games. Lefties and switch-hitters account for only 28 percent of the 82 catchers in major league history who caught at least 1000 games (59 batted right, 18 batted left, and five switch-hit); every other position except shortstop has had more left-handed batters or switch-hitters. Figures at other positions: first base, 63 percent of 1000-game players batted left or both; outfield, 56 percent; second base, 36 percent; third base, 23 percent; shortstop, 18 percent.... Born on April 19, 1968. In baseball that day, Mets rookie Nolan Ryan, in his third major league start, lost 3–2 to the Dodgers, but struck out 11 for the first double-digit strikeout game of his career.

Miscellaneous statistics: Ground outs-to-air outs ratio: 0.57 last season, 3d lowest in A.L.; 0.61 for career.... Grounded into 13 double plays in 130 opportunities (one per 10).... Drove in 13 of 23 runners from third base with less than two outs (57%).... Direction of balls hit to the outfield: 39% to left field, 32% to center, 29% to right.... Base running: Advanced from first base to third on 4 of 19 outfield singles (21%); scored from second on 8 of 10 (80%).... Made 0.72 assists per nine innings at first base.

Comments: Career home-run rate (one every 14.9 at-bats) ranks second among active players to Cecil Fielder (13.5), and stands second in franchise history to Jimmie Foxx (14.6).... Career rate in road games (one every 13.3 at-bats) is the best among active players; home-game rate (one every 17.2 at-bats) ranks 12th among actives.... Even with .201 overall average, Mac hit 51 points higher with runners in scoring position (.238) than at other times. Career breakdown: .281 with runners in scoring position, .231 in other at-bats.... Owns .317 career average in 82 career at-bats with runners in scoring position in Late-Inning Pressure Situations.... Hitless in his last nine at-bats of season, lowering his average to .201, and did not take a turn at bat in team's last two games.... Lowest batting averages in a 20-home-run season: Rob Deer (.179, 25 HR) in 1991; Willie Kirkland (.200, 21) in 1962; McGwire in 1991; Dave Kingman (.203, 24) in 1973; Kingman (.204, 37) in 1982.... There are 222 "team/positions" in majors, including DH but excluding pitcher: nine for each A.L. team, eight for each N.L. team. Only three of those 222 team/positions had a batting average below .200 last year: Tigers right fielders (.190), Padres third basemen (.194), and A's first basemen (.199). The perpetrators: Rob Deer at Detroit, Coolbaugh/Howell/Teufel at San Diego, and McGwire at Oakland.... The low batting average is one thing; the real problem is that Oakland first basemen, with 82 RBIs, had five RBIs fewer than the A.L. average.

Brian McRae
Bats Left and Right

Kansas City Royals	AB	H	2B	3B	HR	RBI	BB	SO	BA	SA	OBA
Season	629	164	28	9	8	64	24	99	.261	.372	.288
vs. Left-Handers	204	60	13	2	2	19	9	16	.294	.407	.326
vs. Right-Handers	425	104	15	7	6	45	15	83	.245	.355	.270
vs. Ground-Ballers	277	72	13	4	3	18	11	43	.260	.368	.286
vs. Fly-Ballers	352	92	15	5	5	46	13	56	.261	.375	.289
Home Games	318	85	16	6	3	29	17	52	.267	.384	.305
Road Games	311	79	12	3	5	35	7	47	.254	.360	.270
Grass Fields	237	64	9	3	3	25	3	33	.270	.371	.278
Artificial Turf	392	100	19	6	5	39	21	66	.255	.372	.294
April	49	7	1	0	1	8	0	11	.143	.224	.137
May	103	29	4	2	3	15	10	13	.282	.447	.345
June	120	33	4	2	0	9	4	21	.275	.342	.296
July	114	34	6	1	2	15	5	18	.298	.421	.325
August	118	32	5	3	0	7	2	15	.271	.364	.295
Sept./Oct.	125	29	8	1	2	10	3	21	.232	.360	.248
Leading Off Inn.	218	67	16	4	1	1	9	33	.307	.431	.335
Runners On	230	55	7	3	5	61	12	35	.239	.361	.274
Bases Empty	399	109	21	6	3	3	12	64	.273	.378	.296
Runners/Scor. Pos.	142	36	5	1	2	52	9	27	.254	.345	.293
Runners On/2 Out	97	21	4	1	3	25	7	21	.216	.371	.269
Scor. Pos./2 Out	71	14	4	0	1	20	6	18	.197	.296	.260
Late-Inning Pressure	91	24	3	1	1	7	5	16	.264	.352	.299
Leading Off	24	9	2	1	0	0	1	2	.375	.542	.400
Runners On	36	8	0	0	1	7	4	4	.222	.306	.293
Runners/Scor. Pos.	22	4	0	0	0	5	3	4	.182	.182	.269

RUNS BATTED IN	From 1B	From 2B	From 3B	Scoring Position
Totals	9/152	27/122	20/53	47/175
Percentage	5.9%	22.1%	37.7%	26.9%

Loves to face: Bill Gullickson (.400, 4-for-10, 1 HR)
Kevin Tapani (.538, 7-for-13, 1 HR)
David Wells (.556, 5-for-9)

Hates to face: Jose Guzman (0-for-8)
Bob Milacki (0-for-6)
Scott Sanderson (0-for-8)

Miscellaneous statistics: Ground outs-to-air outs ratio: 1.31 last season, 1.30 for career.... Grounded into 12 double plays in 104 opportunities (one per 8.7).... Drove in 14 of 26 runners from third base with less than two outs (54%).... Direction of balls hit to the outfield: 34% to left field, 30% to center, 36% to right batting left-handed; 27% to left field, 32% to center, 41% to right batting right-handed.... Base running: Advanced from first base to third on 9 of 19 outfield singles (47%); scored from second on 21 of 23 (91%).... Made 2.80 putouts per nine innings in center field.

Comments: The Royals had a 56–38 record and .596 winning percentage with McRae starting in the leadoff spot, a better percentage than any American League team had over the course of the 1991 season. But Royals went 26–42 with other players in the leadoff spot, a .382 percentage.... April batting average was 4th lowest in the league.... His 22-game hitting streak (July 20–Aug. 13) was the longest in the American League last season.... One of four players in majors last season with at least eight home runs but more triples than homers; others: Roberto Alomar, Steve Finley, and Ray Lankford.... Season statistics in first full season were very similar to rookie numbers of the other second-generation offspring of a Big Red Machiner, Ken Griffey: Griffey batted .261 with 61 RBIs and 16 steals in 127 games in 1989; aided by a rather large difference in home parks, Junior did hit twice as many homers as McRae hit last year.... Only six of his 64 RBIs gave the Royals a lead (9%), the lowest percentage of go-ahead RBIs by any player in the league with at least 50 RBIs last season.... Royals' first-round choice, 17th player selected overall, in 1985 amateur draft. What marked '85 first round was the presence of quality players all through the round: B.J. Surhoff, Will Clark, Bobby Witt, Barry Larkin, Barry Bonds, and Pete Incaviglia were among the first 10 players chosen; Walt Weiss, Tommy Greene, McRae, Joe Magrane, Gregg Jefferies, and Rafael Palmeiro were among the next 12 selections.

Hensley Meulens
Bats Right

New York Yankees	AB	H	2B	3B	HR	RBI	BB	SO	BA	SA	OBA
Season	288	64	8	1	6	29	18	97	.222	.319	.276
vs. Left-Handers	178	42	6	1	5	19	12	54	.236	.365	.297
vs. Right-Handers	110	22	2	0	1	10	6	43	.200	.245	.239
vs. Ground-Ballers	98	18	3	1	1	5	5	39	.184	.265	.231
vs. Fly-Ballers	190	46	5	0	5	24	13	58	.242	.347	.298
Home Games	154	33	5	0	4	16	8	54	.214	.325	.261
Road Games	134	31	3	1	2	13	10	43	.231	.313	.293
Grass Fields	250	51	6	1	5	25	16	82	.204	.296	.261
Artificial Turf	38	13	2	0	1	4	2	15	.342	.474	.375
April	44	9	0	1	0	4	3	16	.205	.250	.255
May	59	13	2	0	3	6	3	23	.220	.407	.258
June	39	11	1	0	0	6	1	12	.282	.308	.300
July	47	9	1	0	2	3	3	18	.191	.340	.255
August	50	11	1	0	0	8	4	14	.220	.240	.281
Sept./Oct.	49	11	3	0	1	2	4	14	.224	.347	.309
Leading Off Inn.	81	17	1	0	2	2	5	31	.210	.296	.264
Runners On	108	29	4	1	3	26	8	36	.269	.407	.325
Bases Empty	180	35	4	0	3	3	10	61	.194	.267	.245
Runners/Scor. Pos.	67	16	2	1	1	22	4	20	.239	.343	.284
Runners On/2 Out	41	10	0	1	1	9	5	17	.244	.366	.354
Scor. Pos./2 Out	28	7	0	1	0	7	3	11	.250	.321	.344
Late-Inning Pressure	36	4	0	0	0	3	0	15	.111	.111	.135
Leading Off	15	1	0	0	0	0	0	7	.067	.067	.067
Runners On	17	3	0	0	0	3	0	8	.176	.176	.222
Runners/Scor. Pos.	11	2	0	0	0	3	0	5	.182	.182	.182

RUNS BATTED IN	From 1B	From 2B	From 3B	Scoring Position
Totals	4/82	12/60	7/25	19/85
Percentage	4.9%	20.0%	28.0%	22.4%

Loves to face: Jim Abbott (.400, 4-for-10)
Scott Erickson (2-for-2, 1 BB)
Jimmy Key (.364, 4-for-11, 1 HR, 4 SO)

Hates to face: Roger Clemens (0-for-3, 3 SO)
Dennis Eckersley (0-for-3, 3 SO)
Greg Hibbard (0-for-9)

Miscellaneous statistics: Ground outs-to-air outs ratio: 1.69 last season, 1.57 for career.... Grounded into 7 double plays in 51 opportunities (one per 7.3).... Drove in 6 of 14 runners from third base with less than two outs (43%).... Direction of balls hit to the outfield: 24% to left field, 40% to center, 36% to right.... Base running: Advanced from first base to third on 4 of 10 outfield singles (40%); scored from second on 7 of 11 (64%).... Made 2.30 putouts per nine innings in left field.

Comments: Struck out 97 times in 313 trips to the plate, the highest single-season rate of strikeouts by any player in Yankees history (minimum: 200 plate appearances). The top five: Meulens (one every 3.2 plate appearances), Steve Balboni (3.4) in 1990, Dan Pasqua (3.7) in 1987, Joel Skinner (3.8) in 1988, Jesse Barfield (3.8) in 1990. Reggie Jackson's top strikeout rate in any of his five years in New York stands no higher than 15th on the all-time list; Mickey Mantle's top rate stands in 29th place. Both Jackson and Mantle took a lot of heat in their day for the frequency of their strikeout totals; today, they might be regarded as contact hitters.... Struck out on 36.4 percent of plate appearances vs. right-handed pitchers, the second-highest single-season rate since 1975 (minimum: 100 at-bats vs. RHP), just a shade behind Rob Deer's record of 36.5 percent set in 1987.... Meulens was not the first player to strike out 100 times in his first 100 games with the Yankees. Jack Clark also did it, as did three pitchers: Johnny Broaca, Bill Bevens, and Stan Bahnsen.... Started all 55 games in which Yankees faced a left-handed starter, but only 23 of 107 against right-handed starters.... Hit five of his six home runs to the opposite field.... One of three Yankees rookies to play at least 80 games last season; others: Pat Kelly and Bernie Williams. Last time Yankees had three 80-game rookies: Hank Bauer, Jerry Coleman, and Cliff Mapes in the magical summer of 1949.

Randy Milligan
Bats Right

Baltimore Orioles	AB	H	2B	3B	HR	RBI	BB	SO	BA	SA	OBA
Season	483	127	17	2	16	70	84	108	.263	.406	.373
vs. Left-Handers	140	32	3	1	5	19	26	35	.229	.371	.347
vs. Right-Handers	343	95	14	1	11	51	58	73	.277	.420	.384
vs. Ground-Ballers	213	64	8	1	8	40	31	41	.300	.460	.394
vs. Fly-Ballers	270	63	9	1	8	30	53	67	.233	.363	.357
Home Games	237	59	9	0	8	33	41	51	.249	.388	.362
Road Games	246	68	8	2	8	37	43	57	.276	.423	.384
Grass Fields	409	103	12	1	13	55	68	91	.252	.381	.360
Artificial Turf	74	24	5	1	3	15	16	17	.324	.541	.440
April	56	11	2	0	0	2	9	17	.196	.232	.303
May	85	23	2	1	3	13	14	23	.271	.424	.374
June	88	30	4	0	6	22	12	18	.341	.591	.420
July	85	20	2	1	3	17	19	11	.235	.388	.377
August	92	24	4	0	1	12	18	18	.261	.337	.382
Sept./Oct.	77	19	3	0	3	4	12	21	.247	.403	.356
Leading Off Inn.	110	27	3	0	5	5	19	27	.245	.409	.357
Runners On	222	56	7	2	5	59	37	56	.252	.369	.361
Bases Empty	261	71	10	0	11	11	47	52	.272	.437	.383
Runners/Scor. Pos.	128	39	4	1	3	53	30	36	.305	.422	.438
Runners On/2 Out	101	27	6	0	3	32	16	32	.267	.416	.378
Scor. Pos./2 Out	65	21	4	0	2	29	13	22	.323	.477	.450
Late-Inning Pressure	73	17	3	1	1	7	16	14	.233	.342	.371
Leading Off	20	3	0	0	0	0	2	6	.150	.150	.227
Runners On	33	7	2	1	0	6	10	5	.212	.333	.395
Runners/Scor. Pos.	17	4	1	0	0	5	8	2	.235	.294	.480

RUNS BATTED IN	From 1B	From 2B	From 3B	Scoring Position
Totals	10/164	24/100	20/53	44/153
Percentage	6.1%	24.0%	37.7%	28.8%

Loves to face: Mark Gubicza (.500, 5-for-10, 1 2B, 1 3B, 2 HR)
Andy Hawkins (.667, 2-for-3, 2 HR, 1 SO)
Bobby Witt (.500, 7-for-14, 1 HR, 7 BB)

Hates to face: Mark Langston (.063, 1-for-16, 3 BB)
Jack Morris (.067, 1-for-15, 1 2B)
Nolan Ryan (0-for-13, 8 SO)

Miscellaneous statistics: Ground outs-to-air outs ratio: 1.12 last season, 1.01 for career.... Grounded into 23 double plays in 103 opportunities (one per 4.5), 4th-worst rate in A.L.... Drove in 13 of 28 runners from third base with less than two outs (46%).... Direction of balls hit to the outfield: 24% to left field, 37% to center, 39% to right.... Base running: Advanced from first base to third on 8 of 37 outfield singles (22%); scored from second on 5 of 13 (38%), 3d-lowest rate in A.L.... Made 0.81 assists per nine innings at first base, 3d-highest rate in A.L.

Comments: His .390 career on-base percentage ranks fifth among active players with at least 1000 plate appearances, behind Wade Boggs (.435), Rickey Henderson (.403), Dave Magadan (.391), and Fred McGriff (.391).... He has averaged one walk every six plate appearances in three years with Orioles. The only player in franchise history with a greater rate of walks was Roy Cullenbine (one every 5.4 PA), who played for the Browns from 1940 to 1942; while with Detroit in 1947, Cullenbine set the major league record of 22 consecutive games drawing at least one walk.... Last season, Randy batted .288 in day games, .255 at night; his career breakdown: .288 in day games, .255 at night.... Started 40 of 42 games in which the Orioles faced a left-handed starter, 92 of 120 against right-handers.... Had the worst fielding percentage among A.L. first basemen who played at least 100 games, averaging one error every 102 chances.... Batting average on artificial turf was 10th highest in the league.... His .345 career average with runners on base in Late-Inning Pressure Situations is the highest among active players (minimum: 25 hits).... Orioles had fewest steals (50) in majors last season. Milligan did his part—he was thrown out on each of five stolen-base attempts, tying Steve Buechele for the biggest oh-fer in the majors. Still, that's only halfway toward the record of Pete "Stop Me Before I Steal Again" Runnels of the 1952 Senators, who went 0-for-10 on stolen-base attempts.

Paul Molitor
Bats Right

Milwaukee Brewers	AB	H	2B	3B	HR	RBI	BB	SO	BA	SA	OBA
Season	665	216	32	13	17	75	77	62	.325	.489	.399
vs. Left-Handers	174	56	8	3	5	17	24	13	.322	.489	.405
vs. Right-Handers	491	160	24	10	12	58	53	49	.326	.489	.397
vs. Ground-Ballers	311	104	13	9	8	41	41	30	.334	.511	.415
vs. Fly-Ballers	354	112	19	4	9	34	36	32	.316	.469	.385
Home Games	315	92	14	8	7	38	39	23	.292	.454	.374
Road Games	350	124	18	5	10	37	38	39	.354	.520	.422
Grass Fields	556	177	25	12	15	67	71	47	.318	.487	.399
Artificial Turf	109	39	7	1	2	8	6	15	.358	.495	.402
April	68	22	6	0	1	5	6	6	.324	.456	.378
May	122	44	4	5	2	10	10	9	.361	.525	.414
June	100	31	7	2	5	15	14	11	.310	.570	.410
July	113	34	3	2	2	11	12	15	.301	.416	.373
August	129	46	9	1	5	20	14	10	.357	.558	.420
Sept./Oct.	133	39	3	3	2	14	21	11	.293	.406	.391
Leading Off Inn.	270	87	12	5	10	18	22	22	.322	.515	.373
Runners On	234	78	10	6	4	62	40	24	.333	.479	.431
Bases Empty	431	138	22	7	13	13	37	38	.320	.494	.381
Runners/Scor. Pos.	138	45	7	3	2	54	31	17	.326	.464	.450
Runners On/2 Out	99	33	5	3	3	33	17	9	.333	.535	.436
Scor. Pos./2 Out	68	23	4	3	1	28	15	7	.338	.529	.464
Late-Inning Pressure	85	26	3	0	3	15	16	9	.306	.447	.422
Leading Off	17	1	0	0	0	0	1	1	.059	.059	.158
Runners On	44	14	2	0	3	15	11	7	.318	.568	.455
Runners/Scor. Pos.	29	10	0	0	2	12	6	6	.345	.552	.457

RUNS BATTED IN	From 1B	From 2B	From 3B	Scoring Position
Totals	12/159	20/105	26/58	46/163
Percentage	7.5%	19.0%	44.8%	28.2%

Loves to face: Jose Guzman (.440, 11-for-25, 1 HR)
Bryan Harvey (4-for-4, 1 BB)
Walt Terrell (.488, 21-for-43, 2 HR)

Hates to face: Luis Aquino (.071, 1-for-14)
Steve Farr (.118, 2-for-17, 2 BB)
Rick Sutcliffe (.050, 1-for-20, 2 BB)

Miscellaneous statistics: Ground outs-to-air outs ratio: 1.08 last season, 1.21 for career.... Grounded into 11 double plays in 107 opportunities (one per 10).... Drove in 15 of 27 runners from third base with less than two outs (56%).... Direction of balls hit to the outfield: 37% to left field, 29% to center, 34% to right.... Base running: Advanced from first base to third on 25 of 63 outfield singles (40%); scored from second on 23 of 34 (68%).... Made 0.71 assists per nine innings at first base.

Comments: A little gerrymandering, anyone? Molly needs just two home runs to join Willie Mays as the only players in major league history with a .300 career batting average, at least 300 steals, and at least 150 home runs.... Reached double figures in doubles, triples, home runs, and steals. Over the last 20 years, only one player as old as Molitor (35) has done that: Jose Cruz (at age 37 in 1984). Ty Cobb was the oldest to do so (at age 38 in 1925).... One of three players to hit .300 or better with runners in scoring position in each of the past six years. The others: Tony Gwynn and Wade Boggs (whose streak is 10 years long).... He has hit for a higher average with runners on base than he has with the bases empty in each of the last eight years.... His .326 average against right-handed pitchers was second highest among right-handed batters in the majors last season (minimum: 100 AB vs. RHP), behind A.L. batting champ Julio Franco.... His .352 average in road games (he hit in 20 straight road games at one point, longest such streak in A.L. last year) was second to Cal Ripken in A.L.; in each of seven previous seasons, Molitor had hit for a higher average at County Stadium than he had on the road.... Became the 8th player in major league history to play at least 50 games at each infield position and in the outfield in his career; among the others: Honus Wagner, Don Money, Chico Salmon, Bill Almon.... His career totals of at-bats and hits (he's 2086-for-6911) are almost exactly the same as his former manager Harvey Kuenn's (2092-for-6913).

Lloyd Moseby

Bats Left

Detroit Tigers	AB	H	2B	3B	HR	RBI	BB	SO	BA	SA	OBA
Season	260	68	15	1	6	35	21	43	.262	.396	.321
vs. Left-Handers	46	11	4	0	1	9	5	11	.239	.391	.327
vs. Right-Handers	214	57	11	1	5	26	16	32	.266	.397	.319
vs. Ground-Ballers	143	37	11	1	1	21	10	22	.259	.371	.312
vs. Fly-Ballers	117	31	4	0	5	14	11	21	.265	.427	.331
Home Games	151	41	8	1	4	25	13	26	.272	.417	.335
Road Games	109	27	7	0	2	10	8	17	.248	.367	.299
Grass Fields	232	59	11	1	6	33	19	39	.254	.388	.315
Artificial Turf	28	9	4	0	0	2	2	4	.321	.464	.367
April	21	4	1	0	0	0	2	3	.190	.238	.261
May	44	12	1	1	0	2	1	4	.273	.341	.289
June	16	4	0	0	0	1	2	3	.250	.250	.316
July	61	18	5	0	3	9	4	10	.295	.525	.343
August	44	11	5	0	1	9	4	7	.250	.432	.327
Sept./Oct.	74	19	3	0	2	14	8	16	.257	.378	.333
Leading Off Inn.	55	14	1	1	0	0	3	12	.255	.309	.293
Runners On	111	30	8	0	3	32	11	14	.270	.423	.333
Bases Empty	149	38	7	1	3	3	10	29	.255	.376	.311
Runners/Scor. Pos.	57	18	4	0	1	26	6	7	.316	.439	.364
Runners On/2 Out	39	11	3	0	1	12	4	4	.282	.436	.364
Scor. Pos./2 Out	23	8	2	0	0	10	2	2	.348	.435	.400
Late-Inning Pressure	44	9	1	0	0	2	3	8	.205	.227	.255
Leading Off	16	4	1	0	0	0	1	3	.250	.313	.294
Runners On	14	2	0	0	0	2	1	2	.143	.143	.200
Runners/Scor. Pos.	7	2	0	0	0	2	1	0	.286	.286	.375

RUNS BATTED IN	From 1B	From 2B	From 3B	Scoring Position
Totals	6/90	10/50	13/25	23/75
Percentage	6.7%	20.0%	52.0%	30.7%

Loves to face: Chris Bosio (.345, 10-for-29, 4 HR)
Joe Grahe (.778, 7-for-9, 1 HR)
Frank Viola (.360, 18-for-50, 4 HR)

Hates to face: Jose Guzman (.100, 2-for-20)
Scott Sanderson (0-for-8)
Dave Stewart (.140, 7-for-50, 7 BB)

Miscellaneous statistics: Ground outs-to-air outs ratio: 1.23 last season, 1.10 for career.... Grounded into 3 double plays in 58 opportunities (one per 19).... Drove in 9 of 16 runners from third base with less than two outs (56%).... Direction of balls hit to the outfield: 29% to left field, 36% to center, 35% to right.... Base running: Advanced from first base to third on 6 of 12 outfield singles (50%); scored from second on 5 of 6 (83%).... Made 2.12 putouts per nine innings in left field.

Comments: One of two major leaguers to make three trips to the disabled list last season; Darren Daulton was the other.... His batting average increase (from .248 in 1990) was illusory, since he rarely saw a left-handed pitcher in 1991. Three straight years of declining averages vs. left-handers have left him as a platoon player, maybe even a sub-platoon player. He started only half of the 118 games in which Tigers faced a right-handed starter last season, and only four of 44 in which they faced a lefty. Last season was the first of his 12-year major league career in which he didn't get at least 100 at-bats vs. lefties.... Started 25 games from third spot in lineup, batting .279 with four homers and 19 RBIs. Tigers went 17–8 with Moseby hitting third, 18–20 in his other starts, 49–50 when he didn't start.... For several years, he was one of the most exciting power/speed players in baseball. He had four years in a row of 15 homers and 30 steals; the only other players ever to do that are Joe Morgan (six years, 1972–77), Bobby Bonds (1972–75), and Rickey Henderson and Juan Samuel (both, like Moseby, 1984–87).... Had five hits in 12 at-bats with bases loaded last year, lifting his career average to .333 in those situations.... Had only one assist in 530⅔ innings in left field, lowest ratio among the 24 left fielders in the majors who played that many innings. Few would guess that there were more assists from left field than from center in the majors last season. Outfield assists breakdown: 332 from right, 244 from left, 232 from center.

Rance Mulliniks

Bats Left

Toronto Blue Jays	AB	H	2B	3B	HR	RBI	BB	SO	BA	SA	OBA
Season	240	60	12	1	2	24	44	44	.250	.333	.364
vs. Left-Handers	12	1	0	0	0	0	0	3	.083	.083	.083
vs. Right-Handers	228	59	12	1	2	24	44	41	.259	.346	.376
vs. Ground-Ballers	133	35	7	1	2	17	21	25	.263	.376	.361
vs. Fly-Ballers	107	25	5	0	0	7	23	19	.234	.280	.366
Home Games	120	30	5	1	1	11	20	25	.250	.333	.355
Road Games	120	30	7	0	1	13	24	19	.250	.333	.372
Grass Fields	85	25	6	0	1	13	20	13	.294	.400	.425
Artificial Turf	155	35	6	1	1	11	24	31	.226	.297	.328
April	33	7	0	1	1	2	8	4	.212	.364	.366
May	5	2	1	0	0	0	1	0	.400	.600	.500
June	54	17	4	0	0	8	16	9	.315	.389	.465
July	61	15	3	0	1	4	8	11	.246	.344	.333
August	53	11	2	0	0	3	8	12	.208	.245	.311
Sept./Oct.	34	8	2	0	0	7	3	8	.235	.294	.289
Leading Off Inn.	53	10	2	1	0	0	11	10	.189	.264	.328
Runners On	97	25	5	0	0	22	20	15	.258	.309	.378
Bases Empty	143	35	7	1	2	2	24	29	.245	.350	.353
Runners/Scor. Pos.	50	20	4	0	0	21	16	7	.400	.480	.529
Runners On/2 Out	33	8	1	0	0	7	8	6	.242	.273	.390
Scor. Pos./2 Out	19	6	1	0	0	7	7	4	.316	.368	.500
Late-Inning Pressure	31	8	0	0	0	3	6	8	.258	.258	.368
Leading Off	6	1	0	0	0	0	2	3	.167	.167	.375
Runners On	11	2	0	0	0	3	3	2	.182	.182	.333
Runners/Scor. Pos.	6	2	0	0	0	3	3	0	.333	.333	.500

RUNS BATTED IN	From 1B	From 2B	From 3B	Scoring Position
Totals	1/70	9/38	12/27	21/65
Percentage	1.4%	23.7%	44.4%	32.3%

Loves to face: Danny Darwin (.406, 13-for-32, 1 HR)
Greg A. Harris (.364, 4-for-11, 1 2B, 1 3B, 1 HR, 4 BB)
Tim Leary (.500, 7-for-14, 4 2B, 1 HR)

Hates to face: Brian Holman (.067, 1-for-15, 3 BB)
Kirk McCaskill (.147, 5-for-34)
Dave Stewart (.040, 1-for-25, 3 BB)

Miscellaneous statistics: Ground outs-to-air outs ratio: 1.94 last season, 5th highest in A.L.; 1.71 for career.... Grounded into 9 double plays in 53 opportunities (one per 5.9).... Drove in 8 of 13 runners from third base with less than two outs (62%).... Direction of balls hit to the outfield: 49% to left field, 32% to center, 19% to right.... Base running: Advanced from first base to third on 3 of 18 outfield singles (17%); scored from second on 4 of 6 (67%).... Made 0.93 assists per nine innings at third base.

Comments: Only had 50 at-bats last season with runners in scoring position, but he had 20 hits; his .400 scoring-position batting average was highest in the majors among players with at least 50 at-bats.... All 73 of his starts last season, and all 298 of his starts since Aug. 21, 1987, have come against right-handed pitchers. His lone hit off a lefty in 1991 came against Bill Krueger, July 7.... Started 70 games as DH last season, most on the team. Jays' DHs combined for fewest home runs (5) and RBIs (56) of any A.L. team; home-run total matches 1974 White Sox for fewest DH homers in a full season.... Directed 43 percent of his hits to the opposite field last season; among A.L. players with at least 60 hits, only Wade Boggs sent a greater portion the other way.... Owns .310 career batting average as a pinch hitter, highest among active players with at least 100 at-bats in that role. A total of 28 major league players have compiled a .300 pinch-hit batting average with at least 100 at-bats; Gordy Coleman is the leader at .333 (40-for-120). Many of their names are forgettable, but four Hall of Famers are among that group: Rod Carew, Al Kaline, Red Schoendienst, and Bill Terry.... In home games last season, Mulliniks had a .250 batting average and a .333 slugging average, with 30 hits in 120 at-bats, 40 total bases, and one home run. He had exactly the same figures in road games. But he's not without a lovable crazy streak: The Ranceter had 11 RBIs at home and 13 on the road. The rascal!

Greg Myers

Bats Left

Toronto Blue Jays	AB	H	2B	3B	HR	RBI	BB	SO	BA	SA	OBA
Season	309	81	22	0	8	36	21	45	.262	.411	.306
vs. Left-Handers	35	6	1	0	1	3	2	7	.171	.286	.211
vs. Right-Handers	274	75	21	0	7	33	19	38	.274	.427	.319
vs. Ground-Ballers	151	39	13	0	2	14	10	23	.258	.384	.302
vs. Fly-Ballers	158	42	9	0	6	22	11	22	.266	.437	.310
Home Games	145	42	14	0	5	20	16	21	.290	.490	.356
Road Games	164	39	8	0	3	16	5	24	.238	.341	.259
Grass Fields	115	22	3	0	2	9	3	21	.191	.270	.210
Artificial Turf	194	59	19	0	6	27	18	24	.304	.495	.360
April	49	12	2	0	1	5	3	7	.245	.347	.283
May	59	18	7	0	1	6	9	7	.305	.475	.397
June	66	20	6	0	1	7	2	7	.303	.439	.324
July	55	11	5	0	1	5	1	12	.200	.345	.207
August	36	9	0	0	3	5	1	5	.250	.500	.270
Sept./Oct.	44	11	2	0	1	8	5	7	.250	.364	.327
Leading Off Inn.	56	22	12	0	2	2	2	5	.393	.714	.414
Runners On	138	29	8	0	3	31	13	20	.210	.333	.273
Bases Empty	171	52	14	0	5	5	8	25	.304	.474	.335
Runners/Scor. Pos.	81	19	5	0	3	30	9	11	.235	.407	.301
Runners On/2 Out	50	8	3	0	1	8	7	6	.160	.280	.263
Scor. Pos./2 Out	35	5	2	0	1	7	4	4	.143	.286	.231
Late-Inning Pressure	41	14	5	0	1	4	2	3	.341	.537	.372
Leading Off	9	3	3	0	0	0	0	0	.333	.667	.333
Runners On	17	5	2	0	0	3	2	1	.294	.412	.368
Runners/Scor. Pos.	9	4	1	0	0	3	2	1	.444	.556	.545

RUNS BATTED IN	From 1B	From 2B	From 3B	Scoring Position
Totals	3/100	10/67	15/36	25/103
Percentage	3.0%	14.9%	41.7%	24.3%

Loves to face: Storm Davis (.375, 3-for-8, 3 2B)
Jeff Montgomery (3-for-3, 2 2B)
Kevin Tapani (.545, 6-for-11)

Hates to face: Roger Clemens (.125, 2-for-16)
Brian Holman (.143, 3-for-21)
Nolan Ryan (.056, 1-for-18, 1 HR, 2 BB)

Miscellaneous statistics: Ground outs-to-air outs ratio: 1.21 last season, 1.31 for career.... Grounded into 13 double plays in 68 opportunities (one per 5.2).... Drove in 12 of 17 runners from third base with less than two outs (71%).... Direction of balls hit to the outfield: 28% to left field, 39% to center, 33% to right.... Base running: Advanced from first base to third on 1 of 13 outfield singles (8%), 4th-lowest rate in A.L.; scored from second on 3 of 10 (30%), lowest rate in majors.... Opposing base stealers: 68-for-93 (73%), 3d-highest rate in A.L.

Comments: Appropriately follows Mulliniks in this section, since he often followed Mully in the Blue Jays lineup. Like his friend, Myers didn't start a single game against a left-handed starter last season; he has a career total of 107 starts, including 91 last season, all against right-handers.... Too bad that some of Rance's clutch hitting ability didn't rub off: Myers had league's 7th-lowest batting average with runners on base, and its 3d lowest with two outs and runners on base.... In his career, Myers has batted .132 in latter category, lowest among active players with at least 100 at-bats in such situations. Blue Jays last season batted only .222 in that category, to rank 24th among 26 teams in majors.... Average production for an American League team from its catchers last season: .252 batting average, 13 home runs, 70 RBIs; Blue Jays' production from their catchers: .255 average, 13 homers, 67 RBIs.... Myers averaged one error every 48 chances, the worst rate of any catcher in the majors who played at least half of his team's games last season. The major league average for catchers: one error every 88 chances.... Myers caught 51 percent of Toronto's innings last season, Borders 48 percent, a couple of rookies one percent. The staff had a 3.57 ERA with Myers, 3.42 with Borders; amazingly, with Myers catching, opponents had a .238 batting average and a .352 slugging average; the same figures held true with Borders back of the plate.

Al Newman

Bats Left and Right

Minnesota Twins	AB	H	2B	3B	HR	RBI	BB	SO	BA	SA	OBA
Season	246	47	5	0	0	19	23	21	.191	.211	.260
vs. Left-Handers	66	16	4	0	0	8	2	7	.242	.303	.265
vs. Right-Handers	180	31	1	0	0	11	21	14	.172	.178	.259
vs. Ground-Ballers	103	19	1	0	0	9	12	10	.184	.194	.265
vs. Fly-Ballers	143	28	4	0	0	10	11	11	.196	.224	.256
Home Games	117	21	3	0	0	10	13	8	.179	.205	.263
Road Games	129	26	2	0	0	9	10	13	.202	.217	.257
Grass Fields	95	22	2	0	0	6	9	11	.232	.253	.298
Artificial Turf	151	25	3	0	0	13	14	10	.166	.185	.237
April	19	3	1	0	0	0	2	2	.158	.211	.238
May	47	11	1	0	0	3	7	3	.234	.255	.327
June	45	8	0	0	0	5	4	3	.178	.178	.245
July	46	11	1	0	0	2	0	2	.239	.261	.239
August	51	10	2	0	0	6	5	6	.196	.235	.276
Sept./Oct.	38	4	0	0	0	3	5	5	.105	.105	.205
Leading Off Inn.	46	8	1	0	0	0	7	5	.174	.196	.283
Runners On	114	25	4	0	0	19	8	8	.219	.254	.270
Bases Empty	132	22	1	0	0	0	15	13	.167	.174	.252
Runners/Scor. Pos.	74	14	3	0	0	19	4	4	.189	.230	.222
Runners On/2 Out	50	8	1	0	0	6	6	5	.160	.180	.250
Scor. Pos./2 Out	38	5	1	0	0	6	3	4	.132	.158	.195
Late-Inning Pressure	43	6	1	0	0	1	9	5	.140	.163	.288
Leading Off	8	1	0	0	0	0	3	1	.125	.125	.364
Runners On	20	3	1	0	0	1	0	2	.150	.200	.150
Runners/Scor. Pos.	17	2	0	0	0	1	0	1	.118	.118	.118

RUNS BATTED IN	From 1B	From 2B	From 3B	Scoring Position
Totals	1/77	5/60	13/32	18/92
Percentage	1.3%	8.3%	40.6%	19.6%

Loves to face: Luis Aquino (.714, 5-for-7)
Greg Cadaret (.400, 4-for-10, 5 BB)
Bobby Witt (.375, 9-for-24, 8 BB)

Hates to face: Dennis Eckersley (0-for-9)
Mark Gubicza (.056, 1-for-18)
Bob Welch (.091, 2-for-22)

Miscellaneous statistics: Ground outs-to-air outs ratio: 1.77 last season, 1.69 for career.... Grounded into 5 double plays in 49 opportunities (one per 10).... Drove in 11 of 17 runners from third base with less than two outs (65%).... Direction of balls hit to the outfield: 35% to left field, 44% to center, 21% to right batting left-handed; 31% to left field, 23% to center, 46% to right batting right-handed.... Base running: Advanced from first base to third on 7 of 16 outfield singles (44%); scored from second on 4 of 7 (57%).... Made 2.69 assists per nine innings at shortstop.

Comments: Became first player ever to play at least 25 games each at second base, third base, and shortstop in four straight years; he did it with a flourish, becoming the seventh guy ever to play *35* at those three positions in one season. The others: Buck Herzog (1916), Frank Frisch (1925), Sparky Adams (1927), Wayne Causey (1965), Jerry Royster (1977), Scott Fletcher (1985).... Last year, a broadcaster (a favorite of ours, actually, who'll remain nameless only because he's not the only one to commit this indiscretion) ripped into a note in the 1991 *Analyst* on Newman's streak. "*Twenty-five* games, at *three* different positions, for *three* straight years—who bothers with this stuff?" he moaned. Well, bucko, if you can't see that this streak defines Al Newman's major league career every bit as much as another defines Cal Ripken's, then you don't know squat about Al Newman. Sometimes you've got to look past the numbers to the essence of the player they describe. Some beat writers make their points with observations about the games or quotes from the players; we use numbers to help identify each player's unique combination of skills. And we're sick and tired of being dissed by those who'd portray us as eggheads who won't look up from our computers long enough to notice the difference between a grass field and artificial turf. We'll just note that there are a few broadcasters out there who, while ridiculing information like ours, couldn't tell the difference between Al and Alfred E.

Matt Nokes

Bats Left

New York Yankees	AB	H	2B	3B	HR	RBI	BB	SO	BA	SA	OBA
Season	456	122	20	0	24	77	25	49	.268	.469	.308
vs. Left-Handers	111	29	1	0	7	23	6	12	.261	.459	.303
vs. Right-Handers	345	93	19	0	17	54	19	37	.270	.472	.310
vs. Ground-Ballers	234	70	16	0	6	39	12	18	.299	.444	.335
vs. Fly-Ballers	222	52	4	0	18	38	13	31	.234	.495	.280
Home Games	200	52	8	0	13	43	12	26	.260	.495	.300
Road Games	256	70	12	0	11	34	13	23	.273	.449	.315
Grass Fields	372	95	14	0	21	67	21	41	.255	.462	.295
Artificial Turf	84	27	6	0	3	10	4	8	.321	.500	.367
April	47	15	5	0	2	9	2	4	.319	.553	.340
May	76	21	2	0	5	11	3	7	.276	.500	.313
June	74	20	3	0	4	12	3	5	.270	.473	.299
July	77	21	3	0	7	23	5	10	.273	.584	.314
August	81	20	4	0	4	10	6	9	.247	.432	.300
Sept./Oct.	101	25	4	0	2	12	6	14	.248	.347	.300
Leading Off Inn.	112	30	2	0	7	7	6	14	.268	.473	.305
Runners On	207	58	11	0	13	66	13	24	.280	.522	.325
Bases Empty	249	64	9	0	11	11	12	25	.257	.426	.294
Runners/Scor. Pos.	125	32	6	0	6	49	12	14	.256	.448	.320
Runners On/2 Out	112	31	7	0	8	37	10	13	.277	.554	.336
Scor. Pos./2 Out	72	19	4	0	4	26	9	10	.264	.486	.346
Late-Inning Pressure	71	19	2	0	1	9	7	13	.268	.338	.342
Leading Off	16	4	0	0	0	0	2	4	.250	.250	.333
Runners On	29	9	1	0	1	9	3	6	.310	.448	.394
Runners/Scor. Pos.	17	5	0	0	1	8	3	4	.294	.471	.429

RUNS BATTED IN	From 1B	From 2B	From 3B	Scoring Position
Totals	19/157	18/96	16/58	34/154
Percentage	12.1%	18.8%	27.6%	22.1%

Loves to face: Mike Boddicker (.359, 14-for-39, 2 HR)
Mike Moore (.385, 10-for-26, 3 HR)
Todd Stottlemyre (.421, 16-for-38, 5 HR)

Hates to face: Erik Hanson (.063, 1-for-16)
Jose Mesa (0-for-12)
Nolan Ryan (.125, 2-for-16)

Miscellaneous statistics: Ground outs-to-air outs ratio: 0.83 last season, 0.93 for career.... Grounded into 6 double plays in 81 opportunities (one per 14).... Drove in 11 of 20 runners from third base with less than two outs (55%).... Direction of balls hit to the outfield: 18% to left field, 28% to center, 54% to right.... Base running: Advanced from first base to third on 2 of 14 outfield singles (14%); scored from second on 7 of 10 (70%).... Opposing base stealers: 99-for-135 (73%), 2d-highest rate in A.L.

Comments: Started 106 of 107 games in which Yankees faced a right-handed starter, but only nine of 55 games against lefties. But his career rate of home runs off left-handed pitchers (one every 19.8 at-bats) is superior to his rate against right-handers (one every 21.2).... Had five multiple-home-run games last season, most by a Yankees player since Don Mattingly had five in 1985; the last Yankees with more than five in a season were Mickey Mantle (eight) and Roger Maris (seven) in 1961.... Among the 51 major league players with 20 home runs last year, Nokes was one of five who averaged more than 10 plate appearances for every strikeout. The leaders: Cal Ripken (one strikeout every 15.6 times up), Lou Whitaker (12.7), Kent Hrbek (11.1), Robin Ventura (10.5), Nokes (10.1).... Yankees catchers ranked first in the majors in home runs (26) and third in the majors in RBIs (90). Don't give Bob Geren too much credit for those numbers.... Yankees' staff had 4.14 ERA with Geren catching, 4.50 with Nokes. The difference was especially pronounced with the Yankees' rookie pitchers, who had a 4.54 ERA with Geren but 6.20 with Nokes. But, hey, if that's the trade-off for 24 dingers, so be it.... Nokes became the first catcher to throw Rickey Henderson out trying to steal twice in one game since Donnie Scott in 1984. You might have missed that one, since it happened on the same day that Rickey broke Lou Brock's record and Nolan Ryan threw his seventh no-hitter. Any other day, it would have been a headline.

Pete O'Brien

Bats Left

Seattle Mariners	AB	H	2B	3B	HR	RBI	BB	SO	BA	SA	OBA
Season	560	139	29	3	17	88	44	61	.248	.402	.300
vs. Left-Handers	179	42	11	0	4	27	11	22	.235	.363	.280
vs. Right-Handers	381	97	18	3	13	61	33	39	.255	.420	.309
vs. Ground-Ballers	247	65	14	1	6	38	12	23	.263	.401	.292
vs. Fly-Ballers	313	74	15	2	11	50	32	38	.236	.403	.305
Home Games	290	69	17	3	12	53	19	30	.238	.441	.279
Road Games	270	70	12	0	5	35	25	31	.259	.359	.321
Grass Fields	207	58	9	0	4	28	17	24	.280	.382	.335
Artificial Turf	353	81	20	3	13	60	27	37	.229	.414	.279
April	81	21	5	0	2	12	5	7	.259	.395	.307
May	96	22	3	1	5	17	10	10	.229	.438	.296
June	94	22	7	0	0	12	8	11	.234	.309	.294
July	102	28	7	2	2	13	1	6	.275	.441	.276
August	98	26	5	0	2	14	11	11	.265	.378	.333
Sept./Oct.	89	20	2	0	6	20	9	16	.225	.449	.290
Leading Off Inn.	132	28	5	1	5	5	7	13	.212	.379	.252
Runners On	266	74	15	0	9	80	24	28	.278	.436	.328
Bases Empty	294	65	14	3	8	8	20	33	.221	.371	.273
Runners/Scor. Pos.	174	50	11	0	7	75	19	22	.287	.471	.342
Runners On/2 Out	140	34	7	0	5	35	10	18	.243	.400	.293
Scor. Pos./2 Out	99	27	5	0	5	35	7	15	.273	.475	.321
Late-Inning Pressure	84	16	2	0	3	15	6	11	.190	.321	.239
Leading Off	25	4	0	0	1	1	0	3	.160	.280	.160
Runners On	36	9	2	0	1	13	4	6	.250	.389	.310
Runners/Scor. Pos.	25	8	2	0	1	13	4	4	.320	.520	.387

RUNS BATTED IN	From 1B	From 2B	From 3B	Scoring Position
Totals	7/188	26/130	38/85	64/215
Percentage	3.7%	20.0%	44.7%	29.8%

Loves to face: Rick Sutcliffe (.455, 5-for-11, 1 HR)
Frank Wills (.313, 5-for-16, 2 HR, 6 BB)
Bobby Witt (.471, 8-for-17, 1 HR)

Hates to face: Mike Flanagan (.152, 5-for-33)
Jaime Navarro (.053, 1-for-19)
Kenny Rogers (0-for-13)

Miscellaneous statistics: Ground outs-to-air outs ratio: 1.08 last season, 0.99 for career.... Grounded into 14 double plays in 103 opportunities (one per 7.4).... Drove in 26 of 45 runners from third base with less than two outs (58%).... Direction of balls hit to the outfield: 27% to left field, 34% to center, 40% to right.... Base running: Advanced from first base to third on 5 of 21 outfield singles (24%); scored from second on 9 of 13 (69%).... Made 0.73 assists per nine innings at first base.

Comments: Finally put the brakes to a historic skid that lasted from 1986 to 1990. He became the first player in major league history to have a decline in both batting average and home-run ratio in each of four consecutive 300 at-bat seasons. In 1986, he hit .290 with a homer every 24 at-bats; by 1990, he was down to .224 and a homer every 73 at-bats. Last year, two things happened: First, O'Brien stopped his streak, boosting his average by 24 points and more than doubling his home run frequency; second, his old Texas buddy, Pete Incaviglia, suffered a fourth consecutive season of similar decline, equaling O'Brien's ignominious record.... Obie's 17 home runs last season were the most by any player who didn't hit at least one to either center field or the opposite field.... At 33, he was the youngest guy in the majors to be the oldest player on his club's active opening-day roster.... Led major league first basemen in fielding percentage, committing an error every 379 chances. Only one other Mariners infielder has ever led A.L. in fielding: Julio Cruz led second basemen in 1978.... On-base percentage leading off innings was 2d lowest in the league.... Mariners started six different players at least 10 times in the cleanup spot, only club in majors to do so last season. They went 7–20 with Jay Buhner there, and 5–15 with Alvin Davis, but they posted a 40–26 record (.607) with O'Brien cleaning up.... Still, they had the fewest cleanup homers of any A.L. team (16). Hello, Kevin Mitchell.

John Olerud
Bats Left

Toronto Blue Jays	AB	H	2B	3B	HR	RBI	BB	SO	BA	SA	OBA
Season	454	116	30	1	17	68	68	84	.256	.438	.353
vs. Left-Handers	83	18	3	1	3	16	17	19	.217	.386	.358
vs. Right-Handers	371	98	27	0	14	52	51	65	.264	.450	.352
vs. Ground-Ballers	231	56	18	0	8	35	40	40	.242	.424	.356
vs. Fly-Ballers	223	60	12	1	9	33	28	44	.269	.453	.350
Home Games	226	61	17	1	7	39	36	36	.270	.447	.374
Road Games	228	55	13	0	10	29	32	48	.241	.430	.332
Grass Fields	172	44	12	0	7	24	25	35	.256	.448	.347
Artificial Turf	282	72	18	1	10	44	43	49	.255	.433	.357
April	61	16	4	0	3	9	10	9	.262	.475	.375
May	77	12	2	0	2	6	11	16	.156	.260	.258
June	70	19	3	1	3	11	8	15	.271	.471	.346
July	79	27	5	0	4	8	5	13	.342	.557	.395
August	80	19	7	0	3	18	14	12	.237	.438	.347
Sept./Oct.	87	23	9	0	2	16	20	19	.264	.437	.394
Leading Off Inn.	116	34	10	0	7	7	15	23	.293	.560	.379
Runners On	194	54	15	1	5	56	37	34	.278	.443	.383
Bases Empty	260	62	15	0	12	12	31	50	.238	.435	.329
Runners/Scor. Pos.	116	27	6	0	3	45	36	24	.233	.362	.396
Runners On/2 Out	93	22	9	1	2	19	16	20	.237	.419	.355
Scor. Pos./2 Out	54	9	3	0	2	13	16	14	.167	.333	.366
Late-Inning Pressure	68	16	6	0	2	9	12	19	.235	.412	.357
Leading Off	19	3	1	0	1	1	1	7	.158	.368	.238
Runners On	25	8	5	0	1	7	7	5	.320	.520	.441
Runners/Scor. Pos.	13	2	1	0	0	6	7	3	.154	.231	.409

RUNS BATTED IN	From 1B	From 2B	From 3B	Scoring Position
Totals	11/133	16/88	24/61	40/149
Percentage	8.3%	18.2%	39.3%	26.8%

Loves to face: Kevin Brown (.429, 6-for-14)
Erik Hanson (.400, 4-for-10, 1 HR)
Ben McDonald (.357, 5-for-14, 2 HR)

Hates to face: Roger Clemens (.059, 1-for-17, 1 2B, 5 BB)
Nolan Ryan (.118, 2-for-17)
Scott Sanderson (0-for-14)

Miscellaneous statistics: Ground outs-to-air outs ratio: 1.29 last season, 1.26 for career.... Grounded into 12 double plays in 85 opportunities (one per 7.1).... Drove in 21 of 36 runners from third base with less than two outs (58%).... Direction of balls hit to the outfield: 37% to left field, 30% to center, 33% to right.... Base running: Advanced from first base to third on 2 of 22 outfield singles (9%), 5th-lowest rate in A.L.; scored from second on 8 of 14 (57%).... Made 0.62 assists per nine innings at first base, 2d-lowest rate in A.L.

Comments: Started 113 of 115 games in which the Blue Jays faced right-handed starters, but only 11 of 47 games in which they faced left-handers.... His May batting average was 5th lowest in the league.... His average hit a bottom of .203 on June 13; from that point to the end of the season, Olerud batted .287.... Ended the regular season with a 66-game errorless streak, the longest by any first baseman last season. But he's not even halfway to the A.L. record of 178 consecutive errorless games at first, set by Mike Hegan over a four-year span from 1970 to 1973.... His 10 sacrifice flies tied him with Alvin Davis for the league lead.... On-base percentage leading off innings was 8th highest in the league, and that's no fluke. He was 29-for-68 reaching base as a leadoff hitter in 1989 and 1990 as well, for a career mark of .395, the 4th highest among active players.... Has attempted to steal four bases in 256 games, and has been caught every time. Two numbers to pique your interest: The most games played by any nonpitcher who never stole a base—906, by Russ Nixon (0-for-7). Among active players, Cecil Fielder is 0-for-3 in 541 games. The most times caught before a runner "broke his maiden": 16, by Pete Runnels. Honorable mention to Bob Nieman, who hit a home run on his first big-league at-bat, but went 0-for-9 before his first stolen base. (Times caught stealing weren't compiled for both leagues until 1950; those figures are limited to players whose careers began since then.)

Joe Orsulak
Bats Left

Baltimore Orioles	AB	H	2B	3B	HR	RBI	BB	SO	BA	SA	OBA
Season	486	135	22	1	5	43	28	45	.278	.358	.321
vs. Left-Handers	64	15	3	0	0	6	4	8	.234	.281	.286
vs. Right-Handers	422	120	19	1	5	37	24	37	.284	.370	.326
vs. Ground-Ballers	216	62	11	0	2	18	15	15	.287	.366	.336
vs. Fly-Ballers	270	73	11	1	3	25	13	30	.270	.352	.308
Home Games	235	65	10	0	3	21	14	23	.277	.357	.322
Road Games	251	70	12	1	2	22	14	22	.279	.359	.320
Grass Fields	406	114	20	1	4	29	25	37	.281	.365	.326
Artificial Turf	80	21	2	0	1	14	3	8	.262	.325	.289
April	45	11	1	0	1	5	4	5	.244	.333	.306
May	76	21	4	0	1	4	3	9	.276	.368	.304
June	99	19	1	0	1	13	5	12	.192	.232	.243
July	90	25	5	0	0	3	3	7	.278	.312	.298
August	99	38	9	1	0	11	6	7	.384	.495	.419
Sept./Oct.	77	21	2	0	2	7	7	5	.273	.377	.345
Leading Off Inn.	91	28	5	1	0	0	3	5	.308	.385	.337
Runners On	223	55	8	0	3	41	13	24	.247	.323	.290
Bases Empty	263	80	14	1	2	2	15	21	.304	.388	.346
Runners/Scor. Pos.	109	26	5	0	1	36	11	11	.239	.312	.312
Runners On/2 Out	91	18	2	0	0	12	6	10	.198	.220	.263
Scor. Pos./2 Out	47	9	1	0	0	12	5	5	.191	.213	.296
Late-Inning Pressure	72	15	3	0	0	4	4	7	.208	.250	.256
Leading Off	20	4	2	0	0	0	0	1	.200	.300	.238
Runners On	29	7	0	0	0	4	3	3	.241	.241	.303
Runners/Scor. Pos.	15	3	0	0	0	4	3	1	.200	.200	.316

RUNS BATTED IN	From 1B	From 2B	From 3B	Scoring Position
Totals	6/158	14/83	18/46	32/129
Percentage	3.8%	16.9%	39.1%	24.8%

Loves to face: Kevin Brown (.429, 6-for-14, 3 2B, 1 HR)
Bill Gullickson (.409, 9-for-22, 5 2B)
Jack McDowell (.474, 9-for-19, 2 HR)

Hates to face: Rick Aguilera (.192, 5-for-26, 0 BB)
Chris Bosio (.176, 3-for-17)
Nolan Ryan (.115, 3-for-26)

Miscellaneous statistics: Ground outs-to-air outs ratio: 0.98 last season, 1.10 for career.... Grounded into 9 double plays in 92 opportunities (one per 10).... Drove in 12 of 22 runners from third base with less than two outs (55%).... Direction of balls hit to the outfield: 30% to left field, 36% to center, 35% to right.... Base running: Advanced from first base to third on 6 of 17 outfield singles (35%); scored from second on 8 of 14 (57%).... Made 2.22 putouts per nine innings in left field, 3d-highest rate in A.L.

Comments: Led the majors with 22 outfield assists last season, seven more than runners-up Jay Buhner, Ken Griffey, Jr., and Marquis Grissom. Over the past 50 years, only three outfielders led the majors by a margin that wide—and what a group it is: Dave Parker (1977), Johnny Callison (1963), and Roberto Clemente (1961).... Orsulak threw out eight runners in his first 30 games, then took a break with only five assists over his next 76 games. But he finished with a spectacular closing kick: nine in his last 26 games.... Add those numbers and you'll see that Orsulak accumulated his 22 assists despite playing only 132 games in the pasture. The last player with that many assists in so few games was Dave Philley in 1948 (22 in 128 games).... Threw out 13 runners from left field and nine from right, leading the Orioles at both positions. His total of 22 was the highest by an Orioles/Browns outfielder since Beau Bell had 22 in 1937.... And it gets even better: Orsulak didn't commit an error all season. Only three players in baseball history had even half as many assists as Orsulak in an errorless season: Carl Yastrzemski (16 in 1977), Ken Berry (13 in 1972), and Mel Ott (13 in 1937).... Started only eight of 42 games in which the Orioles faced left-handed starters, but 110 of 120 games against right-handers.... His August batting average was 2d highest in the majors, and his 21-game hitting streak during the month was the 2d longest in the A.L. last season.

Mike Pagliarulo

Bats Left

Minnesota Twins	AB	H	2B	3B	HR	RBI	BB	SO	BA	SA	OBA
Season	365	102	20	0	6	36	21	55	.279	.384	.322
vs. Left-Handers	16	3	1	0	0	1	3	1	.188	.250	.316
vs. Right-Handers	349	99	19	0	6	35	18	54	.284	.390	.323
vs. Ground-Ballers	163	47	7	0	3	14	10	29	.288	.387	.328
vs. Fly-Ballers	202	55	13	0	3	22	11	26	.272	.381	.318
Home Games	190	54	11	0	4	27	13	32	.284	.405	.332
Road Games	175	48	9	0	2	9	8	23	.274	.360	.312
Grass Fields	136	36	8	0	2	8	6	16	.265	.368	.299
Artificial Turf	229	66	12	0	4	28	15	39	.288	.393	.336
April	45	9	1	0	0	2	0	3	.200	.222	.200
May	67	17	4	0	2	5	2	12	.254	.403	.275
June	55	15	5	0	1	8	5	8	.273	.418	.344
July	58	26	6	0	1	5	7	3	.448	.603	.508
August	68	22	3	0	1	6	3	12	.324	.412	.352
Sept./Oct.	72	13	1	0	1	10	4	17	.181	.236	.237
Leading Off Inn.	88	26	6	0	2	2	3	11	.295	.432	.319
Runners On	153	39	8	0	2	32	13	22	.255	.346	.310
Bases Empty	212	63	12	0	4	4	8	33	.297	.410	.332
Runners/Scor. Pos.	87	17	3	0	1	25	10	18	.195	.264	.273
Runners On/2 Out	65	15	2	0	1	11	7	7	.231	.308	.306
Scor. Pos./2 Out	37	7	1	0	1	9	6	4	.189	.297	.302
Late-Inning Pressure	49	14	4	0	0	5	4	9	.286	.367	.340
Leading Off	11	5	1	0	0	0	2	5	.455	.545	.538
Runners On	24	5	1	0	0	5	1	4	.208	.250	.240
Runners/Scor. Pos.	13	4	1	0	0	4	0	3	.308	.385	.308

RUNS BATTED IN	From 1B	From 2B	From 3B	Scoring Position
Totals	8/116	12/72	10/32	22/104
Percentage	6.9%	16.7%	31.3%	21.2%

Loves to face: Chuck Crim (.833, 5-for-6, 1 SO)
    Mike Henneman (.364, 4-for-11, 2 2B, 1 HR)
    Dave Stewart (.294, 10-for-34, 2 HR)
Hates to face: Jimmy Key (.111, 2-for-18)
    Dan Plesac (0-for-9, 5 SO)
    Bob Welch (.091, 2-for-22, 3 BB)

Miscellaneous statistics: Ground outs-to-air outs ratio: 1.40 last season, 0.95 for career.... Grounded into 9 double plays in 74 opportunities (one per 8.2).... Drove in 9 of 20 runners from third base with less than two outs (45%).... Direction of balls hit to the outfield: 36% to left field, 28% to center, 36% to right.... Base running: Advanced from first base to third on 6 of 19 outfield singles (32%); scored from second on 9 of 15 (60%).... Made 2.44 assists per nine innings at third base, highest rate in A.L.

Comments: Like Candy Maldonado, a free agent after the 1990 season unpursued by his old team, which then found him difficult to replace. Pags had nearly as many hits in part-time play last season as all of San Diego's third basemen combined for the entire season (111).... Started 112 of 120 games in which the Twins faced right-handed starters last season, but he didn't start a single game against a southpaw. Scott Leius was Minnesota's starting third baseman in all 42 games in which they faced left-handed starters.... The Twins allowed an average of 3.86 runs per nine innings with Pags at third base, 4.45 runs per nine innings with Leius there.... Strange, but true: Pags hit for an average 33 points higher in Twins losses (.299) than he did in their victories (.266). The only A.L. player with a larger spread in that direction: Brent Mayne (43 points; .276 and .233).... His batting average was a career high, but his home-run total was a career low. He was batting .300 as late as September 2.... His batting average with runners in scoring position was 10th lowest in the league.... Career average of .154 (12-for-78, 4 HR) as a pinch hitter during the regular season.... Became only the fourth player in postseason history to hit a pinch-hit home run in extra innings. The others: Dusty Rhodes (1954), John Lowenstein (1979), and George Vukovich (1981). All were hit in the 10th inning with the score tied.

Rafael Palmeiro

Bats Left

Texas Rangers	AB	H	2B	3B	HR	RBI	BB	SO	BA	SA	OBA
Season	631	203	49	3	26	88	68	72	.322	.532	.389
vs. Left-Handers	186	51	8	1	9	26	14	26	.274	.473	.333
vs. Right-Handers	445	152	41	2	17	62	54	46	.342	.557	.411
vs. Ground-Ballers	300	96	22	1	10	38	37	38	.320	.500	.395
vs. Fly-Ballers	331	107	27	2	16	50	31	34	.323	.562	.383
Home Games	298	101	22	1	12	43	34	36	.339	.540	.408
Road Games	333	102	27	2	14	45	34	36	.306	.526	.372
Grass Fields	532	177	37	3	23	77	61	62	.333	.543	.402
Artificial Turf	99	26	12	0	3	11	7	10	.263	.475	.315
April	66	21	5	0	2	11	3	6	.318	.485	.338
May	115	38	8	1	2	12	8	14	.330	.470	.376
June	112	34	10	0	5	10	13	11	.304	.527	.376
July	100	39	6	1	8	19	11	15	.390	.710	.456
August	121	39	9	1	5	21	16	11	.322	.537	.407
Sept./Oct.	117	32	11	0	4	15	17	15	.274	.470	.365
Leading Off Inn.	140	47	8	0	5	5	10	15	.336	.500	.384
Runners On	279	83	22	2	12	74	37	38	.297	.520	.375
Bases Empty	352	120	27	1	14	14	31	34	.341	.543	.401
Runners/Scor. Pos.	143	33	12	1	2	49	28	22	.231	.371	.350
Runners On/2 Out	113	33	11	2	4	30	22	17	.292	.531	.416
Scor. Pos./2 Out	71	15	7	1	0	19	20	13	.211	.338	.398
Late-Inning Pressure	93	24	6	0	5	15	11	11	.258	.484	.333
Leading Off	24	9	1	0	0	3	3	3	.375	.417	.444
Runners On	42	8	4	0	3	13	6	6	.190	.500	.286
Runners/Scor. Pos.	25	5	3	0	1	9	5	4	.200	.440	.323

RUNS BATTED IN	From 1B	From 2B	From 3B	Scoring Position
Totals	19/210	18/118	25/60	43/178
Percentage	9.0%	15.3%	41.7%	24.2%

Loves to face: Jim Abbott (.421, 8-for-19, 2 HR)
    Mark Leiter (.600, 6-for-10, 2 2B, 2 HR)
    Frank Tanana (.421, 8-for-19, 2 HR)
Hates to face: Mark Gubicza (.105, 2-for-19)
    Randy Johnson (.071, 1-for-14)
    Jack McDowell (.071, 1-for-14)

Miscellaneous statistics: Ground outs-to-air outs ratio: 0.88 last season, 1.00 for career.... Grounded into 17 double plays in 146 opportunities (one per 8.6).... Drove in 18 of 31 runners from third base with less than two outs (58%).... Direction of balls hit to the outfield: 23% to left field, 34% to center, 43% to right.... Base running: Advanced from first base to third on 13 of 45 outfield singles (29%); scored from second on 20 of 23 (87%).... Made 0.63 assists per nine innings at first base, 3d-lowest rate in A.L.

Comments: The only other player to bat .300 or better and hit double figures in home runs in each of the past two seasons: Edgar Martinez.... Both Palmeiro and teammate Julio Franco raised their career batting averages above the .300 mark last season. Palmeiro started the season at .296, Franco at .297; both are now .302 hitters.... He led the league in doubles while playing his home games on grass. Sound unusual? It shouldn't—it happens all the time in the American League. Over the last nine years, only one player from a team that plays its home games on artificial turf has led the A.L.: George Brett, who shared the lead with Jody Reed in 1990.... What was unusual was his season total in doubles. Only three other active players have hit that many in a season: Wade Boggs (51 in 1989), Don Mattingly (53 in 1986), and Robin Yount (49 in 1980).... Has increased his home-run rate by more than 60 percent in each of the past two seasons; it was one per 70 at-bats in 1989, one per 43 in 1990, and one per 24 last season.... Our projection model suggests that Palmeiro could continue that streak. His chance to hit 30 home runs: 20 percent this season, 38 percent in any season. The odds against him ever reaching the 40 mark: 7-to-1.... One of only four players in Washington/Texas franchise history with a career average of .300 or better (minimum: 1000 AB): Al Oliver (.319), Julio Franco (.318), Palmeiro (.306), Mickey Rivers (.303).

Dean Palmer

Bats Right

Texas Rangers	AB	H	2B	3B	HR	RBI	BB	SO	BA	SA	OBA
Season	268	50	9	2	15	37	32	98	.187	.403	.281
vs. Left-Handers	81	20	3	0	9	16	11	30	.247	.617	.337
vs. Right-Handers	187	30	6	2	6	21	21	68	.160	.310	.256
vs. Ground-Ballers	108	20	2	2	7	13	16	37	.185	.435	.302
vs. Fly-Ballers	160	30	7	0	8	24	16	61	.188	.381	.266
Home Games	114	16	3	1	6	11	19	43	.140	.342	.279
Road Games	154	34	6	1	9	26	13	55	.221	.448	.281
Grass Fields	228	40	8	1	12	28	31	80	.175	.377	.282
Artificial Turf	40	10	1	1	3	9	1	18	.250	.550	.268
April	0	0	0	0	0	0	0	0	—	—	—
May	0	0	0	0	0	0	0	0	—	—	—
June	19	6	0	0	2	8	2	5	.316	.632	.381
July	73	16	2	1	4	8	6	22	.219	.438	.296
August	80	15	3	1	2	6	8	30	.188	.325	.261
Sept./Oct.	96	13	4	0	7	15	16	41	.135	.396	.265
Leading Off Inn.	79	15	3	0	5	5	9	29	.190	.418	.281
Runners On	104	22	1	0	9	31	16	37	.212	.481	.328
Bases Empty	164	28	8	2	6	6	16	61	.171	.354	.249
Runners/Scor. Pos.	56	14	1	0	7	27	9	21	.250	.643	.373
Runners On/2 Out	49	11	1	0	4	18	8	19	.224	.490	.333
Scor. Pos./2 Out	30	10	1	0	4	18	6	12	.333	.767	.444
Late-Inning Pressure	40	10	2	1	4	9	6	20	.250	.650	.348
Leading Off	10	3	2	0	1	1	1	7	.300	.800	.364
Runners On	17	5	0	0	3	8	3	7	.294	.824	.400
Runners/Scor. Pos.	12	3	0	0	3	8	1	5	.250	1.000	.308

RUNS BATTED IN	From 1B	From 2B	From 3B	Scoring Position
Totals	5/75	12/43	5/22	17/65
Percentage	6.7%	27.9%	22.7%	26.2%

Loves to face: Jim Abbott (.400, 2-for-5, 1 HR, 2 BB)
Joe Hesketh (.400, 2-for-5, 1 HR)

Hates to face: Randy Johnson (0-for-6, 6 SO)
Mark Langston (0-for-8, 5 SO)
Dave Stewart (0-for-10)

Miscellaneous statistics: Ground outs-to-air outs ratio: 0.74 last season, 0.75 for career.... Grounded into 4 double plays in 50 opportunities (one per 13).... Drove in 1 of 7 runners from third base with less than two outs (14%).... Direction of balls hit to the outfield: 45% to left field, 34% to center, 20% to right.... Base running: Advanced from first base to third on 5 of 15 outfield singles (33%); scored from second on 4 of 4 (100%).... Made 1.64 assists per nine innings at third base.

Comments: Played 81 games, batted in 80, and struck out in 63. If you eliminate the games in which he failed to bat twice or more, he had only one pair of consecutive games in which he didn't strike out (August 28–31).... His August batting average was 8th lowest in the league, and his average after September 1 was 2d lowest in the majors.... Led A.L. rookies with 98 strikeouts, one more than Hensley Meulens, who came to the plate nine times more than Palmer.... His slugging percentage was 2d highest among A.L. rookies (minimum: 200 ABs).... Didn't hit a home run from August 17 through September 18, then hit seven over the final 18 days of the season to lead the majors over that span. Only three other players had even five: Phil Plantier (6), Rickey Henderson (5), and John Kruk (5).... The only other rookie ever to hit as many as 15 home runs while batting under .200: Mike Schmidt (.196, 18 HRs in 1973).... He was one of three Texas Rangers under the age of 23 to play at least 50 games last season. The others: Juan Gonzalez and Ivan Rodriguez. The most recent clubs to have three position players under 23 years old play that many games were the 1982 Twins (Tom Brunansky, Lenny Faedo, and Kent Hrbek); the 1981 Blue Jays (Danny Ainge, George Bell, and Lloyd Moseby); the 1978 Tigers (Lou Whitaker, Lance Parrish, Alan Trammell); and the 1978 Astros (Terry Puhl, Luis Pujols, and Julio Gonzalez).

Dave Parker

Bats Left

Angels/Blue Jays	AB	H	2B	3B	HR	RBI	BB	SO	BA	SA	OBA
Season	502	120	26	2	11	59	33	98	.239	.365	.288
vs. Left-Handers	133	31	6	1	4	17	3	26	.233	.383	.259
vs. Right-Handers	369	89	20	1	7	42	30	72	.241	.358	.299
vs. Ground-Ballers	259	64	16	1	7	38	14	48	.247	.398	.285
vs. Fly-Ballers	243	56	10	1	4	21	19	50	.230	.329	.292
Home Games	229	49	11	1	6	23	19	39	.214	.349	.273
Road Games	273	71	15	1	5	36	14	59	.260	.377	.301
Grass Fields	404	94	18	1	10	49	25	78	.233	.356	.277
Artificial Turf	98	26	8	1	1	10	8	20	.265	.398	.333
April	77	17	2	1	1	6	2	17	.221	.312	.250
May	95	18	3	0	1	10	8	22	.189	.253	.257
June	103	26	6	1	4	16	6	20	.252	.447	.295
July	94	27	4	0	3	13	6	16	.287	.426	.330
August	89	19	6	0	2	10	6	13	.213	.348	.263
Sept./Oct.	44	13	5	0	0	4	5	10	.295	.409	.367
Leading Off Inn.	108	24	5	1	3	3	8	26	.222	.370	.282
Runners On	232	58	10	0	5	53	13	38	.250	.358	.286
Bases Empty	270	62	16	2	6	6	20	60	.230	.370	.290
Runners/Scor. Pos.	141	36	6	0	4	49	11	21	.255	.383	.303
Runners On/2 Out	107	26	3	0	4	26	6	16	.243	.383	.283
Scor. Pos./2 Out	69	17	2	0	4	25	6	10	.246	.449	.307
Late-Inning Pressure	58	16	4	0	4	9	5	6	.276	.552	.333
Leading Off	17	8	3	0	1	1	2	2	.471	.824	.526
Runners On	17	4	0	0	2	7	2	0	.235	.588	.316
Runners/Scor. Pos.	12	3	0	0	1	5	1	0	.250	.500	.308

RUNS BATTED IN	From 1B	From 2B	From 3B	Scoring Position
Totals	4/165	25/105	19/54	44/159
Percentage	2.4%	23.8%	35.2%	27.7%

Loves to face: Andy Hawkins (.314, 16-for-51, 4 2B, 6 HR)
Eric Show (.362, 17-for-47, 5 HR)
Dave Stewart (.316, 6-for-19, 1 2B, 4 HR)

Hates to face: Danny Darwin (0-for-13)
Steve Howe (0-for-10)
Gregg Olson (0-for-6, 5 SO)

Miscellaneous statistics: Ground outs-to-air outs ratio: 1.13 last season, 1.20 for career.... Grounded into 9 double plays in 98 opportunities (one per 11).... Drove in 14 of 27 runners from third base with less than two outs (52%).... Direction of balls hit to the outfield: 34% to left field, 32% to center, 34% to right.... Base running: Advanced from first base to third on 6 of 26 outfield singles (23%); scored from second on 6 of 13 (46%).

Comments: He has been in an opening-day lineup in each of the last 18 seasons, the longest streak of any player active in 1991, followed by Dwight Evans (17 years), Eddie Murray (15), Dale Murphy, and Lou Whitaker (14 each).... The 1991 Angels were only the fourth team in baseball history to have at least four active players with 200 or more career home runs: Parker, Dave Winfield, Lance Parrish, and Gary Gaetti. The 1971 Cubs had five: Ernie Banks, Ron Santo, Billy Williams, Johnny Callison, and Joe Pepitone. The other clubs with four 200-HR hitters: 1986 Angels (Doug DeCinces, Bobby Grich, George Hendrick, and Reggie Jackson) and the 1986 Red Sox (Tony Armas, Don Baylor, Dwight Evans, and Jim Rice).... Parker has hit for a higher average with runners on base than he has with the bases empty in each of the last nine years, matching Ozzie Smith for the longest current streak of its kind.... Last season represented a 400-to-1 breakdown for Parker at age 39. The last players that old to suffer such extreme breakdowns: Pete Rose in 1983 (still 201 hits short of Cobb's record, he played three more seasons); Willie McCovey, 1978 (hit 15 homers in '79, retired following the 1980 season); Hank Aaron, 1975 (hit 10 HRs in '76, then retired); Willie Mays, 1973 (retired); Minnie Minoso, 1963 (played 30 games in '64, then retired—sort of); Stan Musial, 1963 (retired); and Ted Williams, 1959 (batted .316 with 29 HRs in 1960, then retired).

Lance Parrish

Bats Right

California Angels	AB	H	2B	3B	HR	RBI	BB	SO	BA	SA	OBA
Season	402	87	12	0	19	51	35	117	.216	.388	.285
vs. Left-Handers	105	23	1	0	3	10	12	25	.219	.314	.297
vs. Right-Handers	297	64	11	0	16	41	23	92	.215	.414	.281
vs. Ground-Ballers	187	40	7	0	7	24	15	51	.214	.385	.273
vs. Fly-Ballers	215	47	5	0	12	27	20	66	.219	.409	.296
Home Games	216	49	6	0	9	24	15	51	.227	.380	.280
Road Games	186	38	6	0	10	27	20	66	.204	.398	.292
Grass Fields	335	68	9	0	14	41	27	93	.203	.355	.270
Artificial Turf	67	19	3	0	5	10	8	24	.284	.552	.360
April	64	16	2	0	3	6	9	16	.250	.422	.360
May	78	15	3	0	3	11	6	24	.192	.346	.259
June	36	12	3	0	2	6	2	6	.333	.583	.368
July	82	14	1	0	3	10	9	25	.171	.293	.255
August	77	16	2	0	4	9	5	29	.208	.390	.265
Sept./Oct.	65	14	1	0	4	9	4	17	.215	.415	.257
Leading Off Inn.	83	22	3	0	7	7	6	23	.265	.554	.330
Runners On	164	36	6	0	7	39	14	50	.220	.384	.288
Bases Empty	238	51	6	0	12	12	21	67	.214	.391	.284
Runners/Scor. Pos.	96	24	5	0	3	30	10	29	.250	.396	.318
Runners On/2 Out	79	15	3	0	5	20	8	21	.190	.418	.264
Scor. Pos./2 Out	54	12	3	0	3	16	6	17	.222	.444	.300
Late-Inning Pressure	57	6	1	0	0	3	4	21	.105	.123	.159
Leading Off	13	2	1	0	0	0	1	2	.154	.231	.214
Runners On	17	2	0	0	0	3	1	8	.118	.118	.150
Runners/Scor. Pos.	10	1	0	0	0	3	0	4	.100	.100	.083

RUNS BATTED IN	From 1B	From 2B	From 3B	Scoring Position
Totals	5/121	13/70	14/39	27/109
Percentage	4.1%	18.6%	35.9%	24.8%

Loves to face: Greg Hibbard (.533, 8-for-15, 2 HR)
Kirk McCaskill (.462, 6-for-13, 1 2B, 3 HR)
Roy Smith (.368, 7-for-19, 3 HR)

Hates to face: Alex Fernandez (0-for-10)
Pascual Perez (0-for-13)
David Wells (.077, 1-for-13, 7 SO)

Miscellaneous statistics: Ground outs-to-air outs ratio: 1.08 last season, 1.04 for career.... Grounded into 7 double plays in 75 opportunities (one per 11).... Drove in 10 of 19 runners from third base with less than two outs (53%).... Direction of balls hit to the outfield: 44% to left field, 27% to center, 29% to right.... Base running: Advanced from first base to third on 3 of 28 outfield singles (11%); scored from second on 4 of 7 (57%).... Opposing base stealers: 53-for-92 (58%), 2d-lowest rate in A.L.

Comments: Needs two more RBIs to become the seventh player to catch 1000 games and drive in 1000 runs. The others: Johnny Bench, Yogi Berra, Gary Carter, Bill Dickey, Carlton Fisk, and Gabby Hartnett.... He led major league catchers with 19 passed balls, but his 85-game errorless streak was the longest among A.L. catchers last season.... The Angels' staff posted a 3.50 ERA with Parrish calling the signals, and a 4.02 mark with other catchers (John Orton and Ron Tingley).... He had the most home runs of any player in the majors who didn't hit either a three-run homer or a grand slam last season.... Has hit at least 15 home runs in each of the past 10 seasons.... His strikeout rate increased by 29 percent last season (from one per 4.9 plate appearances to one per 3.8), and his batting average fell by 23 percent (from .268 to .216).... His July batting average was the 6th lowest in the league.... Batting average in road games was 5th lowest in the league.... Batting average in Late-Inning Pressure Situations was lowest in the majors.... He's hit for a lower average in Late-Inning Pressure Situations than he has in other at-bats in each of the last eight years.... Has never walked as many as 50 times in a season. His career high: 49, in 1979.... Having caught 608 games over the past five seasons, he's still keeping pace with most of the younger crowd. The only other players with 600 or more games behind the plate since 1987: Tony Pena (670), Benito Santiago (658), and Mike Scioscia (638).

Dan Pasqua

Bats Left

Chicago White Sox	AB	H	2B	3B	HR	RBI	BB	SO	BA	SA	OBA
Season	417	108	22	5	18	66	62	86	.259	.465	.358
vs. Left-Handers	49	13	2	1	3	8	9	12	.265	.531	.379
vs. Right-Handers	368	95	20	4	15	58	53	74	.258	.457	.355
vs. Ground-Ballers	201	53	11	1	7	26	27	36	.264	.433	.352
vs. Fly-Ballers	216	55	11	4	11	40	35	50	.255	.495	.364
Home Games	196	57	11	3	10	29	36	34	.291	.531	.402
Road Games	221	51	11	2	8	37	26	52	.231	.407	.317
Grass Fields	349	87	18	4	14	52	55	69	.249	.444	.355
Artificial Turf	68	21	4	1	4	14	7	17	.309	.574	.373
April	32	8	0	0	2	5	3	7	.250	.438	.314
May	50	11	3	0	1	5	8	5	.220	.340	.322
June	82	22	4	2	4	13	11	18	.268	.512	.355
July	97	32	7	1	5	21	17	17	.330	.577	.440
August	83	14	2	0	1	5	13	21	.169	.229	.289
Sept./Oct.	73	21	6	2	5	17	10	18	.288	.630	.373
Leading Off Inn.	103	28	6	0	8	8	9	21	.272	.563	.336
Runners On	205	53	9	5	8	56	39	41	.259	.468	.381
Bases Empty	212	55	13	0	10	10	23	45	.259	.462	.335
Runners/Scor. Pos.	111	27	3	5	3	43	22	26	.243	.441	.375
Runners On/2 Out	86	27	5	2	2	21	22	16	.314	.488	.459
Scor. Pos./2 Out	47	14	1	2	1	17	13	8	.298	.468	.459
Late-Inning Pressure	73	19	3	0	2	10	10	17	.260	.384	.349
Leading Off	16	5	0	0	2	2	2	2	.313	.688	.389
Runners On	34	9	2	0	0	8	6	8	.265	.324	.375
Runners/Scor. Pos.	18	6	2	0	0	8	3	5	.333	.444	.429

RUNS BATTED IN	From 1B	From 2B	From 3B	Scoring Position
Totals	15/161	16/86	17/46	33/132
Percentage	9.3%	18.6%	37.0%	25.0%

Loves to face: Scott Erickson (.625, 5-for-8, 1 2B, 3 HR, 2 SO)
Dave Johnson (.667, 6-for-9, 1 2B, 3 HR)
Mike Moore (.423, 22-for-52, 2 HR)

Hates to face: Chris Bosio (.158, 3-for-19)
Nolan Ryan (.100, 2-for-20, 10 SO)
Walt Terrell (.088, 3-for-34, 1 HR, 5 BB)

Miscellaneous statistics: Ground outs-to-air outs ratio: 0.90 last season, 0.81 for career.... Grounded into 9 double plays in 115 opportunities (one per 13).... Drove in 9 of 25 runners from third base with less than two outs (36%), 5th-lowest rate in A.L.... Direction of balls hit to the outfield: 31% to left field, 24% to center, 45% to right.... Base running: Advanced from first base to third on 10 of 23 outfield singles (43%); scored from second on 11 of 15 (73%).... Made 0.71 assists per nine innings at first base.

Comments: Has hit 62 home runs since being traded by the Yankees to the White Sox following the 1988 season. New York's home-run leader during that time: Jesse Barfield, with 60. See the Jay Buhner and Jim Deshaies comments for similar themes.... Started 109 of 114 games in which the White Sox faced right-handed starters, but only five of 48 games against left-handers.... Drove in 21 runs over a 21-game stretch in July.... His August batting average was the 4th lowest in the league.... Career average of .211 (23-for-109, 4 HR) as a pinch hitter.... He has hit for a higher average against ground-ball pitchers than he has against fly-ballers in each of his seven years in the majors. Career breakdown: .277 vs. ground-ballers, .229 vs. fly-ballers.... Last season was the first of his seven-year career in which he compiled a higher batting average vs. left-handed pitchers than vs. right-handers. Previous career BAs: .178 vs. LHP, .264 vs. RHP. He also equaled his career high with three home runs vs. southpaws.... Has batted at least 50 points higher in day games than in night games in each of the past four seasons. During that time: .314 in day games, .229 in night games; only one player has a wider spread in favor of day games: Randy Ready, 114 points (.339 and .225). Rounding out the top five: Craig Biggio, 73 points (.327 and .255); Brady Anderson, 58 points (.261 and .203); and Jeff Reed, 54 points (.276 and .222).

Bill Pecota
Bats Right

Kansas City Royals	AB	H	2B	3B	HR	RBI	BB	SO	BA	SA	OBA
Season	398	114	23	2	6	45	41	45	.286	.399	.356
vs. Left-Handers	128	43	10	0	2	17	17	13	.336	.461	.414
vs. Right-Handers	270	71	13	2	4	28	24	32	.263	.370	.328
vs. Ground-Ballers	182	58	12	1	6	28	18	18	.319	.495	.383
vs. Fly-Ballers	216	56	11	1	0	17	23	27	.259	.319	.333
Home Games	203	60	12	0	4	25	25	20	.296	.414	.378
Road Games	195	54	11	2	2	20	16	25	.277	.385	.332
Grass Fields	133	38	9	2	2	13	10	18	.286	.429	.336
Artificial Turf	265	76	14	0	4	32	31	27	.287	.385	.366
April	17	4	0	0	0	1	4	3	.235	.235	.381
May	79	19	4	0	2	12	5	8	.241	.367	.286
June	29	12	3	0	2	8	2	4	.414	.724	.452
July	74	25	2	0	0	7	4	9	.338	.365	.387
August	96	26	9	1	1	6	12	11	.271	.417	.352
Sept./Oct.	103	28	5	1	1	11	14	10	.272	.369	.359
Leading Off Inn.	77	26	8	0	2	2	5	9	.338	.519	.386
Runners On	174	47	8	1	3	42	23	17	.270	.379	.359
Bases Empty	224	67	15	1	3	3	18	28	.299	.415	.354
Runners/Scor. Pos.	97	31	4	0	2	36	18	12	.320	.423	.431
Runners On/2 Out	64	18	3	0	1	15	13	6	.281	.375	.403
Scor. Pos./2 Out	43	12	3	0	1	15	11	6	.279	.419	.426
Late-Inning Pressure	61	17	5	0	0	5	9	9	.279	.361	.380
Leading Off	12	4	2	0	0	0	2	3	.333	.500	.467
Runners On	28	6	0	0	0	5	5	3	.214	.214	.333
Runners/Scor. Pos.	18	5	0	0	0	5	5	2	.278	.278	.435

RUNS BATTED IN	From 1B	From 2B	From 3B	Scoring Position
Totals	7/119	15/77	17/40	32/117
Percentage	5.9%	19.5%	42.5%	27.4%

Loves to face:

Hates to face: Jose DeLeon (0-for-7)
Mike Jackson (0-for-5)

Miscellaneous statistics: Ground outs-to-air outs ratio: 1.40 last season, 1.21 for career.... Grounded into 12 double plays in 90 opportunities (one per 7.5).... Drove in 13 of 23 runners from third base with less than two outs (57%).... Direction of balls hit to the outfield: 32% to left field, 29% to center, 39% to right.... Base running: Advanced from first base to third on 8 of 22 outfield singles (36%); scored from second on 9 of 11 (82%).... Made 1.87 assists per nine innings at third base.

Comments: Most New Yorkers know as much about Pecota as they do about Bogota, New Jersey. He's unique among active players—a versatile, late-blooming infielder who's played at least 100 games each at second base, third base, and shortstop during a career with the Royals that dates back to 1986. The most recent comparable player would be Art Howe, who now manages the Houston Astros. Both had breakthrough seasons at age 31; Howe batted .293 with seven home runs and 45 RBIs as a 31-year-old in 1978.... Mets manager Jeff Torborg talked of Pecota as a semi-regular starter. But our model projects him as only a .230 hitter in slightly less than 100 games—not to mention what it suggests for Dave Magadan, Pecota's competition at third base. (See page 192.) ... Actually, Pecota would make an ideal right-handed platoonmate for Magadan; his career batting average is 52 points higher vs. left-handers (.287) than vs. right-handers (.235).... His 69-game errorless streak was the longest by any third baseman in the majors last season.... He was one of three major leaguers to start at least one game at all four infield positions and in the outfield last season. The others were Greg Litton and Al Newman.... He's hit for a lower average in Late-Inning Pressure Situations than he has in other at-bats in each of the last six years. Last season marked the first time that he reached the .200 mark in LIPS. Career batting averages: .206 in LIPS, .261 in unpressured ABs.

Tony Pena
Bats Right

Boston Red Sox	AB	H	2B	3B	HR	RBI	BB	SO	BA	SA	OBA
Season	464	107	23	2	5	48	37	53	.231	.321	.291
vs. Left-Handers	106	30	4	0	4	17	9	11	.283	.434	.336
vs. Right-Handers	358	77	19	2	1	31	28	42	.215	.288	.278
vs. Ground-Ballers	212	47	8	1	2	19	19	26	.222	.297	.295
vs. Fly-Ballers	252	60	15	1	3	29	18	27	.238	.341	.288
Home Games	230	51	13	1	2	22	19	27	.222	.313	.290
Road Games	234	56	10	1	3	26	18	26	.239	.329	.293
Grass Fields	381	86	18	2	3	40	36	44	.226	.307	.298
Artificial Turf	83	21	5	0	2	8	1	9	.253	.386	.259
April	67	12	3	0	1	4	1	5	.179	.269	.191
May	86	29	5	1	1	10	7	3	.337	.453	.400
June	76	19	6	1	0	10	8	17	.250	.355	.321
July	84	15	4	0	3	9	6	11	.179	.333	.239
August	73	15	2	0	0	8	2	6	.205	.233	.221
Sept./Oct.	78	17	3	0	0	7	13	11	.218	.256	.337
Leading Off Inn.	102	24	6	1	2	2	13	10	.235	.373	.322
Runners On	223	48	6	1	2	45	14	22	.215	.278	.261
Bases Empty	241	59	17	1	3	3	23	31	.245	.361	.318
Runners/Scor. Pos.	130	31	5	1	0	41	11	12	.238	.292	.297
Runners On/2 Out	106	23	3	0	0	21	4	9	.217	.245	.245
Scor. Pos./2 Out	71	18	3	0	0	21	4	6	.254	.296	.293
Late-Inning Pressure	56	7	1	0	0	4	6	10	.125	.143	.206
Leading Off	7	0	0	0	0	0	4	1	.000	.000	.364
Runners On	30	4	1	0	0	4	1	7	.133	.167	.156
Runners/Scor. Pos.	18	3	1	0	0	4	1	7	.167	.222	.200

RUNS BATTED IN	From 1B	From 2B	From 3B	Scoring Position
Totals	3/164	17/106	23/50	40/156
Percentage	1.8%	16.0%	46.0%	25.6%

Loves to face: Jimmy Key (.400, 6-for-15, 1 HR)
Scott Sanderson (.303, 20-for-66, 4 HR)
David West (.571, 4-for-7, 2 2B, 1 HR)

Hates to face: Kirk McCaskill (.059, 1-for-17)
Nolan Ryan (.161, 5-for-31, 0 BB)
Walt Terrell (.107, 3-for-28)

Miscellaneous statistics: Ground outs-to-air outs ratio: 1.44 last season, 1.61 for career.... Grounded into 23 double plays in 94 opportunities (one per 4.1), 3d-worst rate in A.L.... Drove in 15 of 25 runners from third base with less than two outs (60%).... Direction of balls hit to the outfield: 28% to left field, 30% to center, 41% to right.... Base running: Advanced from first base to third on 3 of 19 outfield singles (16%); scored from second on 11 of 13 (85%).... Opposing base stealers: 81-for-121 (67%).

Comments: Caught the most innings of anyone in the A.L. last season (1156⅔), and ranked third in the majors, behind Benito Santiago (1305⅓) and Craig Biggio (1175⅓).... He was involved in 15 double plays, starting 11 of them. Both figures were tops among major league catchers.... Opposing base stealers were successful in 67 percent of their attempts with Pena behind the plate, but in only 55 percent against John Marzano. The Boston staff posted a slightly lower ERA with Pena (3.98 to 4.17).... Started 127 games from the 8th spot in the batting order, the most of any player in the A.L., and 2d most in the majors to Jose Lind (129).... Of his 107 hits, 41 were to the opposite field (38%), the 6th-highest percentage in the majors (minimum: 60 hits).... His batting average vs. right-handed pitchers was the 7th lowest in the league.... Batting average in Late-Inning Pressure Situations was 2d lowest in the majors.... Hit between 10 and 15 home runs in each of his last five seasons with the Pirates, but hasn't hit more than 10 in five seasons with the Cardinals and Red Sox.... Pena caught 787 games for Pittsburgh, 388 for St. Louis, and needs 18 more to reach the 300 mark with the Red Sox. He would become the seventh player to catch that many games for three different teams; the others: Walker Cooper, Rick Ferrell, Al Lopez, Bob O'Farrell, Darrell Porter, and Wally Schang. (By way of comparison, no infield position has more than six three-team 300-gamers.)

Gary Pettis

Texas Rangers   Bats Left and Right

	AB	H	2B	3B	HR	RBI	BB	SO	BA	SA	OBA
Season	282	61	7	5	0	19	54	91	.216	.277	.341
vs. Left-Handers	77	15	1	1	0	6	14	17	.195	.234	.315
vs. Right-Handers	205	46	6	4	0	13	40	74	.224	.293	.351
vs. Ground-Ballers	136	30	1	4	0	14	18	44	.221	.287	.310
vs. Fly-Ballers	146	31	6	1	0	5	36	47	.212	.267	.368
Home Games	137	29	2	5	0	8	28	41	.212	.299	.343
Road Games	145	32	5	0	0	11	26	50	.221	.255	.339
Grass Fields	237	54	6	5	0	15	50	71	.228	.295	.361
Artificial Turf	45	7	1	0	0	4	4	20	.156	.178	.224
April	38	11	2	0	0	2	8	12	.289	.342	.413
May	51	13	1	0	0	6	6	14	.255	.275	.328
June	62	9	0	1	0	3	13	23	.145	.177	.293
July	30	6	0	3	0	2	8	8	.200	.400	.368
August	57	12	2	1	0	3	13	22	.211	.281	.357
Sept./Oct.	44	10	2	0	0	3	6	12	.227	.273	.320
Leading Off Inn.	70	14	3	2	0	0	20	29	.200	.300	.378
Runners On	128	28	3	2	0	19	16	37	.219	.273	.303
Bases Empty	154	33	4	3	0	0	38	54	.214	.279	.370
Runners/Scor. Pos.	80	18	1	1	0	18	8	24	.225	.262	.292
Runners On/2 Out	55	16	0	1	0	10	7	13	.291	.327	.371
Scor. Pos./2 Out	41	11	0	1	0	10	6	11	.268	.317	.362
Late-Inning Pressure	45	11	1	0	0	4	6	15	.244	.267	.333
Leading Off	9	1	1	0	0	0	2	4	.111	.222	.273
Runners On	20	5	0	0	0	4	3	6	.250	.250	.348
Runners/Scor. Pos.	11	3	0	0	0	4	1	3	.273	.273	.333

RUNS BATTED IN	From 1B	From 2B	From 3B	Scoring Position
Totals	1/81	10/67	8/24	18/91
Percentage	1.2%	14.9%	33.3%	19.8%

Loves to face: Storm Davis (.333, 11-for-33)
                Gene Nelson (.385, 5-for-13)
                David Wells (.500, 6-for-12)
Hates to face: Mike Boddicker (.088, 3-for-34, 6 BB)
                Lee Guetterman (0-for-11)
                Ted Higuera (0-for-22)

Miscellaneous statistics: Ground outs-to-air outs ratio: 1.14 last season, 1.97 for career.... Grounded into 4 double plays in 65 opportunities (one per 16).... Drove in 5 of 12 runners from third base with less than two outs (42%).... Direction of balls hit to the outfield: 48% to left field, 22% to center, 30% to right batting left-handed; 14% to left field, 39% to center, 46% to right batting right-handed.... Base running: Advanced from first base to third on 8 of 17 outfield singles (47%); scored from second on 10 of 12 (83%).... Made 2.85 putouts per nine innings in center field.

Comments: Led off 90 innings last season and drew 20 walks, giving him the highest rate of leadoff walks in the majors last season.... He entered 39 games as a defensive substitute, the most of any player in the league last season. The top five: Pettis (39), Jeff Schaefer (29), Rene Gonzales (27), Vance Law (25), Juan Bell (24).... Has never hit more than five home runs in a season, but last season was the first in which he was shut out.... His total of extra-base hits was also a career low (excluding two season fragments in the early 1980s).... His stolen-base percentage has slid gradually but steadily downward for the past four seasons; year by year since 1987: .828, .815, .741, .717, .690.... He has a career batting average of .237 from each side of the plate. Among the 20 active switch-hitters with at least 4000 plate appearances, only Pettis, Tim Raines, Bill Doran, Tommy Herr, and Alfredo Griffin have career averages of within five points from either side of the plate.... Pettis is one of 321 major leaguers to have played at least 1000 games in the outfield. Only one had a lower career batting average than Pettis's .237 mark: Gorman Thomas, who batted just .225 but out-homered Pettis 268 to 20.... So why has he remained a viable major leaguer for eight seasons (perhaps the nicest thing anyone's ever said about him)? Because among that group of 321, only 16 caught more fly balls per game. Pettis ranks 17th with an average of 2.61 putouts per game—two slots ahead of Rickey Henderson (2.58), two behind Joe DiMaggio (2.62).

Tony Phillips

Detroit Tigers   Bats Left and Right

	AB	H	2B	3B	HR	RBI	BB	SO	BA	SA	OBA
Season	564	160	28	4	17	72	79	95	.284	.438	.371
vs. Left-Handers	154	55	7	0	11	25	32	18	.357	.617	.466
vs. Right-Handers	410	105	21	4	6	47	47	77	.256	.371	.333
vs. Ground-Ballers	279	75	11	0	6	35	41	38	.269	.373	.362
vs. Fly-Ballers	285	85	17	4	11	37	38	57	.298	.502	.380
Home Games	292	86	13	1	9	42	50	43	.295	.438	.398
Road Games	272	74	15	3	8	30	29	52	.272	.438	.341
Grass Fields	474	134	22	3	14	59	72	78	.283	.430	.378
Artificial Turf	90	26	6	1	3	13	7	17	.289	.478	.333
April	75	22	4	1	3	11	9	13	.293	.493	.356
May	92	28	2	0	1	13	21	9	.304	.359	.430
June	97	26	4	1	3	13	15	19	.268	.423	.368
July	106	34	10	1	3	15	8	17	.321	.519	.368
August	79	23	3	0	5	10	14	20	.291	.519	.400
Sept./Oct.	115	27	5	1	2	10	12	17	.235	.348	.313
Leading Off Inn.	216	56	9	1	7	7	32	39	.259	.407	.357
Runners On	194	60	7	3	3	58	29	31	.309	.423	.391
Bases Empty	370	100	21	1	14	14	50	64	.270	.446	.360
Runners/Scor. Pos.	120	38	5	3	1	52	19	24	.317	.433	.397
Runners On/2 Out	80	23	3	2	0	19	16	13	.287	.375	.406
Scor. Pos./2 Out	54	16	2	2	0	18	12	11	.296	.407	.424
Late-Inning Pressure	78	14	2	0	2	7	15	17	.179	.282	.309
Leading Off	22	2	1	0	1	1	5	7	.091	.273	.259
Runners On	30	7	0	0	0	5	7	6	.233	.233	.368
Runners/Scor. Pos.	17	5	0	0	0	5	4	4	.294	.294	.409

RUNS BATTED IN	From 1B	From 2B	From 3B	Scoring Position
Totals	8/119	21/97	26/52	47/149
Percentage	6.7%	21.6%	50.0%	31.5%

Loves to face: Chuck Finley (.321, 9-for-28, 1 HR, 9 BB)
                Frank Viola (.333, 11-for-33, 9 BB)
                Matt Young (.385, 5-for-13, 1 HR, 6 BB)
Hates to face: Mark Eichhorn (.063, 1-for-16)
                Brian Holman (.095, 2-for-21, 2 BB)
                David Wells (.118, 2-for-17)

Miscellaneous statistics: Ground outs-to-air outs ratio: 1.05 last season, 1.14 for career.... Grounded into 8 double plays in 84 opportunities (one per 11).... Drove in 18 of 28 runners from third base with less than two outs (64%).... Direction of balls hit to the outfield: 38% to left field, 36% to center, 26% to right batting left-handed; 55% to left field, 24% to center, 21% to right batting right-handed.... Base running: Advanced from first base to third on 14 of 30 outfield singles (47%); scored from second on 9 of 17 (53%).... Made 2.31 assists per nine innings at third base.

Comments: Established career highs in the big three: batting average, home runs, and RBIs. His previous bests in those categories: .280 (in 1985), 10 HR (in 1987—natch), and 55 RBI (in 1990).... All things considered, his season represented a 70-to-1 breakthrough; only five A.L. players had more extreme breakthroughs last season: Julio Franco (203-to-1), Chili Davis (132-to-1), Cal Ripken (132-to-1), Rafael Palmeiro (86-to-1), and Devon White (86-to-1).... With the help of the DH rule, Phillips was the only player in the majors to start at least one game at seven different positions last season (2B, 3B, SS, LF, CF, RF, and DH). Greg Litton started at six gloved positions in the N.L. (and we don't mean batting gloves).... Phillips became Detroit's ninth different opening-day DH in the last nine years. There have been no repeaters since John Wockenfuss.... Batting average vs. left-handed pitchers was 6th highest in the league, and his 11 home runs vs. southpaws ranked third in the league, behind Cecil Fielder (13) and Cal Ripken (12). Frank Thomas and Dave Winfield shared the third spot with Phillips, who had never before hit more than three home runs vs. left-handers in one season.... His career batting average is 42 points higher from the right side (.284) than from the left (.242).... He has hit for a higher average with runners on base than he has with the bases empty in each of the last six years.

Luis Polonia
Bats Left

California Angels	AB	H	2B	3B	HR	RBI	BB	SO	BA	SA	OBA
Season	604	179	28	8	2	50	52	74	.296	.379	.352
vs. Left-Handers	168	40	8	1	0	17	11	25	.238	.298	.283
vs. Right-Handers	436	139	20	7	2	33	41	49	.319	.411	.377
vs. Ground-Ballers	277	74	8	3	0	19	24	37	.267	.318	.328
vs. Fly-Ballers	327	105	20	5	2	31	28	37	.321	.431	.372
Home Games	303	79	11	4	1	20	30	36	.261	.333	.329
Road Games	301	100	17	4	1	30	22	38	.332	.425	.374
Grass Fields	497	138	19	8	2	41	44	60	.278	.360	.337
Artificial Turf	107	41	9	0	0	9	8	14	.383	.467	.419
April	75	25	2	1	0	7	8	8	.333	.387	.405
May	105	33	5	4	0	10	8	12	.314	.438	.363
June	114	30	3	1	0	15	4	16	.263	.307	.286
July	81	21	3	1	1	5	10	8	.259	.358	.337
August	110	36	8	1	1	9	12	14	.327	.445	.390
Sept./Oct.	119	34	7	0	0	4	10	16	.286	.345	.341
Leading Off Inn.	220	58	10	3	2	2	26	33	.264	.364	.344
Runners On	236	72	11	4	0	48	15	26	.305	.386	.343
Bases Empty	368	107	17	4	2	2	37	48	.291	.375	.357
Runners/Scor. Pos.	132	44	4	2	0	44	12	17	.333	.394	.381
Runners On/2 Out	103	33	5	3	0	23	10	9	.320	.427	.381
Scor. Pos./2 Out	64	23	2	2	0	20	9	7	.359	.453	.438
Late-Inning Pressure	70	22	2	0	0	1	6	12	.314	.343	.368
Leading Off	13	3	1	0	0	0	0	2	.231	.308	.231
Runners On	30	7	0	0	0	1	3	7	.233	.233	.303
Runners/Scor. Pos.	15	3	0	0	0	1	3	4	.200	.200	.333

RUNS BATTED IN	From 1B	From 2B	From 3B	Scoring Position
Totals	6/163	16/109	26/48	42/157
Percentage	3.7%	14.7%	54.2%	26.8%

Loves to face: Kevin Appier (.579, 11-for-19)
Jack Morris (.415, 17-for-41)
Dave Stewart (.500, 10-for-20, 1 HR)
Hates to face: Jose Guzman (.105, 2-for-19, 2 BB)
Ted Higuera (0-for-10)
Charlie Hough (.115, 3-for-26)

Miscellaneous statistics: Ground outs-to-air outs ratio: 1.55 last season, 1.63 for career.... Grounded into 11 double plays in 102 opportunities (one per 9.3).... Drove in 19 of 30 runners from third base with less than two outs (63%).... Direction of balls hit to the outfield: 45% to left field, 35% to center, 20% to right.... Base running: Advanced from first base to third on 25 of 38 outfield singles (66%), 3d-highest rate in A.L.; scored from second on 19 of 20 (95%), 5th-highest rate in A.L.... Made 1.77 putouts per nine innings in left field, lowest rate in A.L.

Comments: Played more innings in left field than any other player in the A.L. last season (1249⅔). (Now there's a scary thought.)... Polonia, Dave Winfield, and Marquis Grissom were the only players to collect five hits in a game twice last season.... Batting average in road games was 4th highest in the league, and he had the A.L.'s highest mark on artificial turf.... Batting average with RISP was 5th highest in the league.... His career average of .336 with two outs and RISP is the highest over the last 17 years.... Career average of .327 (18-for-55, 0 HR) as a pinch hitter.... His career average against fly-ball pitchers (.321) is 4th highest among active players, behind Wade Boggs (.336), Tony Gwynn (.323), and Kirby Puckett (.322).... One of the few batters in baseball with a significantly higher batting average against fly-ball pitchers (.321) than vs. ground-ballers (.279). That 43-point difference (trust us; it's a rounding error) is the 3d largest among active players with at least 1000 career at-bats. Walt Weiss is the reigning champ at 63 points (.285/.222); no one else is close. Jerome Walton is the runner-up (45 points, .286/.242). Rounding out the top five are Delino DeShields (41 points, .282/.240) and Felix Jose (39 points, .302/.263). Four active players with 1000 ABs have hit 40 points better vs. fly-ballers than ground-ballers; by way of comparison, 22 have hit 40 points better in the opposite direction. The widest spread in that direction: 67 points, by Bo Jackson (.288 vs. ground-ballers, .221 vs. fly-ballers).

Kirby Puckett
Bats Right

Minnesota Twins	AB	H	2B	3B	HR	RBI	BB	SO	BA	SA	OBA
Season	611	195	29	6	15	89	31	78	.319	.460	.352
vs. Left-Handers	155	63	8	5	7	24	8	19	.406	.658	.436
vs. Right-Handers	456	132	21	1	8	65	23	59	.289	.393	.324
vs. Ground-Ballers	262	87	14	3	5	35	9	41	.332	.466	.357
vs. Fly-Ballers	349	108	15	3	10	54	22	37	.309	.456	.348
Home Games	328	107	16	4	7	45	16	45	.326	.463	.356
Road Games	283	88	13	2	8	44	15	33	.311	.456	.348
Grass Fields	217	70	10	2	7	38	10	26	.323	.484	.357
Artificial Turf	394	125	19	4	8	51	21	52	.317	.447	.350
April	79	27	2	1	3	10	4	11	.342	.506	.369
May	109	35	5	2	2	14	4	12	.321	.459	.339
June	105	33	6	1	5	18	7	14	.314	.533	.376
July	105	37	4	2	2	19	6	12	.352	.486	.387
August	113	35	5	0	2	12	2	16	.310	.407	.322
Sept./Oct.	100	28	7	0	1	16	8	13	.280	.380	.324
Leading Off Inn.	103	25	5	1	3	3	5	13	.243	.398	.291
Runners On	284	85	9	2	5	79	14	40	.299	.398	.331
Bases Empty	327	110	20	4	10	10	14	38	.336	.514	.371
Runners/Scor. Pos.	153	46	4	2	1	65	13	26	.301	.373	.341
Runners On/2 Out	87	24	1	0	0	19	10	14	.276	.287	.351
Scor. Pos./2 Out	64	17	1	0	0	18	10	11	.266	.281	.365
Late-Inning Pressure	73	28	4	1	1	11	4	14	.384	.507	.423
Leading Off	19	5	1	0	0	0	1	4	.263	.316	.333
Runners On	27	12	2	0	0	10	3	9	.444	.519	.500
Runners/Scor. Pos.	15	7	1	0	0	9	2	3	.467	.533	.529

RUNS BATTED IN	From 1B	From 2B	From 3B	Scoring Position
Totals	12/207	27/112	35/71	62/183
Percentage	5.8%	24.1%	49.3%	33.9%

Loves to face: Mark Knudson (.727, 8-for-11, 1 HR)
Melido Perez (.586, 17-for-29, 2 HR)
Curt Young (.441, 15-for-34, 2 HR)
Hates to face: Danny Darwin (.125, 3-for-24, 0 BB)
Dennis Eckersley (.083, 1-for-12)
Dave Stieb (.200, 12-for-60)

Miscellaneous statistics: Ground outs-to-air outs ratio: 1.44 last season, 1.65 for career.... Grounded into 27 double plays, most in the majors, in 165 opportunities, also a major league high (one per 6.1).... Drove in 29 of 42 runners from third base with less than two outs (69%).... Direction of balls hit to the outfield: 22% to left field, 41% to center, 38% to right.... Base running: Advanced from first base to third on 25 of 41 outfield singles (61%); scored from second on 16 of 23 (70%).... Made 2.56 putouts per nine innings in center field.

Comments: He led the majors with a .406 batting average against left-handed pitchers. Over the past 17 years, only one other A.L. player batted .400 vs. southpaws: Sixto Lezcano (.411 in 1979). Rennie Stennett (.435 in 1977) and Mariano Duncan (.410 in 1990) did it in the National League. Puckett also had a near miss in 1988, when he batted .398 vs. LHPs.... Puckett's career batting average against southpaws (.342) is more than 20 points higher than anyone else's over the past 17 years. The runner-up: Chris Sabo (.321).... Has batted above .300 at the Metrodome in each of his eight seasons in the majors. His career breakdown: .349 at the dome, .291 on the road. Over the past 17 years, only Wade Boggs (.381) has a higher home-game batting average than Puckett.... How good was Hank Aaron? (This may sound like a silly question, but bear with us—we're going somewhere with it.) Last October, Puckett reached the 5000-AB mark with exactly 1600 hits—one more than Aaron had at that point. Puckett, a well-rounded player (sorry—we had to), had 265 doubles, 100 stolen bases, and 98 outfield assists; but Aaron was right there as well: 280 doubles, 73 steals, and 94 assists. So what we have is a player nearly identical to Puckett, a perennial All-Star, at the same stage of his career, except that Aaron (a) was 20 months younger at the time; (b) played until the age of 42 with peak years in his late 30s; and, (c) in the one category in which he significantly differed from Puckett, led at the 5000-AB mark by 147 homers, 270 to 123.

Carlos Quintana — Bats Right

Boston Red Sox	AB	H	2B	3B	HR	RBI	BB	SO	BA	SA	OBA
Season	478	141	21	1	11	71	61	66	.295	.412	.375
vs. Left-Handers	153	52	7	0	5	26	26	21	.340	.484	.436
vs. Right-Handers	325	89	14	1	6	45	35	45	.274	.378	.345
vs. Ground-Ballers	225	61	7	0	3	26	22	31	.271	.342	.341
vs. Fly-Ballers	253	80	14	1	8	45	39	35	.316	.474	.403
Home Games	236	69	10	0	2	30	34	31	.292	.360	.382
Road Games	242	72	11	1	9	41	27	35	.298	.463	.368
Grass Fields	398	116	20	1	6	56	50	54	.291	.392	.371
Artificial Turf	80	25	1	0	5	15	11	12	.313	.512	.396
April	59	18	3	0	1	7	0	9	.305	.407	.317
May	102	33	3	0	2	9	10	10	.324	.412	.384
June	82	23	5	0	2	13	18	13	.280	.415	.416
July	72	17	3	0	2	15	8	8	.236	.361	.305
August	80	27	4	1	3	12	10	15	.338	.525	.411
Sept./Oct.	83	23	3	0	1	15	15	11	.277	.349	.384
Leading Off Inn.	92	38	7	0	3	3	5	13	.413	.587	.443
Runners On	231	65	12	1	6	66	29	21	.281	.420	.357
Bases Empty	247	76	9	0	5	5	32	45	.308	.405	.391
Runners/Scor. Pos.	130	36	6	0	4	58	22	13	.277	.415	.374
Runners On/2 Out	88	26	6	0	2	27	9	7	.295	.432	.361
Scor. Pos./2 Out	52	16	4	0	2	25	6	4	.308	.500	.379
Late-Inning Pressure	53	20	2	0	1	14	8	7	.377	.472	.459
Leading Off	9	4	0	0	0	0	2	1	.444	.444	.545
Runners On	27	13	2	0	1	14	3	1	.481	.667	.533
Runners/Scor. Pos.	21	11	2	0	1	14	0	1	.524	.762	.524

RUNS BATTED IN	From 1B	From 2B	From 3B	Scoring Position
Totals	11/176	20/111	29/54	49/165
Percentage	6.3%	18.0%	53.7%	29.7%

Loves to face: Jim Abbott (.476, 10-for-21)
Jimmy Key (.563, 9-for-16)
David Wells (.400, 6-for-15, 2 HR)

Hates to face: Melido Perez (0-for-11)
Todd Stottlemyre (.083, 1-for-12)
Duane Ward (.091, 1-for-11, 8 SO)

Miscellaneous statistics: Ground outs-to-air outs ratio: 2.26 last season, 2d highest in A.L.; 1.97 for career.... Grounded into 17 double plays in 124 opportunities (one per 7.3).... Drove in 18 of 27 runners from third base with less than two outs (67%).... Direction of balls hit to the outfield: 23% to left field, 39% to center, 38% to right.... Base running: Advanced from first base to third on 7 of 33 outfield singles (21%); scored from second on 10 of 14 (71%).... Made 0.87 assists per nine innings at first base, 2d-highest rate in A.L.

Comments: For the past 60 years, first base has been almost exclusively a power position. Throughout that period, there hasn't been a single long-lasting regular first baseman with as little extra-base power as Carlos Quintana has shown. Since the early 1920s, when the livelier ball transformed Philadelphia's Walter Holke into a late-blooming semi-slugger, only five players have played at least 130 games at first base and accumulated 35 or fewer extra-base hits in consecutive seasons. They were: Dick Siebert (1942–43), Eddie Waitkus (1951–52), Ed Kranepool (1966–67), Mike Hargrove (1982–83), and Quintana, who in 1992 could match Holke's three-year streak (1919–21). Quintana has played 148 and 138 games at first in the last two seasons, with 35 and 33 extra-base hits, respectively. Prior to the Q-man, the last Red Sox first baseman to play as many as 138 games with as few as 35 XBHs was Tony Lupien, in 1943. What must Boomer Scott and Dick Gernert think? ... Let's note that Quintana did raise his home-run total from seven in 1990 to 11 last season. But our projection model rates his chances of hitting 20 home runs at only 8 percent this season, at 20 percent for *any* future season; the odds against his ever hitting 30 or more in a season are 13-to-1.... Led the American League with a .351 batting average in day games. His career batting-average breakdown: .308 in day games, .275 at night.

Tim Raines — Bats Left and Right

Chicago White Sox	AB	H	2B	3B	HR	RBI	BB	SO	BA	SA	OBA
Season	609	163	20	6	5	50	83	68	.268	.345	.359
vs. Left-Handers	208	58	6	1	2	17	21	21	.279	.346	.343
vs. Right-Handers	401	105	14	5	3	33	62	47	.262	.344	.366
vs. Ground-Ballers	286	74	15	2	3	25	38	36	.259	.357	.350
vs. Fly-Ballers	323	89	5	4	2	25	45	32	.276	.334	.367
Home Games	284	72	7	2	1	21	39	30	.254	.303	.348
Road Games	325	91	13	4	4	29	44	38	.280	.382	.368
Grass Fields	519	144	15	5	4	40	73	57	.277	.349	.369
Artificial Turf	90	19	5	1	1	10	10	11	.211	.322	.297
April	62	11	2	0	0	3	7	5	.177	.210	.261
May	109	38	3	3	2	11	20	18	.349	.486	.454
June	98	28	4	2	0	14	12	10	.286	.367	.360
July	99	15	1	0	1	6	17	7	.152	.192	.288
August	121	40	7	1	1	9	16	17	.331	.430	.409
Sept./Oct.	120	31	3	0	1	7	11	11	.258	.308	.326
Leading Off Inn.	270	69	9	1	2	2	26	35	.256	.319	.326
Runners On	183	44	7	3	2	47	40	19	.240	.344	.377
Bases Empty	426	119	13	3	3	3	43	49	.279	.345	.350
Runners/Scor. Pos.	112	32	6	2	0	42	34	12	.286	.375	.450
Runners On/2 Out	89	20	1	2	0	16	17	7	.225	.281	.361
Scor. Pos./2 Out	60	13	1	1	0	15	14	5	.217	.267	.382
Late-Inning Pressure	107	21	2	2	2	11	15	12	.196	.308	.293
Leading Off	32	6	0	0	1	1	0	5	.188	.281	.188
Runners On	44	7	1	1	1	10	12	5	.159	.295	.333
Runners/Scor. Pos.	24	4	1	0	0	7	10	3	.167	.208	.400

RUNS BATTED IN	From 1B	From 2B	From 3B	Scoring Position
Totals	7/120	18/82	20/51	38/133
Percentage	5.8%	22.0%	39.2%	28.6%

Loves to face: Andy Hawkins (.386, 22-for-57, 2 HR)
Eric Show (.364, 16-for-44, 2 HR)
Dave Stewart (.563, 9-for-16, 1 HR)

Hates to face: Rick Aguilera (.138, 4-for-29)
Jack Armstrong (0-for-13)
Mark Davis (.167, 4-for-24)

Miscellaneous statistics: Ground outs-to-air outs ratio: 1.48 last season, 1.23 for career.... Grounded into 7 double plays in 81 opportunities (one per 12).... Drove in 14 of 22 runners from third base with less than two outs (64%).... Direction of balls hit to the outfield: 40% to left field, 28% to center, 32% to right batting left-handed; 33% to left field, 36% to center, 31% to right batting right-handed.... Base running: Advanced from first base to third on 14 of 29 outfield singles (48%); scored from second on 20 of 27 (74%).... Made 2.11 putouts per nine innings in left field.

Comments: He has the highest stolen-base percentage in major league history among players with at least 300 steals (85 percent).... Has stolen at least 30 bases in each of 11 seasons starting with his rookie year of 1981. The only other player to steal 30 or more in each of the last 11 seasons is Rickey, whose streak is 13 years. The longest 30-SB streak ever: 14 years, Lou Brock (1964–77).... Raines stole 51 last season. Since Luis Aparicio's last 50-steal season for Chicago (1961), five different Sox players have reached 50, but none has done it twice. The others: Don Buford (1966), Rudy Law (1983), John Cangelosi (1986), and Gary Redus (1987).... If you remember the noteworthy list of pitchers in his "Loves to Face" section in last year's *Analyst,* and you noticed this year's group, then you won't be surprised that he had the highest batting average in the league against the Athletics last season (.429, 18-for-42).... You may also recall this note from the 1991 edition: "How many players have hit .300 from both sides of the plate (minimum: 1000 career hits)? ... No more than three; at least for the moment, Raines is one." Raines's average from each side dropped from .301 to .298 last season, leaving Tuck Turner and Frankie Frisch as the only contenders. (Anyone out there have play-by-plays for the 1893 Phillies?) ... Career batting average in Late-Inning Pressure Situations (.323) ranks third among active players, behind Tony Gwynn (.335) and Kirby Puckett (.323), and just ahead of Wade Boggs (.332).

Willie Randolph
Bats Right

Milwaukee Brewers	AB	H	2B	3B	HR	RBI	BB	SO	BA	SA	OBA
Season	431	141	14	3	0	54	75	38	.327	.374	.424
vs. Left-Handers	148	53	5	1	0	21	27	10	.358	.405	.457
vs. Right-Handers	283	88	9	2	0	33	48	28	.311	.357	.407
vs. Ground-Ballers	208	57	8	2	0	27	37	18	.274	.332	.381
vs. Fly-Ballers	223	84	6	1	0	27	38	20	.377	.413	.466
Home Games	220	74	10	2	0	31	28	20	.336	.400	.410
Road Games	211	67	4	1	0	23	47	18	.318	.346	.438
Grass Fields	364	120	11	3	0	50	65	28	.330	.376	.428
Artificial Turf	67	21	3	0	0	4	10	10	.313	.358	.403
April	22	5	0	0	0	0	4	1	.227	.227	.346
May	71	21	1	0	0	8	11	9	.296	.310	.390
June	52	24	1	1	0	11	8	6	.462	.519	.533
July	48	11	2	0	0	6	11	4	.229	.271	.373
August	116	43	6	1	0	17	18	9	.371	.440	.449
Sept./Oct.	122	37	4	1	0	12	23	9	.303	.352	.411
Leading Off Inn.	65	14	1	0	0	0	7	3	.215	.231	.292
Runners On	208	78	4	3	0	54	44	21	.375	.423	.478
Bases Empty	223	63	10	0	0	0	31	17	.283	.327	.370
Runners/Scor. Pos.	110	41	2	3	0	52	33	10	.373	.445	.507
Runners On/2 Out	77	27	1	1	0	21	19	5	.351	.390	.479
Scor. Pos./2 Out	49	18	0	1	0	20	17	2	.367	.408	.530
Late-Inning Pressure	70	23	4	0	0	7	7	5	.329	.386	.390
Leading Off	16	2	1	0	0	0	1	0	.125	.188	.176
Runners On	37	12	1	0	0	7	5	5	.324	.351	.405
Runners/Scor. Pos.	17	6	0	0	0	6	4	2	.353	.353	.476

RUNS BATTED IN	From 1B	From 2B	From 3B	Scoring Position
Totals	4/149	19/89	31/48	50/137
Percentage	2.7%	21.3%	64.6%	36.5%

Loves to face: Tom Browning (.533, 8-for-15, 1 HR)
Bruce Hurst (.393, 33-for-84, 1 HR)
John Smiley (.444, 4-for-9, 3 2B)

Hates to face: Doug Drabek (0-for-7)
Bill Swift (.095, 2-for-21, 4 BB)
Ed Whitson (.077, 1-for-13, 1 2B)

Miscellaneous statistics: Ground outs-to-air outs ratio: 1.72 last season, 1.45 for career.... Grounded into 14 double plays in 121 opportunities (one per 8.6).... Drove in 20 of 28 runners from third base with less than two outs (71%).... Direction of balls hit to the outfield: 22% to left field, 39% to center, 39% to right.... Base running: Advanced from first base to third on 16 of 43 outfield singles (37%); scored from second on 18 of 23 (78%).... Made 3.41 assists per nine innings at second base, highest rate in A.L.

Comments: Established a career-high batting average at the age of 37 years, 3 months. Only eight older players set personal bests in this century: Patsy Donovan (.327 at age 38), Charlie Carr (.293 at 37), Dave Shean (.264 at 40), Tris Speaker (.389 at 37), Johnny Cooney (.319 at 40), Pete Suder (.286 at 37), Hank Sauer (.288 at 37), and Mike Schmidt (.293 at 38).... Batting average with runners on base was the highest in the majors last season, and his average with runners in scoring position was best in the A.L.... His average vs. fly-ball pitchers was the 4th highest in the 17-year history of *The Player Analysis,* behind Rod Carew (.424 in 1977), George Brett (.405 in 1980), and Tony Gwynn (.401 in 1987).... One of nine right-handers to hit .300 or better vs. right-handed pitchers last season (minimum: 100 ABs).... One of two players to bat .350 or better vs. left-handers in 1990 and 1991 (minimum: 100 ABs). The other: Dave Henderson.... The Brewers had a 61–49 record with Randolph in the starting lineup (.555), but were 22–30 without him (.423). They allowed 4.33 runs per nine innings when he played second base, 5.11 per nine with Jim Gantner there.... Among major league second basemen, only Delino DeShields (27) committed more errors than Randolph (20).... Batted .419 (18-for-47) against the Yankees, and hit safely in all 12 games against them. He'll return to the Stadium in a Mets uniform on Saturday, April 4, as the 44th to play for both clubs. The only one to play at least 200 games for both: Elliott Maddox.

Jody Reed
Bats Right

Boston Red Sox	AB	H	2B	3B	HR	RBI	BB	SO	BA	SA	OBA
Season	618	175	42	2	5	60	60	53	.283	.382	.349
vs. Left-Handers	165	44	9	0	0	6	16	11	.267	.321	.331
vs. Right-Handers	453	131	33	2	5	54	44	42	.289	.404	.355
vs. Ground-Ballers	284	76	19	0	1	25	26	32	.268	.345	.332
vs. Fly-Ballers	334	99	23	2	4	35	34	21	.296	.413	.363
Home Games	312	82	27	1	3	37	34	27	.263	.385	.336
Road Games	306	93	15	1	2	23	26	26	.304	.379	.362
Grass Fields	530	152	39	1	5	59	54	45	.287	.392	.352
Artificial Turf	88	23	3	1	0	1	6	8	.261	.318	.330
April	66	9	1	0	0	1	4	9	.136	.152	.197
May	108	34	5	1	1	16	11	5	.315	.407	.375
June	90	22	11	0	0	6	8	9	.244	.367	.306
July	112	30	5	0	2	11	9	10	.268	.366	.317
August	115	34	8	1	0	5	7	7	.296	.383	.341
Sept./Oct.	127	46	12	0	2	21	21	13	.362	.504	.460
Leading Off Inn.	132	34	9	1	0	0	8	9	.258	.341	.305
Runners On	267	85	23	1	3	58	35	22	.318	.446	.395
Bases Empty	351	90	19	1	2	2	25	31	.256	.333	.311
Runners/Scor. Pos.	138	42	14	1	0	49	24	10	.304	.420	.400
Runners On/2 Out	93	26	8	0	0	13	10	9	.280	.366	.356
Scor. Pos./2 Out	57	11	5	0	0	11	10	6	.193	.281	.313
Late-Inning Pressure	65	18	3	0	0	7	9	9	.277	.323	.382
Leading Off	23	4	2	0	0	0	2	2	.174	.261	.269
Runners On	19	8	1	0	0	7	4	1	.421	.474	.522
Runners/Scor. Pos.	10	5	1	0	0	7	2	0	.500	.600	.583

RUNS BATTED IN	From 1B	From 2B	From 3B	Scoring Position
Totals	6/199	22/110	27/56	49/166
Percentage	3.0%	20.0%	48.2%	29.5%

Loves to face: Jim Abbott (.435, 10-for-23)
Jack McDowell (.600, 9-for-15)
Scott Sanderson (.556, 10-for-18, 2 HR)

Hates to face: Kevin Appier (.111, 2-for-18)
Mark Langston (.100, 2-for-20)
David Wells (.118, 2-for-17)

Miscellaneous statistics: Ground outs-to-air outs ratio: 0.96 last season, 0.98 for career.... Grounded into 15 double plays in 153 opportunities (one per 10).... Drove in 22 of 33 runners from third base with less than two outs (67%).... Direction of balls hit to the outfield: 52% to left field, 28% to center, 20% to right.... Base running: Advanced from first base to third on 12 of 42 outfield singles (29%); scored from second on 19 of 23 (83%).... Made 3.03 assists per nine innings at second base.

Comments: Wade Boggs has a career average of one double for every 14.3 at-bats, the fifth highest in American League history, but only the second highest on the current Red Sox roster. The all-time A.L. top five (minimum: 100 doubles): Tris Speaker (one 2B every 12.9 at-bats), Earl Webb (13.0), Hank Greenberg (13.1), Reed (13.8), Boggs (14.3). Webb's name might not be familiar, but he holds the all-time single-season record for doubles; he hit 67 for the Red Sox in 1931. (Thank you, Fenway Park.) Tris Speaker holds the career mark (793).... Reed has hit 76 doubles at Fenway over the past three seasons, 70 of them to left field.... Reed may have had the three most similar consecutive seasons in major league history:

Year	G	AB	R	H	2B	3B	HR	RBI	BB	SO	SB	BA
1989	146	524	76	151	42	2	3	40	73	44	4	.288
1990	155	598	70	173	45	0	5	51	75	65	4	.289
1991	153	618	87	175	42	2	5	60	60	53	6	.283

Get out your *Encyclopedia* and we'll give you some challengers. From recent to distant: Eddie Murray, 1977–79; Ken Reitz, 1974–76; Sam Crawford, 1907–09. And with slightly greater variation, check these players who had *four* consecutive like seasons: Jim Sundberg, 1977–80; Fred Schulte, 1931–34; George McBride, 1910–13.... He's the toughest player in the majors to strike out with the bases loaded, having whiffed only once in 55 career plate appearances with the bags full.

Kevin Reimer
Bats Left

Texas Rangers	AB	H	2B	3B	HR	RBI	BB	SO	BA	SA	OBA
Season	394	106	22	0	20	69	33	93	.269	.477	.332
vs. Left-Handers	36	8	1	0	1	4	2	9	.222	.333	.275
vs. Right-Handers	358	98	21	0	19	65	31	84	.274	.492	.338
vs. Ground-Ballers	198	53	12	0	7	29	14	44	.268	.434	.326
vs. Fly-Ballers	196	53	10	0	13	40	19	49	.270	.520	.338
Home Games	184	50	15	0	13	41	16	56	.272	.565	.335
Road Games	210	56	7	0	7	28	17	37	.267	.400	.329
Grass Fields	324	87	19	0	19	65	26	85	.269	.503	.329
Artificial Turf	70	19	3	0	1	4	7	8	.271	.357	.346
April	39	10	2	0	2	6	2	12	.256	.462	.302
May	59	18	6	0	0	9	6	10	.305	.407	.369
June	65	17	2	0	1	8	6	12	.262	.338	.324
July	53	15	6	0	2	7	3	15	.283	.509	.321
August	101	27	3	0	9	25	8	23	.267	.564	.333
Sept./Oct.	77	19	3	0	6	14	8	21	.247	.519	.330
Leading Off Inn.	81	23	7	0	4	4	6	20	.284	.519	.348
Runners On	191	59	11	0	12	61	21	45	.309	.555	.378
Bases Empty	203	47	11	0	8	8	12	48	.232	.404	.284
Runners/Scor. Pos.	101	29	6	0	9	53	16	33	.287	.614	.371
Runners On/2 Out	91	27	3	0	6	28	10	27	.297	.527	.373
Scor. Pos./2 Out	58	16	3	0	5	26	8	22	.276	.586	.373
Late-Inning Pressure	54	20	3	0	2	5	7	7	.370	.537	.443
Leading Off	11	3	0	0	0	0	1	2	.273	.273	.333
Runners On	24	10	2	0	1	4	5	3	.417	.625	.517
Runners/Scor. Pos.	5	1	0	0	0	2	2	1	.200	.200	.429

RUNS BATTED IN	From 1B	From 2B	From 3B	Scoring Position
Totals	13/146	20/84	16/39	36/123
Percentage	8.9%	23.8%	41.0%	29.3%

Loves to face: Kevin Appier (.500, 2-for-4, 1 2B, 1 HR, 3 BB)
Mike Boddicker (.500, 6-for-12)
Roger Clemens (.500, 3-for-6, 3 BB, 2 SO)

Hates to face: Chris Bosio (.083, 1-for-12)
Jack McDowell (0-for-6, 4 SO)
Todd Stottlemyre (.100, 1-for-10)

Miscellaneous statistics: Ground outs-to-air outs ratio: 1.09 last season, 1.01 for career.... Grounded into 10 double plays in 86 opportunities (one per 8.6).... Drove in 13 of 20 runners from third base with less than two outs (65%).... Direction of balls hit to the outfield: 27% to left field, 28% to center, 45% to right.... Base running: Advanced from first base to third on 2 of 20 outfield singles (10%); scored from second on 9 of 12 (75%).... Made 2.15 putouts per nine innings in left field.

Comments: Major league home-run leaders for August through October: Jose Canseco and Howard Johnson, 16; Cecil Fielder, Darryl Strawberry, and Reimer, 15.... The most similar season at the same age as Reimer (27): Al Ferrara (1967). The most similar seasons by eventual 300-HR hitters: Frank Howard (age 24) and Norm Cash (age 25), both in 1960. Both were considerably younger than Reimer, though.... Our model grants him one chance in 17 to hit 30 home runs this season, and about the same odds for hitting 300 in his career.... Of course, to hit those high notes, Reimer will have to be more than a platoon player. He started 104 games last season, all against right-handed pitchers. In fact, every one of his 23 starts prior to 1991 was against a right-hander as well.... He played 464 innings in the outfield, the most of any A.L. player without an assist. He also played 10 games in the outfield without an assist over three previous seasons.... Hit two pinch-hit home runs last season. Among the 17 other players in franchise history who have done that: Rusty Staub (1980), Roy Sievers (1964), and Don Zimmer (1963). Brant Alyea, Don Lock, Tom McCraw, Darrell Porter, and Rick Reichardt share the franchise record (3). What great names!... Only eight of his 69 RBIs gave the Rangers a lead (12%), the 3d-lowest percentage in the league (minimum: 50 RBIs).... Hasn't stolen a base in 215 major league games; he's been caught four times. See the John Olerud comments for more on this.

Harold Reynolds
Bats Left and Right

Seattle Mariners	AB	H	2B	3B	HR	RBI	BB	SO	BA	SA	OBA
Season	631	160	34	6	3	57	72	63	.254	.341	.332
vs. Left-Handers	174	46	7	0	1	16	17	14	.264	.322	.326
vs. Right-Handers	457	114	27	6	2	41	55	49	.249	.348	.334
vs. Ground-Ballers	276	75	20	1	1	25	33	31	.272	.362	.354
vs. Fly-Ballers	355	85	14	5	2	32	39	32	.239	.324	.315
Home Games	314	94	20	5	1	27	42	27	.299	.404	.387
Road Games	317	66	14	1	2	30	30	36	.208	.278	.276
Grass Fields	238	47	10	0	1	24	26	29	.197	.252	.277
Artificial Turf	393	113	24	6	2	33	46	34	.288	.394	.366
April	85	19	5	0	0	11	6	5	.224	.282	.272
May	110	41	6	1	0	9	12	10	.373	.445	.427
June	98	21	7	0	1	7	17	5	.214	.316	.342
July	109	23	6	1	1	12	12	12	.211	.312	.295
August	109	28	4	1	0	7	12	14	.257	.312	.333
Sept./Oct.	120	28	6	3	1	11	13	17	.233	.358	.309
Leading Off Inn.	150	33	8	3	0	0	22	17	.220	.313	.324
Runners On	260	76	16	1	2	56	23	25	.292	.385	.349
Bases Empty	371	84	18	5	1	1	49	38	.226	.310	.320
Runners/Scor. Pos.	146	47	10	1	1	51	15	15	.322	.411	.379
Runners On/2 Out	94	29	5	1	1	24	14	8	.309	.415	.404
Scor. Pos./2 Out	54	23	4	0	1	22	10	3	.426	.556	.523
Late-Inning Pressure	87	24	4	1	1	12	6	11	.276	.379	.313
Leading Off	22	5	0	1	0	0	1	3	.227	.318	.261
Runners On	34	13	4	0	1	12	3	5	.382	.588	.400
Runners/Scor. Pos.	23	10	3	0	1	12	2	2	.435	.696	.429

RUNS BATTED IN	From 1B	From 2B	From 3B	Scoring Position
Totals	5/181	20/119	29/57	49/176
Percentage	2.8%	16.8%	50.9%	27.8%

Loves to face: Chris Bosio (.625, 10-for-16)
Mark Gubicza (.462, 18-for-39)
Mike Henneman (.545, 6-for-11)

Hates to face: Danny Darwin (.071, 1-for-14, 1 2B)
Ted Higuera (.175, 7-for-40)
Dave Stewart (.107, 6-for-56, 5 BB)

Miscellaneous statistics: Ground outs-to-air outs ratio: 0.98 last season, 1.19 for career.... Grounded into 11 double plays in 133 opportunities (one per 12).... Drove in 17 of 32 runners from third base with less than two outs (53%).... Direction of balls hit to the outfield: 28% to left field, 34% to center, 38% to right batting left-handed; 48% to left field, 23% to center, 30% to right batting right-handed.... Base running: Advanced from first base to third on 21 of 32 outfield singles (66%), 4th-highest rate in A.L.; scored from second on 18 of 22 (82%).... Made 2.97 assists per nine innings at second base.

Comments: The Mariners posted a losing record with Reynolds in the leadoff spot (21–27), but they had a record of 61–50 with him in the two-hole.... Led A.L. second basemen in total fielding chances for the 5th consecutive season. Only two other players in league history have done that: Nellie Fox (nine years, 1952–60), and Horace Clarke (five years, 1968–72).... His batting average moved only two points from 1990 to 1991 (from .252 to .254), the least of any player who qualified for the A.L. batting title in both seasons.... His batting average with two outs and runners in scoring position was highest in the majors last season and highest by a Seattle player since Bruce Bochte hit .457 in 1982.... His 25-game Kingdome hitting streak was the longest of any major leaguer in his home ballpark last season.... His total of air outs was the highest in the league.... The next game he plays at second base will be the 1000th of his career.... Reynolds has finally played on a winner. The current player with the longest streak of seasons with losing teams is now Dale Murphy (eight years).... Let's clean up two related errors from the Reynolds comments in last year's edition. The longest streak of losing seasons ever: 16 years, by Cy Williams (1915–30). The longest career spent entirely with losing teams: 12 years, by Dan Meyer (1974–85) and Bruce Bochte (1974–82, 1984–86), both of whom spent five years with the M's.

Ernest Riles
Bats Left

Oakland A's	AB	H	2B	3B	HR	RBI	BB	SO	BA	SA	OBA
Season	281	60	8	4	5	32	31	42	.214	.324	.290
vs. Left-Handers	21	3	0	0	0	1	0	2	.143	.143	.143
vs. Right-Handers	260	57	8	4	5	31	31	40	.219	.338	.301
vs. Ground-Ballers	143	30	4	0	2	15	19	20	.210	.280	.303
vs. Fly-Ballers	138	30	4	4	3	17	12	22	.217	.370	.276
Home Games	148	35	7	1	3	18	18	25	.236	.358	.319
Road Games	133	25	1	3	2	14	13	17	.188	.286	.258
Grass Fields	247	55	8	3	5	29	25	35	.223	.340	.293
Artificial Turf	34	5	0	1	0	3	6	7	.147	.206	.268
April	44	10	0	1	1	2	7	7	.227	.341	.333
May	72	19	1	2	1	13	7	9	.264	.375	.329
June	55	16	4	0	1	7	9	7	.291	.418	.385
July	58	5	1	0	1	5	5	8	.086	.155	.156
August	24	3	1	0	0	0	1	4	.125	.167	.160
Sept./Oct.	28	7	1	1	1	5	2	7	.250	.464	.300
Leading Off Inn.	67	10	1	1	1	1	8	12	.149	.239	.240
Runners On	117	29	3	1	4	31	18	16	.248	.393	.343
Bases Empty	164	31	5	3	1	1	13	26	.189	.274	.249
Runners/Scor. Pos.	72	20	2	1	2	27	9	10	.278	.417	.349
Runners On/2 Out	52	15	2	1	3	18	7	6	.288	.538	.373
Scor. Pos./2 Out	30	10	2	1	1	14	3	3	.333	.567	.394
Late-Inning Pressure	48	12	1	1	2	9	6	12	.250	.438	.327
Leading Off	12	2	0	1	0	0	0	3	.167	.333	.167
Runners On	21	8	1	0	2	9	5	6	.381	.714	.481
Runners/Scor. Pos.	13	5	0	0	1	7	5	4	.385	.615	.526

RUNS BATTED IN	From 1B	From 2B	From 3B	Scoring Position
Totals	5/84	10/59	12/27	22/86
Percentage	6.0%	16.9%	44.4%	25.6%

Loves to face: Scott Bailes (.500, 5-for-10, 1 HR)
Bill Gullickson (.467, 7-for-15, 2 HR)
Terry Mathews (.600, 3-for-5, 2 2B, 1 3B)

Hates to face: Kirk McCaskill (.136, 3-for-22)
Ben McDonald (0-for-7)
Frank Wills (0-for-7)

Miscellaneous statistics: Ground outs-to-air outs ratio: 1.17 last season, 1.41 for career.... Grounded into 8 double plays in 54 opportunities (one per 6.8).... Drove in 6 of 11 runners from third base with less than two outs (55%).... Direction of balls hit to the outfield: 28% to left field, 34% to center, 37% to right.... Base running: Advanced from first base to third on 3 of 7 outfield singles (43%); scored from second on 6 of 6 (100%).... Made 1.87 assists per nine innings at third base.

Comments: Compiled a .270 batting average over his first five seasons in the majors, never batting below .252. But he has batted .200 and .214 in the past two seasons; his combined .209 mark is the 3d lowest in the majors during that period (minimum: 400 AB). See the Dave Valle comments for the bottom five.... That's particularly surprising in that he faced those hated left-handed pitchers only 34 times since 1990, compared to an average of 88 times per season from 1985 through 1990. His career batting averages: .214 vs. left-handers, .268 vs. right-handers (.284 through 1989, .211 since 1990).... His July batting average was the lowest in the majors last season.... Has hit a grand-slam home run in each of the past three seasons, although he's batted with the bags full only 19 times during that period.... Did you realize that all three DiMaggio brothers played for the San Francisco Seals of the Pacific Coast League in the 1930s? Even if you knew that one, you may not know that all three Alou brothers played for both Bay Area major league teams—a remarkable coincidence, we'd say.... Riles is one of 41 players to wear both uniforms since the teams moved west; others still playing there include Dave Henderson, Willie McGee, and Darren Lewis. The eight besides Riles who played at least 100 games for both San Francisco and Oakland: Felipe and Jesus (but not Matty), Dusty, Vida, Kong, Little Joe, and, um, does anyone know any nicknames for Dave Heaverlo or Billy North?

Billy Ripken
Bats Right

Baltimore Orioles	AB	H	2B	3B	HR	RBI	BB	SO	BA	SA	OBA
Season	287	62	11	1	0	14	15	31	.216	.261	.253
vs. Left-Handers	100	27	4	0	0	7	5	9	.270	.310	.302
vs. Right-Handers	187	35	7	1	0	7	10	22	.187	.235	.227
vs. Ground-Ballers	139	29	2	1	0	7	6	12	.209	.237	.240
vs. Fly-Ballers	148	33	9	0	0	7	9	19	.223	.284	.266
Home Games	126	27	5	1	0	8	7	18	.214	.270	.254
Road Games	161	35	6	0	0	6	8	13	.217	.255	.253
Grass Fields	248	53	9	1	0	12	12	29	.214	.258	.248
Artificial Turf	39	9	2	0	0	2	3	2	.231	.282	.286
April	42	8	0	0	0	2	3	4	.190	.190	.244
May	69	14	3	0	0	4	2	7	.203	.246	.222
June	51	15	3	0	0	4	2	7	.294	.353	.315
July	28	4	1	0	0	0	3	2	.143	.179	.226
August	33	8	1	0	0	1	2	7	.242	.273	.286
Sept./Oct.	64	13	3	1	0	3	3	4	.203	.281	.239
Leading Off Inn.	77	18	3	0	0	0	5	6	.234	.273	.280
Runners On	109	21	5	0	0	14	4	12	.193	.239	.217
Bases Empty	178	41	6	1	0	0	11	19	.230	.275	.275
Runners/Scor. Pos.	58	12	3	0	0	13	2	7	.207	.259	.226
Runners On/2 Out	52	14	4	0	0	8	2	8	.269	.346	.296
Scor. Pos./2 Out	28	8	2	0	0	7	2	5	.286	.357	.333
Late-Inning Pressure	22	5	0	0	0	0	1	1	.227	.227	.261
Leading Off	12	4	0	0	0	0	0	0	.333	.333	.333
Runners On	4	0	0	0	0	0	0	0	.000	.000	.000
Runners/Scor. Pos.	1	0	0	0	0	0	0	0	.000	.000	.000

RUNS BATTED IN	From 1B	From 2B	From 3B	Scoring Position
Totals	1/86	5/46	8/24	13/70
Percentage	1.2%	10.9%	33.3%	18.6%

Loves to face: Mark Langston (.375, 9-for-24)
Bill Wegman (.750, 6-for-8)
David Wells (.417, 5-for-12, 1 HR)

Hates to face: Mark Gubicza (.059, 1-for-17, 4 BB)
Jack McDowell (.077, 1-for-13)
Walt Terrell (0-for-13)

Miscellaneous statistics: Ground outs-to-air outs ratio: 1.60 last season, 1.55 for career.... Grounded into 14 double plays in 55 opportunities (one per 3.9), 2d-worst rate in A.L.... Drove in 6 of 15 runners from third base with less than two outs (40%).... Direction of balls hit to the outfield: 28% to left field, 35% to center, 37% to right.... Base running: Advanced from first base to third on 6 of 12 outfield singles (50%); scored from second on 3 of 4 (75%).... Made 3.09 assists per nine innings at second base.

Comments: Hit no home runs and stole no bases, but got 287 at-bats despite a .216 batting average. Over the past 50 years, only three other players batted that often despite no homers, no steals, and a batting average as low as Billy's: Dal Maxvill in 1970 (.201 in 399 ABs), Fred Kendall in 1975 (.199 in 286 ABs), and Houston Jimenez in 1984 (.201 in 298 ABs).... Only three players in franchise history had more at-bats in a homerless season: Mark Belanger (1971, 1973, and 1978), Willie Miranda (1957), and Alan Wiggins (1986).... Was allowed to bat only twice with runners in scoring position in Late-Inning Pressure Situations; he was removed for a pinch hitter four times in those situations.... He's a career .247 hitter who's batted above .290 twice and below .220 twice, but in between only once.... Has batted at least 20 points higher against left-handed pitchers than against right-handers in each of his five seasons. Career batting averages: .277 vs. LHP, .231 vs. RHP.... His 14 career plate appearances against Roger Clemens are the most of any active player who has never been struck out by him.... Six other pairs of brothers played in the majors last season: Roberto and Sandy Alomar, George and Juan Bell, Chris and Tony Gwynn, Al and Mark Leiter, Greg and Mike Maddux, and Melido and Pascual Perez.... In memoriam of *The National*'s "Three of a Kind": Billy Ripken, Ted Kennedy, Steve Albert.

Cal Ripken
Bats Right

Baltimore Orioles	AB	H	2B	3B	HR	RBI	BB	SO	BA	SA	OBA
Season	650	210	46	5	34	114	53	46	.323	.566	.374
vs. Left-Handers	164	57	14	2	12	31	19	15	.348	.677	.411
vs. Right-Handers	486	153	32	3	22	83	34	31	.315	.529	.361
vs. Ground-Ballers	287	86	20	2	13	48	21	23	.300	.519	.349
vs. Fly-Ballers	363	124	26	3	21	66	32	23	.342	.603	.393
Home Games	315	90	19	1	16	52	28	23	.286	.505	.343
Road Games	335	120	27	4	18	62	25	23	.358	.624	.403
Grass Fields	550	173	35	4	31	96	41	42	.315	.562	.364
Artificial Turf	100	37	11	1	3	18	12	4	.370	.590	.426
April	68	23	3	1	5	20	6	6	.338	.632	.408
May	106	37	7	0	7	15	12	6	.349	.613	.412
June	116	43	10	1	5	16	9	7	.371	.603	.417
July	110	27	6	0	5	15	8	7	.245	.436	.300
August	115	38	10	1	4	21	8	8	.330	.539	.370
Sept./Oct.	135	42	10	2	8	27	10	12	.311	.593	.351
Leading Off Inn.	114	36	7	0	9	9	4	4	.316	.614	.345
Runners On	292	94	23	3	13	93	34	22	.322	.555	.388
Bases Empty	358	116	23	2	21	21	19	24	.324	.575	.361
Runners/Scor. Pos.	149	47	13	2	5	70	28	15	.315	.530	.410
Runners On/2 Out	102	31	7	0	5	28	21	5	.304	.520	.432
Scor. Pos./2 Out	55	16	5	0	2	20	18	3	.291	.491	.480
Late-Inning Pressure	89	31	4	1	4	8	13	4	.348	.551	.427
Leading Off	25	12	2	0	2	2	1	1	.480	.800	.500
Runners On	35	9	0	0	0	4	10	2	.257	.257	.413
Runners/Scor. Pos.	19	4	0	0	0	4	9	2	.211	.211	.448

RUNS BATTED IN	From 1B	From 2B	From 3B	Scoring Position
Totals	23/215	23/106	34/65	57/171
Percentage	10.7%	21.7%	52.3%	33.3%

Loves to face: Chuck Crim (.533, 8-for-15, 1 HR)
Frank Viola (.328, 21-for-64, 4 HR)
David Wells (.412, 7-for-17, 2 2B, 3 HR)
Hates to face: Chuck Finley (.179, 7-for-39, 1 HR)
Juan Guzman (0-for-8)
Dan Plesac (.133, 2-for-15)

Miscellaneous statistics: Ground outs-to-air outs ratio: 1.16 last season, 1.01 for career.... Grounded into 19 double plays in 151 opportunities (one per 7.9).... Drove in 25 of 40 runners from third base with less than two outs (63%).... Direction of balls hit to the outfield: 41% to left field, 32% to center, 27% to right.... Base running: Advanced from first base to third on 17 of 37 outfield singles (46%); scored from second on 8 of 12 (67%).... Made 3.33 assists per nine innings at shortstop, 3d-highest rate in A.L.

Comments: Became the eighth player to hit 20 home runs in 10 consecutive seasons starting with his rookie year. The others: Rocky Colavito, Joe DiMaggio, Reggie Jackson, Eddie Mathews (whose 14-year streak was the longest), Frank Robinson, Billy Williams, and Ted Williams.... Played all but 30 of the Orioles' innings at shortstop last season, playing 146 games in their entirety.... As in 1990, he led A.L. shortstops in fielding percentage. No one has done that for three straight years since Luis Aparicio's eight-year streak (1959–66).... His 73-point increase from 1990 to 1991 (.250 to .323) was the largest of any player who qualified for the batting title in both years.... His rate of one strikeout for every 15.6 plate appearances was 7th best in the American League. Over the past 35 years, only one other player had a rate that low in a season of 30 or more home runs: Don Mattingly (in 1985, 1986, and 1987).... First Orioles player to lead the league in total bases or extra-base hits since Frank Robinson won the Triple Crown in 1966.... His total of 85 extra-base hits was one short of the all-time record for shortstops, set by Robin Yount in 1982.... Career total of 1638 games ranks seventh in franchise history. Assuming he plays 162 games this season (has that ever been written of anyone else?), he will move into 4th place, behind Eddie Murray, Mark Belanger, and Brooks Robinson.... His career fielding rate of one error every 45 chances at shortstop is better than Mark Belanger's (one every 43 chances).

Luis Rivera
Bats Right

Boston Red Sox	AB	H	2B	3B	HR	RBI	BB	SO	BA	SA	OBA
Season	414	107	22	3	8	40	35	86	.258	.384	.318
vs. Left-Handers	108	34	10	1	4	16	6	25	.315	.537	.356
vs. Right-Handers	306	73	12	2	4	24	29	61	.239	.330	.305
vs. Ground-Ballers	193	47	11	2	4	20	17	42	.244	.383	.307
vs. Fly-Ballers	221	60	11	1	4	20	18	44	.271	.385	.328
Home Games	204	52	13	0	4	16	23	43	.255	.377	.336
Road Games	210	55	9	3	4	24	12	43	.262	.390	.300
Grass Fields	348	91	18	2	7	35	33	78	.261	.385	.328
Artificial Turf	66	16	4	1	1	5	2	8	.242	.379	.261
April	13	2	0	0	0	1	0	2	.154	.154	.154
May	82	24	7	2	3	14	13	17	.293	.537	.392
June	62	17	4	0	1	4	7	12	.274	.387	.348
July	90	27	6	1	2	7	10	16	.300	.456	.363
August	75	14	2	0	1	4	2	18	.187	.253	.218
Sept./Oct.	92	23	3	0	1	10	3	21	.250	.315	.273
Leading Off Inn.	100	30	7	0	2	2	9	19	.300	.430	.369
Runners On	180	42	11	0	2	34	19	37	.233	.328	.300
Bases Empty	234	65	11	3	6	6	16	49	.278	.427	.332
Runners/Scor. Pos.	109	22	5	0	2	33	17	25	.202	.303	.300
Runners On/2 Out	82	19	3	0	1	16	8	13	.232	.305	.300
Scor. Pos./2 Out	53	12	1	0	1	15	7	9	.226	.302	.317
Late-Inning Pressure	37	8	1	0	1	3	4	9	.216	.324	.293
Leading Off	14	5	1	0	1	1	1	2	.357	.643	.400
Runners On	14	2	0	0	0	2	2	4	.143	.143	.250
Runners/Scor. Pos.	9	1	0	0	0	2	2	4	.111	.111	.273

RUNS BATTED IN	From 1B	From 2B	From 3B	Scoring Position
Totals	3/122	17/92	12/36	29/128
Percentage	2.5%	18.5%	33.3%	22.7%

Loves to face: Alex Fernandez (.462, 6-for-13, 1 HR)
Tim Leary (.700, 7-for-10, 1 HR)
Kenny Rogers (.455, 5-for-11, 3 2B, 1 3B)
Hates to face: Luis Aquino (.100, 2-for-20)
Dave Johnson (.125, 2-for-16)
Nolan Ryan (0-for-10)

Miscellaneous statistics: Ground outs-to-air outs ratio: 1.02 last season, 0.89 for career.... Grounded into 10 double plays in 78 opportunities (one per 7.8).... Drove in 7 of 15 runners from third base with less than two outs (47%).... Direction of balls hit to the outfield: 37% to left field, 28% to center, 35% to right.... Base running: Advanced from first base to third on 10 of 27 outfield singles (37%); scored from second on 12 of 16 (75%).... Made 3.16 assists per nine innings at shortstop.

Comments: His average of one error every 25 chances was the worst of any shortstop in the majors last season (minimum: 100 games). The major league average for shortstops was one error every 32 chances.... He became the first Red Sox shortstop to lead the league in errors since Eddie Bressoud did it in 1962.... At least he cleaned up his act in Late-Inning Pressure Situations, with only one error in 77 chances, compared to eight in 91 chances in LIPS in 1990.... His August batting average was 7th lowest in the league.... Had the same number of extra-base hits as Carlos Quintana, but in 64 fewer at-bats.... Rivera's eight home runs were the most by a Red Sox shortstop since 1980, when Rick Burleson hit eight. The last Boston shortstop to reach double figures: Rico Petrocelli in 1970 (29).... Has stranded one more runner at third base with less than two outs (41) than he's driven in (40) during his six-year career. In Late-Inning Pressure Situations, he's even worse: 5-for-15 (33%).... Rivera and Spike Owen changed jobs, in effect, after the 1988 season. During the three years since they traded places, their offensive performances have been similar, with a slight edge to Rivera. His batting average is six points higher (.247 to .241), he's hit six more home runs, and driven in 12 more runs than Owen. Spike scored nine more runs than Luis, and stole three more bases.

Ivan Rodriguez
Bats Right

Texas Rangers	AB	H	2B	3B	HR	RBI	BB	SO	BA	SA	OBA
Season	280	74	16	0	3	27	5	42	.264	.354	.276
vs. Left-Handers	71	17	6	0	1	9	2	9	.239	.366	.260
vs. Right-Handers	209	57	10	0	2	18	3	33	.273	.349	.282
vs. Ground-Ballers	129	36	10	0	1	14	1	14	.279	.380	.282
vs. Fly-Ballers	151	38	6	0	2	13	4	28	.252	.331	.271
Home Games	135	32	9	0	3	18	2	23	.237	.370	.248
Road Games	145	42	7	0	0	9	3	19	.290	.338	.302
Grass Fields	239	67	14	0	3	26	4	36	.280	.377	.291
Artificial Turf	41	7	2	0	0	1	1	6	.171	.220	.190
April	0	0	0	0	0	0	0	0	—	—	—
May	0	0	0	0	0	0	0	0	—	—	—
June	37	14	2	0	0	4	0	5	.378	.432	.368
July	83	22	6	0	0	6	2	8	.265	.337	.282
August	80	19	4	0	1	8	0	15	.237	.325	.237
Sept./Oct.	80	19	4	0	2	9	3	14	.237	.363	.265
Leading Off Inn.	63	15	2	0	2	2	0	5	.238	.365	.238
Runners On	123	37	9	0	1	25	3	15	.301	.398	.315
Bases Empty	157	37	7	0	2	2	2	27	.236	.318	.245
Runners/Scor. Pos.	51	17	4	0	1	23	1	8	.333	.471	.340
Runners On/2 Out	48	11	3	0	0	10	0	6	.229	.292	.229
Scor. Pos./2 Out	24	7	1	0	0	8	0	3	.292	.333	.292
Late-Inning Pressure	37	8	0	0	0	1	2	7	.216	.216	.256
Leading Off	8	1	0	0	0	0	0	1	.125	.125	.125
Runners On	17	5	0	0	0	1	2	2	.294	.294	.368
Runners/Scor. Pos.	6	1	0	0	0	1	0	1	.167	.167	.167

RUNS BATTED IN	From 1B	From 2B	From 3B	Scoring Position
Totals	3/99	12/43	9/22	21/65
Percentage	3.0%	27.9%	40.9%	32.3%

Loves to face: Chris Bosio (.500, 3-for-6, 2 SO)
Eric King (.500, 3-for-6, 2 2B)

Hates to face: Tom Gordon (0-for-4, 3 SO)

Miscellaneous statistics: Ground outs-to-air outs ratio: 1.57 last season, 1.57 for career.... Grounded into 10 double plays in 66 opportunities (one per 6.6).... Drove in 6 of 12 runners from third base with less than two outs (50%).... Direction of balls hit to the outfield: 30% to left field, 31% to center, 39% to right.... Base running: Advanced from first base to third on 2 of 11 outfield singles (18%); scored from second on 7 of 10 (70%).... Opposing base stealers: 36-for-70 (51%), lowest rate in A.L.

Comments: Last season's pairings of Goose Gossage and Nolan Ryan as batterymates with Rodriguez were the first cases of pitchers in their forties throwing to a catcher in his teens since 1963, when the Angels had a battery of Art Fowler and Ed Kirkpatrick. The only others over the past 40 years: Dizzy Trout to Frank Zupo (1957 Orioles) and Dutch Leonard to Harry Chiti (1952 Cubs). There were only two instances since World War II of a teenage pitcher throwing to a 40-year-old catcher: Bob Miller and Lindy McDaniel to Walker Cooper (1957 Cardinals).... Rodriguez was the 2d-youngest player in the majors last season. Born November 30, 1971, he is nine days older than Todd Van Poppel.... Caught 88 games, one fewer than Frankie Hayes in 1934. Hayes was the only other teenager in baseball history to catch as many as 80 games in a season.... The Rangers had a losing record with Rodriguez starting behind the plate (40–41), but a winning record with each of their other three catchers: Geno Petralli (23–22), John Russell (2–0), and Mike Stanley (20–14).... But as advertised, Ivan easily bested his Rangers competition when it came to opponents' stolen-base percentage: Rodriguez, 51 percent; Petralli, 68 percent; Stanley, 83 percent.... Although he caught only 88 games, his total of 62 assists was only six fewer than the league leader (B. J. Surhoff).... His batting average was 3d highest among A.L. rookies with at least 200 at-bats last season.... Only two of his 27 RBIs gave the Rangers a lead.

Steve Sax
Bats Right

New York Yankees	AB	H	2B	3B	HR	RBI	BB	SO	BA	SA	OBA
Season	652	198	38	2	10	56	41	38	.304	.414	.345
vs. Left-Handers	215	74	20	0	5	20	17	6	.344	.507	.390
vs. Right-Handers	437	124	18	2	5	36	24	32	.284	.368	.322
vs. Ground-Ballers	309	82	11	0	4	24	24	22	.265	.340	.316
vs. Fly-Ballers	343	116	27	2	6	32	17	16	.338	.481	.371
Home Games	327	95	20	1	6	27	25	19	.291	.413	.340
Road Games	325	103	18	1	4	29	16	19	.317	.415	.350
Grass Fields	555	166	33	2	10	48	36	32	.299	.420	.341
Artificial Turf	97	32	5	0	0	8	5	6	.330	.381	.368
April	74	21	1	0	1	11	5	7	.284	.338	.329
May	111	24	6	0	1	8	8	6	.216	.297	.264
June	112	39	7	0	1	8	8	5	.348	.438	.393
July	86	28	7	0	3	8	7	4	.326	.512	.383
August	126	39	7	1	0	9	8	8	.310	.381	.350
Sept./Oct.	143	47	10	1	4	12	5	8	.329	.497	.349
Leading Off Inn.	187	63	12	1	4	4	9	6	.337	.476	.367
Runners On	236	68	13	0	3	49	16	16	.288	.381	.331
Bases Empty	416	130	25	2	7	7	25	22	.313	.433	.353
Runners/Scor. Pos.	132	42	8	0	2	44	10	11	.318	.424	.351
Runners On/2 Out	94	24	8	0	2	19	5	7	.255	.404	.307
Scor. Pos./2 Out	65	16	5	0	1	15	4	7	.246	.369	.290
Late-Inning Pressure	94	22	3	0	1	6	3	7	.234	.298	.255
Leading Off	24	8	0	0	1	1	1	1	.333	.458	.360
Runners On	34	6	1	0	0	5	0	4	.176	.206	.171
Runners/Scor. Pos.	19	2	0	0	0	4	0	2	.105	.105	.100

RUNS BATTED IN	From 1B	From 2B	From 3B	Scoring Position
Totals	5/159	15/103	26/58	41/161
Percentage	3.1%	14.6%	44.8%	25.5%

Loves to face: Roger Clemens (.382, 13-for-34, 1 HR)
Jimmy Key (.476, 10-for-21)
Dave Stewart (.526, 10-for-19)

Hates to face: John Dopson (.087, 2-for-23, 3 BB)
Brian Holman (.152, 5-for-33)
Randy Johnson (.056, 1-for-18, 1 2B, 2 BB)

Miscellaneous statistics: Ground outs-to-air outs ratio: 1.60 last season, 1.94 for career.... Grounded into 15 double plays in 112 opportunities (one per 7.5).... Drove in 20 of 30 runners from third base with less than two outs (67%).... Direction of balls hit to the outfield: 36% to left field, 33% to center, 31% to right.... Base running: Advanced from first base to third on 18 of 43 outfield singles (42%); scored from second on 18 of 20 (90%).... Made 3.06 assists per nine innings at second base.

Comments: Made a spectacular stretch run only to fall two hits short of the 200 mark when he went 0-for-4 in the finale. Had 26 hits in 13 games leading up to that point.... His 44-point increase from 1990 to 1991 (.260 to .304) was the 4th largest of any player who qualified for the batting title in both seasons.... Was batting as low as .231 as late as May 27.... Spent the first two months of the season grounding out to the right side, the next two spanking hits to left field. Contrast these figures: April–May—29 right-side ground outs, 14 hits to left; June–July—16 right-side ground outs, 30 hits to left.... June batting average was 7th highest in the league.... Finished the season with 40 hits and only one strikeout in his last 99 at-bats against left-handed pitchers. His season average vs. southpaws was 8th highest in the league.... Average of one strikeout every 18.6 plate appearances was 2d best in the A.L.... Had more than 600 ABs and fewer than 50 strikeouts in each of his three seasons with the Yankees. Four other Yankees had three-year streaks: Earle Combs (1926–28), Bobby Richardson (6 years, 1961–66), Horace Clarke (1969–71), and Don Mattingly (1984–86)... Had the most ground outs of any player in the majors.... His 71-game errorless streak was the longest by any A.L. second baseman last season. (Of course, you can't make an error on a ball you can't reach.) It equaled the longest by a second baseman in Yankees history, set in 1948 by Snuffy Stirnweiss.

Dick Schofield
Bats Right

California Angels	AB	H	2B	3B	HR	RBI	BB	SO	BA	SA	OBA
Season	427	96	9	3	0	31	50	69	.225	.260	.310
vs. Left-Handers	115	21	1	0	0	8	22	15	.183	.191	.314
vs. Right-Handers	312	75	8	3	0	23	28	54	.240	.285	.309
vs. Ground-Ballers	199	53	3	2	0	14	22	28	.266	.302	.342
vs. Fly-Ballers	228	43	6	1	0	17	28	41	.189	.224	.283
Home Games	211	44	4	1	0	19	22	29	.209	.237	.286
Road Games	216	52	5	2	0	12	28	40	.241	.282	.333
Grass Fields	358	82	8	3	0	29	37	53	.229	.268	.307
Artificial Turf	69	14	1	0	0	2	13	16	.203	.217	.329
April	51	14	0	0	0	2	10	10	.275	.275	.403
May	63	16	4	1	0	9	5	10	.254	.349	.319
June	72	19	2	0	0	6	12	10	.264	.292	.369
July	73	17	2	0	0	6	6	9	.233	.260	.291
August	85	15	0	0	0	3	11	12	.176	.176	.278
Sept./Oct.	83	15	1	2	0	5	6	18	.181	.241	.236
Leading Off Inn.	105	15	0	2	0	0	10	17	.143	.181	.231
Runners On	185	53	5	0	0	31	27	24	.286	.314	.380
Bases Empty	242	43	4	3	0	0	23	45	.178	.219	.255
Runners/Scor. Pos.	110	28	3	0	0	31	21	15	.255	.282	.374
Runners On/2 Out	64	19	2	0	0	15	14	7	.297	.328	.430
Scor. Pos./2 Out	46	13	2	0	0	15	12	4	.283	.326	.431
Late-Inning Pressure	59	12	1	0	0	3	7	12	.203	.220	.299
Leading Off	17	1	0	0	0	0	2	4	.059	.059	.158
Runners On	23	8	1	0	0	3	5	4	.348	.391	.483
Runners/Scor. Pos.	11	3	0	0	0	3	5	1	.273	.273	.500

RUNS BATTED IN	From 1B	From 2B	From 3B	Scoring Position
Totals	0/112	14/82	17/46	31/128
Percentage	0.0%	17.1%	37.0%	24.2%

Loves to face: Allan Anderson (.444, 8-for-18)
Jeff Ballard (.450, 9-for-20, 1 HR)
Matt Young (.357, 5-for-14, 1 HR)
Hates to face: Mark Gubicza (0-for-27)
Tom Henke (0-for-11)
Nolan Ryan (0-for-13, 9 SO)

Miscellaneous statistics: Ground outs-to-air outs ratio: 0.90 last season, 0.92 for career.... Grounded into 3 double plays in 90 opportunities (one per 30).... Drove in 10 of 20 runners from third base with less than two outs (50%).... Direction of balls hit to the outfield: 29% to left field, 29% to center, 43% to right.... Base running: Advanced from first base to third on 7 of 22 outfield singles (32%); scored from second on 11 of 13 (85%).... Made 3.13 assists per nine innings at shortstop.

Comments: His 1060 games are the most of any Angels player who never played a game for another club. His skipper, Buck Rodgers, ranks second on that list (932).... Those two are neck-and-neck at the top of another franchise list: Among the top 30 players in Angels history in terms of at-bats, Schofield and The Skip have the two lowest batting averages and are separated by the margin of a single AB—Schofield, .23210; Rodgers, .23211. (Nice touch, not to embarrass the manager, don't you think?)... Schofield's August batting average was 6th lowest in the league last season.... Of his 96 hits, 39 were to the opposite field (41%), the 4th-highest percentage in the majors (minimum: 60 hits).... Batting average vs. left-handed pitchers was 2d lowest in the league.... He's hit for a higher average against ground-ball pitchers than he has against fly-ballers in each of his nine seasons in the majors. Only one player in *Player Analysis* history had a longer streak (Roy Smalley, 13 years). Schofield's career breakdown: .259 vs. ground-ballers, .213 vs. fly-ballers.... He has driven in only 47 percent of runners from third base with less than two outs during his career, the 3d-lowest rate of any active player (minimum: 150 opportunities).... Bad news: His home-run output has dropped in every season since his career high of 13 in 1986. Worse news: No player has had a longer streak since Curt Blefary (1967–72). Good news: Scho can't go any lower.

Kevin Seitzer
Bats Right

Kansas City Royals	AB	H	2B	3B	HR	RBI	BB	SO	BA	SA	OBA
Season	234	62	11	3	1	25	29	21	.265	.350	.350
vs. Left-Handers	66	22	3	0	1	7	11	3	.333	.424	.429
vs. Right-Handers	168	40	8	3	0	18	18	18	.238	.321	.317
vs. Ground-Ballers	105	28	5	1	1	10	9	11	.267	.362	.328
vs. Fly-Ballers	129	34	6	2	0	15	20	10	.264	.341	.367
Home Games	117	32	7	2	0	15	11	10	.274	.368	.344
Road Games	117	30	4	1	1	10	18	11	.256	.333	.356
Grass Fields	108	29	4	1	1	10	15	9	.269	.352	.358
Artificial Turf	126	33	7	2	0	15	14	12	.262	.349	.343
April	55	10	3	0	0	8	4	8	.182	.236	.258
May	3	1	0	0	0	1	0	0	.333	.333	.333
June	93	26	4	1	1	8	16	5	.280	.376	.385
July	47	14	1	2	0	5	7	7	.298	.404	.389
August	23	6	2	0	0	2	2	0	.261	.348	.320
Sept./Oct.	13	5	1	0	0	1	0	1	.385	.462	.385
Leading Off Inn.	43	10	3	0	0	0	3	7	.233	.302	.298
Runners On	102	30	3	3	0	24	14	6	.294	.382	.381
Bases Empty	132	32	8	0	1	1	15	15	.242	.326	.324
Runners/Scor. Pos.	66	16	2	0	0	23	11	5	.242	.333	.354
Runners On/2 Out	47	11	1	2	0	12	7	3	.234	.340	.333
Scor. Pos./2 Out	35	8	0	2	0	12	4	3	.229	.343	.308
Late-Inning Pressure	41	14	2	0	0	2	4	3	.341	.390	.400
Leading Off	10	4	0	0	0	0	1	2	.400	.400	.455
Runners On	15	3	0	0	0	2	3	1	.200	.200	.333
Runners/Scor. Pos.	11	1	0	0	0	2	3	1	.091	.091	.286

RUNS BATTED IN	From 1B	From 2B	From 3B	Scoring Position
Totals	4/70	7/48	13/29	20/77
Percentage	5.7%	14.6%	44.8%	26.0%

Loves to face: Greg Cadaret (.500, 6-for-12, 1 HR)
Mike Flanagan (.467, 7-for-15, 6 BB)
Erik Hanson (.545, 6-for-11)
Hates to face: Scott Bankhead (0-for-11)
Scott Erickson (0-for-8)
Jack McDowell (.071, 1-for-14, 3 BB)

Miscellaneous statistics: Ground outs-to-air outs ratio: 1.31 last season, 1.44 for career.... Grounded into 4 double plays in 41 opportunities (one per 10).... Drove in 8 of 13 runners from third base with less than two outs (62%).... Direction of balls hit to the outfield: 26% to left field, 36% to center, 38% to right.... Base running: Advanced from first base to third on 9 of 14 outfield singles (64%), 5th-highest rate in A.L.; scored from second on 6 of 7 (86%).... Made 2.20 assists per nine innings at third base.

Comments: Someone get this man a parachute. His once promising career has plummeted, with four consecutive batting-average declines; year by year since his outstanding rookie season of 1987: .323, .304, .281, .275, .265.... The only other players whose averages have fallen in each of the past four seasons (minimum: 200 AB): Scott Fletcher, Andres Galarraga, Pete Incaviglia, and Mitch Webster.... His career batting average still stands at .294, with marks above .290 against both left-handers and right-handers.... Following his sophomore season, our model projected his chances of reaching the 2000-hit mark as one in eight; the odds against that happening now are more than 60-to-1.... The most comparable player at the same age as Seitzer: Ken Oberkfell, following the 1985 season. Three years ago, we'd have suggested Ken Griffey, Sr.... Things could worsen should those trade rumors prove to be true: Seitzer has hit for a higher average at Royals Stadium than he has on the road in each of his six seasons in the majors. Career breakdown: .321 at Royals Stadium, .268 on the road. The only active players who've gained more at home (minimum: 2000 AB): Wade Boggs (71 points, .381/.310); Kirby Puckett (58, .349/.291); and Jerry Browne (57, .297/.240).... Has never hit a triple or a home run in 360 at-bats in Late-Inning Pressure Situations. He's hit one per 42 "unpressured" ABs.... Career average of .556 (15-for-27, 0 HR) as a pinch hitter.

Terry Shumpert

Bats Right

Kansas City Royals	AB	H	2B	3B	HR	RBI	BB	SO	BA	SA	OBA
Season	369	80	16	4	5	34	30	75	.217	.322	.283
vs. Left-Handers	135	28	6	0	2	12	9	25	.207	.296	.277
vs. Right-Handers	234	52	10	4	3	22	21	50	.222	.338	.286
vs. Ground-Ballers	167	31	7	3	0	15	16	34	.186	.263	.262
vs. Fly-Ballers	202	49	9	1	5	19	14	41	.243	.371	.300
Home Games	183	40	8	3	1	16	14	35	.219	.311	.282
Road Games	186	40	8	1	4	18	16	40	.215	.333	.283
Grass Fields	144	30	6	0	4	15	15	32	.208	.333	.286
Artificial Turf	225	50	10	4	1	19	15	43	.222	.316	.280
April	51	9	1	1	0	5	3	13	.176	.235	.218
May	55	14	4	1	0	4	3	9	.255	.364	.300
June	67	12	1	0	3	8	7	12	.179	.328	.253
July	75	18	2	1	1	8	6	9	.240	.333	.305
August	67	20	5	1	0	4	10	17	.299	.403	.397
Sept./Oct.	54	7	3	0	1	5	1	15	.130	.241	.175
Leading Off Inn.	89	19	4	2	2	2	9	23	.213	.371	.307
Runners On	162	34	5	1	1	30	11	30	.210	.272	.264
Bases Empty	207	46	11	3	4	4	19	45	.222	.362	.297
Runners/Scor. Pos.	94	25	3	1	0	27	9	21	.266	.319	.333
Runners On/2 Out	68	16	2	1	0	15	6	11	.235	.294	.316
Scor. Pos./2 Out	48	16	2	1	0	15	4	7	.333	.417	.407
Late-Inning Pressure	36	6	1	1	0	0	4	9	.167	.250	.250
Leading Off	8	2	0	1	0	0	2	2	.250	.500	.400
Runners On	12	0	0	0	0	0	1	3	.000	.000	.077
Runners/Scor. Pos.	5	0	0	0	0	0	0	1	.000	.000	.000

RUNS BATTED IN	From 1B	From 2B	From 3B	Scoring Position
Totals	4/108	13/76	12/40	25/116
Percentage	3.7%	17.1%	30.0%	21.6%

Loves to face: Allan Anderson (.600, 3-for-5, 1 2B, 1 HR)
Dan Gakeler (3-for-3)
Greg A. Harris (.600, 3-for-5, 1 2B, 1 3B)

Hates to face: Rich DeLucia (0-for-5)
Chuck Finley (0-for-8)
Charles Nagy (0-for-5)

Miscellaneous statistics: Ground outs-to-air outs ratio: 0.91 last season, 0.88 for career.... Grounded into 10 double plays in 78 opportunities (one per 7.8).... Drove in 10 of 20 runners from third base with less than two outs (50%).... Direction of balls hit to the outfield: 44% to left field, 31% to center, 25% to right.... Base running: Advanced from first base to third on 9 of 19 outfield singles (47%); scored from second on 12 of 13 (92%).... Made 3.03 assists per nine innings at second base.

Comments: Started 125 games last season, and batted eighth (25) or ninth (98) in 123 of them.... Only five other rookies in the majors started at least three-quarters of the games: Jeff Bagwell (156 starts), Ray Lankford (151), Chuck Knoblauch (141), Luis Gonzalez (137), and Milt Cuyler (136).... Batted .333 with two outs and runners in scoring position, 10th highest in A.L.; but with two outs and a runner on first base only, Shumpert went hitless in 20 at-bats.... Only two of his 34 RBIs gave the Royals a lead (6%), the 3d-lowest percentage of go-ahead RBIs by any player in the majors last season (minimum: 25 RBI).... Struck out at a higher rate than any other regular second baseman in A.L. last season (one every 5.6 times up). League-wide strikeout rate was lower for second basemen than for players at any other position in both A.L. and N.L. last season.... Batted only .153 in day games, the lowest in the majors.... Frank White played 2150 games at second base for Royals; Cookie Rojas played 792. Those players were such mainstays that Shumpert, following his rookie season, already ranks third in team history with 171 games at second base. (He played 27 games there in 1990 but retained rookie status for '91.) Among the 234 team/positions in the majors (9 × 26), he's the only player with fewer than 200 games at a position who ranks among the top three on his team's all-time list. Next lowest: Manny Lee ranks third among Toronto shortstops (a position manned for years by Alfredo Griffin and Tony Fernandez) with 237 games.

Ruben Sierra

Bats Left and Right

Texas Rangers	AB	H	2B	3B	HR	RBI	BB	SO	BA	SA	OBA
Season	661	203	44	5	25	116	56	91	.307	.502	.357
vs. Left-Handers	188	63	15	2	7	32	20	22	.335	.548	.393
vs. Right-Handers	473	140	29	3	18	84	36	69	.296	.484	.342
vs. Ground-Ballers	317	109	22	2	14	64	24	39	.344	.558	.388
vs. Fly-Ballers	344	94	22	3	11	52	32	52	.273	.451	.329
Home Games	328	105	22	4	12	61	18	44	.320	.521	.353
Road Games	333	98	22	1	13	55	38	47	.294	.483	.360
Grass Fields	556	168	35	5	23	98	43	76	.302	.507	.349
Artificial Turf	105	35	9	0	2	18	13	15	.333	.476	.397
April	66	18	5	0	4	13	3	8	.273	.530	.304
May	114	44	4	2	4	21	13	11	.386	.561	.445
June	114	37	9	2	4	22	16	17	.325	.544	.408
July	107	24	6	0	3	16	5	19	.224	.364	.257
August	133	37	9	1	3	18	8	21	.278	.429	.315
Sept./Oct.	127	43	11	0	7	26	11	15	.339	.591	.378
Leading Off Inn.	124	34	9	0	4	4	15	21	.274	.444	.353
Runners On	341	113	21	3	14	105	24	35	.331	.534	.366
Bases Empty	320	90	23	2	11	11	32	56	.281	.469	.347
Runners/Scor. Pos.	187	64	12	3	9	92	18	22	.342	.583	.383
Runners On/2 Out	138	42	6	1	6	37	13	20	.304	.493	.364
Scor. Pos./2 Out	88	24	4	1	3	29	10	13	.273	.443	.347
Late-Inning Pressure	102	29	6	0	3	16	8	15	.284	.431	.333
Leading Off	26	4	1	0	0	0	3	5	.154	.192	.241
Runners On	44	15	2	0	3	16	5	5	.341	.591	.400
Runners/Scor. Pos.	24	8	2	0	1	12	4	4	.333	.542	.414

RUNS BATTED IN	From 1B	From 2B	From 3B	Scoring Position
Totals	19/240	33/139	39/81	72/220
Percentage	7.9%	23.7%	48.1%	32.7%

Loves to face: Randy Johnson (.480, 12-for-25, 1 HR)
Mark Knudson (.556, 5-for-9, 2 2B, 3 HR)
Bill Wegman (.500, 9-for-18, 5 2B, 2 HR)

Hates to face: Ted Higuera (.059, 1-for-17)
Dan Plesac (.150, 3-for-20)
Jeff Shaw (0-for-10)

Miscellaneous statistics: Ground outs-to-air outs ratio: 1.08 last season, 0.92 for career.... Grounded into 17 double plays in 158 opportunities (one per 9.3).... Drove in 26 of 39 runners from third base with less than two outs (67%).... Direction of balls hit to the outfield: 29% to left field, 33% to center, 38% to right batting left-handed; 52% to left field, 30% to center, 18% to right batting right-handed.... Base running: Advanced from first base to third on 14 of 36 outfield singles (39%); scored from second on 13 of 18 (72%).... Made 1.93 putouts per nine innings in right field, 3d-lowest rate in A.L.

Comments: Leads majors with 333 extra-base hits over past five years, two more than Bobby Bonilla and Joe Carter, nine more than Howard Johnson, 11 more than Will Clark. Sierra ranks second over past five years with 531 RBIs, one behind Carter; 986 runs produced (that's runs + RBIs), six behind Clark; and 1498 total bases, 15 behind Kirby Puckett.... Batting average with runners in scoring position: .236 in first three years in majors, .334 in last three years.... Has hit for a higher batting average with runners on base than he has with bases empty in each of six seasons in majors. Career breakdown: .297 with runners on base, .264 with bases empty.... Played 1421 innings in the outfield last season, most in the majors.... His 909 games with Texas are the most among Rangers who have never played a game for anyone else.... Among the 26 current franchises, only Toronto, Houston, and the Senators/Rangers have no 1000-game players who never played with another team.... Ranks third in franchise history with 139 home runs, trailing Frank Howard (246) and Larry Parrish (149); Parrish is the leader since the team settled in Texas in 1972.... One of three Rangers with 200 hits last season, one more than the total of 200-hit players on the other 25 teams combined. Only two other teams in past 50 years had three such players: 1963 Cardinals (Dick Groat, Curt Flood, Bill White) and 1982 Brewers (Robin Yount, Cecil Cooper, Paul Molitor). The '29 Phillies and the '37 Tigers set the record with four 200-hit men.

Joel Skinner
Bats Right

Cleveland Indians	AB	H	2B	3B	HR	RBI	BB	SO	BA	SA	OBA
Season	284	69	14	0	1	24	14	67	.243	.303	.279
vs. Left-Handers	88	27	3	0	0	7	2	19	.307	.341	.319
vs. Right-Handers	196	42	11	0	1	17	12	48	.214	.286	.262
vs. Ground-Ballers	130	33	5	0	0	8	4	32	.254	.292	.281
vs. Fly-Ballers	154	36	9	0	1	16	10	35	.234	.312	.277
Home Games	142	37	9	0	0	15	7	32	.261	.324	.300
Road Games	142	32	5	0	1	9	7	35	.225	.282	.258
Grass Fields	231	62	13	0	1	22	13	47	.268	.338	.308
Artificial Turf	53	7	1	0	0	2	1	20	.132	.151	.148
April	10	3	1	0	0	2	0	4	.300	.400	.300
May	52	17	5	0	1	8	1	7	.327	.481	.333
June	67	14	3	0	0	4	2	19	.209	.254	.229
July	26	4	0	0	0	1	2	9	.154	.154	.214
August	79	17	3	0	0	8	6	17	.215	.253	.279
Sept./Oct.	50	14	2	0	0	1	3	11	.280	.320	.321
Leading Off Inn.	64	15	3	0	1	1	6	20	.234	.328	.300
Runners On	132	31	10	0	0	23	5	29	.235	.311	.264
Bases Empty	152	38	4	0	1	1	9	38	.250	.296	.292
Runners/Scor. Pos.	68	12	3	0	0	19	5	16	.176	.221	.237
Runners On/2 Out	60	15	6	0	0	10	3	10	.250	.350	.297
Scor. Pos./2 Out	31	6	3	0	0	8	3	5	.194	.290	.286
Late-Inning Pressure	42	13	2	0	0	2	1	9	.310	.357	.326
Leading Off	7	3	1	0	0	0	0	3	.429	.571	.429
Runners On	17	4	1	0	0	2	1	4	.235	.294	.278
Runners/Scor. Pos.	8	1	0	0	0	1	1	0	.125	.125	.222

RUNS BATTED IN	From 1B	From 2B	From 3B	Scoring Position
Totals	5/98	7/52	11/33	18/85
Percentage	5.1%	13.5%	33.3%	21.2%

Loves to face: Dave Johnson (.600, 3-for-5, 1 HR)
Bill Wegman (.500, 5-for-10)
Bob Welch (.400, 6-for-15, 1 HR)
Hates to face: Scott Erickson (0-for-8, 7 SO)
Mark Gubicza (0-for-19)
Matt Young (.077, 1-for-13, 7 SO)

Miscellaneous statistics: Ground outs-to-air outs ratio: 2.31 last season, highest in A.L.; 2.05 for career.... Grounded into 8 double plays in 55 opportunities (one per 6.9).... Drove in 9 of 20 runners from third base with less than two outs (45%).... Direction of balls hit to the outfield: 30% to left field, 34% to center, 35% to right.... Base running: Advanced from first base to third on 4 of 13 outfield singles (31%); scored from second on 7 of 11 (64%).... Opposing base stealers: 54-for-82 (66%).

Comments: Home run off Bob Welch on May 5 was the only homer by a Cleveland catcher last season. Other major league teams had an average of 12 home runs by catchers, with no other team having fewer than four. Cleveland catchers also had fewest RBIs (44) in majors, and went 0-for-6 trying to steal bases. (Yes, catchers had the lowest stolen-base rate in the majors last season: 47.9 [92 steals, 100 caught]; percentages for other positions: pitchers 54.5 [6-for-11], first basemen 58.4, third basemen 59.1, shortstops 65.2, right fielders 66.3, center fielders 69.2, left fielders 69.4, second basemen 71.6.) ... Skinner's homer was part of Tribe's unlikely two-day explosion at Oakland last May: 20–6 and 15–6 wins in consecutive games; that tied a team record for runs in consecutive games set in 1923. What we didn't know at the time: Cleveland would finish the season scoring the fewest runs in the majors.... Skinner received the first (and only) intentional walk of his major league career last June 1 when the ol' master of the IBB, Sparky Anderson, resolved the answer to an age-old question: With a runner on third and two outs, would you rather face Joel Skinner or Felix Fermin? (Our answer: yes.) Sparky had Bill Gullickson walk Skinner, then Fermin smacked an RBI single.... Batting average on artificial turf (.132) was lowest in majors last season (minimum: 50 at-bats on that $%#[]&# stuff).... Owns fifth-highest career ratio of ground outs to air outs, and can put the ball on the ground with the best of them: Milt Thompson, Wally Backman, Dave Krieg ...

Luis Sojo
Bats Right

California Angels	AB	H	2B	3B	HR	RBI	BB	SO	BA	SA	OBA
Season	364	94	14	1	3	20	14	26	.258	.327	.295
vs. Left-Handers	114	34	7	1	0	5	5	6	.298	.377	.328
vs. Right-Handers	250	60	7	0	3	15	9	20	.240	.304	.280
vs. Ground-Ballers	166	39	4	0	2	11	3	13	.235	.295	.262
vs. Fly-Ballers	198	55	10	1	1	9	11	13	.278	.354	.322
Home Games	176	42	5	0	1	6	11	11	.239	.284	.287
Road Games	188	52	9	1	2	14	3	15	.277	.367	.303
Grass Fields	305	78	10	0	1	12	14	21	.256	.298	.297
Artificial Turf	59	16	4	1	2	8	0	5	.271	.475	.283
April	54	13	1	1	0	3	1	3	.241	.296	.268
May	56	11	4	0	0	3	2	4	.196	.268	.224
June	47	12	3	0	0	4	2	2	.255	.319	.314
July	69	21	3	0	0	5	1	9	.304	.348	.314
August	78	19	2	0	3	4	5	4	.244	.385	.289
Sept./Oct.	60	18	1	0	0	1	3	4	.300	.317	.354
Leading Off Inn.	81	21	4	0	0	0	7	5	.259	.309	.333
Runners On	170	42	6	1	0	17	3	10	.247	.294	.264
Bases Empty	194	52	8	0	3	3	11	16	.268	.356	.321
Runners/Scor. Pos.	102	23	6	0	0	16	3	6	.225	.284	.248
Runners On/2 Out	77	14	1	0	0	9	1	8	.182	.195	.192
Scor. Pos./2 Out	50	9	1	0	0	9	1	6	.180	.200	.196
Late-Inning Pressure	37	11	0	0	0	1	2	2	.297	.297	.350
Leading Off	10	2	0	0	0	0	2	1	.200	.200	.385
Runners On	19	7	0	0	0	1	0	1	.368	.368	.368
Runners/Scor. Pos.	9	2	0	0	0	1	0	0	.222	.222	.222

RUNS BATTED IN	From 1B	From 2B	From 3B	Scoring Position
Totals	2/122	10/76	5/41	15/117
Percentage	1.6%	13.2%	12.2%	12.8%

Loves to face: Mark Guthrie (.500, 3-for-6, 2 SO)
Charlie Hough (.462, 6-for-13)
Hates to face: Allan Anderson (0-for-11)
Greg A. Harris (0-for-6)
Jose Mesa (0-for-6)

Miscellaneous statistics: Ground outs-to-air outs ratio: 1.27 last season, 1.19 for career.... Grounded into 12 double plays in 84 opportunities (one per 7.0).... Drove in 0 of 14 runners from third base with less than two outs (0%).... Direction of balls hit to the outfield: 41% to left field, 30% to center, 29% to right.... Base running: Advanced from first base to third on 5 of 16 outfield singles (31%); scored from second on 11 of 11 (100%), 3d best in A.L.... Made 3.26 assists per nine innings at second base.

Comments: Led A.L. with 19 sacrifice bunts last season. Ten of those sacrifices came from the second spot in the lineup; in both the A.L. and the N.L. last season, the second spot in the batting order produced more sacrifice bunts than any other spot except the ninth.... Batted .298 vs. left-handers last season; the only Angels with higher marks vs. lefties were Daves Gallagher and Winfield (each hit .300).... Batted .277 in road games but only .239 at home last season. Differences like that must have been a frequent topic of chat on Angels' charter flights last year: Five of his teammates—Dave Gallagher, Donnie Hill, Wally Joyner, Luis Polonia, and Dave Winfield—also hit at least 35 points higher on the road than at home. Result: Angels were the only team in the majors that batted at least 20 points higher in road games (.266) than at home (.243). Since 1975, 91 major league teams have compiled a batting average at least 20 points higher in home games than in road games, but only 13 have hit 20 points better on the road than at home.... Committed only 11 errors in 899⅓ innings; other Angels second basemen combined for 10 errors in 542⅓ innings.... Sojo played 107 games at second base. The last Angels player to appear in 150 or more games in a season there: Bobby Grich in 1979. (Grich was also the last Orioles second baseman to play in 150 or more games; he did that in 1975. But that didn't impress the Hall of Fame voters in January, when they terminated Grich's chances of election in his first year on the ballot.)

Sammy Sosa — Bats Right

Chicago White Sox	AB	H	2B	3B	HR	RBI	BB	SO	BA	SA	OBA
Season	316	64	10	1	10	33	14	98	.203	.335	.240
vs. Left-Handers	128	29	5	0	5	11	8	39	.227	.383	.277
vs. Right-Handers	188	35	5	1	5	22	6	59	.186	.303	.214
vs. Ground-Ballers	128	24	2	1	5	11	9	34	.188	.336	.246
vs. Fly-Ballers	188	40	8	0	5	22	5	64	.213	.335	.236
Home Games	145	27	5	1	3	10	7	44	.186	.297	.222
Road Games	171	37	5	0	7	23	7	54	.216	.368	.256
Grass Fields	264	54	7	1	8	25	13	84	.205	.330	.246
Artificial Turf	52	10	3	0	2	8	1	14	.192	.365	.208
April	54	12	1	1	3	8	4	14	.222	.444	.288
May	95	21	1	0	4	8	3	35	.221	.358	.245
June	81	14	3	0	2	10	4	26	.173	.284	.209
July	25	4	3	0	0	0	0	6	.160	.280	.160
August	14	3	0	0	0	1	2	5	.214	.214	.313
Sept./Oct.	47	10	2	0	1	6	1	12	.213	.319	.245
Leading Off Inn.	87	14	2	0	1	1	3	24	.161	.218	.198
Runners On	132	31	3	1	6	29	8	38	.235	.409	.277
Bases Empty	184	33	7	0	4	4	6	60	.179	.283	.214
Runners/Scor. Pos.	80	19	1	1	5	27	5	25	.237	.463	.279
Runners On/2 Out	52	9	1	1	2	11	2	17	.173	.346	.204
Scor. Pos./2 Out	37	8	1	1	2	11	1	15	.216	.459	.237
Late-Inning Pressure	56	15	2	0	2	3	2	14	.268	.411	.293
Leading Off	20	7	1	0	1	1	0	5	.350	.550	.350
Runners On	22	4	1	0	1	2	2	5	.182	.364	.250
Runners/Scor. Pos.	10	1	0	0	0	0	2	1	.100	.100	.250

RUNS BATTED IN	From 1B	From 2B	From 3B	Scoring Position
Totals	4/95	11/67	8/29	19/96
Percentage	4.2%	16.4%	27.6%	19.8%

Loves to face: Jim Abbott (.368, 7-for-19)
Mike Moore (.462, 6-for-13, 2 2B, 1 3B, 1 HR)
David West (.545, 6-for-11, 2 2B, 1 3B, 1 HR)
Hates to face: Rick Aguilera (0-for-6, 4 SO)
Dave Johnson (.100, 1-for-10)
Nolan Ryan (0-for-16)

Miscellaneous statistics: Ground outs-to-air outs ratio: 1.26 last season, 1.25 for career.... Grounded into 5 double plays in 68 opportunities (one per 14).... Drove in 7 of 17 runners from third base with less than two outs (41%).... Direction of balls hit to the outfield: 44% to left field, 18% to center, 38% to right.... Base running: Advanced from first base to third on 5 of 11 outfield singles (45%); scored from second on 5 of 7 (71%).... Made 2.51 putouts per nine innings in right field, highest rate in majors.

Comments: Became only the second White Sox player in history to hit two home runs in an opening-day game; Minnie Minoso did it in 1960. In fact, Sosa also tied the Sox *career* record for opening-day homers; besides Minoso, only Sherm Lollar and Dick Allen hit two circuit clouts in league lid-lifters (boy, that felt good).... But it was all downhill from there for a player who had reached double figures in doubles, triples, and home runs in 1990. Last year he barely made it in any of them.... Started 76 games last season, but only 16 of those starts came after the All-Star break. He got to visit Vancouver for late July and a good part of August—a beautiful time of year to visit, if you don't have to play in minor league baseball games.... There were 28 right fielders who played at least 400 innings in the majors last season; Sosa, Jose Canseco, and Danny Tartabull were the only three who had more errors than assists.... His 4-for-22 showing last season in Late-Inning Pressure Situations with runners on base actually *raised* his career batting average at such times to .138.... Has averaged one strikeout every 3.8 times up since joining the Sox, second-highest rate in history among players with at least 1000 plate appearances with team. The worst rate belongs to Red Faber, but he was guilty with an explanation: He was a pitcher who won 254 games in a Sox uniform, second most in team history. In fact, Faber had three of Chicago's four wins the last time the Sox won the World Series, in 1917.

Bill Spiers — Bats Left

Milwaukee Brewers	AB	H	2B	3B	HR	RBI	BB	SO	BA	SA	OBA
Season	414	117	13	6	8	54	34	55	.283	.401	.337
vs. Left-Handers	117	26	1	0	2	12	13	16	.222	.282	.305
vs. Right-Handers	297	91	12	6	6	42	21	39	.306	.448	.350
vs. Ground-Ballers	197	49	6	4	4	26	20	26	.249	.381	.317
vs. Fly-Ballers	217	68	7	2	4	28	14	29	.313	.419	.356
Home Games	187	56	6	2	1	24	21	30	.299	.369	.370
Road Games	227	61	7	4	7	30	13	25	.269	.427	.309
Grass Fields	348	105	11	6	6	47	32	45	.302	.420	.361
Artificial Turf	66	12	2	0	2	7	2	10	.182	.303	.203
April	57	16	1	0	3	10	5	9	.281	.456	.339
May	52	11	4	0	0	3	3	10	.212	.288	.255
June	64	15	1	1	0	5	7	10	.234	.281	.319
July	76	18	1	1	2	10	4	12	.237	.355	.265
August	88	34	3	2	1	17	11	8	.386	.500	.450
Sept./Oct.	77	23	3	2	2	9	4	6	.299	.468	.341
Leading Off Inn.	103	19	4	1	0		4	14	.184	.243	.215
Runners On	176	56	7	2	5	51	17	24	.318	.466	.371
Bases Empty	238	61	6	4	3	3	17	31	.256	.353	.311
Runners/Scor. Pos.	103	33	5	2	4	49	9	13	.320	.524	.362
Runners On/2 Out	76	21	1	0	2	14	10	10	.276	.368	.360
Scor. Pos./2 Out	49	11	1	0	2	14	6	6	.224	.367	.309
Late-Inning Pressure	60	21	2	2	1	8	8	8	.350	.500	.429
Leading Off	16	3	0	0	0	0	1	4	.188	.188	.235
Runners On	27	10	2	1	0	7	6	2	.370	.519	.471
Runners/Scor. Pos.	20	6	2	1	0	7	3	2	.300	.500	.375

RUNS BATTED IN	From 1B	From 2B	From 3B	Scoring Position
Totals	5/123	18/74	23/52	41/126
Percentage	4.1%	24.3%	44.2%	32.5%

Loves to face: Roger Clemens (.357, 5-for-14, 1 HR)
Dave Johnson (.500, 8-for-16)
Scott Kamieniecki (3-for-3)
Hates to face: Greg Cadaret (0-for-9)
Jimmy Key (0-for-9)
Kevin Tapani (0-for-9)

Miscellaneous statistics: Ground outs-to-air outs ratio: 1.39 last season, 1.35 for career.... Grounded into 9 double plays in 89 opportunities (one per 10).... Drove in 14 of 24 runners from third base with less than two outs (58%).... Direction of balls hit to the outfield: 33% to left field, 38% to center, 29% to right.... Base running: Advanced from first base to third on 16 of 35 outfield singles (46%); scored from second on 12 of 14 (86%).... Made 2.81 assists per nine innings at shortstop.

Comments: Only Cal Ripken had more RBIs among A.L. shortstops last season, and among A.L. players who started at least half their team's games at short, only Ripken had a higher batting average.... Started 122 games from ninth spot in the batting order, the most by any player in the majors. Dale Sveum started each of the other 40 games for Milwaukee in the nine-hole. That was a productive spot in the Brewers lineup: They led A.L. (and, of course, the majors) with 80 RBIs, 40 extra-base hits, .379 slugging average, and .333 on-base average from the bottom spot in the lineup. Average ninth-spot contribution from other A.L. teams: 49 RBIs, 30 extra-base hits, .323 slugging average, .302 on-base average.... Spiers picked his spots judiciously: He batted .350 in Late-Inning Pressure Situations, but only .250 in other late-inning situations without the necessary close-game component that defines LIPS.... August batting average was highest in the majors.... Has batted .280 at County Stadium, .244 in road games in his three years with Brewers.... As a left-handed-hitting shortstop with some pop, Spiers is a rare bird. How rare? No left-handed hitter (switch-hitters are not included) had had a season of eight homers and 54 RBIs while playing 100 games at shortstop since Dick McAuliffe (23 homers, 56 RBIs) in 1966, his last year as a shortstop. If you include Spiers's .283 batting average, you have to go all the way back to 1935 to find the last such lefty-hitting shortstop, Hall of Famer Arky Vaughan.

Terry Steinbach
Bats Right

Oakland A's	AB	H	2B	3B	HR	RBI	BB	SO	BA	SA	OBA
Season	456	125	31	1	6	67	22	70	.274	.386	.312
vs. Left-Handers	139	37	11	0	3	15	7	17	.266	.410	.302
vs. Right-Handers	317	88	20	1	3	52	15	53	.278	.375	.316
vs. Ground-Ballers	211	60	16	0	0	29	9	33	.284	.360	.323
vs. Fly-Ballers	245	65	15	1	6	38	13	37	.265	.408	.302
Home Games	220	61	19	0	1	31	14	29	.277	.377	.314
Road Games	236	64	12	1	5	36	8	41	.271	.394	.310
Grass Fields	371	104	26	1	4	58	19	52	.280	.388	.315
Artificial Turf	85	21	5	0	2	9	3	18	.247	.376	.297
April	63	18	3	0	1	11	2	17	.286	.381	.333
May	79	23	8	0	2	13	4	7	.291	.468	.329
June	63	19	4	0	2	7	2	6	.302	.460	.333
July	89	29	9	1	0	17	3	11	.326	.449	.337
August	79	19	6	0	1	10	9	12	.241	.354	.311
Sept./Oct.	83	17	1	0	0	9	2	17	.205	.217	.236
Leading Off Inn.	89	20	5	0	1	1	5	14	.225	.315	.274
Runners On	217	60	14	1	3	64	13	29	.276	.392	.317
Bases Empty	239	65	17	0	3	3	9	41	.272	.381	.307
Runners/Scor. Pos.	130	37	7	1	2	60	12	18	.285	.400	.333
Runners On/2 Out	97	22	8	1	0	23	8	19	.227	.330	.299
Scor. Pos./2 Out	66	15	4	1	0	21	7	13	.227	.318	.320
Late-Inning Pressure	79	24	3	0	0	9	4	16	.304	.342	.349
Leading Off	12	1	0	0	0	0	0	3	.083	.083	.083
Runners On	35	10	2	0	0	9	3	9	.286	.343	.350
Runners/Scor. Pos.	19	5	1	0	0	9	3	6	.263	.316	.375

RUNS BATTED IN	From 1B	From 2B	From 3B	Scoring Position
Totals	10/161	19/98	32/63	51/161
Percentage	6.2%	19.4%	50.8%	31.7%

Loves to face: Chris Bosio (.357, 10-for-28, 1 HR)
Chuck Finley (.375, 9-for-24, 1 HR, 0 BB)
Kirk McCaskill (.350, 7-for-20, 1 HR)

Hates to face: Tim Leary (0-for-11)
Steve Olin (0-for-12)
Bobby Witt (0-for-9)

Miscellaneous statistics: Ground outs-to-air outs ratio: 1.32 last season, 1.09 for career.... Grounded into 15 double plays in 99 opportunities (one per 6.6).... Drove in 24 of 35 runners from third base with less than two outs (69%).... Direction of balls hit to the outfield: 35% to left field, 26% to center, 40% to right.... Base running: Advanced from first base to third on 4 of 21 outfield singles (19%); scored from second on 9 of 13 (69%).... Opposing base stealers: 76-for-111 (68%).

Comments: Has caught at least 80 games in each of last five years, a streak that sounds unassuming enough; still, he's the first Athletics catcher to do that—in either Oakland, Kansas City, or Philadelphia—since Mickey Cochrane did it nine years in a row, 1925–33.... Led A.L. catchers with 13 errors last season, one back of major league leader Benito Santiago.... Career batting average with the bases loaded (.466) is 3d highest among active players, behind Pat Tabler (.488) and Tracy Jones (.484). Since going 2-for-9 with bases loaded as a rookie in 1987, Steinbach has 25 hits in his last 49 bases-loaded at-bats. And don't think those pitchers aren't starting to catch on: Steinbach drew three walks in 10 bases-loaded plate appearances last year; in four previous years combined, he drew three walks in 60 times up with bases loaded.... Owns .405 career batting average as a pinch hitter (17-for-42, with four home runs), the best batting average among active players with 40 + pinch-hit at-bats. Aside to local and cable TV producers: The top-five list you're looking for is in Chris James's comments.... Established career highs with 494 plate appearances, 67 RBIs, 38 extra-base hits, and 31 doubles last year, but rate of walks (one every 22.5 times up) and rate of home runs (one every 76 at-bats) were poorest of five-year career.... Batted .321 in day games last season, .255 at night; career breakdown is along the same lines: .292 under sunlight, .258 under moonlight.

Kurt Stillwell
Bats Left and Right

Kansas City Royals	AB	H	2B	3B	HR	RBI	BB	SO	BA	SA	OBA
Season	385	102	17	1	6	51	33	56	.265	.361	.322
vs. Left-Handers	109	29	6	1	1	15	6	17	.266	.367	.304
vs. Right-Handers	276	73	11	0	5	36	27	39	.264	.359	.328
vs. Ground-Ballers	183	47	7	0	1	20	19	25	.257	.311	.324
vs. Fly-Ballers	202	55	10	1	5	31	14	31	.272	.406	.320
Home Games	183	47	10	1	1	24	18	23	.257	.339	.324
Road Games	202	55	7	0	5	27	15	33	.272	.381	.320
Grass Fields	136	39	5	0	4	18	12	25	.287	.412	.340
Artificial Turf	249	63	12	1	2	33	21	31	.253	.333	.311
April	63	20	4	0	1	6	7	12	.317	.429	.380
May	97	21	1	1	1	11	4	15	.216	.278	.245
June	83	22	4	0	2	11	9	13	.265	.386	.333
July	37	7	2	0	1	6	5	6	.189	.324	.279
August	14	4	1	0	0	0	0	3	.286	.357	.286
Sept./Oct.	91	28	5	0	1	17	8	7	.308	.396	.370
Leading Off Inn.	73	19	5	1	2	2	7	10	.260	.438	.333
Runners On	189	54	8	0	4	49	19	25	.286	.392	.344
Bases Empty	196	48	9	1	2	2	14	31	.245	.332	.299
Runners/Scor. Pos.	101	30	5	0	2	44	16	18	.297	.406	.380
Runners On/2 Out	79	25	1	0	3	21	11	7	.316	.443	.400
Scor. Pos./2 Out	46	14	1	0	2	19	10	7	.304	.457	.429
Late-Inning Pressure	69	11	2	0	0	2	9	10	.159	.188	.256
Leading Off	20	2	1	0	0	0	1	3	.100	.150	.143
Runners On	27	4	0	0	0	2	8	5	.148	.148	.343
Runners/Scor. Pos.	16	1	0	0	0	2	8	4	.063	.063	.375

RUNS BATTED IN	From 1B	From 2B	From 3B	Scoring Position
Totals	7/135	20/86	18/41	38/127
Percentage	5.2%	23.3%	43.9%	29.9%

Loves to face: Storm Davis (.625, 5-for-8)
Kirk McCaskill (.391, 9-for-23)
Jack Morris (.417, 10-for-24)

Hates to face: Roger Clemens (.129, 4-for-31, 0 BB)
Gregg Olson (0-for-9, 7 SO)
Nolan Ryan (.125, 4-for-32)

Miscellaneous statistics: Ground outs-to-air outs ratio: 1.02 last season, 0.93 for career.... Grounded into 8 double plays in 92 opportunities (one per 12).... Drove in 15 of 27 runners from third base with less than two outs (56%).... Direction of balls hit to the outfield: 29% to left field, 41% to center, 30% to right batting left-handed; 46% to left field, 24% to center, 30% to right batting right-handed.... Base running: Advanced from first base to third on 4 of 15 outfield singles (27%); scored from second on 10 of 13 (77%).... Made 2.60 assists per nine innings at shortstop, lowest rate in A.L.

Comments: Matched previous season's total of 51 RBIs despite having 121 fewer at-bats in 1991 than in 1990; he did it by making the most of his opportunities with runners in scoring position: He increased his batting average in those situations from .244 in 1990 to .297 last year.... RBI totals last four years: 53, 54, 51, 51; only five other players in baseball history have had between 50 and 55 RBIs for four straight years (including Ozzie Smith, 1988–91).... Has hit for a higher average with runners on base than he has with bases empty in each of six seasons in majors. Career breakdown: .291 with runners on base, .225 with bases empty, the difference between hitting Lou Piniella–style and hitting Paul Casanova–style.... With reasonable production like that from the shortstop spot, how bad must his fielding have been to lead Hal McRae to replace him with David Howard for most of the second half? Stillwell started 71 of Royals' 80 games before the All-Star break, but only seven of their next 61 games. We know this much: Among the 26 shortstops who played the most innings last season, only Luis Rivera had a higher error rate than Stillwell (Rivera, one every 24.6 chances; Stillwell, one every 24.7). And Kurt accepted only 4.2 chances per nine innings, fewest among that same group, compared to Howard's 4.9 rate. And among 25 shortstops who handled at least 50 chances in Late-Inning Pressure Situations last year, Kurt had the highest error rate (one every 21.3 chances). That may not be the full answer but it'll do for now.

Franklin Stubbs
Bats Left

Milwaukee Brewers	AB	H	2B	3B	HR	RBI	BB	SO	BA	SA	OBA
Season	362	77	16	2	11	38	35	71	.213	.359	.282
vs. Left-Handers	87	19	7	0	2	10	1	19	.218	.368	.236
vs. Right-Handers	275	58	9	2	9	28	34	52	.211	.356	.295
vs. Ground-Ballers	155	38	6	1	6	21	13	32	.245	.413	.310
vs. Fly-Ballers	207	39	10	1	5	17	22	39	.188	.319	.262
Home Games	183	40	11	0	8	22	21	41	.219	.410	.304
Road Games	179	37	5	2	3	16	14	30	.207	.307	.259
Grass Fields	297	61	13	0	10	33	31	63	.205	.350	.281
Artificial Turf	65	16	3	2	1	5	4	8	.246	.400	.286
April	56	12	4	0	1	4	4	9	.214	.339	.274
May	86	19	4	0	1	9	9	17	.221	.302	.292
June	56	12	3	0	3	6	4	13	.214	.429	.267
July	74	16	1	2	3	10	7	16	.216	.405	.284
August	73	17	4	0	3	9	10	12	.233	.411	.314
Sept./Oct.	17	1	0	0	0	0	1	4	.059	.059	.158
Leading Off Inn.	86	23	4	1	5	5	4	16	.267	.512	.300
Runners On	168	35	7	0	4	31	21	35	.208	.321	.296
Bases Empty	194	42	9	2	7	7	14	36	.216	.392	.269
Runners/Scor. Pos.	100	15	2	0	4	29	19	26	.150	.290	.286
Runners On/2 Out	76	14	2	0	3	14	12	16	.184	.329	.311
Scor. Pos./2 Out	50	8	1	0	3	13	12	13	.160	.360	.344
Late-Inning Pressure	66	11	2	0	0	1	5	13	.167	.197	.236
Leading Off	21	4	1	0	0	0	1	4	.190	.238	.227
Runners On	25	5	1	0	0	1	2	5	.200	.240	.286
Runners/Scor. Pos.	13	1	1	0	0	1	1	3	.077	.154	.200

RUNS BATTED IN	From 1B	From 2B	From 3B	Scoring Position
Totals	5/127	10/75	12/44	22/119
Percentage	3.9%	13.3%	27.3%	18.5%

Loves to face: Steve Bedrosian (.467, 7-for-15, 2 2B, 3 HR)
Bill Gullickson (.350, 7-for-20, 1 HR)
Greg Hibbard (.500, 5-for-10, 1 HR)

Hates to face: Rick Aguilera (.071, 1-for-14)
Ron Darling (.091, 3-for-33, 1 HR, 6 BB, 19 SO)
Dave Stewart (.083, 1-for-12)

Miscellaneous statistics: Ground outs-to-air outs ratio: 0.81 last season, 0.70 for career. . . . Grounded into 4 double plays in 79 opportunities (one per 20). . . . Drove in 9 of 21 runners from third base with less than two outs (43%). . . . Direction of balls hit to the outfield: 13% to left field, 35% to center, 52% to right. . . . Base running: Advanced from first base to third on 3 of 12 outfield singles (25%); scored from second on 8 of 9 (89%). . . . Made 0.94 assists per nine innings at first base, highest rate in A.L.

Comments: The "Stubbs Across America" Tour took him to Milwaukee last summer, his third team in the past three seasons. . . . Batting average vs. right-handed pitchers was 5th lowest in the league, and the lowest among pure left-handed hitters. Switch-hitting Manny Lee had a lower average. . . . His .160 average with runners in scoring position was lowest in the majors: He went 7-for-50 with less than two outs and 8-for-50 with two outs. . . . Started 95 games last season, but none in Brewers' 25 games after September 10. . . . Has hit for a higher average on artificial turf than he has on grass fields in each of his last six seasons. Career breakdown: .268 on artificial turf, .214 on grass fields. He's like a fish out of water with the Brewers, the team that led the majors in grass-field batting average (.276) last season. . . . One of 14 players in the 30/30 Club over the past two years combined: 34 home runs and a surprising 32 steals (in 42 attempts). . . . Batted .199 in night games; the only other semi-regular players who failed to crack the .200 mark under the lights were Darren Daulton (.187) and Rob Deer (.180). . . . Career pinch hitting: .218 batting average, three home runs in 119 at-bats. Brewers again used fewest pinch hitters in majors last season (78); they did that in each of Tom Trebelhorn's five full years as Milwaukee manager. With Treb replaced by Phil Garner following '91 season, pinch hitting may experience a renaissance in the land of brats and beer.

B. J. Surhoff
Bats Left

Milwaukee Brewers	AB	H	2B	3B	HR	RBI	BB	SO	BA	SA	OBA
Season	505	146	19	4	5	68	26	33	.289	.372	.319
vs. Left-Handers	102	26	2	1	0	11	6	12	.255	.294	.291
vs. Right-Handers	403	120	17	3	5	57	20	21	.298	.392	.326
vs. Ground-Ballers	246	76	11	1	1	34	13	14	.309	.374	.338
vs. Fly-Ballers	259	70	8	3	4	34	13	19	.270	.371	.300
Home Games	236	63	8	3	3	34	14	13	.267	.364	.303
Road Games	269	83	11	1	2	34	12	20	.309	.379	.332
Grass Fields	433	129	18	4	4	55	22	27	.298	.384	.326
Artificial Turf	72	17	1	0	1	13	4	6	.236	.292	.273
April	59	9	0	0	0	3	3	6	.153	.153	.194
May	67	17	1	1	0	10	5	3	.254	.299	.297
June	80	21	2	0	0	8	6	5	.262	.287	.300
July	85	26	6	0	0	14	2	5	.306	.376	.318
August	102	35	7	1	3	14	4	6	.343	.520	.364
Sept./Oct.	112	38	3	2	2	19	6	8	.339	.455	.370
Leading Off Inn.	102	24	3	0	2	2	4	6	.235	.324	.264
Runners On	232	75	8	3	0	63	13	12	.323	.384	.346
Bases Empty	273	71	11	1	5	5	13	21	.260	.363	.294
Runners/Scor. Pos.	134	42	6	3	0	62	9	9	.313	.403	.336
Runners On/2 Out	81	27	4	1	0	19	5	7	.333	.407	.372
Scor. Pos./2 Out	55	16	3	1	0	19	5	5	.291	.382	.350
Late-Inning Pressure	76	22	3	0	2	11	4	8	.289	.408	.321
Leading Off	18	4	0	0	1	1	0	2	.222	.389	.222
Runners On	27	9	3	0	0	9	2	2	.333	.444	.367
Runners/Scor. Pos.	19	5	2	0	0	9	2	1	.263	.368	.318

RUNS BATTED IN	From 1B	From 2B	From 3B	Scoring Position
Totals	5/169	25/109	33/57	58/166
Percentage	3.0%	22.9%	57.9%	34.9%

Loves to face: Scott Sanderson (.833, 5-for-6, 1 HR)
Walt Terrell (.389, 14-for-36, 2 HR)
Bobby Witt (.389, 14-for-36, 2 HR)

Hates to face: Mike Moore (.138, 4-for-29, 4 BB)
Nolan Ryan (.071, 1-for-14)
Bob Welch (.148, 4-for-27, 0 BB)

Miscellaneous statistics: Ground outs-to-air outs ratio: 1.82 last season, 1.34 for career. . . . Grounded into 21 double plays in 132 opportunities (one per 6.3). . . . Drove in 26 of 37 runners from third base with less than two outs (70%). . . . Direction of balls hit to the outfield: 30% to left field, 33% to center, 38% to right. . . . Base running: Advanced from first base to third on 15 of 33 outfield singles (45%); scored from second on 10 of 15 (67%). . . . Opposing base stealers: 86-for-121 (71%), 5th-highest rate in A.L.

Comments: The Brewers had a 67–51 record with Surhoff as starting catcher, a .567 winning percentage—good enough to win the A.L. East last season. Team played only .363 ball with Rick Dempsey starting (16–28), although pitching staff had a lower ERA with Dempsey (3.96) than it did with B.J. (4.26). . . . Percentage of runners driven in from scoring position was 7th highest in A.L.; batting average with two outs and runners on base was also 7th highest in the league. . . . Has had a higher batting average with runners on base than with bases empty in each of five seasons in majors; career breakdown: .297 with runners on base, .251 with bases empty. . . . Had four hits in 10 at-bats with bases loaded last season; Brewers batted .352 with sacks full, second in majors behind Boston's .354 mark. Surhoff, over the last three years, is 14-for-29 with bases loaded; he owns a .392 career mark in those situations. . . . Despite 1991 numbers, owns slightly better career figures vs. left-handed pitchers (.273 batting average, .367 slugging average, .316 on-base average, one home run every 61 at-bats) than vs. right-handers (.270, .363, .315, one every 91). . . . All that catching appears to be taking its toll. He stole only five bases last year, after averaging 16 over his first four seasons. Benito Santiago has also hit the wall: 16 per year over his first three seasons, but a total of 13 over the last two. Makes you appreciate Carlton Fisk all the more for having stolen 17 bases in 1985, at age 38.

Dale Sveum
Bats Left and Right

Milwaukee Brewers	AB	H	2B	3B	HR	RBI	BB	SO	BA	SA	OBA
Season	266	64	19	1	4	43	32	78	.241	.365	.320
vs. Left-Handers	118	29	6	1	2	16	15	35	.246	.364	.331
vs. Right-Handers	148	35	13	0	2	27	17	43	.236	.365	.312
vs. Ground-Ballers	123	32	10	0	1	18	16	27	.260	.366	.348
vs. Fly-Ballers	143	32	9	1	3	25	16	51	.224	.364	.296
Home Games	146	32	10	0	3	21	19	42	.219	.349	.307
Road Games	120	32	9	1	1	22	13	36	.267	.383	.336
Grass Fields	231	54	15	0	3	34	27	67	.234	.338	.312
Artificial Turf	35	10	4	1	1	9	5	11	.286	.543	.372
April	13	0	0	0	0	0	1	5	.000	.000	.071
May	71	20	5	1	3	13	13	19	.282	.507	.393
June	70	12	2	0	0	8	7	26	.171	.200	.244
July	37	10	5	0	1	7	3	10	.270	.486	.326
August	20	4	1	0	0	5	2	6	.200	.250	.273
Sept./Oct.	55	18	6	0	0	10	6	12	.327	.436	.387
Leading Off Inn.	55	13	5	0	2	2	8	18	.236	.436	.333
Runners On	125	34	11	1	1	40	10	30	.272	.400	.321
Bases Empty	141	30	8	0	3	3	22	48	.213	.333	.319
Runners/Scor. Pos.	77	23	7	1	1	39	7	18	.299	.455	.348
Runners On/2 Out	50	14	4	1	1	21	4	13	.280	.460	.333
Scor. Pos./2 Out	38	14	4	1	1	21	3	10	.368	.605	.415
Late-Inning Pressure	52	14	3	1	2	12	5	15	.269	.481	.328
Leading Off	12	3	1	0	2	2	1	4	.250	.833	.308
Runners On	27	8	2	1	0	10	2	7	.296	.444	.333
Runners/Scor. Pos.	18	5	2	1	0	10	1	4	.278	.500	.300

RUNS BATTED IN	From 1B	From 2B	From 3B	Scoring Position
Totals	5/91	18/65	16/36	34/101
Percentage	5.5%	27.7%	44.4%	33.7%

Loves to face: Bill Long (.375, 3-for-8, 1 2B, 1 3B, 1 HR)
Dave Righetti (.429, 3-for-7, 1 HR)
Greg Swindell (.294, 5-for-17, 2 2B, 2 HR, 7 BB)

Hates to face: Bud Black (0-for-9)
Oil Can Boyd (0-for-11)
Bret Saberhagen (.161, 5-for-31, 0 BB)

Miscellaneous statistics: Ground outs-to-air outs ratio: 0.81 last season, 1.02 for career.... Grounded into 8 double plays in 63 opportunities (one per 7.9).... Drove in 12 of 23 runners from third base with less than two outs (52%).... Direction of balls hit to the outfield: 48% to left field, 26% to center, 26% to right batting left-handed; 39% to left field, 33% to center, 29% to right batting right-handed.... Base running: Advanced from first base to third on 4 of 15 outfield singles (27%); scored from second on 4 of 7 (57%).... Made 3.13 assists per nine innings at shortstop.

Comments: Sveum and Bill Spiers combined to play every inning at shortstop for Brewers last season. Only four other positions on any club in the majors were handled exclusively by only two players: Boston catchers (Pena & Marzano), Milwaukee catchers (Surhoff & Dempsey), Toronto second basemen (Alomar & Gonzales), and Cincinnati third basemen (Sabo & Quinones).... Started 37 games against left-handers last season, 38 games vs. right-handers.... Of his 64 hits, 25 were to the opposite field (39%), the 5th-highest percentage in the majors (minimum: 60 hits).... He has hit for a higher average with runners on base than he has with the bases empty in each of his five years in the majors. Career breakdown: .267 with runners on base, .224 with the bases empty. But that's just the tip of the clutch-hitting iceberg. He batted .368 last season with two outs and runners in scoring position; Brewers (.281) led majors in that category. Sveum's .310 career average in that category is 6th highest among active players. Put those conditions into Late-Inning Pressure Situations and he's a .400 hitter, matching Jose Canseco for top average among active players. With two outs and runners on base in LIPS, Sveum's career average (.386) stands alone at the top of active players.... Hit 32 home runs in 852 at-bats in 1986–87, but only 14 in 850 at-bats since 1988. Leaving County Stadium, a tough park for homers, might help: 27 of his 46 home runs have been hit away from Milwaukee.

Danny Tartabull
Bats Right

Kansas City Royals	AB	H	2B	3B	HR	RBI	BB	SO	BA	SA	OBA
Season	484	153	35	3	31	100	65	121	.316	.593	.397
vs. Left-Handers	142	42	9	1	8	22	27	31	.296	.542	.408
vs. Right-Handers	342	111	26	2	23	78	38	90	.325	.614	.392
vs. Ground-Ballers	218	65	18	0	11	44	22	54	.298	.532	.360
vs. Fly-Ballers	266	88	17	3	20	56	43	67	.331	.643	.426
Home Games	226	71	15	2	13	35	30	54	.314	.571	.395
Road Games	258	82	20	1	18	65	35	67	.318	.612	.398
Grass Fields	199	63	14	1	17	55	27	52	.317	.653	.394
Artificial Turf	285	90	21	2	14	45	38	69	.316	.551	.399
April	73	21	7	1	1	10	4	22	.288	.452	.321
May	88	26	4	0	4	14	5	20	.295	.477	.337
June	87	32	5	0	9	25	8	20	.368	.736	.421
July	74	28	7	0	8	19	17	23	.378	.797	.489
August	72	20	7	1	3	14	9	19	.278	.528	.361
Sept./Oct.	90	26	5	1	6	18	22	17	.289	.567	.429
Leading Off Inn.	140	41	9	2	11	11	11	34	.293	.621	.344
Runners On	217	77	18	1	14	83	39	50	.355	.641	.451
Bases Empty	267	76	17	2	17	17	26	71	.285	.554	.348
Runners/Scor. Pos.	124	46	12	1	8	68	31	33	.371	.677	.488
Runners On/2 Out	104	35	5	0	8	35	20	25	.337	.615	.452
Scor. Pos./2 Out	55	19	5	0	4	27	15	15	.345	.655	.500
Late-Inning Pressure	72	24	5	1	6	13	7	16	.333	.681	.392
Leading Off	23	9	1	1	4	4	2	5	.391	1.043	.440
Runners On	24	7	3	0	1	8	2	7	.292	.542	.346
Runners/Scor. Pos.	16	4	2	0	1	8	1	5	.250	.563	.294

RUNS BATTED IN	From 1B	From 2B	From 3B	Scoring Position
Totals	14/150	27/91	28/52	55/143
Percentage	9.3%	29.7%	53.8%	38.5%

Loves to face: Mike Moore (.444, 8-for-18, 4 2B, 1 HR)
Dave Stewart (.438, 14-for-32, 4 HR)
Bob Welch (.367, 11-for-30, 4 HR)

Hates to face: Roger Clemens (.152, 5-for-33)
Tom Henke (.083, 1-for-12, 1 2B, 2 BB, 6 SO)
Nolan Ryan (.059, 1-for-17)

Miscellaneous statistics: Ground outs-to-air outs ratio: 1.13 last season, 1.08 for career.... Grounded into 9 double plays in 91 opportunities (one per 10).... Drove in 22 of 33 runners from third base with less than two outs (67%).... Direction of balls hit to the outfield: 32% to left field, 29% to center, 39% to right.... Base running: Advanced from first base to third on 5 of 20 outfield singles (25%); scored from second on 14 of 22 (64%).... Made 1.65 putouts per nine innings in right field, lowest rate in A.L.

Comments: Leaves Royals Stadium, A.L.'s toughest home-run park, for Yankee Stadium, which is no longer the cause of nightmares for right-handed power hitters: Over past three years, their home run production has been reduced at the Stadium by only five percent. In addition, Tartabull led the majors with 13 opposite-field home runs last season, an encouraging sign for Yankees fans.... But the history is daunting: Over last 40 years, Dave Winfield is the only Yankees right-handed batter to have a 30-homer, 100-RBI season (he did it in both 1982 and 1983); from 1925 to 1950, Joe DiMaggio did it seven times, and Bob Meusel and Joe Gordon once apiece.... Tartabull established personal highs last year in batting average, slugging average, on-base average, and home-run rate.... Led A.L. in slugging average; last player to lead A.L. in slugging and then change teams the following season was Reggie Jackson, who led A.L. with Orioles in 1976 before joining Yankees in 1977.... Percentage of runners driven in from scoring position was 2d highest in A.L. last season, as was his batting average with runners in scoring position.... Batting average vs. right-handed pitchers was 3d highest in majors among right-handed batters last season (minimum: 100 AB vs. RHP).... Hit 18 home runs on the road last season; he led all visiting players with four home runs at both Memorial Stadium and Oakland Coliseum last season, and his three homers at Comiskey tied him for the most by a visiting player there.

Mickey Tettleton

Bats Left and Right

Detroit Tigers	AB	H	2B	3B	HR	RBI	BB	SO	BA	SA	OBA
Season	501	132	17	2	31	89	101	131	.263	.491	.387
vs. Left-Handers	109	27	4	0	9	25	17	32	.248	.532	.349
vs. Right-Handers	392	105	13	2	22	64	84	99	.268	.480	.397
vs. Ground-Ballers	245	70	7	1	18	42	45	57	.286	.498	.396
vs. Fly-Ballers	256	62	10	1	13	47	56	74	.242	.441	.378
Home Games	239	63	7	2	15	44	56	63	.264	.498	.402
Road Games	262	69	10	0	16	45	45	68	.263	.485	.371
Grass Fields	425	115	14	2	26	81	87	113	.271	.496	.394
Artificial Turf	76	17	3	0	5	8	14	18	.224	.461	.344
April	48	9	2	0	2	7	12	13	.188	.354	.344
May	85	28	2	1	5	15	15	22	.329	.553	.430
June	84	22	1	1	7	19	18	19	.262	.548	.396
July	88	24	3	0	6	19	11	27	.273	.511	.354
August	97	23	4	0	6	15	29	26	.237	.464	.409
Sept./Oct.	99	26	5	0	5	14	16	24	.263	.465	.365
Leading Off Inn.	109	27	5	0	5	5	18	29	.248	.431	.359
Runners On	207	57	4	0	17	75	49	50	.275	.541	.408
Bases Empty	294	75	13	2	14	14	52	81	.255	.456	.371
Runners/Scor. Pos.	120	34	3	0	8	57	35	36	.283	.508	.434
Runners On/2 Out	79	17	2	0	4	20	30	17	.215	.392	.431
Scor. Pos./2 Out	52	12	1	0	3	18	24	14	.231	.423	.474
Late-Inning Pressure	92	20	2	0	3	9	7	31	.217	.337	.280
Leading Off	15	2	1	0	0	0	1	7	.133	.200	.188
Runners On	41	7	0	0	1	7	3	15	.171	.244	.227
Runners/Scor. Pos.	20	4	0	0	0	5	1	10	.200	.200	.238

RUNS BATTED IN	From 1B	From 2B	From 3B	Scoring Position
Totals	14/168	23/100	21/48	44/148
Percentage	8.3%	23.0%	43.8%	29.7%

Loves to face: Scott Erickson (.500, 7-for-14)
Lee Guetterman (.333, 5-for-15, 2 HR)
Dan Plesac (.500, 2-for-4, 2 HR, 2 BB)

Hates to face: Dennis Eckersley (0-for-10)
Jack McDowell (0-for-13, 9 SO)
Frank Viola (0-for-14)

Miscellaneous statistics: Ground outs-to-air outs ratio: 0.97 last season, 1.13 for career.... Grounded into 12 double plays in 120 opportunities (one per 10).... Drove in 17 of 32 runners from third base with less than two outs (53%).... Direction of balls hit to the outfield: 16% to left field, 29% to center, 55% to right batting left-handed; 48% to left field, 28% to center, 24% to right batting right-handed.... Base running: Advanced from first base to third on 6 of 23 outfield singles (26%); scored from second on 12 of 18 (67%).... Opposing base stealers: 64-for-104 (62%).

Comments: Set career highs with 89 RBIs and 31 home runs, although he actually had a better home-run ratio in 1989 (26 homers in 411 at-bats) than he had last year.... RBI total was helped by career-high .283 batting average with runners in scoring position; prior to last year, his best average in those situations was a .218 mark in 1986. Even with .283 mark included, he still has lowest career scoring-position batting average among active players (minimum: 500 RISP at-bats): Tettleton .206, Franklin Stubbs .209, Devon White .222, Cory Snyder .223, Dick Schofield .231.... Switch-hitter started 117 of 118 games in which Tigers faced a right-handed starter, but only 22 of 44 vs. lefties.... Owns .221 career batting average in Late-Inning Pressure Situations; it dips to .166 when you add in the phrase, "with runners on base."... His average of one walk every 4.9 times up with bases loaded is 2d highest among active players, behind Jerry Browne.... One of five switch-hitting position players on Tigers last year, the most in any season in franchise history. The others: Milt Cuyler, Tony Phillips, John Shelby, and Tony Bernazard (who played in only six games).... With all his walks, strikeouts, and times hit by pitch, he ranks third in major league history in percentage of plate appearances without putting the ball in play. The all-time POPAWOPBIP (poppa-wop-bip) leaders (minimum: 2000 plate appearances): Rob Deer, 44.9 percent; Bo Jackson, 39.8; Tettleton, 39.2; Ken Phleps, 37.60; Pete Incaviglia, 37.58.

Frank Thomas

Bats Right

Chicago White Sox	AB	H	2B	3B	HR	RBI	BB	SO	BA	SA	OBA
Season	559	178	31	2	32	109	138	112	.318	.553	.453
vs. Left-Handers	170	64	9	0	11	35	42	27	.376	.624	.500
vs. Right-Handers	389	114	22	2	21	74	96	85	.293	.522	.432
vs. Ground-Ballers	264	86	9	1	11	43	57	55	.326	.492	.444
vs. Fly-Ballers	295	92	22	1	21	66	81	57	.312	.607	.460
Home Games	267	99	16	1	24	61	76	60	.371	.708	.509
Road Games	292	79	15	1	8	48	62	52	.271	.411	.399
Grass Fields	470	161	28	2	29	95	119	94	.343	.596	.475
Artificial Turf	89	17	3	0	3	14	19	18	.191	.326	.333
April	64	20	3	1	3	13	11	11	.313	.531	.413
May	87	28	5	0	5	24	30	19	.322	.552	.492
June	107	30	6	0	5	20	23	29	.280	.477	.412
July	99	32	5	0	7	15	25	18	.323	.586	.460
August	110	41	8	1	8	27	24	14	.373	.682	.481
Sept./Oct.	92	27	4	0	4	10	25	21	.293	.467	.444
Leading Off Inn.	87	25	7	0	6	6	23	16	.287	.575	.436
Runners On	263	85	15	1	14	91	68	54	.323	.548	.461
Bases Empty	296	93	16	1	18	18	70	58	.314	.557	.445
Runners/Scor. Pos.	147	51	10	1	7	75	45	32	.347	.571	.497
Runners On/2 Out	81	23	4	0	5	30	35	20	.284	.519	.500
Scor. Pos./2 Out	55	19	4	0	4	28	25	16	.345	.636	.550
Late-Inning Pressure	85	26	3	0	3	8	26	23	.306	.447	.464
Leading Off	19	7	2	0	0	0	2	3	.368	.474	.429
Runners On	33	7	0	0	1	6	13	12	.212	.303	.426
Runners/Scor. Pos.	15	4	0	0	0	4	12	4	.267	.267	.571

RUNS BATTED IN	From 1B	From 2B	From 3B	Scoring Position
Totals	15/197	29/100	33/68	62/168
Percentage	7.6%	29.0%	48.5%	36.9%

Loves to face: Chuck Finley (.556, 5-for-9)
Dave Johnson (.800, 4-for-5, 2 2B, 2 HR)
Randy Johnson (.444, 4-for-9, 1 HR, 6 BB, 5 SO)

Hates to face: Chris Bosio (0-for-5, 3 SO)
Mark Guthrie (.111, 1-for-9, 2 BB)
Nolan Ryan (0-for-8, 7 SO)

Miscellaneous statistics: Ground outs-to-air outs ratio: 1.03 last season, 1.02 for career.... Grounded into 20 double plays in 159 opportunities (one per 8.0).... Drove in 25 of 41 runners from third base with less than two outs (61%).... Direction of balls hit to the outfield: 28% to left field, 35% to center, 37% to right.... Base running: Advanced from first base to third on 14 of 40 outfield singles (35%); scored from second on 10 of 17 (59%).... Made 0.49 assists per nine innings at first base.

Comments: As with Dwight Gooden in 1985, there's good reason to present lots of "youngest since" stuff with Thomas. For example, at age 23, Thomas was the youngest player to walk as many as 138 times since Ted Williams in his .400 season of 1941. But as with Gooden, this unavoidable emphasis on age robs Thomas of much of the acclaim he deserves; the fact is that some of Thomas's accomplishments last season would have been noteworthy *even for a future Hall of Famer in the prime of his career.* The best example: He was the first .300 hitter since Williams (1941–42, 1946–47, and 1949) with that many home runs, RBIs, and walks—regardless of age. Even more impressive: The only other .300 hitter to reach all of those totals was Babe Ruth (six times).... Thomas was the first White Sox player since Dick Allen in 1972 to lead A.L. in walks. His on-base average was the best in the majors in any of the last three years, and the second best in team history (Luke Appling set the mark of .474 in 1936).... Batting average vs. left-handers was 2d best in majors.... Home-game average was second best in majors.... Hit 24 of 32 home runs at Comiskey Park, despite having 25 more at-bats in road games than at home. That's the first time a 30-homer hitter has had a 3-to-1 home–road breakdown since Bob Horner's 32-homer season (25 at home) in 1982. Ken Williams of the Browns hit 32 of 39 homers at Sportsman's Park in 1922; Ralph Kiner hit 31 of 40 at Forbes Field in 1948.... Over the past 17 years, the only other player to bat .370 at home and hit 20 HRs there: Fred Lynn (1979).

Alan Trammell

Detroit Tigers   Bats Right

Detroit Tigers	AB	H	2B	3B	HR	RBI	BB	SO	BA	SA	OBA
Season	375	93	20	0	9	55	37	39	.248	.373	.320
vs. Left-Handers	113	24	6	0	4	17	8	10	.212	.372	.268
vs. Right-Handers	262	69	14	0	5	38	29	29	.263	.374	.341
vs. Ground-Ballers	189	47	14	0	4	25	15	19	.249	.386	.311
vs. Fly-Ballers	186	46	6	0	5	30	22	20	.247	.360	.329
Home Games	218	53	11	0	6	39	22	17	.243	.376	.318
Road Games	157	40	9	0	3	16	15	22	.255	.369	.322
Grass Fields	324	79	17	0	8	49	33	34	.244	.370	.317
Artificial Turf	51	14	3	0	1	6	4	5	.275	.392	.339
April	64	19	6	0	2	12	6	3	.297	.484	.375
May	98	21	7	0	0	9	12	11	.214	.286	.306
June	85	18	2	0	4	9	7	10	.212	.376	.272
July	21	9	1	0	1	4	0	2	.429	.619	.429
August	54	12	1	0	0	9	5	7	.222	.241	.288
Sept./Oct.	53	14	3	0	2	12	7	6	.264	.434	.344
Leading Off Inn.	55	14	2	0	2	2	3	5	.255	.400	.293
Runners On	192	48	13	0	5	51	23	16	.250	.396	.335
Bases Empty	183	45	7	0	4	4	14	23	.246	.350	.303
Runners/Scor. Pos.	112	30	7	0	4	47	11	8	.268	.438	.331
Runners On/2 Out	68	18	4	0	3	22	9	7	.265	.456	.351
Scor. Pos./2 Out	51	13	3	0	3	21	6	5	.255	.490	.333
Late-Inning Pressure	54	8	2	0	1	4	4	7	.148	.241	.207
Leading Off	14	6	1	0	1	1	1	1	.429	.714	.467
Runners On	22	1	1	0	0	3	3	2	.045	.091	.160
Runners/Scor. Pos.	9	0	0	0	0	3	3	1	.000	.000	.250

RUNS BATTED IN	From 1B	From 2B	From 3B	Scoring Position
Totals	7/135	19/88	20/44	39/132
Percentage	5.2%	21.6%	45.5%	29.5%

Loves to face: Tom Gordon (.455, 5-for-11, 2 HR)
Greg A. Harris (.458, 11-for-24, 1 HR)
Mark Langston (.375, 18-for-48, 3 HR)

Hates to face: Luis Aquino (.059, 1-for-17)
Joe Grahe (0-for-7)
Bob Milacki (.077, 2-for-26, 5 BB)

Miscellaneous statistics: Ground outs-to-air outs ratio: 0.86 last season, 0.81 for career.... Grounded into 7 double plays in 112 opportunities (one per 16).... Drove in 15 of 26 runners from third base with less than two outs (58%).... Direction of balls hit to the outfield: 44% to left field, 30% to center, 26% to right.... Base running: Advanced from first base to third on 4 of 13 outfield singles (31%); scored from second on 13 of 13 (100%), best rate in A.L.... Made 3.46 assists per nine innings at shortstop, highest rate in majors.

Comments: Batted third in 71 starts, second in his other 23 starts; Detroit's third-place hitters batted only .237, lowest in majors, and had .317 on-base average, second lowest in majors. Had Trammell and the nine other guys who started in that slot gotten on base more often, big Cecil (who started all 162 games in cleanup spot) would have had even more guys to drive in.... Batting average in Late-Inning Pressure Situations was third lowest in A.L.; Tigers' .218 average in LIPS was worst in majors.... Stole 11 bases in 13 attempts, all of which came with right-handed pitchers on the mound.... At age 33, oldest A.L. shortstop to start at least half of his team's games last season; in the N.L., Ozzie Smith (36) and Alfredo Griffin (34) were older.... Trammell has played 1936 games in majors, all with Detroit; Lou Whitaker has played in 1965, all with Detroit. If both reach the 2000-game plateau (and finish their careers in Detroit), they would join Al Kaline (2834) and Charlie Gehringer (2323) as Tigers who appeared in at least 2000 games and never played for another team. Two other major league teams have three such players: Red Sox (Carl Yastrzemski, Ted Williams, Jim Rice) and Pirates (Roberto Clemente, Willie Stargell, Bill Mazeroski); but Tigers would be the only team with four.... Incidentally, Trammell and Whitaker have played 1722 Major league games together. Is that an all-time record? We'll let you know in the *1993 Analyst.*

Dave Valle

Seattle Mariners   Bats Right

Seattle Mariners	AB	H	2B	3B	HR	RBI	BB	SO	BA	SA	OBA
Season	324	63	8	1	8	32	34	49	.194	.299	.286
vs. Left-Handers	112	26	1	0	6	17	10	14	.232	.402	.320
vs. Right-Handers	212	37	7	1	2	15	24	35	.175	.245	.269
vs. Ground-Ballers	146	36	5	0	5	21	12	20	.247	.384	.319
vs. Fly-Ballers	178	27	3	1	3	11	22	29	.152	.230	.261
Home Games	173	28	4	1	0	8	17	27	.162	.197	.238
Road Games	151	35	4	0	8	24	17	22	.232	.417	.339
Grass Fields	112	31	4	0	7	21	11	16	.277	.500	.359
Artificial Turf	212	32	4	1	1	11	23	33	.151	.193	.248
April	57	13	0	0	2	5	7	9	.228	.333	.333
May	57	4	0	0	1	2	10	9	.070	.123	.221
June	41	3	0	0	0	0	3	7	.073	.073	.174
July	37	8	1	1	1	3	1	6	.216	.378	.237
August	54	12	2	0	2	3	6	8	.222	.370	.295
Sept./Oct.	78	23	5	0	2	19	7	10	.295	.436	.374
Leading Off Inn.	73	15	2	1	1	1	7	14	.205	.301	.310
Runners On	139	23	3	0	4	28	12	20	.165	.273	.242
Bases Empty	185	40	5	1	4	4	22	29	.216	.319	.319
Runners/Scor. Pos.	86	14	3	0	2	24	8	11	.163	.267	.242
Runners On/2 Out	59	12	2	0	1	13	4	10	.203	.288	.277
Scor. Pos./2 Out	38	9	2	0	1	13	3	5	.237	.368	.310
Late-Inning Pressure	39	10	2	1	2	5	2	5	.256	.513	.293
Leading Off	8	2	1	0	0	0	0	0	.250	.500	.250
Runners On	15	4	1	0	1	4	1	2	.267	.533	.313
Runners/Scor. Pos.	6	2	1	0	0	2	0	1	.333	.500	.333

RUNS BATTED IN	From 1B	From 2B	From 3B	Scoring Position
Totals	5/99	7/62	12/37	19/99
Percentage	5.1%	11.3%	32.4%	19.2%

Loves to face: Jeff Ballard (.458, 11-for-24, 3 HR)
Ken Patterson (.600, 3-for-5, 1 3B, 1 HR)
Nolan Ryan (.400, 4-for-10, 2 2B, 1 HR)

Hates to face: Paul Gibson (0-for-7)
Tom Gordon (0-for-9, 5 SO)
Ted Higuera (.080, 2-for-25, 3 BB)

Miscellaneous statistics: Ground outs-to-air outs ratio: 1.82 last season, 1.41 for career.... Grounded into 19 double plays in 66 opportunities (one per 3.5), worst rate in majors.... Drove in 6 of 20 runners from third base with less than two outs (30%), 2d-lowest rate in A.L.... Direction of balls hit to the outfield: 42% to left field, 33% to center, 25% to right.... Base running: Advanced from first base to third on 2 of 14 outfield singles (14%); scored from second on 6 of 10 (60%).... Opposing base stealers: 46-for-77 (60%), 4th-lowest rate in A.L.

Comments: Batting average stood at .128 after game of July 4, but he hit .263 the rest of the way. Raised season average to .196 coming into final game of season, needing 2-for-3 to climb to .200 mark, but he went 0-for-2 against Wilson Alvarez and became the fourth player in Mariners history to bat below .200 in a 300 at-bat season. The others: Leroy Stanton (.182 in 1978), Spike Owen (.196 in 1983), and the patron saint of sub-.200 hitters, Mario Mendoza (.198 in 1979).... Owns the lowest career batting average (.228) among the 37 players who have accumulated at least 1000 at-bats for Mariners. He has also been hit by the most pitches (35).... We welcome all our readers who have been reading the Ernest Riles comments. Here are the lowest batting averages (minimum: 400 at-bats) over the past two years combined. They are: Rob Deer .194, Valle .204, Riles .209, Scott Bradley .215, Bob Geren .215. Those of you reading the Riles comments should now return there; for the rest of our audience, we'll go on with Valle comments.... Has hit for higher average vs. ground-ball pitchers than vs. fly-ball pitchers in each of five full seasons in majors.... Through the end of the 1988 season, he had a .330 career batting average with runners in scoring position; in the three seasons since then, his composite average at those times is .205.... Mariners' staff ERA was 3.65 with Valle behind the plate, 4.05 with Scott Bradley, and 5.12 with Dave Cochrane.

Greg Vaughn
Bats Right

Milwaukee Brewers

	AB	H	2B	3B	HR	RBI	BB	SO	BA	SA	OBA
Season	542	132	24	5	27	98	62	125	.244	.456	.319
vs. Left-Handers	154	35	6	1	5	22	19	35	.227	.377	.307
vs. Right-Handers	388	97	18	4	22	76	43	90	.250	.487	.323
vs. Ground-Ballers	257	59	12	3	10	39	23	51	.230	.416	.290
vs. Fly-Ballers	285	73	12	2	17	59	39	74	.256	.491	.343
Home Games	256	63	16	1	16	54	34	58	.246	.504	.332
Road Games	286	69	8	4	11	44	28	67	.241	.413	.306
Grass Fields	461	118	23	3	27	92	52	100	.256	.495	.328
Artificial Turf	81	14	1	2	0	6	10	25	.173	.235	.264
April	48	13	3	0	5	13	7	11	.271	.646	.375
May	86	22	6	1	3	11	9	20	.256	.453	.326
June	103	24	4	1	7	28	12	21	.233	.495	.313
July	83	15	1	1	3	9	9	24	.181	.325	.255
August	99	24	4	1	4	15	16	22	.242	.424	.342
Sept./Oct.	123	34	6	1	5	22	9	27	.276	.463	.319
Leading Off Inn.	137	34	6	1	9	9	13	29	.248	.504	.318
Runners On	241	64	11	2	13	84	33	55	.266	.490	.345
Bases Empty	301	68	13	3	14	14	29	70	.226	.429	.296
Runners/Scor. Pos.	155	43	9	1	9	74	21	40	.277	.523	.350
Runners On/2 Out	108	25	5	1	6	34	15	29	.231	.463	.325
Scor. Pos./2 Out	76	20	5	1	5	32	11	19	.263	.553	.356
Late-Inning Pressure	89	20	2	0	4	15	12	19	.225	.382	.317
Leading Off	23	5	0	0	2	2	5	6	.217	.478	.357
Runners On	36	10	2	0	1	12	4	5	.278	.417	.350
Runners/Scor. Pos.	22	8	2	0	1	12	3	4	.364	.591	.440

RUNS BATTED IN	From 1B	From 2B	From 3B	Scoring Position
Totals	13/186	24/119	34/68	58/187
Percentage	7.0%	20.2%	50.0%	31.0%

Loves to face: Ron Darling (5-for-5, 1 HR, 1 BB)
Gene Nelson (.444, 4-for-9, 2 HR)
Dave Stewart (.333, 7-for-21, 2 2B, 5 HR, 7 BB)

Hates to face: Roger Clemens (.056, 1-for-18, 10 SO)
Chuck Finley (0-for-11, 7 SO)
Mark Guthrie (0-for-9)

Miscellaneous statistics: Ground outs-to-air outs ratio: 0.63 last season, 5th lowest in A.L.; 0.77 for career.... Grounded into 5 double plays in 121 opportunities (one per 24).... Drove in 24 of 39 runners from third base with less than two outs (62%).... Direction of balls hit to the outfield: 54% to left field, 24% to center, 22% to right.... Base running: Advanced from first base to third on 6 of 22 outfield singles (27%); scored from second on 11 of 12 (92%).... Made 2.43 putouts per nine innings in left field, highest rate in A.L.

Comments: Led majors in batting average with bases loaded last season (minimum: 5 hits); four players hit better than .500: Vaughn (7-for-11), Todd Zeile (6-for-10), Ron Gant (5-for-9), and Willie Randolph (6-for-11).... Had a higher home-run rate vs. right-handed pitchers (one every 17.6 at-bats) than he had vs. lefties (one every 30.8 at-bats) last season. That's not quite as unusual as you might imagine: Nine of the 21 right-handed batters who hit at least 25 homers in 1991 had a better home-run rate against right-handers than against left-handers.... Still, Vaughn had the *lowest* home-run rate off lefties last season among those 21 right-handed sluggers. His career totals are just as diverse: 40 homers in 734 at-bats vs. right-handers (one every 18.4 at-bats), nine in 303 vs. left-handers (one every 33.7 at-bats).... Of his 132 hits, only 11 went to the opposite field (8%), second-lowest percentage in majors (minimum: 60 hits).... Batting average on artificial turf was 5th lowest in the majors.... June RBI total was second highest in majors.... Finished with a rush—driving in 11 runs in a seven-game span to reach 98 with a game and a half to go. But he went hitless over his last eight at-bats of season, leaving 10 runners on base, including six in scoring position. Final at-bat of the season: Roger Clemens struck him out with two runners on base.

Mo Vaughn
Bats Left

Boston Red Sox

	AB	H	2B	3B	HR	RBI	BB	SO	BA	SA	OBA
Season	219	57	12	0	4	32	26	43	.260	.370	.339
vs. Left-Handers	33	7	2	0	0	7	2	8	.212	.273	.257
vs. Right-Handers	186	50	10	0	4	25	24	35	.269	.387	.352
vs. Ground-Ballers	84	24	3	0	1	12	10	15	.286	.357	.371
vs. Fly-Ballers	135	33	9	0	3	20	16	28	.244	.378	.318
Home Games	100	32	8	0	1	16	18	20	.320	.430	.421
Road Games	119	25	4	0	3	16	8	23	.210	.319	.262
Grass Fields	190	49	11	0	3	28	21	39	.258	.363	.332
Artificial Turf	29	8	1	0	1	4	5	4	.276	.414	.382
April	0	0	0	0	0	0	0	0	—	—	—
May	0	0	0	0	0	0	0	0	—	—	—
June	11	3	0	0	1	2	1	3	.273	.545	.308
July	78	19	3	0	2	13	8	17	.244	.359	.318
August	54	16	4	0	1	9	10	3	.296	.426	.394
Sept./Oct.	76	19	5	0	0	8	7	20	.250	.316	.321
Leading Off Inn.	49	12	2	0	2	2	9	9	.245	.408	.362
Runners On	102	33	8	0	1	29	13	18	.324	.431	.392
Bases Empty	117	24	4	0	3	3	13	25	.205	.316	.290
Runners/Scor. Pos.	59	22	5	0	1	28	10	13	.373	.508	.438
Runners On/2 Out	45	14	4	0	0	11	6	7	.311	.400	.392
Scor. Pos./2 Out	31	10	3	0	0	11	5	7	.323	.419	.417
Late-Inning Pressure	31	6	1	0	0	4	1	9	.194	.226	.212
Leading Off	5	1	0	0	0	0	0	0	.200	.200	.200
Runners On	18	4	0	0	0	4	1	6	.222	.222	.250
Runners/Scor. Pos.	10	3	0	0	0	4	1	4	.300	.300	.333

RUNS BATTED IN	From 1B	From 2B	From 3B	Scoring Position
Totals	2/78	12/40	14/29	26/69
Percentage	2.6%	30.0%	48.3%	37.7%

Loves to face: Dave Stewart (.500, 2-for-4, 2 BB)
Walt Terrell (.500, 4-for-8)

Hates to face: Cal Eldred (0-for-5, 3 SO)
Jack Morris (0-for-6)
Scott Sanderson (0-for-6)

Miscellaneous statistics: Ground outs-to-air outs ratio: 1.03 last season, 1.03 for career.... Grounded into 7 double plays in 54 opportunities (one per 7.7).... Drove in 10 of 16 runners from third base with less than two outs (63%).... Direction of balls hit to the outfield: 34% to left field, 39% to center, 27% to right.... Base running: Advanced from first base to third on 1 of 15 outfield singles (7%), 3d-lowest rate in majors; scored from second on 4 of 6 (67%).... Made 0.65 assists per nine innings at first base.

Comments: Top batting averages among A.L. rookies last year (minimum: 200 at-bats): Chuck Knoblauch, .281; Mark Lewis, .264; Ivan Rodriguez, .264; Vaughn, .260; Milt Cuyler, .257. But to call Vaughn just a .260 hitter would be akin to calling Lynne Russell just another newscaster. Vaughn really stood out in key situations. His average with runners on base (.324) was highest among major league rookies last season (minimum: 100 at-bats with ROB); his average with runners in scoring position (.373) was highest among all rookies since Al Pedrique hit .458 and Mickey Brantley .376 in 1987 (minimum: 50 at-bats with RISP).... Started 60 games against right-handers last season, but only three against southpaws.... Boston's first basemen combined for 77 RBIs, third fewest in A.L. last season.... Including Vaughn, 11 of the 26 first-round selections in 1989 amateur draft have already played in majors. Vaughn was the 23d player selected.... Phil Plantier did not bat enough to get into this section, but this seems like a good place to mention that with 11 homers in 148 at-bats, his home-run rate ranked among top-five rookie rates since 1969 (minimum: 10 homers): Sam Horn, one every 11.3 at-bats in 1987; Mark McGwire, one every 11.4 in '87; Kevin Maas, one every 12.1 in 1990; Plantier, one every 13.5 in 1991; Bob Horner, one every 14.0 in 1978.

Robin Ventura
Bats Left

Chicago White Sox	AB	H	2B	3B	HR	RBI	BB	SO	BA	SA	OBA
Season	606	172	25	1	23	100	80	67	.284	.442	.367
vs. Left-Handers	192	50	6	0	5	20	31	29	.260	.370	.364
vs. Right-Handers	414	122	19	1	18	80	49	38	.295	.476	.369
vs. Ground-Ballers	275	79	14	0	10	48	35	20	.287	.447	.365
vs. Fly-Ballers	331	93	11	1	13	52	45	47	.281	.438	.369
Home Games	304	88	13	0	16	58	37	37	.289	.490	.368
Road Games	302	84	12	1	7	42	43	30	.278	.394	.367
Grass Fields	518	147	22	1	23	93	66	57	.284	.463	.366
Artificial Turf	88	25	3	0	0	7	14	10	.284	.318	.375
April	59	19	3	0	2	9	11	5	.322	.475	.429
May	101	21	1	0	0	5	7	15	.208	.218	.266
June	109	34	5	0	2	14	14	6	.312	.413	.387
July	115	41	8	0	12	33	14	9	.357	.739	.431
August	106	30	4	1	5	25	14	11	.283	.481	.358
Sept./Oct.	116	27	4	0	2	14	20	21	.233	.319	.348
Leading Off Inn.	104	25	5	0	4	4	8	12	.240	.404	.301
Runners On	267	81	10	0	12	89	35	26	.303	.476	.375
Bases Empty	339	91	15	1	11	11	45	41	.268	.416	.361
Runners/Scor. Pos.	151	50	7	0	8	77	23	17	.331	.536	.403
Runners On/2 Out	91	25	3	0	4	29	17	6	.275	.440	.389
Scor. Pos./2 Out	59	16	2	0	4	28	12	5	.271	.508	.394
Late-Inning Pressure	111	30	6	1	5	18	7	7	.270	.477	.314
Leading Off	30	10	2	0	1	1	0	1	.333	.500	.333
Runners On	41	8	2	0	2	15	4	3	.195	.390	.267
Runners/Scor. Pos.	25	6	1	0	2	14	3	1	.240	.520	.321

RUNS BATTED IN	From 1B	From 2B	From 3B	Scoring Position
Totals	15/180	32/129	30/63	62/192
Percentage	8.3%	24.8%	47.6%	32.3%

Loves to face: Storm Davis (.667, 4-for-6)
Mike Gardiner (.625, 5-for-8, 1 HR)
Scott Sanderson (.462, 6-for-13, 1 HR)

Hates to face: Tom Gordon (0-for-10)
Jaime Navarro (0-for-7)
Rod Nichols (.077, 1-for-13)

Miscellaneous statistics: Ground outs-to-air outs ratio: 1.49 last season, 1.39 for career.... Grounded into 22 double plays in 137 opportunities (one per 6.2).... Drove in 24 of 36 runners from third base with less than two outs (67%).... Direction of balls hit to the outfield: 42% to left field, 29% to center, 29% to right.... Base running: Advanced from first base to third on 13 of 39 outfield singles (33%); scored from second on 15 of 21 (71%).... Made 2.02 assists per nine innings at third base.

Comments: His 12 home runs during July were the most by any player in majors in any month last season. He ranked seventh in A.L. in batting and second in RBIs during July.... Batting average stood at .303 as late as August 21, but hit .227 the rest of the way to finish at .286. With Frank Thomas batting .318, they came close to becoming the first pair of teammates since Fred Lynn and Jim Rice in 1975 to bat .300 in a season before either's 25th birthday.... Robin batted .284 on grass fields, .284 on artificial turf, .284 in day games, .284 in night games.... First player in White Sox history to drive in 100 runs in a season in which he played at least 100 games at third base; old record: Pete Ward, 94 RBIs in 1964. White Sox (104) and Giants (100) were only major league teams to get 100 RBIs from third base position last year.... Improved slugging average by 124 points from 1990 (.318 to .442), second-largest improvement in majors last season; Cal Ripken slugged .415 in 1990, .566 in 1991.... Of his 172 hits, 41 were directed to opposite field (37%), 6th-highest percentage among A.L. players with at least 60 hits last year.... Batting average with runners in scoring position was 7th highest in A.L.... His average of one error every 24 chances was the worst among A.L. third basemen with at least 100 games last season. Led A.L. third basemen with 18 errors, but that was the lowest total to lead the league in a full season since 1946, when Cecil Travis led with 17.

Omar Vizquel
Bats Left and Right

Seattle Mariners	AB	H	2B	3B	HR	RBI	BB	SO	BA	SA	OBA
Season	426	98	16	4	1	41	45	37	.230	.293	.302
vs. Left-Handers	87	20	4	0	0	11	7	5	.230	.276	.284
vs. Right-Handers	339	78	12	4	1	30	38	32	.230	.298	.306
vs. Ground-Ballers	197	42	9	2	1	16	17	20	.213	.294	.274
vs. Fly-Ballers	229	56	7	2	0	25	28	17	.245	.293	.324
Home Games	206	52	11	4	1	24	21	21	.252	.359	.319
Road Games	220	46	5	0	0	17	24	16	.209	.232	.286
Grass Fields	167	36	3	0	0	13	17	10	.216	.234	.286
Artificial Turf	259	62	13	4	1	28	28	27	.239	.332	.311
April	50	10	1	1	0	4	5	1	.200	.260	.273
May	74	15	2	2	0	7	7	6	.203	.284	.268
June	76	18	4	0	0	6	9	6	.237	.289	.314
July	65	19	2	0	0	5	6	4	.292	.323	.347
August	75	15	2	0	1	8	9	11	.200	.267	.286
Sept./Oct.	86	21	5	1	0	11	9	9	.244	.326	.316
Leading Off Inn.	105	23	5	0	1	1	15	12	.219	.295	.317
Runners On	184	48	8	1	0	40	20	12	.261	.315	.329
Bases Empty	242	50	8	3	1	1	25	25	.207	.277	.281
Runners/Scor. Pos.	109	34	5	1	0	39	13	6	.312	.376	.376
Runners On/2 Out	95	22	2	0	0	18	8	5	.232	.253	.291
Scor. Pos./2 Out	61	19	2	0	0	18	6	4	.311	.344	.373
Late-Inning Pressure	64	18	7	2	0	3	6	6	.281	.453	.343
Leading Off	15	5	3	0	0	0	2	2	.333	.533	.412
Runners On	24	5	2	0	0	3	3	3	.208	.292	.296
Runners/Scor. Pos.	12	1	1	0	0	3	1	1	.083	.167	.154

RUNS BATTED IN	From 1B	From 2B	From 3B	Scoring Position
Totals	3/120	18/93	19/43	37/136
Percentage	2.5%	19.4%	44.2%	27.2%

Loves to face: John Dopson (.571, 4-for-7)
Kirk McCaskill (.316, 6-for-19, 1 HR)
Jaime Navarro (.526, 10-for-19)

Hates to face: Roger Clemens (0-for-12)
Dave Stewart (0-for-13)
Walt Terrell (.059, 1-for-17, 1 2B)

Miscellaneous statistics: Ground outs-to-air outs ratio: 1.40 last season, 1.38 for career.... Grounded into 8 double plays in 82 opportunities (one per 10).... Drove in 11 of 17 runners from third base with less than two outs (65%).... Direction of balls hit to the outfield: 26% to left field, 33% to center, 41% to right batting left-handed; 43% to left field, 23% to center, 34% to right batting right-handed.... Base running: Advanced from first base to third on 5 of 15 outfield singles (33%); scored from second on 8 of 9 (89%).... Made 3.35 assists per nine innings at shortstop, 2d-highest rate in A.L.

Comments: Finished third in fielding among A.L. shortstops last season, averaging a team-record one error every 50.7 chances, behind Cal Ripken (73.3) and Greg Gagne (63.0). Handled 109 chances without an error in Late-Inning Pressure Situations.... Also set team record for shortstops by participating in 105 double plays; ratio of innings to double plays was second best in majors to Alvaro Espinoza.... Started 111 of 120 games in which Mariners faced a right-handed starter, but only 12 of 42 games vs. left-handers.... Mariners quiz: Among all players with at least 1000 at-bats with M's, who is the only player with a lower home-run rate than Omar (who has hit four in 1068 at-bats)? Answer below.... Only two of his 41 RBIs gave Seattle a lead (5%), the lowest percentage of go-ahead RBIs by any player in the majors last season (minimum: 25 RBI).... Seattle had the only infield in the majors last season in which all four regulars played 130 or more games at their positions: Pete O'Brien played 132 games at first, Harold Reynolds 159 at second, Edgar Martinez 144 at third, and Vizquel 138 at short.... Quiz answer: Jack Perconte, two home runs in 1097 at-bats.... Vizquel has been to the plate 1195 times in his major league career and has never been intentionally walked; he's number one on the most-plate-appearances-without-an-IBB list, among active players; that is, unless Ken Williams (1253 plate appearances) gets a job in the bigs this year.

Lou Whitaker
Bats Left

Detroit Tigers	AB	H	2B	3B	HR	RBI	BB	SO	BA	SA	OBA
Season	470	131	26	2	23	78	90	45	.279	.489	.391
vs. Left-Handers	97	24	3	0	2	14	15	15	.247	.340	.354
vs. Right-Handers	373	107	23	2	21	64	75	30	.287	.528	.400
vs. Ground-Ballers	252	71	15	1	11	41	42	17	.282	.480	.384
vs. Fly-Ballers	218	60	11	1	12	37	48	28	.275	.500	.399
Home Games	237	72	13	1	15	51	61	23	.304	.557	.442
Road Games	233	59	13	1	8	27	29	22	.253	.421	.335
Grass Fields	400	118	23	2	20	70	80	36	.295	.512	.409
Artificial Turf	70	13	3	0	3	8	10	9	.186	.357	.289
April	34	10	2	0	4	8	10	3	.294	.706	.444
May	85	17	4	1	1	12	17	8	.200	.306	.337
June	87	23	1	1	5	14	20	10	.264	.471	.400
July	63	27	6	0	2	7	8	4	.429	.619	.486
August	96	26	7	0	8	22	19	14	.271	.594	.388
Sept./Oct.	105	28	6	0	3	15	16	6	.267	.410	.358
Leading Off Inn.	78	18	2	0	2	2	14	8	.231	.333	.348
Runners On	214	65	12	2	12	67	48	21	.304	.547	.421
Bases Empty	256	66	14	0	11	11	42	24	.258	.441	.365
Runners/Scor. Pos.	109	31	7	0	5	47	28	12	.284	.486	.407
Runners On/2 Out	82	20	4	1	4	21	22	10	.244	.463	.410
Scor. Pos./2 Out	50	11	2	0	2	14	13	6	.220	.380	.381
Late-Inning Pressure	70	17	3	0	5	16	19	8	.243	.500	.400
Leading Off	12	5	0	0	1	1	6	2	.417	.667	.611
Runners On	35	8	2	0	2	13	12	5	.229	.457	.417
Runners/Scor. Pos.	23	8	2	0	2	13	7	3	.348	.696	.484

RUNS BATTED IN	From 1B	From 2B	From 3B	Scoring Position
Totals	18/154	16/92	21/44	37/136
Percentage	11.7%	17.4%	47.7%	27.2%

Loves to face: Mike Boddicker (.350, 21-for-60, 3 HR)
Charlie Hough (.348, 23-for-66, 3 HR)
Dave Johnson (.529, 9-for-17, 2 HR)

Hates to face: Jeff Ballard (.063, 1-for-16)
Tom Henke (.042, 1-for-24)
Dave Stieb (.184, 14-for-76)

Miscellaneous statistics: Ground outs-to-air outs ratio: 0.68 last season, 1.07 for career.... Grounded into 3 double plays in 117 opportunities (one per 39).... Drove in 18 of 21 runners from third base with less than two outs (86%), highest rate in majors.... Direction of balls hit to the outfield: 24% to left field, 34% to center, 42% to right.... Base running: Advanced from first base to third on 7 of 25 outfield singles (28%); scored from second on 8 of 10 (80%).... Made 3.06 assists per nine innings at second base.

Comments: Last season was the fourth in which he played at least 100 games at second base with 20+ home runs. The only other players with at least four of those: Joe Gordon and Rogers Hornsby (7), Joe Morgan and Ryne Sandberg (4).... His 42-point increase from 1990 to 1991 (.237 to .279) was the 5th largest of any player who qualified for the batting title in both seasons.... His season represented a 64-to-1 breakthrough at age 33. The only older player with a more extreme breakthrough last season was Ozzie Smith.... As noted above, he led the majors last season in delivering runners from third base with less than two outs. His rate of 86 percent was the best by a Detroit player since we began keeping track in 1975. His career rate: 62 percent.... Started only 11 of 44 games in which the Tigers faced a left-handed starter, 111 of 118 games against right-handers.... He has hit for a higher average against ground-ball pitchers than he has against fly-ballers in each of the last seven years.... He led A.L. second basemen in fielding percentage for the second time in his career, with one error every 155 chances; the league average for second basemen: one per 53 chances.... Here's something to shoot for: No second baseman has led the A.L. in fielding percentage in consecutive seasons since Jerry Adair (1964–65).... Ranks 10th in major league history with 1933 games played at second base, 130 fewer than Nap Lajoie. The only active player above him: Willie Randolph (8th at 2073).

Devon White
Bats Left and Right

Toronto Blue Jays	AB	H	2B	3B	HR	RBI	BB	SO	BA	SA	OBA
Season	642	181	40	10	17	60	55	135	.282	.455	.342
vs. Left-Handers	199	60	15	2	8	20	16	32	.302	.518	.350
vs. Right-Handers	443	121	25	8	9	40	39	103	.273	.427	.339
vs. Ground-Ballers	327	94	21	2	6	23	24	76	.287	.419	.342
vs. Fly-Ballers	315	87	19	8	11	37	31	59	.276	.492	.343
Home Games	326	97	26	6	9	33	25	61	.298	.497	.355
Road Games	316	84	14	4	8	27	30	74	.266	.411	.330
Grass Fields	251	64	11	2	7	22	22	63	.255	.398	.314
Artificial Turf	391	117	29	8	10	38	33	72	.299	.491	.360
April	75	25	9	1	0	13	5	11	.333	.480	.386
May	95	23	4	2	1	11	14	22	.242	.358	.339
June	118	36	9	2	1	6	9	25	.305	.441	.359
July	114	32	4	2	4	9	6	20	.281	.456	.317
August	117	37	8	2	8	15	13	27	.316	.624	.385
Sept./Oct.	123	28	6	1	3	6	8	30	.228	.366	.280
Leading Off Inn.	266	92	22	3	12	12	14	54	.346	.586	.392
Runners On	224	55	11	4	3	46	27	51	.246	.371	.319
Bases Empty	418	126	29	6	14	14	28	84	.301	.500	.355
Runners/Scor. Pos.	128	22	5	1	1	37	18	34	.172	.250	.263
Runners On/2 Out	114	23	2	3	2	18	18	30	.202	.325	.311
Scor. Pos./2 Out	71	10	1	0	0	11	12	21	.141	.155	.265
Late-Inning Pressure	87	29	3	1	0	5	8	23	.333	.391	.389
Leading Off	25	8	2	0	0	0	0	5	.320	.400	.320
Runners On	40	13	0	1	0	5	4	13	.325	.375	.386
Runners/Scor. Pos.	21	3	0	0	0	4	2	9	.143	.143	.217

RUNS BATTED IN	From 1B	From 2B	From 3B	Scoring Position
Totals	9/155	12/102	22/58	34/160
Percentage	5.8%	11.8%	37.9%	21.3%

Loves to face: Joe Hesketh (.556, 5-for-9, 1 HR)
Edwin Nunez (.444, 4-for-9, 2 HR)
Frank Tanana (.429, 9-for-21, 1 HR)

Hates to face: Kevin Brown (.063, 1-for-16)
Roger Clemens (.130, 6-for-46, 0 BB)
Nolan Ryan (.091, 3-for-33, 3 BB)

Miscellaneous statistics: Ground outs-to-air outs ratio: 1.53 last season, 1.46 for career.... Grounded into 7 double plays in 92 opportunities (one per 13).... Drove in 18 of 28 runners from third base with less than two outs (64%).... Direction of balls hit to the outfield: 34% to left field, 31% to center, 36% to right batting left-handed; 44% to left field, 27% to center, 29% to right batting right-handed.... Base running: Advanced from first base to third on 10 of 26 outfield singles (38%); scored from second on 21 of 25 (84%).... Made 2.85 putouts per nine innings in center field, 3d-highest rate in A.L.

Comments: One of three players in majors to reach double figures in doubles, triples, home runs, and stolen bases last season. The others: Mike Devereaux and Paul Molitor. White is the only player to have done that twice in the past three seasons. (He did it in 1989 as well.).... His 65-point increase from 1990 to 1991 (.217 to .282) was the 2d largest of any player who qualified for the batting title in both seasons.... Led the Blue Jays with a .346 batting average leading off innings. Even with only 14 leadoff walks, his on-base percentage in those situations (.392) ranked fifth in the league.... His 17 home runs from the leadoff spot in the batting order was tied for 2d most in the majors. The top five: Rickey Henderson (18), White (17), Paul Molitor (17), Devereaux (16), Brian Downing (15).... Played the most innings of any A.L. center fielder last season (1384).... How do you define "clutch"? White's batting average with runners in scoring position was 5th lowest in the league, but his average in Late-Inning Pressure Situations was 4th highest.... His batting average with runners in scoring position has been lower than his overall batting average in each of his seven seasons in the majors. Career breakdown: .222 with RISP, .265 in other at-bats.... Has driven in fewer than 23 percent of runners from scoring position in each of the past three seasons.

Mark Whiten
Bats Left and Right

Blue Jays/Indians	AB	H	2B	3B	HR	RBI	BB	SO	BA	SA	OBA
Season	407	99	18	7	9	45	30	85	.243	.388	.297
vs. Left-Handers	109	28	7	2	2	10	9	26	.257	.413	.311
vs. Right-Handers	298	71	11	5	7	35	21	59	.238	.379	.291
vs. Ground-Ballers	208	49	13	3	3	21	17	41	.236	.370	.293
vs. Fly-Ballers	199	50	5	4	6	24	13	44	.251	.407	.301
Home Games	197	49	8	5	4	16	16	40	.249	.401	.310
Road Games	210	50	10	2	5	29	14	45	.238	.376	.284
Grass Fields	283	73	13	4	6	31	21	51	.258	.396	.309
Artificial Turf	124	26	5	3	3	14	9	34	.210	.371	.269
April	55	17	2	1	1	14	4	13	.309	.436	.339
May	65	13	2	2	0	4	4	14	.200	.292	.257
June	44	8	2	0	1	2	4	10	.182	.295	.250
July	95	26	5	2	3	12	5	18	.274	.463	.324
August	114	27	7	1	4	12	12	21	.237	.421	.307
Sept./Oct.	34	8	0	1	0	1	1	9	.235	.294	.250
Leading Off Inn.	94	29	6	0	5	5	4	17	.309	.532	.343
Runners On	171	40	8	4	1	37	13	40	.234	.345	.284
Bases Empty	236	59	10	3	8	8	17	45	.250	.419	.306
Runners/Scor. Pos.	95	22	5	1	0	31	9	23	.232	.305	.284
Runners On/2 Out	73	16	2	3	1	12	7	20	.219	.370	.287
Scor. Pos./2 Out	46	6	1	0	0	7	5	14	.130	.152	.216
Late-Inning Pressure	64	14	1	1	2	5	3	14	.219	.359	.261
Leading Off	16	5	0	0	2	2	0	4	.313	.688	.313
Runners On	28	4	1	0	0	3	2	7	.143	.179	.219
Runners/Scor. Pos.	15	3	0	0	0	3	1	4	.200	.200	.235

RUNS BATTED IN	From 1B	From 2B	From 3B	Scoring Position
Totals	7/136	12/79	17/42	29/121
Percentage	5.1%	15.2%	40.5%	24.0%

Loves to face: Kevin Appier (.300, 3-for-10, 2 HR)
Kevin Brown (.455, 5-for-11, 2 HR)
Chuck Finley (.600, 6-for-10)
Hates to face: Alex Fernandez (.100, 1-for-10, 5 SO)
Randy Johnson (0-for-6, 4 SO)
Kirk McCaskill (0-for-7)

Miscellaneous statistics: Ground outs-to-air outs ratio: 1.25 last season, 1.21 for career.... Grounded into 13 double plays in 86 opportunities (one per 6.6).... Drove in 14 of 23 runners from third base with less than two outs (61%).... Direction of balls hit to the outfield: 29% to left field, 33% to center, 38% to right batting left-handed; 47% to left field, 33% to center, 20% to right batting right-handed.... Base running: Advanced from first base to third on 9 of 22 outfield singles (41%); scored from second on 9 of 9 (100%).... Made 2.40 putouts per nine innings in right field, 3d-highest rate in A.L.

Comments: Had a streak of 18 consecutive plate appearances in which he failed to hit the ball out of the infield (May 19–June 5), tying his teammate Chris James for the 2d longest in the A.L. last season. Tim Naehring of the Red Sox had 23 in a row (during an 0-for-39 streak that prompted his season-long demotion to the minors). The longest streak in the majors: 36 PAs without reaching the outfield, by Mike Bielecki (April 13–August 28).... His slugging percentage was 3d highest among A.L. rookies with at least 200 at-bats last season.... Batting average with two outs and runners in scoring position was 4th lowest in the league.... Led all rookie outfielders in assists with 12, despite playing only 109 games. The last rookie outfielders with that many assists: Devon White (16) and Ellis Burks (15) in 1987.... His .237 career batting average in Late-Inning Pressure Situations breaks down like this: .129 with runners on base (4-for-31), .306 with the bases empty (15-for-49).... Most comparable rookie seasons offensively in each of the past five decades: 1980s, Randy Bush; 1970s, Leon Roberts; 1960s, Steve Whitaker; 1950s, George Altman; 1940s, Gil Hodges. Heck, 1-for-5 ain't *that* bad.

Bernie Williams
Bats Left and Right

New York Yankees	AB	H	2B	3B	HR	RBI	BB	SO	BA	SA	OBA
Season	320	76	19	4	3	34	48	57	.237	.350	.336
vs. Left-Handers	104	21	6	0	2	13	17	11	.202	.317	.309
vs. Right-Handers	216	55	13	4	1	21	31	46	.255	.366	.349
vs. Ground-Ballers	155	38	9	2	0	12	22	31	.245	.329	.339
vs. Fly-Ballers	165	38	10	2	3	22	26	26	.230	.370	.333
Home Games	159	42	10	2	1	19	23	22	.264	.371	.355
Road Games	161	34	9	2	2	15	25	35	.211	.329	.317
Grass Fields	276	68	17	4	2	31	42	43	.246	.359	.345
Artificial Turf	44	8	2	0	1	3	6	14	.182	.295	.280
April	0	0	0	0	0	0	0	0	—	—	—
May	0	0	0	0	0	0	0	0	—	—	—
June	0	0	0	0	0	0	0	0	—	—	—
July	71	18	4	1	2	11	15	14	.254	.423	.386
August	125	30	10	1	1	14	17	25	.240	.360	.331
Sept./Oct.	124	28	5	2	0	9	16	18	.226	.298	.310
Leading Off Inn.	104	24	4	1	1	1	20	15	.231	.317	.355
Runners On	122	35	10	1	0	31	17	26	.287	.385	.366
Bases Empty	198	41	9	3	3	3	31	31	.207	.328	.317
Runners/Scor. Pos.	67	23	6	1	0	29	9	12	.343	.463	.405
Runners On/2 Out	54	14	2	1	0	13	7	11	.259	.333	.344
Scor. Pos./2 Out	38	9	1	1	0	12	4	7	.237	.316	.310
Late-Inning Pressure	50	10	2	0	1	8	8	12	.200	.300	.322
Leading Off	11	2	1	0	0	0	3	1	.182	.273	.357
Runners On	24	6	1	0	0	7	2	8	.250	.292	.308
Runners/Scor. Pos.	16	5	1	0	0	7	1	5	.313	.375	.353

RUNS BATTED IN	From 1B	From 2B	From 3B	Scoring Position
Totals	3/86	15/53	13/29	28/82
Percentage	3.5%	28.3%	44.8%	34.1%

Loves to face: Andy Hawkins (.667, 2-for-3, 1 2B, 1 3B, 3 BB)
Eric King (.600, 3-for-5)
Hates to face: Mike Boddicker (0-for-6)
Mark Langston (0-for-6)
Bob Milacki (0-for-8)

Miscellaneous statistics: Ground outs-to-air outs ratio: 1.38 last season, 1.38 for career.... Grounded into 4 double plays in 57 opportunities (one per 14).... Drove in 10 of 16 runners from third base with less than two outs (63%).... Direction of balls hit to the outfield: 37% to left field, 31% to center, 31% to right batting left-handed; 25% to left field, 48% to center, 27% to right batting right-handed.... Base running: Advanced from first base to third on 6 of 18 outfield singles (33%); scored from second on 10 of 11 (91%).... Made 2.74 putouts per nine innings in center field.

Comments: Played every inning of every Yankees game from the time he was recalled (July 7) until the end of the season. No other player played every inning after the All-Star break.... Batted .280 with two home runs in his first 25 games, only .220 with two more homers in his last 80 games.... Despite a late start, he ranked second on the Yankees in walks, and third among A.L. rookies, behind Chuck Knoblauch (59) and Milt Cuyler (52).... Williams's on-base percentage was 4th highest among A.L. rookies with at least 200 at-bats last season.... Williams, Pat Kelly, and Hensley Meulens gave the Yankees three rookies with at least 200 at-bats for only the second time in the past 40 years. The other time, as it happens, was in 1990 (Oscar Azocar, Jim Leyritz, and Kevin Maas).... Was born Friday, September 13, 1968—the day before Denny McLain became baseball's only 30-game winner in the last 50 years.... Williams is the only player in Yankees history born on Friday the 13th. (If that seems like a cheap way of getting Phil Rizzuto to quote our book, you're right.) Among the other players born on Black Cat Day are Dusty Rhodes, Marcel Lachemann, Red Sox prospect Scott Cooper (born in October 1967, the day after Boston lost Game 7 of the 1967 World Series to the Cardinals), and Rodney McCray, the minor leaguer who ran through an outfield wall on highlight films across the country last summer.

Mookie Wilson — Bats Left and Right

Toronto Blue Jays	AB	H	2B	3B	HR	RBI	BB	SO	BA	SA	OBA
Season	241	58	12	4	2	28	8	35	.241	.349	.277
vs. Left-Handers	43	9	2	0	0	1	0	8	.209	.256	.209
vs. Right-Handers	198	49	10	4	2	27	8	27	.247	.369	.291
vs. Ground-Ballers	124	29	8	0	0	13	4	17	.234	.298	.260
vs. Fly-Ballers	117	29	4	4	2	15	4	18	.248	.402	.296
Home Games	115	31	8	1	1	14	3	20	.270	.383	.298
Road Games	126	27	4	3	1	14	5	15	.214	.317	.259
Grass Fields	91	20	3	1	1	8	3	13	.220	.308	.268
Artificial Turf	150	38	9	3	1	20	5	22	.253	.373	.283
April	29	7	0	1	0	2	0	3	.241	.310	.258
May	67	15	3	2	1	12	2	10	.224	.373	.246
June	50	15	5	0	1	9	1	6	.300	.460	.321
July	49	13	1	1	0	2	1	9	.265	.327	.308
August	21	3	2	0	0	0	1	3	.143	.238	.217
Sept./Oct.	25	5	1	0	0	3	3	4	.200	.240	.286
Leading Off Inn.	58	11	3	0	0	0	3	7	.190	.241	.254
Runners On	117	33	6	2	1	27	3	12	.282	.393	.312
Bases Empty	124	25	6	2	1	1	5	23	.202	.306	.244
Runners/Scor. Pos.	68	20	5	2	1	27	3	8	.294	.471	.333
Runners On/2 Out	49	10	2	1	1	12	2	4	.204	.347	.264
Scor. Pos./2 Out	32	6	2	1	1	12	2	3	.188	.406	.257
Late-Inning Pressure	42	11	3	2	0	6	2	7	.262	.429	.326
Leading Off	11	5	1	0	0	0	1	0	.455	.545	.538
Runners On	20	4	2	1	0	6	0	4	.200	.400	.238
Runners/Scor. Pos.	12	3	2	1	0	6	0	3	.250	.583	.250

RUNS BATTED IN	From 1B	From 2B	From 3B	Scoring Position
Totals	3/86	9/54	14/35	23/89
Percentage	3.5%	16.7%	40.0%	25.8%

Loves to face: Brian Holman (.500, 9-for-18, 1 HR)
Rick Honeycutt (.474, 9-for-19, 1 HR)
Charlie Hough (.526, 10-for-19)

Hates to face: Jim Abbott (.091, 1-for-11)
Greg A. Harris (.059, 1-for-17)
Andy Hawkins (.071, 2-for-28, 3 BB)

Miscellaneous statistics: Ground outs-to-air outs ratio: 1.33 last season, 1.63 for career.... Grounded into 4 double plays in 51 opportunities (one per 13).... Drove in 10 of 18 runners from third base with less than two outs (56%).... Direction of balls hit to the outfield: 35% to left field, 36% to center, 29% to right batting left-handed; 38% to left field, 31% to center, 31% to right batting right-handed.... Base running: Advanced from first base to third on 4 of 11 outfield singles (36%); scored from second on 8 of 10 (80%).... Made 1.86 putouts per nine innings in left field.

Comments: Lowest postseason slugging percentages (minimum: 100 plate appearances): Everett Scott, .178; Dave Bancroft, .183; Mookie, .217; Mark Belanger, .238; Frank Crosetti, .261.... Wilson started 60 regular-season games, but only seven after August 4, although he remained on the active roster throughout the season. His last six starts of the regular season were as a designated hitter.... Started 55 games against right-handed pitchers last season, but only five against southpaws.... His rate of one strikeout per 7.4 plate appearances was the best of his career.... His average of one walk every 27 plate appearances since joining the Blue Jays is 2d worst in franchise history. Only Damaso Garcia had a lower rate (one BB every 34.1 PA).... Batted in the .270s in each of his first five full seasons in the majors, between .280 and .300 in each of the next three, and below .270 for each of the last three.... An excellent percentage base stealer, his average has been above 75 percent in nine of the last 10 seasons. The only other players above that mark and with 10 or more steals in each of the last six seasons: Eric Davis, Kirk Gibson, Rickey Henderson, Tim Raines, Ozzie Smith, and Willie Wilson.... As of mid-January, Mookie was still an unsigned free agent. The thought of a Mookie-less baseball season pains us; but if this is the end, the most comparable player in baseball history appears to be Al Bumbry.

Willie Wilson — Bats Left and Right

Oakland A's	AB	H	2B	3B	HR	RBI	BB	SO	BA	SA	OBA
Season	294	70	14	4	0	28	18	43	.238	.313	.290
vs. Left-Handers	99	25	4	0	0	6	6	13	.253	.293	.302
vs. Right-Handers	195	45	10	4	0	22	12	30	.231	.323	.284
vs. Ground-Ballers	147	32	5	3	0	13	10	19	.218	.293	.277
vs. Fly-Ballers	147	38	9	1	0	15	8	24	.259	.333	.304
Home Games	132	33	8	2	0	16	9	19	.250	.341	.303
Road Games	162	37	6	2	0	12	9	24	.228	.290	.280
Grass Fields	239	55	12	3	0	25	13	35	.230	.305	.273
Artificial Turf	55	15	2	1	0	3	5	8	.273	.345	.359
April	51	11	3	2	0	9	4	4	.216	.353	.286
May	52	11	3	1	0	5	2	6	.212	.308	.236
June	57	14	3	0	0	2	4	13	.246	.298	.295
July	53	15	1	0	0	6	5	5	.283	.302	.377
August	32	7	2	1	0	3	1	3	.219	.344	.242
Sept./Oct.	49	12	2	0	0	3	2	12	.245	.286	.275
Leading Off Inn.	66	15	3	0	0	0	5	13	.227	.273	.301
Runners On	128	33	5	4	0	28	7	18	.258	.359	.299
Bases Empty	166	37	9	0	0	0	11	25	.223	.277	.283
Runners/Scor. Pos.	66	19	2	4	0	28	4	9	.288	.439	.333
Runners On/2 Out	47	16	4	2	0	17	2	7	.340	.511	.380
Scor. Pos./2 Out	27	11	2	2	0	17	2	3	.407	.630	.467
Late-Inning Pressure	43	10	3	0	0	4	5	8	.233	.302	.327
Leading Off	10	1	0	0	0	0	2	2	.100	.100	.308
Runners On	16	7	2	0	0	4	2	4	.438	.563	.500
Runners/Scor. Pos.	9	4	1	0	0	4	1	3	.444	.556	.500

RUNS BATTED IN	From 1B	From 2B	From 3B	Scoring Position
Totals	3/96	12/58	13/24	25/82
Percentage	3.1%	20.7%	54.2%	30.5%

Loves to face: Storm Davis (.444, 16-for-36)
Joe Grahe (3-for-3, 1 2B, 1 3B)
Bill Krueger (.556, 5-for-9)

Hates to face: Chris Bosio (.045, 1-for-22)
Roger Clemens (.173, 9-for-52, 0 BB)
Ted Higuera (.118, 4-for-34)

Miscellaneous statistics: Ground outs-to-air outs ratio: 1.81 last season, 1.49 for career.... Grounded into 11 double plays in 67 opportunities (one per 6.1).... Drove in 7 of 11 runners from third base with less than two outs (64%).... Direction of balls hit to the outfield: 43% to left field, 32% to center, 25% to right batting left-handed; 19% to left field, 30% to center, 51% to right batting right-handed.... Base running: Advanced from first base to third on 10 of 18 outfield singles (56%); scored from second on 5 of 6 (83%).... Made 2.82 putouts per nine innings in left field.

Comments: Has stolen 20 bases in each of 14 consecutive seasons starting with his rookie year of 1978. Only two other players in major league history started their careers with streaks that long. This season, Wilson and Ozzie Smith will try to surpass the 14-year streak that Herman Long started as a rookie more than 100 years ago (1889).... He has the 2d-highest stolen-base percentage of any player in major league history who has attempted at least 300 steals. Wilson's rate is 83.6 percent; the all-time leader is Tim Raines (85.0 percent).... Mookie has stolen at least 10 bases with at least a 75 percent success rate in each of the past six seasons. (See the list to your left.) Willie has operated at an even higher level: 20 or more steals at 80 percent or better for six straight years.... Leads active players with 137 career triples, eight more than George Brett.... Has never hit as many as 10 home runs in a season, but last season was the first in which he didn't hit any since 1978, when he batted only 198 times.... Now has career totals of 137 triples and 40 home runs. No player active in the last 50 years had a gap that large; the last was Pie Traynor, who retired in 1937 (164 3Bs, 58 HR).... One of seven major leaguers to start at least 10 games at each of the three outfield positions last season.... Started 13 of Oakland's first 17 games, but started as many as four straight games only once thereafter (June 11–15).

Dave Winfield
Bats Right

California Angels	AB	H	2B	3B	HR	RBI	BB	SO	BA	SA	OBA
Season	568	149	27	4	28	86	56	109	.262	.472	.326
vs. Left-Handers	160	48	9	1	11	27	20	24	.300	.575	.381
vs. Right-Handers	408	101	18	3	17	59	36	85	.248	.431	.304
vs. Ground-Ballers	270	72	16	3	13	38	22	54	.267	.493	.323
vs. Fly-Ballers	298	77	11	1	15	48	34	55	.258	.453	.329
Home Games	271	66	10	1	13	33	25	54	.244	.432	.305
Road Games	297	83	17	3	15	53	31	55	.279	.508	.345
Grass Fields	475	119	21	3	18	53	48	89	.251	.421	.318
Artificial Turf	93	30	6	1	10	33	8	20	.323	.731	.373
April	56	13	4	0	3	14	0	8	.232	.464	.224
May	106	30	7	2	5	15	11	17	.283	.528	.347
June	103	33	5	2	8	24	9	20	.320	.641	.372
July	94	23	4	0	3	7	8	12	.245	.383	.311
August	90	18	2	0	4	8	10	25	.200	.356	.280
Sept./Oct.	119	32	5	0	5	18	18	27	.269	.437	.360
Leading Off Inn.	144	34	6	1	4	4	13	32	.236	.375	.304
Runners On	251	70	14	2	11	69	35	37	.279	.482	.360
Bases Empty	317	79	13	2	17	17	21	72	.249	.464	.298
Runners/Scor. Pos.	139	38	10	1	4	54	23	18	.273	.446	.363
Runners On/2 Out	102	29	6	0	6	26	15	15	.284	.520	.376
Scor. Pos./2 Out	54	15	5	0	2	18	10	7	.278	.481	.391
Late-Inning Pressure	67	13	3	0	3	6	5	22	.194	.373	.250
Leading Off	14	3	1	0	1	1	1	5	.214	.500	.267
Runners On	29	5	2	0	0	3	3	9	.172	.241	.250
Runners/Scor. Pos.	11	3	1	0	0	3	2	3	.273	.364	.385

RUNS BATTED IN	From 1B	From 2B	From 3B	Scoring Position
Totals	12/187	21/106	25/58	46/164
Percentage	6.4%	19.8%	43.1%	28.0%

Loves to face: Lee Guetterman (.857, 6-for-7)
     Rick Sutcliffe (.419, 13-for-31, 5 HR)
     Matt Young (.324, 11-for-34, 2 2B, 5 HR)
Hates to face: Steve Farr (.150, 3-for-20)
     Brian Holman (.091, 1-for-11)
     Randy Johnson (.125, 2-for-16)

Miscellaneous statistics: Ground outs-to-air outs ratio: 1.31 last season, 1.33 for career.... Grounded into 21 double plays in 126 opportunities (one per 6.0).... Drove in 20 of 37 runners from third base with less than two outs (54%).... Direction of balls hit to the outfield: 46% to left field, 36% to center, 18% to right.... Base running: Advanced from first base to third on 10 of 26 outfield singles (38%); scored from second on 8 of 15 (53%).... Made 1.81 putouts per nine innings in right field, 2d-lowest rate in A.L.

Comments: Played 150 games, and turned 40 during the final week of the season. Only three other players that old played as many games: Pete Rose (twice), Honus Wagner (twice), and Darrell Evans.... Became the fifth-oldest player to hit three home runs in a game. The older players: Cap Anson (42 years old in 1894), Stan Musial (41 in 1962), Reggie Jackson (40 in 1986), and Babe Ruth (40 in 1935).... With Winfield playing in the Skydome, keep these facts in mind: *(1)* No player as old as Winfield has ever hit 30 home runs in a season. The oldest was Darrell Evans, who hit 34 in 1987, when he turned 40 on May 26. *(2)* The most home runs by a player as old as Winfield was 29, by Ted Williams in 1960, his final season. (He turned 42 that August 30.)... Last season, Winfield became the oldest player ever to hit for the cycle.... Played over 1100 games for both the Yankees and the Padres. Eddie Collins, Sr., is the only other player in major league history to play that many games for two different clubs. Qualifying at the 1000-game level: Carlton Fisk, Frankie Frisch, Joe Morgan, and Tris Speaker. ... Has grounded into 282 double plays in his career, the most among active players; he could challenge Hank Aaron's major league record of 328 GIDPs.... Made his major league debut for San Diego on June 19, 1973, the day Pete Rose got the 2000th hit of his career. The Padres launched Randy Jones three days earlier.

Robin Yount
Bats Right

Milwaukee Brewers	AB	H	2B	3B	HR	RBI	BB	SO	BA	SA	OBA
Season	503	131	20	4	10	77	54	79	.260	.376	.332
vs. Left-Handers	129	33	5	0	2	18	26	16	.256	.341	.377
vs. Right-Handers	374	98	15	4	8	59	28	63	.262	.388	.314
vs. Ground-Ballers	241	67	8	1	3	30	27	35	.278	.357	.354
vs. Fly-Ballers	262	64	12	3	7	47	27	44	.244	.393	.311
Home Games	250	59	10	3	8	42	26	43	.236	.396	.311
Road Games	253	72	10	1	2	35	28	36	.285	.356	.352
Grass Fields	428	111	16	4	9	67	51	69	.259	.379	.338
Artificial Turf	75	20	4	0	1	10	3	10	.267	.360	.291
April	76	26	5	1	5	17	7	8	.342	.632	.400
May	107	27	4	0	4	16	9	14	.252	.402	.303
June	100	20	3	1	0	10	13	24	.200	.250	.302
July	17	6	1	0	0	0	1	1	.353	.529	.389
August	101	33	6	1	0	17	11	15	.327	.406	.391
Sept./Oct.	102	19	1	0	1	17	13	17	.186	.225	.274
Leading Off Inn.	117	26	6	0	2	2	5	18	.222	.325	.260
Runners On	246	70	11	2	6	73	38	40	.285	.419	.373
Bases Empty	257	61	9	2	4	4	16	39	.237	.335	.287
Runners/Scor. Pos.	145	43	5	2	5	68	25	24	.297	.462	.383
Runners On/2 Out	106	29	2	1	2	26	21	23	.274	.368	.394
Scor. Pos./2 Out	66	19	1	1	2	25	13	14	.288	.424	.405
Late-Inning Pressure	69	15	1	1	4	12	5	12	.217	.435	.276
Leading Off	16	2	0	0	1	1	1	2	.125	.313	.176
Runners On	27	6	1	0	2	10	3	5	.222	.481	.290
Runners/Scor. Pos.	21	3	0	0	2	9	1	4	.143	.429	.174

RUNS BATTED IN	From 1B	From 2B	From 3B	Scoring Position
Totals	10/173	25/106	32/74	57/180
Percentage	5.8%	23.6%	43.2%	31.7%

Loves to face: Mike Flanagan (.443, 35-for-79, 4 HR)
     Jose Guzman (.448, 13-for-29, 2 HR)
     Greg Hibbard (.417, 5-for-12, 1 HR)
Hates to face: Chuck Finley (.171, 6-for-35)
     Bob Milacki (.067, 1-for-15, 3 BB)
     Bob Welch (.138, 4-for-29)

Miscellaneous statistics: Ground outs-to-air outs ratio: 0.82 last season, 0.97 for career.... Grounded into 13 double plays in 122 opportunities (one per 9.4).... Drove in 24 of 47 runners from third base with less than two outs (51%).... Direction of balls hit to the outfield: 26% to left field, 34% to center, 40% to right.... Base running: Advanced from first base to third on 12 of 24 outfield singles (50%); scored from second on 13 of 17 (76%).... Made 2.78 putouts per nine innings in center field.

Comments: With his third at-bat of the 1992 season, Yount will become the 15th player in major league history, and the only active player, to reach the 10,000-AB mark. A 500-AB season would move him into eighth place overall and fourth place among A.L. players, behind Carl Yastrzemski, Ty Cobb, and Brooks Robinson.... The next run he scores will be the 1500th of his career, also the most among active players.... He's the only active player with 2000 or more singles.... Needs 122 hits to become the first player to reach the 3000 mark since Rod Carew got there in 1985.... The Brewers posted a 50–35 record with Yount in the cleanup spot last season (.588), but were 33–44 with other cleanup hitters (.429).... Hit half of his home runs to the opposite field.... His rate of one strike-out every 7.2 plate appearances was the worst of his career.... On-base percentage leading off innings was 4th lowest in the league.... Stole only six bases last season, his lowest total since 1981, when he stole four in 96 games.... All-time Milwaukee RBI leaders: Hank Aaron, 1400; Yount, 1278; Eddie Mathews, 1277; Cecil Cooper, 944; Joe Adcock, 760; Paul Molitor, 701.... Most games played by players who spent their entire careers with a single club: Yastrzemski, 3308; Stan Musial, 3026, Brooks Robinson, 2896; Al Kaline, 2834; Mel Ott, 2732; Yount, 2579; Ernie Banks, 2528; Dave Concepcion, 2488; Roberto Clemente, 2433; Luke Appling, 2422.

Jeff Bagwell
Bats Right

Houston Astros	AB	H	2B	3B	HR	RBI	BB	SO	BA	SA	OBA
Season	554	163	26	4	15	82	75	116	.294	.437	.387
vs. Left-Handers	206	66	10	0	7	37	33	37	.320	.471	.417
vs. Right-Handers	348	97	16	4	8	45	42	79	.279	.417	.369
vs. Ground-Ballers	252	75	10	2	4	40	35	49	.298	.401	.394
vs. Fly-Ballers	305	88	16	2	11	42	41	67	.289	.462	.379
Home Games	274	81	15	2	6	35	36	52	.296	.431	.392
Road Games	280	82	11	2	9	47	39	64	.293	.443	.382
Grass Fields	158	44	2	2	6	30	28	40	.278	.430	.389
Artificial Turf	396	119	24	2	9	52	47	76	.301	.439	.386
April	59	15	3	0	2	8	9	17	.254	.407	.348
May	89	24	2	1	3	11	11	29	.270	.416	.356
June	104	33	7	1	2	11	13	20	.317	.462	.393
July	83	26	5	1	3	14	16	15	.313	.506	.433
August	105	28	4	1	2	20	17	16	.267	.381	.378
Sept./Oct.	114	37	5	0	3	18	9	19	.325	.447	.397
Leading Off Inn.	120	33	8	0	0	0	12	28	.275	.342	.360
Runners On	252	75	8	2	10	77	34	54	.298	.464	.391
Bases Empty	302	88	18	2	5	5	41	62	.291	.414	.383
Runners/Scor. Pos.	154	46	5	2	5	65	23	38	.299	.455	.395
Runners On/2 Out	86	24	3	1	3	26	19	18	.279	.442	.436
Scor. Pos./2 Out	59	16	1	1	1	21	13	14	.271	.373	.427
Late-Inning Pressure	86	35	8	0	3	12	13	21	.407	.605	.505
Leading Off	29	10	4	0	0	0	3	9	.345	.483	.457
Runners On	31	15	2	0	2	11	6	8	.484	.742	.579
Runners/Scor. Pos.	15	6	2	0	0	7	2	6	.400	.533	.500

RUNS BATTED IN	From 1B	From 2B	From 3B	Scoring Position
Totals	11/169	27/124	29/55	56/179
Percentage	6.5%	21.8%	52.7%	31.3%

Loves to face: Jose DeJesus (.667, 6-for-9, 1 HR)
John Franco (2-for-2, 1 BB)
Jose Rijo (.714, 5-for-7)

Hates to face: Frank Castillo (0-for-7)
Paul McClellan (0-for-5)
John Smoltz (.182, 2-for-11)

Miscellaneous statistics: Ground outs-to-air outs ratio: 0.93 last season, 0.93 for career.... Grounded into 12 double plays in 132 opportunities (one per 11).... Drove in 23 of 39 runners from third base with less than two outs (59%).... Direction of balls hit to the outfield: 37% to left field, 29% to center, 35% to right.... Base running: Advanced from first base to third on 14 of 33 outfield singles (42%); scored from second on 9 of 12 (75%).... Made 0.72 assists per nine innings at first base.

Comments: Led major league rookies in batting average, on-base average, hits, RBIs, walks, games (156), starts (151), and plate appearances (650).... He was hit by 13 pitches last season, the most in the majors, and the most by a rookie since Ed Bouchee was coldcocked 14 times in 1957.... Played 155 games at first base, the most by a rookie since George Scott played 158 games there for the 1966 Red Sox.... Ended the year with 48 consecutive errorless games at first base, his longest streak of the season.... Batting average in Late-Inning Pressure Situations was the highest in the majors last season, finishing the season with 30 hits in his last 62 LIPS at-bats. He had the best LIPS batting average by any Houston player since we began keeping track of this category in 1975, and the second-best LIPS average by a rookie. (Scot Thompson of the Cubs batted .413 in LIPS as a rookie in 1979.) The best single-season LIPS average on record: .466 by Manny Trillo in 1981.... Had the league's 7th-highest batting average vs. left-handed pitchers.... Batted .125 with the bases loaded, striking out five times in eight at-bats.... Hit 12 home runs to left field, two to center, one to right.... Batted .212 in 85 first-inning at-bats, .309 in subsequent at-bats.... From our Funky Hitting Streaks Department: Bags hit safely in 22 consecutive games on artificial turf, the longest streak of its kind in the majors last season.

Kevin Bass
Bats Left and Right

San Francisco Giants	AB	H	2B	3B	HR	RBI	BB	SO	BA	SA	OBA
Season	361	84	10	4	10	40	36	56	.233	.366	.307
vs. Left-Handers	113	27	5	0	6	15	5	15	.239	.442	.276
vs. Right-Handers	248	57	5	4	4	25	31	41	.230	.331	.320
vs. Ground-Ballers	162	39	5	3	6	19	18	23	.241	.420	.324
vs. Fly-Ballers	199	45	5	1	4	21	18	33	.226	.322	.293
Home Games	167	35	2	2	5	17	21	35	.210	.335	.298
Road Games	194	49	8	2	5	23	15	21	.253	.392	.315
Grass Fields	249	57	4	4	8	25	26	47	.229	.373	.307
Artificial Turf	112	27	6	0	2	15	10	9	.241	.348	.306
April	74	18	4	1	0	4	6	14	.243	.324	.300
May	78	20	4	0	4	7	6	9	.256	.436	.318
June	52	9	1	0	0	5	6	6	.173	.192	.271
July	25	9	0	0	2	7	3	4	.360	.600	.414
August	56	11	2	0	2	5	4	10	.196	.339	.250
Sept./Oct.	76	17	1	3	2	12	11	13	.224	.395	.330
Leading Off Inn.	76	15	2	2	1	1	4	10	.197	.316	.247
Runners On	156	33	4	1	3	33	22	24	.212	.308	.311
Bases Empty	205	51	6	3	7	7	14	32	.249	.410	.303
Runners/Scor. Pos.	96	19	2	1	3	33	17	16	.198	.333	.316
Runners On/2 Out	76	16	2	0	3	16	12	11	.211	.355	.333
Scor. Pos./2 Out	59	11	1	0	3	16	9	8	.186	.356	.304
Late-Inning Pressure	67	13	1	1	2	11	9	11	.194	.328	.295
Leading Off	20	2	0	0	0	0	2	3	.100	.100	.182
Runners On	26	7	1	1	2	11	5	3	.269	.615	.375
Runners/Scor. Pos.	14	4	0	1	2	11	3	1	.286	.857	.389

RUNS BATTED IN	From 1B	From 2B	From 3B	Scoring Position
Totals	4/113	14/77	12/41	26/118
Percentage	3.5%	18.2%	29.3%	22.0%

Loves to face: Don Carman (.440, 11-for-25, 0 BB)
Neal Heaton (.474, 9-for-19, 3 2B, 3 HR)
Mitch Williams (.500, 3-for-6, 1 2B, 2 HR)

Hates to face: Norm Charlton (0-for-13)
Bill Landrum (0-for-11)
Alejandro Pena (.105, 2-for-19)

Miscellaneous statistics: Ground outs-to-air outs ratio: 1.22 last season, 1.10 for career.... Grounded into 12 double plays in 68 opportunities (one per 5.7).... Drove in 10 of 17 runners from third base with less than two outs (59%).... Direction of balls hit to the outfield: 35% to left field, 32% to center, 32% to right batting left-handed; 38% to left field, 30% to center, 32% to right batting right-handed.... Base running: Advanced from first base to third on 2 of 13 outfield singles (15%); scored from second on 4 of 6 (67%).... Made 1.84 putouts per nine innings in right field, 3d-lowest rate in N.L.

Comments: Enters 1992 with a career total of exactly 1000 hits. There have been 902 players in major league history to reach that level. Two, Dee Fondy and Birdie Tebbetts, finished their careers with exactly 1000 hits. (That's better than Tommie Agee and Gene Alley, who called it a career with 999.)... Had league's second-lowest batting average in both home games (.210) and day games (.188). We knew you'd ask: In home day games he batted .167.... Overall batting average was his lowest since he broke into the majors with one hit in 33 at-bats in 1982.... Batting average with runners on base was 4th lowest in the league, and his average with runners in scoring position was 2d lowest.... Quick quiz: Can you name the only two other players to have played with the Brewers, Astros, and Giants? Hint and answer below.... Giants' starting right fielder in all but one game in April, but started only two games at that position during the last month of the season.... He averaged over 155 games per season from 1985 to 1988, but has averaged only 90 per season since then.... Quiz hint: Both others are former slugging outfielders.... Batted .125 (3-for-24) in 28 games as a pinch hitter.... He's been to the plate 84 times with the bases loaded and has never drawn a force-in walk; among active players, only George Bell (95 plate appearances, no walks) has been more insistent on getting his rips with the bases loaded.... Quiz answer: Ollie Brown and Jeffrey Leonard.

George Bell
Bats Right

Chicago Cubs	AB	H	2B	3B	HR	RBI	BB	SO	BA	SA	OBA
Season	558	159	27	0	25	86	32	62	.285	.468	.323
vs. Left-Handers	208	60	8	0	15	34	17	19	.288	.543	.341
vs. Right-Handers	350	99	19	0	10	52	15	43	.283	.423	.313
vs. Ground-Ballers	236	71	14	0	12	42	8	27	.301	.513	.316
vs. Fly-Ballers	322	88	13	0	13	44	24	35	.273	.435	.329
Home Games	288	77	15	0	9	45	11	30	.267	.413	.294
Road Games	270	82	12	0	16	41	21	32	.304	.526	.354
Grass Fields	411	119	22	0	16	66	22	39	.290	.460	.324
Artificial Turf	147	40	5	0	9	20	10	23	.272	.490	.323
April	81	22	4	0	4	12	2	9	.272	.469	.291
May	93	25	0	0	7	19	6	8	.269	.495	.311
June	105	34	6	0	4	15	9	14	.324	.495	.374
July	97	26	5	0	5	19	3	9	.268	.474	.294
August	107	33	8	0	2	12	7	12	.308	.439	.350
Sept./Oct.	75	19	4	0	3	9	5	10	.253	.427	.300
Leading Off Inn.	139	45	9	0	12	12	9	16	.324	.647	.365
Runners On	255	71	14	0	8	69	10	32	.278	.427	.301
Bases Empty	303	88	13	0	17	17	22	30	.290	.502	.343
Runners/Scor. Pos.	149	35	5	0	6	60	9	24	.235	.389	.272
Runners On/2 Out	125	33	7	0	3	24	6	12	.264	.392	.298
Scor. Pos./2 Out	75	16	4	0	3	22	5	8	.213	.387	.262
Late-Inning Pressure	92	24	4	0	5	17	6	13	.261	.467	.303
Leading Off	21	8	0	0	3	3	1	3	.381	.810	.409
Runners On	45	11	4	0	2	14	2	6	.244	.467	.271
Runners/Scor. Pos.	25	7	1	0	2	14	2	5	.280	.560	.321

RUNS BATTED IN	From 1B	From 2B	From 3B	Scoring Position
Totals	11/185	17/118	33/69	50/187
Percentage	5.9%	14.4%	47.8%	26.7%

Loves to face: Tom Candiotti (.529, 18-for-34, 2 HR)
Neal Heaton (.462, 12-for-26, 4 2B, 4 HR, 0 BB)
Dave Righetti (.393, 11-for-28, 3 2B, 2 3B, 3 HR)
Hates to face: Stan Belinda (0-for-5, 3 SO)
Jeff Innis (0-for-6)
Mike Jackson (0-for-7, 5 SO)

Miscellaneous statistics: Ground outs-to-air outs ratio: 0.70 last season, 0.75 for career.... Grounded into 10 double plays in 102 opportunities (one per 10).... Drove in 26 of 39 runners from third base with less than two outs (67%).... Direction of balls hit to the outfield: 44% to left field, 32% to center, 24% to right.... Base running: Advanced from first base to third on 10 of 30 outfield singles (33%); scored from second on 8 of 12 (67%).... Made 1.88 putouts per nine innings in left field, 3d-lowest rate in N.L.

Comments: He was the only outfielder in the majors to reach double figures in errors last season (10).... Averaged one home run every 22.3 at-bats last season, his best rate since he hit 47 home runs in 1987. So what, you say? After all, it's his first year at Wrigley Field, you say? Surprise: He averaged one homer every 32.0 at-bats inside the friendly confines, one every 16.9 at-bats on the road.... Bell's career rate of walks: one every 19.1 plate appearances. Among the 163 players in major league history with at least 200 home runs, only two walked less frequently than Bell: Tony Armas (one BB every 21.2 PA), and Steve Garvey (one every 19.8).... Has hit for a higher average against ground-ball pitchers than he has against fly-ball pitchers in each of the last six seasons.... Has driven in at least 86 runs in each of the last eight seasons. The last player with a longer streak: Mike Schmidt (1979–87).... Has batted 95 times with the bases loaded during his career, but has never drawn a walk to drive in a run. Since 1975, no other player has had as many bases-loaded opportunities without drawing a walk.... He still has never had a sacrifice bunt in 5,486 plate appearances, and his last triple came in August 1989. He and Paul O'Neill became the 11th and 12th players in major league history to link consecutive triple-less 500 at-bat seasons. No one's ever linked three such seasons in succession.

Jay Bell
Bats Right

Pittsburgh Pirates	AB	H	2B	3B	HR	RBI	BB	SO	BA	SA	OBA
Season	608	164	32	8	16	67	52	99	.270	.428	.330
vs. Left-Handers	194	56	13	5	6	28	26	18	.289	.500	.371
vs. Right-Handers	414	108	19	3	10	39	26	81	.261	.394	.309
vs. Ground-Ballers	280	92	20	5	7	37	28	34	.329	.511	.392
vs. Fly-Ballers	332	72	12	3	9	30	24	67	.217	.352	.272
Home Games	303	85	19	5	7	33	23	49	.281	.446	.332
Road Games	305	79	13	3	9	34	29	50	.259	.410	.327
Grass Fields	160	38	8	3	2	13	13	21	.237	.363	.301
Artificial Turf	448	126	24	5	14	54	39	78	.281	.451	.340
April	71	13	3	1	0	5	4	9	.183	.254	.234
May	87	24	5	0	6	19	8	13	.276	.540	.333
June	106	34	5	3	2	10	8	19	.321	.481	.374
July	119	37	6	0	4	15	9	13	.311	.462	.359
August	114	28	8	1	1	5	8	24	.246	.360	.295
Sept./Oct.	111	28	5	3	3	13	15	21	.252	.432	.349
Leading Off Inn.	99	34	5	3	6	13	6	13	.343	.636	.420
Runners On	254	80	16	4	5	56	22	38	.315	.469	.370
Bases Empty	354	84	16	4	11	11	30	61	.237	.398	.301
Runners/Scor. Pos.	140	40	9	2	4	49	14	22	.286	.464	.344
Runners On/2 Out	108	24	6	2	3	26	11	20	.222	.398	.294
Scor. Pos./2 Out	78	15	4	1	3	24	7	16	.192	.385	.259
Late-Inning Pressure	77	19	4	0	1	6	8	12	.247	.338	.318
Leading Off	20	4	1	0	0	0	1	4	.200	.250	.238
Runners On	32	10	1	0	0	5	4	3	.313	.344	.389
Runners/Scor. Pos.	17	4	1	0	0	5	3	2	.235	.294	.350

RUNS BATTED IN	From 1B	From 2B	From 3B	Scoring Position
Totals	9/168	21/110	21/63	42/173
Percentage	5.4%	19.1%	33.3%	24.3%

Loves to face: Mike Bielecki (.632, 12-for-19)
Jim Clancy (.667, 8-for-12)
Jimmy Jones (.700, 7-for-10, 2 HR)
Hates to face: Tommy Greene (.071, 1-for-14)
Ramon Martinez (0-for-10)
John Smoltz (.056, 1-for-18)

Miscellaneous statistics: Ground outs-to-air outs ratio: 1.04 last season, 1.11 for career.... Grounded into 15 double plays in 140 opportunities (one per 9.3).... Drove in 11 of 21 runners from third base with less than two outs (52%).... Direction of balls hit to the outfield: 41% to left field, 29% to center, 30% to right.... Base running: Advanced from first base to third on 16 of 35 outfield singles (46%); scored from second on 15 of 20 (75%).... Made 3.28 assists per nine innings at shortstop, 3d-highest rate in N.L.

Comments: Bell's 30 sacrifice bunts led the majors last season, making him the first player with 30 or more sac bunts in consecutive seasons since Dick Bartell, who did it in three straight years (1931–33). No player had led the National League in consecutive seasons since Johnny Temple (1957–58). High drama on tap: If Bell leads again this season, he will be the first N.L. player in this century to lead the league for three straight years.... Fifteen of his sacrifices came in the first inning.... First player with 15 home runs and 30 sacrifices in the same season since Johnny Logan's 15 HR, 31 sacrifice bunts in 1956.... His overall batting average was a career high.... His .500 batting average vs. Houston was the highest by any player against any N.L. club last season (25-for-50).... He has hit for a higher average with runners on base than with the bases empty in each of his six seasons in the majors. Career breakdown: .292 with runners on, .227 with the bases empty.... His stolen-base percentage has been exactly .625 in each of the last three seasons.... Started 153 games in the second spot in lineup, the most by any player in the majors last season; only two others made as many as 120 starts from that spot: Roberto Alomar (145), and Ozzie Smith (143).... Bell played 1347⅓ innings at shortstop last season. Only three N.L. players played more innings at any one position: Brett Butler, Mark Grace, and Ryne Sandberg. (You have to guess the positions.)

Rafael Belliard

Bats Right

Atlanta Braves	AB	H	2B	3B	HR	RBI	BB	SO	BA	SA	OBA
Season	353	88	9	2	0	27	22	63	.249	.286	.296
vs. Left-Handers	95	23	2	0	0	4	6	14	.242	.263	.287
vs. Right-Handers	258	65	7	2	0	23	16	49	.252	.295	.300
vs. Ground-Ballers	145	32	3	2	0	14	7	23	.221	.269	.255
vs. Fly-Ballers	208	56	6	0	0	13	15	40	.269	.298	.324
Home Games	173	44	6	2	0	15	10	26	.254	.312	.299
Road Games	180	44	3	0	0	12	12	37	.244	.261	.294
Grass Fields	258	64	8	2	0	19	17	43	.248	.295	.297
Artificial Turf	95	24	1	0	0	8	5	20	.253	.263	.294
April	50	11	1	0	0	5	3	12	.220	.240	.264
May	90	24	3	1	0	10	6	17	.267	.322	.313
June	82	17	1	0	0	3	2	11	.207	.220	.224
July	16	2	0	1	0	2	2	1	.125	.250	.222
August	39	13	0	0	0	3	1	9	.333	.333	.350
Sept./Oct.	76	21	4	0	0	4	8	13	.276	.329	.360
Leading Off Inn.	83	22	2	0	0	0	6	12	.265	.289	.315
Runners On	148	40	4	1	0	27	8	25	.270	.311	.310
Bases Empty	205	48	5	1	0	0	14	38	.234	.268	.286
Runners/Scor. Pos.	78	21	3	1	0	27	5	13	.269	.333	.310
Runners On/2 Out	82	24	2	1	0	16	5	11	.293	.341	.333
Scor. Pos./2 Out	48	14	1	1	0	16	4	5	.292	.354	.346
Late-Inning Pressure	31	5	0	0	0	0	2	8	.161	.161	.212
Leading Off	3	0	0	0	0	0	0	0	.000	.000	.000
Runners On	12	1	0	0	0	0	0	2	.083	.083	.083
Runners/Scor. Pos.	5	1	0	0	0	0	0	0	.200	.200	.200

RUNS BATTED IN	From 1B	From 2B	From 3B	Scoring Position
Totals	2/113	9/59	16/36	25/95
Percentage	1.8%	15.3%	44.4%	26.3%

Loves to face: Mike Bielecki (.417, 5-for-12)
Shawn Boskie (.600, 3-for-5)
Terry Mulholland (.417, 5-for-12)
Hates to face: Tim Belcher (.071, 1-for-14, 1 2B)
Mark Gardner (0-for-7)
Kevin Gross (.091, 1-for-11)

Miscellaneous statistics: Ground outs-to-air outs ratio: 1.55 last season, 1.89 for career.... Grounded into 4 double plays in 62 opportunities (one per 16).... Drove in 7 of 13 runners from third base with less than two outs (54%).... Direction of balls hit to the outfield: 18% to left field, 28% to center, 54% to right.... Base running: Advanced from first base to third on 3 of 12 outfield singles (25%); scored from second on 12 of 14 (86%), 4th-highest rate in N.L.... Made 3.28 assists per nine innings at shortstop, 2d-highest rate in N.L.

Comments: 42 of his 88 hits went to right field (47.7 percent), the highest rate of opposite-field hits by any N.L. player last season (minimum: 60 hits); Wade Boggs led the majors with 48.1 percent. This many be the first time in the history of humankind that batting exploits of Belliard and Boggs are linked.... His only home run in 1404 career at-bats was a three-run shot off Eric Show in 1987. Among active players with at least 1000 at-bats, only Belliard, Al Newman (1 HR, 1861 AB), Lance Johnson (1 HR, 1492 AB), and Felix Fermin (1 HR, 1477 AB) have hit fewer than two home runs.... Streak of 146 consecutive at-bats without an extra-base hit was 2d longest in the majors last season. In 1988, he had a streak of 147 such at-bats.... Eleven extra-base hits may not sound like a lot to you weekend softballers, but it matched his total for the three previous seasons combined.... His longest hitting streak last season was four games; among major leaguers with at least 300 at-bats, Alfredo Griffin was the only other player without a hitting streak of at least five games.... Played 145 games at shortstop, but less than half (72) were complete games.... His 33-game errorless streak was tops among N.L. shortstops last year; six A.L. shortstops had longer streaks.... Last year's moment-by-moment celebration of the 50th anniversary of DiMaggio's streak and Williams's .400 season was only a warm-up; this year baseball celebrates the 50th anniversary of the only Braves' shortstop ever to start the All-Star Game: Eddie Miller did it in 1942.

Craig Biggio

Bats Right

Houston Astros	AB	H	2B	3B	HR	RBI	BB	SO	BA	SA	OBA
Season	546	161	23	4	4	46	53	71	.295	.374	.358
vs. Left-Handers	186	51	10	2	1	11	21	19	.274	.366	.346
vs. Right-Handers	360	110	13	2	3	35	32	52	.306	.378	.364
vs. Ground-Ballers	246	75	10	3	0	24	23	32	.305	.370	.368
vs. Fly-Ballers	304	88	13	1	5	23	30	39	.289	.388	.351
Home Games	277	95	20	3	0	24	27	39	.343	.437	.401
Road Games	269	66	3	1	4	22	26	32	.245	.309	.313
Grass Fields	173	42	2	0	2	15	13	21	.243	.289	.296
Artificial Turf	373	119	21	4	2	31	40	50	.319	.413	.385
April	64	23	1	0	2	5	5	10	.359	.469	.400
May	90	28	6	0	0	7	11	12	.311	.378	.382
June	97	30	4	0	1	4	9	8	.309	.381	.374
July	88	24	1	1	0	10	7	10	.273	.307	.326
August	96	26	7	1	0	9	16	16	.271	.365	.377
Sept./Oct.	111	30	4	2	1	11	5	15	.270	.369	.302
Leading Off Inn.	116	35	7	2	1	1	10	7	.302	.422	.357
Runners On	229	76	8	1	1	43	23	35	.332	.389	.391
Bases Empty	317	85	15	3	3	3	30	36	.268	.363	.333
Runners/Scor. Pos.	125	35	4	0	0	39	16	24	.280	.312	.354
Runners On/2 Out	78	20	7	0	0	17	10	15	.256	.346	.341
Scor. Pos./2 Out	53	14	3	0	0	16	10	12	.264	.321	.381
Late-Inning Pressure	89	19	2	0	0	9	11	18	.213	.236	.307
Leading Off	20	2	0	0	0	0	3	3	.100	.100	.217
Runners On	41	11	2	0	0	9	6	10	.268	.317	.375
Runners/Scor. Pos.	26	8	1	0	0	8	3	7	.308	.346	.379

RUNS BATTED IN	From 1B	From 2B	From 3B	Scoring Position
Totals	5/147	18/94	19/46	37/140
Percentage	3.4%	19.1%	41.3%	26.4%

Loves to face: Steve Avery (.500, 10-for-20)
Orel Hershiser (.577, 15-for-26)
John Wetteland (.625, 5-for-8, 2 HR, 3 SO)
Hates to face: Kevin Gross (.048, 1-for-21)
Dennis Rasmussen (.138, 4-for-29)
Ed Whitson (.100, 2-for-20)

Miscellaneous statistics: Ground outs-to-air outs ratio: 0.91 last season, 1.06 for career.... Grounded into 2 double plays in 113 opportunities (one per 57), 2d-best rate in majors.... Drove in 13 of 20 runners from third base with less than two outs (65%).... Direction of balls hit to the outfield: 42% to left field, 33% to center, 25% to right.... Base running: Advanced from first base to third on 7 of 36 outfield singles (19%); scored from second on 19 of 24 (79%).... Opposing base stealers: 126-for-172 (73%), 3d-highest rate in N.L.

Comments: The only right-handed batter in the majors to hit above .300 against right-handed pitchers in each of the last two seasons.... Caught over 80 percent of the Astros' innings last season. Their staff posted 3.93 ERA throwing to Biggio, 4.31 with other backstops. Opposing base runners, however, found him friendlier than Carl Nichols, against whom they stole only eight bases in 17 attempts (47%).... Became the sixth different Houston catcher to lead the league in passed balls, joining John Bateman, Cliff Johnson, Alan Ashby, Luis Pujols, and Mark Bailey. But most of those guys had the excuse of catching Joe Niekro.... Had the league's highest batting average in home games, and in a related note, the 3d-highest average on artificial turf.... April batting average was the highest in the league.... Batted .397 during the first inning of play, second highest among major leaguers with at least 40 first-inning at-bats last season.... His .328 career batting average in day games is third highest of any player over the last 17 years, behind Rod Carew (.347) and Wade Boggs (.338).... Off-season rumor again has him headed to second base, so we repeat an observation we made a year ago: Only one player played 100 games at both catcher and second base in his major league career: a fellow named Tom Daly, who played from 1887 to 1903. Daly apparently was a weak-armed catcher who after his transition to second base became known for making the long throw to first base underhanded.

Jeff Blauser

Atlanta Braves   Bats Right

	AB	H	2B	3B	HR	RBI	BB	SO	BA	SA	OBA
Season	352	91	14	3	11	54	54	59	.259	.409	.358
vs. Left-Handers	128	39	5	3	4	26	25	20	.305	.484	.416
vs. Right-Handers	224	52	9	0	7	28	29	39	.232	.366	.323
vs. Ground-Ballers	155	41	9	0	4	18	17	20	.265	.400	.339
vs. Fly-Ballers	197	50	5	3	7	36	37	39	.254	.416	.371
Home Games	174	47	6	0	7	32	31	25	.270	.425	.382
Road Games	178	44	8	3	4	22	23	34	.247	.393	.333
Grass Fields	274	69	10	1	10	42	42	42	.252	.405	.350
Artificial Turf	78	22	4	2	1	12	12	17	.282	.423	.385
April	32	9	0	1	1	5	1	2	.281	.438	.303
May	54	11	1	2	1	7	13	6	.204	.352	.362
June	80	24	8	0	3	19	12	9	.300	.512	.394
July	83	22	2	0	3	13	11	14	.265	.398	.347
August	72	18	3	0	2	8	11	16	.250	.375	.349
Sept./Oct.	31	7	0	0	1	2	6	12	.226	.323	.351
Leading Off Inn.	66	12	0	0	2	2	5	9	.182	.273	.239
Runners On	161	51	9	3	4	47	28	26	.317	.484	.418
Bases Empty	191	40	5	0	7	7	26	33	.209	.346	.304
Runners/Scor. Pos.	97	31	6	1	4	43	16	19	.320	.526	.410
Runners On/2 Out	73	24	6	3	1	26	12	13	.329	.534	.424
Scor. Pos./2 Out	52	17	3	1	1	22	7	12	.327	.481	.407
Late-Inning Pressure	63	9	1	0	1	3	8	15	.143	.206	.239
Leading Off	20	3	0	0	1	1	1	3	.150	.300	.190
Runners On	27	5	1	0	0	2	5	9	.185	.222	.313
Runners/Scor. Pos.	13	1	0	0	0	1	4	6	.077	.077	.294

RUNS BATTED IN	From 1B	From 2B	From 3B	Scoring Position
Totals	10/108	20/84	13/32	33/116
Percentage	9.3%	23.8%	40.6%	28.4%

Loves to face: Jim Deshaies (.324, 12-for-37, 2 HR)
Terry Mulholland (.462, 6-for-13, 1 HR)
Mark Portugal (.462, 6-for-13, 3 HR)

Hates to face: Andy Benes (.158, 3-for-19)
Scott Garrelts (.136, 3-for-22, 1 HR)
Bruce Hurst (.162, 6-for-37)

Miscellaneous statistics: Ground outs-to-air outs ratio: 0.81 last season, 0.92 for career.... Grounded into 4 double plays in 79 opportunities (one per 20).... Drove in 7 of 15 runners from third base with less than two outs (47%).... Direction of balls hit to the outfield: 40% to left field, 27% to center, 33% to right.... Base running: Advanced from first base to third on 8 of 22 outfield singles (36%); scored from second on 4 of 6 (67%).... Made 2.59 assists per nine innings at shortstop.

Comments: Owns .290 career batting average vs. left-handers, .246 vs. right-handers, but there's an even wider gap between his career averages against ground-ball pitchers (.293) and fly-ball pitchers (.235). Typical of fly-ball hitters, he has hit for a higher average against ground-ballers than he has against fly-ballers in each of his five seasons in the majors.... Career breakdown: .192 in Late-Inning Pressure Situations, .277 in other at-bats. His 1991 LIPS average was second lowest in N.L., but he hit well in other clutch situations. His average with two outs and runners on base was sixth highest in the league.... Started 39 of 44 games in which Braves faced a left-handed starting pitcher (89%); started 51 of 118 games against right-handers (43%).... Broke a toe on September 3 and started only seven games after that, none during postseason.... Averaged only 4.1 chances accepted per nine innings at shortstop last season; Belliard, playing behind same pitching staff, averaged 4.8. Among 30 major league shortstops who started 50 or more games, only Houston's Andujar Cedeno (3.7) accepted fewer chances per nine innings.... Batted .326 as a second baseman, .243 as a shortstop, and .208 as a third baseman.... Hit all 11 of his home runs to left field.... Committed 13 of his 17 errors in home games, and only two of them in 34 games on artificial surfaces.... Career average of .273 at Atlanta Stadium, .224 on other grass fields, and .281 on artificial turf.

Barry Bonds

Pittsburgh Pirates   Bats Left

	AB	H	2B	3B	HR	RBI	BB	SO	BA	SA	OBA
Season	510	149	28	5	25	116	107	73	.292	.514	.410
vs. Left-Handers	201	57	13	2	7	39	32	30	.284	.473	.385
vs. Right-Handers	309	92	15	3	18	77	75	43	.298	.540	.425
vs. Ground-Ballers	226	66	12	2	4	41	45	27	.292	.416	.402
vs. Fly-Ballers	288	84	16	3	21	75	62	46	.292	.587	.415
Home Games	261	71	8	1	12	51	49	42	.272	.448	.384
Road Games	249	78	20	4	13	65	58	31	.313	.582	.436
Grass Fields	132	37	10	2	5	27	23	18	.280	.500	.375
Artificial Turf	378	112	18	3	20	89	84	55	.296	.519	.422
April	62	11	1	0	2	10	3	15	.177	.290	.212
May	82	23	3	1	3	16	14	9	.280	.451	.400
June	80	26	6	1	5	19	25	9	.325	.613	.481
July	94	34	4	2	6	29	16	11	.362	.638	.447
August	94	27	7	0	6	22	23	15	.287	.553	.417
Sept./Oct.	98	28	7	1	3	20	26	14	.286	.469	.422
Leading Off Inn.	95	28	8	2	0	0	21	12	.295	.421	.432
Runners On	251	82	16	2	17	108	64	37	.327	.421	.448
Bases Empty	259	67	12	3	8	8	43	36	.259	.421	.368
Runners/Scor. Pos.	148	51	10	1	8	87	46	20	.345	.588	.471
Runners On/2 Out	115	34	6	1	7	41	38	14	.296	.548	.474
Scor. Pos./2 Out	77	24	3	0	4	33	29	8	.312	.506	.500
Late-Inning Pressure	72	23	7	0	2	15	13	12	.319	.500	.419
Leading Off	11	3	1	0	0	0	2	0	.273	.364	.385
Runners On	35	13	4	0	2	15	8	7	.371	.657	.477
Runners/Scor. Pos.	18	7	2	0	0	10	6	3	.389	.500	.520

RUNS BATTED IN	From 1B	From 2B	From 3B	Scoring Position
Totals	16/201	30/114	45/72	75/186
Percentage	8.0%	26.3%	62.5%	40.3%

Loves to face: Andy Benes (.600, 3-for-5, 2 HR, 4 BB)
Tom Browning (.353, 12-for-34, 5 HR, 11 BB)
Bruce Hurst (.440, 11-for-25, 2 HR)

Hates to face: Mike Bielecki (.063, 2-for-32, 6 BB)
Jeff Brantley (0-for-10)
Dennis Martinez (.200, 15-for-75, 1 HR)

Miscellaneous statistics: Ground outs-to-air outs ratio: 0.74 last season, 0.84 for career.... Grounded into 8 double plays in 126 opportunities (one per 16).... Drove in 34 of 43 runners from third base with less than two outs (79%), 4th-highest rate in N.L.... Direction of balls hit to the outfield: 30% to left field, 32% to center, 37% to right.... Base running: Advanced from first base to third on 20 of 35 outfield singles (57%); scored from second on 10 of 16 (63%).... Made 2.18 putouts per nine innings in left field.

Comments: Only three players in Pirates history—Willie Stargell, Ralph Kiner, and Roberto Clemente—have hit 200 home runs. Bonds already ranks sixth on the team list with 142; if he's still with Bucs as you read this he could pass Frank Thomas I (163) and Dave Parker (166) this year.... His back-to-back seasons of 114 and 116 RBIs are almost unprecedented in team history; Kiner had four straight years of at least 118 RBIs (1947–50).... Percentage of runners driven in from scoring position (40.3%) led N.L.; yearly RBI percentage since 1987: 15.2, 26.1, 26.7, 37.1, 40.3.... Also had league's top walk rate last year; his walk rate has also increased each year since 1987.... Led majors with 1295⅔ innings in left field; had 13 assists from there, tying Joe Orsulak for the major league lead.... Owns .097 career batting average (6-for-62) with two outs and runners in scoring position in Late-Inning Pressure Situations, lowest since 1975 (minimum: 50 such at-bats).... Hitless in his last 22 at-bats with runners on base in postseason play (last six at-bats in 1990, all 16 in 1991), tying all-time record streak set by Gene Tenace (1973–82).... Did not drive in a run in Championship Series; only three times previously had a player with 100 + regular-season RBIs been blanked in a seven-game postseason series: Reds' Frank McCormick (127 regular-season RBIs) in 1940 World Series, Tommy Herr (110) in 1985 World Series, and Jim Rice (110) in 1986 World Series.... See Pirates essay, page 70, for more on same subject.

Bobby Bonilla
Bats Left and Right

Pittsburgh Pirates	AB	H	2B	3B	HR	RBI	BB	SO	BA	SA	OBA
Season	577	174	44	6	18	100	90	67	.302	.492	.391
vs. Left-Handers	232	66	13	1	14	47	25	23	.284	.530	.349
vs. Right-Handers	345	108	31	5	4	53	65	44	.313	.467	.418
vs. Ground-Ballers	249	72	14	2	4	37	33	20	.289	.410	.368
vs. Fly-Ballers	331	102	30	4	14	63	58	48	.308	.550	.407
Home Games	285	88	25	3	9	51	49	29	.309	.512	.408
Road Games	292	86	19	3	9	49	41	38	.295	.473	.374
Grass Fields	155	44	5	2	4	21	14	23	.284	.419	.339
Artificial Turf	422	130	39	4	14	79	76	44	.308	.519	.409
April	73	23	6	0	3	17	11	5	.315	.521	.407
May	93	29	6	0	3	15	12	10	.312	.473	.383
June	83	18	9	1	1	9	14	11	.217	.386	.327
July	112	37	4	2	6	23	10	13	.330	.563	.379
August	106	40	13	1	3	20	19	9	.377	.604	.465
Sept./Oct.	110	27	6	2	2	16	24	19	.245	.391	.375
Leading Off Inn.	138	38	10	2	3	3	13	11	.275	.442	.342
Runners On	293	94	23	1	11	93	52	38	.321	.519	.412
Bases Empty	284	80	21	5	7	7	38	29	.282	.465	.368
Runners/Scor. Pos.	159	49	12	1	6	75	36	23	.308	.509	.413
Runners On/2 Out	134	40	9	0	6	39	27	18	.299	.500	.420
Scor. Pos./2 Out	76	21	4	0	3	29	17	13	.276	.447	.409
Late-Inning Pressure	73	21	6	1	3	12	16	9	.288	.521	.407
Leading Off	23	7	2	0	0	0	1	5	.304	.391	.333
Runners On	31	7	2	0	2	11	9	4	.226	.484	.381
Runners/Scor. Pos.	16	4	1	0	2	10	7	2	.250	.688	.440

RUNS BATTED IN	From 1B	From 2B	From 3B	Scoring Position
Totals	18/213	20/111	44/80	64/191
Percentage	8.5%	18.0%	55.0%	33.5%

Loves to face: Mike Bielecki (.375, 12-for-32, 4 HR)
Tom Browning (.390, 16-for-41, 4 2B, 1 3B, 8 HR)
Jose Rijo (.400, 8-for-20, 3 HR)
Hates to face: Craig Lefferts (.059, 1-for-17)
Bob Ojeda (.214, 12-for-56)
Zane Smith (.188, 6-for-32)

Miscellaneous statistics: Ground outs-to-air outs ratio: 0.89 last season, 0.91 for career.... Grounded into 14 double plays in 143 opportunities (one per 10).... Drove in 33 of 44 runners from third base with less than two outs (75%).... Direction of balls hit to the outfield: 34% to left field, 29% to center, 38% to right batting left-handed; 51% to left field, 27% to center, 23% to right batting right-handed.... Base running: Advanced from first base to third on 18 of 38 outfield singles (47%); scored from second on 12 of 21 (57%).... Made 1.95 putouts per nine innings in right field; made 2.32 assists per nine innings at third base, 2d-highest rate in N.L.

Comments: Before last season, you could safely say that Bo hit better vs. right-handed pitchers than vs. left-handers. Breakdown through 1990: .286 batting average, one homer every 25.2 at-bats vs. RHP; .268 average, one every 32.3 at-bats vs. LHP. In 1991 he still hit better for average vs. right-handers, but 14 of 18 home runs came off lefties. New switch-hitting teammates Eddie Murray and Howard Johnson have both had a tougher time vs. left-handers than vs. right-handers for several years running.... Has hit for higher average in day games than at night in each of six years in majors; last season's disparity (.340 day, .288 night) was widest of career.... Career batting average breakdown: .301 in day games, .275 at night; also .301 on grass fields, .275 on rugs.... Increased walks from 45 (in 1990) to 90 while cutting whiffs from 103 (in 1990) to 67. Only two other players in major league history had increased walks and reduced whiffs by 35 or more in the same season: Adolfo Phillips (43/135 in 1966, 80/93 in 1967) and Frank Howard (54/141 in 1968, 102/96 in 1969).... Okay, fielding percentage for outfielders is not an absolute measure of ability, but consider this: Bonilla has averaged one error every 38.9 outfield chances, considerably worse than the major league average of one error every 59 chances. But his average compares *favorably* to other Mets' outfielders: Daryl Boston (38.3), Howard Johnson (40.5), Vince Coleman (37.0). It could be dangerous out there.

Daryl Boston
Bats Left

New York Mets	AB	H	2B	3B	HR	RBI	BB	SO	BA	SA	OBA
Season	255	70	16	4	4	21	30	42	.275	.416	.350
vs. Left-Handers	31	6	3	0	1	1	0	11	.194	.387	.194
vs. Right-Handers	224	64	13	4	3	20	30	31	.286	.420	.369
vs. Ground-Ballers	110	33	4	3	1	14	13	12	.300	.418	.371
vs. Fly-Ballers	146	38	12	1	3	7	17	30	.260	.418	.337
Home Games	135	33	11	2	2	13	19	26	.244	.400	.338
Road Games	120	37	5	2	2	8	11	16	.308	.433	.364
Grass Fields	173	44	13	2	2	15	21	29	.254	.387	.333
Artificial Turf	82	26	3	2	2	6	9	13	.317	.476	.385
April	26	5	0	1	0	2	2	3	.192	.269	.250
May	22	3	1	0	0	0	1	3	.136	.182	.174
June	49	14	8	0	0	5	5	9	.286	.449	.352
July	39	10	3	0	1	2	8	6	.256	.410	.383
August	59	18	0	1	0	5	4	11	.305	.339	.344
Sept./Oct.	60	20	4	2	3	7	10	10	.333	.617	.429
Leading Off Inn.	72	25	10	1	1	1	13	8	.347	.556	.447
Runners On	88	22	5	1	1	18	12	15	.250	.364	.337
Bases Empty	167	48	11	3	3	3	18	27	.287	.443	.357
Runners/Scor. Pos.	52	15	3	0	1	16	9	9	.288	.404	.387
Runners On/2 Out	38	6	2	0	0	5	5	8	.158	.211	.256
Scor. Pos./2 Out	24	4	2	0	0	5	4	5	.167	.250	.286
Late-Inning Pressure	43	11	2	2	1	4	6	5	.256	.465	.347
Leading Off	10	3	2	0	0	0	3	0	.300	.500	.462
Runners On	15	4	0	1	0	3	3	2	.267	.400	.389
Runners/Scor. Pos.	8	2	0	0	0	1	3	2	.250	.250	.455

RUNS BATTED IN	From 1B	From 2B	From 3B	Scoring Position
Totals	3/61	6/43	8/15	14/58
Percentage	4.9%	14.0%	53.3%	24.1%

Loves to face: Mike Morgan (.375, 6-for-16, 3 2B, 2 HR)
Bryn Smith (.700, 7-for-10)
Bob Tewksbury (.563, 9-for-16)
Hates to face: Mike LaCoss (0-for-7)
Greg Maddux (.143, 3-for-21)
Jose Rijo (.083, 1-for-12, 2 BB)

Miscellaneous statistics: Ground outs-to-air outs ratio: 1.03 last season, 0.93 for career.... Grounded into 2 double plays in 40 opportunities (one per 20).... Drove in 7 of 9 runners from third base with less than two outs (78%).... Direction of balls hit to the outfield: 24% to left field, 28% to center, 49% to right.... Base running: Advanced from first base to third on 5 of 12 outfield singles (42%); scored from second on 7 of 9 (78%).... Made 2.52 putouts per nine innings in center field.

Comments: Could also learn to love Houston hurler Xavier Hernandez. Last season, Boston had two home runs in two at-bats vs. Hernandez; he hit two homers in 253 at-bats against everyone else.... Home run off Wally Ritchie in his final at-bat of season was only his second in 287 at-bats in majors vs. lefties. The other was off Mark Thurmond in 1986.... Used as a defensive substitute 40 times last season, 3d most of any player in majors.... Career pinch-hitting: .215 batting average (20-for-93), two home runs.... Started 57 games last season, all against right-handed starters.... Batted .303 in 35 games from the top spot in lineup; other Mets (are you listening, Vince?) combined for a .245 average from that spot.... Combine Boston's 1991 efforts against lefties and Dave Gallagher's performance against right-handers and you get a .290 batting average in slightly over 300 at-bats. Is that enough for Jeff Torborg? Both players were released by White Sox in 1990, when Torborg was the manager.... Hitless in 22 career at-bats with two outs and the bases loaded.... He has hit for a lower batting average in Late-Inning Pressure Situations than he has in other at-bats in each of his eight seasons in the majors. Career breakdown: .203 in LIPS, .259 in other at-bats.... Batted 42 points higher in Mets' losses (.294) than he did in Mets' victories. Among players with at least 250 at-bats last season, only ten hit for a higher average in losing efforts than in victories. Of them, Boston had the largest difference.

Glenn Braggs
Bats Right

Cincinnati Reds	AB	H	2B	3B	HR	RBI	BB	SO	BA	SA	OBA
Season	250	65	10	0	11	39	23	46	.260	.432	.323
vs. Left-Handers	124	35	6	0	5	23	14	22	.282	.452	.352
vs. Right-Handers	126	30	4	0	6	16	9	24	.238	.413	.292
vs. Ground-Ballers	125	33	8	0	6	18	11	24	.264	.472	.326
vs. Fly-Ballers	125	32	2	0	5	21	12	22	.256	.392	.319
Home Games	120	36	6	0	8	23	9	19	.300	.550	.346
Road Games	130	29	4	0	3	16	14	27	.223	.323	.301
Grass Fields	91	19	3	0	1	8	9	17	.209	.275	.284
Artificial Turf	159	46	7	0	10	31	14	29	.289	.522	.345
April	26	3	0	0	1	3	6	5	.115	.231	.281
May	46	10	2	0	4	8	10	8	.217	.522	.351
June	43	10	1	0	2	10	6	11	.233	.395	.327
July	48	15	3	0	1	4	0	10	.313	.438	.313
August	87	27	4	0	3	14	1	12	.310	.460	.322
Sept./Oct.	0	0	0	0	0	0	0	0	.000	.000	.000
Leading Off Inn.	56	17	3	0	4	4	8	13	.304	.571	.391
Runners On	120	32	6	0	3	31	10	18	.267	.392	.313
Bases Empty	130	33	4	0	8	8	13	28	.254	.469	.331
Runners/Scor. Pos.	63	19	3	0	1	26	8	9	.302	.397	.360
Runners On/2 Out	52	13	0	0	0	8	5	6	.250	.250	.316
Scor. Pos./2 Out	32	9	0	0	0	8	4	2	.281	.281	.361
Late-Inning Pressure	44	11	1	0	1	4	4	11	.250	.341	.327
Leading Off	10	2	0	0	0	0	1	3	.200	.200	.273
Runners On	20	5	1	0	0	3	2	5	.250	.300	.318
Runners/Scor. Pos.	8	3	0	0	0	3	2	2	.375	.375	.500

RUNS BATTED IN	From 1B	From 2B	From 3B	Scoring Position
Totals	4/84	8/47	16/30	24/77
Percentage	4.8%	17.0%	53.3%	31.2%

Loves to face: Steve Avery (.529, 9-for-17, 2 HR)
Bret Saberhagen (.423, 11-for-26, 1 HR, 0 BB)
Zane Smith (.412, 7-for-17, 1 HR)
Hates to face: Scott Garrelts (.100, 1-for-10)
Greg W. Harris (0-for-7)
Dennis Rasmussen (.111, 2-for-18, 2 BB)

Miscellaneous statistics: Ground outs-to-air outs ratio: 1.67 last season, 1.27 for career.... Grounded into 4 double plays in 51 opportunities (one per 13).... Drove in 12 of 19 runners from third base with less than two outs (63%).... Direction of balls hit to the outfield: 43% to left field, 30% to center, 27% to right.... Base running: Advanced from first base to third on 4 of 12 outfield singles (33%); scored from second on 5 of 6 (83%).... Made 2.27 putouts per nine innings in left field.

Comments: Started 39 of 55 games (71%) in which the Reds were opposed by a left-handed starter, 22 of 107 games (21%) in which they faced a right-hander; nevertheless, he ended up with more at-bats vs. right-handers than vs. left-handers.... Averaged one strikeout every 6.1 plate appearances last season, the lowest rate of his career. With a decrease in strikeouts came an increase in power: His average of one homer every 22.7 at-bats was the best of his career.... Stolen base rate (11-of-14) was also the best of his career.... Spent the final 41 days of the season on the disabled list with a bad hamstring; he had batted .320 over his previous 26 games.... Batted .284 through the first six innings of play, .221 from the seventh inning on.... Has batted over .300 with runners in scoring position in three of the past four years.... Averages one home run every 33.4 at-bats, but he's homerless in 43 career at-bats with the bases loaded.... Committed four errors in slightly over 400 innings of play in left field last season. Ten other Cincinnati left fielders combined for two errors in over 1000 innings.... Career rate of errors (one every 27.8 chances) is third highest among active outfielders (minimum: 500 games); Pete Incaviglia (one every 27.2 chances) and Lonnie Smith (one every 27.6 chances) are more error-prone. Honorable mention to Bo Jackson (one every 24.8 chances), who would lead the parade except that he has played only 464 games in the outfield.

Sid Bream
Bats Left

Atlanta Braves	AB	H	2B	3B	HR	RBI	BB	SO	BA	SA	OBA
Season	265	67	12	0	11	45	25	31	.253	.423	.313
vs. Left-Handers	40	6	0	0	1	7	0	9	.150	.225	.150
vs. Right-Handers	225	61	12	0	10	38	25	22	.271	.458	.339
vs. Ground-Ballers	101	26	7	0	2	13	12	11	.257	.386	.333
vs. Fly-Ballers	164	41	5	0	9	32	13	20	.250	.445	.300
Home Games	115	31	5	0	3	21	8	15	.270	.391	.310
Road Games	150	36	7	0	8	24	17	16	.240	.447	.315
Grass Fields	186	48	9	0	6	31	18	21	.258	.403	.317
Artificial Turf	79	19	3	0	5	14	7	10	.241	.468	.302
April	54	13	6	0	2	8	5	7	.241	.463	.305
May	80	23	3	0	5	20	6	13	.287	.512	.330
June	44	15	2	0	2	6	3	4	.341	.523	.375
July	0	0	0	0	0	0	0	0	.000	.000	.000
August	10	2	1	0	0	0	2	1	.200	.300	.333
Sept./Oct.	77	14	0	0	2	11	9	6	.182	.260	.264
Leading Off Inn.	61	16	3	0	2	2	7	7	.262	.410	.338
Runners On	115	27	6	0	5	39	15	13	.235	.417	.313
Bases Empty	150	40	6	0	6	6	10	18	.267	.427	.313
Runners/Scor. Pos.	78	20	4	0	4	36	12	10	.256	.462	.340
Runners On/2 Out	45	8	1	0	2	12	5	8	.178	.333	.260
Scor. Pos./2 Out	35	7	1	0	2	12	4	7	.200	.400	.282
Late-Inning Pressure	29	6	0	0	0	2	0	4	.207	.207	.207
Leading Off	12	3	0	0	0	0	0	1	.250	.250	.250
Runners On	9	1	0	0	0	2	0	1	.111	.111	.111
Runners/Scor. Pos.	6	1	0	0	0	2	0	1	.167	.167	.167

RUNS BATTED IN	From 1B	From 2B	From 3B	Scoring Position
Totals	6/85	11/64	17/37	28/101
Percentage	7.1%	17.2%	45.9%	27.7%

Loves to face: Kevin Gross (.364, 16-for-44, 4 HR)
Ramon Martinez (.364, 4-for-11, 1 2B, 3 HR)
Wally Ritchie (.750, 3-for-4, 1 2B, 1 HR)
Hates to face: Tim Belcher (.095, 2-for-21, 3 BB)
Sid Fernandez (.063, 1-for-16)
Ed Whitson (.118, 2-for-17)

Miscellaneous statistics: Ground outs-to-air outs ratio: 0.97 last season, 1.00 for career.... Grounded into 8 double plays in 56 opportunities (one per 7.0).... Drove in 13 of 17 runners from third base with less than two outs (76%).... Direction of balls hit to the outfield: 30% to left field, 29% to center, 41% to right.... Base running: Advanced from first base to third on 4 of 13 outfield singles (31%); scored from second on 7 of 8 (88%).... Made 0.70 assists per nine innings at first base.

Comments: Started 70 of 118 games in which Braves faced a right-handed starter, but only two of 44 against southpaws. Started 45 of team's first 61 games, but only 27 of last 101.... Averaged one home run every 24.1 at-bats, the best rate of his career. But don't attribute that to the Launching Pad in Atlanta: He hit only three homers in 115 at-bats there (one every 38.3 AB), but hit eight (one every 18.8 at-bats) on the road.... Had the lowest strikeout rate of his career, averaging one whiff every 9.6 times to the plate.... Hit a pinch-hit home run in his first at-bat on return to Three Rivers Stadium last May 10.... Managed only one extra-base hit in 40 at-bats vs. left-handers last season, but it was a grand-slam homer off Pittsburgh's Bob Patterson, the first granny of his career. Then in the Championship Series, he poled a long homer off lefty Rosario Rodriguez.... Also hit another grand-slam homer last year, off Ramon Martinez.... At one time, covered tremendous ground at first base; among all first basemen in major league history (minimum: 500 games played), he stands third in assists-to-games ratio: Mark Grace is the leader (560 assists in 588 games), followed by Darrell Evans (752 in 856), Bream (640 in 734), Bill Buckner (1351 in 1555), Buddy Hassett (649 in 751), and Keith Hernandez (1682, a major league record, in 2014).... Spent only two days on the active roster in between 37- and 24-day stints on the disabled list after having "loose bodies" removed from his right knee.

Hubie Brooks
Bats Right

New York Mets	AB	H	2B	3B	HR	RBI	BB	SO	BA	SA	OBA
Season	357	85	11	1	16	50	44	62	.238	.409	.324
vs. Left-Handers	121	30	5	0	5	17	18	13	.248	.413	.343
vs. Right-Handers	236	55	6	1	11	33	26	49	.233	.407	.315
vs. Ground-Ballers	158	35	5	1	7	19	19	26	.222	.399	.311
vs. Fly-Ballers	202	51	7	0	9	31	25	36	.252	.421	.335
Home Games	172	41	6	1	4	22	27	28	.238	.355	.340
Road Games	185	44	5	0	12	28	17	34	.238	.459	.309
Grass Fields	270	68	9	1	10	37	32	47	.252	.404	.330
Artificial Turf	87	17	2	0	6	13	12	15	.195	.425	.307
April	58	14	4	0	3	7	8	8	.241	.466	.343
May	86	22	1	1	4	14	6	20	.256	.430	.301
June	76	24	3	0	6	19	17	9	.316	.592	.438
July	93	18	1	0	2	6	10	12	.194	.269	.279
August	44	7	2	0	1	4	3	13	.159	.273	.213
Sept./Oct.	0	0	0	0	0	0	0	0	.000	.000	.000
Leading Off Inn.	82	26	5	0	5	5	1	11	.317	.561	.333
Runners On	162	34	5	1	4	38	35	34	.210	.327	.348
Bases Empty	195	51	6	0	12	12	9	28	.262	.477	.301
Runners/Scor. Pos.	99	21	3	1	2	33	26	23	.212	.323	.367
Runners On/2 Out	64	12	1	0	2	15	12	14	.188	.297	.325
Scor. Pos./2 Out	46	8	1	0	2	15	10	11	.174	.326	.321
Late-Inning Pressure	61	14	2	0	2	5	8	17	.230	.361	.319
Leading Off	15	4	1	0	1	1	0	4	.267	.533	.267
Runners On	25	4	1	0	0	3	6	7	.160	.200	.323
Runners/Scor. Pos.	12	1	0	0	0	3	4	3	.083	.083	.313

RUNS BATTED IN	From 1B	From 2B	From 3B	Scoring Position
Totals	6/111	13/79	15/44	28/123
Percentage	5.4%	16.5%	34.1%	22.8%

Loves to face: Dennis Cook (.444, 4-for-9, 1 HR, 4 BB)
Rick Honeycutt (.579, 11-for-19)
Scott Scudder (.600, 3-for-5, 1 2B, 1 HR)

Hates to face: Steve Bedrosian (.171, 7-for-41, 1 HR)
Bob Kipper (.111, 1-for-9)
Walt Terrell (.125, 2-for-16)

Miscellaneous statistics: Ground outs-to-air outs ratio: 1.10 last season, 1.35 for career.... Grounded into 7 double plays in 82 opportunities (one per 12).... Drove in 9 of 16 runners from third base with less than two outs (56%).... Direction of balls hit to the outfield: 34% to left field, 28% to center, 37% to right.... Base running: Advanced from first base to third on 7 of 18 outfield singles (39%); scored from second on 8 of 11 (73%).... Made 1.89 putouts per nine innings in right field.

Comments: Slipped to a career low in batting average and hits. Batting average with runners in scoring position, always a strength, was also a career low. Batting average with runners on base was 3d lowest in the league.... Batted over .310 vs. left-handers in each of four seasons, 1985–88, but has fallen to .284, .240, and .248 vs. lefties in the three seasons since.... Only player in majors to steal home twice last year, but don't go off conjuring an image of Jackie Robinson beating Whitey Ford's pitch and sliding in under Yogi Berra's glove. Each of Hubie's efforts came as part of a double steal.... Has played in 1454 games in majors, all in N.L., to rank 10th in games among active players who have never played in the American League. Those with more: Gary Carter, Andre Dawson, Dale Murphy, Garry Templeton, Ozzie Smith, Tim Wallach, Ryne Sandberg, Pedro Guerrero, and Rafael Ramirez.... Has not had a sacrifice bunt since 1983.... He has hit at least one grand-slam home run in six of the last seven seasons; owns .341 career batting average with the bags full (47-for-138, 7 HR). His career rate of one homer every 19.7 at-bats with the bases loaded is more than double his rate at other times (one every 40.2 AB).... Drew only one walk in 84 innings as leadoff batter, lowest rate in N.L. (minimum: 50 leadoff PA).... He has been an opening-day starter in each of the last 11 years.... Both Brooks and new teammate Von Hayes arrive in Anaheim with 139 career home runs to their credit. We say Hayes will be leading after the '92 results are in.

Steve Buechele
Bats Right

Rangers/Pirates	AB	H	2B	3B	HR	RBI	BB	SO	BA	SA	OBA
Season	530	139	22	3	22	85	49	97	.262	.440	.331
vs. Left-Handers	131	39	7	1	9	26	22	23	.298	.573	.404
vs. Right-Handers	399	100	15	2	13	59	27	74	.251	.396	.305
vs. Ground-Ballers	228	61	11	1	9	40	21	45	.268	.443	.336
vs. Fly-Ballers	302	78	11	2	13	45	28	52	.258	.437	.327
Home Games	251	69	14	1	9	32	24	42	.275	.446	.343
Road Games	279	70	8	2	13	53	25	55	.251	.434	.320
Grass Fields	397	106	18	1	16	60	34	64	.267	.438	.331
Artificial Turf	133	33	4	2	6	25	15	33	.248	.444	.331
April	51	13	3	0	2	3	5	5	.255	.431	.333
May	85	26	1	0	6	17	8	15	.306	.529	.362
June	92	22	6	1	3	13	13	21	.239	.424	.333
July	91	24	2	1	4	15	8	17	.264	.440	.337
August	102	26	5	0	3	18	5	12	.255	.392	.300
Sept./Oct.	109	28	5	1	4	19	10	27	.257	.431	.328
Leading Off Inn.	114	31	6	0	2	2	6	18	.272	.377	.314
Runners On	239	69	11	3	12	75	25	35	.289	.510	.362
Bases Empty	291	70	11	0	10	10	24	62	.241	.381	.305
Runners/Scor. Pos.	149	45	7	3	8	66	21	21	.302	.550	.392
Runners On/2 Out	103	27	4	2	5	33	14	13	.262	.485	.361
Scor. Pos./2 Out	66	18	3	2	3	29	13	9	.273	.515	.407
Late-Inning Pressure	88	22	3	1	1	15	7	20	.250	.341	.313
Leading Off	18	3	1	0	0	0	2	4	.167	.222	.250
Runners On	44	12	1	1	0	14	4	8	.273	.341	.333
Runners/Scor. Pos.	30	9	1	1	0	14	4	4	.300	.400	.382

RUNS BATTED IN	From 1B	From 2B	From 3B	Scoring Position
Totals	13/174	27/122	23/58	50/180
Percentage	7.5%	22.1%	39.7%	27.8%

Loves to face: John Candelaria (.381, 8-for-21, 1 HR)
Tony Castillo (.750, 3-for-4, 1 HR)
Bret Saberhagen (.478, 11-for-23, 1 HR)

Hates to face: Mike Jackson (0-for-8)
Dennis Martinez (0-for-5)
Bill Swift (0-for-13)

Miscellaneous statistics: Ground outs-to-air outs ratio: 0.92 last season, 1.10 for career.... Grounded into 14 double plays in 115 opportunities (one per 8.2).... Drove in 16 of 33 runners from third base with less than two outs (48%).... Direction of balls hit to the outfield: 39% to left field, 34% to center, 27% to right.... Base running: Advanced from first base to third on 9 of 30 outfield singles (30%); scored from second on 11 of 16 (69%).... Made 2.28 assists per nine innings at third base.

Comments: With 22 home runs and 85 RBIs (combining totals in both leagues), he hit four more homers than Bobby Bonilla and had two more RBIs than Andy Van Slyke.... Career batting average: .270 vs. left-handers, .228 vs. right-handers.... Had only three errors in 329 chances over 111 games with Texas to break Don Money's one-season A.L. record for lowest rate of errors (one every 94.4 chances) set in 1974. But Bue booted four of 90 chances with Bucs, dropping his overall *major league* rate to one every 59.9 chances. All of which means that Money still owns the *major league* record for one season, even though Buechele holds the *American League* mark.... Career rate (one error every 33 chances) is best among active third basemen (minimum: 200 games). Last season, major league third basemen averaged one error every 21 chances.... Pirates used nine players at third base last season, tying A's for most in the majors. Buechele, Bobby Bonilla, Jeff King, and John Wehner all started at least 25 games there.... Hit 18 home runs for Texas prior to the trade, only the 10th time in major league history that an in-season trade sent a player away from a team for whom he had hit so many homers. The most home runs ever hit by a player for a single club before an in-season deal was 20, by Frank Robinson (1974 Angels) and Rico Carty (1978 Blue Jays). Others traded after hitting 18 or more for one club: Johnny Mize (1949), Vic Wertz (1952), Bob Oliver (1972), Deron Johnson (1975), Ron Kittle (1986), Fred Lynn (1988), and Dale Murphy (1990).

Brett Butler   Bats Left

Los Angeles Dodgers	AB	H	2B	3B	HR	RBI	BB	SO	BA	SA	OBA
Season	615	182	13	5	2	38	108	79	.296	.343	.401
vs. Left-Handers	256	72	2	3	0	14	49	41	.281	.313	.397
vs. Right-Handers	359	110	11	2	2	24	59	38	.306	.365	.404
vs. Ground-Ballers	262	84	7	1	1	27	42	33	.321	.366	.415
vs. Fly-Ballers	353	98	6	4	1	11	66	46	.278	.326	.390
Home Games	295	92	7	2	2	22	59	29	.312	.369	.425
Road Games	320	90	6	3	0	16	49	50	.281	.319	.377
Grass Fields	451	137	10	2	2	34	79	50	.304	.348	.406
Artificial Turf	164	45	3	3	0	4	29	29	.274	.329	.387
April	76	24	2	0	1	6	7	11	.316	.382	.369
May	103	25	2	1	0	5	22	15	.243	.282	.381
June	109	34	1	1	0	4	18	14	.312	.339	.409
July	98	33	1	1	0	11	19	9	.337	.367	.444
August	111	39	3	2	1	10	21	13	.351	.441	.451
Sept./Oct.	118	27	4	0	0	2	21	17	.229	.263	.345
Leading Off Inn.	280	85	7	4	1	1	44	34	.304	.368	.398
Runners On	174	54	4	1	1	37	37	22	.310	.362	.427
Bases Empty	441	128	9	4	1	1	71	57	.290	.336	.390
Runners/Scor. Pos.	110	34	3	1	1	36	30	15	.309	.382	.451
Runners On/2 Out	91	26	1	1	0	17	21	13	.286	.319	.420
Scor. Pos./2 Out	65	18	0	1	0	16	17	10	.277	.308	.427
Late-Inning Pressure	91	31	2	1	1	11	18	12	.341	.418	.450
Leading Off	22	8	0	1	0	0	5	1	.364	.455	.481
Runners On	45	16	1	0	1	11	6	5	.356	.444	.431
Runners/Scor. Pos.	32	11	1	0	1	11	5	4	.344	.469	.432

RUNS BATTED IN	From 1B	From 2B	From 3B	Scoring Position
Totals	2/112	11/88	23/49	34/137
Percentage	1.8%	12.5%	46.9%	24.8%

Loves to face: Neal Heaton (.500, 6-for-12)
Mike Morgan (.459, 17-for-37, 0 SO)
John Smoltz (.438, 14-for-32)

Hates to face: Zane Smith (.174, 4-for-23)
Scott Terry (.143, 2-for-14)
Randy Tomlin (.111, 1-for-9)

Miscellaneous statistics: Ground outs-to-air outs ratio: 1.90 last season, 5th highest in N.L.; 1.30 for career.... Grounded into 3 double plays in 73 opportunities (one per 24).... Drove in 15 of 25 runners from third base with less than two outs (60%).... Direction of balls hit to the outfield: 49% to left field, 37% to center, 15% to right.... Base running: Advanced from first base to third on 27 of 47 outfield singles (57%); scored from second on 18 of 24 (75%).... Made 2.38 putouts per nine innings in center field.

Comments: Led the league in runs scored for the second time in his career, becoming the first player since Arky Vaughan to lead the league in that category as a member of two different clubs. Vaughan did it in 1936 and 1940 with Pirates and in 1943 with Dodgers.... Butler has led the majors in singles in each of the last two seasons. No one had done that since Matty Alou (1969–70), and no player has done it in three straight years since Nellie Fox had a four-year streak, 1954–57.... His streak of 167 consecutive at-bats without an extra-base hit was the longest in the majors last season.... Became the first everyday leadoff batter to lead the National League in walks since Joe Morgan did it for Houston in 1965.... Played 161 games in the outfield without an error, one game shy of Rocky Colavito's single-season major league record set in 1965. Butler enters 1992 with an errorless streak of 186 games, 56 games shy of Doug Dascenzo's specious National League record.... Stole 12 bases in 18 attempts (67%) on artificial turf, 26 bases in 48 attempts (54%) on dirt infields.... Led the majors with 61 infield hits last season.... Has scored 100 runs in a season six times: twice with Cleveland, thrice with the Giants, and last year with the Dodgers. It was reported here last year that Joe Carter could (in 1991) become the first player to drive in 100 runs in a season for three different teams. And so he did. Butler became the first player in the postwar era to score 100 runs for three different teams.

Ivan Calderon   Bats Right

Montreal Expos	AB	H	2B	3B	HR	RBI	BB	SO	BA	SA	OBA
Season	470	141	22	3	19	75	53	64	.300	.481	.368
vs. Left-Handers	161	57	9	1	11	31	20	22	.354	.627	.423
vs. Right-Handers	309	84	13	2	8	44	33	42	.272	.405	.339
vs. Ground-Ballers	207	66	11	2	8	36	22	32	.319	.507	.386
vs. Fly-Ballers	268	78	11	1	12	41	31	32	.291	.474	.357
Home Games	224	69	8	2	7	29	26	35	.308	.455	.374
Road Games	246	72	14	1	12	46	27	29	.293	.504	.362
Grass Fields	132	39	7	1	5	21	13	18	.295	.477	.360
Artificial Turf	338	102	15	2	14	54	40	46	.302	.482	.370
April	76	21	3	0	3	15	5	10	.276	.434	.325
May	91	30	1	1	4	20	11	13	.330	.495	.387
June	109	35	11	0	2	12	14	17	.321	.477	.397
July	77	23	2	1	3	10	11	11	.299	.468	.378
August	99	26	5	1	6	15	10	9	.263	.515	.333
Sept./Oct.	18	6	0	0	1	3	2	4	.333	.500	.400
Leading Off Inn.	77	21	6	0	5	5	11	10	.273	.545	.371
Runners On	217	70	9	3	7	63	17	26	.323	.488	.357
Bases Empty	253	71	13	0	12	12	36	38	.281	.474	.377
Runners/Scor. Pos.	145	44	5	2	5	57	14	16	.303	.469	.343
Runners On/2 Out	70	14	2	0	2	10	8	7	.200	.314	.282
Scor. Pos./2 Out	52	9	2	0	2	10	6	4	.173	.327	.259
Late-Inning Pressure	79	29	6	0	5	12	10	15	.367	.633	.435
Leading Off	15	5	3	0	1	1	2	1	.333	.733	.412
Runners On	31	10	2	0	1	8	6	6	.323	.484	.410
Runners/Scor. Pos.	20	5	1	0	1	8	3	5	.250	.450	.320

RUNS BATTED IN	From 1B	From 2B	From 3B	Scoring Position
Totals	5/131	15/108	36/66	51/174
Percentage	3.8%	13.9%	54.5%	29.3%

Loves to face: Dennis Rasmussen (.400, 6-for-15, 3 HR)
Curt Schilling (3-for-3, 2 BB)
Trevor Wilson (.429, 3-for-7, 2 HR)

Hates to face: Juan Berenguer (.100, 2-for-20, 2 BB)
Tom Candiotti (.053, 1-for-19, 5 BB)
Dave Righetti (.133, 2-for-15)

Miscellaneous statistics: Ground outs-to-air outs ratio: 1.11 last season, 1.00 for career.... Grounded into 7 double plays in 96 opportunities (one per 14).... Drove in 33 of 46 runners from third base with less than two outs (72%).... Direction of balls hit to the outfield: 29% to left field, 34% to center, 37% to right.... Base running: Advanced from first base to third on 2 of 11 outfield singles (18%); scored from second on 12 of 15 (80%).... Made 2.22 putouts per nine innings in left field.

Comments: Had 75 RBIs and 31 steals; in 1990 he had 74 RBIs and 32 steals. But there's a significant difference: He had 607 at-bats in 1990, only 470 last year.... Ranked third in the league with 32 go-ahead RBIs. Think about that: 43 percent of his RBIs put his team in front. No other player in the majors had such a high ratio of go-ahead RBIs. The top five (minimum: 15 go-aheads): Calderon, Carlos Baerga (26 of 69), Julio Franco (29 of 78), Dan Gladden (19 of 52), Fred McGriff (38 of 106).... Had N.L.'s third-highest batting average vs. left-handed pitchers; career breakdown: .300 vs. lefties, .266 vs. righties.... Has put together back-to-back seasons of more than 30 stolen bases after having only 29 steals in 502 games prior to 1990.... The distribution of balls hit to the outfield matched his 1990 output almost exactly. He puts a lot of balls in play to the opposite field, but he has no opposite-field home runs in either of the last two seasons. Last year, he hit 17 home runs to left field, two to center.... Batted .367 in Late-Inning Pressure Situations, 4th best in N.L., after batting .206, .208, and .211 in those situations over the three previous years.... Has .281 career average with runners in scoring position that breaks down as follows: .328 with less than two outs, .208 with two outs. He's 2-for-23 lifetime with two outs and the bases loaded.... Elbow problem limited him to pinch-hitting after September 4. Four hits in his final nine at-bats of the season lifted his batting average to exactly .300, a career high.

Ken Caminiti — Bats Left and Right

Houston Astros	AB	H	2B	3B	HR	RBI	BB	SO	BA	SA	OBA
Season	574	145	30	3	13	80	46	85	.253	.383	.312
vs. Left-Handers	232	72	14	2	9	44	12	27	.310	.504	.347
vs. Right-Handers	342	73	16	1	4	36	34	58	.213	.301	.289
vs. Ground-Ballers	267	56	15	1	5	31	22	41	.210	.330	.274
vs. Fly-Ballers	310	90	15	2	8	49	25	44	.290	.429	.346
Home Games	289	73	18	2	9	48	22	52	.253	.422	.307
Road Games	285	72	12	1	4	32	24	33	.253	.344	.316
Grass Fields	177	46	6	1	3	14	12	22	.260	.356	.314
Artificial Turf	397	99	24	2	10	66	34	63	.249	.395	.311
April	71	19	3	0	1	8	4	7	.268	.352	.316
May	106	24	2	1	2	9	10	11	.226	.321	.297
June	90	19	4	0	3	8	7	18	.211	.356	.263
July	95	27	6	2	4	25	7	11	.284	.516	.340
August	108	29	9	0	2	22	12	21	.269	.407	.344
Sept./Oct.	104	27	6	0	1	8	6	17	.260	.346	.306
Leading Off Inn.	138	34	8	0	1	1	5	23	.246	.326	.293
Runners On	279	77	15	2	9	76	29	36	.276	.441	.340
Bases Empty	295	68	15	1	4	4	17	49	.231	.329	.284
Runners/Scor. Pos.	156	45	11	1	4	63	22	22	.288	.449	.368
Runners On/2 Out	112	31	6	2	3	25	13	10	.277	.446	.352
Scor. Pos./2 Out	65	19	5	1	2	22	10	8	.292	.492	.387
Late-Inning Pressure	92	30	3	0	3	9	5	18	.326	.457	.361
Leading Off	24	9	1	0	0	0	1	5	.375	.417	.400
Runners On	41	12	1	0	2	8	4	7	.293	.463	.356
Runners/Scor. Pos.	25	6	0	0	1	6	4	5	.240	.360	.345

RUNS BATTED IN	From 1B	From 2B	From 3B	Scoring Position
Totals	14/212	25/121	28/66	53/187
Percentage	6.6%	20.7%	42.4%	28.3%

Loves to face: Bob Ojeda (.636, 7-for-11, 1 HR)
Alejandro Pena (.500, 6-for-12, 1 HR)
Trevor Wilson (.333, 6-for-18, 2 2B, 3 HR)

Hates to face: Tim Belcher (.118, 4-for-34, 0 BB)
Norm Charlton (0-for-22)
Dwight Gooden (.077, 1-for-13)

Miscellaneous statistics: Ground outs-to-air outs ratio: 1.08 last season, 1.00 for career.... Grounded into 18 double plays in 139 opportunities (one per 7.7).... Drove in 20 of 37 runners from third base with less than two outs (54%).... Direction of balls hit to the outfield: 25% to left field, 32% to center, 43% to right batting left-handed; 43% to left field, 27% to center, 30% to right batting right-handed.... Base running: Advanced from first base to third on 7 of 25 outfield singles (28%); scored from second on 13 of 17 (76%).... Made 2.02 assists per nine innings at third base.

Comments: Had the league's 8th-highest batting average vs. left-handed pitchers and the 6th lowest vs. right-handers. There's a 62-point discrepancy in his career averages (.285 vs. left-handers, .223 vs. right-handers), the second-largest difference among active switch-hitters with at least 1500 at-bats. The perennial winner of the "Why Switch-Hit At All?" Award is, of course, Wally Backman, whose career average vs. left-handers (.165) is 131 points lower than his average vs. righties (.296).... Batting average in Late-Inning Pressure Situations was 8th highest in league. Astros, ninth in N.L. in overall batting average, ranked third in league in LIPS (.260).... Career breakdown: .234 with the bases empty, .261 with runners on base, .277 with runners in scoring position.... Career average at the Astrodome (.263) is 32 points higher than his road average (.231). He also has more home runs in the dome (16) than elsewhere (15).... Averaged one strikeout every 7.4 plate appearances, the lowest rate of his career.... Started a 5–4–3 ground-ball triple play on April 16, replicating something he did the previous September. ESPN won our first annual "Worst 'First-Since' Note of the Year" Award with its observation that night that Houston's triple play was the first by the team since Sept. 21, 1990. All the way from September 1990 to April 1991 without making a single triple play? Incredible: *18 entire games without a triple play!*

Casey Candaele — Bats Left and Right

Houston Astros	AB	H	2B	3B	HR	RBI	BB	SO	BA	SA	OBA
Season	461	121	20	7	4	50	40	49	.262	.362	.319
vs. Left-Handers	158	45	7	1	1	13	15	15	.285	.361	.347
vs. Right-Handers	303	76	13	6	3	37	25	34	.251	.363	.305
vs. Ground-Ballers	209	57	8	2	1	24	16	21	.273	.344	.322
vs. Fly-Ballers	252	64	12	5	3	26	24	28	.254	.377	.318
Home Games	235	69	11	5	1	33	26	27	.294	.396	.361
Road Games	226	52	9	2	3	17	14	22	.230	.327	.274
Grass Fields	135	32	5	0	2	11	7	15	.237	.319	.273
Artificial Turf	326	89	15	7	2	39	33	34	.273	.380	.338
April	45	12	3	3	0	8	6	5	.267	.467	.346
May	77	18	4	1	0	7	4	9	.234	.312	.272
June	96	23	5	0	1	11	9	12	.240	.323	.302
July	79	26	3	2	3	8	10	10	.329	.532	.404
August	93	22	4	1	0	7	7	9	.237	.301	.290
Sept./Oct.	71	20	1	0	0	9	4	4	.282	.296	.316
Leading Off Inn.	113	29	6	2	1	1	12	12	.257	.372	.328
Runners On	206	62	11	3	1	47	16	24	.301	.398	.347
Bases Empty	255	59	9	4	3	3	24	25	.231	.333	.297
Runners/Scor. Pos.	112	34	6	2	1	45	15	16	.304	.420	.377
Runners On/2 Out	100	28	4	2	0	22	9	11	.280	.360	.339
Scor. Pos./2 Out	62	18	2	2	0	21	9	7	.290	.387	.380
Late-Inning Pressure	96	27	6	1	0	15	11	11	.281	.365	.355
Leading Off	27	7	1	1	0	0	4	3	.259	.370	.355
Runners On	45	12	2	0	0	15	5	6	.267	.311	.340
Runners/Scor. Pos.	25	12	2	0	0	15	5	4	.480	.560	.567

RUNS BATTED IN	From 1B	From 2B	From 3B	Scoring Position
Totals	6/151	21/98	19/44	40/142
Percentage	4.0%	21.4%	43.2%	28.2%

Loves to face: Rick Mahler (.583, 7-for-12, 1 HR)
Jamie Moyer (.462, 6-for-13, 4 2B)
Bob Ojeda (.429, 9-for-21)

Hates to face: Jeff Brantley (0-for-7)
Sid Fernandez (0-for-8)
Dwight Gooden (.167, 4-for-24)

Miscellaneous statistics: Ground outs-to-air outs ratio: 0.95 last season, 1.15 for career.... Grounded into 5 double plays in 88 opportunities (one per 18).... Drove in 13 of 19 runners from third base with less than two outs (68%).... Direction of balls hit to the outfield: 30% to left field, 36% to center, 34% to right batting left-handed; 27% to left field, 39% to center, 34% to right batting right-handed.... Base running: Advanced from first base to third on 3 of 16 outfield singles (19%); scored from second on 9 of 12 (75%).... Made 3.12 assists per nine innings at second base.

Comments: Played 109 games at second base last season, the first time in his major league career that he's stayed in one spot long enough to accumulate 100 games there. Still, he was the only N.L. player to start at least two games at five different positions (2B, 3B, LF, CF, RF) last season.... One of six N.L. players to bat over .300 with runners in scoring position in each of the last two seasons (minimum: 50 AB with RISP in each season).... Batting average with runners in scoring position in Late-Inning Pressure Situations was 2d highest among N.L. players with at least 15 at-bats in those situations. Shawon Dunston went 10-for-20 in those pressure-packed at-bats to lead league.... Owns a higher career batting average on grass fields (.272) than he does on artificial turf (.253).... There's a 57-point gap between his career batting averages from the right (.295) and left (.238) sides of the plate. Among active switch-hitters with at least 1500 plate appearances, only Wally Backman and Ken Caminiti have larger differences. Astros also have a third switch-hitter who's at least 50 points better from the right side in Gerald Young.... Houston's second basemen batted only .231 last season, lowest team batting average for second basemen in the league. Candaele (.264 as a second baseman) wasn't really to blame, but neither of the real culprits, Mark McLemore or Andy Mota, accumulated enough at-bats to earn a spot in this section of the book. Sorry, Casey, we'll try to make it up to you in the '93 edition.

Mark Carreon

New York Mets   Bats Right

New York Mets	AB	H	2B	3B	HR	RBI	BB	SO	BA	SA	OBA
Season	254	66	6	0	4	21	12	26	.260	.331	.297
vs. Left-Handers	165	40	4	0	3	14	8	15	.242	.321	.286
vs. Right-Handers	89	26	2	0	1	7	4	11	.292	.348	.319
vs. Ground-Ballers	102	27	4	0	1	9	6	5	.265	.333	.303
vs. Fly-Ballers	153	39	2	0	3	12	6	21	.255	.327	.292
Home Games	155	39	4	0	3	15	9	15	.252	.335	.299
Road Games	99	27	2	0	1	6	3	11	.273	.323	.294
Grass Fields	184	46	4	0	3	17	10	17	.250	.321	.294
Artificial Turf	70	20	2	0	1	4	2	9	.286	.357	.306
April	31	10	1	0	2	3	4	3	.323	.548	.400
May	25	7	1	0	1	1	0	4	.280	.440	.280
June	54	12	0	0	0	3	2	9	.222	.222	.250
July	32	7	1	0	0	5	4	4	.219	.250	.306
August	49	9	0	0	1	2	2	2	.184	.245	.231
Sept./Oct.	63	21	3	0	0	7	0	4	.333	.381	.338
Leading Off Inn.	48	12	0	0	1	1	1	5	.250	.313	.265
Runners On	126	34	4	0	3	17	7	14	.270	.302	.311
Bases Empty	128	32	2	0	1	4	5	12	.250	.359	.284
Runners/Scor. Pos.	80	18	2	0	0	17	6	11	.225	.250	.284
Runners On/2 Out	58	16	1	0	0	10	1	10	.276	.293	.300
Scor. Pos./2 Out	38	10	1	0	0	10	0	7	.263	.289	.282
Late-Inning Pressure	54	15	2	0	2	5	0	7	.278	.426	.286
Leading Off	10	5	0	0	0	0	0	1	.500	.500	.500
Runners On	28	6	1	0	0	3	0	5	.214	.250	.233
Runners/Scor. Pos.	17	3	0	0	0	3	0	4	.176	.176	.211

RUNS BATTED IN	From 1B	From 2B	From 3B	Scoring Position
Totals	0/92	7/63	10/30	17/93
Percentage	0.0%	11.1%	33.3%	18.3%

Loves to face: Rheal Cormier (.417, 5-for-12, 1 HR)
                 Neal Heaton (.600, 6-for-10, 2 HR)

Hates to face: Paul Assenmacher (0-for-7, 4 SO)
                 Tom Glavine (.083, 1-for-12)
                 Craig Lefferts (.100, 1-for-10, 5 SO)

Miscellaneous statistics: Ground outs-to-air outs ratio: 1.13 last season, 0.95 for career.... Grounded into 13 double plays in 55 opportunities (one per 4.2), 3d-worst rate in N.L.... Drove in 4 of 13 runners from third base with less than two outs (31%).... Direction of balls hit to the outfield: 34% to left field, 39% to center, 26% to right.... Base running: Advanced from first base to third on 4 of 14 outfield singles (29%); scored from second on 2 of 2 (100%).... Made 2.05 putouts per nine innings in left field.

Comments: Started 43 of 64 games in which Mets faced a left-handed starter, but only 10 of 97 games vs. right-handers.... Had only one hit in 20 first-inning at-bats, and only one hit in 22 at-bats while in games as a right fielder. One of these statistics might be vaguely relevant.... He needs 82 more games to match his father's career total of 354 games. Camilo Carreon caught for the White Sox, Indians, and Orioles from 1959 to 1966.... Career average of .258 at Shea Stadium, .276 on other grass fields, and .291 on artificial turf.... He's hit for a higher average with runners on base than he has with the bases empty in each of his five seasons in the majors. But 17 of his 21 home runs have come with the bases empty.... Career pinch-hitting: .290 batting average (27-for-93) with eight home runs. Among active players, only Candy Maldonado (nine) has more career pinch-hit homers. Carreon had three pinch homers last year and Mets led majors in that category with eight.... That pinch-hit batting average is pretty good; consider that in the National League last season, the overall batting average for pinch hitters was only .216. Manny Mota, the player with the all-time career record for pinch hits (150), had a career pinch-hit batting average of .297. The best pinch-hit batting average by any player in major league history (minimum: 100 at-bats): .333 by Gordon Coleman (40-for-120) of the Indians and Reds.

Gary Carter

Los Angeles Dodgers   Bats Right

Los Angeles Dodgers	AB	H	2B	3B	HR	RBI	BB	SO	BA	SA	OBA
Season	248	61	14	0	6	26	22	26	.246	.375	.323
vs. Left-Handers	151	38	9	0	3	14	18	16	.252	.371	.347
vs. Right-Handers	97	23	5	0	3	12	4	10	.237	.381	.282
vs. Ground-Ballers	100	21	4	0	1	8	9	12	.210	.280	.298
vs. Fly-Ballers	148	40	10	0	5	18	13	14	.270	.439	.339
Home Games	125	27	2	0	3	11	11	17	.216	.304	.298
Road Games	123	34	12	0	3	15	11	9	.276	.447	.348
Grass Fields	185	44	8	0	5	19	15	19	.238	.362	.314
Artificial Turf	63	17	6	0	1	7	7	7	.270	.413	.347
April	11	1	0	0	0	1	1	1	.091	.091	.167
May	38	8	2	0	2	7	6	4	.211	.421	.326
June	48	13	2	0	1	5	3	3	.271	.375	.327
July	66	18	6	0	2	8	4	9	.273	.455	.338
August	48	14	3	0	1	4	1	5	.292	.417	.320
Sept./Oct.	37	7	1	0	0	2	7	4	.189	.216	.333
Leading Off Inn.	57	16	4	0	2	2	1	5	.281	.456	.305
Runners On	109	27	7	0	1	21	10	11	.248	.339	.328
Bases Empty	139	34	7	0	5	5	12	15	.245	.403	.318
Runners/Scor. Pos.	69	18	6	0	1	19	7	9	.261	.362	.346
Runners On/2 Out	52	13	4	0	1	11	8	4	.250	.385	.381
Scor. Pos./2 Out	39	9	3	0	1	10	6	4	.231	.385	.362
Late-Inning Pressure	52	13	4	0	2	4	6	8	.250	.442	.328
Leading Off	14	6	1	0	1	0	2	2	.429	.714	.429
Runners On	23	2	2	0	0	2	4	3	.087	.174	.222
Runners/Scor. Pos.	14	1	1	0	0	2	3	3	.071	.143	.235

RUNS BATTED IN	From 1B	From 2B	From 3B	Scoring Position
Totals	2/79	7/49	11/36	18/85
Percentage	2.5%	14.3%	30.6%	21.2%

Loves to face: Atlee Hammaker (.433, 13-for-30, 1 HR, 0 BB)
                 Bruce Hurst (.400, 4-for-10, 2 2B, 1 HR)
                 Mike Maddux (.800, 4-for-5, 1 SO)

Hates to face: Tim Burke (.148, 4-for-27, 0 BB)
                 Jose DeLeon (.191, 9-for-47)
                 Dave Smith (.059, 1-for-17)

Miscellaneous statistics: Ground outs-to-air outs ratio: 0.97 last season, 0.79 for career.... Grounded into 11 double plays in 44 opportunities (one per 4.0), 2d-worst rate in N.L.... Drove in 7 of 13 runners from third base with less than two outs (54%).... Direction of balls hit to the outfield: 47% to left field, 32% to center, 21% to right.... Base running: Advanced from first base to third on 6 of 19 outfield singles (32%); scored from second on 3 of 7 (43%).... Opposing base stealers: 59-for-87 (68%).

Comments: One of six players in history who played for the Mets, Giants, and Dodgers. How many can you name? Answer below.... Career total of 2201 games ranks ninth among active players, but it's the most by any active player who has spent his entire career in the National League.... Total of 1971 games behind the plate ranks third in major league history behind Bob Boone (2225) and Carlton Fisk (2147). Carter doesn't have to look over his shoulder yet. His closest active pursuer is Lance Parrish, 324 games behind Gary.... Needs seven more home runs as a catcher to become fourth to reach 300 at that position. If he gets a little closer, remember that when he approached 300 overall home runs he stalled out, going homerless for two months.... Carter caught 1257 games for Expos, more than twice as many as any other catcher in team history (Mike Fitzgerald, 559, is second).... Started 43 of 68 games (63%) in which Dodgers faced a left-handed starter, only 16 of 94 vs. right-handers.... Others who played for Mets, Giants, and Dodgers: Duke Snider, Ron Hunt, Joe Pignatano, Alex Trevino, Mike Vail.... Hitless in 15 at-bats with the bases loaded over the last two years. Last season, he batted with the bags full nine times and failed to drive in a single run.... We last saw the Kid in an Expos' uniform on Sept. 30, 1984. In that game against New York, Jeff Reardon saved a win for Bill Gullickson, Dan Driessen homered for Montreal, and Carter stole a base and had the game-winning RBI.

Andujar Cedeno · Bats Right

Houston Astros	AB	H	2B	3B	HR	RBI	BB	SO	BA	SA	OBA
Season	251	61	13	2	9	36	9	74	.243	.418	.270
vs. Left-Handers	80	17	4	0	0	10	1	24	.213	.262	.220
vs. Right-Handers	171	44	9	2	9	26	8	50	.257	.491	.293
vs. Ground-Ballers	103	17	2	0	3	16	3	28	.165	.272	.193
vs. Fly-Ballers	148	44	11	2	6	20	6	46	.297	.520	.325
Home Games	134	30	7	2	4	21	5	41	.224	.396	.250
Road Games	117	31	6	0	5	15	4	33	.265	.444	.293
Grass Fields	87	23	4	0	5	14	3	22	.264	.483	.293
Artificial Turf	164	38	9	2	4	22	6	52	.232	.384	.257
April	0	0	0	0	0	0	0	0	—	—	—
May	0	0	0	0	0	0	0	0	—	—	—
June	0	0	0	0	0	0	0	0	—	—	—
July	20	5	1	1	0	2	1	6	.250	.400	.286
August	117	28	5	0	4	18	3	34	.239	.385	.256
Sept./Oct.	114	28	7	1	5	16	5	34	.246	.456	.281
Leading Off Inn.	59	10	3	0	2	2	1	19	.169	.322	.183
Runners On	114	29	5	2	4	31	6	32	.254	.439	.287
Bases Empty	137	32	8	0	5	5	3	42	.234	.401	.255
Runners/Scor. Pos.	67	17	1	2	3	28	5	19	.254	.463	.297
Runners On/2 Out	48	11	2	1	1	9	4	14	.229	.375	.288
Scor. Pos./2 Out	35	8	0	1	1	8	4	11	.229	.371	.308
Late-Inning Pressure	41	9	4	0	2	2	2	15	.220	.463	.256
Leading Off	10	2	1	0	1	1	0	3	.200	.600	.200
Runners On	14	1	0	0	0	0	2	6	.071	.071	.188
Runners/Scor. Pos.	7	0	0	0	0	0	1	3	.000	.000	.125

RUNS BATTED IN	From 1B	From 2B	From 3B	Scoring Position
Totals	4/80	10/55	13/24	23/79
Percentage	5.0%	18.2%	54.2%	29.1%

Loves to face: Joe Boever (4-for-4)
Paul McClellan (.500, 2-for-4, 2 HR)
John Smoltz (.571, 4-for-7)

Hates to face: Steve Avery (0-for-6)
Chris Nabholz (0-for-3, 3 SO)
Jose Rijo (0-for-6)

Miscellaneous statistics: Ground outs-to-air outs ratio: 1.10 last season, 1.08 for career. . . . Grounded into 3 double plays in 56 opportunities (one per 19). . . . Drove in 12 of 17 runners from third base with less than two outs (71%). . . . Direction of balls hit to the outfield: 43% to left field, 34% to center, 23% to right. . . . Base running: Advanced from first base to third on 5 of 11 outfield singles (45%); scored from second on 8 of 8 (100%). . . . Made 2.34 assists per nine innings at shortstop, lowest rate in majors.

Comments: Memories of the '91 pennant race: Cedeno made six errors over three games in Atlanta on the season's final weekend as the Braves won their struggle with the Dodgers for the N.L. West title. . . . Averaged one error every 14.3 chances in 66 games with Astros; only one N.L. shortstop (minimum: 50 games) over the past 10 years has had a higher rate of errors: Kurt Stillwell, one error every 11.6 chances in 51 games in 1987. . . . Selected as shortstop on the *Baseball America* AAA All-Star team. One other Tucson player, outfielder Kenny Lofton, was selected to that team, but was traded to Cleveland in the off-season. . . . Astros rookies' total of games played was 793, the most in the majors, and more than double the major league average. Of those 793 game appearances, 550 were starts, an average of over three rookies in the starting lineup every game. . . . Cedeno's total of 67 games ranked fourth among rookies on the club, behind Jeff Bagwell, Luis Gonzalez, and Al Osuna. . . . Let's hope Andujar's role models are not Joaquin and Cesar. . . . Cedeno was the youngest player to appear in at least 50 National League games last season. The Astros also had Jeff Juden, the youngest player to appear in *any* National League games last season. Juden was born on Jan. 19, 1971, the day after George McGovern announced his intention to run against President Nixon in 1972. Cedeno arrived on Aug. 21, 1969, the day after the Beatles' final session together at Abbey Road Studios.

Rick Cerone · Bats Right

New York Mets	AB	H	2B	3B	HR	RBI	BB	SO	BA	SA	OBA
Season	227	62	13	0	2	16	30	24	.273	.357	.360
vs. Left-Handers	111	35	8	0	0	8	11	13	.315	.387	.377
vs. Right-Handers	116	27	5	0	2	8	19	11	.233	.328	.346
vs. Ground-Ballers	103	28	4	0	2	5	13	13	.272	.369	.359
vs. Fly-Ballers	124	34	9	0	0	11	17	11	.274	.347	.362
Home Games	123	36	9	0	1	12	14	10	.293	.390	.365
Road Games	104	26	4	0	1	4	16	14	.250	.317	.355
Grass Fields	172	49	12	0	1	12	21	15	.285	.372	.363
Artificial Turf	55	13	1	0	1	4	9	9	.236	.309	.354
April	26	10	3	0	1	4	0	2	.385	.615	.407
May	44	10	4	0	0	3	6	3	.227	.318	.320
June	49	10	1	0	0	3	12	5	.204	.224	.361
July	46	14	1	0	0	2	7	5	.304	.326	.396
August	49	15	3	0	0	3	4	6	.306	.367	.358
Sept./Oct.	13	3	1	0	1	1	1	3	.231	.538	.286
Leading Off Inn.	60	20	4	0	1	7	4	3	.333	.450	.403
Runners On	88	20	4	0	0	14	19	15	.227	.273	.370
Bases Empty	139	42	9	0	2	2	11	9	.302	.410	.353
Runners/Scor. Pos.	49	10	1	0	0	12	17	10	.204	.224	.418
Runners On/2 Out	40	8	3	0	0	8	8	7	.200	.275	.347
Scor. Pos./2 Out	24	5	1	0	0	6	7	5	.208	.250	.406
Late-Inning Pressure	33	12	3	0	1	1	3	3	.364	.545	.417
Leading Off	11	4	1	0	0	0	0	1	.364	.455	.364
Runners On	11	2	1	0	0	0	3	2	.182	.273	.357
Runners/Scor. Pos.	3	0	0	0	0	0	2	2	.000	.000	.400

RUNS BATTED IN	From 1B	From 2B	From 3B	Scoring Position
Totals	3/73	5/43	6/19	11/62
Percentage	4.1%	11.6%	31.6%	17.7%

Loves to face: Neal Heaton (.400, 6-for-15, 1 HR)
Charlie Leibrandt (.385, 10-for-26, 1 HR)
Nolan Ryan (.379, 11-for-29, 2 HR)

Hates to face: Charlie Hough (.100, 2-for-20)
Mark Langston (.120, 3-for-25, 3 BB)
Dennis Martinez (.059, 1-for-17)

Miscellaneous statistics: Ground outs-to-air outs ratio: 1.21 last season, 0.98 for career. . . . Grounded into 9 double plays in 47 opportunities (one per 5.2). . . . Drove in 4 of 12 runners from third base with less than two outs (33%). . . . Direction of balls hit to the outfield: 37% to left field, 27% to center, 37% to right. . . . Base running: Advanced from first base to third on 1 of 12 outfield singles (8%), 5th-lowest rate in N.L.; scored from second on 3 of 6 (50%). . . . Opposing base stealers: 39-for-71 (55%), 2d-lowest rate in N.L.

Comments: Mets' catching situation was, shall we say, unsteady last season; for a while it seemed that the pitchers, depending on their individual clout, selected to whom they would throw. Doc got first choice, and had Charlie O'Brien catch over 70 percent of his innings. Frank Viola preferred Cerone, who caught 73 percent of his innings. Mackey Sasser caught Gooden in only five starts and never caught any of Viola's. . . . Cerone caught 39.9 percent of the Mets' innings, followed by O'Brien (34%), Sasser (16%), and Todd Hundley (10%). Mets' pitchers had 3.12 ERA with Hundley, 3.36 with Cerone, 3.52 with O'Brien, 4.45 with Sasser. . . . In the majors last year, 17 catchers caught at least half of their team's innings; three teams (Mets, Cubs, Expos) split the job so that no catcher caught even 40 percent of its innings. . . . Carlton Fisk, Rick Dempsey, Ernie Whitt, Ron Hassey, and Gary Carter are all older, but among them, only Fisk caught more games than Cerone last season. . . . Averaged one walk every 8.6 times up last season, best rate of his career. In 1990 he had his worst rate, one walk every 29.2 times up, with Yankees. . . . He stole a base last season, the fifth of his career to go along with the 20 times he's been caught stealing. Records on times caught stealing, and therefore records of stolen-base percentage, are incomplete in baseball history. But among players for whom we have complete data, Cerone's 5-for-25 ranks as the worst in history; former infielder Luis Gomez was 6-for-28, ex-outfielder Bob Nieman was 10-for-40.

Wes Chamberlain

Bats Right

Philadelphia Phillies	AB	H	2B	3B	HR	RBI	BB	SO	BA	SA	OBA
Season	383	92	16	3	13	50	31	73	.240	.399	.300
vs. Left-Handers	140	38	8	1	7	26	16	18	.271	.493	.350
vs. Right-Handers	243	54	8	2	6	24	15	55	.222	.346	.270
vs. Ground-Ballers	193	46	4	3	6	23	13	30	.238	.383	.290
vs. Fly-Ballers	190	46	12	0	7	27	18	43	.242	.416	.311
Home Games	211	56	9	1	9	32	15	37	.265	.445	.317
Road Games	172	36	7	2	4	18	16	36	.209	.343	.280
Grass Fields	94	20	4	0	3	12	6	19	.213	.351	.260
Artificial Turf	289	72	12	3	10	38	25	54	.249	.415	.313
April	5	1	0	0	0	0	0	0	.200	.200	.200
May	0	0	0	0	0	0	0	0	.000	.000	.000
June	58	19	4	0	1	6	2	8	.328	.448	.361
July	73	19	5	0	3	12	3	12	.260	.452	.289
August	116	31	3	2	6	18	16	24	.267	.483	.356
Sept./Oct.	131	22	4	1	3	14	10	29	.168	.282	.232
Leading Off Inn.	69	16	1	1	1	1	5	10	.232	.319	.293
Runners On	179	46	6	2	11	48	13	36	.257	.497	.311
Bases Empty	204	46	10	1	2	2	18	37	.225	.314	.291
Runners/Scor. Pos.	97	24	4	1	6	36	11	21	.247	.495	.330
Runners On/2 Out	58	13	3	1	5	16	5	9	.224	.569	.286
Scor. Pos./2 Out	29	6	2	0	3	10	5	4	.207	.586	.324
Late-Inning Pressure	56	15	3	0	1	3	5	12	.268	.375	.328
Leading Off	12	3	0	0	0	0	2	3	.250	.250	.357
Runners On	26	7	0	0	0	2	1	4	.269	.269	.296
Runners/Scor. Pos.	17	4	0	0	0	2	1	3	.235	.235	.278

RUNS BATTED IN	From 1B	From 2B	From 3B	Scoring Position
Totals	11/126	11/69	15/39	26/108
Percentage	8.7%	15.9%	38.5%	24.1%

Loves to face: Greg W. Harris (.500, 3-for-6, 2 HR)
Jimmy Jones (3-for-3, 2 2B)
John Smiley (.400, 4-for-10, 2 HR)
Hates to face: Brian Barnes (.071, 1-for-14, 2 BB)
Chris Haney (0-for-8)
Omar Olivares (0-for-6)

Miscellaneous statistics: Ground outs-to-air outs ratio: 1.01 last season, 1.06 for career.... Grounded into 8 double plays in 91 opportunities (one per 11).... Drove in 13 of 28 runners from third base with less than two outs (46%).... Direction of balls hit to the outfield: 42% to left field, 29% to center, 29% to right.... Base running: Advanced from first base to third on 10 of 24 outfield singles (42%); scored from second on 2 of 4 (50%).... Made 2.09 putouts per nine innings in left field.

Comments: Even though Mickey Morandini got a huge head start, Chamberlain came back to lead Phillies rookies in at-bats and games, and became the first Phillies rookie to play at least 100 games since Chris James in 1987.... Started 96 games last season to finish tied for fourth among N.L. rookies.... Batted .271 vs. left-handers and .222 vs. right-handers. Last year, the Phillies had the lowest overall batting average (.241) in N.L., but they had the league's second-best average (.261) vs. left-handers. Phils' .230 mark vs. right-handers was lowest in the majors by any team over last 10 years.... Had the league's 7th-lowest batting average vs. right-handed pitchers, 5th-lowest average in road games, and the 1st-lowest average in day games (.182).... Batted .184 during 76 first-inning at-bats, .254 thereafter.... Started season with Phillies but was sent to Scranton after making only one start in first two weeks of the season. Recalled after Von Hayes's injury.... He's a career .277 hitter in the minors, .245 in the majors.... Career breakdown: .269 at The Vet, .219 in other stadiums with artificial turf, and .211 on grass fields.... His ground outs-to-air outs ratio was much higher on grass fields (1.48) than on artificial turf (0.89). The major league G/A ratio last season was just about the same on grass fields (1.15) as on the rugs (1.13).... Born April 13, 1966, opening day for the Phillies that year. John Herrnstein drove in the winning run in a 12-inning victory at St. Louis.

Jerald Clark

Bats Right

San Diego Padres	AB	H	2B	3B	HR	RBI	BB	SO	BA	SA	OBA
Season	369	84	16	0	10	47	31	90	.228	.352	.295
vs. Left-Handers	126	22	3	0	4	13	10	31	.175	.294	.239
vs. Right-Handers	243	62	13	0	6	34	21	59	.255	.383	.324
vs. Ground-Ballers	184	47	10	0	6	29	14	34	.255	.408	.315
vs. Fly-Ballers	185	37	6	0	4	18	17	56	.200	.297	.275
Home Games	195	41	9	0	8	29	14	43	.210	.379	.270
Road Games	174	43	7	0	2	18	17	47	.247	.322	.323
Grass Fields	282	64	12	0	8	40	20	74	.227	.355	.284
Artificial Turf	87	20	4	0	2	7	11	16	.230	.345	.330
April	73	21	3	0	3	13	8	16	.288	.452	.366
May	21	5	1	0	0	3	1	7	.238	.286	.304
June	68	20	5	0	4	15	12	4	.294	.544	.410
July	91	18	3	0	2	8	4	25	.198	.297	.232
August	67	14	3	0	1	6	4	16	.209	.299	.260
Sept./Oct.	49	6	1	0	0	2	2	22	.122	.143	.167
Leading Off Inn.	89	19	5	0	1	1	8	24	.213	.303	.286
Runners On	168	44	8	0	6	43	9	35	.262	.417	.308
Bases Empty	201	40	8	0	4	4	22	55	.199	.299	.284
Runners/Scor. Pos.	89	21	2	0	3	36	3	16	.236	.360	.280
Runners On/2 Out	76	23	7	0	3	20	5	13	.303	.513	.354
Scor. Pos./2 Out	50	14	2	0	2	18	1	10	.280	.440	.308
Late-Inning Pressure	66	12	1	0	0	6	4	19	.182	.197	.225
Leading Off	14	3	1	0	0	0	2	3	.214	.286	.313
Runners On	33	7	0	0	0	6	1	7	.212	.212	.229
Runners/Scor. Pos.	18	4	0	0	0	6	1	3	.222	.222	.250

RUNS BATTED IN	From 1B	From 2B	From 3B	Scoring Position
Totals	7/141	15/73	15/32	30/105
Percentage	5.0%	20.5%	46.9%	28.6%

Loves to face: Doug Drabek (2-for-2, 1 BB)
Jason Grimsley (1-for-1, 1 HR, 2 BB)
Mike Morgan (.417, 5-for-12, 1 HR)
Hates to face: Danny Jackson (0-for-10)
Charlie Leibrandt (0-for-9)
Jose Rijo (0-for-9, 5 SO)

Miscellaneous statistics: Ground outs-to-air outs ratio: 1.19 last season, 1.03 for career.... Grounded into 10 double plays in 89 opportunities (one per 8.9).... Drove in 13 of 18 runners from third base with less than two outs (72%).... Direction of balls hit to the outfield: 38% to left field, 33% to center, 28% to right.... Base running: Advanced from first base to third on 7 of 17 outfield singles (41%); scored from second on 2 of 5 (40%).... Made 1.82 putouts per nine innings in left field, 2d-lowest rate in N.L.

Comments: If you just looked at his batting statistics against left- and right-handed pitchers, you'd swear that he's one of those left-handed batters who get to play against some meatball left-handers but who sit against the tough ones. In reality, Clark's a right-handed hitter who, to this point in his career, has one of the most extreme "backward" tendencies of any batter we've seen. Career breakdown: .263 vs. right-handers, .182 vs. left-handers. That's the lowest batting average vs. lefties by any active right-handed batter (minimum: 200 AB vs. LHP); that doesn't count Wally Backman, a switch-hitter with a .165 career mark vs. lefties.... Last year's average vs. lefties was the league's 3d lowest; he also had the 3d-lowest average in home games.... Batting average in Late-Inning Pressure Situations was 8th lowest in the league.... Career breakdown: .204 at Jack Murphy Stadium, .278 on other grass fields, .244 on artificial turf. Eleven of his 16 career home runs have been hit in San Diego.... He was batting .280 at the All-Star break, but posted a .175 average during the second half.... Batted over .300 at every stop in his minor league career, posting a career average of .310 in the bushes.... Stole two bases in three attempts last season. Padres ranked 10th in N.L. with 101 stolen bases; their outfielders had only 37 steals in 63 tries, league lows in both steals and success rates.

Will Clark
Bats Left

San Francisco Giants	AB	H	2B	3B	HR	RBI	BB	SO	BA	SA	OBA
Season	565	170	32	7	29	116	51	91	.301	.536	.359
vs. Left-Handers	197	47	11	2	9	40	14	35	.239	.452	.291
vs. Right-Handers	368	123	21	5	20	76	37	56	.334	.582	.394
vs. Ground-Ballers	257	85	14	4	13	53	27	38	.331	.568	.392
vs. Fly-Ballers	308	85	18	3	16	63	24	53	.276	.510	.330
Home Games	283	80	20	4	17	47	25	51	.283	.562	.344
Road Games	282	90	12	3	12	69	26	40	.319	.511	.373
Grass Fields	410	121	22	6	21	74	35	72	.295	.532	.353
Artificial Turf	155	49	10	1	8	42	16	19	.316	.548	.374
April	77	25	4	2	4	21	10	9	.325	.584	.402
May	103	24	2	0	5	15	9	19	.233	.398	.289
June	78	26	1	2	3	20	4	12	.333	.513	.361
July	90	29	6	0	7	18	8	11	.322	.622	.384
August	118	41	14	2	7	28	11	16	.347	.678	.408
Sept./Oct.	99	25	5	1	3	14	9	24	.253	.414	.312
Leading Off Inn.	103	27	3	1	2	2	5	13	.262	.369	.303
Runners On	253	84	13	5	18	105	29	31	.332	.636	.395
Bases Empty	312	86	19	2	11	11	22	60	.276	.455	.327
Runners/Scor. Pos.	151	51	7	3	10	84	24	15	.338	.623	.419
Runners On/2 Out	76	25	4	0	5	24	8	11	.329	.579	.393
Scor. Pos./2 Out	46	13	1	0	3	18	8	6	.283	.500	.389
Late-Inning Pressure	81	25	5	2	2	20	11	13	.309	.494	.387
Leading Off	27	10	2	0	0	0	0	2	.370	.444	.370
Runners On	33	14	3	2	2	20	7	3	.424	.818	.512
Runners/Scor. Pos.	21	7	0	1	2	17	6	1	.333	.714	.464

RUNS BATTED IN	From 1B	From 2B	From 3B	Scoring Position
Totals	20/172	36/116	31/55	67/171
Percentage	11.6%	31.0%	56.4%	39.2%

Loves to face: Ramon Martinez (.400, 12-for-30, 3 HR)
Pete Smith (.417, 10-for-24, 3 HR)
Scott Terry (.600, 6-for-10)

Hates to face: Norm Charlton (.067, 1-for-15, 2 BB)
Mike Harkey (0-for-9)
Terry Mulholland (.071, 2-for-28, 1 HR, 0 BB)

Miscellaneous statistics: Ground outs-to-air outs ratio: 0.86 last season, 0.85 for career.... Grounded into 5 double plays in 124 opportunities (one per 25).... Drove in 25 of 34 runners from third base with less than two outs (74%).... Direction of balls hit to the outfield: 37% to left field, 29% to center, 34% to right.... Base running: Advanced from first base to third on 5 of 16 outfield singles (31%); scored from second on 12 of 15 (80%).... Made 0.80 assists per nine innings at first base.

Comments: Led N.L. in slugging, but his percentage was the lowest to lead N.L. since Johnny Mize's .521 mark in 1942.... Mize was also the last Giants first baseman to lead N.L. in fielding, as Clark did last year; but that doesn't exactly represent a lack of talent at first base: 14 Giants started the All-Star Game for N.L. between 1948 and 1990.... Will's 64-game errorless streak was the longest by any first baseman in the N.L. last season.... Collected three or more hits in 18 games last season, tying Tony Fernandez for league lead.... Owns .320 career average with two outs and runners on base, second highest among active players behind Wade Boggs (.330).... Batting average vs. left-handers (.239) was a career low; he had topped .300 against them in four of his previous five seasons. Career breakdown: .306 vs. right-handers, .294 vs. lefties; .310 at Candlestick, .303 on other grass fields, .284 on artificial turf.... Hit 10 home runs to the opposite field last season, second in majors to Danny Tartabull's 13.... One of three major leaguers with 90+ RBIs in each of the last five seasons. The others: Joe Carter, who has a six-year streak, and Ruben Sierra.... Stole nine bases in 33 attempts (27%) over his first two years in the majors, but has stolen 29 bases in 37 attempts (78%) since then.... What happens to this guy with the bases loaded? Career numbers: .212 batting average (14-for-66), no walks, 18 strikeouts.

Vince Coleman
Bats Left and Right

New York Mets	AB	H	2B	3B	HR	RBI	BB	SO	BA	SA	OBA
Season	278	71	7	5	1	17	39	47	.255	.327	.347
vs. Left-Handers	105	26	3	0	1	4	9	11	.248	.305	.307
vs. Right-Handers	173	45	4	5	0	13	30	36	.260	.341	.369
vs. Ground-Ballers	127	33	4	2	0	11	17	22	.260	.323	.347
vs. Fly-Ballers	155	40	4	3	1	6	22	25	.258	.342	.350
Home Games	107	25	3	0	0	5	22	16	.234	.262	.364
Road Games	171	46	4	5	1	12	17	31	.269	.368	.335
Grass Fields	189	46	5	1	0	10	34	35	.243	.280	.359
Artificial Turf	89	25	2	4	1	7	5	12	.281	.427	.319
April	73	16	2	2	0	5	14	13	.219	.301	.345
May	93	28	1	1	0	6	16	18	.301	.333	.404
June	50	12	2	2	1	5	4	6	.240	.420	.296
July	22	7	0	0	0	0	1	7	.318	.318	.348
August	35	7	1	0	0	1	4	3	.200	.229	.282
Sept./Oct.	5	1	0	0	0	0	0	0	.200	.400	.200
Leading Off Inn.	110	27	4	1	0	0	18	19	.245	.300	.352
Runners On	85	23	2	2	0	16	12	14	.271	.341	.361
Bases Empty	193	48	5	3	1	1	27	33	.249	.321	.341
Runners/Scor. Pos.	57	16	2	1	0	15	8	12	.281	.351	.369
Runners On/2 Out	38	12	0	1	0	6	6	5	.316	.368	.409
Scor. Pos./2 Out	26	7	0	0	0	5	4	4	.269	.269	.367
Late-Inning Pressure	44	10	1	1	0	4	8	5	.227	.295	.346
Leading Off	12	2	1	0	0	0	2	2	.167	.250	.286
Runners On	15	3	0	1	0	4	4	1	.200	.333	.368
Runners/Scor. Pos.	10	2	0	0	0	3	1	1	.200	.200	.273

RUNS BATTED IN	From 1B	From 2B	From 3B	Scoring Position
Totals	1/51	6/44	9/24	15/68
Percentage	2.0%	13.6%	37.5%	22.1%

Loves to face: Tim Belcher (.556, 10-for-18)
Zane Smith (.442, 23-for-52)
Ed Whitson (.395, 15-for-38)

Hates to face: Dennis Martinez (.196, 11-for-56)
Randy Tomlin (.071, 1-for-14)
Bob Walk (.207, 12-for-58, 1 HR)

Miscellaneous statistics: Ground outs-to-air outs ratio: 1.48 last season, 1.48 for career.... Grounded into 3 double plays in 34 opportunities (one per 11).... Drove in 6 of 13 runners from third base with less than two outs (46%).... Direction of balls hit to the outfield: 52% to left field, 21% to center, 27% to right batting left-handed; 21% to left field, 37% to center, 42% to right batting right-handed.... Base running: Advanced from first base to third on 8 of 14 outfield singles (57%); scored from second on 9 of 10 (90%), 2d-highest rate in N.L.... Made 1.97 putouts per nine innings in center field, lowest rate in majors.

Comments: It appeared we'd witnessed the passing of the baton when Coleman out-stole Rickey Henderson by more than 100 bases in his first four seasons (407–301). And while Coleman ranks second in the majors in the three years since then, it's Rickey who's on top for that period, by a 200–179 margin.... Durability is part of the problem. After playing over 150 games in each of his first four seasons, Coleman has played in 145, 124, and 72 games over the past three.... Stole 10 bases in 12 attempts (83%) on artificial turf, 27 bases in 39 attempts (69%) on dirt infields. His career numbers aren't as lopsided: 84 percent on artificial turf, 76 percent on dirt. Blame a bad hammy for his career-low stolen base total (37); blame the dirt for his career-low percentage (73%).... Also likes artificial turf as a hitter. Career batting averages: .270 on turf, .251 on grass.... His average of one walk every 8.2 plate appearances was the best rate of his career, after posting a career worst rate in 1990 (one per 15.4).... He has driven in 21.8 percent of runners from scoring position during his career. That's the absolute lowest rate of any player with as many opportunities as Coleman over the last 17 years.... Career total of 586 stolen bases is tied with Maury Wills for 7th in N.L. history. Ahead of him are Lou Brock (938), Billy Hamilton (797), Max Carey (738), Honus Wagner (722), Joe Morgan (681), and Tim Raines (634).

Kal Daniels

Los Angeles Dodgers — Bats Left

	AB	H	2B	3B	HR	RBI	BB	SO	BA	SA	OBA
Season	461	115	15	1	17	73	63	116	.249	.397	.337
vs. Left-Handers	206	52	8	0	6	36	19	52	.252	.379	.309
vs. Right-Handers	255	63	7	1	11	37	44	64	.247	.412	.359
vs. Ground-Ballers	214	52	8	0	6	26	28	43	.243	.364	.329
vs. Fly-Ballers	247	63	7	1	11	47	35	73	.255	.425	.344
Home Games	242	60	7	0	12	48	31	63	.248	.426	.332
Road Games	219	55	8	1	5	25	32	53	.251	.365	.343
Grass Fields	357	89	12	1	15	61	49	94	.249	.415	.338
Artificial Turf	104	26	3	0	2	12	14	22	.250	.337	.333
April	66	14	3	0	2	18	5	13	.212	.348	.260
May	72	20	2	0	2	9	2	21	.278	.389	.303
June	88	25	1	0	6	14	14	20	.284	.500	.379
July	45	13	4	0	2	5	12	13	.289	.511	.439
August	91	19	1	0	1	10	17	23	.209	.253	.327
Sept./Oct.	99	24	4	1	4	17	13	26	.242	.424	.330
Leading Off Inn.	96	29	5	0	1	1	9	21	.302	.385	.368
Runners On	206	56	5	1	11	67	33	55	.272	.466	.363
Bases Empty	255	59	10	0	6	6	30	61	.231	.341	.315
Runners/Scor. Pos.	127	37	2	1	9	61	25	32	.291	.535	.392
Runners On/2 Out	85	27	2	1	8	33	18	21	.318	.647	.437
Scor. Pos./2 Out	56	19	0	1	7	29	13	13	.339	.750	.464
Late-Inning Pressure	66	16	2	0	0	8	6	22	.242	.273	.301
Leading Off	14	7	1	0	0	0	2	4	.500	.571	.563
Runners On	28	6	0	0	0	8	3	9	.214	.214	.281
Runners/Scor. Pos.	20	6	0	0	0	8	2	6	.300	.300	.348

RUNS BATTED IN	From 1B	From 2B	From 3B	Scoring Position
Totals	11/154	19/99	26/57	45/156
Percentage	7.1%	19.2%	45.6%	28.8%

Loves to face: Mike Bielecki (.375, 6-for-16, 1 HR)
Tim Burke (.714, 5-for-7)
Greg Maddux (.471, 8-for-17, 2 HR)

Hates to face: Kelly Downs (.091, 2-for-22)
Dennis Martinez (.091, 3-for-33, 1 HR, 3 BB)
Ed Whitson (.108, 4-for-37, 2 2B, 1 HR)

Miscellaneous statistics: Ground outs-to-air outs ratio: 1.50 last season, 1.53 for career.... Grounded into 9 double plays in 101 opportunities (one per 11).... Drove in 19 of 33 runners from third base with less than two outs (58%).... Direction of balls hit to the outfield: 40% to left field, 32% to center, 28% to right.... Base running: Advanced from first base to third on 11 of 24 outfield singles (46%); scored from second on 7 of 15 (47%), 3d-lowest rate in N.L.... Made 1.90 putouts per nine innings in left field.

Comments: Daniels and Juan Samuel are only the sixth and seventh players in franchise history to strike out at least 100 times in consecutive seasons. The only three-year streak: Frank Howard (1962–64)—and don't tell him *we* said so.... One of five N.L. players to qualify for the batting title without putting together a hitting streak of longer than six games.... Hit nine of his 17 home runs to the opposite field.... Hit 15 of his 17 home runs in Dodgers victories.... Posted the league's 4th-lowest batting average in day games (.202).... Batted .302 in the first inning, .243 thereafter.... Has hit four grand-slam homers over the past two seasons (three in 1990, one last year).... Career slugging percentage of .544 vs. right-handed pitchers is the 3d highest in the majors over the last 17 years, behind Fred McGriff and his good buddy Darryl Strawberry.... Career on-base percentage of .394 leading off innings is 5th highest during that same period.... Career batting average of .327 as a pinch hitter (16-for-49, 0 HR).... Career breakdown: .248 with one home run every 39 at-bats against left-handed pitchers; .308, one HR every 18 AB vs. right-handers.... Stole 68 bases over his first three seasons, compared to 19 in three seasons since then. Had knee surgery in both 1987 and 1989.... From the "Something Has to Give" Dept.: Neither Daniels, Strawberry, Brett Butler, nor Eric Davis has ever played a major league game at any position other than the outfield. Boys and girls, can you say "No-trade clause"?

Doug Dascenzo

Chicago Cubs — Bats Left and Right

	AB	H	2B	3B	HR	RBI	BB	SO	BA	SA	OBA
Season	239	61	11	0	1	18	24	26	.255	.314	.327
vs. Left-Handers	87	26	4	0	0	8	5	7	.299	.345	.340
vs. Right-Handers	152	35	7	0	1	10	19	19	.230	.296	.320
vs. Ground-Ballers	111	30	6	0	0	7	10	10	.270	.324	.336
vs. Fly-Ballers	128	31	5	0	1	11	14	16	.242	.305	.319
Home Games	125	29	5	0	0	8	13	12	.232	.272	.309
Road Games	114	32	6	0	1	10	11	14	.281	.360	.346
Grass Fields	175	48	7	0	1	13	18	20	.274	.331	.349
Artificial Turf	64	13	4	0	0	5	6	6	.203	.266	.268
April	40	9	2	0	0	5	6	3	.225	.275	.326
May	42	15	2	0	1	4	3	4	.357	.476	.413
June	50	15	4	0	0	2	6	6	.300	.380	.375
July	43	4	1	0	0	4	4	6	.093	.116	.170
August	29	5	2	0	0	0	2	4	.172	.241	.226
Sept./Oct.	35	13	0	0	0	3	3	3	.371	.371	.425
Leading Off Inn.	76	20	5	0	1	1	8	8	.263	.368	.341
Runners On	96	23	3	0	0	17	10	7	.240	.271	.315
Bases Empty	143	38	8	0	1	1	14	19	.266	.343	.335
Runners/Scor. Pos.	60	10	0	0	0	16	7	5	.167	.167	.261
Runners On/2 Out	39	7	0	0	0	3	7	3	.179	.179	.319
Scor. Pos./2 Out	30	5	0	0	0	3	5	3	.167	.167	.306
Late-Inning Pressure	52	16	5	0	0	8	4	6	.308	.404	.362
Leading Off	14	6	2	0	0	0	1	2	.429	.571	.500
Runners On	25	7	2	0	0	8	3	2	.280	.360	.345
Runners/Scor. Pos.	15	3	0	0	0	7	1	1	.200	.200	.235

RUNS BATTED IN	From 1B	From 2B	From 3B	Scoring Position
Totals	1/63	5/49	11/26	16/75
Percentage	1.6%	10.2%	42.3%	21.3%

Loves to face: Tom Browning (.556, 5-for-9)
Dennis Rasmussen (.412, 7-for-17)
Zane Smith (.375, 6-for-16)

Hates to face: Jose DeLeon (.053, 1-for-19, 1 2B)
Doug Drabek (.067, 1-for-15, 2 BB)
Jose Rijo (0-for-12)

Miscellaneous statistics: Ground outs-to-air outs ratio: 1.53 last season, 1.20 for career.... Grounded into 3 double plays in 45 opportunities (one per 15).... Drove in 10 of 15 runners from third base with less than two outs (67%).... Direction of balls hit to the outfield: 40% to left field, 25% to center, 35% to right batting left-handed; 36% to left field, 46% to center, 18% to right batting right-handed.... Base running: Advanced from first base to third on 6 of 15 outfield singles (40%); scored from second on 6 of 7 (86%).... Made 2.44 putouts per nine innings in center field.

Comments: Like crosstown rival Lance Johnson, an outfielder without power. He's played more than 250 games in the outfield, but hit only three home runs. Over the past 50 years, only one OF reached the 250-game mark without a single home run: Greg Gross.... Broke Curt Flood's N.L. record of 226 consecutive errorless games in the outfield. But because he's a frequently used defensive replacement, that record is somewhat tainted; Dascenzo started only 140 of those games, and completed just 104.... He has committed two errors since then, but his career rate of one error every 232 chances in the outfield is still the best among active players (minimum: 250 games). If Dascenzo can maintain that pace until the 1000-game mark, he'll supplant Terry Puhl (one error every 147 chances) as the all-time leader in fielding percentage among outfielders.... Played 519 innings in the outfield, the most of any player without an assist last season. (He also failed to get an assist in four innings as a pitcher.)... Had only 18 RBIs, but seven of them were go-ahead RBIs. (See the Mariners essay for more on this.)... Batted .308 in Late-Inning Pressure Situations last season, .241 at other times.... Made 17 appearances as a pinch runner last season, 4th most in the league, behind Geronimo Pena (31), Ced Landrum (26), and Gerald Young (19).... Career batting average of .077 as a pinch hitter (3-for-39, 0 HR).... He's another poor excuse for a switch-hitter, with a career average of .277 from the right side of the plate, but only .197 from the left.

Darren Daulton

Bats Left

Philadelphia Phillies	AB	H	2B	3B	HR	RBI	BB	SO	BA	SA	OBA
Season	285	56	12	0	12	42	41	66	.196	.365	.297
vs. Left-Handers	96	14	4	0	2	9	9	31	.146	.250	.224
vs. Right-Handers	189	42	8	0	10	33	32	35	.222	.423	.332
vs. Ground-Ballers	134	26	5	0	4	17	12	33	.194	.321	.260
vs. Fly-Ballers	155	31	7	0	8	25	29	34	.200	.400	.326
Home Games	152	32	9	0	8	23	24	38	.211	.428	.320
Road Games	133	24	3	0	4	19	17	28	.180	.293	.271
Grass Fields	77	18	2	0	3	10	11	20	.234	.377	.330
Artificial Turf	208	38	10	0	9	32	30	46	.183	.361	.285
April	64	13	5	0	0	8	7	17	.203	.281	.292
May	14	1	0	0	0	0	4	7	.071	.071	.278
June	30	5	0	0	2	5	4	5	.167	.367	.250
July	77	16	2	0	4	12	14	15	.208	.390	.330
August	86	17	3	0	5	15	11	18	.198	.407	.287
Sept./Oct.	14	4	2	0	1	2	1	4	.286	.643	.333
Leading Off Inn.	56	10	3	0	5	5	9	14	.179	.500	.292
Runners On	117	27	5	0	2	32	19	24	.231	.325	.331
Bases Empty	168	29	7	0	10	10	22	42	.173	.393	.272
Runners/Scor. Pos.	62	18	3	0	1	29	14	7	.290	.387	.402
Runners On/2 Out	38	9	1	0	0	11	10	8	.237	.263	.396
Scor. Pos./2 Out	25	6	1	0	0	11	8	4	.240	.280	.424
Late-Inning Pressure	48	10	3	0	1	9	7	16	.208	.333	.304
Leading Off	10	2	1	0	1	1	3	4	.200	.600	.385
Runners On	21	7	2	0	0	8	2	5	.333	.429	.375
Runners/Scor. Pos.	6	4	1	0	0	7	2	1	.667	.833	.667

RUNS BATTED IN	From 1B	From 2B	From 3B	Scoring Position
Totals	4/88	10/54	16/27	26/81
Percentage	4.5%	18.5%	59.3%	32.1%

Loves to face: John Burkett (.714, 5-for-7)
David Cone (.238, 5-for-21, 1 2B, 3 HR, 9 BB)
Darryl Kile (2-for-2, 2 HR, 1 BB)

Hates to face: Bill Landrum (0-for-10)
John Smoltz (0-for-19)
Ed Whitson (.063, 1-for-16)

Miscellaneous statistics: Ground outs-to-air outs ratio: 0.81 last season, 0.83 for career.... Grounded into 4 double plays in 70 opportunities (one per 18).... Drove in 11 of 13 runners from third base with less than two outs (85%).... Direction of balls hit to the outfield: 12% to left field, 32% to center, 56% to right.... Base running: Advanced from first base to third on 1 of 12 outfield singles (8%), 5th-lowest rate in N.L.; scored from second on 5 of 6 (83%).... Opposing base stealers: 84-for-102 (82%), highest rate in majors.

Comments: Since 1969, only two Phillies have posted lower batting averages in a season of at least 250 at-bats: Steve Jeltz (.187 in 1988) and Mike Schmidt (.196 in 1973).... Daulton caught about half the innings for Philadelphia last season, but the club's staff posted a far higher ERA of 4.05 with him behind the plate than with their other catchers there (3.68). Steve Lake (4.22) and Darrin Fletcher (2.94) split most of the remaining innings.... Opponents stole an average of one base every 8.5 innings against Daulton, one every 11.1 innings against other Phillies catchers (Lake, one per 11.9; Fletcher, one per 8.5).... Had the league's 4th-lowest batting average in home games, the 2d-lowest average on artificial turf, and the lowest average in night games (.187), and against left-handed pitchers.... Had a streak of 40 consecutive hitless at-bats against southpaws, the longest in the 12 years we've kept track.... Daulton and two teammates, John Kruk and Dale Murphy, were among six opponents who hit three HRs at Wrigley Field last season. The others: Orlando Merced, Luis Gonzalez, and Andy Van Slyke.... Has stolen 12 bases in 13 attempts over the past two seasons, raising his career average to 78 percent (21-for-27).... With Von Hayes headed west, Daulton is the only member of the current Phillies who played for them as far back as 1983.... Difference between his career batting averages against ground- and fly-ball pitchers (.255 and .188, respectively) is much greater than that between left- and right-handed opponents (.202 and .226).

Eric Davis

Bats Right

Cincinnati Reds	AB	H	2B	3B	HR	RBI	BB	SO	BA	SA	OBA
Season	285	67	10	0	11	33	48	92	.235	.386	.353
vs. Left-Handers	105	24	5	0	3	11	20	31	.229	.362	.359
vs. Right-Handers	180	43	5	0	8	22	28	61	.239	.400	.349
vs. Ground-Ballers	117	26	4	0	3	13	23	38	.222	.333	.355
vs. Fly-Ballers	172	43	6	0	8	20	25	55	.250	.424	.355
Home Games	140	34	6	0	5	18	30	47	.243	.393	.376
Road Games	145	33	4	0	6	15	18	45	.228	.379	.329
Grass Fields	87	22	2	0	4	7	14	27	.253	.414	.375
Artificial Turf	198	45	8	0	7	26	34	65	.227	.374	.343
April	37	10	4	0	0	1	8	9	.270	.378	.400
May	78	17	1	0	7	13	17	23	.218	.500	.378
June	46	13	1	0	1	5	7	17	.283	.370	.389
July	72	20	2	0	2	9	7	21	.278	.389	.346
August	10	3	1	0	0	1	3	3	.300	.400	.429
Sept./Oct.	42	4	1	0	1	4	6	19	.095	.190	.208
Leading Off Inn.	69	17	2	0	4	6	6	16	.246	.449	.316
Runners On	129	30	6	0	5	27	27	42	.233	.395	.365
Bases Empty	156	37	4	0	6	6	21	50	.237	.378	.343
Runners/Scor. Pos.	69	15	3	0	2	21	19	21	.217	.348	.378
Runners On/2 Out	59	17	2	0	3	13	15	17	.288	.475	.440
Scor. Pos./2 Out	31	9	1	0	1	9	12	9	.290	.419	.488
Late-Inning Pressure	42	7	1	0	3	6	9	17	.167	.405	.327
Leading Off	10	1	0	0	1	1	1	1	.100	.400	.182
Runners On	21	5	1	0	2	5	5	10	.238	.571	.407
Runners/Scor. Pos.	9	3	1	0	1	3	3	3	.333	.778	.500

RUNS BATTED IN	From 1B	From 2B	From 3B	Scoring Position
Totals	4/92	9/59	9/23	18/82
Percentage	4.3%	15.3%	39.1%	22.0%

Loves to face: Don Carman (.571, 8-for-14, 1 2B, 5 HR)
Jim Deshaies (.333, 14-for-42, 6 HR)
John Smoltz (.556, 10-for-18, 4 HR)

Hates to face: David Cone (.167, 3-for-18, 1 HR, 9 SO)
Sid Fernandez (.143, 3-for-21)
Greg Maddux (.184, 7-for-38)

Miscellaneous statistics: Ground outs-to-air outs ratio: 1.13 last season, 1.05 for career.... Grounded into 4 double plays in 61 opportunities (one per 15).... Drove in 5 of 13 runners from third base with less than two outs (38%).... Direction of balls hit to the outfield: 29% to left field, 42% to center, 28% to right.... Base running: Advanced from first base to third on 7 of 20 outfield singles (35%); scored from second on 6 of 6 (100%).... Made 2.59 putouts per nine innings in center field.

Comments: Last season's average of one home run per 25.9 at-bats was a career low, but he leaves Cincinnati with a career mark of one HR per 16.1 ABs, the best in franchise history (minimum: 50 HR). The last player to leave Cincinnati while leading in that category was Frank Robinson, who went on to hit 262 home runs for other clubs.... Thirteen players have hit at least 100 home runs for other teams after leaving the Reds (the most of any N.L. team): Joe Adcock (305), Robinson (262), Hank Sauer (242), Lee May (207), Ken Williams (196), Hal McRae (169), Deron Johnson (147), George McQuinn (135), Eddie Joost (123), Frank Thomas the Elder (111), Tommy Harper (102), George Foster (100), and Tony Gonzalez (100).... Career home-run rate against left-handed pitchers (one per 14.5 AB) is 4th highest among active players, behind Cecil Fielder, Rob Deer, and Jose Canseco.... Had the highest stolen-base percentage in the N.L. last season (.875, 14-for-16; minimum: 15 attempts). Needs 16 more attempts to qualify for all-time lead, and his current mark of 87.0 percent is higher than that of record holder Tim Raines (85.0%).... Since his first full season with the Reds in 1986, Davis has played in 743 of 971 games (77%), an average of 124 games per season.... Career average of .246 (one HR every 19.5 AB) at Dodger Stadium.... He will become only the second player in major league history to reach the 200-HR mark without playing more than 135 games in a season. The other: Dave Kingman.

Andre Dawson
Chicago Cubs — Bats Right

	AB	H	2B	3B	HR	RBI	BB	SO	BA	SA	OBA
Season	563	153	21	4	31	104	22	80	.272	.488	.302
vs. Left-Handers	223	66	8	1	16	47	7	27	.296	.556	.319
vs. Right-Handers	340	87	13	3	15	57	15	53	.256	.444	.291
vs. Ground-Ballers	233	62	6	3	12	41	13	32	.266	.472	.306
vs. Fly-Ballers	330	91	15	1	19	63	9	48	.276	.500	.299
Home Games	280	82	11	1	22	59	11	38	.293	.575	.328
Road Games	283	71	10	3	9	45	11	42	.251	.403	.277
Grass Fields	405	112	13	3	25	80	15	54	.277	.509	.306
Artificial Turf	158	41	8	1	6	24	7	26	.259	.437	.292
April	79	26	4	1	5	17	6	10	.329	.595	.376
May	88	22	4	2	4	12	3	11	.250	.477	.298
June	91	25	2	0	2	13	0	16	.275	.363	.275
July	84	24	4	0	7	26	4	13	.286	.583	.312
August	111	26	1	1	5	15	4	17	.234	.396	.263
Sept./Oct.	110	30	6	0	8	21	5	13	.273	.545	.304
Leading Off Inn.	142	31	6	1	5	5	4	23	.218	.380	.250
Runners On	265	77	7	2	19	92	13	31	.291	.547	.319
Bases Empty	298	76	14	2	12	12	9	49	.255	.436	.286
Runners/Scor. Pos.	158	47	4	2	12	76	12	18	.297	.576	.339
Runners On/2 Out	131	37	2	2	7	39	7	14	.282	.489	.319
Scor. Pos./2 Out	83	25	1	2	5	35	7	9	.301	.542	.356
Late-Inning Pressure	103	22	3	0	5	12	4	23	.214	.388	.255
Leading Off	28	3	2	0	0	0	1	9	.107	.179	.167
Runners On	44	10	0	0	3	10	3	8	.227	.432	.271
Runners/Scor. Pos.	23	5	0	0	2	8	2	3	.217	.478	.269

RUNS BATTED IN	From 1B	From 2B	From 3B	Scoring Position
Totals	16/194	28/123	29/69	57/192
Percentage	8.2%	22.8%	42.0%	29.7%

Loves to face: Stan Belinda (.500, 4-for-8, 4 HR)
John Smiley (.447, 17-for-38, 4 HR, 0 BB)
Randy Tomlin (.545, 6-for-11, 2 HR)
Hates to face: Norm Charlton (.077, 1-for-13)
Jay Howell (.077, 1-for-13, 1 2B)
John Smoltz (.050, 1-for-20)

Miscellaneous statistics: Ground outs-to-air outs ratio: 0.89 last season, 0.99 for career.... Grounded into 10 double plays in 114 opportunities (one per 11).... Drove in 17 of 31 runners from third base with less than two outs (55%).... Direction of balls hit to the outfield: 40% to left field, 31% to center, 29% to right.... Base running: Advanced from first base to third on 7 of 29 outfield singles (24%); scored from second on 5 of 9 (56%).... Made 1.83 putouts per nine innings in right field, 2d-lowest rate in N.L.

Comments: Has driven in 100 or more runs three times in five seasons for the Cubs (including each of the last two), compared to once in 10 full seasons with Montreal.... Only three players in Cubs history have had three or more consecutive 100-RBI seasons: Hack Wilson (1926–30), Ernie Banks (1957–60), and unofficially Cap Anson (1885–87 and 1889–91).... Rate of one home run every 17.9 at-bats since joining the Cubs ranks fourth in franchise history, behind Dave Kingman (12.6), Hank Sauer (16.0), and Hack Wilson (16.6), and just ahead of Ernie Banks (18.4).... Had a streak of 27 consecutive hitless at-bats in Late-Inning Pressure Situations, the longest of any N.L. player last season.... His on-base percentage leading off innings was the 2d lowest in the league.... Was the only visiting player to hit three home runs at Busch Stadium last season.... Has hit for a higher average in day games than he has in night games in 15 of his 16 years in the majors, with career marks of .304 (one HR every 18.5 AB) in day games, .265 (one HR every 26.0 AB) at night.... He has had at least 45 extra-base hits in 15 straight seasons. Only a few other players have done that: Hank Aaron (18 years), Stan Musial (16), Willie Mays, Mel Ott, and Honus Wagner (15 each).... One of three active players with at least 2000 games in the outfield: Dave Winfield (2411), Dwight Evans (2146), and Dawson (2099). Things that make you go "Hmmmm": Two of those three never played a home game on artificial turf. (So far.)

Steve Decker
San Francisco Giants — Bats Right

	AB	H	2B	3B	HR	RBI	BB	SO	BA	SA	OBA
Season	233	48	7	1	5	24	16	44	.206	.309	.262
vs. Left-Handers	86	19	2	1	3	13	2	11	.221	.372	.231
vs. Right-Handers	147	29	5	0	2	11	14	33	.197	.272	.279
vs. Ground-Ballers	101	18	2	0	1	8	9	17	.178	.228	.248
vs. Fly-Ballers	132	30	5	1	4	16	7	27	.227	.371	.273
Home Games	112	27	5	1	4	19	9	16	.241	.411	.304
Road Games	121	21	2	0	1	5	7	28	.174	.215	.221
Grass Fields	177	36	6	1	5	23	13	27	.203	.333	.262
Artificial Turf	56	12	1	0	0	1	3	17	.214	.232	.262
April	63	15	1	0	4	8	8	16	.238	.444	.319
May	55	8	2	0	1	5	1	9	.145	.236	.158
June	51	13	3	0	0	5	2	11	.255	.314	.304
July	25	6	1	0	0	2	3	3	.240	.280	.333
August	0	0	0	0	0	0	0	0	.000	.000	.000
Sept./Oct.	39	6	0	1	0	4	2	5	.154	.205	.195
Leading Off Inn.	52	9	2	0	1	1	3	7	.173	.269	.232
Runners On	102	24	5	1	2	21	8	21	.235	.363	.293
Bases Empty	131	24	2	0	3	3	8	23	.183	.267	.236
Runners/Scor. Pos.	58	8	0	1	1	16	5	14	.138	.224	.194
Runners On/2 Out	48	10	2	1	1	11	4	8	.208	.354	.296
Scor. Pos./2 Out	36	5	0	1	1	10	3	6	.139	.278	.205
Late-Inning Pressure	48	10	1	0	2	4	1	10	.208	.354	.224
Leading Off	10	1	0	0	0	0	0	2	.100	.100	.100
Runners On	19	4	1	0	0	2	0	4	.211	.263	.211
Runners/Scor. Pos.	8	0	0	0	0	1	0	3	.000	.000	.000

RUNS BATTED IN	From 1B	From 2B	From 3B	Scoring Position
Totals	6/75	6/50	7/24	13/74
Percentage	8.0%	12.0%	29.2%	17.6%

Loves to face: Shawn Boskie (.750, 3-for-4)
Mark Portugal (3-for-3)
Dennis Rasmussen (.571, 4-for-7)
Hates to face: Tim Belcher (0-for-6)
Bob Ojeda (0-for-5)
John Smiley (0-for-7)

Miscellaneous statistics: Ground outs-to-air outs ratio: 0.73 last season, 0.74 for career.... Grounded into 7 double plays in 50 opportunities (one per 7.1).... Drove in 5 of 11 runners from third base with less than two outs (45%).... Direction of balls hit to the outfield: 39% to left field, 33% to center, 28% to right.... Base running: Advanced from first base to third on 2 of 6 outfield singles (33%); scored from second on 2 of 3 (67%).... Opposing base stealers: 49-for-77 (64%).

Comments: Rookie catchers haven't been the Giants' thing. The only two to catch as many as 100 games were Bob Schmidt (1958) and Dave Rader (1972). Tom Haller holds the franchise record for home runs by a rookie catcher with 18 (1962); Schmidt, who hit 14, was the only other one in double figures.... Giants' catching was split between Decker (40 percent of all innings), Kirt Manwaring (33%), and Terry Kennedy (27%). Their staff ERA was considerably higher with Kennedy (4.50) than with either Decker (3.77) or Manwaring (3.99).... Opposing runners stole one base for every 11.8 innings vs. Decker, one per 13.5 innings vs. Manwaring, one per 8.9 vs. Kennedy.... N.L. home-run leaders on the morning of April 22 were Kevin Mitchell (6) and Decker (4). At that point, Decker had hit seven homers in his first 94 big league at-bats, but he hit only one more in 193 ABs thereafter.... His batting average during the month of May was the lowest in the league.... Collected only one hit in 23 at-bats against the Braves.... Since divisional play began in 1969, only three Giants have posted lower batting averages in a season of at least 250 plate appearances: Matt Williams (.188 in 1987, .202 in 1989), Bob Melvin (.199 in 1987), and Dave Kingman (.203 in 1973).... Had a career batting average of .305 in more than 1000 minor league at-bats, compared to .223 in the bigs (287 ABs).

Delino DeShields
Bats Left

Montreal Expos	AB	H	2B	3B	HR	RBI	BB	SO	BA	SA	OBA
Season	563	134	15	4	10	51	95	151	.238	.332	.347
vs. Left-Handers	189	41	2	0	3	14	33	58	.217	.275	.338
vs. Right-Handers	374	93	13	4	7	37	62	93	.249	.361	.352
vs. Ground-Ballers	248	52	9	2	4	21	51	73	.210	.310	.343
vs. Fly-Ballers	320	83	6	2	7	31	44	79	.259	.356	.349
Home Games	238	63	9	1	3	15	44	64	.265	.349	.379
Road Games	325	71	6	3	7	36	51	87	.218	.320	.324
Grass Fields	173	35	2	2	4	19	29	49	.202	.306	.314
Artificial Turf	390	99	13	2	6	32	66	102	.254	.344	.362
April	73	21	1	2	2	6	12	15	.288	.438	.388
May	94	16	1	0	3	5	21	25	.170	.277	.328
June	102	29	5	0	2	17	22	31	.284	.392	.408
July	90	23	3	0	0	3	13	20	.256	.289	.350
August	105	30	5	1	1	11	14	22	.286	.381	.375
Sept./Oct.	99	15	0	1	2	9	13	38	.152	.232	.241
Leading Off Inn.	219	50	6	2	6	6	33	56	.228	.356	.335
Runners On	180	47	5	1	3	44	30	43	.261	.350	.358
Bases Empty	383	87	10	3	7	7	65	108	.227	.324	.342
Runners/Scor. Pos.	108	27	4	1	1	40	21	26	.250	.333	.358
Runners On/2 Out	81	14	2	1	0	11	19	22	.173	.222	.330
Scor. Pos./2 Out	58	9	2	1	0	11	14	15	.155	.224	.319
Late-Inning Pressure	92	19	3	0	1	10	14	29	.207	.272	.311
Leading Off	25	4	0	0	1	1	1	5	.160	.280	.192
Runners On	41	8	0	0	0	9	7	14	.195	.195	.313
Runners/Scor. Pos.	25	6	0	0	0	9	7	6	.240	.240	.406

RUNS BATTED IN	From 1B	From 2B	From 3B	Scoring Position
Totals	3/111	11/82	27/54	38/136
Percentage	2.7%	13.4%	50.0%	27.9%

Loves to face: Tim Belcher (.800, 4-for-5)
Scott Garrelts (.444, 4-for-9, 1 HR)
Ramon Martinez (.462, 6-for-13, 1 HR)

Hates to face: Tom Browning (0-for-11)
Omar Olivares (.118, 2-for-17, 3 BB)
Trevor Wilson (0-for-13)

Miscellaneous statistics: Ground outs-to-air outs ratio: 1.80 last season, 1.79 for career.... Grounded into 6 double plays in 85 opportunities (one per 14).... Drove in 23 of 29 runners from third base with less than two outs (79%), 3d-highest rate in N.L.... Direction of balls hit to the outfield: 40% to left field, 36% to center, 23% to right.... Base running: Advanced from first base to third on 13 of 32 outfield singles (41%); scored from second on 12 of 18 (67%).... Made 2.81 assists per nine innings at second base, 3d-lowest rate in N.L.

Comments: Became the first player to steal at least 40 bases in both his rookie and sophomore seasons (42 and 56, respectively) since Vince Coleman (1985–86). Six others have done so over the past 15 years, but when Omar Moreno became the first of them in 1978, he broke a 61-year drought dating back to Benny Kauff (1914–15).... His 151 strikeouts were the most in the National League, breaking ex-Expos teammate Andres Galarraga's three-year hold on the title. Between Mike Schmidt and Juan Samuel, Philadelphia batters had a share of the strikeout lead for five straight years from 1983 through 1987.... Led major league second basemen with 27 errors.... Career average of one error every 34 chances at second base is worst among active players (minimum: 200 games). Last season's league average: one error per 55 chances at second base.... Batted .287 in the first inning, .224 thereafter.... Batting average on grass fields was 5th lowest in the league.... Batting average during May was the 5th lowest in the league.... Hitless in nine career at-bats as a pinch hitter.... Career batting average of .199 in Late-Inning Pressure Situations, .274 in other at-bats.... Career average of .289 at Olympic Stadium, .263 in other ballparks with artificial turf, and .220 on grass fields.... Ended the season at age 22, two stolen bases short of the 100 mark for his career. For a list of the youngest players to reach that plateau, see the Roberto Alomar comments.

Bill Doran
Bats Left and Right

Cincinnati Reds	AB	H	2B	3B	HR	RBI	BB	SO	BA	SA	OBA
Season	361	101	12	2	6	35	46	39	.280	.374	.359
vs. Left-Handers	80	21	4	1	2	8	13	8	.262	.412	.362
vs. Right-Handers	281	80	8	1	4	27	33	31	.285	.363	.358
vs. Ground-Ballers	186	46	7	0	3	20	24	17	.247	.333	.330
vs. Fly-Ballers	177	56	5	2	3	15	22	22	.316	.418	.390
Home Games	169	50	8	1	3	18	26	14	.296	.408	.390
Road Games	192	51	4	1	3	17	20	25	.266	.344	.330
Grass Fields	120	33	1	1	3	13	12	12	.275	.375	.336
Artificial Turf	241	68	11	1	3	22	34	27	.282	.373	.370
April	48	16	3	0	0	2	10	2	.333	.396	.441
May	14	1	0	0	0	1	0	2	.071	.071	.071
June	72	27	3	1	2	13	12	6	.375	.528	.459
July	95	24	3	0	3	8	9	12	.253	.379	.317
August	71	13	1	1	0	4	9	8	.183	.225	.272
Sept./Oct.	61	20	2	0	1	7	6	9	.328	.410	.388
Leading Off Inn.	96	28	2	0	4	4	19	15	.292	.438	.409
Runners On	141	43	6	1	1	30	15	7	.305	.383	.365
Bases Empty	220	58	6	1	5	5	31	32	.264	.368	.355
Runners/Scor. Pos.	82	22	4	1	0	28	9	5	.268	.341	.330
Runners On/2 Out	60	16	1	0	1	10	8	3	.267	.333	.353
Scor. Pos./2 Out	41	8	1	0	0	8	5	2	.195	.220	.283
Late-Inning Pressure	74	16	3	0	1	7	10	9	.216	.297	.302
Leading Off	15	5	1	0	0	0	3	2	.333	.400	.444
Runners On	28	3	1	0	0	6	5	3	.107	.143	.229
Runners/Scor. Pos.	16	2	0	0	0	6	4	2	.125	.125	.273

RUNS BATTED IN	From 1B	From 2B	From 3B	Scoring Position
Totals	2/91	12/61	15/36	27/97
Percentage	2.2%	19.7%	41.7%	27.8%

Loves to face: Tom Glavine (.435, 10-for-23)
Craig Lefferts (.467, 14-for-30)
Mike Maddux (.455, 5-for-11, 1 HR)

Hates to face: David Cone (.156, 5-for-32)
Dennis Martinez (.133, 4-for-30)
Bob Ojeda (.063, 1-for-16)

Miscellaneous statistics: Ground outs-to-air outs ratio: 0.95 last season, 1.07 for career.... Grounded into 4 double plays in 60 opportunities (one per 15).... Drove in 12 of 20 runners from third base with less than two outs (60%).... Direction of balls hit to the outfield: 29% to left field, 35% to center, 37% to right batting left-handed; 61% to left field, 26% to center, 13% to right batting right-handed.... Base running: Advanced from first base to third on 3 of 21 outfield singles (14%); scored from second on 7 of 10 (70%).... Made 2.66 assists per nine innings at second base, 2d-lowest rate in N.L.

Comments: Started 44 games in the leadoff spot for the Reds, the most of any player on the team last season. Cincinnati used 10 different players in that role, tying them with the Pirates and Rangers for the most in the majors last year. The Reds were 16–28 with Doran, 58–60 with others.... Doran had the best fielding percentage among the three players who shared second base for the Reds last season. See the Mariano Duncan comments for runs-allowed rates by each.... April batting average was 4th highest in the league.... Stole only five bases last season, snapping a streak of eight consecutive seasons in double figures.... Stolen-base rate over the past two seasons is 68 percent (28-for-41), compared to 85 percent over two previous seasons (39-for-46).... Over the last two seasons, has batted 35 points higher from the left side (.301) than from the right side (.266), but there's only a four-point difference between his career averages (.272 and .268, respectively).... Career average of .156 (27-for-173) with runners in scoring position in Late-Inning Pressure Situations is 2d lowest in *Player Analysis* history (minimum: 100 ABs). The worst RISP/LIPS average belongs to Barry Bonds (.154).... Played only 88 games at second base last season, snapping a streak of eight consecutive 100-plus years dating back to his rookie season (1983). Only one player in N.L. history had a longer streak starting as a rookie: Billy Herman (12 years, 1932–43).

Mariano Duncan   Bats Right

Cincinnati Reds	AB	H	2B	3B	HR	RBI	BB	SO	BA	SA	OBA
Season	333	86	7	4	12	40	12	57	.258	.411	.288
vs. Left-Handers	140	44	6	2	5	19	7	22	.314	.493	.347
vs. Right-Handers	193	42	1	2	7	21	5	35	.218	.352	.244
vs. Ground-Ballers	155	41	5	2	4	19	6	24	.265	.400	.295
vs. Fly-Ballers	179	45	2	2	8	21	6	33	.251	.419	.283
Home Games	167	52	4	2	10	25	5	25	.311	.539	.333
Road Games	166	34	3	2	2	15	7	32	.205	.283	.243
Grass Fields	91	21	1	2	2	12	2	16	.231	.352	.253
Artificial Turf	242	65	6	2	10	28	10	41	.269	.434	.301
April	33	5	1	0	1	2	0	9	.152	.273	.200
May	96	23	2	3	0	10	3	13	.240	.323	.267
June	38	7	1	0	1	2	4	6	.184	.289	.262
July	24	6	0	0	1	3	0	6	.250	.375	.240
August	41	18	2	1	3	11	1	9	.439	.756	.452
Sept./Oct.	101	27	1	0	6	12	4	14	.267	.455	.292
Leading Off Inn.	71	13	3	0	2	2	3	13	.183	.310	.227
Runners On	127	36	1	3	4	32	1	17	.283	.433	.293
Bases Empty	206	50	6	1	8	8	11	40	.243	.398	.284
Runners/Scor. Pos.	73	25	0	3	2	28	0	9	.342	.507	.346
Runners On/2 Out	66	15	0	2	2	14	0	13	.227	.379	.239
Scor. Pos./2 Out	42	12	0	2	1	12	0	8	.286	.452	.302
Late-Inning Pressure	46	9	0	1	0	3	1	13	.196	.239	.213
Leading Off	10	2	0	0	0	0	0	2	.200	.200	.200
Runners On	22	3	0	1	0	3	1	6	.136	.227	.174
Runners/Scor. Pos.	9	2	0	1	0	3	0	3	.222	.444	.222

RUNS BATTED IN	From 1B	From 2B	From 3B	Scoring Position
Totals	3/83	9/60	16/29	25/89
Percentage	3.6%	15.0%	55.2%	28.1%

Loves to face: Tom Browning (.370, 10-for-27, 2 HR, 0 BB)
Sid Fernandez (.440, 11-for-25)
John Franco (.533, 8-for-15, 4 SO)
Hates to face: John Burkett (.077, 1-for-13)
Dwight Gooden (.063, 1-for-16, 1 HR, 8 SO)
Les Lancaster (0-for-10)

Miscellaneous statistics: Ground outs-to-air outs ratio: 1.28 last season, 1.27 for career.... Grounded into 0 double plays in 48 opportunities, best in majors.... Drove in 13 of 16 runners from third base with less than two outs (81%), highest rate in N.L.... Direction of balls hit to the outfield: 33% to left field, 33% to center, 34% to right.... Base running: Advanced from first base to third on 6 of 14 outfield singles (43%); scored from second on 3 of 4 (75%).... Made 2.73 assists per nine innings at second base.

Comments: Made 356 plate appearances without grounding into a double play, the highest total in Reds history.... The Reds allowed an average of 3.81 runs per nine innings with Duncan at second base, far better than with Bill Doran (4.65) or Luis Quinones (4.44) there.... Started 41 of 55 games in which the Reds faced left-handed starting pitchers, 44 of 107 games in which they faced right-handers.... A reformed switch-hitter now batting exclusively right-handed, his career average of .310 vs. left-handed pitchers is 7th highest among active players. But his career mark is only .215 vs. right-handers. Duncan batted left-handed against opposing righties from 1985 to 1987 and compiled a .209 mark, compared to .224 mark against them right-handed.... Had the league's 3d-lowest batting average in road games.... He owns a career average of .274 on artificial turf, but only .235 on grass fields.... Has a career batting average of .250 at Veterans Stadium.... Has batted .285 over the past two seasons, 50 points higher than his previous career mark. Has also raised his home-run rate from one per 65 at-bats during the 1980s to one per 35 ABs during the '90s.... Duncan's breakthrough season in 1990 represented nearly a 1500-to-1 departure from his prior career performance, the third-most extreme over the past three seasons, topped only by Kevin Mitchell in 1989 and Terry Pendleton in 1991.

Shawon Dunston   Bats Right

Chicago Cubs	AB	H	2B	3B	HR	RBI	BB	SO	BA	SA	OBA
Season	492	128	22	7	12	50	23	64	.260	.407	.292
vs. Left-Handers	194	45	7	2	5	19	10	23	.232	.366	.269
vs. Right-Handers	298	83	15	5	7	31	13	41	.279	.433	.308
vs. Ground-Ballers	194	54	12	2	3	18	10	22	.278	.407	.313
vs. Fly-Ballers	298	74	10	5	9	32	13	42	.248	.406	.280
Home Games	237	70	10	3	7	26	10	30	.295	.451	.329
Road Games	255	58	12	4	5	24	13	34	.227	.365	.258
Grass Fields	339	95	14	5	10	39	15	45	.280	.440	.312
Artificial Turf	153	33	8	2	2	11	8	19	.216	.333	.248
April	68	16	2	0	2	7	5	6	.235	.353	.286
May	88	19	3	1	4	8	2	15	.216	.409	.245
June	98	25	4	2	2	12	3	13	.255	.398	.282
July	76	14	4	0	1	5	6	10	.184	.276	.241
August	82	35	6	3	1	11	4	13	.427	.610	.438
Sept./Oct.	80	19	3	1	2	7	3	7	.237	.375	.262
Leading Off Inn.	130	38	8	0	4	4	7	18	.292	.446	.338
Runners On	193	48	7	5	3	41	8	27	.249	.383	.268
Bases Empty	299	80	15	2	9	9	15	37	.268	.421	.309
Runners/Scor. Pos.	107	29	3	4	1	35	7	15	.271	.402	.280
Runners On/2 Out	78	19	2	2	1	12	3	9	.244	.359	.280
Scor. Pos./2 Out	49	11	1	2	0	10	3	8	.224	.327	.269
Late-Inning Pressure	98	37	6	2	2	11	6	10	.378	.541	.425
Leading Off	30	15	4	0	0	0	4	2	.500	.633	.571
Runners On	34	14	2	1	1	10	1	3	.412	.618	.444
Runners/Scor. Pos.	20	10	1	1	1	10	1	3	.500	.800	.524

RUNS BATTED IN	From 1B	From 2B	From 3B	Scoring Position
Totals	5/136	10/89	23/47	33/136
Percentage	3.7%	11.2%	48.9%	24.3%

Loves to face: Cris Carpenter (.500, 6-for-12)
Mike Maddux (.333, 6-for-18, 3 2B, 1 HR)
Scott Terry (.368, 7-for-19, 2 HR)
Hates to face: Jose DeLeon (.170, 8-for-47, 0 BB)
Tom Glavine (.111, 2-for-18)
Zane Smith (.147, 5-for-34)

Miscellaneous statistics: Ground outs-to-air outs ratio: 0.71 last season, 0.98 for career.... Grounded into 9 double plays in 87 opportunities (one per 10).... Drove in 19 of 29 runners from third base with less than two outs (66%).... Direction of balls hit to the outfield: 35% to left field, 38% to center, 26% to right.... Base running: Advanced from first base to third on 12 of 13 outfield singles (92%), highest rate in majors; scored from second on 6 of 6 (100%).... Made 2.89 assists per nine innings at shortstop.

Comments: The only National League player to qualify for the batting championship in each of the past two seasons with an on-base average below .300 in both. Gary Gaetti, whose streak is three years long, is the only A.L. player to do so.... Among qualifying batters, Dunston had the 3d-smallest differential between his 1990 and 1991 batting averages (.262, .260), behind Barry Larkin (.301, .302) and Harold Reynolds (.252, .254).... His streak of 155 consecutive plate appearances without a walk was the longest in the majors last season (May 1–June 19). His closest competition was Ozzie Guillen, who had a streak of 150.... Among active players who have batted at least 2000 times, only Guillen has walked more infrequently than Dunston, who has a career average of one for every 25.8 plate appearances. To put that in perspective, Ferguson Jenkins averaged one walk every 24.6 times up for the Cubs.... Chicago knows good shortstops. Dunston's career average of one error every 31 chances for the Cubs is better than Don Kessinger's (one per 28), but not as good as Larry Bowa's (42) or Ernie Banks's (33).... Batting average in Late-Inning Pressure Situations was 3d highest in the majors last season....Career batting average is only one point higher vs. right-handers (.258) than left-handers (.257), but his slugging percentage is considerably higher against lefties (.417 to .386).... Attention CBS, ESPN, and WGN: Would someone please put the JUGS gun on one of his throws from deep shortstop? Inquiring minds want to know.

Len Dykstra

Bats Left

Philadelphia Phillies	AB	H	2B	3B	HR	RBI	BB	SO	BA	SA	OBA
Season	246	73	13	5	3	12	37	20	.297	.427	.391
vs. Left-Handers	94	29	6	3	2	6	16	13	.309	.500	.414
vs. Right-Handers	152	44	7	2	1	6	21	7	.289	.382	.376
vs. Ground-Ballers	127	38	4	3	1	9	16	12	.299	.402	.382
vs. Fly-Ballers	123	35	9	2	2	3	21	8	.285	.439	.389
Home Games	118	38	7	2	3	6	20	10	.322	.492	.424
Road Games	128	35	6	3	0	6	17	10	.273	.367	.359
Grass Fields	81	22	4	1	0	4	12	9	.272	.346	.366
Artificial Turf	165	51	9	4	3	8	25	11	.309	.467	.403
April	82	26	7	2	2	6	17	2	.317	.524	.434
May	14	3	0	0	0	0	3	0	.214	.214	.353
June	0	0	0	0	0	0	0	0	.000	.000	.000
July	56	18	0	0	0	1	4	6	.321	.321	.377
August	94	26	6	3	1	5	13	12	.277	.436	.364
Sept./Oct.	0	0	0	0	0	0	0	0	.000	.000	.000
Leading Off Inn.	109	33	5	2	2	2	17	7	.303	.440	.397
Runners On	67	18	4	2	1	10	14	7	.269	.433	.402
Bases Empty	179	55	9	3	2	2	23	13	.307	.425	.386
Runners/Scor. Pos.	32	8	0	1	0	7	12	4	.250	.313	.455
Runners On/2 Out	26	4	0	0	0	4	8	2	.154	.154	.353
Scor. Pos./2 Out	19	4	0	0	0	4	8	2	.211	.211	.444
Late-Inning Pressure	42	14	4	0	1	3	8	4	.333	.500	.440
Leading Off	12	2	0	0	1	1	3	2	.167	.417	.333
Runners On	20	7	3	0	0	2	5	2	.350	.500	.480
Runners/Scor. Pos.	7	3	0	0	0	2	5	0	.429	.429	.667

RUNS BATTED IN	From 1B	From 2B	From 3B	Scoring Position
Totals	3/53	2/23	4/14	6/37
Percentage	5.7%	8.7%	28.6%	16.2%

Loves to face: Paul Assenmacher (.583, 7-for-12, 1 HR, 3 SO)
David Cone (.389, 7-for-18, 1 HR)
Bob Walk (.424, 14-for-33)

Hates to face: Norm Charlton (0-for-9)
Doug Drabek (.159, 7-for-44)
Bruce Hurst (.071, 1-for-14)

Miscellaneous statistics: Ground outs-to-air outs ratio: 0.79 last season, 0.98 for career.... Grounded into 1 double play in 40 opportunities (one per 40), 5th-best rate in N.L.... Drove in 1 of 4 runners from third base with less than two outs (25%).... Direction of balls hit to the outfield: 28% to left field, 38% to center, 35% to right.... Base running: Advanced from first base to third on 7 of 12 outfield singles (58%), 5th-highest rate in N.L.; scored from second on 6 of 10 (60%).... Made 2.75 putouts per nine innings in center field, 3d-highest rate in N.L.

Comments: Has scored 193 runs in 302 games for the Phillies. Only one Phillies player of the past 40 years had a higher rate: Dick Allen (697 runs in 1070 games).... Among players with at least 20 stolen bases last season, Dykstra had the highest success rate (.857, 24-for-28).... First player to steal 85 percent or better in consecutive 20-steal seasons since Eric Davis (1986–88).... Career stolen base percentage (.809) ranks seventh among active players (minimum: 100 SB). He falls between Rickey Henderson (.813) and Ozzie Smith (.806).... Had 15 hits in his first 35 at-bats after his return from the disabled list.... Phillies allowed 3.91 runs per nine innings with Dykstra in center field, compared to 4.35 with other center fielders. (Then again, the most frequent starter there during Dykstra's absences was DH-in-waiting Von Hayes.)... Batted from the first spot in the order in all but one of his starts.... Average of one walk every 7.7 plate appearances was the best of his career.... Batting average vs. left-handed pitchers was a career high. His career mark against lefties (.259) is 32 points lower than his mark against right-handers (.291).... Drove in only 16 percent of runners from scoring position, less than half his rate in 1990 (33%).... Had no sacrifices in 284 plate appearances—bunts or flies. For the record, since 1954, when sacrifice flies became an official statistic, more than 50 players who batted at least that often had no sacs. The most no-sac PAs: 633, by Graig Nettles in 1970 and Nick Esasky in 1989.

Kevin Elster

Bats Right

New York Mets	AB	H	2B	3B	HR	RBI	BB	SO	BA	SA	OBA
Season	348	84	16	2	6	36	40	53	.241	.351	.318
vs. Left-Handers	159	47	9	0	1	14	17	16	.296	.371	.362
vs. Right-Handers	189	37	7	2	5	22	23	37	.196	.333	.282
vs. Ground-Ballers	167	41	6	1	4	20	16	21	.246	.365	.310
vs. Fly-Ballers	181	43	10	1	2	16	24	32	.238	.337	.325
Home Games	181	48	11	0	3	14	19	24	.265	.376	.335
Road Games	167	36	5	2	3	22	21	29	.216	.323	.300
Grass Fields	232	62	14	1	3	21	24	29	.267	.375	.335
Artificial Turf	116	22	2	1	3	15	16	24	.190	.302	.286
April	39	12	1	1	2	8	5	4	.308	.538	.378
May	42	10	1	0	1	5	7	6	.238	.333	.340
June	67	13	6	0	0	9	5	11	.194	.284	.250
July	51	9	2	0	1	2	5	11	.176	.275	.263
August	64	19	2	0	2	7	6	10	.297	.422	.357
Sept./Oct.	85	21	4	1	0	5	12	11	.247	.318	.333
Leading Off Inn.	63	14	1	0	1	1	10	8	.222	.286	.329
Runners On	157	40	8	1	2	32	17	22	.255	.357	.324
Bases Empty	191	44	8	1	4	4	23	31	.230	.346	.313
Runners/Scor. Pos.	85	23	4	1	2	31	13	10	.271	.412	.359
Runners On/2 Out	82	16	3	1	2	17	9	11	.195	.329	.275
Scor. Pos./2 Out	50	11	2	1	2	17	8	6	.220	.420	.328
Late-Inning Pressure	48	7	0	0	0	3	11	9	.146	.146	.305
Leading Off	4	0	0	0	0	0	3	2	.000	.000	.429
Runners On	24	4	0	0	0	3	6	4	.167	.167	.333
Runners/Scor. Pos.	15	3	0	0	0	3	5	2	.200	.200	.400

RUNS BATTED IN	From 1B	From 2B	From 3B	Scoring Position
Totals	5/116	11/71	14/33	25/104
Percentage	4.3%	15.5%	42.4%	24.0%

Loves to face: Doug Drabek (.370, 10-for-27, 2 HR)
Neal Heaton (.400, 6-for-15)
Bruce Hurst (.421, 8-for-19)

Hates to face: Jim Deshaies (.063, 1-for-16, 2 BB)
Kevin Gross (.154, 4-for-26, 0 BB)
Charlie Leibrandt (.125, 2-for-16)

Miscellaneous statistics: Ground outs-to-air outs ratio: 0.82 last season, 0.79 for career.... Grounded into 4 double plays in 70 opportunities (one per 18).... Drove in 10 of 14 runners from third base with less than two outs (71%).... Direction of balls hit to the outfield: 35% to left field, 32% to center, 33% to right.... Base running: Advanced from first base to third on 3 of 14 outfield singles (21%); scored from second on 5 of 5 (100%).... Made 3.11 assists per nine innings at shortstop.

Comments: Career batting average of .224 is 3d lowest in franchise history among players with at least 1000 at-bats, ahead of Duffy Dyer (.219) and Dave Kingman (.219).... Started 52 of 64 games in which the Mets faced left-handed starting pitchers (81%), 46 of 97 games in which they faced right-handers (47%).... Among the 1991 Mets, only Garry Templeton (.337) and Rick Cerone (.315) had higher averages vs. left-handed pitchers.... Had the league's 4th-lowest batting average on artificial turf, and the 2d-lowest average against right-handed pitchers.... Batting average in Late-Inning Pressure Situations was 4th lowest in the league.... Rate of one walk per 9.9 plate appearances was the best of his career.... New York allowed more runs per nine innings with Elster at shortstop (4.16) than with either Howard Johnson (3.88) or Garry Templeton (3.87).... Was involved in an average of one double play every 22.2 innings at shortstop, the lowest average of any N.L. shortstop last season (minimum: 50 games); the major league average for shortstops is one double play every 15.5 innings. Who's more to blame: a pitching staff that struck out more than 1000 batters, or second baseman Gregg Jefferies?...Career fielding average of one error every 34.3 chances at shortstop is the best in Mets' history, slightly better than either Roy McMillan (one every 33.9 chances) or Bud Harrelson (33.5). Harrelson's error rate was much higher as a manager.

Mike Felder   Bats Left and Right

San Francisco Giants	AB	H	2B	3B	HR	RBI	BB	SO	BA	SA	OBA
Season	348	92	10	6	0	18	30	31	.264	.328	.325
vs. Left-Handers	107	29	5	1	0	4	7	8	.271	.336	.316
vs. Right-Handers	241	63	5	5	0	14	23	23	.261	.324	.328
vs. Ground-Ballers	159	41	2	3	0	7	14	10	.258	.308	.318
vs. Fly-Ballers	189	51	8	3	0	11	16	21	.270	.344	.330
Home Games	168	48	5	3	0	10	13	13	.286	.351	.337
Road Games	180	44	5	3	0	8	17	18	.244	.306	.313
Grass Fields	270	78	7	5	0	17	21	26	.289	.352	.342
Artificial Turf	78	14	3	1	0	1	9	5	.179	.244	.264
April	29	12	1	0	0	1	3	4	.414	.448	.469
May	101	31	4	5	0	8	4	13	.307	.446	.333
June	89	21	0	1	0	1	10	3	.236	.258	.320
July	57	11	3	0	0	6	5	4	.193	.246	.258
August	16	3	0	0	0	0	1	0	.188	.188	.235
Sept./Oct.	56	14	2	0	0	2	7	7	.250	.286	.333
Leading Off Inn.	153	37	4	1	0	0	10	19	.242	.281	.288
Runners On	102	31	3	2	0	18	14	6	.304	.373	.393
Bases Empty	246	61	7	4	0	0	16	25	.248	.309	.294
Runners/Scor. Pos.	61	17	3	1	0	17	9	3	.279	.361	.371
Runners On/2 Out	42	12	1	1	0	9	6	2	.286	.357	.375
Scor. Pos./2 Out	29	7	1	1	0	9	4	1	.241	.345	.333
Late-Inning Pressure	60	12	2	0	0	6	13	7	.200	.233	.351
Leading Off	23	4	1	0	0	0	3	5	.174	.217	.269
Runners On	21	6	0	0	0	6	8	1	.286	.286	.500
Runners/Scor. Pos.	14	3	0	0	0	6	6	1	.214	.214	.450

RUNS BATTED IN	From 1B	From 2B	From 3B	Scoring Position
Totals	2/65	7/47	9/25	16/72
Percentage	3.1%	14.9%	36.0%	22.2%

Loves to face: Dennis Martinez (.400, 4-for-10)
Jose Rijo (.538, 7-for-13)
John Smoltz (.625, 5-for-8)
Hates to face: Andy Benes (0-for-6, 2 BB)
Jose DeLeon (0-for-6, 1 BB)
Bruce Hurst (.100, 1-for-10)

Miscellaneous statistics: Ground outs-to-air outs ratio: 1.56 last season, 1.45 for career.... Grounded into 1 double play in 50 opportunities (one per 50), 3d-best rate in N.L.... Drove in 6 of 11 runners from third base with less than two outs (55%).... Direction of balls hit to the outfield: 21% to left field, 42% to center, 37% to right batting left-handed; 55% to left field, 23% to center, 23% to right batting right-handed.... Base running: Advanced from first base to third on 3 of 13 outfield singles (23%); scored from second on 13 of 16 (81%).... Made 2.27 putouts per nine innings in left field.

Comments: Most at-bats without a home run among N.L. players last season: Otis Nixon (401), Rafael Belliard (353), Alfredo Griffin (350), Felder (348).... Had the league's lowest batting average on artificial turf.... He was the only player in the majors to start at least 20 games at each of the three outfield positions.... Career stolen base percentage of .796 is 11th best among active players with at least 100 stolen bases.... Has pinch-run 42 times over the past three seasons, stealing at least 20 bases in each without batting as many as 400 times in any of them. Does anyone remember Larry Lintz?...Has grounded into only one double play over the last two seasons. As you might expect, it occurred while batting right-handed. Felder hasn't grounded into a double play batting left-handed in 72 opportunities since August 19, 1989. Last season, right-handed batters grounded into an average of one double play every 9.0 opportunities; left-handers averaged one every 11.1 opportunities.... Career batting average of .277 vs. ground-ball pitchers, .229 vs. fly-ball pitchers, running counter to the trend that most ground-ball hitters have a higher average against fly-ball pitchers than against ground-ballers.

Tony Fernandez   Bats Left and Right

San Diego Padres	AB	H	2B	3B	HR	RBI	BB	SO	BA	SA	OBA
Season	558	152	27	5	4	38	55	74	.272	.360	.337
vs. Left-Handers	184	48	7	1	2	13	17	22	.261	.342	.323
vs. Right-Handers	374	104	20	4	2	25	38	52	.278	.369	.344
vs. Ground-Ballers	289	76	15	3	1	17	29	29	.263	.346	.330
vs. Fly-Ballers	269	76	12	2	3	21	26	45	.283	.375	.345
Home Games	271	79	13	2	1	17	30	38	.292	.365	.362
Road Games	287	73	14	3	3	21	25	36	.254	.355	.313
Grass Fields	402	111	16	3	4	26	43	59	.276	.361	.345
Artificial Turf	156	41	11	2	0	12	12	15	.263	.359	.315
April	88	23	3	1	0	7	6	18	.261	.318	.309
May	108	30	6	3	1	5	15	14	.278	.417	.366
June	98	32	5	0	1	3	11	10	.327	.408	.394
July	72	12	4	0	0	4	7	10	.167	.222	.241
August	110	31	5	1	2	12	8	13	.282	.400	.328
Sept./Oct.	82	24	4	0	0	7	8	9	.293	.341	.356
Leading Off Inn.	114	35	6	1	1	1	12	11	.307	.404	.373
Runners On	212	65	10	3	1	35	19	24	.307	.396	.362
Bases Empty	346	87	17	2	3	3	36	50	.251	.338	.322
Runners/Scor. Pos.	117	36	4	2	1	33	11	17	.308	.402	.364
Runners On/2 Out	83	21	3	2	1	23	7	14	.253	.373	.311
Scor. Pos./2 Out	61	17	3	1	1	22	4	10	.279	.410	.323
Late-Inning Pressure	76	19	2	0	0	5	8	11	.250	.276	.321
Leading Off	18	6	0	0	0	0	4	2	.333	.333	.455
Runners On	29	8	1	0	0	5	2	7	.276	.310	.323
Runners/Scor. Pos.	18	5	1	0	0	5	1	3	.278	.333	.316

RUNS BATTED IN	From 1B	From 2B	From 3B	Scoring Position
Totals	5/134	13/89	16/43	29/132
Percentage	3.7%	14.6%	37.2%	22.0%

Loves to face: John Candelaria (.500, 11-for-22)
Jim Deshaies (4-for-4, 1 BB)
Curt Schilling (.750, 3-for-4, 2 2B, 1 3B)
Hates to face: Bud Black (.193, 11-for-57)
Tom Candiotti (.154, 6-for-39)
Bret Saberhagen (.205, 8-for-39)

Miscellaneous statistics: Ground outs-to-air outs ratio: 1.39 last season, 1.30 for career.... Grounded into 12 double plays in 101 opportunities (one per 8.4).... Drove in 8 of 17 runners from third base with less than two outs (47%)....Direction of balls hit to the outfield: 33% to left field, 32% to center, 36% to right batting left-handed; 38% to left field, 29% to center, 33% to right batting right-handed.... Base running: Advanced from first base to third on 19 of 31 outfield singles (61%), 4th-highest rate in N.L.; scored from second on 7 of 12 (58%).... Made 3.14 assists per nine innings at shortstop.

Comments: The all-time fielding percentage leaders at shortstop, as they have been traditionally expressed: Larry Bowa (.980), Fernandez (.979), Ozzie Smith (.978), Cal Ripken, Jr. (.978), Spike Owen (.978). Now by fielding chances per error, which clarifies the differences between the players: Bowa (one error per 49.2 chances), Fernandez (48.4), Smith (46.4), Ripken (45.1), and Owen (44.5).... Fernandez averaged one error every 35 chances last season, compared to one per 87 chances in 1990, and one every 124 chances the year before that. (Blame it on San Diego's grass field, his adjustment to batters in a new league, or even inconsistent official scoring, but you can't blame it on a change of first baseman.)... Collected three or more hits in 18 games last season, tying Will Clark for the league lead.... June batting average was 5th highest in the league, but his average during July was 2d lowest.... Batted .349 in Padres victories, .183 in losses.... Last season's batting average in Late-Inning Pressure Situations was the lowest of his career. He has a career mark of .319 in LIPS, .282 in other at-bats.... Fernandez turns 30 at the end of June. Shortstop is the youngest position in the majors (their average age last season was 28 years, 3 months), and has been in each of the past 11 years. But 15 shortstops in major league history played at least 1000 games there after turning 30, including Honus Wagner (who played 1671 games there after turning 30) and one active player: Ozzie (1053 and counting).

Steve Finley — Bats Left

Houston Astros	AB	H	2B	3B	HR	RBI	BB	SO	BA	SA	OBA
Season	596	170	28	10	8	54	42	65	.285	.406	.331
vs. Left-Handers	184	46	6	1	1	16	11	25	.250	.310	.290
vs. Right-Handers	412	124	22	9	7	38	31	40	.301	.449	.350
vs. Ground-Ballers	271	75	9	8	4	21	24	28	.277	.413	.334
vs. Fly-Ballers	328	95	19	2	4	34	18	38	.290	.396	.325
Home Games	300	82	15	8	0	20	17	36	.273	.377	.309
Road Games	296	88	13	2	8	34	25	29	.297	.436	.353
Grass Fields	183	60	10	1	5	19	12	21	.328	.475	.367
Artificial Turf	413	110	18	9	3	35	30	44	.266	.375	.316
April	64	13	2	1	0	3	6	8	.203	.266	.268
May	100	35	8	2	3	12	8	9	.350	.560	.391
June	100	27	3	0	2	8	11	9	.270	.360	.342
July	95	33	5	3	1	10	4	7	.347	.495	.380
August	113	30	5	3	1	14	7	17	.265	.389	.308
Sept./Oct.	124	32	5	1	1	7	6	15	.258	.339	.290
Leading Off Inn.	201	70	11	5	3	3	8	24	.348	.498	.376
Runners On	184	48	9	2	3	49	17	19	.261	.380	.314
Bases Empty	412	122	19	8	5	5	25	46	.296	.417	.339
Runners/Scor. Pos.	103	32	5	2	3	46	15	12	.311	.485	.379
Runners On/2 Out	82	24	5	2	3	27	9	10	.293	.512	.363
Scor. Pos./2 Out	58	19	4	2	3	26	9	9	.328	.621	.418
Late-Inning Pressure	81	20	2	0	0	8	6	10	.247	.272	.292
Leading Off	21	4	0	0	0	0	2	3	.190	.190	.261
Runners On	27	10	1	0	0	8	2	2	.370	.407	.387
Runners/Scor. Pos.	17	6	1	0	0	8	2	1	.353	.412	.381

RUNS BATTED IN	From 1B	From 2B	From 3B	Scoring Position
Totals	5/130	21/87	20/38	41/125
Percentage	3.8%	24.1%	52.6%	32.8%

Loves to face: David Cone (.667, 6-for-9)
Ramon Martinez (3-for-3, 1 2B, 1 HR)
Mike Morgan (.471, 8-for-17, 2 HR)

Hates to face: Mark Gardner (0-for-11)
Jim Gott (0-for-7, 2 BB)
Greg Swindell (0-for-10)

Miscellaneous statistics: Ground outs-to-air outs ratio: 1.33 last season, 1.44 for career.... Grounded into 8 double plays in 94 opportunities (one per 12).... Drove in 14 of 19 runners from third base with less than two outs (74%).... Direction of balls hit to the outfield: 28% to left field, 32% to center, 41% to right.... Base running: Advanced from first base to third on 19 of 41 outfield singles (46%); scored from second on 15 of 24 (63%).... Made 2.52 putouts per nine innings in center field.

Comments: Total of 212 ground-outs was 5th highest in the league, behind Brett Butler, Tony Gwynn, Mark Grace, and Ozzie Smith.... Was the only player to start all 100 games in which the Astros faced right-handed starting pitchers.... Ranked fourth in the N.L. with 29 infield hits.... Had three or more hits in 16 games, the 3d-highest total in the National League.... Batting average on grass fields was 2d highest in the league.... Batting average with runners in scoring position was 10th highest in the league, and his mark during the month of May was 7th highest.... Career batting average of .115 as a pinch-hitter (3-for-26, 0 HR).... His relatively low RBI total resulted primarily from a lack of opportunities. Among players who qualified for the N.L. batting title, only Robby Thompson batted with fewer runners in scoring position (118) than Finley (125). Finley's percentage of runners driven in from scoring position was 11th highest in the league, falling between Ryne Sandberg and Howard Johnson.... Of his 54 RBIs, 14 gave the Astros a lead. Compare that to Casey Candaele, who drove in 50 runs but had only five go-ahead RBIs.... Has increased his batting average and walk rate, and decreased his strikeout rate in each of the past two seasons. The only other player to do that: Carlos Quintana.... Have the Astros ever made a better deal than Glenn Davis for Finley, Pete Harnisch, and Curt Schilling? Certainly not one that was immediately and widely characterized by the media as a franchise sell-off.

Andres Galarraga — Bats Right

Montreal Expos	AB	H	2B	3B	HR	RBI	BB	SO	BA	SA	OBA
Season	375	82	13	2	9	33	23	86	.219	.336	.268
vs. Left-Handers	128	23	1	2	6	17	7	35	.180	.359	.222
vs. Right-Handers	247	59	12	0	3	16	16	51	.239	.324	.291
vs. Ground-Ballers	182	41	8	1	4	16	8	43	.225	.346	.258
vs. Fly-Ballers	197	42	5	1	5	17	15	43	.213	.325	.276
Home Games	152	34	6	1	3	14	7	37	.224	.336	.258
Road Games	223	48	7	1	6	19	16	49	.215	.336	.274
Grass Fields	111	24	5	0	3	10	6	29	.216	.342	.256
Artificial Turf	264	58	8	2	6	23	17	57	.220	.333	.272
April	64	15	3	0	1	2	7	15	.234	.328	.319
May	77	21	5	0	2	9	2	14	.273	.416	.291
June	0	0	0	0	0	0	0	0	.000	.000	.000
July	67	13	1	1	0	4	6	14	.194	.239	.260
August	82	14	1	0	1	5	2	21	.171	.220	.200
Sept./Oct.	85	19	3	1	5	13	6	22	.224	.459	.275
Leading Off Inn.	84	16	3	0	3	3	5	19	.190	.333	.236
Runners On	176	35	5	1	3	27	13	46	.199	.290	.258
Bases Empty	199	47	8	1	6	6	10	40	.236	.377	.276
Runners/Scor. Pos.	98	17	2	1	1	21	11	28	.173	.245	.264
Runners On/2 Out	76	12	2	0	2	10	6	22	.158	.263	.220
Scor. Pos./2 Out	46	5	0	0	1	7	5	15	.109	.174	.196
Late-Inning Pressure	68	11	2	0	0	4	4	20	.162	.191	.208
Leading Off	18	2	1	0	0	0	2	6	.111	.167	.200
Runners On	33	8	1	0	0	4	2	8	.242	.273	.286
Runners/Scor. Pos.	17	4	1	0	0	4	2	4	.235	.294	.316

RUNS BATTED IN	From 1B	From 2B	From 3B	Scoring Position
Totals	5/117	9/72	10/45	19/117
Percentage	4.3%	12.5%	22.2%	16.2%

Loves to face: Joe Boever (.471, 8-for-17, 2 HR, 5 SO)
Kelly Downs (.440, 11-for-25, 3 HR)
Zane Smith (.414, 12-for-29, 2 HR)

Hates to face: Tim Belcher (.222, 6-for-27, 0 BB, 13 SO)
Greg Maddux (.167, 8-for-48, 1 HR, 0 BB)
Roger McDowell (.111, 2-for-18)

Miscellaneous statistics: Ground outs-to-air outs ratio: 1.39 last season, 1.48 for career.... Grounded into 6 double plays in 66 opportunities (one per 11).... Drove in 8 of 27 runners from third base with less than two outs (30%), 2d-lowest rate in majors.... Direction of balls hit to the outfield: 35% to left field, 30% to center, 35% to right.... Base running: Advanced from first base to third on 7 of 21 outfield singles (33%); scored from second on 6 of 7 (86%).... Made 0.83 assists per nine innings at first base.

Comments: Why are all the kings of swing in the American League? Galarraga's career average of one strikeout every 4.3 plate appearances is the highest among last season's National League players (minimum: 1000 AB), but there were no fewer than 12 batters with higher career strikeout rates: Bo Jackson, Rob Deer, John Russell, Pete Incaviglia, Jay Buhner, Sammy Sosa, Cory Snyder, Joel Skinner, Ron Kittle, Cecil Fielder, Mickey Tettleton, and Jose Canseco.... Well, okay, Rick Reuschel was active briefly with the Giants, and *he* had a higher SO rate than Galarraga.... Had the league's 7th-lowest batting average in road games, the 2d-lowest average in night games (.214), the 4th lowest against left-handed pitchers, and the 5th lowest in Late-Inning Pressure Situations. His batting average with runners in scoring position was the lowest in the league.... Galarraga and Bernard Gilkey were the only two regular N.L. players to bat below .200 with runners on base last season. This season, they could hit back-to-back in the Cardinals' lineup.... Among players with at least 100 opportunities last season, only California's Luis Sojo drove in a lower percentage of runners from scoring position than Galarraga.... Career batting average of .148 as a pinch-hitter (4-for-27, 1 HR).... Career average of .259 (50-for-193, 5 HR) at Busch Stadium.... Yearly batting averages since 1987: .305, .302, .257, .256, .219.... Has only one sacrifice bunt in 3366 career plate appearances, and that was in 1986.

Ron Gant

Bats Right

Atlanta Braves	AB	H	2B	3B	HR	RBI	BB	SO	BA	SA	OBA
Season	561	141	35	3	32	105	71	104	.251	.496	.338
vs. Left-Handers	164	47	16	0	10	37	25	23	.287	.567	.383
vs. Right-Handers	397	94	19	3	22	68	46	81	.237	.466	.318
vs. Ground-Ballers	225	50	11	1	9	36	25	45	.222	.400	.302
vs. Fly-Ballers	336	91	24	2	23	69	46	59	.271	.560	.362
Home Games	258	72	16	1	18	52	36	52	.279	.558	.370
Road Games	303	69	19	2	14	53	35	52	.228	.442	.310
Grass Fields	411	107	23	3	26	80	46	77	.260	.521	.338
Artificial Turf	150	34	12	0	6	25	25	27	.227	.427	.337
April	68	11	6	0	1	7	8	9	.162	.294	.250
May	90	22	3	0	9	19	8	17	.244	.578	.310
June	91	23	7	1	3	11	6	16	.253	.451	.306
July	92	32	7	1	7	22	11	21	.348	.674	.423
August	107	25	4	0	8	23	16	19	.234	.495	.336
Sept./Oct.	113	28	8	1	4	23	22	22	.248	.442	.367
Leading Off Inn.	121	36	8	1	10	10	10	15	.298	.628	.356
Runners On	281	66	20	2	14	87	41	53	.235	.470	.331
Bases Empty	280	75	15	1	18	18	30	51	.268	.521	.345
Runners/Scor. Pos.	172	45	16	2	6	69	29	29	.262	.483	.362
Runners On/2 Out	126	22	5	1	3	22	21	27	.175	.302	.293
Scor. Pos./2 Out	82	16	3	1	1	17	15	15	.195	.293	.320
Late-Inning Pressure	74	16	2	1	4	16	12	11	.216	.432	.341
Leading Off	18	3	0	1	2	2	3	2	.167	.611	.318
Runners On	37	9	2	0	2	14	7	5	.243	.459	.378
Runners/Scor. Pos.	23	8	1	0	2	13	4	3	.348	.652	.444

RUNS BATTED IN	From 1B	From 2B	From 3B	Scoring Position
Totals	19/191	26/126	28/74	54/200
Percentage	9.9%	20.6%	37.8%	27.0%

Loves to face: Terry Mulholland (.400, 8-for-20, 2 HR)
Omar Olivares (.800, 4-for-5, 1 2B, 2 HR)
Mark Portugal (.471, 8-for-17, 1 HR)
Hates to face: Doug Drabek (.130, 3-for-23, 1 HR, 3 BB)
Kevin Gross (.118, 2-for-17)
Bryn Smith (.095, 2-for-21, 1 2B, 1 HR)

Miscellaneous statistics: Ground outs-to-air outs ratio: 0.64 last season, 3d lowest in N.L.; 0.70 for career.... Grounded into 6 double plays in 131 opportunities (one per 22).... Drove in 21 of 39 runners from third base with less than two outs (54%).... Direction of balls hit to the outfield: 63% to left field, 27% to center, 11% to right.... Base running: Advanced from first base to third on 7 of 17 outfield singles (41%); scored from second on 18 of 20 (90%), 2d-highest rate in N.L.... Made 2.35 putouts per nine innings in center field, 3d-lowest rate in N.L.

Comments: Déjà vu: Had 34 doubles, three triples, and 32 homers in 1990. His totals of doubles, triples, and homers against right-handed pitchers last season were exactly the same as in the previous year.... So how did his RBI total increase from 84 in 1990 to 105 in 1991, despite a 52-point drop in batting average and virtually the same total of extra-base hits? Once again, it's a matter of opportunities. Gant batted with 166 men in scoring position in 1990, but last season he had 200 opportunities, the 2d-highest total in the league; Benito Santiago had 214.... Led the majors with 22 game-winning RBIs.... Batted .279 in 226 at-bats from the cleanup spot, but only .215 in 163 at-bats from the 3d spot in the order.... His batting average with two outs and runners on base was the 6th lowest in the league.... Led visiting players with four home runs at Candlestick Park last season.... Despite a career average of .317 in 41 at-bats with the bases loaded, and a career average of one home run every 22 at-bats, he has never hit a grand slam.... This season, Gant could become the fourth player in franchise history to hit 30 home runs in three consecutive seasons. The others: Hank Aaron (1957–63, 1965–67, and 1969–73), Eddie Mathews (1963–61), and Dale Murphy (1982–85). (Nice group, eh?) Wally Berger and Bob Horner also had two straight 30-HR seasons.... Gant is also the third player with 30 HRs and 30 steals in consecutive seasons. Willie Mays (1956–57) and Bobby Bonds (1977–78) also did it; neither did it three years in a row.

Bernard Gilkey

Bats Right

St. Louis Cardinals	AB	H	2B	3B	HR	RBI	BB	SO	BA	SA	OBA
Season	268	58	7	2	5	20	39	33	.216	.313	.316
vs. Left-Handers	137	26	5	0	2	9	20	15	.190	.270	.297
vs. Right-Handers	131	32	2	2	3	11	19	18	.244	.359	.336
vs. Ground-Ballers	135	27	5	1	2	11	16	16	.200	.296	.288
vs. Fly-Ballers	133	31	2	1	3	9	23	17	.233	.331	.344
Home Games	149	32	4	1	2	10	21	14	.215	.295	.316
Road Games	119	26	3	1	3	10	18	19	.218	.336	.317
Grass Fields	47	13	1	0	3	7	7	8	.277	.489	.364
Artificial Turf	221	45	6	2	2	13	32	25	.204	.276	.306
April	77	20	1	1	1	5	12	11	.260	.338	.360
May	71	14	3	0	2	5	15	7	.197	.324	.337
June	37	9	0	1	0	2	2	3	.243	.297	.282
July	50	9	1	0	0	3	6	9	.180	.200	.276
August	27	3	1	0	0	2	2	3	.111	.148	.172
Sept./Oct.	6	3	1	0	2	3	2	0	.500	1.667	.556
Leading Off Inn.	79	21	4	0	4	4	8	5	.266	.468	.341
Runners On	112	22	2	1	0	15	22	16	.196	.232	.324
Bases Empty	156	36	5	1	5	5	17	17	.231	.372	.310
Runners/Scor. Pos.	62	13	2	1	0	15	19	13	.210	.274	.386
Runners On/2 Out	38	6	1	1	0	9	12	5	.158	.237	.360
Scor. Pos./2 Out	29	5	1	1	0	9	10	5	.172	.276	.385
Late-Inning Pressure	37	10	1	0	1	5	9	5	.270	.378	.404
Leading Off	7	3	1	0	1	1	3	1	.429	1.000	.600
Runners On	15	4	0	0	0	4	4	2	.267	.267	.400
Runners/Scor. Pos.	12	3	0	0	0	4	4	2	.250	.250	.412

RUNS BATTED IN	From 1B	From 2B	From 3B	Scoring Position
Totals	0/82	5/53	10/28	15/81
Percentage	0.0%	9.4%	35.7%	18.5%

Loves to face: Shawn Boskie (.500, 3-for-6, 1 HR)
Chris Hammond (.750, 3-for-4)
Terry Mulholland (.429, 6-for-14)
Hates to face: Norm Charlton (0-for-6)
Zane Smith (.100, 1-for-10, 9 ground outs)
Mitch Williams (0-for-5)

Miscellaneous statistics: Ground outs-to-air outs ratio: 1.09 last season, 1.18 for career.... Grounded into 14 double plays in 61 opportunities (one per 4.4), 4th-worst rate in N.L.... Drove in 4 of 8 runners from third base with less than two outs (50%).... Direction of balls hit to the outfield: 33% to left field, 32% to center, 35% to right.... Base running: Advanced from first base to third on 5 of 9 outfield singles (56%); scored from second on 7 of 10 (70%).... Made 2.44 putouts per nine innings in left field, 2d-highest rate in majors.

Comments: Had the National League's 7th-lowest batting average vs. left-handed pitchers.... Batting average with runners on base was the lowest in the league.... Eight of his 20 RBIs gave the Cardinals a lead.... Add together the number of games by all Cardinals rookies last season and you get 443, the 2d-highest total among N.L. clubs, behind Houston (793). The most games among St. Louis rookies last year: Ray Lankford (151), Geronimo Pena (104), and Gilkey (81).... St. Louis's rookies accumulated 1270 plate appearances, the team's highest total since 1976, when Jose Cruz, Jerry Mumphrey, and Garry Templeton were frosh.... One of three rookie batters (minimum: 100 PA) with more walks than strikeouts. The others: Chuck Knoblauch and Darren Lewis. Gilkey averaged one walk every 8.0 plate appearances, compared to a league average for rookies of one per 12.1 PAs. His strikeout rate (one per 9.4) was also considerably better than the league average for rookies (one per 5.1).... Grounded into 14 double plays, the most of any rookie in the majors.... Unusual for a rookie outfielder to play this much despite such a low batting average. Since 1969, only four rookies had as many ABs as Gilkey, as many games in the outfield (74), and a batting average that low: Paul Householder (.211 in 1982), Doug Frobel (.203 in 1984), Brady Anderson (.212 in 1988), and Jay Buhner (.215 in 1988).... Made only one error in 171 chances last season, after leading his league in outfield errors twice in six years in the minors.

Luis Gonzalez

Bats Left

Houston Astros	AB	H	2B	3B	HR	RBI	BB	SO	BA	SA	OBA
Season	473	120	28	9	13	69	40	101	.254	.433	.320
vs. Left-Handers	122	21	7	1	1	13	12	31	.172	.270	.257
vs. Right-Handers	351	99	21	8	12	56	28	70	.282	.490	.342
vs. Ground-Ballers	212	55	14	3	7	28	13	44	.259	.453	.307
vs. Fly-Ballers	264	65	14	6	6	41	28	59	.246	.413	.329
Home Games	227	62	15	6	4	32	20	41	.273	.445	.339
Road Games	246	58	13	3	9	37	20	60	.236	.423	.303
Grass Fields	148	37	6	1	6	25	12	35	.250	.426	.309
Artificial Turf	325	83	22	8	7	44	28	66	.255	.437	.325
April	61	9	3	1	0	3	4	19	.148	.230	.212
May	94	27	8	3	6	23	5	18	.287	.628	.317
June	85	19	7	1	1	5	11	15	.224	.365	.327
July	84	23	3	1	3	16	8	16	.274	.440	.347
August	76	19	3	2	2	11	5	21	.250	.421	.318
Sept./Oct.	73	23	4	1	1	11	7	12	.315	.438	.375
Leading Off Inn.	90	19	3	1	4	4	6	15	.211	.400	.268
Runners On	246	64	15	7	5	61	26	57	.260	.439	.331
Bases Empty	227	56	13	2	8	8	14	44	.247	.427	.308
Runners/Scor. Pos.	136	37	9	2	3	50	18	40	.272	.434	.356
Runners On/2 Out	114	27	7	1	4	24	17	30	.237	.421	.336
Scor. Pos./2 Out	70	14	4	0	2	17	13	23	.200	.343	.325
Late-Inning Pressure	67	18	4	1	0	9	5	9	.269	.358	.342
Leading Off	10	2	0	0	0	0	0	0	.200	.200	.273
Runners On	33	10	2	1	0	9	4	7	.303	.424	.385
Runners/Scor. Pos.	18	7	1	0	0	8	3	5	.389	.444	.478

RUNS BATTED IN	From 1B	From 2B	From 3B	Scoring Position
Totals	14/183	24/112	18/48	42/160
Percentage	7.7%	21.4%	37.5%	26.3%

Loves to face: Dwight Gooden (.667, 4-for-6)
Greg Maddux (.583, 7-for-12, 3 HR)
Mitch Williams (2-for-2, 1 HP)

Hates to face: Steve Avery (.071, 1-for-14, 1 2B)
Bryn Smith (.083, 1-for-12)
John Smoltz (.091, 1-for-11, 2 BB)

Miscellaneous statistics: Ground outs-to-air outs ratio: 0.86 last season, 0.85 for career.... Grounded into 9 double plays in 113 opportunities (one per 13).... Drove in 16 of 24 runners from third base with less than two outs (67%).... Direction of balls hit to the outfield: 25% to left field, 37% to center, 38% to right.... Base running: Advanced from first base to third on 6 of 19 outfield singles (32%); scored from second on 7 of 10 (70%).... Made 2.43 putouts per nine innings in left field, 3d-highest rate in majors.

Comments: Led major league rookies in extra-base hits (50), marking the fourth consecutive season in which a National League rookie led the majors. The others: Ron Gant (1988), Gregg Jefferies (1989), and David Justice (1990). Gonzalez also led all rookies in doubles.... Came within one triple of becoming only the sixth rookie in the past 30 years to reach double figures in all three extra-base-hit categories. The others form an impressive list: Dick Allen (1964), Joe Morgan (1965), Gary Matthews (1973), Juan Samuel (1984), and Ruben Sierra (1986).... Gonzalez and Bagwell gave Houston two rookies with at least 502 plate appearances for the first time in the team's history (surprising if you've read the Astros essay). In fact, only two Astros rookies qualified for the batting title over the past 16 years: Bill Doran (1983) and Craig Biggio (1989).... Had the league's 2d-lowest batting average vs. left-handed pitchers.... April batting average was 5th lowest in the league.... Despite playing regularly throughout the season, he never hit safely in more than six consecutive games.... Hit three home runs at Wrigley Field, tying five others for the most among visiting players.... Sixteen of his 69 RBIs gave the Astros a lead, and nine of them proved to be game winners.... Highlight of a miserable year against left-handed pitchers was a home run off of Cincinnati's Chris Hammond.

Mark Grace

Bats Left

Chicago Cubs	AB	H	2B	3B	HR	RBI	BB	SO	BA	SA	OBA
Season	619	169	28	5	8	58	70	53	.273	.373	.346
vs. Left-Handers	252	68	7	3	2	19	23	33	.270	.345	.333
vs. Right-Handers	367	101	21	2	6	39	47	20	.275	.392	.355
vs. Ground-Ballers	256	62	9	3	4	32	32	22	.242	.348	.321
vs. Fly-Ballers	363	107	19	2	4	26	38	31	.295	.391	.365
Home Games	322	93	18	1	5	32	38	28	.289	.398	.364
Road Games	297	76	10	4	3	26	32	25	.256	.347	.327
Grass Fields	453	128	22	2	7	41	49	42	.283	.386	.352
Artificial Turf	166	41	6	3	1	17	21	11	.247	.337	.332
April	71	19	4	1	1	12	10	3	.268	.394	.365
May	105	30	8	0	2	10	10	9	.286	.419	.348
June	105	29	3	1	1	11	11	12	.276	.352	.339
July	101	25	6	1	2	6	16	6	.248	.386	.347
August	119	40	5	1	0	11	10	13	.336	.395	.385
Sept./Oct.	118	26	2	1	2	8	13	10	.220	.305	.301
Leading Off Inn.	117	26	2	0	2	2	10	10	.222	.291	.289
Runners On	244	75	15	4	2	52	28	15	.307	.426	.371
Bases Empty	375	94	13	1	6	6	42	38	.251	.339	.329
Runners/Scor. Pos.	131	30	6	2	1	46	23	10	.229	.328	.333
Runners On/2 Out	83	18	5	1	0	16	16	5	.217	.301	.350
Scor. Pos./2 Out	59	10	3	1	0	9	13	5	.169	.254	.329
Late-Inning Pressure	98	25	3	0	1	9	16	7	.255	.316	.362
Leading Off	28	5	0	0	1	1	4	1	.179	.286	.281
Runners On	36	9	3	0	0	8	9	3	.250	.333	.404
Runners/Scor. Pos.	24	5	0	0	0	7	8	3	.208	.208	.412

RUNS BATTED IN	From 1B	From 2B	From 3B	Scoring Position
Totals	7/177	14/93	29/63	43/156
Percentage	4.0%	15.1%	46.0%	27.6%

Loves to face: Scott Garrelts (.579, 11-for-19, 1 HR)
Jose Rijo (.462, 12-for-26, 1 HR)
Bob Walk (.462, 12-for-26)

Hates to face: Juan Agosto (.077, 1-for-13)
John Franco (0-for-12)
Mitch Williams (0-for-9)

Miscellaneous statistics: Ground outs-to-air outs ratio: 1.16 last season, 1.24 for career.... Grounded into 6 double plays in 133 opportunities (one per 22).... Drove in 27 of 37 runners from third base with less than two outs (73%).... Direction of balls hit to the outfield: 34% to left field, 32% to center, 34% to right.... Base running: Advanced from first base to third on 12 of 40 outfield singles (30%), highest rate in majors; scored from second on 11 of 14 (79%).... Made 1.07 assists per nine innings at first base, highest rate in majors.

Comments: Was the only National League player to appear in each of his team's games last season, starting 155 and coming off the bench five times. Because the Cubs played only 160 games, Brett Butler led the league with 161.... His total of 703 plate appearances was the most by a Cubs player since Bill Buckner had 709 in 1982.... Discounting the 1981 season, Grace's total of 619 at-bats was the lowest to lead the National League since Maury Wills led with 613 in 1961, the last year of the 154-game schedule.... Ended the season with 52 consecutive errorless games at first base, the longest streak of his career.... He is one of four active players to drive in over 70 percent of runners from third base with less than two outs during his career. The top four: David Justice (71.4%), Grace (71.2%), Wade Boggs (70.3%), and Tony Gwynn (70.2%).... Career average of .313 at Wrigley Field, .282 on other grass fields, .280 on artificial turf.... Has a career average of .394 (13-for-33) with only one strikeout in 41 plate appearances with the bases loaded. Among active players who have batted at least 40 times with the bags full, only Jody Reed has a lower strikeout rate (one SO in 70 PA).... On the heels of consecutive .300 seasons, Grace's 1991 figures represented the most extreme breakdown by a Cubs starter since Ivan DeJesus batted .196 in 1981.... One year ago, we'd have rated his chances of reaching 2500 hits as one in 20; at this point, it's 45-to-1.... His career track parallels Kevin Seitzer's very closely.

Alfredo Griffin
Bats Left and Right

Los Angeles Dodgers	AB	H	2B	3B	HR	RBI	BB	SO	BA	SA	OBA
Season	350	85	6	2	0	27	22	49	.243	.271	.286
vs. Left-Handers	148	40	1	1	0	9	10	19	.270	.291	.319
vs. Right-Handers	202	45	5	1	0	18	12	30	.223	.257	.261
vs. Ground-Ballers	151	41	4	2	0	16	7	21	.272	.325	.304
vs. Fly-Ballers	199	44	2	0	0	11	15	28	.221	.231	.272
Home Games	158	32	2	0	0	11	11	20	.203	.215	.247
Road Games	192	53	4	2	0	16	11	29	.276	.318	.319
Grass Fields	249	59	5	1	0	18	15	33	.237	.265	.278
Artificial Turf	101	26	1	1	0	9	7	16	.257	.287	.306
April	61	13	0	0	0	3	1	9	.213	.213	.222
May	38	10	1	1	0	5	6	4	.263	.342	.356
June	88	21	1	0	0	6	3	13	.239	.250	.261
July	82	22	3	1	0	6	6	13	.268	.329	.322
August	14	3	0	0	0	1	1	2	.214	.214	.267
Sept./Oct.	67	16	1	0	0	6	5	8	.239	.254	.288
Leading Off Inn.	88	15	2	0	0	0	5	16	.170	.193	.215
Runners On	137	40	1	2	0	27	12	12	.292	.328	.342
Bases Empty	213	45	5	0	0	0	10	37	.211	.235	.247
Runners/Scor. Pos.	80	21	0	1	0	26	8	10	.262	.287	.319
Runners On/2 Out	60	13	0	1	0	9	7	8	.217	.250	.299
Scor. Pos./2 Out	40	9	0	1	0	9	6	7	.225	.275	.326
Late-Inning Pressure	53	17	2	0	0	4	2	10	.321	.358	.345
Leading Off	13	3	1	0	0	0	1	3	.231	.308	.286
Runners On	24	8	0	0	0	4	1	3	.333	.333	.360
Runners/Scor. Pos.	17	4	0	0	0	4	1	3	.235	.235	.278

RUNS BATTED IN	From 1B	From 2B	From 3B	Scoring Position
Totals	2/105	7/65	18/43	25/108
Percentage	1.9%	10.8%	41.9%	23.1%

Loves to face: Bud Black (.533, 16-for-30, 0 BB)
Tom Candiotti (.700, 7-for-10)
Dave Righetti (.474, 9-for-19)

Hates to face: Kelly Downs (.083, 2-for-24, 0 BB)
Charlie Leibrandt (.167, 8-for-48)
Dennis Martinez (.131, 8-for-61, 1 HR)

Miscellaneous statistics: Ground outs-to-air outs ratio: 1.33 last season, 1.15 for career.... Grounded into 5 double plays in 71 opportunities (one per 14).... Drove in 13 of 24 runners from third base with less than two outs (54%).... Direction of balls hit to the outfield: 32% to left field, 26% to center, 42% to right batting left-handed; 18% to left field, 44% to center, 39% to right batting right-handed.... Base running: Advanced from first base to third on 10 of 13 outfield singles (77%), 2d-highest rate in majors; scored from second on 3 of 5 (60%).... Made 3.36 assists per nine innings at shortstop, highest rate in N.L.

Comments: His longest hitting streak of the season was four games. Among major leaguers with at least 300 at-bats, only one other didn't hit in five consecutive games: Rafael Belliard.... Among N.L. players who didn't hit a home run, only Otis Nixon (401) and Belliard (353) had more at-bats than Griffin, who has only one home run in 1317 at-bats over the last three years.... Had the league's lowest batting average in home games.... Posted the 9th-lowest average in the National League against right-handed pitchers.... Every one of his plate appearances came from the eighth spot in the batting order.... Has hit for a higher average on artificial turf than on grass fields in each of the last six seasons.... There's a difference of only two points between his career batting averages from the right and left sides of the plate (.251 and .249, respectively).... His career average against ground-ball pitchers (.258) is 15 points higher than his mark vs. fly-ballers (.243).... He has hit for a higher average with runners on base than with the bases empty in each of the last seven seasons.... Drew 40 walks as a rookie, and that remains his career high. Once drew only four bases on balls in over 400 plate appearances for the Blue Jays (1984). But he improved his rate from one BB every 24 plate appearances in 12 seasons in the A.L. to one per 17 times up during four seasons with the Dodgers.... His streak of 13 consecutive opening-day starts seems to be in final jeopardy.

Marquis Grissom
Bats Right

Montreal Expos	AB	H	2B	3B	HR	RBI	BB	SO	BA	SA	OBA
Season	558	149	23	9	6	39	34	89	.267	.373	.310
vs. Left-Handers	211	60	11	1	3	18	18	35	.284	.389	.341
vs. Right-Handers	347	89	12	8	3	21	16	54	.256	.363	.291
vs. Ground-Ballers	262	75	12	4	3	24	12	28	.286	.397	.318
vs. Fly-Ballers	296	74	11	5	3	15	22	61	.250	.351	.304
Home Games	233	65	7	3	3	18	15	41	.279	.373	.323
Road Games	325	84	16	6	3	21	19	48	.258	.372	.301
Grass Fields	181	47	3	3	1	12	7	27	.260	.326	.291
Artificial Turf	377	102	20	6	5	27	27	62	.271	.395	.319
April	35	8	2	0	1	6	1	9	.229	.371	.250
May	118	36	5	1	4	9	10	19	.305	.466	.359
June	112	30	3	1	0	7	9	17	.268	.313	.322
July	91	18	2	1	0	7	7	18	.198	.242	.263
August	91	22	6	4	1	4	4	12	.242	.429	.274
Sept./Oct.	111	35	5	2	0	6	3	14	.315	.396	.333
Leading Off Inn.	147	33	7	3	1	1	13	25	.224	.333	.287
Runners On	214	63	6	2	3	36	14	33	.294	.383	.338
Bases Empty	344	86	17	7	3	3	20	56	.250	.366	.293
Runners/Scor. Pos.	125	36	4	1	3	34	13	23	.288	.408	.355
Runners On/2 Out	78	27	4	1	3	27	7	10	.346	.538	.400
Scor. Pos./2 Out	57	20	3	1	3	26	6	8	.351	.596	.413
Late-Inning Pressure	93	17	1	0	2	10	6	16	.183	.258	.232
Leading Off	32	5	0	0	0	0	2	5	.156	.156	.206
Runners On	39	10	1	0	1	9	1	7	.256	.359	.275
Runners/Scor. Pos.	26	6	1	0	1	9	1	7	.231	.385	.259

RUNS BATTED IN	From 1B	From 2B	From 3B	Scoring Position
Totals	7/138	14/106	12/37	26/143
Percentage	5.1%	13.2%	32.4%	18.2%

Loves to face: Bruce Hurst (.500, 9-for-18)
John Smiley (.381, 8-for-21, 1 HR)
Ed Whitson (.571, 4-for-7, 1 HR)

Hates to face: Tommy Greene (.083, 1-for-12, 1 2B)
Bob Ojeda (.133, 2-for-15)
Pete Schourek (0-for-6)

Miscellaneous statistics: Ground outs-to-air outs ratio: 1.27 last season, 1.21 for career.... Grounded into 8 double plays in 97 opportunities (one per 12).... Drove in 5 of 16 runners from third base with less than two outs (31%), 3d-lowest rate in N.L.... Direction of balls hit to the outfield: 35% to left field, 30% to center, 36% to right.... Base running: Advanced from first base to third on 6 of 16 outfield singles (38%); scored from second on 11 of 18 (61%).... Made 2.71 putouts per nine innings in center field.

Comments: The first player in over a decade other than Vince Coleman or Tim Raines to lead the N.L. in stolen bases. Over the past 40 years, only four players who led the N.L. in that category failed to do so more than once: Pee Wee Reese, Bobby Tolan, Frank Taveras, and Ron LeFlore (who had won another stolen-base title, albeit in the American League).... Three different Expos players have stolen 70 or more bases in a single season (Grissom, LeFlore, and Raines), the most of any team over the 23 years since the franchise began operation.... Stole 52 bases in 67 attempts on artificial turf (78%), 24 bases in 26 attempts on dirt infields (92%).... Stole 13 bases against the Braves last season, and is a perfect 14-for-14 against them in his career. He also has 13 steals in 13 career attempts against the Cubs, all of which occurred last season.... Was the only N.L. player to collect five hits in two separate games. Two A.L. players also did that: Luis Polonia and Dave Winfield.... Batting average in Late-Inning Pressure Situations was 9th lowest in the league. But in a different kind of pressure situation—that is, with two outs and runners on base—his average was the highest.... Ranked third in the N.L. with 34 infield hits.... Shared the league lead in assists among outfielders with Felix Jose (15). Grissom's 13 assists as a center fielder led the N.L.... Slugging percentage has increased but walk rate and on-base average have decreased in each of the past two seasons.

Pedro Guerrero
Bats Right

St. Louis Cardinals	AB	H	2B	3B	HR	RBI	BB	SO	BA	SA	OBA
Season	427	116	12	1	8	70	37	46	.272	.361	.326
vs. Left-Handers	160	41	5	1	0	15	17	14	.256	.300	.326
vs. Right-Handers	267	75	7	0	8	55	20	32	.281	.397	.327
vs. Ground-Ballers	194	59	7	0	3	27	16	20	.304	.387	.358
vs. Fly-Ballers	233	57	5	1	5	43	21	26	.245	.339	.300
Home Games	216	61	7	0	4	42	21	23	.282	.370	.340
Road Games	211	55	5	1	4	28	16	23	.261	.351	.311
Grass Fields	118	28	1	1	0	10	9	14	.237	.263	.289
Artificial Turf	309	88	11	0	8	60	28	32	.285	.398	.340
April	79	22	3	0	2	13	10	7	.278	.392	.360
May	90	27	4	1	1	18	5	6	.300	.400	.330
June	90	22	0	0	1	13	12	9	.244	.278	.324
July	30	11	1	0	3	9	1	3	.367	.700	.387
August	40	7	0	0	0	2	3	9	.175	.175	.227
Sept./Oct.	98	27	4	0	1	15	6	12	.276	.347	.321
Leading Off Inn.	113	28	3	1	2	2	12	17	.248	.345	.320
Runners On	206	62	6	0	4	66	15	21	.301	.388	.341
Bases Empty	221	54	6	1	4	4	22	25	.244	.335	.313
Runners/Scor. Pos.	142	50	6	0	3	64	14	11	.352	.458	.396
Runners On/2 Out	91	22	2	0	1	18	5	10	.242	.297	.289
Scor. Pos./2 Out	61	16	2	0	1	18	5	5	.262	.344	.328
Late-Inning Pressure	65	15	0	0	1	9	6	9	.231	.277	.292
Leading Off	22	6	0	0	1	1	4	3	.273	.409	.385
Runners On	30	6	0	0	0	8	0	4	.200	.200	.194
Runners/Scor. Pos.	19	5	0	0	0	8	0	3	.263	.263	.250

RUNS BATTED IN	From 1B	From 2B	From 3B	Scoring Position
Totals	2/129	27/99	33/76	60/175
Percentage	1.6%	27.3%	43.4%	34.3%

Loves to face: Tom Glavine (.455, 10-for-22, 2 HR)
    Dennis Rasmussen (.733, 11-for-15)
    Ed Whitson (.368, 21-for-57, 6 HR)
Hates to face: Scott Garrelts (.087, 2-for-23, 6 BB)
    Orel Hershiser (.063, 1-for-16)
    Bob Ojeda (.095, 2-for-21, 4 BB)

Miscellaneous statistics: Ground outs-to-air outs ratio: 1.14 last season, 0.88 for career.... Grounded into 12 double plays in 80 opportunities (one per 6.7).... Drove in 25 of 41 runners from third base with less than two outs (61%).... Direction of balls hit to the outfield: 30% to left field, 39% to center, 31% to right.... Base running: Advanced from first base to third on 3 of 26 outfield singles (12%); scored from second on 2 of 6 (33%).... Made 0.64 assists per nine innings at first base.

Comments: When he broke his leg on July 7, he ranked fourth in the N.L. with 53 RBIs, with 17 in his last 13 games. Finished the season in 29th place in the league rankings, but only 12 players drove in more runs during the periods that Guerrero was active.... Over the past four seasons, has driven in 37 percent of runners from scoring position, the highest rate in the majors.... Has a career average of one error every 82 chances at first base. Among active players, only Gerald Perry has a higher error rate at first (minimum: 500 games). Enter Andres Galarraga: The Big Cat has averaged one error every 131 chances, virtually the same as last season's major league average for that position (one error every 128 chances).... Batting average with runners in scoring position was 2d highest in the league.... He was the Cardinals' cleanup hitter in each of the 111 games he started last season. The Cardinals were 56–55 with Guerrero in the starting lineup, 28–23 without him.... Averaged one home run every 53 at-bats last season, by far the lowest rate of his career. You can't blame it all on Busch Stadium; he split his home runs equally between home and road games.... His career average is higher against right-handed pitchers (.303) than it is against left-handers (.299). He's one of only three active right-handed batters with a career average of .300 or better vs. RHP (minimum: 200 AB). The others: Kirby Puckett (.312) and Brian Harper (.302).

Tony Gwynn
Bats Left

San Diego Padres	AB	H	2B	3B	HR	RBI	BB	SO	BA	SA	OBA
Season	530	168	27	11	4	62	34	19	.317	.432	.355
vs. Left-Handers	211	62	7	4	2	19	13	7	.294	.393	.332
vs. Right-Handers	319	106	20	7	2	43	21	12	.332	.458	.370
vs. Ground-Ballers	274	93	15	5	1	32	16	7	.339	.442	.375
vs. Fly-Ballers	256	75	12	6	3	30	18	12	.293	.422	.335
Home Games	244	75	13	4	1	21	17	12	.307	.406	.348
Road Games	286	93	14	7	3	41	17	7	.325	.455	.361
Grass Fields	371	119	20	7	3	37	29	16	.321	.437	.367
Artificial Turf	159	49	7	4	1	25	5	3	.308	.421	.325
April	82	28	4	3	0	13	6	3	.341	.463	.378
May	116	42	9	4	2	21	8	3	.362	.560	.403
June	110	40	6	1	0	12	3	4	.364	.436	.374
July	95	24	3	1	0	5	6	4	.253	.305	.294
August	104	30	4	2	2	11	10	5	.288	.423	.351
Sept./Oct.	23	4	1	0	0	0	1	0	.174	.217	.208
Leading Off Inn.	99	22	4	0	1	1	4	4	.222	.293	.252
Runners On	231	85	13	5	2	60	20	8	.368	.494	.410
Bases Empty	299	83	14	6	2	2	14	11	.278	.385	.310
Runners/Scor. Pos.	129	49	8	4	1	55	16	6	.380	.527	.433
Runners On/2 Out	73	25	8	3	0	17	7	2	.342	.534	.400
Scor. Pos./2 Out	46	17	6	2	0	16	6	2	.370	.587	.442
Late-Inning Pressure	76	25	2	0	1	5	5	6	.329	.395	.366
Leading Off	21	6	1	0	0	0	0	1	.286	.333	.286
Runners On	32	12	0	0	1	5	5	4	.375	.469	.447
Runners/Scor. Pos.	17	5	0	0	0	3	4	2	.294	.294	.409

RUNS BATTED IN	From 1B	From 2B	From 3B	Scoring Position
Totals	6/155	29/110	23/39	52/149
Percentage	3.9%	26.4%	59.0%	34.9%

Loves to face: Jeff Brantley (.643, 9-for-14)
    Barry Jones (.800, 4-for-5, 2 2B, 1 HR)
    John Smoltz (.515, 17-for-33, 2 HR)
Hates to face: Dwight Gooden (.214, 12-for-56)
    Dennis Martinez (.194, 6-for-31, 0 BB)
    Omar Olivares (0-for-7)

Miscellaneous statistics: Ground outs-to-air outs ratio: 1.83 last season, 1.72 for career.... Grounded into 11 double plays in 114 opportunities (one per 10).... Drove in 20 of 26 runners from third base with less than two outs (77%), 5th-highest rate in N.L.... Direction of balls hit to the outfield: 39% to left field, 35% to center, 26% to right.... Base running: Advanced from first base to third on 9 of 28 outfield singles (32%); scored from second on 13 of 16 (81%).... Made 2.23 putouts per nine innings in right field, 2d-highest rate in N.L.

Comments: In each of the last eight years, Gwynn has accumulated more than 500 at-bats and batted no lower than .309. Only five other players in this century had streaks that long: Stan Musial (14 years, 1943–57); Paul Waner (12, 1926–37); Tris Speaker (9, 1909–17); Roberto Clemente (8, 1960–67); Lou Gehrig (8, 1930–37).... This season, could become first N.L. player since Musial (1941–58) to hit .300 or better in 10 straight seasons. Gwynn and Wade Boggs (who has a 10-year A.L. streak) have become the Musial and Ted Williams of their era, sort of. The Man and the Splinter had concurrent 17-year streaks that ended in 1958.... First player to strike out fewer than 20 times in 500 or more at-bats since Bill Buckner and Rich Dauer in 1980.... Average of one strikeout every 29.9 plate appearances was by far the best in the majors last season. Boggs was the only other major leaguer to average over 20 PAs per strikeout.... Hit safely in 30 consecutive San Diego victories, the longest streak of its kind in the majors last season.... Career batting average of .335 in Late-Inning Pressure Situations is the highest of any player in the 17-year history of *The Player Analysis*.... Career total of 1335 games is 2d highest among active players who've spent their entire careers with a single N.L. club. Tim Wallach's 1617 games with Montreal tops that list.... Over the past four seasons, has driven in 35.5 percent of runners from scoring position, the second-highest rate in the majors, behind Pedro Guerrero (36.7%).

Lenny Harris
Bats Left

Los Angeles Dodgers	AB	H	2B	3B	HR	RBI	BB	SO	BA	SA	OBA
Season	429	123	16	1	3	38	37	32	.287	.350	.349
vs. Left-Handers	87	21	0	0	1	9	6	8	.241	.276	.309
vs. Right-Handers	342	102	16	1	2	29	31	24	.298	.368	.359
vs. Ground-Ballers	181	47	4	0	3	22	12	19	.260	.331	.315
vs. Fly-Ballers	248	76	12	1	0	16	25	13	.306	.363	.373
Home Games	211	58	6	0	1	17	18	18	.275	.318	.341
Road Games	218	65	10	1	2	21	19	14	.298	.381	.357
Grass Fields	313	83	11	1	2	28	24	24	.265	.326	.323
Artificial Turf	116	40	5	0	1	10	13	8	.345	.414	.417
April	39	10	0	0	0	3	3	2	.256	.256	.310
May	63	23	2	0	0	3	9	7	.365	.397	.444
June	90	25	2	1	1	11	7	7	.278	.356	.337
July	61	13	3	0	0	6	5	6	.213	.262	.284
August	88	28	7	0	1	7	6	5	.318	.432	.361
Sept./Oct.	88	24	2	0	1	8	7	5	.273	.330	.340
Leading Off Inn.	94	29	1	0	0	0	6	8	.309	.319	.356
Runners On	195	56	6	1	3	38	17	16	.287	.374	.350
Bases Empty	234	67	10	0	0	0	20	16	.286	.329	.348
Runners/Scor. Pos.	100	28	0	1	2	32	11	11	.280	.360	.345
Runners On/2 Out	84	19	3	0	1	13	7	5	.226	.298	.293
Scor. Pos./2 Out	53	10	0	0	1	12	6	5	.189	.245	.271
Late-Inning Pressure	62	19	3	0	0	6	11	4	.306	.355	.421
Leading Off	20	7	1	0	0	0	5	0	.350	.400	.480
Runners On	26	9	2	0	0	6	5	3	.346	.423	.471
Runners/Scor. Pos.	10	4	0	0	0	4	5	2	.400	.400	.563

RUNS BATTED IN	From 1B	From 2B	From 3B	Scoring Position
Totals	6/157	15/81	14/33	29/114
Percentage	3.8%	18.5%	42.4%	25.4%

Loves to face: Jose DeLeon (.421, 8-for-19)
Mark Gardner (.467, 7-for-15, 1 HR)
Jose Rijo (.409, 9-for-22)

Hates to face: Jose DeJesus (0-for-11)
Doug Drabek (.059, 1-for-17)
Dennis Martinez (.200, 5-for-25, 0 BB)

Miscellaneous statistics: Ground outs-to-air outs ratio: 1.94 last season, 4th highest in N.L.; 1.82 for career.... Grounded into 16 double plays in 111 opportunities (one per 6.9).... Drove in 10 of 16 runners from third base with less than two outs (63%).... Direction of balls hit to the outfield: 41% to left field, 29% to center, 30% to right.... Base running: Advanced from first base to third on 14 of 28 outfield singles (50%); scored from second on 14 of 18 (78%).... Made 1.78 assists per nine innings at third base, 3d-lowest rate in N.L.

Comments: Only 10 other N.L. players batted .280 or higher in each of the past two seasons. Of the 11, only Harris, Willie McGee, and Bip Roberts failed to make the All-Star team in either season.... Was the only player to start each of the 94 games in which the Dodgers faced right-handed starting pitchers; started only 18 of 68 games against southpaws.... Last season's batting average against lefties was a career high, but his career figures still favor heavily right-handers: .230 vs. LHP, .292 vs. RHP.... August batting average was 6th highest in the league.... Had a streak of 15 consecutive plate appearances in which he batted with runners on base (August 16–20), the 2d longest in the majors.... Batted .366 in the first inning, .278 in subsequent at-bats.... Total of 12 sacrifice bunts ranked fifth in the league, second among nonpitchers behind Jay Bell (30).... Had the league's 2d-highest average on artificial turf, but that's not a career-long trend. He owns career averages of .263 at Dodger Stadium, .305 on other grass fields, and .288 on artificial turf.... Harris played slightly more than half the Dodgers' innings at third base, committing an average of one error every 17.6 chances. Mike Sharperson played half the remaining time, with only one error per 52 chances. Note well: Harris made one error per 13 chances on grass fields, but one per 76 on artificial turf. The major league averages for third basemen are one per 19 and one per 25, respectively.

Billy Hatcher
Bats Right

Cincinnati Reds	AB	H	2B	3B	HR	RBI	BB	SO	BA	SA	OBA
Season	442	116	25	3	4	41	26	55	.262	.360	.312
vs. Left-Handers	130	36	7	1	1	11	8	20	.277	.369	.324
vs. Right-Handers	312	80	18	2	3	30	18	35	.256	.356	.307
vs. Ground-Ballers	222	57	13	1	2	19	12	29	.257	.351	.298
vs. Fly-Ballers	224	59	12	2	2	22	14	26	.263	.362	.320
Home Games	216	58	16	1	2	17	16	24	.269	.380	.323
Road Games	226	58	9	2	2	24	10	31	.257	.341	.300
Grass Fields	129	34	5	1	1	12	4	19	.264	.341	.287
Artificial Turf	313	82	20	2	3	29	22	36	.262	.367	.322
April	46	6	0	0	0	4	1	7	.130	.130	.184
May	64	20	4	1	1	7	3	6	.313	.453	.348
June	95	28	9	1	2	7	6	14	.295	.474	.346
July	79	24	4	0	1	11	3	14	.304	.392	.325
August	72	14	2	0	0	4	8	9	.194	.222	.275
Sept./Oct.	86	24	6	1	0	8	5	5	.279	.372	.333
Leading Off Inn.	123	27	7	0	0	0	9	23	.220	.276	.289
Runners On	161	48	10	2	1	38	13	15	.298	.404	.352
Bases Empty	281	68	15	1	3	3	13	40	.242	.335	.288
Runners/Scor. Pos.	94	32	6	2	0	35	9	12	.340	.447	.387
Runners On/2 Out	81	26	6	1	1	26	7	9	.321	.457	.382
Scor. Pos./2 Out	57	20	5	1	0	23	6	9	.351	.474	.413
Late-Inning Pressure	73	23	2	1	0	9	2	6	.315	.370	.346
Leading Off	24	5	0	0	0	0	2	5	.208	.208	.296
Runners On	26	12	2	0	0	9	0	1	.462	.538	.444
Runners/Scor. Pos.	17	8	2	0	0	9	0	1	.471	.588	.444

RUNS BATTED IN	From 1B	From 2B	From 3B	Scoring Position
Totals	4/102	19/79	14/32	33/111
Percentage	3.9%	24.1%	43.8%	29.7%

Loves to face: Bill Landrum (.600, 9-for-15)
Ramon Martinez (.529, 9-for-17)
Alejandro Pena (.444, 8-for-18, 1 HR)

Hates to face: Jim Deshaies (.067, 1-for-15)
Dennis Martinez (.063, 1-for-16)
Ed Whitson (.107, 3-for-28, 1 HR, 0 BB)

Miscellaneous statistics: Ground outs-to-air outs ratio: 1.31 last season, 1.22 for career.... Grounded into 9 double plays in 71 opportunities (one per 7.9).... Drove in 6 of 10 runners from third base with less than two outs (60%).... Direction of balls hit to the outfield: 28% to left field, 37% to center, 36% to right.... Base running: Advanced from first base to third on 10 of 24 outfield singles (42%); scored from second on 9 of 11 (82%).... Made 2.14 putouts per nine innings in left field.

Comments: His batting average with two outs and runners on base was the 9th highest in the league.... April batting average was 4th lowest in the league.... Although he did not hit an opposite field home run last season, 12 of his 25 doubles were hit to right field.... Lou Piniella wrote 11 different left fielders onto his lineup cards last season; in order of innings played, they were Hatcher, Glenn Braggs, Carmelo Martinez, Chris Jones, Todd Benzinger, Bill Doran, Eric Davis, Mariano Duncan, Herm Winningham, Stan Jefferson, and Hal Morris. No other N.L. club used more than seven.... Batted .210 in 124 at-bats from the leadoff slot in the batting order, but he hit .307 in 166 at-bats from the two hole. Even so, the Reds were 16–13 with Hatcher batting leadoff, the best record they posted with any of the 10 players who started in that position.... Carries the mark of a career leadoff hitter—he's scored more runs than he's driven in in each of his eight seasons. Among the others who wore that tag throughout their careers: Lou Brock, Bert Campaneris, and Willie Keeler, who all had 19-year runs.... Stole only 11 bases in 20 attempts last season (55%), after averaging more than 35 steals per season with a success rate of over 75 percent for the previous five years.... Hitless in nine at-bats with the bases loaded since joining the Reds in 1990. He drove in only one of 27 base runners in those at-bats.... Has a career average of one home run per 46 at-bats in day games, but only one per 119 ABs at night.

Charlie Hayes
Bats Right

Philadelphia Phillies	AB	H	2B	3B	HR	RBI	BB	SO	BA	SA	OBA
Season	460	106	23	1	12	53	16	75	.230	.363	.257
vs. Left-Handers	190	49	14	0	4	22	6	30	.258	.395	.283
vs. Right-Handers	270	57	9	1	8	31	10	45	.211	.341	.239
vs. Ground-Ballers	231	50	11	1	5	26	8	34	.216	.338	.246
vs. Fly-Ballers	232	56	12	0	7	27	8	41	.241	.384	.266
Home Games	248	65	16	1	6	34	10	36	.262	.407	.292
Road Games	212	41	7	0	6	19	6	39	.193	.311	.216
Grass Fields	118	21	3	0	4	11	6	20	.178	.305	.218
Artificial Turf	342	85	20	1	8	42	10	55	.249	.383	.271
April	77	19	4	0	3	14	2	14	.247	.416	.266
May	97	16	3	1	2	7	4	16	.165	.278	.198
June	62	13	2	0	1	5	3	15	.210	.290	.242
July	35	5	2	0	0	1	2	4	.143	.200	.189
August	113	31	8	0	4	14	0	17	.274	.451	.274
Sept./Oct.	76	22	4	0	2	12	5	9	.289	.421	.341
Leading Off Inn.	86	23	5	0	4	4	3	14	.267	.465	.292
Runners On	218	49	15	0	5	46	7	37	.225	.362	.251
Bases Empty	242	57	8	1	7	7	9	38	.236	.364	.263
Runners/Scor. Pos.	109	26	6	0	4	38	4	21	.239	.404	.263
Runners On/2 Out	94	23	8	0	3	26	4	15	.245	.426	.276
Scor. Pos./2 Out	50	15	3	0	2	20	1	12	.300	.480	.314
Late-Inning Pressure	99	32	5	1	4	11	4	15	.323	.515	.350
Leading Off	29	10	1	0	3	3	1	3	.345	.690	.367
Runners On	38	13	4	0	0	7	3	7	.342	.447	.390
Runners/Scor. Pos.	20	5	0	0	0	5	1	6	.250	.300	.286

RUNS BATTED IN	From 1B	From 2B	From 3B	Scoring Position
Totals	10/158	16/86	15/42	31/128
Percentage	6.3%	18.6%	35.7%	24.2%

Loves to face: Tom Glavine (.381, 8-for-21, 1 HR)
Kevin Gross (.462, 6-for-13, 1 HR)
Randy Tomlin (.600, 6-for-10)

Hates to face: Tim Burke (0-for-11)
David Cone (.063, 1-for-16, 1 2B)
Greg Maddux (.087, 2-for-23)

Miscellaneous statistics: Ground outs-to-air outs ratio: 1.11 last season, 1.01 for career.... Grounded into 13 double plays in 95 opportunities (one per 7.3).... Drove in 8 of 17 runners from third base with less than two outs (47%).... Direction of balls hit to the outfield: 31% to left field, 36% to center, 32% to right.... Base running: Advanced from first base to third on 4 of 18 outfield singles (22%); scored from second on 4 of 8 (50%).... Made 2.04 assists per nine innings at third base.

Comments: Only three players have appeared in 250 games for both the Yankees and Phillies: Nick Etten, Oscar Gamble, and Bill Robinson.... His average of one walk every 30 times up was the worst of any N.L. player with at least 400 plate appearances last season. His career average of one walk every 26 plate appearances is about the same as Shawon Dunston's.... Started 51 of 62 games in which the Phillies faced left-handed starting pitchers, 59 of 100 games against right-handers.... Posted the 5th-lowest average in the National League against right-handed pitchers.... Batting average during May was the 4th lowest in the league.... Had the league's lowest batting average in road games, and the 2d-lowest average on grass fields; career marks are balanced on grass (.246) and turf (.247).... Raised his extra-base-hit total from 30 to 36, but hit 35 fewer singles than in 1990.... His 1991 breakdown against ground-ball and fly-ball pitchers was much different than his previous career averages. Even with last season included, he still favors ground-ball pitchers (.269) to fly-ballers (.223).... His fielding percentage at third base has shown improvement: one error every 11 chances in 1989, one every 23 in 1990, and one per 24 last season.... Career batting average of .381 as a pinch-hitter (8-for-21, 0 HR).... Year by year batting averages in Late-Inning Pressure Situations since 1989: .238, .275, .323.... Similar career tracks: Best case—Jim Davenport; worst case—Jeff Hamilton; best guess—Ken McMullen. All were third basemen with similar career statistics at a comparable age.

Von Hayes
Bats Left

Philadelphia Phillies	AB	H	2B	3B	HR	RBI	BB	SO	BA	SA	OBA
Season	284	64	15	1	0	21	31	42	.225	.285	.303
vs. Left-Handers	90	24	4	1	0	8	11	15	.267	.333	.355
vs. Right-Handers	194	40	11	0	0	13	20	27	.206	.263	.278
vs. Ground-Ballers	135	29	5	1	0	8	15	24	.215	.267	.299
vs. Fly-Ballers	153	36	10	0	0	13	16	19	.235	.301	.306
Home Games	99	20	4	0	0	5	17	14	.202	.242	.319
Road Games	185	44	11	1	0	16	14	28	.238	.308	.294
Grass Fields	105	26	5	0	0	10	6	16	.248	.295	.289
Artificial Turf	179	38	10	1	0	11	25	26	.212	.279	.311
April	68	13	4	0	0	8	12	11	.191	.250	.306
May	102	23	6	0	0	2	7	13	.225	.284	.282
June	47	13	2	1	0	8	6	7	.277	.362	.364
July	0	0	0	0	0	0	0	0	.000	.000	.000
August	0	0	0	0	0	0	0	0	—	—	—
Sept./Oct.	67	15	3	0	0	3	6	11	.224	.269	.288
Leading Off Inn.	88	22	5	0	0	0	5	14	.250	.307	.290
Runners On	114	22	4	1	0	21	12	16	.193	.246	.276
Bases Empty	170	42	11	0	0	0	19	26	.247	.312	.323
Runners/Scor. Pos.	67	12	2	1	0	21	7	7	.179	.239	.241
Runners On/2 Out	38	4	3	0	0	5	6	5	.105	.184	.227
Scor. Pos./2 Out	27	3	2	0	0	5	4	2	.111	.185	.226
Late-Inning Pressure	42	11	1	0	0	7	7	7	.262	.286	.392
Leading Off	9	3	1	0	0	0	1	2	.333	.444	.400
Runners On	17	2	0	0	0	0	2	2	.118	.118	.286
Runners/Scor. Pos.	9	0	0	0	0	0	1	2	.000	.000	.100

RUNS BATTED IN	From 1B	From 2B	From 3B	Scoring Position
Totals	2/84	6/56	13/28	19/84
Percentage	2.4%	10.7%	46.4%	22.6%

Loves to face: Ron Darling (.333, 23-for-69, 4 HR)
Tim Leary (.500, 10-for-20)
Rick Sutcliffe (.441, 26-for-59, 5 HR)

Hates to face: Jack Morris (.067, 1-for-15)
Nolan Ryan (.135, 5-for-37, 1 HR, 6 BB)
Bob Welch (.194, 7-for-36)

Miscellaneous statistics: Ground outs-to-air outs ratio: 0.97 last season, 1.19 for career.... Grounded into 6 double plays in 66 opportunities (one per 11).... Drove in 12 of 15 runners from third base with less than two outs (80%), 2d-highest rate in N.L.... Direction of balls hit to the outfield: 21% to left field, 35% to center, 44% to right.... Base running: Advanced from first base to third on 9 of 19 outfield singles (47%); scored from second on 7 of 11 (64%).... Made 2.86 putouts per nine innings in center field.

Comments: Became the first player in major league history with at least 250 at-bats and no home runs coming off a season of more than 10 homers. (Hayes hit 17 in 1990.) Near misses: Jim Holt hit 11 homers in 1973, then went 0-for-239 ABs in 1974; four players were shut out following seasons of exactly 10 HRs—Bill Shindle (1891), Jimmy Canavan (1892), Taffy Wright (1942), and Snuffy Stirnweiss (1946).... Carries westward a streak of 336 consecutive at-bats without a home run. That's by far the longest drought of his career, more than twice as long as his previous mark for home-run futility (158 ABs, 1985–86).... And by the way, in 1989 Hayes hit 26 home runs.... Posted the 3d-lowest average in the National League against right-handed pitchers.... Batting average with runners in scoring position and percentage of runners driven in from scoring position were both career lows.... Was all over the Phillies lineup card last season, starting 71 games in seven different batting-order positions, with at least 10 starts each batting first, second, third, and fifth.... Has averaged only 116 games over the last four years, compared to 149 over the previous six years.... Last season, Hayes became the ninth different opening-day starter in left field for the Phillies in the last nine years. Who'll be number 10?...Ends his career in Philadelphia with 1208 games for the Phillies, ranking 20th in franchise history.... Four fewer players will need first initials on their uniforms as the result of the Kyle Abbott-for-Von Hayes deal.

Tommy Herr
Bats Left and Right

Mets/Giants	AB	H	2B	3B	HR	RBI	BB	SO	BA	SA	OBA
Season	215	45	8	1	1	21	45	28	.209	.270	.344
vs. Left-Handers	83	18	3	1	0	14	18	11	.217	.277	.356
vs. Right-Handers	132	27	5	0	1	7	27	17	.205	.265	.335
vs. Ground-Ballers	86	18	1	1	0	9	16	13	.209	.244	.330
vs. Fly-Ballers	131	27	7	0	1	12	30	16	.206	.282	.352
Home Games	100	19	3	0	0	7	20	15	.190	.220	.322
Road Games	115	26	5	1	1	14	25	13	.226	.313	.362
Grass Fields	145	31	3	0	1	10	27	21	.214	.255	.335
Artificial Turf	70	14	5	1	0	11	18	7	.200	.300	.360
April	55	11	6	0	0	5	17	6	.200	.309	.378
May	51	13	0	0	1	5	9	5	.255	.314	.367
June	21	1	0	0	0	1	2	3	.048	.048	.130
July	27	4	1	0	0	3	4	7	.148	.185	.258
August	20	6	1	0	0	1	2	4	.300	.350	.364
Sept./Oct.	41	10	0	1	0	6	11	3	.244	.293	.404
Leading Off Inn.	43	8	3	0	1	1	8	5	.186	.326	.314
Runners On	92	21	2	1	0	20	23	10	.228	.272	.376
Bases Empty	123	24	6	0	1	1	22	18	.195	.268	.317
Runners/Scor. Pos.	58	13	2	1	0	20	17	7	.224	.293	.390
Runners On/2 Out	39	9	1	1	0	9	12	5	.231	.308	.412
Scor. Pos./2 Out	26	6	1	1	0	9	11	4	.231	.346	.459
Late-Inning Pressure	42	8	1	1	0	3	10	8	.190	.262	.346
Leading Off	13	1	1	0	0	0	5	2	.077	.154	.333
Runners On	19	4	0	1	0	3	4	5	.211	.316	.348
Runners/Scor. Pos.	11	1	0	1	0	3	4	4	.091	.273	.333

RUNS BATTED IN	From 1B	From 2B	From 3B	Scoring Position
Totals	1/60	9/47	10/27	19/74
Percentage	1.7%	19.1%	37.0%	25.7%

Loves to face: Jose DeLeon (.364, 8-for-22, 11 BB)
Neal Heaton (.440, 11-for-25, 0 BB)
Doug Sisk (.556, 10-for-18)
Hates to face: Scott Garrelts (.087, 2-for-23)
Zane Smith (.158, 6-for-38)
Rick Sutcliffe (.152, 7-for-46)

Miscellaneous statistics: Ground outs-to-air outs ratio: 1.27 last season, 1.27 for career.... Grounded into 4 double plays in 46 opportunities (one per 12).... Drove in 7 of 12 runners from third base with less than two outs (58%).... Direction of balls hit to the outfield: 42% to left field, 26% to center, 32% to right batting left-handed; 34% to left field, 31% to center, 34% to right batting right-handed.... Base running: Advanced from first base to third on 3 of 12 outfield singles (25%); scored from second on 4 of 8 (50%).... Made 2.79 assists per nine innings at second base.

Comments: Played 72 games at second base last season, the highest single-season total in major league history for a player who didn't commit an error. The previous high was 61 games by Pepe Frias in 1978.... Made his last error in his final game of the 1990 season. His streak of 72 errorless games at second base was the longest in the majors last season, only 51 games shy of Ryne Sandberg's all-time record.... The Mets used five players at second base last season, and by mid-December all had been dealt out of the organization: Herr, Jeff Gardner, Gregg Jefferies, Keith Miller, and Tim Teufel.... His average of one walk every 5.9 plate appearances was the best of his career; his previous career rate was one walk per 10 PAs.... Was the only player in the National League to draw walks in five consecutive plate appearances last season (Sept. 30–Oct. 2).... Spent his first nine seasons with the Cardinals, but has split time between two teams in three of the past four years.... Career average of .272 from the right-side of the plate, .271 from the left-side. Now that's a real switch-hitter! Among the 48 switch-hitters active in 1991 with at least 1500 career plate appearances, only nine had a difference of five points or less between batting averages from each side of the plate: Herr, Bill Doran, Alfredo Griffin, Gregg Jefferies, Jose Oquendo, Gary Pettis, Tim Raines, John Shelby, and Mickey Tettleton.

Thomas Howard
Bats Left and Right

San Diego Padres	AB	H	2B	3B	HR	RBI	BB	SO	BA	SA	OBA
Season	281	70	12	3	4	22	24	57	.249	.356	.309
vs. Left-Handers	28	8	0	1	1	2	5	5	.286	.464	.394
vs. Right-Handers	253	62	12	2	3	20	19	52	.245	.344	.299
vs. Ground-Ballers	135	38	4	2	1	13	13	21	.281	.363	.349
vs. Fly-Ballers	146	32	8	1	3	9	11	36	.219	.349	.272
Home Games	140	36	4	1	4	14	11	29	.257	.386	.316
Road Games	141	34	8	2	0	8	13	28	.241	.326	.303
Grass Fields	204	52	8	2	4	18	14	41	.255	.373	.306
Artificial Turf	77	18	4	1	0	4	10	16	.234	.312	.318
April	1	0	0	0	0	0	0	0	.000	.000	.000
May	42	9	1	1	0	2	3	10	.214	.286	.261
June	78	23	3	1	1	6	7	7	.295	.397	.360
July	50	11	2	0	0		8	12	.220	.260	.328
August	45	9	3	0	1	5	1	10	.200	.333	.217
Sept./Oct.	65	18	3	1	2	9	5	18	.277	.446	.329
Leading Off Inn.	84	17	4	1	0		4	14	.202	.274	.239
Runners On	107	29	5	1	2	20	14	27	.271	.393	.352
Bases Empty	174	41	7	2	2		10	30	.236	.333	.281
Runners/Scor. Pos.	70	20	3	0	2	19	11	20	.286	.414	.378
Runners On/2 Out	52	13	2	0	0	9	7	11	.250	.288	.339
Scor. Pos./2 Out	38	12	2	0	0	9	6	10	.316	.368	.400
Late-Inning Pressure	57	12	1	0	1	6	3	13	.211	.281	.250
Leading Off	12	2	0	0	0	0	0	2	.167	.167	.167
Runners On	25	7	1	0	1	6	1	6	.280	.440	.308
Runners/Scor. Pos.	16	6	1	0	1	6	0	4	.375	.625	.375

RUNS BATTED IN	From 1B	From 2B	From 3B	Scoring Position
Totals	3/73	9/60	6/21	15/81
Percentage	4.1%	15.0%	28.6%	18.5%

Loves to face: Les Lancaster (.333, 2-for-6, 1 2B, 1 HR)
Hates to face: John Burkett (0-for-5)
Pete Harnisch (0-for-6, 4 SO)
Pete Smith (0-for-5)

Miscellaneous statistics: Ground outs-to-air outs ratio: 1.60 last season, 1.56 for career.... Grounded into 4 double plays in 42 opportunities (one per 11).... Drove in 2 of 7 runners from third base with less than two outs (29%).... Direction of balls hit to the outfield: 45% to left field, 28% to center, 27% to right batting left-handed; 14% to left field, 43% to center, 43% to right batting right-handed.... Base running: Advanced from first base to third on 7 of 14 outfield singles (50%); scored from second on 5 of 7 (71%).... Made 2.97 putouts per nine innings in center field.

Comments: One of seven players to start at least 10 games in each of the three outfield positions. Howard was one of five to pick up an assist at each of those three positions. The others: Skeeter Barnes, Greg Briley, Dave Gallagher, and Otis Nixon.... Ranked fifth among N.L. rookies with 106 games.... One of three switch-hitting rookies to accumulate at least 200 plate appearances in the National League last season. The others: Geronimo Pena and Orlando Merced.... Career batting average of .265 at San Diego Stadium, .243 on other grass fields, .237 on artificial turf.... Career average of .307 as a minor leaguer, .252 as a major leaguer.... In the A's essay of the 1991 *Analyst*, we wrote that the 1986 free-agent draft best illustrated the point that baseball draft becomes a crapshoot before the first round ends. The first six picks in 1986 were Jeff King, Greg Swindell, Matt Williams, Kevin Brown, Kent Mercker, and Gary Sheffield. Among the 20 players chosen later in that round, Howard (the 11th selection overall) has the most major league hits (82). The most successful have been Scott Scudder (who won 15 games for Cincinnati over the past three years) and Greg McMurtry (who caught 63 passes for New England). The only other first-round selection to play even 100 games in the bigs: Luis Alicea, who broke in with 93 games for St. Louis in 1988 but has played only 56 games in three seasons since.

Jack Howell
Bats Left

Angels/Padres	AB	H	2B	3B	HR	RBI	BB	SO	BA	SA	OBA
Season	241	50	5	1	8	23	29	44	.207	.336	.293
vs. Left-Handers	29	3	1	0	0	0	1	10	.103	.138	.133
vs. Right-Handers	212	47	4	1	8	23	28	34	.222	.363	.313
vs. Ground-Ballers	133	31	4	0	6	19	11	22	.233	.398	.292
vs. Fly-Ballers	108	19	1	1	2	4	18	22	.176	.259	.294
Home Games	117	24	2	0	3	12	15	19	.205	.299	.295
Road Games	124	26	3	1	5	11	14	25	.210	.371	.290
Grass Fields	178	35	3	0	7	19	21	31	.197	.331	.281
Artificial Turf	63	15	2	1	1	4	8	13	.238	.349	.324
April	19	5	2	0	1	2	5	2	.263	.526	.417
May	8	1	0	0	0	1	1	0	.125	.125	.222
June	48	10	0	0	1	4	5	8	.208	.271	.283
July	7	1	0	0	0	0	0	2	.143	.143	.143
August	79	15	1	0	3	8	4	19	.190	.316	.229
Sept./Oct.	80	18	2	1	3	8	14	13	.225	.387	.340
Leading Off Inn.	52	9	1	0	3	3	8	10	.173	.365	.283
Runners On	107	27	1	0	4	19	9	19	.252	.374	.310
Bases Empty	134	23	4	1	4	4	20	25	.172	.306	.279
Runners/Scor. Pos.	48	14	1	0	1	13	6	9	.292	.375	.370
Runners On/2 Out	37	8	0	0	3	11	2	9	.216	.459	.256
Scor. Pos./2 Out	19	5	0	0	1	7	2	4	.263	.421	.333
Late-Inning Pressure	33	12	1	0	2	5	4	4	.364	.576	.432
Leading Off	8	5	0	0	2	2	1	1	.625	1.375	.667
Runners On	12	5	0	0	0	3	1	1	.417	.417	.462
Runners/Scor. Pos.	7	4	0	0	0	3	1	1	.571	.571	.625

RUNS BATTED IN	From 1B	From 2B	From 3B	Scoring Position
Totals	3/82	4/37	8/19	12/56
Percentage	3.7%	10.8%	42.1%	21.4%

Loves to face: Chris Bosio (.389, 7-for-18, 1 HR)
Bob Milacki (.333, 4-for-12, 1 HR, 4 BB)
Dave Stieb (.440, 11-for-25, 3 HR)

Hates to face: Storm Davis (.067, 1-for-15, 3 BB, 8 SO)
Charlie Hough (.045, 1-for-22, 5 BB)
Dave Righetti (0-for-10, 9 SO)

Miscellaneous statistics: Ground outs-to-air outs ratio: 1.05 last season, 1.02 for career.... Grounded into 2 double plays in 60 opportunities (one per 30).... Drove in 5 of 11 runners from third base with less than two outs (45%).... Direction of balls hit to the outfield: 36% to left field, 39% to center, 26% to right.... Base running: Advanced from first base to third on 7 of 23 outfield singles (30%); scored from second on 3 of 5 (60%).... Made 2.33 assists per nine innings at third base.

Comments: Started at least one game at five different positions for the Angels last season (1B, 2B, 3B, LF, RF), but played only third base for the Padres. San Francisco's Greg Litton was the only N.L. player to start at more positions; he played Howell's five spots and shortstop too.... The Padres allowed fewer runs per nine innings with Howell at third base (3.46) than they did with Scott Coolbaugh (3.90), Tim Teufel (4.09), or Jim Presley (4.60). (What's this infatuation the Padres have with American League third basemen?)...Three home runs at Dodger Stadium last season tied him with Steve Finley for the most home runs by a visiting player there. (That exacta paid $8437.60.)... Howell played 533 games at third base for the Angels, 2d most in franchise history behind Doug DeCinces.... Career batting average of .297 as a pinch hitter (19-for-64, 3 HR).... Started 38 games in which Padres faced right-handed starting pitchers, but made only one start against a southpaw.... Has batted below .200 against left-handed pitchers in five of his seven seasons in the majors, and his .175 career mark vs. LHP is the lowest in *Player Analysis* history (minimum: 500 AB).... Career batting average of .256 with one home run every 23 at-bats vs. right-handers.

Brian Hunter
Bats Right

Atlanta Braves	AB	H	2B	3B	HR	RBI	BB	SO	BA	SA	OBA
Season	271	68	16	1	12	50	17	48	.251	.450	.296
vs. Left-Handers	121	33	4	0	6	22	6	17	.273	.455	.305
vs. Right-Handers	150	35	12	1	6	28	11	31	.233	.447	.288
vs. Ground-Ballers	100	25	5	1	4	18	4	16	.250	.440	.276
vs. Fly-Ballers	171	43	11	0	8	32	13	32	.251	.456	.306
Home Games	141	38	7	1	7	33	12	22	.270	.482	.331
Road Games	130	30	9	0	5	17	5	26	.231	.415	.255
Grass Fields	208	53	12	1	10	41	13	37	.255	.466	.300
Artificial Turf	63	15	4	0	2	9	4	11	.238	.397	.279
April	0	0	0	0	0	0	0	0	—	—	—
May	2	0	0	0	0	0	1	0	.000	.000	.333
June	39	13	2	0	4	11	3	6	.333	.692	.381
July	78	19	4	1	3	17	2	10	.244	.436	.262
August	97	21	4	0	3	14	9	20	.216	.351	.284
Sept./Oct.	55	15	6	0	2	8	2	12	.273	.491	.298
Leading Off Inn.	57	14	2	0	5	5	2	9	.246	.544	.271
Runners On	128	39	10	1	5	43	8	21	.305	.516	.345
Bases Empty	143	29	6	0	7	7	9	27	.203	.392	.250
Runners/Scor. Pos.	91	29	7	1	3	37	7	13	.319	.516	.360
Runners On/2 Out	51	12	2	1	1	15	5	6	.235	.373	.304
Scor. Pos./2 Out	42	9	2	1	0	13	5	3	.214	.310	.298
Late-Inning Pressure	41	9	5	0	2	5	2	8	.220	.488	.256
Leading Off	6	2	1	0	1	1	0	1	.333	1.000	.333
Runners On	22	4	2	0	1	4	2	6	.182	.409	.250
Runners/Scor. Pos.	13	1	1	0	1	2	5	.077	.154	.200

RUNS BATTED IN	From 1B	From 2B	From 3B	Scoring Position
Totals	6/88	13/67	19/46	32/113
Percentage	6.8%	19.4%	41.3%	28.3%

Loves to face: Danny Jackson (.563, 9-for-16, 2 HR)

Hates to face: Frank Castillo (0-for-5, 3 SO)
Norm Charlton (0-for-5)
Bob Tewksbury (0-for-6)

Miscellaneous statistics: Ground outs-to-air outs ratio: 0.81 last season, 0.81 for career.... Grounded into 6 double plays in 60 opportunities (one per 10).... Drove in 11 of 19 runners from third base with less than two outs (58%).... Direction of balls hit to the outfield: 67% to left field, 18% to center, 15% to right.... Base running: Advanced from first base to third on 4 of 8 outfield singles (50%); scored from second on 5 of 5 (100%).... Made 0.70 assists per nine innings at first base.

Comments: Had the highest slugging percentage among major league rookies last season.... Twelve of his RBIs were go-ahead runs, and 11 of them turned out to be game winners.... His batting average for the Braves last season was higher than the career mark he accumulated over five seasons in the minors (.248).... Hit for a higher average in Braves losses (.269) than he did in their victories (.240). Of 309 players with at least 200 plate appearances last season, only 19 had higher BAs in losses than in wins.... Ended the regular-season with 32 consecutive errorless games at first base, his longest streak of the season.... Hunter and Sid Bream both played in 85 games at first base; the Braves allowed 3.86 runs per nine innings with Hunter there, and 3.84 runs with Bream.... Started 33 of 44 games in which the Braves faced left-handed starting pitchers, only 31 of 118 games against right-handers.... Homered in Game 7 of the N.L.C.S. Only two younger players have hit home runs in postseason "rubber matches": Mickey Mantle (20 years old, 1952) and George Brett (23 years, 4 months, 1976 A.L.C.S.). Hunter was 23 years, 7 months at the time.... The latest player to join the list of players who bat right-handed and throw lefty. Only three other position players did so last season: Rickey Henderson, Mark Carreon, and Luis Medina. The most famous retired member: Hal Chase. Among the others: Cleon Jones and many noted pitchers including Carl Hubbell and Sandy Koufax.

Darrin Jackson
Bats Right

San Diego Padres	AB	H	2B	3B	HR	RBI	BB	SO	BA	SA	OBA
Season	359	94	12	1	21	49	27	66	.262	.476	.315
vs. Left-Handers	163	43	5	0	11	26	12	24	.264	.497	.311
vs. Right-Handers	196	51	7	1	10	23	15	42	.260	.459	.318
vs. Ground-Ballers	179	52	8	1	10	26	16	26	.291	.514	.345
vs. Fly-Ballers	180	42	4	0	11	23	11	40	.233	.439	.284
Home Games	174	45	3	1	12	24	13	29	.259	.494	.317
Road Games	185	49	9	0	9	25	14	37	.265	.459	.312
Grass Fields	274	76	7	1	20	44	21	47	.277	.529	.332
Artificial Turf	85	18	5	0	1	5	6	19	.212	.306	.258
April	21	7	1	0	1	2	2	3	.333	.524	.375
May	38	5	2	0	1	3	8	8	.132	.263	.283
June	43	12	0	0	4	8	1	8	.279	.558	.289
July	42	14	1	0	4	7	3	3	.333	.643	.378
August	92	21	3	1	4	11	5	22	.228	.413	.268
Sept./Oct.	123	35	5	0	7	18	8	22	.285	.496	.336
Leading Off Inn.	122	37	7	0	8	8	5	18	.303	.557	.331
Runners On	124	33	2	0	6	34	12	19	.266	.427	.333
Bases Empty	235	61	10	1	15	15	15	47	.260	.502	.304
Runners/Scor. Pos.	79	21	2	0	4	30	9	13	.266	.443	.344
Runners On/2 Out	57	14	1	0	2	13	8	12	.246	.368	.348
Scor. Pos./2 Out	37	10	1	0	2	13	6	7	.270	.459	.386
Late-Inning Pressure	57	8	1	0	2	5	7	11	.140	.263	.234
Leading Off	20	2	0	0	1	1	2	6	.100	.250	.182
Runners On	20	5	1	0	0	3	3	2	.250	.300	.348
Runners/Scor. Pos.	13	4	1	0	0	3	2	1	.308	.385	.400

RUNS BATTED IN	From 1B	From 2B	From 3B	Scoring Position
Totals	4/90	9/60	15/39	24/99
Percentage	4.4%	15.0%	38.5%	24.2%

Loves to face: Danny Jackson (.563, 9-for-16, 2 HR)
Bob Patterson (.750, 3-for-4, 2 HR, 1 SO)
Bob Scanlan (3-for-3, 1 HR)
Hates to face: John Franco (0-for-10)
Ramon Martinez (.100, 1-for-10)
Terry Mulholland (.063, 1-for-16)

Miscellaneous statistics: Ground outs-to-air outs ratio: 0.94 last season, 0.93 for career.... Grounded into 5 double plays in 58 opportunities (one per 12).... Drove in 9 of 19 runners from third base with less than two outs (47%).... Direction of balls hit to the outfield: 52% to left field, 26% to center, 22% to right.... Base running: Advanced from first base to third on 8 of 17 outfield singles (47%); scored from second on 9 of 15 (60%).... Made 2.87 putouts per nine innings in center field, highest rate in N.L.

Comments: Averaged one home run every 17.1 at-bats, the 4th-highest rate in the National League last season, behind Kevin Mitchell (13.7), Howard Johnson (14.8), and Fred McGriff (17.0).... Only two other players in N.L. history hit more than 20 home runs with fewer than 50 RBIs: Gary Matthews (21 HR, 46 RBI in 1986) and Art Shamsky (21 HR, 47 RBI in 1966).... Batting average in Late-Inning Pressure Situations was the lowest in the league, dropping his career mark from .185 to .167—the 2d lowest among active players (minimum: 100 AB). The bottom three: Jeff King (.159), Jackson, and Junior Felix (.169).... Was the only National League player to start at least one game in eight different spots in the batting order. Shane Mack did it in the A.L., but of course he had all nine spots available.... Led the league with six home runs against the Giants.... Hit three home runs at Atlanta Stadium, tying Joe Oliver, Tim Wallach, and Kevin Bass for the most by any visiting player there during the regular season.... Batted 102 points higher vs. ground-ball pitchers than vs. fly-ballers in 1990 to go with last season's 68-point spread. But prior to 1990, Jackson hit 37 points higher against fly-ball pitchers than vs. ground-ballers (.258 to .221). Career batting average of .274 vs. left-handers, .234 vs. right-handers.... Career batting average of .198 as a pinch-hitter (16-for-81, 4 HR).

Gregg Jefferies
Bats Left and Right

New York Mets	AB	H	2B	3B	HR	RBI	BB	SO	BA	SA	OBA
Season	486	132	19	2	9	62	47	38	.272	.374	.336
vs. Left-Handers	174	51	10	1	1	18	15	9	.293	.379	.353
vs. Right-Handers	312	81	9	1	8	44	32	29	.260	.372	.328
vs. Ground-Ballers	216	59	8	0	3	20	17	16	.273	.352	.331
vs. Fly-Ballers	274	74	12	2	6	43	30	23	.270	.394	.340
Home Games	244	72	10	1	5	28	30	21	.295	.406	.371
Road Games	242	60	9	1	4	34	17	17	.248	.343	.300
Grass Fields	364	101	14	1	7	44	33	30	.277	.379	.355
Artificial Turf	122	31	5	1	2	18	14	8	.254	.361	.341
April	52	10	4	0	0	8	10	6	.192	.269	.333
May	57	21	3	0	0	10	1	6	.368	.421	.379
June	97	25	4	0	5	14	10	7	.258	.454	.324
July	70	20	2	1	2	15	8	3	.286	.429	.354
August	103	22	2	1	2	7	5	10	.214	.311	.248
Sept./Oct.	107	34	4	0	0	8	13	6	.318	.355	.397
Leading Off Inn.	97	31	4	0	3	3	7	3	.320	.454	.365
Runners On	222	64	8	1	4	57	23	19	.288	.387	.351
Bases Empty	264	68	11	1	5	5	24	19	.258	.364	.324
Runners/Scor. Pos.	124	38	6	1	1	50	18	8	.306	.395	.386
Runners On/2 Out	84	19	2	1	1	17	5	11	.226	.310	.270
Scor. Pos./2 Out	54	13	2	1	0	15	4	4	.241	.315	.293
Late-Inning Pressure	69	16	1	0	1	5	14	6	.232	.290	.369
Leading Off	15	2	0	0	0	0	4	2	.133	.133	.316
Runners On	34	10	1	0	1	5	4	2	.294	.412	.368
Runners/Scor. Pos.	19	3	1	0	0	3	2	1	.158	.211	.238

RUNS BATTED IN	From 1B	From 2B	From 3B	Scoring Position
Totals	6/156	21/92	26/56	47/148
Percentage	3.8%	22.8%	46.4%	31.8%

Loves to face: Mark Langston (.333, 2-for-6, 1 2B, 1 HR)
Tim Leary (.500, 3-for-6, 2 2B, 1 HR)
Scott Scudder (.600, 3-for-5)
Hates to face: Ken Dayley (0-for-6)
Bill Gullickson (0-for-5)

Miscellaneous statistics: Ground outs-to-air outs ratio: 0.88 last season, 0.86 for career.... Grounded into 12 double plays in 106 opportunities (one per 8.8).... Drove in 21 of 30 runners from third base with less than two outs (70%).... Direction of balls hit to the outfield: 28% to left field, 32% to center, 39% to right batting left-handed; 37% to left field, 40% to center, 23% to right batting right-handed.... Base running: Advanced from first base to third on 3 of 23 outfield singles (13%); scored from second on 13 of 18 (72%).... Made 2.60 assists per nine innings at second base, lowest rate in majors.

Comments: Career average of one strikeout every 14.0 plate appearances is 5th best in Mets history, behind Felix Millan (32.1), Doug Flynn (15.1), Rusty Staub (14.5), and Ron Hunt (14.2).... Doubled in Vince Coleman from second base in his first at-bat of the 1991 season, after finishing 1990 hitless in his last 37 at-bats with runners in scoring position.... Was involved in an average of one double play every 41 innings at second base, the lowest rate in the majors last season (minimum: 20 games). The major league average for that position is one DP every 14.4 innings.... Has been successful on 84 percent of his stolen-base attempts over the last two seasons (37-for-44).... Of his 42 career home runs, 29 have been solo shots.... Has hit for a lower average in Late-Inning Pressure Situations than in other at-bats in each of his three full seasons in the majors.... Difference of 33 points between his batting averages from the left and right side of the plate was atypical of his previous career performance. His career batting average is four points higher against left-handers (.277) than it is against right-handers (.273).... Career batting average of .301 vs. ground-ball pitchers, .252 vs. fly-ballers.... Career breakdown: .306 at Shea Stadium, .266 on other grass fields, .227 on artificial turf. That poor average on turf combined with Jefferies's tendency to hit the ball in the air could make his transition to cavernous Royals Stadium a tough one.

Howard Johnson

Bats Left and Right

New York Mets	AB	H	2B	3B	HR	RBI	BB	SO	BA	SA	OBA
Season	564	146	34	4	38	117	78	120	.259	.535	.342
vs. Left-Handers	217	55	9	1	14	40	24	59	.253	.498	.320
vs. Right-Handers	347	91	25	3	24	77	54	61	.262	.559	.355
vs. Ground-Ballers	244	75	15	3	19	59	30	52	.307	.627	.371
vs. Fly-Ballers	323	71	19	1	19	58	48	69	.220	.461	.317
Home Games	280	75	12	3	21	64	38	60	.268	.557	.347
Road Games	284	71	22	1	17	53	40	60	.250	.514	.337
Grass Fields	400	102	19	4	27	82	56	81	.255	.525	.339
Artificial Turf	164	44	15	0	11	35	22	39	.268	.561	.349
April	57	12	2	0	4	14	8	15	.211	.456	.290
May	96	26	6	1	7	21	9	17	.271	.573	.324
June	89	21	5	1	6	20	22	13	.236	.517	.384
July	93	27	7	0	5	16	17	13	.290	.527	.386
August	106	25	4	1	6	15	5	24	.236	.462	.277
Sept./Oct.	123	35	10	1	10	31	17	38	.285	.626	.364
Leading Off Inn.	144	41	8	0	16	16	16	22	.285	.674	.356
Runners On	265	68	15	1	15	94	39	64	.257	.491	.335
Bases Empty	299	78	19	3	23	39	39	56	.261	.575	.348
Runners/Scor. Pos.	152	42	11	0	6	74	28	30	.276	.467	.359
Runners On/2 Out	110	26	8	0	5	31	17	25	.236	.445	.339
Scor. Pos./2 Out	71	17	5	0	3	26	15	13	.239	.437	.372
Late-Inning Pressure	87	22	5	0	7	17	14	25	.253	.552	.350
Leading Off	23	5	1	0	1	1	5	4	.217	.391	.357
Runners On	43	11	2	0	4	14	6	16	.256	.581	.333
Runners/Scor. Pos.	21	5	1	0	1	8	5	9	.238	.429	.357

RUNS BATTED IN	From 1B	From 2B	From 3B	Scoring Position
Totals	15/201	27/129	37/68	64/197
Percentage	7.5%	20.9%	54.4%	32.5%

Loves to face: Kevin Gross (.377, 23-for-61, 5 HR)
Greg Maddux (.339, 19-for-56, 5 HR)
Ramon Martinez (.350, 7-for-20, 4 2B, 2 HR)

Hates to face: Tom Browning (.103, 4-for-39, 2 HR)
Jose DeJesus (0-for-16)
John Smiley (.103, 4-for-39)

Miscellaneous statistics: Ground outs-to-air outs ratio: 0.44 last season, lowest in majors; 0.56 for career.... Grounded into 4 double plays in 133 opportunities (one per 33).... Drove in 31 of 45 runners from third base with less than two outs (69%).... Direction of balls hit to the outfield: 19% to left field, 29% to center, 51% to right batting left-handed; 57% to left field, 30% to center, 13% to right batting right-handed.... Base running: Advanced from first base to third on 12 of 30 outfield singles (40%); scored from second on 11 of 15 (73%).... Made 1.77 assists per nine innings at third base, 2d-lowest rate in N.L.

Comments: Became the first player in Mets history to lead the league in RBIs. No New York player had led his league in both home runs and RBIs since Roger Maris did it in 1961; no New Yorker led the N.L. in both categories since Johnny Mize did it for the Giants in 1947.... Ranks 2d in the National League with 157 home runs over the past five seasons, 15 fewer than Darryl Strawberry.... Has had three seasons of more than 35 home runs. Only three other active players have done that: Jose Canseco, Dale Murphy, and Strawberry.... Played 152 complete games last season, to lead the N.L.... Led the major leagues with 31 errors despite playing his last 30 games in the outfield. Began the season as the Mets' everyday shortstop—every day until the third week of the season as it turned out—before moving to third base.... He was the only everyday player in the majors last season who had twice as many fly outs as ground outs. His career ratio of ground outs-to-air outs (0.56) is the lowest of any player over the last 17 years.... Year after year, he's consistent from the left side of the plate, but he's alternated good and bad seasons from the right side. Batting averages batting right-handed year by year since 1986: .213, .289, .183, .278, .208, .253.... It was actually reported in one publication that Howard Johnson tied the National League record for sacrifice flies by a switch-hitter. My God, we've created a monster!

Ricky Jordan

Bats Right

Philadelphia Phillies	AB	H	2B	3B	HR	RBI	BB	SO	BA	SA	OBA
Season	301	82	21	3	9	49	14	49	.272	.452	.304
vs. Left-Handers	126	39	12	0	4	19	6	15	.310	.500	.338
vs. Right-Handers	175	43	9	3	5	30	8	34	.246	.417	.280
vs. Ground-Ballers	138	42	12	0	3	24	9	21	.304	.457	.353
vs. Fly-Ballers	163	40	9	3	6	25	5	28	.245	.448	.262
Home Games	158	47	9	2	5	27	4	21	.297	.475	.317
Road Games	143	35	12	1	4	22	10	28	.245	.427	.291
Grass Fields	78	20	7	0	4	15	7	17	.256	.500	.318
Artificial Turf	223	62	14	3	5	34	7	32	.278	.435	.299
April	34	10	5	1	1	5	3	5	.294	.588	.351
May	89	26	3	1	4	18	4	13	.292	.483	.320
June	68	17	8	0	0	7	5	9	.250	.368	.307
July	43	11	2	1	2	6	1	6	.256	.488	.273
August	39	8	2	0	1	9	1	10	.205	.333	.220
Sept./Oct.	28	10	1	0	1	4	0	6	.357	.500	.357
Leading Off Inn.	66	18	3	0	4	4	2	11	.273	.500	.294
Runners On	145	43	11	2	4	44	7	25	.297	.483	.323
Bases Empty	156	39	10	1	5	5	7	24	.250	.423	.287
Runners/Scor. Pos.	89	27	7	1	4	42	7	17	.303	.539	.337
Runners On/2 Out	62	15	4	2	0	13	1	13	.242	.371	.254
Scor. Pos./2 Out	42	9	1	1	0	11	1	9	.214	.286	.233
Late-Inning Pressure	69	15	2	1	0	5	5	12	.217	.275	.276
Leading Off	13	5	1	0	0	0	0	2	.385	.462	.385
Runners On	34	6	1	0	0	5	4	8	.176	.206	.275
Runners/Scor. Pos.	22	2	1	0	0	5	4	5	.091	.136	.222

RUNS BATTED IN	From 1B	From 2B	From 3B	Scoring Position
Totals	7/110	14/71	19/35	33/106
Percentage	6.4%	19.7%	54.3%	31.1%

Loves to face: Tom Browning (.471, 8-for-17, 1 HR)
John Costello (.700, 7-for-10, 1 HR)
Ramon Martinez (.429, 6-for-14, 1 HR)

Hates to face: Doug Drabek (.063, 1-for-16, 1 2B)
Greg Maddux (.207, 6-for-29)
John Smoltz (.167, 3-for-18)

Miscellaneous statistics: Ground outs-to-air outs ratio: 1.24 last season, 1.15 for career.... Grounded into 11 double plays in 70 opportunities (one per 6.4).... Drove in 13 of 22 runners from third base with less than two outs (59%).... Direction of balls hit to the outfield: 33% to left field, 32% to center, 35% to right.... Base running: Advanced from first base to third on 3 of 10 outfield singles (30%); scored from second on 8 of 10 (80%).... Made 0.55 assists per nine innings at first base, 2d-lowest rate in majors.

Comments: Has batted over .300 against left-handed pitchers in three of his four seasons in the majors. But despite a career average of .304 against southpaws, he started only 33 of 62 games in which the Phillies faced southpaw starters. He actually started more games against right-handers, against whom he owns a .260 career average.... Has walked only 57 times in four seasons with Philadelphia, and more than a quarter of them have been intentional (15).... Among active players with at least 1500 plate appearances, Jordan's career average of one walk every 26 times to the plate is 4th lowest, behind Alvaro Espinoza (one BB every 34 PA), Ozzie Guillen (33), and Brian Harper (29).... One of four active players with at least 1000 career plate appearances, but no sacrifice bunts. The others: George Bell, Cecil Fielder, and Randy Milligan.... Has played 365 games in the field, all at first base.... Career batting average of .326 as a pinch-hitter (15-for-46, 0 HR).... Has hit a grand slam in each of the last two seasons, and has batted .433 (13-for-30) with the bases loaded over the last three. No Phillies player has hit grand slams in three consecutive seasons since Mike Schmidt did it from 1979 through 1981.... Was born May 26, 1965, the day after Muhammad Ali made his first defense of the heavyweight title, knocking out Sonny Liston in the first round.

Felix Jose

St. Louis Cardinals — Bats Left and Right

	AB	H	2B	3B	HR	RBI	BB	SO	BA	SA	OBA
Season	568	173	40	6	8	77	50	113	.305	.438	.360
vs. Left-Handers	262	78	18	2	2	30	23	51	.298	.405	.354
vs. Right-Handers	306	95	22	4	6	47	27	62	.310	.467	.365
vs. Ground-Ballers	251	66	16	3	2	29	18	52	.263	.375	.314
vs. Fly-Ballers	317	107	24	3	6	48	32	61	.338	.489	.395
Home Games	280	83	16	5	3	39	25	48	.296	.421	.353
Road Games	288	90	24	1	5	38	25	65	.313	.455	.367
Grass Fields	163	44	12	1	3	22	6	41	.270	.411	.294
Artificial Turf	405	129	28	5	5	55	44	72	.319	.449	.385
April	79	28	9	2	2	15	9	5	.354	.595	.422
May	92	30	8	0	0	10	14	24	.326	.413	.421
June	91	29	6	1	0	14	5	17	.319	.407	.354
July	94	25	7	0	1	10	7	21	.266	.372	.311
August	96	28	6	0	0	9	8	21	.292	.354	.343
Sept./Oct.	116	33	4	3	5	19	7	25	.284	.500	.323
Leading Off Inn.	132	37	10	0	1	1	5	24	.280	.379	.307
Runners On	270	87	20	5	5	74	29	50	.322	.489	.384
Bases Empty	298	86	20	1	3	3	21	63	.289	.393	.338
Runners/Scor. Pos.	143	49	13	3	3	68	23	31	.343	.538	.424
Runners On/2 Out	113	35	3	4	3	26	10	18	.310	.487	.366
Scor. Pos./2 Out	71	20	1	3	3	25	9	12	.282	.507	.363
Late-Inning Pressure	86	33	9	0	3	8	10	17	.384	.593	.443
Leading Off	16	6	3	0	0	0	0	4	.375	.563	.375
Runners On	41	13	2	0	2	7	7	6	.317	.512	.408
Runners/Scor. Pos.	15	5	1	0	1	5	5	1	.333	.600	.476

RUNS BATTED IN	From 1B	From 2B	From 3B	Scoring Position
Totals	11/193	22/101	36/71	58/172
Percentage	5.7%	21.8%	50.7%	33.7%

Loves to face: Tommy Greene (.615, 8-for-13, 4 2B, 1 3B)
Chris Nabholz (.636, 7-for-11, 3 SO)
John Smiley (.444, 8-for-18)

Hates to face: Steve Avery (0-for-12)
Tom Glavine (0-for-9)
Greg Maddux (0-for-9)

Miscellaneous statistics: Ground outs-to-air outs ratio: 1.49 last season, 1.46 for career.... Grounded into 12 double plays in 132 opportunities (one per 11).... Drove in 24 of 37 runners from third base with less than two outs (65%).... Direction of balls hit to the outfield: 37% to left field, 29% to center, 34% to right batting left-handed; 25% to left field, 34% to center, 41% to right batting right-handed.... Base running: Advanced from first base to third on 9 of 30 outfield singles (30%); scored from second on 10 of 15 (67%).... Made 1.84 putouts per nine innings in right field.

Comments: Has batted .300 since joining the Cardinals in the deal that sent Willie McGee to Oakland in August 1990. In just over 400 at-bats with the Athletics, Jose had a career average of .255.... Batted .325 with runners in scoring position in 1990, for a two-year mark of .335, the 5th highest in the majors (minimum: 200 AB).... April batting average was 2d highest in the league; he was among league's top 10 every day from April 21 through the end of the season.... Ranked second in the league with 51 multiple-hit games, behind Terry Pendleton (52). Jose's four games with four or more hits tied the N.L. MVP for the league lead in that category.... Batting average in Late-Inning Pressure Situations was 2d highest in the majors.... Had the league's 3d-highest batting average on artificial turf. He has a career mark of .304 on synthetics, .264 on grass.... He was the only player in the majors to hit safely in eight consecutive at-bats last season.... Had 21 consecutive plate appearances with the bases empty (Sept. 4–10), the 2d longest streak in the majors.... Led N.L. right fielders with 15 assists; tied Marquis Grissom for the lead among all N.L. outfielders.... His career batting average is 25 points higher from the right side (.299) than from the left (.274), but his HR rate is twice as high batting left-handed (one per 45 at-bats) as right-handed (one per 97).

David Justice

Atlanta Braves — Bats Left

	AB	H	2B	3B	HR	RBI	BB	SO	BA	SA	OBA
Season	396	109	25	1	21	87	65	81	.275	.503	.377
vs. Left-Handers	155	43	6	1	7	39	14	24	.277	.465	.333
vs. Right-Handers	241	66	19	0	14	48	51	57	.274	.527	.403
vs. Ground-Ballers	149	40	5	1	6	33	20	31	.268	.436	.355
vs. Fly-Ballers	247	69	20	0	15	54	45	50	.279	.543	.391
Home Games	175	47	12	1	11	41	30	39	.269	.537	.371
Road Games	221	62	13	0	10	46	35	42	.281	.475	.382
Grass Fields	273	79	18	1	16	61	42	55	.289	.538	.383
Artificial Turf	123	30	7	0	5	26	23	26	.244	.423	.365
April	69	16	4	0	2	10	7	17	.232	.377	.299
May	97	37	9	0	5	28	11	16	.381	.629	.450
June	70	17	4	1	4	13	12	20	.243	.500	.361
July	0	0	0	0	0	0	0	0	.000	.000	.000
August	50	12	4	0	3	10	8	9	.240	.500	.345
Sept./Oct.	110	27	4	0	7	26	27	19	.245	.473	.386
Leading Off Inn.	107	25	7	0	7	7	5	22	.234	.495	.268
Runners On	196	62	12	1	11	77	43	37	.316	.556	.435
Bases Empty	200	47	13	0	10	10	22	44	.235	.450	.314
Runners/Scor. Pos.	124	43	10	1	6	66	34	24	.347	.589	.479
Runners On/2 Out	86	21	2	0	3	19	28	20	.244	.372	.435
Scor. Pos./2 Out	50	10	1	0	1	14	25	12	.200	.280	.474
Late-Inning Pressure	56	14	4	0	3	12	12	15	.250	.482	.382
Leading Off	12	3	2	0	0	0	2	2	.250	.417	.357
Runners On	27	7	1	0	2	11	6	6	.259	.519	.394
Runners/Scor. Pos.	17	7	1	0	2	11	5	3	.412	.824	.545

RUNS BATTED IN	From 1B	From 2B	From 3B	Scoring Position
Totals	11/132	26/96	29/52	55/148
Percentage	8.3%	27.1%	55.8%	37.2%

Loves to face: Kevin Gross (.600, 3-for-5, 1 HR)
Vicente Palacios (.600, 3-for-5, 2 2B, 1 HR)
Bill Sampen (.429, 3-for-7, 2 HR)

Hates to face: Jose DeLeon (.083, 1-for-12, 1 2B)
Jose Rijo (.063, 1-for-16, 4 BB)
Ed Whitson (.071, 1-for-14)

Miscellaneous statistics: Ground outs-to-air outs ratio: 0.80 last season, 0.69 for career.... Grounded into 4 double plays in 83 opportunities (one per 21).... Drove in 26 of 34 runners from third base with less than two outs (76%).... Direction of balls hit to the outfield: 17% to left field, 33% to center, 50% to right.... Base running: Advanced from first base to third on 5 of 25 outfield singles (20%); scored from second on 8 of 10 (80%).... Made 1.92 putouts per nine innings in right field.

Comments: Justice has 50 home runs in 886 career at-bats. Most HRs in first 1000 ABs for Braves: Bob Horner, 71; Eddie Mathews, 65; Jeff Burroughs, 62; Davey Johnson, 58; Earl Williams, 56. Where's the original Hammer? He had only 40; but remember, Aaron broke in at age 20 and didn't play in the Launching Pad until much later. (Now let's see if M.C. has the same staying power as Hank.)... His seven errors in right field were the most in the league.... Led the league in RBIs during May.... Batting average with runners in scoring position was 3d highest in the league.... Career average of .231 with the bases empty, .331 with runners on base.... He has driven in 71.4 percent of runners from third base with less than two outs in his career, the highest rate among active players. He was walked intentionally in that situation in the 8th inning of Game 7—a no-brainer, but nonetheless a move that may have won the Series for Minnesota.... Over 42 percent of Justice's hits have been for extra bases, 9th-highest rate among active players (minimum: 1000 plate appearances). More than half his hits at Atlanta Stadium have been for extra bases.... Career breakdown: .293 at Atlanta Stadium, .278 on other grass fields, .246 on artificial turf.... Still hasn't played a full season, having appeared in only 109 regular-season games last year, and 127 the year before. His career statistics prorated over 162 games are 32 homers and 108 RBIs.

John Kruk
Bats Left

Philadelphia Phillies	AB	H	2B	3B	HR	RBI	BB	SO	BA	SA	OBA
Season	538	158	27	6	21	92	67	100	.294	.483	.367
vs. Left-Handers	202	60	12	2	4	35	18	38	.297	.436	.350
vs. Right-Handers	336	98	15	4	17	57	49	62	.292	.512	.378
vs. Ground-Ballers	240	69	11	2	6	28	40	44	.287	.425	.390
vs. Fly-Ballers	302	90	16	4	16	65	27	56	.298	.536	.347
Home Games	276	79	17	1	8	48	35	50	.286	.442	.363
Road Games	262	79	10	5	13	44	32	50	.302	.527	.372
Grass Fields	138	36	2	2	9	23	14	26	.261	.500	.323
Artificial Turf	400	122	25	4	12	69	53	74	.305	.478	.383
April	77	24	2	0	4	20	6	9	.312	.494	.353
May	84	23	5	1	1	12	12	16	.274	.393	.350
June	99	28	2	4	5	22	10	15	.283	.535	.349
July	75	18	4	1	3	7	8	17	.240	.440	.313
August	82	25	4	0	3	14	18	17	.305	.463	.427
Sept./Oct.	121	40	10	0	5	17	13	26	.331	.537	.393
Leading Off Inn.	135	45	7	1	4	4	14	25	.333	.489	.396
Runners On	244	72	13	2	10	81	36	40	.295	.488	.376
Bases Empty	294	86	14	4	11	11	31	60	.293	.480	.360
Runners/Scor. Pos.	131	36	6	0	5	65	27	27	.275	.435	.381
Runners On/2 Out	96	27	8	0	6	31	20	17	.281	.552	.405
Scor. Pos./2 Out	53	16	3	0	4	24	15	10	.302	.585	.456
Late-Inning Pressure	92	27	3	2	1	12	16	22	.293	.402	.394
Leading Off	25	7	1	0	0	0	2	9	.280	.320	.333
Runners On	40	12	2	0	0	11	10	7	.300	.350	.431
Runners/Scor. Pos.	21	7	2	0	0	11	7	4	.333	.429	.483

RUNS BATTED IN	From 1B	From 2B	From 3B	Scoring Position
Totals	16/189	23/106	32/57	55/163
Percentage	8.5%	21.7%	56.1%	33.7%

Loves to face: Brian Barnes (.667, 6-for-9, 1 HR)
Jose DeLeon (.500, 11-for-22, 1 HR)
Bob Walk (.433, 13-for-30, 1 HR)
Hates to face: Kelly Downs (.129, 4-for-31, 1 HR)
Bob Patterson (0-for-11)
Zane Smith (.118, 2-for-17)

Miscellaneous statistics: Ground outs-to-air outs ratio: 0.95 last season, 1.46 for career.... Grounded into 11 double plays in 128 opportunities (one per 12).... Drove in 28 of 43 runners from third base with less than two outs (65%).... Direction of balls hit to the outfield: 42% to left field, 34% to center, 25% to right.... Base running: Advanced from first base to third on 11 of 32 outfield singles (34%); scored from second on 11 of 17 (65%).... Made 0.54 assists per nine innings at first base, lowest rate in majors.

Comments: Batting average from September 1 on was 3d highest in the league.... Batted .366 in Phillies' victories, .219 in their losses.... Batted .239 in 88 at-bats during the first inning, .304 thereafter.... Among the players who qualified for the N.L. batting title in each of the last two seasons, Kruk had the 3d-smallest differential between his 1990 and 1991 batting averages (.287, .284). Has batted between .291 and .313 in five of six seasons in the majors; the exception: .241 in 1988.... Stole seven bases in seven attempts last season. Career average: 67 percent (45-for-67).... Led the league with a .459 average against his ex-mates, the Padres.... Hit for a higher average against left-handers than right-handers for the first time in his six seasons in the majors. Career breakdown: .260 (with one home run every 56 at-bats) vs. left-handers, .305 (one HR every 30 AB) vs. right-handers.... Has hit for a higher average on artificial turf than he has on grass fields in each of his six seasons in the majors.... Ended last season with 43 consecutive error-less games at first base, his longest streak of the season. Career rate of one error every 237 chances at first base is the best of any active player (minimum: 200 games).... Was hit with a pitch for the first time in his career last season (August 21). Among players whose careers started after 1920, only three avoided pitched balls in each of their first 2000 plate appearances: Kruk, U. L. Washington, and Mickey Mantle.

Ray Lankford
Bats Left

St. Louis Cardinals	AB	H	2B	3B	HR	RBI	BB	SO	BA	SA	OBA
Season	566	142	23	15	9	69	41	114	.251	.392	.301
vs. Left-Handers	220	52	11	7	0	26	16	48	.236	.350	.290
vs. Right-Handers	346	90	12	8	9	43	25	66	.260	.419	.308
vs. Ground-Ballers	233	62	7	5	6	27	20	42	.266	.416	.325
vs. Fly-Ballers	333	80	16	10	3	42	21	72	.240	.375	.284
Home Games	283	67	10	10	4	33	23	53	.237	.385	.294
Road Games	283	75	13	5	5	36	18	61	.265	.399	.308
Grass Fields	143	39	9	3	3	25	10	32	.273	.441	.321
Artificial Turf	423	103	14	12	6	44	31	82	.243	.376	.295
April	55	14	1	2	0	3	4	6	.255	.345	.305
May	95	23	5	0	0	10	2	13	.242	.295	.258
June	92	23	3	4	0	12	10	16	.250	.370	.327
July	80	21	2	2	2	13	6	18	.262	.412	.307
August	118	25	5	5	1	14	4	30	.212	.364	.238
Sept./Oct.	126	36	7	2	6	17	15	31	.286	.516	.362
Leading Off Inn.	179	47	6	2	4	4	11	43	.263	.385	.305
Runners On	228	67	12	11	3	63	23	36	.294	.482	.357
Bases Empty	338	75	11	4	6	6	18	78	.222	.331	.261
Runners/Scor. Pos.	133	38	5	8	1	54	17	20	.286	.466	.364
Runners On/2 Out	84	28	5	5	1	22	10	12	.333	.548	.411
Scor. Pos./2 Out	55	16	0	4	0	17	8	5	.291	.436	.391
Late-Inning Pressure	73	22	2	2	1	13	7	14	.301	.425	.363
Leading Off	17	5	0	0	0	0	5	.294	.294	.294	
Runners On	36	11	1	2	0	12	3	7	.306	.444	.359
Runners/Scor. Pos.	20	9	1	2	0	12	2	4	.450	.700	.500

RUNS BATTED IN	From 1B	From 2B	From 3B	Scoring Position
Totals	10/149	24/110	26/63	50/173
Percentage	6.7%	21.8%	41.3%	28.9%

Loves to face: John Franco (3-for-3)
Tommy Greene (.375, 6-for-16, 2 2B, 1 3B, 1 HR)
Pete Harnisch (.400, 4-for-10, 1 HR)
Hates to face: Doug Drabek (.125, 2-for-16)
Bob Patterson (0-for-7)
Zane Smith (.143, 2-for-14)

Miscellaneous statistics: Ground outs-to-air outs ratio: 1.15 last season, 1.12 for career.... Grounded into 4 double plays in 109 opportunities (one per 27).... Drove in 17 of 32 runners from third base with less than two outs (53%).... Direction of balls hit to the outfield: 37% to left field, 35% to center, 28% to right.... Base running: Advanced from first base to third on 7 of 15 outfield singles (47%); scored from second on 12 of 17 (71%).... Made 2.71 putouts per nine innings in center field.

Comments: Led the major leagues with 15 triples last season. No player has led the N.L. in that category in consecutive seasons since Garry Templeton did it for three straight years for the Cardinals from 1977 to 1979. The last player to lead the major leagues in triples twice in a row was George Brett (1975–76).... Only two rookies in the past 50 years have had as many triples in a season: Juan Samuel (19 in 1984) and Jim Gilliam (17 in 1953).... Led major league rookies in at-bats with one more than Chuck Knoblauch.... The Cardinals looked at him briefly in the leadoff position in May and June, and he took the spot on a full-time basis in late July. St. Louis's leadoff slot had a .305 on-base percentage, 2d lowest in the league.... Stole 44 bases, most by a rookie since Chris Sabo stole 46 in 1988.... Total of eight infield hits seems a little low for a left-handed speedster, and it is. Five other left-handers stole as many as 30 bases; they had an average of 33 infield hits, ranging from Barry Bonds's 12 to Brett Butler's 61.... His batting average with two outs and runners on base was the 3d highest in the league.... His six errors in center field tied Ron Gant for the most in the league.... Has a career batting average of .239 at Busch Stadium, .257 in other stadiums with artificial turf, and .290 on grass fields.... Has hit 12 career home runs, all against right-handed pitchers.

Barry Larkin
Bats Right

Cincinnati Reds	AB	H	2B	3B	HR	RBI	BB	SO	BA	SA	OBA
Season	464	140	27	4	20	69	55	64	.302	.506	.378
vs. Left-Handers	135	44	7	2	8	23	28	15	.326	.585	.436
vs. Right-Handers	329	96	20	2	12	46	27	49	.292	.474	.351
vs. Ground-Ballers	217	71	17	2	3	30	17	25	.327	.465	.376
vs. Fly-Ballers	251	71	10	2	18	40	38	39	.283	.554	.381
Home Games	242	79	17	2	16	48	30	37	.326	.612	.404
Road Games	222	61	10	2	4	21	25	27	.275	.392	.349
Grass Fields	128	34	5	1	2	11	10	17	.266	.367	.324
Artificial Turf	336	106	22	3	18	58	45	47	.315	.560	.397
April	69	15	1	0	3	7	4	11	.217	.362	.260
May	29	11	3	2	2	6	2	3	.379	.828	.424
June	92	34	5	0	9	23	23	12	.370	.717	.496
July	76	19	4	0	1	8	7	15	.250	.342	.313
August	120	36	6	2	4	18	12	12	.300	.483	.368
Sept./Oct.	78	25	8	0	1	7	7	11	.321	.462	.376
Leading Off Inn.	100	29	8	0	5	5	9	15	.290	.520	.349
Runners On	192	61	10	2	8	57	32	25	.318	.516	.414
Bases Empty	272	79	17	2	12	12	23	39	.290	.500	.350
Runners/Scor. Pos.	111	32	4	2	3	45	16	16	.288	.441	.377
Runners On/2 Out	64	19	3	1	3	21	13	10	.297	.516	.416
Scor. Pos./2 Out	49	13	3	1	2	19	9	8	.265	.490	.379
Late-Inning Pressure	70	17	2	1	1	6	3	16	.243	.343	.284
Leading Off	12	3	0	0	0	0	0	0	.250	.250	.250
Runners On	35	7	1	1	1	6	3	10	.200	.371	.263
Runners/Scor. Pos.	24	4	1	1	1	6	1	6	.167	.417	.200

RUNS BATTED IN	From 1B	From 2B	From 3B	Scoring Position
Totals	11/129	14/84	24/46	38/130
Percentage	8.5%	16.7%	52.2%	29.2%

Loves to face: Jim Deshaies (.400, 12-for-30, 5 HR)
Zane Smith (.429, 15-for-35, 3 HR)
Ed Whitson (.485, 16-for-33, 1 HR)
Hates to face: David Cone (.176, 6-for-34)
Ramon Martinez (.125, 2-for-16, 1 3B)
Mark Portugal (.091, 1-for-11)

Miscellaneous statistics: Ground outs-to-air outs ratio: 1.41 last season, 1.15 for career.... Grounded into 7 double plays in 109 opportunities (one per 16).... Drove in 16 of 26 runners from third base with less than two outs (62%).... Direction of balls hit to the outfield: 30% to left field, 29% to center, 41% to right.... Base running: Advanced from first base to third on 15 of 27 outfield singles (56%); scored from second on 13 of 19 (68%).... Made 3.24 assists per nine innings at shortstop.

Comments: The 1991 Reds were only the fourth team in major league history with a shortstop and third baseman who both had slugging averages of .500 or higher. (Chris Sabo had a .505 mark.) The others: 1930 Giants—Travis Jackson and Fred Lindstrom; 1940 Red Sox—Joe Cronin and Jim Tabor; and 1948 Indians—Lou Boudreau and Ken Keltner.... First shortstop to hit .300 or better in three consecutive seasons since Harvey Kuenn (four years, 1953–56; minimum: 80 games at SS).... Became only the third shortstop in major league history to hit three home runs in a game. The others: Ernie Banks (1955 and 1957) and Freddie Patek (1980).... Won the N.L. triple crown for June, leading the league in batting average, home runs, and RBIs for the month.... Hit safely in 22 consecutive home games, the longest streak in the league last season.... Had a streak of 35 consecutive plate appearances in which he batted without a runner in scoring position (August 14–23), the longest streak in the N.L. last season.... Career batting average of .315 vs. left-handed pitchers is 5th highest among active players. One of the four players ahead of him is teammate Sabo (.321).... Career strikeout rate against southpaws (one every 20.3 plate appearances) is 2d best among active players, topped only by Felix Fermin.... Career stolen-base percentage of .821 is 4th highest among active players (minimum: 100 SB). He trails Eric Davis (.870), Tim Raines (.850), and Willie Wilson (.836), holding a slight edge over Vince Coleman (.820).

Mike LaValliere
Bats Left

Pittsburgh Pirates	AB	H	2B	3B	HR	RBI	BB	SO	BA	SA	OBA
Season	336	97	11	2	3	41	33	27	.289	.360	.351
vs. Left-Handers	54	12	2	1	0	14	3	9	.222	.296	.259
vs. Right-Handers	282	85	9	1	3	27	30	18	.301	.372	.368
vs. Ground-Ballers	142	42	2	1	0	14	12	10	.296	.324	.348
vs. Fly-Ballers	197	55	9	1	3	27	21	18	.279	.381	.348
Home Games	163	54	5	1	1	22	20	13	.331	.393	.400
Road Games	173	43	6	1	2	19	13	14	.249	.329	.304
Grass Fields	83	19	4	0	2	11	5	6	.229	.349	.286
Artificial Turf	253	78	7	2	1	30	28	21	.308	.364	.372
April	49	10	1	0	1	10	2	2	.204	.286	.235
May	55	16	1	1	0	5	7	5	.291	.345	.359
June	49	17	2	0	1	1	7	4	.347	.449	.439
July	68	20	4	0	1	10	5	6	.294	.397	.351
August	56	16	0	0	0	5	6	6	.286	.286	.349
Sept./Oct.	59	18	3	1	0	10	6	4	.305	.390	.358
Leading Off Inn.	88	23	4	0	0	0	8	5	.261	.307	.330
Runners On	146	35	4	2	1	39	17	17	.240	.315	.310
Bases Empty	190	62	7	0	2	2	16	10	.326	.395	.385
Runners/Scor. Pos.	95	25	4	2	1	39	13	12	.263	.379	.336
Runners On/2 Out	71	15	0	1	0	12	7	7	.211	.239	.282
Scor. Pos./2 Out	48	11	0	1	0	12	4	6	.229	.271	.288
Late-Inning Pressure	31	6	1	0	0	2	5	3	.194	.226	.324
Leading Off	13	3	1	0	0	0	0	0	.231	.308	.286
Runners On	10	1	0	0	0	2	5	3	.100	.100	.400
Runners/Scor. Pos.	7	1	0	0	0	2	4	3	.143	.143	.455

RUNS BATTED IN	From 1B	From 2B	From 3B	Scoring Position
Totals	2/108	16/70	20/46	36/116
Percentage	1.9%	22.9%	43.5%	31.0%

Loves to face: Juan Agosto (.500, 5-for-10)
Kelly Downs (.500, 11-for-22)
John Smoltz (.533, 8-for-15, 1 HR)
Hates to face: David Cone (.167, 5-for-30)
Ken Hill (.100, 1-for-10)
Scott Terry (.100, 1-for-10)

Miscellaneous statistics: Ground outs-to-air outs ratio: 1.13 last season, 1.04 for career.... Grounded into 10 double plays in 59 opportunities (one per 5.9).... Drove in 15 of 25 runners from third base with less than two outs (60%).... Direction of balls hit to the outfield: 35% to left field, 43% to center, 22% to right.... Base running: Advanced from first base to third on 1 of 14 outfield singles (7%), 2d-lowest rate in N.L.; scored from second on 4 of 13 (31%), lowest rate in N.L.... Opposing base stealers: 90-for-129 (70%).

Comments: Pirates catchers compiled a .301 batting average last season, the highest of all 26 teams.... Started only three of 53 games in which the Pirates faced left-handed starting pitchers, but 97 of 109 games against right-handers. Career batting-average breakdown: .237 vs. LHP, .279 vs. RHP.... Led major league catchers with one error in 612 chances last season. Only one catcher in N.L. history ever posted a lower single-season error rate (minimum: 100 games): Wes Westrum, who committed only one error in 680 chances for the Giants in 1950. Lavalliere ended the season with a 93-game errorless streak, the longest by any catcher last season.... Only five of his 41 RBIs gave the Pirates a lead, compared to Steve Buechele, who drove in 16 runs with Pittsburgh, but had six go-ahead RBIs.... Had two infield hits last season, matching his combined total for the previous two years.... Has driven in over 30 percent of runners from scoring position in each of the last four years.... Has never poked more than 20 extra-base hits in a season.... Career batting average of .429 (18-for-42) with the bases loaded is 4th highest among active players.... Career batting average of .194 as a pinch-hitter (7-for-36, 0 HR).... Has thrown out four of eight opposing base stealers in six postseason games. Best postseason average (minimum: 10 attempts): Johnny Bench, whose opponents were 6-for-21.

Mark Lemke

Bats Left and Right

Atlanta Braves	AB	H	2B	3B	HR	RBI	BB	SO	BA	SA	OBA
Season	269	63	11	2	2	23	29	27	.234	.312	.305
vs. Left-Handers	114	29	7	1	0	11	11	7	.254	.333	.313
vs. Right-Handers	155	34	4	1	2	12	18	20	.219	.297	.299
vs. Ground-Ballers	104	20	2	1	0	8	12	10	.192	.231	.276
vs. Fly-Ballers	165	43	9	1	2	15	17	17	.261	.364	.323
Home Games	132	37	8	0	2	14	14	13	.280	.386	.345
Road Games	137	26	3	2	0	9	15	14	.190	.241	.266
Grass Fields	197	51	9	2	2	19	22	17	.259	.355	.329
Artificial Turf	72	12	2	0	0	4	7	10	.167	.194	.237
April	19	5	2	0	0	1	2	4	.263	.368	.318
May	26	7	1	0	0	4	6	2	.269	.308	.394
June	28	6	2	1	0	3	3	3	.214	.357	.290
July	46	9	0	0	1	5	4	6	.196	.261	.260
August	53	16	2	0	1	4	5	8	.302	.396	.356
Sept./Oct.	97	20	4	1	0	6	9	4	.206	.268	.271
Leading Off Inn.	51	15	4	1	0	0	5	7	.294	.412	.357
Runners On	122	27	3	1	0	21	13	10	.221	.262	.288
Bases Empty	147	36	8	1	2	2	16	17	.245	.354	.319
Runners/Scor. Pos.	74	17	1	1	0	20	6	5	.230	.270	.274
Runners On/2 Out	43	10	0	0	0	8	7	3	.233	.233	.340
Scor. Pos./2 Out	32	8	0	0	0	8	5	3	.250	.250	.351
Late-Inning Pressure	47	16	1	1	0	7	6	5	.340	.404	.415
Leading Off	12	3	1	0	0	0	2	2	.250	.333	.357
Runners On	20	7	0	1	0	7	2	2	.350	.450	.409
Runners/Scor. Pos.	14	7	0	1	0	7	1	0	.500	.643	.533

RUNS BATTED IN	From 1B	From 2B	From 3B	Scoring Position
Totals	1/86	9/57	11/30	20/87
Percentage	1.2%	15.8%	36.7%	23.0%

Loves to face: Randy Myers (.600, 3-for-5)
Wally Whitehurst (.750, 3-for-4)
Hates to face: Tim Belcher (0-for-13)
Bruce Hurst (.125, 2-for-16)
Bob Tewksbury (0-for-7)

Miscellaneous statistics: Ground outs-to-air outs ratio: 1.22 last season, 1.17 for career.... Grounded into 9 double plays in 65 opportunities (one per 7.2).... Drove in 7 of 17 runners from third base with less than two outs (41%).... Direction of balls hit to the outfield: 22% to left field, 39% to center, 39% to right batting left-handed; 40% to left field, 31% to center, 29% to right batting right-handed.... Base running: Advanced from first base to third on 4 of 11 outfield singles (36%); scored from second on 6 of 9 (67%).... Made 3.05 assists per nine innings at second base.

Comments: Hit three triples in 24 at-bats in the World Series, compared to three in 621 career ABs in regular-season play. Of the five other players who had at least three threes in a Series, four did so in the first Series (1903): Buck Freeman, Tommy Leach (4), Freddy Parent, and Chick Stahl; the fifth was Billy Johnson in 1947.... Was brought into 46 games as a defensive replacement during the regular season, 2d most in the majors, behind Jose Vizcaino (52).... The Braves allowed an average of 3.36 runs per nine innings while Lemke was at second base, more than a run per game less than with either Jeff Blauser or Jeff Treadway there (4.44 runs per nine innings combined).... Committed an average of one error every 47 chances, compared to an average of one per 25 by Treadway.... Drove in seven of 15 runners from scoring position in Late-Inning Pressure Situations last season (47%), 3d-highest rate among N.L. players (minimum: 10 opportunities), behind the big boys, Barry Bonds and Will Clark.... Career batting average is .199 with the bases empty, but .263 with runners on base.... Another noteworthy career breakdown: .244 at Atlanta Stadium, .243 on other grass fields, .176 on artificial turf.... Has a career total of one stolen base in seven attempts.... Hasn't been hit with a pitch in 698 career plate appearances.... How much longer can he keep doing this? Chuck Cottier and Doug Flynn made pretty good careers out of the same stuff, and our projection model gives him between 300 and 400 more games.

Darren Lewis

Bats Right

San Francisco Giants	AB	H	2B	3B	HR	RBI	BB	SO	BA	SA	OBA
Season	222	55	5	3	1	15	36	30	.248	.311	.358
vs. Left-Handers	75	21	4	1	1	6	12	8	.280	.400	.386
vs. Right-Handers	147	34	1	2	0	9	24	22	.231	.265	.343
vs. Ground-Ballers	104	28	0	3	1	9	16	13	.269	.356	.367
vs. Fly-Ballers	118	27	5	0	0	6	20	17	.229	.271	.350
Home Games	121	28	2	0	0	6	21	15	.231	.248	.354
Road Games	101	27	3	3	1	9	15	15	.267	.386	.362
Grass Fields	165	37	3	1	1	9	26	22	.224	.273	.337
Artificial Turf	57	18	2	2	0	6	10	8	.316	.421	.418
April	0	0	0	0	0	0	0	0	—	—	—
May	0	0	0	0	0	0	0	0	—	—	—
June	0	0	0	0	0	0	0	0	—	—	—
July	62	21	4	1	0	5	11	10	.339	.435	.446
August	96	24	1	2	1	7	10	12	.250	.333	.327
Sept./Oct.	64	10	0	0	0	3	15	8	.156	.156	.316
Leading Off Inn.	86	22	1	2	1	1	16	15	.256	.349	.373
Runners On	84	25	3	0	0	14	12	9	.298	.333	.398
Bases Empty	138	30	2	3	1	1	24	21	.217	.297	.333
Runners/Scor. Pos.	48	11	1	0	0	13	10	8	.229	.250	.373
Runners On/2 Out	36	9	1	0	0	8	6	5	.250	.278	.372
Scor. Pos./2 Out	25	6	1	0	0	8	5	4	.240	.280	.387
Late-Inning Pressure	27	8	1	1	0	4	4	6	.296	.407	.387
Leading Off	6	1	0	1	0	0	0	2	.167	.500	.167
Runners On	14	5	1	0	0	4	3	4	.357	.429	.471
Runners/Scor. Pos.	11	4	1	0	0	4	2	3	.364	.455	.462

RUNS BATTED IN	From 1B	From 2B	From 3B	Scoring Position
Totals	1/54	3/36	10/23	13/59
Percentage	1.9%	8.3%	43.5%	22.0%

Loves to face: Brian Barnes (3-for-3, 2 2B)
Tom Browning (.667, 4-for-6)
Kent Mercker (1-for-1, 4 BB)
Hates to face: Steve Avery (0-for-6)
Kip Gross (0-for-8)
Alejandro Pena (0-for-3, 2 SO)

Miscellaneous statistics: Ground outs-to-air outs ratio: 1.74 last season, 1.66 for career.... Grounded into 1 double play in 43 opportunities (one per 43), 4th-best rate in N.L.... Drove in 5 of 10 runners from third base with less than two outs (50%).... Direction of balls hit to the outfield: 22% to left field, 26% to center, 52% to right.... Base running: Advanced from first base to third on 4 of 19 outfield singles (21%); scored from second on 6 of 9 (67%).... Made 2.82 putouts per nine innings in center field, 2d-highest rate in N.L.

Comments: Fantasy Draft Alert—list of comparable players in Rookies and Prospects Section suggests this guy has a future; four of five had productive careers, and the fifth, Steve Finley, is on his way. Also among the 20 most-comparable rookies of the past 30 years: Kevin Bass, Len Dykstra, Ken Griffey Sr., Gene Locklear, Bip Roberts.... Batted .340 in 81 games for Phoenix last season before his midseason call-up to the Giants.... Started 54 games last season, all as a center fielder, and all from the leadoff slot in the Giants batting order.... Reached base safely in 21 of the first 22 games in which he started.... Batted .326 in 43 first-inning at-bats, .229 thereafter.... Lewis, Chuck Knoblauch, and Bernard Gilkey were the only rookies to bat at least 200 times last season and walk more often than they struck out. Over the last 30 years, only two other San Francisco rookies did that: Chuck Hiller (1961) and Steve Ontiveros (1974).... Was 1-for-13 with runners in scoring position for the Athletics in 1990, giving him a career mark of .197 with RISP.... One of the "pair of minor leaguers" acquired by the Giants for Ernest Riles. Looks like one more notch in Al Rosen's belt.... Hey, box-score readers, remember "Ru.Jones," who played for Seattle during the 1980s, and his teammate "Ri.Jones"? Darren and Dan Lewis, a first baseman in the Giants' system, could become the Ruppert and Rick of the 1990s.

Jose Lind
Bats Right

Pittsburgh Pirates	AB	H	2B	3B	HR	RBI	BB	SO	BA	SA	OBA
Season	502	133	16	6	3	54	30	56	.265	.339	.306
vs. Left-Handers	167	45	2	1	2	15	14	20	.269	.329	.326
vs. Right-Handers	335	88	14	5	1	39	16	36	.263	.343	.295
vs. Ground-Ballers	237	67	6	4	2	28	15	24	.283	.367	.325
vs. Fly-Ballers	268	66	10	2	1	26	15	33	.246	.310	.285
Home Games	262	64	7	5	2	30	17	32	.244	.332	.290
Road Games	240	69	9	1	1	24	13	24	.287	.346	.323
Grass Fields	137	38	4	0	0	12	6	12	.277	.307	.310
Artificial Turf	365	95	12	6	3	42	24	44	.260	.351	.304
April	64	17	2	0	1	6	3	8	.266	.344	.294
May	70	18	3	1	1	9	3	4	.257	.371	.284
June	71	17	0	0	1	8	6	8	.239	.282	.299
July	88	25	3	1	0	6	6	5	.284	.341	.337
August	99	24	4	2	0	7	5	16	.242	.323	.271
Sept./Oct.	110	32	4	2	0	18	7	15	.291	.364	.336
Leading Off Inn.	108	23	2	1	1	1	3	12	.213	.278	.234
Runners On	243	65	11	4	1	52	19	24	.267	.358	.319
Bases Empty	259	68	5	2	2	2	11	32	.263	.320	.293
Runners/Scor. Pos.	118	33	5	1	1	47	15	8	.280	.364	.355
Runners On/2 Out	92	27	4	2	1	19	14	9	.293	.413	.387
Scor. Pos./2 Out	44	13	3	1	1	17	13	1	.295	.477	.456
Late-Inning Pressure	62	15	0	0	0	3	3	9	.242	.242	.277
Leading Off	17	4	0	0	0	0	1	1	.235	.235	.278
Runners On	25	6	0	0	0	3	1	4	.240	.240	.269
Runners/Scor. Pos.	14	2	0	0	0	3	0	3	.143	.143	.143

RUNS BATTED IN	From 1B	From 2B	From 3B	Scoring Position
Totals	8/190	14/89	29/59	43/148
Percentage	4.2%	15.7%	49.2%	29.1%

Loves to face: Shawn Boskie (.500, 5-for-10)
Don Carman (.500, 11-for-22, 1 HR)
Rob Dibble (.833, 5-for-6)

Hates to face: Scott Garrelts (0-for-12)
Jose Rijo (.105, 2-for-19)
Ed Whitson (.056, 1-for-18)

Miscellaneous statistics: Ground outs-to-air outs ratio: 1.49 last season, 1.41 for career.... Grounded into 20 double plays in 127 opportunities (one per 6.4).... Drove in 25 of 40 runners from third base with less than two outs (63%).... Direction of balls hit to the outfield: 24% to left field, 35% to center, 41% to right.... Base running: Advanced from first base to third on 5 of 17 outfield singles (29%); scored from second on 10 of 12 (83%).... Made 3.17 assists per nine innings at second base, 3d-highest rate in N.L.

Comments: Has played at least 150 games in each of the last four seasons. Only three players in team history have had five-year streaks: Gus Suhr (6 years, 1932–37), Ralph Kiner (1947–51), and Johnny Ray (1982–86).... Grounded into 20 double plays last season, one fewer than league-leader Benito Santiago. He has grounded into 40 double plays over the last two seasons, 2d most in the N.L., behind Dale Murphy (42).... Last year marked the first season in which he hit for a higher average on grass fields than on artificial turf. Career averages: .261 at Three Rivers Stadium, .277 on other turfed fields, .238 on grass fields.... Stole seven bases in 11 attempts last season after going 23-for-24 over the previous two years.... His 640 games at second base rank sixth in Pirates history. Bill Mazeroski played more than twice as many games there than any other player in the history of the franchise. (And this seems an appropriate time to point out that 16 years ago, the Bucs traded a 21-year-old prospect named Willie Randolph for Doc Medich, and threw in Dock Ellis and Ken Brett to boot. Ouch!)...Lind's career average of one error every 73 chances at second base is the best in franchise history.... Career averages against left- and right-handed pitchers are virtually identical (.258, .259), but there's a 15-point gap between his averages against ground-ball and fly-ball pitchers (.251, .266).

Dave Magadan
Bats Left

New York Mets	AB	H	2B	3B	HR	RBI	BB	SO	BA	SA	OBA
Season	418	108	23	0	4	51	83	50	.258	.342	.378
vs. Left-Handers	151	37	4	0	0	12	24	14	.245	.272	.347
vs. Right-Handers	267	71	19	0	4	39	59	36	.266	.382	.395
vs. Ground-Ballers	176	46	7	0	3	21	37	21	.261	.352	.384
vs. Fly-Ballers	246	62	16	0	1	30	46	29	.252	.329	.369
Home Games	202	49	10	0	2	25	38	27	.243	.322	.358
Road Games	216	59	13	0	2	26	45	23	.273	.361	.398
Grass Fields	300	74	17	0	3	39	54	35	.247	.333	.357
Artificial Turf	118	34	6	0	1	12	29	15	.288	.364	.430
April	63	17	3	0	0	8	18	12	.270	.317	.427
May	88	22	6	0	2	14	12	8	.250	.386	.340
June	79	17	5	0	1	9	19	8	.215	.316	.363
July	82	25	4	0	1	12	16	8	.305	.390	.420
August	90	26	4	0	0	8	15	14	.289	.333	.383
Sept./Oct.	16	1	1	0	0	0	3	1	.063	.125	.211
Leading Off Inn.	73	21	6	0	0	0	16	9	.288	.370	.422
Runners On	184	52	9	0	2	49	35	17	.283	.364	.388
Bases Empty	234	56	14	0	2	2	48	33	.239	.325	.371
Runners/Scor. Pos.	103	30	5	0	1	45	21	8	.291	.369	.394
Runners On/2 Out	72	24	4	0	1	22	16	3	.333	.431	.461
Scor. Pos./2 Out	50	19	3	0	1	21	9	2	.380	.500	.483
Late-Inning Pressure	63	11	3	0	0	6	16	11	.175	.222	.342
Leading Off	18	3	2	0	0	0	5	6	.167	.278	.348
Runners On	26	6	1	0	0	6	3	1	.231	.269	.310
Runners/Scor. Pos.	14	5	1	0	0	6	3	0	.357	.429	.471

RUNS BATTED IN	From 1B	From 2B	From 3B	Scoring Position
Totals	5/120	18/82	24/49	42/131
Percentage	4.2%	22.0%	49.0%	32.1%

Loves to face: Tim Belcher (.500, 7-for-14)
Dennis Martinez (.364, 12-for-33, 1 HR)
Ed Whitson (.421, 8-for-19, 1 HR)

Hates to face: Bud Black (.077, 1-for-13)
Jose DeJesus (.133, 2-for-15, 1 3B)
Jose Rijo (.063, 1-for-16, 3 BB)

Miscellaneous statistics: Ground outs-to-air outs ratio: 1.13 last season, 1.16 for career.... Grounded into 5 double plays in 96 opportunities (one per 19).... Drove in 19 of 26 runners from third base with less than two outs (73%).... Direction of balls hit to the outfield: 40% to left field, 34% to center, 26% to right.... Base running: Advanced from first base to third on 10 of 33 outfield singles (30%); scored from second on 11 of 13 (85%), 5th-highest rate in N.L.... Made 0.79 assists per nine innings at first base.

Comments: Three of the six toughest N.L. batters to strike out last season were Mets: Gregg Jefferies (3d, one per 14.2 plate appearances), Kevin McReynolds (5th, 12.6), and Magadan (6th, 10.3).... Had the league's 6th-lowest batting average in both day games (.207) and Late-Inning Pressure Situations.... Batting average with two outs and runners in scoring position was the league's best.... One of five N.L. players to qualify for the batting title without a hitting streak longer than six games.... Projection model likes his chances for a rebound almost as much as Dikembe Motumbo's; best guess for 1992 is .292, with one chance in three of hitting .300 or better.... Career batting average of .331 with runners on base is 4th highest over last 17 years, behind Wade Boggs (.350), Rod Carew (.348), and Tony Gwynn (.346).... Career on-base percentage (.391) ranks third among active players (minimum: 1000 AB), behind Wade Boggs (.435) and Rickey Henderson (.403).... Career batting average (.294) ranks second in Mets history, behind Keith Hernandez (.297).... Has driven in 34 percent of runners from scoring position, 7th-highest rate among active players.... Career total of 145 games at third base amounts to about a season's worth, and his error rate there (one per 33 chances) is better than Tim Wallach's 1991 league-leading figure (one per 30). Howard Johnson, the Mets' most regular third baseman (that's on the field; this ain't no Ex-Lax ad!) had an average of one error per 14 chances during that time.

Carmelo Martinez

Bats Right

Pirates/K.C./Reds	AB	H	2B	3B	HR	RBI	BB	SO	BA	SA	OBA
Season	275	61	11	0	10	36	43	64	.222	.371	.324
vs. Left-Handers	131	29	7	0	2	16	23	32	.221	.321	.335
vs. Right-Handers	144	32	4	0	8	20	20	32	.222	.417	.313
vs. Ground-Ballers	143	34	7	0	5	20	24	31	.238	.392	.343
vs. Fly-Ballers	132	27	4	0	5	16	19	33	.205	.348	.303
Home Games	130	28	4	0	5	15	18	28	.215	.362	.307
Road Games	145	33	7	0	5	21	25	36	.228	.379	.339
Grass Fields	102	25	6	0	5	19	14	27	.245	.451	.333
Artificial Turf	173	36	5	0	5	17	29	37	.208	.324	.319
April	16	4	0	0	0	0	1	2	.250	.250	.294
May	66	11	2	0	1	6	17	15	.167	.242	.337
June	49	13	3	0	3	10	8	10	.265	.510	.368
July	18	4	1	0	1	2	3	1	.222	.444	.333
August	81	18	3	0	3	9	8	23	.222	.370	.289
Sept./Oct.	45	11	2	0	2	9	6	13	.244	.422	.321
Leading Off Inn.	72	16	2	0	6	6	13	15	.222	.500	.341
Runners On	115	25	7	0	2	28	13	27	.217	.330	.290
Bases Empty	160	36	4	0	8	8	30	37	.225	.400	.347
Runners/Scor. Pos.	68	15	6	0	1	25	8	16	.221	.353	.291
Runners On/2 Out	40	9	3	0	0	9	5	11	.225	.300	.311
Scor. Pos./2 Out	24	6	2	0	0	8	3	5	.250	.333	.333
Late-Inning Pressure	49	9	2	0	1	2	6	17	.184	.286	.273
Leading Off	16	3	0	0	1	1	1	7	.188	.375	.235
Runners On	16	2	1	0	0	1	3	5	.125	.188	.263
Runners/Scor. Pos.	8	1	1	0	0	1	2	3	.125	.250	.300

RUNS BATTED IN	From 1B	From 2B	From 3B	Scoring Position
Totals	7/83	8/51	11/29	19/80
Percentage	8.4%	15.7%	37.9%	23.8%

Loves to face: John Burkett (.444, 4-for-9, 1 HR)
Atlee Hammaker (.421, 8-for-19, 4 HR, 9 BB)
Bob Ojeda (.455, 10-for-22, 1 HR)

Hates to face: Norm Charlton (0-for-11)
Rob Dibble (0-for-9, 5 SO)
Doug Drabek (.067, 1-for-15, 3 BB)

Miscellaneous statistics: Ground outs-to-air outs ratio: 0.82 last season, 0.85 for career.... Grounded into 7 double plays in 55 opportunities (one per 7.9).... Drove in 9 of 21 runners from third base with less than two outs (43%).... Direction of balls hit to the outfield: 43% to left field, 33% to center, 24% to right.... Base running: Advanced from first base to third on 3 of 19 outfield singles (16%), including 2d-worst rate in A.L. (0-for-10); scored from second on 10 of 16 (63%).... Made 0.77 assists per nine innings at first base.

Comments: Century 21's Bert Blyleven has nothing on this guy; Martinez played for two different clubs in 1990, and three last season—Pittsburgh (11 games), Kansas City (44), and Cincinnati (53).... Five teams have given up on this guy over the last three seasons. Can he hold on to a job until expansion?...Drove in three runs on June 11, in Kansas City's 55th game of the season, marking the first time all season that a Royals first baseman drove in more than one run in any game. They had only five RBIs over their first 50 games from that position.... For the second straight season his batting average vs. left-handed pitchers was a career low. At least in 1990 he hit five home runs in 90 at-bats against southpaws; last season, there was no trace of power.... Last season's strikeout rate (one every 5.0 plate appearances) was his worst since 1983, when he broke into the majors with 29 games for the Cubs.... Hadn't grounded into a double play in 24 opportunities with Cincinnati before hitting into a twin-killing in his final plate appearance of the season.... Has hit for a higher average on grass fields than on artificial turf in each of the last five seasons. Has also hit for a higher average against ground-ball pitchers than vs. fly-ballers in each of those seasons.... Over the past three seasons, he's stranded 37 of 60 runners at third base with less than two outs (62%), the third-worst rate in the majors (minimum: 50 opportunities), behind Rob Deer (63%) and Dave Valle (62%).

Dave Martinez

Bats Left

Montreal Expos	AB	H	2B	3B	HR	RBI	BB	SO	BA	SA	OBA
Season	396	117	18	5	7	42	20	54	.295	.419	.332
vs. Left-Handers	93	22	6	1	0	8	5	22	.237	.323	.287
vs. Right-Handers	303	95	12	4	7	34	15	32	.314	.449	.346
vs. Ground-Ballers	171	49	8	2	3	19	9	29	.287	.409	.328
vs. Fly-Ballers	230	71	11	3	4	23	11	25	.309	.435	.340
Home Games	173	49	9	2	3	21	8	19	.283	.410	.315
Road Games	223	68	9	3	4	21	12	35	.305	.426	.345
Grass Fields	110	32	2	3	3	13	5	19	.291	.445	.325
Artificial Turf	286	85	16	2	4	29	15	35	.297	.409	.334
April	58	12	1	1	0	5	4	8	.207	.259	.258
May	37	10	1	1	1	7	2	5	.270	.432	.300
June	92	24	6	1	1	11	3	12	.261	.380	.281
July	74	26	3	0	1	3	4	7	.351	.432	.385
August	72	25	5	1	2	8	2	8	.347	.528	.382
Sept./Oct.	63	20	2	1	2	8	5	14	.317	.476	.371
Leading Off Inn.	86	22	2	1	1	1	4	7	.256	.337	.289
Runners On	149	45	7	3	0	35	12	18	.302	.389	.359
Bases Empty	247	72	11	2	7	7	8	36	.291	.437	.314
Runners/Scor. Pos.	96	29	3	1	0	31	9	13	.302	.354	.369
Runners On/2 Out	61	17	3	0	0	14	4	8	.279	.328	.333
Scor. Pos./2 Out	48	15	2	0	0	13	3	8	.313	.354	.365
Late-Inning Pressure	67	12	1	0	0	6	4	9	.179	.194	.243
Leading Off	16	3	0	0	0	0	1	1	.188	.188	.235
Runners On	23	5	1	0	0	6	1	3	.217	.261	.345
Runners/Scor. Pos.	20	5	1	0	0	6	3	2	.250	.300	.385

RUNS BATTED IN	From 1B	From 2B	From 3B	Scoring Position
Totals	5/92	14/77	16/37	30/114
Percentage	5.4%	18.2%	43.2%	26.3%

Loves to face: Mike Bielecki (.308, 8-for-26, 3 HR)
Frank Castillo (2-for-2, 2 HR, 1 BB)
Jose DeJesus (.444, 8-for-18, 2 HR)

Hates to face: Paul Assenmacher (.067, 1-for-15)
Shawn Boskie (.125, 2-for-16)
Alejandro Pena (.077, 1-for-13)

Miscellaneous statistics: Ground outs-to-air outs ratio: 0.84 last season, 0.97 for career.... Grounded into 3 double plays in 64 opportunities (one per 21).... Drove in 11 of 18 runners from third base with less than two outs (61%).... Direction of balls hit to the outfield: 34% to left field, 35% to center, 32% to right.... Base running: Advanced from first base to third on 8 of 19 outfield singles (42%); scored from second on 7 of 12 (58%).... Made 2.36 putouts per nine innings in right field.

Comments: His seven home runs were the most by any player who hit all solo HRs. Career totals: 28 solo shots, eight with runners on.... Posted the league's 5th-highest batting average vs. right-handed pitchers.... Batting average in Late-Inning Pressure Situations was 7th lowest in the league.... Averaged one walk every 21.4 times to the plate last season, the worst rate of his career, and the fourth straight season in which his rate decreased.... One of seven major leaguers to start at least 10 games in each of the three outfield positions last season.... Batted .325 as a right fielder, .297 as a left fielder, and .237 as a center fielder. Does anyone believe those numbers represent anything more than coincidence?...Started only 11 of 53 games in which the Expos faced left-handed starters, but managed to accumulate over 100 plate appearances vs. southpaws for the first time in his career.... Career batting averages: .221 vs. left-handers, .279 vs. right-handers. Of his 36 career home runs, only four have been hit against lefties.... He has a career batting average of .275 at Riverfront Stadium (19-for-69, 2 HR).... Batting averages year by year since 1988: .255, .274, .279, .295. The only other players to raise their mark in each of the last three seasons (minimum: 300 AB): Craig Biggio, Dale Murphy, B. J. Surhoff, and Jeff Treadway.

Willie McGee
Bats Left and Right

San Francisco Giants	AB	H	2B	3B	HR	RBI	BB	SO	BA	SA	OBA
Season	497	155	30	3	4	43	34	74	.312	.408	.357
vs. Left-Handers	154	52	11	0	2	20	10	24	.338	.448	.380
vs. Right-Handers	343	103	19	3	2	23	24	50	.300	.391	.347
vs. Ground-Ballers	238	66	7	1	3	20	18	35	.277	.353	.331
vs. Fly-Ballers	259	89	23	2	1	23	16	39	.344	.459	.381
Home Games	222	60	12	0	2	20	12	29	.270	.351	.306
Road Games	275	95	18	3	2	23	22	45	.345	.455	.397
Grass Fields	363	103	17	2	4	32	22	59	.284	.375	.323
Artificial Turf	134	52	13	1	0	11	12	15	.388	.500	.446
April	57	19	1	1	2	4	2	11	.333	.491	.356
May	111	33	9	1	1	10	5	16	.297	.423	.325
June	91	32	6	0	1	5	13	9	.352	.451	.434
July	1	0	0	0	0	0	0	0	.000	.000	.000
August	114	31	7	1	0	15	8	15	.272	.351	.325
Sept./Oct.	123	40	7	0	0	9	6	23	.325	.382	.357
Leading Off Inn.	110	26	7	0	2	2	6	21	.236	.355	.282
Runners On	180	61	9	1	1	40	19	21	.339	.417	.401
Bases Empty	317	94	21	2	3	3	15	53	.297	.404	.330
Runners/Scor. Pos.	105	36	8	0	0	35	16	16	.343	.400	.427
Runners On/2 Out	71	24	4	0	0	17	8	7	.338	.394	.412
Scor. Pos./2 Out	49	17	2	0	0	16	7	7	.347	.388	.439
Late-Inning Pressure	78	26	5	0	1	8	6	16	.333	.436	.376
Leading Off	19	5	1	0	0	0	2	6	.263	.316	.333
Runners On	31	11	1	0	0	7	3	5	.355	.387	.400
Runners/Scor. Pos.	24	8	1	0	0	7	3	5	.333	.375	.393

RUNS BATTED IN	From 1B	From 2B	From 3B	Scoring Position
Totals	6/112	13/79	20/47	33/126
Percentage	5.4%	16.5%	42.6%	26.2%

Loves to face: Rob Dibble (.500, 5-for-10)
Darryl Kile (.667, 6-for-9)
Bob Ojeda (.382, 13-for-34, 5 2B, 1 3B, 3 HR)
Hates to face: Tom Browning (.132, 5-for-38, 1 HR)
John Candelaria (.136, 3-for-22, 1 HR)
Bruce Hurst (.118, 2-for-17, 3 BB)

Miscellaneous statistics: Ground outs-to-air outs ratio: 3.31 last season, highest in majors; 2.34 for career.... Grounded into 11 double plays in 80 opportunities (one per 7.3).... Drove in 13 of 28 runners from third base with less than two outs (46%).... Direction of balls hit to the outfield: 48% to left field, 31% to center, 21% to right batting left-handed; 18% to left field, 28% to center, 54% to right batting right-handed.... Base running: Advanced from first base to third on 14 of 31 outfield singles (45%); scored from second on 9 of 13 (69%).... Made 2.43 putouts per nine innings in center field.

Comments: Has batted .300 or better from each side of the plate in each of the last two seasons.... Had the league's highest batting average in day games (.348), on the road, on artificial turf, and against fly-ball pitchers.... McGee's ground outs-to-air outs ratio was well above 3.00; only three other regular starters had ratios above 2.00. Over the past 17 years, only one other player had more than three ground outs for every fly out: Felix Fermin (3.24 in 1989). McGee's career rate is the 3d highest of any player over the last 17 years, behind Milt Thompson and Wally Backman.... Hit safely in 25 consecutive road games, the longest streak in the majors last season.... Ranked fourth in the N.L. with 29 infield hits.... Laid down eight sacrifice bunts for Roger Craig, after having a career total of seven in nine years with St. Louis and one month with Oakland.... Tied Brett Butler for the N.L. lead in double plays by an outfielder with 3, the lowest total ever to lead either league.... In his first full season playing home games on natural grass, McGee produced the most lopsided breakdown in 10 seasons in the majors. Career batting averages: .301 on artificial turf, .293 on grass fields.... Felix Jose now looks like a hefty price for the Athletics to have paid to rent McGee for the 1990 postseason. That draft pick Oakland received as compensation for losing McGee as a Type-A free agent had better pan out. (Remember his name—Mike Neill, an outfielder from Villanova who led the Class-A Northwest League with a .350 batting average last summer.)

Fred McGriff
Bats Left

San Diego Padres	AB	H	2B	3B	HR	RBI	BB	SO	BA	SA	OBA
Season	528	147	19	1	31	106	105	135	.278	.494	.396
vs. Left-Handers	213	58	7	1	14	48	39	56	.272	.512	.380
vs. Right-Handers	315	89	12	0	17	58	66	79	.283	.483	.406
vs. Ground-Ballers	275	78	12	0	12	49	57	75	.284	.458	.399
vs. Fly-Ballers	253	69	7	1	19	57	48	60	.273	.534	.391
Home Games	239	67	7	0	18	53	60	68	.280	.536	.426
Road Games	289	80	12	1	13	53	45	67	.277	.460	.369
Grass Fields	387	111	14	0	25	79	78	101	.287	.517	.405
Artificial Turf	141	36	5	1	6	27	27	34	.255	.433	.371
April	72	23	2	0	2	8	17	22	.319	.431	.444
May	104	29	3	1	9	22	15	27	.279	.587	.372
June	78	17	3	0	4	20	23	16	.218	.410	.396
July	86	26	4	0	4	10	14	20	.302	.488	.400
August	96	22	2	0	7	24	18	31	.229	.469	.339
Sept./Oct.	92	30	5	0	5	22	18	19	.326	.543	.438
Leading Off Inn.	136	29	2	0	10	10	19	37	.213	.449	.310
Runners On	248	75	11	1	14	89	65	66	.302	.524	.439
Bases Empty	280	72	8	0	17	17	40	69	.257	.468	.352
Runners/Scor. Pos.	143	39	6	1	8	73	52	38	.273	.497	.453
Runners On/2 Out	106	27	3	1	2	17	35	33	.255	.358	.440
Scor. Pos./2 Out	55	10	1	1	0	11	28	18	.182	.236	.458
Late-Inning Pressure	65	18	2	0	3	7	24	20	.277	.446	.467
Leading Off	22	7	1	0	2	2	3	8	.318	.636	.400
Runners On	25	5	0	0	0	4	14	9	.200	.200	.475
Runners/Scor. Pos.	11	1	0	0	0	4	11	5	.091	.091	.522

RUNS BATTED IN	From 1B	From 2B	From 3B	Scoring Position
Totals	18/184	18/94	39/74	57/168
Percentage	9.8%	19.1%	52.7%	33.9%

Loves to face: Jimmy Jones (.385, 5-for-13, 3 HR)
Dennis Martinez (.556, 5-for-9, 1 HR)
Terry Mulholland (.600, 6-for-10, 2 HR)
Hates to face: John Candelaria (.048, 1-for-21, 2 BB)
Pete Harnisch (.067, 1-for-15)
Darryl Kile (0-for-4, 3 SO)

Miscellaneous statistics: Ground outs-to-air outs ratio: 1.30 last season, 1.12 for career.... Grounded into 14 double plays in 125 opportunities (one per 8.9).... Drove in 32 of 49 runners from third base with less than two outs (65%).... Direction of balls hit to the outfield: 38% to left field, 29% to center, 34% to right.... Base running: Advanced from first base to third on 6 of 42 outfield singles (14%); scored from second on 12 of 20 (60%).... Made 0.58 assists per nine innings at first base, 3d-lowest rate in N.L.

Comments: Averaged one homer every 17.0 at-bats last season, third-best rate in N.L., but poorest of his career.... Made huge strides vs. left-handers last season, finishing with a better home-run rate vs. lefties (one every 15.2 at-bats) than vs. righties (one every 18.5). Through 1990, his homer rate vs. lefties was one every 30.1 at-bats.... Career home-run rate vs. right-handed pitchers (one every 13.6 at-bats) is the best by any player since 1975.... The only player to hit at least 30 home runs in each of the last four seasons. Only two other active players have had four straight 30-homer seasons at any time in their careers: Mark McGwire and Dale Murphy. Since 1969, only Mike Schmidt (nine years in a row, 1979–87) has had a longer streak.... Career slugging percentage (.522) ranks second among active players to ex-Toronto teammate Cecil Fielder's .527 mark (minimum: 1000 AB). McGriff's .391 on-base percentage ranks fourth among the same group, and his career rate of one walk every 6.5 times up is second to Randy Milligan.... Led majors last season with 38 go-ahead RBIs and 26 intentional walks.... Started 11 double plays, the most by any N.L. first baseman.... Had higher batting average with runners on base than with bases empty last season for first time in five years in majors. Career breakdown: .287 with bases empty, .267 with runners on base, .247 with runners in scoring position.... Has batted below .200 with two outs and runners in scoring position in four of last five years, with only eight homers in 267 at-bats.

Kevin McReynolds

Bats Right

New York Mets	AB	H	2B	3B	HR	RBI	BB	SO	BA	SA	OBA
Season	522	135	32	1	16	74	49	46	.259	.416	.322
vs. Left-Handers	189	49	10	1	6	21	14	17	.259	.418	.311
vs. Right-Handers	333	86	22	0	10	53	35	29	.258	.414	.329
vs. Ground-Ballers	223	59	15	1	3	24	25	18	.265	.381	.341
vs. Fly-Ballers	301	76	17	0	13	50	24	28	.252	.439	.306
Home Games	236	56	12	1	7	33	17	14	.237	.386	.289
Road Games	286	79	20	0	9	41	32	32	.276	.441	.349
Grass Fields	361	88	21	1	10	48	29	32	.244	.391	.299
Artificial Turf	161	47	11	0	6	26	20	14	.292	.472	.372
April	47	6	3	0	1	6	3	3	.128	.255	.180
May	88	29	8	0	2	13	10	6	.330	.489	.394
June	97	33	9	0	4	18	9	8	.340	.557	.398
July	104	25	5	0	3	15	9	10	.240	.375	.301
August	90	21	2	1	2	7	7	10	.233	.344	.283
Sept./Oct.	96	21	5	0	4	15	11	9	.219	.396	.306
Leading Off Inn.	130	27	6	1	3	3	9	9	.208	.338	.259
Runners On	220	59	14	0	9	67	28	18	.268	.455	.350
Bases Empty	302	76	18	1	7	7	21	28	.252	.387	.300
Runners/Scor. Pos.	143	44	12	0	7	62	19	14	.308	.538	.383
Runners On/2 Out	105	28	7	0	6	35	18	13	.267	.505	.384
Scor. Pos./2 Out	75	21	6	0	4	30	14	12	.280	.520	.400
Late-Inning Pressure	82	26	7	0	6	22	7	11	.317	.622	.371
Leading Off	17	1	0	0	0	0	0	2	.059	.059	.059
Runners On	32	12	3	0	5	21	6	4	.375	.938	.474
Runners/Scor. Pos.	21	9	2	0	4	19	6	3	.429	1.095	.556

RUNS BATTED IN	From 1B	From 2B	From 3B	Scoring Position
Totals	10/140	27/110	21/52	48/162
Percentage	7.1%	24.5%	40.4%	29.6%

Loves to face: Rick Honeycutt (.500, 15-for-30, 1 HR)
Mark Langston (.500, 4-for-8, 1 HR)
Bruce Ruffin (.424, 14-for-33, 3 HR)

Hates to face: Ron Darling (.143, 3-for-21)
Mark Davis (.100, 3-for-30)
Jeff Reardon (.111, 1-for-9, 5 SO)

Miscellaneous statistics: Ground outs-to-air outs ratio: 0.57 last season, 2d lowest in N.L.; 0.73 for career. . . . Grounded into 8 double plays in 93 opportunities (one per 12). . . . Drove in 12 of 22 runners from third base with less than two outs (55%). . . . Direction of balls hit to the outfield: 45% to left field, 28% to center, 27% to right. . . . Base running: Advanced from first base to third on 8 of 24 outfield singles (33%); scored from second on 15 of 18 (83%). . . . Made 2.16 putouts per nine innings in left field.

Comments: Has declined in batting average, RBIs, and steals in each of three consecutive 500 at-bat seasons. Only one other player in history experienced three such years of successive declines: Eddie Mathews (1962–64). . . . Made 225 outs in the air last season, the most by any player in the majors. Second place: Howard Johnson (220). . . . Has batted major league high .541 (20-for-37) with five home runs with the bases loaded over the past four years. . . . Had 59 outfield assists in five seasons with Mets, tying Rusty Staub for second most in team history, five behind Cleon Jones. . . . On-base percentage leading off innings was 3d lowest in N.L. last season. . . . April batting average was 2d lowest in N.L., ahead of only Mark McLemore (.075). June batting average was 4th highest in league. . . . Averaged one strikeout every 12.6 plate appearances last year, best rate of his career. . . . He'll be playing home games on artificial turf for first time in his career. Career breakdown: .281 on plastic, .264 on grass. . . . Hit for a higher average in road games than he did at Shea Stadium in each of five years with Mets. . . . Has played no fewer than 143 games in each of the last eight seasons. That won't keep the ghost of Lou Gehrig pacing the floors at night, but only three other players have done that: Cal Ripken (of course), Wade Boggs, and Dale Murphy. . . . Did we miss something or was "team chemistry" cited as a factor in both the trade that brought Big Mac to the Mets in 1986 and the trade that sent him away in 1991?

Orlando Merced

Bats Left and Right

Pittsburgh Pirates	AB	H	2B	3B	HR	RBI	BB	SO	BA	SA	OBA
Season	411	113	17	2	10	50	64	81	.275	.399	.373
vs. Left-Handers	53	11	3	1	0	6	3	10	.208	.302	.263
vs. Right-Handers	358	102	14	1	10	44	61	71	.285	.413	.388
vs. Ground-Ballers	181	50	8	0	3	15	27	36	.276	.370	.368
vs. Fly-Ballers	230	63	9	2	7	35	37	45	.274	.422	.377
Home Games	192	49	9	1	5	22	35	41	.255	.391	.370
Road Games	219	64	8	1	5	28	29	40	.292	.406	.376
Grass Fields	105	34	3	1	3	17	8	17	.324	.457	.368
Artificial Turf	306	79	14	1	7	33	56	64	.258	.379	.375
April	22	7	0	1	0	3	6	5	.318	.409	.464
May	69	25	6	0	4	12	10	14	.362	.623	.450
June	66	10	1	0	0	2	8	16	.152	.167	.240
July	82	26	3	1	2	12	16	14	.317	.451	.429
August	90	24	6	0	1	11	12	17	.267	.367	.353
Sept./Oct.	82	21	1	0	3	10	12	15	.256	.378	.351
Leading Off Inn.	170	40	8	1	0	0	30	26	.235	.294	.350
Runners On	150	48	8	1	6	46	15	36	.320	.507	.383
Bases Empty	261	65	9	1	4	4	49	45	.249	.337	.368
Runners/Scor. Pos.	95	31	7	1	6	46	10	25	.326	.611	.387
Runners On/2 Out	74	24	7	0	3	27	11	16	.324	.541	.412
Scor. Pos./2 Out	55	19	6	0	3	27	7	12	.345	.618	.419
Late-Inning Pressure	49	11	3	0	2	7	12	9	.224	.408	.371
Leading Off	14	4	1	0	0	0	5	3	.286	.357	.474
Runners On	21	7	2	0	2	7	3	3	.333	.714	.400
Runners/Scor. Pos.	11	3	1	0	2	7	2	3	.273	.909	.357

RUNS BATTED IN	From 1B	From 2B	From 3B	Scoring Position
Totals	7/97	17/75	16/40	33/115
Percentage	7.2%	22.7%	40.0%	28.7%

Loves to face: Dave Smith (2-for-2, 2 HR, 2 BB)
John Smoltz (.500, 5-for-10, 1 HR)
Bob Tewksbury (.538, 7-for-13, 1 HR)

Hates to face: John Burkett (.111, 1-for-9)
Les Lancaster (0-for-8)
Scott Terry (0-for-6)

Miscellaneous statistics: Ground outs-to-air outs ratio: 1.88 last season, 1.81 for career. . . . Grounded into 6 double plays in 61 opportunities (one per 10). . . . Drove in 8 of 17 runners from third base with less than two outs (47%). . . . Direction of balls hit to the outfield: 31% to left field, 38% to center, 31% to right batting left-handed; 41% to left field, 18% to center, 41% to right batting right-handed. . . . Base running: Advanced from first base to third on 12 of 27 outfield singles (44%); scored from second on 10 of 16 (63%). . . . Made 0.62 assists per nine innings at first base.

Comments: Eight major league rookies started more games than Merced last year, but none scored more runs; he tied Ray Lankford with 83 runs scored, tops among rookies. . . . Batting average was 3d highest among rookies last season, behind the two award winners, Jeff Bagwell and Chuck Knoblauch. . . . The overall N.L. batting average for rookies last season was .231; Pirates rookies combined for a league-high .275 mark. Merced accounted for over 70 percent of the at-bats by Bucs rookies last season; their only other rookie with more than 25 at-bats was John Wehner, who hit .340 in 106 at-bats. . . . Hit 71 points higher with runners on base than with bases empty; his .324 mark with two outs and runners on base was 7th highest in the league. . . . Switch-hitter started 95 of 109 games in which Bucs faced a right-hander, but only one of 53 vs. left-handers. . . . Batted .200 in 80 at-bats in first inning, .293 in other at-bats. . . . Jim Leyland regularly batted his first basemen in leadoff spot (Merced and Gary Redus); Paul Molitor was the only other player in majors with 10 or more starts as a leadoff first baseman last season. . . . Had 10 go-ahead RBIs last year; in all 10 cases, Pirates held the lead the rest of the game, transforming each go-ahead RBI into a game-winning RBI. Merced tried to work that magic by hitting a leadoff home run in his first postseason start, Game 3 of the Championship Series at Atlanta. But that lead didn't even last an inning; Braves scored four times in first at-bat and won, 10–3.

Keith Miller

Bats Right

New York Mets	AB	H	2B	3B	HR	RBI	BB	SO	BA	SA	OBA
Season	275	77	22	1	4	23	23	44	.280	.411	.345
vs. Left-Handers	146	36	11	0	1	7	9	26	.247	.342	.297
vs. Right-Handers	129	41	11	1	3	16	14	18	.318	.488	.397
vs. Ground-Ballers	105	23	5	1	1	6	15	11	.219	.314	.333
vs. Fly-Ballers	170	54	17	0	3	17	8	33	.318	.471	.354
Home Games	158	46	12	0	2	10	13	23	.291	.405	.354
Road Games	117	31	10	1	2	13	10	21	.265	.419	.333
Grass Fields	186	51	14	0	2	13	18	30	.274	.382	.346
Artificial Turf	89	26	8	1	2	10	5	14	.292	.472	.344
April	17	4	2	0	0	0	2	2	.235	.353	.316
May	24	11	2	0	1	2	1	6	.458	.667	.480
June	6	2	0	0	0	0	0	1	.333	.333	.333
July	50	14	5	0	0	5	0	6	.280	.380	.294
August	58	10	1	0	1	4	6	13	.172	.241	.262
Sept./Oct.	120	36	12	1	2	12	14	16	.300	.467	.384
Leading Off Inn.	96	20	5	0	2	2	8	15	.208	.323	.276
Runners On	96	33	13	0	0	19	10	15	.344	.479	.413
Bases Empty	179	44	9	1	4	4	13	29	.246	.374	.308
Runners/Scor. Pos.	58	20	6	0	0	18	5	9	.345	.448	.400
Runners On/2 Out	41	18	5	0	0	15	6	6	.439	.561	.511
Scor. Pos./2 Out	28	12	3	0	0	14	2	3	.429	.536	.467
Late-Inning Pressure	34	10	2	0	1	4	8	5	.294	.441	.429
Leading Off	7	1	0	0	0	0	2	2	.143	.143	.333
Runners On	13	6	1	0	0	3	4	2	.462	.538	.588
Runners/Scor. Pos.	5	4	1	0	0	3	1	0	.800	1.000	.833

RUNS BATTED IN	From 1B	From 2B	From 3B	Scoring Position
Totals	2/57	10/50	7/23	17/73
Percentage	3.5%	20.0%	30.4%	23.3%

Loves to face: Jack Armstrong (.600, 3-for-5)
Bruce Ruffin (.467, 7-for-15, 4 2B, 1 3B)
Hates to face: Mark Langston (.083, 1-for-12, 1 2B)

Miscellaneous statistics: Ground outs-to-air outs ratio: 0.69 last season, 5th lowest in N.L.; 1.17 for career.... Grounded into 2 double plays in 36 opportunities (one per 18).... Drove in 2 of 11 runners from third base with less than two outs (18%).... Direction of balls hit to the outfield: 48% to left field, 31% to center, 21% to right.... Base running: Advanced from first base to third on 6 of 12 outfield singles (50%); scored from second on 8 of 10 (80%).... Made 3.16 assists per nine innings at second base.

Comments: His .318 batting average vs. right-handed pitchers was the highest among right-handed batters in N.L. (minimum: 100 AB vs. RHP). Career breakdown: .268 vs. left-handers, .260 vs. right-handers.... Had streak of 30 consecutive hitless at-bats vs. left-handed pitchers last year, longest streak by a Mets batter since Darryl Strawberry had 0-for-33 drought vs. southpaws in 1986.... Started 35 of 64 games in which the Mets faced a left-handed starter, only 27 of 97 vs. right-handers.... Started at four positions last season (2B, 3B, LF, RF), and appeared as a defensive substitiute at another two (CF, SS).... Has increased his total of games in each of five seasons in majors, but still hasn't cracked the 100-game plateau.... Batted .224 in 58 at-bats during the first inning, .295 thereafter.... He started more games after August 29 than he had started all season until then.... K.C.-bound career breakdown: .248 batting average on grass fields, .291 on artificial turf.... Batted .345 with runners in scoring position last season, after hitting .187 at those times prior to 1990.... Has had a higher batting average in Late-Inning Pressure Situations than in other at-bats in each of his five seasons in the majors.... Owns career stolen base percentage of .772 (44-for-57), despite going 0-for-5 in 1988.... Miller-for-Pecota part of Mets-Royals deal was looked upon as a swap of utility men, but Miller is more than three years younger.

Kevin Mitchell

Bats Right

San Francisco Giants	AB	H	2B	3B	HR	RBI	BB	SO	BA	SA	OBA
Season	371	95	13	1	27	69	43	57	.256	.515	.338
vs. Left-Handers	114	31	4	0	7	22	17	7	.272	.491	.370
vs. Right-Handers	257	64	9	1	20	47	26	50	.249	.525	.323
vs. Ground-Ballers	173	46	4	1	14	36	15	25	.266	.543	.335
vs. Fly-Ballers	198	49	9	0	13	33	28	32	.247	.490	.341
Home Games	190	46	7	1	9	30	17	26	.242	.432	.307
Road Games	181	49	6	0	18	39	26	31	.271	.602	.370
Grass Fields	273	66	8	1	18	45	25	39	.242	.476	.314
Artificial Turf	98	29	5	0	9	24	18	18	.296	.622	.402
April	67	18	2	0	7	16	8	3	.269	.612	.346
May	50	12	1	0	3	5	13	7	.240	.440	.397
June	15	7	2	0	3	8	2	2	.467	1.200	.529
July	92	24	2	0	6	18	6	19	.261	.478	.306
August	105	28	5	1	6	18	11	17	.267	.505	.347
Sept./Oct.	42	6	1	0	2	4	3	9	.143	.310	.217
Leading Off Inn.	87	25	3	0	7	7	8	15	.287	.563	.361
Runners On	179	43	7	0	12	54	25	25	.240	.480	.330
Bases Empty	192	52	6	1	15	15	18	32	.271	.547	.346
Runners/Scor. Pos.	99	24	3	0	6	39	19	13	.242	.455	.358
Runners On/2 Out	85	18	3	0	3	15	15	11	.212	.353	.330
Scor. Pos./2 Out	48	9	2	0	2	11	12	7	.188	.313	.350
Late-Inning Pressure	55	8	2	0	1	5	10	15	.145	.236	.284
Leading Off	16	4	1	0	0	0	1	3	.250	.313	.294
Runners On	24	3	1	0	0	4	6	8	.125	.167	.313
Runners/Scor. Pos.	12	2	1	0	0	4	5	2	.167	.250	.421

RUNS BATTED IN	From 1B	From 2B	From 3B	Scoring Position
Totals	13/125	13/69	16/46	29/115
Percentage	10.4%	18.8%	34.8%	25.2%

Loves to face: Jack Armstrong (.400, 4-for-10, 2 2B, 2 HR)
Joe Hesketh (.583, 7-for-12, 1 HR)
Rick Honeycutt (.500, 6-for-12, 2 2B, 2 HR)
Hates to face: Walt Terrell (.091, 1-for-11, 1 HR)
Bill Gullickson (.154, 4-for-26, 2 HR)
Rick Sutcliffe (.192, 5-for-26, 1 HR)

Miscellaneous statistics: Ground outs-to-air outs ratio: 0.71 last season, 0.76 for career.... Grounded into 6 double plays in 78 opportunities (one per 13).... Drove in 14 of 28 runners from third base with less than two outs (50%).... Direction of balls hit to the outfield: 36% to left field, 26% to center, 38% to right.... Base running: Advanced from first base to third on 3 of 21 outfield singles (14%); scored from second on 6 of 10 (60%).... Made 2.05 putouts per nine innings in left field.

Comments: Averaged one home run every 15.5 at-bats during his five years with Giants. In team history dating to 1883, only Willie McCovey (one every 15.4 at-bats) hit them out with greater frequency.... Averaged one strike-out every 7.4 plate appearances last season, lowest rate of his career.... Batting average in Late-Inning Pressure Situations was 3d lowest in the league, and follows a season in which he batted .351 in those situations.... Home-run rate last season (one every 13.7 at-bats) was best in N.L.; his career average (one per 17.0 at-bats) ranks seventh among 80 active players with at least 100 home runs.... There's no denying that a guy who hits 109 home runs over three seasons is a run producer, but his career percentage of teammates driven in from scoring position (27.4%) is no better than that of Dante Bichette, Ernest Riles, or new teammate Jay Buhner.... Next stop, Alaska? As Mitchell continues to move up the West Coast, keep in mind that over the last five years, the Kingdome has increased home-run output by 26 percent over other A.L. parks; Candlestick Park stands in the middle of the N.L. pack in its effect on home runs (2 percent increase). All other things being equal, that should increase Mitchell's home run output by about 13 percent. Something to keep in mind this spring when someone will inevitably say, "He could hit 70 in that ballpark." With the Giants, Mitchell averaged 32 homers for every 500 at-bats; a more logical prediction, given the Kingdome factor, would be 36.

Mickey Morandini

Bats Left

Philadelphia Phillies	AB	H	2B	3B	HR	RBI	BB	SO	BA	SA	OBA
Season	325	81	11	4	1	20	29	45	.249	.317	.313
vs. Left-Handers	65	12	0	0	0	3	3	11	.185	.185	.221
vs. Right-Handers	260	69	11	4	1	17	26	34	.265	.350	.334
vs. Ground-Ballers	166	39	4	2	1	11	14	20	.235	.301	.301
vs. Fly-Ballers	159	42	7	2	0	9	15	25	.264	.333	.326
Home Games	166	39	4	3	1	10	14	22	.235	.313	.295
Road Games	159	42	7	1	0	10	15	23	.264	.321	.331
Grass Fields	84	26	5	1	0	9	6	7	.310	.393	.356
Artificial Turf	241	55	6	3	1	11	23	38	.228	.290	.299
April	15	4	0	0	0	0	1	4	.267	.267	.313
May	46	13	1	0	0	3	4	4	.283	.304	.353
June	91	22	3	0	1	12	9	15	.242	.308	.307
July	61	14	4	1	0	3	5	4	.230	.328	.284
August	53	13	1	1	0	0	5	7	.245	.302	.322
Sept./Oct.	59	15	2	2	0	2	5	11	.254	.356	.313
Leading Off Inn.	84	24	4	0	0	0	9	12	.286	.333	.362
Runners On	125	30	2	2	1	20	8	16	.240	.312	.281
Bases Empty	200	51	9	2	0	0	21	29	.255	.320	.332
Runners/Scor. Pos.	64	17	0	1	1	19	4	10	.266	.344	.300
Runners On/2 Out	50	13	0	1	1	14	3	9	.260	.360	.302
Scor. Pos./2 Out	35	10	0	1	1	14	1	7	.286	.429	.306
Late-Inning Pressure	49	11	1	0	0	4	7	.224	.245	.296	
Leading Off	15	5	1	0	0	0	2	0	.333	.400	.444
Runners On	19	4	0	0	0	0	0	5	.211	.211	.211
Runners/Scor. Pos.	9	1	0	0	0	0	0	4	.111	.111	.111

RUNS BATTED IN	From 1B	From 2B	From 3B	Scoring Position
Totals	2/84	7/52	10/22	17/74
Percentage	2.4%	13.5%	45.5%	23.0%

Loves to face: Mike Bielecki (.400, 4-for-10)
Kelly Downs (.800, 4-for-5)
Bryn Smith (.333, 3-for-9, 2 2B)

Hates to face: Dennis Martinez (0-for-12)
Mike Morgan (.083, 1-for-12)
Jose Rijo (.083, 1-for-12, 1 3B)

Miscellaneous statistics: Ground outs-to-air outs ratio: 1.40 last season, 1.41 for career.... Grounded into 7 double plays in 63 opportunities (one per 9.0).... Drove in 5 of 6 runners from third base with less than two outs (83%).... Direction of balls hit to the outfield: 39% to left field, 32% to center, 29% to right.... Base running: Advanced from first base to third on 9 of 20 outfield singles (45%); scored from second on 5 of 9 (56%).... Made 2.98 assists per nine innings at second base.

Comments: The Phillies allowed fewer runs per nine innings with Morandini at second base (3.98) than they did with either Randy Ready (4.48) or Wally Backman (4.26).... Started 76 of 100 games in which they faced a right-handed starter, but only nine of 62 vs. lefties. Owns a .175 career average vs. left-handers, with one extra-base hit (a double) in 80 at-bats.... Had only 16 extra-base hits in 325 at-bats last season; Phillies had a total of 31 extra-base hits from second basemen last season, tying Pirates and Astros for fewest in N.L.... Special quiz for Phillies fans: Who are the three second basemen in team history who started the All-Star Game?...Batted .338 in the lower levels of Phillies' minor league system in 1989, but his batting average over two seasons with AAA Scranton was only .261, and his career average in the majors is .248.... He's reached base in 11 of 22 leadoff plate appearances in Late-Inning Pressure Situations, but he has never driven in a runner from scoring position in LIPS (0-for-10).... Quiz answer: Emil Verban (1947), Granny Hamner (1954), and Manny Trillo (1982) were Phillies second basemen who started an All-Star Game.... He'll turn 26 years old in April, and was the Phillies' 5th-round pick in the 1988 draft. The only position players from that draft who have made an impact on the major league level thus far are Robin Ventura, Luis Gonzalez, and Marquis Grissom. Hoping to join them: Morandini, Tino Martinez, Pat Kelly, and Mark Lewis.

Hal Morris

Bats Left

Cincinnati Reds	AB	H	2B	3B	HR	RBI	BB	SO	BA	SA	OBA
Season	478	152	33	1	14	59	46	61	.318	.479	.374
vs. Left-Handers	103	26	8	1	1	12	6	25	.252	.379	.288
vs. Right-Handers	375	126	25	0	13	47	40	36	.336	.507	.397
vs. Ground-Ballers	208	71	18	1	4	31	17	23	.341	.495	.389
vs. Fly-Ballers	274	82	15	0	10	29	29	39	.299	.464	.362
Home Games	238	76	20	1	9	33	21	31	.319	.525	.370
Road Games	240	76	13	0	5	26	25	30	.317	.433	.378
Grass Fields	130	48	10	0	4	20	15	15	.369	.538	.430
Artificial Turf	348	104	23	1	10	39	31	46	.299	.457	.352
April	53	19	7	0	2	9	0	5	.358	.604	.352
May	95	30	6	1	2	14	7	11	.316	.463	.365
June	79	21	5	0	1	7	5	14	.266	.367	.302
July	80	29	7	0	3	11	14	9	.363	.563	.453
August	76	23	3	0	2	7	6	8	.303	.421	.349
Sept./Oct.	95	30	5	0	4	11	14	14	.316	.495	.400
Leading Off Inn.	99	32	6	0	2	2	3	13	.323	.444	.343
Runners On	203	60	14	1	2	47	27	36	.296	.404	.367
Bases Empty	275	92	19	0	12	12	19	25	.335	.535	.380
Runners/Scor. Pos.	116	33	7	1	1	41	21	20	.284	.388	.375
Runners On/2 Out	89	26	5	0	1	22	13	18	.292	.382	.382
Scor. Pos./2 Out	59	19	4	0	1	21	11	12	.322	.441	.429
Late-Inning Pressure	71	23	0	0	2	5	5	13	.324	.408	.368
Leading Off	17	6	0	0	0	0	1	4	.353	.353	.389
Runners On	27	8	0	0	0	3	4	6	.296	.296	.387
Runners/Scor. Pos.	15	4	0	0	0	3	4	2	.267	.267	.421

RUNS BATTED IN	From 1B	From 2B	From 3B	Scoring Position
Totals	7/143	14/94	24/49	38/143
Percentage	4.9%	14.9%	49.0%	26.6%

Loves to face: John Burkett (.471, 8-for-17, 2 HR)
Scott Garrelts (.500, 6-for-12, 1 HR)
Greg Maddux (.615, 8-for-13)

Hates to face: Pete Harnisch (.111, 1-for-9)
Darryl Kile (0-for-6)
Bob Tewksbury (0-for-12)

Miscellaneous statistics: Ground outs-to-air outs ratio: 1.20 last season, 1.28 for career.... Grounded into 4 double plays in 100 opportunities (one per 25).... Drove in 16 of 28 runners from third base with less than two outs (57%).... Direction of balls hit to the outfield: 40% to left field, 28% to center, 32% to right.... Base running: Advanced from first base to third on 6 of 22 outfield singles (27%); scored from second on 11 of 17 (65%).... Made 0.84 assists per nine innings at first base, 3d-highest rate in N.L.

Comments: Lost the batting title to Terry Pendleton by slightly more than .001; Morris went 3-for-3 vs. Andy Benes on the final day of the season to draw within one hit of the title, but lefty reliever Rich Rodriguez got him to fly out on his final at-bat.... Posted the highest batting average vs. right-handed pitchers in the N.L. and the highest on grass fields in the majors.... Started 102 of 107 games in which Reds faced right-handed starters, 19 of 55 in which they faced lefties. Why? Try his .346 career average vs. right-handers, .230 vs. left-handers. Of his 21 career home runs, 20 have been hit off right-handers.... Has seven hits in 15 career at-bats with the bases loaded. As a team, Reds batted only .238 with bases full last season; Dodgers (.213) were only team in majors with a lower bases-loaded batting average.... In two years with Reds he has batted .326 at Riverfront, .327 on the road.... Career batting average in Late-Inning Pressure Situations is only .259, compared to .332 in other at-bats. He has driven in only 11 percent of runners from scoring position in LIPS, compared to 29 percent of runners from scoring position at other times.... One of four active players to hit .300 or better in both his rookie and sophomore seasons (minimum: 300 AB). The others: Wade Boggs, Mike Greenwell, and Kevin Seitzer. Last N.L. player to do it: Ken Oberkfell (1979–80).... Traded by Yankees to Reds for Tim Leary in December 1989. Since then, Morris's average is .327, Leary's .310 (13–29).

Dale Murphy

Bats Right

Philadelphia Phillies	AB	H	2B	3B	HR	RBI	BB	SO	BA	SA	OBA
Season	544	137	33	1	18	81	48	93	.252	.415	.309
vs. Left-Handers	192	57	13	0	5	25	17	33	.297	.443	.351
vs. Right-Handers	352	80	20	1	13	56	31	60	.227	.401	.286
vs. Ground-Ballers	254	62	16	1	5	37	25	42	.244	.374	.309
vs. Fly-Ballers	294	76	17	0	13	44	23	54	.259	.449	.308
Home Games	279	78	21	0	9	54	29	48	.280	.452	.343
Road Games	265	59	12	1	9	27	19	45	.223	.377	.272
Grass Fields	157	32	4	1	6	13	12	25	.204	.357	.257
Artificial Turf	387	105	29	0	12	68	36	68	.271	.439	.329
April	75	22	2	0	4	13	5	16	.293	.480	.333
May	90	21	5	0	3	11	7	15	.233	.389	.283
June	83	22	4	1	4	13	8	14	.265	.482	.326
July	86	17	5	0	1	9	9	14	.198	.291	.274
August	98	23	7	0	4	13	11	19	.235	.429	.312
Sept./Oct.	112	32	10	0	2	22	8	15	.286	.429	.325
Leading Off Inn.	126	34	11	0	6	6	12	18	.270	.500	.333
Runners On	257	63	15	1	6	69	24	47	.245	.381	.302
Bases Empty	287	74	18	0	12	12	24	46	.258	.446	.315
Runners/Scor. Pos.	155	37	10	0	4	63	18	30	.239	.381	.306
Runners On/2 Out	105	25	6	0	3	27	8	22	.238	.381	.292
Scor. Pos./2 Out	72	19	5	0	3	26	6	16	.264	.458	.338
Late-Inning Pressure	97	23	4	0	6	18	7	19	.237	.464	.286
Leading Off	25	7	0	0	3	3	1	6	.280	.640	.308
Runners On	46	9	4	0	1	13	4	11	.196	.348	.255
Runners/Scor. Pos.	28	6	3	0	1	13	3	6	.214	.429	.281

RUNS BATTED IN	From 1B	From 2B	From 3B	Scoring Position
Totals	9/187	15/112	39/78	54/190
Percentage	4.8%	13.4%	50.0%	28.4%

Loves to face: Atlee Hammaker (.442, 19-for-43, 5 HR)
Bob Ojeda (.500, 13-for-26, 1 HR)
Bob Patterson (.500, 2-for-4, 2 HR)
Hates to face: Rob Dibble (.158, 3-for-19, 10 SO)
Greg Maddux (.065, 2-for-31)
Mike Morgan (.185, 5-for-27, 0 BB)

Miscellaneous statistics: Ground outs-to-air outs ratio: 1.38 last season, 1.27 for career. . . . Grounded into 20 double plays in 133 opportunities (one per 6.7). . . . Drove in 27 of 44 runners from third base with less than two outs (61%). . . . Direction of balls hit to the outfield: 38% to left field, 31% to center, 32% to right. . . . Base running: Advanced from first base to third on 8 of 23 outfield singles (35%); scored from second on 8 of 12 (67%). . . . Made 2.09 putouts per nine innings in right field.

Comments: With 396 home runs, ranks third among active players behind Dave Winfield (406) and Eddie Murray (398). Murph has hit 198 with runners on base and 198 solo shots. . . . Needs 12 home runs to pass Duke Snider (407) and move into 10th place in N.L. history. . . . Has played in 150 or more games in each of 10 consecutive seasons. Cal Ripken also has a 10-year streak of 150 games; only Willie Mays (13), Pete Rose (12), Billy Williams (12), Lou Brock (11), Nellie Fox (11), and Ron Santo (11) have done it in the past. Why not Lou Gehrig? In 1935, Yankees played only 149 games (five scheduled games were canceled), leaving Old Biscuit Pants no way to get to 150. . . . Posted the league's 5th-lowest batting average in day games (.205). . . . Played the most innings among N.L. outfielders not involved in a double play last season. . . . He broke a streak of at least 100 strikeouts in nine straight seasons, third-longest streak in major league history. Last year, he averaged one strikeout every 6.4 plate appearances, his lowest strikeout rate in any of his 14 full seasons in majors. . . . But the increased contact came at a price: decreased power. His home-run rate in 1991 (one every 30.2 at-bats) was a career low. . . . Has batted below .230 against right-handed pitchers in each of the past four years. . . . He and Lou Whitaker both have streaks of 14 consecutive years as opening-day starters. For a list of longer streaks among active players, read the Eddie Murray comments.

Eddie Murray

Bats Left and Right

Los Angeles Dodgers	AB	H	2B	3B	HR	RBI	BB	SO	BA	SA	OBA
Season	576	150	23	1	19	96	55	74	.260	.403	.321
vs. Left-Handers	254	55	10	0	6	40	20	30	.217	.327	.269
vs. Right-Handers	322	95	13	1	13	56	35	44	.295	.463	.361
vs. Ground-Ballers	243	63	10	0	5	37	26	32	.259	.362	.326
vs. Fly-Ballers	333	87	13	1	14	59	29	42	.261	.432	.317
Home Games	282	76	9	1	11	50	35	41	.270	.426	.347
Road Games	294	74	14	0	8	46	20	33	.252	.381	.295
Grass Fields	419	116	13	1	16	73	46	49	.277	.427	.343
Artificial Turf	157	34	10	0	3	23	9	25	.217	.338	.257
April	50	15	3	0	2	5	9	2	.300	.480	.407
May	100	30	5	0	4	22	7	14	.300	.470	.339
June	105	24	6	0	2	20	10	12	.229	.343	.291
July	99	17	4	0	1	12	11	20	.172	.242	.248
August	111	29	3	0	4	13	9	16	.261	.396	.317
Sept./Oct.	111	35	2	1	6	24	9	10	.315	.514	.364
Leading Off Inn.	149	33	3	0	5	5	3	17	.221	.342	.237
Runners On	276	75	13	1	9	86	40	41	.272	.424	.355
Bases Empty	300	75	10	0	10	10	15	33	.250	.383	.286
Runners/Scor. Pos.	155	40	9	0	5	75	34	23	.258	.413	.376
Runners On/2 Out	126	34	5	0	5	37	18	21	.270	.429	.361
Scor. Pos./2 Out	76	21	4	0	3	32	17	12	.276	.447	.409
Late-Inning Pressure	84	21	3	1	3	17	10	9	.250	.417	.320
Leading Off	18	3	0	0	1	1	0	1	.167	.333	.167
Runners On	47	14	2	1	2	16	9	6	.298	.511	.390
Runners/Scor. Pos.	24	5	1	0	1	13	8	4	.208	.375	.371

RUNS BATTED IN	From 1B	From 2B	From 3B	Scoring Position
Totals	14/204	27/119	36/75	63/194
Percentage	6.9%	22.7%	48.0%	32.5%

Loves to face: Jose DeLeon (.414, 12-for-29, 4 HR)
Kevin Gross (.412, 7-for-17, 1 HR, 6 BB)
Ed Whitson (.429, 12-for-28, 4 HR)
Hates to face: Bruce Hurst (.149, 10-for-67, 4 HR)
Mike Morgan (.118, 4-for-34, 7 BB)
Randy Myers (.067, 1-for-15, 2 BB)

Miscellaneous statistics: Ground outs-to-air outs ratio: 1.09 last season, 1.04 for career. . . . Grounded into 17 double plays in 137 opportunities (one per 8.1). . . . Drove in 23 of 36 runners from third base with less than two outs (64%). . . . Direction of balls hit to the outfield: 35% to left field, 26% to center, 40% to right batting left-handed; 44% to left field, 33% to center, 23% to right batting right-handed. . . . Base running: Advanced from first base to third on 6 of 34 outfield singles (18%); scored from second on 6 of 18 (33%), 2d-lowest rate in N.L. . . . Made 0.89 assists per nine innings at first base, 2d-highest rate in N.L.

Comments: He has driven in at least 75 runs in all 15 seasons in majors from start of career, tying major league record set by Hall-of-Famer Al Simmons (1924–38). The only other players with 75-RBI streaks as long at any time during a career: Hank Aaron (19 years, 1955–73) and Mel Ott (15 years, 1928–42). . . . Needs two home runs to reach 400 for his career; coupled with 2502 hits, he would become 15th player in history with both 400 homers and 2500 hits. Twelve of the others are already enshrined in Cooperstown; the other two (Reggie Jackson and Dave Winfield) are not yet eligible. . . . Has driven in over 38 percent of runners from scoring position in Late-Inning Pressure Situations during his career; among active players, only Jose Canseco has a higher rate. . . . He has been in the starting lineup on opening day in each of the last 15 seasons, third-longest current streak in the majors, behind Dwight Evans (17 years) and Dave Parker (18 years). . . . On-base percentage leading off innings was the lowest in N.L. . . . Career total of 2060 games at first base leads active players and stands seventh on the all-time list; needs only 77 more games to move past Lou Gehrig into the third place. The all-time record: 2377 games by turn-of-the-century first baseman Jake Beckley. . . . Had 14 grand-slam homers over his first 10 seasons and appeared to be a serious threat to Gehrig's record of 23 career slams. But he has had only one home run in 44 bases-loaded at-bats over the past five years.

Otis Nixon

Bats Left and Right

Atlanta Braves	AB	H	2B	3B	HR	RBI	BB	SO	BA	SA	OBA
Season	401	119	10	1	0	26	47	40	.297	.327	.371
vs. Left-Handers	95	29	5	0	0	7	14	7	.305	.358	.400
vs. Right-Handers	306	90	5	1	0	19	33	33	.294	.317	.362
vs. Ground-Ballers	174	60	5	1	0	11	16	12	.345	.385	.401
vs. Fly-Ballers	227	59	5	0	0	15	31	28	.260	.282	.349
Home Games	207	68	8	0	0	15	26	18	.329	.367	.404
Road Games	194	51	2	1	0	11	21	22	.263	.284	.335
Grass Fields	280	90	10	0	0	20	35	30	.321	.357	.396
Artificial Turf	121	29	0	1	0	6	12	10	.240	.256	.311
April	21	5	0	0	0	2	4	1	.238	.238	.360
May	69	27	5	0	0	5	10	4	.391	.464	.463
June	96	28	1	0	0	3	6	11	.292	.302	.346
July	102	37	2	0	0	6	13	13	.363	.382	.435
August	78	11	1	0	0	5	9	8	.141	.154	.227
Sept./Oct.	35	11	1	1	0	5	5	3	.314	.400	.390
Leading Off Inn.	172	57	2	0	0	0	20	16	.331	.343	.404
Runners On	120	33	3	1	0	26	14	13	.275	.317	.348
Bases Empty	281	86	7	0	0	0	33	27	.306	.331	.381
Runners/Scor. Pos.	77	24	3	1	0	26	9	9	.312	.377	.378
Runners On/2 Out	40	13	1	0	0	10	8	4	.325	.350	.449
Scor. Pos./2 Out	32	12	1	0	0	10	5	4	.375	.406	.474
Late-Inning Pressure	48	15	2	1	0	3	10	4	.313	.396	.431
Leading Off	12	5	1	0	0	0	0	2	.417	.500	.417
Runners On	19	6	0	1	0	3	4	2	.316	.421	.435
Runners/Scor. Pos.	10	4	0	1	0	3	3	1	.400	.600	.538

RUNS BATTED IN	From 1B	From 2B	From 3B	Scoring Position
Totals	1/69	14/65	11/27	25/92
Percentage	1.4%	21.5%	40.7%	27.2%

Loves to face: Jose DeLeon (.294, 5-for-17, 7 BB)
Ken Hill (.600, 6-for-10)
John Smiley (.300, 9-for-30)

Hates to face: Tom Browning (.083, 2-for-24, 3 BB)
Doug Drabek (.095, 2-for-21)
Ramon Martinez (0-for-9)

Miscellaneous statistics: Ground outs-to-air outs ratio: 1.57 last season, 1.45 for career.... Grounded into 5 double plays in 60 opportunities (one per 12).... Drove in 8 of 14 runners from third base with less than two outs (57%).... Direction of balls hit to the outfield: 36% to left field, 43% to center, 21% to right batting left-handed; 38% to left field, 44% to center, 19% to right batting right-handed.... Base running: Advanced from first base to third on 11 of 24 outfield singles (46%); scored from second on 17 of 21 (81%).... Made 2.01 putouts per nine innings in right field.

Comments: Captured regular job with .391 batting average in May, second in N.L. behind teammate Terry Pendleton.... Led league in batting for the month of July. He hit .345 over three-month span before suffering through August with league's lowest batting average. Suspended by Commissioner's office as repeat drug offender on September 16; Lonnie Smith took his spot in the lineup.... Entered last season with a career average of .228, having never accumulated as many as 300 at-bats in any season.... Had one of five hitting streaks of 20 or more games in majors last season: Brett Butler (23), Brian McRae (22), Joe Orsulak (21), Nixon (20), and Chuck Knoblauch (20).... His on-base percentage leading off innings was 3d highest in the league.... Helped Braves amass 199 hits, 84 stolen bases, 127 runs scored, and .298 batting average from the leadoff spot, each the best in the league. Average leadoff performance for N.L. teams: 174 hits, 40 steals, 104 runs, .261 batting average.... Over past two seasons, has had slightly higher stolen-base percentage vs. left-handed pitchers (82 percent, 51-for-62) than vs. right-handers (76 percent, 71-for-94). Ranked second in N.L. with 42 infield hits.... One of seven players to start at least ten games in each of the three outfield positions.... Braves outfielders led N.L. in runs (324) and home runs (67) last season. Nixon contributed 81 runs scored but not a single home run.

Joe Oliver

Bats Right

Cincinnati Reds	AB	H	2B	3B	HR	RBI	BB	SO	BA	SA	OBA
Season	269	58	11	0	11	41	18	53	.216	.379	.265
vs. Left-Handers	131	30	5	0	8	27	15	24	.229	.450	.308
vs. Right-Handers	138	28	6	0	3	14	3	29	.203	.312	.220
vs. Ground-Ballers	145	33	7	0	5	23	6	23	.228	.379	.258
vs. Fly-Ballers	124	25	4	0	6	18	12	30	.202	.379	.272
Home Games	145	29	6	0	7	17	11	27	.200	.386	.256
Road Games	124	29	5	0	4	24	7	26	.234	.371	.275
Grass Fields	78	18	2	0	4	19	4	19	.231	.410	.268
Artificial Turf	191	40	9	0	7	22	14	34	.209	.366	.263
April	32	5	2	0	0	1	3	9	.156	.219	.229
May	31	6	1	0	0	0	1	7	.194	.226	.219
June	35	10	3	0	1	3	4	6	.286	.457	.359
July	56	13	2	0	3	10	2	7	.232	.429	.259
August	66	11	2	0	4	14	6	15	.167	.379	.236
Sept./Oct.	49	13	1	0	3	13	2	9	.265	.469	.294
Leading Off Inn.	71	14	2	0	2	2	2	16	.197	.310	.219
Runners On	112	26	5	0	8	38	9	22	.232	.491	.289
Bases Empty	157	32	6	0	3	3	9	31	.204	.299	.247
Runners/Scor. Pos.	62	16	4	0	5	32	8	13	.258	.565	.343
Runners On/2 Out	44	10	4	0	3	18	7	8	.227	.523	.333
Scor. Pos./2 Out	27	7	3	0	2	16	6	5	.259	.593	.394
Late-Inning Pressure	46	11	0	0	0	2	5	7	.239	.239	.314
Leading Off	11	3	0	0	0	0	1	3	.273	.273	.333
Runners On	16	2	0	0	0	2	2	2	.125	.125	.222
Runners/Scor. Pos.	8	2	0	0	0	2	1	1	.250	.250	.333

RUNS BATTED IN	From 1B	From 2B	From 3B	Scoring Position
Totals	7/79	11/46	12/29	23/75
Percentage	8.9%	23.9%	41.4%	30.7%

Loves to face: Steve Avery (.462, 6-for-13, 1 HR)
Charlie Leibrandt (.333, 6-for-18, 2 HR)
Zane Smith (.391, 9-for-23, 3 HR)

Hates to face: John Burkett (0-for-9)
Jose DeLeon (.083, 1-for-12)
Bob Ojeda (.056, 1-for-18)

Miscellaneous statistics: Ground outs-to-air outs ratio: 1.07 last season, 0.88 for career.... Grounded into 14 double plays in 50 opportunities (one per 3.6), worst rate in N.L.... Drove in 8 of 16 runners from third base with less than two outs (50%).... Direction of balls hit to the outfield: 44% to left field, 29% to center, 27% to right.... Base running: Advanced from first base to third on 0 of 3 outfield singles (0%); scored from second on 1 of 5 (20%).... Opposing base stealers: 70-for-98 (71%).

Comments: Potential lobbyist for more day games: He owns a .314 career batting average in day games compared to .210 at night. Perspective on that disparity: Don Mattingly is a .314 career hitter; Steve Jeltz is a .210 career hitter.... Started 51 of 55 games in which Reds faced a left-handed starter, 27 of 107 in which they faced right-handers.... Caught 47 percent of Reds' innings last season; Jeff Reed caught 48 percent. Theirs was the most even distribution of innings between the top two catchers on any club in the majors last season. A close second: K.C.'s Mike Macfarlane and Brent Mayne.... Reds pitchers had 3.57 ERA with Reed catching, 3.98 with Oliver.... Reds catchers made 19 errors last season (Oliver had 11); only the Cubs (20) had more.... August batting average was 2d lowest in the league.... Nine of his 11 home runs were hit from the 8th spot in lineup, the most by any N.L. player. Mike Gallego led A.L. with 10 such homers. Including five homers by other 8th-place hitters, Reds had 14 from that spot in order to lead majors.... Career total of 784 at-bats is third highest among active players who have never hit a triple, behind Craig Worthington (1105) and Sam Horn (836).... Led the league with six home runs and 21 RBIs against the Braves last season; no other player drove in more than 13 runs vs. Atlanta. (Despite that, Jack Lang assures us that no Atlanta writer voted for Oliver as the league's MVP.)

Greg Olson
Bats Right

Atlanta Braves	AB	H	2B	3B	HR	RBI	BB	SO	BA	SA	OBA
Season	411	99	25	0	6	44	44	48	.241	.345	.316
vs. Left-Handers	100	29	8	0	2	17	10	12	.290	.430	.348
vs. Right-Handers	311	70	17	0	4	27	34	36	.225	.318	.306
vs. Ground-Ballers	172	40	9	0	4	21	15	18	.233	.355	.302
vs. Fly-Ballers	239	59	16	0	2	23	29	30	.247	.339	.327
Home Games	202	58	11	0	6	31	15	18	.287	.431	.330
Road Games	209	41	14	0	0	13	29	30	.196	.263	.303
Grass Fields	306	76	18	0	6	34	29	34	.248	.366	.312
Artificial Turf	105	23	7	0	0	10	15	14	.219	.286	.328
April	22	11	2	0	0	1	1	3	.500	.591	.522
May	54	11	0	0	1	7	5	6	.204	.259	.279
June	73	17	5	0	2	7	6	5	.233	.384	.300
July	76	20	5	0	2	12	9	8	.263	.408	.337
August	71	18	4	0	1	9	9	9	.254	.352	.333
Sept./Oct.	115	22	9	0	0	8	14	17	.191	.270	.282
Leading Off Inn.	103	24	5	0	3	3	10	14	.233	.369	.301
Runners On	160	45	11	0	2	40	21	15	.281	.387	.364
Bases Empty	251	54	14	0	4	4	23	33	.215	.319	.284
Runners/Scor. Pos.	92	27	5	0	1	33	19	10	.293	.380	.400
Runners On/2 Out	74	25	5	0	0	21	15	7	.338	.405	.449
Scor. Pos./2 Out	51	19	3	0	0	19	13	5	.373	.431	.500
Late-Inning Pressure	63	12	2	0	0	6	8	10	.190	.222	.284
Leading Off	20	2	0	0	0	0	4	3	.100	.100	.250
Runners On	24	7	2	0	0	6	3	5	.292	.375	.345
Runners/Scor. Pos.	15	5	2	0	0	6	2	3	.333	.467	.368

RUNS BATTED IN	From 1B	From 2B	From 3B	Scoring Position
Totals	6/112	18/71	14/39	32/110
Percentage	5.4%	25.4%	35.9%	29.1%

Loves to face: Tim Belcher (.222, 2-for-9, 1 HR, 6 BB)
    Mark Gardner (.667, 4-for-6)
    Zane Smith (.444, 4-for-9)

Hates to face: Andy Benes (.077, 1-for-13, 2 BB)
    Mike Morgan (0-for-9)
    Vicente Palacios (0-for-7)

Miscellaneous statistics: Ground outs-to-air outs ratio: 1.40 last season, 1.34 for career.... Grounded into 13 double plays in 71 opportunities (one per 5.5).... Drove in 8 of 18 runners from third base with less than two outs (44%).... Direction of balls hit to the outfield: 40% to left field, 32% to center, 28% to right.... Base running: Advanced from first base to third on 4 of 18 outfield singles (22%); scored from second on 10 of 17 (59%).... Opposing base stealers: 95-for-132 (72%).

Comments: Caught just under 70 percent of the Braves' innings during the regular season, but caught 127⅓ of 128⅓ innings during postseason.... Olson caught all but two of Tom Glavine's 246⅔ innings during the season.... Down the stretch Olson was an ironman, starting all 32 games from September 1 until the title clinching on October 5.... Braves pitchers had a 3.30 ERA with Olson, 3.93 with other catchers. Opponents' stolen-base percentage was virtually the same with Olson (72%) as with other guys (71%).... His .338 batting average with two outs and runners on base was the second highest in N.L.; Marquis Grissom (.346) was the leader. Game-winning double in ninth inning of Game Six of Championship Series, which drove in the only run of game, came in exactly that situation.... Also ranked second in N.L. with .373 average with two outs and runners in scoring position; Dave Magadan (.380) was the leader there.... Has only two hits in 17 career at-bats with the bases loaded, but both of them went for extra bases (a home run and a double).... Career breakdowns: .223 with the bases empty, .290 with runners on base; .303 vs. left-handers, .221 vs. right-handers; .287 (10 HR) at Atlanta Stadium, .213 (3 HR) on the road.... One of four N.L. players who went homerless on the road last season in at least 200 at-bats: Brett Butler (320 AB), Tom Pagnozzi (238), Olson (209), and Bip Roberts (201). None of the other players had more than three homers in their own ballparks, while Olson hit six in Atlanta.

Paul O'Neill
Bats Left

Cincinnati Reds	AB	H	2B	3B	HR	RBI	BB	SO	BA	SA	OBA
Season	532	136	36	0	28	91	73	107	.256	.481	.346
vs. Left-Handers	169	34	9	0	3	15	11	52	.201	.308	.254
vs. Right-Handers	363	102	27	0	25	76	62	55	.281	.562	.385
vs. Ground-Ballers	242	66	20	0	10	36	33	41	.273	.479	.361
vs. Fly-Ballers	294	71	17	0	18	55	40	67	.241	.483	.332
Home Games	268	76	21	0	20	59	32	45	.284	.586	.361
Road Games	264	60	15	0	8	32	41	62	.227	.375	.331
Grass Fields	161	46	9	0	8	26	24	38	.286	.491	.378
Artificial Turf	371	90	27	0	20	65	49	69	.243	.477	.332
April	61	13	4	0	4	7	10	11	.213	.475	.324
May	80	23	5	0	6	18	12	12	.287	.575	.380
June	97	27	8	0	5	22	12	16	.278	.515	.364
July	80	17	4	0	2	6	18	18	.213	.338	.284
August	99	26	7	0	6	20	19	25	.263	.515	.381
Sept./Oct.	115	30	8	0	5	18	12	25	.261	.461	.328
Leading Off Inn.	109	25	8	0	5	5	11	19	.229	.440	.306
Runners On	252	67	15	0	16	79	47	52	.266	.516	.380
Bases Empty	280	69	21	0	12	12	26	55	.246	.450	.313
Runners/Scor. Pos.	149	39	9	0	7	60	36	30	.262	.463	.403
Runners On/2 Out	120	33	3	0	9	40	24	28	.275	.525	.396
Scor. Pos./2 Out	76	21	3	0	4	30	17	15	.276	.474	.409
Late-Inning Pressure	70	13	3	0	2	7	17	25	.186	.314	.345
Leading Off	15	2	1	0	1	1	5	5	.133	.400	.350
Runners On	35	5	1	0	1	6	9	13	.143	.257	.318
Runners/Scor. Pos.	21	2	1	0	0	4	7	10	.095	.143	.321

RUNS BATTED IN	From 1B	From 2B	From 3B	Scoring Position
Totals	18/177	21/117	24/58	45/175
Percentage	10.2%	17.9%	41.4%	25.7%

Loves to face: Scott Garrelts (.387, 12-for-31, 3 HR)
    Mike Harkey (.625, 5-for-8, 2 HR)
    Jay Howell (.800, 8-for-10, 2 2B, 1 3B, 2 HR)

Hates to face: Andy Benes (.176, 3-for-17, 3 BB, 9 SO)
    Tom Glavine (.050, 1-for-20)
    Bob Walk (.083, 1-for-12, 3 BB)

Miscellaneous statistics: Ground outs-to-air outs ratio: 0.83 last season, 0.92 for career.... Grounded into 8 double plays in 107 opportunities (one per 13).... Drove in 15 of 29 runners from third base with less than two outs (52%).... Direction of balls hit to the outfield: 30% to left field, 32% to center, 39% to right.... Base running: Advanced from first base to third on 9 of 19 outfield singles (47%); scored from second on 8 of 12 (67%).... Made 2.15 putouts per nine innings in right field, 3d-highest rate in N.L.

Comments: Fizzled vs. left-handers in 1991 after showing promise (.259) against them in Reds' championship season.... Had the league's 10th-lowest batting average in a career-high 181 plate appearances vs. left-handers last year. Started 38 of 55 games in which Reds faced left-handed starters.... Career numbers: .281, one homer every 30 at-bats, vs. right-handed pitchers; .212, one homer every 51 at-bats, vs. left-handers.... Five N.L. batters had extra-base hits in four consecutive at-bats last season, but O'Neill was the only player with two such streaks.... Amassed 64 extra-base hits last season to lead N.L. right fielders. Remember that Andre Dawson and Darryl Strawberry play that position.... Committed only two errors in 316 chances to lead N.L. right fielders in fielding for the second consecutive season. Career totals: 40 assists, 16 errors; last two seasons: 25 assists, four errors.... Led the league with six home runs against the Cubs and 18 RBIs against the Dodgers.... With the departure of Eric Davis, O'Neill and Tom Browning are the only players remaining from the 1985 Reds.... Career breakdown: .280 at Riverfront Stadium, .245 in road games. Has hit 57 of 82 career homers at Riverfront.... Reds outfielders combined for a .248 batting average last season, the lowest of any N.L. club. The league average for outfielders was .263.

67

3834

Jose Oquendo — Bats Left and Right

St. Louis Cardinals

	AB	H	2B	3B	HR	RBI	BB	SO	BA	SA	OBA
Season	366	88	11	4	1	26	67	48	.240	.301	.357
vs. Left-Handers	150	36	8	1	1	15	29	21	.240	.327	.365
vs. Right-Handers	216	52	3	3	0	11	38	27	.241	.282	.352
vs. Ground-Ballers	166	38	5	3	0	11	26	22	.229	.295	.332
vs. Fly-Ballers	200	50	6	1	1	15	41	26	.250	.305	.377
Home Games	184	48	3	2	0	14	32	19	.261	.299	.372
Road Games	182	40	8	2	1	12	35	29	.220	.302	.342
Grass Fields	96	16	2	0	0	8	24	15	.167	.188	.331
Artificial Turf	270	72	9	4	1	18	43	33	.267	.341	.367
April	60	12	2	2	0	5	13	8	.200	.300	.338
May	48	7	0	1	1	5	5	5	.146	.250	.226
June	73	20	1	0	0	4	21	9	.274	.288	.436
July	61	20	3	1	0	1	13	8	.328	.410	.453
August	83	23	5	0	0	13	9	14	.277	.337	.340
Sept./Oct.	41	6	0	0	0	2	6	4	.146	.146	.255
Leading Off Inn.	96	21	4	0	0	0	12	12	.219	.260	.306
Runners On	133	34	4	1	0	25	40	14	.256	.301	.424
Bases Empty	233	54	7	3	1	1	27	34	.232	.300	.312
Runners/Scor. Pos.	80	20	3	1	0	25	29	12	.250	.313	.438
Runners On/2 Out	60	11	2	1	0	9	21	7	.183	.250	.395
Scor. Pos./2 Out	43	8	2	1	0	9	17	7	.186	.279	.417
Late-Inning Pressure	54	16	1	1	0	5	11	6	.296	.352	.418
Leading Off	14	4	1	0	0	0	4	1	.286	.357	.444
Runners On	21	6	0	0	0	5	4	1	.286	.286	.407
Runners/Scor. Pos.	13	2	0	0	0	5	3	1	.154	.154	.294

RUNS BATTED IN	From 1B	From 2B	From 3B	Scoring Position
Totals	1/90	4/53	20/49	24/102
Percentage	1.1%	7.5%	40.8%	23.5%

Loves to face: Tom Browning (.400, 10-for-25, 2 HR, 0 SO)
Norm Charlton (.417, 5-for-12, 1 HR)
Ed Whitson (.409, 9-for-22)
Hates to face: Dwight Gooden (.077, 2-for-26)
Bruce Hurst (.148, 4-for-27)
Bill Landrum (0-for-10)

Miscellaneous statistics: Ground outs-to-air outs ratio: 1.10 last season, 1.02 for career.... Grounded into 5 double plays in 75 opportunities (one per 15).... Drove in 14 of 23 runners from third base with less than two outs (61%).... Direction of balls hit to the outfield: 36% to left field, 36% to center, 28% to right batting left-handed; 37% to left field, 27% to center, 37% to right batting right-handed.... Base running: Advanced from first base to third on 6 of 19 outfield singles (32%); scored from second on 8 of 8 (100%).... Made 3.44 assists per nine innings at second base, highest rate in majors.

Comments: Career rate of one error every 132 chances at second base is the lowest among all players in major league history with at least 500 games there. In the record books, career fielding-percentage leaders are based on a minimum of 1000 games, so Oquendo (546 games at second base) does not qualify. The official record holder is Ryne Sandberg, with one error every 98 chances.... Owned the lowest batting average in the major leagues on grass fields last season, after batting above .300 on grass in three of the previous four seasons.... Had a streak of 29 consecutive hitless at-bats vs. left-handed pitchers, the 3d longest in the majors. Career batting averages: .263 vs. LHP, .260 vs. RHP. He has 11 career HRs off southpaws, and one off Doug Bair.... Curious: Oquendo has hit exactly one home run in each of the last three seasons. Over the past 15 years, only one other player has had a three-year streak (400 or more plate appearances): Wally Backman (1984–86). Curiouser: Don Kessinger had a streak of seven seasons in even-numbered years only (1966–78). Anyone remember Bud Abbott's "Kangaroo Straight?"...Stole 10 bases in 11 attempts for the Mets in 1984, but has only 15 steals in 36 attempts since then.... When Al Osuna hit him with a pitch last July 24, it ended a streak of 2651 consecutive times up without being hit by a pitch; Oquendo was last hit by a pitch in April 1984 while with the Mets. Properly incensed, Oquendo enacted revenge on Osuna the next time up by getting the game-winning hit in the bottom of the ninth.

Spike Owen — Bats Left and Right

Montreal Expos

	AB	H	2B	3B	HR	RBI	BB	SO	BA	SA	OBA
Season	424	108	22	8	3	26	42	61	.255	.366	.321
vs. Left-Handers	200	61	18	2	1	12	14	25	.305	.430	.350
vs. Right-Handers	224	47	4	6	2	14	28	36	.210	.308	.296
vs. Ground-Ballers	207	55	7	3	2	10	20	26	.266	.357	.329
vs. Fly-Ballers	221	53	15	5	1	16	22	36	.240	.367	.308
Home Games	161	34	6	1	1	7	19	26	.211	.280	.291
Road Games	263	74	16	7	2	19	23	35	.281	.418	.339
Grass Fields	141	37	6	4	1	12	13	22	.262	.383	.323
Artificial Turf	283	71	16	4	2	14	29	39	.251	.357	.320
April	55	13	2	1	0	3	2	6	.236	.309	.263
May	79	16	3	0	1	6	13	14	.203	.278	.323
June	63	11	4	2	0	1	11	8	.175	.302	.297
July	63	18	5	0	1	5	5	6	.286	.413	.333
August	54	16	2	2	0	5	5	13	.296	.407	.344
Sept./Oct.	110	34	6	3	1	6	6	14	.309	.445	.342
Leading Off Inn.	93	27	4	3	1	1	10	10	.290	.430	.359
Runners On	164	38	7	3	1	24	20	26	.232	.329	.309
Bases Empty	260	70	15	5	2	2	22	35	.269	.388	.329
Runners/Scor. Pos.	93	20	5	1	0	20	18	19	.215	.290	.330
Runners On/2 Out	69	11	2	1	1	6	13	17	.159	.261	.293
Scor. Pos./2 Out	40	4	1	0	0	3	12	14	.100	.125	.308
Late-Inning Pressure	71	22	4	0	2	6	8	12	.310	.451	.380
Leading Off	17	9	1	0	1	1	4	4	.529	.765	.619
Runners On	28	8	1	0	1	5	2	5	.286	.429	.333
Runners/Scor. Pos.	14	3	1	0	0	3	2	4	.214	.286	.313

RUNS BATTED IN	From 1B	From 2B	From 3B	Scoring Position
Totals	4/110	8/69	11/36	19/105
Percentage	3.6%	11.6%	30.6%	18.1%

Loves to face: Juan Agosto (.455, 5-for-11, 1 HR, 6 ground outs)
Tom Browning (.476, 10-for-21)
Ed Whitson (.444, 8-for-18, 2 HR)
Hates to face: Mike Bielecki (0-for-20)
Tom Candiotti (.032, 1-for-31, 2 BB)
Orel Hershiser (0-for-13)

Miscellaneous statistics: Ground outs-to-air outs ratio: 0.96 last season, 1.14 for career.... Grounded into 11 double plays in 71 opportunities (one per 6.5).... Drove in 10 of 20 runners from third base with less than two outs (50%).... Direction of balls hit to the outfield: 32% to left field, 40% to center, 28% to right batting left-handed; 45% to left field, 28% to center, 26% to right batting right-handed.... Base running: Advanced from first base to third on 8 of 20 outfield singles (40%); scored from second on 7 of 12 (58%).... Made 3.17 assists per nine innings at shortstop.

Comments: Doesn't look too scary at the plate—except, of course, by comparison to Brian Barnes or Chris Nabholz on deck. That's why only three N.L. players were issued more intentional passes than Owen's 48 over the past three seasons: Barry Bonds (62), Eddie Murray (62), and Kevin Mitchell (49).... No other player in major league history has had at least 250 at-bats in each of his first nine seasons in the majors despite batting below .260 in each. In fact, only six other players have had such a streak for nine straight years at any time during their careers, including a current streak by Tom Brunansky. The others: 11 years by George McBride (1905–16) and Jim Hegan (1946–56), nine years by Doug Rader (1969–1977), Aurelio Rodriguez (1969–1977), and Roger Metzger (1971–1979).... Had the league's 4th-lowest batting average in home games.... Another bogus switch-hitter: He had the league's 9th-highest average vs. left-handed pitchers, but the 4th-lowest mark against right-handers. Career breakdown: .272 from the right side of the plate, .225 from the left.... Started 51 of 53 games in which the Expos faced left-handed starting pitchers, only 68 of 108 games against right-handers.... Made only three errors in 393 chances on artificial turf; his rate on grass fields was more than three times as high (one per 36 chances).... Batting average with two outs and runners in scoring position was the lowest in the league, marking the third time in the past four years he's hit .100 or lower in those situations. His career average: .188.

Tom Pagnozzi

Bats Right

St. Louis Cardinals	AB	H	2B	3B	HR	RBI	BB	SO	BA	SA	OBA
Season	459	121	24	5	2	57	36	63	.264	.351	.319
vs. Left-Handers	201	51	11	2	2	25	18	29	.254	.358	.311
vs. Right-Handers	258	70	13	3	0	32	18	34	.271	.345	.326
vs. Ground-Ballers	212	47	12	0	2	22	18	30	.222	.307	.286
vs. Fly-Ballers	247	74	12	5	0	35	18	33	.300	.389	.348
Home Games	221	50	11	2	2	23	23	29	.226	.321	.306
Road Games	238	71	13	3	0	34	13	34	.298	.378	.332
Grass Fields	124	33	6	2	0	21	7	21	.266	.347	.311
Artificial Turf	335	88	18	3	2	36	29	42	.263	.352	.323
April	63	15	1	0	0	4	3	9	.238	.254	.265
May	79	22	6	1	1	14	9	8	.278	.418	.367
June	89	21	3	1	1	13	2	11	.236	.326	.250
July	76	18	2	2	0	8	9	12	.237	.316	.322
August	83	21	7	1	0	6	6	13	.253	.361	.300
Sept./Oct.	69	24	5	0	0	12	7	10	.348	.420	.416
Leading Off Inn.	118	32	5	1	0	0	11	12	.271	.331	.333
Runners On	208	57	13	3	1	56	18	36	.274	.380	.330
Bases Empty	251	64	11	2	1	1	18	27	.255	.327	.310
Runners/Scor. Pos.	134	35	9	2	1	53	14	25	.261	.381	.325
Runners On/2 Out	74	18	4	1	0	13	9	16	.243	.324	.341
Scor. Pos./2 Out	50	10	3	0	0	11	7	10	.200	.260	.310
Late-Inning Pressure	77	15	2	0	0	3	8	13	.195	.221	.267
Leading Off	23	5	1	0	0	0	4	2	.217	.261	.333
Runners On	34	6	1	0	0	3	4	6	.176	.206	.256
Runners/Scor. Pos.	18	2	0	0	0	3	4	4	.111	.111	.261

RUNS BATTED IN	From 1B	From 2B	From 3B	Scoring Position
Totals	8/137	15/90	32/78	47/168
Percentage	5.8%	16.7%	41.0%	28.0%

Loves to face: Dwight Gooden (.529, 9-for-17)
Terry Mulholland (.438, 7-for-16)
Randy Tomlin (.500, 6-for-12)
Hates to face: Tom Glavine (.091, 1-for-11, 1 2B)
Bill Landrum (0-for-9)
Zane Smith (.056, 1-for-18, 2 BB)

Miscellaneous statistics: Ground outs-to-air outs ratio: 1.35 last season, 1.13 for career.... Grounded into 10 double plays in 105 opportunities (one per 11).... Drove in 27 of 56 runners from third base with less than two outs (48%).... Direction of balls hit to the outfield: 20% to left field, 36% to center, 44% to right.... Base running: Advanced from first base to third on 2 of 27 outfield singles (7%), 3d-lowest rate in N.L.; scored from second on 8 of 13 (62%).... Opposing base stealers: 86-for-156 (55%), 3d-lowest rate in N.L.

Comments: Only player with at least 10 at-bats vs. Gooden to top the .500 mark during Doc's nine seasons.... Pagnozzi and Rich Gedman combined to catch 1407⅓ of 1435⅓ innings for the Cardinals last season; no N.L. club had two catchers who accounted for more. Either John Marzano or Tony Pena caught every pitch for the Red Sox; B. J. Surhoff and Rick Dempsey did the same for the Brewers.... One of four N.L. catchers to work at least 1000 innings last season. The others: Benito Santiago, Craig Biggio, and Greg Olson.... Although the stolen-base rate against Gedman (75%, one every 8.4 innings) couldn't compare to Pagnozzi's (55%, one every 13.4 innings), St. Louis's staff ERA was higher with Pagnozzi (3.75) behind the plate than with Gedman there (3.33).... One of five N.L. players to qualify for the batting title without putting together a hitting streak of longer than six games.... Among right-handed batters that qualified for the N.L. batting title last season, only four others had higher batting averages against right-handed pitchers than against lefties: Craig Biggio, Juan Samuel, Shawon Dunston, and Tim Wallach. That's no fluke; all but Wallach have career averages that skew the same way.... Stole nine bases in 140 games, compared to two steals in 229 games prior to 1991. The last Cardinals catcher to steal as many as nine bases: Tim McCarver (1966).... Hit the first five triples of his career; was 0-for-543 through 1990.... Should someone put Mike LaValliere in touch with Pags's speed coach?

Terry Pendleton

Bats Left and Right

Atlanta Braves	AB	H	2B	3B	HR	RBI	BB	SO	BA	SA	OBA
Season	586	187	34	8	22	86	43	70	.319	.517	.363
vs. Left-Handers	177	53	10	3	4	23	15	9	.299	.458	.351
vs. Right-Handers	409	134	24	5	18	63	28	61	.328	.543	.368
vs. Ground-Ballers	230	88	16	4	4	28	17	22	.383	.539	.422
vs. Fly-Ballers	356	99	18	4	18	58	26	48	.278	.503	.325
Home Games	285	97	18	3	13	48	18	30	.340	.561	.377
Road Games	301	90	16	5	9	38	25	40	.299	.475	.350
Grass Fields	426	139	27	4	18	69	30	47	.326	.535	.367
Artificial Turf	160	48	7	4	4	17	13	23	.300	.469	.351
April	47	11	3	0	2	6	10	4	.234	.426	.362
May	83	34	7	2	3	14	7	3	.410	.651	.446
June	96	29	6	1	2	12	5	17	.302	.448	.337
July	100	36	7	0	5	21	6	10	.360	.580	.385
August	126	32	3	2	4	14	5	18	.254	.405	.280
Sept./Oct.	134	45	8	3	6	19	10	18	.336	.575	.386
Leading Off Inn.	114	43	11	3	5	5	5	12	.377	.658	.403
Runners On	280	89	15	2	9	73	23	32	.318	.482	.361
Bases Empty	306	98	19	6	13	13	20	38	.320	.549	.364
Runners/Scor. Pos.	169	54	9	1	7	66	17	19	.320	.509	.368
Runners On/2 Out	84	27	5	0	4	24	9	8	.321	.524	.387
Scor. Pos./2 Out	57	16	3	0	2	19	7	7	.281	.439	.359
Late-Inning Pressure	76	24	7	0	0	10	6	9	.316	.408	.361
Leading Off	18	8	2	0	0	0	1	2	.444	.556	.474
Runners On	36	13	3	0	0	10	3	5	.361	.444	.400
Runners/Scor. Pos.	20	8	2	0	0	10	3	2	.400	.500	.458

RUNS BATTED IN	From 1B	From 2B	From 3B	Scoring Position
Totals	8/177	30/137	26/55	56/192
Percentage	4.5%	21.9%	47.3%	29.2%

Loves to face: Jose DeLeon (.550, 11-for-20)
Roger McDowell (.367, 11-for-30, 3 HR)
Zane Smith (.458, 22-for-48, 1 HR)
Hates to face: Pat Combs (.091, 1-for-11)
Terry Mulholland (.167, 4-for-24)
Trevor Wilson (.111, 2-for-18)

Miscellaneous statistics: Ground outs-to-air outs ratio: 1.14 last season, 1.24 for career.... Grounded into 16 double plays in 141 opportunities (one per 8.8).... Drove in 19 of 32 runners from third base with less than two outs (59%).... Direction of balls hit to the outfield: 32% to left field, 31% to center, 37% to right batting left-handed; 26% to left field, 32% to center, 42% to right batting right-handed.... Base running: Advanced from first base to third on 6 of 29 outfield singles (21%); scored from second on 19 of 24 (79%).... Made 2.45 assists per nine innings at third base, highest rate in majors.

Comments: The 1990s' candidate for Comeback Player of the Century. He batted .230 with six home runs in 1990, and last year became the first player in major league history to increase his batting average by at least 80 points and his home run total by at least 15 from one year to the next (minimum: 400 AB each season). Al Simmons had come closest, with a 76-point, 16-HR increase (1924–25).... First Braves player to win the league batting title or lead the league in hits since Ralph Garr in 1974. Pendleton's .319 average was the 2d lowest ever to lead the N.L., six points higher than Tony Gwynn's in 1988.... Batting average vs. ground-ball pitchers was 3d highest in the N.L. over the last 17 years.... Averaged one strikeout every seven times up batting left-handed, but his rate of one SO per 22 PAs vs. left-handers was 2d best in the league, behind Tony Gwynn.... Had seven sacrifice bunts, more than any other MVP (other than pitchers) since Brooks Robinson gave himself up eight times in 1964.... Errors year by year since 1988: 12, 15, 19, 24. Last season, he committed 16 of his 24 errors in home games, and averaged one error per 16 chances on grass, one per 62 on turf.... The five greatest breakthrough seasons in baseball history (defined in the Braves essay): Harry Heilmann, 1921 (.394, 19 HR, 139 RBI); Jim Hickman, 1970 (.315, 32 HR, 115 RBI); Robin Yount, 1982 (.331, 29 HR, 114 RBI); Eddie Joost, 1949 (.263, 23 HR, 81 RBI); Babe Ruth, 1920 (.376, 54 HR, 137 RBI).

Gerald Perry
Bats Left

St. Louis Cardinals	AB	H	2B	3B	HR	RBI	BB	SO	BA	SA	OBA
Season	242	58	8	4	6	36	22	34	.240	.380	.300
vs. Left-Handers	104	25	3	2	2	13	7	14	.240	.365	.286
vs. Right-Handers	138	33	5	2	4	23	15	20	.239	.391	.310
vs. Ground-Ballers	100	21	3	2	0	14	8	8	.210	.280	.264
vs. Fly-Ballers	142	37	5	2	6	22	14	26	.261	.451	.325
Home Games	130	24	1	4	1	15	11	15	.185	.277	.246
Road Games	112	34	7	0	5	21	11	19	.304	.500	.360
Grass Fields	62	19	5	0	1	10	1	10	.306	.435	.308
Artificial Turf	180	39	3	4	5	26	21	24	.217	.361	.297
April	12	3	0	1	1	6	4	1	.250	.667	.412
May	22	4	1	0	0	5	2	5	.182	.227	.240
June	28	9	2	1	2	7	1	5	.321	.679	.333
July	77	19	3	0	3	7	6	12	.247	.403	.301
August	63	17	1	2	0	8	7	7	.270	.349	.343
Sept./Oct.	40	6	1	0	0	3	2	4	.150	.175	.190
Leading Off Inn.	48	7	1	0	1	1	2	4	.146	.229	.180
Runners On	111	34	5	4	2	32	13	18	.306	.477	.370
Bases Empty	131	24	3	0	4	4	9	16	.183	.298	.236
Runners/Scor. Pos.	72	23	4	3	0	27	12	12	.319	.458	.402
Runners On/2 Out	39	6	3	1	0	7	6	10	.154	.282	.267
Scor. Pos./2 Out	29	5	3	1	0	7	6	7	.172	.345	.314
Late-Inning Pressure	58	13	0	1	2	12	8	8	.224	.362	.318
Leading Off	9	0	0	0	0	0	0	0	.000	.000	.000
Runners On	24	8	0	1	1	11	7	6	.333	.542	.484
Runners/Scor. Pos.	16	5	0	0	0	8	6	4	.313	.313	.500

RUNS BATTED IN	From 1B	From 2B	From 3B	Scoring Position
Totals	4/71	10/57	16/33	26/90
Percentage	5.6%	17.5%	48.5%	28.9%

Loves to face: Danny Cox (.579, 11-for-19)
Scott Garrelts (.385, 5-for-13, 3 HR)
Dennis Rasmussen (.444, 8-for-18, 2 HR)

Hates to face: Steve Avery (0-for-9)
David Cone (.091, 2-for-22, 4 BB)
Roger McDowell (.071, 1-for-14, 1 2B)

Miscellaneous statistics: Ground outs-to-air outs ratio: 1.18 last season, 1.46 for career.... Grounded into 2 double plays in 54 opportunities (one per 27).... Drove in 12 of 16 runners from third base with less than two outs (75%).... Direction of balls hit to the outfield: 31% to left field, 44% to center, 25% to right.... Base running: Advanced from first base to third on 5 of 10 outfield singles (50%); scored from second on 6 of 6 (100%).... Made 0.59 assists per nine innings at first base.

Comments: Started only 10 games before the All-Star break, 40 during the second half of the season.... Made 48 appearances as a pinch hitter, 7th most in the league. Those with more: Chris Gwynn (64), Stan Javier (59), Eric Bullock (57), Mike Kingery (55), Dwight Smith (50), and Wally Backman (49).... His on-base percentage leading off innings (.180) was the lowest in the N.L. (minimum: 50 PA).... Career-long preference for grass fields (.275) over artificial turf (.246) helped produce the largest home/road disparity in the majors last season.... Has had a higher batting average with runners on base than with the bases empty in each of the past five seasons. His averages during that period: .301 and .240; only six players had wider spreads in that direction.... Batting average vs. left-handed pitchers, year by year since 1989: .337, .209, .240; vs. right-handers: .198, .272, .239. Career averages create an illusion of consistency: .256 vs. LHP, .268 vs. RHP.... Has stolen 42 bases over the past three seasons. Seems like light years since he stole the same number in one season for the Braves (1987), then batted .300 for them a year later.... Following the 1988 season, our projection model made him odds-on to reach the 1000-hit mark; with 727 hits to date, his chances are now 28 percent and falling.... With Perry and Pedro Guerrero backing up Andres Galarraga in St. Louis, our only question is this: Which one is the DH?

Randy Ready
Bats Right

Philadelphia Phillies	AB	H	2B	3B	HR	RBI	BB	SO	BA	SA	OBA
Season	205	51	10	1	1	20	47	25	.249	.322	.385
vs. Left-Handers	147	39	10	1	1	18	39	17	.265	.367	.418
vs. Right-Handers	58	12	0	0	0	2	8	8	.207	.207	.294
vs. Ground-Ballers	91	24	7	0	1	9	25	11	.264	.374	.420
vs. Fly-Ballers	114	27	3	1	0	11	22	14	.237	.281	.355
Home Games	108	27	5	1	1	10	30	11	.250	.343	.414
Road Games	97	24	5	0	0	10	17	14	.247	.299	.350
Grass Fields	49	10	3	0	0	7	13	7	.204	.265	.359
Artificial Turf	156	41	7	1	1	13	34	18	.263	.340	.394
April	35	9	0	0	0	3	7	5	.257	.257	.381
May	31	11	3	0	0	5	10	2	.355	.452	.512
June	10	3	0	0	0	1	1	2	.300	.300	.364
July	24	2	0	0	0	0	2	3	.083	.083	.185
August	45	9	2	1	1	8	17	6	.200	.356	.394
Sept./Oct.	60	17	5	0	0	3	10	7	.283	.367	.386
Leading Off Inn.	49	9	3	0	0	0	7	4	.184	.245	.298
Runners On	87	22	4	1	0	19	25	14	.253	.322	.405
Bases Empty	118	29	6	0	1	1	22	11	.246	.322	.369
Runners/Scor. Pos.	52	13	2	0	0	16	14	7	.250	.288	.386
Runners On/2 Out	36	9	2	1	0	7	9	9	.250	.361	.400
Scor. Pos./2 Out	25	5	1	0	0	5	5	7	.200	.240	.333
Late-Inning Pressure	42	8	0	0	0	3	13	6	.190	.190	.375
Leading Off	9	1	0	0	0	0	3	0	.111	.111	.333
Runners On	22	4	0	0	0	3	6	5	.182	.182	.345
Runners/Scor. Pos.	14	3	0	0	0	3	4	1	.214	.214	.368

RUNS BATTED IN	From 1B	From 2B	From 3B	Scoring Position
Totals	3/62	8/46	8/17	16/63
Percentage	4.8%	17.4%	47.1%	25.4%

Loves to face: Ken Dayley (.500, 4-for-8, 1 HR)
Bob Kipper (.375, 3-for-8, 2 2B, 5 BB)
Jeff Montgomery (3-for-3, 1 HR)

Hates to face: Terry Leach (0-for-5, 3 SO)
Dave Stieb (0-for-6)
Frank Tanana (1-for-8)

Miscellaneous statistics: Ground outs-to-air outs ratio: 0.78 last season, 0.83 for career.... Grounded into 5 double plays in 51 opportunities (one per 10).... Drove in 7 of 11 runners from third base with less than two outs (64%).... Direction of balls hit to the outfield: 40% to left field, 32% to center, 29% to right.... Base running: Advanced from first base to third on 5 of 18 outfield singles (28%); scored from second on 2 of 2 (100%).... Made 2.75 assists per nine innings at second base.

Comments: Started 51 of 62 games in which the Phillies faced left-handed starting pitchers, but only three of 100 games against right-handers.... Rate of one walk per 5.5 plate appearances was a career best.... Stopped the bleeding by raising his batting average by five points over his 1990 mark, snapping a streak of three consecutive declines. But his mark against right-handers continues to drop; year by year since 1987: .286, .250, .240, .236, .207.... His 58 at-bats vs. right-handed pitchers were the most of any player without an extra-base hit against them last season. Over the last two years, he has had only one extra-base hit (a double) in 147 at-bats against right-handers.... Hit eight home runs in 187 at-bats for the Phillies in 1989, but has since hit only two home runs in 422 at-bats.... He has hit for a higher average against ground-ball pitchers than against fly-ballers in each of the last five seasons.... Has hit for a higher average in day games than in night games in each of the last six. His .310 career mark in day games is 12th highest among active players (minimum: 500 AB), behind all of the names you would expect, plus Jim Eisenreich.... Has two hits in 21 career at-bats with two outs and the bases loaded.... His 1987 season (.309, 12 HR) is one of the most extreme career years among active players—if by "career year" you mean a single season out of context with the entire career viewed in retrospect. For the most outstanding career years, see the Brook Jacoby comments.

Gary Redus
Bats Right

Pittsburgh Pirates	AB	H	2B	3B	HR	RBI	BB	SO	BA	SA	OBA
Season	252	62	12	2	7	24	28	39	.246	.393	.324
vs. Left-Handers	173	43	7	2	5	15	15	27	.249	.399	.302
vs. Right-Handers	79	19	5	0	2	9	13	12	.241	.380	.368
vs. Ground-Ballers	122	34	8	1	5	16	16	14	.279	.484	.366
vs. Fly-Ballers	133	28	4	1	2	8	13	25	.211	.301	.282
Home Games	125	35	8	2	3	11	12	18	.280	.448	.353
Road Games	127	27	4	0	4	13	16	21	.213	.339	.297
Grass Fields	80	17	2	0	4	9	9	11	.213	.387	.283
Artificial Turf	172	45	10	2	3	15	19	28	.262	.395	.344
April	39	9	2	0	0	1	4	3	.231	.282	.318
May	39	7	0	0	0	1	4	5	.179	.179	.256
June	38	11	4	0	2	4	1	7	.289	.553	.317
July	45	14	3	1	2	8	8	7	.311	.556	.418
August	35	8	0	0	3	6	4	8	.229	.486	.300
Sept./Oct.	56	13	3	1	0	4	7	9	.232	.321	.313
Leading Off Inn.	107	30	6	1	3	3	9	14	.280	.439	.336
Runners On	77	16	2	0	1	18	11	12	.208	.273	.309
Bases Empty	175	46	10	2	6	6	17	27	.263	.446	.332
Runners/Scor. Pos.	49	7	0	0	1	18	10	7	.143	.204	.292
Runners On/2 Out	38	8	0	0	1	10	6	4	.211	.289	.348
Scor. Pos./2 Out	30	6	0	0	1	10	6	2	.200	.300	.368
Late-Inning Pressure	45	12	1	0	1	6	7	9	.267	.356	.377
Leading Off	11	4	0	0	0	0	1	2	.364	.364	.417
Runners On	21	6	0	0	0	5	5	3	.286	.286	.444
Runners/Scor. Pos.	13	3	0	0	0	5	5	1	.231	.231	.474

RUNS BATTED IN	From 1B	From 2B	From 3B	Scoring Position
Totals	1/48	4/44	12/25	16/69
Percentage	2.1%	9.1%	48.0%	23.2%

Loves to face: Chris Hammond (.462, 6-for-13)
Terry Mulholland (.300, 6-for-20, 4 2B, 2 HR)
Bob Ojeda (.304, 7-for-23, 2 HR, 9 BB)

Hates to face: Dwight Gooden (.067, 1-for-15, 1 2B)
Danny Jackson (0-for-18)
Alejandro Pena (.063, 1-for-16)

Miscellaneous statistics: Ground outs-to-air outs ratio: 0.73 last season, 0.68 for career.... Grounded into 0 double plays in 32 opportunities.... Drove in 8 of 13 runners from third base with less than two outs (62%).... Direction of balls hit to the outfield: 43% to left field, 31% to center, 26% to right.... Base running: Advanced from first base to third on 5 of 7 outfield singles (71%); scored from second on 8 of 10 (80%).... Made 0.61 assists per nine innings at first base.

Comments: If a .250 batting average is your idea of a Brand X ballplayer, meet Mr. X. Last season marked the seventh time that Redus has compiled an average between .245 and .255 (in at least 200 ABs). Only two other players had even six such seasons: Tommy Corcoran (1890–1907) and Terry Turner (1901–19).... Became the first player in the 17 years of *The Player Analysis* to hit for a higher average with the bases empty than with runners on base in seven consecutive seasons.... Started 49 of 53 games in which the Pirates faced left-handed starting pitchers, seven of 109 vs. right-handers.... Stole 17 bases in 20 attempts to keep his career success rate above 80 percent (.804). Only five active players have higher percentages (minimum: 300 attempts).... The only active players with a higher career ratio of air outs to ground outs than Redus are Howard Johnson, Rob Deer, Mark McGwire, and Luis Quinones (minimum: 1000 PA).... True to form for fly-ball hitters, his career average against ground-ball pitchers (.269) is considerably higher than his average against fly-ball types (.225).... Has grounded into one double play over the last two seasons—during the regular season, that is. He grounded into a big one in Game 6 of the 1991 N.L.C.S.... Needs 12 more games to reach the 1000 mark, although he's never played more than 130 in a season. Of the 1062 thousand-gamers, 62 reached that level without playing more than 130 games in any season (including, of course, Hoyt Wilhelm and Kent Tekulve).

Jeff Reed
Bats Left

Cincinnati Reds	AB	H	2B	3B	HR	RBI	BB	SO	BA	SA	OBA
Season	270	72	15	2	3	31	23	38	.267	.370	.321
vs. Left-Handers	26	5	2	0	0	5	3	6	.192	.269	.281
vs. Right-Handers	244	67	13	2	3	26	20	32	.275	.381	.326
vs. Ground-Ballers	111	27	4	2	2	13	11	12	.243	.369	.306
vs. Fly-Ballers	161	46	11	0	1	18	14	26	.286	.373	.341
Home Games	115	30	9	2	1	15	13	19	.261	.400	.336
Road Games	155	42	6	0	2	16	10	19	.271	.348	.310
Grass Fields	92	25	3	0	1	7	6	10	.272	.337	.316
Artificial Turf	178	47	12	2	2	24	17	28	.264	.388	.323
April	29	7	0	0	0	2	6	5	.241	.241	.361
May	57	18	2	0	1	5	2	9	.316	.404	.344
June	60	16	5	0	1	12	9	7	.267	.400	.357
July	26	10	2	0	0	5	2	4	.385	.462	.414
August	42	6	2	0	0	0	2	6	.143	.190	.182
Sept./Oct.	56	15	4	2	1	7	2	7	.268	.464	.288
Leading Off Inn.	68	22	3	1	1	1	5	10	.324	.441	.370
Runners On	105	25	4	1	2	30	13	15	.238	.352	.315
Bases Empty	165	47	11	1	1	1	10	23	.285	.382	.326
Runners/Scor. Pos.	59	12	1	1	1	25	10	11	.203	.305	.307
Runners On/2 Out	52	11	0	0	2	12	8	6	.212	.327	.328
Scor. Pos./2 Out	33	6	0	0	1	10	6	6	.182	.273	.325
Late-Inning Pressure	37	10	1	0	0	3	3	6	.270	.297	.310
Leading Off	16	6	0	0	0	0	1	1	.375	.375	.412
Runners On	10	2	0	0	0	3	1	4	.200	.200	.231
Runners/Scor. Pos.	5	1	0	0	0	3	1	3	.200	.200	.250

RUNS BATTED IN	From 1B	From 2B	From 3B	Scoring Position
Totals	6/72	7/43	15/37	22/80
Percentage	8.3%	16.3%	40.5%	27.5%

Loves to face: Andy Benes (.417, 5-for-12, 1 HR)
Greg Maddux (.324, 11-for-34, 1 HR)
Dennis Martinez (.286, 4-for-14, 1 HR)

Hates to face: David Cone (.095, 2-for-21, 3 BB)
Paul McClellan (0-for-7)
Mike Morgan (.154, 2-for-13)

Miscellaneous statistics: Ground outs-to-air outs ratio: 1.29 last season, 1.23 for career.... Grounded into 6 double plays in 43 opportunities (one per 7.2).... Drove in 11 of 17 runners from third base with less than two outs (65%).... Direction of balls hit to the outfield: 38% to left field, 29% to center, 33% to right.... Base running: Advanced from first base to third on 1 of 9 outfield singles (11%); scored from second on 6 of 12 (50%), 4th-lowest rate in N.L.... Opposing base stealers: 57-for-85 (67%).

Comments: The Reds posted a better ERA with Reed behind the plate (3.57) than they did with Joe Oliver (3.98). Of the five pitchers on the staff who accumulated at least 100 innings last season, only Scott Scudder posted a higher ERA with Reed than with Oliver.... Their opponents also had a lower stolen-base percentage against Reed than Oliver (67 percent and 71 percent, respectively).... No longer a pushover at the plate: He's batted .261 over the past two seasons, compared to .222 from 1984 through 1989. Total of 20 extra-base hits last season was a career high. But he still lacks long-ball power; three homers last season equaled his career high.... Had never before batted higher than .236 against right-handed pitchers.... Started 77 games last season, all against right-handed pitchers. He has started 135 games against right-handers since his last start against a southpaw (September 16, 1989 vs. Jim Deshaies).... Has never accumulated more than 52 plate appearances vs. left-handers in any season. His two career home runs against southpaws were both hit in 1990 (against Don Carman and Derek Lilliquist).... His .270 average in Late-Inning Pressure Situations came immediately after a season in which he was 0-for-17 in LIPS.... Career average of .244 with the bases empty, .219 with runners on base. He has batted below .200 with two outs and runners on base in six of his eight seasons in the majors.

Bip Roberts — Bats Left and Right

San Diego Padres	AB	H	2B	3B	HR	RBI	BB	SO	BA	SA	OBA
Season	424	119	13	3	3	32	37	71	.281	.347	.342
vs. Left-Handers	118	30	3	1	0	8	7	13	.254	.297	.302
vs. Right-Handers	306	89	10	2	3	24	30	58	.291	.366	.357
vs. Ground-Ballers	214	64	7	2	3	14	14	26	.299	.393	.341
vs. Fly-Ballers	210	55	6	1	0	18	23	45	.262	.300	.343
Home Games	223	64	4	1	3	17	12	32	.287	.354	.331
Road Games	201	55	9	2	0	15	25	39	.274	.338	.354
Grass Fields	311	88	7	3	3	26	18	45	.283	.354	.328
Artificial Turf	113	31	6	0	0	6	19	26	.274	.327	.376
April	76	20	2	1	0	6	9	12	.263	.316	.349
May	100	27	4	1	0	6	10	16	.270	.330	.345
June	77	20	2	1	0	7	5	17	.260	.312	.313
July	65	20	2	0	1	7	6	11	.308	.385	.361
August	52	18	2	0	2	3	4	12	.346	.500	.393
Sept./Oct.	54	14	1	0	0	3	3	3	.259	.278	.293
Leading Off Inn.	177	49	6	0	1	1	18	26	.277	.328	.354
Runners On	122	36	5	3	1	30	10	25	.295	.410	.341
Bases Empty	302	83	8	0	2	2	27	46	.275	.321	.342
Runners/Scor. Pos.	79	25	5	1	1	28	9	18	.316	.443	.374
Runners On/2 Out	62	20	4	1	1	15	7	11	.323	.468	.391
Scor. Pos./2 Out	49	16	4	0	1	14	7	10	.327	.469	.411
Late-Inning Pressure	58	18	1	0	1	6	5	11	.310	.379	.375
Leading Off	14	5	0	0	0	0	2	0	.357	.357	.438
Runners On	23	8	1	0	1	6	1	7	.348	.522	.375
Runners/Scor. Pos.	15	4	1	0	1	6	1	7	.267	.533	.313

RUNS BATTED IN	From 1B	From 2B	From 3B	Scoring Position
Totals	2/74	12/61	15/36	27/97
Percentage	2.7%	19.7%	41.7%	27.8%

Loves to face: Kip Gross (.800, 4-for-5, 2 HR)
Greg Maddux (.400, 6-for-15, 6 BB)
Dennis Martinez (.500, 14-for-28, 0 BB)

Hates to face: Dwight Gooden (.176, 3-for-17)
Pete Harnisch (0-for-6, 4 SO)
Mike LaCoss (.133, 2-for-15)

Miscellaneous statistics: Ground outs-to-air outs ratio: 2.01 last season, 3d highest in N.L.; 1.62 for career.... Grounded into 6 double plays in 48 opportunities (one per 8.0).... Drove in 9 of 13 runners from third base with less than two outs (69%).... Direction of balls hit to the outfield: 56% to left field, 30% to center, 15% to right batting left-handed; 31% to left field, 29% to center, 41% to right batting right-handed.... Base running: Advanced from first base to third on 5 of 26 outfield singles (19%); scored from second on 18 of 28 (64%).... Made 2.96 assists per nine innings at second base.

Comments: Ranks sixth in the National League with a .298 batting average over the past three years.... His acquisition solves Cincinnati's left-field problem; or his versatility could be the catalyst for continued changes. Career games by position: 2B, 173; LF, 118; 3B, 95; SS, 32; CF, 30; RF, 19.... Career average of .310 (27-for-87, 1 HR) at Riverfront Stadium, .322 on other fields with artificial turf, .282 on grass fields.... Was tough to double-up last season, and he'll be even tougher in 1991. He hasn't grounded into a double play on artificial turf in 32 opportunities over the last two years.... Stole 10 bases in 12 attempts on artificial turf, but was only 16-for-25 on dirt infields. Career figures: 32-for-40 on turf (80%), 75-for-115 on dirt (65%).... Career breakdown: .271 batting right-handed, .304 batting left-handed. Among active switch-hitters with at least 1500 plate appearances, Roberts has the highest career batting average from the left side. Only two others have career averages above .300 batting left-handed: Willie McGee and Roberto Alomar.... Made 104 of his 105 starts last season from the leadoff spot in the Padres batting order. The only exception: one start batting eighth, in his first game back from the disabled list (Sept. 10).... Leaves the Padres with a career batting average of .291, the 2d highest in franchise history (minimum: 1000 AB). Do we have to tell you who's first? (Hint: It's not Jack Clark.)

Chris Sabo — Bats Right

Cincinnati Reds	AB	H	2B	3B	HR	RBI	BB	SO	BA	SA	OBA
Season	582	175	35	3	26	88	44	79	.301	.505	.354
vs. Left-Handers	193	69	17	1	9	29	16	23	.358	.596	.412
vs. Right-Handers	389	106	18	2	17	59	28	56	.272	.460	.325
vs. Ground-Ballers	290	89	17	1	11	45	21	36	.307	.486	.361
vs. Fly-Ballers	296	87	19	2	15	44	23	43	.294	.524	.347
Home Games	298	101	24	2	15	45	25	37	.339	.584	.393
Road Games	284	74	11	1	11	43	19	42	.261	.423	.314
Grass Fields	176	50	6	1	7	28	12	25	.284	.449	.333
Artificial Turf	406	125	29	2	19	60	32	54	.308	.530	.363
April	72	16	2	0	2	6	6	10	.222	.333	.291
May	99	26	3	0	4	7	12	20	.263	.414	.339
June	89	28	7	2	5	21	12	15	.315	.607	.404
July	88	30	6	1	5	17	5	9	.341	.602	.383
August	114	40	11	0	5	14	4	14	.351	.579	.375
Sept./Oct.	120	35	6	0	5	23	5	11	.292	.467	.325
Leading Off Inn.	156	44	8	1	8	8	17	22	.282	.500	.356
Runners On	260	81	18	1	12	74	20	31	.312	.527	.366
Bases Empty	322	94	17	2	14	14	24	48	.292	.488	.345
Runners/Scor. Pos.	144	44	8	1	8	64	15	18	.306	.542	.346
Runners On/2 Out	114	31	4	1	8	34	11	15	.272	.535	.391
Scor. Pos./2 Out	60	16	2	1	5	27	9	9	.267	.583	.371
Late-Inning Pressure	88	20	3	0	2	8	5	12	.227	.330	.274
Leading Off	18	3	1	0	0	0	2	0	.167	.167	.250
Runners On	39	7	1	0	2	8	1	5	.179	.359	.214
Runners/Scor. Pos.	19	3	0	0	2	8	1	2	.158	.474	.227

RUNS BATTED IN	From 1B	From 2B	From 3B	Scoring Position
Totals	12/189	20/113	30/61	50/174
Percentage	6.3%	17.7%	49.2%	28.7%

Loves to face: Steve Avery (.500, 9-for-18, 1 HR)
John Burkett (.455, 10-for-22, 1 HR)
Dwight Gooden (.471, 8-for-17)

Hates to face: David Cone (.118, 2-for-17, 2 BB, 8 SO)
Sid Fernandez (.067, 1-for-15, 1 2B, 2 BB)
Wally Whitehurst (0-for-8)

Miscellaneous statistics: Ground outs-to-air outs ratio: 0.72 last season, 0.74 for career.... Grounded into 13 double plays in 113 opportunities (one per 8.7).... Drove in 21 of 34 runners from third base with less than two outs (62%).... Direction of balls hit to the outfield: 49% to left field, 30% to center, 20% to right.... Base running: Advanced from first base to third on 17 of 24 outfield singles (71%), 3d-highest rate in majors; scored from second on 10 of 13 (77%).... Made 1.76 assists per nine innings at third base, lowest rate in N.L.

Comments: Became the first N.L. third baseman since Mike Schmidt in 1981 to hit 25 or more home runs while batting .300 or better. Three N.L. third basemen did so during the 1970s: Tony Perez (1970), and Bob Horner and Larry Parrish (both 1979). Five third basemen accounted for eight such seasons in the 1960s: Ron Santo (three times), Dick Allen (twice), and Ken Boyer, Don Demeter, and Eddie Mathews (once). Boyer and Mathews also did so in the 1950s (twice each); Andy Pafko and and Whitey Kurowski in the 1940s; and Mel Ott in the 1930s.... Had the league's 3d-highest batting average in home games and the league's 2d-highest mark vs. left-handed pitchers. He batted .391 vs. lefties at Riverfront Stadium.... He has a career average of only .257 vs. right-handers, but his career mark of .321 vs. left-handers is 2d highest among active players, behind Kirby Puckett (.342). The scary part is that he keeps getting better. His yearly averages vs. southpaws: .286, .290, .327, .358.... Ranked second in the league with a .331 batting average after the All-Star break.... He's quite a homey, sporting a career average of .295 with one home run every 24 at-bats at Riverfront Stadium, compared to a .261 average with one HR per 37 ABs on the road.... His .236 batting average in day games last season was a career high, but he's never hit below .280 at night. Career averages: .229 in day games, .296 in night games. No wonder he appeared on "Late Night with David Letterman." But he seems like a natural for the Costas show.

Luis Salazar

Bats Right

Chicago Cubs	AB	H	2B	3B	HR	RBI	BB	SO	BA	SA	OBA
Season	333	86	14	1	14	38	15	45	.258	.432	.292
vs. Left-Handers	166	45	8	0	10	25	8	18	.271	.500	.309
vs. Right-Handers	167	41	6	1	4	13	7	27	.246	.365	.276
vs. Ground-Ballers	125	35	6	1	2	10	6	18	.280	.392	.313
vs. Fly-Ballers	208	51	8	0	12	28	9	27	.245	.457	.280
Home Games	165	43	11	0	8	20	4	22	.261	.473	.278
Road Games	168	43	3	1	6	18	11	23	.256	.393	.306
Grass Fields	236	63	12	1	11	30	10	29	.267	.466	.297
Artificial Turf	97	23	2	0	3	8	5	16	.237	.351	.282
April	15	2	0	0	1	1	1	2	.133	.333	.188
May	43	14	1	0	3	6	3	6	.326	.558	.370
June	67	17	2	0	2	7	7	10	.254	.373	.333
July	53	17	4	0	3	4	0	8	.321	.566	.321
August	75	21	4	1	2	9	1	6	.280	.440	.289
Sept./Oct.	80	15	3	0	3	11	3	13	.188	.338	.217
Leading Off Inn.	76	25	3	1	6	6	1	7	.329	.632	.338
Runners On	138	34	8	0	5	29	8	23	.246	.413	.288
Bases Empty	195	52	6	1	9	9	7	22	.267	.446	.296
Runners/Scor. Pos.	73	14	4	0	3	24	3	13	.192	.370	.224
Runners On/2 Out	59	17	3	0	3	14	5	11	.288	.492	.344
Scor. Pos./2 Out	33	7	2	0	1	10	1	5	.212	.364	.235
Late-Inning Pressure	59	20	2	0	3	10	5	4	.339	.525	.391
Leading Off	16	6	0	0	1	1	1	2	.375	.563	.412
Runners On	23	6	2	0	1	8	2	1	.261	.478	.320
Runners/Scor. Pos.	14	3	2	0	0	6	2	0	.214	.357	.313

RUNS BATTED IN	From 1B	From 2B	From 3B	Scoring Position
Totals	6/103	8/53	10/29	18/82
Percentage	5.8%	15.1%	34.5%	22.0%

Loves to face: Bud Black (.500, 9-for-18, 3 HR)
Scott Garrelts (.333, 5-for-15, 2 HR)
Terry Mulholland (.333, 6-for-18, 2 HR)

Hates to face: Steve Avery (.083, 1-for-12)
Neal Heaton (.143, 3-for-21)
John Smoltz (0-for-9)

Miscellaneous statistics: Ground outs-to-air outs ratio: 0.98 last season, 1.08 for career.... Grounded into 8 double plays in 64 opportunities (one per 8.0).... Drove in 6 of 13 runners from third base with less than two outs (46%).... Direction of balls hit to the outfield: 42% to left field, 31% to center, 27% to right.... Base running: Advanced from first base to third on 1 of 10 outfield singles (10%); scored from second on 3 of 5 (60%).... Made 2.01 assists per nine innings at third base.

Comments: What team started an infield including Salazar at third base, Bryan Little at second base, and Joe DeSa at first base on August 29, 1985? Hint below.... He was involved in an average of one double play every 135 innings at third base, the worst rate by far among the 26 players with at least 500 innings there last season. The major league average: one DP per 49 innings at third. Note also that the Cubs' staff had the highest ratio of ground outs to air outs in the majors last season (1.34), perhaps balanced by the fact that among N.L. teams only the Cardinals faced fewer right-handed batters than Chicago's predominantly right-handed staff.... Started 47 of 64 games in which the Cubs faced left-handed starting pitchers, 35 of 96 games against right-handers.... He averaged one home run every 24 at-bats last season, nearly 40 percent higher than his previous best rate (one per 33 AB in 1985).... Was 0-for-3 on stolen-base attempts last season. Has stolen only 13 bases over his last six seasons, compared to an average of 17 per year for his first six. The missing link: a knee injury on Sept. 23, 1985 that required extensive surgery.... Career batting average of .352 with runners in scoring position in Late-Inning Pressure Situations is 2d highest among active players, behind Jose Canseco (.373).... Hint: The starting shortstop was Ozzie Guillen. That should give it away.

Juan Samuel

Bats Right

Los Angeles Dodgers	AB	H	2B	3B	HR	RBI	BB	SO	BA	SA	OBA
Season	594	161	22	6	12	58	49	133	.271	.389	.328
vs. Left-Handers	250	63	11	2	7	27	14	59	.252	.396	.294
vs. Right-Handers	344	98	11	4	5	31	35	74	.285	.384	.352
vs. Ground-Ballers	249	62	6	4	5	28	22	63	.249	.365	.311
vs. Fly-Ballers	345	99	16	2	7	30	27	70	.287	.406	.340
Home Games	295	75	12	1	4	26	25	67	.254	.342	.315
Road Games	299	86	10	5	8	32	24	66	.288	.435	.342
Grass Fields	450	121	16	4	9	46	34	103	.269	.382	.322
Artificial Turf	144	40	6	2	3	12	15	30	.278	.410	.348
April	83	25	4	1	4	15	3	14	.301	.518	.326
May	94	33	6	0	1	12	12	22	.351	.447	.421
June	110	34	2	0	3	12	9	24	.309	.409	.355
July	104	23	2	1	2	6	4	20	.221	.317	.250
August	91	19	1	2	0	7	12	26	.209	.264	.308
Sept./Oct.	112	27	7	2	2	6	9	27	.241	.393	.309
Leading Off Inn.	105	24	2	1	3	3	13	22	.229	.352	.314
Runners On	255	73	10	3	5	51	21	52	.286	.408	.344
Bases Empty	339	88	12	3	7	7	28	81	.260	.375	.316
Runners/Scor. Pos.	129	32	6	1	2	41	19	28	.248	.357	.346
Runners On/2 Out	95	25	4	1	1	18	9	18	.263	.358	.333
Scor. Pos./2 Out	64	17	3	0	1	17	8	13	.266	.359	.347
Late-Inning Pressure	82	20	3	1	1	13	12	24	.244	.341	.337
Leading Off	24	4	0	0	0	0	5	8	.167	.167	.310
Runners On	38	12	3	1	1	13	5	9	.316	.526	.386
Runners/Scor. Pos.	25	7	2	0	1	11	5	7	.280	.480	.387

RUNS BATTED IN	From 1B	From 2B	From 3B	Scoring Position
Totals	10/186	19/111	17/58	36/169
Percentage	5.4%	17.1%	29.3%	21.3%

Loves to face: Mike Bielecki (.500, 9-for-18, 2 HR)
Bud Black (.533, 8-for-15, 2 HR)
Jeff Robinson D. (.419, 13-for-31, 2 HR)

Hates to face: Steve Avery (0-for-18)
Sid Fernandez (.111, 6-for-54, 3 2B, 1 HR)
Craig Lefferts (.091, 2-for-22, 2 BB)

Miscellaneous statistics: Ground outs-to-air outs ratio: 1.45 last season, 1.14 for career.... Grounded into 8 double plays in 135 opportunities (one per 17).... Drove in 12 of 30 runners from third base with less than two outs (40%), 5th-lowest rate in N.L.... Direction of balls hit to the outfield: 26% to left field, 28% to center, 46% to right. ...Base running: Advanced from first base to third on 6 of 23 outfield singles (26%); scored from second on 16 of 19 (84%).... Made 3.02 assists per nine innings at second base.

Comments: Played over 1300 innings at second base, 2d most in the league to Ryne Sandberg.... Ranked seventh in the league with a .313 batting average at the All-Star break, prompting complaints about the fans' selection of Sandberg to the All-Star team. That should be enough for Congress to impose a moratorium on criticism of voting process. The fans might not be perfect, but they got that one right.... Samuel batted .224 during the second half, the 4th-lowest average in the league.... Has danced nearly every dance for the past eight years, playing at least 137 games in each. The only other players to do that in the N.L.: Kevin McReynolds and Dale Murphy.... Has a streak of eight straight seasons with 120 or more strikeouts, the longest in major league history. Bobby Bonds (1969–75) and Dale Murphy (1984–90) had seven-year streaks.... Samuel has another fairly unusual streak: eight straight seasons with at least 10 home runs and 20 stolen bases. That matches Don Baylor (1972–79) for the 2d longest streak ever behind Daddy Bonds again, who had an 11-year streak from 1969 through 1979.... "Extra: Old Dog Learns New Trick"—Samuel has executed 17 sacrifice bunts over the past three seasons (including a career-high 10 in 1991), compared to only three from 1983 through 1988.... One of two players to drive in less than 22 percent of runners from scoring position for three straight seasons (minimum: 100 opportunities in each). The other: Robby Thompson.

Ryne Sandberg

Bats Right

Chicago Cubs	AB	H	2B	3B	HR	RBI	BB	SO	BA	SA	OBA
Season	585	170	32	2	26	100	87	89	.291	.485	.379
vs. Left-Handers	209	75	19	0	8	27	39	23	.359	.565	.456
vs. Right-Handers	376	95	13	2	18	73	48	66	.253	.441	.335
vs. Ground-Ballers	238	73	16	1	14	42	33	41	.307	.559	.387
vs. Fly-Ballers	347	97	16	1	12	58	54	48	.280	.435	.374
Home Games	291	90	14	2	15	54	43	39	.309	.526	.394
Road Games	294	80	18	0	11	46	44	50	.272	.446	.364
Grass Fields	409	124	22	2	22	78	62	57	.303	.528	.390
Artificial Turf	176	46	10	0	4	22	25	32	.261	.386	.353
April	84	17	3	0	1	2	10	9	.202	.274	.287
May	103	35	9	0	6	20	9	15	.340	.602	.386
June	103	33	5	1	5	18	15	10	.320	.534	.407
July	79	26	5	0	4	19	22	13	.329	.544	.476
August	110	26	2	0	5	17	13	26	.236	.391	.315
Sept./Oct.	106	33	8	1	5	24	18	16	.311	.547	.402
Leading Off Inn.	88	24	7	1	4	4	18	16	.273	.511	.402
Runners On	254	86	17	1	14	88	51	36	.339	.579	.436
Bases Empty	331	84	15	1	12	12	36	53	.254	.414	.331
Runners/Scor. Pos.	135	46	9	1	8	70	31	15	.341	.600	.440
Runners On/2 Out	96	27	4	0	2	22	15	19	.281	.385	.378
Scor. Pos./2 Out	57	14	2	0	1	18	10	10	.246	.333	.358
Late-Inning Pressure	92	24	2	1	2	13	18	17	.261	.370	.375
Leading Off	16	3	0	0	0	0	7	3	.188	.188	.435
Runners On	45	15	1	1	2	13	9	10	.333	.533	.429
Runners/Scor. Pos.	24	10	0	1	1	10	4	2	.417	.625	.467

RUNS BATTED IN	From 1B	From 2B	From 3B	Scoring Position
Totals	17/172	23/107	34/65	57/172
Percentage	9.9%	21.5%	52.3%	33.1%

Loves to face: Bob Ojeda (.458, 11-for-24, 3 HR)
Scott Terry (.407, 11-for-27, 3 2B, 5 HR, 0 BB)
Randy Tomlin (.667, 6-for-9, 1 HR)

Hates to face: Larry Andersen (.081, 3-for-37, 0 BB)
Rob Dibble (.071, 1-for-14, 7 SO)
Bryn Smith (.147, 11-for-75, 2 HR, 12 BB)

Miscellaneous statistics: Ground outs-to-air outs ratio: 1.05 last season, 1.12 for career.... Grounded into 9 double plays in 132 opportunities (one per 15).... Drove in 26 of 38 runners from third base with less than two outs (68%).... Direction of balls hit to the outfield: 41% to left field, 27% to center, 32% to right.... Base running: Advanced from first base to third on 17 of 38 outfield singles (45%); scored from second on 14 of 19 (74%).... Made 3.37 assists per nine innings at second base, 2d-highest rate in N.L.

Comments: Became the fourth second baseman ever with 60 extra-base hits in three consecutive seasons. The record is four, held by—you're not going to believe this—Juan Samuel (1984–87). Others with three-year streaks: Charlie Gehringer (1932–34) and Rogers Hornsby (twice).... The only other players with 60 or more XBH in each of the past three seasons: Howard Johnson and Bobby Bonilla, whose streak is four years.... Led N.L. second basemen in fielding percentage last season, becoming the first player since Red Schoendienst to do that four times.... Had the league's highest batting average vs. left-handed pitchers.... Drove in exactly 100 runs in each of the last two seasons, and reached that figure in his final at-bat in both years.... Sandberg and Andre Dawson both had at least 100 RBIs in each of the last two seasons, as did Barry Bonds and Bobby Bonilla. The last pair of N.L. teammates to reach 100 in consecutive seasons: Johnny Bench and Tony Perez (three years, 1973–75).... Sometimes our projections suggest something we find a little, shall we say, curious. The model indicates that Sandberg has reached the turning point, calling for only 12 home runs and a .258 batting average this season, and citing as support mediocre seasons by Ken Boyer (1964), Amos Otis (1979), Gary Matthews (1982), and Dusty Baker (1982). All were comparable offensive players to Sandberg, coming off seasons similar to Ryno's 1991 performance at about the same age. Sandberg is 32 years old. We'll see.

Benito Santiago

Bats Right

San Diego Padres	AB	H	2B	3B	HR	RBI	BB	SO	BA	SA	OBA
Season	580	155	22	3	17	87	23	114	.267	.403	.296
vs. Left-Handers	204	58	12	2	8	35	10	41	.284	.480	.318
vs. Right-Handers	376	97	10	1	9	52	13	73	.258	.362	.284
vs. Ground-Ballers	290	82	14	3	11	51	11	44	.283	.466	.307
vs. Fly-Ballers	290	73	8	0	6	36	12	70	.252	.341	.286
Home Games	287	70	8	0	6	34	8	49	.244	.334	.267
Road Games	293	85	14	3	11	53	15	65	.290	.471	.325
Grass Fields	441	122	16	3	15	68	14	83	.277	.429	.300
Artificial Turf	139	33	6	0	2	19	9	31	.237	.324	.286
April	84	25	3	0	2	12	1	15	.298	.405	.306
May	97	17	1	0	3	11	3	26	.175	.278	.204
June	101	29	5	1	2	13	4	19	.287	.416	.308
July	85	21	5	0	4	9	3	19	.247	.447	.275
August	103	26	2	2	2	13	5	22	.252	.369	.294
Sept./Oct.	110	37	6	0	4	29	7	13	.336	.500	.378
Leading Off Inn.	107	32	1	1	3	3	5	18	.299	.411	.342
Runners On	290	79	14	2	7	77	12	56	.272	.407	.294
Bases Empty	290	76	8	1	10	10	11	58	.262	.400	.298
Runners/Scor. Pos.	170	47	8	1	6	72	8	39	.276	.441	.297
Runners On/2 Out	130	34	8	1	2	32	3	27	.262	.385	.274
Scor. Pos./2 Out	91	23	6	1	1	28	3	22	.253	.374	.277
Late-Inning Pressure	100	31	3	0	2	13	3	17	.310	.400	.330
Leading Off	23	5	0	0	1	1	1	5	.217	.348	.250
Runners On	53	18	3	0	0	11	2	8	.340	.396	.364
Runners/Scor. Pos.	29	9	1	0	0	10	1	5	.310	.345	.333

RUNS BATTED IN	From 1B	From 2B	From 3B	Scoring Position
Totals	8/232	28/131	34/83	62/214
Percentage	3.4%	21.4%	41.0%	29.0%

Loves to face: Steve Avery (.444, 4-for-9, 1 HR, 3 SO)
Tom Browning (.385, 15-for-39, 1 HR)
Zane Smith (.385, 10-for-26, 4 HR)

Hates to face: Norm Charlton (.063, 1-for-16, 2 BB)
Doug Drabek (.050, 1-for-20, 1 3B)
Sid Fernandez (.074, 2-for-27, 0 BB)

Miscellaneous statistics: Ground outs-to-air outs ratio: 0.89 last season, 0.89 for career.... Grounded into 21 double plays in 142 opportunities (one per 6.8).... Drove in 25 of 44 runners from third base with less than two outs (57%).... Direction of balls hit to the outfield: 44% to left field, 30% to center, 26% to right.... Base running: Advanced from first base to third on 11 of 20 outfield singles (55%); scored from second on 7 of 9 (78%).... Opposing base stealers: 93-for-150 (62%).

Comments: Led the majors with 151 games behind the plate last season, the 13th-highest total in major league history, and the highest since Gary Carter caught 153 games for the Expos in 1982.... Led N.L. catchers in errors for the fourth time in his five-year career. The record for most seasons leading the league is seven, by Ivy Wingo from 1912 to 1921. The last catcher to lead as many as four times was John Bateman.... Had exactly 100 assists last season, the most by a catcher in either league. Tom Pagnozzi had 81, and no other catcher had more than 64. Santiago's total looks impressive, but consider this: Thirty of those assists came as the result of dropped third strikes and subsequent 2–3 putouts.... What do you think is the single-season record for assists by a catcher? Would you believe *two hundred fourteen!*—by Pat Moran, who caught just 107 games for the 1903 Boston Braves. Guess they dropped *a lot* of third strikes in those days.... Led the N.L. in batting from September 1 to the end of the 1991 season.... Batted .159 in the first inning (lowest in the N.L.; minimum: 40 AB), .276 thereafter.... Grounded into 21 double plays, to lead the N.L.... Stole only 13 bases over the past two seasons; averaged 16 per year from 1987 through 1989.... Career average of one walk every 22.5 plate appearances is 4th lowest in Padres history (minimum: 1000 PA), behind Ivan Murrell (30), Tito Fuentes (27), and Luis Salazar (25).... Career batting average of .321 in Late-Inning Pressure Situations is 6th highest over the last 17 years.

Mike Scioscia

Bats Left

Los Angeles Dodgers	AB	H	2B	3B	HR	RBI	BB	SO	BA	SA	OBA
Season	345	91	16	2	8	40	47	32	.264	.391	.353
vs. Left-Handers	106	20	2	0	3	13	11	12	.189	.292	.276
vs. Right-Handers	239	71	14	2	5	27	36	20	.297	.435	.388
vs. Ground-Ballers	150	36	8	1	2	20	21	16	.240	.347	.337
vs. Fly-Ballers	195	55	8	1	6	20	26	16	.282	.426	.366
Home Games	163	47	9	0	3	22	26	15	.288	.399	.380
Road Games	182	44	7	2	5	18	21	17	.242	.385	.329
Grass Fields	250	73	14	2	5	33	34	21	.292	.424	.372
Artificial Turf	95	18	2	0	3	7	13	11	.189	.305	.306
April	63	20	3	1	1	9	7	4	.317	.444	.380
May	57	11	2	0	2	6	14	6	.193	.333	.361
June	58	18	7	0	0	7	7	7	.310	.431	.388
July	24	7	1	0	0	5	2	2	.292	.333	.333
August	67	13	0	0	1	4	11	10	.194	.239	.308
Sept./Oct.	76	22	3	1	4	9	6	3	.289	.513	.345
Leading Off Inn.	90	23	2	1	5	5	8	6	.256	.467	.323
Runners On	146	40	8	1	0	32	24	15	.274	.342	.371
Bases Empty	199	51	8	1	8	8	23	17	.256	.427	.339
Runners/Scor. Pos.	87	24	6	1	0	31	15	9	.276	.368	.368
Runners On/2 Out	62	14	2	1	0	12	12	7	.226	.290	.360
Scor. Pos./2 Out	40	8	2	1	0	12	6	6	.200	.300	.304
Late-Inning Pressure	52	15	0	0	2	6	11	7	.288	.404	.424
Leading Off	14	5	0	0	1	1	3	1	.357	.571	.500
Runners On	21	4	0	0	0	4	7	4	.190	.190	.400
Runners/Scor. Pos.	12	1	0	0	0	4	5	3	.083	.083	.333

RUNS BATTED IN	From 1B	From 2B	From 3B	Scoring Position
Totals	5/113	10/68	17/37	27/105
Percentage	4.4%	14.7%	45.9%	25.7%

Loves to face: Kelly Downs (.450, 18-for-40)
Lee Smith (.438, 7-for-16, 1 HR)
John Smoltz (.333, 9-for-27, 3 HR, 0 SO)

Hates to face: Juan Agosto (.059, 1-for-17)
Larry Andersen (0-for-15)
David Cone (.156, 5-for-32)

Miscellaneous statistics: Ground outs-to-air outs ratio: 0.84 last season, 1.04 for career.... Grounded into 5 double plays in 77 opportunities (one per 15).... Drove in 12 of 20 runners from third base with less than two outs (60%).... Direction of balls hit to the outfield: 36% to left field, 23% to center, 41% to right.... Base running: Advanced from first base to third on 4 of 20 outfield singles (20%); scored from second on 4 of 7 (57%).... Opposing base stealers: 82-for-112 (73%), 4th-highest rate in N.L.

Comments: Let's play word association: "Dodgers"—Did anyone say "Scioscia?" Only 12 players have appeared in more games for the team on either coast; of these, the only ones to bleed cerulean for their entire careers were Bill Russell (2181), Pee Wee Reese (2166), Jim Gilliam (1956), Carl Furillo (1806), and Jackie Robinson (1382). Scioscia has played 1324 games.... Of the players most often used by Los Angeles at each of the eight nonpitching positions last season, only Scioscia was a product of the Dodgers system.... Has batted in the .250s or .260s in each of the past six seasons with at least 400 plate appearances in each, the longest such streak in major league history. Does that make him consistent or mediocre?...Both.... Dodgers' ERA was considerably higher with Scioscia behind the plate (3.20) than it was with Gary Carter there (2.79). Among six Dodger hurlers with at least 100 innings, Orel Hershiser and Mike Morgan posted lower ERAs with Scioscia than with the Kid.... Had the league's 3d-lowest batting average on artificial turf, and 6th lowest against left-handed pitchers.... Career average of one strikeout every 16.9 plate appearances is 5th best among active players (minimum: 1500 PA), behind Tony Gwynn (20.8), Don Mattingly (18.3), Ozzie Smith (17.8), and Felix Fermin (17.5).... Career average of .275 on grass fields, .227 on artificial turf.... Career batting average of .229 in Late-Inning Pressure Situations.

Mike Sharperson

Bats Right

Los Angeles Dodgers	AB	H	2B	3B	HR	RBI	BB	SO	BA	SA	OBA
Season	216	60	11	2	2	20	25	24	.278	.375	.355
vs. Left-Handers	158	51	10	2	2	15	18	19	.323	.449	.392
vs. Right-Handers	58	9	1	0	0	5	7	5	.155	.172	.258
vs. Ground-Ballers	97	28	8	0	0	8	8	12	.289	.371	.349
vs. Fly-Ballers	119	32	3	2	2	12	17	12	.269	.378	.360
Home Games	97	32	4	0	1	9	13	11	.330	.402	.409
Road Games	119	28	7	2	1	11	12	13	.235	.353	.311
Grass Fields	168	49	10	0	2	13	18	19	.292	.387	.364
Artificial Turf	48	11	1	2	0	7	7	5	.229	.333	.327
April	29	5	1	0	0	3	2	2	.172	.207	.250
May	5	0	0	0	0	0	1	0	.000	.000	.167
June	23	9	1	0	0	5	4	4	.391	.565	.481
July	39	14	2	1	0	3	6	4	.359	.462	.444
August	44	9	2	1	0	2	5	6	.205	.295	.286
Sept./Oct.	76	23	5	0	1	7	7	8	.303	.408	.361
Leading Off Inn.	47	13	1	0	0	0	4	5	.277	.298	.333
Runners On	97	27	4	2	0	18	7	11	.278	.361	.333
Bases Empty	119	33	7	0	2	2	18	13	.277	.387	.372
Runners/Scor. Pos.	58	12	0	1	0	16	5	7	.207	.241	.270
Runners On/2 Out	38	9	0	0	0	6	3	4	.237	.237	.293
Scor. Pos./2 Out	29	6	0	0	0	6	2	3	.207	.207	.258
Late-Inning Pressure	42	13	1	1	0	6	6	5	.310	.381	.383
Leading Off	10	1	0	0	0	0	1	1	.100	.100	.182
Runners On	23	9	0	1	0	6	1	3	.391	.478	.417
Runners/Scor. Pos.	17	6	0	0	0	5	1	2	.353	.353	.389

RUNS BATTED IN	From 1B	From 2B	From 3B	Scoring Position
Totals	3/68	5/47	10/25	15/72
Percentage	4.4%	10.6%	40.0%	20.8%

Loves to face: Danny Jackson (.474, 9-for-19)
Randy Myers (.273, 3-for-11, 1 2B, 2 3B, 4 BB)
John Smiley (.444, 4-for-9, 1 HR)

Hates to face: Bud Black (.182, 2-for-11)
Kelly Downs (0-for-5)
Greg W. Harris (0-for-5)

Miscellaneous statistics: Ground outs-to-air outs ratio: 1.32 last season, 1.30 for career.... Grounded into 2 double plays in 54 opportunities (one per 27).... Drove in 7 of 13 runners from third base with less than two outs (54%).... Direction of balls hit to the outfield: 30% to left field, 32% to center, 37% to right.... Base running: Advanced from first base to third on 3 of 16 outfield singles (19%); scored from second on 2 of 4 (50%).... Made 1.59 assists per nine innings at third base.

Comments: As part of a platoon with Lenny Harris, Sharperson played only 68 games at third base. But among third basemen with 50 or more games, his rate of one error per 52 chances was second best in team history behind Randy Jackson, who made two errors in 270 chances in 1956. The team record for true qualifiers is one per 44 chances, set by Ron Cey in 1979.... Sharperson's 58-game errorless streak at third base was the longest in the National League last season. The 3d longest was 36 games by his platoon partner, Lenny Harris.... One of seven players in the majors to start at least one game at each of the four infield positions last season.... Had the league's 6th-highest batting average vs. left-handed pitchers, raising his career average to .308—one point lower than Tony Gwynn's career mark against southpaws, four points higher than Wade Boggs's. Sharperson's career average vs. right-handers is only .236.... There's also a huge gap between his career averages against fly-ball pitchers (.244) and ground-ball pitchers (.315).... And there's more: Career average of .299 at Dodger Stadium, .288 on other grass fields, .226 on artificial turf.... Career average of .227 in Late-Inning Pressure Situations, .286 in other at-bats.... Has career batting averages above .300 in May, June, and July (both separately and combined), but he has a .247 mark before and after.... Give the Blue Jays credit for patience and foresight. They traded Sharperson to the Dodgers for Juan Guzman in 1987, and didn't see any dividends until last season.

Don Slaught
Bats Right

Pittsburgh Pirates	AB	H	2B	3B	HR	RBI	BB	SO	BA	SA	OBA
Season	220	65	17	1	1	29	21	32	.295	.395	.363
vs. Left-Handers	126	33	10	0	0	11	14	20	.262	.341	.345
vs. Right-Handers	94	32	7	1	1	18	7	12	.340	.468	.388
vs. Ground-Ballers	122	38	12	0	0	19	9	16	.311	.410	.361
vs. Fly-Ballers	99	27	5	1	1	10	12	16	.273	.374	.363
Home Games	118	38	11	0	0	15	9	19	.322	.415	.372
Road Games	102	27	6	1	1	14	12	13	.265	.373	.353
Grass Fields	61	15	5	0	1	7	5	9	.246	.377	.303
Artificial Turf	159	50	12	1	0	22	16	23	.314	.403	.385
April	25	8	3	0	0	3	2	3	.320	.440	.370
May	36	8	2	1	0	7	3	2	.222	.333	.282
June	43	8	1	0	0	3	4	9	.186	.209	.255
July	27	6	2	0	0	2	1	5	.222	.296	.276
August	34	12	3	0	1	8	4	7	.353	.529	.410
Sept./Oct.	55	23	6	0	0	6	7	6	.418	.527	.500
Leading Off Inn.	48	19	6	0	1	1	3	5	.396	.583	.442
Runners On	108	26	7	1	0	28	12	16	.241	.324	.314
Bases Empty	112	39	10	0	1	1	9	16	.348	.464	.411
Runners/Scor. Pos.	67	19	6	1	0	27	10	9	.284	.403	.372
Runners On/2 Out	49	9	3	1	0	13	6	7	.184	.286	.273
Scor. Pos./2 Out	32	8	3	1	0	13	6	2	.250	.406	.368
Late-Inning Pressure	31	9	3	1	1	7	5	6	.290	.548	.389
Leading Off	14	5	1	0	1	1	2	2	.357	.643	.438
Runners On	12	3	2	1	0	6	1	4	.250	.583	.308
Runners/Scor. Pos.	8	2	1	1	0	5	1	1	.250	.625	.333

RUNS BATTED IN	From 1B	From 2B	From 3B	Scoring Position
Totals	3/65	12/46	13/42	25/88
Percentage	4.6%	26.1%	31.0%	28.4%

Loves to face: Dennis Martinez (.500, 8-for-16)
Bob McClure (.500, 7-for-14)
Bob Ojeda (.412, 7-for-17)
Hates to face: Juan Agosto (0-for-7)
Juan Berenguer (.118, 2-for-17, 2 BB)
Dave Righetti (0-for-14)

Miscellaneous statistics: Ground outs-to-air outs ratio: 1.45 last season, 0.96 for career.... Grounded into 6 double plays in 44 opportunities (one per 7.3).... Drove in 9 of 22 runners from third base with less than two outs (41%).... Direction of balls hit to the outfield: 35% to left field, 44% to center, 21% to right.... Base running: Advanced from first base to third on 0 of 13 outfield singles (0%), worst in majors; scored from second on 1 of 4 (25%).... Opposing base stealers: 42-for-69 (61%).

Comments: The Bucs' staff ERA was more than a half-run lower with Slaught behind the plate (3.04) than with Mike LaValliere catching (3.55). Among five Pirates pitchers with at least 100 innings last season, only Bob Walk had a lower ERA with Spanky than with Sluggo.... Opposing base stealers also had a rougher time against Slaught (61 percent, one every 12.1 innings) than against LaValliere (70 percent, one every 9.5 innings).... His only home run of the season (August 31 off of Jose Melendez) ended a 0-for-323 drought. Prior to last season, Slaught had a career average of one home run every 48 at-bats.... Had three game-winning RBIs in extra innings last season, tying David Justice, John Kruk, Dale Murphy, and pinch-hitter Ken Oberkfell for the N.L. lead.... His .340 batting average against right-handed pitchers was the highest of any right-handed batter in the majors with at least 75 at-bats against like pitchers last season. Of course, that's a little over his head; he has career marks of .288 vs. LHP, .263 vs. RHP.... In two seasons with the Pirates, he has started 98 games vs. left-handers, 16 against right-handers.... Of his last 27 home runs, 23 have been solo shots.... Has played 917 major league games, pretty evenly split among four teams: Kansas City, 250; Texas, 292; Yankees, 214; and Pittsburgh, 161.... Opponents have stolen 16 bases in 19 attempts in 78 innings of postseason catching.

Lonnie Smith
Bats Right

Atlanta Braves	AB	H	2B	3B	HR	RBI	BB	SO	BA	SA	OBA
Season	353	97	19	1	7	44	50	64	.275	.394	.377
vs. Left-Handers	115	39	9	1	0	11	18	22	.339	.435	.435
vs. Right-Handers	238	58	10	0	7	33	32	42	.244	.374	.348
vs. Ground-Ballers	153	42	7	0	3	20	27	25	.275	.379	.388
vs. Fly-Ballers	200	55	12	1	4	24	23	39	.275	.405	.368
Home Games	193	56	10	0	6	31	23	35	.290	.435	.374
Road Games	160	41	9	1	1	13	27	29	.256	.344	.380
Grass Fields	280	78	14	0	7	37	39	48	.279	.404	.376
Artificial Turf	73	19	5	1	0	7	11	16	.260	.356	.379
April	1	0	0	0	0	0	0	0	.000	.000	.000
May	59	17	3	0	2	10	12	15	.288	.441	.432
June	80	19	3	1	1	10	8	11	.237	.338	.311
July	65	20	4	0	2	11	13	13	.308	.462	.430
August	58	19	4	0	0	4	4	9	.328	.397	.391
Sept./Oct.	90	22	5	0	2	9	13	16	.244	.367	.349
Leading Off Inn.	113	35	6	1	3	3	13	22	.310	.460	.400
Runners On	139	40	7	0	3	40	20	22	.288	.403	.384
Bases Empty	214	57	12	1	4	4	30	42	.266	.388	.372
Runners/Scor. Pos.	96	28	5	0	1	36	15	16	.292	.375	.386
Runners On/2 Out	52	17	3	0	1	18	9	9	.327	.442	.435
Scor. Pos./2 Out	39	15	3	0	1	18	8	5	.385	.538	.489
Late-Inning Pressure	46	10	3	0	0	1	8	10	.217	.283	.357
Leading Off	17	6	2	0	0	0	2	3	.353	.471	.476
Runners On	18	4	1	0	0	1	3	4	.222	.278	.333
Runners/Scor. Pos.	10	1	0	0	0	1	2	3	.100	.100	.250

RUNS BATTED IN	From 1B	From 2B	From 3B	Scoring Position
Totals	3/87	17/73	17/35	34/108
Percentage	3.4%	23.3%	48.6%	31.5%

Loves to face: Ken Hill (.600, 6-for-10)
Terry Mulholland (.538, 14-for-26, 0 BB)
Bob Walk (.647, 11-for-17, 3 HR)
Hates to face: Jose DeLeon (.133, 4-for-30, 4 BB)
Ramon Martinez (0-for-12)
Bill Swift (.188, 3-for-16)

Miscellaneous statistics: Ground outs-to-air outs ratio: 0.85 last season, 1.01 for career.... Grounded into 4 double plays in 58 opportunities (one per 15).... Drove in 11 of 20 runners from third base with less than two outs (55%).... Direction of balls hit to the outfield: 38% to left field, 27% to center, 35% to right.... Base running: Advanced from first base to third on 12 of 21 outfield singles (57%); scored from second on 9 of 14 (64%).... Made 1.67 putouts per nine innings in left field, lowest rate in majors.

Comments: Let's just say for openers that we thought the replay was—to borrow a term from NFL lingo—inconclusive, and that with nobody out, there's a chance (just a *chance*, mind you) that Lonnie might have been held at third base. Does there always have to be a goat? There's a whole school of sportswriters who seem to look for the "choker" in every game. According to these second-guessers, contests are never won, they're only lost. Sure the play made for great speculation, and it always will. But what a way to remember perhaps the greatest Series of our time.... His on-base average leading off innings was the 4th highest in the league.... Among players with at least 1000 career plate appearances in a Braves uniform, Smith's .386 on-base average ranks fifth, behind Billy Hamilton (.453), Bob Elliott (.398), Rico Carty (.388), and Jimmy Bannon (.387).... Has been hit by 83 pitches in his career, the 3d-highest total among active players, behind two graybeards: Carlton Fisk (141) and Brian Downing (121).... There's a 52-point gap between his career batting averages against ground-ball (.317, 6th highest among active players) and fly-ball pitchers (.265).... Has hit for a higher average in home games than on the road in each of his four seasons with the Braves, and in two seasons prior to that with Kansas City.... Has hit for a lower average in Late-Inning Pressure Situations than in other at-bats in each of the last 10 seasons. Over the past 17 years, the only player with a longer streak was Jim Rice (11 years).

Ozzie Smith
Bats Left and Right

St. Louis Cardinals	AB	H	2B	3B	HR	RBI	BB	SO	BA	SA	OBA
Season	550	157	30	3	3	50	83	36	.285	.367	.380
vs. Left-Handers	248	65	18	2	3	25	35	20	.262	.387	.356
vs. Right-Handers	302	92	12	1	0	25	48	16	.305	.351	.399
vs. Ground-Ballers	242	69	12	2	0	21	37	15	.285	.351	.379
vs. Fly-Ballers	308	88	18	1	3	29	46	21	.286	.380	.380
Home Games	291	94	19	1	2	28	46	18	.323	.416	.416
Road Games	259	63	11	2	1	22	37	18	.243	.313	.338
Grass Fields	132	26	7	1	0	7	14	11	.197	.265	.274
Artificial Turf	418	131	23	2	3	43	69	25	.313	.400	.411
April	69	18	2	0	0	4	12	4	.261	.290	.373
May	93	36	5	0	0	13	14	6	.387	.441	.467
June	85	24	7	1	0	12	15	7	.282	.388	.390
July	88	23	3	0	0	4	16	7	.261	.295	.375
August	101	28	3	2	2	9	15	6	.277	.406	.371
Sept./Oct.	114	28	10	0	1	8	11	6	.246	.360	.312
Leading Off Inn.	103	28	4	1	0	0	23	6	.272	.330	.405
Runners On	217	65	14	2	2	49	28	13	.300	.410	.381
Bases Empty	333	92	16	1	1	1	55	23	.276	.339	.379
Runners/Scor. Pos.	139	38	6	2	1	43	23	9	.273	.367	.374
Runners On/2 Out	78	17	4	1	1	15	16	3	.218	.333	.351
Scor. Pos./2 Out	58	11	1	1	1	14	14	2	.190	.293	.347
Late-Inning Pressure	69	18	0	1	0	11	14	6	.261	.290	.388
Leading Off	16	4	0	0	0	0	6	2	.250	.250	.455
Runners On	28	10	0	1	0	11	6	3	.357	.429	.472
Runners/Scor. Pos.	17	8	0	1	0	11	5	1	.471	.588	.565

RUNS BATTED IN	From 1B	From 2B	From 3B	Scoring Position
Totals	5/122	19/113	23/53	42/166
Percentage	4.1%	16.8%	43.4%	25.3%

Loves to face: Larry Andersen (.500, 7-for-14, 8 BB)
     Tim Crews (.600, 6-for-10, 1 HR)
     Pete Schourek (.556, 5-for-9)
Hates to face: Tom Browning (.143, 6-for-42)
     Sid Fernandez (.122, 6-for-49, 5 BB)
     Mark Portugal (0-for-8)

Miscellaneous statistics: Ground outs-to-air outs ratio: 1.46 last season, 1.54 for career.... Grounded into 8 double plays in 92 opportunities (one per 12).... Drove in 17 of 30 runners from third base with less than two outs (57%).... Direction of balls hit to the outfield: 30% to left field, 34% to center, 36% to right batting left-handed; 33% to left field, 25% to center, 42% to right batting right-handed.... Base running: Advanced from first base to third on 18 of 41 outfield singles (44%); scored from second on 22 of 29 (76%).... Made 2.78 assists per nine innings at shortstop, 3d-lowest rate in N.L.

Comments: Led N.L. shortstops in fielding percentage for the seventh time, tying the league record of Jack Glasscock, who won his seventh league fielding title almost 100 years ago (1894).... Also led N.L. shortstops in double plays for the fifth time, tying Dick Groat's record.... Career total of 2056 games at shortstop is the most of any active player, and ranks ninth on the all-time list. He is 162 games behind the third-place total of Luke Appling, 166 games behind Larry Bowa's N.L. record, and 525 games shy of Luis Aparicio's all-time record.... With 1474 of those games at shortstop played for the Cardinals, Ozzie needs only 19 games to pass Marty Marion as the club's all-time leader at that position.... He has hit for a higher average with runners on base than he has with the bases empty in each of the last nine years, matching Dave Parker for the longest current streak in the majors.... Last season's batting average and walk rate (one per 7.7 PAs) were the 2d highest of his career, and the season represented a 76-to-1 breakthrough at age 36. (Breakthroughs are defined in the Braves essay.) The last player that old with such an extreme breakthrough was Mickey Vernon, when he batted .310 with 15 homers in 1956 at age 37 (minimum: 400 AB). Before that, it was Tris Speaker and Zack Wheat in 1925.... With so much else in the package, Ozzie's base stealing is often overlooked. But his first steal of 1992 will be the 500th of his career. See the Willie Wilson comments for more.

Darryl Strawberry
Bats Left

Los Angeles Dodgers	AB	H	2B	3B	HR	RBI	BB	SO	BA	SA	OBA
Season	505	134	22	4	28	99	75	125	.265	.491	.361
vs. Left-Handers	228	63	9	2	11	43	34	59	.276	.478	.370
vs. Right-Handers	277	71	13	2	17	56	41	66	.256	.502	.353
vs. Ground-Ballers	215	60	8	3	12	44	30	58	.279	.512	.368
vs. Fly-Ballers	290	74	14	1	16	55	45	67	.255	.476	.355
Home Games	257	73	12	2	14	54	38	55	.284	.510	.374
Road Games	248	61	10	2	14	45	37	70	.246	.472	.347
Grass Fields	367	99	18	3	20	71	55	85	.270	.499	.364
Artificial Turf	138	35	4	1	8	28	20	40	.254	.471	.350
April	69	17	6	1	1	7	11	17	.246	.406	.357
May	82	17	2	0	6	17	19	27	.207	.451	.356
June	32	7	1	0	0	2	3	6	.219	.250	.286
July	93	27	2	2	6	17	13	21	.290	.548	.377
August	106	32	5	0	9	28	16	29	.302	.604	.395
Sept./Oct.	123	34	6	1	6	28	13	25	.276	.488	.341
Leading Off Inn.	91	17	3	0	4	4	14	24	.187	.352	.295
Runners On	252	76	11	2	15	86	37	63	.302	.540	.389
Bases Empty	253	58	11	2	13	13	38	62	.229	.443	.332
Runners/Scor. Pos.	158	45	4	2	9	72	24	40	.285	.506	.376
Runners On/2 Out	89	20	3	1	5	27	11	28	.225	.449	.324
Scor. Pos./2 Out	61	12	1	1	3	22	9	18	.197	.393	.319
Late-Inning Pressure	74	20	3	0	3	15	15	22	.270	.432	.389
Leading Off	16	3	1	0	1	1	4	3	.188	.438	.350
Runners On	40	15	2	0	2	14	8	13	.375	.575	.469
Runners/Scor. Pos.	23	9	0	2	2	13	6	8	.391	.652	.500

RUNS BATTED IN	From 1B	From 2B	From 3B	Scoring Position
Totals	15/167	30/118	26/59	56/177
Percentage	9.0%	25.4%	44.1%	31.6%

Loves to face: Cris Carpenter (2-for-2, 2 HR)
     Rick Mahler (.447, 21-for-47, 5 HR)
     Bob Walk (.400, 8-for-20, 1 2B, 4 HR)
Hates to face: Alejandro Pena (0-for-13)
     Zane Smith (.159, 7-for-44, 1 HR)
     Trevor Wilson (0-for-13)

Miscellaneous statistics: Ground outs-to-air outs ratio: 0.92 last season, 0.93 for career.... Grounded into 8 double plays in 129 opportunities (one per 16).... Drove in 20 of 35 runners from third base with less than two outs (57%).... Direction of balls hit to the outfield: 28% to left field, 30% to center, 42% to right.... Base running: Advanced from first base to third on 14 of 28 outfield singles (50%); scored from second on 10 of 12 (83%).... Made 1.59 putouts per nine innings in right field, lowest rate in majors.

Comments: Has hit at least 26 home runs in every season of his nine-year career. Only six players in major league history have had longer streaks of 25 or more: Babe Ruth (15 years), Willie Mays (13), Jimmie Foxx (12), Lou Gehrig (12), Eddie Mathews (11), and Reggie Jackson (10). Among them only Mathews's streak, like Darryl's, started as a rookie.... Leads the majors with 280 home runs during his nine seasons, 12 more than runner-up Dale Murphy and 36 more than anyone else. That's no big surprise (except to semiprofessional Darryl bashers). This *is* surprising (except if you read the Dodgers essay in the 1991 *Analyst*): He also leads the majors in home runs against left-handed pitching during that time (91).... Led the majors with 69 RBIs after the All-Star break last season.... His 10 home runs and 27 RBIs against the Astros were the most by any player against any club last season, and his six homers at the Astrodome were the most by any visiting player at any ballpark.... Straw was the only visiting player to hit three home runs at Shea Stadium last year.... Batted .361 (35-for-97, 4 HR) in the first inning, .243 thereafter.... Has stolen only 36 bases over the past three seasons. He averaged 28 over his first six years.... It boils down to this: Strawberry, Tomas Sandstrom, Tony Granato, and Bree Walker to L.A. for Mark Messier (via Edmonton for Bernie Nicholls), the Grammys, and Pat Riley.

Garry Templeton
Bats Left and Right

Padres/Mets	AB	H	2B	3B	HR	RBI	BB	SO	BA	SA	OBA
Season	276	61	10	2	3	26	10	38	.221	.304	.246
vs. Left-Handers	96	33	4	2	1	13	6	10	.344	.458	.379
vs. Right-Handers	180	28	6	0	2	13	4	28	.156	.222	.172
vs. Ground-Ballers	126	28	5	0	1	13	3	15	.222	.286	.237
vs. Fly-Ballers	150	33	5	2	2	13	7	23	.220	.320	.253
Home Games	138	35	7	1	2	18	9	20	.254	.362	.299
Road Games	138	26	3	1	1	8	1	18	.188	.246	.190
Grass Fields	197	41	8	1	3	21	9	29	.208	.305	.242
Artificial Turf	79	20	2	1	0	5	1	9	.253	.304	.256
April	36	5	0	1	0	0	1	7	.139	.194	.162
May	21	6	1	0	1	6	0	2	.286	.476	.273
June	65	18	3	0	1	7	2	8	.277	.369	.299
July	64	11	2	0	1	5	3	7	.172	.250	.206
August	53	10	2	1	0	6	0	9	.189	.264	.185
Sept./Oct.	37	11	2	0	0	2	4	5	.297	.351	.366
Leading Off Inn.	60	18	2	1	1	1	1	9	.300	.417	.311
Runners On	117	23	6	1	2	25	5	13	.197	.316	.224
Bases Empty	159	38	4	1	1	1	5	25	.239	.296	.262
Runners/Scor. Pos.	73	15	3	0	1	20	4	9	.205	.288	.237
Runners On/2 Out	52	8	4	1	1	9	4	7	.154	.327	.214
Scor. Pos./2 Out	36	6	3	0	1	8	3	6	.167	.333	.231
Late-Inning Pressure	56	11	4	0	1	5	3	10	.196	.321	.237
Leading Off	16	4	1	0	0	0	0	2	.250	.313	.250
Runners On	21	3	2	0	1	5	5	2	.143	.381	.250
Runners/Scor. Pos.	12	3	2	0	1	5	3	1	.250	.667	.400

RUNS BATTED IN	From 1B	From 2B	From 3B	Scoring Position
Totals	5/84	7/58	11/35	18/93
Percentage	6.0%	12.1%	31.4%	19.4%

Loves to face: Danny Darwin (.524, 11-for-21, 3 HR)
Terry Mulholland (.409, 9-for-22)
Fernando Valenzuela (.341, 30-for-88, 2 HR)

Hates to face: Dennis Martinez (.080, 2-for-25, 0 BB)
Mike Scott (.171, 13-for-76)
John Smoltz (.095, 2-for-21)

Miscellaneous statistics: Ground outs-to-air outs ratio: 1.34 last season, 1.62 for career.... Grounded into 10 double plays in 51 opportunities (one per 5.1).... Drove in 8 of 18 runners from third base with less than two outs (44%).... Direction of balls hit to the outfield: 36% to left field, 31% to center, 33% to right batting left-handed; 32% to left field, 28% to center, 40% to right batting right-handed.... Base running: Advanced from first base to third on 2 of 10 outfield singles (20%); scored from second on 5 of 6 (83%).... Made 3.31 assists per nine innings at shortstop.

Comments: Enters 1992 with 1964 career games at shortstop. Only 11 players in major league history have played 2000 games at that position. Templeton needs 64 games to match Roy McMillen's career total and break into the top 10.... Prior to 1991, two games at third base were his only appearances at a position other than shortstop. But last season, he played 15 games at third base for the Padres and for the Mets, who also used him at first base (25) and in right field (2).... Drew only one walk in 61 plate appearances leading off innings, the 3d-lowest rate in the league (minimum: 50 PA), behind Hubie Brooks and Luis Salazar.... His batting average with two outs and runners on base was the lowest in the league.... Although his overall batting average was the lowest of his career, his average from the right side of the plate was his highest since 1979. Over the last three seasons, he has a .295 average batting right-handed, .219 from the left side.... If it's all over, Templeton had a pretty good run. He broke in with the Cardinals in 1976 at age 20. A year later he became the 3d-youngest player in National League history to play as many as 150 games at shortstop, behind Travis Jackson and Chris Speier. He batted .300 or better in three of his first four full seasons and was pointed in the direction of Cooperstown when a series of injuries and the famous "This one's for you" finger incident derailed him in the early 1980s. Still, he ought to be remembered for a lot more than the other side of the Ozzie trade.

Tim Teufel
Bats Right

Mets/Padres	AB	H	2B	3B	HR	RBI	BB	SO	BA	SA	OBA
Season	341	74	16	0	12	44	51	77	.217	.370	.319
vs. Left-Handers	132	36	8	0	7	27	23	22	.273	.492	.378
vs. Right-Handers	209	38	8	0	5	17	28	55	.182	.292	.280
vs. Ground-Ballers	175	35	4	0	6	20	26	42	.200	.326	.302
vs. Fly-Ballers	166	39	12	0	6	24	25	35	.235	.416	.337
Home Games	162	37	10	0	6	24	28	33	.228	.401	.344
Road Games	179	37	6	0	6	20	23	44	.207	.341	.296
Grass Fields	246	47	12	0	8	34	40	57	.191	.337	.300
Artificial Turf	95	27	4	0	4	10	11	20	.284	.453	.358
April	13	1	0	0	0	0	1	0	.077	.077	.143
May	21	3	0	0	1	2	1	8	.143	.286	.182
June	78	25	5	0	2	14	18	15	.321	.462	.448
July	67	10	3	0	0	2	8	15	.149	.194	.240
August	58	16	2	0	5	13	10	15	.276	.569	.377
Sept./Oct.	104	19	6	0	4	13	13	24	.183	.356	.277
Leading Off Inn.	82	19	3	0	2	2	8	19	.232	.341	.300
Runners On	147	32	7	0	8	40	21	34	.218	.429	.316
Bases Empty	194	42	9	0	4	4	30	43	.216	.325	.321
Runners/Scor. Pos.	94	20	5	0	6	35	15	23	.213	.457	.315
Runners On/2 Out	70	15	4	0	4	16	9	18	.214	.443	.304
Scor. Pos./2 Out	52	10	3	0	2	12	8	13	.192	.365	.300
Late-Inning Pressure	65	15	3	0	3	10	8	15	.231	.415	.315
Leading Off	18	5	1	0	1	1	0	3	.278	.500	.278
Runners On	26	9	2	0	2	9	6	4	.346	.654	.469
Runners/Scor. Pos.	15	5	1	0	0	4	3	2	.333	.400	.421

RUNS BATTED IN	From 1B	From 2B	From 3B	Scoring Position
Totals	7/101	13/76	12/34	25/110
Percentage	6.9%	17.1%	35.3%	22.7%

Loves to face: Juan Berenguer (.667, 4-for-6, 1 HR)
Tom Browning (.439, 18-for-41, 4 HR)
Greg Maddux (.381, 8-for-21, 2 HR)

Hates to face: Bud Black (.067, 1-for-15, 2 BB)
Dwight Gooden (0-for-7)
Zane Smith (.174, 8-for-46)

Miscellaneous statistics: Ground outs-to-air outs ratio: 0.92 last season, 1.06 for career.... Grounded into 8 double plays in 70 opportunities (one per 8.8).... Drove in 10 of 18 runners from third base with less than two outs (56%).... Direction of balls hit to the outfield: 40% to left field, 40% to center, 19% to right.... Base running: Advanced from first base to third on 3 of 18 outfield singles (17%); scored from second on 7 of 13 (54%), 5th-lowest rate in N.L.... Made 2.42 assists per nine innings at second base.

Comments: Batted .308 with 14 home runs in 299 at-bats in 1987, one of the most outstanding examples of a "career year" among active players. See the Brook Jacoby comments for more on career years.... Had the league's lowest batting average against right-handed pitchers last season, the lowest in July, and the lowest after the All-Star break (.199).... His average of one walk every 7.8 plate appearances was the highest rate of his career.... Stole nine bases in 12 attempts; was 1-for-5 over the previous three seasons.... Had only 16 games of major league experience at third base before the Padres used him there 48 times.... Teufel got more at-bats in four months with the Padres than he had in any of his full seasons in New York. Total of 28 extra-base hits was his highest since that outstanding 1987 season.... Had only one hit in 22 at-bats against the team that traded him away.... Has driven in only 20.8 percent of runners from scoring position over the past four seasons, the 5th-lowest rate in the majors during that time (minimum: 300 opportunities).... Teufel's departure left the Mets with only four players from their 1986 World Series roster: Dwight Gooden, Sid Fernandez, Howard Johnson, and Kevin Elster. Actually, that's one more than the Red Sox have left (Wade Boggs, Roger Clemens, and Mike Greenwell).

Milt Thompson
Bats Left

St. Louis Cardinals	AB	H	2B	3B	HR	RBI	BB	SO	BA	SA	OBA
Season	326	100	16	5	6	34	32	53	.307	.442	.368
vs. Left-Handers	74	16	3	0	1	6	3	17	.216	.297	.247
vs. Right-Handers	252	84	13	5	5	28	29	36	.333	.484	.401
vs. Ground-Ballers	146	42	7	3	3	22	13	26	.288	.438	.346
vs. Fly-Ballers	180	58	9	2	3	12	19	27	.322	.444	.385
Home Games	159	45	6	4	4	21	16	22	.283	.447	.347
Road Games	167	55	10	1	2	13	16	31	.329	.437	.388
Grass Fields	101	38	8	1	1	9	12	18	.376	.505	.442
Artificial Turf	225	62	8	4	5	25	20	35	.276	.413	.333
April	24	10	1	0	0	3	7	3	.417	.458	.548
May	33	14	0	1	1	3	3	6	.424	.576	.472
June	78	25	6	4	1	15	6	8	.321	.538	.365
July	51	15	2	0	0	5	2	6	.294	.333	.321
August	57	17	3	0	3	5	8	9	.298	.509	.385
Sept./Oct.	83	19	4	0	1	3	6	21	.229	.313	.281
Leading Off Inn.	75	33	7	0	3	3	6	6	.440	.653	.481
Runners On	144	37	4	3	1	29	19	28	.257	.347	.341
Bases Empty	182	63	12	2	5	5	13	25	.346	.516	.390
Runners/Scor. Pos.	86	19	3	3	0	26	15	18	.221	.326	.333
Runners On/2 Out	48	12	2	2	0	13	8	10	.250	.375	.357
Scor. Pos./2 Out	34	8	2	2	0	13	6	8	.235	.412	.350
Late-Inning Pressure	66	16	3	2	1	9	7	15	.242	.394	.311
Leading Off	14	5	3	0	1	1	1	1	.357	.786	.400
Runners On	34	7	0	2	0	8	6	7	.206	.324	.317
Runners/Scor. Pos.	21	5	0	2	0	8	4	3	.238	.429	.346

RUNS BATTED IN	From 1B	From 2B	From 3B	Scoring Position
Totals	7/103	9/65	12/35	21/100
Percentage	6.8%	13.8%	34.3%	21.0%

Loves to face: John Burkett (.462, 6-for-13, 1 HR)
David Cone (.391, 18-for-46, 1 HR)
Roger McDowell (.524, 11-for-21)

Hates to face: Orel Hershiser (.143, 5-for-35, 5 BB)
Dennis Martinez (.138, 4-for-29)
Mitch Williams (0-for-7, 5 SO)

Miscellaneous statistics: Ground outs-to-air outs ratio: 2.46 last season, 2d highest in majors; 2.35 for career, highest by any player in majors since 1975.... Grounded into 4 double plays in 71 opportunities (one per 18).... Drove in 7 of 21 runners from third base with less than two outs (33%), 4th-lowest rate in N.L.... Direction of balls hit to the outfield: 36% to left field, 29% to center, 35% to right.... Base running: Advanced from first base to third on 11 of 21 outfield singles (52%); scored from second on 10 of 15 (67%).... Made 2.55 putouts per nine innings in left field, highest rate in majors.

Comments: Best work came leading off innings: .440 batting average and .481 on-base average were both best in majors among batters who led off at least 75 innings.... Batting average with runners in scoring position was 9th lowest in the league.... Owns .377 career average with two outs and runners on base in Late-Inning Pressure Situations, 3d highest among active players, behind Dale Sveum (.386) and Scott Bradley (.380).... Last season's stolen base percentage (64%) was the lowest of his career, down from over 83 percent in 1990.... Stole 11 bases in 16 attempts on artificial turf, five bases in nine attempts on dirt infields; had 15 steals vs. right-handed pitchers, only one against a lefty.... His playing time against left-handers is diminishing, from 222 plate appearances in 1989, to 129 in 1990, to 77 last season. That's a big deal for a player on the Cardinals, who last year faced more left-handed starters (72) than any team in the majors. Milt started only nine of those 72 games.... Career batting average: .295 vs. right-handers, only .224 vs. southpaws. Of his 33 career home runs, only two have come against left-handers, including a shot off Bob Kipper last season.... In three seasons with St. Louis, he has hit more home runs at Busch Stadium (9) than he has on the road (7).... His eight assists from the outfield were a career high. Cardinals outfielders had 41 assists last season, one shy of league-leading Astros.

Robby Thompson
Bats Right

San Francisco Giants	AB	H	2B	3B	HR	RBI	BB	SO	BA	SA	OBA
Season	492	129	24	5	19	48	63	95	.262	.447	.352
vs. Left-Handers	135	38	8	1	7	16	20	26	.281	.511	.378
vs. Right-Handers	357	91	16	4	12	32	43	69	.255	.423	.342
vs. Ground-Ballers	221	59	9	4	8	18	34	37	.267	.452	.372
vs. Fly-Ballers	271	70	15	1	11	30	29	58	.258	.443	.336
Home Games	241	71	13	4	11	26	38	43	.295	.519	.399
Road Games	251	58	11	1	8	22	25	52	.231	.378	.305
Grass Fields	362	99	19	4	15	37	51	67	.273	.472	.369
Artificial Turf	130	30	5	1	4	11	12	28	.231	.377	.303
April	73	17	3	2	3	6	8	16	.233	.452	.317
May	83	24	6	0	4	7	13	16	.289	.506	.388
June	69	16	4	0	2	9	7	12	.232	.377	.329
July	89	25	3	1	5	9	9	19	.281	.506	.347
August	105	32	7	1	3	10	13	16	.305	.476	.381
Sept./Oct.	73	15	1	1	2	7	13	16	.205	.329	.333
Leading Off Inn.	125	29	6	1	5	5	16	27	.232	.416	.333
Runners On	181	41	8	1	4	33	24	37	.227	.348	.322
Bases Empty	311	88	16	4	15	15	39	58	.283	.505	.370
Runners/Scor. Pos.	96	22	4	0	2	28	13	22	.229	.333	.324
Runners On/2 Out	73	18	4	1	2	16	13	12	.247	.411	.360
Scor. Pos./2 Out	44	11	3	0	1	13	6	9	.250	.386	.340
Late-Inning Pressure	74	24	6	0	1	8	12	14	.324	.446	.425
Leading Off	17	7	3	0	0	0	3	4	.412	.588	.500
Runners On	32	9	0	0	0	7	7	6	.281	.281	.425
Runners/Scor. Pos.	22	7	0	0	0	7	3	4	.318	.318	.423

RUNS BATTED IN	From 1B	From 2B	From 3B	Scoring Position
Totals	5/133	10/71	14/47	24/118
Percentage	3.8%	14.1%	29.8%	20.3%

Loves to face: Paul Assenmacher (.600, 6-for-10)
Mike Maddux (.667, 6-for-9, 1 HR)
Bob Ojeda (.412, 14-for-34, 2 HR)

Hates to face: Tim Burke (.118, 2-for-17)
Jay Howell (.133, 2-for-15, 9 SO)
Ramon Martinez (.138, 4-for-29, 0 BB)

Miscellaneous statistics: Ground outs-to-air outs ratio: 0.98 last season, 1.00 for career.... Grounded into 5 double plays in 98 opportunities (one per 20).... Drove in 9 of 22 runners from third base with less than two outs (41%).... Direction of balls hit to the outfield: 52% to left field, 24% to center, 24% to right.... Base running: Advanced from first base to third on 16 of 28 outfield singles (57%); scored from second on 10 of 15 (67%).... Made 3.00 assists per nine innings at second base.

Comments: With his final game of last season, he passed Tito Fuentes on the Giants' all-time list of games played at second base. Thompson has now played 843 games there, 750 fewer than all-time franchise leader, Larry Doyle.... Has played at least 132 games in each of his six seasons with the Giants. In the history of the Giants by the bay, only two players have had longer streaks: Willie Mays (11 years, 1958–68), and Orlando Cepeda (7 years, 1958–64).... Hit safely in 14 consecutive San Francisco losses, the longest streak of its kind in the National League last season.... His average of one walk every 9.1 plate appearances was the best rate of his career, as was his strikeout rate (one every 6.0 PA).... His 19 home runs last season ranked second to Ryne Sandberg among N.L. second basemen. His transformation to power hitter was gradual and steady, not sudden; Thompson's home-run rate, year by year since 1988: one every 68 at-bats, followed by 42, 33, and 26.... Career average of .274 at Candlestick, .251 on other grass fields, .233 on artificial turf.... No walks in 61 plate appearances with the bases loaded.... Has driven in 22.4 percent of runners from scoring position during his career, the 4th-lowest rate of the last 17 years (minimum: 750 opportunities). The bottom five: Frank Taveras (20.8%), Vince Coleman (21.8%), Jose Uribe (21.8%), Thompson (22.4%), Johnnie LeMaster (22.8%).... That should blow away those Taveras comeback rumors.

Dickie Thon

Bats Right

Philadelphia Phillies	AB	H	2B	3B	HR	RBI	BB	SO	BA	SA	OBA
Season	539	136	18	4	9	44	25	84	.252	.351	.283
vs. Left-Handers	205	53	7	2	2	14	14	23	.259	.341	.306
vs. Right-Handers	334	83	11	2	7	30	11	61	.249	.356	.269
vs. Ground-Ballers	261	67	5	1	5	24	16	39	.257	.341	.296
vs. Fly-Ballers	280	69	13	3	4	20	10	46	.246	.357	.271
Home Games	270	73	8	2	4	25	12	44	.270	.359	.299
Road Games	269	63	10	2	5	19	13	40	.234	.342	.268
Grass Fields	155	38	7	1	1	7	7	22	.245	.323	.278
Artificial Turf	384	98	11	3	8	37	18	62	.255	.362	.286
April	60	16	2	0	1	5	5	15	.267	.350	.309
May	93	22	3	0	1	6	4	15	.237	.301	.268
June	93	23	1	3	2	5	7	15	.247	.387	.300
July	77	16	2	1	0	3	4	9	.208	.260	.247
August	114	34	8	0	3	20	2	13	.298	.447	.308
Sept./Oct.	102	25	2	0	2	5	3	17	.245	.324	.267
Leading Off Inn.	134	36	2	1	4	4	3	21	.269	.388	.285
Runners On	214	46	11	1	3	38	11	29	.215	.318	.249
Bases Empty	325	90	7	3	6	6	14	55	.277	.372	.307
Runners/Scor. Pos.	118	26	9	0	0	29	8	12	.220	.297	.262
Runners On/2 Out	91	20	6	0	1	17	6	15	.220	.319	.268
Scor. Pos./2 Out	57	13	5	0	0	14	6	7	.228	.316	.302
Late-Inning Pressure	103	26	3	0	3	9	3	20	.252	.369	.271
Leading Off	33	6	2	0	1	1	0	8	.182	.333	.182
Runners On	37	11	1	0	1	7	1	3	.297	.405	.308
Runners/Scor. Pos.	20	4	1	0	0	5	1	0	.200	.250	.227

RUNS BATTED IN	From 1B	From 2B	From 3B	Scoring Position
Totals	8/152	13/97	14/41	27/138
Percentage	5.3%	13.4%	34.1%	19.6%

Loves to face: Eric Show (.391, 9-for-23, 2 2B, 1 3B, 3 HR)
Mark Davis (.375, 6-for-16, 1 HR)
Scott Sanderson (.417, 5-for-12, 1 HR)

Hates to face: Mark Langston (0-for-8, 5 SO)
Scott Scudder (0-for-7)
Frank Viola (.200, 7-for-35, 1 HR, 0 BB)

Miscellaneous statistics: Ground outs-to-air outs ratio: 1.05 last season, 1.11 for career.... Grounded into 9 double plays in 94 opportunities (one per 10).... Drove in 9 of 18 runners from third base with less than two outs (50%).... Direction of balls hit to the outfield: 34% to left field, 33% to center, 32% to right.... Base running: Advanced from first base to third on 6 of 19 outfield singles (32%); scored from second on 11 of 16 (69%).... Made 2.90 assists per nine innings at shortstop.

Comments: Thon's no longer seeing double, but you might think you are by looking at his season statistics above. Compare the top line to his figures for 1990: 141-for-552, 20 2B, 4 3B, 8 HR, 48 RBI, 37 BB, 77 SO. His averages across the board: .255, .350, and .305.... Turned 33 during the 1991 season and started 143 games at shortstop. Only two older players started as many as 140 games at either third base, shortstop, or second base last season: Ozzie Smith and Tim Wallach. Wade Boggs, active major leaguer closest in age to Thon, started 139 games at third base.... Played 1277 innings at shortstop, 2d most in the league behind Jay Bell.... Batting average with runners on base was 5th lowest in the league.... Has driven in less than 20 percent of runners from scoring position in Late-Inning Pressure Situations in four of the last five years.... The move from Veterans Stadium to Arlington should be a smooth transition. He has a career average of .264 on grass fields, .266 on artificial turf.... Thon hasn't played an American League game in more than a decade, so let's debrief him: The Twins, Blue Jays, White Sox, and Orioles have new ballparks, but the Rangers still play at Arlington Stadium. The Jays are good; the Yankees are not. And that 45-year-old on the mound (whom you might recognize from your days with the Angels) is your ace, not the batting-practice pitcher.

Jeff Treadway

Bats Left

Atlanta Braves	AB	H	2B	3B	HR	RBI	BB	SO	BA	SA	OBA
Season	306	98	17	2	3	32	23	19	.320	.418	.368
vs. Left-Handers	20	5	0	0	0	0	0	2	.250	.250	.250
vs. Right-Handers	286	93	17	2	3	32	23	17	.325	.430	.376
vs. Ground-Ballers	135	41	8	1	3	15	13	13	.304	.444	.362
vs. Fly-Ballers	171	57	9	1	0	17	10	6	.333	.398	.373
Home Games	159	42	7	1	1	12	18	8	.264	.340	.343
Road Games	147	56	10	1	2	20	5	11	.381	.503	.399
Grass Fields	218	64	11	1	2	16	19	12	.294	.381	.353
Artificial Turf	88	34	6	1	1	16	4	7	.386	.511	.409
April	49	16	0	1	2	9	3	1	.327	.490	.358
May	39	14	1	1	0	2	3	1	.359	.436	.409
June	50	17	4	0	0	3	4	8	.340	.420	.389
July	57	18	5	0	1	9	8	1	.316	.456	.400
August	67	20	4	0	0	5	4	5	.299	.358	.333
Sept./Oct.	44	13	3	0	0	4	1	3	.295	.364	.326
Leading Off Inn.	55	15	1	0	1	1	3	4	.273	.345	.322
Runners On	124	42	7	1	2	31	11	8	.339	.460	.384
Bases Empty	182	56	10	1	1	1	12	11	.308	.390	.357
Runners/Scor. Pos.	66	22	3	0	1	27	8	4	.333	.424	.390
Runners On/2 Out	38	12	3	1	0	12	3	3	.316	.447	.366
Scor. Pos./2 Out	25	7	2	0	0	11	3	2	.280	.360	.357
Late-Inning Pressure	37	12	0	1	0	6	1	2	.324	.378	.333
Leading Off	8	3	0	0	0	0	0	0	.375	.375	.375
Runners On	17	5	0	1	0	6	0	1	.294	.412	.278
Runners/Scor. Pos.	10	3	0	0	0	5	0	0	.300	.300	.273

RUNS BATTED IN	From 1B	From 2B	From 3B	Scoring Position
Totals	4/90	13/49	12/29	25/78
Percentage	4.4%	26.5%	41.4%	32.1%

Loves to face: Tom Browning (.400, 6-for-15, 1 HR)
David Cone (.409, 9-for-22, 2 HR)
Orel Hershiser (.350, 7-for-20, 1 HR)

Hates to face: John Burkett (.125, 3-for-24)
Scott Garrelts (.179, 5-for-28)
Dave Smith (0-for-10)

Miscellaneous statistics: Ground outs-to-air outs ratio: 0.68 last season, 4th lowest in N.L.; 0.87 for career.... Grounded into 8 double plays in 67 opportunities (one per 8.4).... Drove in 8 of 18 runners from third base with less than two outs (44%).... Direction of balls hit to the outfield: 29% to left field, 29% to center, 41% to right.... Base running: Advanced from first base to third on 10 of 18 outfield singles (56%); scored from second on 9 of 14 (64%).... Made 2.95 assists per nine innings at second base.

Comments: His batting average has increased in every season since 1988: .252, .277, .283, .320.... Has batted .290 in three seasons with Atlanta after hitting .252 as a rookie with the Reds in 1988.... Started 85 games last season, all against right-handed starting pitchers. He had only 20 plate appearances against southpaws last season, down from a career-high 131 in 1990.... Started only once in Atlanta's last 15 regular-season games (the meaningless finale at that) because of an injury to his right hand, and started only twice in 14 postseason games.... Average of one strikeout every 17.7 times to the plate last season was the best rate of his career. He drew more walks than strikeouts for the first time.... Had a .397 batting average during the first inning, the highest in the majors (minimum: 40 AB). He batted .298 later in the game.... Drove in 32 runs last season, 10 of which were go-ahead RBIs. Compare that to Rafael Belliard, who had 27 RBIs, only two of which gave the Braves a lead.... His .333 batting average with runners in scoring position was down eight points from his 1990 mark. Only two other major leaguers hit as high as .333 with RISP in each of the last two seasons (minimum: 50 AB each season): Barry Bonds and Frank Thomas.... Career batting average of .350 as a pinch hitter (14-for-40, 0 HR).... Committed 12 errors in home games, but only three on the road.... Looking more and more like the Rance Mulliniks of the 1990s.

Jose Uribe
Bats Left and Right

San Francisco Giants	AB	H	2B	3B	HR	RBI	BB	SO	BA	SA	OBA
Season	231	51	8	4	1	12	20	33	.221	.303	.283
vs. Left-Handers	60	15	2	1	0	3	7	8	.250	.317	.328
vs. Right-Handers	171	36	6	3	1	9	13	25	.211	.298	.266
vs. Ground-Ballers	124	22	5	1	0	6	11	19	.177	.234	.244
vs. Fly-Ballers	107	29	3	3	1	6	9	14	.271	.383	.328
Home Games	115	27	3	2	0	7	9	16	.235	.296	.290
Road Games	116	24	5	2	1	5	11	17	.207	.310	.276
Grass Fields	160	30	5	2	0	8	15	22	.188	.244	.257
Artificial Turf	71	21	3	2	1	4	5	11	.296	.437	.342
April	22	2	0	0	0	0	3	4	.091	.091	.200
May	33	6	0	0	1	3	6	10	.182	.273	.308
June	35	7	1	2	0	2	3	3	.200	.343	.263
July	24	5	1	1	0	1	1	2	.208	.333	.240
August	79	25	6	1	0	5	6	6	.316	.418	.365
Sept./Oct.	38	6	0	0	0	1	1	8	.158	.158	.179
Leading Off Inn.	56	12	3	0	1	1	6	11	.214	.321	.290
Runners On	84	22	2	3	0	11	11	8	.262	.357	.347
Bases Empty	147	29	6	1	1	1	9	25	.197	.272	.244
Runners/Scor. Pos.	52	13	2	2	0	10	8	6	.250	.365	.350
Runners On/2 Out	33	7	1	1	0	5	10	4	.212	.303	.395
Scor. Pos./2 Out	22	6	1	1	0	5	8	4	.273	.409	.467
Late-Inning Pressure	21	5	1	0	0	0	5	8	.238	.286	.385
Leading Off	10	2	1	0	0	0	2	4	.200	.300	.333
Runners On	5	2	0	0	0	0	1	1	.400	.400	.500
Runners/Scor. Pos.	5	2	0	0	0	0	1	1	.400	.400	.400

RUNS BATTED IN	From 1B	From 2B	From 3B	Scoring Position
Totals	2/56	4/39	5/19	9/58
Percentage	3.6%	10.3%	26.3%	15.5%

Loves to face: Larry Andersen (.313, 5-for-16, 1 HR)
Tim Burke (.429, 6-for-14, 1 HR)
Jose DeLeon (.455, 10-for-22)

Hates to face: Doug Drabek (.100, 2-for-20)
Bob Walk (.120, 3-for-25)
Ed Whitson (.086, 3-for-35)

Miscellaneous statistics: Ground outs-to-air outs ratio: 1.00 last season, 1.04 for career. . . . Grounded into 2 double plays in 33 opportunities (one per 17). . . . Drove in 2 of 5 runners from third base with less than two outs (40%). . . . Direction of balls hit to the outfield: 29% to left field, 31% to center, 40% to right batting left-handed; 29% to left field, 25% to center, 46% to right batting right-handed. . . . Base running: Advanced from first base to third on 6 of 9 outfield singles (67%); scored from second on 3 of 3 (100%). . . . Made 3.16 assists per nine innings at shortstop.

Comments: The Giants used seven different players at shortstop last season. (Only the A's used as many.) In order of innings played, they were: Uribe, Dave Anderson, Mike Benjamin, Tony Perezchica, Royce Clayton, Greg Litton, and Matt Williams. . . . Uribe and Rob Thompson have been San Francisco's regular middle-infield tandem team each of the last six seasons, making them the longest-running DP-combo in Giants history. . . . Started 75 games last season, once again all from the 8th slot in the order. He has occupied that position in each of his last 377 starts, and in 830 of 867 for his career. . . . Had only one game last season in which he drove in more than one run. . . . Batted nearly 100 points higher against fly-ball pitchers than against ground-ballers last season, a drastic departure from his previous career performance. Even including 1991, his career average against ground-ballers (.257) is considerably higher than his average against fly-ballers (.224). . . . Has hit for a higher average with runners on base than he has with the bases empty in each of his seven seasons with the Giants. . . . Has a career average of .172 with the bases loaded (10-for-58, no extra-base hits), and it's even worse with two outs and the bags full (.094, 3-for-32). . . . It's our guess that more people know the name on the back of Uribe's uniform when he made his major league debut in 1984 ("Gonzalez"; he changed his name a year later) than the team name shown on the front ("Cardinals"; he was traded to the Giants after the season).

Andy Van Slyke
Bats Left

Pittsburgh Pirates	AB	H	2B	3B	HR	RBI	BB	SO	BA	SA	OBA
Season	491	130	24	7	17	83	71	85	.265	.446	.355
vs. Left-Handers	185	36	9	2	4	23	23	40	.195	.330	.287
vs. Right-Handers	306	94	15	5	13	60	48	45	.307	.516	.396
vs. Ground-Ballers	220	59	9	3	6	39	27	34	.268	.418	.346
vs. Fly-Ballers	274	71	15	4	11	44	45	51	.259	.464	.361
Home Games	265	60	9	4	9	46	37	44	.226	.392	.319
Road Games	226	70	15	3	8	37	34	41	.310	.509	.397
Grass Fields	119	33	4	1	4	16	14	22	.277	.429	.353
Artificial Turf	372	97	20	6	13	67	57	63	.261	.452	.356
April	67	17	2	1	4	16	8	9	.254	.493	.321
May	86	19	2	2	2	10	18	11	.221	.360	.358
June	80	16	3	0	0	6	7	17	.200	.237	.273
July	71	25	4	3	5	25	18	14	.352	.704	.467
August	94	24	5	1	4	16	9	21	.255	.457	.317
Sept./Oct.	93	29	8	0	2	10	11	13	.312	.462	.387
Leading Off Inn.	91	17	6	1	2	2	12	15	.187	.341	.288
Runners On	224	65	8	6	9	75	30	37	.290	.500	.366
Bases Empty	267	65	16	1	8	8	41	48	.243	.401	.346
Runners/Scor. Pos.	132	37	6	2	1	55	23	26	.280	.379	.365
Runners On/2 Out	58	12	0	2	2	14	10	12	.207	.379	.324
Scor. Pos./2 Out	39	9	0	1	1	11	8	7	.231	.359	.362
Late-Inning Pressure	60	16	3	0	1	7	6	11	.267	.367	.319
Leading Off	11	1	1	0	0	0	2	2	.091	.182	.231
Runners On	26	7	0	0	1	7	2	5	.269	.385	.290
Runners/Scor. Pos.	14	3	0	0	0	5	2	2	.214	.214	.263

RUNS BATTED IN	From 1B	From 2B	From 3B	Scoring Position
Totals	15/155	21/105	30/59	51/164
Percentage	9.7%	20.0%	50.8%	31.1%

Loves to face: Jason Grimsley (.714, 5-for-7, 1 HR)
Jimmy Jones (.400, 10-for-25, 3 HR)
Roger McDowell (.455, 10-for-22, 2 HR)

Hates to face: Randy Myers (.111, 3-for-27)
Bob Ojeda (.173, 9-for-52, 1 HR)
Lee Smith (.040, 1-for-25, 1 HR, 4 BB)

Miscellaneous statistics: Ground outs-to-air outs ratio: 0.78 last season, 0.89 for career. . . . Grounded into 5 double plays in 123 opportunities (one per 25). . . . Drove in 27 of 40 runners from third base with less than two outs (68%). . . . Direction of balls hit to the outfield: 25% to left field, 28% to center, 48% to right. . . . Base running: Advanced from first base to third on 12 of 30 outfield singles (40%); scored from second on 16 of 16 (100%), best in majors. . . . Made 2.16 putouts per nine innings in center field, 2d-lowest rate in majors.

Comments: The Bonilla-Van Slyke-Bonds outfield went out on a high note: Bucs outfielders (occasionally including others) led the majors with 315 RBIs. No other team reached the 300 mark. . . . Were it not for his defense, Van Slyke would be a platoon player. He had the league's 8th-highest average against right-handers last season, but the 8th-lowest mark vs. left-handers. Last season marked the third time that Van Slyke has failed to crack the .200 mark vs. southpaws. His career averages: .219 vs. LHP, .290 vs. RHP. . . . All but one of his 129 starts came from the 3d spot in the batting order. The Bucs were 82–46 with Van Slyke batting third, 16–18 with others. . . . Hit the most home runs of any N.L. player who didn't hit a three-run or grand-slam homer last season. . . . His strike-out rate has improved in each of the last four seasons; year by year since 1987: one SO per 5.18 PA, then 5.24, 5.3, 6.4, and 6.8. . .Has batted .262 over the past three seasons, with an average of 12 home runs and 13 stolen bases per year. For the three previous years, his figures were .285, 20 HR, and 28 SB. . . . Career batting average of .201 with runners in scoring position in Late-Inning Pressure Situations, the 8th-lowest mark among active players (minimum: 100 AB), but 47 points higher than Barry Bonds's average. . . . Has reached base on catchers' interference 13 times in his career, more than twice as often as any other active player.

Chico Walker
Bats Left and Right

Chicago Cubs	AB	H	2B	3B	HR	RBI	BB	SO	BA	SA	OBA
Season	374	96	10	1	6	34	33	57	.257	.337	.315
vs. Left-Handers	119	25	2	1	3	12	8	17	.210	.319	.256
vs. Right-Handers	255	71	8	0	3	22	25	40	.278	.345	.342
vs. Ground-Ballers	152	43	4	1	2	18	7	15	.283	.362	.313
vs. Fly-Ballers	222	53	6	0	4	16	26	42	.239	.320	.316
Home Games	200	54	5	1	4	19	17	27	.270	.365	.324
Road Games	174	42	5	0	2	15	16	30	.241	.305	.304
Grass Fields	278	75	7	1	6	31	25	41	.270	.367	.328
Artificial Turf	96	21	3	0	0	3	8	16	.219	.250	.276
April	10	2	0	0	0	0	1	0	.200	.200	.273
May	38	13	0	0	1	4	5	8	.342	.421	.419
June	51	12	3	0	0	3	5	11	.235	.294	.304
July	93	31	3	1	1	12	8	13	.333	.419	.379
August	100	21	3	0	2	8	6	9	.210	.300	.255
Sept./Oct.	82	17	1	0	2	7	8	16	.207	.293	.275
Leading Off Inn.	132	29	4	0	1	1	7	17	.220	.273	.259
Runners On	126	35	3	0	4	32	21	23	.278	.397	.373
Bases Empty	248	61	7	1	2	2	12	34	.246	.306	.281
Runners/Scor. Pos.	84	24	2	0	2	28	18	18	.286	.381	.400
Runners On/2 Out	62	10	0	0	2	10	14	15	.161	.258	.316
Scor. Pos./2 Out	46	6	0	0	0	6	12	13	.130	.130	.310
Late-Inning Pressure	89	29	4	0	1	11	11	20	.326	.404	.396
Leading Off	16	5	1	0	0	0	0	4	.313	.375	.313
Runners On	40	13	1	0	1	11	10	12	.325	.425	.451
Runners/Scor. Pos.	28	9	1	0	0	9	8	9	.321	.357	.459

RUNS BATTED IN	From 1B	From 2B	From 3B	Scoring Position
Totals	3/78	11/65	14/36	25/101
Percentage	3.8%	16.9%	38.9%	24.8%

Loves to face: Tim Burke (.714, 5-for-7)
Mark Gardner (.333, 4-for-12, 2 HR)
Ramon Martinez (.375, 3-for-8)
Hates to face: Brian Barnes (0-for-12)
Tom Browning (.077, 1-for-13)
Dwight Gooden (.063, 1-for-16)

Miscellaneous statistics: Ground outs-to-air outs ratio: 1.00 last season, 1.16 for career. . . . Grounded into 3 double plays in 50 opportunities (one per 17). . . . Drove in 12 of 16 runners from third base with less than two outs (75%). . . . Direction of balls hit to the outfield: 35% to left field, 40% to center, 25% to right batting left-handed; 32% to left field, 42% to center, 27% to right batting right-handed. . . . Base running: Advanced from first base to third on 4 of 20 outfield singles (20%); scored from second on 9 of 14 (64%). . . . Made 1.65 assists per nine innings at third base.

Comments: Although his first tour of duty with the Cubs lasted three seasons (1985–87), he played more games for Chicago last season (124) than over his previous stint with the club (96 games). . . . His on-base percentage leading off innings was the 4th lowest in the league. . . . Led N.L. pinch hitters with a .406 batting average (13-for-32; minimum: 20 AB). . . . Batting average in Late-Inning Pressure Situations was the 8th highest in the league, but he has only one hit in 17 career at-bats with runners in scoring position in LIPS. . . . Other career batting-average breakdowns: .213 vs. left-handers, .245 vs. right-handers; .275 vs. ground-ball pitchers, .205 vs. fly-ballers; .215 with runners in scoring position, .141 with two outs and RISP. . . . Hit six home runs in 374 at-bats last season, compared to two in 377 ABs prior to 1991. . . . When Walker hit his first home run of the 1991 season, which was his first in the majors since 1986, we were asked if the five-year gap was an all-time record. Actually, it wasn't even the longest homerless streak of Walker's own career! His only home run prior to 1986 was in 1980, while playing for the Red Sox. For the record, these are the longest home-run gaps in major league history: 14 seasons, by Nick Altrock (1904–18) and Ralph Winegarner (1935–49). Last season, Warren Cromartie snapped a streak that spanned eight years (not including one day for crossing the International Date Line).

Larry Walker
Bats Left

Montreal Expos	AB	H	2B	3B	HR	RBI	BB	SO	BA	SA	OBA
Season	487	141	30	2	16	64	42	102	.290	.458	.349
vs. Left-Handers	160	46	9	0	4	25	13	39	.287	.419	.352
vs. Right-Handers	327	95	21	2	12	39	29	63	.291	.477	.348
vs. Ground-Ballers	215	65	16	1	6	26	21	40	.302	.470	.372
vs. Fly-Ballers	276	79	15	1	10	38	22	62	.286	.457	.339
Home Games	187	51	14	0	5	24	14	46	.273	.428	.330
Road Games	300	90	16	2	11	40	28	56	.300	.477	.361
Grass Fields	156	45	4	1	8	26	20	28	.288	.481	.367
Artificial Turf	331	96	26	1	8	38	22	74	.290	.447	.341
April	55	10	2	1	0	3	6	11	.182	.255	.258
May	91	22	3	0	4	8	11	22	.242	.407	.320
June	78	20	4	0	2	10	10	24	.256	.385	.356
July	42	13	2	1	3	12	2	8	.310	.619	.341
August	101	38	13	0	4	12	7	12	.376	.624	.427
Sept./Oct.	120	38	6	0	3	19	6	25	.317	.442	.349
Leading Off Inn.	133	43	11	1	3	3	9	28	.323	.489	.366
Runners On	196	58	12	1	9	57	18	36	.296	.505	.357
Bases Empty	291	83	18	1	7	7	24	66	.285	.426	.344
Runners/Scor. Pos.	119	32	9	1	2	41	16	26	.269	.412	.355
Runners On/2 Out	87	20	4	1	2	18	10	18	.230	.368	.309
Scor. Pos./2 Out	60	13	4	1	0	14	10	13	.217	.317	.329
Late-Inning Pressure	84	24	4	2	3	11	10	14	.286	.488	.375
Leading Off	24	5	1	1	0	0	6	6	.208	.333	.367
Runners On	32	11	2	1	2	10	2	8	.344	.656	.417
Runners/Scor. Pos.	23	7	1	1	0	6	1	7	.304	.435	.385

RUNS BATTED IN	From 1B	From 2B	From 3B	Scoring Position
Totals	12/142	14/95	22/51	36/146
Percentage	8.5%	14.7%	43.1%	24.7%

Loves to face: John Burkett (.412, 7-for-17, 3 HR)
Mike Hartley (.571, 4-for-7, 1 2B, 1 3B, 1 HR)
Omar Olivares (.533, 8-for-15)
Hates to face: Paul Assenmacher (.077, 1-for-13)
Mark Portugal (0-for-8)
Bryn Smith (.071, 1-for-14)

Miscellaneous statistics: Ground outs-to-air outs ratio: 1.35 last season, 1.45 for career. . . . Grounded into 7 double plays in 87 opportunities (one per 12). . . . Drove in 15 of 22 runners from third base with less than two outs (68%). . . . Direction of balls hit to the outfield: 38% to left field, 32% to center, 30% to right. . . . Base running: Advanced from first base to third on 13 of 30 outfield singles (43%); scored from second on 7 of 13 (54%), 5th-lowest rate in N.L. . . . Made 2.48 putouts per nine innings in right field, highest rate in N.L.

Comments: Raised his average from .241 in 1990. That 49-point increase was the largest by any rookie from the class of '90 (minimum: 250 AB each season). The last sophomore to raise his rookie-season average by that much was Pete O'Brien, from .237 to .287 in 1984 (minimum: 400 AB each). The largest second-season increase ever was 76 points by Al Simmons in 1925 (.308 to .384). . . . Quietly led the National League with a .338 batting average after the All-Star break. . . . The Expos used nine different players at first base last season, the most of any team in the league. The departed Andres Galarraga played 105 games there, followed by Walker (39 games), Tom Foley (31), and six others with fewer than 10 games. . . . Montreal also started eight different players in right field, tied with the Giants for the most of any N.L. team. In order of innings, they were: Walker, Dave Martinez, Ken Williams, Junior Noboa, Marquis Grissom, Mike Fitzgerald, Nikco Riesgo, and Eric Bullock. . . . Started the last two games of the season in center field, his only starts at that position. . . . Career batting-average breakdowns: .272 with the bases empty, .249 with runners on base, .233 with runners in scoring position; .224 in day games, .276 at night. . . . He has a career mark of .257 at Olympic Stadium, .247 on other artificial surfaces, .286 on grass fields. . . . Career batting average of .100 as a pinch hitter (2-for-20, 1 HR).

Tim Wallach
Bats Right

Montreal Expos	AB	H	2B	3B	HR	RBI	BB	SO	BA	SA	OBA
Season	577	130	22	1	13	73	50	100	.225	.334	.292
vs. Left-Handers	185	41	8	0	5	21	18	29	.222	.346	.293
vs. Right-Handers	392	89	14	1	8	52	32	71	.227	.329	.292
vs. Ground-Ballers	265	47	7	1	3	27	20	56	.177	.245	.234
vs. Fly-Ballers	317	84	15	0	10	47	30	44	.265	.407	.337
Home Games	230	49	9	0	5	23	26	36	.213	.317	.303
Road Games	347	81	13	1	8	50	24	64	.233	.346	.285
Grass Fields	165	39	4	0	4	22	15	36	.236	.333	.304
Artificial Turf	412	91	18	1	9	51	35	64	.221	.335	.287
April	81	17	2	0	1	4	1	13	.210	.272	.220
May	100	22	3	0	2	11	16	19	.220	.310	.339
June	112	32	4	0	5	20	11	17	.286	.455	.360
July	75	17	4	0	2	12	9	14	.227	.360	.302
August	104	19	5	1	2	11	7	22	.183	.308	.241
Sept./Oct.	105	23	4	0	1	15	6	15	.219	.286	.263
Leading Off Inn.	161	39	7	0	3	3	5	22	.242	.342	.265
Runners On	256	57	8	1	5	65	33	49	.223	.320	.319
Bases Empty	321	73	14	0	8	8	17	51	.227	.346	.268
Runners/Scor. Pos.	168	40	4	1	3	58	26	37	.238	.327	.347
Runners On/2 Out	126	23	4	0	3	26	21	26	.183	.286	.304
Scor. Pos./2 Out	84	17	2	0	2	23	19	18	.202	.298	.350
Late-Inning Pressure	96	20	2	0	1	7	13	16	.208	.260	.309
Leading Off	27	6	1	0	1	1	1	3	.222	.370	.250
Runners On	40	9	0	0	0	6	9	7	.225	.225	.380
Runners/Scor. Pos.	30	6	0	0	0	6	6	5	.200	.200	.351

RUNS BATTED IN	From 1B	From 2B	From 3B	Scoring Position
Totals	9/155	23/119	28/75	51/194
Percentage	5.8%	19.3%	37.3%	26.3%

Loves to face: Tom Browning (.356, 16-for-45, 3 HR)
Tom Glavine (.294, 10-for-34, 2 2B, 5 HR)
Greg W. Harris (.500, 6-for-12, 2 HR)
Hates to face: Sid Fernandez (.167, 7-for-42, 0 BB)
Omar Olivares (.063, 1-for-16)
Wally Whitehurst (0-for-10)

Miscellaneous statistics: Ground outs-to-air outs ratio: 0.82 last season, 0.84 for career.... Grounded into 12 double plays in 99 opportunities (one per 8.3).... Drove in 18 of 34 runners from third base with less than two outs (53%).... Direction of balls hit to the outfield: 31% to left field, 38% to center, 31% to right.... Base running: Advanced from first base to third on 3 of 20 outfield singles (15%); scored from second on 7 of 12 (58%).... Made 2.11 assists per nine innings at third base, 3d-highest rate in N.L.

Comments: Wallach is the Expos' all-time leader in games (1617), at-bats (5992), doubles (331), RBIs (846), strike-outs (919), and GIDPs (142).... Posted the the league's 2d-lowest batting average in night games last season (.214).... His on-base percentage leading off innings was the 5th lowest in the league.... He started 127 games in the cleanup spot for Montreal. The Expos tried seven different players in that lineup position, the most in the league, but kept coming back to Wallach.... Batting average decreased 71 points from 1990 to 1991, the 2d-largest decrease among major league players who qualified for the batting title in both seasons. The largest drop belonged to George Brett (74 points).... Led N.L. third basemen in fielding percentage for the first time in his career. He averaged one error every 31 chances, compared to a league average of one per 20 chances.... Ended the season with a 32-game errorless streak, his longest of the season.... Career total of 1539 games at third base ranks third among active players, behind George Brett (1689) and Carney Lansford (1601), who combined to play only four games at that position last season.... Career total of 1617 games is the most of any active N.L. player who has spent his entire major league career with a single club. Seven active players have spent longer careers entirely with the same American League teams, but that's not skewed by the DH rule. Of those seven, only two now play primarily as a DH: Paul Molitor and George Brett.

Jerome Walton
Bats Right

Chicago Cubs	AB	H	2B	3B	HR	RBI	BB	SO	BA	SA	OBA
Season	270	59	13	1	5	17	19	55	.219	.330	.275
vs. Left-Handers	128	25	6	0	0	6	10	23	.195	.242	.261
vs. Right-Handers	142	34	7	1	5	11	9	32	.239	.408	.288
vs. Ground-Ballers	107	19	2	0	1	4	4	29	.178	.224	.212
vs. Fly-Ballers	163	40	11	1	4	13	15	26	.245	.399	.313
Home Games	120	27	6	0	3	6	10	21	.225	.350	.286
Road Games	150	32	7	1	2	11	9	34	.213	.313	.265
Grass Fields	166	37	7	0	4	8	11	32	.223	.337	.280
Artificial Turf	104	22	6	1	1	9	8	23	.212	.317	.265
April	49	13	3	0	1	4	1	9	.265	.388	.288
May	61	14	5	0	0	2	1	13	.230	.311	.238
June	63	16	1	0	1	2	5	9	.254	.317	.319
July	30	6	3	0	1	3	3	8	.200	.400	.294
August	37	5	0	0	1	4	2	8	.135	.216	.175
Sept./Oct.	30	5	1	1	1	2	7	8	.167	.367	.324
Leading Off Inn.	117	28	8	0	5	5	5	22	.239	.436	.270
Runners On	89	17	1	1	0	12	5	18	.191	.225	.235
Bases Empty	181	42	12	0	5	5	14	37	.232	.381	.294
Runners/Scor. Pos.	52	9	1	0	0	11	4	13	.173	.192	.233
Runners On/2 Out	39	5	0	0	0	4	2	10	.128	.128	.209
Scor. Pos./2 Out	26	3	0	0	0	2	3	7	.115	.115	.207
Late-Inning Pressure	49	9	0	1	1	6	4	11	.184	.286	.241
Leading Off	12	2	0	0	1	1	0	4	.167	.417	.167
Runners On	20	6	0	1	0	5	1	6	.300	.400	.318
Runners/Scor. Pos.	12	3	0	0	0	4	1	4	.250	.250	.286

RUNS BATTED IN	From 1B	From 2B	From 3B	Scoring Position
Totals	1/55	4/44	7/16	11/60
Percentage	1.8%	9.1%	43.8%	18.3%

Loves to face: Bill Landrum (.364, 4-for-11, 2 HR)
Dennis Martinez (.364, 4-for-11, 2 2B, 1 HR)
John Smiley (.400, 8-for-20, 2 HR)
Hates to face: Xavier Hernandez (0-for-8)
Roger McDowell (0-for-8)
Zane Smith (.091, 1-for-11)

Miscellaneous statistics: Ground outs-to-air outs ratio: 1.41 last season, 1.44 for career.... Grounded into 7 double plays in 34 opportunities (one per 4.9).... Drove in 6 of 9 runners from third base with less than two outs (67%).... Direction of balls hit to the outfield: 38% to left field, 32% to center, 31% to right.... Base running: Advanced from first base to third on 4 of 16 outfield singles (25%); scored from second on 4 of 7 (57%).... Made 2.65 putouts per nine innings in center field.

Comments: Started 34 of 64 games in which the Cubs faced left-handed starting pitchers, 25 of 96 games against right-handers.... He started only 15 games after the All-Star break.... Despite playing 123 games last season, he came to the plate only 298 times. He was used as a defensive replacement 32 times, as a pinch hitter 27 times, and as a pinch runner five times. Only two other major leaguers played in as many as 120 games without accumulating at least 300 plate appearances: Stan Javier and Daryl Boston.... Batting average in Late-Inning Pressure Situations was 10th lowest in the league. He had only one hit in 15 at-bats in extra innings.... Had the league's 6th-lowest batting average in road games, and the 9th lowest vs. left-handed pitchers.... He has hit 12 career home runs, all of them solo shots. Leadoff batters have a disproportionate number of at-bats with the bases empty, but that's no excuse. Walton has a career average of one home run every 65 at-bats with the bases empty, but no home runs in 353 career ABs with runners on.... Career average of .279 on grass fields (including .281 at Wrigley), .236 on artificial turf.... Has anyone's stock dropped as drastically as Walton's over the last two years? He batted .293 en route to the Rookie of the Year Award in 1989, but followed that with season averages of .263 and .219. The only other players with consecutive batting-average declines that large were Jerry Browne and Franklin Stubbs.

Matt Williams
Bats Right

San Francisco Giants	AB	H	2B	3B	HR	RBI	BB	SO	BA	SA	OBA
Season	589	158	24	5	34	98	33	128	.268	.499	.310
vs. Left-Handers	165	46	8	0	7	25	9	34	.279	.455	.315
vs. Right-Handers	424	112	16	5	27	73	24	94	.264	.517	.309
vs. Ground-Ballers	276	72	12	0	17	46	12	62	.261	.489	.295
vs. Fly-Ballers	313	86	12	5	17	52	21	66	.275	.508	.324
Home Games	289	83	12	3	17	46	16	60	.287	.526	.327
Road Games	300	75	12	2	17	52	17	68	.250	.473	.294
Grass Fields	444	126	19	3	24	71	20	92	.284	.502	.317
Artificial Turf	145	32	5	2	10	27	13	36	.221	.490	.290
April	78	21	2	.1	3	15	5	13	.269	.436	.310
May	111	20	4	1	2	8	1	19	.180	.288	.195
June	91	23	7	0	5	18	7	20	.253	.495	.310
July	91	31	3	1	11	21	4	24	.341	.758	.378
August	106	27	6	1	4	13	8	30	.255	.443	.304
Sept./Oct.	112	36	2	1	9	23	8	22	.321	.598	.368
Leading Off Inn.	130	40	4	3	9	9	9	23	.308	.592	.366
Runners On	279	77	10	1	15	79	14	63	.276	.480	.308
Bases Empty	310	81	14	4	19	19	19	65	.261	.516	.312
Runners/Scor. Pos.	148	36	3	1	4	55	12	35	.243	.358	.292
Runners On/2 Out	134	43	7	1	7	35	8	27	.321	.545	.368
Scor. Pos./2 Out	74	22	2	1	3	26	7	15	.297	.473	.366
Late-Inning Pressure	87	20	4	0	3	11	4	14	.230	.379	.272
Leading Off	16	4	0	0	2	2	1	3	.250	.625	.294
Runners On	44	9	2	0	1	9	2	8	.205	.318	.239
Runners/Scor. Pos.	23	3	0	0	0	6	2	5	.130	.130	.200

RUNS BATTED IN	From 1B	From 2B	From 3B	Scoring Position
Totals	16/214	19/113	29/66	48/179
Percentage	7.5%	16.8%	43.9%	26.8%

Loves to face: Shawn Boskie (.375, 6-for-16, 2 2B, 2 HR)
John Smiley (.429, 9-for-21, 4 HR)
Ed Whitson (.387, 12-for-31, 3 HR, 0 BB)

Hates to face: Greg W. Harris (0-for-13)
Dennis Martinez (.100, 2-for-20, 1 3B)
Mark Portugal (.094, 3-for-32)

Miscellaneous statistics: Ground outs-to-air outs ratio: 0.90 last season, 0.94 for career.... Grounded into 11 double plays in 115 opportunities (one per 10).... Drove in 21 of 32 runners from third base with less than two outs (66%).... Direction of balls hit to the outfield: 43% to left field, 27% to center, 30% to right.... Base running: Advanced from first base to third on 3 of 22 outfield singles (14%); scored from second on 11 of 17 (65%).... Made 2.00 assists per nine innings at third base.

Comments: Led the National League with 67 home runs over the past two seasons, and shared second place in RBIs with Bobby Bonilla at 220, 10 fewer than Barry Bonds.... Batted .273 over the past two seasons, compared to .198 from 1987 through 1989.... Led the league with 22 home runs after the All-Star break, during which time he batted .301. His 11 home runs during July were the most by any N.L. player in any month.... His streak of 32 consecutive hitless at-bats vs. right-handed pitchers (April 30–May 13) was the longest by any nonpitcher in the majors last season. Charlie Leibrandt had a streak of 40 hitless at-bats against righties.... His career total of home runs (101) is almost as high as his total of walks (104). In fact, over the last four seasons, Williams has more homers (93) than walks (88). Last year, he became the 19th player in history to hit at least 30 homers with fewer BBs than HRs; Dave Kingman did it four times, Tony Armas three times, and Ernie Banks, Andre Dawson, and Bob Horner each did it twice. Williams almost did it in 1990, when he had equal amounts in the two categories (30).... Has a career batting average of .199 with one home run every 37 at-bats in Late-Inning Pressure Situations, compared to .253 with one HR per 17 ABs at other times.... He has a career average of .270 (one HR every 14 AB) in day games, .229 (one HR every 24 AB) at night.

Eric Yelding
Bats Right

Houston Astros	AB	H	2B	3B	HR	RBI	BB	SO	BA	SA	OBA
Season	276	67	11	1	1	20	13	46	.243	.301	.276
vs. Left-Handers	97	29	3	1	0	5	6	15	.299	.351	.337
vs. Right-Handers	179	38	8	0	1	15	7	31	.212	.274	.242
vs. Ground-Ballers	128	32	6	0	0	8	8	17	.250	.297	.294
vs. Fly-Ballers	152	36	5	2	1	12	5	29	.237	.316	.259
Home Games	137	31	3	0	0	10	5	28	.226	.248	.252
Road Games	139	36	8	1	1	10	8	18	.259	.353	.299
Grass Fields	72	17	3	0	0	3	5	9	.236	.278	.286
Artificial Turf	204	50	8	1	1	17	8	37	.245	.309	.272
April	68	13	3	1	0	2	2	12	.191	.265	.214
May	85	26	5	0	1	10	2	16	.306	.400	.322
June	84	19	2	0	0	9	6	13	.226	.250	.290
July	39	9	1	0	0	1	1	5	.231	.256	.250
August	0	0	0	0	0	0	0	0	.000	.000	.000
Sept./Oct.	0	0	0	0	0	0	0	0	—	—	—
Leading Off Inn.	74	16	2	1	0	0	5	11	.216	.270	.266
Runners On	109	30	4	0	0	19	5	13	.275	.312	.304
Bases Empty	167	37	7	1	1	1	8	33	.222	.293	.257
Runners/Scor. Pos.	63	15	3	0	0	18	4	11	.238	.286	.279
Runners On/2 Out	51	14	1	0	0	6	3	6	.275	.294	.315
Scor. Pos./2 Out	32	6	1	0	0	6	3	5	.188	.219	.257
Late-Inning Pressure	47	13	1	0	0	5	3	8	.277	.298	.320
Leading Off	6	1	0	0	0	0	1	1	.167	.167	.286
Runners On	20	7	1	0	0	5	2	1	.350	.400	.409
Runners/Scor. Pos.	9	4	1	0	0	5	1	1	.444	.556	.500

RUNS BATTED IN	From 1B	From 2B	From 3B	Scoring Position
Totals	1/70	5/49	13/24	18/73
Percentage	1.4%	10.2%	54.2%	24.7%

Loves to face: Steve Avery (.556, 5-for-9, 3 2B)
Pat Combs (.385, 5-for-13)
Jose DeJesus (.462, 6-for-13)

Hates to face: Jose DeLeon (.100, 1-for-10, 5 SO)
Greg Maddux (.115, 3-for-26)
Jose Rijo (.100, 1-for-10)

Miscellaneous statistics: Ground outs-to-air outs ratio: 1.14 last season, 1.28 for career.... Grounded into 4 double plays in 44 opportunities (one per 11).... Drove in 10 of 13 runners from third base with less than two outs (77%).... Direction of balls hit to the outfield: 35% to left field, 33% to center, 31% to right.... Base running: Advanced from first base to third on 6 of 11 outfield singles (55%); scored from second on 6 of 7 (86%).... Made 2.55 assists per nine innings at shortstop, 2d-lowest rate in majors.

Comments: Yelding played 40.4 percent of the Astros' innings at shortstop last season, compared to 39.7 percent by Andujar Cedeno, 19 percent by Rafael Ramirez, and a few innings from Dave Rohde. Both Yelding and Cedeno committed 18 errors, and Ramirez contributed six for a major league high total of 42 errors at shortstop, despite having the fewest fielding chances there. Of the four teams with the highest error rates at shortstop, Houston is the only one that plays its home games on artificial turf. The major league error rate for shortstops is roughly one quarter higher on grass fields (one per 29 chances) than on turf (one per 37).... Drove in 25 percent of runners from scoring position last season despite stranding 19 runners in a row to start the season. After breaking his early-season drought, he drove in 33 percent.... No home runs in 374 career at-bats vs. left-handers, but his career batting average is 51 points higher against southpaws (.278) than northpaws (.227).... Has only one extra-base hit in 131 career at-bats in Late-Inning Pressure Situations—a ninth-inning game-winning double off John Franco last June 14.... Yelding was sent to Tucson in July, and his season ended on August 11 at Las Vegas when a pitch by Adam Peterson hit him in the face, breaking his nose and cheekbone. Yelding hadn't been hit by a pitch since August 6, 1989 (by Jeff Brantley).

Todd Zeile

Bats Right

St. Louis Cardinals	AB	H	2B	3B	HR	RBI	BB	SO	BA	SA	OBA
Season	565	158	36	3	11	81	62	94	.280	.412	.353
vs. Left-Handers	237	72	15	1	5	33	26	44	.304	.439	.375
vs. Right-Handers	328	86	21	2	6	48	36	50	.262	.393	.337
vs. Ground-Ballers	254	74	17	2	2	27	27	33	.291	.398	.365
vs. Fly-Ballers	311	84	19	1	9	54	35	61	.270	.424	.343
Home Games	279	83	20	2	7	50	33	40	.297	.459	.374
Road Games	286	75	16	1	4	31	29	54	.262	.367	.331
Grass Fields	149	40	12	0	0	12	11	30	.268	.349	.325
Artificial Turf	416	118	24	3	11	69	51	64	.284	.435	.362
April	63	20	3	1	1	12	5	10	.317	.444	.377
May	93	30	7	1	1	10	11	19	.323	.452	.396
June	102	24	7	0	1	10	9	14	.235	.333	.301
July	100	26	5	1	4	14	11	15	.260	.450	.333
August	108	31	4	0	2	18	8	14	.287	.380	.339
Sept./Oct.	99	27	10	0	2	17	18	22	.273	.434	.380
Leading Off Inn.	125	41	8	0	3	3	16	18	.328	.464	.408
Runners On	255	75	18	2	2	72	32	39	.294	.404	.369
Bases Empty	310	83	18	1	9	9	30	55	.268	.419	.338
Runners/Scor. Pos.	158	48	10	1	1	64	28	30	.304	.399	.402
Runners On/2 Out	109	30	10	0	0	29	13	21	.275	.367	.358
Scor. Pos./2 Out	80	20	7	0	0	27	13	14	.250	.338	.362
Late-Inning Pressure	87	27	3	1	1	7	10	16	.310	.402	.384
Leading Off	22	11	3	0	1	1	5	2	.500	.773	.607
Runners On	37	11	0	1	0	6	4	7	.297	.351	.357
Runners/Scor. Pos.	19	4	0	0	0	5	4	5	.211	.211	.333

RUNS BATTED IN	From 1B	From 2B	From 3B	Scoring Position
Totals	12/159	28/125	30/71	58/196
Percentage	7.5%	22.4%	42.3%	29.6%

Loves to face: Jose DeJesus (.429, 3-for-7, 1 HR, 4 BB)
Roger McDowell (.500, 5-for-10, 4 2B, 3 SO)
Bob Patterson (.444, 4-for-9, 2 2B, 1 HR)

Hates to face: Tom Browning (.063, 1-for-16)
Bob Ojeda (.067, 1-for-15)
Zane Smith (.111, 2-for-18, 1 3B, 2 BB)

Miscellaneous statistics: Ground outs-to-air outs ratio: 1.32 last season, 1.13 for career.... Grounded into 15 double plays in 107 opportunities (one per 7.1).... Drove in 20 of 35 runners from third base with less than two outs (57%).... Direction of balls hit to the outfield: 44% to left field, 33% to center, 22% to right.... Base running: Advanced from first base to third on 12 of 31 outfield singles (39%); scored from second on 13 of 21 (62%).... Made 1.97 assists per nine innings at third base.

Comments: Became only the fourth player in major league history to have 100-game seasons at both catcher and third base. The others: Duke Farrell, Johnny Bench, and Zeile's current manager Joe Torre.... Total of 1325⅓ innings at third base was the highest in the league, and 2d highest in the majors behind Gary Gaetti (1339⅔).... Committed the most errors (25) of any third baseman in the majors last season. Of the other catchers-turned-third basemen mentioned above, only Torre led the league in errors at the hot corner (1971).... Increased his batting average 36 points from 1990 to 1991, the largest increase of any player who qualified for the N.L. batting title in both seasons.... Had the league's 10th-highest batting average vs. left-handed pitchers.... Had the league's highest on-base percentage leading off innings.... Stole 14 bases in 18 attempts on artificial turf, but only three bases in 10 attempts on dirt infields.... Career batting average of .278 at Busch Stadium, .261 on other artificial surfaces, and .236 on grass fields.... Career averages of .300 in day games, .250 at night.... Hitless in eight career at-bats as a pinch hitter.... Has driven in only 18 percent of runners from scoring position in Late-Inning Pressure Situations, compared to 26 percent at other times.... Statistical profile is quite similar to those of two other young third basemen of recent seasons: Brook Jacoby through 1985 and Kelly Gruber through 1988.

PITCHER SECTION

The Pitcher Section is an alphabetical listing of every pitcher who either faced 500 batters, started 15 games, or finished 25 games in relief in the major leagues last season. Pitchers who pitched in both leagues are listed in the league where they finished the season.

Column Headings Information

Jim Abbott

California Angels	W-L	ERA	AB	H	HR	BB	SO	BA	SA	OBA

W-L	Won-Lost Record
ERA	Earned Run Average
AB	At-Bats
H	Hits
HR	Home Runs
BB	Bases on Balls
SO	Strikeouts
BA	Batting Average
SA	Slugging Average
OBA	On-Base Average

In addition to the traditional statistics used to evaluate pitchers—won-lost record, ERA, walks, and strikeouts—this section provides the batting performance of the league against each pitcher. This enables us to break down his performance into the same types of categories used to measure batters' performance. We can identify those pitchers with huge platoon differentials, or those who give up a lot of hits and home runs but can bear down with runners on base and avoid giving up the clutch run-scoring hit. (Bear in mind that overall batting average increases with runners on base, as a result of the altered defensive alignment and the effects of pitching out of the stretch position. This makes any pitcher who holds opponents to a lower average with runners on all the more impressive.)

Season Summary Information

Season										
Season	10-14	4.51	833	246	16	72	105	.295	.401	.353
vs. Left-Handers			110	35	3	15	20	.318	.436	.398
vs. Right-Handers			723	211	13	57	85	.292	.396	.345
vs. Ground-Ballers			410	114	8	35	54	.278	.366	.334
vs. Fly-Ballers			423	132	8	37	51	.312	.435	.370
Home Games	4-7	4.75	437	138	9	31	46	.316	.421	.362
Road Games	6-7	4.25	396	108	7	41	59	.273	.379	.343
Grass Fields	8-11	4.54	702	209	14	60	89	.298	.400	.354
Artificial Turf	2-3	4.32	131	37	2	12	16	.282	.405	.347
April	0-1	6.06	62	21	0	9	5	.339	.419	.425
May	2-3	5.01	163	47	3	18	22	.288	.393	.359
June	3-2	4.35	145	40	1	14	20	.276	.338	.340
July	2-3	2.63	143	37	4	8	16	.259	.371	.299
August	2-3	6.08	155	51	4	12	20	.329	.458	.375
Sept./Oct.	1-2	3.83	165	50	4	11	22	.303	.430	.354

Each pitcher's performance for the season is broken down into a variety of special categories. The first line given for each pitcher is his season total. This is followed by a breakdown of his performance against left- and right-handed hitters, against ground-ball and

fly-ball hitters (defined by whether their ground outs-to-air outs ratio is above or below the league average), in home and road games, on grass fields and artificial turf, and by month (regular season October games are combined with September). For pitchers who pitched with more than one team, all totals are combined; the "home" totals for Tom Candiotti, for example, include all games pitched in Cleveland while with the Indians, and in Toronto while with the Blue Jays.

Leading Off Inn.	206	61	6	19	20	.296	.442	.358
Bases Empty	474	139	10	35	53	.293	.407	.344
Runners On	359	107	6	37	52	.298	.393	.363
Runners/Scor. Pos.	182	52	1	29	29	.286	.352	.379
Runners On/2 Out	146	39	4	20	28	.267	.384	.363
Scor. Pos./2 Out	83	19	1	17	14	.229	.301	.366

Following these breakdowns, each pitcher's performance is divided into specific game situations. Totals are given for each pitcher against batters who lead off an inning (for relievers, this would not include the first batter faced if not leading off an inning), with bases empty and runners on base, with runners in scoring position (on second or third, or both), with runners on base and two out, and with runners in scoring position and two out.

Late-Inning Pressure	61	16	2	2	7	.262	.377	.286
Leading Off	19	4	1	0	3	.211	.368	.211
Runners On	12	5	0	1	1	.417	.417	.462
Runners/Scor. Pos.	7	3	0	1	1	.429	.429	.500

The next group shows the pitcher's performance in Late-Inning Pressure Situations (LIPS). These are the flip side of the batters' pressure situations: any at-bats in the seventh inning or later, with the score tied, or the pitcher's team leading by one, two, or three runs (or four if there are two or more runners on base).

The statistics for Late-Inning Pressure Situations are then broken down for each pitcher's performance when the hitter is leading off an inning, batting with runners on base, or with runners in scoring position.

First 9 Batters	268	81	4	24	36	.302	.410	.360
Second 9 Batters	264	72	3	22	32	.273	.348	.328
All Batters Thereafter	301	93	9	26	37	.309	.439	.368

The last set of breakdowns tracks a pitcher's performance through each appearance by listing the opponents' record in his first time through the batting order, his second time through, and all at-bats thereafter. This spotlights those pitchers who get stronger as the game progresses, as well as those who breeze through the first time around but falter on repeated viewing.

Following the statistics for each pitcher is a list of batters he "loves and hates to face." The stats listed for each match-up include all regular-season games since 1975 inclusive. Next are miscellaneous statistics given in text form; these include: the pitcher's ground outs-to-air outs ratio; the number of double- play grounders he induced and the number of opportunities he faced (runner on first, less than two out); the number of doubles and triples he allowed in his innings pitched; and the performance of opposing base-stealers, along with his totals of pickoffs and balks. In addition, for starting pitchers there are his totals of first-inning runs allowed, and the batting support per start given him by his team. For relievers, the number of inherited runners he stranded and allowed to score are given.

As with batters, for purposes of comparison the league totals in all these categories are listed in the introduction to the Team Section (see page 2).

Jim Abbott
Throws Left

California Angels	W-L	ERA	AB	H	HR	BB	SO	BA	SA	OBA
Season	18-11	2.89	909	222	14	73	158	.244	.336	.302
vs. Left-Handers			142	43	3	9	25	.303	.430	.348
vs. Right-Handers			767	179	11	64	133	.233	.318	.293
vs. Ground-Ballers			424	96	2	30	82	.226	.281	.280
vs. Fly-Ballers			485	126	12	43	76	.260	.384	.320
Home Games	8-7	2.57	472	109	7	35	78	.231	.311	.285
Road Games	10-4	3.25	437	113	7	38	80	.259	.362	.320
Grass Fields	15-9	2.60	777	184	12	59	139	.237	.314	.293
Artificial Turf	3-2	4.78	132	38	2	14	19	.288	.462	.351
April	0-4	6.00	95	31	2	9	15	.326	.463	.389
May	4-0	1.96	133	32	1	8	17	.241	.293	.282
June	2-1	3.43	157	39	5	15	32	.248	.389	.314
July	3-2	2.66	164	38	1	9	34	.232	.293	.277
August	5-1	1.99	164	36	1	15	27	.220	.299	.282
Sept./Oct.	4-3	2.65	196	46	4	17	33	.235	.327	.299
Leading Off Inn.			237	58	4	16	40	.245	.342	.292
Bases Empty			551	136	8	44	92	.247	.332	.305
Runners On			358	86	6	29	66	.240	.341	.297
Runners/Scor. Pos.			193	45	5	19	38	.233	.358	.292
Runners On/2 Out			155	32	2	15	26	.206	.284	.281
Scor. Pos./2 Out			88	17	1	11	17	.193	.250	.283
Late-Inning Pressure			83	25	4	8	16	.301	.458	.363
Leading Off			24	7	1	1	4	.292	.417	.320
Runners On			31	10	2	5	3	.323	.516	.417
Runners/Scor. Pos.			19	6	2	3	3	.316	.632	.409
First 9 Batters			275	64	4	26	46	.233	.331	.299
Second 9 Batters			275	60	1	23	55	.218	.258	.277
All Batters Thereafter			359	98	9	24	57	.273	.398	.323

Loves to face: Scott Fletcher (.063, 1-for-16)

Chris James (0-for-15)

Pat Tabler (0-for-13)

Hates to face: George Brett (.600, 12-for-20, 3 HR)

Dave Henderson (.529, 9-for-17, 1 2B, 5 HR)

Rafael Palmeiro (.421, 8-for-19, 2 HR)

Miscellaneous statistics: Ground outs-to-air outs ratio: 1.83 last season, 4th highest in A.L.; 1.76 for career.... Induced 22 double plays in 162 opportunities (one per 7.4).... Allowed 35 doubles, 3 triples in 243 innings.... Allowed 12 first-inning runs in 34 starts (3.18 ERA).... Batting support: 4.21 runs per start.... Opposing base stealers: 12-for-26 (46%); 7 pickoffs, 4 balks (tied for most in A.L.).

Comments: One of three Angels left-handers to win 15 or more games last season. Braves also had three lefties win 15 last year, but it had been done only three times previously in major league history.... Lost his first four starts of the season, and finished season with three losses in his last five decisions. In between he went 16–4.... Only A.L. pitcher to lose four games in April.... Home-game ERA was 3d lowest in the league.... One of five pitchers tied for A.L. lead in road victories (10).... Defeated every opposing A.L. club except Oakland last season.... Balked four times, tying Denis Boucher for the league lead.... Faced 128 consecutive batters without allowing an extra-base hit in late August and early September; that was the 2d-longest such streak in majors last season: Mike Timlin had a 139-batter streak from June 1 to July 19.... Career breakdown of opponents' batting average: .315 by left-handed batters, .262 by right-handers. In each of three seasons in majors, lefties have hit over .300; he's the only left-hander in the majors for whom that is true.... Did not walk any of the last 51 batters he faced leading off innings.... Has started 96 games without ever making a relief appearance.... Recorded more air outs than ground outs in only three of his 34 starts last season.... Led A.L. pitchers with 65 chances accepted; he made errors on two additional chances (one a wild pickoff throw, the other a wild throw to third on a bunt).

Rick Aguilera
Throws Right

Minnesota Twins	W-L	ERA	AB	H	HR	BB	SO	BA	SA	OBA
Season	4-5	2.35	240	44	3	30	61	.183	.275	.274
vs. Left-Handers			136	25	2	19	36	.184	.272	.285
vs. Right-Handers			104	19	1	11	25	.183	.279	.259
vs. Ground-Ballers			104	23	1	17	20	.221	.308	.328
vs. Fly-Ballers			136	21	2	13	41	.154	.250	.230
Home Games	2-0	1.00	119	14	2	12	36	.118	.202	.203
Road Games	2-5	3.82	121	30	1	18	25	.248	.347	.340
Grass Fields	2-4	4.05	98	25	1	15	20	.255	.367	.348
Artificial Turf	2-1	1.28	142	19	2	15	41	.134	.211	.220
April	0-1	1.17	29	6	0	3	10	.207	.276	.281
May	1-1	2.20	53	10	0	11	13	.189	.245	.318
June	1-1	4.63	40	10	2	8	8	.250	.475	.367
July	0-1	2.53	41	9	0	1	10	.220	.293	.256
August	2-0	0.82	38	5	0	2	10	.132	.132	.175
Sept./Oct.	0-1	2.31	39	4	1	5	10	.103	.231	.205
Leading Off Inn.			48	5	0	8	10	.104	.125	.232
Bases Empty			127	21	2	14	30	.165	.228	.254
Runners On			113	23	1	16	31	.204	.327	.295
Runners/Scor. Pos.			64	13	0	12	21	.203	.297	.316
Runners On/2 Out			56	11	0	8	16	.196	.286	.297
Scor. Pos./2 Out			39	9	0	6	13	.231	.333	.333
Late-Inning Pressure			201	38	2	24	50	.189	.279	.275
Leading Off			41	5	0	7	9	.122	.146	.250
Runners On			95	21	0	13	23	.221	.337	.306
Runners/Scor. Pos.			53	13	0	9	15	.245	.358	.338
First 9 Batters			229	41	3	29	60	.179	.275	.271
Second 9 Batters			11	3	0	1	1	.273	.273	.333
All Batters Thereafter			0	0	0	0	0	—	—	—

Loves to face: Dave Henderson (.071, 1-for-14, 8 SO)

Tim Raines (.138, 4-for-29)

Franklin Stubbs (.071, 1-for-14)

Hates to face: Mark McGwire (.429, 3-for-7, 1 2B, 2 HR)

Paul Molitor (.571, 4-for-7, 1 HR)

Lance Parrish (.385, 5-for-13, 1 HR)

Miscellaneous statistics: Ground outs-to-air outs ratio: 0.63 last season, 1.09 for career.... Induced 6 double plays in 52 opportunities (one per 8.7).... Allowed 9 doubles, 2 triples in 69 innings.... Saved 42 games in 51 opportunities (82%).... Stranded 28 inherited runners, allowed 9 to score (76%).... Opposing base stealers: 7-for-7 (100%); 0 pickoffs, 0 balks.

Comments: Faced 11 batters with bases loaded last season, the most by any major league pitcher who didn't allow a hit, walk, or hit batsman with the bags full.... Has held opponents to .111 career average with bases loaded: four singles and one double in 45 at-bats. Top five active pitchers with bases loaded (ranked by opponents' batting average; minimum: 50 batters faced): Jeff Brantley .091, Aguilera .111, Bryan Harvey .127, Oil Can Boyd .133, Jesse Orosco .139.... Ended the regular season by holding opponents hitless in their last 26 at-bats leading off innings.... Allowed only three home runs last season; each of them came in the 6⅔ innings he spent with Lenny Webster catching. He allowed no homers in 62⅔ innings with Junior Ortiz or Brian Harper calling the signals.... Career breakdown of strikeouts per nine innings: 6.06 as a starting pitcher, 8.65 in relief.... Became the first "pitcher" to pinch-hit in World Series since Don Drysdale batted for Sandy Koufax in 1965. Pitchers have been hitless in 15 pinch-hit at-bats during World Series play since Jack Bentley went 2-for-3 in that role for 1923 Giants. Among those who have tried: Larry Sherry (1959 Dodgers), Tommy Byrne (1955 and 1956 Yankees), Bob Lemon (1954 Indians), Johnny Sain (1952 Yankees), Red Ruffing (1932, 1936, and 1942 Yankees), and, before Bentley, Babe Ruth (1915 Red Sox). The last pitcher with a World Series pinch-hit RBI: Joe Bush of Yankees in 1923, when pinch-hitting pitchers apparently were baseball's answer to the Charleston.

Allan Anderson   Throws Left

Minnesota Twins	W-L	ERA	AB	H	HR	BB	SO	BA	SA	OBA
Season	5-11	4.96	527	148	24	42	51	.281	.474	.336
vs. Left-Handers			111	25	2	6	5	.225	.315	.265
vs. Right-Handers			416	123	22	36	46	.296	.517	.354
vs. Ground-Ballers			226	59	11	12	17	.261	.456	.298
vs. Fly-Ballers			301	89	13	30	34	.296	.488	.364
Home Games	2-4	4.52	263	69	12	16	30	.262	.437	.310
Road Games	3-7	5.40	264	79	12	26	21	.299	.511	.361
Grass Fields	1-5	5.07	188	52	6	20	17	.277	.452	.343
Artificial Turf	4-6	4.89	339	96	18	22	34	.283	.487	.332
April	1-2	4.06	113	27	3	12	6	.239	.363	.310
May	0-2	6.66	100	34	3	7	10	.340	.530	.382
June	3-2	2.87	149	40	8	6	14	.268	.463	.304
July	0-2	8.77	59	19	7	6	6	.322	.712	.394
August	0-0	8.00	36	12	2	3	6	.333	.528	.381
Sept./Oct.	1-3	4.26	70	16	1	8	9	.229	.371	.308
Leading Off Inn.			135	34	7	5	17	.252	.459	.284
Bases Empty			337	93	14	21	40	.276	.451	.324
Runners On			190	55	10	21	11	.289	.516	.356
Runners/Scor. Pos.			107	26	6	14	7	.243	.449	.326
Runners On/2 Out			89	24	2	7	8	.270	.416	.323
Scor. Pos./2 Out			59	13	1	6	7	.220	.322	.292
Late-Inning Pressure			15	7	1	2	0	.467	.800	.556
Leading Off			6	3	1	0	0	.500	1.333	.500
Runners On			6	2	0	2	0	.333	.333	.500
Runners/Scor. Pos.			3	1	0	1	0	.333	.333	.500
First 9 Batters			215	65	10	15	21	.302	.512	.350
Second 9 Batters			187	50	11	16	19	.267	.481	.325
All Batters Thereafter			125	33	3	11	11	.264	.400	.329

Loves to face: George Brett (.143, 4-for-28, 0 BB)
Mark McGwire (.115, 3-for-26, 3 BB)
Frank Thomas (0-for-9)

Hates to face: Jose Canseco (.375, 9-for-24, 2 2B, 5 HR)
Joe Carter (.333, 6-for-18, 5 HR)
Travis Fryman (.750, 6-for-8, 2 2B, 2 HR)

Miscellaneous statistics: Ground outs-to-air outs ratio: 1.10 last season, 1.15 for career.... Induced 9 double plays in 94 opportunities (one per 10).... Allowed 26 doubles, 2 triples in 134⅓ innings.... Allowed 15 first-inning runs in 22 starts (6.14 ERA).... Batting support: 3.68 runs per start, 7th-lowest average in A.L.... Opposing base stealers: 14-for-20 (70%); 5 pickoffs, 0 balks.

Comments: Not a single pitcher from the Twins' 1987 postseason roster appeared on their roster in last season's postseason. How rare is that? There are 127 teams that have made two postseason appearances within five years. Only four of them turned their staff over completely: the Red Sox (1912–15), Yankees (1952–55), Angels (1979–82), and Twins (1987–91). Anderson, who did not pitch in postseason in either 1987 or 1991, was the only regular-season link to Twins' 1987 staff; he was optioned to Kenosha with Tom Edens on August 31, making room for Jarvis Brown and Paul Sorrento.... Struck out only five first-inning batters in 22 innings of work, the lowest rate of any A.L. pitcher last season.... One of five major league pitchers to average fewer than 3.5 strikeouts per nine innings in at least 100 innings pitched last season: Jeff Ballard (2.69), Walt Terrell (3.29), Greg Hibbard (3.29), Anderson (3.42), and Dan Petry (3.46).... In each of last three seasons, Anderson's total of innings pitched has decreased, while the number of home runs he allowed has increased. Yearly totals since 1988: 14 homers in 202⅓ innings; 15 HR in 196⅔; 20 in 188⅔; 24 in 134⅓. The 22 home runs he allowed to right-handed batters were 2d most in A.L. to Mark Langston (29).... Career rate of 9.91 hits allowed per nine innings is 2d highest among active pitchers with at least 750 innings pitched. The highest rate belongs to Bruce Ruffin (9.92).

Kevin Appier   Throws Right

Kansas City Royals	W-L	ERA	AB	H	HR	BB	SO	BA	SA	OBA
Season	13-10	3.42	803	205	13	61	158	.255	.357	.307
vs. Left-Handers			403	108	8	37	61	.268	.395	.327
vs. Right-Handers			400	97	5	24	97	.243	.320	.287
vs. Ground-Ballers			430	117	4	24	75	.272	.358	.311
vs. Fly-Ballers			373	88	9	37	83	.236	.357	.303
Home Games	5-5	2.79	360	83	4	28	74	.231	.333	.285
Road Games	8-5	3.97	443	122	9	33	84	.275	.377	.326
Grass Fields	7-5	3.93	367	103	8	26	73	.281	.387	.327
Artificial Turf	6-5	3.03	436	102	5	35	85	.234	.333	.291
April	1-3	4.64	89	30	3	7	13	.337	.483	.385
May	2-2	3.18	123	29	2	6	16	.236	.350	.275
June	1-2	3.89	151	36	3	12	28	.238	.338	.293
July	3-0	3.09	124	31	1	7	31	.250	.315	.286
August	3-2	2.72	151	35	2	13	34	.232	.338	.295
Sept./Oct.	3-1	3.48	165	44	2	16	36	.267	.364	.330
Leading Off Inn.			202	42	2	15	38	.208	.292	.266
Bases Empty			482	108	6	33	98	.224	.305	.277
Runners On			321	97	7	28	60	.302	.436	.352
Runners/Scor. Pos.			179	51	3	22	37	.285	.397	.353
Runners On/2 Out			133	34	4	20	29	.256	.406	.353
Scor. Pos./2 Out			85	22	2	16	20	.259	.376	.376
Late-Inning Pressure			58	17	0	1	6	.293	.328	.305
Leading Off			16	3	0	1	2	.188	.188	.235
Runners On			20	7	0	0	2	.350	.450	.350
Runners/Scor. Pos.			9	3	0	0	1	.333	.556	.333
First 9 Batters			280	77	2	18	56	.275	.346	.318
Second 9 Batters			253	67	6	23	52	.265	.407	.324
All Batters Thereafter			270	61	5	20	50	.226	.322	.281

Loves to face: Rob Deer (0-for-10)
Gary Gaetti (.077, 1-for-13)
Pete O'Brien (0-for-16)

Hates to face: Julio Franco (.429, 6-for-14, 1 HR)
Chris James (.500, 7-for-14, 1 HR)
Luis Polonia (.579, 11-for-19)

Miscellaneous statistics: Ground outs-to-air outs ratio: 1.01 last season, 1.08 for career.... Induced 12 double plays in 145 opportunities (one per 12).... Allowed 41 doubles, 1 triple in 207⅔ innings.... Allowed 14 first-inning runs in 31 starts (2.90 ERA).... Batting support: 4.71 runs per start.... Opposing base stealers: 10-for-18 (56%); 1 pickoff, 1 balk.

Comments: One of three A.L. pitchers to throw shutouts in consecutive starts last season. The others: Jack McDowell and Scott Erickson.... Has nine complete games in 60 career starts, six of them shutouts.... Appier and Chuck Finley are the only pitchers who shut out the Red Sox in both 1990 and 1991. (Finley also shut them out in 1989.) ... Opponents' on-base percentage leading off innings was 4th lowest in A.L., right behind the big boys: Ryan, Clemens, and McDowell.... Dropped from the Royals' rotation after a 1–4 start, he then lost his first relief appearance before posting 12–5 mark the rest of the way.... Averaged 5.56 strikeouts per nine innings during the first half of the season, but increased that to 8.09 strikeouts per nine innings after the All-Star break.... Allowed 18 unearned runs last season, 2d most of any pitcher in majors, but they provided the margin of defeat in only one of his losses.... Has not allowed a first-inning home run in 55 starts since June 1, 1990, when Jose Canseco and Mark McGwire got him back-to-back.... Opponents have a career average of .287 with runners on base, .242 with the bases empty.... Has allowed only two hits in 29 at-bats with bases loaded, including a grand slam by Mel Hall in 1989. With bases loaded and two outs, opponents are hitless in 18 at-bats.... Tim Raines stole three bases in three attempts against him, while he held the rest of the league below 50 percent (7-for-15).

Luis Aquino
Throws Right

Kansas City Royals	W-L	ERA	AB	H	HR	BB	SO	BA	SA	OBA
Season	8-4	3.44	601	152	10	47	80	.253	.374	.308
vs. Left-Handers			289	76	2	26	42	.263	.367	.318
vs. Right-Handers			312	76	8	21	38	.244	.381	.299
vs. Ground-Ballers			273	71	1	15	34	.260	.333	.300
vs. Fly-Ballers			328	81	9	32	46	.247	.409	.314
Home Games	3-1	3.13	297	74	4	24	38	.249	.347	.307
Road Games	5-3	3.74	304	78	6	23	42	.257	.401	.309
Grass Fields	4-3	3.79	276	74	6	20	40	.268	.428	.316
Artificial Turf	4-1	3.15	325	78	4	27	40	.240	.329	.302
April	0-0	7.82	51	16	3	4	4	.314	.569	.373
May	0-0	1.74	41	9	1	5	6	.220	.341	.304
June	1-1	2.91	134	36	2	10	17	.269	.343	.315
July	4-1	1.09	127	28	0	4	25	.220	.291	.242
August	1-0	2.76	103	20	1	10	15	.194	.301	.263
Sept./Oct.	2-2	5.50	145	43	3	14	13	.297	.469	.364
Leading Off Inn.			146	35	0	11	18	.240	.349	.293
Bases Empty			354	87	3	27	53	.246	.345	.301
Runners On			247	65	7	20	27	.263	.417	.318
Runners/Scor. Pos.			136	31	4	15	17	.228	.360	.291
Runners On/2 Out			115	31	2	9	12	.270	.383	.328
Scor. Pos./2 Out			67	13	1	8	10	.194	.254	.280
Late-Inning Pressure			56	15	1	6	8	.268	.411	.339
Leading Off			15	3	0	0	3	.200	.333	.200
Runners On			23	6	0	5	2	.261	.348	.393
Runners/Scor. Pos.			12	3	0	5	0	.250	.417	.471
First 9 Batters			275	64	4	26	37	.233	.338	.303
Second 9 Batters			190	58	5	10	24	.305	.468	.342
All Batters Thereafter			136	30	1	11	19	.221	.316	.273

Loves to face: Manny Lee (0-for-12)
Luis Rivera (.100, 2-for-20)
Alan Trammell (.059, 1-for-17)

Hates to face: Pete O'Brien (.500, 7-for-14)
Dan Pasqua (.364, 4-for-11, 2 HR)
Lou Whitaker (.462, 6-for-13)

Miscellaneous statistics: Ground outs-to-air outs ratio: 0.95 last season, 0.99 for career.... Induced 9 double plays in 102 opportunities (one per 11).... Allowed 33 doubles, 5 triples in 157 innings.... Allowed 11 first-inning runs in 18 starts (4.00 ERA).... Batting support: 4.72 runs per start.... Record of 6–4, 3.85 ERA as a starter; 2–0, 2.34 ERA in 20 relief appearances.... Stranded 9 inherited runners, allowed 7 to score (56%).... Opposing base stealers: 10-for-16 (63%); 2 pickoffs, 0 balks.

Comments: Started five games before the All-Star break, but was used exclusively in that role after July 25. Career breakdown: 13–13 (3.80 ERA) as a starter; 7–1 (2.85 ERA) in relief.... Led A.L. in ERA during July, but his ERA during September/October was 8th highest in the league.... Converted each of his three save opportunities last season, the only saves of his career.... Opponents have a career batting average of .222 in day games, .277 in night games. That contributes to a career record of 8–1 in day games, 12–13 at night.... Something to watch for: Aquino's ground outs-to-air outs ratio decreases as the game goes on. It's 1.14 in his first pass through the order, 1.07 in his second pass, and only 0.57 thereafter. A by-product: he did not induce a double-play grounder in 19 opportunities after his second pass though the lineup.... Career rate of one home run allowed every 16 innings breaks down this way: one every 19.7 innings at Royals Stadium, one every 14 innings elsewhere. Helped by their home park, Royals have allowed fewest home runs in A.L. in six of last seven years.... Three of his six complete games have been shutouts, a burgeoning trend; in the American League last season, slightly more than 25 percent of complete games were shutouts.... What do Ferguson Jenkins and Luis Aquino have in common? They were both involved in trades, 12 years apart, for Juan Beniquez.

Don August
Throws Right

Milwaukee Brewers	W-L	ERA	AB	H	HR	BB	SO	BA	SA	OBA
Season	9-8	5.47	551	166	18	47	62	.301	.450	.358
vs. Left-Handers			302	96	10	27	20	.318	.477	.375
vs. Right-Handers			249	70	8	20	42	.281	.418	.336
vs. Ground-Ballers			273	87	13	18	23	.319	.516	.362
vs. Fly-Ballers			278	79	5	29	39	.284	.385	.354
Home Games	8-5	4.13	303	78	8	20	30	.257	.373	.309
Road Games	1-3	7.34	248	88	10	27	32	.355	.544	.415
Grass Fields	9-6	4.86	454	130	14	33	48	.286	.430	.337
Artificial Turf	0-2	8.72	97	36	4	14	14	.371	.546	.446
April	1-2	7.62	53	18	5	0	8	.340	.660	.352
May	3-0	2.79	104	23	2	8	14	.221	.279	.281
June	2-1	4.26	116	29	3	14	8	.250	.336	.331
July	2-2	6.33	111	37	2	8	10	.333	.441	.383
August	1-1	5.86	118	39	5	14	14	.331	.542	.396
Sept./Oct.	0-2	10.80	49	20	1	3	8	.408	.653	.442
Leading Off Inn.			141	48	4	8	16	.340	.482	.380
Bases Empty			307	97	8	24	31	.316	.443	.371
Runners On			244	69	10	23	31	.283	.459	.341
Runners/Scor. Pos.			131	43	7	13	17	.328	.557	.381
Runners On/2 Out			102	31	6	7	14	.304	.549	.349
Scor. Pos./2 Out			66	21	3	4	9	.318	.545	.357
Late-Inning Pressure			32	12	3	6	3	.375	.656	.474
Leading Off			11	4	1	0	1	.364	.636	.364
Runners On			11	4	2	4	1	.364	.909	.533
Runners/Scor. Pos.			5	2	1	3	1	.400	1.000	.625
First 9 Batters			219	70	7	18	31	.320	.470	.373
Second 9 Batters			190	59	5	13	22	.311	.447	.353
All Batters Thereafter			142	37	6	16	9	.261	.423	.340

Loves to face: Brian Downing (0-for-12)
Carney Lansford (.077, 1-for-13)
Danny Tartabull (0-for-10)

Hates to face: Mel Hall (.583, 7-for-12, 1 HR)
Dave Henderson (.421, 8-for-19, 4 2B, 1 HR)
Rance Mulliniks (.545, 6-for-11, 1 HR)

Miscellaneous statistics: Ground outs-to-air outs ratio: 1.42 last season, 1.31 for career.... Induced 16 double plays in 127 opportunities (one per 7.9).... Allowed 22 doubles, 3 triples in 138⅓ innings.... Allowed 18 first-inning runs in 23 starts (6.65 ERA).... Batting support: 5.30 runs per start, 4th-highest average in A.L.... Opposing base stealers: 18-for-22 (82%); 1 pickoff, 0 balks.

Comments: The only A.L. starter who had a winning record last season despite an ERA over 4.00 in 100 or more innings. Think about that: His ERA was almost one-and-a-half runs higher than any other A.L. starting pitcher who had a winning record. Seven other pitchers had ERAs as high as August's in at least 100 innings, and they combined for a .357 winning percentage. Since 1969, 84 pitchers have had seasons of 100+ innings in which their ERA was as high as August's; of those 84, only six others had winning records, most recently Jeff M. Robinson (10–9, 5.96 ERA) in 1990.... August also posted a .500 record (12–12) in 1989, despite a 5.31 ERA. Career record is four games over .500 (34–30), with a 4.64 ERA.... Strikeout rate during the first inning (6.26 per nine innings) was his highest in any inning.... Despite his high ground outs-to-air outs ratio, he failed to induce any double-play grounders in 34 opportunities over his last eight appearances.... Ground-ball pitchers do well against ground-ball hitters, but not this one. Ground-ball hitters have a .311 career batting average vs. August; fly-ball hitters have a .263 mark.... Although he came to spring training as a nonroster player, he managed to spend a full season in the big leagues for the first time in his career. That might have been considered a longshot after his first outing, when he allowed six runs in one inning pitched at the Skydome in April.

Jeff Ballard   Throws Left

Baltimore Orioles	W-L	ERA	AB	H	HR	BB	SO	BA	SA	OBA
Season	6-12	5.60	506	153	16	28	37	.302	.478	.340
vs. Left-Handers			88	16	1	6	13	.182	.284	.232
vs. Right-Handers			418	137	15	22	24	.328	.519	.363
vs. Ground-Ballers			237	62	6	11	15	.262	.392	.292
vs. Fly-Ballers			269	91	10	17	22	.338	.554	.381
Home Games	0-8	5.93	186	57	7	12	18	.306	.478	.350
Road Games	6-4	5.42	320	96	9	16	19	.300	.478	.333
Grass Fields	5-11	5.35	425	126	13	22	31	.296	.456	.333
Artificial Turf	1-1	6.98	81	27	3	6	6	.333	.593	.375
April	2-2	4.40	117	27	4	8	11	.231	.385	.286
May	1-4	3.63	139	38	2	6	13	.273	.388	.299
June	1-2	7.82	110	39	5	6	8	.355	.600	.388
July	2-3	6.26	114	37	4	6	5	.325	.509	.361
August	0-0	0.00	0	0	0	0	0	.000	.000	.000
Sept./Oct.	0-1	11.12	26	12	1	2	0	.462	.731	.500
Leading Off Inn.			123	32	6	7	5	.260	.480	.311
Bases Empty			297	77	11	14	22	.259	.424	.297
Runners On			209	76	5	14	15	.364	.555	.398
Runners/Scor. Pos.			113	43	5	11	10	.381	.611	.425
Runners On/2 Out			81	30	0	4	4	.370	.469	.400
Scor. Pos./2 Out			47	19	0	4	1	.404	.468	.451
Late-Inning Pressure			10	4	0	3	0	.400	.800	.538
Leading Off			4	1	0	0	0	.250	.250	.250
Runners On			5	2	0	2	0	.400	.800	.571
Runners/Scor. Pos.			5	2	0	2	0	.400	.800	.571
First 9 Batters			207	60	4	15	16	.290	.430	.344
Second 9 Batters			174	54	7	9	15	.310	.506	.341
All Batters Thereafter			125	39	5	4	6	.312	.520	.331

Loves to face: George Brett (.130, 3-for-23, 1 HR)
Mike Gallego (.067, 1-for-15, 1 2B)
Lou Whitaker (.063, 1-for-16)

Hates to face: Brian Downing (.444, 8-for-18, 1 HR)
Kirby Puckett (.563, 9-for-16, 1 HR)
Dave Valle (.458, 11-for-24, 3 HR)

Miscellaneous statistics: Ground outs-to-air outs ratio: 1.09 last season, 1.08 for career.... Induced 11 double plays in 101 opportunities (one per 9.2).... Allowed 33 doubles, 4 triples in 123⅔ innings.... Allowed 24 first-inning runs in 22 starts (8.31 ERA, 2d highest in A.L.)... Batting support: 3.82 runs per start, 9th-lowest average in A.L.... Opposing base stealers: 1-for-5 (20%); 0 pickoffs, 1 balk.

Comments: First-inning troubles even extended to his strong suit, control: Nine walks in 21⅔ first innings pitched translates to 3.74 walks per nine innings, his highest rate in any inning. Each of the two batters he hit last season were also in the first inning.... Opponents batted a rousing .381 with runners in scoring position, the highest batting average vs. any pitcher in the past 11 years (minimum: 100 at-bats with RISP). As a group, Baltimore pitchers allowed a .303 batting average in those situations last year, only the fourth time since 1975 that a staff has allowed a .300 batting average at the worst possible time.... Opposing base runners stole one base in 123⅔ innings. The only pitcher in the majors who pitched more innings without allowing at least two steals was Boston's Greg Harris (one steal in 173 innings). The only player to steal against Ballard last season was Minnesota's Dan Gladden.... Had a record of 18–8 in 1989, but is 18–43 for the rest of his career.... He's the bottom man on a couple of pretty lengthy lists. His career rate of 10.51 hits allowed per nine innings is the highest among active pitchers with at least 500 innings. Moreover, his career rate of 2.81 strikeouts per nine innings is the lowest among that same group of pitchers. No pitcher whose career extended into the 1960s or later had a strikeout rate as low.... Yet with all of that, he has held a future Hall of Famer to a .130 career batting average (3-for-23) with six strikeouts. George Brett, here's your Hub Pruett.

Mike Boddicker   Throws Right

Kansas City Royals	W-L	ERA	AB	H	HR	BB	SO	BA	SA	OBA
Season	12-12	4.08	692	188	13	59	79	.272	.408	.340
vs. Left-Handers			355	107	7	29	22	.301	.470	.365
vs. Right-Handers			337	81	6	30	57	.240	.341	.314
vs. Ground-Ballers			340	81	3	20	31	.238	.321	.293
vs. Fly-Ballers			352	107	10	39	48	.304	.491	.383
Home Games	7-8	4.07	423	111	7	29	50	.262	.402	.325
Road Games	5-4	4.11	269	77	6	30	29	.286	.416	.362
Grass Fields	4-3	4.35	202	59	6	25	23	.292	.441	.376
Artificial Turf	8-9	3.98	490	129	7	34	56	.263	.394	.325
April	2-2	2.03	109	20	2	9	10	.183	.294	.250
May	1-2	5.56	83	24	2	11	9	.289	.410	.379
June	3-2	2.48	131	28	1	9	16	.214	.298	.285
July	2-1	6.30	128	41	4	8	11	.320	.523	.370
August	3-2	3.00	155	49	3	13	21	.316	.465	.380
Sept./Oct.	1-3	7.06	86	26	1	9	12	.302	.442	.381
Leading Off Inn.			172	56	3	14	18	.326	.436	.386
Bases Empty			385	109	5	40	46	.283	.418	.358
Runners On			307	79	8	19	33	.257	.394	.316
Runners/Scor. Pos.			182	45	1	13	25	.247	.335	.317
Runners On/2 Out			127	33	2	10	10	.260	.386	.347
Scor. Pos./2 Out			88	20	0	9	7	.227	.307	.333
Late-Inning Pressure			51	14	0	3	4	.275	.294	.351
Leading Off			14	4	0	0	2	.286	.286	.375
Runners On			21	5	0	1	1	.238	.238	.304
Runners/Scor. Pos.			13	3	0	1	1	.231	.231	.286
First 9 Batters			230	61	3	22	27	.265	.417	.337
Second 9 Batters			228	63	5	17	23	.276	.412	.335
All Batters Thereafter			234	64	5	20	29	.274	.393	.347

Loves to face: Pat Borders (0-for-8)
Jack Clark (0-for-16)
Mike Greenwell (0-for-9)

Hates to face: Carney Lansford (.423, 22-for-52, 4 HR)
Mark McGwire (.269, 7-for-26, 4 HR, 12 BB)
Geno Petralli (.444, 16-for-36, 2 HR)

Miscellaneous statistics: Ground outs-to-air outs ratio: 1.21 last season, 1.32 for career.... Induced 18 double plays in 147 opportunities (one per 8.2).... Allowed 41 doubles, 7 triples in 180⅔ innings.... Allowed 11 first-inning runs in 29 starts (3.54 ERA).... Batting support: 4.24 runs per start.... Opposing base stealers: 17-for-27 (63%); 4 pickoffs, 2 balks.

Comments: One of two pitchers (Bruce Hurst is the other) to have won at least 10 games in each of the last nine seasons. That's the longest current streak in the majors.... Opponents' on-base percentage leading off innings was the highest in the majors.... Left-handers' .301 batting average was a career high.... Pitched 180⅔ innings in 29 starts, breaking a streak of seven consecutive years with at least 30 starts and 200 innings pitched. He would have reached those levels if not for his poor finish and Rickey Henderson, who lined a ball off of Boddicker's knee on September 25. X rays proved negative, but the bruise ended Boddicker's season, after he had lasted fewer than five innings per game over his last six starts.... Has 7–1 career record against his former teams (5–1 vs. Baltimore and 2–0 vs. Boston since leaving).... Has faced 109 batters in 1983 innings without allowing a grand-slam home run. He hasn't even allowed a grand-slam triple.... Hit 13 batters last year, tying Kevin Brown of Texas for major league lead. Has a career average of one batter hit for every 26.4 innings pitched; by way of comparison, Don Drysdale averaged one bull's-eye for every 22.3 innings.... The Winder took particular pleasure in plunking Houston's Don Wilson (on the "If-You-Hit-One-of-Mine, I'll-Hit-Two-of-Yours Theory"). With no opposing pitchers to target, Boddicker has gotten his licks in on Kent Hrbek—four times, in fact, more than any other active batter.

Tom Bolton

Throws Left

Boston Red Sox	W-L	ERA	AB	H	HR	BB	SO	BA	SA	OBA
Season	8-9	5.24	441	136	16	51	64	.308	.485	.378
vs. Left-Handers			81	20	2	5	11	.247	.395	.295
vs. Right-Handers			360	116	14	46	53	.322	.506	.396
vs. Ground-Ballers			189	51	5	21	25	.270	.402	.341
vs. Fly-Ballers			252	85	11	30	39	.337	.548	.406
Home Games	5-5	4.68	261	84	10	24	33	.322	.498	.376
Road Games	3-4	6.04	180	52	6	27	31	.289	.467	.381
Grass Fields	7-9	5.50	416	132	16	48	60	.317	.502	.386
Artificial Turf	1-0	1.29	25	4	0	3	4	.160	.200	.250
April	2-0	1.47	70	16	0	4	9	.229	.314	.270
May	3-2	5.40	136	38	8	19	26	.279	.515	.369
June	2-3	5.84	106	39	4	11	9	.368	.566	.424
July	0-2	5.28	60	23	2	10	7	.383	.533	.465
August	0-0	0.00	9	0	0	0	3	.000	.000	.000
Sept./Oct.	1-2	9.88	60	20	2	7	10	.333	.500	.397
Leading Off Inn.			114	33	3	6	22	.289	.430	.325
Bases Empty			258	81	7	21	39	.314	.457	.366
Runners On			183	55	9	30	25	.301	.525	.394
Runners/Scor. Pos.			97	26	5	19	16	.268	.474	.375
Runners On/2 Out			75	25	4	16	7	.333	.613	.451
Scor. Pos./2 Out			47	13	3	14	6	.277	.553	.443
Late-Inning Pressure			23	11	1	0	0	.478	.739	.478
Leading Off			8	5	1	0	0	.625	1.125	.625
Runners On			7	1	0	0	0	.143	.143	.143
Runners/Scor. Pos.			3	1	0	0	0	.333	.333	.333
First 9 Batters			185	54	4	22	30	.292	.443	.367
Second 9 Batters			158	55	8	15	23	.348	.544	.400
All Batters Thereafter			98	27	4	14	11	.276	.469	.366

Loves to face: Shane Mack (0-for-6)
Tim Raines (0-for-7)
Willie Wilson (0-for-5, 4 SO)

Hates to face: Alvin Davis (.545, 6-for-11, 1 HR)
Julio Franco (.714, 5-for-7, 1 HR)
Roberto Kelly (.357, 5-for-14, 1 HR)

Miscellaneous statistics: Ground outs-to-air outs ratio: 1.91 last season, 1.44 for career.... Induced 18 double plays in 104 opportunities (one per 5.8), 4th-best rate in A.L.... Allowed 22 doubles, 4 triples in 110 innings.... Allowed 13 first-inning runs in 19 starts (5.68 ERA).... Batting support: 4.11 runs per start.... Opposing base stealers: 5-for-7 (71%); 1 pickoff, 0 balks.

Comments: Allowed one home run in 19 first innings of his starts, but an average of one homer every 5.3 innings thereafter.... His season followed the same pattern: no home runs allowed in his first 26 innings, but one every 5.3 innings after that. The only left-handers to homer against him were both Yankees: Mel Hall and Kevin Maas.... Career won–lost breakdown: 13–7 at home, 7–14 on the road.... A welcome sight to hitters in Late-Inning Pressure Situations: Opponents have a .378 career average in 98 at-bats in those situations; as subsets of that category, opponents have hit .439 with runners on base and .625 (10-for-16) with runners in scoring position. He hasn't been allowed to face too many hitters in LIPS; on the basis of these figures, why would he? ... Ground outs-to-air outs ratio was 5th highest among A.L. pitchers with at least 100 innings. Bolton had a streak of four straight starts in which he induced at least two double-play grounders.... Bolton (19 starts), Joe Hesketh (17), Matt Young (16), and Kevin Morton (15) all took a turn in the Boston rotation last year; all are left-handed. But their total of 67 starts is nowhere near the Red Sox record for starts by left-handed pitchers in one season. In 1951, five lefties started 106 of Boston's 154 games: Mel Parnell (29), Chuck Stobbs (25), Mickey McDermott (19), Bill Wight (17), and Leo Kiely (16).

Chris Bosio

Throws Right

Milwaukee Brewers	W-L	ERA	AB	H	HR	BB	SO	BA	SA	OBA
Season	14-10	3.25	766	187	15	58	117	.244	.350	.302
vs. Left-Handers			418	105	6	30	53	.251	.347	.303
vs. Right-Handers			348	82	9	28	64	.236	.353	.300
vs. Ground-Ballers			353	87	2	25	40	.246	.312	.297
vs. Fly-Ballers			413	100	13	33	77	.242	.383	.306
Home Games	5-6	3.83	379	105	8	26	58	.277	.404	.328
Road Games	9-4	2.74	387	82	7	32	59	.212	.297	.277
Grass Fields	13-9	3.30	684	165	14	50	108	.241	.351	.298
Artificial Turf	1-1	2.91	82	22	1	8	9	.268	.341	.337
April	3-2	2.00	130	28	2	16	19	.215	.292	.311
May	1-3	2.87	137	31	4	5	24	.226	.365	.257
June	2-2	5.28	113	29	4	11	20	.257	.416	.325
July	1-1	3.24	96	28	1	10	12	.292	.385	.364
August	3-1	3.66	155	44	2	6	24	.284	.394	.317
Sept./Oct.	4-1	2.87	135	27	2	10	18	.200	.259	.253
Leading Off Inn.			201	47	6	13	29	.234	.408	.280
Bases Empty			470	112	9	31	76	.238	.349	.291
Runners On			296	75	6	27	41	.253	.351	.318
Runners/Scor. Pos.			152	40	3	12	20	.263	.349	.314
Runners On/2 Out			119	24	3	13	16	.202	.311	.280
Scor. Pos./2 Out			70	14	3	8	9	.200	.343	.282
Late-Inning Pressure			58	17	1	6	3	.293	.362	.359
Leading Off			16	7	1	2	0	.438	.688	.500
Runners On			29	6	0	2	3	.207	.207	.258
Runners/Scor. Pos.			11	4	0	1	2	.364	.364	.417
First 9 Batters			271	63	6	13	53	.232	.332	.272
Second 9 Batters			250	57	4	21	41	.228	.316	.294
All Batters Thereafter			245	67	5	24	23	.273	.404	.342

Loves to face: Wade Boggs (.161, 5-for-31)
Jim Eisenreich (.105, 2-for-19)
Willie Wilson (.045, 1-for-22)

Hates to face: Kirk Gibson (.385, 5-for-13, 3 2B, 1 HR)
Lloyd Moseby (.345, 10-for-29, 4 HR)
Harold Reynolds (.625, 10-for-16)

Miscellaneous statistics: Ground outs-to-air outs ratio: 1.29 last season, 1.29 for career.... Induced 22 double plays in 155 opportunities (one per 7.0).... Allowed 28 doubles, 4 triples in 204⅔ innings.... Allowed 8 first-inning runs in 32 starts (2.25 ERA).... Batting support: 4.97 runs per start, 8th-highest average in A.L.... Opposing base stealers: 9-for-13 (69%); 2 pickoffs, 0 balks.

Comments: Another guy who has got going what George Bush might call "that Saberhagen thing"—a winning record in odd-numbered years (1987, 1989, 1991) and a losing record in even-numbered years (1986, 1988, 1990). Sabes has crossed the .500 line in seven consecutive seasons, tying a major league record.... Oh, well, here's one constant for Bosio: Opponents have hit for a higher average with runners on base than with the bases empty in each of his six seasons in the majors. Career breakdown: .276 with runners on, .248 with bases empty.... Has walked fewer than three batters per nine innings in each of his five major league seasons of 100 or more innings. Career rate: 2.3 walks per nine innings, 11th lowest among active pitchers (minimum: 500 innings).... Owns a 16–4 career record in April, 35–52 in warmer months.... Has allowed only one first-inning home run over his last 35 starts.... Has pitched at least one shutout in each of the last five seasons; Roger Clemens (eight), Charlie Leibrandt (seven), and Dennis Martinez (seven) have longer streaks; Doug Drabek and Greg Maddux also have five-year streaks.... Opponents' overall batting average was a career low.... Tell us the truth now. Is there another publication that'll give you the all-time Brewers leaders in errors by pitchers? Jim Slaton (21), Jaime Cocanower (14), Bosio (13), Moose Haas (13), Bill Wegman (12), Bob McClure (12).

Oil Can Boyd

Throws Right

Expos/Rangers	W-L	ERA	AB	H	HR	BB	SO	BA	SA	OBA
Season	8-15	4.59	708	196	21	57	115	.277	.448	.329
vs. Left-Handers			367	97	5	32	56	.264	.395	.322
vs. Right-Handers			341	99	16	25	59	.290	.504	.337
vs. Ground-Ballers			310	93	7	21	47	.300	.452	.343
vs. Fly-Ballers			398	103	14	36	68	.259	.445	.318
Home Games	5-5	3.23	377	92	7	27	69	.244	.379	.295
Road Games	3-10	6.26	331	104	14	30	46	.314	.526	.367
Grass Fields	4-9	5.55	332	97	13	23	53	.292	.473	.338
Artificial Turf	4-6	3.79	376	99	8	34	62	.263	.426	.321
April	0-3	6.26	88	30	2	9	9	.341	.534	.394
May	2-3	2.79	141	31	4	8	30	.220	.376	.260
June	2-1	3.86	119	34	2	15	22	.286	.412	.366
July	2-3	3.79	134	31	3	14	27	.231	.396	.302
August	0-2	7.77	103	36	4	7	13	.350	.534	.391
Sept./Oct.	2-3	4.75	123	34	6	4	14	.276	.488	.299
Leading Off Inn.			176	40	5	14	30	.227	.398	.284
Bases Empty			422	117	11	34	66	.277	.436	.331
Runners On			286	79	10	23	49	.276	.465	.326
Runners/Scor. Pos.			163	47	8	18	30	.288	.500	.351
Runners On/2 Out			128	37	4	9	19	.289	.484	.336
Scor. Pos./2 Out			75	22	4	8	8	.293	.547	.361
Late-Inning Pressure			27	10	0	1	3	.370	.630	.393
Leading Off			8	4	0	0	0	.500	.875	.500
Runners On			13	5	0	0	2	.385	.692	.385
Runners/Scor. Pos.			8	2	0	0	1	.250	.375	.250
First 9 Batters			252	59	5	24	40	.234	.373	.301
Second 9 Batters			250	66	5	19	48	.264	.388	.314
All Batters Thereafter			206	71	11	14	27	.345	.612	.383

Loves to face: Tom Brunansky (.120, 3-for-25)
Ozzie Guillen (.192, 5-for-26)
Pete Incaviglia (0-for-11, 8 SO)

Hates to face: Jose Canseco (.429, 9-for-21, 1 2B, 5 HR)
Dave Henderson (.478, 11-for-23, 2 HR)
Carney Lansford (.441, 15-for-34, 2 HR, 0 SO)

Miscellaneous statistics: Ground outs-to-air outs ratio: 0.87 last season, 0.96 for career.... Induced 10 double plays in 117 opportunities (one per 12).... Allowed 44 doubles, 7 triples in 182⅓ innings.... Allowed 8 first-inning runs in 31 starts (2.32 ERA).... Batting support: 3.48 runs per start.... Opposing base stealers: 14-for-26 (54%); 0 pickoffs, 4 balks.

Comments: 6–8 with 3.52 ERA in 19 starts with Expos, 2–7 with 6.68 ERA in 12 starts with Rangers. He lasted fewer than six innings in seven of his 12 starts with the Rangers.... Has not allowed a first-inning home run in 43 starts, since July 26, 1990.... For the fourth time in the past five years, he allowed a higher batting average to right-handed batters than to lefties. Career breakdown: .280 by right-handers, .255 by left-handers. His home-run rate also contravenes the usual rules: Right-handed batters have averaged one homer every 24.9 at-bats, lefties one every 43 at-bats.... Tough trivia: Boyd is one of three players to appear in a game for the Red Sox, Expos, and Rangers. Who are the other two? Keep reading but no peeking.... Cardinals had a tough time running on him. In one game, both Ray Lankford and Bernard Gilkey were caught attempting to steal; in another game, both Ozzie Smith and Felix Jose were gunned down.... His only complete game of the year was a five-hit shutout of the Giants in his swan song with Montreal.... He may never again be the workhorse he was when he accumulated 272⅓ innings for Boston in 1985, but he has started 31 games in each of the last two seasons following a three-year period (1987–89) in which he started only 40 games total.... Trivia answer: Larry Parrish and Greg Harris.... Maybe the Blue Jays should have picked up the Can instead of Candy: Boyd owns a career record of 8–1 vs. the Twins, having won his last seven decisions against them.

Kevin Brown

Throws Right

Texas Rangers	W-L	ERA	AB	H	HR	BB	SO	BA	SA	OBA
Season	9-12	4.40	821	233	17	90	96	.284	.404	.362
vs. Left-Handers			410	112	8	47	51	.273	.395	.349
vs. Right-Handers			411	121	9	43	45	.294	.414	.375
vs. Ground-Ballers			404	113	12	44	40	.280	.428	.357
vs. Fly-Ballers			417	120	5	46	56	.288	.381	.367
Home Games	4-5	4.14	436	124	11	45	45	.284	.429	.358
Road Games	5-7	4.70	385	109	6	45	51	.283	.377	.367
Grass Fields	9-10	4.61	715	202	16	79	82	.283	.407	.362
Artificial Turf	0-2	2.96	106	31	1	11	14	.292	.387	.361
April	2-1	4.38	89	21	2	9	6	.236	.393	.310
May	2-2	7.04	100	40	1	15	8	.400	.500	.478
June	2-2	3.46	150	35	0	19	21	.233	.293	.339
July	1-3	3.92	170	48	7	15	27	.282	.447	.346
August	2-2	3.51	128	37	3	14	14	.289	.406	.372
Sept./Oct.	0-2	5.08	184	52	4	18	20	.283	.408	.350
Leading Off Inn.			200	53	2	19	27	.265	.375	.335
Bases Empty			436	122	11	46	55	.280	.420	.358
Runners On			385	111	6	44	41	.288	.387	.367
Runners/Scor. Pos.			231	59	2	27	26	.255	.338	.341
Runners On/2 Out			140	36	2	17	15	.257	.357	.350
Scor. Pos./2 Out			91	20	0	10	8	.220	.264	.317
Late-Inning Pressure			70	25	2	10	8	.357	.557	.444
Leading Off			22	6	0	1	3	.273	.409	.304
Runners On			26	10	0	6	4	.385	.423	.515
Runners/Scor. Pos.			17	6	0	5	4	.353	.353	.522
First 9 Batters			258	66	2	31	34	.256	.329	.342
Second 9 Batters			254	70	6	29	31	.276	.402	.355
All Batters Thereafter			309	97	9	30	31	.314	.469	.384

Loves to face: Gary Gaetti (.050, 1-for-20)
Ozzie Guillen (0-for-22)
Devon White (.063, 1-for-16)

Hates to face: George Brett (.529, 9-for-17, 1 HR, 8 ground outs)
Lance Johnson (.526, 10-for-19)
Dave Winfield (.389, 7-for-18, 3 HR)

Miscellaneous statistics: Ground outs-to-air outs ratio: 2.52 last season, highest in majors; 2.51 for career.... Induced 30 double plays in 202 opportunities (one per 6.7).... Allowed 40 doubles, 4 triples in 210⅔ innings.... Allowed 18 first-inning runs in 33 starts (4.09 ERA).... Batting support: 4.91 runs per start.... Opposing base stealers: 5-for-16 (31%, 3d-lowest rate in A.L.); 5 pickoffs, 3 balks (3d most in A.L.).

Comments: He's tough to steal against, has a great pickoff move, and gets plenty of double-play grounders. Put that all together, and he might as well intentionally walk opposing leadoff batters just to get a runner on first base! ... The five runners he picked off were no slouches: Gary Sheffield, Lance Johnson, Rickey Henderson, Mike Devereaux, and Ken Griffey, Jr.... Call him Oil Can Brown: Another right-hander who has allowed a higher batting average to right-handed batters than to left-handed batters in each of the past three years.... Did not allow a home run in the first inning last season despite facing 139 batters; that's the most batters faced by any pitcher in the majors who did not allow a first-inning dinger.... Yearly winning percentages are on a downward spiral since 1989 (.571, .545, .429); not coincidentally, his ERA is on the rise (3.35, 3.60, 4.40).... Hit 13 batters (including Joey Cora twice in one game) to tie Mike Boddicker for the most in the majors.... Had 12 no-decision starts, second most among A.L. pitchers, behind Dave Stewart (13).... Some titles just aren't as impressive as they used to be: Middle Linebacker, King of England, Democratic Presidential Nominee, Yankee Killer; nevertheless, Brown has a 7–1 mark against the one-time Bombers, compared to 28–31 against other teams.

Greg Cadaret

Throws Left

New York Yankees	W-L	ERA	AB	H	HR	BB	SO	BA	SA	OBA
Season	8-6	3.62	447	110	8	59	105	.246	.365	.335
vs. Left-Handers			118	29	0	12	25	.246	.305	.313
vs. Right-Handers			329	81	8	47	80	.246	.386	.342
vs. Ground-Ballers			206	52	1	19	48	.252	.325	.317
vs. Fly-Ballers			241	58	7	40	57	.241	.398	.349
Home Games	4-3	4.72	226	62	7	35	51	.274	.434	.371
Road Games	4-3	2.52	221	48	1	24	54	.217	.294	.296
Grass Fields	7-5	3.78	363	86	7	54	82	.237	.361	.336
Artificial Turf	1-1	2.91	84	24	1	5	23	.286	.381	.326
April	1-3	5.40	44	9	0	6	15	.205	.250	.300
May	0-0	1.06	57	12	0	11	7	.211	.281	.338
June	1-0	3.04	87	20	2	12	22	.230	.333	.323
July	1-1	4.67	68	20	1	5	13	.294	.441	.347
August	3-1	4.73	121	30	5	11	32	.248	.438	.313
Sept./Oct.	2-1	2.75	70	19	0	14	16	.271	.343	.388
Leading Off Inn.			103	23	2	13	29	.223	.330	.322
Bases Empty			242	59	3	31	60	.244	.339	.335
Runners On			205	51	5	28	45	.249	.395	.335
Runners/Scor. Pos.			112	33	2	19	26	.295	.446	.388
Runners On/2 Out			89	21	1	15	19	.236	.281	.346
Scor. Pos./2 Out			60	15	0	12	12	.250	.250	.375
Late-Inning Pressure			91	20	0	15	24	.220	.242	.327
Leading Off			23	5	0	4	5	.217	.261	.333
Runners On			44	7	0	7	13	.159	.159	.269
Runners/Scor. Pos.			21	5	0	2	5	.238	.238	.292
First 9 Batters			331	74	6	45	80	.224	.332	.315
Second 9 Batters			78	23	0	10	18	.295	.372	.382
All Batters Thereafter			38	13	2	4	7	.342	.632	.409

Loves to face: Kent Hrbek (.063, 1-for-16, 2 BB)
Bill Spiers (0-for-9)
Devon White (.105, 2-for-19)

Hates to face: Mike Greenwell (.350, 7-for-20, 2 HR)
Al Newman (.400, 4-for-10, 5 BB)
B. J. Surhoff (.471, 8-for-17)

Miscellaneous statistics: Ground outs-to-air outs ratio: 1.22 last season, 1.12 for career.... Induced 14 double plays in 100 opportunities (one per 7.1).... Allowed 21 doubles, 4 triples in 121⅔ innings.... Stranded 28 inherited runners, allowed 14 to score (67%).... Opposing base stealers: 11-for-19 (58%); 1 pickoff, 1 balk.

Comments: Has never allowed a home run to a left-handed batter in 149 at-bats at Yankee Stadium. The last left-hander to homer against him was Mike Greenwell, who hit an inside-the-park grand slam at Fenway in September 1990. The last lefty to take him over a wall was Alvin Davis at the Kingdome in May 1990.... Cadaret and bullpen partner John Habyan combined to face 255 left-handed batters without allowing a home run last season.... Made a cameo appearance in the starting rotation for the third straight season. Career breakdown: 8–9 (4.87 ERA) as a starter, 21–10 (3.41 ERA) in relief.... One of only 15 pitchers to have a record of .500 or better in each of the last five years. Longest streak: eight years by Roger Clemens, Dwight Gooden, and Orel Hershiser.... Came into bases-loaded situations four times and stranded all 12 runners.... Started five double plays as a fielder last season, the most among A.L. pitchers. Yankees pitchers led majors by taking part (as fielders) in 23 double plays and by starting 18.... Opponents have a career average of .280 with runners in scoring position, compared to .249 average in other at-bats. However, with runners in scoring position in Late-Inning Pressure Situations—yes, those dreaded RISP in LIPS situations—he has held batters to a .221 average.... Don't look now, but with 118 games in relief, Cadaret is creeping up on some legendary Yankees relief pitchers: Ryne Duren (131 relief appearances in Pinstripes), Pedro Ramos (129), Luis Arroyo (127).

Tom Candiotti

Throws Right

Indians/Blue Jays	W-L	ERA	AB	H	HR	BB	SO	BA	SA	OBA
Season	13-13	2.65	887	202	12	73	167	.228	.337	.288
vs. Left-Handers			449	109	6	35	63	.243	.354	.295
vs. Right-Handers			438	93	6	38	104	.212	.320	.280
vs. Ground-Ballers			407	92	2	31	73	.226	.314	.282
vs. Fly-Ballers			480	110	10	42	94	.229	.356	.292
Home Games	6-6	3.11	419	103	5	35	84	.246	.370	.303
Road Games	7-7	2.25	468	99	7	38	83	.212	.308	.274
Grass Fields	9-7	2.80	479	101	7	35	88	.211	.313	.265
Artificial Turf	4-6	2.47	408	101	5	38	79	.248	.365	.313
April	2-1	1.24	104	21	1	8	19	.202	.279	.259
May	4-1	3.14	162	38	2	11	35	.235	.327	.279
June	1-5	2.34	163	37	4	11	35	.227	.356	.277
July	2-3	2.15	140	33	0	11	26	.236	.329	.301
August	2-1	2.68	159	33	3	16	29	.208	.314	.277
Sept./Oct.	2-2	3.83	159	40	2	16	23	.252	.396	.324
Leading Off Inn.			224	46	3	19	46	.205	.308	.270
Bases Empty			539	128	8	43	106	.237	.364	.299
Runners On			348	74	4	30	61	.213	.296	.271
Runners/Scor. Pos.			211	40	3	24	36	.190	.275	.266
Runners On/2 Out			166	31	2	21	30	.187	.265	.286
Scor. Pos./2 Out			111	20	2	18	19	.180	.279	.305
Late-Inning Pressure			86	18	0	7	22	.209	.279	.281
Leading Off			22	4	0	3	9	.182	.318	.308
Runners On			32	7	0	2	10	.219	.219	.257
Runners/Scor. Pos.			20	3	0	2	6	.150	.150	.217
First 9 Batters			269	64	3	31	57	.238	.342	.321
Second 9 Batters			277	59	3	17	47	.213	.307	.255
All Batters Thereafter			341	79	6	25	63	.232	.358	.286

Loves to face: Ivan Calderon (.053, 1-for-19, 5 BB)
Tony Fernandez (.154, 6-for-39)
Spike Owen (.032, 1-for-31, 2 BB)

Hates to face: George Bell (.529, 18-for-34, 2 HR)
Alfredo Griffin (.700, 7-for-10)
Fred McGriff (.381, 8-for-21, 8 BB)

Miscellaneous statistics: Ground outs-to-air outs ratio: 0.98 last season, 1.23 for career.... Induced 9 double plays in 121 opportunities (one per 13).... Allowed 41 doubles, 10 triples (tied for most in majors) in 238 innings.... Allowed 17 first-inning runs in 34 starts (4.01 ERA).... Batting support: 3.59 runs per start, 5th-lowest average in A.L.... Opposing base stealers: 26-for-34 (76%), 3d-most steals in A.L.; 4 pickoffs, 0 balks.

Comments: Since the DH rule was adopted in 1973, only one other A.L. pitcher (we're talking about ERA qualifiers here) had a single-season ERA as low as Candiotti's without posting a winning record: Andy Hassler, 7–11 despite a 2.61 ERA for the 1974 Angels.... Among regular A.L. starters, only Juan Guzman (.162) held opponents to a lower batting average with runners in scoring position.... Led A.L. starters in a couple of diverse categories: road-game ERA (2.25) and home-run rate (one every 19.8 innings).... Has topped 200 innings in each of the last six years; only Frank Viola (nine) has a longer current streak.... Toronto acquired two Candy Men (Maldonado and Candiotti) who were teammates in Cleveland in 1990. Other recent examples of the "outhouse-to-penthouse" syndrome: In 1990, Tom Brunansky and Willie McGee went from last-place Cardinals to teams that met in the A.L. playoffs. Most renowned case: In 1969, Donn Clendenon went from expansion Expos to World Series MVP with Miracle Mets.... What made Candy's two-team act odd: He had a winning record for the last-place team (7–6) and a losing mark for the first-place team (6–7), with approximately the same run support from both.... He sure did have his favorite catchers: With Indians, he had 3.15 ERA in 60 innings with Joel Skinner, but 0.94 in 48 innings with Sandy Alomar; with Jays, 4.26 ERA in 80⅓ innings with Pat Borders, but 0.91 in 49⅓ innings with Greg Myers.... Now we'll see if Mike Scioscia can block knuckleballs as well as he does base runners.

Roger Clemens — Throws Right

Boston Red Sox

	W-L	ERA	AB	H	HR	BB	SO	BA	SA	OBA
Season	18-10	2.62	993	219	15	65	241	.221	.328	.270
vs. Left-Handers			563	123	3	47	121	.218	.302	.279
vs. Right-Handers			430	96	12	18	120	.223	.363	.258
vs. Ground-Ballers			464	111	4	30	107	.239	.334	.287
vs. Fly-Ballers			529	108	11	35	134	.204	.323	.255
Home Games	8-5	2.59	526	120	9	35	132	.228	.337	.278
Road Games	10-5	2.66	467	99	6	30	109	.212	.319	.260
Grass Fields	16-8	2.52	857	182	12	53	213	.212	.309	.261
Artificial Turf	2-2	3.28	136	37	3	12	28	.272	.449	.325
April	4-0	0.28	109	17	0	5	34	.156	.174	.191
May	3-2	3.80	167	35	1	10	46	.210	.287	.253
June	2-3	1.94	156	37	2	11	26	.237	.365	.288
July	2-2	3.19	160	42	4	13	36	.262	.381	.320
August	3-1	2.70	189	41	4	18	49	.217	.370	.288
Sept./Oct.	4-2	3.00	212	47	4	8	50	.222	.335	.253
Leading Off Inn.			263	59	3	12	72	.224	.316	.258
Bases Empty			635	132	8	35	168	.208	.307	.253
Runners On			358	87	7	30	73	.243	.366	.299
Runners/Scor. Pos.			199	46	3	25	32	.231	.332	.306
Runners On/2 Out			152	32	3	16	30	.211	.329	.290
Scor. Pos./2 Out			97	21	2	14	14	.216	.330	.315
Late-Inning Pressure			101	15	0	10	31	.149	.198	.225
Leading Off			28	3	0	3	10	.107	.143	.194
Runners On			31	8	0	3	8	.258	.290	.324
Runners/Scor. Pos.			20	4	0	2	7	.200	.200	.273
First 9 Batters			288	69	8	18	72	.240	.385	.290
Second 9 Batters			302	62	4	12	78	.205	.311	.236
All Batters Thereafter			403	88	3	35	91	.218	.300	.280

Loves to face: Mark McGwire (.036, 1-for-28, 1 2B, 3 BB)
Greg Vaughn (.056, 1-for-18, 10 SO)
Devon White (.130, 6-for-46, 0 BB)

Hates to face: Geno Petralli (.394, 13-for-33, 2 HR)
Alan Trammell (.353, 18-for-51, 2 HR)
Lou Whitaker (.351, 20-for-57, 2 HR)

Miscellaneous statistics: Ground outs-to-air outs ratio: 1.23 last season, 1.03 for career.... Induced 17 double plays in 163 opportunities (one per 10).... Allowed 46 doubles (5th most in majors), 8 triples (3d most in A.L.) in 271⅓ innings.... Allowed 20 first-inning runs in 35 starts (4.11 ERA).... Batting support: 4.49 runs per start.... Opposing base stealers: 23-for-39 (59%); 4 pickoffs, 0 balks.

Comments: Became the first pitcher in major league history with a .600 winning percentage and 200 strikeouts for six years in a row. Four pitchers, Hall of Famers all, had five-year streaks: John Clarkson (1885–89), Walter Johnson (1911–15), Sandy Koufax (1962–66), and Tom Seaver (1969–73).... Career winning percentage ranks fourth in A.L. history among pitchers with at least 150 decisions: Spud Chandler (.717, 109–43); Whitey Ford (.690, 236–106); Vic Raschi (.689, 124–56); Clemens (.687, 134–61); Lefty Grove (.682, 300–140).... Among active starters with at least 300 innings pitched, his career ERA (2.85) ranks second to Orel Hershiser (2.77).... Clemens and Gooden are the only pitchers with a winning record in each of the last eight years.... He's 5–9 vs. Oakland, his only losing record vs. any club (he's also 0–1 vs. A's in postseason). Conversely, he has won eight straight decisions vs. Toronto.... His first-inning ERA (4.11) was his highest in any inning.... Because of his velocity, you might think that some of the home runs he allowed would be hit to the opposite field. Not so: All 15 homers last season were pulled.... Did not walk any of the last 77 leadoff batters he faced.... Had two stretches of seven starts in which he was unbeatable: 6–0 with 0.95 ERA in first seven starts; 6–0 with 1.33 ERA in seven starts, Aug. 26–Sept. 26. During latter stretch, he held opponents hitless in 30 consecutive at-bats in Late-Inning Pressure Situations.... The rest of the year he was actually ordinary: 6–10, 3.76.

Chuck Crim — Throws Right

Milwaukee Brewers

	W-L	ERA	AB	H	HR	BB	SO	BA	SA	OBA
Season	8-5	4.63	377	115	9	25	39	.305	.416	.351
vs. Left-Handers			184	54	7	16	19	.293	.446	.355
vs. Right-Handers			193	61	2	9	20	.316	.389	.347
vs. Ground-Ballers			167	53	4	8	14	.317	.425	.350
vs. Fly-Ballers			210	62	5	17	25	.295	.410	.351
Home Games	5-2	5.07	208	65	5	15	26	.313	.423	.359
Road Games	3-3	4.10	169	50	4	10	13	.296	.408	.341
Grass Fields	7-4	4.76	319	101	7	21	33	.317	.426	.363
Artificial Turf	1-1	4.02	58	14	2	4	6	.241	.362	.286
April	1-1	4.50	61	13	2	4	7	.213	.311	.262
May	2-2	7.41	69	20	2	9	8	.290	.435	.372
June	1-1	1.54	49	15	0	1	3	.306	.347	.333
July	1-1	6.00	56	22	1	2	5	.393	.464	.417
August	2-0	5.31	81	23	4	6	8	.284	.481	.333
Sept./Oct.	1-0	1.88	61	22	0	3	8	.361	.426	.391
Leading Off Inn.			84	20	1	3	11	.238	.333	.264
Bases Empty			200	55	5	10	20	.275	.400	.313
Runners On			177	60	4	15	19	.339	.435	.392
Runners/Scor. Pos.			110	40	3	15	12	.364	.482	.441
Runners On/2 Out			84	23	2	7	11	.274	.381	.337
Scor. Pos./2 Out			58	18	2	7	9	.310	.448	.394
Late-Inning Pressure			127	38	2	7	10	.299	.378	.341
Leading Off			33	8	1	0	2	.242	.394	.242
Runners On			56	21	0	3	6	.375	.375	.407
Runners/Scor. Pos.			33	13	0	3	4	.394	.394	.444
First 9 Batters			339	102	7	22	34	.301	.404	.344
Second 9 Batters			38	13	2	3	5	.342	.526	.405
All Batters Thereafter			0	0	0	0	0	—	—	—

Loves to face: Julio Franco (.143, 3-for-21)
Brian Harper (0-for-10)
Manny Lee (.091, 1-for-11)

Hates to face: John Olerud (.500, 3-for-6, 1 2B, 2 HR)
Cal Ripken (.533, 8-for-15, 1 HR)
Alan Trammell (.526, 10-for-19)

Miscellaneous statistics: Ground outs-to-air outs ratio: 1.17 last season, 1.42 for career.... Induced 7 double plays in 72 opportunities (one per 10).... Allowed 15 doubles, 0 triples in 91⅓ innings.... Stranded 27 inherited runners, allowed 15 to score (64%).... Opposing base stealers: 12-for-13 (92%); 0 pickoffs, 3 balks (3d most in A.L.).

Comments: Leaves Brewers ranked third in franchise history in games pitched (332), behind Jim Slaton (364) and Bob McClure (352), and 11 ahead of Dan Plesac (321).... Holds team record for career wins in relief (32).... One of two pitchers (Juan Agosto is the other) to appear in at least 65 games in each of the last four seasons. That's one year short of the major league record shared by Jack Baldschun (1961–65), Pedro Borbon (1973–77), Rollie Fingers (1974–78), Gary Lavelle (1975–79), and Lee Smith (1982–86).... Only runner caught stealing against him: Oakland's Willie Wilson.... Opponents' batting average, year by year, since 1988: .247, .259, .261, .305.... Among all major league right-handed pitchers who faced at least 200 right-handed batters, only Tim Leary (.322) allowed a higher batting average to righties than Crim.... Led A.L. relievers with three balks.... Allowed nine of 59 home runs allowed by Brewers relievers last season; Brewers and Rangers shared major league lead in that category—although Oakland's relievers had the highest ratio of home runs to innings.... Traded to Angels, the team that used its relief pitchers for fewer innings than any team in the majors last season. Relievers pitched only 27.7 percent of Angels' innings, lowest rate in majors. A lot of folks would lay some green that relief pitchers log more innings in N.L. than in DH-using A.L., but uh-uh: In the N.L. last season, 31.8 percent of innings were thrown by bullpen; in A.L., 32.6 percent.

Ron Darling

Throws Right

Mets/Expos/A's	W-L	ERA	AB	H	HR	BB	SO	BA	SA	OBA
Season	8-15	4.26	727	185	22	71	129	.254	.414	.325
vs. Left-Handers			391	93	8	37	76	.238	.358	.303
vs. Right-Handers			336	92	14	34	53	.274	.479	.351
vs. Ground-Ballers			340	82	4	24	58	.241	.347	.290
vs. Fly-Ballers			387	103	18	47	71	.266	.473	.354
Home Games	3-9	5.40	347	100	10	39	59	.288	.473	.360
Road Games	5-6	3.28	380	85	12	32	70	.224	.361	.293
Grass Fields	6-11	4.52	544	141	18	54	100	.259	.432	.330
Artificial Turf	2-4	3.53	183	44	4	17	29	.240	.361	.311
April	1-2	3.86	80	22	1	4	12	.275	.338	.326
May	1-0	4.06	120	30	5	8	20	.250	.442	.308
June	2-3	5.09	134	38	2	11	18	.284	.463	.340
July	1-3	4.22	123	31	7	10	19	.252	.472	.311
August	3-1	3.55	133	33	3	18	26	.248	.376	.338
Sept./Oct.	0-6	4.62	137	31	4	20	34	.226	.372	.325
Leading Off Inn.			183	50	4	12	35	.273	.372	.332
Bases Empty			423	104	14	41	75	.246	.411	.321
Runners On			304	81	8	30	54	.266	.418	.330
Runners/Scor. Pos.			179	52	5	22	28	.291	.464	.363
Runners On/2 Out			123	30	3	17	18	.244	.398	.340
Scor. Pos./2 Out			84	26	3	12	9	.310	.536	.402
Late-Inning Pressure			33	10	2	1	6	.303	.576	.324
Leading Off			10	1	0	0	2	.100	.100	.100
Runners On			8	4	0	0	1	.500	.750	.500
Runners/Scor. Pos.			5	2	0	0	1	.400	.800	.400
First 9 Batters			257	66	3	20	46	.257	.339	.313
Second 9 Batters			244	60	6	25	41	.246	.385	.324
All Batters Thereafter			226	59	13	26	42	.261	.531	.340

Loves to face: Joe Carter (0-for-8)
Kevin McReynolds (.143, 3-for-21)
Franklin Stubbs (.091, 3-for-33, 1 HR, 6 BB, 19 SO)

Hates to face: Jack Clark (.360, 9-for-25, 3 HR, 10 SO)
Von Hayes (.333, 23-for-69, 4 HR)
Greg Vaughn (5-for-5, 1 HR, 1 BB)

Miscellaneous statistics: Ground outs-to-air outs ratio: 1.14 last season, 1.08 for career.... Induced 10 double plays in 141 opportunities (one per 14).... Allowed 30 doubles, 10 triples (most in majors) in 194⅓ innings.... Allowed 10 first-inning runs in 32 starts (2.81 ERA).... Batting support: 3.41 runs per start, 6th-lowest average in majors.... Opposing base stealers: 24-for-27 (89%); 4 pickoffs, 5 balks (2d most in majors).

Comments: Enjoyed five consecutive seasons (1984–88) with double-digit wins and single-digit losses, one year shy of Whitey Ford's all-time record. But it's been downhill from there: 14–14 in 1989, 7–9 and 8–15 the last two years.... Won his first three decisions in A.L. to even his 1991 record at 8–8, but then lost his last seven.... Accomplished in one year what only three others have done in their entire careers—pitching for Mets, Expos, and A's. Others: Ray Burris, Mike Torrez, Don Shaw (the winning pitcher in the first game the Expos ever played).... Has not allowed a first-inning home run in 47 starts since July 1990.... Many pitchers can't find the plate early, but Darling's first-inning rate of walks (2.25 per nine innings) was his lowest in any inning.... We'd like to measure his control in the ninth inning, but no can do: In 32 starts he never got past the eighth (most starts by any pitcher in majors last year without making the ninth).... Led major league pitchers with six errors in 1991, including five on wild pickoff throws to second base. Of his 15 errors since 1988, 11 have been wild pickoff throws.... Won 99 games with Mets, fourth-highest total in team history. He had one shot at #100 in a Mets uniform, but lost to Padres, 2–1, on July 14.... Three other pitchers in baseball history have finished their work with a given team with a "99" in the wins column—but none had done it since Detroit said so long to Twilight Ed Killian back in 1910.... Darling was 1–5 in day games last year; so much for being a matinee idol.

Storm Davis

Throws Right

Kansas City Royals	W-L	ERA	AB	H	HR	BB	SO	BA	SA	OBA
Season	3-9	4.96	458	140	11	46	53	.306	.437	.367
vs. Left-Handers			227	76	6	26	30	.335	.498	.402
vs. Right-Handers			231	64	5	20	23	.277	.377	.333
vs. Ground-Ballers			240	72	5	19	25	.300	.421	.351
vs. Fly-Ballers			218	68	6	27	28	.312	.454	.384
Home Games	2-3	4.12	212	60	2	18	18	.283	.344	.338
Road Games	1-6	5.73	246	80	9	28	35	.325	.516	.392
Grass Fields	1-4	4.26	154	45	7	17	22	.292	.468	.364
Artificial Turf	2-5	5.31	304	95	4	29	31	.313	.421	.369
April	2-1	3.60	100	26	2	5	8	.260	.340	.299
May	0-4	6.28	114	37	2	15	11	.325	.500	.394
June	0-2	1.50	66	14	2	5	11	.212	.333	.268
July	1-0	2.66	90	24	0	7	12	.267	.289	.320
August	0-2	10.32	50	21	3	8	7	.420	.660	.500
Sept./Oct.	0-0	11.74	38	18	2	6	4	.474	.737	.545
Leading Off Inn.			100	33	2	8	9	.330	.460	.385
Bases Empty			234	71	5	15	29	.303	.432	.348
Runners On			224	69	6	31	24	.308	.442	.386
Runners/Scor. Pos.			131	39	2	25	10	.298	.405	.400
Runners On/2 Out			96	29	3	10	9	.302	.406	.368
Scor. Pos./2 Out			63	21	2	7	5	.333	.429	.400
Late-Inning Pressure			75	23	2	9	6	.307	.427	.381
Leading Off			16	5	0	1	1	.313	.375	.353
Runners On			41	13	2	7	3	.317	.463	.417
Runners/Scor. Pos.			29	8	1	7	3	.276	.379	.417
First 9 Batters			299	98	8	32	39	.328	.472	.392
Second 9 Batters			98	27	1	8	7	.276	.388	.324
All Batters Thereafter			61	15	2	6	7	.246	.344	.319

Loves to face: Randy Bush (.103, 4-for-39)
Pete Incaviglia (.056, 1-for-18, 3 BB)
Joel Skinner (.077, 1-for-13, 7 SO)

Hates to face: Greg Gagne (.458, 11-for-24, 2 HR)
Ruben Sierra (.297, 11-for-37, 2 2B, 5 HR)
Willie Wilson (.444, 16-for-36)

Miscellaneous statistics: Ground outs-to-air outs ratio: 1.14 last season, 1.10 for career.... Induced 16 double plays in 120 opportunities (one per 7.5).... Allowed 21 doubles, 3 triples in 114⅓ innings.... Stranded 20 inherited runners, allowed 11 to score (65%).... Opposing base stealers: 2-for-4 (50%); 0 pickoffs, 0 balks.

Comments: Opponents' batting average was the highest of his career, but part of a natural progression. His opponents' average in three-year groups: 1983–85, .246; 1986–88, .273; 1989–91, .291.... Left-handed batters strafed him for a .335 average; among major league pitchers who faced at least 200 left-handed batters, only Dave Johnson (.405) and Jeff M. Robinson (.350) allowed a higher batting average.... Average of 4.17 strikeouts per nine innings was the lowest of his career.... Made nine starts followed by 42 relief appearances last year.... One of three A.L. pitchers to record both a save and a shutout last season. The others: Luis Aquino and Rod Nichols.... Has not allowed a first-inning home run in any of his last 50 starts.... Allowed two grand-slam home runs, raising his career total to five.... Career breakdown: 43–49 during the first half of the season, 59–32 after the All-Star break.... Completed eight of 28 starts for Birds in 1985, but has completed only five of 133 since.... Threw only one wild pitch in 114⅓ innings last season, after averaging one every 15 innings over previous three years.... Like his pagemate Darling, Storm finished 1991 with 102 major league wins. (Darling is 102–79, Davis 102–81.) Among others in Club 102: Bryn Smith, Wild Bill Hallahan, Don Cardwell, and Twilight Ed Killian, who ties an *Analyst* record by getting into two notes on the same page 81 years after his retirement.

Rich DeLucia

Seattle Mariners   Throws Right

	W-L	ERA	AB	H	HR	BB	SO	BA	SA	OBA
Season	12-13	5.09	678	176	31	78	98	.260	.457	.333
vs. Left-Handers			320	92	11	54	34	.287	.453	.386
vs. Right-Handers			358	84	20	24	64	.235	.461	.282
vs. Ground-Ballers			307	78	7	35	39	.254	.388	.324
vs. Fly-Ballers			371	98	24	43	59	.264	.515	.341
Home Games	7-4	4.72	331	80	18	31	48	.242	.456	.306
Road Games	5-9	5.46	347	96	13	47	50	.277	.458	.358
Grass Fields	4-8	5.65	272	73	12	39	39	.268	.463	.356
Artificial Turf	8-5	4.72	406	103	19	39	59	.254	.453	.317
April	2-2	5.26	92	26	5	14	16	.283	.500	.373
May	3-0	3.74	128	35	4	12	25	.273	.422	.336
June	1-3	5.40	105	22	6	22	17	.210	.438	.346
July	3-1	3.86	121	28	3	10	16	.231	.339	.286
August	2-2	3.38	121	29	7	5	13	.240	.463	.268
Sept./Oct.	1-5	9.64	111	36	6	15	11	.324	.604	.397
Leading Off Inn.			182	48	10	14	28	.264	.500	.316
Bases Empty			435	106	20	39	67	.244	.439	.307
Runners On			243	70	11	39	31	.288	.490	.375
Runners/Scor. Pos.			125	34	6	26	21	.272	.464	.364
Runners On/2 Out			102	27	4	12	18	.265	.451	.342
Scor. Pos./2 Out			55	11	1	10	14	.200	.291	.323
Late-Inning Pressure			21	8	2	1	3	.381	.762	.409
Leading Off			7	3	1	0	1	.429	1.000	.429
Runners On			8	2	1	0	1	.250	.625	.250
Runners/Scor. Pos.			3	0	0	0	0	.000	.000	.000
First 9 Batters			249	63	9	29	44	.253	.414	.328
Second 9 Batters			233	56	11	30	30	.240	.446	.324
All Batters Thereafter			196	57	11	19	24	.291	.526	.353

Loves to face: Albert Belle (0-for-6)
Travis Fryman (0-for-8)
Sammy Sosa (0-for-6)

Hates to face: Rob Deer (.571, 4-for-7, 2 2B, 1 HR, 2 SO)
Cecil Fielder (.333, 3-for-9, 3 HR)
Dave Henderson (.417, 5-for-12, 2 HR, 7 fly outs)

Miscellaneous statistics: Ground outs-to-air outs ratio: 0.61 last season, 3d lowest in A.L.; 0.62 for career.... Induced 13 double plays in 140 opportunities (one per 11).... Allowed 35 doubles, 3 triples in 182 innings.... Allowed 30 first-inning runs in 31 starts (8.13 ERA, 3d highest in A.L.).... Batting support: 5.00 runs per start, 6th-highest average in A.L.... Opposing base stealers: 4-for-13 (31%, 2d-lowest rate in A.L.); 1 pickoff, 0 balks.

Comments: Led major league rookie pitchers in wins; among rookies, only Charles Nagy (33) started more games than DeLucia (31).... Allowed 31 home runs to lead A.L. (one behind Tom Browning's major league high). No other rookie allowed more than 18 homers.... Rate of gopher balls increased throughout the game: Opponents averaged a homer every 28 at-bats during his first pass through the lineup, every 22 at-bats the second time through, and every 18 at-bats thereafter.... Had a 6.43 ERA over the first three innings, 3.86 in subsequent innings.... Started 31 games last season without ever pitching into the ninth inning (the most of any pitcher in the A.L.).... Allowed at least one extra-base hit in all but one of his appearances.... Spent his entire season with the Mariners after appearing with four different clubs in the Mariners' chain the previous year.... His nine losses in road games tied him for 2d most in the league.... Breakdown against left- and right-handed batters suggests aggressiveness vs. right-handers, tentativeness vs. lefties: DeLucia struck out 50 more right-handed batters than he walked, but he walked 19 more left-handed batters than he struck out.... Born on Oct. 7, 1964, the day the World Series opened. (Ray Sadecki beat Whitey Ford in Ford's 22d and final Series start.) Turned 26 years of age in final week of season; he's older than rotation-mates Erik Hanson and Brian Holman.

Dennis Eckersley

Oakland A's   Throws Right

	W-L	ERA	AB	H	HR	BB	SO	BA	SA	OBA
Season	5-4	2.96	288	60	11	9	87	.208	.365	.235
vs. Left-Handers			150	34	5	6	34	.227	.353	.261
vs. Right-Handers			138	26	6	3	53	.188	.377	.206
vs. Ground-Ballers			132	33	3	2	34	.250	.364	.267
vs. Fly-Ballers			156	27	8	7	53	.173	.365	.209
Home Games	5-1	1.83	139	23	3	7	49	.165	.273	.211
Road Games	0-3	4.17	149	37	8	2	38	.248	.450	.258
Grass Fields	5-3	2.52	236	44	8	9	74	.186	.331	.220
Artificial Turf	0-1	5.40	52	16	3	0	13	.308	.519	.308
April	0-1	4.00	32	6	2	0	6	.188	.438	.188
May	1-0	2.13	53	15	2	0	16	.283	.472	.283
June	0-0	0.69	46	5	1	1	13	.109	.196	.128
July	0-1	4.85	53	14	3	3	17	.264	.434	.316
August	2-0	1.35	49	9	0	3	16	.184	.245	.231
Sept./Oct.	2-2	4.80	55	11	3	2	19	.200	.400	.228
Leading Off Inn.			64	17	3	1	16	.266	.469	.277
Bases Empty			171	40	5	3	47	.234	.386	.251
Runners On			117	20	6	6	40	.171	.333	.211
Runners/Scor. Pos.			78	12	3	5	28	.154	.282	.205
Runners On/2 Out			56	9	5	2	17	.161	.446	.190
Scor. Pos./2 Out			39	7	3	2	13	.179	.436	.220
Late-Inning Pressure			250	50	9	7	78	.200	.352	.225
Leading Off			56	12	2	1	16	.214	.375	.228
Runners On			98	16	5	5	33	.163	.327	.204
Runners/Scor. Pos.			66	9	2	5	24	.136	.242	.197
First 9 Batters			285	59	10	9	86	.207	.354	.234
Second 9 Batters			3	1	1	0	1	.333	1.333	.333
All Batters Thereafter			0	0	0	0	0	—	—	—

Loves to face: Dan Gladden (.143, 3-for-21)
Al Newman (0-for-9)
Mickey Tettleton (0-for-10)

Hates to face: Tom Brunansky (.391, 9-for-23, 2 HR)
Carlton Fisk (.304, 14-for-46, 3 HR)
Kent Hrbek (.375, 9-for-24, 4 2B, 2 HR)

Miscellaneous statistics: Ground outs-to-air outs ratio: 0.58 last season, 0.71 for career.... Induced 0 double plays in 45 opportunities.... Allowed 8 doubles, 2 triples in 76 innings.... Saved 43 games in 51 opportunities (84%), 3d-highest rate in A.L.... Stranded 22 inherited runners, allowed 9 to score (71%).... Opposing base stealers: 8-for-9 (89%); 1 pickoff, 0 balks.

Comments: Now has 188 career saves to complement his 100 complete games. No other pitcher has reached the 100 mark in both categories; in fact, among pitchers with 100 *starts*, only five others have reached triple figures in saves: Dave Giusti (145), Ron Kline (108), Ron Reed (103), Ellis Kinder (102), and Firpo Marberry (101)—all of whom built part or all of their save totals before the category was officially compiled starting in 1969.... Over the past 30 years, only five other pitchers had at least twelve wins for six straight seasons starting as rookies: Dean Chance, Tom Seaver, Dennis Leonard, Fernando Valenzuela, and Ron Darling.... Career record of 150–129 (3.71 ERA) as a starter, 24–15 (2.05 ERA) in relief.... Holds the Athletics franchise record for fewest walks per nine innings (1.00) and most strikeouts per nine innings (9.06). No other club has the same leader in both categories.... Averaged more than 10 strikeouts per nine innings last season for the first time in his career. His previous high was 9.05, set 15 years earlier.... Walked Bill Spiers to lead off an inning on September 3, breaking a streak of 166 consecutive leadoff batters faced without a walk dating back to September 1988. In five years with Oakland, he has walked only three of 337 leadoff batters.... Oakland's bullpen posted the highest ERA in the league (4.74) along with the league's worst home-run rate (one every eight innings). Eckersley and Gene Nelson were the home-run culprits, allowing a total of 23.

Scott Erickson

Throws Right

Minnesota Twins	W-L	ERA	AB	H	HR	BB	SO	BA	SA	OBA
Season	20-8	3.18	762	189	13	71	108	.248	.364	.314
vs. Left-Handers			417	123	8	45	40	.295	.424	.363
vs. Right-Handers			345	66	5	26	68	.191	.290	.255
vs. Ground-Ballers			358	85	0	31	54	.237	.296	.303
vs. Fly-Ballers			404	104	13	40	54	.257	.423	.324
Home Games	10-3	3.53	370	97	8	29	51	.262	.403	.318
Road Games	10-5	2.86	392	92	5	42	57	.235	.327	.311
Grass Fields	9-2	2.51	300	68	4	31	41	.227	.327	.304
Artificial Turf	11-6	3.62	462	121	9	40	67	.262	.387	.322
April	2-2	2.03	113	29	1	12	15	.257	.345	.333
May	5-0	1.36	172	35	3	13	29	.203	.273	.261
June	5-1	2.18	166	37	2	11	30	.223	.307	.270
July	2-0	5.49	76	24	2	11	5	.316	.513	.416
August	2-3	9.45	88	30	2	7	9	.341	.511	.381
Sept./Oct.	4-2	3.02	147	34	3	17	20	.231	.381	.315
Leading Off Inn.			195	50	5	15	35	.256	.390	.313
Bases Empty			437	114	6	46	70	.261	.371	.335
Runners On			325	75	7	25	38	.231	.354	.286
Runners/Scor. Pos.			162	38	2	21	25	.235	.346	.314
Runners On/2 Out			129	24	2	13	16	.186	.271	.266
Scor. Pos./2 Out			73	13	0	13	12	.178	.205	.302
Late-Inning Pressure			64	16	1	6	9	.250	.375	.314
Leading Off			16	5	0	4	3	.313	.438	.450
Runners On			29	6	1	1	1	.207	.345	.233
Runners/Scor. Pos.			14	3	0	1	1	.214	.286	.267
First 9 Batters			259	64	3	22	51	.247	.332	.308
Second 9 Batters			243	60	4	23	30	.247	.374	.315
All Batters Thereafter			260	65	6	26	27	.250	.385	.321

Loves to face: Jack Clark (0-for-10)
Jeff Huson (0-for-11)
Joel Skinner (0-for-8, 7 SO)

Hates to face: Alex Cole (.636, 7-for-11)
Dan Pasqua (.625, 5-for-8, 1 2B, 3 HR, 2 SO)
Ruben Sierra (.467, 7-for-15, 1 HR)

Miscellaneous statistics: Ground outs-to-air outs ratio: 2.12 last season, 2d highest in A.L.; 2.02 for career.... Induced 22 double plays in 162 opportunities (one per 7.4).... Allowed 39 doubles, 5 triples in 204 innings.... Allowed 11 first-inning runs in 32 starts (3.13 ERA).... Batting support: 5.38 runs per start, 3d-highest average in A.L.... Opposing base stealers: 4-for-14 (29%, lowest rate in A.L.); 1 pickoff, 0 balks.

Comments: Won 20 games during the season, but was winless in three postseason starts. Only five other pitchers did that: Joaquin Andujar (1985), Ed Figueroa (1978), Vida Blue (winless in four postseason starts in 1973), Lefty Williams (1919), and Christy Mathewson (1912).... Won 19 of his first 25 career decisions, two short of the highest total in this century. (The only pitcher in the last 50 years to start his career with a 21–4 mark: Wes Stock.) Two other pitchers went 19–6 or better in their first 25 decisions for the Twins/Senators: Hall of Famer Stan Coveleski (who joined Washington in 1925 at age 36; 20–5) and Monte Weaver (who won 22 games for the Senators as a rookie in 1932; 19–6).... Highest winning percentages among active pitchers (minimum: 40 decisions): Dwight Gooden, .714 (132–53); Erickson, .700 (28–12); Mike Henneman, .700 (49–21); Roger Clemens, .687 (134–61); Ramon Martinez, .629 (44–26).... Has allowed only one first-inning home run in 49 career starts. He started his career with 31 starts without allowing a first-inning earned run. That streak was broken by the White Sox on June 29, the same game that snapped his 12-game winning streak and was the turning point of his season: 12–2, 1.39 before; 8–6, 5.54 after.... Ground outs-to-air outs ratio decreased as the game progressed: 2.49 on his first pass through the order, 2.18 on his second, and 1.81 after that.... Among A.L. pitchers who started at least 20 games last season, two of the three with the highest run support were the league's only two 20-game winners.

Steve Farr

Throws Right

New York Yankees	W-L	ERA	AB	H	HR	BB	SO	BA	SA	OBA
Season	5-5	2.19	260	57	4	20	60	.219	.312	.288
vs. Left-Handers			116	28	2	11	23	.241	.345	.333
vs. Right-Handers			144	29	2	9	37	.201	.285	.248
vs. Ground-Ballers			119	24	1	5	24	.202	.277	.252
vs. Fly-Ballers			141	33	3	15	36	.234	.340	.316
Home Games	3-3	2.56	146	30	3	9	37	.205	.315	.256
Road Games	2-2	1.72	114	27	1	11	23	.237	.307	.326
Grass Fields	5-4	2.15	233	52	4	16	54	.223	.318	.282
Artificial Turf	0-1	2.45	27	5	0	4	6	.185	.259	.333
April	0-1	3.72	37	8	1	7	9	.216	.378	.341
May	2-0	1.98	52	13	0	4	13	.250	.327	.316
June	0-0	0.00	45	6	0	1	11	.133	.133	.152
July	0-0	0.00	29	4	0	1	8	.138	.138	.167
August	1-3	6.75	52	14	2	4	10	.269	.462	.356
Sept./Oct.	2-1	0.77	45	12	1	3	9	.267	.356	.327
Leading Off Inn.			59	15	0	1	15	.254	.339	.279
Bases Empty			146	32	1	6	33	.219	.288	.255
Runners On			114	25	3	14	27	.219	.342	.326
Runners/Scor. Pos.			64	12	2	10	17	.188	.313	.325
Runners On/2 Out			54	14	3	10	12	.259	.444	.385
Scor. Pos./2 Out			34	6	2	7	8	.176	.353	.333
Late-Inning Pressure			177	40	3	16	41	.226	.316	.305
Leading Off			39	9	0	1	11	.231	.282	.268
Runners On			79	17	2	11	18	.215	.329	.333
Runners/Scor. Pos.			42	6	1	7	13	.143	.238	.294
First 9 Batters			252	54	3	18	60	.214	.298	.277
Second 9 Batters			8	3	1	2	0	.375	.750	.545
All Batters Thereafter			0	0	0	0	0	—	—	—

Loves to face: Carlton Fisk (.095, 2-for-21, 1 HR, 11 SO)
Brian Harper (0-for-8)
Mickey Tettleton (.071, 1-for-14, 2 BB, 9 SO)

Hates to face: Harold Reynolds (.474, 9-for-19)
Cal Ripken (.364, 8-for-22, 1 HR)
Ruben Sierra (.500, 8-for-16, 1 HR, 6 SO)

Miscellaneous statistics: Ground outs-to-air outs ratio: 1.25 last season, 1.11 for career.... Induced 8 double plays in 51 opportunities (one per 6.4).... Allowed 12 doubles, 0 triples in 70 innings.... Saved 23 games in 30 opportunities (77%).... Stranded 23 inherited runners, allowed 8 to score (74%).... Opposing base stealers: 2-for-4 (50%); 0 pickoffs, 0 balks.

Comments: At age 34, Farr became the oldest Yankees pitcher ever to make as many as 60 relief appearances in a season—by a whisker. He was six days older at the end of the season than Lindy McDaniel was for the finale in 1970, when he relieved in 62 games. Luis Arroyo was two months younger when he made 65 relief appearances in 1961.... Pitched in save situations in only five of his first 18 appearances. That's not to say he wasn't the stopper—he just had nothing to stop. New York's bullpen had only one save opportunity in the club's first 23 games.... Opponents had only two hits in 29 at-bats with runners on base during a 27-inning scoreless streak (May 29–August 2), the longest by any reliever in the majors last season. He then allowed seven earned runs in his next seven appearances, of which he lost three. Murmurs of a "tired arm" were heard, but his strong finish silenced them.... Allowed 2.57 walks per nine innings, the lowest rate of his career.... Didn't walk any of the last 47 batters he faced leading off innings.... Has held opposing batters below the .200 mark with runners in scoring position three times in the last six years.... Started 16 games as a 27-year-old rookie for the Indians in 1984, but only 12 more in seven seasons since then. Still, last season was only the third in which he pitched exclusively out of the bullpen.... Career record of 10–11 (3.77 ERA) as a starter, 32–29 (3.06 ERA) in relief.

Alex Fernandez
Throws Right

Chicago White Sox	W-L	ERA	AB	H	HR	BB	SO	BA	SA	OBA
Season	9-13	4.51	719	186	16	88	145	.259	.388	.337
vs. Left-Handers			330	83	4	42	64	.252	.355	.331
vs. Right-Handers			389	103	12	46	81	.265	.416	.342
vs. Ground-Ballers			350	89	3	33	59	.254	.337	.316
vs. Fly-Ballers			369	97	13	55	86	.263	.436	.355
Home Games	5-7	4.48	349	80	7	36	70	.229	.355	.298
Road Games	4-6	4.53	370	106	9	52	75	.286	.419	.372
Grass Fields	8-13	4.78	645	167	15	72	132	.259	.392	.331
Artificial Turf	1-0	2.21	74	19	1	16	13	.257	.351	.385
April	2-2	8.55	83	27	3	16	20	.325	.494	.436
May	0-2	4.80	112	27	3	19	23	.241	.366	.346
June	2-3	4.71	135	34	2	13	29	.252	.326	.315
July	1-0	4.08	108	29	4	7	14	.269	.491	.314
August	1-5	4.66	143	39	1	10	29	.273	.399	.314
Sept./Oct.	3-1	2.25	138	30	3	23	30	.217	.312	.325
Leading Off Inn.			182	50	4	24	31	.275	.401	.365
Bases Empty			421	101	8	46	81	.240	.363	.318
Runners On			298	85	8	42	64	.285	.423	.362
Runners/Scor. Pos.			157	42	4	27	35	.268	.382	.354
Runners On/2 Out			109	25	3	24	28	.229	.358	.368
Scor. Pos./2 Out			71	13	2	16	20	.183	.282	.333
Late-Inning Pressure			42	10	3	6	10	.238	.476	.333
Leading Off			14	3	2	1	6	.214	.643	.267
Runners On			13	2	0	2	3	.154	.231	.267
Runners/Scor. Pos.			3	1	0	2	1	.333	.667	.600
First 9 Batters			266	74	4	28	62	.278	.398	.345
Second 9 Batters			232	56	6	28	45	.241	.401	.325
All Batters Thereafter			221	56	6	32	38	.253	.362	.340

Loves to face: Jose Canseco (.083, 1-for-12, 2 BB, 8 SO)
Junior Felix (0-for-7, 5 SO)
Lance Parrish (0-for-10)

Hates to face: Tom Brunansky (.400, 6-for-15, 2 HR)
Travis Fryman (.714, 5-for-7)
Luis Rivera (.462, 6-for-13, 1 HR)

Miscellaneous statistics: Ground outs-to-air outs ratio: 0.90 last season, 0.93 for career.... Induced 13 double plays in 162 opportunities (one per 12).... Allowed 33 doubles, 6 triples in 191⅔ innings.... Allowed 13 first-inning runs in 32 starts (3.38 ERA).... Batting support: 3.63 runs per start, 6th-lowest average in A.L.... Opposing base stealers: 15-for-26 (58%); 2 pickoffs, 1 balk.

Comments: Over the past 60 years, only two pitchers younger than Fernandez started as many as 20 games for the White Sox: Britt Burns and Rich Dotson both started 32 games at the age of 21 in 1980.... Teammates Ramon Garcia (15 starts) and Wilson Alvarez (9) were both younger than Fernandez. (Still are.) The last team with three pitchers that young who all made at least nine starts was the expansion Blue Jays in 1977 (Jeff Byrd, Jim Clancy, and Jerry Garvin).... ERA was 2d highest in the majors during the month of April.... Pitched 27 innings at the old Comiskey Park in 1990 without allowing a home run. He allowed seven homers in 96⅓ innings at the new one last season.... None of the four home runs he allowed to left-handed batters were hit by the usual suspects; Fernandez got nailed by Wade Boggs, Jamie Quirk, Kurt Stillwell, and Randy Bush.... Strikeout rate during the first inning of play was his highest in any inning (31 SO in 32 IP). He averaged 8.13 strikeouts per nine innings on his first pass through the batting order, 6.39 the second time through, and 5.73 thereafter.... Had a record of 2–4 with a 7.32 ERA in day games.... Opponents were batting .345 with runners in scoring position at the All-Star break, but batted only .178 with RISP during the second half.... Opponents have a career average of .289 with runners on base, .239 with the bases empty.... Opponents have nine hits in 19 career at-bats with the bases loaded (.474).... Has completed five of 45 career starts, but none have been shutouts.

Chuck Finley
Throws Left

California Angels	W-L	ERA	AB	H	HR	BB	SO	BA	SA	OBA
Season	18-9	3.80	839	205	23	101	171	.244	.385	.330
vs. Left-Handers			109	28	4	13	22	.257	.422	.336
vs. Right-Handers			730	177	19	88	149	.242	.379	.329
vs. Ground-Ballers			392	99	6	35	75	.253	.367	.319
vs. Fly-Ballers			447	106	17	66	96	.237	.400	.340
Home Games	9-3	3.03	444	99	14	50	103	.223	.360	.307
Road Games	9-6	4.73	395	106	9	51	68	.268	.413	.356
Grass Fields	13-9	4.05	688	174	22	81	148	.253	.404	.337
Artificial Turf	5-0	2.74	151	31	1	20	23	.205	.298	.298
April	4-0	2.45	101	16	1	12	24	.158	.267	.248
May	4-2	4.54	159	46	4	20	41	.289	.396	.379
June	3-1	3.82	127	31	3	21	31	.244	.362	.360
July	3-2	4.39	155	40	6	16	26	.258	.471	.329
August	2-2	3.38	126	31	4	11	19	.246	.421	.312
Sept./Oct.	2-2	3.77	171	41	5	21	30	.240	.357	.323
Leading Off Inn.			216	49	5	21	35	.227	.333	.304
Bases Empty			506	122	15	56	98	.241	.395	.320
Runners On			333	83	8	45	73	.249	.369	.345
Runners/Scor. Pos.			181	48	5	25	42	.265	.414	.352
Runners On/2 Out			142	41	6	22	35	.289	.493	.395
Scor. Pos./2 Out			95	28	4	14	22	.295	.505	.385
Late-Inning Pressure			93	20	2	13	25	.215	.312	.311
Leading Off			28	5	1	4	9	.179	.321	.281
Runners On			30	4	0	5	8	.133	.167	.257
Runners/Scor. Pos.			6	2	0	3	2	.333	.500	.556
First 9 Batters			271	58	5	30	54	.214	.325	.302
Second 9 Batters			254	74	8	31	47	.291	.469	.371
All Batters Thereafter			314	73	10	40	70	.232	.369	.321

Loves to face: Jerry Browne (.050, 1-for-20, 1 2B)
Mike Devereaux (.080, 2-for-25)
Greg Vaughn (0-for-11, 7 SO)

Hates to face: Mel Hall (5-for-5)
Candy Maldonado (.583, 7-for-12, 2 HR, 3 SO)
Mike Stanley (.480, 12-for-25)

Miscellaneous statistics: Ground outs-to-air outs ratio: 1.00 last season, 1.06 for career.... Induced 21 double plays in 178 opportunities (one per 8.5).... Allowed 43 doubles, 3 triples in 227⅓ innings.... Allowed 23 first-inning runs in 34 starts (6.15 ERA).... Batting support: 4.79 runs per start.... Opposing base stealers: 15-for-29 (52%); 0 pickoffs, 3 balks (3d most in A.L.).

Comments: He needed three wins over his last five starts to reach 20 victories, but went 1–1 with three no-decisions.... Lost his last three starts of 1990, but never lost two in a row in 1991. In fact, Finley was the only A.L. pitcher with at least 20 starts who didn't have at least a two-game losing streak.... Became the third Angels pitcher to win at least 16 games in three consecutive seasons. The others: Clyde Wright (1970–72) and Nolan Ryan (1972–74).... Has won 50 of his last 75 decisions, after a 16–25 start.... Career winning percentage of .569 (66–50) is highest in Angels history (minimum: 50 decisions).... Never started a game in his minor league career, and made his first 57 major league appearances out of the bullpen. But since his first start, in September 1987, he has appeared in 129 games, all as a starter, and has more wins than any other A.L. pitcher except Stewart, Clemens, and Welch.... Career records: 61–43 with a 3.27 ERA as a starter; 5–7, 3.92 in relief.... Left-handed batters drove in only eight runs against Finley last season, four on solo home runs. No left-handed batter had homered against him in either 1989 or 1990.... He was the only left-handed pitcher to throw a complete game against the Red Sox last season, and it was a shutout. He has shut Boston out in each of the last three seasons, becoming the first pitcher to do that since Frank Tanana (1974–76).... He has a career record of 36–19 against Eastern Division clubs, but is only 30–31 within his own division (including 1–7 vs. Oakland).

Ramon Garcia
Throws Right

Chicago White Sox	W-L	ERA	AB	H	HR	BB	SO	BA	SA	OBA
Season	4-4	5.40	294	79	13	31	40	.269	.449	.340
vs. Left-Handers			135	37	4	19	18	.274	.422	.359
vs. Right-Handers			159	42	9	12	22	.264	.472	.324
vs. Ground-Ballers			126	40	6	17	17	.317	.516	.403
vs. Fly-Ballers			168	39	7	14	23	.232	.399	.292
Home Games	2-2	6.40	173	47	9	19	20	.272	.486	.344
Road Games	2-2	4.05	121	32	4	12	20	.264	.397	.336
Grass Fields	4-3	5.00	271	73	11	27	37	.269	.443	.338
Artificial Turf	0-1	9.95	23	6	2	4	3	.261	.522	.370
April	0-0	—	0	0	0	0	0	—	—	—
May	0-0	5.14	21	2	1	4	4	.095	.238	.240
June	0-3	4.91	108	29	5	6	21	.269	.472	.310
July	2-0	4.05	100	27	5	13	10	.270	.440	.360
August	2-0	7.43	57	19	1	6	4	.333	.474	.391
Sept./Oct.	0-1	18.00	8	2	1	2	1	.250	.625	.400
Leading Off Inn.			80	23	5	7	9	.287	.587	.345
Bases Empty			191	51	9	18	31	.267	.466	.333
Runners On			103	28	4	13	9	.272	.417	.353
Runners/Scor. Pos.			46	16	3	9	4	.348	.543	.448
Runners On/2 Out			39	9	2	9	3	.231	.385	.375
Scor. Pos./2 Out			18	6	2	5	2	.333	.667	.478
Late-Inning Pressure			14	5	1	2	1	.357	.643	.471
Leading Off			5	2	0	1	0	.400	.600	.500
Runners On			4	1	1	1	0	.250	1.000	.400
Runners/Scor. Pos.			3	1	1	1	0	.333	1.333	.500
First 9 Batters			115	36	8	16	14	.313	.565	.394
Second 9 Batters			101	23	3	8	19	.228	.356	.284
All Batters Thereafter			78	20	2	7	7	.256	.397	.330

Loves to face: Tom Brunansky (0-for-6)
Jeff Huson (0-for-5)

Hates to face: Julio Franco (.556, 5-for-9, 1 HR)
Brian Harper (.600, 3-for-5, 1 HR)
Cal Ripken (3-for-3, 1 HR)

Miscellaneous statistics: Ground outs-to-air outs ratio: 0.89 last season, 0.89 for career.... Induced 7 double plays in 50 opportunities (one per 7.1).... Allowed 14 doubles, 0 triples in 78⅓ innings.... Allowed 12 first-inning runs in 15 starts (6.91 ERA).... Batting support: 5.67 runs per start.... Opposing base stealers: 4-for-9 (44%); 1 pickoff, 2 balks.

Comments: Three of the four youngest pitchers to start at least 15 games last season pitched for Chicago teams: Garcia, teammate Alex Fernandez, and Frank Castillo of the Cubs. (Atlanta's Steve Avery was the fourth.) But the youngest White Sox starter last season wasn't Fernandez or Garcia; it was 21-year-old Wilson Alvarez, who started nine games, including a no-hitter against Baltimore in August.... But all things considered, last season's Sox rotation was their oldest since 1987; their 1990 staff was the league's youngest since 1980, when Chicago unveiled Britt Burns and Richard Dotson, among others.... Alvarez pitched the most innings of any major league pitcher who didn't allow a stolen base last season; opposing base runners were 0-for-4 in 56⅓ innings.... Garcia pitched into the ninth inning in only one of his 15 starts, while failing to last three innings three times.... Allowed a grand-slam home run to Mike Gallego in his major league debut on May 31.... Allowed an average of one home run per six innings, fueled by a streak of eight consecutive starts in which he allowed at least one (June 15–July 27). Among A.L. pitchers with as many innings as Garcia, only Rich DeLucia, Jim Acker, Allan Anderson, and Dave Johnson had higher home-run rates.... Pitched 78⅓ innings over 16 games, but did not appear in a day game.

Mike Gardiner
Throws Right

Boston Red Sox	W-L	ERA	AB	H	HR	BB	SO	BA	SA	OBA
Season	9-10	4.85	511	140	18	47	91	.274	.438	.333
vs. Left-Handers			247	64	4	22	39	.259	.364	.317
vs. Right-Handers			264	76	14	25	52	.288	.508	.348
vs. Ground-Ballers			248	68	6	25	41	.274	.407	.339
vs. Fly-Ballers			263	72	12	22	50	.274	.468	.328
Home Games	4-5	4.30	296	81	10	27	50	.274	.432	.332
Road Games	5-5	5.60	215	59	8	20	41	.274	.447	.335
Grass Fields	7-9	4.73	441	120	15	41	79	.272	.433	.333
Artificial Turf	2-1	5.60	70	20	3	6	12	.286	.471	.338
April	0-0	—	0	0	0	0	0	—	—	—
May	1-0	2.57	26	6	0	2	5	.231	.231	.286
June	2-2	5.52	118	34	3	11	24	.288	.424	.344
July	0-3	4.15	72	22	3	10	9	.306	.458	.390
August	3-1	5.45	143	38	8	11	28	.266	.503	.318
Sept./Oct.	3-4	4.50	152	40	4	13	25	.263	.414	.319
Leading Off Inn.			125	38	6	18	19	.304	.512	.392
Bases Empty			299	77	10	28	61	.258	.418	.321
Runners On			212	63	8	19	30	.297	.467	.350
Runners/Scor. Pos.			114	32	4	10	15	.281	.465	.331
Runners On/2 Out			72	15	3	9	13	.208	.389	.296
Scor. Pos./2 Out			50	11	3	6	7	.220	.480	.304
Late-Inning Pressure			7	3	1	0	2	.429	.857	.429
Leading Off			2	0	0	0	1	.000	.000	.000
Runners On			2	2	1	0	0	1.000	2.500	1.000
Runners/Scor. Pos.			1	1	1	0	0	1.000	4.000	1.000
First 9 Batters			179	35	4	19	41	.196	.291	.273
Second 9 Batters			182	55	6	13	31	.302	.495	.345
All Batters Thereafter			150	50	8	15	19	.333	.547	.392

Loves to face: Gary Gaetti (.100, 1-for-10, 1 2B)
Wally Joyner (0-for-8)
Joel Skinner (0-for-5)

Hates to face: Mark McGwire (.429, 3-for-7, 3 HR)
Frank Thomas (.750, 6-for-8, 2 HR)
Robin Ventura (.625, 5-for-8, 1 HR)

Miscellaneous statistics: Ground outs-to-air outs ratio: 1.14 last season, 1.19 for career.... Induced 11 double plays in 118 opportunities (one per 11).... Allowed 26 doubles, 2 triples in 130 innings.... Allowed 6 first-inning runs in 22 starts (1.64 ERA, 3d lowest in A.L.).... Batting support: 4.86 runs per start.... Opposing base stealers: 11-for-16 (69%); 1 pickoff, 0 balks.

Comments: Spent most of the 1989 season as a reliever in the Mariners organization before being returned to a starting role in 1990, when he was the Eastern League's Pitcher of the Year.... Made his major league debut at Fenway Park, in a Mariners uniform, in September 1990.... Won seven of eight decisions at Pawtucket last season before his late-May call-up.... Became the fifth rookie pitcher since 1969 to start as many as 22 games for the Red Sox. The others: Dana Kiecker (1990), Al Nipper (1984), Lynn McGlothen (1972), and Mike Nagy (1969).... Didn't reach the ninth inning in any of his starts last season, nor in three for Seattle in 1990.... Opponents batted only .122 during the first inning, the lowest mark against any A.L. starter, but hit .300 from the second inning on.... Didn't allow a stolen base in 58⅓ innings over his last 10 starts. Two runners were caught during that time, another was picked off.... The 70th Canadian-born pitcher to appear in a major league game. He proved his loyalty to the team that signs his paychecks by defeating the Blue Jays in his only appearance against them. Among other pitchers born in the True North: Ferguson Jenkins, John Hiller, Ron Taylor, Claude Raymond, Ken MacKenzie, and Reggie Cleveland. Active Canadian pitchers include Kirk McCaskill, Denis Boucher, and Steve Wilson.

Paul Gibson
Throws Left

Detroit Tigers	W-L	ERA	AB	H	HR	BB	SO	BA	SA	OBA
Season	5-7	4.59	377	112	10	48	52	.297	.424	.379
vs. Left-Handers			113	39	6	11	12	.345	.549	.405
vs. Right-Handers			264	73	4	37	40	.277	.371	.368
vs. Ground-Ballers			193	60	1	18	25	.311	.378	.371
vs. Fly-Ballers			184	52	9	30	27	.283	.473	.387
Home Games	4-3	4.08	205	59	4	25	34	.288	.390	.365
Road Games	1-4	5.23	172	53	6	23	18	.308	.465	.395
Grass Fields	4-6	4.83	292	91	7	37	42	.312	.438	.390
Artificial Turf	1-1	3.86	85	21	3	11	10	.247	.376	.343
April	2-1	0.00	47	9	0	6	11	.191	.191	.278
May	0-1	3.46	92	18	3	8	17	.196	.348	.267
June	1-2	9.90	49	21	2	6	5	.429	.592	.491
July	1-1	7.04	66	24	2	10	4	.364	.470	.462
August	1-2	6.75	78	28	2	13	8	.359	.513	.451
Sept./Oct.	0-0	1.54	45	12	1	5	7	.267	.422	.333
Leading Off Inn.			79	22	2	9	14	.278	.418	.360
Bases Empty			182	51	4	20	30	.280	.390	.358
Runners On			195	61	6	28	22	.313	.456	.398
Runners/Scor. Pos.			117	35	1	21	15	.299	.376	.400
Runners On/2 Out			86	22	1	15	10	.256	.349	.366
Scor. Pos./2 Out			64	15	1	12	9	.234	.313	.355
Late-Inning Pressure			152	46	6	15	20	.303	.454	.363
Leading Off			36	11	1	4	6	.306	.444	.375
Runners On			74	22	5	6	9	.297	.514	.346
Runners/Scor. Pos.			40	10	1	4	6	.250	.325	.311
First 9 Batters			331	98	10	43	49	.296	.429	.380
Second 9 Batters			46	14	0	5	3	.304	.391	.373
All Batters Thereafter			0	0	0	0	0	—	—	—

Loves to face: George Bell (0-for-11)
Mike Felder (0-for-12)
Hates to face: Tony Fernandez (.353, 6-for-17, 2 2B, 2 3B, 6 BB)

Miscellaneous statistics: Ground outs-to-air outs ratio: 0.78 last season, 0.82 for career.... Induced 13 double plays in 104 opportunities (one per 8.0).... Allowed 10 doubles, 4 triples in 96 innings.... Stranded 43 inherited runners, allowed 26 to score (62%).... Opposing base stealers: 5-for-10 (50%); 3 pickoffs, 0 balks.

Comments: His opening-day victory was the first opening-day decision by a Tigers reliever since Pete Burnside in 1960.... Through the end of May he had stranded 25 of 28 inherited runners (89%). But after June 1, Gibson's inheritance tax took a big bite out of the Tigers starters' income: He allowed 23 to score, and stranded only 18 (44%).... That slump coincided with an inability to retire left-handed hitters. Opposing lefties batted .171 through June 5, but .423 for the remainder of the year. Left-handers had hit only eight home runs in 400 career at-bats against Gibson through early June, then six more in a span of only 52 ABs.... Last season marked the first time that opposing left-handers drove in more runs than right-handed batters. Prior to 1991: RHB—98, LHB—52.... Opponents have an overall career batting average of .266, but have batted only .197 with two outs and runners in scoring position.... Rate of hits allowed per nine innings has increased steadily since his rookie season of 1988: 8.12, 8.80, 9.15, 10.50.... That problem's compounded by annual increases in walk rates; walks per nine innings year by year: 3.33, 3.89, 4.07, 4.50.... And then there's his home-run rate. Guess what? Home runs per nine innings, year by year: 0.59, 0.75, 0.92, 0.94.... Has faced 62 batters with the bases loaded over four seasons without walking in a run.

Tom Gordon
Throws Right

Kansas City Royals	W-L	ERA	AB	H	HR	BB	SO	BA	SA	OBA
Season	9-14	3.87	585	129	16	87	167	.221	.357	.324
vs. Left-Handers			302	75	4	42	81	.248	.344	.340
vs. Right-Handers			283	54	12	45	86	.191	.371	.307
vs. Ground-Ballers			292	75	3	41	79	.257	.342	.350
vs. Fly-Ballers			293	54	13	46	88	.184	.372	.299
Home Games	2-8	4.00	345	77	8	46	93	.223	.362	.318
Road Games	7-6	3.70	240	52	8	41	74	.217	.350	.332
Grass Fields	5-4	3.60	200	44	6	33	62	.220	.345	.332
Artificial Turf	4-10	4.02	385	85	10	54	105	.221	.364	.320
April	1-1	0.47	68	12	0	7	25	.176	.235	.253
May	3-1	2.33	135	26	3	13	28	.193	.296	.264
June	0-4	6.53	124	35	5	21	31	.282	.532	.399
July	2-3	8.38	74	17	5	22	24	.230	.473	.398
August	3-2	1.48	89	21	1	7	30	.236	.315	.299
Sept./Oct.	0-3	4.44	95	18	2	17	29	.189	.253	.310
Leading Off Inn.			141	30	3	15	35	.213	.319	.288
Bases Empty			333	82	11	38	88	.246	.402	.325
Runners On			252	47	5	49	79	.187	.298	.322
Runners/Scor. Pos.			152	30	5	28	51	.197	.382	.324
Runners On/2 Out			106	13	2	24	31	.123	.179	.285
Scor. Pos./2 Out			69	9	2	15	23	.130	.217	.286
Late-Inning Pressure			104	25	2	11	31	.240	.298	.319
Leading Off			31	10	0	1	6	.323	.323	.344
Runners On			33	4	0	7	15	.121	.121	.293
Runners/Scor. Pos.			16	1	0	4	7	.063	.063	.250
First 9 Batters			300	59	3	46	95	.197	.257	.309
Second 9 Batters			151	40	8	25	37	.265	.510	.365
All Batters Thereafter			134	30	5	16	35	.224	.410	.311

Loves to face: Dave Henderson (0-for-12, 9 SO)
Roberto Kelly (0-for-11)
Harold Reynolds (.087, 2-for-23, 5 BB)
Hates to face: Juan Gonzalez (.417, 5-for-12, 2 2B, 1 3B, 1 HR)
Ken Griffey, Jr. (.389, 7-for-18, 3 HR)
Ozzie Guillen (.615, 8-for-13)

Miscellaneous statistics: Ground outs-to-air outs ratio: 1.07 last season, 1.14 for career.... Induced 8 double plays in 134 opportunities (one per 17), worst rate in A.L.... Allowed 16 doubles, 8 triples (3d most in A.L.) in 158 innings.... Allowed 6 first-inning runs in 14 starts (2.57 ERA).... Batting support: 4.50 runs per start.... Record of 5–7, 4.77 ERA as a starter; 4–7, 2.73 ERA in 31 relief appearances.... Stranded 11 inherited runners, allowed 6 to score (65%).... Opposing base stealers: 9-for-16 (56%); 0 pickoffs, 0 balks.

Comments: According to rosters published by the clubs, Gordon and Montreal's Brian Barnes are both five-nine and they share the distinction of being the shortest pitchers to appear in a game during the 1991 season.... One of five A.L. pitchers to allow two grand-slam home runs last season. His teammate Storm Davis was another.... April ERA was 2d lowest in the majors.... Made the last of his 14 starts on July 19.... Gordon was the pitcher of decision in six consecutive relief appearances from late July to mid-August.... Career record of 24–27 (4.14 ERA) as a starter, 14–9 (2.82 ERA) in relief.... Career average of 8.68 strikeouts per nine innings is the highest in Royals franchise history, just ahead of Jeff Montgomery (8.28). His average of 4.72 walks per nine innings is also the highest in franchise history (minimum: 300 innings).... Ranks fifth in the American League with 495 strikeouts over the past three seasons.... Has walked the leadoff batter in 56 of 516 innings over the past three years (one per 9.2), the 5th-highest total in the A.L. during that time (minimum: 300 BFP).... Career total of 532 innings is 2d highest among pitchers active in 1991 who have never been called for a balk. The highest total belongs to teammate Steve Crawford (562⅔).... Opponents have a career batting average of .265 on grass fields, .227 at Royals Stadium, and .182 on other artificial surfaces.

Mark Gubicza

Throws Right

Kansas City Royals	W-L	ERA	AB	H	HR	BB	SO	BA	SA	OBA
Season	9-12	5.68	545	168	10	42	89	.308	.424	.361
vs. Left-Handers			258	84	3	28	43	.326	.438	.394
vs. Right-Handers			287	84	7	14	46	.293	.411	.330
vs. Ground-Ballers			266	83	3	20	37	.312	.395	.363
vs. Fly-Ballers			279	85	7	22	52	.305	.452	.359
Home Games	4-6	5.21	266	75	2	18	48	.282	.380	.332
Road Games	5-6	6.15	279	93	8	24	41	.333	.466	.388
Grass Fields	3-3	6.12	175	55	5	17	23	.314	.434	.374
Artificial Turf	6-9	5.48	370	113	5	25	66	.305	.419	.355
April	0-0	—	0	0	0	0	0	—	—	—
May	1-3	4.70	92	27	1	6	18	.293	.370	.343
June	2-1	5.60	73	23	0	6	8	.315	.356	.363
July	3-1	6.00	130	39	6	9	22	.300	.515	.359
August	2-2	4.25	139	38	0	8	24	.273	.338	.315
Sept./Oct.	1-5	8.20	111	41	3	13	17	.369	.514	.430
Leading Off Inn.			131	37	2	7	17	.282	.412	.324
Bases Empty			294	82	5	26	46	.279	.391	.342
Runners On			251	86	5	16	43	.343	.462	.384
Runners/Scor. Pos.			150	47	4	11	30	.313	.453	.361
Runners On/2 Out			109	42	3	13	17	.385	.541	.455
Scor. Pos./2 Out			76	27	3	9	13	.355	.539	.424
Late-Inning Pressure			6	0	0	0	2	.000	.000	.000
Leading Off			2	0	0	0	1	.000	.000	.000
Runners On			0	0	0	0	0	—	—	—
Runners/Scor. Pos.			0	0	0	0	0	—	—	—
First 9 Batters			213	56	3	18	41	.263	.352	.325
Second 9 Batters			205	68	4	14	28	.332	.449	.375
All Batters Thereafter			127	44	3	10	20	.346	.504	.400

Loves to face: Rafael Palmeiro (.105, 2-for-19)
Dick Schofield (0-for-27)
Joel Skinner (0-for-19)

Hates to face: Wade Boggs (.364, 20-for-55, 1 HR, 17 BB)
Don Mattingly (.377, 23-for-61, 3 HR)
Randy Milligan (.500, 5-for-10, 1 2B, 1 3B, 2 HR)

Miscellaneous statistics: Ground outs-to-air outs ratio: 2.10 last season, 3d highest in A.L.; 1.69 for career.... Induced 14 double plays in 111 opportunities (one per 7.9).... Allowed 27 doubles, 3 triples in 133 innings.... Allowed 19 first-inning runs in 26 starts (6.31 ERA).... Batting support: 4.15 runs per start.... Opposing base stealers: 18-for-24 (75%); 1 pickoff, 0 balks.

Comments: Pitched at least 240 innings in three consecutive seasons (1987–89), but a total of only 227 in two years since.... Opponents' batting average has increased by at least 20 points in every year since 1988: .234, .259, .283, .308. The only other pitcher ever to suffer three straight 20-point increases in seasons of 15 or more starts: Burt Hooton (1972–74).... Career total of 97 wins ranks fifth in Royals history, but he ranks third in losses (86).... Last season, Gubicza had the highest single-season ERA ever by a Royals pitcher (minimum: 100 IP). Other Royals pitchers with ERAs in the fives: Rich Gale (5.64 in 1979, 5.38 in 1981), Larry Gura (5.18 in 1984), Charlie Leibrandt (5.14 in 1989), and Dennis Leonard (5.10 in 1982).... Didn't reach the ninth inning in any of his 26 starts. Has completed only two of 42 starts over the past two seasons, compared to a 26-for-106 mark from 1987 through 1989 ... At Tiger Stadium in July, he allowed three home runs in a game for only the third time in his career.... All three home runs that he allowed to left-handed batters were hit in road games. He hasn't surrendered a home run to a left-hander in Royals Stadium since Tony Phillips hit one in Gubicza's final appearance of the 1990 season.... Career average of one home run allowed per 17.3 innings pitched is 3d best among active players (minimum: 1500 IP). Only Orel Hershiser (one HR every 20.2 innings) and Doc Gooden (19.7) have better rates.

Lee Guetterman

Throws Left

New York Yankees	W-L	ERA	AB	H	HR	BB	SO	BA	SA	OBA
Season	3-4	3.68	340	91	6	25	35	.268	.388	.320
vs. Left-Handers			97	17	2	7	13	.175	.289	.250
vs. Right-Handers			243	74	4	18	22	.305	.428	.348
vs. Ground-Ballers			156	38	1	14	15	.244	.353	.314
vs. Fly-Ballers			184	53	5	11	20	.288	.418	.325
Home Games	2-1	4.18	200	55	5	17	25	.275	.405	.336
Road Games	1-3	2.97	140	36	1	8	10	.257	.364	.296
Grass Fields	3-2	3.57	292	78	6	22	34	.267	.397	.320
Artificial Turf	0-2	4.38	48	13	0	3	1	.271	.333	.321
April	0-0	1.35	24	6	0	1	3	.250	.292	.280
May	1-0	1.42	48	9	1	3	2	.188	.333	.231
June	1-1	3.60	42	12	0	2	2	.286	.381	.318
July	0-0	2.60	62	15	1	3	4	.242	.323	.277
August	0-1	8.27	69	24	3	9	7	.348	.536	.432
Sept./Oct.	1-2	3.24	95	25	1	7	17	.263	.379	.314
Leading Off Inn.			75	20	1	3	4	.267	.400	.304
Bases Empty			180	51	3	9	17	.283	.417	.328
Runners On			160	40	3	16	18	.250	.356	.311
Runners/Scor. Pos.			95	22	3	10	11	.232	.358	.294
Runners On/2 Out			67	13	1	9	9	.194	.284	.289
Scor. Pos./2 Out			46	9	1	6	6	.196	.283	.288
Late-Inning Pressure			93	28	3	4	9	.301	.452	.337
Leading Off			21	5	0	0	3	.238	.333	.273
Runners On			44	12	1	2	3	.273	.386	.292
Runners/Scor. Pos.			24	6	1	1	2	.250	.417	.259
First 9 Batters			313	83	6	2C	33	.265	.387	.312
Second 9 Batters			27	8	0	5	2	.296	.407	.406
All Batters Thereafter			0	0	0	0	0	—	—	—

Loves to face: Ellis Burks (.133, 2-for-15)
Dan Gladden (.077, 1-for-13)
Gary Pettis (0-for-11)

Hates to face: Gary Gaetti (.526, 10-for-19)
Mike Greenwell (.533, 8-for-15, 1 HR)
Dave Winfield (.857, 6-for-7)

Miscellaneous statistics: Ground outs-to-air outs ratio: 2.15 last season, 1.76 for career.... Induced 11 double plays in 76 opportunities (one per 6.9).... Allowed 19 doubles, 2 triples in 88 innings.... Stranded 23 inherited runners, allowed 10 to score (70%).... Opposing base stealers: 4-for-7 (57%); 1 pickoff, 0 balks.

Comments: He's listed at 6 feet, 8 inches. Only two players active in 1991 are taller: Terry Bross (six-nine) and Randy Johnson (six-ten).... Career strikeout rate of just a shade over four per nine innings does not seem to fit his big frame. Of 63 pitchers in major league history listed in the *Encyclopedia* at six-six or taller (minimum: 100 IP), only 13 had lower rates than Guetterman, four of whom have pitched since 1980: Glenn Abbott (3.39), Mike Barlow (3.39), Bob Scanlan (3.57), and Dave Frost (3.63).... Prior to last season, only six pitchers in team history had made as many as 64 appearances in any season—Guetterman's lowest total since 1989. Dave Righetti, Sparky Lyle, Goose Gossage are the obvious ones, and your dads might guess Luis Arroyo and Pedro Ramos. But Dooley Womack? (Didn't he later star in *The Dukes of Hazzard*?) ... Had an ERA of 1.59 a few days after the All-Star break, but posted a 4.99 mark after that.... One of five A.L. pitchers to allow two grand slams last season. Only one pitcher in Yankees history ever allowed three in a single season (Dennis Rasmussen in 1984).... Hit three batters with pitches last season, equaling his combined total for the previous four seasons.... Committed three errors, contributing to a league-high total of 19 errors by Yankees pitchers.... Opponents have an overall career batting average of .278, but it's only .214 with two outs and runners in scoring position.... Career record of 6–0 vs. the Brewers.

Bill Gullickson
Throws Right

Detroit Tigers	W-L	ERA	AB	H	HR	BB	SO	BA	SA	OBA
Season	20-9	3.90	890	256	22	44	91	.288	.435	.321
vs. Left-Handers			487	134	15	25	35	.275	.444	.312
vs. Right-Handers			403	122	7	19	56	.303	.424	.333
vs. Ground-Ballers			451	132	8	16	32	.293	.428	.316
vs. Fly-Ballers			439	124	14	28	59	.282	.442	.326
Home Games	10-4	4.95	418	123	17	23	47	.294	.483	.331
Road Games	10-5	3.01	472	133	5	21	44	.282	.392	.313
Grass Fields	15-7	4.09	675	191	18	40	70	.283	.434	.323
Artificial Turf	5-2	3.27	215	65	4	4	21	.302	.437	.317
April	2-0	4.37	88	27	2	7	8	.307	.466	.351
May	3-2	5.00	149	50	4	5	11	.336	.510	.350
June	4-2	2.91	179	48	4	9	16	.268	.380	.302
July	4-2	5.40	145	48	5	8	15	.331	.517	.368
August	3-1	2.75	139	35	5	7	17	.252	.432	.297
Sept./Oct.	4-2	3.58	190	48	2	8	24	.253	.353	.285
Leading Off Inn.			233	61	3	4	25	.262	.352	.274
Bases Empty			544	152	13	18	60	.279	.425	.307
Runners On			346	104	9	26	31	.301	.451	.342
Runners/Scor. Pos.			184	57	5	24	20	.310	.429	.375
Runners On/2 Out			149	49	6	20	16	.329	.490	.408
Scor. Pos./2 Out			96	31	3	19	11	.323	.438	.435
Late-Inning Pressure			61	20	1	6	5	.328	.443	.397
Leading Off			16	5	0	1	2	.313	.438	.353
Runners On			32	12	1	3	2	.375	.469	.429
Runners/Scor. Pos.			16	8	1	2	1	.500	.688	.556
First 9 Batters			295	81	10	12	31	.275	.437	.307
Second 9 Batters			284	70	4	12	30	.246	.370	.276
All Batters Thereafter			311	105	8	20	30	.338	.492	.375

Loves to face: Albert Belle (.100, 1-for-10)
Greg Briley (0-for-7)
B. J. Surhoff (.077, 1-for-13)

Hates to face: Jack Clark (.318, 14-for-44, 4 HR)
Brian McRae (.400, 4-for-10, 1 HR)
Kirby Puckett (.462, 6-for-13)

Miscellaneous statistics: Ground outs-to-air outs ratio: 1.02 last season, 0.92 for career.... Induced 22 double plays in 144 opportunities (one per 6.5).... Allowed 51 doubles (most in majors), 7 triples in 226⅓ innings.... Allowed 19 first-inning runs in 35 starts (4.76 ERA).... Batting support: 5.66 runs per start, highest average in majors.... Opposing base stealers: 15-for-23 (65%); 1 pickoff, 0 balks.

Comments: Since 1961, there have been 121 American League 20-game winners. Only two had higher ERAs than Gullickson: Denny McLain (20–14, 3.92 ERA in 1966) and Paul Splittorff (20–11, 3.98 ERA in 1973).... The last 20-game winner to strike out as few batters as Gullickson was Tommy John in 1980 (78).... Over the past 10 seasons, 13 other pitchers made 25+ starts and had ERAs and strikeout rates between 3.50 and 4.00. None won more than 15 games; their combined record was 155–136 (.533). But of the 92 pitchers whose run support was between 5.50 and 6.00 runs per start, 13 had at least 15 wins (including four 20-game winners). Their combined record: 428–235 (.646).... On August 18 vs. Toronto, he allowed back-to-back homers to Devon White and Roberto Alomar to lead off the first inning, then hit Joe Carter in the head and was ejected. No pitcher had allowed homers to the first two batters since Rick Reuschel launched Nike's "Bo Knows" campaign in the 1989 All-Star Game.... His longest losing streak of the season came in May when he lost back-to-back starts.... Has made 302 consecutive starts since last appearing in relief for the Expos in 1980. Only three pitchers have made more consecutive starts since their last relief appearance: Nolan Ryan (555), Jack Morris (431), and Frank Viola (317).... Strikeout rate fell by roughly one per nine innings from rookie season of 1980 (7.66) through 1985 (3.38), then rebounded slightly (4.68 for 1986–87). But his 3.52 mark in two seasons since his return from Japan is the 3d lowest in the majors during that time (minimum: 50 GS).

Jose Guzman
Throws Right

Texas Rangers	W-L	ERA	AB	H	HR	BB	SO	BA	SA	OBA
Season	13-7	3.08	636	152	10	84	125	.239	.341	.330
vs. Left-Handers			283	69	6	47	52	.244	.367	.353
vs. Right-Handers			353	83	4	37	73	.235	.320	.311
vs. Ground-Ballers			300	65	4	38	53	.217	.303	.308
vs. Fly-Ballers			336	87	6	46	72	.259	.375	.350
Home Games	5-3	3.86	228	57	5	27	42	.250	.355	.327
Road Games	8-4	2.64	408	95	5	57	83	.233	.333	.332
Grass Fields	13-4	2.63	521	116	7	61	102	.223	.315	.307
Artificial Turf	0-3	5.22	115	36	3	23	23	.313	.461	.429
April	0-0	—	0	0	0	0	0	—	—	—
May	0-1	3.97	42	13	1	10	3	.310	.405	.434
June	3-2	2.91	158	37	6	18	35	.234	.405	.311
July	3-1	2.08	131	29	1	21	28	.221	.290	.333
August	3-1	4.13	136	39	1	14	26	.287	.390	.358
Sept./Oct.	4-2	3.02	169	34	1	21	33	.201	.266	.295
Leading Off Inn.			159	43	4	16	29	.270	.384	.341
Bases Empty			356	92	7	44	69	.258	.371	.342
Runners On			280	60	3	40	56	.214	.304	.316
Runners/Scor. Pos.			154	25	0	26	35	.162	.208	.283
Runners On/2 Out			120	25	2	21	24	.208	.308	.331
Scor. Pos./2 Out			79	12	0	14	18	.152	.203	.280
Late-Inning Pressure			65	13	2	7	17	.200	.338	.278
Leading Off			19	4	1	2	3	.211	.421	.286
Runners On			21	4	0	3	6	.190	.238	.292
Runners/Scor. Pos.			7	1	0	0	2	.143	.286	.143
First 9 Batters			196	47	3	26	45	.240	.337	.326
Second 9 Batters			196	53	3	25	31	.270	.378	.359
All Batters Thereafter			244	52	4	33	49	.213	.316	.311

Loves to face: Gary Gaetti (.111, 3-for-27)
Darryl Hamilton (.077, 1-for-13)
Steve Sax (.125, 2-for-16)

Hates to face: Kent Hrbek (.400, 10-for-25, 3 HR)
Danny Tartabull (.371, 13-for-35, 3 HR)
Robin Yount (.448, 13-for-29, 2 HR)

Miscellaneous statistics: Ground outs-to-air outs ratio: 1.26 last season, 1.29 for career.... Induced 11 double plays in 137 opportunities (one per 12).... Allowed 33 doubles, 1 triple in 169⅔ innings.... Allowed 9 first-inning runs in 25 starts (3.24 ERA).... Batting support: 4.92 runs per start, 10th-highest average in A.L.... Opposing base stealers: 12-for-25 (48%); 2 pickoffs, 1 balk.

Comments: No other pitcher in the last 50 years spent two full seasons out of the majors due to injury, but won at least 10 games immediately before and after the hiatus. During that time, five won in double figures on both sides of two-year gaps unrelated to injuries: Bill Gullickson (in Japan 1988–89), and four who missed time in military service—Vinegar Bend Mizell (1954–55), and Kirby Higbe, Johnny Vander Meer, and Schoolboy Rowe (all serving during 1944–45).... Didn't miss a turn in the rotation after returning to the Rangers in late May.... Allowed 4.46 walks per nine innings for the season, the highest rate of his career (a full walk per nine innings above his previous career rate—3.45).... Allowed four home runs to right-handed batters, but none over his last 17 starts.... Opponents' batting average with runners in scoring position was the lowest in the majors.... Threw back-to-back complete games twice last season, including his final two appearances of the year.... What changed since he last pitched in 1988? Well, that was the "Year of the Balk," and Guzman was called for 12 of them. He balked only once last season.... In Texas Rangers history, only Charlie Hough, Ferguson Jenkins, and Bobby Witt have started more games on the mound than Guzman.... The "Guzman" entry went off at 1000-to-1 but almost took the bronze medal in the Surname Sweepstakes. Six pitchers named Smith took the gold with a total of 40 wins, followed by the two Martinezes (31), the two McDowells (26), and the three Guzmans (24).

Juan Guzman — Throws Right

Toronto Blue Jays	W-L	ERA	AB	H	HR	BB	SO	BA	SA	OBA
Season	10-3	2.99	497	98	6	66	123	.197	.268	.294
vs. Left-Handers			238	46	1	36	49	.193	.239	.299
vs. Right-Handers			259	52	5	30	74	.201	.293	.289
vs. Ground-Ballers			238	52	2	34	45	.218	.290	.319
vs. Fly-Ballers			259	46	4	32	78	.178	.247	.270
Home Games	5-1	3.82	230	47	5	34	62	.204	.309	.310
Road Games	5-2	2.28	267	51	1	32	61	.191	.232	.279
Grass Fields	3-1	2.38	159	30	1	20	41	.189	.226	.282
Artificial Turf	7-2	3.28	338	68	5	46	82	.201	.287	.299
April	0-0	—	0	0	0	0	0	—	—	—
May	0-0	—	0	0	0	0	0	—	—	—
June	2-2	3.09	84	16	1	10	18	.190	.250	.274
July	1-0	2.76	104	20	1	15	24	.192	.250	.298
August	2-0	3.89	127	27	2	20	35	.213	.315	.322
Sept./Oct.	5-1	2.45	182	35	2	21	46	.192	.253	.279
Leading Off Inn.			119	25	2	22	26	.210	.277	.343
Bases Empty			275	53	3	43	67	.193	.251	.308
Runners On			222	45	3	23	56	.203	.288	.275
Runners/Scor. Pos.			116	23	2	15	30	.198	.284	.279
Runners On/2 Out			94	20	1	11	24	.213	.330	.295
Scor. Pos./2 Out			59	11	1	10	15	.186	.305	.304
Late-Inning Pressure			34	7	1	6	10	.206	.324	.325
Leading Off			7	2	1	3	1	.286	.714	.500
Runners On			17	2	0	1	5	.118	.118	.167
Runners/Scor. Pos.			10	2	0	0	3	.200	.200	.200
First 9 Batters			179	34	3	24	50	.190	.285	.286
Second 9 Batters			171	33	2	21	36	.193	.257	.286
All Batters Thereafter			147	31	1	21	37	.211	.259	.312

Loves to face: Joe Orsulak (0-for-9)
Tony Phillips (0-for-6, 4 SO)
Cal Ripken (0-for-8)

Hates to face: Jack Clark (1-for-1, 1 3B, 2 BB)
Bob Melvin (.571, 4-for-7, 1 HR)

Miscellaneous statistics: Ground outs-to-air outs ratio: 0.93 last season, 0.93 for career.... Induced 7 double plays in 110 opportunities (one per 16), 2d-worst rate in A.L.... Allowed 13 doubles, 2 triples in 138⅔ innings.... Allowed 14 first-inning runs in 23 starts (5.48 ERA).... Batting support: 4.78 runs per start.... Opposing base stealers: 11-for-17 (65%); 0 pickoffs, 0 balks.

Comments: Had a 10-game winning streak snapped in his final regular-season appearance, which amounted to a three-inning tune-up for the playoffs. No A.L. rookie had a longer winning streak since 1963, when Rookie of the Year Gary Peters won 11 straight decisions for the White Sox.... No rookie starter posted a higher winning percentage in as many decisions since Wayne Simpson went 14-3 for Cincinnati in 1970 (.824). The last rookie starter to do it in the A.L. was Mike Nagy of the Red Sox, with a 12–2 mark in 1969 (.857).... Led major league rookies in strikeouts (123), and had the lowest ERA of any rookie starter (minimum: 100 IP).... Even though he didn't debut until June 7, only four rookie pitchers started more games: Charles Nagy (33), Rich DeLucia (31), Brian Barnes (27), and Omar Olivares (24).... Had the best home-run rate in road games in the American League (minimum: 50 IP).... The only home run by an opposing left-handed batter was hit by Paul Sorrento in late September.... Committed three errors in only 17 chances. Among pitchers with at least 100 innings pitched, only Randy Johnson had a higher error rate (five errors in 28 chances).... Ten of his 23 starts resulted in no decision. Someone noted that if the Blue Jays had not blown his leads, Guzman would have finished the year at 19–2. But Guzman pitched the five innings required for a victory only 17 times. End of research.... Has made 113 starts in pro ball and never pitched a shutout (majors or minors).

Erik Hanson — Throws Right

Seattle Mariners	W-L	ERA	AB	H	HR	BB	SO	BA	SA	OBA
Season	8-8	3.81	676	182	16	56	143	.269	.414	.323
vs. Left-Handers			355	85	10	18	84	.239	.411	.275
vs. Right-Handers			321	97	6	38	59	.302	.417	.374
vs. Ground-Ballers			337	79	3	23	64	.234	.326	.285
vs. Fly-Ballers			339	103	13	33	79	.304	.501	.361
Home Games	4-5	4.25	350	100	12	19	80	.286	.463	.318
Road Games	4-3	3.36	326	82	4	37	63	.252	.362	.329
Grass Fields	3-2	2.97	253	61	4	29	53	.241	.364	.319
Artificial Turf	5-6	4.33	423	121	12	27	90	.286	.444	.326
April	2-1	3.28	134	33	3	16	30	.246	.381	.329
May	1-1	5.52	61	22	2	4	15	.361	.557	.394
June	1-1	2.63	49	11	0	4	9	.224	.286	.283
July	2-2	4.06	150	44	4	5	29	.293	.447	.310
August	1-2	4.28	157	43	5	14	30	.274	.420	.335
Sept./Oct.	1-1	3.27	125	29	2	13	30	.232	.384	.300
Leading Off Inn.			174	42	5	8	34	.241	.402	.275
Bases Empty			399	108	10	31	82	.271	.421	.323
Runners On			277	74	6	25	61	.267	.404	.324
Runners/Scor. Pos.			150	35	3	20	34	.233	.373	.309
Runners On/2 Out			111	27	1	16	25	.243	.333	.339
Scor. Pos./2 Out			72	13	1	14	19	.181	.278	.314
Late-Inning Pressure			51	11	0	8	7	.216	.255	.311
Leading Off			13	2	0	3	3	.154	.231	.313
Runners On			29	5	0	2	4	.172	.172	.212
Runners/Scor. Pos.			17	2	0	1	1	.118	.118	.200
First 9 Batters			229	66	11	13	49	.288	.498	.325
Second 9 Batters			213	59	3	21	46	.277	.408	.340
All Batters Thereafter			234	57	2	22	48	.244	.338	.307

Loves to face: Jose Canseco (0-for-16)
Rob Deer (0-for-16, 9 SO)
Matt Nokes (.063, 1-for-16)

Hates to face: Wade Boggs (.391, 9-for-23, 5 2B, 0 SO)
Ellis Burks (.579, 11-for-19, 2 HR)
Paul Molitor (.458, 11-for-24, 1 HR)

Miscellaneous statistics: Ground outs-to-air outs ratio: 1.11 last season, 1.20 for career.... Induced 16 double plays in 132 opportunities (one per 8.3).... Allowed 36 doubles, 7 triples in 174⅔ innings.... Allowed 11 first-inning runs in 27 starts (3.33 ERA).... Batting support: 4.67 runs per start.... Opposing base stealers: 11-for-21 (52%); 0 pickoffs, 1 balk.

Comments: One of 14 A.L. pitchers to make two trips to the disabled list last season. Other "must avoids" on fantasy draft day: Brad Arnsberg, Scott Bankhead, Steve Crawford, Mark Davis, Danny Darwin, Ken Dayley, Rich Gossage, Ted Higuera, Ben McDonald, Pascual Perez, Rudy Seanez, Mike Witt, and Nolan Ryan.... Okay, we'll make an exception—you can draft Ryan (and, if the winter-league squirrels are right, Seanez).... Allowed one home run every 22 at-bats during his first pass through the batting order, one every 100 ABs thereafter. He pitched a total of 47.2 innings without allowing a home run in the sixth inning or later.... Reduced his total of leadoff walks from 19 in 1990 to eight last season, three of which came in the same game (August 4).... Threw 14 wild pitches last season, one fewer than league leader Jack Morris.... Has a career record of 16-7 on grass, 21–18 on artificial surfaces.... Has allowed 42 home runs: 26 at the Kingdome, 16 on the road.... Opponents are hitless in 14 career at-bats with—fanfare, please—two outs and runners in scoring position in Late-Inning Pressure Situations.... Has faced 35 batters with the bases loaded, the 2d most among active pitchers who've never walked in a run or allowed a grand slam. The most: 95, by Steve Crawford of all people.... Career record of 4–0 vs. the Athletics.

Greg A. Harris
Throws Right

Boston Red Sox	W-L	ERA	AB	H	HR	BB	SO	BA	SA	OBA
Season	11-12	3.85	645	157	13	69	127	.243	.363	.318
vs. Left-Handers			303	74	5	34	58	.244	.353	.322
vs. Right-Handers			342	83	8	35	69	.243	.371	.314
vs. Ground-Ballers			330	81	7	28	62	.245	.361	.303
vs. Fly-Ballers			315	76	6	41	65	.241	.365	.332
Home Games	4-6	3.80	262	66	5	31	55	.252	.355	.327
Road Games	7-6	3.88	383	91	8	38	72	.238	.368	.312
Grass Fields	10-9	3.95	500	127	11	55	100	.254	.368	.326
Artificial Turf	1-3	3.51	145	30	2	14	27	.207	.345	.291
April	1-2	3.63	83	23	2	11	13	.277	.482	.367
May	0-3	5.20	106	29	1	10	20	.274	.358	.331
June	3-2	4.24	127	28	2	14	29	.220	.323	.301
July	3-4	4.30	140	33	3	8	25	.236	.364	.275
August	3-0	1.09	85	15	1	12	21	.176	.247	.290
Sept./Oct.	1-1	4.05	104	29	4	14	19	.279	.413	.361
Leading Off Inn.			155	34	4	18	29	.219	.361	.316
Bases Empty			374	85	6	40	71	.227	.326	.309
Runners On			271	72	7	29	56	.266	.413	.330
Runners/Scor. Pos.			139	41	3	20	28	.295	.446	.369
Runners On/2 Out			116	26	3	15	23	.224	.371	.313
Scor. Pos./2 Out			66	16	2	11	11	.242	.439	.351
Late-Inning Pressure			92	19	1	15	21	.207	.283	.318
Leading Off			23	4	1	5	1	.174	.391	.321
Runners On			35	8	0	9	11	.229	.286	.386
Runners/Scor. Pos.			17	5	0	8	3	.294	.412	.520
First 9 Batters			339	77	9	31	76	.227	.345	.296
Second 9 Batters			185	43	1	20	32	.232	.314	.303
All Batters Thereafter			121	37	3	18	19	.306	.488	.397

Loves to face: Jose Canseco (0-for-14, 9 SO)
                Gene Larkin (.083, 1-for-12)
                Mookie Wilson (.059, 1-for-17)

Hates to face: Albert Belle (.375, 3-for-8, 3 HR)
                Pat Tabler (.500, 9-for-18, 1 HR)
                Alan Trammell (.458, 11-for-24, 1 HR)

Miscellaneous statistics: Ground outs-to-air outs ratio: 1.39 last season, 1.34 for career.... Induced 17 double plays in 135 opportunities (one per 7.9).... Allowed 30 doubles, 4 triples in 173 innings.... Allowed 9 first-inning runs in 21 starts (3.86 ERA).... Batting support: 3.76 runs per start, 8th-lowest average in A.L.... Record of 7–10, 4.55 ERA as a starter; 4–2, 2.24 ERA in 32 relief appearances.... Stranded 17 inherited runners, allowed 9 to score (65%).... Opposing base stealers: 1-for-7 (14%); 3 pickoffs, 1 balk.

Comments: Joe Hesketh, Roger Clemens, and Harris all ranked among the league's top-10 ERAs after the All-Star break (3.00, 3.01, and 3.07, respectively).... He was the toughest pitcher in baseball to steal against, allowing only one stolen base (Kelly Gruber) in 173 innings. In 1990, runners stole 15 bases in 22 attempts against him... Only one active pitcher has more career starts than Harris (96) without ever throwing a shutout: Todd Stottlemyre (101).... Career record of 29–36 (4.52 ERA) as a starter, 30–30 (2.89 ERA) in relief.... Only two other A.L. pitchers over the last 10 years have had seasons in which they accumulated more than 20 starts and more than 20 relief appearances: John Cerutti (1987) and Lary Sorensen (1984). Harris became the fifth pitcher in Red Sox history to do it. The others: Jack Wilson (1937), Ellis Kinder (1950), Jim Lonborg (1966), and Sonny Siebert (1969).... Harris was the only pitcher to beat the Athletics three times last season.... Harris posted an 0–3 record against both the Twins and the Rangers last season. Maybe it has something to do with those old Washington Senators franchises.... One of five active players to appear in at least one game for seven different clubs. The others: Juan Berenguer, John Candelaria (8), Goose Gossage, and Dan Schatzeder (9). Who is the only player that's been a teammate of Harris's for three different teams? Answer on page 257.

Bryan Harvey
Throws Right

California Angels	W-L	ERA	AB	H	HR	BB	SO	BA	SA	OBA
Season	2-4	1.60	286	51	6	17	101	.178	.266	.225
vs. Left-Handers			164	30	4	11	62	.183	.293	.233
vs. Right-Handers			122	21	2	6	39	.172	.230	.215
vs. Ground-Ballers			132	25	1	7	41	.189	.250	.230
vs. Fly-Ballers			154	26	5	10	60	.169	.279	.222
Home Games	2-2	2.06	145	28	3	11	47	.193	.276	.253
Road Games	0-2	1.14	141	23	3	6	54	.163	.255	.196
Grass Fields	2-3	1.99	226	38	6	16	78	.168	.265	.224
Artificial Turf	0-1	0.00	60	13	0	1	23	.217	.267	.230
April	1-0	0.87	35	6	1	1	8	.171	.257	.216
May	0-1	1.64	43	10	0	3	14	.233	.256	.277
June	0-0	0.66	49	8	1	1	21	.163	.265	.180
July	1-2	4.09	40	6	2	2	15	.150	.325	.190
August	0-0	0.64	48	7	1	1	20	.146	.229	.163
Sept./Oct.	0-1	1.93	71	14	1	9	23	.197	.268	.284
Leading Off Inn.			58	11	2	4	16	.190	.362	.242
Bases Empty			150	30	4	6	48	.200	.307	.231
Runners On			136	21	2	11	53	.154	.221	.220
Runners/Scor. Pos.			90	13	2	9	36	.144	.222	.225
Runners On/2 Out			63	8	2	6	25	.127	.238	.214
Scor. Pos./2 Out			41	5	2	6	15	.122	.268	.250
Late-Inning Pressure			228	43	4	15	80	.189	.263	.240
Leading Off			46	7	1	4	13	.152	.283	.220
Runners On			109	19	1	9	42	.174	.220	.240
Runners/Scor. Pos.			69	11	1	7	26	.159	.203	.241
First 9 Batters			283	50	6	17	100	.177	.265	.224
Second 9 Batters			3	1	0	0	1	.333	.333	.333
All Batters Thereafter			0	0	0	0	0	—	—	—

Loves to face: Jim Gantner (0-for-6)
                Mike Greenwell (0-for-10)
                Kent Hrbek (0-for-9)

Hates to face: Jesse Barfield (.333, 3-for-9, 2 HR, 4 SO)
                Randy Milligan (.500, 2-for-4, 1 HR)
                Paul Molitor (4-for-4, 1 BB)

Miscellaneous statistics: Ground outs-to-air outs ratio: 1.73 last season, 0.87 for career.... Induced 3 double plays in 51 opportunities (one per 17).... Allowed 7 doubles, 0 triples in 78⅔ innings.... Saved 46 games in 52 opportunities (88%), 2d-highest rate in A.L.... Stranded 27 inherited runners, allowed 10 to score (73%).... Opposing base stealers: 12-for-12 (100%); 0 pickoffs, 2 balks.

Comments: Has compiled three of the six highest save totals in franchise history over the past three years (25, 25, and 46, respectively).... He walked 6.71 batters per nine innings in 1989, lowered that to 4.90 in 1990, and then posted a mark of 1.94 last season. His decline of 2.95 walks per nine last season was the largest by a relief pitcher since 1975, when Gene Garber dropped his rate from 5.21 to 2.21 (minimum: 60 IP in relief in both seasons).... Only two other pitchers have raised their strikeout totals while lowering their walk totals in each of the past two seasons: the Gregs, Maddux and Swindell.... After allowing three inherited runners to score on a Randy Milligan grand slam in July, Harvey stranded 15 of 16 inherited runners the rest of the year.... Allowed the most stolen bases of any A.L. pitcher who did not catch a thief last season.... Opposing batters have only 10 hits in 104 career at-bats—look out, here it comes again—with two outs and runners in scoring position in Late-Inning Pressure Situations.... Has held fly-ball hitters below the .190 mark in four consecutive seasons. Their career batting average vs. Harvey is .177, the lowest vs. any pitcher over the past 17 years, and 41 points lower than that of ground-ball hitters (.218).... Only three players in major league history have a career average of more than 10 strikeouts per nine innings (minimum: 200 IP): Rob Dibble (12.22), Harvey (10.68), and Tom Henke (10.30). What a segue!...

Tom Henke

Throws Right

Toronto Blue Jays	W-L	ERA	AB	H	HR	BB	SO	BA	SA	OBA
Season	0-2	2.32	179	33	4	11	53	.184	.307	.232
vs. Left-Handers			95	17	3	8	24	.179	.347	.243
vs. Right-Handers			84	16	1	3	29	.190	.262	.218
vs. Ground-Ballers			81	15	0	4	19	.185	.235	.224
vs. Fly-Ballers			98	18	4	7	34	.184	.367	.238
Home Games	0-1	2.31	82	17	2	5	25	.207	.317	.253
Road Games	0-1	2.33	97	16	2	6	28	.165	.299	.214
Grass Fields	0-1	2.55	62	9	2	5	19	.145	.290	.209
Artificial Turf	0-1	2.20	117	24	2	6	34	.205	.316	.244
April	0-0	0.00	7	2	0	0	1	.286	.286	.286
May	0-0	0.00	13	0	0	1	4	.000	.000	.071
June	0-0	2.19	42	7	1	3	11	.167	.262	.222
July	0-0	1.80	38	8	0	1	8	.211	.289	.231
August	0-2	4.50	50	9	3	2	21	.180	.420	.212
Sept./Oct.	0-0	1.17	29	7	0	4	8	.241	.345	.333
Leading Off Inn.			47	9	0	1	12	.191	.255	.208
Bases Empty			117	21	1	5	36	.179	.265	.213
Runners On			62	12	3	6	17	.194	.387	.265
Runners/Scor. Pos.			36	8	2	4	11	.222	.444	.300
Runners On/2 Out			29	6	1	2	5	.207	.345	.258
Scor. Pos./2 Out			19	3	1	2	3	.158	.316	.238
Late-Inning Pressure			130	22	2	5	42	.169	.269	.200
Leading Off			36	8	0	0	11	.222	.306	.222
Runners On			40	7	2	4	12	.175	.350	.250
Runners/Scor. Pos.			24	6	2	3	8	.250	.542	.333
First 9 Batters			177	32	3	11	52	.181	.288	.229
Second 9 Batters			2	1	1	0	1	.500	2.000	.500
All Batters Thereafter			0	0	0	0	0	—	—	—

Loves to face: Dave Bergman (0-for-16)
Mel Hall (0-for-14)
Lou Whitaker (.042, 1-for-24)

Hates to face: Wade Boggs (.400, 4-for-10, 6 BB)
Don Mattingly (.389, 7-for-18, 2 HR)
Luis Polonia (.500, 4-for-8, 2 2B, 1 3B)

Miscellaneous statistics: Ground outs-to-air outs ratio: 0.83 last season, 0.74 for career.... Induced 4 double plays in 26 opportunities (one per 6.5).... Allowed 8 doubles, 1 triple in 50⅓ innings.... Saved 32 games in 36 opportunities (89%), highest rate in majors.... Stranded 12 inherited runners, allowed 3 to score (80%).... Opposing base stealers: 2-for-2 (100%); 1 pickoff, 0 balks.

Comments: Like Harvey, Henke's a once-wild pitcher who has improved his control remarkably. Walks per nine innings over the course of his career: 1982–84 with Texas—4.80; 1985–88, his first four seasons with Toronto—2.73; year by year since then—2.53, 2.29, 1.97.... Walked only one of the last 72 right-handed batters he faced last season, and didn't walk any of the last 38 leadoff batters he faced.... Among the nine A.L. pitchers with 30 or more saves, Henke was the least likely to enter a game with runners on; he inherited runners in only seven of his 49 appearances (despite the fact that he disposed of most of them).... Henke and Duane Ward became only the third pair of teammates with 20 or more saves in the same season. The others: Greg Minton and Gary Lavelle (1983 Giants) and Roger McDowell and Jesse Orosco (1986 Mets). If you believe in saves before 1969, click your heels and add Eddie Fisher and Hoyt Wilhelm of the '65 White Sox to the list.... Toronto is the only team with two relievers in double figures in saves for three straight years (Henke and Ward in all three). The Cubs are the only other team to do it in both 1990 and 1991.... Henke is one of 16 pitchers in major league history to appear in at least 400 games, all as a reliever. Among active pitchers who've never started, only Jeff Reardon (751) and John Franco (500) have appeared in more games than Henke (430).... Career ERA of 2.68 ranks fourth among active pitchers, behind Franco (2.53), Tim Burke (2.62), and Dave Smith (2.67; minimum: 500 IP).

Mike Henneman

Throws Right

Detroit Tigers	W-L	ERA	AB	H	HR	BB	SO	BA	SA	OBA
Season	10-2	2.88	314	81	2	34	61	.258	.344	.326
vs. Left-Handers			127	34	0	23	17	.268	.339	.373
vs. Right-Handers			187	47	2	11	44	.251	.348	.290
vs. Ground-Ballers			144	33	0	15	28	.229	.299	.298
vs. Fly-Ballers			170	48	2	19	33	.282	.382	.349
Home Games	7-0	1.95	188	43	2	17	41	.229	.309	.291
Road Games	3-2	4.28	126	38	0	17	20	.302	.397	.374
Grass Fields	10-1	2.71	273	71	2	28	53	.260	.341	.325
Artificial Turf	0-1	3.97	41	10	0	6	8	.244	.366	.333
April	2-0	0.69	45	10	0	5	8	.222	.267	.294
May	3-1	2.18	75	21	0	9	11	.280	.320	.353
June	0-1	6.00	56	15	1	9	9	.268	.446	.369
July	3-0	1.72	61	13	0	5	13	.213	.262	.269
August	1-0	3.09	45	14	1	5	11	.311	.378	.324
Sept./Oct.	1-0	4.32	32	8	0	1	9	.250	.438	.265
Leading Off Inn.			66	20	0	3	7	.303	.379	.333
Bases Empty			146	41	0	13	28	.281	.336	.340
Runners On			168	40	2	21	33	.238	.351	.314
Runners/Scor. Pos.			102	25	1	13	23	.245	.373	.317
Runners On/2 Out			80	16	0	12	17	.200	.300	.304
Scor. Pos./2 Out			55	12	0	10	12	.218	.345	.338
Late-Inning Pressure			206	53	1	20	42	.257	.316	.319
Leading Off			40	11	0	2	6	.275	.325	.310
Runners On			115	27	1	12	22	.235	.296	.300
Runners/Scor. Pos.			73	18	1	9	15	.247	.342	.318
First 9 Batters			296	77	2	33	61	.260	.351	.329
Second 9 Batters			18	4	0	1	0	.222	.222	.263
All Batters Thereafter			0	0	0	0	0	—	—	—

Loves to face: Joe Carter (.067, 1-for-15)
Bo Jackson (0-for-9)
Carney Lansford (0-for-10)

Hates to face: Don Mattingly (.438, 7-for-16)
Kirby Puckett (.500, 4-for-8)
Harold Reynolds (.545, 6-for-11)

Miscellaneous statistics: Ground outs-to-air outs ratio: 1.40 last season, 1.34 for career.... Induced 10 double plays in 81 opportunities (one per 8.1).... Allowed 17 doubles, 2 triples in 84⅓ innings.... Saved 21 games in 25 opportunities (84%), 4th-highest rate in A.L.... Stranded 33 inherited runners, allowed 8 to score (80%), 3d-highest rate in A.L.... Opposing base stealers: 3-for-5 (60%); 0 pickoffs, 0 balks.

Comments: Henneman is the first player in history with at least eight relief wins in five straight years. Other relievers with four-year streaks: Pedro Borbon (1972–75), Mark Clear (1979–82), Rollie Fingers (1974–77), Willie Hernandez (1983–86), Jim Kern (1976–79), Mike Marshall (1972–75), Jesse Orosco (1983–86), Dick Radatz (1962–65), Bob Stanley (1981–84), and Kent Tekulve (1977–80).... Henneman's total of 49 relief wins is already the third highest in Tigers' history, behind only those of John Hiller (72) and Aurelio Lopez (51).... Career record of 49–21 makes him one of two pitchers in history with at least 60 decisions in relief and a winning percentage of .700 or better. The other is Hugh Casey, the pitcher on the mound when Mickey Owen attained baseball infamy in the 1941 World Series. Casey had a career record of 51–20 as a reliever (.718).... Had a 4–0 record against Texas last season to raise his career record to 8–0 against them.... Career record of 7–0 vs. Seattle.... Hasn't allowed a home run to a left-handed batter since Dan Pasqua smoked him in 1989.... Opponents have a career average of .206 with runners in scoring position, compared to .259 in other at-bats. Opponents' career average with RISP drops to .185 with two outs.... Only two runners were thrown out attempting to steal against him all season, and they were caught in consecutive innings (Brian Harper and Dan Gladden on May 11).... Induced only one double-play grounder in his last 39 opportunities.

Doug Henry
Throws Right

Milwaukee Brewers	W-L	ERA	AB	H	HR	BB	SO	BA	SA	OBA
Season	2-1	1.00	120	16	1	14	28	.133	.208	.221
vs. Left-Handers			60	8	0	8	14	.133	.233	.229
vs. Right-Handers			60	8	1	6	14	.133	.183	.212
vs. Ground-Ballers			47	5	0	5	9	.106	.149	.185
vs. Fly-Ballers			73	11	1	9	19	.151	.247	.244
Home Games	1-0	0.53	55	6	0	7	20	.109	.145	.210
Road Games	1-1	1.42	65	10	1	7	8	.154	.262	.230
Grass Fields	2-0	0.86	106	14	1	11	25	.132	.208	.212
Artificial Turf	0-1	1.93	14	2	0	3	3	.143	.214	.278
April	0-0	—	0	0	0	0	0	—	—	—
May	0-0	—	0	0	0	0	0	—	—	—
June	0-0	—	0	0	0	0	0	—	—	—
July	1-0	3.00	19	4	1	2	3	.211	.474	.286
August	1-1	1.04	60	8	0	9	15	.133	.183	.239
Sept./Oct.	0-0	0.00	41	4	0	3	10	.098	.122	.159
Leading Off Inn.			27	2	1	2	8	.074	.222	.138
Bases Empty			70	11	1	7	19	.157	.257	.234
Runners On			50	5	0	7	9	.100	.140	.203
Runners/Scor. Pos.			29	4	0	5	6	.138	.172	.250
Runners On/2 Out			26	2	0	3	5	.077	.115	.172
Scor. Pos./2 Out			17	2	0	2	4	.118	.176	.211
Late-Inning Pressure			80	11	0	10	21	.138	.175	.228
Leading Off			18	1	0	1	5	.056	.111	.105
Runners On			33	4	0	5	6	.121	.152	.225
Runners/Scor. Pos.			17	3	0	4	4	.176	.176	.304
First 9 Batters			120	16	1	14	28	.133	.208	.221
Second 9 Batters			0	0	0	0	0	—	—	—
All Batters Thereafter			0	0	0	0	0	—	—	—

Loves to face: John Olerud (0-for-2, 2 SO)

Hates to face:

Miscellaneous statistics: Ground outs-to-air outs ratio: 0.60 last season, 0.60 for career.... Induced 1 double play in 23 opportunities (one per 23).... Allowed 6 doubles, 0 triples in 36 innings.... Saved 15 games in 18 opportunities (83%), 5th-highest rate in A.L.... Stranded 14 inherited runners, allowed 3 to score (82%).... Opposing base stealers: 0-for-1 (0%); 0 pickoffs, 0 balks.

Comments: If you gave up 16 hits in 36 innings, you wouldn't hate to face anyone either.... Although he didn't debut until after the All-Star break, he still had the most saves (15) by any major league rookie last season. Houston's Al Osuna was runner-up with 12; Oakland's Steve Chitren finished second among A.L. rookies with four.... Converted all 12 save opportunities from August 18 to the end of the season.... From September 20 until the season's end, Henry appeared in eight games, retiring 25 of the 27 batters he faced, allowing one single and one walk.... Of his last 25 appearances, 21 came in Late-Inning Pressure Situations.... Allowed only one of the last 23 leadoff batters he faced to reach base safely. That was a particular relief to the Brewers, whose pitchers allowed the highest on-base average leading off innings (.330) in the league last season.... Craig Grebeck's home run on July 19 was the only extra-base hit he allowed to a right-handed batter.... Made his professional debut in 1986, and his major league debut, at the age of 27, last year. He's two weeks younger than Walt Weiss, one month older than Ozzie Guillen.... Brewers' 8th-round pick in the 1985 amateur draft, the same draft in which the White Sox selected Bobby Thigpen in the fourth round.... No longer considered a rookie in 1992. Although he's still under the limit of 50 innings pitched, he lost his rookie status by accumulating more than 45 days on the Brewers' active roster prior to September 1. He was called up on July 14, accumulating 49 days of service by August 31.

Joe Hesketh
Throws Left

Boston Red Sox	W-L	ERA	AB	H	HR	BB	SO	BA	SA	OBA
Season	12-4	3.29	568	142	19	53	104	.250	.424	.313
vs. Left-Handers			87	21	2	12	18	.241	.391	.327
vs. Right-Handers			481	121	17	41	86	.252	.430	.310
vs. Ground-Ballers			257	53	5	24	43	.206	.327	.273
vs. Fly-Ballers			311	89	14	29	61	.286	.505	.345
Home Games	7-1	2.04	258	60	7	24	53	.233	.364	.298
Road Games	5-3	4.35	310	82	12	29	51	.265	.474	.325
Grass Fields	9-4	3.09	475	117	16	48	87	.246	.415	.314
Artificial Turf	3-0	4.26	93	25	3	5	17	.269	.473	.303
April	0-0	3.86	31	7	0	5	9	.226	.290	.333
May	2-0	4.15	59	15	3	13	9	.254	.475	.384
June	0-1	4.08	68	19	4	11	16	.279	.500	.380
July	2-1	2.93	118	32	4	5	22	.271	.475	.301
August	5-1	3.55	143	33	6	6	20	.231	.427	.260
Sept./Oct.	3-1	2.45	149	36	2	13	28	.242	.356	.301
Leading Off Inn.			145	41	6	10	26	.283	.497	.329
Bases Empty			333	97	12	30	56	.291	.486	.350
Runners On			235	45	7	23	48	.191	.336	.261
Runners/Scor. Pos.			134	19	4	20	33	.142	.276	.248
Runners On/2 Out			92	16	3	14	21	.174	.315	.283
Scor. Pos./2 Out			59	9	1	14	17	.153	.237	.315
Late-Inning Pressure			39	6	0	7	8	.154	.231	.283
Leading Off			11	0	0	2	1	.000	.000	.154
Runners On			11	2	0	3	5	.182	.364	.357
Runners/Scor. Pos.			7	0	0	2	4	.000	.000	.222
First 9 Batters			260	60	5	20	58	.231	.342	.285
Second 9 Batters			179	43	8	20	30	.240	.464	.313
All Batters Thereafter			129	39	6	13	16	.302	.535	.366

Loves to face: Carlos Baerga (0-for-9)
                 Albert Belle (0-for-8)
                 Don Mattingly (0-for-7)

Hates to face: Glenn Davis (.308, 4-for-13, 1 2B, 3 HR)
                 Randy Milligan (.714, 5-for-7, 1 HR, 2 SO)
                 Kevin Mitchell (.583, 7-for-12, 1 HR)

Miscellaneous statistics: Ground outs-to-air outs ratio: 1.47 last season, 1.24 for career.... Induced 19 double plays in 106 opportunities (one per 5.6), 2d-best rate in A.L.... Allowed 32 doubles, 5 triples in 153⅓ innings.... Allowed 4 first-inning runs in 17 starts (2.12 ERA, 5th lowest in A.L.).... Batting support: 4.88 runs per start.... Record of 10-4, 3.19 ERA as a starter; 2-0, 3.53 ERA in 22 relief appearances.... Stranded 12 inherited runners, allowed 11 to score (52%).... Opposing base stealers: 7-for-15 (47%); 5 pickoffs, 0 balks.

Comments: The unlikeliest of pitchers to lead Boston's second-half surge, but his 10-3 record after the All-Star break was better than Roger Clemens's second-half record (7-5).... Only three other A.L. pitchers reached double-digit wins in the second half: Kevin Tapani (11-2), Bill Wegman (11-4), and Jim Abbott (11-5).... Key to success: He held opponents to .142 batting average with runners in scoring position, lowest in A.L. last season and fourth lowest since we began keeping track in 1975 (minimum: 125 batters faced). The top five: Mitch Williams (.108 in 1991), Mark Davis (.123 in 1989), Jim Deshaies (.140 in 1986), Hesketh, and Goose Gossage (.143 in 1978).... Hesketh had allowed a .340 scoring-position batting average in 1989, .305 in 1990.... Before making his first start on June 30, he had allowed 11 of the last 16 runners he inherited as an incoming reliever to score. Starting him looked safer.... Walked only one batter during the first inning of his 17 starts, the lowest rate among major league pitchers last season.... Did not allow a home run to a left-handed batter in 122 innings after June 5.... Longest outing last season: eight innings, on two occasions. Has not thrown a complete game in 39 major league starts since July 28, 1985, when he shut out Cincinnati while pitching for Montreal.... Owns a 28-17 career record with 3.17 ERA as a starting pitcher. Only seven active pitchers have lower ERAs with career records at least 10 games over .500 as starters: Belcher, Clemens, Cone, Erickson, Gooden, Hershiser, and Ryan.

Greg Hibbard — Throws Left

Chicago White Sox	W-L	ERA	AB	H	HR	BB	SO	BA	SA	OBA
Season	11-11	4.31	737	196	23	57	71	.266	.402	.320
vs. Left-Handers			120	30	5	4	10	.250	.392	.283
vs. Right-Handers			617	166	18	53	61	.269	.404	.326
vs. Ground-Ballers			333	85	9	18	29	.255	.372	.293
vs. Fly-Ballers			404	111	14	39	42	.275	.426	.341
Home Games	4-5	3.44	340	92	9	28	29	.271	.406	.327
Road Games	7-6	5.10	397	104	14	29	42	.262	.398	.313
Grass Fields	9-9	4.00	601	161	17	49	58	.268	.399	.324
Artificial Turf	2-2	5.77	136	35	6	8	13	.257	.412	.299
April	2-0	1.55	99	19	1	13	14	.192	.273	.286
May	1-3	4.43	160	43	3	12	12	.269	.387	.320
June	3-3	5.18	173	54	10	7	14	.312	.509	.339
July	1-2	5.58	118	30	6	8	11	.254	.432	.302
August	1-2	6.41	75	22	1	12	7	.293	.387	.386
Sept./Oct.	3-1	3.06	112	28	2	5	13	.250	.348	.292
Leading Off Inn.			192	51	4	17	11	.266	.354	.325
Bases Empty			454	111	12	37	39	.244	.352	.303
Runners On			283	85	11	20	32	.300	.481	.346
Runners/Scor. Pos.			144	51	8	13	17	.354	.611	.403
Runners On/2 Out			114	41	8	9	7	.360	.640	.407
Scor. Pos./2 Out			68	34	6	7	4	.500	.868	.547
Late-Inning Pressure			52	14	1	4	1	.269	.385	.321
Leading Off			16	4	1	2	0	.250	.438	.333
Runners On			14	3	0	1	1	.214	.357	.267
Runners/Scor. Pos.			6	3	0	1	1	.500	.833	.571
First 9 Batters			260	63	6	18	32	.242	.354	.296
Second 9 Batters			244	74	8	25	18	.303	.455	.365
All Batters Thereafter			233	59	9	14	21	.253	.399	.296

Loves to face: Felix Fermin (.056, 1-for-18, 2 BB)
    Gary Gaetti (0-for-18)
    Hensley Meulens (0-for-9)

Hates to face: Harold Baines (.700, 7-for-10, 1 HR)
    Lance Parrish (.533, 8-for-15, 2 HR)
    Ruben Sierra (.304, 7-for-23, 2 2B, 1 3B, 2 HR)

Miscellaneous statistics: Ground outs-to-air outs ratio: 1.57 last season, 1.41 for career.... Induced 27 double plays in 154 opportunities (one per 5.7), 3d-best rate in A.L.... Allowed 27 doubles, 2 triples in 194 innings.... Allowed 18 first-inning runs in 29 starts (4.97 ERA).... Batting support: 4.97 runs per start, 9th-highest average in A.L.... Opposing base stealers: 6-for-14 (43%); 1 pickoff, 0 balks.

Comments: The only pitcher in the majors last season with at least 20 decisions, but no winning streak or losing streak longer than two games.... Opponents batted .354 with runners in scoring position to rank among five highest averages allowed by A.L. pitchers in those situations (minimum: 100 RISP at-bats): Jeff Ballard .381, Chuck Crim .364, Hibbard .354, Jose Mesa .352, Tim Leary .339.... Getting the third out was a monumental problem. With runners in scoring position and two outs—a decisive moment when a hit usually means a run but an out kills a rally—Hibbard's performance was the worst in recorded history. He allowed 34 hits in 68 such at-bats; that .500 batting average was the highest by any pitcher in any season since we began keeping track of the category in 1975 (minimum: 30 at-bats). The old record: Bob Shirley allowed a .481 batting average (25-for-52) in 1975.... Had never allowed a home run to a left-handed batter before last season, but allowed five last season. Current tally: Hibbard has allowed two home runs in six at-bats by Kevin Maas, and three home runs in 275 career at-bats by all other left-handed batters.... Carlton Fisk caught more than 85 percent of the innings pitched by Hibbard last season.... His 11 wins last season ranked second on the staff. Only two teams in this century (1981 excluded) have won a pennant or division title without getting at least a dozen wins from two different pitchers: the 1982 Braves and the 1987 Cardinals.

Shawn Hillegas — Throws Right

Cleveland Indians	W-L	ERA	AB	H	HR	BB	SO	BA	SA	OBA
Season	3-4	4.34	300	67	7	46	66	.223	.340	.324
vs. Left-Handers			142	32	1	20	34	.225	.289	.315
vs. Right-Handers			158	35	6	26	32	.222	.386	.332
vs. Ground-Ballers			133	32	1	14	30	.241	.323	.305
vs. Fly-Ballers			167	35	6	32	36	.210	.353	.338
Home Games	3-2	3.07	196	38	2	30	47	.194	.281	.296
Road Games	0-2	6.91	104	29	5	16	19	.279	.452	.377
Grass Fields	3-4	3.95	264	57	6	40	58	.216	.333	.333
Artificial Turf	0-0	7.20	36	10	1	6	8	.278	.389	.386
April	0-0	1.17	27	4	0	2	7	.148	.148	.207
May	0-0	2.03	46	10	1	6	14	.217	.348	.308
June	2-1	2.13	42	5	0	11	13	.119	.143	.309
July	0-1	9.00	55	14	4	12	9	.255	.473	.382
August	1-1	4.76	63	17	1	8	14	.270	.381	.351
Sept./Oct.	0-1	4.91	67	17	1	7	9	.254	.388	.312
Leading Off Inn.			66	13	1	5	17	.197	.288	.254
Bases Empty			150	30	2	22	32	.200	.280	.302
Runners On			150	37	5	24	34	.247	.400	.344
Runners/Scor. Pos.			88	18	4	17	21	.205	.398	.319
Runners On/2 Out			71	16	3	11	13	.225	.394	.337
Scor. Pos./2 Out			47	8	3	9	9	.170	.404	.316
Late-Inning Pressure			105	22	3	22	27	.210	.333	.341
Leading Off			25	7	1	3	9	.280	.400	.357
Runners On			58	10	1	10	15	.172	.276	.286
Runners/Scor. Pos.			31	4	1	6	10	.129	.290	.256
First 9 Batters			247	55	6	43	56	.223	.336	.336
Second 9 Batters			46	10	1	3	10	.217	.348	.260
All Batters Thereafter			7	2	0	0	0	.286	.429	.286

Loves to face: Alvaro Espinoza (.083, 1-for-12)
    Greg Gagne (0-for-9)
    Jamie Quirk (0-for-8)

Hates to face: Alvin Davis (.667, 4-for-6, 1 HR, 4 BB)
    Roberto Kelly (.545, 6-for-11)
    Don Mattingly (.444, 4-for-9, 2 HR)

Miscellaneous statistics: Ground outs-to-air outs ratio: 0.74 last season, 0.76 for career.... Induced 6 double plays in 80 opportunities (one per 13).... Allowed 12 doubles, 1 triple in 83 innings.... Stranded 29 inherited runners, allowed 17 to score (63%).... Opposing base stealers: 6-for-9 (67%); 1 pickoff, 0 balks.

Comments: Memo re: relief pitching statistics, specifically "inherited runners." It can be an oversimplification to treat all inherited-runner situations with absolute equality; after all, inheriting a runner on third base with none out is inherently different from inheriting a runner on first with two outs. But sometimes the total figures make a valuable point, and such is the case with last year's Indians. Hillegas allowed 17 inherited runners to score while stranding 29. Do you think that ratio is good or bad? Actually, in the majors as a whole last season, there were about two inherited runners stranded for every one allowed to score; the exact rate was 65 percent. (We don't include a third classification of inherited runners—those bequeathed to subsequent relievers—in either the "stranded" or "scored" categories.) So Hillegas's rate (63 percent stranded) is a bit worse than average, but it was far and away the best on the Indians, the team that had the worst inherited-runners numbers in the majors last season. As a team, Cleveland's relievers stranded only 54 percent of the runners they inherited. To put that number in perspective, here are the five worst such rates in the majors last season: Indians, 54.2%; Cubs, 58.8%; Blue Jays, 61.2%; Mets, 61.6%; Red Sox, 62.0%.

Brian Holman — Throws Right

Seattle Mariners	W-L	ERA	AB	H	HR	BB	SO	BA	SA	OBA
Season	13-14	3.69	743	199	16	77	108	.268	.392	.343
vs. Left-Handers			391	111	6	46	48	.284	.394	.362
vs. Right-Handers			352	88	10	31	60	.250	.389	.322
vs. Ground-Ballers			356	76	3	33	44	.213	.289	.287
vs. Fly-Ballers			387	123	13	44	64	.318	.486	.394
Home Games	9-7	2.65	441	106	5	32	74	.240	.333	.296
Road Games	4-7	5.28	302	93	11	45	34	.308	.477	.407
Grass Fields	3-5	5.05	229	72	8	35	23	.314	.472	.413
Artificial Turf	10-9	3.12	514	127	8	42	85	.247	.356	.310
April	2-2	2.83	102	27	3	13	13	.265	.382	.353
May	3-3	3.40	146	36	3	17	23	.247	.356	.335
June	2-3	5.81	121	32	1	16	19	.264	.339	.364
July	2-2	2.16	130	36	1	9	13	.277	.369	.324
August	2-3	4.67	140	40	7	16	22	.286	.529	.363
Sept./Oct.	2-1	3.21	104	28	1	6	18	.269	.356	.315
Leading Off Inn.			182	54	5	21	20	.297	.412	.379
Bases Empty			401	115	9	44	53	.287	.414	.364
Runners On			342	84	7	33	55	.246	.365	.319
Runners/Scor. Pos.			172	39	3	23	31	.227	.326	.320
Runners On/2 Out			135	33	6	20	24	.244	.437	.342
Scor. Pos./2 Out			88	20	2	14	19	.227	.352	.333
Late-Inning Pressure			42	7	1	2	7	.167	.262	.222
Leading Off			12	4	0	2	2	.333	.333	.429
Runners On			16	1	0	0	3	.063	.125	.063
Runners/Scor. Pos.			2	1	0	0	0	.500	1.000	.500
First 9 Batters			238	70	5	23	32	.294	.429	.367
Second 9 Batters			242	66	4	24	35	.273	.405	.342
All Batters Thereafter			263	63	7	30	41	.240	.346	.323

Loves to face: Jim Gantner (.067, 1-for-15)
Tony Phillips (.095, 2-for-21, 2 BB)
Steve Sax (.152, 5-for-33)

Hates to face: Rickey Henderson (.385, 5-for-13, 1 HR, 6 BB)
Carlos Martinez (.778, 7-for-9, 1 HR)
Rafael Palmeiro (.667, 8-for-12)

Miscellaneous statistics: Ground outs-to-air outs ratio: 1.38 last season, 1.22 for career.... Induced 21 double plays in 186 opportunities (one per 8.9).... Allowed 36 doubles, 4 triples in 195⅓ innings.... Allowed 13 first-inning runs in 30 starts (3.60 ERA).... Batting support: 3.47 runs per start, 4th-lowest average in A.L.... Opposing base stealers: 4-for-9 (44%); 2 pickoffs, 1 balk.

Comments: 2.65 ERA at the Kingdome (6th lowest in home games in the A.L.), 5.28 in road games. Is this the same Kingdome that we've known and loved? Actually, last year's distribution of runs in Mariners games was closer than you might think: 693 runs were scored in 81 games in Seattle, 683 were scored in team's 81 road games. Over past five years, Kingdome ranks sixth among 26 stadiums in its effect on run scoring, but its effect is closer to stadiums in Milwaukee and Texas than it is to Atlanta Stadium or Wrigley Field. Seattle pitchers had 3.48 ERA in their own home park, second lowest such ERA in A.L. behind Toronto's 3.16 at Skydome.... Holman, Greg Swindell, and Charlie Hough were the only A.L. starters with sub-.500 records despite ERAs under 4.00 (minimum: 100 innings).... Stood at 13–13 on Sept. 10 after three straight wins, but lost his final decision in quest for first winning record. Missed his final two starts with a rotator cuff tear, which may keep him out for part of 1992.... Opponents have an overall career batting average of .264, but it's only .207 with two outs and runners in scoring position.... Opponents batted only .190 with RISP after the All-Star break.... Dave Valle caught over 80 percent of innings pitched by Holman, compared to just below 60 percent of innings by other guys.... Opponents on-base average leading off innings was 2d highest in A.L., behind Mike Boddicker.... Chosen with the second of the Expos' two first-round picks in 1983 amateur draft. Holman was 16th pick, Roger Clemens was 19th.

Charlie Hough — Throws Right

Chicago White Sox	W-L	ERA	AB	H	HR	BB	SO	BA	SA	OBA
Season	9-10	4.02	729	167	21	94	107	.229	.381	.320
vs. Left-Handers			355	84	8	44	48	.237	.375	.323
vs. Right-Handers			374	83	13	50	59	.222	.388	.317
vs. Ground-Ballers			316	72	11	28	34	.228	.402	.294
vs. Fly-Ballers			413	95	10	66	73	.230	.366	.339
Home Games	5-5	3.38	391	89	12	41	59	.228	.373	.307
Road Games	4-5	4.76	338	78	9	53	48	.231	.391	.334
Grass Fields	7-7	3.81	568	127	15	81	88	.224	.366	.323
Artificial Turf	2-3	4.78	161	40	6	13	19	.248	.435	.309
April	0-1	7.94	20	5	0	8	7	.250	.300	.484
May	1-1	4.01	128	31	4	12	22	.242	.422	.313
June	4-1	3.13	160	28	7	24	22	.175	.338	.289
July	1-3	3.16	152	33	5	17	17	.217	.355	.297
August	1-2	7.04	125	39	5	18	15	.312	.528	.395
Sept./Oct.	2-2	3.10	144	31	0	15	24	.215	.306	.289
Leading Off Inn.			185	43	5	18	23	.232	.389	.314
Bases Empty			428	97	13	58	67	.227	.381	.329
Runners On			301	70	8	36	40	.233	.382	.308
Runners/Scor. Pos.			149	30	4	23	19	.201	.336	.289
Runners On/2 Out			132	27	4	15	21	.205	.364	.300
Scor. Pos./2 Out			76	12	2	8	12	.158	.250	.247
Late-Inning Pressure			65	18	4	10	8	.277	.492	.364
Leading Off			18	4	0	3	3	.222	.222	.333
Runners On			20	6	1	3	1	.300	.550	.360
Runners/Scor. Pos.			9	1	1	1	0	.111	.444	.167
First 9 Batters			237	45	7	34	40	.190	.325	.292
Second 9 Batters			226	61	5	20	34	.270	.434	.326
All Batters Thereafter			266	61	9	40	33	.229	.387	.340

Loves to face: Roberto Alomar (0-for-12)
Brian Harper (0-for-10)
Luis Polonia (.115, 3-for-26)

Hates to face: Joe Carter (.298, 14-for-47, 6 HR)
Dwight Evans (.312, 24-for-77, 4 HR)
Lou Whitaker (.348, 23-for-66, 3 HR)

Miscellaneous statistics: Ground outs-to-air outs ratio: 0.96 last season, 1.03 for career.... Induced 12 double plays in 155 opportunities (one per 13).... Allowed 28 doubles, 10 triples (tied for most in majors) in 199⅓ innings.... Allowed 15 first-inning runs in 29 starts (3.41 ERA).... Batting support: 4.17 runs per start.... Opposing base stealers: 10-for-19 (53%); 4 pickoffs, 1 balk.

Comments: 1991 was a streak breaker. Item One: Hough's streak of nine 30-start seasons (sorry, we don't cut any slack for those two relief appearances in addition to 29 starts, even if you were 43 years old); Cy Young's record of 19 is safe. Item Two: Hough's streak of nine consecutive years with 10+ wins and 10+ losses; Pud Galvin and Kid Nichols, both of whom started before 1900, had 14 years in a row and more recently, Phil Niekro had 13.... The sole survivor: Hough now has 10 consecutive seasons with at least 10 losses, the longest streak of that kind since Jerry Koosman's 11-year run (1971–81).... By virtue of his years as a reliever with the Dodgers, Hough leads active pitchers with 776 games, nine more than Nolan Ryan. He's the only pitcher in major league history to start 350 games and relieve in 350 games.... You make the call: either Carlton Fisk wanted no part of the Hough knuckler, or he just has something against pitchers in their forties (Fisk is 10 days older than Hough). Whatever, those two ancient warriors didn't team up for a single inning last year; Hough's batterymates were Ron Karkovice (66 percent of innings), and Don Wakamatsu (34%). Pudge caught 62 percent of the innings by the rest of the staff.... Opponents batted .198 during the first inning, .234 thereafter.... The only two pitchers to shut out the Orioles last season were Charlie Hough and Wilson Alvarez.... His final win of 1991 moved him into baseball's all-time top 100 in wins. Needs five wins to reach 200 for his career, a plateau reached by 89 other pitchers.

Mike Jackson

Throws Right

Seattle Mariners	W-L	ERA	AB	H	HR	BB	SO	BA	SA	OBA
Season	7-7	3.25	319	64	5	34	74	.201	.298	.290
vs. Left-Handers			119	30	2	17	23	.252	.387	.355
vs. Right-Handers			200	34	3	17	51	.170	.245	.249
vs. Ground-Ballers			156	34	1	13	30	.218	.288	.282
vs. Fly-Ballers			163	30	4	21	44	.184	.307	.296
Home Games	3-2	2.64	166	25	3	9	39	.151	.277	.203
Road Games	4-5	3.95	153	39	2	25	35	.255	.320	.374
Grass Fields	3-2	3.77	111	23	2	19	31	.207	.279	.333
Artificial Turf	4-5	2.97	208	41	3	15	43	.197	.308	.264
April	1-2	3.86	40	8	0	4	4	.200	.225	.304
May	3-0	0.95	65	9	2	2	18	.138	.262	.176
June	0-0	4.26	44	6	3	3	15	.136	.341	.191
July	0-2	4.85	55	17	0	9	8	.309	.473	.406
August	2-0	0.00	59	10	0	5	13	.169	.169	.246
Sept./Oct.	1-3	7.20	56	14	0	11	16	.250	.321	.391
Leading Off Inn.			70	13	0	7	15	.186	.229	.260
Bases Empty			175	32	4	12	36	.183	.280	.239
Runners On			144	32	1	22	38	.222	.319	.345
Runners/Scor. Pos.			87	19	1	18	23	.218	.299	.376
Runners On/2 Out			61	14	0	9	14	.230	.328	.347
Scor. Pos./2 Out			41	8	0	7	11	.195	.244	.340
Late-Inning Pressure			208	44	3	20	49	.212	.317	.287
Leading Off			50	11	0	3	13	.220	.280	.264
Runners On			86	22	0	12	23	.256	.360	.360
Runners/Scor. Pos.			54	12	0	12	17	.222	.278	.373
First 9 Batters			310	62	5	30	73	.200	.297	.283
Second 9 Batters			9	2	0	4	1	.222	.333	.462
All Batters Thereafter			0	0	0	0	0	—	—	—

Loves to face: Steve Buechele (0-for-8)
George Bell (0-for-7, 5 SO)
Casey Candaele (.100, 1-for-10)

Hates to face: Dave Martinez (.667, 4-for-6)
Rafael Palmeiro (.778, 7-for-9, 2 HR)

Miscellaneous statistics: Ground outs-to-air outs ratio: 1.09 last season, 0.78 for career.... Induced 5 double plays in 77 opportunities (one per 15).... Allowed 10 doubles, 3 triples in 88⅔ innings.... Saved 14 games in 23 opportunities (61%).... Stranded 40 inherited runners, allowed 10 to score (80%), 4th-highest rate in A.L.... Opposing base stealers: 5-for-5 (100%); 0 pickoffs, 0 balks.

Comments: So close and yet so far: Jackson needed just 11 games to become the Mariners' all-time leader in pitching appearances. Who holds that record? Would you believe Ed Vande Berg? ... Most decisions by A.L. relievers last season: Mike Timlin (15, 10–5); Jackson (14, 7–7); Chuck Crim (13, 8–5); Joe Klink (13, 10–3); Duane Ward (13, 7–6).... Lowered his average of walks per nine innings from 5.12 in 1990 to 3.45 last season.... Eleven of his 34 walks were intentional.... Held opponents to sub-.200 batting average with two outs and runners in scoring position for fourth time in past five years. Mariners led A.L. in that category, holding foes to a .212 mark in those spots.... Took over as team's stopper in June, but four straight unconverted save opportunities returned him to middle relief. Saves by month: April (1), May (3), June (9), July (0), August (1), Sept./Oct. (0).... Only two pitchers held right-handed batters to a lower average than Jackson did last season (minimum: 200 at-bats by RHB): Nolan Ryan (.157) and Todd Frohwirth (.169). That's nothing new: M.J. has held righties below .200 mark three times in past five years.... Consider this list of the highest strikeout rates vs. right-handed batters by active pitchers (minimum: 1000 RHB faced): Tom Henke, 29.1 strikeouts per 100 batters; David Cone, 29.0; Jose DeLeon, 27.1; Roger Clemens, 26.4; Lee Smith, 26.3; Nolan Ryan (since 1975), 26.0; Jackson, 25.8.

Jeff Johnson

Throws Left

New York Yankees	W-L	ERA	AB	H	HR	BB	SO	BA	SA	OBA
Season	6-11	5.95	512	156	15	33	62	.305	.453	.351
vs. Left-Handers			52	12	1	7	7	.231	.308	.344
vs. Right-Handers			460	144	14	26	55	.313	.470	.352
vs. Ground-Ballers			226	67	7	15	22	.296	.460	.347
vs. Fly-Ballers			286	89	8	18	40	.311	.448	.355
Home Games	2-6	5.57	258	83	8	9	26	.322	.473	.348
Road Games	4-5	6.35	254	73	7	24	36	.287	.433	.354
Grass Fields	4-9	5.83	423	131	11	27	56	.310	.452	.357
Artificial Turf	2-2	6.55	89	25	4	6	6	.281	.461	.323
April	0-0	—	0	0	0	0	0	—	—	—
May	0-0	—	0	0	0	0	0	—	—	—
June	1-3	4.25	115	29	3	7	11	.252	.374	.295
July	3-0	2.78	123	33	2	5	13	.268	.350	.297
August	1-5	10.87	114	43	4	7	16	.377	.570	.422
Sept./Oct.	1-3	6.64	160	51	6	14	22	.319	.506	.379
Leading Off Inn.			128	36	6	7	15	.281	.453	.319
Bases Empty			298	84	9	12	34	.282	.413	.318
Runners On			214	72	6	21	28	.336	.509	.394
Runners/Scor. Pos.			128	42	3	15	16	.328	.469	.392
Runners On/2 Out			86	27	2	13	9	.314	.488	.410
Scor. Pos./2 Out			61	20	1	10	6	.328	.475	.431
Late-Inning Pressure			29	7	1	2	3	.241	.345	.290
Leading Off			9	3	1	1	1	.333	.667	.400
Runners On			6	2	0	0	0	.333	.333	.333
Runners/Scor. Pos.			2	1	0	0	0	.500	.500	.500
First 9 Batters			195	60	4	10	23	.308	.415	.340
Second 9 Batters			177	51	4	11	20	.288	.429	.339
All Batters Thereafter			140	45	7	12	19	.321	.536	.382

Loves to face: Joe Carter (.154, 2-for-13)
Billy Ripken (0-for-6)
Pat Tabler (.111, 1-for-9)

Hates to face: Glenallen Hill (.667, 4-for-6, 1 HR)
Edgar Martinez (3-for-3, 1 2B, 1 HR)
Devon White (.455, 5-for-11, 1 HR)

Miscellaneous statistics: Ground outs-to-air outs ratio: 1.74 last season, 1.74 for career.... Induced 13 double plays in 105 opportunities (one per 8.1).... Allowed 21 doubles, 5 triples in 127 innings.... Allowed 19 first-inning runs in 23 starts (6.65 ERA).... Batting support: 4.09 runs per start.... Opposing base stealers: 18-for-22 (82%); 4 pickoffs, 1 balk.

Comments: Made 23 starts last season to finish third among A.L. rookies behind Charles Nagy (33) and Rich DeLucia (31).... Johnson and Wade Taylor made their major league debuts within five days in June, the first time since 1944 that Yanks had two starting pitchers make their debuts in the same week. Johnson and Taylor became only third pair of rookie pitchers in last 75 years to start at least 20 games apiece for Yankees. The others: Johnny Broaca and Johnny Murphy in 1934, Doug Drabek and Bob Tewksbury in 1986.... Did not walk more than three batters in a game, and didn't walk more than two in any of his first 20 starts. Of course it helped that he didn't pitch more than six innings in 14 of 23 starts (including 10 in a row at one point).... Averaged 2.34 walks per nine innings, 2d-lowest rate among A.L. rookies to Mike Mussina (2.16).... Opponents averaged one steal every 7.1 innings vs. Johnson, highest frequency of steals vs. any left-handed pitcher in A.L.... Yankees fans can either skip the following note or risk prolonged depression. The highest ERAs among pitchers with at least 100 innings in 1991: Tim Leary (6.49), Wade Taylor (6.27), Jose Mesa (5.97), Johnson (5.95). You have to go back 52 years to find the last major league team with three pitchers who made 15 starts and had ERAs of 5.95 or higher: the 1939 Philadelphia Athletics, with the infamous trio of Cotton Pipper, Buck Ross, and Nelson Potter. Potter eventually righted himself and in 1944 overcame a 10-day suspension for throwing a spitter to win 19 games for A.L. champion Browns.

Randy Johnson
Throws Left

Seattle Mariners	W-L	ERA	AB	H	HR	BB	SO	BA	SA	OBA
Season	13-10	3.98	708	151	15	152	228	.213	.325	.358
vs. Left-Handers			85	18	2	15	25	.212	.306	.337
vs. Right-Handers			623	133	13	137	203	.213	.327	.361
vs. Ground-Ballers			329	73	9	61	102	.222	.359	.351
vs. Fly-Ballers			379	78	6	91	126	.206	.296	.364
Home Games	6-5	3.92	376	85	7	72	114	.226	.332	.355
Road Games	7-5	4.05	332	66	8	80	114	.199	.316	.361
Grass Fields	7-3	4.43	237	45	6	61	87	.190	.312	.361
Artificial Turf	6-7	3.74	471	106	9	91	141	.225	.331	.357
April	2-2	4.94	96	24	2	22	22	.250	.375	.387
May	1-3	4.46	123	28	1	32	44	.228	.325	.396
June	3-1	3.38	94	17	5	29	36	.181	.362	.384
July	3-1	2.97	137	25	2	25	46	.182	.255	.311
August	3-2	3.00	122	26	3	12	40	.213	.328	.292
Sept./Oct.	1-1	5.21	136	31	2	32	40	.228	.331	.382
Leading Off Inn.			172	35	4	37	53	.203	.314	.357
Bases Empty			392	74	8	81	132	.189	.296	.340
Runners On			316	77	7	71	96	.244	.361	.379
Runners/Scor. Pos.			190	45	4	43	62	.237	.353	.370
Runners On/2 Out			129	27	4	29	41	.209	.341	.358
Scor. Pos./2 Out			96	20	4	20	30	.208	.375	.350
Late-Inning Pressure			59	12	0	6	16	.203	.271	.288
Leading Off			17	3	0	0	3	.176	.235	.176
Runners On			21	5	0	4	7	.238	.333	.360
Runners/Scor. Pos.			12	2	0	1	5	.167	.250	.231
First 9 Batters			232	42	5	56	83	.181	.302	.353
Second 9 Batters			230	45	6	47	73	.196	.309	.338
All Batters Thereafter			246	64	4	49	72	.260	.362	.382

Loves to face: Rob Deer (.105, 2-for-19, 10 SO)
Craig Grebeck (0-for-13)
Ed Sprague (0-for-9, 5 SO)

Hates to face: Bob Melvin (.526, 10-for-19)
Ruben Sierra (.480, 12-for-25, 1 HR)
Frank Thomas (.444, 4-for-9, 1 HR, 6 BB, 5 SO)

Miscellaneous statistics: Ground outs-to-air outs ratio: 1.10 last season, 1.00 for career.... Induced 22 double plays in 191 opportunities (one per 8.7).... Allowed 32 doubles, 1 triple in 201⅓ innings.... Allowed 13 first-inning runs in 33 starts (3.27 ERA).... Batting support: 4.67 runs per start.... Opposing base stealers: 18-for-27 (67%); 4 pickoffs, 2 balks.

Comments: Averaged 10.2 strikeouts per nine innings; only five others in major league history reached a double-digit strikeout rate in a season of 200 or more innings: Nolan Ryan (seven times), Sandy Koufax, Sam McDowell, Dwight Gooden, and Mike Scott.... Led majors in walks for second year in a row; his total of 152 was 32 higher than a year earlier. Also led majors in leadoff walks for second straight year, though he cut his total from 39 to 37.... Career rate of 5.55 walks per nine innings is 4th highest among active pitchers (minimum: 500 innings); his 1991 rate of 6.79 was highest among pitchers with at least 100 innings. Only one pitcher in the last 40 years had a season in which he qualified for the ERA title and had a higher walk rate: Toothpick Sam Jones walked 6.88 batters per nine innings for the 1955 Cubs.... Held opposing batters hitless in 30 consecutive at-bats with runners in scoring position, June 15–July 28.... Threw a one-hit shutout vs. Oakland in his best outing of the season; also allowed only one hit in his worst outing of the season—a four-inning stint at Milwaukee in which he walked ten.... At six feet, 10 inches, Johnson is taller than eight of the 12 players on the Seattle SuperSonics opening-night roster.... The tallest pitcher in major league history has never faced any of the shortest active batters (Jarvis Brown, Warren Newson, or Bip Roberts, all listed at 5'7''). Gap of one foot, three inches wouldn't come close to the record of two feet, five inches set when Bob Cain pitched to Eddie Gaedel in 1951.

Doug Jones
Throws Right

Cleveland Indians	W-L	ERA	AB	H	HR	BB	SO	BA	SA	OBA
Season	4-8	5.54	272	87	7	17	48	.320	.496	.357
vs. Left-Handers			132	45	4	9	20	.341	.530	.380
vs. Right-Handers			140	42	3	8	28	.300	.464	.336
vs. Ground-Ballers			119	37	2	6	17	.311	.445	.344
vs. Fly-Ballers			153	50	5	11	31	.327	.536	.367
Home Games	1-4	6.41	116	38	1	5	24	.328	.448	.352
Road Games	3-4	4.91	156	49	6	12	24	.314	.532	.361
Grass Fields	4-7	4.94	248	78	4	14	43	.315	.460	.348
Artificial Turf	0-1	12.60	24	9	3	3	5	.375	.875	.444
April	0-2	5.00	39	12	2	1	8	.308	.462	.317
May	1-2	11.74	38	16	2	3	7	.421	.763	.463
June	0-2	6.23	36	11	1	3	5	.306	.472	.359
July	0-1	7.50	24	6	2	4	4	.250	.667	.345
August	0-0	—	0	0	0	0	0			
Sept./Oct.	3-1	3.66	135	42	0	6	24	.311	.407	.340
Leading Off Inn.			61	12	2	12		.197	.344	.222
Bases Empty			136	44	4	7	21	.324	.493	.357
Runners On			136	43	3	10	27	.316	.500	.358
Runners/Scor. Pos.			80	26	2	6	13	.325	.550	.364
Runners On/2 Out			61	18	1	3	10	.295	.443	.328
Scor. Pos./2 Out			39	11	0	1	6	.282	.410	.300
Late-Inning Pressure			81	35	4	3	12	.432	.778	.452
Leading Off			18	5	1	1	2	.278	.500	.316
Runners On			43	18	2	2	8	.419	.837	.444
Runners/Scor. Pos.			24	12	1	2	2	.500	1.042	.538
First 9 Batters			174	58	7	12	29	.333	.546	.372
Second 9 Batters			34	10	0	4	7	.294	.324	.368
All Batters Thereafter			64	19	0	1	12	.297	.453	.308

Loves to face: Paul Molitor (.100, 2-for-20)
Lloyd Moseby (.158, 3-for-19)
Ruben Sierra (.071, 1-for-14)

Hates to face: Kent Hrbek (.500, 7-for-14, 2 HR)
Mark McGwire (.467, 7-for-15, 1 HR)
Cal Ripken (.556, 10-for-18, 1 HR)

Miscellaneous statistics: Ground outs-to-air outs ratio: 1.61 last season, 1.34 for career.... Induced 5 double plays in 58 opportunities (one per 12).... Allowed 23 doubles, 2 triples in 63⅓ innings.... Stranded 4 inherited runners, allowed 9 to score (31%).... Opposing base stealers: 4-for-4 (100%); 0 pickoffs, 0 balks.

Comments: What a difference a year makes. In July 1990, Jones was named to the A.L. All-Star squad for the third consecutive year. In July 1991, with his ERA at 7.47, he was shipped to the minors.... Like Dan Plesac and Randy Myers, Jones sought to remedy his problems by moving into the starting rotation after appearing in his first 271 major league games as a reliever. He won each of his first three starts, and even came within one out of a complete game in his debut as a starter, after posting a 1–7 record in relief. He averaged 7.75 innings in his four starts; other Indians starters averaged 6.34 innings per start.... Opponents have an overall career batting average of .258, but they're batting .201 with two outs and runners in scoring position.... Recorded five saves in April and one in his final game of the season (Oct. 5), but had only one save in between.... Allowed 23 earned runs in 22⅔ innings over a 23-game span before being sent down (April 30–July 16).... Yearly ERAs since 1988: 2.27, 2.34, 2.56, 5.54.... Opponents batted over 100 points higher against him last season than they did in 1990 (.218).... Career rate of 2.10 walks per nine innings is about the same as Jimmy Key's or Dennis Eckersley's, but Jones has pitched far fewer innings.... Opponents batted .432 in Late-Inning Pressure Situations, highest average vs. any pitcher in majors this season (minimum: 75 batters faced in LIPS). And it wasn't close for second: Jones .432, Texas's Kevin Brown .357, Gene Nelson .353, Dave Smith .307, Storm Davis .307.

Jimmy Key — Throws Left

Toronto Blue Jays	W-L	ERA	AB	H	HR	BB	SO	BA	SA	OBA
Season	16-12	3.05	815	207	12	44	125	.254	.347	.293
vs. Left-Handers			112	32	2	6	19	.286	.357	.325
vs. Right-Handers			703	175	10	38	106	.249	.346	.288
vs. Ground-Ballers			384	115	2	17	51	.299	.367	.331
vs. Fly-Ballers			431	92	10	27	74	.213	.329	.260
Home Games	7-8	3.43	441	120	6	27	66	.272	.365	.316
Road Games	9-4	2.64	374	87	6	17	59	.233	.326	.266
Grass Fields	9-4	2.59	356	82	5	16	59	.230	.320	.263
Artificial Turf	7-8	3.43	459	125	7	28	66	.272	.368	.316
April	4-0	1.86	101	18	1	8	16	.178	.228	.234
May	3-2	2.87	149	38	1	11	32	.255	.315	.311
June	3-1	2.08	158	43	1	3	20	.272	.342	.286
July	1-3	4.88	125	37	3	4	17	.296	.472	.318
August	3-3	3.03	145	37	4	9	20	.255	.372	.299
Sept./Oct.	2-3	3.68	137	34	2	9	20	.248	.336	.297
Leading Off Inn.			207	50	1	9	27	.242	.304	.276
Bases Empty			484	112	5	22	78	.231	.300	.269
Runners On			331	95	7	22	47	.287	.417	.327
Runners/Scor. Pos.			176	36	3	16	26	.205	.313	.264
Runners On/2 Out			138	35	1	12	23	.254	.326	.313
Scor. Pos./2 Out			83	16	1	10	11	.193	.289	.280
Late-Inning Pressure			55	12	0	3	7	.218	.236	.259
Leading Off			16	2	0	1	2	.125	.125	.176
Runners On			16	5	0	1	1	.313	.375	.353
Runners/Scor. Pos.			6	1	0	1	0	.167	.333	.286
First 9 Batters			273	70	6	15	44	.256	.374	.298
Second 9 Batters			277	76	3	10	41	.274	.365	.297
All Batters Thereafter			265	61	3	19	40	.230	.302	.284

Loves to face: Ellis Burks (.091, 2-for-22)
Henry Cotto (.111, 3-for-27, 0 BB)
Kevin Maas (0-for-10)

Hates to face: Dave Henderson (.417, 20-for-48, 3 HR)
Rickey Henderson (.377, 26-for-69, 5 HR)
Carlos Quintana (.563, 9-for-16)

Miscellaneous statistics: Ground outs-to-air outs ratio: 0.99 last season, 1.20 for career.... Induced 14 double plays in 158 opportunities (one per 11).... Allowed 36 doubles, 2 triples in 209⅓ innings.... Allowed 19 first-inning runs in 33 starts (3.82 ERA).... Batting support: 4.18 runs per start.... Opposing base stealers: 6-for-8 (75%); 1 pickoff, 0 balks.

Comments: One of six active pitchers with at least 100 wins and a winning percentage of .600 or better: Dwight Gooden (.714, 132–53); Roger Clemens (.687, 134–61); Orel Hershiser (.613, 106–67); Bob Welch (.606, 188–122); John Candelaria (.606, 175–114); Key (.602, 103–68).... Key and Frank Viola are the only two pitchers to win at least 12 games in each of the last seven seasons.... Winning pitcher in the All-Star Game, which was played in his home ballpark. Oddly, the last pitcher to do that was also pitching for a Canadian team: Steve Rogers in the 1982 game at Montreal.... But he was hardly the pitcher after the All-Star break (6–8, 4.02 ERA) that he was during the first half (10–4, 2.23). Result: the Jays' leading winner during the regular season didn't start until Game 3 of the League Championship Series. Curiously, the same also applied to the Twins' leading winner, Scott Erickson, and for similar reasons.... Breakdown of Key's work over the last two years: 19–6, 2.81 ERA with Greg Myers catching, 10–13, 4.40 ERA with Pat Borders.... Faced 131 consecutive batters without a walk last June, the second-longest streak in A.L. last season, behind Mark Eichhorn (146). Key has averaged fewer than two walks per nine innings in each of last three years. His career rate of 2.10 walks per nine innings is 5th best among active pitchers (minimum: 1000 innings).... Hadn't allowed a home run to a left-handed batter until mid-September, when both Ken Griffey, Jr., and Pete O'Brien took him deep.... Career record from September 1 on: 21–10.

Eric King — Throws Right

Cleveland Indians	W-L	ERA	AB	H	HR	BB	SO	BA	SA	OBA
Season	6-11	4.60	594	166	7	44	59	.279	.384	.328
vs. Left-Handers			326	93	5	26	33	.285	.393	.334
vs. Right-Handers			268	73	2	18	26	.272	.373	.321
vs. Ground-Ballers			273	78	2	19	20	.286	.377	.327
vs. Fly-Ballers			321	88	5	25	39	.274	.389	.330
Home Games	2-7	5.95	268	89	3	22	26	.332	.440	.378
Road Games	4-4	3.57	326	77	4	22	33	.236	.337	.286
Grass Fields	6-8	4.97	497	144	7	37	52	.290	.398	.338
Artificial Turf	0-3	3.67	97	22	0	7	7	.227	.309	.280
April	2-2	4.55	110	30	1	1	14	.273	.364	.277
May	2-2	6.06	138	38	5	13	17	.275	.413	.331
June	0-1	5.93	56	19	0	7	0	.339	.411	.415
July	0-1	2.25	29	6	0	0	4	.207	.310	.200
August	1-2	3.55	127	34	0	10	17	.268	.370	.329
Sept./Oct.	1-3	4.13	134	39	1	13	7	.291	.388	.351
Leading Off Inn.			150	38	2	11	17	.253	.380	.309
Bases Empty			338	89	5	20	34	.263	.367	.306
Runners On			256	77	2	24	25	.301	.406	.355
Runners/Scor. Pos.			137	40	1	16	11	.292	.401	.356
Runners On/2 Out			95	23	2	11	12	.242	.379	.321
Scor. Pos./2 Out			52	13	1	9	7	.250	.423	.361
Late-Inning Pressure			23	9	1	2	0	.391	.783	.462
Leading Off			7	3	1	2	0	.429	1.143	.600
Runners On			6	3	0	0	0	.500	1.000	.500
Runners/Scor. Pos.			4	2	0	0	0	.500	1.000	.500
First 9 Batters			203	48	1	17	32	.236	.310	.295
Second 9 Batters			203	58	1	10	13	.286	.369	.315
All Batters Thereafter			188	60	5	17	14	.319	.479	.378

Loves to face: George Brett (.150, 3-for-20)
Dave Henderson (.100, 2-for-20)
Harold Reynolds (.138, 4-for-29)

Hates to face: Jesse Barfield (.333, 7-for-21, 2 2B, 3 HR)
Don Mattingly (.400, 10-for-25, 1 HR)
Tony Phillips (.417, 10-for-24)

Miscellaneous statistics: Ground outs-to-air outs ratio: 1.11 last season, 1.18 for career.... Induced 9 double plays in 133 opportunities (one per 15), 4th-worst rate in A.L.... Allowed 33 doubles, 4 triples in 150⅔ innings.... Allowed 13 first-inning runs in 24 starts (4.50 ERA).... Batting support: 4.58 runs per start.... Opposing base stealers: 8-for-11 (73%); 0 pickoffs, 2 balks.

Comments: The three teams for which he has pitched—the Tigers, White Sox, and Indians—are all original A.L. franchises. There have been 16 others in major league history who have pitched for each of those clubs, but King is the only one to hurl a shutout for each of them.... Averaged 3.52 strikeouts per nine innings last season, the lowest rate of his career; at one point he faced 104 batters between strikeouts, the longest such streak in the majors last season.... Allowed only one home run over his last 91 innings pitched.... Career records as starter and as reliever are very similar: 38–32 (3.87 ERA) in 99 starts; 10–7 (3.74 ERA) in 87 relief appearances.... His only relief appearance in 1991 was disastrous: He entered with the bases loaded and proceeded to allow all three runners to score.... Opponents have an overall career batting average of .245, but they've hit just .203 with two outs and runners in scoring position.... Despite a 6–11 season, his career winning percentage of .552 (48–39) still fits into the overall scheme of things as a little better than Dennis Martinez's and a little worse than Bruce Hurst's.... Has only eight complete games in his career, but five are shutouts.... Contrary to appearances, his contract does not mandate a 25-game work year. King has pitched in exactly 25 games in each of the past three years after pitching in 23 games in 1988. Maybe it's just a trial balloon: Could this be the next benefit sought by the Players Association in collective bargaining?

Bill Krueger
Throws Left

Seattle Mariners	W-L	ERA	AB	H	HR	BB	SO	BA	SA	OBA
Season	11-8	3.60	672	194	15	60	91	.289	.418	.346
vs. Left-Handers			140	43	2	10	19	.307	.414	.351
vs. Right-Handers			532	151	13	50	72	.284	.419	.345
vs. Ground-Ballers			315	110	8	23	32	.349	.505	.392
vs. Fly-Ballers			357	84	7	37	59	.235	.342	.308
Home Games	7-3	3.73	362	100	10	31	52	.276	.420	.331
Road Games	4-5	3.44	310	94	5	29	39	.303	.416	.364
Grass Fields	3-3	2.35	216	65	3	22	30	.301	.389	.365
Artificial Turf	8-5	4.21	456	129	12	38	61	.283	.432	.337
April	0-0	5.68	30	12	0	1	5	.400	.467	.419
May	1-2	4.91	110	35	4	15	11	.318	.500	.398
June	4-1	2.12	118	26	1	12	18	.220	.305	.288
July	4-0	1.19	140	33	3	11	24	.236	.357	.294
August	1-4	6.54	135	48	2	11	21	.356	.489	.409
Sept./Oct.	1-1	3.50	139	40	5	10	12	.288	.432	.329
Leading Off Inn.			175	51	8	8	21	.291	.474	.330
Bases Empty			396	118	13	23	58	.298	.447	.340
Runners On			276	76	2	37	33	.275	.377	.355
Runners/Scor. Pos.			147	38	0	24	15	.259	.367	.352
Runners On/2 Out			111	30	1	20	11	.270	.378	.386
Scor. Pos./2 Out			73	17	0	16	6	.233	.342	.378
Late-Inning Pressure			37	14	3	4	5	.378	.730	.439
Leading Off			11	2	0	1	1	.182	.182	.250
Runners On			12	4	0	2	2	.333	.500	.429
Runners/Scor. Pos.			7	2	0	1	1	.286	.429	.375
First 9 Batters			264	74	4	22	27	.280	.383	.334
Second 9 Batters			222	63	6	22	35	.284	.405	.347
All Batters Thereafter			186	57	5	16	29	.306	.484	.363

Loves to face: Ellis Burks (0-for-11)
Junior Felix (0-for-12)
Mel Hall (0-for-12)

Hates to face: Brian Downing (.385, 10-for-26, 4 HR)
Mike Greenwell (.625, 10-for-16)
Cal Ripken (.378, 14-for-37, 3 HR)

Miscellaneous statistics: Ground outs-to-air outs ratio: 1.11 last season, 1.10 for career.... Induced 19 double plays in 144 opportunities (one per 7.6).... Allowed 34 doubles, 4 triples in 175 innings.... Allowed 17 first-inning runs in 25 starts (5.04 ERA). He had an ERA of 3.20 in subsequent innings of his starts.... Batting support: 4.00 runs per start.... Opposing base stealers: 11-for-16 (69%); 6 pickoffs, 1 balk.

Comments: Andy Warhol would have been impressed: Krueger had more than 15 minutes of fame last year; for two months he was, gulp, the best pitcher in baseball. He won eight of nine decisions in 11 appearances in June and July, tying Bill Gullickson, Mark Langston, Jack McDowell, and Jack Morris for the major league lead; his 1.64 ERA during the middle months was the lowest in the majors.... Set career highs in wins, starts (25), and innings (175).... Average of 3.09 walks per nine innings last season was the lowest of his career.... His ERA stood at 2.88 in mid-August to rank among top 10 in A.L., and he threatened to break Erik Hanson's single-season team record ERA of 3.24, set a year earlier. But his last nine starts produced a 1–3 record and a 5.40 ERA, and Hanson's name is still in the record book.... Has yielded only three home runs in 327 at-bats to left-handed batters over the last three seasons: Harold Baines in 1990, and Kevin Maas and Kent Hrbek last year.... Complete game loss at Texas on Sept. 30 was his first CG in majors in just under six years.... Enters 1992 with a streak of 120 games since last committing an error in April 1986.... Has started 114 games in majors but has never pitched a shutout. All-time leaders in that category: Roy Mahaffey (128), Al Nipper (124), Roger Erickson (117), Krueger (114), and Coldwater Jim Hughey (113). Other active contenders: Todd Stottlemyre (101) and Boston's Greg Harris (96).

Mark Langston
Throws Left

California Angels	W-L	ERA	AB	H	HR	BB	SO	BA	SA	OBA
Season	19-8	3.00	884	190	30	96	183	.215	.360	.291
vs. Left-Handers			129	28	1	14	27	.217	.295	.294
vs. Right-Handers			755	162	29	82	156	.215	.371	.291
vs. Ground-Ballers			406	88	7	42	74	.217	.313	.289
vs. Fly-Ballers			478	102	23	54	109	.213	.400	.294
Home Games	9-3	3.33	460	103	18	45	105	.224	.389	.294
Road Games	10-5	2.64	424	87	12	51	78	.205	.328	.289
Grass Fields	15-7	3.07	761	167	27	82	162	.219	.373	.295
Artificial Turf	4-1	2.55	123	23	3	14	21	.187	.276	.270
April	1-1	4.38	90	23	3	12	20	.256	.411	.346
May	5-1	3.30	168	37	4	19	29	.220	.345	.298
June	5-0	3.19	134	26	6	13	31	.194	.366	.265
July	3-3	3.42	194	43	10	16	42	.222	.438	.281
August	1-2	2.08	118	24	3	18	17	.203	.305	.307
Sept./Oct.	4-1	2.10	180	37	4	18	44	.206	.294	.276
Leading Off Inn.			226	53	6	31	43	.235	.354	.327
Bases Empty			558	122	18	69	108	.219	.355	.306
Runners On			326	68	12	27	75	.209	.368	.267
Runners/Scor. Pos.			150	34	8	19	44	.227	.440	.303
Runners On/2 Out			137	25	7	8	37	.182	.380	.228
Scor. Pos./2 Out			68	12	4	7	19	.176	.382	.253
Late-Inning Pressure			81	20	3	10	18	.247	.383	.326
Leading Off			21	5	0	6	5	.238	.286	.407
Runners On			26	5	1	2	5	.192	.346	.241
Runners/Scor. Pos.			7	0	0	1	2	.000	.000	.111
First 9 Batters			276	52	10	30	56	.188	.341	.268
Second 9 Batters			271	62	7	30	62	.229	.365	.306
All Batters Thereafter			337	76	13	36	65	.226	.371	.299

Loves to face: Henry Cotto (.059, 1-for-17)
Kelly Gruber (.080, 2-for-25)
Jody Reed (.100, 2-for-20)

Hates to face: Brian Downing (.346, 18-for-52, 4 HR)
Dave Henderson (.471, 16-for-34, 3 HR)
Alan Trammell (.375, 18-for-48, 3 HR)

Miscellaneous statistics: Ground outs-to-air outs ratio: 0.73 last season, 4th lowest in A.L.; 0.99 for career.... Induced 16 double plays in 164 opportunities (one per 10).... Allowed 34 doubles, 2 triples in 246⅓ innings.... Allowed 9 first-inning runs in 34 starts (2.38 ERA).... Batting support: 4.29 runs per start.... Opposing base stealers: 10-for-25 (40%, 5th-lowest rate in A.L.); 9 pickoffs (2d most in A.L.), 0 balks.

Comments: Equaled his career high of 19 wins set in 1987. No pitcher in major league history has won 19 games in three different seasons without ever having a 20-win season. Langston joins Paul Dean, Jim Bibby, and Jack Billingham as the only non-20-game winners with two 19-win seasons.... Left-handed batters drove in only seven runs all season against Langston, with three of them coming on a single swing of John Olerud's bat.... Has held lefties to a .199 career batting average. Five active pitchers have held lefties to lower career averages (minimum: 400 LHB faced), but they're all relievers.... One of three active pitchers with at least 1500 innings pitched and an average of more than four walks per nine innings: Nolan Ryan (4.68); Langston (4.24); and Charlie Hough (4.02). Among the same group of pitchers, Langston's career rate of 7.96 strikeouts per nine innings ranks fourth, behind Ryan (9.61), Roger Clemens (8.40), and Dwight Gooden (8.09).... Had a record of only 3–4 in his seven complete games. Leaguewide, A.L. pitchers won only 66 percent of complete games; N.L. pitchers won 85 percent of CGs. The Angels were the only team in the majors that had a losing record in games in which their starter went all the way (8–10).... Has averaged 34.5 starts and 248.2 innings over the past six years, ranking third in both categories; Tom Browning and Frank Viola have both averaged 35.7 starts, while Roger Clemens (258.8) and Viola (249.1) have averaged more innings.

Tim Leary

Throws Right

New York Yankees	W-L	ERA	AB	H	HR	BB	SO	BA	SA	OBA
Season	4-10	6.49	481	150	20	57	83	.312	.511	.388
vs. Left-Handers			267	81	9	30	42	.303	.491	.371
vs. Right-Handers			214	69	11	27	41	.322	.537	.408
vs. Ground-Ballers			223	70	5	23	29	.314	.466	.378
vs. Fly-Ballers			258	80	15	34	54	.310	.550	.397
Home Games	1-4	5.75	217	62	9	26	39	.286	.465	.363
Road Games	3-6	7.13	264	88	11	31	44	.333	.549	.408
Grass Fields	3-8	5.92	409	125	15	48	75	.306	.482	.380
Artificial Turf	1-2	9.87	72	25	5	9	8	.347	.681	.429
April	2-0	4.67	103	27	2	8	28	.262	.398	.319
May	1-4	5.00	142	42	5	22	19	.296	.472	.390
June	1-3	8.89	119	42	8	12	15	.353	.647	.417
July	0-1	12.54	44	20	1	5	8	.455	.591	.510
August	0-1	5.09	63	15	3	8	12	.238	.444	.329
Sept./Oct.	0-1	7.71	10	4	1	2	1	.400	.700	.538
Leading Off Inn.			114	31	6	14	22	.272	.491	.357
Bases Empty			272	77	12	31	52	.283	.496	.359
Runners On			209	73	8	26	31	.349	.531	.425
Runners/Scor. Pos.			118	40	6	23	20	.339	.568	.452
Runners On/2 Out			81	21	2	19	14	.259	.407	.406
Scor. Pos./2 Out			50	13	1	17	10	.260	.420	.456
Late-Inning Pressure			12	2	1	3	3	.167	.167	.231
Leading Off			4	1	0	0	2	.250	.250	.250
Runners On			2	1	0	0	0	.500	.500	.500
Runners/Scor. Pos.			1	0	0	0	0	.000	.000	.000
First 9 Batters			196	71	8	26	37	.362	.571	.442
Second 9 Batters			163	46	4	12	31	.282	.429	.335
All Batters Thereafter			122	33	8	19	15	.270	.525	.369

Loves to face: George Brett (.056, 1-for-18, 2 BB)
Greg Briley (.056, 1-for-18, 2 BB)
Gary Gaetti (.056, 1-for-18)

Hates to face: Jose Canseco (.391, 9-for-23, 3 HR)
Joe Carter (.636, 7-for-11, 3 HR)
Luis Rivera (.700, 7-for-10, 1 HR)

Miscellaneous statistics: Ground outs-to-air outs ratio: 1.13 last season, 1.30 for career.... Induced 13 double plays in 98 opportunities (one per 7.5).... Allowed 32 doubles, 2 triples in 120⅔ innings.... Allowed 15 first-inning runs in 18 starts (7.50 ERA, 5th highest in A.L.).... Batting support: 4.78 runs per start.... Opposing base stealers: 10-for-15 (67%); 0 pickoffs, 0 balks.

Comments: Only four pitchers in the postwar era (that's WWII, for you young'ns) have had seasons of at least 120 innings with ERAs as high as Leary had in 1991: Karl Drews, 1949 Browns (6.62); John Butcher, 1986 Twins/Indians (6.56); Dick Starr, 1951 Browns/Senators (6.51); and Ken Schrom, 1987 Indians (6.50).... Last season, Leary was an opening-day pitcher for the first, and probably last, time in his career. He became the Yankees' seventh different opening-day starter in the last seven years. His predecessors: 1990, Dave LaPoint; 1989, Tommy John; 1988, Rick Rhoden; 1987, Dennis Rasmussen; 1986, Ron Guidry; 1985, Phil Niekro. No American League team had done that since the Indians (1977–83) and the White Sox (1976–83).... With apologies to Geraldo, now it can be told: Leary's 1988 season was a fluke. His 17–11 record with the Dodgers that year represents the only winning season of his major league career. In three seasons since then, his record is 21–43, a .328 winning percentage.... His won-lost records over the last three years are 8–14, 9–19, and 4–10. The last pitcher to suffer through three consecutive years of .364 or worse (minimum: 10 losses each year) was Jesse Jefferson, who had four such years, 1977–80. But get this: the all-time record in that category is five years, *and it's held by a pitcher immortalized in the Hall of Fame.* Red Ruffing started his career with records of 9–18, 6–15, 5–13, 10–25, and 9–22 from 1925 to 1929. He was traded to the Yankees during the 1930 season, and was elected to the Hall on the basis of his 231–124 mark over 15 years in New York.

Mark Leiter

Throws Right

Detroit Tigers	W-L	ERA	AB	H	HR	BB	SO	BA	SA	OBA
Season	9-7	4.21	511	125	16	50	103	.245	.397	.316
vs. Left-Handers			230	55	9	26	33	.239	.417	.322
vs. Right-Handers			281	70	7	24	70	.249	.381	.311
vs. Ground-Ballers			222	54	6	31	33	.243	.356	.340
vs. Fly-Ballers			289	71	10	19	70	.246	.429	.297
Home Games	4-3	4.11	278	64	8	28	58	.230	.374	.301
Road Games	5-4	4.33	233	61	8	22	45	.262	.425	.333
Grass Fields	8-5	4.01	471	115	13	43	96	.244	.389	.310
Artificial Turf	1-2	6.35	40	10	3	7	7	.250	.500	.375
April	1-1	16.20	5	1	0	2	2	.200	.200	.500
May	1-0	2.16	86	18	1	19	23	.209	.267	.358
June	0-0	13.50	17	3	2	4	4	.176	.588	.333
July	0-1	5.06	105	26	5	8	17	.248	.429	.304
August	5-0	2.93	124	34	4	7	22	.274	.435	.311
Sept./Oct.	2-5	4.44	174	43	4	10	35	.247	.402	.293
Leading Off Inn.			122	26	4	12	28	.213	.369	.289
Bases Empty			302	69	10	31	66	.228	.401	.304
Runners On			209	56	6	19	37	.268	.392	.332
Runners/Scor. Pos.			120	36	4	16	18	.300	.467	.375
Runners On/2 Out			100	22	2	12	23	.220	.330	.316
Scor. Pos./2 Out			60	14	1	11	11	.233	.367	.361
Late-Inning Pressure			30	8	1	3	4	.267	.467	.343
Leading Off			6	1	0	2	3	.167	.333	.375
Runners On			15	3	0	1	1	.200	.200	.278
Runners/Scor. Pos.			13	3	0	1	1	.231	.231	.267
First 9 Batters			242	50	6	29	53	.207	.318	.304
Second 9 Batters			146	36	5	16	31	.247	.384	.319
All Batters Thereafter			123	39	5	5	19	.317	.569	.336

Loves to face: Harold Baines (0-for-7)
Jim Gantner (0-for-5)
Leo Gomez (.111, 1-for-9, 5 SO)

Hates to face: George Brett (.500, 3-for-6, 1 2B, 2 HR)
Gary Gaetti (.857, 6-for-7, 1 HR)
Rafael Palmeiro (.600, 6-for-10, 2 2B, 2 HR)

Miscellaneous statistics: Ground outs-to-air outs ratio: 0.77 last season, 0.78 for career.... Induced 8 double plays in 98 opportunities (one per 12).... Allowed 20 doubles, 5 triples in 134⅔ innings.... Allowed 1 first-inning run in 15 starts (0.60 ERA, lowest in majors).... Batting support: 4.93 runs per start.... Record of 7–6, 4.30 ERA as a starter; 2–1, 4.01 ERA in 23 relief appearances.... Stranded 19 inherited runners, allowed 14 to score (58%).... Opposing base stealers: 6-for-12 (50%); 2 pickoffs, 0 balks.

Comments: Mark and Al were one of only three pairs of brothers to pitch in the majors last season. The others: Pascual & Melido Perez, Mike & Greg Maddux. Don't you just know that the Niekros root against all of them? ... His second-inning ERA was the same as his first-inning ERA (one earned run in 15 innings). He posted a 1.98 ERA over the first four innings of his starts, but an 8.45 ERA from the fifth inning on.... Oldest rookie pitcher to appear in at least 25 games last season. He was born in April 1963, almost four months before veteran Jose Oquendo.... One of only four A.L. rookie pitchers to post winning records last season (minimum: 10 decisions). Others: Mike Timlin (11–6), Jose Guzman (10–3), and Kevin Morton (6–5).... Averaged 6.88 strikeouts per nine innings, good enough to rank 21st among 135 major league pitchers with at least 100 innings last season. But on the Tigers' put-the-ball-in-play pitching staff, that rate was Koufaxian. Consider the strikeout rates of their other starters: Frank Tanana, 4.43, to rank 111th; Bill Gullickson, 3.62, to rank 126th; Walt Terrell, 3.29, to rank 134th.... Of course, the Tigers pitchers never got to face the greatest assemblage of strikeout batters seen in some time—namely, the Tigers hitters. In a city consumed by the balance-of-trade deficit, the 446-strikeout difference between the strikeouts by Detroit hitters (1185) and Detroit pitchers (739) represented the greatest balance-of-strikeout deficit in major league history.

Kirk McCaskill — Throws Right

California Angels	W-L	ERA	AB	H	HR	BB	SO	BA	SA	OBA
Season	10-19	4.26	681	193	19	66	71	.283	.435	.347
vs. Left-Handers			351	110	11	22	24	.313	.467	.355
vs. Right-Handers			330	83	8	44	47	.252	.400	.338
vs. Ground-Ballers			332	87	5	23	28	.262	.358	.311
vs. Fly-Ballers			349	106	14	43	43	.304	.507	.378
Home Games	4-10	4.08	347	94	9	27	38	.271	.415	.320
Road Games	6-9	4.45	334	99	10	39	33	.296	.455	.373
Grass Fields	7-17	4.10	566	155	15	56	55	.274	.415	.339
Artificial Turf	3-2	5.08	115	38	4	10	16	.330	.530	.383
April	2-2	2.84	93	20	3	14	12	.215	.366	.318
May	3-3	4.09	131	37	5	10	12	.282	.473	.338
June	2-4	3.76	145	41	2	14	20	.283	.407	.344
July	1-4	4.19	144	40	2	12	12	.278	.347	.329
August	2-4	6.23	122	41	5	12	8	.336	.557	.387
Sept./Oct.	0-2	4.50	46	14	2	4	7	.304	.500	.385
Leading Off Inn.			166	47	7	19	13	.283	.464	.357
Bases Empty			390	107	10	44	34	.274	.413	.349
Runners On			291	86	9	22	37	.296	.464	.343
Runners/Scor. Pos.			157	42	5	18	25	.268	.446	.335
Runners On/2 Out			122	34	3	11	17	.279	.426	.343
Scor. Pos./2 Out			73	19	3	10	11	.260	.466	.357
Late-Inning Pressure			35	7	2	3	4	.200	.371	.263
Leading Off			11	3	1	0	1	.273	.545	.273
Runners On			10	2	1	0	2	.200	.500	.200
Runners/Scor. Pos.			1	1	1	0	0	1.000	4.000	1.000
First 9 Batters			239	62	3	27	24	.259	.360	.336
Second 9 Batters			238	74	9	20	21	.311	.500	.360
All Batters Thereafter			204	57	7	19	26	.279	.446	.344

Loves to face: Jerry Browne (.056, 1-for-18, 3 BB)
Tony Pena (.059, 1-for-17)
John Shelby (0-for-10)
Hates to face: Jose Canseco (.324, 12-for-37, 4 HR)
Kirk Gibson (.526, 10-for-19, 4 HR)
Lance Parrish (.462, 6-for-13, 1 2B, 3 HR)

Miscellaneous statistics: Ground outs-to-air outs ratio: 1.74 last season, 5th highest in A.L.; 1.20 for career.... Induced 22 double plays in 131 opportunities (one per 6.0), 5th-best rate in A.L.... Allowed 36 doubles, 5 triples in 177⅔ innings.... Allowed 10 first-inning runs in 30 starts (1.80 ERA, 4th lowest in A.L.).... Batting support: 2.93 runs per start, lowest average in majors.... Opposing base stealers: 8-for-14 (57%); 1 pickoff, 0 balks.

Comments: Became the majors' fifth 19-game loser since Brian Kingman last broke the 20-game barrier in 1980. Like several others, McCaskill went out wimping. He lost his 18th game on Sept. 4, but took the mound only once after that (Sept. 27). Among the other 19-game losers since 1980 (Jose DeLeon, 1985 & 1990; Matt Young, 1985; Mike Moore, 1987; Tim Leary, 1990), only Moore took it like a man and started a game after his 19th loss, winning his last two starts to raise his record to 9-19.... Despite 19 losses, McCaskill was undefeated against the three clubs with the best records in the league last season: the Twins (2-0), Blue Jays (1-0), and White Sox (1-0).... May have been the unluckiest pitcher in the majors last season, with the Angels scoring fewer than three runs in 17 of his 30 starts; he had a record of 2-14 in those 17 starts.... One of three major league pitchers to start at least 30 games without lasting longer than eight innings in any of them. The others: Ron Darling (32) and Rich DeLucia (31).... His high ground outs-to-air outs ratio helped the Angels staff lead A.L. in that department with a 1.29 GAR. But in a year in which McCaskill greatly increased his tendency to throw ground balls, the anomaly is that his home-run rate was his highest in four years. He allowed nine homers in 174⅓ innings in 1990 (one every 19.4 innings), and 19 in 177⅔ innings last season (one every 9.4 innings).

Ben McDonald — Throws Right

Baltimore Orioles	W-L	ERA	AB	H	HR	BB	SO	BA	SA	OBA
Season	6-8	4.84	483	126	16	43	85	.261	.418	.321
vs. Left-Handers			256	55	8	26	50	.215	.348	.285
vs. Right-Handers			227	71	8	17	35	.313	.498	.362
vs. Ground-Ballers			223	66	7	21	37	.296	.457	.357
vs. Fly-Ballers			260	60	9	22	48	.231	.385	.290
Home Games	2-4	3.70	276	75	6	12	50	.272	.399	.302
Road Games	4-4	6.41	207	51	10	31	35	.246	.444	.343
Grass Fields	5-8	4.75	419	110	12	38	75	.263	.408	.323
Artificial Turf	1-0	5.51	64	16	4	5	10	.250	.484	.304
April	0-1	12.27	35	15	1	4	4	.429	.686	.487
May	2-2	5.47	91	18	3	12	15	.198	.374	.288
June	0-0	0.00	0	0	0	0	0	.000	.000	.000
July	2-2	4.66	149	39	8	10	31	.262	.456	.311
August	1-3	3.80	160	43	2	16	24	.269	.363	.333
Sept./Oct.	1-0	3.46	48	11	2	1	11	.229	.375	.245
Leading Off Inn.			124	24	3	9	24	.194	.355	.248
Bases Empty			307	69	9	25	58	.225	.362	.283
Runners On			176	57	7	18	27	.324	.517	.384
Runners/Scor. Pos.			88	28	3	16	18	.318	.511	.411
Runners On/2 Out			76	23	2	10	11	.303	.434	.384
Scor. Pos./2 Out			40	15	1	8	7	.375	.550	.479
Late-Inning Pressure			30	7	2	3	6	.233	.500	.303
Leading Off			10	2	0	0	3	.200	.300	.200
Runners On			7	4	1	0	0	.571	1.143	.571
Runners/Scor. Pos.			3	2	0	0	0	.667	.667	.667
First 9 Batters			170	41	6	16	27	.241	.418	.307
Second 9 Batters			156	42	2	16	35	.269	.365	.335
All Batters Thereafter			157	43	8	11	23	.274	.471	.321

Loves to face: Greg Brock (0-for-7)
Pete O'Brien (0-for-7)
Lance Parrish (0-for-11)
Hates to face: Rickey Henderson (.500, 6-for-12, 2 HR)
Matt Nokes (.571, 4-for-7, 1 2B, 2 HR)
John Olerud (.357, 5-for-14, 2 HR)

Miscellaneous statistics: Ground outs-to-air outs ratio: 0.96 last season, 0.94 for career.... Induced 11 double plays in 73 opportunities (one per 6.6).... Allowed 22 doubles, 3 triples in 126⅓ innings.... Allowed 14 first-inning runs in 21 starts (5.57 ERA).... Batting support: 4.67 runs per start.... Opposing base stealers: 14-for-17 (82%); 1 pickoff, 0 balks.

Comments: Won the first five starts of his major league career in 1990, but made 21 starts without winning two of them in a row in 1991.... Averaged more than a full inning less per start last season (6.02) than he did in 1990 (7.26).... His 4.84 ERA is not a pretty sight, but understand that the final figure was the *lowest* that his ERA stood at any time last season. Orioles finished with highest ERA in A.L. for the second time in the last four years after playing their first 34 years in Baltimore without that indignity.... One of seven right-handed pitchers in the majors last season against whom right-handed batters hit above .300 (minimum: 200 AB). Of those seven, only Tim Leary (.322) allowed a higher average than McDonald. In 252⅓ innings in the majors, right-handed batters have hit .275, lefties only .200.... Why was this man smiling at the closing of Memorial Stadium? Opponents had a career batting average of .249 against him there, .217 on the road.... Opponents have a career average of .269 with runners on base, .217 with the bases empty.... Has faced over 1000 batters in his major league career, but has hit only one with a pitch. At least he picked on a guy his own size—Jose Canseco.... The amateur draft of 1989 produced two major leaguers within three months: McDonald and John Olerud. But in only two years, a few other players from that draft have made names for themselves: Scott Erickson, Chuck Knoblauch, Frank Thomas, Mo Vaughn, and Jeff Bagwell. Pretty talented group.

Jack McDowell Throws Right

Chicago White Sox	W-L	ERA	AB	H	HR	BB	SO	BA	SA	OBA
Season	17-10	3.41	930	212	19	82	191	.228	.347	.292
vs. Left-Handers			485	109	7	42	84	.225	.324	.289
vs. Right-Handers			445	103	12	40	107	.231	.373	.295
vs. Ground-Ballers			478	109	5	39	88	.228	.328	.288
vs. Fly-Ballers			452	103	14	43	103	.228	.367	.297
Home Games	10-6	3.89	524	134	12	48	101	.256	.382	.318
Road Games	7-4	2.82	406	78	7	34	90	.192	.303	.260
Grass Fields	15-8	3.22	827	186	17	76	177	.225	.346	.292
Artificial Turf	2-2	5.00	103	26	2	6	14	.252	.359	.295
April	4-1	2.97	130	24	4	13	31	.185	.308	.259
May	1-2	5.08	157	47	4	20	32	.299	.465	.379
June	4-1	2.01	169	28	1	14	33	.166	.225	.228
July	4-1	2.59	149	31	3	7	26	.208	.315	.245
August	2-3	3.98	161	42	2	11	35	.261	.398	.318
Sept./Oct.	2-2	4.06	164	40	5	17	34	.244	.372	.315
Leading Off Inn.			244	49	5	18	55	.201	.320	.259
Bases Empty			577	117	9	52	123	.203	.300	.272
Runners On			353	95	10	30	68	.269	.425	.325
Runners/Scor. Pos.			193	52	4	20	42	.269	.404	.335
Runners On/2 Out			152	36	6	12	34	.237	.408	.293
Scor. Pos./2 Out			94	22	2	10	21	.234	.362	.308
Late-Inning Pressure			77	17	1	8	19	.221	.338	.294
Leading Off			23	6	1	1	4	.261	.522	.292
Runners On			28	7	0	3	8	.250	.321	.323
Runners/Scor. Pos.			15	5	0	2	4	.333	.467	.412
First 9 Batters			277	54	5	33	57	.195	.300	.284
Second 9 Batters			281	75	5	21	60	.267	.388	.319
All Batters Thereafter			372	83	9	28	74	.223	.352	.278

Loves to face: Darryl Hamilton (.118, 2-for-17)
Mickey Tettleton (0-for-13, 9 SO)
Walter Weiss (.059, 1-for-17)

Hates to face: Chuck Knoblauch (.667, 6-for-9)
Joe Orsulak (.474, 9-for-19, 2 HR)
Jody Reed (.600, 9-for-15)

Miscellaneous statistics: Ground outs-to-air outs ratio: 0.80 last season, 0.93 for career.... Induced 12 double plays in 165 opportunities (one per 14), 5th-worst rate in A.L.... Allowed 44 doubles, 5 triples in 253⅔ innings.... Allowed 15 first-inning runs in 35 starts (3.86 ERA).... Batting support: 5.09 runs per start, 5th-highest average in A.L.... Opposing base stealers: 22-for-32 (69%); 8 pickoffs, 1 balk.

Comments: Youngest A.L. pitcher to start on opening day last season, and the White Sox' sixth different opening-day starter in the last six years.... He should treat his teammates the same way quarterbacks treat their offensive linemen and buy them watches at the end of the year (Rolexes, no doubt). Besides being supported with more than five runs per outing, McDowell was charged with only one unearned run all season.... Made 78 major league starts before pitching his first shutout on June 25, then threw back-to-back shutouts in September.... His eight pickoffs tied him with Jack Armstrong for major league lead among right-handed pitchers.... Will any pitcher ever again reach the 300-inning mark in a season? Consider this: McDowell tied for the A.L. lead in starts (35) and led the league in complete games (15) and still only accumulated 253⅔ innings, second in A.L. behind Roger Clemens (271⅓). The last 300-inning man in the majors (maybe forever): Steve Carlton in 1980.... Rate of walks per nine innings has decreased in each of his full seasons in the majors: 3.86, 3.38, 2.91.... Has issued only two intentional walks over the last two years; he purposely passed Wade Boggs twice in one game last May.... Opponents have a career batting average of .217 in day games, .242 at night. You would think it would be the other way around, given his rock-star reputation.... His R.E.M. style was a pleasant surprise, considering some of the other musical acts that athletes have foisted on us. Anyone for some old Smokin' Joe Frazier tunes?

Jose Mesa Throws Right

Baltimore Orioles	W-L	ERA	AB	H	HR	BB	SO	BA	SA	OBA
Season	6-11	5.97	492	151	11	62	64	.307	.449	.385
vs. Left-Handers			258	78	4	34	23	.302	.407	.380
vs. Right-Handers			234	73	7	28	41	.312	.496	.390
vs. Ground-Ballers			227	64	3	26	30	.282	.370	.357
vs. Fly-Ballers			265	87	8	36	34	.328	.517	.408
Home Games	2-8	5.68	227	67	4	34	32	.295	.405	.385
Road Games	4-3	6.23	265	84	7	28	32	.317	.487	.385
Grass Fields	5-10	5.58	402	121	8	50	57	.301	.428	.378
Artificial Turf	1-1	7.77	90	30	3	12	7	.333	.544	.417
April	1-3	3.33	89	22	1	11	17	.247	.360	.330
May	3-2	4.47	171	48	3	22	15	.281	.404	.363
June	0-3	11.84	87	35	3	11	8	.402	.609	.475
July	0-0	0.00	0	0	0	0	0	.000	.000	.000
August	1-0	5.54	48	10	3	4	12	.208	.396	.278
Sept./Oct.	1-3	7.04	97	36	1	14	12	.371	.495	.446
Leading Off Inn.			123	42	5	14	9	.341	.496	.409
Bases Empty			271	77	5	35	30	.284	.395	.370
Runners On			221	74	6	27	34	.335	.516	.403
Runners/Scor. Pos.			122	43	4	19	18	.352	.557	.428
Runners On/2 Out			89	22	2	10	20	.247	.360	.323
Scor. Pos./2 Out			55	13	2	7	11	.236	.400	.323
Late-Inning Pressure			7	2	0	1	0	.286	.429	.375
Leading Off			2	0	0	1	0	.000	.000	.333
Runners On			2	1	0	0	0	.500	.500	.500
Runners/Scor. Pos.			2	1	0	0	0	.500	.500	.500
First 9 Batters			175	50	3	27	25	.286	.400	.382
Second 9 Batters			165	56	7	19	23	.339	.570	.412
All Batters Thereafter			152	45	1	16	16	.296	.375	.359

Loves to face: Mike Greenwell (.111, 2-for-18)
Edgar Martinez (0-for-8)
Matt Nokes (0-for-12)

Hates to face: Wade Boggs (.556, 10-for-18)
Kevin Maas (.700, 7-for-10)
Danny Tartabull (.833, 5-for-6, 3 2B)

Miscellaneous statistics: Ground outs-to-air outs ratio: 0.90 last season, 0.92 for career.... Induced 9 double plays in 113 opportunities (one per 13).... Allowed 33 doubles, 2 triples in 123⅔ innings.... Allowed 20 first-inning runs in 23 starts (7.83 ERA, 4th highest in A.L.).... Batting support: 4.87 runs per start.... Opposing base stealers: 12-for-17 (71%); 0 pickoffs, 0 balks.

Comments: Allowed 15.72 base runners per nine innings, the 3d-highest rate among A.L. pitchers last season (minimum: 100 IP). Only Wade Taylor (15.78) and Tim Leary (15.74) had higher rates.... Battery breakdown: 4.31 ERA, with base stealers successful in seven of 12 attempts in 77⅓ innings with Chris Hoiles; 8.54 ERA, with base stealers 4-for-4 in 39 innings with Bob Melvin.... One of three Orioles starters with a first-inning ERA above 7.00. The others: Jeff Robinson (12.23), Dave Johnson (7.71), and Jeff Ballard (8.31). No team allowed more first-inning runs than Baltimore (134).... Walked 19 batters during the first inning. His rate of walks in the opening frame was 2d highest in the majors, behind Bobby Witt's.... Opponents batted .352 with runners in scoring position, the 4th-highest mark in the A.L. (minimum: 100 AB), but not the highest on the Orioles. See the Greg Hibbard comments for the top five.... Opponents have a career average of .326 with runners in scoring position, compared to a .273 average in other at-bats.... This guy led the Southern League in innings pitched in 1987, then underwent surgery on his throwing elbow twice over the next two years limiting him to 38 innings. But when he returned from a 15-day stay on the disabled list with an inflammation of that elbow, he pitched a three-hit victory over Texas for one of his two complete games in 35 career starts.

Bob Milacki — Throws Right

Baltimore Orioles	W-L	ERA	AB	H	HR	BB	SO	BA	SA	OBA
Season	10-9	4.01	692	175	17	53	108	.253	.383	.305
vs. Left-Handers			360	92	5	28	56	.256	.350	.307
vs. Right-Handers			332	83	12	25	52	.250	.419	.303
vs. Ground-Ballers			351	89	2	21	47	.254	.336	.296
vs. Fly-Ballers			341	86	15	32	61	.252	.431	.314
Home Games	4-4	5.16	333	98	10	18	50	.294	.450	.328
Road Games	6-5	3.05	359	77	7	35	58	.214	.320	.285
Grass Fields	8-6	4.04	558	143	14	46	83	.256	.384	.311
Artificial Turf	2-3	3.89	134	32	3	7	25	.239	.381	.278
April	1-0	0.00	16	1	0	2	1	.063	.063	.167
May	0-2	5.48	85	25	5	12	10	.294	.494	.378
June	3-0	3.52	144	37	1	11	26	.257	.361	.310
July	2-3	4.91	117	24	2	10	17	.205	.333	.269
August	2-2	3.51	160	43	7	5	23	.269	.456	.291
Sept./Oct.	2-2	4.00	170	45	2	13	31	.265	.341	.314
Leading Off Inn.			178	53	7	14	26	.298	.472	.352
Bases Empty			418	103	11	33	67	.246	.380	.303
Runners On			274	72	6	20	41	.263	.387	.308
Runners/Scor. Pos.			136	45	4	14	23	.331	.478	.381
Runners On/2 Out			102	26	3	11	14	.255	.402	.327
Scor. Pos./2 Out			55	14	1	8	9	.255	.364	.349
Late-Inning Pressure			46	9	2	6	4	.196	.391	.288
Leading Off			14	3	1	4	2	.214	.500	.389
Runners On			12	1	0	1	1	.083	.167	.154
Runners/Scor. Pos.			4	1	0	1	0	.250	.500	.400
First 9 Batters			244	65	5	27	40	.266	.381	.339
Second 9 Batters			244	59	5	10	41	.242	.357	.268
All Batters Thereafter			204	51	7	16	27	.250	.417	.305

Loves to face: Sandy Alomar, Jr. (0-for-10)
Gary Pettis (0-for-11, 7 SO)
Alan Trammell (.077, 2-for-26, 5 BB)

Hates to face: George Brett (.458, 11-for-24)
Carlos Martinez (.500, 9-for-18, 5 2B, 1 HR)
Rafael Palmeiro (.583, 7-for-12, 1 HR)

Miscellaneous statistics: Ground outs-to-air outs ratio: 1.25 last season, 1.10 for career.... Induced 18 double plays in 148 opportunities (one per 8.2).... Allowed 39 doubles, 0 triples in 184 innings.... Allowed 17 first-inning runs in 26 starts (5.61 ERA).... Batting support: 4.04 runs per start.... Opposing base stealers: 12-for-18 (67%); 0 pickoffs, 2 balks.

Comments: Walked more batters than he struck out in 1990, but had more than twice as many strikeouts as walks last season. His rate of walks per nine innings dropped from 4.06 to 2.59; his strikeout rate rose from 3.99 to 5.28. The last pitcher to both increase his strikeout rate and decrease his walk rate by at least 1.25 in the same season was Mark Langston in 1986 (minimum: 100 IP both seasons).... Orioles starters averaged only 5.56 innings per game, 2d-lowest mark in the A.L., but Milacki was one of Baltimore's marathoners, with an average of 6.26 innings per start, second on the team to Mike Mussina (7.26).... Home-game ERA was the highest of any regular A.L. starter.... Ended the season with 43 consecutive innings without allowing a home run, the longest streak of his career.... Career record of 10–2 during September, 21–27 in all other months combined.... Opponents have a career batting average of .221 in day games, .261 at night.... Career records of 5–0 vs. New York, 0–3 vs. Boston.... Has pitched eight complete games in 89 career starts, five for shutouts.... Allowed six triples in 1989, but none since. Among pitchers who didn't allow a triple in either 1990 or 1991, none faced even half as many batters as Milacki did during that time (1352). That's likely to change at Camden Yards.

Jeff Montgomery — Throws Right

Kansas City Royals	W-L	ERA	AB	H	HR	BB	SO	BA	SA	OBA
Season	4-4	2.90	338	83	6	28	77	.246	.355	.305
vs. Left-Handers			168	44	4	15	33	.262	.399	.323
vs. Right-Handers			170	39	2	13	44	.229	.312	.288
vs. Ground-Ballers			144	34	1	14	29	.236	.313	.304
vs. Fly-Ballers			194	49	5	14	48	.253	.387	.307
Home Games	3-3	3.44	191	49	4	12	46	.257	.377	.306
Road Games	1-1	2.23	147	34	2	16	31	.231	.327	.305
Grass Fields	1-1	2.01	115	27	2	10	21	.235	.322	.296
Artificial Turf	3-3	3.38	223	56	4	18	56	.251	.372	.310
April	1-1	1.74	40	9	1	0	13	.225	.375	.225
May	0-1	4.91	58	15	0	6	14	.259	.310	.328
June	0-2	6.27	78	28	3	6	11	.359	.538	.405
July	0-0	1.59	64	16	0	6	15	.250	.297	.314
August	2-0	0.68	47	8	0	4	11	.170	.255	.250
Sept./Oct.	1-0	1.13	51	7	2	6	13	.137	.275	.228
Leading Off Inn.			67	16	2	8	12	.239	.418	.320
Bases Empty			160	41	3	15	33	.256	.400	.324
Runners On			178	42	3	13	44	.236	.315	.289
Runners/Scor. Pos.			122	27	2	9	31	.221	.295	.276
Runners On/2 Out			85	24	1	10	22	.282	.329	.365
Scor. Pos./2 Out			62	16	0	7	17	.258	.258	.343
Late-Inning Pressure			249	59	4	19	54	.237	.325	.294
Leading Off			52	13	2	4	10	.250	.423	.304
Runners On			130	29	2	9	30	.223	.292	.275
Runners/Scor. Pos.			85	19	2	7	21	.224	.318	.284
First 9 Batters			309	74	4	27	73	.239	.337	.303
Second 9 Batters			29	9	2	1	4	.310	.552	.333
All Batters Thereafter			0	0	0	0	0	—	—	—

Loves to face: Jesse Barfield (0-for-8)
Dave Henderson (0-for-7, 4 SO)
Dave Winfield (0-for-7, 4 SO)

Hates to face: Scott Bradley (.400, 4-for-10, 1 HR)
Kent Hrbek (.500, 5-for-10, 1 HR)
Kirby Puckett (.429, 6-for-14)

Miscellaneous statistics: Ground outs-to-air outs ratio: 1.54 last season, 1.21 for career.... Induced 7 double plays in 64 opportunities (one per 9.1).... Allowed 15 doubles, 2 triples in 90 innings.... Saved 33 games in 41 opportunities (80%).... Stranded 24 inherited runners, allowed 17 to score (59%).... Opposing base stealers: 4-for-4 (100%); 0 pickoffs, 0 balks.

Comments: Made his major league debut on August 1, 1987, in relief of Bill Scherrer, who had taken over for Bill Gullickson. What team was it? Answer below.... ERA of 2.44 with Kansas City is lowest in Royals history among pitchers with at least 300 innings.... His percentage of inherited runners stranded (59%) was the worst among the nine A.L. pitchers to save at least 30 games last season. He was credited with saves in five games in which he allowed inherited runners to score.... How often do you see a relief pitcher allow three home runs in the same game, at Royals Stadium no less? That's what Montgomery did on June 23; the sluggers were Chris Hoiles, Tim Hulett, and Brady Anderson. (Hoiles and Hulett were the only right-handed batters to homer against Montgomery for the season.)... No runners were caught stealing with him on the mound last season, and only four attempted to steal. Opponents were 14-for-17 in 1990.... Opponents' batting average has increased in each of the last two seasons (.198, .228, .246) while Montgomery's strikeout rate has decreased (9.20 per nine innings, 8.97, 7.70).... Collected eight of his 33 saves against the Brewers.... Career batting average of .255 by opposing left-handed batters, .208 by opposing right-handers.... Has made 258 consecutive appearances in relief since his only career start in 1987.... Montgomery pitched for the Cincinnati Reds in 1987 (14 appearances, including that sole start).

Mike Moore

Throws Right

Oakland A's	W-L	ERA	AB	H	HR	BB	SO	BA	SA	OBA
Season	17-8	2.96	768	176	11	105	153	.229	.318	.324
vs. Left-Handers			394	90	4	56	65	.228	.307	.322
vs. Right-Handers			374	86	7	49	88	.230	.329	.327
vs. Ground-Ballers			352	82	4	44	60	.233	.315	.319
vs. Fly-Ballers			416	94	7	61	93	.226	.320	.328
Home Games	11-3	2.14	415	81	6	54	81	.195	.277	.291
Road Games	6-5	4.00	353	95	5	51	72	.269	.365	.363
Grass Fields	14-8	3.00	644	147	10	91	122	.228	.321	.327
Artificial Turf	3-0	2.73	124	29	1	14	31	.234	.298	.312
April	3-0	2.52	92	24	0	14	16	.261	.283	.358
May	4-2	6.06	133	39	3	19	24	.293	.406	.383
June	2-4	3.09	164	33	2	27	29	.201	.287	.314
July	0-1	2.40	49	9	1	10	10	.184	.265	.344
August	3-1	2.61	155	37	4	11	36	.239	.374	.289
Sept./Oct.	5-0	1.46	175	34	1	24	38	.194	.263	.294
Leading Off Inn.			192	42	5	30	40	.219	.333	.327
Bases Empty			448	101	10	58	98	.225	.337	.320
Runners On			320	75	1	47	55	.234	.291	.331
Runners/Scor. Pos.			181	38	0	33	34	.210	.260	.329
Runners On/2 Out			127	24	0	20	23	.189	.213	.299
Scor. Pos./2 Out			92	15	0	15	17	.163	.185	.280
Late-Inning Pressure			44	14	0	6	9	.318	.386	.412
Leading Off			14	6	0	4	3	.429	.500	.556
Runners On			17	5	0	2	3	.294	.353	.400
Runners/Scor. Pos.			9	3	0	1	2	.333	.444	.455
First 9 Batters			265	57	3	28	63	.215	.294	.294
Second 9 Batters			242	53	3	45	45	.219	.293	.341
All Batters Thereafter			261	66	5	32	45	.253	.364	.338

Loves to face: Brady Anderson (.059, 1-for-17, 2 BB)
Paul Molitor (.159, 7-for-44)
Gary Pettis (.152, 10-for-66)

Hates to face: Rob Deer (.371, 13-for-35, 4 HR)
Mike Greenwell (.565, 13-for-23, 0 SO)
Dan Pasqua (.423, 22-for-52, 2 HR)

Miscellaneous statistics: Ground outs-to-air outs ratio: 1.42 last season, 1.27 for career.... Induced 19 double plays in 178 opportunities (one per 9.4).... Allowed 35 doubles, 0 triples in 210 innings.... Allowed 14 first-inning runs in 33 starts (3.82 ERA).... Batting support: 3.97 runs per start, 10th-lowest average in A.L.... Opposing base stealers: 19-for-31 (61%); 0 pickoffs, 0 balks.

Comments: Good enough to accumulate 100 victories, but not good enough to have a winning record for his career. Only four other active pitchers meet those specifications: Pascual Perez (114–115), Walt Terrell (104–114), Danny Darwin (114–115), and Jim Clancy (140–167). There are 90 other pitchers in major league history who have done that, but only two reached 200 wins: Jack Powell (246–255) and Bobo Newsom (211–222).... Returned from a 17-day stint on the disabled list on August 6, then compiled an 8–1 record with a 1.99 ERA over his last 13 starts. He led the A.L. with a 1.99 ERA after the All-Star break, and his Sept./Oct. ERA of 1.46 was the best in the majors, as was his ERA in home games (2.14). Only Jack Morris won more home games than Moore.... Among A.L. pitchers, only Randy Johnson had a higher rate of walks to batters leading off innings (one per 7.4 innings). That's been a career-long problem for Moore; he's walked an average of 19 leadoff batters per season during his 10-year career.... Held opponents to nine hits in their last 80 at-bats with runners in scoring position (.113).... Walks per nine innings year by year since 1988: 2.48, 3.09, 3.79, 4.50. The only other pitcher with an increase of at least one-half walk per nine innings in three consecutive seasons of 30 starts was Bob Caruthers, exactly 100 years earlier.... Has started at least 32 games in each of the last eight seasons. Only one other pitcher has a current streak that long: Frank Viola (nine years).... Hasn't balked in 651 innings over three seasons with the A's.

Jack Morris

Throws Right

Minnesota Twins	W-L	ERA	AB	H	HR	BB	SO	BA	SA	OBA
Season	18-12	3.43	922	226	18	92	163	.245	.347	.315
vs. Left-Handers			456	128	9	58	63	.281	.393	.359
vs. Right-Handers			466	98	9	34	100	.210	.303	.269
vs. Ground-Ballers			417	106	7	36	58	.254	.341	.314
vs. Fly-Ballers			505	120	11	56	105	.238	.352	.315
Home Games	13-3	3.31	495	120	7	42	85	.242	.337	.304
Road Games	5-9	3.57	427	106	11	50	78	.248	.358	.326
Grass Fields	4-9	3.88	395	100	11	47	74	.253	.370	.332
Artificial Turf	14-3	3.10	527	126	7	45	89	.239	.330	.301
April	2-3	5.34	131	42	1	16	25	.321	.397	.397
May	3-2	3.80	157	36	4	23	28	.229	.382	.324
June	6-0	2.25	169	36	3	15	25	.213	.290	.276
July	2-2	5.20	105	28	4	7	17	.267	.429	.316
August	2-3	3.83	174	45	3	13	33	.259	.345	.316
Sept./Oct.	3-2	1.74	186	39	3	18	35	.210	.290	.278
Leading Off Inn.			235	58	3	18	41	.247	.340	.303
Bases Empty			556	137	8	47	106	.246	.345	.309
Runners On			366	89	10	45	57	.243	.350	.323
Runners/Scor. Pos.			214	57	9	33	37	.266	.407	.358
Runners On/2 Out			165	45	6	25	28	.273	.418	.372
Scor. Pos./2 Out			113	33	6	20	15	.292	.478	.403
Late-Inning Pressure			98	27	1	10	16	.276	.367	.343
Leading Off			29	6	0	3	4	.207	.241	.281
Runners On			31	9	1	5	5	.290	.387	.389
Runners/Scor. Pos.			18	6	1	4	3	.333	.500	.455
First 9 Batters			291	75	5	19	50	.258	.337	.306
Second 9 Batters			268	63	7	32	40	.235	.347	.318
All Batters Thereafter			363	88	6	41	73	.242	.355	.319

Loves to face: Mike Devereaux (.067, 1-for-15)
Von Hayes (.067, 1-for-15)
Randy Milligan (.067, 1-for-15, 1 2B)

Hates to face: Wade Boggs (.365, 27-for-74)
George Brett (.333, 25-for-75, 5 HR)
Kent Hrbek (.293, 22-for-75, 7 HR)

Miscellaneous statistics: Ground outs-to-air outs ratio: 1.15 last season, 1.13 for career.... Induced 23 double plays in 168 opportunities (one per 7.3).... Allowed 28 doubles, 6 triples in 246⅔ innings.... Allowed 27 first-inning runs in 35 starts (5.91 ERA).... Batting support: 4.83 runs per start.... Opposing base stealers: 32-for-40 (80%), most steals in A.L.; 0 pickoffs, 1 balk.

Comments: Became the second pitcher to start on opening day, the All-Star Game, an L.C.S. opener, and the World Series opener. The other was Dave Stewart (1989).... His 12th consecutive opening-day start tied a record shared by Robin Roberts (1950–61) and Tom Seaver (1968–79). Steve Carlton started 14 of 15 openers for the Phillies from 1972 through 1986; Jim Kaat started their '76 opener.... His 10-inning complete-game win in the World Series finale broke a string of 30 consecutive incomplete games by Twins pitchers in postseason play. The Reds have a current streak of 29 straight postseason games in which they've used their bullpen.... Has thrown at least nine complete games in each of the last 13 seasons. Talk about a dying art—no pitcher has had a streak that long since Steve Carlton (1967–82); and the last A.L. pitcher with a 13-year streak was Detroit's Tommy Bridges (1931–43).... Led the majors with 13 victories in home games; in his 14 years with Detroit, he never won more than 11 games at Tiger Stadium. But his nine road losses tied him for 2d most in the league.... Has started an A.L.-record 431 games since his last relief appearance, but the major league record for consecutive starting assignments belongs to Nolan Ryan—555 games across two leagues and still going.... Batting average by opposing right-handers was his lowest in any full season in the majors, and the lowest of any A.L. starter last season.... Needs 84 wins to reach 300, but only 10 pitchers in major league history won that many games after their 37th birthdays, including two active pitchers: Nolan Ryan and Charlie Hough.

Kevin Morton
Throws Left

Boston Red Sox	W-L	ERA	AB	H	HR	BB	SO	BA	SA	OBA
Season	6-5	4.59	328	93	9	40	45	.284	.448	.356
vs. Left-Handers			41	11	2	6	8	.268	.463	.375
vs. Right-Handers			287	82	7	34	37	.286	.446	.354
vs. Ground-Ballers			145	47	1	15	13	.324	.421	.380
vs. Fly-Ballers			183	46	8	25	32	.251	.470	.338
Home Games	4-2	4.91	173	52	7	21	29	.301	.509	.376
Road Games	2-3	4.25	155	41	2	19	16	.265	.381	.335
Grass Fields	5-4	5.00	260	72	9	30	39	.277	.465	.348
Artificial Turf	1-1	3.00	68	21	0	10	6	.309	.382	.387
April	0-0	—	0	0	0	0	0	—	—	—
May	0-0	—	0	0	0	0	0	—	—	—
June	0-0	—	0	0	0	0	0	—	—	—
July	2-2	6.00	99	31	4	12	17	.313	.535	.386
August	1-1	2.88	89	22	1	11	13	.247	.337	.327
Sept./Oct.	3-2	4.82	140	40	4	17	15	.286	.457	.354
Leading Off Inn.			83	27	5	9	7	.325	.578	.391
Bases Empty			192	59	7	15	22	.307	.505	.361
Runners On			136	34	2	25	23	.250	.368	.351
Runners/Scor. Pos.			69	19	1	19	12	.275	.406	.400
Runners On/2 Out			55	17	2	8	11	.309	.491	.397
Scor. Pos./2 Out			32	10	1	7	6	.313	.500	.436
Late-Inning Pressure			2	1	1	0	0	.500	2.000	.500
Leading Off			1	0	0	0	0	.000	.000	.000
Runners On			0	0	0	0	0	—	—	—
Runners/Scor. Pos.			0	0	0	0	0	—	—	—
First 9 Batters			120	40	4	16	14	.333	.517	.407
Second 9 Batters			108	24	0	12	17	.222	.287	.298
All Batters Thereafter			100	29	5	12	14	.290	.540	.357

Loves to face: Andy Allanson (0-for-6)
Travis Fryman (0-for-5, 3 SO)
Tony Phillips (.125, 1-for-8)

Hates to face: Juan Gonzales (.667, 2-for-3, 1 2B, 1 HR, 1 SO)
Jim Leyritz (3-for-3)
Shane Mack (4-for-4, 1 BB)

Miscellaneous statistics: Ground outs-to-air outs ratio: 1.03 last season, 1.03 for career.... Induced 9 double plays in 73 opportunities (one per 8.1).... Allowed 23 doubles, 2 triples in 86⅓ innings.... Allowed 13 first-inning runs in 15 starts (5.52 ERA).... Batting support: 6.00 runs per start.... Opposing base stealers: 4-for-6 (67%); 2 pickoffs, 1 balk.

Comments: Rankings for batting support in the section of miscellaneous statistics are based on 20 starts. Morton had the highest run support in the majors among pitchers who started at least 15 games.... Threw a complete-game five-hitter in his major league debut, but didn't reach the ninth inning in any other start. No Boston pitcher has thrown a shutout in his debut since Billy Rohr's near no-hitter against the Yankees in 1967.... Struck out nine batters in his debut, but didn't fan more than four batters in any game after that.... Morton and Mike Gardiner are the fourth pair of Red Sox rookie pitchers in the last 30 years to start at least 15 games each. The others: Roger Clemens and Al Nipper (1984); Lynn McGlothen and John Curtis (1972); Dave Morehead and Bob Heffner (1963).... Selected in the 1989 June free-agent draft as compensation for San Diego's signing of Bruce Hurst.... In a doubleheader on August 13, Cleveland's Charles Nagy started the opener, and Morton started the nightcap. Both are former Big East Pitchers of the Year. The conference is known almost exclusively for its basketball; 32 active NBA players attended Big East schools. But Big East baseball, which started conference play only in 1985, was represented by nine major leaguers last season. Besides Morton (from Seton Hall) and Nagy (Connecticut), they are: Craig Biggio (Seton Hall/Astros), Terry Bross (St. John's/Mets), Roberto Hernandez (Connecticut/White Sox), Rafael Novoa (Villanova/Giants), Wayne Rosenthal (St. John's/Rangers), Gary Scott (Villanova/Cubs), and Mo Vaughn (Seton Hall/Red Sox).

Rob Murphy
Throws Left

Seattle Mariners	W-L	ERA	AB	H	HR	BB	SO	BA	SA	OBA
Season	0-1	3.00	188	47	4	19	34	.250	.410	.322
vs. Left-Handers			74	15	2	1	9	.203	.351	.224
vs. Right-Handers			114	32	2	18	25	.281	.447	.379
vs. Ground-Ballers			86	21	2	6	17	.244	.349	.301
vs. Fly-Ballers			102	26	2	13	17	.255	.461	.339
Home Games	0-0	1.40	93	19	0	10	16	.204	.280	.282
Road Games	0-1	4.84	95	28	4	9	18	.295	.537	.362
Grass Fields	0-1	5.00	76	22	4	7	14	.289	.526	.349
Artificial Turf	0-0	1.80	112	25	0	12	20	.223	.330	.304
April	0-0	1.42	25	7	0	3	3	.280	.480	.357
May	0-0	2.92	46	11	1	3	8	.239	.370	.286
June	0-0	3.09	46	11	2	5	12	.239	.457	.327
July	0-0	2.08	34	7	1	4	5	.206	.324	.289
August	0-0	1.17	29	7	0	2	6	.241	.345	.290
Sept./Oct.	0-1	27.00	8	4	0	2	0	.500	.750	.600
Leading Off Inn.			33	8	2	5	3	.242	.515	.342
Bases Empty			88	18	2	9	13	.205	.330	.286
Runners On			100	29	2	10	21	.290	.480	.355
Runners/Scor. Pos.			64	16	1	9	16	.250	.375	.342
Runners On/2 Out			43	10	0	6	7	.233	.326	.327
Scor. Pos./2 Out			30	6	0	6	6	.200	.233	.333
Late-Inning Pressure			52	12	0	6	10	.231	.269	.310
Leading Off			6	0	0	2	1	.000	.000	.250
Runners On			32	8	0	3	9	.250	.281	.314
Runners/Scor. Pos.			21	4	0	2	7	.190	.190	.261
First 9 Batters			188	47	4	19	34	.250	.410	.322
Second 9 Batters			0	0	0	0	0	—	—	—
All Batters Thereafter			0	0	0	0	0	—	—	—

Loves to face: Bill Doran (0-for-10)
Dale Murphy (0-for-13)
Darryl Strawberry (.100, 1-for-10, 7 SO)

Hates to face: Mark McGwire (.750, 3-for-4, 1 2B, 2 HR, 1 SO)
Kirby Puckett (.571, 4-for-7, 1 HR)
Terry Steinbach (.750, 3-for-4, 1 2B, 1 HR)

Miscellaneous statistics: Ground outs-to-air outs ratio: 0.67 last season, 1.12 for career.... Induced 2 double plays in 40 opportunities (one per 20).... Allowed 12 doubles, 3 triples in 48 innings.... Stranded 19 inherited runners, allowed 15 to score (56%).... Opposing base stealers: 5-for-5 (100%); 0 pickoffs, 0 balks.

Comments: Four years ago, Murphy set a major league record by appearing in 76 games without a victory. In 1990, he made 68 appearances without a win, and last season he was 0-for-57. Since the time of Adam and Eve, only eight men or women have pitched in as many as 57 games in a winless season; no one except Murphy has done it more than once. The list of others: Arnold Earley (57), Dan Osinski (61), and Wes Stock (62) in 1965; Dave Campbell, 1977 (65); Pat Clements, 1986 (65); Tom Henke, 1987 (72); Jeff Innis, 1991 (69).... Started his career with a 14–5 record over three seasons, but has a record of 5–20 since then, including 0–7 over the last two years. He is winless in his last 129 games, the longest streak in major league history.... Compiled a 6.32 ERA in 1990; his highest mark in five other full seasons was 3.08 (1988)—not bad considering that the three ballparks he's called home are Riverfront Stadium, Fenway Park, and the Kingdome, the third-, fourth-, and sixth-best hitters parks on the current list (page 335).... Career batting averages: .221 by opposing left-handed batters, .261 by right-handers.... Opponents have a career batting average of .273 on grass fields, .224 on artificial surfaces.... Has faced 61 batters with the bases loaded but has never walked in a run.... Did you know they played pro ball in Vermont? That's where Murphy made the last start of his career in 1984. He's made 398 appearances in the bigs, all in relief.... Committed two errors in his last 24 games, one more than he made in 374 games before that.

Charles Nagy — Throws Right

Cleveland Indians	W-L	ERA	AB	H	HR	BB	SO	BA	SA	OBA
Season	10-15	4.13	828	228	15	66	109	.275	.403	.330
vs. Left-Handers			460	133	7	37	62	.289	.417	.341
vs. Right-Handers			368	95	8	29	47	.258	.386	.316
vs. Ground-Ballers			404	114	4	29	42	.282	.396	.331
vs. Fly-Ballers			424	114	11	37	67	.269	.410	.329
Home Games	6-5	3.56	360	92	3	25	55	.256	.347	.309
Road Games	4-10	4.59	468	136	12	41	54	.291	.447	.346
Grass Fields	10-10	4.07	673	184	12	49	85	.273	.389	.325
Artificial Turf	0-5	4.38	155	44	3	17	24	.284	.465	.352
April	1-1	1.57	98	19	1	10	17	.194	.265	.266
May	0-4	6.42	136	39	4	15	15	.287	.441	.361
June	2-4	3.41	154	46	1	12	26	.299	.390	.353
July	3-1	1.42	139	34	0	10	9	.245	.338	.291
August	2-1	6.82	139	46	5	12	22	.331	.525	.390
Sept./Oct.	2-4	5.05	162	44	4	7	20	.272	.420	.300
Leading Off Inn.			206	56	3	16	35	.272	.393	.324
Bases Empty			464	132	5	36	68	.284	.399	.336
Runners On			364	96	10	30	41	.264	.409	.323
Runners/Scor. Pos.			208	50	6	21	30	.240	.380	.310
Runners On/2 Out			142	33	3	12	14	.232	.352	.301
Scor. Pos./2 Out			86	18	3	12	11	.209	.349	.320
Late-Inning Pressure			58	16	0	4	7	.276	.310	.323
Leading Off			17	5	0	1	1	.294	.353	.333
Runners On			19	6	0	3	2	.316	.368	.409
Runners/Scor. Pos.			9	2	0	3	1	.222	.222	.417
First 9 Batters			264	83	5	26	38	.314	.466	.376
Second 9 Batters			268	71	6	14	35	.265	.410	.306
All Batters Thereafter			296	74	4	26	36	.250	.341	.310

Loves to face: Rickey Henderson (0-for-9)
Manny Lee (0-for-13)
Pete O'Brien (.071, 1-for-14)

Hates to face: Ken Griffey, Jr. (.455, 5-for-11, 2 2B, 1 3B, 1 HR)
Kelly Gruber (.545, 6-for-11, 3 2B, 2 HR)
Luis Polonia (.750, 6-for-8)

Miscellaneous statistics: Ground outs-to-air outs ratio: 1.47 last season, 1.41 for career.... Induced 22 double plays in 177 opportunities (one per 8.0).... Allowed 45 doubles, 8 triples (3d most in A.L.) in 211⅓ innings.... Allowed 26 first-inning runs in 33 starts (7.09 ERA).... Batting support: 3.24 runs per start, 2d-lowest average in majors.... Opposing base stealers: 23-for-30 (77%); 0 pickoffs, 2 balks.

Comments: Pitched 45⅔ innings in 1990 to barely maintain his rookie status for last season; 50 innings is the maximum. Good thing, too, or it would've been considerably more difficult to fill this space.... Led major league rookie pitchers in games started (33), complete games (6), innings, and losses.... One of four rookies to pitch a shutout last season. The others: Wilson Alvarez (a no-hitter), Mike Remlinger, and Pete Schourek.... Only three Indians rookies pitched more innings over the past 50 years: Dick Tidrow (237 in 1972), Gene Bearden (230 in 1952), and Herb Score (227 in 1955).... Nagy became the third Cleveland rookie to lose as many as 15 games in a season, joining Jim Bagby Sr. (16–16 in 1916) and Tidrow (14–15 in 1972).... His 10 losses in road games were the most of any A.L. pitcher.... Compiled a 1.67 ERA over his first five starts, followed by an 8.03 mark over his next five, and a 1.85 ERA from starts 11 through 15.... His August ERA was the 2d highest in the A.L. (minimum: 30 IP).... Albert Belle may not have turned cartwheels over the new Cleveland Stadium dimensions, but Nagy mustn't have been displeased. He allowed five home runs in 38 innings there in 1990, compared to only three in 93⅔ innings last season.... Was born May 5, 1967, a date associated with one of the greatest trivia questions of all-time: 559 fans attended the White Sox game in Cleveland that night; name them.

Jaime Navarro — Throws Right

Milwaukee Brewers	W-L	ERA	AB	H	HR	BB	SO	BA	SA	OBA
Season	15-12	3.92	908	237	18	73	114	.261	.370	.318
vs. Left-Handers			480	130	13	43	52	.271	.392	.328
vs. Right-Handers			428	107	5	30	62	.250	.346	.305
vs. Ground-Ballers			435	105	2	23	53	.241	.297	.284
vs. Fly-Ballers			473	132	16	50	61	.279	.438	.347
Home Games	9-3	3.58	435	111	7	34	60	.255	.345	.312
Road Games	6-9	4.24	473	126	11	39	54	.266	.393	.323
Grass Fields	13-8	3.63	728	181	14	59	92	.249	.349	.305
Artificial Turf	2-4	5.23	180	56	4	14	22	.311	.456	.367
April	1-0	6.27	78	30	1	7	13	.385	.526	.437
May	4-2	2.59	184	43	3	7	26	.234	.332	.259
June	2-2	4.25	139	35	4	14	18	.252	.381	.316
July	1-4	4.19	176	51	2	15	21	.290	.364	.351
August	4-2	6.03	135	37	4	15	14	.274	.452	.349
Sept./Oct.	3-2	2.53	196	41	4	15	22	.209	.286	.271
Leading Off Inn.			224	54	6	17	38	.241	.357	.303
Bases Empty			528	140	10	37	76	.265	.373	.318
Runners On			380	97	8	36	38	.255	.366	.317
Runners/Scor. Pos.			212	54	5	22	19	.255	.382	.317
Runners On/2 Out			163	42	4	18	19	.258	.411	.335
Scor. Pos./2 Out			103	28	4	13	12	.272	.485	.359
Late-Inning Pressure			99	25	5	8	9	.253	.444	.309
Leading Off			29	6	2	1	4	.207	.448	.233
Runners On			32	7	1	5	3	.219	.344	.308
Runners/Scor. Pos.			16	4	1	2	0	.250	.500	.300
First 9 Batters			281	64	3	23	43	.228	.320	.285
Second 9 Batters			263	69	6	22	31	.262	.376	.325
All Batters Thereafter			364	104	9	28	40	.286	.404	.337

Loves to face: Albert Belle (0-for-9, 5 SO)
Felix Fermin (.071, 1-for-14)
Pete O'Brien (.053, 1-for-19)

Hates to face: Julio Franco (.563, 9-for-16)
Steve Sax (.476, 10-for-21)
Omar Vizquel (.526, 10-for-19)

Miscellaneous statistics: Ground outs-to-air outs ratio: 1.33 last season, 1.23 for career.... Induced 20 double plays in 177 opportunities (one per 8.9).... Allowed 39 doubles, 3 triples in 234 innings.... Allowed 11 first-inning runs in 34 starts (2.91 ERA).... Batting support: 4.59 runs per start.... Opposing base stealers: 23-for-30 (77%); 0 pickoffs, 0 balks.

Comments: Shared third place in the American League in complete games with Jack Morris (10). Only Jack McDowell (15) and Roger Clemens (10) had more.... Only two starting pitchers in the American League had winning records with ERAs higher than Navarro's (minimum: 20 GS): Don August (9–8, 5.40) and Randy Johnson (13–10, 3.98).... Allowed three or fewer earned runs in six of his 12 losses.... Among A.L. pitchers, only Kevin Brown and Jim Abbott recorded more outs on ground balls than Navarro, whose ratio of ground outs to air outs was much higher in the first inning (2.07) than it was thereafter (1.24).... His nine road losses tied him for 2d most in the league.... Defeated the Orioles three times to raise his career record against them to 6–0.... Rickey Henderson ran wild on him, stealing seven bases in seven attempts against Navarro. Rickey's teammates were 4-for-4; all other teams combined were only 12-for-19.... Didn't commit a balk in 237 innings last season, after leading the league with five in 149⅓ innings in 1990.... Pitched more innings last season than his father Julio totaled in six seasons in the majors (212).... Has allowed only six home runs in 923 at-bats by opposing ground-ballers over the past three years (one per 154). His rate against fly-ball hitters is more than four times that (one per 35 ABs). The A.L. home-run rate is roughly twice as high for fly-ball hitters (one per 31) as for ground-ballers (one per 59).... Opponents have a career batting average of .264 on grass fields, and .323 on artificial surfaces.

Rod Nichols

Throws Right

Cleveland Indians	W-L	ERA	AB	H	HR	BB	SO	BA	SA	OBA
Season	2-11	3.54	532	145	6	30	76	.273	.344	.316
vs. Left-Handers			272	81	2	20	34	.298	.375	.349
vs. Right-Handers			260	64	4	10	42	.246	.312	.281
vs. Ground-Ballers			245	74	3	13	28	.302	.363	.337
vs. Fly-Ballers			287	71	3	17	48	.247	.328	.299
Home Games	1-7	4.08	296	87	3	22	35	.294	.351	.348
Road Games	1-4	2.89	236	58	3	8	41	.246	.335	.275
Grass Fields	2-9	3.29	484	128	6	28	69	.264	.333	.311
Artificial Turf	0-2	6.35	48	17	0	2	7	.354	.458	.373
April	0-0	—	0	0	0	0	0	—	—	—
May	0-3	2.83	111	27	1	6	19	.243	.306	.288
June	0-3	4.50	122	34	4	8	17	.279	.426	.333
July	1-2	4.33	109	37	0	5	14	.339	.376	.356
August	1-2	3.09	119	29	1	7	15	.244	.294	.291
Sept./Oct.	0-1	2.55	71	18	0	4	11	.254	.296	.312
Leading Off Inn.			136	35	1	1	21	.257	.309	.279
Bases Empty			303	83	3	11	46	.274	.333	.313
Runners On			229	62	3	19	30	.271	.358	.321
Runners/Scor. Pos.			119	33	1	15	16	.277	.353	.348
Runners On/2 Out			100	24	1	8	15	.240	.320	.296
Scor. Pos./2 Out			57	18	1	7	8	.316	.439	.391
Late-Inning Pressure			63	9	1	1	8	.143	.190	.169
Leading Off			17	2	0	0	4	.118	.118	.167
Runners On			21	3	0	1	1	.143	.143	.143
Runners/Scor. Pos.			9	1	0	0	0	.111	.111	.111
First 9 Batters			234	68	3	12	40	.291	.363	.329
Second 9 Batters			167	49	2	9	17	.293	.377	.341
All Batters Thereafter			131	28	1	9	19	.214	.267	.262

Loves to face: Carlton Fisk (.150, 3-for-20)

Luis Rivera (0-for-6, 4 SO)

Robin Ventura (.077, 1-for-13)

Hates to face: Jose Canseco (.313, 5-for-16, 1 2B, 3 HR)

Ozzie Guillen (.462, 6-for-13)

Cal Ripken (.385, 5-for-13, 2 HR)

Miscellaneous statistics: Ground outs-to-air outs ratio: 0.74 last season, 5th lowest in A.L.; 0.73 for career.... Induced 10 double plays in 107 opportunities (one per 11).... Allowed 18 doubles, 1 triple in 137⅓ innings.... Allowed 9 first-inning runs in 16 starts (4.50 ERA).... Batting support: 2.25 runs per start.... Record of 2–10, 3.98 ERA as a starter; 0–1, 2.48 ERA in 15 relief appearances.... Stranded 6 inherited runners, allowed 11 to score (35%).... Opposing base stealers: 16-for-24 (67%); 0 pickoffs, 0 balks.

Comments: Only two pitchers in the majors were supported by an average of fewer than three runs per game: Nichols, and 19-game loser Kirk McCaskill (minimum: 15 GS).... Allowed an average of one home run every 22.9 innings, 3d-best rate among A.L. pitchers (minimum: 100 IP). As you can see by the statistics above, he was just as effective keeping the ball inside the park on the road as he was at spacious Cleveland Stadium.... His rates of both walks and strikeouts were higher during the first inning than any other. He walked six batters and struck out 16 in the first innings of 16 starts, compared to rates of 1.88 and 4.43 per nine innings thereafter.... Walked only one of 140 batters leading off innings, the best rate in the A.L. last season (minimum 100 leadoff BFPs).... Allowed nine consecutive leadoff batters to reach base (July 23–August 2), matching his new teammate Scott Scudder for the longest streak in the majors last season.... Despite his 2–10 record as a starter, he allowed more than four earned runs in only one of his 16 starts.... Has career records of 7–22 as a starter (4.60 ERA), 0–5 in relief (3.41).... His combined record of 7–27 leaves him one loss above the .200 mark. Only six pitchers in major league history with at least as many decisions as Nichols compiled winning percentages below .200; the only one to pitch within the last 75 years: Ken Reynolds, .194 (7–29).

Steve Olin

Throws Right

Cleveland Indians	W-L	ERA	AB	H	HR	BB	SO	BA	SA	OBA
Season	3-6	3.36	223	61	2	23	38	.274	.354	.344
vs. Left-Handers			103	34	1	12	10	.330	.417	.400
vs. Right-Handers			120	27	1	11	28	.225	.300	.295
vs. Ground-Ballers			100	25	2	8	22	.250	.350	.306
vs. Fly-Ballers			123	36	0	15	16	.293	.358	.374
Home Games	0-1	3.80	81	20	0	10	11	.247	.333	.337
Road Games	3-5	3.09	142	41	2	13	27	.289	.366	.348
Grass Fields	3-5	3.23	202	53	1	21	35	.262	.337	.335
Artificial Turf	0-1	5.40	21	8	1	2	3	.381	.524	.435
April	2-1	2.84	47	10	0	3	5	.213	.277	.260
May	0-2	10.80	31	11	0	3	4	.355	.452	.429
June	0-0	0.00	0	0	0	0	0	.000	.000	.000
July	0-0	1.54	42	9	0	4	11	.214	.286	.283
August	0-3	3.27	52	17	1	4	11	.327	.442	.375
Sept./Oct.	1-0	1.88	51	14	1	9	7	.275	.333	.383
Leading Off Inn.			48	10	0	4	10	.208	.229	.269
Bases Empty			112	28	0	9	22	.250	.286	.306
Runners On			111	33	2	14	16	.297	.423	.381
Runners/Scor. Pos.			66	21	1	13	10	.318	.409	.438
Runners On/2 Out			45	9	0	6	5	.200	.244	.294
Scor. Pos./2 Out			29	4	0	5	2	.138	.138	.265
Late-Inning Pressure			134	34	1	14	29	.254	.313	.324
Leading Off			31	6	0	3	8	.194	.194	.265
Runners On			59	17	1	10	12	.288	.390	.391
Runners/Scor. Pos.			39	12	0	9	9	.308	.359	.438
First 9 Batters			211	57	2	21	35	.270	.355	.339
Second 9 Batters			12	4	0	2	3	.333	.333	.429
All Batters Thereafter			0	0	0	0	0	—	—	—

Loves to face: Randy Bush (0-for-6)

Sam Horn (0-for-4, 3 SO)

Terry Steinbach (0-for-12)

Hates to face: Harold Baines (5-for-5, 1 BB)

Juan Gonzalez (3-for-3, 2 2B)

Roberto Kelly (.400, 4-for-10, 2 HR)

Miscellaneous statistics: Ground outs-to-air outs ratio: 2.44 last season, 2.89 for career.... Induced 9 double plays in 62 opportunities (one per 6.9).... Allowed 10 doubles, 1 triple in 56⅓ innings.... Saved 17 games in 22 opportunities (77%).... Stranded 14 inherited runners, allowed 12 to score (54%), 5th-lowest rate in A.L.... Opposing base stealers: 3-for-5 (60%); 0 pickoffs, 0 balks.

Comments: Didn't get his first save opportunity until July 19; his total of 17 saves ranked sixth in the American League after the All-Star break—pretty impressive pitching for a club that lost 105 games. Second-half or late-season saves have often been a great angle for fantasy-league drafts. Among those who ranked among their league leaders prior to breakthrough saves seasons were Dennis Eckersley and Jim Gott in 1987 and Mike Schooler and Bryan Harvey in 1988. They saved an average of 15 games in those seasons (five before the All-Star break, 10 after, including five in September), but more than doubled that average the next year to 34.... Doug Jones's collapse gave Olin the opportunity to pitch in Late-Inning Pressure Situations. Over 60 percent of the batters Olin faced last season came up during LIPS, compared to only 12 percent in 1990.... Allowed an average of one home run every 28.2 innings last season, 9th best among A.L. pitchers with at least 50 innings. Before you attribute that to Cleveland Stadium, you should know that his home-run rate over his previous two seasons with the Indians was even better (one HR every 32 IP).... His ground outs-to-air outs ratio was high throughout the season, but over the last six weeks he must have been rolling the ball up to the plate, recording only five outs in the air over his last 18 innings.... Seven of the 23 walks he issued were intentional.... Career batting average of .316 by opposing left-handed batters, .235 by opposing right-handers.... Opponents have a career average of .300 with runners in scoring position, compared to a .254 average in other at-bats.

Gregg Olson — Throws Right

Baltimore Orioles	W-L	ERA	AB	H	HR	BB	SO	BA	SA	OBA
Season	4-6	3.18	282	74	1	29	72	.262	.305	.332
vs. Left-Handers			139	32	1	17	39	.230	.266	.316
vs. Right-Handers			143	42	0	12	33	.294	.343	.348
vs. Ground-Ballers			135	30	0	16	38	.222	.237	.307
vs. Fly-Ballers			147	44	1	13	34	.299	.367	.356
Home Games	3-1	3.15	126	31	1	19	33	.246	.294	.349
Road Games	1-5	3.20	156	43	0	10	39	.276	.314	.317
Grass Fields	3-3	2.76	218	54	1	23	55	.248	.284	.322
Artificial Turf	1-3	4.80	64	20	0	6	17	.313	.375	.366
April	0-0	1.42	22	6	0	0	4	.273	.318	.273
May	0-1	3.00	46	12	1	7	13	.261	.326	.358
June	1-2	4.91	55	12	0	7	18	.218	.236	.302
July	0-1	3.07	61	16	0	2	15	.262	.295	.286
August	2-0	3.00	51	17	0	7	7	.333	.373	.414
Sept./Oct.	1-2	2.57	47	11	0	6	15	.234	.298	.333
Leading Off Inn.			62	13	1	1	8	.210	.306	.222
Bases Empty			137	34	1	8	35	.248	.307	.295
Runners On			145	40	0	21	37	.276	.303	.365
Runners/Scor. Pos.			94	25	0	18	25	.266	.298	.381
Runners On/2 Out			67	21	0	12	14	.313	.358	.418
Scor. Pos./2 Out			54	15	0	10	11	.278	.333	.391
Late-Inning Pressure			199	52	1	18	54	.261	.312	.324
Leading Off			46	9	1	0	6	.196	.326	.196
Runners On			94	28	0	13	24	.298	.304	.380
Runners/Scor. Pos.			62	17	0	11	17	.274	.323	.378
First 9 Batters			270	73	1	27	68	.270	.315	.338
Second 9 Batters			12	1	0	2	4	.083	.083	.214
All Batters Thereafter			0	0	0	0	0			

Loves to face: Kurt Stillwell (0-for-9, 7 SO)
Pete Incaviglia (0-for-7, 6 SO)
Ruben Sierra (0-for-8)

Hates to face: Dwight Evans (.600, 3-for-5, 2 HR)
Brian Harper (.571, 4-for-7, 3 SO)
Danny Tartabull (.556, 5-for-9)

Miscellaneous statistics: Ground outs-to-air outs ratio: 1.07 last season, 0.96 for career.... Induced 5 double plays in 64 opportunities (one per 13).... Allowed 5 doubles, 2 triples in 73⅔ innings.... Saved 31 games in 40 opportunities (78%).... Stranded 18 inherited runners, allowed 12 to score (60%).... Opposing base stealers: 13-for-14 (93%); 0 pickoffs, 1 balk.

Comments: A right-handed pitcher who's been far more effective against left-handed batters throughout his four-year career. Opposing right-handers have outhit lefties .257 to .185. The only pitcher to hold left-handed batters to a lower mark over the past 17 years: Bryan Harvey, another right-hander (.177).... No opposing right-hander has homered against him since Mark McGwire did it in August 1990.... Allowed only one home run in 73⅔ innings last season, the best rate among A.L. pitchers (minimum: 50 IP). In the other major league, only Scott Terry had a lower rate (one HR in 80⅓ IP).... Allowed more earned runs (14) in 22 innings with Bob Melvin as a batterymate than he did in 42⅔ innings with Chris Hoiles behind the plate (11). ERA breakdown: 2.32 with Hoiles, 5.73 with Melvin.... Needs 11 saves to pass Tippy Martinez as the Orioles' all-time leader in that category.... Finished the 1991 season five saves short of the 100 mark for his career. He should become the youngest player to reach that plateau, and by an incredibly wide margin. Olson will be 25 years, 5 months on opening day; the youngest pitchers to reach the 100-save mark (years/months): Bruce Sutter (26/7), Bobby Thigpen (26/8), and Lee Smith (27/7).... Had a career record of 11–1 in the Birds' old nest.... Orioles had a 3–16 record in games that were tied after eight innings—an extreme case that prompts a common-sense question: Wouldn't a team improve its chances in such games if they didn't reserve closers like Olson almost exclusively for late-lead situations?

Melido Perez — Throws Right

Chicago White Sox	W-L	ERA	AB	H	HR	BB	SO	BA	SA	OBA
Season	8-7	3.12	495	111	15	52	128	.224	.352	.299
vs. Left-Handers			223	45	6	24	66	.202	.332	.279
vs. Right-Handers			272	66	9	28	62	.243	.368	.315
vs. Ground-Ballers			226	56	5	20	50	.248	.350	.308
vs. Fly-Ballers			269	55	10	32	78	.204	.353	.291
Home Games	2-3	3.61	232	57	8	23	56	.246	.397	.316
Road Games	6-4	2.70	263	54	7	29	72	.205	.314	.283
Grass Fields	7-6	3.27	433	96	13	47	108	.222	.351	.299
Artificial Turf	1-1	2.08	62	15	2	5	20	.242	.355	.294
April	1-0	4.41	64	13	2	10	15	.203	.359	.311
May	0-4	4.81	131	33	7	18	31	.252	.443	.342
June	2-0	1.69	70	14	0	6	15	.200	.243	.273
July	3-0	2.20	100	22	3	6	20	.220	.340	.262
August	0-0	1.53	59	10	0	4	19	.169	.169	.222
Sept./Oct.	2-3	3.50	71	19	3	8	28	.268	.451	.342
Leading Off Inn.			111	20	4	16	31	.180	.351	.289
Bases Empty			284	64	10	29	77	.225	.370	.299
Runners On			211	47	5	23	51	.223	.327	.298
Runners/Scor. Pos.			117	26	2	16	30	.222	.299	.313
Runners On/2 Out			94	21	2	10	22	.223	.309	.298
Scor. Pos./2 Out			58	13	1	7	13	.224	.310	.308
Late-Inning Pressure			115	28	3	9	29	.243	.339	.298
Leading Off			30	6	1	4	5	.200	.300	.294
Runners On			47	11	1	4	11	.234	.340	.294
Runners/Scor. Pos.			22	5	0	2	4	.227	.273	.292
First 9 Batters			286	64	7	30	78	.224	.325	.299
Second 9 Batters			135	30	5	14	36	.222	.400	.295
All Batters Thereafter			74	17	3	8	14	.230	.365	.305

Loves to face: Harold Baines (.130, 3-for-23, 4 BB)
Dan Gladden (.115, 3-for-26)
Carlos Quintana (0-for-11)

Hates to face: Jose Canseco (.409, 9-for-22, 2 HR)
Gene Larkin (.368, 7-for-19, 2 HR)
Kirby Puckett (.586, 17-for-29, 2 HR)

Miscellaneous statistics: Ground outs-to-air outs ratio: 1.24 last season, 0.91 for career.... Induced 10 double plays in 88 opportunities (one per 8.8).... Allowed 16 doubles, 1 triple in 135⅔ innings.... Stranded 22 inherited runners, allowed 14 to score (61%).... Opposing base stealers: 15-for-20 (75%); 1 pickoff, 1 balk.

Comments: Strikeout rate has increased each season; SOs per nine innings, year by year since 1987: 4.35, 6.30, 6.92, 7.36, 8.49.... During his four seasons with the White Sox, he had an average of 7.17 strikeouts per nine innings, the highest in franchise history among pitchers with at least 300 innings. Terry Forster (7.13) is the only other Chisox pitcher with an average above seven. Goose Gossage averaged only 6.45 SOs per nine while with Chicago.... Perez had pitched in 109 games for the White Sox, all as a starter, when Jeff Torborg demoted him to the bullpen in late May. He made 41 appearances after that, all in relief.... Won his first six decisions out of the bullpen.... Melido has a career total of 45 wins, brother Pascual has 67. In baseball history, only six pairs of brothers have each won 50 games: Jesse and Virgil Barnes (153 and 61); Harry and Stan Coveleski (81 and 215); Dizzy and Paul Dean (150 and 50); Bob and Ken Forsch (168 and 114); Joe and Phil Niekro (221 and 318); Gaylord and Jim Perry (314 and 215).... Last year at this time, the Perez brothers were one of two pairs of brothers to have both pitched no-hitters. Now the Forsches stand alone—thanks to the clarification of the definition of a "no-hitter." (And you thought only Andy Hawkins could lose a no-hitter!) ... Speaking of Pascual, he's pitched only 87⅔ innings over the past two seasons, but remains quite effective when he's out there, compiling a 2.87 mark. And over the past five seasons, his ERA of 2.81 ranks third in the majors, behind Orel Hershiser (2.70) and Roger Clemens (2.74; minimum: 500 IP).

Dan Plesac
Throws Left

Milwaukee Brewers	W-L	ERA	AB	H	HR	BB	SO	BA	SA	OBA
Season	2-7	4.29	350	92	12	39	61	.263	.434	.336
vs. Left-Handers			64	19	4	7	12	.297	.516	.361
vs. Right-Handers			286	73	8	32	49	.255	.416	.330
vs. Ground-Ballers			137	40	4	15	20	.292	.460	.362
vs. Fly-Ballers			213	52	8	24	41	.244	.418	.320
Home Games	0-4	5.63	184	49	6	27	38	.266	.429	.352
Road Games	2-3	2.84	166	43	6	12	23	.259	.440	.317
Grass Fields	2-6	4.63	306	81	11	38	57	.265	.438	.343
Artificial Turf	0-1	2.13	44	11	1	1	4	.250	.409	.283
April	0-1	4.82	39	14	2	1	5	.359	.667	.375
May	0-0	0.00	15	2	0	3	3	.133	.133	.278
June	0-1	3.18	38	7	1	3	8	.184	.289	.244
July	0-2	2.45	52	11	2	8	10	.212	.365	.333
August	1-1	4.74	71	17	4	9	11	.239	.465	.321
Sept./Oct.	1-2	5.73	135	41	3	15	24	.304	.452	.365
Leading Off Inn.			80	24	4	9	13	.300	.512	.378
Bases Empty			174	51	10	25	29	.293	.511	.385
Runners On			176	41	2	14	32	.233	.358	.286
Runners/Scor. Pos.			83	20	0	11	14	.241	.361	.320
Runners On/2 Out			73	9	0	7	16	.123	.151	.220
Scor. Pos./2 Out			37	5	0	5	8	.135	.162	.273
Late-Inning Pressure			55	16	4	6	8	.291	.582	.365
Leading Off			12	5	2	2	1	.417	.917	.500
Runners On			32	7	1	2	6	.219	.438	.278
Runners/Scor. Pos.			12	3	0	2	2	.250	.500	.375
First 9 Batters			228	54	8	25	36	.237	.421	.316
Second 9 Batters			78	27	4	11	16	.346	.513	.415
All Batters Thereafter			44	11	0	3	9	.250	.364	.286

Loves to face: Tom Brunansky (.091, 1-for-11)
      Mike Pagliarulo (0-for-9, 5 SO)
      Cal Ripken (.133, 2-for-15)

Hates to face: Jesse Barfield (.444, 4-for-9, 1 HR)
      Brian Harper (.600, 6-for-10, 3 HR)
      Don Mattingly (.400, 6-for-15, 1 HR)

Miscellaneous statistics: Ground outs-to-air outs ratio: 0.79 last season, 0.85 for career.... Induced 7 double plays in 86 opportunities (one per 12).... Allowed 20 doubles, 2 triples in 92⅓ innings.... Allowed 5 first-inning runs in 10 starts (3.60 ERA).... Batting support: 5.30 runs per start.... Record of 2–3, 4.69 ERA as a starter; 0–4, 3.86 ERA in 35 relief appearances.... Stranded 18 inherited runners, allowed 4 to score (82%).... Opposing base stealers: 4-for-9 (44%); 0 pick-offs, 1 balk.

Comments: Plesac is trying to make an unprecedented transition from the bullpen to the starting rotation. He had pitched in relief 311 times without a start before making his last 10 appearances of the 1991 season as a starter. Thirty-three other pitchers in major league history began their careers with at least 300 relief appearances and no starts; only seven of them made even one start later in their careers. The only one prior to Plesac to make more than five starts was Hoyt Wilhelm, who led the A.L. in ERA in 1959 as a starter for the Baltimore Orioles.... Plesac had never pitched more than 4⅓ innings in any relief appearance before going five in his debut as a starter (August 10), but he has one thing in his favor: He made 61 starts in his three seasons in the minors, only one relief appearance.... He lasted fewer than six innings in seven of his 10 starts.... Was unsuccessful in three of his last four save opportunities before the big switch.... Opponents grounded into only two double plays in 48 opportunities in his 10 starts.... Hasn't won at County Stadium since August 1990.... All season we heard how he had lost a couple miles off his fastball (which we take to mean miles *per hour*). His strikeout numbers certainly support that. He averaged 5.95 whiffs per nine innings, considerably lower than his previous career average (8.49), which was almost identical to his 1990 mark (8.48).... Hasn't committed an error in his last 235 games (since July 1987).

Eric Plunk
Throws Right

New York Yankees	W-L	ERA	AB	H	HR	BB	SO	BA	SA	OBA
Season	2-5	4.76	448	128	18	62	103	.286	.478	.371
vs. Left-Handers			223	65	10	35	44	.291	.502	.385
vs. Right-Handers			225	63	8	27	59	.280	.453	.357
vs. Ground-Ballers			205	55	3	24	37	.268	.385	.343
vs. Fly-Ballers			243	73	15	38	66	.300	.556	.393
Home Games	2-2	4.35	243	68	8	37	51	.280	.453	.375
Road Games	0-3	5.26	205	60	10	25	52	.293	.507	.366
Grass Fields	2-5	4.93	399	114	16	58	90	.286	.476	.374
Artificial Turf	0-0	3.18	49	14	2	4	13	.286	.490	.340
April	0-1	9.82	36	16	2	9	7	.444	.667	.532
May	0-1	5.70	90	22	3	12	22	.244	.411	.337
June	0-0	2.45	43	10	0	4	9	.233	.256	.292
July	2-0	3.46	56	19	1	6	12	.339	.429	.403
August	0-1	4.13	114	30	7	15	31	.263	.561	.349
Sept./Oct.	0-2	4.76	109	31	5	16	22	.284	.495	.376
Leading Off Inn.			96	24	3	16	16	.250	.448	.363
Bases Empty			229	67	11	30	42	.293	.524	.377
Runners On			219	61	7	32	61	.279	.429	.365
Runners/Scor. Pos.			148	41	2	25	44	.277	.399	.373
Runners On/2 Out			96	27	2	15	25	.281	.396	.378
Scor. Pos./2 Out			69	20	0	14	17	.290	.362	.410
Late-Inning Pressure			25	9	1	4	6	.360	.560	.448
Leading Off			7	2	0	3	2	.286	.429	.500
Runners On			10	3	0	1	1	.300	.400	.364
Runners/Scor. Pos.			7	3	0	0	1	.429	.571	.429
First 9 Batters			263	70	7	37	75	.266	.426	.355
Second 9 Batters			127	40	9	17	19	.315	.598	.393
All Batters Thereafter			58	18	2	8	9	.310	.448	.394

Loves to face: Cal Ripken (.087, 2-for-23, 1 HR, 3 BB)
      Ruben Sierra (.136, 3-for-22, 1 2B, 1 3B, 10 SO)
      Danny Tartabull (.053, 1-for-19, 1 2B, 2 BB)

Hates to face: Rickey Henderson (.267, 4-for-15, 1 HR, 12 BB)
      Wally Joyner (.692, 9-for-13, 3 HR)
      Paul Molitor (.636, 7-for-11, 1 HR)

Miscellaneous statistics: Ground outs-to-air outs ratio: 0.61 last season, 2d lowest in A.L.; 0.84 for career.... Induced 7 double plays in 96 opportunities (one per 14).... Allowed 22 doubles, 5 triples in 111⅔ innings.... Stranded 13 inherited runners, allowed 11 to score (54%).... Opposing base stealers: 28-for-31 (90%), 2d-most steals in A.L.; 1 pickoff, 2 balks.

Comments: Compare the stolen-base numbers above to his 1990 figures, when opponents were 4-for-12 in 72⅔ innings.... One of four pitchers in major league history to start at least 40 games without completing any. The list: Steve Bedrosian (46 starts), Shawn Hillegas (42), Plunk (41), and Scott Scudder (41).... The 1991 Yankees had six pitchers with a career total of 140 career starts and no complete games among them: Plunk (41), Dave Eiland (27), Jeff Johnson (23), Wade Taylor (22), John Habyan (18), and Scott Kamienicki (9). Love those pitch counts.... Struck out 20 batters in the first and second innings of his eight starts, but had only 18 SOs in 29 innings after that.... Career record of 9–16 (4.99 ERA) as a starter, 22–13 (3.54 ERA) in relief.... Opponents have a career batting average of .218 in day games, .248 at night. Over the past two years, Plunk is 7–1 in day games, 1–7 at night.... Career average of 5.75 walks per nine innings is 3d highest among active pitchers (minimum: 500 IP).... Only one pitcher in Yankees' history had a higher strikeout rate than Plunk (minimum: 250 IP). The top five: Goose Gossage (8.65 per nine innings); Plunk (8.00); Al Downing (7.49); Dave Righetti (7.45); Steve Hamilton (7.22).... Most career wins by pitchers named Eric: Show, 101; Rasmussen, 50; King, 48; Erickson, 34; Plunk, 31. (Our judges ruled that Rasmussen would be credited for games he won even when he was known as Harry.)

Jeff Reardon
Throws Right

Boston Red Sox	W-L	ERA	AB	H	HR	BB	SO	BA	SA	OBA
Season	1-4	3.03	229	54	9	16	44	.236	.419	.286
vs. Left-Handers			127	38	7	10	17	.299	.528	.348
vs. Right-Handers			102	16	2	6	27	.157	.284	.209
vs. Ground-Ballers			103	23	3	11	16	.223	.369	.298
vs. Fly-Ballers			126	31	6	5	28	.246	.460	.276
Home Games	1-2	3.62	123	29	7	9	25	.236	.480	.286
Road Games	0-2	2.33	106	25	2	7	19	.236	.349	.287
Grass Fields	1-4	3.35	186	43	8	14	38	.231	.435	.284
Artificial Turf	0-0	1.64	43	11	1	2	6	.256	.349	.298
April	0-0	1.04	33	7	0	5	5	.212	.333	.333
May	0-1	4.35	38	8	2	1	7	.211	.368	.225
June	0-1	3.00	35	8	2	1	6	.229	.400	.250
July	0-0	3.48	38	7	3	1	8	.184	.447	.205
August	0-1	3.75	51	16	1	4	12	.314	.490	.357
Sept./Oct.	1-1	2.00	34	8	1	4	6	.235	.441	.316
Leading Off Inn.			48	6	0	1	7	.125	.229	.143
Bases Empty			135	32	7	4	25	.237	.467	.259
Runners On			94	22	2	12	19	.234	.351	.321
Runners/Scor. Pos.			61	13	2	10	12	.213	.377	.315
Runners On/2 Out			48	9	0	8	13	.188	.208	.304
Scor. Pos./2 Out			31	4	0	7	8	.129	.161	.289
Late-Inning Pressure			188	44	7	12	37	.234	.415	.282
Leading Off			41	4	0	0	7	.098	.195	.098
Runners On			73	17	2	10	17	.233	.370	.329
Runners/Scor. Pos.			47	11	2	8	11	.234	.426	.339
First 9 Batters			229	54	9	16	44	.236	.419	.286
Second 9 Batters			0	0	0	0	0	—	—	—
All Batters Thereafter			0	0	0	0	0	—	—	—

Loves to face: Jose Canseco (.111, 1-for-9)
Kevin McReynolds (.111, 1-for-9, 5 SO)
Robin Yount (.125, 1-for-8, 4 SO)
Hates to face: Randy Bush (2-for-2, 2 HR)
Kelly Gruber (.500, 5-for-10, 1 HR)
Danny Tartabull (.375, 3-for-8, 1 3B, 1 HR, 3 BB)

Miscellaneous statistics: Ground outs-to-air outs ratio: 0.61 last season, 0.54 for career.... Induced 2 double plays in 31 opportunities (one per 16).... Allowed 11 doubles, 2 triples in 59⅓ innings.... Saved 40 games in 50 opportunities (80%).... Stranded 14 inherited runners, allowed 4 to score (78%).... Opposing base stealers: 3-for-4 (75%); 0 pickoffs, 0 balks.

Comments: The first pitcher in baseball history to save 20 or more games in 10 straight seasons. Bruce Sutter had a nine-year streak (1977–85); Lee Smith and Dave Righetti have current streaks of nine and eight, respectively.... Reardon could become the first pitcher to save 100 games for three different teams. He had 152 saves for Montreal and 104 for Twins; his current total for the Red Sox is 61. Two other pitchers qualify at the 50 level: Rollie Fingers (Athletics, 136; Padres, 108; and Brewers, 97) and Lee Smith (Cubs, 180; Cardinals, 74; and Red Sox, 58).... Leads active pitchers in relief appearances (751, and no starts), saves (327), relief wins (63), and relief losses (69). Lee Smith ranks second to him in each of those categories (with 711, 312, 61, and 60, respectively).... The turning point of Boston's season came on September 22 when Reardon allowed a two-out, two-strike, ninth-inning, game-tying home run to Roberto Kelly. A victory in that game would have put the Sox into a first-place tie with the Blue Jays, capping a comeback from 11½ games down. Boston lost that game in the 10th, and never recovered.... Walked the first leadoff batter he faced last season, and then didn't walk another for the rest of the season.... Reardon's the only player who's been a teammate of Greg A. Harris for three different clubs (Mets, Expos, Red Sox). Reardon left the Mets nine days after Harris's big-league debut; he was traded to the Expos for (shield your eyes, Mets fans) Ellis Valentine.

Jeff M. Robinson
Throws Right

Baltimore Orioles	W-L	ERA	AB	H	HR	BB	SO	BA	SA	OBA
Season	4-9	5.18	412	119	12	51	65	.289	.434	.375
vs. Left-Handers			214	75	11	31	28	.350	.570	.437
vs. Right-Handers			198	44	1	20	37	.222	.288	.306
vs. Ground-Ballers			214	64	6	21	30	.299	.467	.372
vs. Fly-Ballers			198	55	6	30	35	.278	.399	.378
Home Games	3-3	3.78	268	72	5	28	40	.269	.381	.347
Road Games	1-6	7.90	144	47	7	23	25	.326	.535	.426
Grass Fields	4-7	4.89	361	102	8	42	53	.283	.402	.365
Artificial Turf	0-2	7.30	51	17	4	9	12	.333	.667	.443
April	1-2	4.02	60	17	1	9	8	.283	.383	.377
May	2-2	3.74	135	39	3	12	27	.289	.422	.356
June	0-2	5.40	131	37	6	17	19	.282	.481	.382
July	1-3	7.89	86	26	2	13	11	.302	.419	.394
August	0-0	0.00	0	0	0	0	0	.000	.000	.000
Sept./Oct.	0-0		0	0	0	0	0	—	—	—
Leading Off Inn.			104	20	4	9	13	.192	.346	.263
Bases Empty			236	65	6	28	36	.275	.398	.364
Runners On			176	54	6	23	29	.307	.483	.390
Runners/Scor. Pos.			90	27	3	19	20	.300	.478	.427
Runners On/2 Out			78	25	3	12	14	.321	.538	.418
Scor. Pos./2 Out			42	14	2	9	10	.333	.619	.462
Late-Inning Pressure			24	6	0	3	2	.250	.333	.333
Leading Off			8	0	0	1	0	.000	.000	.111
Runners On			4	3	0	0	0	.750	1.000	.750
Runners/Scor. Pos.			2	2	0	0	0	1.000	1.500	1.000
First 9 Batters			159	51	6	22	28	.321	.497	.413
Second 9 Batters			138	35	4	16	22	.254	.391	.344
All Batters Thereafter			115	33	2	13	15	.287	.400	.359

Loves to face: Joe Orsulak (0-for-10)
Tony Pena (0-for-9)
Dick Schofield (.100, 2-for-20)
Hates to face: Chili Davis (.400, 8-for-20, 3 HR)
Kent Hrbek (.375, 9-for-24, 2 2B, 5 HR)
Terry Steinbach (.500, 8-for-16, 1 HR)

Miscellaneous statistics: Ground outs-to-air outs ratio: 0.93 last season, 1.01 for career.... Induced 12 double plays in 82 opportunities (one per 6.8).... Allowed 22 doubles, 1 triple in 104⅓ innings.... Allowed 24 first-inning runs in 19 starts (12.23 ERA, highest in majors).... Batting support: 3.58 runs per start.... Opposing base stealers: 10-for-15 (67%); 0 pickoffs, 0 balks.

Comments: Robinson provides the best evidence that any pitcher can thrive in the majors if his run support is good enough. (This will duplicate some of the material in the Orioles essay, but it's important stuff.) During his four years with Detroit, only two pitchers received better support than Robinson. The top three from 1987 through 1990 (minimum: 50 GS): Mike Smithson, 5.53; Roy Smith, 5.50; and Robinson, 5.30. That support allowed Robinson to compile a 36–26 record despite a 4.65 ERA. Only one pitcher in major league history with an ERA above 4.50 had a higher winning percentage than Jeff Robinson's during that period: Erv Brame, who compiled a 52–37 record for the Pittsburgh Pirates from 1928 through 1932 despite a 4.77 ERA. Last season, Robinson's support dropped a notch, and so did he—to Triple-A.... Lasted fewer than five innings in eight of his 19 starts.... Had the highest first-inning ERA in the league in each of the last two seasons.... Career home-run rates: one per 24 at-bats on his first pass through the batting order, one per 35 ABs thereafter.... Career ERA of 4.74 is 2d highest among pitchers active in 1991 (minimum: 500 IP), ahead of only Scott Bailes (4.76).... Traded even-up for Mickey Tettleton in January 1991. Seven months later, Robinson was in the minors, Tettleton was on his way to a 30-home-run season.... It's always a bad sign when a player is sent down in midseason and not recalled in September. On the bright side (unless you live in Denver or Miami), expansion's only a year away.

Kenny Rogers   Throws Left

Texas Rangers	W-L	ERA	AB	H	HR	BB	SO	BA	SA	OBA
Season	10-10	5.42	430	121	14	61	73	.281	.444	.375
vs. Left-Handers			98	22	3	16	19	.224	.357	.342
vs. Right-Handers			332	99	11	45	54	.298	.470	.385
vs. Ground-Ballers			206	59	2	29	27	.286	.379	.372
vs. Fly-Ballers			224	62	12	32	46	.277	.504	.376
Home Games	6-5	5.59	186	50	5	31	36	.269	.403	.383
Road Games	4-5	5.29	244	71	9	30	37	.291	.475	.368
Grass Fields	7-9	5.81	347	94	13	51	65	.271	.435	.370
Artificial Turf	3-1	3.80	83	27	1	10	8	.325	.482	.392
April	0-3	13.11	50	19	3	8	8	.380	.640	.483
May	4-1	4.60	128	40	3	20	13	.313	.500	.403
June	0-3	8.10	81	26	5	10	13	.321	.531	.402
July	2-0	2.65	57	10	2	6	18	.175	.281	.266
August	3-1	3.00	77	17	1	9	16	.221	.299	.303
Sept./Oct.	1-2	3.38	37	9	0	8	5	.243	.351	.375
Leading Off Inn.			97	26	0	9	13	.268	.320	.330
Bases Empty			226	65	7	24	39	.288	.460	.359
Runners On			204	56	7	37	34	.275	.426	.390
Runners/Scor. Pos.			119	35	6	32	22	.294	.487	.444
Runners On/2 Out			89	20	3	17	17	.225	.371	.367
Scor. Pos./2 Out			59	14	3	16	13	.237	.424	.416
Late-Inning Pressure			114	25	4	14	24	.219	.368	.313
Leading Off			28	6	0	5	5	.214	.250	.333
Runners On			45	8	1	7	7	.178	.267	.296
Runners/Scor. Pos.			26	2	0	5	6	.077	.077	.219
First 9 Batters			283	73	9	42	56	.258	.403	.359
Second 9 Batters			84	24	2	12	11	.286	.440	.378
All Batters Thereafter			63	24	3	7	6	.381	.635	.443

Loves to face: Mike Greenwell (.077, 1-for-13, 1 2B)
       Ozzie Guillen (.071, 1-for-14)
       Pete O'Brien (0-for-13)

Hates to face: Luis Rivera (.455, 5-for-11, 3 2B, 1 3B)
       Pat Tabler (.429, 3-for-7, 1 HR, 3 BB)
       Robin Yount (.571, 4-for-7)

Miscellaneous statistics: Ground outs-to-air outs ratio: 1.14 last season, 1.04 for career.... Induced 11 double plays in 118 opportunities (one per 11).... Allowed 22 doubles, 3 triples in 109⅔ innings.... Stranded 35 inherited runners, allowed 9 to score (80%).... Opposing base stealers: 1-for-4 (25%); 3 pickoffs, 1 balk.

Comments: Had 20 wins and 20 saves over the past two seasons. In this era of relief specialization, no other pitcher reached 20 in both categories for 1990–91. The only 20/20 pitcher for 1989–90 was Detroit's Mike Henneman (who was one in 1988–89 as well).... Held opposing base runners much better than in 1990, when he allowed six stolen bases in seven attempts.... One steal in 109⅔ innings was the 3d-lowest rate in the majors, behind Greg A. Harris (one in 173 innings) and Jeff Ballard (one in 123⅔ innings).... Posted a 6.42 ERA in 40⅔ innings with Geno Petralli behind the plate, and a 3.21 ERA in 42 innings with Ivan Rodriguez as a batterymate.... Career record of 5–6 (6.17 ERA) as a starter, 18–14 (3.40 ERA) in relief.... Stranded 22 of the first 23 runners he inherited.... Led major league pitchers with 40 appearances after the All-Star break.... Has appeared in fewer games but pitched more innings each season of his career. Year by year, starting with 1989: 73 games, 73⅔ innings; 69 and 97⅔; 63 and 109⅔. He pitched exclusively in relief as a rookie, made three starts in 1990 and nine last season.... He has some other interesting yearly progressions. Earned run average: 2.93, 3.13, 5.42. Strikeouts per nine innings: 7.70, 6.82, 5.99.... Career batting average of .206 by opposing left-handed batters, .276 by opposing right-handers.

Jeff Russell   Throws Right

Texas Rangers	W-L	ERA	AB	H	HR	BB	SO	BA	SA	OBA
Season	6-4	3.29	301	71	11	26	52	.236	.365	.295
vs. Left-Handers			145	35	2	17	20	.241	.297	.317
vs. Right-Handers			156	36	9	9	32	.231	.429	.273
vs. Ground-Ballers			155	39	4	14	24	.252	.342	.314
vs. Fly-Ballers			146	32	7	12	28	.219	.390	.275
Home Games	2-1	3.00	143	33	6	9	29	.231	.371	.275
Road Games	4-3	3.57	158	38	5	17	23	.241	.361	.313
Grass Fields	3-3	3.11	239	57	8	18	44	.238	.360	.287
Artificial Turf	3-1	4.02	62	14	3	8	8	.226	.387	.324
April	0-0	0.00	33	3	0	0	9	.091	.091	.088
May	1-0	4.41	63	16	4	4	7	.254	.476	.294
June	1-1	4.20	55	15	2	7	7	.273	.418	.349
July	1-2	1.98	48	7	1	6	14	.146	.229	.250
August	0-1	2.92	48	12	2	4	7	.250	.396	.308
Sept./Oct.	3-0	5.25	54	18	2	5	8	.333	.444	.390
Leading Off Inn.			55	13	1	6	13	.236	.309	.311
Bases Empty			148	33	4	10	29	.223	.311	.277
Runners On			153	38	7	16	23	.248	.418	.312
Runners/Scor. Pos.			101	20	1	9	13	.198	.238	.254
Runners On/2 Out			70	18	6	8	13	.257	.543	.333
Scor. Pos./2 Out			46	10	1	5	8	.217	.283	.294
Late-Inning Pressure			238	51	9	23	42	.214	.345	.282
Leading Off			44	8	1	5	12	.182	.273	.265
Runners On			115	25	5	16	17	.217	.374	.304
Runners/Scor. Pos.			79	11	0	9	12	.139	.152	.217
First 9 Batters			300	71	11	26	52	.237	.367	.296
Second 9 Batters			1	0	0	0	0	.000	.000	.000
All Batters Thereafter			0	0	0	0	0	—	—	—

Loves to face: Joe Carter (.071, 1-for-14)
       Gary Gaetti (.056, 1-for-18)
       Dan Gladden (.133, 4-for-30, 0 BB)

Hates to face: George Brett (.400, 6-for-15, 3 HR)
       Ellis Burks (.500, 9-for-18, 2 HR)
       Mike Greenwell (.583, 7-for-12, 2 HR)

Miscellaneous statistics: Ground outs-to-air outs ratio: 1.44 last season, 1.23 for career.... Induced 10 double plays in 65 opportunities (one per 6.5).... Allowed 6 doubles, 0 triples in 79⅓ innings.... Saved 30 games in 40 opportunities (75%).... Stranded 26 inherited runners, allowed 18 to score (59%).... Opposing base stealers: 1-for-1 (100%); 0 pickoffs, 0 balks.

Comments: Shared major league lead by allowing nine home runs in Late-Inning Pressure Situations. Dennis Eckersley also allowed nine.... Allowed one stolen base in 79 innings, the 4th-best rate among major league pitchers. Russell and Kenny Rogers, who had the league's 7th-best rate, made the Rangers' bullpen the toughest in the majors to steal against, allowing the fewest total steals (25) and the lowest rate of steals (one every 21.2 innings).... The only home runs he allowed to left-handed batters were by Chili Davis and Kent Hrbek in back-to-back games (Sept. 12–13).... From the time he joined the Rangers in 1985, Russell's home-run rate improved in every season until 1991. Innings per home run, year by year starting with 1985: 6.2, 7.5, 10.8, 12.6, 18.2, 25.3, 7.2.... Has allowed only one triple in 366 innings over the past four seasons.... Has posted winning records in five of the last six seasons, but his career record remains well below the .500 mark (46–57) on account of his 10–23 mark with Cincinnati in 1983 and 1984.... Washington/Texas franchise leaders in relief wins: Steve Foucault (26), Ron Kline (26), Casey Cox (25), Darold Knowles (25), Danny Darwin (24), Jeff Russell (24).... Career record of 22–39 (4.47 ERA) as a starter, 24–18 (3.28 ERA) in relief.... Career record of 5–0 vs. the Athletics.... Averaged 5.57 hits per nine innings in 1989, compared to 9.20 before and 8.08 since.... Averaged 9.54 strikeouts per nine innings in 1989, compared to 5.07 before and 5.85 since.... Maybe someone else was wearing Russell's uniform in '89.

Nolan Ryan

Throws Right

Texas Rangers	W-L	ERA	AB	H	HR	BB	SO	BA	SA	OBA
Season	12-6	2.91	594	102	12	72	203	.172	.285	.263
vs. Left-Handers			345	63	5	34	105	.183	.281	.257
vs. Right-Handers			249	39	7	38	98	.157	.289	.271
vs. Ground-Ballers			304	50	4	29	95	.164	.263	.237
vs. Fly-Ballers			290	52	8	43	108	.179	.307	.290
Home Games	10-4	3.08	448	75	12	53	157	.167	.297	.256
Road Games	2-2	2.40	146	27	0	19	46	.185	.247	.286
Grass Fields	11-4	2.81	490	80	12	56	172	.163	.284	.250
Artificial Turf	1-2	3.41	104	22	0	16	31	.212	.288	.325
April	2-2	3.94	107	23	3	10	37	.215	.336	.280
May	1-2	3.09	76	8	1	11	30	.105	.224	.227
June	1-0	1.20	105	17	2	6	30	.162	.267	.212
July	3-1	3.00	125	19	6	20	48	.152	.352	.272
August	2-1	3.75	44	10	0	7	12	.227	.273	.333
Sept./Oct.	3-0	3.00	137	25	0	18	46	.182	.234	.277
Leading Off Inn.			163	26	3	15	64	.160	.276	.230
Bases Empty			403	59	8	48	162	.146	.258	.242
Runners On			191	43	4	24	41	.225	.340	.305
Runners/Scor. Pos.			118	27	4	20	28	.229	.381	.329
Runners On/2 Out			86	16	3	13	19	.186	.302	.300
Scor. Pos./2 Out			57	13	3	10	14	.228	.404	.353
Late-Inning Pressure			58	7	1	6	25	.121	.207	.203
Leading Off			18	1	1	1	10	.056	.222	.105
Runners On			12	2	0	1	1	.167	.167	.231
Runners/Scor. Pos.			2	1	0	1	0	.500	.500	.667
First 9 Batters			208	40	7	29	71	.192	.356	.296
Second 9 Batters			207	36	2	21	70	.174	.256	.250
All Batters Thereafter			179	26	3	22	62	.145	.235	.239

Loves to face: Jesse Barfield (0-for-12, 10 SO)
Rob Deer (0-for-14, 10 SO)
Sammy Sosa (0-for-16)

Hates to face: George Brett (.362, 25-for-69)
Jack Clark (.250, 11-for-44, 4 2B, 1 3B, 4 HR)
Kevin Maas (.429, 3-for-7, 2 HR)

Miscellaneous statistics: Ground outs-to-air outs ratio: 0.61 last season, lowest in A.L.; 1.02 for career. . . . Induced 7 double plays in 71 opportunities (one per 10). . . . Allowed 25 doubles, 3 triples in 173 innings. . . . Allowed 12 first-inning runs in 27 starts (3.67 ERA). . . . Batting support: 4.70 runs per start. . . . Opposing base stealers: 24-for-32 (75%), 4th-most steals in A.L.; 2 pickoffs, 0 balks.

Comments: His last three no-hitters have all been against eventual division winners (1981 Dodgers, 1990 Athletics, 1991 Blue Jays). Perhaps teams will be fighting for the honor/omen of who will be next. . . . ERA breakdown: 4.33 in 43⅔ innings with Geno Petralli catching, 2.74 in 75⅔ innings with Ivan Rodriguez, 1.83 in 39⅓ innings with Mike Stanley. . . . Did not allow a home run in any of his last nine starts, matching his longest single-season streak since 1981, when he did not allow a home run in his first 14 starts of the season while with Houston. . . . Ryan has made 85 errors in his career, the most by any pitcher in this century, but has none in the past two years. . . . An appearance in Baltimore's new stadium will give him a total of 35 different parks in which he has pitched a major league game. . . . The only man to play for each of the four original expansion franchises of 1961-62 (Mets, Angels, Astros, and Senators/Rangers). . . . One of five pitchers in major league history to win 100 or more games for two teams. The others are Hall of Famers: John Clarkson, Cy Young, Grover Alexander, Lefty Grove. . . . The oldest player in the majors (born 1/31/47), but two older players appeared in spring training games last season: comeback Hall of Famer Jim Palmer (10/15/45) with Baltimore and rookie Tom Selleck (1/29/45) with Detroit. . . . Rangers drew an average of close to 4000 more fans in Ryan's home appearances than they did in other home games. He made 20 of his 27 starts, including 10 of his last 12, at Arlington Stadium. Hmmmmm.

Bret Saberhagen

Throws Right

Kansas City Royals	W-L	ERA	AB	H	HR	BB	SO	BA	SA	OBA
Season	13-8	3.07	724	165	12	45	136	.228	.327	.280
vs. Left-Handers			354	76	9	27	68	.215	.333	.270
vs. Right-Handers			370	89	3	18	68	.241	.322	.290
vs. Ground-Ballers			359	93	3	18	65	.259	.334	.298
vs. Fly-Ballers			365	72	9	27	71	.197	.321	.263
Home Games	7-3	2.76	338	70	3	25	62	.207	.278	.270
Road Games	6-5	3.36	386	95	9	20	74	.246	.370	.290
Grass Fields	2-5	4.37	264	71	7	16	47	.269	.424	.317
Artificial Turf	11-3	2.38	460	94	5	29	89	.204	.272	.260
April	1-3	3.34	125	36	2	9	19	.288	.384	.346
May	5-0	2.30	170	37	1	7	25	.218	.288	.251
June	0-0	4.50	50	13	1	4	8	.260	.400	.315
July	1-2	6.55	85	25	2	11	18	.294	.424	.378
August	3-1	0.88	136	20	1	7	31	.147	.199	.188
Sept./Oct.	3-2	3.64	158	34	5	7	35	.215	.361	.271
Leading Off Inn.			185	40	3	14	32	.216	.303	.279
Bases Empty			449	97	9	28	86	.216	.323	.270
Runners On			275	68	3	17	50	.247	.335	.298
Runners/Scor. Pos.			144	38	3	8	28	.264	.403	.310
Runners On/2 Out			113	25	2	8	22	.221	.345	.273
Scor. Pos./2 Out			68	14	2	4	14	.206	.382	.250
Late-Inning Pressure			93	21	1	5	19	.226	.301	.270
Leading Off			25	6	0	1	4	.240	.320	.269
Runners On			33	7	0	3	9	.212	.242	.289
Runners/Scor. Pos.			18	4	0	0	6	.222	.278	.250
First 9 Batters			226	46	1	21	46	.204	.265	.283
Second 9 Batters			228	50	5	10	43	.219	.316	.256
All Batters Thereafter			270	69	6	14	47	.256	.389	.299

Loves to face: Todd Benzinger (0-for-5, 3 SO)
Dale Sveum (.161, 5-for-31, 0 BB)

Hates to face: George Bell (.372, 16-for-43, 5 HR)
Steve Buechele (.478, 11-for-23, 1 HR)
Fred McGriff (.414, 12-for-29, 2 HR)

Miscellaneous statistics: Ground outs-to-air outs ratio: 1.04 last season, 1.10 for career. . . . Induced 14 double plays in 144 opportunities (one per 10). . . . Allowed 28 doubles, 4 triples in 196⅓ innings. . . . Allowed 7 first-inning runs in 28 starts (1.61 ERA, 2d lowest in A.L.). . . . Batting support: 4.61 runs per start. . . . Opposing base stealers: 9-for-18 (50%); 5 pickoffs, 1 balk.

Comments: Has allowed higher batting average to right-handed batters than to left-handed batters in each of the past six years. Career breakdown: .260 by right-handers, .237 by left-handers. . . . The only pitcher to win three games vs. Minnesota last season; his 1.05 ERA against the world champs was also the best in the league. . . . His July ERA was 2d highest in A.L., but his August ERA was lowest in majors. . . . Has not allowed a first-inning home run in 43 starts, since May 1, 1990. . . . Allowed one home run for every 66.5 opponents' at-bats in eight years at Royals Stadium; one for every 39.4 at-bats in other A.L. parks. Shea Stadium does not retard homers as much as Royals Stadium does, but Shea is a better overall pitchers' park. . . . Career rate of 1.79 walks per nine innings is lowest among active pitchers (minimum: 1500 innings). . . . Retains the 5th-lowest walk rate since 1920, when the live-ball era began (minimum: 200 GS)—but barely. The six best: Grover Alexander, 1.31; Red Lucas, 1.61; Fritz Peterson, 1.730; Robin Roberts, 1.731; Saberhagen, 1.794; Pete Donohue, 1.797. . . . In eight years in majors, Saberhagen owns a winning record in every odd-numbered year and a losing record in every even-numbered year. Composite records: 74-30 in odd years, 36-48 in even years. Lindy McDaniel and Dave Wickersham also crossed over the .500 line seven straight years, but a losing record this season would make Saberhagen the all-time king of flip-flop. Could a career in politics be in his future?

Scott Sanderson

Throws Right

New York Yankees	W-L	ERA	AB	H	HR	BB	SO	BA	SA	OBA
Season	16-10	3.81	795	200	22	29	130	.252	.405	.279
vs. Left-Handers			437	114	15	17	74	.261	.437	.290
vs. Right-Handers			358	86	7	12	56	.240	.366	.265
vs. Ground-Ballers			374	94	5	11	57	.251	.353	.276
vs. Fly-Ballers			421	106	17	18	73	.252	.451	.282
Home Games	7-6	4.66	364	102	13	16	55	.280	.456	.310
Road Games	9-4	3.12	431	98	9	13	75	.227	.362	.252
Grass Fields	14-9	3.97	670	173	21	26	105	.258	.419	.286
Artificial Turf	2-1	2.97	125	27	1	3	25	.216	.328	.240
April	1-1	6.33	92	29	4	3	11	.315	.533	.344
May	5-1	2.27	145	32	1	5	22	.221	.303	.247
June	2-1	3.69	125	37	2	2	21	.296	.400	.302
July	2-4	6.02	158	43	8	7	22	.272	.475	.302
August	4-1	3.43	145	29	5	9	38	.200	.393	.252
Sept./Oct.	2-2	2.02	130	30	2	3	16	.231	.362	.248
Leading Off Inn.			206	53	6	9	28	.257	.408	.295
Bases Empty			508	130	13	19	83	.256	.406	.285
Runners On			287	70	9	10	47	.244	.404	.267
Runners/Scor. Pos.			153	41	4	6	31	.268	.431	.291
Runners On/2 Out			127	35	5	4	19	.276	.465	.298
Scor. Pos./2 Out			75	25	4	3	15	.333	.587	.359
Late-Inning Pressure			38	6	0	0	4	.158	.184	.158
Leading Off			11	1	0	0	0	.091	.091	.091
Runners On			10	3	0	0	3	.300	.400	.300
Runners/Scor. Pos.			3	0	0	0	1	.000	.000	.000
First 9 Batters			291	81	6	8	47	.278	.405	.297
Second 9 Batters			282	68	8	13	50	.241	.372	.276
All Batters Thereafter			222	51	8	8	33	.230	.446	.259

Loves to face: Greg Briley (0-for-17)
Tom Brunansky (.048, 1-for-21, 1 2B)
John Olerud (0-for-14)

Hates to face: Scott Fletcher (.583, 7-for-12, 2 HR)
Jody Reed (.556, 10-for-18, 2 HR)
B. J. Surhoff (.833, 5-for-6, 1 HR)

Miscellaneous statistics: Ground outs-to-air outs ratio: 0.83 last season, 0.79 for career.... Induced 19 double plays in 114 opportunities (one per 6.0).... Allowed 46 doubles (5th most in majors), 5 triples in 208 innings.... Allowed 15 first-inning runs in 34 starts (3.71 ERA).... Batting support: 4.59 runs per start.... Opposing base stealers: 16-for-23 (70%); 0 pickoffs, 1 balk.

Comments: A.L.'s best and worst records in 1990 belonged to A's and Yankees; Sanderson became first pitcher in A.L. history to start regularly for team with best record, and then join the team with worst record during following off-season. You'd never guess by looking at his won-lost records: 17–11 in 1990, 16–10 last year.... How many other pitchers have had records of 16–10 (or better) for teams that finished 71–91 (or worse)? Among pitchers with at least 30 starts there have been 13 others, but only five over past 50 years: Ned Garver (20–12 for 52–102 Browns in 1951), Camilo Pascual (17–10 for 63–91 Senators in 1959), Steve Carlton (27–10 for 59–97 Phillies in 1972), Randy Jones (20–12 for 71–91 Padres in 1975), and Mario Soto (18–7 for 70–92 Reds in 1984).... Sanderson matched top win total by a Yankees right-hander since Ed Figueroa won 20 in 1978. Others to win 16 since then: Phil Niekro (1984 & 1985) and Rick Rhoden (1987).... Career record: 74–54 before All-Star break, 57–56 after.... Had no-hit bid spoiled in ninth inning in Yankees debut, April 10. Twelve no-hit tries were spoiled in ninth inning over previous two years, but Sanderson's was one of only three last year.... Posted 4.52 ERA over first three innings of his starts, 3.16 from fourth inning on.... Pitched team's only two complete-game shutouts, and two of club's major league record-low three complete games in 1991. After his one-hit shutout of Angels on July 11, Yankees finished season with 83 straight incomplete games, another major league record.

Joe Slusarski

Throws Right

Oakland A's	W-L	ERA	AB	H	HR	BB	SO	BA	SA	OBA
Season	5-7	5.27	427	121	14	52	60	.283	.436	.364
vs. Left-Handers			253	75	7	22	29	.296	.443	.350
vs. Right-Handers			174	46	7	30	31	.264	.425	.383
vs. Ground-Ballers			212	65	5	23	19	.307	.429	.370
vs. Fly-Ballers			215	56	9	29	41	.260	.442	.359
Home Games	2-3	5.36	170	46	5	17	24	.271	.394	.342
Road Games	3-4	5.21	257	75	9	35	36	.292	.463	.378
Grass Fields	5-5	5.09	338	95	9	45	47	.281	.405	.369
Artificial Turf	0-2	5.96	89	26	5	7	13	.292	.551	.344
April	1-0	2.08	62	15	1	11	7	.242	.306	.365
May	0-2	6.97	87	26	5	6	19	.299	.540	.351
June	1-2	6.75	74	21	0	14	13	.284	.365	.402
July	1-0	0.75	44	8	0	3	3	.182	.205	.234
August	0-2	7.71	94	29	5	9	9	.309	.532	.369
Sept./Oct.	2-1	4.50	66	22	3	9	9	.333	.515	.408
Leading Off Inn.			103	22	2	13	13	.214	.301	.308
Bases Empty			249	66	8	30	32	.265	.422	.346
Runners On			178	55	6	22	28	.309	.455	.388
Runners/Scor. Pos.			102	29	4	14	20	.284	.461	.377
Runners On/2 Out			69	16	1	11	16	.232	.333	.346
Scor. Pos./2 Out			47	11	1	8	12	.234	.362	.357
Late-Inning Pressure			13	5	1	2	1	.385	.615	.467
Leading Off			2	1	1	1	0	.500	2.000	.667
Runners On			8	2	0	1	0	.250	.250	.333
Runners/Scor. Pos.			6	1	0	1	0	.167	.167	.286
First 9 Batters			159	46	6	18	25	.289	.459	.361
Second 9 Batters			154	41	3	17	26	.266	.377	.349
All Batters Thereafter			114	34	5	17	9	.298	.482	.389

Loves to face: Pete O'Brien (0-for-6)
Jody Reed (0-for-5)
Sammy Sosa (0-for-4, 4 SO)

Hates to face: Ken Griffey, Jr. (.500, 3-for-6, 2 HR)
Danny Tartabull (1-for-1, 1 HR, 2 BB)
Greg Vaughn (.667, 2-for-3, 1 2B, 1 HR, 3 BB)

Miscellaneous statistics: Ground outs-to-air outs ratio: 1.11 last season, 1.11 for career.... Induced 11 double plays in 97 opportunities (one per 8.8).... Allowed 17 doubles, 3 triples in 109⅓ innings.... Allowed 8 first-inning runs in 19 starts (3.79 ERA).... Batting support: 5.21 runs per start.... Opposing base stealers: 5-for-10 (50%); 1 pickoff, 0 balks.

Comments: One of 40 pitchers who made major league debut as a starter in 1991; Slusarski pitched seven shutout innings to beat the Twins on April 11. Those 40 pitchers went a combined 15–13 in their debut games, but 82–118 after that.... Allowed 14 home runs in 109⅓ innings, third-highest rate on team behind Gene Nelson (12 in 48⅔) and Dennis Eckersley (11 in 76). A's allowed the most home runs in the majors last season, no mean feat given the homer-killing Oakland Coliseum. It marked first time since team moved there in 1968 that A's had led even their league in home runs allowed.... Held opponents to .194 batting average during first inning, 4th lowest in A.L. (minimum: 50 AB), but five of 13 hits he allowed in opening frame were homers.... All five steals vs. Slusarski came with Jamie Quirk catching, even though Quirk caught only 35 of his 109⅓ innings.... Started 19 games, third-highest total by an Oakland rookie since 1980; Chris Codiroli started 31 in 1983 and Tim Birtsas 25 in 1985.... Walked a major league season high five consecutive batters over course of two games in June.... In a disappointing 1991 season, at least A's took a look at some young starting pitchers. In 1990, they had only three starts from pitchers under 30 years of age (two by Todd Burns and one by Reggie Harris). No other team in A.L. history had fewer than 10 games started by pitchers under the age of 30. Slusarski (24 years old in 1991), Kirk Dressendorfer (22), and Todd Van Poppel (19) combined for 27 starts last year.

Dave Stewart

Throws Right

Oakland A's	W-L	ERA	AB	H	HR	BB	SO	BA	SA	OBA
Season	11-11	5.18	880	245	24	105	144	.278	.428	.356
vs. Left-Handers			444	134	8	46	51	.302	.428	.361
vs. Right-Handers			436	111	16	59	93	.255	.429	.350
vs. Ground-Ballers			410	133	4	41	50	.324	.441	.383
vs. Fly-Ballers			470	112	20	64	94	.238	.417	.333
Home Games	8-3	4.21	442	118	10	45	72	.267	.389	.334
Road Games	3-8	6.18	438	127	14	60	72	.290	.468	.377
Grass Fields	11-6	4.59	732	192	20	85	120	.262	.406	.338
Artificial Turf	0-5	8.47	148	53	4	20	24	.358	.541	.440
April	2-2	6.75	133	39	4	14	19	.293	.451	.367
May	1-0	2.22	88	24	1	13	11	.273	.341	.359
June	2-2	7.09	155	43	7	21	23	.277	.471	.367
July	3-1	4.01	181	41	3	18	37	.227	.359	.294
August	2-3	5.79	145	46	5	21	18	.317	.517	.401
Sept./Oct.	1-3	4.74	178	52	4	18	36	.292	.416	.360
Leading Off Inn.			216	54	7	19	34	.250	.431	.319
Bases Empty			500	133	13	54	72	.266	.406	.342
Runners On			380	112	11	51	72	.295	.458	.373
Runners/Scor. Pos.			222	64	7	33	44	.288	.468	.369
Runners On/2 Out			165	45	6	26	37	.273	.442	.375
Scor. Pos./2 Out			104	30	4	17	23	.288	.500	.393
Late-Inning Pressure			50	15	2	15	13	.300	.420	.463
Leading Off			13	2	1	4	5	.154	.385	.353
Runners On			20	5	0	8	5	.250	.250	.467
Runners/Scor. Pos.			10	3	0	3	2	.300	.300	.467
First 9 Batters			264	84	4	35	47	.318	.455	.401
Second 9 Batters			273	60	3	25	47	.220	.311	.285
All Batters Thereafter			343	101	17	45	50	.294	.501	.374

Loves to face: Rance Mulliniks (.040, 1-for-25, 3 BB)
Geno Petralli (.056, 1-for-18)
Harold Reynolds (.107, 6-for-56, 5 BB)
Hates to face: Tim Raines (.563, 9-for-16, 1 HR)
Danny Tartabull (.438, 14-for-32, 4 HR)
Greg Vaughn (.333, 7-for-21, 2 2B, 5 HR, 7 BB)

Miscellaneous statistics: Ground outs-to-air outs ratio: 1.01 last season, 0.86 for career.... Induced 19 double plays in 182 opportunities (one per 10).... Allowed 44 doubles, 8 triples (3d most in A.L.) in 226 innings.... Allowed 27 first-inning runs in 35 starts (6.94 ERA).... Batting support: 5.63 runs per start (2d-highest average in majors).... Opposing base stealers: 23-for-32 (72%); 0 pickoffs, 0 balks.

Comments: Loss to Mariners on April 19 was portent of a disappointing season; that loss broke a streak of 20 consecutive wins during April, and also broke a streak of 14 consecutive wins vs. Seattle.... Encountered troubles left and right last year: Opposing left-handed batters batted .302 (compared to .207 the year before); right-handed batters took him deep 16 times (compared to eight in 1990).... Had 13 starts in which he received no decision, most in A.L.; those 13 no-decisions matched his total for previous three years combined.... Even though his streak of four 20-win seasons was snapped, his 95 wins over past five years are still tops in majors. Only five pitchers are even within 20 wins of that total: Roger Clemens (94), Bob Welch (88), Frank Viola (87), Mark Langston (79), and Doug Drabek (77).... Opponents' batting average was the highest of his career. His ERA more than doubled from 1990 to 1991 (2.56 to 5.18). The increase of 2.62 earned runs per nine innings was the largest ever by a pitcher making at least 30 starts in both seasons.... Set major league single-season record of 16 balks in 1988, but hasn't been called for one since.... Opponents have a career average of .228 with runners in scoring position, compared to a .255 average in other at-bats. Opponents' average with RISP drops to .203 with two outs.... Became only the third pitcher in the three-city history of the franchise to start as many as 35 games in at least five consecutive seasons. The others: Vida Blue (1973–77) and Catfish Hunter (six years, 1969–74).

Todd Stottlemyre

Throws Right

Toronto Blue Jays	W-L	ERA	AB	H	HR	BB	SO	BA	SA	OBA
Season	15-8	3.78	826	194	21	75	116	.235	.356	.305
vs. Left-Handers			422	102	11	40	51	.242	.355	.310
vs. Right-Handers			404	92	10	35	65	.228	.356	.300
vs. Ground-Ballers			366	76	4	31	50	.208	.276	.276
vs. Fly-Ballers			460	118	17	44	66	.257	.420	.328
Home Games	9-3	3.96	437	99	12	28	51	.227	.362	.285
Road Games	6-5	3.58	389	95	9	47	65	.244	.350	.327
Grass Fields	4-4	3.68	296	71	7	37	48	.240	.345	.325
Artificial Turf	11-4	3.84	530	123	14	38	68	.232	.362	.293
April	2-0	3.91	85	19	1	12	17	.224	.329	.330
May	3-1	3.07	151	31	3	15	27	.205	.305	.274
June	4-2	2.78	171	41	5	8	19	.240	.357	.280
July	1-1	4.20	118	27	2	14	20	.229	.347	.321
August	2-2	5.35	147	44	6	11	14	.299	.469	.354
Sept./Oct.	3-2	3.80	154	32	4	15	19	.208	.318	.289
Leading Off Inn.			207	52	6	18	24	.251	.382	.323
Bases Empty			487	112	9	46	67	.230	.329	.308
Runners On			339	82	12	29	49	.242	.395	.301
Runners/Scor. Pos.			170	40	4	21	23	.235	.371	.310
Runners On/2 Out			152	39	5	17	20	.257	.382	.335
Scor. Pos./2 Out			85	17	1	15	10	.200	.271	.320
Late-Inning Pressure			65	21	2	4	9	.323	.492	.362
Leading Off			20	8	1	0	1	.400	.750	.400
Runners On			24	8	1	0	5	.333	.458	.333
Runners/Scor. Pos.			9	1	0	0	1	.111	.111	.111
First 9 Batters			270	57	9	27	42	.211	.333	.297
Second 9 Batters			273	57	5	25	38	.209	.315	.281
All Batters Thereafter			283	80	7	23	36	.283	.417	.337

Loves to face: Joe Carter (0-for-11)
Scott Fletcher (.056, 1-for-18, 2 BB)
Kent Hrbek (.067, 1-for-15, 1 2B, 2 BB)
Hates to face: George Brett (.611, 11-for-18)
Mel Hall (.563, 18-for-32, 1 HR)
Matt Nokes (.421, 16-for-38, 5 HR)

Miscellaneous statistics: Ground outs-to-air outs ratio: 0.93 last season, 0.95 for career.... Induced 10 double plays in 150 opportunities (one per 15), 3d-worst rate in A.L.... Allowed 27 doubles, 5 triples in 219 innings.... Allowed 19 first-inning runs in 34 starts (5.03 ERA).... Batting support: 4.26 runs per start.... Opposing base stealers: 24-for-27 (89%), including 18 steals in a row to start season, 4th-most steals in A.L.; 0 pickoffs, 0 balks.

Comments: Only three pairs of fathers and sons have ever pitched in the postseason: the Jim Bagbys Senior (1920) & Junior (1946); Dizzy Trout (1940, 1945) and Steve Trout (1984); and the Stottlemyres, Mel Senior (1964) and Todd (1989, 1991). The Bagbys remain the only father and son pitchers in World Series play.... Posted 2.30 ERA in 70⅓ innings with Pat Borders catching, 4.48 in 148⅔ innings with Greg Myers.... Allowed seven first-inning home runs, matching Rich DeLucia for the most in the majors.... His 11 no-decision starts were 3d most among A.L. pitchers.... Yearly opponents' batting averages since his 1988 debut: .283, .282, .274, .235.... Career breakdown of those figures: .294 by left-handed batters, .234 by right-handers. Last year was the first time in Todd's four years in majors that he held lefty batters below .300 mark.... Opponents have an overall career average of .264, but only a .210 mark with two outs and runners in scoring position.... Pitched over 200 innings, but no player had a sacrifice bunt against him. Only one other pitcher in the majors, Joe Slusarski, pitched even 100 innings without allowing a sacrifice bunt.... Has started 101 games, but has never thrown a shutout. The all-time record for that kind of thing is held by Roy Mahaffey (128 starts). Bill Krueger has the most among active pitchers (114).... Todd's father, Mel, is the only pitcher in the history of major league baseball to have two sons play in the majors.

Bill Swift
Throws Right

Seattle Mariners	W-L	ERA	AB	H	HR	BB	SO	BA	SA	OBA
Season	1-2	1.99	330	74	3	26	48	.224	.276	.283
vs. Left-Handers			123	29	1	9	15	.236	.276	.288
vs. Right-Handers			207	45	2	17	33	.217	.275	.280
vs. Ground-Ballers			141	32	1	11	23	.227	.255	.283
vs. Fly-Ballers			189	42	2	15	25	.222	.291	.283
Home Games	1-2	1.65	158	34	1	10	27	.215	.253	.262
Road Games	0-0	2.31	172	40	2	16	21	.233	.297	.302
Grass Fields	0-0	1.70	136	29	1	9	17	.213	.250	.267
Artificial Turf	1-2	2.19	194	45	2	17	31	.232	.294	.294
April	0-0	6.75	7	3	0	1	2	.429	.714	.500
May	0-1	2.38	78	16	2	4	13	.205	.282	.244
June	1-0	3.24	64	17	1	5	7	.266	.313	.319
July	0-1	1.15	59	13	0	5	10	.220	.220	.292
August	0-0	0.00	54	8	0	6	4	.148	.185	.233
Sept./Oct.	0-0	2.45	68	17	0	5	12	.250	.309	.301
Leading Off Inn.			73	20	1	3	13	.274	.370	.303
Bases Empty			157	40	2	13	25	.255	.331	.312
Runners On			173	34	1	13	23	.197	.225	.257
Runners/Scor. Pos.			99	18	1	12	13	.182	.222	.277
Runners On/2 Out			74	16	1	7	6	.216	.284	.293
Scor. Pos./2 Out			51	8	1	7	6	.157	.235	.271
Late-Inning Pressure			150	38	0	12	27	.253	.287	.309
Leading Off			36	10	0	1	9	.278	.333	.297
Runners On			75	17	0	6	12	.227	.240	.284
Runners/Scor. Pos.			41	7	0	5	6	.171	.195	.261
First 9 Batters			320	72	3	25	48	.225	.278	.283
Second 9 Batters			10	2	0	1	0	.200	.200	.273
All Batters Thereafter			0	0	0	0	0	—	—	—

Loves to face: Steve Buechele (0-for-13)
Willie Randolph (.095, 2-for-21, 4 BB)
Lonnie Smith (.188, 3-for-16)

Hates to face: Tony Fernandez (.545, 6-for-11)
Rich Gedman (.750, 9-for-12)
Fred McGriff (.500, 5-for-10, 1 HR)

Miscellaneous statistics: Ground outs-to-air outs ratio: 4.73 last season, 2.88 for career.... Induced 19 double plays in 90 opportunities (one per 4.7).... Allowed 6 doubles, 1 triple in 90⅓ innings.... Saved 17 games in 23 opportunities (74%).... Stranded 41 inherited runners, allowed 17 to score (71%).... Opposing base stealers: 1-for-2 (50%); 0 pickoffs, 1 balk.

Comments: Even pitching half his games in the King-dome, the A.L.'s top home-run park, this ground-ball pitcher extraordinaire has held home runs to a minimum. In each of his six seasons in the majors, he has pitched at least 90 innings, and has never had a home-run rate of one every 15 innings. No pitcher has had a six-year streak of that type since his new teammate, Dave Righetti, did it with the Yankees, 1981–86.... In his first 10 appearances of 1991, he recorded 34 outs on ground balls and only one in the air.... Biggest positive development of '91: Swift held left-handed batters to a .236 batting average. Prior to that, lefties had hit .321 off him. Even with last year's figure included, lefties still own a .313 career mark vs. Swift; only two other pitchers active in the majors in 1991 have allowed a .300 career average to lefties: Steve Crawford (.316) and Roy Smith (.306).... Owns career rate of only 3.46 strikeouts per nine innings, lowest among active pitchers with 750 or more innings; his 1991 strikeout rate (4.78) was a career high.... In the rich history of the Seattle Mariners, only Ed Vande Berg (272) and Mike Jackson (262) pitched in more games than Swift (253).... Ended season with 10 scoreless innings to drop his ERA below 2.00 over 71 games. The 70-Game, Below-2.00-ERA Club seems as if it should be a rather exclusive fraternity, but it's no Shoal Creek. Membership has grown to 24, including the 1991 admissions of Swift, Chuck McElroy, and Mark Eichhorn.

Greg Swindell
Throws Left

Cleveland Indians	W-L	ERA	AB	H	HR	BB	SO	BA	SA	OBA
Season	9-16	3.48	916	241	21	31	169	.263	.393	.287
vs. Left-Handers			153	42	1	7	28	.275	.373	.309
vs. Right-Handers			763	199	20	24	141	.261	.397	.283
vs. Ground-Ballers			436	112	8	15	73	.257	.362	.279
vs. Fly-Ballers			480	129	13	16	96	.269	.421	.294
Home Games	7-9	2.52	570	139	10	18	107	.244	.333	.267
Road Games	2-7	5.21	346	102	11	13	62	.295	.491	.320
Grass Fields	8-13	3.18	805	208	17	28	151	.258	.373	.284
Artificial Turf	1-3	5.65	111	33	4	3	18	.297	.541	.313
April	0-3	2.91	137	34	1	8	28	.248	.307	.295
May	2-2	2.72	153	39	3	2	25	.255	.392	.263
June	2-1	2.94	187	49	4	6	33	.262	.390	.289
July	2-3	4.04	138	35	6	4	36	.254	.442	.275
August	2-3	3.79	130	37	1	5	19	.285	.392	.307
Sept./Oct.	1-4	4.50	171	47	6	6	28	.275	.427	.294
Leading Off Inn.			242	63	5	2	45	.260	.388	.272
Bases Empty			578	143	8	14	116	.247	.344	.269
Runners On			338	98	13	17	53	.290	.476	.317
Runners/Scor. Pos.			190	47	4	13	33	.247	.368	.284
Runners On/2 Out			140	37	2	5	24	.264	.407	.290
Scor. Pos./2 Out			87	21	1	5	16	.241	.379	.283
Late-Inning Pressure			104	27	0	3	18	.260	.308	.278
Leading Off			30	4	0	0	5	.133	.167	.133
Runners On			31	5	0	2	6	.161	.194	.206
Runners/Scor. Pos.			13	1	0	2	3	.077	.077	.188
First 9 Batters			284	69	6	5	69	.243	.380	.261
Second 9 Batters			270	67	4	15	49	.248	.341	.285
All Batters Thereafter			362	105	11	11	51	.290	.442	.309

Loves to face: Steve Finley (0-for-10)
Willie Randolph (.188, 6-for-32)
Gary Redus (0-for-10)

Hates to face: George Bell (.375, 9-for-24, 3 HR)
Fred McGriff (.385, 5-for-13, 1 HR, 6 BB, 6 SO)
Luis Salazar (.600, 6-for-10)

Miscellaneous statistics: Ground outs-to-air outs ratio: 0.75 last season, 0.76 for career.... Induced 15 double plays in 158 opportunities (one per 11).... Allowed 48 doubles (2d most in majors), 4 triples in 238 innings.... Allowed 20 first-inning runs in 33 starts (4.36 ERA).... Batting support: 3.42 runs per start, 3d-lowest average in A.L.... Opposing base stealers: 9-for-20 (45%); 9 pickoffs (2d most in A.L.), 1 balk.

Comments: Walked only two of 246 batters faced leading off innings, and ended the season with a streak of 137 leadoff batters faced without a walk. Among pitchers who have thrown at least 200 innings in a season since 1975, only Rick Langford of the 1982 A's had a lower rate of leadoff walks (one in 246 innings); Zane Smith came close in 1991 (two in 233 innings).... Career average of 1.95 walks per nine innings is 2d lowest among active pitchers with at least 1000 innings, behind only Bret Saberhagen (1.79), but Swindell is gaining. His yearly walk rate since 1989: 2.49, 1.97, 1.17.... Since his major league debut in 1986, Swindell has posted a winning percentage of .522 (60–55), but Indians have had only a .418 pecentage (308–428) in games in which he wasn't involved in the decision.... ERA in home games was second lowest in A.L., but his nine losses at Cleveland Stadium were second most by any pitcher in his home ballpark. Indians scored fewer than three runs in 13 of his 20 home starts, and exactly three runs in another three starts.... Has allowed a .293 career batting average on artificial turf, not good news for Riverfront fans.... Had lowest ERA among A.L. starters with losing records (minimum: 100 innings). The last pitcher with as poor a won-lost record as Swindell in a 30-start season with a sub-3.50 ERA: Nolan Ryan (8–16, 2.76) in 1987. Contributing factor was his defensive support, or lack thereof. Swindell was charged with 20 unearned runs, the most against any pitcher in the majors last season.

Frank Tanana — Throws Left

Detroit Tigers	W-L	ERA	AB	H	HR	BB	SO	BA	SA	OBA
Season	13-12	3.77	818	217	26	78	107	.265	.412	.327
vs. Left-Handers			159	37	5	11	25	.233	.371	.282
vs. Right-Handers			659	180	21	67	82	.273	.422	.338
vs. Ground-Ballers			375	108	10	26	37	.288	.413	.334
vs. Fly-Ballers			443	109	16	52	70	.246	.411	.322
Home Games	7-5	4.10	452	122	14	49	62	.270	.416	.341
Road Games	6-7	3.35	366	95	12	29	45	.260	.407	.311
Grass Fields	13-11	3.72	772	203	24	73	102	.263	.408	.325
Artificial Turf	0-1	4.63	46	14	2	5	5	.304	.478	.365
April	1-2	3.71	136	40	5	9	15	.294	.426	.338
May	1-2	7.77	92	31	8	14	10	.337	.641	.425
June	3-2	1.21	155	29	3	14	30	.187	.277	.251
July	2-1	4.38	93	28	0	8	11	.301	.366	.350
August	4-1	3.73	155	43	7	14	16	.277	.471	.331
Sept./Oct.	2-4	4.06	187	46	3	19	25	.246	.374	.319
Leading Off Inn.			208	64	13	15	23	.308	.548	.354
Bases Empty			486	139	20	40	54	.286	.463	.342
Runners On			332	78	6	38	53	.235	.337	.308
Runners/Scor. Pos.			186	38	3	26	30	.204	.290	.293
Runners On/2 Out			141	37	3	16	22	.262	.390	.342
Scor. Pos./2 Out			92	21	1	12	11	.228	.315	.324
Late-Inning Pressure			35	14	0	8	3	.400	.429	.489
Leading Off			8	1	0	3	0	.125	.125	.364
Runners On			18	10	0	2	1	.556	.611	.545
Runners/Scor. Pos.			10	4	0	2	1	.400	.400	.429
First 9 Batters			270	77	11	23	45	.285	.470	.341
Second 9 Batters			250	60	7	27	29	.240	.360	.311
All Batters Thereafter			298	80	8	28	33	.268	.403	.329

Loves to face: Jim Gantner (.143, 6-for-42)
Ozzie Guillen (.182, 8-for-44, 0 BB)
Harold Reynolds (.193, 11-for-57)

Hates to face: Rickey Henderson (.367, 33-for-90, 9 HR)
Paul Molitor (.380, 27-for-71, 3 HR)
Kirby Puckett (.391, 18-for-46, 3 HR)

Miscellaneous statistics: Ground outs-to-air outs ratio: 0.93 last season, 0.99 for career.... Induced 17 double plays in 169 opportunities (one per 10).... Allowed 34 doubles, 4 triples in 217⅓ innings.... Allowed 17 first-inning runs in 33 starts (4.68 ERA).... Batting support: 4.79 runs per start.... Opposing base stealers: 17-for-31 (55%); 7 pickoffs, 1 balk.

Comments: The starting pitcher in the first game ever played in both the Kingdome and new Comiskey Park, becoming the sixth pitcher in this century, and only the second in the last 80 years, to start inaugural major league games at two different parks. Thanks to expansion, Camilo Pascual did it within a six-day span in 1961 (Metropolitan Stadium and L.A.'s Wrigley Field). Bill Carrick, Joe McGinnity, Cy Young, and Eddie Plank did it during the 19-aughts. (What name do you give to the first decade of a century, anyway? We hope there's a committee out there working on this. And is it two thousand or twenty hundred?) But Tanana topped them all: Not only did he open two parks, he threw shutouts in both games! You want more? O.K., remember the last game at Memorial Stadium? That's right, Tanana beat the Birds 4–1.... Allowed 13 home runs leading off innings; no other pitcher in majors allowed more than 10.... One of ten pitchers in history to start at least 100 games for each of three different major league teams.... What makes Tanana a rare bird is that he has enjoyed winning, 30-start seasons in which his rate of strikeouts per nine innings has ranged from a high of 9.42 (in 1975) to a low of 4.43 (in 1990). In between, he has also had winning seasons with his strikeout rate in the eights, sevens, sixes, and fives. Think about it: He has been a winner in 30-start seasons with his strikeout rate in six different whole-number categories. Only one other pitcher in major league history has done that: another thinking man's pitcher, Tom Seaver.

Kevin Tapani — Throws Right

Minnesota Twins	W-L	ERA	AB	H	HR	BB	SO	BA	SA	OBA
Season	16-9	2.99	917	225	23	40	135	.245	.382	.277
vs. Left-Handers			520	122	8	16	69	.235	.342	.257
vs. Right-Handers			397	103	15	24	66	.259	.433	.302
vs. Ground-Ballers			437	119	8	13	52	.272	.389	.295
vs. Fly-Ballers			480	106	15	27	83	.221	.375	.260
Home Games	10-5	2.79	494	117	12	25	80	.237	.372	.274
Road Games	6-4	3.22	423	108	11	15	55	.255	.392	.279
Grass Fields	5-1	2.82	266	66	6	9	31	.248	.372	.272
Artificial Turf	11-8	3.06	651	159	17	31	104	.244	.386	.278
April	2-0	2.10	111	26	2	4	23	.234	.324	.267
May	0-6	5.35	156	46	6	10	22	.295	.506	.335
June	3-1	1.56	145	29	3	2	19	.200	.283	.211
July	3-0	2.76	177	48	2	6	17	.271	.395	.293
August	5-0	2.63	171	35	5	10	20	.205	.345	.250
Sept./Oct.	3-2	3.48	157	41	5	8	34	.261	.414	.293
Leading Off Inn.			237	65	10	12	29	.274	.498	.312
Bases Empty			582	150	18	26	94	.258	.419	.292
Runners On			335	75	5	14	41	.224	.316	.251
Runners/Scor. Pos.			186	38	1	8	23	.204	.263	.230
Runners On/2 Out			145	28	1	5	18	.193	.248	.220
Scor. Pos./2 Out			84	15	0	4	12	.179	.202	.216
Late-Inning Pressure			71	18	1	2	10	.254	.338	.280
Leading Off			21	6	0	1	3	.286	.381	.318
Runners On			21	7	1	1	2	.333	.524	.348
Runners/Scor. Pos.			5	2	0	1	0	.400	.400	.429
First 9 Batters			285	51	5	15	43	.179	.274	.221
Second 9 Batters			296	86	7	7	38	.291	.446	.305
All Batters Thereafter			336	88	11	18	54	.262	.417	.300

Loves to face: Scott Bradley (.059, 1-for-17)
Alvin Davis (.091, 2-for-22)
Candy Maldonado (0-for-10)

Hates to face: Jose Canseco (.375, 6-for-16, 3 HR)
Edgar Martinez (.500, 7-for-14)
Brian McRae (.538, 7-for-13, 1 HR)

Miscellaneous statistics: Ground outs-to-air outs ratio: 1.16 last season, 1.08 for career.... Induced 15 double plays in 129 opportunities (one per 8.6).... Allowed 48 doubles (2d most in majors), 4 triples in 244 innings.... Allowed 9 first-inning runs in 34 starts (2.38 ERA).... Batting support: 4.85 runs per start.... Opposing base stealers: 18-for-21 (86%); 0 pickoffs, 3 balks (3d most in A.L.).

Comments: Formula for success, easy to describe but difficult to achieve: Step One, don't let batters reach base; Step Two, when they do get on base, keep them there. Tapani followed the formula in 1991. He allowed only 9.85 base runners per nine innings (the only other A.L. starters with rates below 10 were Nolan Ryan and Roger Clemens); he then took care of the guys who did reach by holding opponents to a .204 batting average with runners in scoring position.... In 67 career starts during the regular season, he has never walked more than three batters in a game. Averaged 1.48 walks per nine innings last season, 4th-lowest rate in majors.... Career breakdown: 19-9 at home, 11-10 on road.... Six losses in May were the most by any A.L. pitcher in any month, matched by Angels' Joe Grahe in August. Had six-game losing streak in May and nine-game winning streak extending into September. Only two other A.L. pitchers had both a winning streak and a losing streak of even five games in length—Kevin Appier and David Wells—both of whom won seven straight and lost five straight.... Tapani went 11–2 with 2.84 ERA after All-Star break. Jack Morris was 7–6 (3.18) and Scott Erickson 8–5 (5.20) during second half.... Committed one of only five errors made by Twins pitchers last season, lowest total by any staff (1981 excluded) since White Sox made only four errors in 1964. Only two other teams in this century had pitching staffs that made as few as four errors in a season: 1948 Cardinals and 1958 White Sox.

Wade Taylor

Throws Right

New York Yankees	W-L	ERA	AB	H	HR	BB	SO	BA	SA	OBA
Season	7-12	6.27	459	144	13	53	72	.314	.477	.388
vs. Left-Handers			206	67	6	31	29	.325	.485	.415
vs. Right-Handers			253	77	7	22	43	.304	.470	.365
vs. Ground-Ballers			213	69	3	22	29	.324	.446	.392
vs. Fly-Ballers			246	75	10	31	43	.305	.504	.385
Home Games	5-6	5.34	249	81	6	19	36	.325	.454	.373
Road Games	2-6	7.33	210	63	7	34	36	.300	.505	.404
Grass Fields	7-11	6.55	410	131	12	48	62	.320	.483	.395
Artificial Turf	0-1	4.05	49	13	1	5	10	.265	.429	.327
April	0-0	—	0	0	0	0	0	—	—	—
May	0-0	—	0	0	0	0	0	—	—	—
June	3-2	6.39	99	27	2	11	16	.273	.384	.351
July	2-4	6.55	132	46	4	15	21	.348	.523	.421
August	2-1	5.16	112	34	4	12	17	.304	.455	.365
Sept./Oct.	0-5	6.99	116	37	3	15	18	.319	.526	.403
Leading Off Inn.			114	42	3	11	16	.368	.570	.429
Bases Empty			236	72	4	29	40	.305	.449	.393
Runners On			223	72	9	24	32	.323	.507	.383
Runners/Scor. Pos.			127	41	2	11	14	.323	.433	.363
Runners On/2 Out			76	20	1	9	11	.263	.382	.349
Scor. Pos./2 Out			50	14	1	4	3	.280	.440	.345
Late-Inning Pressure			2	2	1	0	0	1.000	2.500	1.000
Leading Off			1	1	0	0	0	1.000	1.000	1.000
Runners On			1	1	1	0	0	1.000	4.000	1.000
Runners/Scor. Pos.			0	0	0	0	0	—	—	—
First 9 Batters			172	52	6	22	28	.302	.459	.395
Second 9 Batters			158	50	4	19	25	.316	.487	.385
All Batters Thereafter			129	42	3	12	19	.326	.488	.381

Loves to face: Cecil Fielder (0-for-5)
Dan Gladden (0-for-7)
Rickey Henderson (0-for-7)

Hates to face: Carlos Baerga (3-for-3, 1 HR)
Mike Bordick (3-for-3)
Joe Orsulak (.600, 3-for-5, 1 2B, 1 HR)

Miscellaneous statistics: Ground outs-to-air outs ratio: 1.34 last season, 1.34 for career.... Induced 17 double plays in 123 opportunities (one per 7.2).... Allowed 28 doubles, 4 triples in 116⅓ innings.... Allowed 11 first-inning runs in 22 starts (4.57 ERA).... Batting support: 4.14 runs per start.... Opposing base stealers: 12-for-18 (67%); 4 pickoffs, 3 balks (3d most in A.L.).

Comments: The purest records are those that are set without the setter even knowing it, since such records are free from outside influences. Whenever a player is aware of a record or an achievement, that awareness may consciously or subconsciously alter his style of play; the record is then compromised in some small degree. This subtlety is at the root of our distaste for consecutive-game streaks and similar records. Last year, Taylor set a record that he didn't know about: He had the highest ERA in baseball history by any rookie making 20 or more starts. His 6.266 ERA just nosed out Jim Walkup of the 1935 Browns, whose ERA was 6.265. In fact, Walkup was the only other 20-start rookie with an ERA of 6.00 or higher. Had Taylor or Stump (or to use his formal title, manager Stump) known that he needed to retire just one more batter to avoid that distinction, that might have been arranged, though perhaps not confidently.... Allowed 15.78 base runners per nine innings, highest rate among major league pitchers with at least 100 innings last season.... Only the second Yankee pitcher over last 25 years to win each of his first two major league games. The other: Scott Nielsen in 1986.... Combined record of Yanks' rookie pitchers, by month: June, 6–6 (4.66 ERA); July, 7–6 (4.37); August, 3–7 (8.13); Sept./Oct., 1–9 (6.66).... Three pitchers from last year's rotation produced the three highest individual ERAs in Yankees history among pitchers with at least 15 starts: Tim Leary, 6.49; Taylor, 6.27; Jeff Johnson, 5.95. The old record: Dave LaPoint's 5.62 in 1989.

Walt Terrell

Throws Right

Detroit Tigers	W-L	ERA	AB	H	HR	BB	SO	BA	SA	OBA
Season	12-14	4.24	853	257	16	79	80	.301	.433	.358
vs. Left-Handers			461	141	9	50	31	.306	.440	.371
vs. Right-Handers			392	116	7	29	49	.296	.423	.343
vs. Ground-Ballers			414	124	8	34	30	.300	.428	.350
vs. Fly-Ballers			439	133	8	45	50	.303	.437	.366
Home Games	9-7	4.84	442	138	13	36	38	.312	.452	.360
Road Games	3-7	3.62	411	119	3	43	42	.290	.411	.357
Grass Fields	12-12	4.02	769	225	15	72	76	.293	.414	.351
Artificial Turf	0-2	6.52	84	32	1	7	4	.381	.607	.424
April	0-3	3.60	122	38	2	9	13	.311	.467	.356
May	2-2	5.45	146	47	1	14	10	.322	.452	.379
June	2-3	3.98	153	46	3	11	14	.301	.425	.341
July	3-1	3.82	129	38	3	12	12	.295	.442	.357
August	3-1	4.31	146	40	4	20	18	.274	.397	.359
Sept./Oct.	2-4	4.20	157	48	3	13	13	.306	.420	.358
Leading Off Inn.			219	70	3	11	18	.320	.479	.352
Bases Empty			487	146	10	32	53	.300	.456	.344
Runners On			366	111	6	47	27	.303	.402	.376
Runners/Scor. Pos.			208	65	3	34	18	.313	.423	.397
Runners On/2 Out			149	44	2	18	14	.295	.376	.371
Scor. Pos./2 Out			87	26	1	16	9	.299	.368	.408
Late-Inning Pressure			63	17	1	6	7	.270	.333	.333
Leading Off			20	5	0	0	2	.250	.250	.250
Runners On			23	5	0	3	1	.217	.217	.308
Runners/Scor. Pos.			10	3	0	1	1	.300	.300	.364
First 9 Batters			278	76	4	25	30	.273	.399	.331
Second 9 Batters			270	86	5	24	21	.319	.437	.372
All Batters Thereafter			305	95	7	30	29	.311	.459	.372

Loves to face: Dan Pasqua (.088, 3-for-34, 1 HR, 5 BB)
Tony Pena (.107, 3-for-28)
Omar Vizquel (.059, 1-for-17, 1 2B)

Hates to face: Wade Boggs (.404, 23-for-57, 2 HR)
Brian Downing (.483, 14-for-29, 1 HR)
Paul Molitor (.488, 21-for-43, 2 HR)

Miscellaneous statistics: Ground outs-to-air outs ratio: 1.28 last season, 1.39 for career.... Induced 35 double plays in 190 opportunities (one per 5.4), best rate in majors.... Allowed 48 doubles (2d most in majors), 8 triples (3d most in A.L.) in 218⅔ innings.... Allowed 12 first-inning runs in 33 starts (3.27 ERA).... Batting support: 4.73 runs per start.... Opposing base stealers: 6-for-11 (55%); 0 pickoffs, 0 balks.

Comments: One of four pitchers active in 1991 with at least 100 career wins but a sub-.500 record: Jim Clancy (140–167), Mike Moore (115–130), Walt Terrell (104–114), and Danny Darwin (114–115). Darwin's career ERA is 3.46; the other three guys are in the fours.... On a more positive if less compelling note, here are the five pitchers active in 1991 with the lowest error rates: Jim Acker (one error every 115.5 chances), Frank Tanana (53.8), Mike Flanagan (51.7), Terrell (50.3), Dan Petry (50.3).... Do kids still argue about which league is better? A strong exhibit in defense of the Senior Circuit: Terrell's career record is 26–43 in N.L., 78–71 in A.L.; he has a winning record for both the Yankees and Tigers, and a losing record with the Mets, Padres, and Pirates.... Another way to look at his career: He's 48–21 (3.40 ERA) at Tiger Stadium, 56–93 (4.51) elsewhere.... Averaged 3.29 strikeouts per nine innings last season, the lowest rate of his career; his opponents' batting average, meanwhile, was a career high.... He compiled an 8–1 record with a 3.23 ERA over the two-month period immediately following the All-Star break. It was during that period that Detroit erased an eight-game Toronto lead.... He has strong roots in New York sports aside from pitching for both the Mets and Yankees. He's been in trades involving Ron Darling, Lee Mazzilli, Howard Johnson, and Mike Pagliarulo, and attended Morehead State University, alma mater of Giants' quarterback Phil Simms.

Bobby Thigpen
Throws Right

Chicago White Sox	W-L	ERA	AB	H	HR	BB	SO	BA	SA	OBA
Season	7-5	3.49	257	63	10	38	47	.245	.409	.348
vs. Left-Handers			124	32	6	21	18	.258	.468	.363
vs. Right-Handers			133	31	4	17	29	.233	.353	.333
vs. Ground-Ballers			119	35	3	17	19	.294	.429	.391
vs. Fly-Ballers			138	28	7	21	28	.203	.391	.311
Home Games	5-2	4.59	128	35	5	17	22	.273	.438	.363
Road Games	2-3	2.48	129	28	5	21	25	.217	.380	.333
Grass Fields	6-4	3.67	226	53	9	34	43	.235	.398	.336
Artificial Turf	1-1	2.16	31	10	1	4	4	.323	.484	.432
April	0-0	4.35	39	8	2	7	9	.205	.410	.326
May	3-1	3.07	52	10	3	13	11	.192	.404	.364
June	1-1	5.79	35	12	2	5	5	.343	.600	.429
July	3-1	1.62	54	11	1	6	7	.204	.259	.295
August	0-1	2.38	43	10	1	3	9	.233	.349	.277
Sept./Oct.	0-1	6.14	34	12	1	4	6	.353	.529	.425
Leading Off Inn.			46	8	1	7	8	.174	.239	.296
Bases Empty			113	30	5	12	20	.265	.434	.346
Runners On			144	33	5	26	27	.229	.389	.349
Runners/Scor. Pos.			88	19	2	20	19	.216	.341	.363
Runners On/2 Out			65	15	2	18	14	.231	.400	.412
Scor. Pos./2 Out			49	13	2	16	12	.265	.469	.463
Late-Inning Pressure			207	51	8	34	39	.246	.401	.359
Leading Off			37	5	0	7	8	.135	.135	.289
Runners On			117	29	5	23	23	.248	.419	.372
Runners/Scor. Pos.			73	18	2	17	17	.247	.370	.389
First 9 Batters			253	62	10	38	47	.245	.407	.347
Second 9 Batters			4	1	0	0	0	.250	.500	.400
All Batters Thereafter			0	0	0	0	0	—	—	—

Loves to face: George Brett (.067, 1-for-15, 2 BB)
Jim Gantner (0-for-11)
Geno Petralli (.071, 1-for-14)

Hates to face: Julio Franco (.636, 7-for-11, 1 HR)
Mel Hall (.462, 6-for-13, 2 HR)
Ruben Sierra (.313, 5-for-16, 2 HR)

Miscellaneous statistics: Ground outs-to-air outs ratio: 1.15 last season, 0.92 for career.... Induced 4 double plays in 77 opportunities (one per 19).... Allowed 8 doubles, 2 triples in 69⅔ innings.... Saved 30 games in 39 opportunities (77%).... Stranded 27 inherited runners, allowed 12 to score (69%).... Opposing base stealers: 8-for-13 (62%); 1 pickoff, 0 balks.

Comments: Third pitcher in A.L. history to record 30 or more saves in four consecutive seasons. Dennis Eckersley, owner of a concurrent streak, and Dan Quisenberry (1982–85) are the others to do it. Jeff Reardon and John Franco share the major league record with five-year streaks.... Among the nine A.L. pitchers with 30 or more saves last season, Thigpen was the one most likely to be called into a game with runners on base; he inherited at least one runner in 31 of his 67 appearances.... Allowed 13.6 base runners per nine innings last season, the highest rate among the 18 major league pitchers with 20 or more saves. Among that same group, only Mitch Williams (6.32) allowed more walks per nine innings than Thigpen (4.91), with no other pitcher over four, and only Craig Lefferts (3.91) had a higher ERA than Thigpen. Thig's rates of base runners and walks were career highs, as was his average of allowing one home run every seven innings.... Walked Greg Vaughn, Rick Dempsey, and Willie Randolph in the same game in July, but did not walk any of 56 right-handed batters he faced after that.... Has limited opponents to lower batting average with runners on base than with bases empty in each of his five 50-game seasons in majors. Career breakdowns: .250 with bases empty, .224 with runners on base; .255 in Chicago, .213 on road.... Needs 15 relief appearances to pass Hoyt Wilhelm (358) as all-time team leader in that category. Red Faber holds team record for games pitched (669, including 484 starts).

Duane Ward
Throws Right

Toronto Blue Jays	W-L	ERA	AB	H	HR	BB	SO	BA	SA	OBA
Season	7-6	2.77	386	80	3	33	132	.207	.262	.271
vs. Left-Handers			187	36	3	21	76	.193	.278	.275
vs. Right-Handers			199	44	0	12	56	.221	.246	.266
vs. Ground-Ballers			169	37	0	16	62	.219	.266	.282
vs. Fly-Ballers			217	43	3	17	70	.198	.258	.262
Home Games	5-4	3.14	225	46	1	15	81	.204	.244	.257
Road Games	2-2	2.23	161	34	2	18	51	.211	.286	.289
Grass Fields	1-2	2.16	121	27	1	13	33	.223	.298	.296
Artificial Turf	6-4	3.04	265	53	2	20	99	.200	.245	.259
April	0-1	3.09	46	12	1	2	19	.261	.391	.306
May	0-1	1.69	55	10	0	6	14	.182	.182	.266
June	1-1	2.66	78	12	1	10	28	.154	.205	.244
July	2-0	2.95	68	14	1	4	27	.206	.309	.250
August	3-2	4.43	79	21	0	6	21	.266	.316	.318
Sept./Oct.	1-1	1.56	60	11	0	5	23	.183	.183	.246
Leading Off Inn.			94	20	1	2	38	.213	.277	.229
Bases Empty			232	44	1	10	93	.190	.237	.223
Runners On			154	36	2	23	39	.234	.299	.333
Runners/Scor. Pos.			100	28	2	15	23	.280	.370	.372
Runners On/2 Out			72	19	1	14	16	.264	.347	.398
Scor. Pos./2 Out			50	14	1	11	9	.280	.380	.429
Late-Inning Pressure			239	50	1	18	76	.209	.234	.268
Leading Off			59	13	0	0	23	.220	.237	.220
Runners On			96	20	1	14	21	.208	.240	.316
Runners/Scor. Pos.			60	15	1	8	12	.250	.300	.347
First 9 Batters			364	75	3	31	127	.206	.261	.269
Second 9 Batters			22	5	0	2	5	.227	.273	.292
All Batters Thereafter			0	0	0	0	0	—	—	—

Loves to face: Jose Canseco (0-for-10)
Carlos Quintana (.091, 1-for-11, 8 SO)
Steve Sax (.143, 2-for-14)

Hates to face: Mike Greenwell (.500, 7-for-14)
Ken Griffey, Jr. (.556, 5-for-9, 1 HR)
Rickey Henderson (.474, 9-for-19)

Miscellaneous statistics: Ground outs-to-air outs ratio: 1.39 last season, 1.86 for career.... Induced 8 double plays in 73 opportunities (one per 9.1).... Allowed 10 doubles, 1 triple in 107⅓ innings.... Saved 23 games in 35 opportunities (66%).... Stranded 26 inherited runners, allowed 10 to score (72%).... Opposing base stealers: 7-for-11 (64%); 0 pickoffs, 0 balks.

Comments: Twenty-three saves last season were the most ever by a pitcher who did not lead his club in that category. The old record: 21 by Jesse Orosco with 1986 Mets.... Only player to have pitched 100 or more innings in relief in each of the last four years. Last pitcher to do that: Dan Quisenberry (1982–85); major league record: seven years, Rollie Fingers (1972–78). But closers usually don't pitch 100 innings in a season anymore. Ward generally serves as setup man for Tom Henke when Henke is healthy; he was the only one of the 18 major league pitchers with 20 or more saves last year to reach 100 innings.... Allowed an average of one home run every 35.8 innings pitched, the best rate among A.L. pitchers last season (minimum: 100 innings).... Has not allowed a home run to a right-handed batter since Tom Brunansky hit a big one during 1990 pennant race (Sept. 29). No other pitcher in the majors faced as many right-handers without allowing them a home run last season.... Held opposing batters hitless in 32 consecutive at-bats with runners on base, April 25–May 30.... Opponents' batting average, year by year since his first full season in 1988: .245, .230, .221, .207.... Rate of walks per nine innings (2.77) was lowest of his career; rate of strikeouts per nine innings (11.07) was his highest. Total of 132 strikeouts in relief was 12th highest in major league history; of the 11 others, only Rob Dibble had a rate of strikeouts as high as Ward's (Dibble averaged 12.82 in 1989 and 12.49 in 1990).

Bill Wegman
Throws Right

Milwaukee Brewers	W-L	ERA	AB	H	HR	BB	SO	BA	SA	OBA
Season	15-7	2.84	728	176	16	40	89	.242	.356	.286
vs. Left-Handers			384	85	6	26	33	.221	.307	.271
vs. Right-Handers			344	91	10	14	56	.265	.410	.303
vs. Ground-Ballers			342	84	5	18	32	.246	.339	.292
vs. Fly-Ballers			386	92	11	22	57	.238	.370	.281
Home Games	7-4	2.62	382	91	8	21	51	.238	.325	.285
Road Games	8-3	3.09	346	85	8	19	38	.246	.390	.287
Grass Fields	14-5	2.53	655	155	14	36	80	.237	.347	.281
Artificial Turf	1-2	5.68	73	21	2	4	9	.288	.438	.333
April	0-0	—	0	0	0	0	0	—	—	—
May	1-1	5.16	85	24	2	7	9	.282	.376	.344
June	2-2	3.23	118	30	2	6	16	.254	.364	.302
July	3-2	2.76	156	36	3	8	16	.231	.346	.267
August	4-1	2.47	158	42	5	8	13	.266	.405	.305
Sept./Oct.	5-1	2.03	211	44	4	11	35	.209	.313	.253
Leading Off Inn.			192	51	9	9	22	.266	.443	.299
Bases Empty			466	116	12	24	55	.249	.386	.293
Runners On			262	60	4	16	34	.229	.302	.275
Runners/Scor. Pos.			147	34	2	11	24	.231	.293	.282
Runners On/2 Out			119	26	2	5	19	.218	.303	.250
Scor. Pos./2 Out			72	16	1	4	14	.222	.292	.263
Late-Inning Pressure			85	19	4	4	18	.224	.388	.267
Leading Off			25	6	1	0	3	.240	.400	.240
Runners On			29	5	2	1	8	.172	.379	.200
Runners/Scor. Pos.			15	1	1	1	7	.067	.267	.125
First 9 Batters			223	49	4	20	27	.220	.305	.292
Second 9 Batters			228	53	5	10	25	.232	.346	.267
All Batters Thereafter			277	74	7	10	37	.267	.404	.298

Loves to face: Alvin Davis (.107, 3-for-28)
Dwight Evans (.067, 1-for-15, 2 BB)
Lou Whitaker (.128, 6-for-47, 3 2B, 1 HR)

Hates to face: Ellis Burks (.615, 8-for-13, 1 HR)
Kent Hrbek (.406, 13-for-32, 4 HR)
Ruben Sierra (.500, 9-for-18, 5 2B, 2 HR)

Miscellaneous statistics: Ground outs-to-air outs ratio: 1.36 last season, 0.93 for career.... Induced 17 double plays in 117 opportunities (one per 6.9).... Allowed 29 doubles, 3 triples in 193⅓ innings.... Allowed 19 first-inning runs in 28 starts (3.25 ERA).... Batting support: 5.00 runs per start, 6th-highest average in A.L.... Opposing base stealers: 10-for-17 (59%); 2 pickoffs, 0 balks.

Comments: The only pitcher in the majors to throw complete games in four consecutive appearances last season. That streak was followed by his shortest outing of the year: two-thirds of an inning in which he allowed eight runs, which nonetheless lowered his ERA, since all were unearned.... He won 11 games after the All-Star break, tying Kevin Tapani and Jim Abbott for the A.L. lead.... Not bad timing for a guy entering a winter of free-agent eligibility. He re-signed with Brewers for four years, at over two million per.... In three previous 25-start seasons in majors (1986–88), his ERAs read 5.13, 4.24, and 4.12. His 1991 ERA was almost two runs lower than his previous career average (4.63). Elbow problems had limited him to fewer than 100 innings (majors and minors) over the previous two seasons combined.... Allowed less than one home run for every nine innings pitched for first time in his major league career.... Career average of 2.13 walks per nine innings is 3d lowest in team history, behind Lary Sorensen (1.82) and Mike Caldwell (1.98).... Allowed 15 unearned runs last season, tied with teammate Jaime Navarro for 3d most among A.L. pitchers.... Averaged 4.14 strikeouts per nine innings last season. Only three of the 28 major league pitchers who won at least 15 games last season had strikeout rates below 4.5 (meaning less than one strikeout every other inning); Brewers had two of them, Wegman and Jaime Navarro (4.38). Bill Gullickson won 20 games with a 3.62 strikeout rate, becoming the first 20-game winner with fewer than 100 strikeouts since Tommy John in 1980.

Bob Welch
Throws Right

Oakland A's	W-L	ERA	AB	H	HR	BB	SO	BA	SA	OBA
Season	12-13	4.58	835	220	25	91	101	.263	.404	.341
vs. Left-Handers			430	117	8	51	49	.272	.377	.348
vs. Right-Handers			405	103	17	40	52	.254	.432	.334
vs. Ground-Ballers			405	100	6	39	41	.247	.343	.318
vs. Fly-Ballers			430	120	19	52	60	.279	.460	.362
Home Games	8-7	3.60	464	112	9	43	65	.241	.351	.309
Road Games	4-6	5.87	371	108	16	48	36	.291	.469	.380
Grass Fields	11-9	3.85	675	172	17	71	91	.255	.381	.330
Artificial Turf	1-4	7.88	160	48	8	20	10	.300	.500	.388
April	3-1	1.80	145	31	2	6	13	.214	.262	.265
May	1-2	5.63	150	39	7	21	16	.260	.460	.353
June	3-2	3.82	125	26	2	12	13	.208	.312	.286
July	1-1	4.98	137	45	7	10	24	.328	.533	.373
August	3-3	4.69	149	39	3	15	15	.262	.376	.331
Sept./Oct.	1-4	7.11	129	40	4	27	20	.310	.481	.434
Leading Off Inn.			203	56	10	27	19	.276	.478	.364
Bases Empty			484	122	15	50	52	.252	.382	.328
Runners On			351	98	10	41	49	.279	.433	.359
Runners/Scor. Pos.			190	59	4	29	33	.311	.447	.396
Runners On/2 Out			143	41	2	22	24	.287	.392	.389
Scor. Pos./2 Out			86	25	1	16	16	.291	.384	.408
Late-Inning Pressure			70	19	2	5	10	.271	.443	.338
Leading Off			18	7	2	2	1	.389	.833	.450
Runners On			32	5	0	3	6	.156	.281	.250
Runners/Scor. Pos.			15	2	0	2	6	.133	.200	.235
First 9 Batters			280	72	6	29	37	.257	.361	.332
Second 9 Batters			258	76	7	35	29	.295	.434	.381
All Batters Thereafter			297	72	12	27	35	.242	.418	.314

Loves to face: Brady Anderson (0-for-13)
Wade Boggs (.037, 1-for-27, 1 2B, 3 BB)
Al Newman (.091, 2-for-22)

Hates to face: Glenn Davis (.467, 14-for-30, 2 HR)
Danny Tartabull (.367, 11-for-30, 4 HR)
Lou Whitaker (.333, 11-for-33, 5 2B, 3 HR)

Miscellaneous statistics: Ground outs-to-air outs ratio: 0.91 last season, 0.93 for career.... Induced 17 double plays in 179 opportunities (one per 11).... Allowed 34 doubles, 4 triples in 220 innings.... Allowed 16 first-inning runs in 35 starts (4.11 ERA).... Batting support: 4.34 runs per start.... Opposing base stealers: 12-for-28 (43%); 3 pickoffs, 2 balks.

Comments: From August 12, 1989, to August 12, 1991, Welch made 71 regular-season starts without so much as a two-game losing streak. Dwight Gooden, who has the highest winning percentage among active pitchers, has never made more than 44 straight starts without a two-game losing streak. Roger Clemens's longest such streak: 48 starts.... Among pitchers in franchise history with at least 100 decisions, only Lefty Grove (.714, 195–78) has a higher winning percentage than Welch (.670, 73–36).... Welch walked more leadoff batters last season than he did in the two previous years combined. Opponents' leadoff on-base average was 4th highest among regular A.L. starters.... Averaged 3.72 walks per nine innings, a career high; also allowed home runs more frequently (one every 8.8 innings) than ever before.... After finally dropping two games in a row in August, he lost four straight in September; his ERA from September 1 on was highest in the league.... Became the third straight A.L. Cy Young winner to post a losing record the following season.... One improvement from 1990 to 1991 was holding runners on base; allowed 10 steals in 17 attempts in 1990.... Among regular A.L. pitchers, only Dave Stewart (6.18) had a higher ERA in road games than Welch. Oakland's ERA in road games, an important category to remove the illusions created by the conditions of a particular home stadium, was 5.13, highest in the majors.

Dave Wells — Throws Left

Toronto Blue Jays	W-L	ERA	AB	H	HR	BB	SO	BA	SA	OBA
Season	15-10	3.72	747	188	24	49	106	.252	.403	.297
vs. Left-Handers			130	27	3	6	14	.208	.315	.246
vs. Right-Handers			617	161	21	43	92	.261	.421	.308
vs. Ground-Ballers			364	95	9	23	51	.261	.404	.304
vs. Fly-Ballers			383	93	15	26	55	.243	.402	.291
Home Games	6-5	4.81	331	89	16	24	49	.269	.462	.316
Road Games	9-5	2.88	416	99	8	25	57	.238	.356	.283
Grass Fields	7-5	3.11	313	72	7	19	47	.230	.364	.275
Artificial Turf	8-5	4.17	434	116	17	30	59	.267	.431	.313
April	1-3	5.16	90	26	3	6	7	.289	.478	.330
May	5-1	1.73	139	28	2	9	31	.201	.302	.255
June	3-0	2.91	126	26	3	9	20	.206	.333	.257
July	3-1	3.52	146	32	7	13	15	.219	.390	.286
August	1-4	5.93	127	41	7	7	17	.323	.543	.353
Sept./Oct.	2-1	4.31	119	35	2	5	16	.294	.403	.320
Leading Off Inn.			191	47	3	14	34	.246	.325	.298
Bases Empty			463	118	12	33	70	.255	.387	.306
Runners On			284	70	12	16	36	.246	.430	.283
Runners/Scor. Pos.			133	33	5	14	17	.248	.406	.307
Runners On/2 Out			125	33	5	7	13	.264	.440	.303
Scor. Pos./2 Out			66	16	2	6	8	.242	.364	.306
Late-Inning Pressure			90	21	2	4	18	.233	.322	.266
Leading Off			22	5	1	2	7	.227	.364	.292
Runners On			30	8	1	0	6	.267	.400	.267
Runners/Scor. Pos.			11	3	0	0	2	.273	.273	.273
First 9 Batters			289	73	10	26	42	.253	.401	.314
Second 9 Batters			227	51	7	10	35	.225	.383	.256
All Batters Thereafter			231	64	7	13	29	.277	.424	.315

Loves to face: Carlos Baerga (0-for-11)
Henry Cotto (.063, 1-for-16)
Lance Parrish (.077, 1-for-13, 7 SO)

Hates to face: Chili Davis (.435, 10-for-23, 3 HR)
Dwight Evans (.500, 10-for-20, 2 HR)
Cal Ripken (.412, 7-for-17, 2 2B, 3 HR)

Miscellaneous statistics: Ground outs-to-air outs ratio: 0.80 last season, 0.88 for career.... Induced 11 double plays in 130 opportunities (one per 12).... Allowed 37 doubles, 2 triples in 198⅓ innings.... Allowed 10 first-inning runs in 28 starts (2.89 ERA).... Batting support: 4.32 runs per start.... Opposing base stealers: 8-for-21 (38%, 4th-lowest rate in A.L.); 13 pickoffs (most in majors), 3 balks (3d most in A.L.).

Comments: His major league–leading total of 13 pickoffs was higher than the team total of seven different clubs.... Opposing base runners were caught stealing in eight straight attempts in April and May.... His first 28 appearances were all as a starter, but he was moved to the bullpen in mid-September and stayed there through the playoffs.... Career record of 24–17 (3.62 ERA) as a starter, 16–11 (3.15 ERA) in relief.... Had a seven-game winning streak snapped by a July 29 loss that started a five-game losing streak. Only two other A.L. pitchers had both winning and losing streaks of at least five games last season, Kevin Tapani and Kevin Appier.... Opponents batted only .190 during the first inning of his starts.... Batters leading off an inning had only a .298 on-base average; Blue Jays led A.L. in that category, allowing only a .297 on-base average in those situations.... Opponents have a career average of .226 with runners in scoring position, compared to a .250 average in other at-bats.... Ranked among the league's top 10 in road-game ERA, but among the bottom five in ERA at home. Admittedly, Skydome is a hitter's park, but that's a little extreme.... Among A.L. pitchers, only Mark Langston (27) and Allan Anderson (22) gave up more home runs to right-handed batters. That should be expected from Wells; the combination of being a fly-ball pitcher and having good control in a home-run park inevitably leads to the long ball. Just ask Tom Browning.

Bobby Witt — Throws Right

Texas Rangers	W-L	ERA	AB	H	HR	BB	SO	BA	SA	OBA
Season	3-7	6.09	331	84	4	74	82	.254	.356	.388
vs. Left-Handers			151	35	2	37	40	.232	.331	.381
vs. Right-Handers			180	49	2	37	42	.272	.378	.394
vs. Ground-Ballers			156	42	1	34	35	.269	.359	.396
vs. Fly-Ballers			175	42	3	40	47	.240	.354	.381
Home Games	0-5	6.30	147	42	1	30	40	.286	.361	.402
Road Games	3-2	5.92	184	42	3	44	42	.228	.353	.377
Grass Fields	1-7	6.40	267	71	2	60	68	.266	.363	.399
Artificial Turf	2-0	4.91	64	13	2	14	14	.203	.328	.342
April	1-2	3.76	94	21	1	22	20	.223	.309	.368
May	2-1	4.64	118	26	2	30	32	.220	.331	.373
June	0-0	0.00	0	0	0	0	0	.000	.000	.000
July	0-0	—	0	0	0	0	0			
August	0-3	9.64	95	30	1	17	21	.316	.453	.421
Sept./Oct.	0-1	10.50	24	7	0	5	9	.292	.292	.414
Leading Off Inn.			76	22	0	16	18	.289	.368	.413
Bases Empty			164	41	2	40	41	.250	.341	.400
Runners On			167	43	2	34	41	.257	.371	.376
Runners/Scor. Pos.			106	27	1	22	30	.255	.368	.371
Runners On/2 Out			72	17	1	14	20	.236	.333	.360
Scor. Pos./2 Out			53	14	1	13	17	.264	.396	.409
Late-Inning Pressure			7	2	0	4	4	.286	.286	.545
Leading Off			2	1	0	1	1	.500	.500	.667
Runners On			4	1	0	2	3	.250	.250	.500
Runners/Scor. Pos.			4	1	0	1	3	.250	.250	.400
First 9 Batters			118	28	0	30	33	.237	.314	.388
Second 9 Batters			111	35	2	24	23	.315	.414	.434
All Batters Thereafter			102	21	2	20	26	.206	.343	.336

Loves to face: Gary Gaetti (.120, 3-for-25)
Matt Nokes (.154, 4-for-26)
Terry Steinbach (0-for-9)

Hates to face: Wade Boggs (.345, 10-for-29, 15 BB)
Randy Milligan (.500, 7-for-14, 1 HR, 7 BB)
B. J. Surhoff (.389, 14-for-36, 2 HR)

Miscellaneous statistics: Ground outs-to-air outs ratio: 0.97 last season, 0.95 for career.... Induced 5 double plays in 85 opportunities (one per 17).... Allowed 18 doubles, 2 triples in 88⅔ innings.... Allowed 9 first-inning runs in 16 starts (3.94 ERA).... Batting support: 5.31 runs per start.... Opposing base stealers: 18-for-22 (82%); 0 pickoffs, 0 balks.

Comments: Suffered wildness relapse during injury-interrupted 1991 season, as rate of walks per nine innings increased from 4.46 (in 1990) to 7.51. Remember, we're talking about the guy who had the highest and third-highest single-season walk rates in baseball history (minimum: 25 starts in a season) back in 1986 (8.16) and 1987 (8.81). (Tommy Byrne had an 8.22 walk rate in 1949; he's the only other pitcher with a rate of eight or more in a 25-start season.)... Among 917 pitchers in major league history with least 1000 innings pitched, only nine averaged five or more walks per nine innings over their careers, and only Byrne (6.85 for his career) averaged more than six. Witt (6.26 career rate) needs 20 more innings to reach the 1000 mark and keep Byrne company.... Witt's career ERA is 4.63; no active pitcher with 1000 or more innings has a career ERA over 4.35.... Averaged 7.88 walks per nine innings during first inning last year, highest by any A.L. starter.... Returned from 66-day stay on D.L. to post some very poor numbers: 0–4, 9.82 ERA in 29⅓ innings. But even after returning from his rotator cuff problem, he still struck out more than a batter per inning.... Only Charlie Hough (313) and Ferguson Jenkins (190) have started more games for the Texas/Washington franchise than Witt (157).... Who says it's hard to repeat? Texas pitchers have led A.L. in walks in five of Witt's six seasons with team (Tigers led in 1990); meanwhile, Phillies have led N.L. in same category in each of last four years.

Matt Young

Throws Left

Boston Red Sox	W-L	ERA	AB	H	HR	BB	SO	BA	SA	OBA
Season	3-7	5.18	346	92	4	53	69	.266	.335	.365
vs. Left-Handers			51	13	1	7	8	.255	.353	.356
vs. Right-Handers			295	79	3	46	61	.268	.332	.366
vs. Ground-Ballers			148	41	2	24	26	.277	.372	.376
vs. Fly-Ballers			198	51	2	29	43	.258	.308	.357
Home Games	2-3	4.53	172	42	1	30	33	.244	.297	.356
Road Games	1-4	5.86	174	50	3	23	36	.287	.374	.374
Grass Fields	3-7	5.33	293	80	3	46	61	.273	.334	.373
Artificial Turf	0-0	4.40	53	12	1	7	8	.226	.340	.317
April	0-1	3.55	87	16	1	17	14	.184	.264	.314
May	3-2	4.75	117	32	1	20	29	.274	.325	.377
June	0-0	—	0	0	0	0	0	—	—	—
July	0-0	—	0	0	0	0	0	—	—	—
August	0-2	5.76	107	33	1	9	21	.308	.383	.362
Sept./Oct.	0-2	10.13	35	11	1	7	5	.314	.400	.455
Leading Off Inn.			84	23	1	14	15	.274	.357	.378
Bases Empty			188	50	2	25	41	.266	.330	.352
Runners On			158	42	2	28	28	.266	.342	.379
Runners/Scor. Pos.			92	27	1	19	16	.293	.370	.417
Runners On/2 Out			62	16	1	11	15	.258	.339	.370
Scor. Pos./2 Out			41	13	1	10	9	.317	.439	.451
Late-Inning Pressure			22	7	0	6	1	.318	.364	.483
Leading Off			8	3	0	1	0	.375	.500	.444
Runners On			9	2	0	3	1	.222	.222	.462
Runners/Scor. Pos.			2	0	0	2	0	.000	.000	.600
First 9 Batters			143	30	2	15	35	.210	.273	.289
Second 9 Batters			122	36	2	18	26	.295	.385	.385
All Batters Thereafter			81	26	0	20	8	.321	.370	.455

Loves to face: Ozzie Guillen (0-for-17)
Ron Karkovice (0-for-9, 5 SO)
Joel Skinner (.077, 1-for-13, 7 SO)

Hates to face: Tony Phillips (.385, 5-for-13, 1 HR, 6 BB)
Alan Trammell (.375, 12-for-32, 1 HR)
Dave Winfield (.324, 11-for-34, 2 2B, 5 HR)

Miscellaneous statistics: Ground outs-to-air outs ratio: 2.67 last season, 1.81 for career.... Induced 11 double plays in 94 opportunities (one per 8.5).... Allowed 12 doubles, 0 triples in 88⅔ innings.... Allowed 7 first-inning runs in 16 starts (2.81 ERA).... Batting support: 3.94 runs per start.... Opposing base stealers: 8-for-11 (73%); 0 pickoffs, 0 balks.

Comments: Career percentage of .388 (54–85) is the lowest among active pitchers with at least 100 decisions. Curiously, that's the same career won-lost record compiled by former pitcher and current Expos executive Bill Stoneman, who spiced it up a bit with a pair of no-hitters. The all-time worst career record (minimum: 100 decisions) belongs to Coldwater Jim Hughey (29–80, .266), who went a cool 4–30 for the Cleveland Spiders in 1899; among pitchers active since World War II, Jesse Jefferson (39–81, .325) has the worst record.... Young has had more losses than wins in seven of his eight big league seasons.... Opponents have career .305 batting average vs. Young in Late-Inning Pressure Situations, highest against any active pitcher (minimum: 500 batters faced in LIPS).... Career ERA of 4.33 is 2d highest among active pitchers with at least 1000 innings pitched; only Neal Heaton (4.35) stands worse.... Home run by Wally Joyner in August was the only one hit off Young by a left-handed batter since Jose Cruz connected in April 1987. Jose Cruz? Was that in the American League or the Senior League?... He has not pitched for the same team in consecutive seasons since 1985–86. His itinerary: Seattle (1983–86); Los Angeles (1987); Oakland (1989, after spending all of 1988 on the disabled list); Seattle (again in 1990); and Boston (1991).... Has lost each of his last nine decisions against the Athletics. To paraphrase the old saying, "If you can't beat 'em, don't leave 'em."

Jack Armstrong

Cincinnati Reds   Throws Right

Cincinnati Reds	W-L	ERA	AB	H	HR	BB	SO	BA	SA	OBA
Season	7-13	5.48	540	158	25	54	93	.293	.491	.354
vs. Left-Handers			297	83	13	35	35	.279	.481	.355
vs. Right-Handers			243	75	12	19	58	.309	.502	.352
vs. Ground-Ballers			261	80	8	28	49	.307	.456	.370
vs. Fly-Ballers			279	78	17	26	44	.280	.523	.338
Home Games	4-8	6.38	255	74	14	30	44	.290	.510	.360
Road Games	3-5	4.66	285	84	11	24	49	.295	.474	.348
Grass Fields	3-3	4.47	196	57	10	17	29	.291	.490	.347
Artificial Turf	4-10	6.04	344	101	15	37	64	.294	.491	.357
April	1-1	4.24	62	14	4	4	14	.226	.435	.273
May	3-2	4.09	119	32	3	10	26	.269	.378	.318
June	1-3	6.26	115	39	5	15	16	.339	.574	.409
July	1-3	6.29	91	26	6	12	16	.286	.538	.369
August	0-1	12.60	20	6	4	2	2	.300	.950	.391
Sept./Oct.	1-3	5.18	133	41	3	11	19	.308	.444	.356
Leading Off Inn.			132	34	9	13	24	.258	.515	.329
Bases Empty			334	89	15	30	60	.266	.446	.329
Runners On			206	69	10	24	33	.335	.563	.392
Runners/Scor. Pos.			114	41	7	15	20	.360	.596	.406
Runners On/2 Out			86	26	2	12	16	.302	.419	.394
Scor. Pos./2 Out			54	19	2	7	9	.352	.481	.426
Late-Inning Pressure			18	5	0	1	5	.278	.389	.316
Leading Off			5	0	0	1	1	.000	.000	.167
Runners On			6	2	0	0	1	.333	.333	.333
Runners/Scor. Pos.			4	1	0	0	1	.250	.250	.250
First 9 Batters			210	62	8	20	41	.295	.471	.359
Second 9 Batters			188	54	9	21	33	.287	.489	.352
All Batters Thereafter			142	42	8	13	19	.296	.521	.348

Loves to face: Glenn Davis (.100, 1-for-10, 1 2B, 3 BB)
               Tim Raines (0-for-13)

Hates to face: Roberto Alomar (.455, 5-for-11)
               Jack Clark (.333, 2-for-6, 2 HR, 3 BB, 3 SO)
               Kevin Mitchell (.400, 4-for-10, 2 2B, 2 HR)

Miscellaneous statistics: Ground outs-to-air outs ratio: 0.76 last season, 0.80 for career.... Induced 7 double plays in 108 opportunities (one per 15).... Allowed 24 doubles, 4 triples in 139⅔ innings.... Allowed 21 first-inning runs in 24 starts (7.13 ERA, 5th highest in N.L.).... Batting support: 3.88 runs per start.... Opposing base stealers: 12-for-20 (60%); 8 pickoffs (3d most in N.L.), 1 balk.

Comments: Has a record of 8–19 since starting the 1990 All-Star Game.... Owns career records of 5–1 in April and 7–4 in May, but he's 13–27 in all other months combined.... Opponents have a .292 career batting average with runners on base, .241 with the bases empty.... Allowed an average of one home run every 5.6 innings last season, the highest rate in the league among pitchers with 75 or more innings. That came as a surprise after 1990, when he allowed only nine home runs all season, an average of one every 18.4 innings pitched. The fences have come back in at Cleveland Stadium this year, so who knows what to expect next? ... From July 6 through the end of last season, he posted a 1–7 record; opponents batted .480 (24-for-50) with runners in scoring position.... Opposing right-handers hit for a higher average than left-handers for the first time in his career, but the walk-to-strikeout ratio remained consistent with his past performance. Career breakdown: .274, 117 BB, 117 SO by left-handed batters; .245, 55 BB, 154 SO by right-handed batters.... Maybe a change of leagues can change his luck on the west coast. In four seasons with Cincinnati, he never won a game west of Houston, going 0–9 in California.... Of the ten major league pitchers with the highest ERAs last season (minimum: 100 IP), nine were American Leaguers; Armstrong was the other. Welcome to the DH world, Jack.

Paul Assenmacher

Chicago Cubs   Throws Left

Chicago Cubs	W-L	ERA	AB	H	HR	BB	SO	BA	SA	OBA
Season	7-8	3.24	381	85	10	31	117	.223	.357	.284
vs. Left-Handers			134	24	1	10	49	.179	.261	.247
vs. Right-Handers			247	61	9	21	68	.247	.409	.304
vs. Ground-Ballers			166	38	4	14	54	.229	.331	.287
vs. Fly-Ballers			215	47	6	17	63	.219	.377	.282
Home Games	4-2	2.07	223	44	6	13	69	.197	.318	.247
Road Games	3-6	4.97	158	41	4	18	48	.259	.411	.333
Grass Fields	5-4	2.63	287	59	8	20	93	.206	.345	.260
Artificial Turf	2-4	5.25	94	26	2	11	24	.277	.394	.355
April	0-0	2.30	56	8	1	3	17	.143	.250	.186
May	2-2	5.06	64	17	1	5	19	.266	.375	.329
June	1-2	3.94	56	13	0	13	21	.232	.286	.361
July	0-0	2.70	55	15	2	1	17	.273	.473	.286
August	4-1	2.01	77	15	4	5	25	.195	.364	.241
Sept./Oct.	0-3	3.72	73	17	2	4	18	.233	.384	.291
Leading Off Inn.			83	18	3	6	33	.217	.373	.270
Bases Empty			217	48	7	11	71	.221	.369	.259
Runners On			164	37	3	20	46	.226	.341	.314
Runners/Scor. Pos.			104	27	2	16	28	.260	.385	.357
Runners On/2 Out			77	18	2	8	24	.234	.351	.322
Scor. Pos./2 Out			52	14	2	8	15	.269	.423	.377
Late-Inning Pressure			247	56	6	21	73	.227	.340	.292
Leading Off			51	11	2	4	21	.216	.353	.273
Runners On			114	25	2	13	31	.219	.307	.308
Runners/Scor. Pos.			68	19	2	11	16	.279	.412	.381
First 9 Batters			364	81	9	28	114	.223	.352	.277
Second 9 Batters			17	4	1	3	3	.235	.471	.409
All Batters Thereafter			0	0	0	0	0	—	—	—

Loves to face: Barry Bonds (.115, 3-for-26, 2 2B, 3 BB)
               Dave Martinez (.067, 1-for-15)
               Milt Thompson (.067, 1-for-15, 1 2B)

Hates to face: Eric Davis (.625, 5-for-8, 2 HR, 2 SO)
               Len Dykstra (.583, 7-for-12, 1 HR, 3 SO)
               Mike Scioscia (.467, 7-for-15)

Miscellaneous statistics: Ground outs-to-air outs ratio: 0.83 last season, 1.19 for career.... Induced 3 double plays in 79 opportunities (one per 26), worst rate in majors.... Allowed 13 doubles, 4 triples in 102⅔ innings.... Saved 15 games in 32 opportunities (47%).... Stranded 26 inherited runners, allowed 21 to score (55%), 4th-lowest rate in N.L.... Opposing base stealers: 8-for-13 (62%); 1 pickoff, 0 balks.

Comments: Pitched 102⅔ innings in 75 games last season, after throwing 103 in 74 games the year before. In first four years in majors (1986–89), he averaged fewer than 70 innings in 60 games per season.... For the first time in his career, more than half of the batters he faced came in Late-Inning Pressure Situations.... Opponents have a .208 career batting average with two outs and runners on base, compared to a .243 overall average.... Walk rate (2.72 per nine innings) was the lowest of his career, while his strikeout rate (10.26 per nine innings) was a career high.... He's one of six active pitchers to strike out at least one-quarter of the left-handed batters he has faced during his career. The others: left-handers Sid Fernandez and Randy Myers and right-handers Rob Dibble, Bryan Harvey, and Tom Henke.... Has allowed only two home runs to left-handed batters over the last three seasons; Len Dykstra was the only lefty to take him deep last season.... Extended his errorless streak to 322 games before committing the only error of his career, nine games into the 1991 season. He was only 10 games shy of Rob Murphy's record for consecutive errorless games at the start of a career.... Okay, armchair managers, the bases are loaded and you need a strikeout. Who you gonna call? Assenmacher. He has fanned 29 of 82 batters faced with the bases loaded, the highest bases-loaded strikeout rate among active pitchers. And he's never allowed a grand-slam home run.

Steve Avery

Throws Left

Atlanta Braves	W-L	ERA	AB	H	HR	BB	SO	BA	SA	OBA
Season	18-8	3.38	788	189	21	65	137	.240	.372	.299
vs. Left-Handers			164	30	3	12	33	.183	.287	.237
vs. Right-Handers			624	159	18	53	104	.255	.394	.315
vs. Ground-Ballers			372	89	7	27	73	.239	.347	.294
vs. Fly-Ballers			416	100	14	38	64	.240	.394	.303
Home Games	9-5	3.75	399	100	9	33	66	.251	.356	.311
Road Games	9-3	3.01	389	89	12	32	71	.229	.388	.286
Grass Fields	14-7	3.39	565	137	14	46	95	.242	.365	.301
Artificial Turf	4-1	3.36	223	52	7	19	42	.233	.390	.292
April	2-1	2.86	78	17	2	9	12	.218	.372	.295
May	4-1	3.38	139	36	3	15	23	.259	.381	.329
June	1-3	4.73	129	38	4	11	20	.295	.465	.348
July	4-0	2.87	131	24	4	11	21	.183	.290	.250
August	3-3	4.97	123	39	5	9	27	.317	.520	.364
Sept./Oct.	4-0	2.25	188	35	3	10	34	.186	.261	.235
Leading Off Inn.			210	54	6	13	36	.257	.419	.300
Bases Empty			502	112	11	37	83	.223	.347	.279
Runners On			286	77	10	28	54	.269	.416	.332
Runners/Scor. Pos.			163	41	5	18	36	.252	.387	.319
Runners On/2 Out			122	35	5	13	21	.287	.459	.360
Scor. Pos./2 Out			75	20	2	9	16	.267	.387	.345
Late-Inning Pressure			47	8	0	4	6	.170	.170	.250
Leading Off			11	3	0	2	2	.273	.273	.385
Runners On			22	3	0	2	3	.136	.136	.208
Runners/Scor. Pos.			9	2	0	2	0	.222	.222	.364
First 9 Batters			286	58	6	24	64	.203	.322	.263
Second 9 Batters			274	56	6	22	46	.204	.321	.263
All Batters Thereafter			228	75	9	19	27	.329	.496	.386

Loves to face: Felix Jose (0-for-12)
                 Juan Samuel (0-for-18)
                 Darryl Strawberry (.071, 1-for-14)

Hates to face: Craig Biggio (.500, 10-for-20)
                 Glenn Braggs (.529, 9-for-17, 2 HR)
                 Chris Sabo (.500, 9-for-18, 1 HR)

Miscellaneous statistics: Ground outs-to-air outs ratio: 1.28 last season, 1.29 for career.... Induced 17 double plays in 134 opportunities (one per 7.9).... Allowed 33 doubles, 4 triples in 210⅓ innings.... Allowed 18 first-inning runs in 35 starts (4.37 ERA).... Batting support: 5.26 runs per start, 3d-highest average in N.L.... Opposing base stealers: 21-for-32 (66%); 2 pickoffs, 1 balk.

Comments: At age 21, became third-youngest left-hander in this century to win 18 or more games in a season: Babe Ruth (age 20, 1915) and Johnny Lush (age 20, 1906) rank one-two on that list.... Raised his record from eight games below .500 in 1990 (3–11) to 10 above last season. That net gain of plus-18 was the largest by a Braves pitcher since Warren Spahn went from 14–19 in 1952 to 23–7 in '53.... First pitcher in major league history to win a pair of 1–0 decisions in the same postseason series. He did that en route to an L.C.S. record 16⅓ consecutive scoreless innings. Those two wins made Avery, at 21 years and six months, the second-youngest pitcher in major league history to win two games (by *any* score) in a postseason series; the youngest: Paul Dean of the Cardinals in 1934 (21 years, two months).... Twice during postseason play, Bobby Cox removed Avery while he was pitching a shutout. Three times during the regular season, he took a shutout into the ninth inning only to give up a run.... Opponents batted .204 during his first two passes through the batting order, but .329 thereafter.... Has held left-handed batters to a .204 career batting average; right-handers have hit .274.... Owns 5–0 career record and 0.99 ERA against the Dodgers; he's 16–19 with a 4.64 ERA against the rest of the league.... He can hit, too: first pitcher to have a three-hit game and a four-hit game in the same season since 1970, when Mike Torrez did it while with St. Louis.

Brian Barnes

Throws Left

Montreal Expos	W-L	ERA	AB	H	HR	BB	SO	BA	SA	OBA
Season	5-8	4.22	580	135	16	84	117	.233	.371	.333
vs. Left-Handers			104	25	3	22	19	.240	.413	.380
vs. Right-Handers			476	110	13	62	98	.231	.361	.322
vs. Ground-Ballers			254	62	7	31	55	.244	.382	.330
vs. Fly-Ballers			326	73	9	53	62	.224	.362	.336
Home Games	1-5	4.24	250	57	5	32	59	.228	.348	.314
Road Games	4-3	4.21	330	78	11	52	58	.236	.388	.348
Grass Fields	3-0	3.92	155	35	4	26	24	.226	.342	.346
Artificial Turf	2-8	4.33	425	100	12	58	93	.235	.381	.329
April	0-0	—	0	0	0	0	0	—	—	—
May	0-2	8.38	76	23	2	11	14	.303	.500	.396
June	0-1	3.65	133	31	4	18	34	.233	.353	.329
July	2-0	4.09	79	21	3	13	15	.266	.443	.362
August	1-2	2.63	144	25	4	17	25	.174	.292	.270
Sept./Oct.	2-3	4.43	148	35	3	25	29	.236	.358	.349
Leading Off Inn.			148	35	5	17	24	.236	.385	.323
Bases Empty			344	78	9	46	64	.227	.349	.325
Runners On			236	57	7	38	53	.242	.403	.345
Runners/Scor. Pos.			133	31	4	17	33	.233	.383	.318
Runners On/2 Out			109	29	4	18	32	.266	.459	.370
Scor. Pos./2 Out			72	19	3	11	22	.264	.472	.361
Late-Inning Pressure			24	6	0	6	6	.250	.292	.308
Leading Off			9	2	0	0	3	.222	.333	.222
Runners On			6	2	0	0	1	.333	.333	.333
Runners/Scor. Pos.			4	2	0	0	1	.500	.500	.500
First 9 Batters			211	42	4	27	52	.199	.308	.296
Second 9 Batters			205	49	5	28	36	.239	.356	.333
All Batters Thereafter			164	44	7	29	29	.268	.470	.379

Loves to face: Wes Chamberlain (.071, 1-for-14, 2 BB)
                 Billy Hatcher (0-for-7)
                 Chico Walker (0-for-12)

Hates to face: Barry Bonds (.667, 4-for-6, 2 2B, 2 HR)
                 John Kruk (.667, 6-for-9, 1 HR)
                 Barry Larkin (.429, 3-for-7, 1 HR, 3 BB)

Miscellaneous statistics: Ground outs-to-air outs ratio: 1.06 last season, 1.15 for career.... Induced 10 double plays in 118 opportunities (one per 12).... Allowed 24 doubles, 4 triples in 160 innings.... Allowed 8 first-inning runs in 27 starts (2.67 ERA).... Batting support: 3.44 runs per start, 5th-lowest average in N.L.... Opposing base stealers: 20-for-28 (71%); 7 pickoffs, 1 balk.

Comments: Finished only two innings shy of qualifying for the ERA title, which isn't to say he would have won it, or even ranked among the league leaders. But he would have become only the seventh rookie in Expos' history to pitch that many innings. The most recent: John Dopson in 1988. As it was, only three rookie pitchers accumulated 162 innings last year: Charles Nagy, Rich DeLucia, and Omar Olivares.... Among pitchers with as many innings as Barnes last season, only Jose DeJesus and Randy Johnson walked more batters per nine innings.... Barnes, a left-hander, has walked more left-handed batters in his career than he has struck out (22 BB, 21 SO).... Had no decisions in 14 of his 27 starts last season.... Led N.L. pitchers with a 1.63 ERA against the Cubs last season.... Opponents batted .174 during the first inning of his starts, 2d lowest among N.L. pitchers last season.... Spent the first 27 days of the season on the disabled list, and posted a record of 0–3 with eight no-decisions over his first 11 starts. He did not win his first game until after the All-Star break.... He allowed three triples in his season debut, and one in his season finale, but none in 26 games in between.... Led N.L. pitchers with 7 walks (as a batter) last season.... Listed at five feet, nine inches, Barnes and Tom Gordon were the shortest pitchers in the majors last season. (That's according to heights listed on rosters put out by the teams themselves. No, the Elias Bureau is not yet sending its men and women into the locker rooms, tape measures in hand.)

Tim Belcher   Throws Right

Los Angeles Dodgers	W-L	ERA	AB	H	HR	BB	SO	BA	SA	OBA
Season	10-9	2.62	789	189	10	75	156	.240	.318	.306
vs. Left-Handers			445	122	4	46	82	.274	.342	.343
vs. Right-Handers			344	67	6	29	74	.195	.288	.258
vs. Ground-Ballers			338	83	1	34	73	.246	.284	.313
vs. Fly-Ballers			451	106	9	41	83	.235	.344	.301
Home Games	7-4	2.67	456	111	9	34	102	.243	.331	.296
Road Games	3-5	2.56	333	78	1	41	54	.234	.300	.319
Grass Fields	9-6	2.51	649	154	10	57	137	.237	.317	.299
Artificial Turf	1-3	3.16	140	35	0	18	19	.250	.321	.340
April	3-1	0.91	108	20	1	7	21	.185	.259	.233
May	2-3	4.76	119	38	2	17	17	.319	.437	.410
June	2-0	1.45	156	32	1	17	36	.205	.250	.283
July	0-3	5.90	119	36	2	10	17	.303	.412	.357
August	2-1	1.16	168	34	2	11	37	.202	.274	.251
Sept./Oct.	1-1	3.06	119	29	2	13	28	.244	.311	.316
Leading Off Inn.			200	51	3	16	35	.255	.340	.313
Bases Empty			447	111	6	38	88	.248	.331	.309
Runners On			342	78	4	37	68	.228	.301	.303
Runners/Scor. Pos.			192	42	3	22	43	.219	.318	.298
Runners On/2 Out			143	35	1	21	31	.245	.336	.341
Scor. Pos./2 Out			93	19	0	13	22	.204	.280	.302
Late-Inning Pressure			86	24	0	10	14	.279	.372	.351
Leading Off			24	8	0	2	3	.333	.458	.385
Runners On			36	7	0	7	9	.194	.250	.318
Runners/Scor. Pos.			19	3	0	3	4	.158	.263	.261
First 9 Batters			270	57	2	17	72	.211	.256	.257
Second 9 Batters			235	52	4	25	39	.221	.302	.298
All Batters Thereafter			284	80	4	33	45	.282	.391	.357

Loves to face: Sid Bream (.095, 2-for-21)
Ken Caminiti (.118, 4-for-34, 0 BB)
Mark Lemke (0-for-13)

Hates to face: Vince Coleman (.556, 10-for-18)
Howard Johnson (.375, 6-for-16, 2 2B, 2 HR, 10 fly outs)
Dave Magadan (.500, 7-for-14)

Miscellaneous statistics: Ground outs-to-air outs ratio: 1.13 last season, 0.83 for career.... Induced 15 double plays in 172 opportunities (one per 11).... Allowed 26 doubles, 3 triples in 209⅓ innings.... Allowed 16 first-inning runs in 33 starts (2.76 ERA).... Batting support: 3.73 runs per start.... Opposing base stealers: 17-for-27 (63%); 0 pickoffs, 0 balks.

Comments: Among major leaguers who qualified for the ERA title in 1991, only Jose DeJesus, Jose Rijo, and Dennis Martinez had lower home-run rates than Belcher.... He has not allowed more than one homer in any of his last 47 starts. We'll see how those figures hold up now that he'll be pitching half of his games in the major leagues' top home-run park over the past five years (yes, Riverfront Stadium; see the Reds essay) instead of Dodger Stadium, which stands 21st on that list.... Opponents have batted either .217 or .240 against him in each of his five years in the majors. Yearly averages: .240, .217, .217, .240, .240.... Walked 3.22 batters per nine innings last season, the highest rate of his career.... His April ERA was 2d lowest in the league; his August ERA was the lowest.... Has held batters to a .180 career average with runners on base in Late-Inning Pressure Situations, 2d lowest among active pitchers behind Mike Boddicker (.168).... Finished the Dodgers phase of his career with a 2.99 ERA, becoming the 14th Dodgers pitcher with 800 or more innings and a sub-3.00 ERA.... He was the unsigned number-one pick of the Twins in 1983, before signing with the Yankees in 1984. Oakland then selected him in the free-agent compensation pool and traded him to the Dodgers in the Rick Honeycutt deal. Now he's been dealt to the Reds. His high-profile name has been associated with so many clubs that it's easy to forget that he's spent his entire major league career, until now, with Los Angeles.

Stan Belinda   Throws Right

Pittsburgh Pirates	W-L	ERA	AB	H	HR	BB	SO	BA	SA	OBA
Season	7-5	3.45	272	50	10	35	71	.184	.327	.283
vs. Left-Handers			123	25	4	14	25	.203	.325	.298
vs. Right-Handers			149	25	6	21	46	.168	.329	.272
vs. Ground-Ballers			113	23	2	16	30	.204	.292	.313
vs. Fly-Ballers			165	28	8	20	42	.170	.345	.263
Home Games	2-1	1.94	141	23	3	9	38	.163	.262	.229
Road Games	5-4	5.15	131	27	7	26	33	.206	.397	.335
Grass Fields	2-2	5.30	66	14	4	13	19	.212	.409	.346
Artificial Turf	5-3	2.87	206	36	6	22	52	.175	.301	.262
April	1-1	6.23	32	6	1	5	10	.188	.344	.316
May	2-0	4.61	47	9	1	8	13	.191	.298	.328
June	0-0	0.00	37	6	0	2	13	.162	.216	.205
July	0-1	5.17	54	11	5	10	13	.204	.500	.333
August	0-2	2.12	59	8	1	5	14	.136	.186	.203
Sept./Oct.	4-1	2.77	43	10	2	5	8	.233	.419	.306
Leading Off Inn.			60	7	2	6	21	.117	.250	.197
Bases Empty			158	25	6	17	46	.158	.304	.253
Runners On			114	25	4	18	25	.219	.360	.324
Runners/Scor. Pos.			81	15	3	14	20	.185	.321	.303
Runners On/2 Out			56	10	3	6	11	.179	.375	.270
Scor. Pos./2 Out			39	8	2	4	8	.205	.410	.295
Late-Inning Pressure			142	25	4	19	39	.176	.303	.282
Leading Off			33	2	0	2	14	.061	.061	.114
Runners On			63	14	3	11	13	.222	.413	.347
Runners/Scor. Pos.			45	9	2	7	11	.200	.378	.321
First 9 Batters			265	50	10	35	68	.189	.336	.290
Second 9 Batters			7	0	0	0	3	.000	.000	.000
All Batters Thereafter			0	0	0	0	0	—	—	—

Loves to face: George Bell (0-for-5, 3 SO)
Kevin Elster (0-for-5, 3 SO)
Terry Pendleton (.143, 1-for-7)

Hates to face: Andre Dawson (.500, 4-for-8, 4 HR)
Hal Morris (.571, 4-for-7, 2 2B, 1 HR)
Todd Zeile (.222, 2-for-9, 1 2B, 1 HR, 4 BB)

Miscellaneous statistics: Ground outs-to-air outs ratio: 0.60 last season, 0.73 for career.... Induced 2 double plays in 50 opportunities (one per 25).... Allowed 5 doubles, 2 triples in 78⅓ innings.... Saved 16 games in 22 opportunities (73%).... Stranded 25 inherited runners, allowed 13 to score (66%).... Opposing base stealers: 13-for-16 (81%); 0 pickoffs, 0 balks.

Comments: Sort of the Rob Deer of pitchers. Held opponents to .184 batting average last season but allowed 10 home runs in 78⅓ innings. Since 1969, that's the 2d-lowest batting average against any pitcher (minimum: 50 innings) who had given up home runs at a rate of one or more per nine innings; the lowest: .181 against Jeff Gray last season.... The only N.L. relief pitcher to yield more home runs was Mike Hartley (11).... Had 16 saves, one fewer than team leader Bill Landrum, but had only two after August 28; of those 16 saves, 13 came at home.... Allowed only 5.74 hits per nine innings, the 2d-lowest one-season rate in team history among pitchers who threw at least 60 innings. Only Goose Gossage (5.28 in 1977) had a lower rate.... Among pitchers who faced at least 175 right-handed batters last season, only Nolan Ryan held righties to a lower batting average than Belinda. But he's no slouch against lefties either. Career breakdown: .209 by left-handed batters, .212 by right-handers.... Opponents have a career average of .235 at Three Rivers, .204 on other artificial surfaces, and .159 on grass fields. They've hit .259 in day games, .193 in night games.... He has been charged with only one unearned run in his entire career, and that was back in September of 1989. He has never committed an error in 123 appearances. Of course, that's kind of a bogus distinction for a relief pitcher—after all, he's had only 16 fielding chances in those 123 games.

Andy Benes Throws Right

San Diego Padres	W-L	ERA	AB	H	HR	BB	SO	BA	SA	OBA
Season	15-11	3.03	836	194	23	59	167	.232	.358	.285
vs. Left-Handers			466	107	13	32	93	.230	.354	.281
vs. Right-Handers			370	87	10	27	74	.235	.362	.289
vs. Ground-Ballers			362	75	5	16	81	.207	.265	.241
vs. Fly-Ballers			474	119	18	43	86	.251	.428	.316
Home Games	6-5	3.73	434	117	13	35	94	.270	.412	.327
Road Games	9-6	2.33	402	77	10	24	73	.192	.299	.238
Grass Fields	10-7	3.16	584	142	18	39	121	.243	.382	.293
Artificial Turf	5-4	2.74	252	52	5	20	46	.206	.302	.265
April	0-2	3.86	90	24	3	11	30	.267	.422	.347
May	2-4	3.70	157	40	4	14	29	.255	.376	.318
June	2-2	5.02	144	41	6	13	22	.285	.451	.346
July	1-2	2.10	114	24	3	6	18	.211	.325	.250
August	5-0	2.40	144	23	3	6	31	.160	.257	.199
Sept./Oct.	5-1	1.64	187	42	4	9	37	.225	.337	.260
Leading Off Inn.			219	52	5	11	32	.237	.370	.277
Bases Empty			534	123	14	32	105	.230	.363	.275
Runners On			302	71	9	27	62	.235	.348	.301
Runners/Scor. Pos.			154	30	3	18	35	.195	.279	.285
Runners On/2 Out			125	25	2	14	32	.200	.288	.291
Scor. Pos./2 Out			74	12	1	11	22	.162	.243	.287
Late-Inning Pressure			91	19	1	10	24	.209	.253	.287
Leading Off			27	5	0	1	6	.185	.185	.214
Runners On			33	6	1	4	9	.182	.273	.270
Runners/Scor. Pos.			11	3	0	1	3	.273	.273	.333
First 9 Batters			268	50	7	23	60	.187	.302	.255
Second 9 Batters			278	62	7	15	55	.223	.360	.264
All Batters Thereafter			290	82	9	21	52	.283	.407	.331

Loves to face: Jay Bell (.100, 1-for-10)
               Greg Olson (.077, 1-for-13, 2 BB)
               Mike Simms (0-for-8)

Hates to face: Bobby Bonilla (.545, 6-for-11, 1 HR)
               Brett Butler (.391, 9-for-23)
               Matt Williams (.368, 7-for-19, 2 HR)

Miscellaneous statistics: Ground outs-to-air outs ratio: 0.72 last season, 3d lowest in N.L.; 0.75 for career.... Induced 11 double plays in 154 opportunities (one per 14).... Allowed 24 doubles, 6 triples in 223 innings.... Allowed 13 first-inning runs in 33 starts (3.55 ERA).... Batting support: 3.24 runs per start, 2d-lowest average in majors.... Opposing base stealers: 10-for-21 (48%); 0 pickoffs, 4 balks (3d most in N.L.).

Comments: Note to managers: Don't bother playing lefty/righty against Benes. Left-handers have a .234 career batting average and a .362 slugging percentage, while right-handers have marks of .233 and .365, respectively.... Has held opponents to .195 career batting average on his first pass through the lineup, .212 on his second pass, and .295 thereafter. Among active starting pitchers, only Sid Fernandez has held batters to a lower average during his first time through.... Last year, Benes held foes to a .168 average in the first inning, lowest among N.L. pitchers.... Opponents have a career average of .181 with two outs and runners in scoring position, compared to an overall mark of .234.... Struck out 25 batters without allowing a walk over a stretch of four games, the 2d-longest such streak in the league last season, one strikeout shy of Bob Patterson's league-high streak.... Had a 4–10 record with a 4.18 ERA as of July 15, but went 11–1 with a 1.77 ERA the rest of the way.... His 1.92 ERA after the All-Star break was the best in the majors.... Walked 4.19 batters per nine innings in his rookie season, but has lowered that to 3.23 and 2.38 in two seasons since then.... Finished the season hitless in his last 50 at-bats, the longest one-season hitless streak in the majors in the last 10 years. This is the same guy who was 6-for-24 with a home run in his rookie season. Padres pitchers batted .086 last season, the worst in the N.L.

Juan Berenguer Throws Right

Atlanta Braves	W-L	ERA	AB	H	HR	BB	SO	BA	SA	OBA
Season	0-3	2.24	228	43	5	20	53	.189	.303	.261
vs. Left-Handers			106	21	1	15	22	.198	.255	.303
vs. Right-Handers			122	22	4	5	31	.180	.344	.221
vs. Ground-Ballers			106	25	4	8	23	.236	.387	.297
vs. Fly-Ballers			122	18	1	12	30	.148	.230	.230
Home Games	0-1	2.76	114	22	2	8	30	.193	.307	.254
Road Games	0-2	1.71	114	21	3	12	23	.184	.298	.268
Grass Fields	0-2	2.68	153	29	3	12	41	.190	.301	.259
Artificial Turf	0-1	1.31	75	14	2	8	12	.187	.307	.265
April	0-0	2.38	44	10	1	6	9	.227	.364	.333
May	0-1	2.29	74	14	1	8	16	.189	.270	.286
June	0-2	2.51	46	8	2	4	8	.174	.348	.235
July	0-0	0.75	36	3	0	2	10	.083	.083	.128
August	0-0	3.86	28	8	1	0	10	.286	.500	.286
Sept./Oct.	0-0	0.00	0	0	0	0	0	.000	.000	.000
Leading Off Inn.			53	11	1	6	12	.208	.321	.288
Bases Empty			131	23	3	13	28	.176	.290	.260
Runners On			97	20	2	7	25	.206	.320	.262
Runners/Scor. Pos.			55	8	0	7	17	.145	.164	.234
Runners On/2 Out			41	4	1	3	13	.098	.171	.178
Scor. Pos./2 Out			25	2	0	3	9	.080	.080	.179
Late-Inning Pressure			119	20	3	15	29	.168	.294	.270
Leading Off			31	5	1	4	6	.161	.290	.257
Runners On			47	9	1	7	15	.191	.298	.291
Runners/Scor. Pos.			32	4	0	7	11	.125	.125	.275
First 9 Batters			217	41	5	18	51	.189	.309	.258
Second 9 Batters			11	2	0	2	2	.182	.182	.308
All Batters Thereafter			0	0	0	0	0	—	—	—

Loves to face: Ivan Calderon (.100, 2-for-20, 2 BB)
               Mike Heath (.053, 1-for-19, 3 BB)
               Benito Santiago (0-for-4, 4 SO)

Hates to face: George Bell (.353, 6-for-17, 1 HR)
               Sid Bream (.750, 3-for-4, 1 2B, 1 HR)
               Dale Murphy (.500, 2-for-4, 2 HR)

Miscellaneous statistics: Ground outs-to-air outs ratio: 0.62 last season, 0.63 for career.... Induced 3 double plays in 48 opportunities (one per 16).... Allowed 7 doubles, 2 triples in 64⅓ innings.... Saved 17 games in 20 opportunities (85%), 4th-highest rate in N.L.... Stranded 24 inherited runners, allowed 1 to score (96%), highest rate in majors.... Opposing base stealers: 3-for-4 (75%); 0 pickoffs, 0 balks.

Comments: Has faced 131 major league batters with the bases loaded but has never allowed a grand-slam home run; that's the highest such total of batters by any active pitcher who has never been slammed.... Career breakdown: 26–35 (3.94 ERA) in 93 starts, 37–22 (3.66 ERA) in 350 relief appearances.... He's pitched with seven clubs during his career, posting a record of 33–13 with the Twins and 30–44 with the others.... Had 17 saves in 49 games last year; prior to 1991, had only 14 saves in 301 relief appearances.... Left-handed batters drove in only two runs against him last season: a two-out bunt single by Jeff Reed in April and a solo home run by Stan Javier in June. Berenguer held left-handed batters to four hits in 30 at-bats with runners in scoring position.... Averaged 2.80 walks per nine innings last season, the lowest of his 14-year career, as was his opponents' batting average.... Although he pitched in both the L.C.S. and the World Series for the 1987 Twins, last year was the second time that Berenguer looked on from the bench as his club advanced into the World Series. He was a member of the 1984 Tigers, but did not play in either the Championship Series or the World Series. Last season, he was not included on the Braves' postseason roster.... Not a bad career for a player released by the Blue Jays 10 years ago.... How long will it be before no one in the world remembers what a "second-look" free agent was?

Mike Bielecki

Throws Right

Cubs/Braves	W-L	ERA	AB	H	HR	BB	SO	BA	SA	OBA
Season	13-11	4.46	653	171	18	56	75	.262	.420	.319
vs. Left-Handers			345	95	10	36	37	.275	.426	.343
vs. Right-Handers			308	76	8	20	38	.247	.412	.292
vs. Ground-Ballers			261	64	7	26	31	.245	.395	.314
vs. Fly-Ballers			392	107	11	30	44	.273	.436	.323
Home Games	8-7	4.74	367	101	12	21	35	.275	.436	.315
Road Games	5-4	4.12	286	70	6	35	40	.245	.399	.325
Grass Fields	9-9	4.76	479	127	14	33	50	.265	.422	.313
Artificial Turf	4-2	3.67	174	44	4	23	25	.253	.414	.337
April	4-1	2.70	92	18	2	9	10	.196	.337	.267
May	3-1	3.91	90	20	3	14	13	.222	.356	.324
June	1-4	6.86	84	26	3	9	11	.310	.488	.376
July	3-1	3.82	127	37	2	8	13	.291	.386	.333
August	1-1	4.82	147	42	6	7	13	.286	.524	.323
Sept./Oct.	1-3	5.04	113	28	2	9	15	.248	.389	.298
Leading Off Inn.			161	50	5	13	12	.311	.503	.369
Bases Empty			385	99	13	28	38	.257	.429	.311
Runners On			268	72	5	28	37	.269	.407	.331
Runners/Scor. Pos.			160	42	1	23	22	.262	.375	.344
Runners On/2 Out			97	21	1	14	18	.216	.320	.315
Scor. Pos./2 Out			65	12	0	14	13	.185	.277	.329
Late-Inning Pressure			50	12	1	9	8	.240	.320	.361
Leading Off			12	3	1	1	3	.250	.500	.357
Runners On			22	7	0	6	4	.318	.364	.448
Runners/Scor. Pos.			15	4	0	4	2	.267	.333	.400
First 9 Batters			290	71	7	25	33	.245	.386	.304
Second 9 Batters			209	62	7	17	23	.297	.498	.346
All Batters Thereafter			154	38	4	14	19	.247	.377	.312

Loves to face: Todd Benzinger (0-for-12)
Barry Bonds (.063, 2-for-32, 6 BB)
Spike Owen (0-for-20)

Hates to face: Jay Bell (.632, 12-for-19)
Bobby Bonilla (.375, 12-for-32, 4 HR)
Juan Samuel (.500, 9-for-18, 2 HR)

Miscellaneous statistics: Ground outs-to-air outs ratio: 1.43 last season, 1.20 for career.... Induced 15 double plays in 127 opportunities (one per 8.5).... Allowed 31 doubles, 9 triples (tied for most in N.L.) in 173⅔ innings.... Allowed 16 first-inning runs in 25 starts (5.76 ERA).... Batting support: 4.76 runs per start, 8th-highest average in N.L.... Record of 10–8, 4.41 ERA as a starter; 3–3, 4.74 ERA in 16 relief appearances.... Stranded 6 inherited runners, allowed 7 to score (46%).... Opposing base stealers: 17-for-26 (65%); 4 pickoffs, 0 balks.

Comments: The only N.L. pitcher to start at least 25 games and not pitch past the eighth inning in any of them.... Had the highest ERA of any N.L. pitcher who had a winning record and pitched at least 162 innings.... Opponents batted .309 against him during the first inning, the highest in any inning against him. His first-inning strikeout rate (1.80 per nine innings) was his lowest in any frame, and the lowest in the majors last season.... Shared major league lead in victories at the end of April with Smiley, Clemens, Finley, Key, and McDowell.... Opponents' on-base percentage leading off innings was the 2d highest in the league.... ERA in home games was the highest of any N.L. pitcher (minimum: 81 innings). That's all a result of his time in Wrigley Field. He did not pitch a home game in Atlanta after the Braves acquired him on September 29.... Became the 12th pitcher in history to play for the Pirates, Cubs, and Braves. The most well known among them: Don Cardwell, Burleigh Grimes, and Juan Pizarro.... Career ERA as a reliever (3.28) is a full run lower than his career mark as a starter (4.28).... Has walked only one of 60 batters faced with the bases loaded during his career.... Collected three game-winning RBIs last season, the most by any pitcher in the majors.... Lowest batting averages in major league history (minimum: 200 AB): Ron Herbel, .029 (6-for-206); Don Carman, .057 (12-for-209); Dean Chance, .066 (44-for-662); Bielecki, .074 (18-for-243).

Bud Black

Throws Left

San Francisco Giants	W-L	ERA	AB	H	HR	BB	SO	BA	SA	OBA
Season	12-16	3.99	800	201	25	71	104	.251	.396	.313
vs. Left-Handers			175	48	6	15	20	.274	.406	.326
vs. Right-Handers			625	153	19	56	84	.245	.394	.309
vs. Ground-Ballers			339	90	10	29	48	.265	.392	.323
vs. Fly-Ballers			461	111	15	42	56	.241	.399	.305
Home Games	8-7	2.81	406	92	8	31	48	.227	.325	.282
Road Games	4-9	5.28	394	109	17	40	56	.277	.470	.343
Grass Fields	11-11	3.35	671	161	18	58	87	.240	.367	.302
Artificial Turf	1-5	7.67	129	40	7	13	17	.310	.550	.370
April	1-3	5.09	129	31	6	16	21	.240	.411	.322
May	4-2	1.89	164	31	2	14	23	.189	.274	.257
June	1-1	3.97	126	36	4	11	14	.286	.437	.341
July	2-2	3.49	109	27	4	9	9	.248	.394	.308
August	2-5	6.35	138	41	4	11	19	.297	.435	.349
Sept./Oct.	2-3	3.86	134	35	5	10	18	.261	.455	.313
Leading Off Inn.			206	49	6	16	18	.238	.345	.293
Bases Empty			511	122	12	34	72	.239	.348	.290
Runners On			289	79	13	37	32	.273	.481	.350
Runners/Scor. Pos.			153	40	5	25	14	.261	.355	.355
Runners On/2 Out			121	28	5	21	15	.231	.413	.345
Scor. Pos./2 Out			75	16	3	16	4	.213	.373	.352
Late-Inning Pressure			50	13	0	7	8	.260	.320	.351
Leading Off			12	3	0	2	1	.250	.250	.357
Runners On			24	8	0	3	2	.333	.458	.407
Runners/Scor. Pos.			16	5	0	1	2	.313	.500	.353
First 9 Batters			273	68	4	23	36	.249	.348	.307
Second 9 Batters			266	71	11	21	31	.267	.444	.318
All Batters Thereafter			261	62	10	27	37	.238	.398	.314

Loves to face: Luis Gonzalez (.111, 1-for-9)
Dave Magadan (.077, 1-for-13)
Dale Sveum (0-for-9)

Hates to face: Joe Oliver (.571, 4-for-7, 1 2B, 2 HR)
Luis Salazar (.500, 9-for-18, 3 HR)
Juan Samuel (.533, 8-for-15, 2 HR)

Miscellaneous statistics: Ground outs-to-air outs ratio: 1.06 last season, 1.08 for career.... Induced 20 double plays in 148 opportunities (one per 7.4), 5th-best rate in N.L.... Allowed 31 doubles, 5 triples in 214⅓ innings.... Allowed 20 first-inning runs in 34 starts (4.50 ERA).... Batting support: 3.71 runs per start.... Opposing base stealers: 14-for-25 (56%); 6 pickoffs, 6 balks (most in majors).

Comments: For second consecutive year, has allowed a higher batting average to left-handed batters than to right-handed batters. In 1990, lefties out-hit righties, .269 to .224. In each of the two previous years, he held lefties below the .180 mark.... Each of his first three wins was a shutout.... Threw shutouts in consecutive starts against Mets last season; his 0.95 ERA vs. New York was a league low.... His streak of 26 consecutive scoreless innings in May was the 2d longest by any N.L. pitcher last season.... Led N.L. with 16 losses, becoming first Giants pitcher to lead the league in losses since Ray Sadecki shared the honor with Claude Osteen in 1968. No Giants pitcher had led the league solo since Dave Koslo did it for the Polo Grounders in 1946.... Also led N.L. with 6 balks last season. His career total of 30 balks stands fifth among active pitchers. (Bob Welch leads with 42; the all-time record is 89 by Steve Carlton.)... Has pitched for five clubs in his career, four in the last four years.... One of 14 pitchers to throw at least 200 innings in each of the last three years.... Issued eight intentional walks for Roger Craig last season, more than he had in his previous four years combined.... Handled 52 fielding chances without an error last season, and hasn't committed an error since May 7, 1990.... Came to the plate 80 times last season, the most by any major leaguer who didn't draw a walk.

Joe Boever
Throws Right

Philadelphia Phillies	W-L	ERA	AB	H	HR	BB	SO	BA	SA	OBA
Season	3-5	3.84	368	90	10	54	89	.245	.383	.336
vs. Left-Handers			171	44	4	30	41	.257	.380	.361
vs. Right-Handers			197	46	6	24	48	.234	.386	.314
vs. Ground-Ballers			156	42	4	21	25	.269	.410	.352
vs. Fly-Ballers			215	50	6	33	64	.233	.367	.329
Home Games	2-1	3.17	200	45	2	28	46	.225	.315	.317
Road Games	1-4	4.67	168	45	8	26	43	.268	.464	.359
Grass Fields	1-2	2.70	109	24	4	15	32	.220	.367	.310
Artificial Turf	2-3	4.35	259	66	6	39	57	.255	.390	.348
April	1-1	3.44	68	16	2	11	17	.235	.368	.338
May	2-3	3.74	83	19	2	9	22	.229	.337	.301
June	0-1	5.30	69	18	3	16	14	.261	.478	.391
July	0-0	1.59	43	10	0	6	6	.233	.302	.327
August	0-0	3.86	60	16	3	10	17	.267	.433	.371
Sept./Oct.	0-0	4.50	45	11	0	2	13	.244	.356	.265
Leading Off Inn.			83	19	3	7	19	.229	.361	.289
Bases Empty			206	48	7	21	53	.233	.364	.304
Runners On			162	42	3	33	36	.259	.407	.373
Runners/Scor. Pos.			97	25	2	26	21	.258	.423	.395
Runners On/2 Out			83	22	0	20	17	.265	.337	.408
Scor. Pos./2 Out			57	15	0	15	10	.263	.351	.417
Late-Inning Pressure			109	28	4	22	29	.257	.404	.382
Leading Off			26	6	0	6	5	.231	.269	.375
Runners On			50	11	2	14	14	.220	.380	.391
Runners/Scor. Pos.			28	6	1	10	7	.214	.393	.421
First 9 Batters			347	85	10	50	83	.245	.386	.335
Second 9 Batters			21	5	0	4	6	.238	.333	.360
All Batters Thereafter			0	0	0	0	0	—	—	—

Loves to face: Jeff Hamilton (0-for-8)
              Tommy Herr (0-for-9)
              Robby Thompson (.071, 1-for-14)

Hates to face: Jeff Blauser (.800, 4-for-5, 2 2B, 1 HR, 1 SO)
              Andujar Cedeno (4-for-4)
              Mike Scioscia (.667, 4-for-6, 4 BB)

Miscellaneous statistics: Ground outs-to-air outs ratio: 0.72 last season, 0.80 for career.... Induced 2 double plays in 70 opportunities (one per 35).... Allowed 15 doubles, 3 triples in 98⅓ innings.... Stranded 20 inherited runners, allowed 15 to score (57%).... Opposing base stealers: 12-for-14 (86%); 1 pickoff, 1 balk.

Comments: Although he saved 35 games over the two previous seasons, he appeared in 68 games without registering one last year. That's one game shy of the all-time single-season record for appearances by a relief pitcher without any saves. Norm Charlton set the mark in 1989, and Jeff Innis matched it last season.... Boever entered only one game in a save situation, but he walked the first batter he faced, who turned out to be the only batter he faced.... Career record of 11–25 gives him the lowest winning percentage (.306) among active pitchers with at least 35 decisions.... Dig in, boys: Boever has faced 1493 batters in his major league career and has hit only two of them. He has never hit a left-handed batter in 763 chances to do so.... Career lefty/righty breakdown is almost the exact inverse of his 1991 numbers. Career: .259 by right-handers, .237 by left-handers. Moreover, right-handers have hit home runs at three times the rate that lefties have (RHB: one every 27 at-bats; LHB: one every 81 at-bats).... The gap is much wider between ground- and fly-ball hitters than between left- and right-handed batters. Career numbers: .275 by ground-ball hitters, .226 by fly-ballers.... He's a member of the I've-Never-Started-a-Game-in-the-Majors Club. Officers: Kent Tekulve, President (1050 games); Sparky Lyle, Vice President (899); Jeff Reardon, Secretary (751); Dan Quisenberry, Treasurer (674). There are 37 card-carrying members (minimum: 250 games needed for membership).

Shawn Boskie
Throws Right

Chicago Cubs	W-L	ERA	AB	H	HR	BB	SO	BA	SA	OBA
Season	4-9	5.23	511	150	14	52	62	.294	.456	.361
vs. Left-Handers			291	93	10	36	27	.320	.526	.393
vs. Right-Handers			220	57	4	16	35	.259	.364	.315
vs. Ground-Ballers			224	64	4	18	33	.286	.402	.340
vs. Fly-Ballers			287	86	10	34	29	.300	.498	.376
Home Games	3-5	5.43	264	85	8	34	27	.322	.511	.401
Road Games	1-4	5.04	247	65	6	18	35	.263	.397	.316
Grass Fields	3-8	6.10	367	118	12	41	40	.322	.510	.390
Artificial Turf	1-1	3.23	144	32	2	11	22	.222	.319	.283
April	2-1	2.25	104	25	1	9	10	.240	.308	.302
May	0-3	5.73	128	41	1	12	19	.320	.422	.371
June	1-3	5.81	127	36	2	12	12	.283	.449	.355
July	0-1	24.00	18	11	2	1	1	.611	1.278	.619
August	1-0	0.00	37	6	0	4	8	.162	.189	.244
Sept./Oct.	0-1	7.33	97	31	8	14	12	.320	.619	.411
Leading Off Inn.			117	41	5	18	14	.350	.650	.445
Bases Empty			271	82	8	26	39	.303	.498	.370
Runners On			240	68	6	26	23	.283	.408	.350
Runners/Scor. Pos.			145	37	4	14	14	.255	.386	.313
Runners On/2 Out			94	26	4	9	14	.277	.457	.346
Scor. Pos./2 Out			58	13	3	6	11	.224	.414	.297
Late-Inning Pressure			23	7	0	3	1	.304	.391	.407
Leading Off			6	4	0	1	0	.667	.833	.714
Runners On			12	1	0	2	1	.083	.083	.267
Runners/Scor. Pos.			5	1	0	1	0	.200	.200	.429
First 9 Batters			209	56	5	22	35	.268	.397	.333
Second 9 Batters			171	50	3	11	18	.292	.421	.344
All Batters Thereafter			131	44	6	19	9	.336	.595	.424

Loves to face: Dave Martinez (.125, 2-for-16)
              Tim Teufel (0-for-5, 4 SO)
              Jose Uribe (0-for-10)

Hates to face: Bobby Bonilla (.600, 6-for-10)
              Orlando Merced (3-for-3)
              Matt Williams (.375, 6-for-16, 2 2B, 2 HR)

Miscellaneous statistics: Ground outs-to-air outs ratio: 1.01 last season, 1.04 for career.... Induced 9 double plays in 126 opportunities (one per 14).... Allowed 29 doubles, 6 triples in 129 innings.... Allowed 16 first-inning runs in 20 starts (7.20 ERA, 4th highest in N.L.).... Batting support: 4.10 runs per start.... Opposing base stealers: 4-for-6 (67%); 1 pickoff, 1 balk.

Comments: Warning: Please keep impressionable children and pets away from these comments. Reader discretion is advised. With our legal responsibilities out of the way, and knowing that only mature adults are still with us, we can begin. But it won't be pretty. Boskie ranked last among N.L. pitchers last season (minimum: 100 innings) in hits allowed (10.5) and base runners allowed (14.4) per nine innings, opponents' batting average (.294), and opponents' on-base average (.361).... Leadoff batters reached base in almost 45 percent of innings he started last season, the highest rate against any pitcher in majors who faced at least 100 leadoff batters.... Boskie and Jack Armstrong were the only two N.L. pitchers with ERAs over 5.00 in at least 100 innings last season.... Boskie allowed at least one home run in each of his last seven starts (spread over a June 17–Oct. 5 span); he didn't last more than 5⅓ innings in any of those starts.... Career opponents' batting average: .301 by left-handed batters, .256 by right-handers.... Opponents have .302 career average at Wrigley Field, .316 on other grass fields, and .224 on artificial turf. He's allowed a career rate of one home run every 32.9 at-bats at Wrigley, one every 55.9 at-bats elsewhere.... Okay, the rough part is over, you can bring the kids and pets back in.... Appeared in eight games in relief and stranded 10 of 11 inherited runners.... One of three pitchers to hit a triple last season. The others: Steve Avery and Charlie Leibrandt.

Jeff Brantley
Throws Right

San Francisco Giants	W-L	ERA	AB	H	HR	BB	SO	BA	SA	OBA
Season	5-2	2.45	346	78	8	52	81	.225	.338	.332
vs. Left-Handers			185	38	3	36	42	.205	.286	.338
vs. Right-Handers			161	40	5	16	39	.248	.398	.324
vs. Ground-Ballers			157	39	1	20	41	.248	.331	.335
vs. Fly-Ballers			189	39	7	32	40	.206	.344	.329
Home Games	2-0	2.14	156	36	2	19	34	.231	.321	.320
Road Games	3-2	2.70	190	42	6	33	47	.221	.353	.341
Grass Fields	4-0	2.45	247	60	4	31	58	.243	.328	.333
Artificial Turf	1-2	2.45	99	18	4	21	23	.182	.364	.328
April	0-1	3.60	36	9	1	5	8	.250	.444	.326
May	0-0	2.12	58	14	3	10	16	.241	.414	.371
June	3-0	1.20	56	15	0	10	10	.268	.304	.373
July	0-0	5.54	47	10	2	8	7	.213	.362	.345
August	2-1	0.93	68	12	1	12	18	.176	.279	.300
Sept./Oct.	0-0	2.57	81	18	1	7	22	.222	.296	.292
Leading Off Inn.			74	15	3	11	13	.203	.405	.322
Bases Empty			182	48	7	20	42	.264	.429	.343
Runners On			164	30	1	32	39	.183	.238	.320
Runners/Scor. Pos.			119	19	1	23	32	.160	.210	.297
Runners On/2 Out			74	13	1	17	21	.176	.284	.344
Scor. Pos./2 Out			57	8	1	14	17	.140	.228	.329
Late-Inning Pressure			202	51	5	34	40	.252	.337	.360
Leading Off			43	11	3	9	7	.256	.512	.396
Runners On			98	16	0	22	19	.163	.163	.311
Runners/Scor. Pos.			65	9	0	14	14	.138	.138	.284
First 9 Batters			340	78	8	49	79	.229	.344	.332
Second 9 Batters			6	0	0	3	2	.000	.000	.333
All Batters Thereafter			0	0	0	0	0	—	—	—

Loves to face: Barry Bonds (0-for-10)
Mariano Duncan (.083, 1-for-12)
Barry Larkin (.100, 1-for-10)
Hates to face: Tony Gwynn (.643, 9-for-14)
Paul O'Neill (.429, 3-for-7, 2 HR, 6 BB)
Luis Quinones (.667, 6-for-9)

Miscellaneous statistics: Ground outs-to-air outs ratio: 0.72 last season, 1.08 for career.... Induced 6 double plays in 79 opportunities (one per 13).... Allowed 13 doubles, 1 triple in 95⅓ innings.... Saved 15 games in 19 opportunities (79%).... Stranded 27 inherited runners, allowed 11 to score (71%).... Opposing base stealers: 17-for-19 (89%); 0 pickoffs, 0 balks.

Comments: Has held opponents to .155 and .160 batting average with runners in scoring position in last two years. Among pitchers who faced at least 100 batters in a season in those situations, he's the only pitcher to hold batters to .160 or below in each of the past two years.... Has held opponents to .130 career average (19-for-136) with runners in scoring position in Late-Inning Pressure Situations.... Opponents' yearly batting averages since he broke into the majors in 1988: .275, .271, .240, .225. Although batting average was a career low and strikeout rate (7.65 per nine innings) was a career high, he walked a career-high 4.91 batters per nine innings; his previous career average: 3.34 walks per nine.... Opponents have a career average of .246 at Candlestick Park, .285 on other grass fields, and .216 on artificial surfaces.... Half of the eight homers he allowed last season were hit within a span of 15 batters.... Owns .773 career winning percentage (17–5) in relief, highest among active relief pitchers with at least 20 decisions.... Held opponents to one hit in 16 at-bats with the bases loaded, after holding them 0-for-14 in 1990. That reduced opponents' career batting average with bases loaded to .091 (4-for-44), the lowest bases-loaded average against any pitcher over the last 17 years (minimum: 50 PA). One of those hits was a grand-slam homer by Paul O'Neill in 1989.

Tom Browning
Throws Left

Cincinnati Reds	W-L	ERA	AB	H	HR	BB	SO	BA	SA	OBA
Season	14-14	4.18	906	241	32	56	115	.266	.427	.309
vs. Left-Handers			212	43	4	19	41	.203	.344	.269
vs. Right-Handers			694	198	28	37	74	.285	.452	.321
vs. Ground-Ballers			427	94	6	22	69	.220	.307	.258
vs. Fly-Ballers			507	152	27	35	50	.300	.525	.345
Home Games	10-4	3.50	449	104	18	33	57	.232	.399	.283
Road Games	4-10	4.94	457	137	14	23	58	.300	.455	.335
Grass Fields	3-4	3.68	292	79	7	15	35	.271	.404	.309
Artificial Turf	11-10	4.41	614	162	25	41	80	.264	.438	.309
April	3-1	2.33	134	26	5	2	16	.194	.336	.203
May	3-3	4.38	150	36	6	11	19	.240	.400	.290
June	4-0	3.79	137	34	4	18	24	.248	.401	.333
July	1-3	6.38	155	52	10	8	15	.335	.606	.367
August	2-1	2.72	161	43	2	5	22	.267	.354	.293
Sept./Oct.	1-6	5.53	169	50	5	12	19	.296	.450	.344
Leading Off Inn.			227	56	10	12	26	.247	.410	.287
Bases Empty			556	141	22	33	68	.254	.417	.298
Runners On			350	100	10	23	47	.286	.443	.326
Runners/Scor. Pos.			174	56	4	17	24	.322	.460	.365
Runners On/2 Out			157	41	4	16	24	.261	.389	.333
Scor. Pos./2 Out			89	23	2	12	15	.258	.360	.347
Late-Inning Pressure			59	18	2	2	7	.305	.458	.328
Leading Off			19	5	1	0	1	.263	.421	.263
Runners On			17	5	0	1	2	.294	.353	.333
Runners/Scor. Pos.			7	3	0	1	1	.429	.429	.429
First 9 Batters			302	78	11	19	43	.258	.444	.300
Second 9 Batters			297	76	9	19	42	.256	.391	.297
All Batters Thereafter			307	87	12	18	30	.283	.446	.328

Loves to face: Jeff Hamilton (.107, 3-for-28, 0 BB)
Howard Johnson (.103, 4-for-39, 2 HR)
Todd Zeile (.063, 1-for-16)
Hates to face: Barry Bonds (.353, 12-for-34, 5 HR, 11 BB)
Bobby Bonilla (.390, 16-for-41, 4 2B, 1 3B, 8 HR)
Tim Teufel (.439, 18-for-41, 4 HR)

Miscellaneous statistics: Ground outs-to-air outs ratio: 0.72 last season, 2d lowest in N.L.; 0.65 for career.... Induced 13 double plays in 154 opportunities (one per 12).... Allowed 40 doubles (5th most in N.L.), 5 triples in 230⅓ innings.... Allowed 25 first-inning runs in 36 starts (6.25 ERA).... Batting support: 4.83 runs per start, 7th-highest average in N.L.... Opposing base stealers: 21-for-27 (78%); 2 pickoffs, 1 balk.

Comments: One of four N.L. opening-day starters who finished last season without a winning record. The others, Danny Jackson (1–5), Mike Scott (0–2), and Ed Whitson (4–6), all had their seasons shortened by injury.... His 6.25 first-inning ERA was his highest in any inning, despite a first-inning strikeout rate of 5.50 batters per nine innings, also his highest in any inning.... Carried a 13–8 record into September, but lost six of his last seven starts.... Has reached double figures in wins in each of the past seven years. That may seem a rather modest feat, but only four others have done it (Boddicker and Hurst, nine years; Viola, eight; Key, seven).... He's completed only three of 71 starts over the last two years, but he's the only N.L. pitcher to start at least 35 games in each of the last four seasons.... Career total of 255 starts ranks ninth in Reds' history. Another 35-start season would put him into fifth place behind Eppa Rixey (356), Paul Derringer (322), Dolf Luque (319), and Bucky Walters (296).... Among major league pitchers who qualified for the ERA title, only Seattle's Rich DeLucia allowed home runs at a greater rate than Browning. Over the last five years, Tom has allowed 91 homers at home, 59 on road.... Among active pitchers with at least 750 innings, only John Cerutti, Curt Young, and Bill Wegman have higher career home-run rates.... Owns a winning career record against every opposing club in his league; Dwight Gooden is the only other active pitcher with that distinction (minimum: 20 decisions).

Tim Burke

Throws Right

Expos/Mets	W-L	ERA	AB	H	HR	BB	SO	BA	SA	OBA
Season	6-7	3.36	385	96	8	26	59	.249	.369	.301
vs. Left-Handers			192	57	2	15	20	.297	.417	.346
vs. Right-Handers			193	39	6	11	39	.202	.321	.257
vs. Ground-Ballers			180	45	1	8	28	.250	.317	.289
vs. Fly-Ballers			205	51	7	18	31	.249	.415	.313
Home Games	2-2	2.16	183	40	3	12	27	.219	.339	.268
Road Games	4-5	4.53	202	56	5	14	32	.277	.396	.332
Grass Fields	4-5	3.81	226	57	6	12	37	.252	.376	.289
Artificial Turf	2-2	2.80	159	39	2	14	22	.245	.358	.318
April	2-1	3.97	40	9	1	4	4	.225	.400	.333
May	1-1	3.63	63	13	1	6	13	.206	.286	.275
June	0-1	5.40	51	16	1	2	6	.314	.431	.352
July	1-2	3.21	60	17	1	4	9	.283	.400	.328
August	0-2	3.47	89	23	1	4	12	.258	.348	.287
Sept./Oct.	2-0	1.61	82	18	3	6	15	.220	.378	.270
Leading Off Inn.			93	29	3	4	11	.312	.484	.340
Bases Empty			212	54	5	10	33	.255	.387	.291
Runners On			173	42	3	16	26	.243	.347	.313
Runners/Scor. Pos.			99	26	3	13	17	.263	.414	.356
Runners On/2 Out			62	12	2	6	13	.194	.323	.286
Scor. Pos./2 Out			38	8	2	5	8	.211	.421	.333
Late-Inning Pressure			187	45	3	15	28	.241	.374	.302
Leading Off			44	14	1	2	4	.318	.455	.348
Runners On			92	18	1	8	17	.196	.326	.272
Runners/Scor. Pos.			55	12	1	8	12	.218	.382	.333
First 9 Batters			365	92	8	26	55	.252	.375	.307
Second 9 Batters			20	4	0	0	4	.200	.250	.200
All Batters Thereafter			0	0	0	0	0	—	—	—

Loves to face: Gary Carter (.148, 4-for-27, 0 BB)
Len Dykstra (.077, 1-for-13, 2 BB)
Charlie Hayes (0-for-11)

Hates to face: Pedro Guerrero (.450, 9-for-20, 2 HR)
Lonnie Smith (.625, 5-for-8)
Jose Uribe (.429, 6-for-14, 1 HR)

Miscellaneous statistics: Ground outs-to-air outs ratio: 1.58 last season, 1.51 for career.... Induced 14 double plays in 92 opportunities (one per 6.6), 3d-best rate in N.L.... Allowed 16 doubles, 3 triples in 101⅔ innings.... Stranded 27 inherited runners, allowed 12 to score (69%).... Opposing base stealers: 8-for-9 (89%); 0 pickoffs, 0 balks.

Comments: 2.62 career ERA stands second among active pitchers (minimum: 500 IP); it also ranks second in his own bullpen behind John Franco (2.53), who could diabolically widen that gap by occasionally allowing runners inherited from Burke to score.... Had 4.41 ERA in 37 games with Montreal, 2.75 in 35 games with New York.... The 95-point gap between last season's batting averages of opposing left- and right-handed batters is the largest of his career, but he's approached it several times (75 points in 1990, 65 in 1988, 84 in 1986, 87 in 1985). Career breakdown: .272 by left-handed batters, .201 by right-handers. Owns a stellar strikeout/walk ratio of 3.7 vs. right-handed batters, but only 1.3 vs. lefties.... Allowed a grand-slam homer to Pedro Guerrero as a rookie in 1985, but hasn't allowed one in 73 at-bats since 1986.... Opponents hit for a higher average on grass fields than on artificial turf for the first time in his career.... Threw to eight different catchers last season; opponents stole seven bases in 11⅔ innings with Mike Fitzgerald catching, and only one in 90 innings with other guys behind the dish.... Burke and Roger McDowell have pitched in at least 55 games in each of the last seven seasons since breaking into the majors together in 1985. Only one other pitcher in major league history has appeared in that many games in each of his first seven seasons: Craig Lefferts, who had an eight-year streak snapped last season, when he appeared in 54.

John Burkett

Throws Right

San Francisco Giants	W-L	ERA	AB	H	HR	BB	SO	BA	SA	OBA
Season	12-11	4.18	804	223	19	60	131	.277	.392	.332
vs. Left-Handers			467	137	14	39	72	.293	.441	.347
vs. Right-Handers			337	86	5	21	59	.255	.323	.312
vs. Ground-Ballers			378	93	8	29	66	.246	.344	.307
vs. Fly-Ballers			426	130	11	31	65	.305	.434	.355
Home Games	6-6	3.54	421	102	10	25	72	.242	.349	.291
Road Games	6-5	4.90	383	121	9	35	59	.316	.439	.375
Grass Fields	7-9	3.73	590	156	14	39	93	.264	.366	.318
Artificial Turf	5-2	5.43	214	67	5	21	38	.313	.463	.371
April	2-2	3.66	120	33	1	9	18	.275	.358	.326
May	0-1	3.50	139	39	3	12	27	.281	.396	.344
June	2-1	2.41	126	26	4	14	28	.206	.325	.291
July	3-1	3.89	159	44	4	9	23	.277	.396	.312
August	2-3	7.45	125	43	4	7	18	.344	.496	.381
Sept./Oct.	3-3	4.91	135	38	3	9	27	.281	.378	.345
Leading Off Inn.			195	59	7	14	29	.303	.451	.352
Bases Empty			436	116	13	35	75	.266	.394	.334
Runners On			368	107	6	25	56	.291	.389	.331
Runners/Scor. Pos.			197	63	2	16	36	.320	.396	.360
Runners On/2 Out			154	43	3	16	19	.279	.390	.355
Scor. Pos./2 Out			97	28	0	9	15	.289	.330	.349
Late-Inning Pressure			51	11	2	6	4	.216	.333	.293
Leading Off			13	5	0	1	0	.385	.385	.429
Runners On			26	3	1	3	4	.115	.231	.200
Runners/Scor. Pos.			10	1	0	2	2	.100	.100	.231
First 9 Batters			276	73	6	23	52	.264	.366	.332
Second 9 Batters			268	86	5	18	52	.321	.433	.365
All Batters Thereafter			260	64	8	19	27	.246	.377	.297

Loves to face: Joe Oliver (0-for-9)
Garry Templeton (0-for-11)
Jeff Treadway (.125, 3-for-24)

Hates to face: Hal Morris (.471, 8-for-17, 2 HR)
Chris Sabo (.455, 10-for-22, 1 HR)
Larry Walker (.412, 7-for-17, 3 HR)

Miscellaneous statistics: Ground outs-to-air outs ratio: 1.12 last season, 1.27 for career.... Induced 14 double plays in 183 opportunities (one per 13).... Allowed 31 doubles, 2 triples in 206⅔ innings.... Allowed 21 first-inning runs in 34 starts (4.76 ERA).... Batting support: 3.71 runs per start.... Opposing base stealers: 17-for-33 (52%); 3 pickoffs, 0 balks.

Comments: 1991 ERA by batterymate: 2.97 with Terry Kennedy (in 57⅔ innings), 3.07 with Steve Decker (99⅔), and 7.84 with Kirt Manwaring (49⅓). That Burkett-Manwaring ERA was the highest among all N.L. pitcher-catcher combinations with at least 30 innings together last season.... Only one of the 19 home runs he allowed came on a pitch called (or at least signaled) by Kennedy.... Finished with the 2d-highest ERA among N.L. pitchers with winning records who qualified for the ERA title. The last qualifying Giants pitcher with a winning record and an ERA as high as Burkett's was Sam McDowell (10–8, 4.34 ERA in 1972). The only other San Francisco pitchers to do it: Jack Sanford in 1961, and Mike McCormick in 1958.... Has pitched more than 200 innings in each of last two years; in 1991, for first time since 1980, the Giants had three 200-inning pitchers.... Hit 10 batters with pitches last season, most in N.L.... Sixteen base runners were caught stealing with Burkett on the mound, 2d most by any pitcher in the majors. Opponents stole only eight bases in 21 attempts before the All-Star break, but were 9-for-12 during the second half.... Opponents' on-base average leading off innings was 3d highest in N.L.... Opponents have a career average of .249 at Candlestick Park, .279 on other grass fields, and .297 on artificial surfaces.... As a batter, he had a streak of 34 consecutive plate appearances in which he failed to reach base, the longest streak in the majors last season.

Frank Castillo — Throws Right

Chicago Cubs	W-L	ERA	AB	H	HR	BB	SO	BA	SA	OBA
Season	6-7	4.35	425	107	5	33	73	.252	.351	.304
vs. Left-Handers			273	77	5	27	49	.282	.392	.344
vs. Right-Handers			152	30	0	6	24	.197	.276	.226
vs. Ground-Ballers			160	38	2	11	20	.237	.350	.283
vs. Fly-Ballers			265	69	3	22	53	.260	.351	.316
Home Games	3-3	3.73	188	42	4	12	43	.223	.324	.266
Road Games	3-4	4.87	237	65	1	21	30	.274	.371	.333
Grass Fields	4-4	4.48	248	63	4	18	51	.254	.359	.301
Artificial Turf	2-3	4.18	177	44	1	15	22	.249	.339	.307
April	0-0	—	0	0	0	0	0	—	—	—
May	0-0	—	0	0	0	0	0	—	—	—
June	0-0	2.25	27	5	0	1	2	.185	.259	.214
July	3-2	3.99	184	48	1	11	32	.261	.332	.301
August	2-0	1.47	63	12	0	3	12	.190	.254	.224
Sept./Oct.	1-5	6.63	151	42	4	18	27	.278	.430	.353
Leading Off Inn.			107	21	0	10	19	.196	.290	.265
Bases Empty			254	56	4	14	51	.220	.343	.261
Runners On			171	51	1	19	22	.298	.363	.363
Runners/Scor. Pos.			105	31	1	16	12	.295	.362	.379
Runners On/2 Out			63	13	1	6	7	.206	.302	.275
Scor. Pos./2 Out			44	8	1	5	6	.182	.295	.265
Late-Inning Pressure			43	8	0	2	8	.186	.209	.222
Leading Off			12	3	0	2	3	.250	.250	.357
Runners On			15	3	0	0	3	.200	.267	.200
Runners/Scor. Pos.			4	0	0	0	0	.000	.000	.000
First 9 Batters			136	37	1	14	27	.272	.375	.336
Second 9 Batters			131	30	0	10	21	.229	.298	.282
All Batters Thereafter			158	40	4	9	25	.253	.373	.293

Loves to face: Jay Bell (.100, 1-for-10)
Felix Jose (0-for-6)
Rafael Ramirez (0-for-7)

Hates to face: Dave Martinez (2-for-2, 2 HR, 1 BB)
Ozzie Smith (3-for-3, 3 BB)
Andy Van Slyke (.556, 5-for-9, 1 HR)

Miscellaneous statistics: Ground outs-to-air outs ratio: 1.19 last season, 1.19 for career.... Induced 5 double plays in 91 opportunities (one per 18).... Allowed 23 doubles, 2 triples in 111⅔ innings.... Allowed 11 first-inning runs in 18 starts (5.29 ERA).... Batting support: 3.83 runs per start.... Opposing base stealers: 7-for-11 (64%); 1 pickoff, 1 balk.

Comments: 22-year-old made 18 starts after being recalled late in June; the only younger pitchers with 15 or more starts in the majors last season were 21-year-old Steve Avery (35 starts), 21-year-old Ramon Garcia (15), and Alex Fernandez (32), who turned 22 during the summer.... He was 4–2 with a 3.48 ERA when placed on the disabled list on August 11 (strained right shoulder), but posted a 2–5 record with a 5.55 ERA after his return. His ERA after September 1 was 2d highest in the league.... Right-handed batters had 152 at-bats against him, the most against any N.L. pitcher who did not allow a home run to a righty swinger last season.... Allowed only one home run in 61 innings outside of Wrigley Field. Among N.L. pitchers with at least 50 innings on the road last season, only Tim Belcher had a lower home-run rate (one HR in 88 IP).... Opponents batted .319 during the first two innings of his starts, but only .221 subsequently.... Among the 26 major league clubs last season, only Cleveland had a higher total of innings pitched by rookies than the Cubs. Castillo, Bob Scanlan, and Chuck McElroy were three of the six N.L. rookies to pitch at least 100 innings last season, and became the first trio of Cubs rookies to reach the 100-inning barrier since 1966. The 1991 freshmen will be hard pressed to match the careers of the rookie Cubs from that season—Ferguson Jenkins, Bill Hands, and Ken Holtzman.

David Cone — Throws Right

New York Mets	W-L	ERA	AB	H	HR	BB	SO	BA	SA	OBA
Season	14-14	3.29	868	204	13	73	241	.235	.329	.296
vs. Left-Handers			545	135	7	50	123	.248	.345	.311
vs. Right-Handers			323	69	6	23	118	.214	.303	.270
vs. Ground-Ballers			452	99	4	34	124	.219	.285	.272
vs. Fly-Ballers			416	105	9	39	117	.252	.377	.321
Home Games	6-7	3.91	439	112	6	36	118	.255	.353	.314
Road Games	8-7	2.68	429	92	7	37	123	.214	.305	.278
Grass Fields	8-11	3.94	583	147	11	44	152	.252	.358	.307
Artificial Turf	6-3	2.03	285	57	2	29	89	.200	.270	.274
April	2-1	5.25	94	32	0	12	18	.340	.426	.417
May	3-2	2.20	163	36	2	7	43	.221	.276	.254
June	2-2	2.52	133	28	1	13	38	.211	.278	.291
July	3-2	3.14	160	33	3	8	45	.206	.394	.253
August	2-3	5.03	141	45	0	12	33	.319	.383	.368
Sept./Oct.	2-4	2.82	177	30	2	20	64	.169	.266	.251
Leading Off Inn.			222	58	2	15	63	.261	.356	.311
Bases Empty			514	120	4	42	141	.233	.319	.295
Runners On			354	84	9	31	100	.237	.345	.297
Runners/Scor. Pos.			206	47	7	24	64	.228	.359	.305
Runners On/2 Out			164	41	5	18	46	.250	.384	.324
Scor. Pos./2 Out			108	28	5	14	30	.259	.444	.344
Late-Inning Pressure			81	19	0	3	19	.235	.284	.262
Leading Off			22	8	0	1	5	.364	.409	.391
Runners On			31	8	0	1	6	.258	.258	.281
Runners/Scor. Pos.			21	3	0	1	5	.143	.286	.182
First 9 Batters			271	54	5	26	99	.199	.288	.274
Second 9 Batters			269	72	2	25	70	.268	.349	.333
All Batters Thereafter			328	78	6	22	72	.238	.348	.282

Loves to face: Charlie Hayes (.063, 1-for-16, 1 2B)
Rafael Ramirez (.067, 1-for-15)
Jeff Reed (.095, 2-for-21, 3 BB)

Hates to face: Darren Daulton (.238, 5-for-21, 3 HR, 9 BB)
Len Dykstra (.389, 7-for-18, 1 HR)
Milt Thompson (.391, 18-for-46, 1 HR)

Miscellaneous statistics: Ground outs-to-air outs ratio: 0.91 last season, 0.85 for career.... Induced 8 double plays in 154 opportunities (one per 19).... Allowed 29 doubles, 7 triples in 232⅔ innings.... Allowed 16 first-inning runs in 34 starts (4.24 ERA).... Batting support: 3.85 runs per start.... Opposing base stealers: 27-for-40 (68%), 4th-most steals in N.L.; 2 pickoffs, 1 balk.

Comments: Became only third pitcher in major league history with two consecutive seasons striking out more than nine batters per nine innings while walking fewer than three (minimum: 100 innings). The others: Sandy Koufax (1964–65) and Luis Tiant (1967–68). Cone's rates: 9.9 strikeouts, 2.8 walks in 1990; 9.3 and 2.8 in 1991. But here's the bottom line: Sandy was 45–13, Looie was 33–18, Coney, 28–24.... His .620 career winning percentage (67–41) is 4th highest among active pitchers with at least 100 decisions, behind Dwight Gooden (.714, 132–53), Roger Clemens (.687, 134–61), and Ted Higuera (.622, 92–56).... Winning percentage has fallen in every season since 20–3 mark in 1988; last year was his third in a row with 14 wins, while losses have climbed from 8 to 10 to 14.... Had 3.76 ERA over first four innings of work, 2.65 from fifth inning on.... For second straight year, first-inning strikeout rate was his highest in any inning. But so was his home run rate (one HR every 25.8 at-bats in first inning, one every 92.4 AB after that).... Had three strikeouts in an inning 17 times in 1991, most in the majors; struck out the side six times, most in N.L. (Note: "Struck out the side" means three up, three down, three strikeouts; the phrase is often misused to represent "three strikeouts in an inning," when such an inning might have also included three home runs.)... Has led the N.L. in strikeouts in each of the last two seasons. Last pitcher to lead N.L. three years in a row: Warren Spahn (1949–51).... ERA breakdown: 2.89 with Charlie O'Brien catching, 3.08 with Rick Cerone, 4.16 with Mackey Sasser.

Danny Cox   Throws Right

Philadelphia Phillies	W-L	ERA	AB	H	HR	BB	SO	BA	SA	OBA
Season	4-6	4.57	380	98	14	39	46	.258	.426	.323
vs. Left-Handers			189	51	7	24	15	.270	.450	.346
vs. Right-Handers			191	47	7	15	31	.246	.403	.300
vs. Ground-Ballers			171	51	6	19	23	.298	.450	.363
vs. Fly-Ballers			209	47	8	20	23	.225	.407	.291
Home Games	2-4	4.41	182	44	6	19	25	.242	.385	.309
Road Games	2-2	4.72	198	54	8	20	21	.273	.465	.336
Grass Fields	2-1	3.86	125	27	5	15	16	.216	.392	.301
Artificial Turf	2-5	4.95	255	71	9	24	30	.278	.443	.335
April	0-0	1.29	24	3	1	1	4	.125	.292	.160
May	1-1	3.60	73	17	2	9	13	.233	.370	.313
June	2-0	6.60	55	14	1	7	4	.255	.382	.344
July	0-3	5.65	55	17	3	10	6	.309	.509	.403
August	1-2	5.08	133	39	5	9	13	.293	.481	.333
Sept./Oct.	0-0	2.92	40	8	2	3	6	.200	.375	.250
Leading Off Inn.			92	19	2	13	8	.207	.304	.305
Bases Empty			227	54	9	30	26	.238	.396	.327
Runners On			153	44	5	9	20	.288	.471	.318
Runners/Scor. Pos.			95	26	4	5	13	.274	.474	.290
Runners On/2 Out			69	17	4	4	10	.246	.493	.297
Scor. Pos./2 Out			43	9	3	2	7	.209	.465	.244
Late-Inning Pressure			10	0	0	1	3	.000	.000	.083
Leading Off			2	0	0	1	0	.000	.000	.333
Runners On			4	0	0	0	2	.000	.000	.000
Runners/Scor. Pos.			2	0	0	0	1	.000	.000	.000
First 9 Batters			166	37	5	15	24	.223	.361	.283
Second 9 Batters			138	44	9	14	10	.319	.565	.381
All Batters Thereafter			76	17	0	10	12	.224	.316	.307

Loves to face: George Bell (0-for-7)
        Will Clark (.130, 3-for-23)
        Mark Grace (.100, 1-for-10)
Hates to face: Gerald Perry (.579, 11-for-19)
        Darryl Strawberry (.417, 15-for-36, 1 HR)
        Matt Williams (.571, 4-for-7, 1 2B, 2 HR)

Miscellaneous statistics: Ground outs-to-air outs ratio: 1.20 last season, 1.37 for career.... Induced 6 double plays in 61 opportunities (one per 10).... Allowed 16 doubles, 3 triples in 102⅓ innings.... Allowed 7 first-inning runs in 17 starts (3.71 ERA).... Batting support: 4.88 runs per start.... Opposing base stealers: 11-for-18 (61%); 0 pickoffs, 1 balk.

Comments: Made 17 starts, second most among major league pitchers who never made it into the eighth inning last season. He went seven full innings on four occasions, including his Phillies debut on April 27. The only pitcher with more starts than Cox without pitching into the eighth inning was another guy nursing his way back from arm problems, Orel Hershiser.... After Cox missed the entire 1989 and 1990 seasons, last year could be considered the start of his "second career." It's only fitting that he started 1991 with a clean slate: a new team and a career record of exactly .500 (56–56). He wavered around the .500 mark until dropping his final two decisions.... Owns a 24–16 career record in starts following losing starts, but a 14–28 record in starts following winning starts.... His last six appearances of the year were out of the bullpen. He had made only two relief appearances previously, both in 1984.... Walked 3.43 batters per nine innings, the highest rate of his career.... Also had the highest home-run rate of his career, allowing one every 7.3 innings, but that had to be expected with his move from cavernous Busch Stadium.... Even before his injuries, this six-foot four-inch, 230-pounder was never a strikeout pitcher: His career strikeout rate is just 4.46 per nine innings. That's not only shy of the standards set by six-foot six-inch Dick Radatz (9.68), but it doesn't even measure up to the modest career rate of five-foot six-inch Bobby Shantz (4.98).

Jose DeJesus   Throws Right

Philadelphia Phillies	W-L	ERA	AB	H	HR	BB	SO	BA	SA	OBA
Season	10-9	3.42	655	147	7	128	118	.224	.318	.353
vs. Left-Handers			376	87	1	89	65	.231	.309	.377
vs. Right-Handers			279	60	6	39	53	.215	.330	.318
vs. Ground-Ballers			270	51	1	61	48	.189	.252	.342
vs. Fly-Ballers			385	96	6	67	70	.249	.364	.361
Home Games	4-5	3.39	280	67	2	54	52	.239	.329	.363
Road Games	6-4	3.44	375	80	5	74	66	.213	.309	.346
Grass Fields	3-2	3.61	159	26	3	37	25	.164	.264	.328
Artificial Turf	7-7	3.35	496	121	4	91	93	.244	.335	.362
April	0-1	5.40	70	15	1	20	9	.214	.300	.402
May	1-1	3.45	58	14	0	13	10	.241	.293	.380
June	4-1	3.23	146	34	1	23	24	.233	.322	.341
July	2-1	2.10	119	25	2	18	19	.210	.319	.312
August	3-0	3.49	143	34	1	28	36	.238	.329	.364
Sept./Oct.	0-5	3.71	119	25	2	26	20	.210	.319	.349
Leading Off Inn.			161	37	2	27	22	.230	.348	.344
Bases Empty			348	75	4	67	57	.216	.307	.345
Runners On			307	72	3	61	61	.235	.329	.362
Runners/Scor. Pos.			191	39	2	41	42	.204	.288	.346
Runners On/2 Out			134	30	1	24	25	.224	.313	.346
Scor. Pos./2 Out			89	18	1	19	17	.202	.270	.349
Late-Inning Pressure			58	15	1	8	6	.259	.397	.343
Leading Off			16	4	0	3	1	.250	.438	.368
Runners On			24	7	0	3	3	.292	.375	.357
Runners/Scor. Pos.			16	3	0	1	2	.188	.250	.222
First 9 Batters			214	49	2	52	41	.229	.322	.385
Second 9 Batters			197	44	2	35	41	.223	.310	.341
All Batters Thereafter			244	54	3	41	36	.221	.320	.333

Loves to face: Eric Anthony (0-for-10)
        Lenny Harris (0-for-11)
        Howard Johnson (0-for-16)
Hates to face: Jeff Bagwell (.667, 6-for-9, 1 HR)
        Bip Roberts (.357, 5-for-14, 6 BB)
        Todd Zeile (.429, 3-for-7, 1 HR, 4 BB)

Miscellaneous statistics: Ground outs-to-air outs ratio: 1.04 last season, 1.10 for career.... Induced 17 double plays in 157 opportunities (one per 9.2).... Allowed 32 doubles, 4 triples in 181⅔ innings.... Allowed 10 first-inning runs in 29 starts (2.79 ERA).... Batting support: 3.72 runs per start.... Opposing base stealers: 19-for-30 (63%); 0 pickoffs, 0 balks.

Comments: Allowed one home run for every 26 innings last season, the best rate among major league pitchers who qualified for the ERA title. Very impressive when you consider that The Vet has no significant negative effect on four-baggers. Gregg Jefferies was the only one of the 477 left-handed batters he faced to take him deep.... Has held ground-ball hitters to a .200 career average, the lowest among active pitchers (minimum: 500 PA), while fly-ball hitters have a .237 career mark against him.... Opponents have a .172 career average on grass fields, .239 on artificial surfaces; .237 in day games, .218 at night.... Six major league pitchers had both winning and losing streaks of at least five games last season. Three of those six had their streaks back-to-back: DeJesus, David Wells, and John Burkett.... As a batter, he struck out in nine consecutive plate appearances vs. right-handed pitchers, the longest streak in the majors last season.... Led N.L. in walks with 44 more than runner-up Brian Barnes—or 52 percent more. Only two other pitchers in N.L. history led the league by more than 50 percent: "Toothpick Sam" Jones over Bob Buhl, 185–109 in 1955 and Phil Niekro over J. R. Richard 164–104 in 1977.... Walked an average of 6.34 batters every nine innings. Among all pitchers in N.L. history with at least one inning for each game played by their teams, only two had higher rates: William (Adonis) Terry, 6.97 for Pittsburgh and Chicago in 1894; and Toothpick Sam Jones again, 6.88 walks for the Cubs in 1955. DeJesus's rate is the highest ever by a player without a nickname.

Jose DeLeon

Throws Right

St. Louis Cardinals	W-L	ERA	AB	H	HR	BB	SO	BA	SA	OBA
Season	5-9	2.71	603	144	15	61	118	.239	.378	.313
vs. Left-Handers			326	82	9	43	44	.252	.408	.339
vs. Right-Handers			277	62	6	18	74	.224	.343	.281
vs. Ground-Ballers			264	65	5	22	47	.246	.375	.304
vs. Fly-Ballers			339	79	10	39	71	.233	.381	.319
Home Games	3-4	2.42	333	78	6	33	65	.234	.348	.309
Road Games	2-5	3.07	270	66	9	28	53	.244	.415	.318
Grass Fields	1-3	2.56	116	26	2	4	22	.224	.328	.252
Artificial Turf	4-6	2.75	487	118	13	57	96	.242	.390	.327
April	1-2	2.22	101	20	2	11	25	.198	.307	.287
May	1-2	4.28	101	26	4	18	19	.257	.455	.372
June	1-2	3.05	144	32	4	8	31	.222	.361	.261
July	2-2	2.38	135	38	1	11	19	.281	.407	.342
August	0-1	2.17	103	25	4	11	20	.243	.398	.322
Sept./Oct.	0-0	0.00	19	3	0	2	4	.158	.158	.238
Leading Off Inn.			158	35	6	15	34	.222	.392	.289
Bases Empty			377	92	12	40	73	.244	.411	.323
Runners On			226	52	3	21	45	.230	.323	.296
Runners/Scor. Pos.			124	21	2	11	27	.169	.250	.241
Runners On/2 Out			100	18	1	8	24	.180	.270	.248
Scor. Pos./2 Out			63	9	1	6	13	.143	.238	.229
Late-Inning Pressure			22	8	1	2	1	.364	.727	.417
Leading Off			8	3	0	2	1	.375	.500	.500
Runners On			8	2	1	0	0	.250	.750	.250
Runners/Scor. Pos.			4	1	0	0	0	.250	.500	.250
First 9 Batters			215	49	5	24	48	.228	.344	.310
Second 9 Batters			213	55	3	16	45	.258	.390	.313
All Batters Thereafter			175	40	7	21	25	.229	.406	.317

Loves to face: Todd Benzinger (.067, 1-for-15, 1 2B)
Doug Dascenzo (.053, 1-for-19, 1 2B)
Terry Kennedy (.081, 3-for-37, 1 HR, 5 BB)

Hates to face: Barry Bonds (.400, 10-for-25, 3 HR)
Eddie Murray (.414, 12-for-29, 4 HR)
Terry Pendleton (.550, 11-for-20)

Miscellaneous statistics: Ground outs-to-air outs ratio: 0.81 last season, 0.78 for career.... Induced 8 double plays in 110 opportunities (one per 14).... Allowed 29 doubles, 5 triples in 162⅔ innings.... Allowed 14 first-inning runs in 28 starts (3.90 ERA).... Batting support: 4.00 runs per start.... Opposing base stealers: 12-for-24 (50%); 0 pickoffs, 1 balk.

Comments: Has held right-handed batters to a .189 career batting average, lowest vs. any pitcher since 1975 (minimum: 600 RHB faced). Last year's .224 mark was actually a career high.... Averaged 8.09 strikeouts per nine innings in four seasons with Pirates, highest in their history among pitchers with at least 400 innings; with the Cardinals, his average is 7.63, third in Redbirds' history. Last year's rate (6.53) was a career low.... Breakdown by batterymate: 1.70 ERA in 53 innings with Rich Gedman, 3.20 in 109⅔ innings with Tom Pagnozzi.... Who was the last ERA qualifier to finish four games below .500 with an ERA as low as DeLeon's? Teammate Joe Magrane (2.18 ERA and 5–9 record) in 1988. But over the last 30 years, only three other N.L. pitchers finished four-below with ERAs as low as DeLeon's: Don Sutton, 1968 (11–15, 2.60); Ken Johnson, 1963 (11–17, 2.65); Larry Jackson, 1963 (14–18, 2.55).... Among life's mysteries: proving the existence of the afterlife, stopping "12:00" from blinking ad nauseam on your VCR, and explaining DeLeon's 73–105 career record. Consider that his career average of hits allowed per nine innings is only 7.33, to rank 13th in major league history among pitchers with 200 or more starts. Among the top 30 pitchers on that list, only one other pitcher possesses a sub-.500 record (Johnny Vander Meer, 119–121). To find a pitcher with a poorer career record than DeLeon's, you have to go down to the 225th spot on the hits list; there you encounter one Dupee Shaw (83–121 in a career that ended in 1888).

Jim Deshaies

Throws Left

Houston Astros	W-L	ERA	AB	H	HR	BB	SO	BA	SA	OBA
Season	5-12	4.98	602	156	19	72	98	.259	.430	.336
vs. Left-Handers			104	29	4	19	18	.279	.471	.386
vs. Right-Handers			498	127	15	53	80	.255	.422	.324
vs. Ground-Ballers			284	77	6	33	47	.271	.398	.348
vs. Fly-Ballers			318	79	13	39	51	.248	.459	.325
Home Games	2-3	3.72	228	50	4	27	37	.219	.342	.300
Road Games	3-9	5.83	374	106	15	45	61	.283	.484	.358
Grass Fields	2-6	6.66	205	61	11	28	30	.298	.537	.377
Artificial Turf	3-6	4.19	397	95	8	44	68	.239	.375	.314
April	0-2	6.43	84	25	1	10	10	.298	.452	.368
May	2-3	5.94	128	36	5	23	20	.281	.492	.386
June	0-2	4.62	141	31	6	17	22	.220	.397	.300
July	2-1	3.45	105	25	1	6	12	.238	.343	.277
August	0-4	4.76	122	31	4	15	31	.254	.426	.338
Sept./Oct.	1-0	5.40	22	8	2	1	3	.364	.636	.391
Leading Off Inn.			154	37	3	14	17	.240	.351	.308
Bases Empty			377	85	9	41	64	.225	.347	.303
Runners On			225	71	10	31	34	.316	.569	.388
Runners/Scor. Pos.			133	35	5	27	25	.263	.511	.371
Runners On/2 Out			92	23	1	19	11	.250	.413	.330
Scor. Pos./2 Out			60	13	0	9	12	.217	.367	.319
Late-Inning Pressure			46	13	0	8	4	.283	.348	.382
Leading Off			12	1	0	2	0	.083	.083	.214
Runners On			20	8	0	3	2	.400	.500	.458
Runners/Scor. Pos.			9	2	0	3	1	.222	.333	.385
First 9 Batters			207	54	7	29	37	.261	.425	.347
Second 9 Batters			216	56	8	20	34	.259	.454	.322
All Batters Thereafter			179	46	4	23	27	.257	.408	.338

Loves to face: Kevin Elster (.063, 1-for-16, 2 BB)
Billy Hatcher (.067, 1-for-15)
Charlie Hayes (.105, 2-for-19)

Hates to face: Eric Davis (.333, 14-for-42, 6 HR)
Barry Larkin (.400, 12-for-30, 5 HR)
Randy Ready (.429, 6-for-14, 1 HR, 6 BB)

Miscellaneous statistics: Ground outs-to-air outs ratio: 0.59 last season, lowest in majors; 0.62 for career.... Induced 12 double plays in 107 opportunities (one per 8.9).... Allowed 36 doubles, 5 triples in 161 innings.... Allowed 32 first-inning runs in 28 starts (10.67 ERA, highest in N.L.).... Batting support: 3.39 runs per start, 3d-lowest average in N.L.... Opposing base stealers: 21-for-35 (60%); 9 pickoffs (2d most in N.L.), 5 balks (2d most in majors).

Comments: Traded by Yankees to Houston in September 1985; has won 61 games in six seasons in N.L., a modest enough total, but more than double the total of any Yankees pitchers since the trade. Yankees' leaders: Tommy John (29), Rick Rhoden (28), Dennis Rasmussen (27).... Opponents hit .360 during the first inning, second highest among N.L. pitchers last season.... Had not allowed a first-inning homer in 43 consecutive starts through late April, then yielded six in his next 24 starts. Six home runs during the opening frame tied Tom Browning for the most off any pitcher in the league.... One of 19 different pitchers to lose a game for Houston last season, one shy of the major league record shared by seven teams, most recently the 1990 Giants.... Had .583 winning percentage (49–35) and 3.36 ERA from 1986 to 1989, but he's 12–24 (.333) with 4.30 ERA over the last two years.... Only the best left-handed batters stay in the lineup against Deshaies, which may explain left-handers' .269 career batting average off him (right-handed batters have hit only .232).... Opponents have .222 career batting average in the Astrodome, .253 elsewhere.... His career batting average ranks among the worst in major league history among players with at least 300 at-bats. The bottom five: Dean Chance (.066), Bill Hands (.078), Lee Stange (.079), Deshaies (.080, 27-for-338), Wilbur Wood (.084). All Deshaies needs to take the top spot is an 0-for-69 streak.... Hitless in 20 career at-bats with the bases loaded, including 17 whiffs.

Rob Dibble — Throws Right

Cincinnati Reds	W-L	ERA	AB	H	HR	BB	SO	BA	SA	OBA
Season	3-5	3.17	301	67	5	25	124	.223	.322	.280
vs. Left-Handers			173	34	2	14	75	.197	.272	.255
vs. Right-Handers			128	33	3	11	49	.258	.391	.312
vs. Ground-Ballers			127	25	1	11	50	.197	.268	.257
vs. Fly-Ballers			175	42	4	14	74	.240	.360	.295
Home Games	1-4	5.26	152	38	5	16	60	.250	.395	.320
Road Games	2-1	1.26	149	29	0	9	64	.195	.248	.237
Grass Fields	2-1	1.95	99	22	0	7	39	.222	.303	.271
Artificial Turf	1-4	3.79	202	45	5	18	85	.223	.332	.284
April	0-0	2.53	42	11	0	1	21	.262	.262	.279
May	0-0	0.00	45	5	0	4	21	.111	.156	.184
June	0-0	1.69	53	9	1	7	22	.170	.283	.258
July	1-1	5.00	35	13	0	2	9	.371	.457	.395
August	2-2	3.86	76	15	3	7	32	.197	.342	.265
Sept./Oct.	0-2	6.75	50	14	1	4	19	.280	.440	.333
Leading Off Inn.			60	14	0	8	25	.233	.300	.324
Bases Empty			155	33	2	13	67	.213	.316	.274
Runners On			146	34	3	12	57	.233	.329	.286
Runners/Scor. Pos.			104	23	3	8	39	.221	.337	.270
Runners On/2 Out			68	14	2	6	28	.206	.294	.270
Scor. Pos./2 Out			53	10	2	5	20	.189	.302	.259
Late-Inning Pressure			219	54	4	16	87	.247	.356	.295
Leading Off			44	10	0	6	21	.227	.295	.320
Runners On			105	29	3	8	36	.276	.390	.322
Runners/Scor. Pos.			78	21	3	6	25	.269	.410	.314
First 9 Batters			294	64	5	24	123	.218	.320	.274
Second 9 Batters			7	3	0	1	1	.429	.429	.500
All Batters Thereafter			0	0	0	0	0	—	—	—

Loves to face: Andres Galarraga (0-for-7, 7 SO)
Carmelo Martinez (0-for-9, 5 SO)
Ryne Sandberg (.071, 1-for-14, 7 SO)
Hates to face: Pedro Guerrero (.455, 5-for-11)
Jose Lind (.833, 5-for-6)
Willie McGee (.500, 5-for-10)

Miscellaneous statistics: Ground outs-to-air outs ratio: 1.09 last season, 0.98 for career. . . . Induced 1 double play in 63 opportunities (one per 63). . . . Allowed 9 doubles, 3 triples in 82⅓ innings. . . . Saved 31 games in 35 opportunities (89%), 2d-highest rate in N.L. . . . Stranded 34 inherited runners, allowed 8 to score (81%), 4th-highest rate in N.L. . . . Opposing base stealers: 16-for-21 (76%); 0 pickoffs, 0 balks.

Comments: Career average of 12.22 strikeouts per nine innings is almost two strikeouts higher than anyone else in major league history (minimum: 300 innings). Tom Henke (10.30) is the only other pitcher to average more than ten, and only five others have averages of nine or more. . . . Over the last three years, he has posted the three highest single-season rates of strikeouts per nine innings ever attained by pitchers with at least 75 innings: 13.55 last season for the Gold, 12.82 in 1989 for the Silver, and 12.49 in 1990 for the Bronze. . . . He has fanned 33 percent of the right-handed batters he has faced, and 35 percent of the left-handed batters. . . . Opponents have .195 career batting average, which falls off to .179 with runners in scoring position and .127 with two outs and runners in scoring position. . . . However, opponents have hit for a higher average in Late-Inning Pressure Situations than in other at-bats in each of his four years in the majors. Career breakdown: .229 in LIPS, .148 at other times. . . . Right-handed batters had never hit higher than .200 off him before last year. . . . He has hit only one batter with a pitch over the last two years (Ozzie Smith in 1990). Doug Dascenzo doesn't count; we said "with a pitch." . . . Anyone else a little tired of this "nicest guy in the world off the field" stuff?

Doug Drabek — Throws Right

Pittsburgh Pirates	W-L	ERA	AB	H	HR	BB	SO	BA	SA	OBA
Season	15-14	3.07	894	245	16	62	142	.274	.385	.321
vs. Left-Handers			530	152	8	41	59	.287	.391	.337
vs. Right-Handers			364	93	8	21	83	.255	.376	.298
vs. Ground-Ballers			464	120	9	36	71	.259	.379	.313
vs. Fly-Ballers			452	133	8	26	74	.294	.398	.331
Home Games	9-8	2.40	488	131	8	30	87	.268	.371	.310
Road Games	6-6	3.91	406	114	8	32	55	.281	.401	.335
Grass Fields	2-4	5.77	196	59	4	16	27	.301	.434	.357
Artificial Turf	13-10	2.37	698	186	12	46	115	.266	.371	.311
April	1-4	4.15	122	35	3	11	11	.287	.418	.351
May	2-3	2.75	136	33	1	8	20	.243	.301	.288
June	3-1	2.25	154	47	2	12	29	.305	.396	.353
July	4-2	3.98	153	40	5	15	26	.261	.418	.325
August	3-1	2.84	145	41	3	5	15	.283	.386	.309
Sept./Oct.	2-3	2.72	184	49	2	11	41	.266	.386	.305
Leading Off Inn.			226	69	3	14	36	.305	.407	.346
Bases Empty			526	150	11	34	85	.285	.409	.332
Runners On			368	95	5	28	57	.258	.351	.306
Runners/Scor. Pos.			209	51	3	26	35	.244	.325	.320
Runners On/2 Out			149	31	1	20	32	.208	.275	.302
Scor. Pos./2 Out			98	22	1	19	21	.224	.296	.350
Late-Inning Pressure			59	26	2	4	5	.441	.627	.485
Leading Off			16	10	0	2	1	.625	.813	.667
Runners On			33	13	2	2	4	.394	.636	.417
Runners/Scor. Pos.			19	6	2	2	2	.316	.632	.364
First 9 Batters			287	88	4	20	42	.307	.394	.348
Second 9 Batters			289	69	5	18	52	.239	.360	.285
All Batters Thereafter			318	88	7	24	48	.277	.399	.329

Loves to face: Ricky Jordan (.063, 1-for-16, 1 2B)
Otis Nixon (.095, 2-for-21)
Benito Santiago (.050, 1-for-20, 1 3B)
Hates to face: Brett Butler (.444, 16-for-36, 1 HR)
Kevin Elster (.370, 10-for-27, 2 HR)
Tony Gwynn (.406, 13-for-32)

Miscellaneous statistics: Ground outs-to-air outs ratio: 1.26 last season, 1.09 for career. . . . Induced 15 double plays in 168 opportunities (one per 11). . . . Allowed 41 doubles (3d most in N.L.), 5 triples in 234⅔ innings. . . . Allowed 21 first-inning runs in 35 starts (4.63 ERA). . . . Batting support: 4.37 runs per start. . . . Opposing base stealers: 29-for-44 (66%), 3d-most steals in N.L.; 4 pickoffs, 0 balks.

Comments: Owns 1.15 career ERA in postseason play, 7th best in history, and lowest among active pitchers (minimum: 30 innings). Harry Brecheen (0.83) is the all-time leader, Babe Ruth (0.87) stands second, and Sandy Koufax (1.01) is fourth. Orel Hershiser (1.71) is the only other active pitcher below the 2.00 mark. . . . Opponents have a career average of .216 with two outs and runners in scoring position, compared to an overall average of .246. . . . Career batting average of .261 by opposing left-handed batters, .227 by right-handers. . . . He failed to induce a double-play grounder in any of 26 opportunities during the opening frame. . . . His ERA was more than a run per game lower with Don Slaught catching (2.34) than with Mike LaValliere catching (3.45). The same was true for Zane Smith and Randy Tomlin. In 1990, Drabek had 2.06 ERA with Slaught, 4.01 with LaV. . . . Opponents' batting average was a career high, and increased almost 50 points from his Cy Young season. Yearly averages since 1986: .251, .247, .239, .238, .225, .274. . . . The last Pirates pitcher to lose as many as 14 games with an ERA as low as Drabek's was Dock Ellis, who posted a 12–14 record despite a 3.05 ERA in 1973. . . . Drabek has four straight winning seasons under his belt. The last Pirates pitcher to have five straight winning seasons of at least 15 decisions: Jim Rooker (1973–77). The club record is nine in a row by Sam Leever (1900–08).

Jeff Fassero

Throws Left

Montreal Expos	W-L	ERA	AB	H	HR	BB	SO	BA	SA	OBA
Season	2-5	2.44	199	39	1	17	42	.196	.266	.263
vs. Left-Handers			70	17	0	5	19	.243	.329	.293
vs. Right-Handers			129	22	1	12	23	.171	.233	.246
vs. Ground-Ballers			87	16	1	9	21	.184	.253	.268
vs. Fly-Ballers			112	23	0	8	21	.205	.277	.258
Home Games	2-2	2.17	96	15	0	13	24	.156	.188	.257
Road Games	0-3	2.73	103	24	1	4	18	.233	.340	.269
Grass Fields	0-1	1.38	51	12	1	1	6	.235	.353	.250
Artificial Turf	2-4	2.76	148	27	0	16	36	.182	.236	.267
April	0-0	—	0	0	0	0	0	—	—	—
May	0-1	4.50	5	2	0	1	1	.400	.400	.500
June	1-0	1.20	52	7	1	3	14	.135	.288	.182
July	0-0	1.20	49	5	0	4	11	.102	.122	.170
August	1-3	2.77	51	12	0	5	9	.235	.275	.304
Sept./Oct.	0-1	5.23	42	13	0	4	7	.310	.381	.383
Leading Off Inn.			44	13	0	4	7	.295	.364	.354
Bases Empty			97	20	0	9	19	.206	.258	.274
Runners On			102	19	1	8	23	.186	.275	.252
Runners/Scor. Pos.			75	16	1	7	16	.213	.307	.280
Runners On/2 Out			39	4	0	1	11	.103	.128	.125
Scor. Pos./2 Out			29	4	0	1	9	.138	.172	.167
Late-Inning Pressure			93	24	0	8	16	.258	.269	.324
Leading Off			20	9	0	2	1	.450	.450	.500
Runners On			56	13	0	3	13	.232	.250	.283
Runners/Scor. Pos.			41	11	0	2	10	.268	.293	.302
First 9 Batters			198	39	1	17	41	.197	.268	.264
Second 9 Batters			1	0	0	0	0	.000	.000	.000
All Batters Thereafter			0	0	0	0	0	—	—	—

Loves to face: Fred McGriff (0-for-4)
Andy Van Slyke (0-for-5)
Hates to face: Jay Bell (2-for-2, 1 BB)
Len Dykstra (.667, 2-for-3, 1 SO)

Miscellaneous statistics: Ground outs-to-air outs ratio: 1.78 last season, 1.78 for career.... Induced 4 double plays in 50 opportunities (one per 13).... Allowed 7 doubles, 2 triples in 55⅓ innings.... Stranded 21 inherited runners, allowed 10 to score (68%).... Opposing base stealers: 3-for-4 (75%); 0 pickoffs, 0 balks.

Comments: Held right-handed batters to .171 batting average, lowest mark by righties against any left-handed pitcher in the majors last season (minimum: 100 at-bats by RHB). That was also the lowest average by right-handed batters against any major league rookie.... Allowed only one home run in 55⅓ innings pitched, the second-lowest rate among N.L. pitchers with at least 50 innings. That homer was hit by Greg Olson at Atlanta in Fassero's fourth appearance.... Ranked third among major league rookies with eight saves, behind Doug Henry (15) and Al Osuna (12). Fassero and Mel Rojas became the first rookie teammates with at least five saves apiece since Mitch Williams and Dale Mohorcic did it for Texas in 1986.... Had exactly two saves in every month from June through September.... ERA stood at 1.79 on September 22, but over his final four appearances he allowed five earned runs in five innings.... Brian Barnes (160), Chris Haney (84⅔), and Fassero (55⅓) combined for 300 innings pitched last season; Montreal's total of 385⅓ innings by rookies was 3d highest in N.L., behind Chicago (398⅔) and Houston (393).... Expos rookie pitchers combined for a 13–24 record, 2d worst in the league to Philadelphia's rookies, who posted a 4–14 record. Only the Astros rookies (23–29) combined to lose more games than Montreal's.... Oldest rookie pitcher in the majors to appear in at least 25 games last season. He's only three days younger than David Cone.

John Franco

Throws Left

New York Mets	W-L	ERA	AB	H	HR	BB	SO	BA	SA	OBA
Season	5-9	2.93	225	61	2	18	45	.271	.360	.328
vs. Left-Handers			53	18	0	4	7	.340	.415	.397
vs. Right-Handers			172	43	2	14	38	.250	.343	.306
vs. Ground-Ballers			95	21	0	7	28	.221	.263	.275
vs. Fly-Ballers			133	40	2	11	18	.301	.421	.359
Home Games	1-4	3.00	111	32	2	10	20	.288	.405	.347
Road Games	4-5	2.86	114	29	0	8	25	.254	.316	.309
Grass Fields	2-5	2.15	150	39	2	12	25	.260	.353	.315
Artificial Turf	3-4	4.58	75	22	0	6	20	.293	.373	.354
April	0-1	1.50	21	4	0	5	5	.190	.238	.346
May	1-2	0.00	52	12	0	3	7	.231	.288	.273
June	0-3	12.00	30	13	0	3	7	.433	.533	.485
July	1-0	0.00	31	9	0	2	7	.290	.290	.333
August	2-1	2.03	48	11	1	0	12	.229	.354	.229
Sept./Oct.	1-2	5.40	43	12	1	5	7	.279	.442	.367
Leading Off Inn.			45	11	1	1	12	.244	.311	.261
Bases Empty			94	28	1	4	25	.298	.372	.327
Runners On			131	33	1	14	20	.252	.351	.329
Runners/Scor. Pos.			86	21	1	11	13	.244	.360	.337
Runners On/2 Out			58	18	0	5	13	.310	.362	.365
Scor. Pos./2 Out			44	11	0	3	5	.250	.295	.298
Late-Inning Pressure			195	54	2	12	41	.277	.379	.322
Leading Off			40	11	1	1	10	.275	.350	.293
Runners On			113	28	1	10	19	.248	.363	.315
Runners/Scor. Pos.			75	17	1	7	13	.227	.360	.301
First 9 Batters			223	61	2	18	44	.274	.363	.331
Second 9 Batters			2	0	0	0	1	.000	.000	.000
All Batters Thereafter			0	0	0	0	0	—	—	—

Loves to face: Delino DeShields (0-for-6, 4 SO)
Mark Grace (0-for-12)
Darrin Jackson (0-for-10)
Hates to face: Mariano Duncan (.533, 8-for-15, 4 SO)
Ray Lankford (3-for-3)
Terry Pendleton (.538, 7-for-13)

Miscellaneous statistics: Ground outs-to-air outs ratio: 2.66 last season, 1.90 for career.... Induced 6 double plays in 59 opportunities (one per 10).... Allowed 8 doubles, 3 triples in 55⅓ innings.... Saved 30 games in 35 opportunities (86%), 3d-highest rate in N.L.... Stranded 17 inherited runners, allowed 8 to score (68%).... Opposing base stealers: 4-for-6 (67%); 1 pickoff, 0 balks.

Comments: Reached 30 saves for the fifth consecutive season, tying major league record set by Jeff Reardon (1985–89).... His 2.53 career ERA is the 2d lowest in history among relief pitchers with at least 500 innings pitched. The six best: Hoyt Wilhelm (2.50), Franco (2.53), Billy O'Dell (2.59), Danny Darwin (2.61), Dave Smith (2.64), Tim Burke (2.66). Remember, that only includes innings pitched in relief.... Opponents' batting average was a career high; that can be traced to his awful performance against left-handed batters. Annual averages by opposing lefties since 1988: .137, .200, .228, .340. Only two lefty pitchers allowed southpaw swingers to hit for a higher average last year (minimum: 50 AB): Neal Heaton (.354) and Paul Gibson (.345), hardly company that Franco usually keeps.... Only two Mets relievers have lost more than nine games in a season: Skip Lockwood (13 in 1978) and Neil Allen (10 in 1980).... Has pitched at least 50 games in each of his first eight years in the majors, including a career-low 52 games last season. Only two pitchers in history had longer streaks of 50-game seasons starting with their first year in the majors: Craig Lefferts (9 years, 1983–91) and Ron Perranoski (10 years, 1961–70).... For a career-long closer, he doesn't close out his seasons very well: Franco's ERA from Sept. 1 to the end of the season has been above 5.00 in five of his eight years in the majors. Over the past three years, his September/October ERA is 5.86 in 35⅓ innings.

Mark Gardner

Throws Right

Montreal Expos	W-L	ERA	AB	H	HR	BB	SO	BA	SA	OBA
Season	9-11	3.85	604	139	17	75	107	.230	.356	.318
vs. Left-Handers			381	87	10	51	61	.228	.352	.321
vs. Right-Handers			223	52	7	24	46	.233	.363	.313
vs. Ground-Ballers			261	55	2	30	50	.211	.268	.296
vs. Fly-Ballers			343	84	15	45	57	.245	.423	.335
Home Games	4-4	2.51	231	52	3	30	46	.225	.294	.323
Road Games	5-7	4.69	373	87	14	45	61	.233	.394	.315
Grass Fields	1-6	6.39	215	61	11	23	36	.284	.484	.351
Artificial Turf	8-5	2.57	389	78	6	52	71	.201	.285	.300
April	0-0	—	0	0	0	0	0			
May	0-2	4.43	82	23	3	8	18	.280	.439	.341
June	3-2	4.11	114	32	3	12	14	.281	.386	.354
July	2-3	1.66	147	24	1	21	29	.163	.211	.281
August	3-2	2.75	141	34	2	13	22	.241	.326	.303
Sept./Oct.	1-2	7.44	120	26	8	21	24	.217	.483	.333
Leading Off Inn.			155	43	2	21	27	.277	.368	.371
Bases Empty			370	77	6	45	63	.208	.289	.297
Runners On			234	62	11	30	44	.265	.462	.351
Runners/Scor. Pos.			125	35	7	19	28	.280	.496	.374
Runners On/2 Out			90	24	5	13	22	.267	.522	.365
Scor. Pos./2 Out			55	14	2	9	15	.255	.436	.369
Late-Inning Pressure			51	13	0	9	9	.255	.314	.367
Leading Off			17	5	0	3	4	.294	.353	.400
Runners On			17	4	0	4	0	.235	.235	.381
Runners/Scor. Pos.			5	1	0	3	0	.200	.200	.500
First 9 Batters			215	38	6	24	46	.177	.288	.266
Second 9 Batters			209	53	6	24	35	.254	.373	.333
All Batters Thereafter			180	48	5	27	26	.267	.417	.362

Loves to face: Steve Finley (0-for-11)
Rich Gedman (0-for-8)
Milt Thompson (.111, 2-for-18)

Hates to face: Andre Dawson (.368, 7-for-19, 4 2B, 2 HR)
Pedro Guerrero (.455, 5-for-11, 2 HR)
Felix Jose (.375, 3-for-8, 1 2B, 2 HR, 3 BB)

Miscellaneous statistics: Ground outs-to-air outs ratio: 0.77 last season, 0.84 for career.... Induced 8 double plays in 120 opportunities (one per 15).... Allowed 21 doubles, 2 triples in 168⅓ innings.... Allowed 13 first-inning runs in 27 starts (4.33 ERA).... Batting support: 3.52 runs per start, 9th-lowest average in N.L.... Opposing base stealers: 13-for-30 (43%); 1 pickoff, 1 balk.

Comments: Has compiled a 16–20 record over the past two seasons despite a 3.64 ERA. No other pitcher had winning percentages of .450 or lower in each of the last two seasons despite ERAs below four.... More base runners were caught stealing with Gardner on the mound (17) than any other pitcher in the majors.... Had a 2.99 ERA at the end of August, but his mark from September 1 on was the highest in the league.... Opponents' on-base percentage leading off innings was the highest in the league.... He was 4–0 vs. Houston last season, to raise his career mark to 5–0 against the Astros with a 0.72 ERA. Against the rest of the league he's 11–23 with a 4.27 ERA.... Opponents have a career batting average of .271 in day games, .213 in night games. Career record: 3–11 in day games, 13–12 at night.... His no-hit bid on July 26 was ruined by a single by Lenny Harris in the 10th inning. The subsequent controversy led to the commissioner's ruling on what is and what isn't a no-hitter. Now we're not here to crucify Harvey Haddix; he may have pitched the greatest game in baseball history. But when you look under his "hits" column in the box score, you won't find a zero; that means it's not a no-hitter. Would anyone argue that a pitcher should be awarded a shutout in a game in which he allows no runs through nine innings, but is scored upon in an extra frame? Think of that as a "no-runner," and you'll see why Fay Vincent ruled as he did.

Tom Glavine

Throws Left

Atlanta Braves	W-L	ERA	AB	H	HR	BB	SO	BA	SA	OBA
Season	20-11	2.55	905	201	17	69	192	.222	.330	.277
vs. Left-Handers			171	50	4	17	38	.292	.433	.354
vs. Right-Handers			734	151	13	52	154	.206	.307	.259
vs. Ground-Ballers			416	97	10	32	88	.233	.351	.287
vs. Fly-Ballers			489	104	7	37	104	.213	.313	.268
Home Games	10-4	2.71	395	90	13	28	78	.228	.372	.279
Road Games	10-7	2.44	510	111	4	41	114	.218	.298	.276
Grass Fields	17-6	2.55	652	148	16	45	125	.227	.350	.276
Artificial Turf	3-5	2.57	253	53	1	24	67	.209	.281	.280
April	2-2	2.39	96	20	0	6	26	.208	.260	.262
May	6-0	1.76	172	35	6	6	33	.203	.337	.230
June	3-2	2.17	171	38	2	8	39	.222	.304	.257
July	3-1	2.87	137	32	4	8	29	.234	.372	.275
August	3-3	1.71	150	30	1	18	28	.200	.280	.284
Sept./Oct.	3-3	4.22	179	46	4	23	37	.257	.397	.338
Leading Off Inn.			240	47	6	10	45	.196	.321	.231
Bases Empty			587	124	13	33	124	.211	.324	.254
Runners On			318	77	4	36	68	.242	.343	.316
Runners/Scor. Pos.			172	43	2	28	35	.250	.331	.348
Runners On/2 Out			132	25	2	21	34	.189	.265	.301
Scor. Pos./2 Out			79	13	0	17	20	.165	.190	.313
Late-Inning Pressure			95	22	1	5	13	.232	.337	.267
Leading Off			25	1	0	0	5	.040	.080	.040
Runners On			27	6	0	4	3	.222	.259	.313
Runners/Scor. Pos.			18	4	0	3	2	.222	.278	.318
First 9 Batters			280	68	7	20	75	.243	.386	.294
Second 9 Batters			276	50	4	26	60	.181	.261	.253
All Batters Thereafter			349	83	6	23	57	.238	.341	.283

Loves to face: Shawon Dunston (.111, 2-for-18)
Jeff Hamilton (.167, 4-for-24)
Paul O'Neill (.050, 1-for-20)

Hates to face: Kal Daniels (.417, 10-for-24)
Lloyd McClendon (.529, 9-for-17, 2 HR)
Tim Wallach (.294, 10-for-34, 2 2B, 5 HR)

Miscellaneous statistics: Ground outs-to-air outs ratio: 1.35 last season, 1.31 for career.... Induced 19 double plays in 148 opportunities (one per 7.8).... Allowed 35 doubles, 6 triples in 246⅔ innings.... Allowed 20 first-inning runs in 34 starts (4.76 ERA).... Batting support: 4.56 runs per start.... Opposing base stealers: 18-for-28 (64%); 7 pickoffs, 2 balks.

Comments: Became the fifth pitcher to win the N.L. Cy Young Award coming off a losing season. Two of the others were relievers: Bruce Sutter (1979) and Mark Davis (1989); two were starters: Mike McCormick (1967) and John Denny (1983).... It's a good thing for Glavine that voters cast their ballots for the Cy Young Award before the start of postseason play. He tied the all-time record of three losses in one postseason shared by Lefty Williams (1919), Don Sutton (1978), George Frazier (1981), Charlie Leibrandt (1985), Doc Gooden (1986), Calvin Schiraldi (1986), and Danny Cox (1987).... Became the first N.L. pitcher to start the All-Star Game and then go on to a 20-win season since Randy Jones in 1976.... Led the majors in wins during May.... His 154 strikeouts vs. right-handers led the N.L. by plenty; Terry Mulholland ranked second at 123.... Opponents' on-base percentage leading off innings was the lowest in the league.... Allowed at least one run during the first inning of each of his last six starts during the regular season. Earlier in the year, he had a streak of 16 starts in which he didn't allow a first-inning run.... Greg Olson was his batterymate for all but two of his 246⅔ innings.... Has won his last seven decisions against the Phillies. His lifetime record against the Astros is 0–8.... Opponents have hit for a higher average with runners on base than with the bases empty in each of his five seasons in the majors. Career breakdown: .275 with runners on, .242 with bases empty.

Dwight Gooden

Throws Right

New York Mets	W-L	ERA	AB	H	HR	BB	SO	BA	SA	OBA
Season	13-7	3.60	721	185	12	56	150	.257	.369	.311
vs. Left-Handers			412	104	4	42	75	.252	.345	.321
vs. Right-Handers			309	81	8	14	75	.262	.401	.298
vs. Ground-Ballers			382	103	2	36	78	.270	.343	.334
vs. Fly-Ballers			367	88	11	21	79	.240	.392	.281
Home Games	9-3	3.55	401	98	9	29	85	.244	.359	.298
Road Games	4-4	3.66	320	87	3	27	65	.272	.381	.328
Grass Fields	12-4	3.30	539	132	12	40	112	.245	.358	.299
Artificial Turf	1-3	4.57	182	53	0	16	38	.291	.401	.347
April	3-1	2.43	134	27	2	8	39	.201	.284	.245
May	2-3	4.75	170	53	3	11	29	.312	.453	.357
June	2-2	5.80	158	47	6	10	24	.297	.506	.341
July	4-0	2.15	137	29	1	13	36	.212	.270	.283
August	2-1	2.43	122	29	0	14	22	.238	.279	.314
Sept./Oct.	0-0	0.00	0	0	0	0	0	.000	.000	.000
Leading Off Inn.			183	55	5	12	34	.301	.464	.347
Bases Empty			414	107	7	33	82	.258	.377	.316
Runners On			307	78	5	23	68	.254	.358	.304
Runners/Scor. Pos.			184	51	3	17	44	.277	.380	.335
Runners On/2 Out			126	30	1	10	29	.238	.317	.299
Scor. Pos./2 Out			83	20	1	7	21	.241	.325	.308
Late-Inning Pressure			65	15	0	3	20	.231	.246	.265
Leading Off			18	5	0	0	6	.278	.278	.278
Runners On			24	6	0	1	9	.250	.250	.280
Runners/Scor. Pos.			10	3	0	0	3	.300	.300	.300
First 9 Batters			218	50	2	21	46	.229	.317	.298
Second 9 Batters			225	59	4	16	53	.262	.387	.311
All Batters Thereafter			278	76	6	19	51	.273	.396	.322

Loves to face: Ken Caminiti (.077, 1-for-13)
Jose Oquendo (.077, 2-for-26)
Gary Redus (.067, 1-for-15, 1 2B)
Hates to face: Sid Bream (.333, 17-for-51, 2 HR)
Chris Sabo (.471, 8-for-17)
Ozzie Smith (.368, 25-for-68)

Miscellaneous statistics: Ground outs-to-air outs ratio: 1.73 last season, 1.31 for career.... Induced 15 double plays in 130 opportunities (one per 8.7).... Allowed 33 doubles, 6 triples in 190 innings.... Allowed 12 first-inning runs in 27 starts (3.67 ERA).... Batting support: 5.04 runs per start, 6th-highest average in N.L.... Opposing base stealers: 33-for-49 (67%), 2d-most steals in majors; 1 pickoff, 2 balks.

Comments: Needs 10 wins in his first 15 decisions to surpass Lefty Grove's total of 141 victories in his first 200 decisions, the highest in this century.... Last season's winning percentage of .650 was the lowest of his eight-year career. Only one other pitcher in baseball history has ever had a streak of eight seasons with a winning percentage no lower than .650: Vic Raschi, whose lowest mark through his first eight seasons was .677 in 1949 (21–10). After his eighth season, Raschi was sold by the Yankees to the Cardinals; he was out of baseball two years later, after losing seasons in both 1954 and 1955.... Struck out the side only once last season.... Charlie O'Brien caught each of Gooden's last 10 starts, and was his batterymate in over 70 percent of his innings for the season. Doc posted a 3.38 ERA with O'Brien behind the plate, 4.13 with Rick Cerone or Mackey Sasser.... Opponents' on-base percentage leading off innings was the 5th highest in the league.... Has a winning career record against every opposing N.L. club, and has won his last 11 decisions against both the Dodgers (14–1 overall) and the Cubs (23–3).... The Mets have scored an average of 4.88 runs in his 236 career starts, the best support in the N.L. during that time (minimum: 100 GS). Rounding out the top five: Shane Rawley (4.63), Mike Krukow (4.60), Bob Walk (4.56), and Tom Browning (4.56).... Pitched 19 shutouts in his first 134 starts (one per seven); only two in his last 102.

Jim Gott

Throws Right

Los Angeles Dodgers	W-L	ERA	AB	H	HR	BB	SO	BA	SA	OBA
Season	4-3	2.96	282	63	5	32	73	.223	.312	.304
vs. Left-Handers			142	27	2	17	36	.190	.268	.277
vs. Right-Handers			140	36	3	15	37	.257	.357	.331
vs. Ground-Ballers			130	28	3	12	38	.215	.331	.280
vs. Fly-Ballers			152	35	2	20	35	.230	.296	.324
Home Games	1-0	2.68	132	23	2	21	41	.174	.250	.286
Road Games	3-3	3.23	150	40	3	11	32	.267	.367	.321
Grass Fields	3-2	2.68	184	38	3	26	47	.207	.277	.303
Artificial Turf	1-1	3.51	98	25	2	6	26	.255	.378	.305
April	0-0	2.53	37	6	0	6	7	.162	.162	.279
May	0-0	2.25	45	10	0	8	12	.222	.244	.340
June	1-2	6.35	24	7	0	8	6	.292	.417	.469
July	1-1	3.27	44	12	1	2	8	.273	.364	.304
August	1-0	3.57	63	14	3	6	19	.222	.429	.286
Sept./Oct.	1-0	1.89	69	14	1	2	21	.203	.261	.236
Leading Off Inn.			69	19	0	10	20	.275	.290	.367
Bases Empty			172	41	1	11	42	.238	.279	.284
Runners On			110	22	4	21	31	.200	.364	.331
Runners/Scor. Pos.			72	12	1	14	23	.167	.292	.307
Runners On/2 Out			53	11	3	12	15	.208	.434	.364
Scor. Pos./2 Out			42	8	1	10	12	.190	.333	.358
Late-Inning Pressure			51	15	0	12	17	.294	.353	.429
Leading Off			10	4	0	4	3	.400	.400	.571
Runners On			31	8	0	8	11	.258	.355	.410
Runners/Scor. Pos.			26	7	0	6	9	.269	.385	.406
First 9 Batters			268	59	3	32	71	.220	.291	.305
Second 9 Batters			14	4	2	0	2	.286	.714	.286
All Batters Thereafter			0	0	0	0	0	—	—	—

Loves to face: Ken Caminiti (.077, 1-for-13)
Andre Dawson (.136, 3-for-22, 3 BB)
Dwight Gooden (0-for-8)
Hates to face: Kal Daniels (.444, 4-for-9, 3 HR, 3 SO)
Eric Davis (.357, 5-for-14, 2 2B, 2 HR, 5 SO)
Juan Samuel (.455, 5-for-11, 1 HR)

Miscellaneous statistics: Ground outs-to-air outs ratio: 1.56 last season, 1.33 for career.... Induced 6 double plays in 52 opportunities (one per 8.7).... Allowed 6 doubles, 2 triples in 76 innings.... Stranded 14 inherited runners, allowed 6 to score (70%).... Opposing base stealers: 8-for-8 (100%); 0 pickoffs, 3 balks.

Comments: He might hate to face those guys, and as long as he stays with the Dodgers he won't have to. (Just don't ask him to pitch B.P.)... Tough trivia: Gott is one of two players in major league history to play at least one game for the Blue Jays, Giants, Pirates, and Dodgers. Who is the other? Answer below.... Saved 34 games for the Pirates in 1988, then missed almost all of the 1989 season following elbow surgery. Has only five saves in 105 appearances for the Dodgers in two seasons since then.... Raised his strikeout rate from 6.39 in 1990 (his first season following surgery) to 8.64 last season.... Opponents' overall batting average last season was the lowest of his career.... Batting average by opposing left-handed batters was the lowest vs. any right-handed pitcher in the league (minimum: 150 BFP). Only two other N.L. right-handers held opposing lefties under the .200 mark: Alejandro Pena and Rob Dibble. Gott's career breakdown: .261 by left-handers, .246 by right-handers.... Until last season, he had walked only one of 69 batters faced with the bases loaded. But he walked in two runs in 1991, including an RBI-walk by Kent Mercker.... Hasn't committed an error in his last 201 games.... Career record of 26–38 (4.59 ERA) in 96 starts, 16–18 (3.04 ERA) in 266 relief appearances.... Opponents have a career average of .193 with two outs and runners in scoring position, compared to an overall mark of .253.... The trivia answer: Al Oliver.

Tommy Greene   Throws Right

Philadelphia Phillies	W-L	ERA	AB	H	HR	BB	SO	BA	SA	OBA
Season	13-7	3.38	768	177	19	66	154	.230	.361	.290
vs. Left-Handers			453	116	12	45	82	.256	.404	.321
vs. Right-Handers			315	61	7	21	72	.194	.298	.244
vs. Ground-Ballers			358	66	4	30	77	.184	.271	.248
vs. Fly-Ballers			410	111	15	36	77	.271	.439	.327
Home Games	6-4	3.31	402	95	10	34	89	.236	.351	.296
Road Games	7-3	3.45	366	82	9	32	65	.224	.372	.283
Grass Fields	2-1	4.94	121	29	6	13	17	.240	.430	.316
Artificial Turf	11-6	3.11	647	148	13	53	137	.229	.348	.285
April	0-0	4.79	71	18	0	6	6	.254	.394	.293
May	4-0	0.29	101	12	0	11	30	.119	.139	.212
June	1-1	3.19	162	40	6	10	33	.247	.414	.287
July	2-3	4.00	133	32	5	15	24	.241	.398	.320
August	2-2	3.96	151	38	4	15	31	.252	.384	.317
Sept./Oct.	4-1	4.15	150	37	4	9	30	.247	.380	.290
Leading Off Inn.			192	34	4	18	40	.177	.281	.251
Bases Empty			491	102	14	41	107	.208	.336	.273
Runners On			277	75	5	25	47	.271	.404	.319
Runners/Scor. Pos.			152	43	2	16	29	.283	.414	.330
Runners On/2 Out			127	23	1	15	28	.181	.291	.268
Scor. Pos./2 Out			76	14	1	10	20	.184	.316	.279
Late-Inning Pressure			57	12	2	5	13	.211	.351	.274
Leading Off			16	1	1	3	7	.063	.250	.211
Runners On			16	4	0	0	2	.250	.375	.250
Runners/Scor. Pos.			5	1	0	0	1	.200	.400	.200
First 9 Batters			273	57	4	25	58	.209	.315	.271
Second 9 Batters			237	60	8	20	41	.253	.418	.316
All Batters Thereafter			258	60	7	21	55	.233	.357	.287

Loves to face: Jay Bell (.071, 1-for-14)
Marquis Grissom (.083, 1-for-12, 1 2B)
Milt Thompson (.133, 2-for-15)

Hates to face: Barry Bonds (.444, 4-for-9, 1 2B, 2 HR)
Felix Jose (.615, 8-for-13, 4 2B, 1 3B)
Ray Lankford (.375, 6-for-16, 2 2B, 1 3B, 1 HR)

Miscellaneous statistics: Ground outs-to-air outs ratio: 0.80 last season, 0.84 for career.... Induced 9 double plays in 125 opportunities (one per 14).... Allowed 35 doubles, 4 triples in 207⅔ innings.... Allowed 8 first-inning runs in 27 starts (2.77 ERA).... Batting support: 4.15 runs per start.... Opposing base stealers: 18-for-25 (72%); 1 pickoff, 1 balk.

Comments: Pitched two shutouts against the Expos last season, including a no-hitter, limiting them to one earned run in 32 innings pitched (0.28 ERA).... His streak of 28.2 consecutive shutout innings, which included back-to-back shutouts against Montreal, was the longest streak by any N.L. pitcher last season, and helped him post the major leagues' lowest ERA during May. Only one pitcher in the majors had a lower ERA in any month (Clemens, 0.28 in April).... Strange breakdown of opponents' batting with runners in scoring position: .358 with less than two outs, .185 with two outs.... Hasn't allowed a first-inning home run in his last 30 starts, dating back to September 1990.... Didn't allow more than four runs in any of his starts, but did allow seven runs in a 7⅔ inning relief appearance in April.... Career record of 16–12 (3.59 ERA) in 40 starts, 1–0 (4.93 ERA) in 15 relief appearances.... Career batting average of .202 by opposing ground-ball hitters is 2d lowest among active pitchers (minimum: 500 BFP), behind teammate Jose DeJesus; opposing fly-ballers have a career mark of .267.... Career batting average of .269 by opposing left-handed batters, .191 by right-handers.... Opponents have a career average of .264 with runners on base, .218 with the bases empty.... Greene was traded from Atlanta with Dale Murphy for Jeff Parrett, Jim Vatcher, and Victor Rosario. Braves staff would be pretty scary had they not thrown Greene into that deal.

Kevin Gross   Throws Right

Los Angeles Dodgers	W-L	ERA	AB	H	HR	BB	SO	BA	SA	OBA
Season	10-11	3.58	447	123	10	50	95	.275	.380	.348
vs. Left-Handers			233	73	6	35	42	.313	.446	.400
vs. Right-Handers			214	50	4	15	53	.234	.308	.288
vs. Ground-Ballers			200	64	3	19	37	.320	.415	.374
vs. Fly-Ballers			247	59	7	31	58	.239	.352	.327
Home Games	7-3	2.79	232	59	5	21	58	.254	.353	.313
Road Games	3-8	4.47	215	64	5	29	37	.298	.409	.385
Grass Fields	8-7	3.27	336	90	6	35	77	.268	.357	.336
Artificial Turf	2-4	4.55	111	33	4	15	18	.297	.450	.383
April	1-3	8.27	66	23	2	9	21	.348	.500	.421
May	2-1	2.25	78	18	1	11	14	.231	.346	.330
June	1-1	3.38	40	13	0	4	5	.325	.375	.386
July	2-1	1.31	76	16	1	7	23	.211	.276	.277
August	2-3	3.47	86	21	3	10	15	.244	.360	.323
Sept./Oct.	2-2	3.65	101	32	3	9	17	.317	.426	.373
Leading Off Inn.			114	32	7	8	22	.281	.491	.328
Bases Empty			266	68	8	25	61	.256	.380	.320
Runners On			181	55	2	25	34	.304	.381	.387
Runners/Scor. Pos.			95	32	1	17	19	.337	.411	.432
Runners On/2 Out			82	18	1	13	16	.220	.305	.326
Scor. Pos./2 Out			46	10	1	8	11	.217	.326	.333
Late-Inning Pressure			111	33	1	11	26	.297	.351	.366
Leading Off			28	6	1	4	7	.214	.393	.313
Runners On			38	16	0	5	7	.421	.421	.500
Runners/Scor. Pos.			20	12	0	4	3	.600	.600	.680
First 9 Batters			279	79	5	34	68	.283	.380	.364
Second 9 Batters			112	30	4	10	24	.268	.402	.323
All Batters Thereafter			56	14	1	6	3	.250	.339	.317

Loves to face: Craig Biggio (.048, 1-for-21)
Kevin Elster (.154, 4-for-26, 0 BB)
Ron Gant (.118, 2-for-17)

Hates to face: Sid Bream (.364, 16-for-44, 4 HR)
Howard Johnson (.377, 23-for-61, 5 HR)

Miscellaneous statistics: Ground outs-to-air outs ratio: 1.45 last season, 0.99 for career.... Induced 6 double plays in 97 opportunities (one per 16).... Allowed 13 doubles, 2 triples in 115⅔ innings.... Allowed 6 first-inning runs in 10 starts (5.40 ERA).... Batting support: 3.80 runs per start.... Record of 4–5, 4.13 ERA as a starter; 6–6, 3.13 ERA in 36 relief appearances.... Stranded 5 inherited runners, allowed 3 to score (63%).... Opposing base stealers: 15-for-21 (71%); 1 pickoff, 0 balks.

Comments: Career record of 77–93 (4.11 ERA) in 231 starts, 13–8 (2.75 ERA) in 80 relief appearances.... Appeared in more games out of the bullpen than as a starter for the first time since his second year in the majors (1984).... Earned three saves within eight days (June 29–July 6), his only saves of the season and his first since 1984.... Averaged 7.39 strikeouts per nine innings, the highest rate of his career.... The only pitcher to lose more than 10 games in each of the last seven seasons. (Other than Gross, only Charlie Leibrandt has even a six-year streak.) But it ain't as bad as it sounds; he's only 12 games below .500 for the period.... Gross's streak of five consecutive losing seasons has followed him from Philadelphia to Montreal to Los Angeles. Only four other pitchers have had losing records in each of the last five seasons: Jamie Moyer, Dan Plesac, Bruce Ruffin, and Pete Smith. The major league record for consecutive losing seasons is 10 by Bill Bailey (1908–22) and Ron Kline (1952–63).... Only six runners were caught stealing against him last season, but three came in the same game in April against the Braves.... Batting average of opposing right-handers has decreased in recent years, but last year's mark by left-handers was a career high.... Has a history of keeping the ball in the park with runners on base. Opponents have averaged one home run every 32 at-bats with the bases empty, but with runners on base they hit one every 72 ABs.

Chris Hammond

Throws Left

Cincinnati Reds	W-L	ERA	AB	H	HR	BB	SO	BA	SA	OBA
Season	7-7	4.06	368	92	4	48	50	.250	.340	.339
vs. Left-Handers			98	18	1	13	14	.184	.255	.286
vs. Right-Handers			270	74	3	35	36	.274	.370	.358
vs. Ground-Ballers			165	39	0	21	28	.236	.291	.324
vs. Fly-Ballers			203	53	4	27	22	.261	.379	.351
Home Games	3-3	4.73	175	46	2	26	26	.263	.366	.360
Road Games	4-4	3.50	193	46	2	22	24	.238	.316	.319
Grass Fields	1-1	4.20	55	15	1	5	7	.273	.364	.333
Artificial Turf	6-6	4.04	313	77	3	43	43	.246	.335	.340
April	3-0	1.64	80	18	0	7	9	.225	.250	.287
May	0-3	6.43	81	20	1	10	11	.247	.333	.337
June	3-2	4.66	105	27	3	20	14	.257	.400	.381
July	1-2	3.86	96	27	0	11	15	.281	.375	.352
August	0-0	0.00	0	0	0	0	0	.000	.000	.000
Sept./Oct.	0-0	0.00	6	0	0	0	1	.000	.000	.000
Leading Off Inn.			93	24	2	13	13	.258	.376	.349
Bases Empty			211	50	2	27	33	.237	.318	.326
Runners On			157	42	2	21	17	.268	.369	.356
Runners/Scor. Pos.			84	25	0	15	10	.298	.381	.406
Runners On/2 Out			66	18	0	9	7	.273	.333	.368
Scor. Pos./2 Out			44	11	0	7	7	.250	.318	.365
Late-Inning Pressure			12	2	1	2	1	.167	.417	.286
Leading Off			4	1	1	1	1	.250	1.000	.400
Runners On			4	1	0	0	0	.250	.250	.250
Runners/Scor. Pos.			0	0	0	0	0	—	—	—
First 9 Batters			150	34	0	21	26	.227	.260	.324
Second 9 Batters			131	35	2	16	16	.267	.359	.351
All Batters Thereafter			87	23	2	11	8	.264	.448	.347

Loves to face: Ken Caminiti (.125, 1-for-8)
Fred McGriff (0-for-6)
Carl Nichols (0-for-4, 4 SO)

Hates to face: Barry Bonds (.417, 5-for-12, 1 HR)
Bernard Gilkey (.750, 3-for-4)
Gary Redus (.462, 6-for-13)

Miscellaneous statistics: Ground outs-to-air outs ratio: 1.62 last season, 1.66 for career.... Induced 13 double plays in 83 opportunities (one per 6.4).... Allowed 17 doubles, 2 triples in 99⅔ innings.... Allowed 6 first-inning runs in 18 starts (3.00 ERA).... Batting support: 3.28 runs per start.... Opposing base stealers: 8-for-11 (73%); 3 pickoffs, 0 balks.

Comments: Returned on September 1 from a 36-day stay on the disabled list, but pitched only once (2 innings in relief) before being shut down for the season.... Started 18 games but lasted into the eighth inning only once, never retiring a batter in that frame.... All of his wins and losses came in streaks—three wins, followed by five losses, four wins, and two losses.... Pitched just under 100 innings to rank seventh among N.L. rookies. Reds rookies pitched a total of 298 innings last season, 4th most among N.L. staffs, behind the Cubs (398⅔), Astros (393), and Expos (385⅓).... Didn't commit a balk last season after being called for three in only 11 innings during the proverbial cup o' Joe in 1990.... Average of one home run allowed every 24.9 innings was the best of any rookie pitcher in the majors.... Didn't allow a home run during the first three innings of any of his 18 starts last season.... Opponents have a career average of .209 during his first pass through the batting order, .289 thereafter. He has allowed only one home run in 172 at-bats during that first look.... Minor league record was 42–13 from 1988 through 1990, with a 2.39 ERA and an average of 7.69 strikeouts per nine innings. (The first of those three seasons was at the Double-A level, the last two at Triple-A.) Major league career figures: 7–9, 4.30 ERA, 4.38 SO per nine IP.

Chris Haney

Throws Left

Montreal Expos	W-L	ERA	AB	H	HR	BB	SO	BA	SA	OBA
Season	3-7	4.04	336	94	6	43	51	.280	.405	.362
vs. Left-Handers			60	11	0	14	12	.183	.250	.347
vs. Right-Handers			276	83	6	29	39	.301	.438	.366
vs. Ground-Ballers			143	39	0	16	25	.273	.364	.344
vs. Fly-Ballers			193	55	6	27	26	.285	.435	.376
Home Games	3-2	2.42	169	40	1	16	27	.237	.302	.303
Road Games	0-5	5.85	167	54	5	27	24	.323	.509	.418
Grass Fields	0-2	6.35	74	26	3	13	8	.351	.514	.448
Artificial Turf	3-5	3.46	262	68	3	30	43	.260	.374	.337
April	0-0	—	0	0	0	0	0	—	—	—
May	0-0	—	0	0	0	0	0	—	—	—
June	0-2	5.40	37	10	2	4	8	.270	.486	.349
July	1-2	3.31	65	22	1	7	7	.338	.415	.403
August	1-0	3.62	126	30	1	21	20	.238	.333	.347
Sept./Oct.	1-3	4.50	108	32	2	11	16	.296	.454	.361
Leading Off Inn.			79	21	1	9	14	.266	.367	.348
Bases Empty			177	49	2	22	28	.277	.390	.360
Runners On			159	45	4	21	23	.283	.421	.365
Runners/Scor. Pos.			93	26	1	16	11	.280	.376	.382
Runners On/2 Out			68	21	2	10	9	.309	.485	.397
Scor. Pos./2 Out			42	15	0	8	3	.357	.476	.460
Late-Inning Pressure			9	2	0	0	1	.222	.222	.222
Leading Off			3	0	0	0	1	.000	.000	.000
Runners On			1	1	0	0	0	1.000	1.000	1.000
Runners/Scor. Pos.			0	0	0	0	0	—	—	—
First 9 Batters			127	37	3	14	25	.291	.433	.364
Second 9 Batters			121	34	1	19	16	.281	.364	.379
All Batters Thereafter			88	23	2	10	10	.261	.420	.337

Loves to face: Wes Chamberlain (0-for-8)
Darren Daulton (0-for-6)
Mariano Duncan (0-for-5)

Hates to face: Jeff Blauser (2-for-2, 1 HR, 1 BB)
Howard Johnson (.800, 4-for-5, 2 HR)
Dale Murphy (.750, 3-for-4, 2 2B)

Miscellaneous statistics: Ground outs-to-air outs ratio: 1.28 last season, 1.28 for career.... Induced 5 double plays in 75 opportunities (one per 15).... Allowed 20 doubles, 2 triples in 84⅔ innings.... Allowed 12 first-inning runs in 16 starts (5.63 ERA).... Batting support: 3.19 runs per start.... Opposing base stealers: 8-for-14 (57%); 3 pickoffs, 0 balks.

Comments: Haney, who started 16 games, and Brian Barnes, who started 27, became the fourth pair of Expos rookies to start 15 games apiece in the same season. The 1969 Expos had a trio—Jerry Robertson, Mike Wegener, and Steve Renko. Other pairs: Bill Gullickson and Charlie Lea (1980), and John Dopson and Brian Holman (1988).... Allowed six home runs, all to right-handed batters. Opposing left-handers managed only three extra-base hits, all off the bats of All-Stars: doubles by Mark Grace and Brett Butler, and a triple by Lenny Dykstra.... Held opposing left-handed hitters to only one hit in their last 23 at-bats.... Threw nine wild pitches in only 84 innings. Among N.L. rookies, only Philadelphia's Jason Grimsley threw more wild ones (14).... Opponents had three hits in 10 at-bats with the bases loaded, with each of the hits going for extra bases, including a grand-slam home run by Jeff Blauser.... Among N.L. pitchers who started at least 15 games last season, only Steve Avery, Frank Castillo, and Darryl Kile are younger than Haney.... Minor league experience consists of 180⅔ innings over two seasons.... Haney's father, Larry, a former major league catcher who played for several teams including the Seattle Pilots, was Milwaukee's pitching coach last season. Only three other teams had pitching coaches who weren't pitchers during their playing days; all were catchers. The others: Dave Duncan (Oakland), Mike Roarke (San Diego), and Norm Sherry (San Francisco).

Pete Harnisch

Houston Astros — Throws Right

Houston Astros	W-L	ERA	AB	H	HR	BB	SO	BA	SA	OBA
Season	12-9	2.70	796	169	14	83	172	.212	.313	.288
vs. Left-Handers			457	107	10	55	88	.234	.352	.319
vs. Right-Handers			339	62	4	28	84	.183	.260	.247
vs. Ground-Ballers			373	78	6	42	86	.209	.300	.292
vs. Fly-Ballers			423	91	8	41	86	.215	.324	.285
Home Games	7-4	2.41	432	87	6	34	102	.201	.306	.261
Road Games	5-5	3.05	364	82	8	49	70	.225	.321	.320
Grass Fields	4-1	1.92	207	43	2	27	41	.208	.275	.305
Artificial Turf	8-8	2.98	589	126	12	56	131	.214	.326	.282
April	1-0	1.05	88	14	0	17	21	.159	.227	.295
May	2-3	3.43	145	31	2	14	23	.214	.297	.282
June	2-3	2.06	154	31	5	15	34	.201	.338	.272
July	1-1	3.00	140	33	3	12	24	.236	.343	.292
August	2-1	2.70	147	31	1	17	39	.211	.299	.304
Sept./Oct.	4-1	3.66	122	29	3	8	31	.238	.344	.288
Leading Off Inn.			201	45	4	21	40	.224	.358	.304
Bases Empty			465	102	11	45	101	.219	.342	.294
Runners On			331	67	3	38	71	.202	.272	.281
Runners/Scor. Pos.			203	38	2	32	47	.187	.251	.292
Runners On/2 Out			146	29	0	19	36	.199	.240	.291
Scor. Pos./2 Out			104	18	0	16	27	.173	.212	.283
Late-Inning Pressure			58	9	0	11	18	.155	.207	.286
Leading Off			19	6	0	3	2	.316	.474	.409
Runners On			21	1	0	5	10	.048	.048	.222
Runners/Scor. Pos.			10	1	0	4	4	.100	.100	.333
First 9 Batters			268	58	3	20	59	.216	.295	.271
Second 9 Batters			248	52	3	37	53	.210	.306	.317
All Batters Thereafter			280	59	8	26	60	.211	.336	.278

Loves to face: Rich Gedman (0-for-10)
  Fred McGriff (.067, 1-for-15)
  Benito Santiago (0-for-9)
Hates to face: Tony Fernandez (.421, 8-for-19)
  Ray Lankford (.400, 4-for-10, 1 HR)
  Gerald Perry (.417, 5-for-12, 1 HR)

Miscellaneous statistics: Ground outs-to-air outs ratio: 0.75 last season, 4th lowest in N.L.; 0.75 for career.... Induced 6 double plays in 145 opportunities (one per 24), 3d-worst rate in majors.... Allowed 28 doubles, 5 triples in 216⅔ innings.... Allowed 14 first-inning runs in 33 starts (3.00 ERA).... Batting support: 3.45 runs per start, 6th-lowest average in N.L.... Opposing base stealers: 27-for-33 (82%), 4th-most steals in N.L.; 0 pickoffs, 2 balks.

Comments: Opponents' overall batting average was the lowest off any pitcher who qualified for the N.L. ERA title.... Pitched 21 innings against the Padres without allowing a run.... Walked four consecutive batters in his N.L. debut, and won that game despite walking eight in five innings. No other N.L. pitcher walked four in a row in a game all season.... Opponents had only one hit in 21 at-bats with runners on base in Late-Inning Pressure Situations.... Lost a streak of 73 consecutive starts without allowing a first-inning home run when Eddie Murray connected on September 11.... His ground out-to-air out ratio declines sharply over the course of the game. Career figures: 1.04 during his first pass through the batting order, 0.67 in his second pass, and 0.59 thereafter.... Opponents have a career average of .181 with two outs and runners in scoring position, compared to an overall .239 average.... Career batting average of .258 by opposing left-handed batters, .214 by right-handers.... His control has improved in each of his seasons in the majors. Walks per nine innings year-by-year: 6.23, 5.57, 4.10, 3.45. That's not the only linear progression found in his yearly statistics. Harnisch is just the 10th pitcher in major league history to increase his win and strikeout totals and decrease his ERA in three consecutive seasons. The only other pitcher to do so in the past 25 years: Chuck Finley (1988–90).

Greg W. Harris

San Diego Padres — Throws Right

San Diego Padres	W-L	ERA	AB	H	HR	BB	SO	BA	SA	OBA
Season	9-5	2.23	498	116	16	27	95	.233	.363	.273
vs. Left-Handers			309	78	12	16	64	.252	.398	.288
vs. Right-Handers			189	38	4	11	31	.201	.307	.248
vs. Ground-Ballers			222	49	3	8	43	.221	.306	.250
vs. Fly-Ballers			276	67	13	19	52	.243	.409	.291
Home Games	5-2	1.85	268	60	8	11	48	.224	.343	.254
Road Games	4-3	2.70	230	56	8	16	47	.243	.387	.294
Grass Fields	8-4	2.15	404	93	12	20	73	.230	.349	.267
Artificial Turf	1-1	2.63	94	23	4	7	22	.245	.426	.297
April	1-1	2.30	59	12	2	1	9	.203	.322	.217
May	0-0	0.00	0	0	0	0	0	.000	.000	.000
June	0-0	—	0	0	0	0	0	—	—	—
July	1-2	3.19	120	32	4	9	21	.267	.433	.313
August	2-1	1.67	154	35	3	9	32	.227	.325	.270
Sept./Oct.	5-1	2.08	165	37	7	8	33	.224	.364	.264
Leading Off Inn.			130	29	5	7	23	.223	.392	.263
Bases Empty			328	80	10	15	59	.244	.375	.277
Runners On			170	36	6	12	36	.212	.341	.265
Runners/Scor. Pos.			96	15	2	11	27	.156	.229	.245
Runners On/2 Out			84	18	4	9	16	.214	.393	.290
Scor. Pos./2 Out			52	6	1	9	13	.115	.192	.246
Late-Inning Pressure			62	13	2	4	11	.210	.339	.258
Leading Off			19	2	0	0	4	.105	.158	.105
Runners On			15	2	0	1	2	.133	.133	.188
Runners/Scor. Pos.			7	1	0	1	2	.143	.143	.250
First 9 Batters			159	43	6	7	34	.270	.415	.301
Second 9 Batters			156	31	2	10	30	.199	.276	.249
All Batters Thereafter			183	42	8	10	31	.230	.393	.269

Loves to face: Todd Benzinger (.063, 1-for-16)
  Matt Williams (0-for-13)
  Gerald Young (.077, 1-for-13)
Hates to face: Tom Pagnozzi (3-for-3, 2 2B)
  Darryl Strawberry (.350, 7-for-20, 3 HR)
  Tim Wallach (.500, 6-for-12, 2 HR)

Miscellaneous statistics: Ground outs-to-air outs ratio: 1.13 last season, 1.17 for career.... Induced 3 double plays in 69 opportunities (one per 23), 5th-worst rate in majors.... Allowed 17 doubles, 0 triples in 133 innings.... Allowed 8 first-inning runs in 20 starts (3.79 ERA).... Batting support: 3.65 runs per start.... Opposing base stealers: 13-for-21 (62%); 0 pickoffs, 0 balks.

Comments: Compiled a 2.60 ERA as a rookie in 1989, and a 2.30 mark as a sophomore. The last pitcher with a 2.60 mark or lower in each of his first three seasons was Dick Radatz (1962–64). The four prior to that were Hod Eller, Walter Johnson, Carl Mays, and Babe Ruth.... Career ERA of 2.34 is 2d lowest among active pitchers (minimum: 300 IP). No other pitcher in Padres history has an ERA below 2.80; others under 3.00: Gaylord Perry, Gary Lucas, Lance McCullers, and Dave Roberts.... Spent 72 days on the disabled list with tendinitis in his elbow, but a little more than a month after his return he threw back-to-back complete-game shutouts.... Won five of his last six starts, losing only a 1–0 decision to the Braves on September 11. The only other N.L. pitchers to win as many as five games after September 1: Chris Nabholz and Andy Benes.... Career record of 13–9 (2.51 ERA) in 29 starts, 14–13 (2.19 ERA) in 123 relief appearances.... Career record of 7–0 against the Astros, 20–22 against everyone else.... Career batting average of .197 by opposing right-handed batters is 5th lowest in *Player Analysis* history (minimum: 600 BFP).... Opponents' career average of .202 in day games is the lowest of any pitcher over the last 17 years; at night, opponents have hit .231.... Opponents have a career on-base percentage of .251 leading off innings, the 3d lowest in *Player Analysis* history, behind Tim Crews (.245) and Erik Hanson (.247).

Dwayne Henry · Throws Right

Houston Astros	W-L	ERA	AB	H	HR	BB	SO	BA	SA	OBA
Season	3-2	3.19	233	51	7	39	51	.219	.361	.333
vs. Left-Handers			133	30	4	25	30	.226	.368	.350
vs. Right-Handers			100	21	3	14	21	.210	.350	.310
vs. Ground-Ballers			114	17	0	18	29	.149	.193	.269
vs. Fly-Ballers			119	34	7	21	22	.286	.521	.394
Home Games	3-1	3.26	132	29	5	26	32	.220	.402	.348
Road Games	0-1	3.10	101	22	2	13	19	.218	.307	.313
Grass Fields	0-1	1.45	60	9	1	7	13	.150	.217	.250
Artificial Turf	3-1	3.86	173	42	6	32	38	.243	.410	.361
April	2-0	0.75	34	3	0	5	6	.088	.088	.205
May	0-0	5.06	36	10	2	12	9	.278	.556	.440
June	0-0	5.63	33	10	0	6	6	.303	.394	.410
July	0-0	1.50	37	6	1	6	12	.162	.270	.279
August	1-2	3.78	64	17	2	6	10	.266	.422	.338
Sept./Oct.	0-0	3.24	29	5	2	4	8	.172	.379	.294
Leading Off Inn.			56	16	3	6	16	.286	.500	.355
Bases Empty			136	27	5	16	41	.199	.360	.283
Runners On			97	24	2	23	10	.247	.361	.395
Runners/Scor. Pos.			68	17	1	21	7	.250	.368	.430
Runners On/2 Out			36	8	2	9	3	.222	.444	.404
Scor. Pos./2 Out			28	5	1	9	2	.179	.357	.410
Late-Inning Pressure			65	14	1	12	12	.215	.292	.346
Leading Off			16	4	1	3	3	.250	.438	.368
Runners On			24	6	0	6	0	.250	.292	.419
Runners/Scor. Pos.			17	5	0	5	0	.294	.353	.478
First 9 Batters			227	51	7	39	50	.225	.370	.341
Second 9 Batters			6	0	0	0	1	.000	.000	.000
All Batters Thereafter			0	0	0	0	0	—	—	—

Loves to face: Craig Biggio (0-for-6)
Lenny Harris (0-for-6, 2 BB)
Stan Javier (0-for-5)

Hates to face: Eddie Murray (.455, 5-for-11, 1 HR)
Benito Santiago (2-for-2, 1 HR, 1 BB)
Darryl Strawberry (1-for-1, 1 HR, 2 BB)

Miscellaneous statistics: Ground outs-to-air outs ratio: 0.60 last season, 0.74 for career.... Induced 3 double plays in 57 opportunities (one per 19).... Allowed 10 doubles, 1 triple in 67⅔ innings.... Stranded 16 inherited runners, allowed 17 to score (48%), lowest rate in N.L.... Opposing base stealers: 7-for-10 (70%); 1 pickoff, 0 balks.

Comments: For Justin Wilson fans, a trivia quiz with a southern flavor. Judging by his resume, Henry seems destined to play for the Florida Marlins. He is one of three pitchers in history to appear in at least one game for Texas, Houston, and Atlanta. Who are the other two? Answer below.... Henry has pitched in eight major league seasons, but has never accumulated more than 67⅔ innings in any year. Only two pitchers in major league history played in more seasons without ever pitching that many innings in any one of them. One was Ed Glynn, who had a 10-year career (we're *serious*—1975–83, 1985), playing for the Tigers, Mets, Indians, and Expos. His career high was 60 innings. The other was George Boehler, whose nine-year career lasted from 1912 to 1926; career high: 63.... Henry's career total of only 183⅔ innings pitched represents less than 23 per year. Last season was his first full year with a major league club.... Picked up a save in his debut with the Astros on April 12 and converted his next opportunity as well, but didn't enter a game in a save situation after May 5.... He was used during Late-Inning Pressure Situations only once over a span of 22 appearances from mid-May through the end of July.... Career average of .214 by opposing ground-ball hitters, .267 by fly-ballers.... Career average of 6.03 walks per nine innings is 3d highest among pitchers active in 1991 (minimum: 150 IP), behind Mitch Williams (6.76) and Bobby Witt (6.26).... Trivia answer: Joe Hoerner and Mike Marshall.

Orel Hershiser · Throws Right

Los Angeles Dodgers	W-L	ERA	AB	H	HR	BB	SO	BA	SA	OBA
Season	7-2	3.46	433	112	3	32	73	.259	.330	.316
vs. Left-Handers			208	59	2	18	27	.284	.375	.345
vs. Right-Handers			225	53	1	14	46	.236	.289	.289
vs. Ground-Ballers			183	33	0	16	42	.180	.224	.249
vs. Fly-Ballers			250	79	3	16	31	.316	.408	.367
Home Games	3-2	3.27	242	61	0	22	37	.252	.306	.318
Road Games	4-0	3.70	191	51	3	10	36	.267	.361	.314
Grass Fields	5-2	3.79	350	93	3	25	60	.266	.340	.321
Artificial Turf	2-0	2.08	83	19	0	7	13	.229	.289	.297
April	0-0	—	0	0	0	0	0	—	—	—
May	0-1	9.00	20	9	0	3	4	.450	.450	.522
June	2-1	2.83	134	36	1	14	30	.269	.343	.338
July	1-0	5.40	92	24	1	3	16	.261	.337	.352
August	2-0	4.18	94	26	1	1	13	.277	.383	.296
Sept./Oct.	2-0	1.04	93	17	0	3	17	.183	.226	.216
Leading Off Inn.			111	30	0	2	17	.270	.306	.296
Bases Empty			236	65	1	13	36	.275	.347	.319
Runners On			197	47	2	19	37	.239	.310	.314
Runners/Scor. Pos.			105	29	1	16	20	.276	.333	.374
Runners On/2 Out			80	19	0	10	14	.237	.287	.330
Scor. Pos./2 Out			53	13	0	9	10	.245	.302	.355
Late-Inning Pressure			9	2	0	0	2	.222	.222	.222
Leading Off			3	0	0	0	1	.000	.000	.000
Runners On			4	0	0	0	0	.000	.000	.000
Runners/Scor. Pos.			0	0	0	0	0	—	—	—
First 9 Batters			173	47	2	9	29	.272	.353	.311
Second 9 Batters			160	37	1	14	29	.231	.300	.303
All Batters Thereafter			100	28	0	9	15	.280	.340	.345

Loves to face: Pedro Guerrero (.063, 1-for-16)
Spike Owen (0-for-13)
Benito Santiago (.176, 6-for-34, 0 BB)

Hates to face: Craig Biggio (.577, 15-for-26)
Bobby Bonilla (.321, 9-for-28, 2 HR)
Andy Van Slyke (.310, 13-for-42, 2 HR)

Miscellaneous statistics: Ground outs-to-air outs ratio: 1.62 last season, 2.07 for career.... Induced 8 double plays in 102 opportunities (one per 13).... Allowed 18 doubles, 2 triples in 112 innings.... Allowed 12 first-inning runs in 21 starts (5.14 ERA).... Batting support: 5.62 runs per start, highest average in N.L.... Opposing base stealers: 11-for-13 (85%); 2 pickoffs, 4 balks (3d most in N.L.).

Comments: Pitched an average of 5.33 innings per start last season, the lowest average in the N.L. (minimum: 20 GS).... Ended the season with a 6-game winning streak—over 15 starts.... Made 21 starts, but never reached the eighth inning.... Allowed one home run per 37.3 innings, the best rate of any pitcher with at least 100 innings.... Streak of 141 consecutive batters without a walk was the longest by any N.L. pitcher last season.... His average of 2.57 walks per nine innings last season was lower than his career mark prior to his shoulder reconstruction (2.66).... The Dodgers defense is often criticized, but not by Orel. Dodgers infielders made three errors in 313 chances behind Hershiser last season. The only N.L. pitchers with better infield support: Mike Bielecki (4 in 500 chances), Chris Nabholz (3 in 366 chances), and John Smiley (5 in 527 chances). Hershiser didn't allow an unearned run.... Has won 11 consecutive decisions against the Braves.... Has pitched in the majors for nine years without posting a losing record in any season. That's the longest streak by any pitcher at the start of a career since 1982, when Tom Seaver's 15-year streak was snapped, as was a nine-year streak by, believe it or not, Doug ("the Fidrych") Bird.... Over the last two seasons (which amounts to less than 140 innings) opposing fly-ball hitters have out-hit ground-ball hitters by a 144-point margin, .321 to .177.... Has pitched 58 postseason innings without allowing a home run, an all-time record.

Ken Hill   Throws Right

St. Louis Cardinals	W-L	ERA	AB	H	HR	BB	SO	BA	SA	OBA
Season	11-10	3.57	656	147	15	67	121	.224	.346	.299
vs. Left-Handers			367	87	8	37	62	.237	.341	.307
vs. Right-Handers			289	60	7	30	59	.208	.353	.288
vs. Ground-Ballers			286	63	3	30	53	.220	.283	.300
vs. Fly-Ballers			370	84	12	37	68	.227	.395	.298
Home Games	6-4	3.18	308	63	3	34	60	.205	.276	.291
Road Games	5-6	3.94	348	84	12	33	61	.241	.408	.306
Grass Fields	4-3	3.28	225	50	7	18	39	.222	.351	.279
Artificial Turf	7-7	3.72	431	97	8	49	82	.225	.343	.309
April	2-1	3.54	77	23	2	10	9	.299	.429	.374
May	3-1	3.29	143	28	6	9	27	.196	.350	.243
June	2-3	3.27	119	30	1	10	25	.252	.303	.305
July	1-2	6.32	107	26	3	17	21	.243	.439	.352
August	0-2	5.59	36	10	1	3	6	.278	.444	.366
Sept./Oct.	3-1	1.85	174	30	2	18	33	.172	.259	.254
Leading Off Inn.			165	31	6	19	26	.188	.315	.283
Bases Empty			402	82	9	43	76	.204	.301	.287
Runners On			254	65	6	24	45	.256	.417	.317
Runners/Scor. Pos.			130	33	5	16	26	.254	.446	.325
Runners On/2 Out			109	29	3	12	16	.266	.459	.350
Scor. Pos./2 Out			67	17	3	9	12	.254	.493	.351
Late-Inning Pressure			47	10	1	7	10	.213	.383	.327
Leading Off			12	1	0	2	3	.083	.083	.267
Runners On			15	4	0	2	2	.267	.600	.353
Runners/Scor. Pos.			3	0	0	1	0	.000	.000	.250
First 9 Batters			237	44	3	26	50	.186	.266	.270
Second 9 Batters			227	54	7	22	40	.238	.374	.310
All Batters Thereafter			192	49	5	19	31	.255	.411	.322

Loves to face: Ken Caminiti (.118, 2-for-17, 3 BB)
            Shawon Dunston (.125, 2-for-16)
            Dale Murphy (0-for-12)
Hates to face: Len Dykstra (.600, 6-for-10, 1 HR)
            Ron Gant (.313, 5-for-16, 2 HR)
            Lonnie Smith (.600, 6-for-10)

Miscellaneous statistics: Ground outs-to-air outs ratio: 1.03 last season, 1.25 for career.... Induced 11 double plays in 128 opportunities (one per 12).... Allowed 23 doubles, 6 triples in 181⅓ innings.... Allowed 9 first-inning runs in 30 starts (2.70 ERA).... Batting support: 3.83 runs per start.... Opposing base stealers: 19-for-30 (63%); 0 pickoffs, 1 balk.

Comments: Became the second pitcher in Cardinals history to start as many as 30 games in a season without completing one. The other: Jose DeLeon (32 GS in 1990). Career totals: 3 CGs in 78 starts.... Had a streak of 22⅔ consecutive scoreless innings in September, the 5th-longest streak in the league last season. His ERA for September/October was 3d best in the league—particularly encouraging for a guy who came off a three-week stay on the disabled list on September 1.... Opposing base runners stole seven bases in eight attempts with Rich Gedman catching, 12 in 22 attempts with Tom Pagnozzi.... Allowed 7.3 hits per nine innings, the 4th-lowest rate in the N.L., behind Pete Harnisch (7.02), Jose Rijo (7.27), and Jose DeJesus (7.28).... Led the National League with 99 walks in 1989, but has reduced his rate per nine innings substantially in both seasons since then; year by year: 4.53, 3.78, 3.33.... Opponents' career breakdown: .212 during his first pass through the order, .253 during his second pass, and .275 in subsequent at-bats.... Has allowed one home run per 26.6 innings at Busch Stadium, one per 11.2 innings elsewhere.... Opponents have a career average of .228 on grass fields, .241 at Busch Stadium, and .271 on other fields with artificial surfaces.... Has lost each of his last three starts at his new home, Olympic Stadium. Career record there: 1–3 with a 4.18 ERA.... Opponents have a career average of .262 with runners on base, .232 with the bases empty.

Jay Howell   Throws Right

Los Angeles Dodgers	W-L	ERA	AB	H	HR	BB	SO	BA	SA	OBA
Season	6-5	3.18	183	39	3	11	40	.213	.328	.259
vs. Left-Handers			97	17	1	7	21	.175	.289	.234
vs. Right-Handers			86	22	2	4	19	.256	.372	.289
vs. Ground-Ballers			72	11	1	1	15	.153	.222	.162
vs. Fly-Ballers			111	28	2	10	25	.252	.396	.317
Home Games	6-2	2.84	113	26	1	6	26	.230	.292	.273
Road Games	0-3	3.72	70	13	2	5	14	.186	.386	.237
Grass Fields	6-2	2.28	154	32	1	7	37	.208	.279	.245
Artificial Turf	0-3	8.22	29	7	2	4	3	.241	.586	.324
April	0-0	2.35	32	9	0	0	10	.281	.364	.273
May	0-1	2.25	58	11	2	1	13	.190	.345	.203
June	2-1	3.60	34	7	0	2	6	.206	.294	.243
July	2-0	0.00	5	0	0	2	0	.000	.000	.286
August	1-2	3.65	42	9	1	4	10	.214	.333	.292
Sept./Oct.	1-1	9.00	11	3	0	2	1	.273	.364	.385
Leading Off Inn.			45	14	2	2	9	.311	.533	.340
Bases Empty			109	23	2	4	23	.211	.339	.246
Runners On			74	16	1	7	17	.216	.311	.277
Runners/Scor. Pos.			49	10	1	5	12	.204	.327	.268
Runners On/2 Out			31	6	0	2	6	.194	.194	.242
Scor. Pos./2 Out			22	4	0	2	5	.182	.182	.250
Late-Inning Pressure			136	25	2	10	29	.184	.272	.243
Leading Off			34	11	2	2	6	.324	.588	.361
Runners On			55	8	0	7	13	.145	.182	.238
Runners/Scor. Pos.			38	5	0	5	11	.132	.158	.227
First 9 Batters			179	38	3	11	37	.212	.330	.259
Second 9 Batters			4	1	0	0	3	.250	.250	.250
All Batters Thereafter			0	0	0	0	0	—	—	—

Loves to face: Ken Caminiti (0-for-10)
            Andre Dawson (.077, 1-for-13, 1 2B)
            Robby Thompson (.133, 2-for-15, 9 SO)
Hates to face: George Bell (.556, 5-for-9, 1 HR)
            Glenn Braggs (.600, 3-for-5, 1 HR)
            Paul O'Neill (.800, 8-for-10, 2 2B, 1 3B, 2 HR)

Miscellaneous statistics: Ground outs-to-air outs ratio: 0.72 last season, 1.00 for career.... Induced 1 double play in 36 opportunities (one per 36).... Allowed 8 doubles, 2 triples in 51 innings.... Saved 16 games in 20 opportunities (80%).... Stranded 10 inherited runners, allowed 5 to score (67%).... Opposing base stealers: 3-for-4 (75%); 0 pickoffs, 0 balks.

Comments: The Dodgers posted a 12–15 record during his stay on the disabled list (June 20–July 23), blowing leads in the eighth inning or later in three of those losses. How many games did the Braves win by? ... Averaged fewer than two walks per nine innings for the first time in his career.... It's hard for a relief pitcher to earn a lot of saves without compiling a losing record; they usually enter games in can't-win situations. But Howell has saved at least 15 games and won at least as many as he's lost for four straight seasons. The only other pitcher with a current streak that long: Dennis Eckersley. No pitcher has ever had a five-year streak.... Has saved 81 games for the Dodgers. Howell ranks second in Dodgers history, behind Jim Brewer (105), or fourth if you include pre-1969 saves, behind Brewer (125), Ron Perranoski (101), and Clem Labine (83).... Has faced 81 batters with the bases loaded, but has never allowed a grand-slam home run.... When a pitcher spends parts of two straight seasons on the disabled list, we would generally recommend a hands-off policy for fantasy-league GMs. But that might not be the case with Howell, whose left knee put him on the D.L. in 1990, and his right knee in 1991. He's run out of knees, so 1992 could be the year he becomes the first pitcher in Dodgers history to save 30 games.... Warning: Only one pitcher as old as Howell has ever saved as many as 30—Dennis Eckersley (43 in 1991).

Bruce Hurst

Throws Left

San Diego Padres	W-L	ERA	AB	H	HR	BB	SO	BA	SA	OBA
Season	15-8	3.29	835	201	17	59	141	.241	.340	.292
vs. Left-Handers			136	24	1	13	31	.176	.221	.247
vs. Right-Handers			699	177	16	46	110	.253	.363	.301
vs. Ground-Ballers			341	77	4	16	62	.226	.290	.260
vs. Fly-Ballers			494	124	13	43	79	.251	.374	.313
Home Games	7-5	3.34	469	103	12	36	92	.220	.328	.278
Road Games	8-3	3.22	366	98	5	23	49	.268	.355	.310
Grass Fields	10-6	3.54	644	154	15	47	111	.239	.348	.292
Artificial Turf	5-2	2.45	191	47	2	12	30	.246	.314	.293
April	2-0	2.17	103	21	5	8	26	.204	.359	.268
May	3-2	3.95	171	47	2	14	27	.275	.357	.332
June	4-2	2.49	169	36	3	12	20	.213	.302	.265
July	3-1	3.86	135	30	4	9	24	.222	.333	.269
August	3-1	3.28	176	43	1	11	32	.244	.324	.291
Sept./Oct.	0-2	4.35	81	24	2	5	12	.296	.407	.333
Leading Off Inn.			209	37	5	18	38	.177	.301	.242
Bases Empty			509	114	13	39	95	.224	.334	.281
Runners On			326	87	4	20	46	.267	.350	.310
Runners/Scor. Pos.			169	44	4	12	26	.260	.373	.306
Runners On/2 Out			142	34	1	8	24	.239	.282	.285
Scor. Pos./2 Out			87	20	1	6	12	.230	.299	.280
Late-Inning Pressure			96	20	1	8	13	.208	.292	.269
Leading Off			27	2	0	3	6	.074	.111	.167
Runners On			30	8	0	3	3	.267	.400	.333
Runners/Scor. Pos.			11	2	0	1	1	.182	.273	.250
First 9 Batters			254	62	4	19	57	.244	.335	.295
Second 9 Batters			247	54	9	17	40	.219	.364	.272
All Batters Thereafter			334	85	4	23	44	.254	.326	.304

Loves to face: Todd Benzinger (.143, 3-for-21)
Jeff Blauser (.162, 6-for-37)
Len Dykstra (.071, 1-for-14)

Hates to face: Barry Bonds (.440, 11-for-25, 2 HR)
David Hollins (4-for-4, 1 HR, 1 BB)
Willie Randolph (.393, 33-for-84, 1 HR)

Miscellaneous statistics: Ground outs-to-air outs ratio: 1.25 last season, 1.17 for career.... Induced 14 double plays in 158 opportunities (one per 11).... Allowed 30 doubles, 1 triple in 221⅔ innings.... Allowed 11 first-inning runs in 31 starts (2.61 ERA).... Batting support: 4.35 runs per start.... Opposing base stealers: 11-for-17 (65%); 7 pickoffs, 1 balk.

Comments: A loss in his final appearance of the season gave him his only two-game losing streak of the year. He left that September 17 game with stiffness in his elbow, and didn't pitch after that.... His first-inning strikeout rate (8.71 per nine innings) was his highest in any frame.... Benito Santiago caught every inning that Hurst pitched last season.... Average of 2.40 walks per nine innings was the lowest of his career.... Strikeout rate has declined in every season since he posted a career-high 8.62 mark in 1986. Year by year since then: 7.16, 6.90, 6.58, 6.52, 5.72. Only two pitchers have had longer streaks in seasons of 25 or more starts: Bob Feller (seven years, 1947–53) and Mickey Lolich (six, 1970–75).... Huge difference between 1991 batting averages of opposing left- and right-handers is not indicative of his career performance. Career breakdown: .260 by left-handers, .264 by right-handers.... Winning percentage of .594 as a member of the Padres is 2d highest in franchise history (minimum: 50 decisions), behind Gaylord Perry (.660, 33–17).... Fourth player in Padres history to post a winning record in three consecutive seasons, joining Ed Whitson (1988–90); Dave Dravecky (4 years, 1982–85); and Eric Show (5 years, 1982–86).... Hurst and Mike Boddicker are the only pitchers to win at least 10 games in each of the last nine seasons. The last pitcher with a 10-year streak was Jack Morris (1979–88), and the last with a longer streak than that was Nolan Ryan (16 years, 1971–86).

Jeff Innis

Throws Right

New York Mets	W-L	ERA	AB	H	HR	BB	SO	BA	SA	OBA
Season	0-2	2.66	302	66	2	23	47	.219	.291	.270
vs. Left-Handers			124	31	1	10	17	.250	.331	.301
vs. Right-Handers			178	35	1	13	30	.197	.264	.247
vs. Ground-Ballers			136	32	0	9	17	.235	.287	.281
vs. Fly-Ballers			166	34	2	14	30	.205	.295	.261
Home Games	0-2	2.59	166	30	1	12	27	.181	.265	.231
Road Games	0-0	2.75	136	36	1	11	20	.265	.324	.318
Grass Fields	0-2	2.43	232	45	2	18	38	.194	.276	.248
Artificial Turf	0-0	3.50	70	21	0	5	9	.300	.343	.342
April	0-1	6.00	18	4	0	2	4	.222	.222	.273
May	0-0	1.17	27	3	1	1	4	.111	.222	.143
June	0-0	2.04	61	12	0	5	10	.197	.279	.258
July	0-0	2.41	68	17	0	4	13	.250	.324	.292
August	0-0	3.57	70	20	1	8	12	.286	.386	.346
Sept./Oct.	0-1	2.12	58	10	0	3	4	.172	.207	.213
Leading Off Inn.			69	19	1	4	14	.275	.377	.315
Bases Empty			170	36	2	7	26	.212	.306	.243
Runners On			132	30	0	16	21	.227	.273	.301
Runners/Scor. Pos.			92	18	0	15	18	.196	.239	.295
Runners On/2 Out			62	10	0	7	14	.161	.242	.246
Scor. Pos./2 Out			49	6	0	7	12	.122	.184	.232
Late-Inning Pressure			33	10	0	2	9	.303	.364	.343
Leading Off			8	4	0	1	2	.500	.625	.556
Runners On			15	6	0	1	4	.400	.467	.438
Runners/Scor. Pos.			13	5	0	1	4	.385	.462	.429
First 9 Batters			287	61	2	21	45	.213	.289	.262
Second 9 Batters			15	5	0	2	2	.333	.333	.412
All Batters Thereafter			0	0	0	0	0	—	—	—

Loves to face: Andres Galarraga (.077, 1-for-13)
Otis Nixon (0-for-6)
Benito Santiago (0-for-6)

Hates to face: Will Clark (.600, 3-for-5, 1 HR)
Paul O'Neill (.750, 3-for-4, 1 2B, 1 HR, 1 SO)
Andy Van Slyke (.500, 3-for-6, 1 HR)

Miscellaneous statistics: Ground outs-to-air outs ratio: 3.04 last season, 2.45 for career.... Induced 6 double plays in 62 opportunities (one per 10).... Allowed 10 doubles, 3 triples in 84⅔ innings.... Stranded 35 inherited runners, allowed 19 to score (65%).... Opposing base stealers: 6-for-11 (55%); 0 pickoffs, 0 balks.

Comments: Led the N.L. in relief appearances after the All-Star break.... Tied the record for most appearances without recording a save (69), set by Norm Charlton in 1989. He didn't win a game either, and only two pitchers in history have pitched in more games in a winless season: Rob Murphy (76 games in 1988) and Tom Henke (72 games in 1987). Innis shattered the previous mark for most games without a win *or* a save (since 1969) by Beamon-like dimensions (Dave Tomlin, 49 games in 1976).... Pitched in Late-Inning Pressure Situations in only 12 of his 69 appearances (17 percent).... Allowed only two home runs in 84⅔ innings, the 3d-lowest rate of any N.L. pitcher (minimum: 50 IP).... Career total of one save in 144 relief appearances. Only two other relief pitchers have pitched in more games with no more than one save: Dave Rucker (one save in 196 games) and Greg Booker (one save in 157 games).... Opponents have a career average of .206 at Shea Stadium, .272 on other grass fields, and .263 on artificial surfaces.... Huge margins between the career averages of right- and left-handed batters, as well as ground-ball and fly-ball hitters. Breakdowns: .289 by left-handers, .204 by right-handers; .276 by ground-ballers, .203 by fly-ballers.... While we're at it: .246 with the bases empty, .224 with runners on base, .193 with runners in scoring position.... "Big Fish, Small Pond" theory: Innis's two career wins rank him fifth in major league history among I-Men. The leaders: Bert Inks (27) and Ham Iburg (11).

Barry Jones — Throws Right

Montreal Expos

	W-L	ERA	AB	H	HR	BB	SO	BA	SA	OBA
Season	4-9	3.35	309	76	8	33	46	.246	.369	.318
vs. Left-Handers			141	36	2	21	15	.255	.369	.348
vs. Right-Handers			168	40	6	12	31	.238	.369	.291
vs. Ground-Ballers			139	32	1	14	18	.230	.309	.299
vs. Fly-Ballers			173	44	7	20	30	.254	.410	.332
Home Games	1-2	2.70	131	30	2	15	23	.229	.305	.311
Road Games	3-7	3.88	178	46	6	18	23	.258	.416	.323
Grass Fields	1-4	4.57	77	19	4	12	8	.247	.455	.344
Artificial Turf	3-5	2.96	232	57	4	21	38	.246	.341	.309
April	0-0	2.77	48	12	2	8	5	.250	.438	.357
May	2-2	2.61	64	9	2	7	9	.141	.250	.225
June	1-3	6.43	54	19	1	2	9	.352	.463	.362
July	0-2	4.22	36	8	2	6	5	.222	.417	.333
August	0-1	0.00	53	10	0	5	10	.189	.208	.267
Sept./Oct.	1-1	5.14	54	18	1	5	8	.333	.481	.390
Leading Off Inn.			67	17	2	8	10	.254	.388	.333
Bases Empty			165	34	2	18	26	.206	.273	.284
Runners On			144	42	6	15	20	.292	.479	.356
Runners/Scor. Pos.			89	28	4	9	13	.315	.494	.366
Runners On/2 Out			68	22	4	8	10	.324	.544	.395
Scor. Pos./2 Out			44	14	3	4	8	.318	.568	.375
Late-Inning Pressure			160	46	4	18	27	.287	.438	.357
Leading Off			37	12	1	5	6	.324	.459	.405
Runners On			76	26	3	9	11	.342	.579	.404
Runners/Scor. Pos.			49	17	2	6	8	.347	.551	.397
First 9 Batters			304	75	8	31	44	.247	.372	.316
Second 9 Batters			5	1	0	2	2	.200	.200	.429
All Batters Thereafter			0	0	0	0	0	—	—	—

Loves to face: Will Clark (0-for-6)
Andre Dawson (.182, 2-for-11)
Tim Teufel (0-for-6, 4 SO)
Hates to face: George Bell (.500, 5-for-10, 1 HR)
Vince Coleman (.556, 5-for-9)
Tony Gwynn (.800, 4-for-5, 2 2B, 1 HR)

Miscellaneous statistics: Ground outs-to-air outs ratio: 1.65 last season, 1.70 for career.... Induced 12 double plays in 61 opportunities (one per 5.1).... Allowed 10 doubles, 2 triples in 88⅔ innings.... Saved 13 games in 17 opportunities (76%).... Stranded 34 inherited runners, allowed 17 to score (67%).... Opposing base stealers: 8-for-14 (57%); 2 pickoffs, 1 balk.

Comments: Became the fourth different Expos pitcher to lead the league in appearances, joining Mike Marshall (1972–74), Dale Murray (1976), and Tim Burke (1985).... Saved only nine games in 204 appearances over the previous five years before earning 13 in 77 games last season.... Allowed only two home runs in 74 innings in 1990.... Threw 13 wild pitches in 82⅓ innings in 1988, but has uncorked (a technical term) only two wild ones in 193 innings since then.... Walked more left-handed batters than he struck out not only last season, but over his career (78 BB, 67 SO). Has walked an equal number of right-handed batters, but struck out more than twice as many (146).... Career record of 16–8 with a 2.35 ERA with the White Sox, but 10–18 with a 3.63 ERA in his N.L. career.... Jones is the only player to pitch for the Pirates, White Sox, and Expos. Three position players have played for those three teams: Bill Almon, Miguel Dilone, and Vance Law.... Started all 14 games in which he appeared for Watertown (Class A) in his first year of professional ball (1984). But since then, his only starting assignments have come as part of a rehabilitation assignment with Sarasota in 1989. He has appeared in 281 major league games, all in relief.... Opponents have a career average of only .216 on grass fields, but they have a .273 mark on artificial surfaces.

Jimmy Jones — Throws Right

Houston Astros

	W-L	ERA	AB	H	HR	BB	SO	BA	SA	OBA
Season	6-8	4.39	530	143	9	51	88	.270	.374	.336
vs. Left-Handers			348	105	6	37	57	.302	.414	.371
vs. Right-Handers			182	38	3	14	31	.209	.297	.268
vs. Ground-Ballers			274	75	3	22	48	.274	.361	.329
vs. Fly-Ballers			256	68	6	29	40	.266	.387	.344
Home Games	4-3	3.08	362	82	4	35	64	.227	.293	.297
Road Games	2-5	7.62	168	61	5	16	24	.363	.548	.422
Grass Fields	0-3	6.48	103	32	4	11	17	.311	.495	.383
Artificial Turf	6-5	3.92	427	111	5	40	71	.260	.344	.325
April	2-1	2.59	95	22	2	7	14	.232	.337	.284
May	2-1	2.85	155	35	2	15	27	.226	.290	.298
June	0-3	6.75	96	33	1	13	8	.344	.490	.423
July	2-2	5.11	100	29	2	6	19	.290	.380	.333
August	0-1	5.91	84	24	2	10	20	.286	.429	.362
Sept./Oct.	0-0	0.00	0	0	0	0	0	.000	.000	.000
Leading Off Inn.			130	31	2	11	20	.238	.338	.303
Bases Empty			296	80	6	27	51	.270	.361	.335
Runners On			234	63	3	24	37	.269	.389	.337
Runners/Scor. Pos.			125	36	0	16	22	.288	.400	.364
Runners On/2 Out			96	21	0	16	20	.219	.292	.336
Scor. Pos./2 Out			63	13	0	12	14	.206	.302	.333
Late-Inning Pressure			38	6	0	5	9	.158	.158	.256
Leading Off			10	2	0	3	2	.200	.200	.385
Runners On			16	2	0	2	3	.125	.125	.222
Runners/Scor. Pos.			10	2	0	1	2	.200	.200	.273
First 9 Batters			200	54	6	19	33	.270	.385	.336
Second 9 Batters			174	48	2	21	34	.276	.362	.354
All Batters Thereafter			156	41	1	11	21	.263	.372	.315

Loves to face: Kevin Bass (.150, 3-for-20)
Chris Sabo (.158, 3-for-19)
Robby Thompson (.067, 1-for-15, 2 BB)
Hates to face: Jay Bell (.700, 7-for-10, 2 HR)
Fred McGriff (.385, 5-for-13, 3 HR)
Andy Van Slyke (.400, 10-for-25, 3 HR)

Miscellaneous statistics: Ground outs-to-air outs ratio: 1.91 last season, 4th highest in N.L.; 1.63 for career.... Induced 9 double plays in 112 opportunities (one per 12).... Allowed 18 doubles, 5 triples in 135⅓ innings.... Allowed 11 first-inning runs in 22 starts (4.50 ERA).... Batting support: 3.59 runs per start, 10th-lowest average in N.L.... Opposing base stealers: 18-for-24 (75%); 0 pickoffs, 0 balks.

Comments: Opponents batted .330 during the first inning of his starts, .255 thereafter.... Walked the leadoff batter only once in the last 60 innings he started.... Struck out 5.85 batters per nine innings, a career high.... Opponents' career breakdown: .278 overall; .260 with the bases empty, .303 with runners on base, .325 with runners in scoring position.... During six major league seasons, Jones has played for last-place clubs—and bad ones at that, with at least 95 losses—three times: the 1987 Padres, 1990 Yankees, and 1991 Astros. All things considered, his career record of 29–32 doesn't look that bad. In fact, his winning percentage (.475) is 23 points higher than that of his teammates (.452).... In 1988, Jones was traded from San Diego to New York along with Lance McCullers and Stan Jefferson in exchange for Jack Clark. A lopsided deal? Excuse us, we forgot to mention that the Yanks sweetened the pot with Pat Clements.... Jones was the Padres' first-round selection, and the third choice overall, in the 1982 free-agent draft. He was picked after Shawon Dunston and the human trivia answer, Augie Schmidt, and before Dwight Gooden, Bret Saberhagen, Jimmy Key, and Tom Browning—not to mention Jose Canseco, Alvin Davis, Terry Pendleton, and Vince Coleman. The Padres selected Mitch Williams in the eighth round of that draft.

Darryl Kile

Throws Right

Houston Astros	W-L	ERA	AB	H	HR	BB	SO	BA	SA	OBA
Season	7-11	3.69	585	144	16	84	100	.246	.393	.344
vs. Left-Handers			343	90	7	56	64	.262	.399	.365
vs. Right-Handers			242	54	9	28	36	.223	.384	.314
vs. Ground-Ballers			269	59	1	42	54	.219	.283	.324
vs. Fly-Ballers			320	87	15	42	47	.272	.488	.363
Home Games	4-5	3.36	289	68	2	45	49	.235	.336	.341
Road Games	3-6	4.03	296	76	14	39	51	.257	.449	.347
Grass Fields	1-3	4.23	173	43	9	22	27	.249	.445	.333
Artificial Turf	6-8	3.47	412	101	7	62	73	.245	.371	.348
April	0-1	8.16	59	16	3	9	9	.271	.508	.368
May	0-0	3.09	45	12	1	10	3	.267	.400	.414
June	2-1	1.80	125	25	2	19	18	.200	.320	.304
July	2-4	3.86	104	30	4	11	22	.288	.471	.359
August	2-2	3.86	113	30	3	18	21	.265	.398	.376
Sept./Oct.	1-3	3.68	139	31	3	17	27	.223	.345	.308
Leading Off Inn.			134	31	4	21	26	.231	.388	.335
Bases Empty			303	74	9	48	57	.244	.403	.351
Runners On			282	70	7	36	43	.248	.383	.336
Runners/Scor. Pos.			181	40	5	29	31	.221	.354	.321
Runners On/2 Out			125	30	4	15	19	.240	.392	.336
Scor. Pos./2 Out			94	21	3	12	18	.223	.351	.311
Late-Inning Pressure			31	9	1	6	4	.290	.581	.395
Leading Off			9	2	0	2	1	.222	.333	.364
Runners On			11	3	1	2	2	.273	.818	.357
Runners/Scor. Pos.			9	2	1	2	3	.222	.667	.333
First 9 Batters			265	69	8	34	48	.260	.415	.350
Second 9 Batters			181	43	3	26	29	.238	.348	.336
All Batters Thereafter			139	32	5	24	23	.230	.410	.343

Loves to face: Hal Morris (0-for-6)
    Robby Thompson (.100, 1-for-10)
    Matt Williams (.071, 1-for-14, 1 HR)
Hates to face: Darren Daulton (2-for-2, 2 HR, 1 BB)
    Willie McGee (.667, 6-for-9)
    Eddie Murray (.500, 4-for-8, 1 HR)

Miscellaneous statistics: Ground outs-to-air outs ratio: 1.09 last season, 1.09 for career.... Induced 7 double plays in 139 opportunities (one per 20).... Allowed 28 doubles, 5 triples in 153⅔ innings.... Allowed 9 first-inning runs in 22 starts (2.86 ERA).... Batting support: 4.14 runs per start.... Record of 7–9, 3.07 ERA as a starter; 0–2, 6.93 ERA in 15 relief appearances.... Stranded 4 inherited runners, allowed 2 to score (67%).... Opposing base stealers: 12-for-15 (80%); 0 pickoffs, 4 balks (3d most in N.L.).

Comments: Hitless in 38 at-bats last season, the 8th-highest total in major league history by a player without a hit. Bob Buhl holds the record: 0-for-70 in 1962; he's followed by Bill Wight (61 AB in 1960), Ron Herbel (47 in 1964), Karl Drews (46 in 1949), Ernie Koob (41 in 1916), Randy Tate (41 in 1975), and Ed Rakow (39 in 1964). Herbel was hitless over the first 55 at-bats of his major league career.... Didn't reach the ninth inning in any of his 22 starts.... Faced 50 consecutive batters with runners on base without allowing a hit (June 8–29), the longest such streak in the 13 seasons we've kept track.... Opponents batted .195 during the first inning, the 5th lowest among N.L. pitchers. His first-inning strikeout rate (8.59 per nine innings) was his highest in any frame.... Led N.L. rookies with 11 losses, which might pass for a mark of honor. Consecutive leaders in the 1960s included Tug McGraw (1965), Ken Holtzman (1966), Tom Seaver (1967), and Nolan Ryan (1968). Dwight Gooden and Ron Darling shared the lead in 1984. Other recent (and admittedly more typical) leaders were Pete Smith (1988), Ken Hill (1989), and Pat Combs (1990).... Kile was one of eight different rookies to lose at least one game for Houston last season. Astros' rookies combined for a 23–29 record, which represents both the most wins and the most losses by any N.L. staff. The roll call: Ryan Bowen (6–4), Chris Gardner (1–2), Jeff Juden (0–2), Kile (7–11), Rob Mallicoat (0–2), Al Osuna (7–6), Dean Wilkins (2–1), and Brian Williams (0–1).

Les Lancaster

Throws Right

Chicago Cubs	W-L	ERA	AB	H	HR	BB	SO	BA	SA	OBA
Season	9-7	3.52	587	150	13	49	102	.256	.376	.315
vs. Left-Handers			310	81	6	33	46	.261	.374	.335
vs. Right-Handers			277	69	7	16	56	.249	.379	.292
vs. Ground-Ballers			262	60	4	22	50	.229	.328	.295
vs. Fly-Ballers			325	90	9	27	52	.277	.415	.331
Home Games	7-2	3.46	310	77	8	21	57	.248	.381	.293
Road Games	2-5	3.59	277	73	5	28	45	.264	.372	.339
Grass Fields	8-4	3.63	417	110	10	34	77	.264	.398	.321
Artificial Turf	1-3	3.25	170	40	3	15	25	.235	.324	.301
April	0-0	4.11	56	11	2	4	7	.196	.357	.250
May	2-1	2.53	84	21	3	3	14	.250	.405	.273
June	2-1	2.57	133	33	1	15	26	.248	.338	.329
July	3-2	5.71	157	44	6	10	26	.280	.433	.325
August	2-3	2.91	85	22	1	3	15	.259	.376	.284
Sept./Oct.	0-0	2.08	72	19	0	14	14	.264	.306	.389
Leading Off Inn.			144	32	3	9	27	.222	.313	.273
Bases Empty			350	90	6	22	62	.257	.357	.305
Runners On			237	60	7	27	40	.253	.405	.330
Runners/Scor. Pos.			134	42	6	17	23	.313	.530	.389
Runners On/2 Out			107	22	0	18	10	.206	.280	.274
Scor. Pos./2 Out			69	18	0	5	11	.261	.362	.311
Late-Inning Pressure			121	36	1	6	25	.298	.355	.331
Leading Off			32	8	0	2	7	.250	.250	.294
Runners On			43	15	1	4	9	.349	.488	.404
Runners/Scor. Pos.			23	10	1	3	5	.435	.652	.500
First 9 Batters			376	91	9	33	76	.242	.375	.304
Second 9 Batters			112	29	3	9	12	.259	.393	.314
All Batters Thereafter			99	30	1	7	14	.303	.364	.361

Loves to face: Mariano Duncan (0-for-10)
    Barry Larkin (0-for-8)
    Orlando Merced (0-for-8)
Hates to face: Bobby Bonilla (.571, 4-for-7, 7 BB, 2 SO)
    Dale Murphy (.364, 8-for-22, 2 HR)
    Darryl Strawberry (.429, 9-for-21, 2 HR)

Miscellaneous statistics: Ground outs-to-air outs ratio: 1.01 last season, 1.01 for career.... Induced 6 double plays in 119 opportunities (one per 20).... Allowed 26 doubles, 3 triples in 156 innings.... Allowed 7 first-inning runs in 11 starts (5.73 ERA).... Batting support: 4.91 runs per start.... Record of 5–3, 4.48 ERA as a starter; 4–4, 2.69 ERA in 53 relief appearances.... Stranded 23 inherited runners, allowed 18 to score (56%), 5th-lowest rate in N.L.... Opposing base stealers: 14-for-28 (50%); 1 pickoff, 2 balks.

Comments: The departure of Rick Sutcliffe leaves Lancaster and Greg Maddux as the senior members of the Cubs' pitching staff. No one else has pitched for Chicago in every season since 1987.... ERA breakdown by battery-mate: 2.20 in 45 innings with Hector Villanueva, 3.19 in 42⅓ innings with Damon Berryhill, and 4.82 in 61⅔ innings with Rick Wilkins.... Lancaster's total of 194 relief appearances ranks ninth in the history of the Cubs franchise. This season, he could pass Turk Lown (211) and Phil Regan (245). The franchise record is 452, held by Lee Smith.... The only pitcher with both a complete game and a save in each of the past two seasons. The last pitcher to do that for three years in a row: Jerry Koosman (four years, 1980–83).... Has appeared as both a starter and a reliever in four of his five seasons in the majors. Career records: 16–7 (4.54 ERA) in 38 starts, 18–16 (3.29 ERA) in 194 relief appearances.... Has never committed an error in 232 career games. He's handled more chances (117) than any pitcher in major league history who never committed an error.... Opposing fly-ball hitters have batted 26 points higher than ground-ballers (.276 and .249, respectively).... Opponents have a career average of .219 with two outs and runners in scoring position, compared to an overall average of .263.... Opponents have a career average of .357 (20-for-56) with the bases loaded, including three home runs.

Bill Landrum

Throws Right

Pittsburgh Pirates	W-L	ERA	AB	H	HR	BB	SO	BA	SA	OBA
Season	4-4	3.18	301	76	4	19	45	.252	.329	.296
vs. Left-Handers			139	38	2	13	19	.273	.360	.336
vs. Right-Handers			162	38	2	6	26	.235	.302	.260
vs. Ground-Ballers			122	29	3	5	18	.238	.328	.268
vs. Fly-Ballers			183	48	1	14	27	.262	.328	.313
Home Games	1-1	1.80	132	26	0	6	23	.197	.220	.232
Road Games	3-3	4.35	169	50	4	13	22	.296	.414	.344
Grass Fields	3-2	4.81	98	30	4	7	14	.306	.449	.349
Artificial Turf	1-2	2.42	203	46	0	12	31	.227	.271	.270
April	0-0	0.00	36	6	0	1	7	.167	.222	.189
May	0-0	2.45	55	11	0	2	7	.200	.273	.228
June	1-0	3.48	48	18	0	1	5	.375	.417	.388
July	0-2	5.52	61	19	2	6	8	.311	.443	.368
August	1-2	1.80	52	7	0	4	12	.135	.135	.196
Sept./Oct.	2-0	5.56	49	15	2	5	6	.306	.449	.370
Leading Off Inn.			65	15	3	1	7	.231	.415	.242
Bases Empty			160	39	4	3	27	.244	.344	.258
Runners On			141	37	0	16	18	.262	.312	.335
Runners/Scor. Pos.			82	23	0	13	9	.280	.354	.375
Runners On/2 Out			74	25	0	11	7	.338	.392	.424
Scor. Pos./2 Out			48	15	0	9	5	.313	.396	.421
Late-Inning Pressure			162	41	3	12	25	.253	.333	.305
Leading Off			34	7	2	0	4	.206	.412	.206
Runners On			77	20	0	10	11	.260	.286	.345
Runners/Scor. Pos.			48	9	0	8	5	.188	.208	.304
First 9 Batters			291	72	4	19	44	.247	.326	.293
Second 9 Batters			10	4	0	0	1	.400	.400	.400
All Batters Thereafter			0	0	0	0	0	—	—	—

Loves to face: Kevin Bass (0-for-11)
Darren Daulton (0-for-10)
Jose Oquendo (0-for-10)
Hates to face: Billy Hatcher (.600, 9-for-15)
Dave Magadan (.714, 5-for-7)
Jerome Walton (.364, 4-for-11, 2 HR)

Miscellaneous statistics: Ground outs-to-air outs ratio: 0.91 last season, 1.22 for career.... Induced 3 double plays in 54 opportunities (one per 18).... Allowed 7 doubles, 2 triples in 76⅓ innings.... Saved 17 games in 23 opportunities (74%).... Stranded 24 inherited runners, allowed 10 to score (71%).... Opposing base stealers: 9-for-10 (90%); 1 pickoff, 2 balks.

Comments: Had a stretch of 36 games in which he allowed only two of 22 inherited runners to score.... Had 15 saves by the end of June, but only two more for the rest of the season, and none after August 29. Rosario Rodriguez led the Bucs' bullpen with five saves after September 1.... Landrum's total of 30 saves over the last two seasons ranks 26th among major league pitchers, but it was enough to lead the division-winning Pirates in each of the last two seasons (13 in 1990, 17 last season). The lowest save totals for pitchers who led division winners (excluding 1981): Doug Corbett, 1982 Angels (8); Eric King, 1987 Tigers (9); Grant Jackson and Bob Reynolds, 1973 Orioles (9). The fewest to lead an N.L. division winner was 12, by Dave Giusti (1974 Pirates) and Scott Garrelts (1987 Giants).... Landrum's career high in saves is 26 in 1989, when the Pirates finished in fifth place.... You can get carried away with relief pitchers' ERAs, but this is rather striking. Landrum compiled a 5.16 ERA in 90⅔ innings over three seasons with the Reds and Cubs (1986–88), compared to 2.32 in three seasons of full-time work with the Pirates.... Landrum didn't make his breakthrough with Pittsburgh until he was 30 years old. He ain't been around long, but Landrum's two weeks older than Von Hayes.

Craig Lefferts

Throws Left

San Diego Padres	W-L	ERA	AB	H	HR	BB	SO	BA	SA	OBA
Season	1-6	3.91	260	74	5	14	48	.285	.408	.318
vs. Left-Handers			64	18	1	3	16	.281	.422	.309
vs. Right-Handers			196	56	4	11	32	.286	.403	.321
vs. Ground-Ballers			104	27	3	5	26	.260	.394	.292
vs. Fly-Ballers			156	47	2	9	22	.301	.417	.335
Home Games	0-5	3.46	156	41	3	9	29	.263	.391	.302
Road Games	1-1	4.61	104	33	2	5	19	.317	.433	.342
Grass Fields	0-6	3.91	191	54	3	12	32	.283	.408	.321
Artificial Turf	1-0	3.93	69	20	2	2	16	.290	.406	.310
April	0-1	4.32	32	9	0	2	6	.281	.438	.324
May	0-1	4.82	70	18	4	7	11	.257	.457	.321
June	0-2	4.63	43	12	0	0	4	.279	.326	.273
July	0-0	3.68	25	6	0	3	5	.240	.400	.345
August	1-1	4.66	42	16	0	0	6	.381	.452	.372
Sept./Oct.	0-1	1.35	48	13	1	2	16	.271	.354	.288
Leading Off Inn.			51	17	0	3	6	.333	.392	.370
Bases Empty			120	38	3	8	21	.317	.458	.359
Runners On			140	36	2	6	27	.257	.364	.283
Runners/Scor. Pos.			70	20	0	5	16	.286	.357	.321
Runners On/2 Out			60	15	0	1	14	.250	.317	.262
Scor. Pos./2 Out			26	7	0	1	8	.269	.346	.296
Late-Inning Pressure			186	52	4	10	29	.280	.403	.315
Leading Off			38	11	0	3	4	.289	.368	.341
Runners On			97	24	2	3	17	.247	.351	.269
Runners/Scor. Pos.			42	13	0	3	9	.310	.357	.347
First 9 Batters			250	72	5	14	47	.288	.412	.322
Second 9 Batters			10	2	0	0	1	.200	.300	.200
All Batters Thereafter			0	0	0	0	0	—	—	—

Loves to face: Bobby Bonilla (.059, 1-for-17)
Mark Carreon (.100, 1-for-10, 5 SO)
Juan Samuel (.091, 2-for-22, 2 BB)
Hates to face: Bill Doran (.467, 14-for-30)
Howard Johnson (.429, 6-for-14, 6 BB, 5 SO)
Willie McGee (.379, 11-for-29, 1 HR, 0 BB)

Miscellaneous statistics: Ground outs-to-air outs ratio: 0.91 last season, 0.84 for career.... Induced 4 double plays in 72 opportunities (one per 18).... Allowed 11 doubles, 3 triples in 69 innings.... Saved 23 games in 35 opportunities (66%).... Stranded 18 inherited runners, allowed 9 to score (67%).... Opposing base stealers: 6-for-10 (60%); 1 pickoff, 1 balk.

Comments: Walked an average of 1.83 batters per nine innings, the lowest rate of his career, but last season was the first time in his nine major league seasons that he allowed more than one hit per inning (9.65 per nine).... Pitched in Late-Inning Pressure Situations in 46 of 54 appearances.... One of six pitchers in major league history to appear in at least 50 games in nine consecutive seasons. Only two, Ron Perranoski and Lee Smith, had 10-year streaks. Others with nine: Roy Face, Rollie Fingers, and Jesse Orosco. Lefferts's streak spans his entire career.... Hasn't committed an error in 265 games since August 1987. Don't get excited yet; he's still a couple seasons away from Lee Smith's all-time record of 417 consecutive errorless games by a pitcher. (You can bet that no starting pitcher will ever break that record.)... Has a career record of 0–7 vs. the Mets, 9–1 vs. the Dodgers.... Lefferts's 348 games in a Padres uniform is the most by any pitcher in franchise history. Eric Show is the only other Padres pitcher with at least 300 games.... Who's the best reliever ever to pitch for the Cubs, Giants, and Padres? Sorry, Craig, but we've got to go with Goose Gossage on this one.... Opponents have a career average of .180 with two outs and runners in scoring position, compared to an overall average of .242.... Opponents have a career batting average of .218 in day games, .256 in night games.... One of two pitchers with at least 20 saves for N.L. teams in each of the past two seasons. The other: John Franco.

Charlie Leibrandt
Throws Left

Atlanta Braves	W-L	ERA	AB	H	HR	BB	SO	BA	SA	OBA
Season	15-13	3.49	864	212	18	56	128	.245	.363	.292
vs. Left-Handers			190	52	2	13	31	.274	.389	.319
vs. Right-Handers			674	160	16	43	97	.237	.356	.285
vs. Ground-Ballers			396	105	7	16	58	.265	.374	.292
vs. Fly-Ballers			468	107	11	40	70	.229	.355	.293
Home Games	6-8	4.35	388	105	11	28	55	.271	.420	.318
Road Games	9-5	2.81	476	107	7	28	73	.225	.317	.271
Grass Fields	10-11	3.33	635	154	15	36	93	.243	.364	.284
Artificial Turf	5-2	3.94	229	58	3	20	35	.253	.362	.316
April	2-2	2.97	125	33	1	9	21	.264	.344	.321
May	2-2	2.77	148	38	3	6	20	.257	.358	.284
June	3-1	2.55	127	23	1	10	10	.181	.268	.237
July	2-4	7.31	133	47	3	9	18	.353	.511	.403
August	4-2	2.63	150	34	5	7	29	.227	.367	.259
Sept./Oct.	2-2	3.31	181	37	5	15	30	.204	.337	.264
Leading Off Inn.			225	50	6	12	27	.222	.329	.262
Bases Empty			546	128	8	31	77	.234	.317	.278
Runners On			318	84	10	25	51	.264	.443	.316
Runners/Scor. Pos.			170	48	8	19	25	.282	.518	.350
Runners On/2 Out			134	23	3	16	22	.172	.269	.260
Scor. Pos./2 Out			80	13	2	14	14	.162	.287	.287
Late-Inning Pressure			73	16	1	3	5	.219	.274	.250
Leading Off			21	5	1	1	2	.238	.429	.273
Runners On			25	5	0	0	2	.200	.200	.200
Runners/Scor. Pos.			11	4	0	0	0	.364	.364	.364
First 9 Batters			292	66	6	21	49	.226	.336	.281
Second 9 Batters			296	76	8	17	52	.257	.402	.298
All Batters Thereafter			276	70	4	18	27	.254	.351	.299

Loves to face: Kevin Elster (.125, 2-for-16)
Darryl Strawberry (.143, 2-for-14)
Tim Wallach (0-for-12)

Hates to face: Brett Butler (.389, 14-for-36, 2 HR)
Mark Davidson (.417, 10-for-24, 0 SO)
Ryne Sandberg (.462, 6-for-13, 2 HR)

Miscellaneous statistics: Ground outs-to-air outs ratio: 1.22 last season, 1.17 for career.... Induced 6 double plays in 145 opportunities (one per 24), 3d-worst rate in majors.... Allowed 38 doubles, 5 triples in 229⅔ innings.... Allowed 13 first-inning runs in 36 starts (2.50 ERA, 5th lowest in N.L.).... Batting support: 4.00 runs per start.... Opposing base stealers: 35-for-46 (76%), most steals in majors; 12 pickoffs (most in N.L.), 3 balks.

Comments: Has made seven postseason starts without a victory, tying the all-time record held by Ed Figueroa. (Only two others have made even six starts without a win: Doyle Alexander and Doc Gooden.) But Leibrandt pitched into the seventh inning in five of those seven starts, lost one of them 1–0, and blew ninth-inning shutouts in two others.... That's okay; Leibrandt won Game 7 of the 1985 N.L.C.S. with a 5⅓-inning relief stint.... Had never allowed a postseason home run until Game 1 of the 1991 World Series, when Greg Gagne took him deep. Then came Kirby Puckett in Game 6.... ERA in home games was 2d highest among qualifying N.L. pitchers.... July ERA was 2d highest in the league, behind that of John Smoltz (7.85).... Ended the regular season by retiring the last 23 batters he faced leading off innings, matching Andy Benes for the longest streak in the N.L. last season.... Allowed five hits, including two HRs, in eight ABs with the bases loaded.... One of two pitchers to lose more than 10 games in each of the last six seasons. Kevin Gross, whose streak is seven years long, is the other.... One of three pitchers with shutouts in each of the last seven seasons. The others: Roger Clemens, whose streak extends to eight years, and Dennis Martinez. Dave Stieb's 12-year streak came to an end last season.... At the plate, he was hitless in 40 at-bats against right-handed pitchers last season.

Greg Maddux
Throws Right

Chicago Cubs	W-L	ERA	AB	H	HR	BB	SO	BA	SA	OBA
Season	15-11	3.35	979	232	18	66	198	.237	.345	.288
vs. Left-Handers			587	148	14	44	113	.252	.378	.306
vs. Right-Handers			392	84	4	22	85	.214	.296	.262
vs. Ground-Ballers			407	93	4	28	88	.229	.305	.284
vs. Fly-Ballers			572	139	14	38	110	.243	.374	.292
Home Games	7-5	3.45	479	118	10	36	94	.246	.374	.301
Road Games	8-6	3.26	500	114	8	30	104	.228	.318	.276
Grass Fields	12-8	3.40	688	162	15	49	139	.235	.353	.290
Artificial Turf	3-3	3.24	291	70	3	17	59	.241	.326	.285
April	2-1	3.76	95	23	0	7	20	.242	.305	.294
May	3-2	3.00	177	38	6	13	31	.215	.367	.272
June	1-3	4.01	164	39	5	14	43	.238	.384	.309
July	2-0	3.95	171	47	2	7	33	.275	.351	.307
August	3-2	3.92	156	43	3	16	30	.276	.410	.341
Sept./Oct.	4-3	2.20	216	42	2	9	41	.194	.264	.228
Leading Off Inn.			252	59	5	16	45	.234	.333	.288
Bases Empty			610	134	8	41	125	.220	.305	.273
Runners On			369	98	10	25	73	.266	.412	.313
Runners/Scor. Pos.			211	55	4	18	46	.261	.398	.318
Runners On/2 Out			158	40	7	13	28	.253	.456	.314
Scor. Pos./2 Out			97	21	4	9	20	.216	.402	.290
Late-Inning Pressure			122	37	2	7	25	.303	.418	.344
Leading Off			32	10	0	1	5	.313	.375	.333
Runners On			49	20	1	6	11	.408	.571	.474
Runners/Scor. Pos.			35	14	1	6	7	.400	.629	.476
First 9 Batters			295	57	5	26	73	.193	.302	.260
Second 9 Batters			306	71	6	21	56	.232	.343	.290
All Batters Thereafter			378	104	7	19	69	.275	.381	.310

Loves to face: Charlie Hayes (.087, 2-for-23)
Dale Murphy (.065, 2-for-31)
Eric Yelding (.115, 3-for-26)

Hates to face: Luis Gonzalez (.583, 7-for-12, 3 HR)
Tony Gwynn (.559, 19-for-34, 0 SO)
Howard Johnson (.339, 19-for-56, 5 HR)

Miscellaneous statistics: Ground outs-to-air outs ratio: 1.88 last season, 5th highest in N.L.; 1.93 for career.... Induced 14 double plays in 164 opportunities (one per 12).... Allowed 34 doubles, 9 triples (tied for most in N.L.) in 263 innings.... Allowed 13 first-inning runs in 37 starts (2.68 ERA).... Batting support: 4.22 runs per start.... Opposing base stealers: 25-for-32 (78%); 5 pickoffs, 3 balks.

Comments: The only National League pitcher to win at least 15 games in each of the last four seasons, and the first Cubs pitcher to do so since Ferguson Jenkins (1967–72). The team record: eight years in a row, by Three Finger Brown (1904–11).... Led all major league pitchers with 37 starts, and led N.L. pitchers with 263 innings. The last Cubs pitcher to lead the league in innings pitched was Jenkins in 1971, but before that you have to go all the way back to Charlie Root in 1927.... Led the National League with 100 three-up, three-down innings.... Fell two strike-outs shy of the 200 mark. Since 1900, only four Cubs pitchers have reached 200: Long Tom Hughes (1901), Orval Overall (1909), Ken Holtzman (1970), and Fergie Jenkins (1967–71).... Posted a 2.33 ERA in 108⅓ innings with Hector Villanueva behind the plate, 4.07 in 154⅔ innings with other catchers.... Had a streak of 36 consecutive batters faced with runners in scoring position without allowing a hit (May 17–June 11).... Ended the season with a streak of 21 starts in which he did not allow a home run to a right-handed batter.... Lost 14 of his first 16 career decisions in day games, but has raised that mark to 38–39. His night-game record: 37–25.... Opponents have a career average of .276 with runners on base, .244 with the bases empty.... Career batting average of .274 by opposing left-handed batters, .236 by right-handers.

Mike Maddux   Throws Right

San Diego Padres	W-L	ERA	AB	H	HR	BB	SO	BA	SA	OBA
Season	7-2	2.46	353	78	4	27	57	.221	.300	.277
vs. Left-Handers			171	42	0	13	27	.246	.298	.296
vs. Right-Handers			182	36	4	14	30	.198	.302	.259
vs. Ground-Ballers			144	28	0	9	21	.194	.229	.245
vs. Fly-Ballers			209	50	4	18	36	.239	.349	.298
Home Games	5-1	1.75	175	31	1	12	29	.177	.229	.234
Road Games	2-1	3.23	178	47	3	15	28	.264	.371	.318
Grass Fields	6-1	2.86	259	57	4	19	43	.220	.320	.275
Artificial Turf	1-1	1.37	94	21	0	8	14	.223	.245	.282
April	2-1	3.86	56	18	1	5	9	.321	.500	.371
May	0-0	3.06	64	18	0	7	8	.281	.297	.347
June	1-0	1.40	68	12	1	1	9	.176	.265	.188
July	1-0	0.00	38	3	0	5	7	.079	.079	.186
August	1-1	6.75	55	17	2	4	8	.309	.491	.356
Sept./Oct.	2-0	0.82	72	10	0	5	16	.139	.153	.205
Leading Off Inn.			88	23	4	6	14	.261	.477	.316
Bases Empty			213	47	4	12	35	.221	.324	.265
Runners On			140	31	0	15	22	.221	.264	.293
Runners/Scor. Pos.			92	17	0	10	16	.185	.217	.260
Runners On/2 Out			57	5	0	8	11	.088	.088	.200
Scor. Pos./2 Out			41	3	0	6	7	.073	.073	.191
Late-Inning Pressure			85	18	1	8	17	.212	.259	.284
Leading Off			20	4	1	4	5	.200	.350	.360
Runners On			34	9	0	2	5	.265	.294	.297
Runners/Scor. Pos.			21	7	0	0	3	.333	.381	.318
First 9 Batters			308	64	3	23	50	.208	.286	.263
Second 9 Batters			44	14	1	4	6	.318	.409	.375
All Batters Thereafter			1	0	0	0	1	.000	.000	.000

Loves to face: Jay Bell (0-for-8)
Barry Bonds (.150, 3-for-20, 2 2B)
Andy Van Slyke (.100, 1-for-10)
Hates to face: Sid Bream (.462, 6-for-13)
Mark Grace (.471, 8-for-17, 1 HR)
Robby Thompson (.667, 6-for-9, 1 HR)

Miscellaneous statistics: Ground outs-to-air outs ratio: 2.22 last season, 2.05 for career.... Induced 7 double plays in 65 opportunities (one per 9.3).... Allowed 10 doubles, 3 triples in 98⅔ innings.... Stranded 35 inherited runners, allowed 9 to score (80%), 5th-highest rate in N.L.... Opposing base stealers: 5-for-12 (42%, 5th-lowest rate in N.L.); 1 pickoff, 0 balks.

Comments: Among N.L. pitchers with as many innings pitched as Maddux, only Zane Smith, Roger McDowell, and Wally Whitehurst had higher ground outs-to-air outs ratio: ios. Maddux's average peaked at 4.17 on May 18, but was only 1.83 after that. He induced only three DP grounders in 39 opportunities after that turning point.... ERA and opponents' batting average were both career lows—particularly impressive in a season in which he also set a career high in innings pitched. Career record prior to 1991: 10–14, with a 4.68 ERA.... Opposing base stealers were 0-for-3 in Late-Inning Pressure Situations.... Allowed only four of 24 inherited runners to score after May 17.... Total of 171 at-bats by left-handed batters is the most against any pitcher who did not allow a home run to a lefty swinger last season.... Held right-handed batters hitless in 36 consecutive plate appearances, the longest streak by any N.L. pitcher last season (June 17–July 31).... Right-handers outslugged left-handers, despite the fact that left-handers had a higher batting average, both last season and throughout his career.... Career record of 8–13 (4.88 ERA) in 36 starts, 9–3 (3.17 ERA) in 103 relief appearances.... Had only one save in 40 relief appearances prior to 1991.... Opponents have a career average of .212 with two outs and runners in scoring position, compared to an overall average of .267.... Has held opposing ground-ball hitters under .200 in each of the last two seasons.

Dennis Martinez   Throws Right

Montreal Expos	W-L	ERA	AB	H	HR	BB	SO	BA	SA	OBA
Season	14-11	2.39	829	187	9	62	123	.226	.311	.282
vs. Left-Handers			489	114	4	51	73	.233	.301	.304
vs. Right-Handers			340	73	5	11	50	.215	.326	.247
vs. Ground-Ballers			396	81	3	25	66	.205	.275	.254
vs. Fly-Ballers			457	107	6	39	62	.234	.328	.297
Home Games	7-4	2.16	359	86	5	21	51	.240	.340	.280
Road Games	7-7	2.57	470	101	4	41	72	.215	.289	.283
Grass Fields	4-2	2.51	238	52	3	20	36	.218	.311	.284
Artificial Turf	10-9	2.35	591	135	6	42	87	.228	.311	.281
April	3-2	1.23	132	23	0	11	23	.174	.220	.241
May	3-2	3.48	162	46	4	8	23	.284	.426	.318
June	3-1	1.37	171	38	2	15	27	.222	.298	.289
July	2-1	2.13	138	30	0	9	17	.217	.246	.265
August	1-3	4.09	126	29	2	12	19	.230	.365	.297
Sept./Oct.	2-2	2.36	100	21	1	7	14	.210	.290	.269
Leading Off Inn.			218	49	1	7	28	.225	.289	.249
Bases Empty			511	117	6	25	70	.229	.315	.266
Runners On			318	70	3	37	53	.220	.305	.305
Runners/Scor. Pos.			193	38	1	33	38	.197	.285	.316
Runners On/2 Out			143	31	2	17	28	.217	.308	.309
Scor. Pos./2 Out			101	20	1	16	22	.198	.277	.314
Late-Inning Pressure			108	24	1	7	8	.222	.287	.276
Leading Off			30	4	0	1	1	.133	.133	.161
Runners On			39	10	0	2	4	.256	.308	.293
Runners/Scor. Pos.			17	5	0	1	1	.294	.412	.333
First 9 Batters			252	53	4	19	43	.210	.298	.264
Second 9 Batters			256	51	1	17	44	.199	.285	.255
All Batters Thereafter			321	83	4	26	36	.259	.343	.317

Loves to face: Gary Carter (.071, 2-for-28, 0 BB)
Kal Daniels (.091, 3-for-33, 1 HR, 3 BB)
Rich Gedman (0-for-20)
Hates to face: Bip Roberts (.500, 14-for-28)
Ryne Sandberg (.358, 19-for-53, 4 HR)
Don Slaught (.500, 8-for-16)

Miscellaneous statistics: Ground outs-to-air outs ratio: 1.38 last season, 1.21 for career.... Induced 14 double plays in 144 opportunities (one per 10).... Allowed 32 doubles, 6 triples in 222 innings.... Allowed 15 first-inning runs in 31 starts (3.48 ERA).... Batting support: 3.48 runs per start, 7th-lowest average in N.L.... Opposing base stealers: 22-for-26 (85%); 4 pickoffs, 0 balks.

Comments: Established a career low in ERA more than four months after turning 36. Over the past 30 years, only one other pitcher that old set a personal best (considering only seasons of 20 or more starts): Joe Niekro in 1982 (2.47). The oldest pitcher ever to do so was Hall of Famer Ted Lyons, with a league-leading 2.10 mark in 1942 at age 41.... Martinez posted a 2.17 ERA in 153⅓ innings with Ron Hassey behind the plate, 2.88 in 68⅔ innings with other batterymates.... Average of one home run allowed every 24.7 innings, also the best of his career, was 3d best among pitchers who qualified for the 1991 ERA title. Prior to 1991, Martinez allowed a career average of one HR every 10.2 innings.... Joins Steve Rogers as the only members of the Expos to lead the league in ERA.... Total of 69 wins with the Expos ranks fourth in franchise history, behind Steve Rogers (158), Bryn Smith (81), and Bill Gullickson (72).... Shared the league lead in complete games with Tom Glavine at nine, the lowest total ever to lead either league.... Pitched 25 innings against the Dodgers last season without allowing an earned run.... Matchup of Martinez and Tom Browning on August 28 was the first between pitchers who had previously thrown perfect games since 1966, when Sandy Koufax defeated Jim Bunning.... Had a 1–5 record in games in which he was charged with an unearned run.... Among pitchers active at the end of 1991, only Nolan Ryan (733), Frank Tanana (553), and Jack Morris (443) have started more games than Martinez (410).

Ramon Martinez — Throws Right

Los Angeles Dodgers	W-L	ERA	AB	H	HR	BB	SO	BA	SA	OBA
Season	17-13	3.27	828	190	18	69	150	.229	.337	.293
vs. Left-Handers			453	102	7	48	81	.225	.318	.302
vs. Right-Handers			375	88	11	21	69	.235	.360	.282
vs. Ground-Ballers			385	90	4	34	75	.234	.301	.299
vs. Fly-Ballers			443	100	14	35	75	.226	.368	.288
Home Games	9-4	2.91	386	82	7	37	85	.212	.288	.282
Road Games	8-9	3.59	442	108	11	32	65	.244	.380	.302
Grass Fields	14-10	3.26	660	154	15	53	125	.233	.336	.295
Artificial Turf	3-3	3.30	168	36	3	16	25	.214	.339	.285
April	3-1	2.17	109	21	2	5	21	.193	.284	.233
May	5-1	3.07	157	36	3	12	28	.229	.344	.284
June	2-1	2.61	135	29	2	13	26	.215	.296	.293
July	4-2	1.24	161	36	0	8	21	.224	.261	.257
August	1-4	6.37	123	35	5	8	21	.285	.455	.331
Sept./Oct.	2-4	4.85	143	33	6	23	33	.231	.392	.349
Leading Off Inn.			207	45	4	17	37	.217	.329	.286
Bases Empty			505	106	9	41	96	.210	.311	.276
Runners On			323	84	9	28	54	.260	.378	.319
Runners/Scor. Pos.			190	45	4	14	36	.237	.332	.287
Runners On/2 Out			145	32	4	17	24	.221	.338	.302
Scor. Pos./2 Out			102	18	2	9	19	.176	.275	.243
Late-Inning Pressure			79	11	1	7	17	.139	.190	.218
Leading Off			19	3	0	5	3	.158	.211	.360
Runners On			28	2	1	1	8	.071	.179	.103
Runners/Scor. Pos.			10	0	0	1	4	.000	.000	.091
First 9 Batters			270	62	9	21	55	.230	.367	.293
Second 9 Batters			261	61	4	24	48	.234	.349	.301
All Batters Thereafter			297	67	5	24	47	.226	.300	.286

Loves to face: Jay Bell (0-for-10)
Lonnie Smith (0-for-12)
Robby Thompson (.138, 4-for-29, 0 BB)
Hates to face: Will Clark (.400, 12-for-30, 3 HR)
Billy Hatcher (.529, 9-for-17)
Howard Johnson (.350, 7-for-20, 4 2B, 2 HR)

Miscellaneous statistics: Ground outs-to-air outs ratio: 0.76 last season, 5th lowest in N.L.; 0.79 for career.... Induced 6 double plays in 149 opportunities (one per 25), 2d-worst rate in majors.... Allowed 33 doubles, 1 triple in 220⅓ innings.... Allowed 15 first-inning runs in 33 starts (3.27 ERA).... Batting support: 4.45 runs per start.... Opposing base stealers: 16-for-25 (64%); 3 pick-offs, 0 balks.

Comments: Won 10 of his first 12 starts, but only seven of 21 after that. Posted a 3–8 record with a 5.50 ERA after August 1, compared to 14–5 record with a 2.25 ERA through the end of July.... His August ERA was 3d highest in the league (minimum: 25 IP).... Needed only six wins in his last 12 starts to become the first Dodgers pitcher since Sandy Koufax (1965–66) to win 20 games in back-to-back seasons. In 25 years since then, 10 Dodgers pitchers have won 20 games, but none could repeat. The last N.L. pitcher to do that was Joaquin Andujar (1984–85).... Total of 37 wins over past two seasons is highest in National League. Doug Drabek shared the lead with Martinez.... Career average of 7.41 strikeouts per nine innings is 2d highest in Dodgers' history, behind Koufax (9.27 per nine innings; minimum: 500 IP).... Struck out 8.56 batters per nine innings in 1990, but only 6.13 last season.... Over the first three years of his career, opponents had batted no higher than .194 during his first pass through the order.... Opponents' career batting average (.223) is 5th lowest among active pitchers (minimum: 2000 AB), although it has increased slightly in each of his seasons in the majors; year by year since 1988: .216, .219, .221, .229.... Has won his last seven decisions against the Padres.... Opponents have a career average of .241 with runners on base, .213 with the bases empty.... Opponents have a career average of .204 at Dodger Stadium, .250 on other grass fields, and .238 on artificial surfaces.

Roger McDowell — Throws Right

Phillies/Dodgers	W-L	ERA	AB	H	HR	BB	SO	BA	SA	OBA
Season	9-9	2.93	381	100	4	48	50	.262	.357	.346
vs. Left-Handers			197	53	2	36	25	.269	.371	.381
vs. Right-Handers			184	47	2	12	25	.255	.342	.303
vs. Ground-Ballers			149	40	1	13	16	.268	.342	.329
vs. Fly-Ballers			232	60	3	35	34	.259	.366	.356
Home Games	5-5	3.48	202	60	3	21	24	.297	.421	.364
Road Games	4-4	2.36	179	40	1	27	26	.223	.285	.325
Grass Fields	5-4	3.06	188	48	4	23	25	.255	.383	.333
Artificial Turf	4-5	2.81	193	52	0	25	25	.269	.332	.357
April	3-0	0.98	67	13	1	6	9	.194	.284	.260
May	0-1	1.88	50	11	0	8	5	.220	.240	.328
June	0-4	5.48	90	30	0	16	11	.333	.433	.440
July	0-1	5.40	22	7	0	2	3	.318	.364	.375
August	2-2	3.27	77	19	2	7	13	.247	.390	.302
Sept./Oct.	4-1	1.77	75	20	1	9	9	.267	.373	.345
Leading Off Inn.			87	24	0	6	12	.276	.402	.323
Bases Empty			192	54	4	14	24	.281	.422	.330
Runners On			189	46	0	34	26	.243	.291	.360
Runners/Scor. Pos.			132	30	0	29	17	.227	.258	.367
Runners On/2 Out			81	21	0	15	8	.259	.333	.388
Scor. Pos./2 Out			64	15	0	13	5	.234	.281	.380
Late-Inning Pressure			223	54	3	38	27	.242	.327	.350
Leading Off			57	16	0	5	8	.281	.351	.339
Runners On			104	22	0	25	13	.212	.250	.359
Runners/Scor. Pos.			69	11	0	24	10	.159	.174	.368
First 9 Batters			366	95	4	44	46	.260	.358	.341
Second 9 Batters			15	5	0	4	4	.333	.333	.450
All Batters Thereafter			0	0	0	0	0	—	—	—

Loves to face: Craig Biggio (.091, 1-for-11)
Andres Galarraga (.111, 2-for-18)
Gerald Perry (.071, 1-for-14, 1 2B)
Hates to face: Terry Pendleton (.367, 11-for-30, 3 HR)
Milt Thompson (.524, 11-for-21)
Andy Van Slyke (.455, 10-for-22, 2 HR)

Miscellaneous statistics: Ground outs-to-air outs ratio: 2.45 last season, 2.95 for career.... Induced 10 double plays in 97 opportunities (one per 10).... Allowed 20 doubles, 2 triples in 101⅓ innings.... Saved 10 games in 20 opportunities (50%).... Stranded 26 inherited runners, allowed 14 to score (65%).... Opposing base stealers: 12-for-16 (75%); 0 pickoffs, 0 balks.

Comments: Issued 20 intentional walks last season, the most in the majors, and six more than runner-up Scott Terry. That's almost as many as the White Sox' entire staff (25), and accounts for McDowell's deceptive career-high average of 4.26 walks per nine innings.... Has pitched at least 100 innings in three of the last seven years. Only one other N.L. relief pitcher has done that: Jeff D. Robinson, who pitched 100 innings in relief for the Pirates and Giants from 1986 through 1988.... Had the most decisions of any reliever in the majors last season, and tied John Franco and Barry Jones for most losses.... Lost each of his last six decisions in a Phillies uniform.... Career average of one home run per 23.8 innings is third best among pitchers active in 1991—or should we say barely breathing. The leaders: Doug Sisk, who earned a nice postseason bonus after he spent the last four months of the season on Atlanta's disabled list (one HR per 34.5 IP), and Joe Magrane, who spent the entire season on St. Louis's D.L. (one per 25.8 IP).... Career ground outs-to-air outs ratio: io is the highest among active pitchers (minimum: 1000 BFP). In the 17-year history of *The Player Analysis,* only Doug Corbett had a higher ratio.... One of only three pitchers in major league history to appear in a game for the Mets, Phillies, and Dodgers. The others: Roger Craig and Pat Zachry.

Kent Mercker — Throws Left

Atlanta Braves	W-L	ERA	AB	H	HR	BB	SO	BA	SA	OBA
Season	5-3	2.58	266	56	5	35	62	.211	.316	.303
vs. Left-Handers			72	14	1	13	20	.194	.250	.318
vs. Right-Handers			194	42	4	22	42	.216	.340	.297
vs. Ground-Ballers			124	25	1	22	28	.202	.242	.318
vs. Fly-Ballers			142	31	4	13	34	.218	.380	.288
Home Games	4-1	2.48	131	30	2	19	30	.229	.321	.331
Road Games	1-2	2.68	135	26	3	16	32	.193	.311	.275
Grass Fields	4-3	2.87	196	45	4	27	43	.230	.342	.323
Artificial Turf	1-0	1.80	70	11	1	8	19	.157	.243	.244
April	0-1	1.86	32	4	1	4	8	.125	.219	.222
May	2-1	1.46	45	11	2	2	13	.244	.422	.277
June	2-1	2.53	38	9	0	9	9	.237	.342	.388
July	0-0	2.63	52	11	1	7	9	.212	.288	.305
August	0-0	8.31	20	8	1	2	5	.400	.600	.455
Sept./Oct.	1-0	2.38	79	13	0	11	18	.165	.228	.264
Leading Off Inn.			61	11	0	12	15	.180	.279	.315
Bases Empty			143	31	1	26	38	.217	.322	.337
Runners On			123	25	4	9	24	.203	.309	.259
Runners/Scor. Pos.			66	16	3	8	12	.242	.379	.325
Runners On/2 Out			54	10	3	6	12	.185	.352	.267
Scor. Pos./2 Out			31	6	2	6	6	.194	.387	.324
Late-Inning Pressure			77	20	3	9	23	.260	.429	.341
Leading Off			18	4	0	1	6	.222	.389	.263
Runners On			36	10	2	5	10	.278	.444	.372
Runners/Scor. Pos.			24	8	1	4	6	.333	.458	.433
First 9 Batters			217	44	4	31	55	.203	.304	.304
Second 9 Batters			43	12	1	2	5	.279	.419	.304
All Batters Thereafter			6	0	0	2	2	.000	.000	.250

Loves to face: Craig Biggio (0-for-7)
Tony Fernandez (0-for-6)
Stan Javier (0-for-3, 3 SO)
Hates to face: Darren Lewis (1-for-1, 4 BB)
Andy Van Slyke (2-for-2, 1 2B, 1 HR)
John Wehner (.750, 3-for-4)

Miscellaneous statistics: Ground outs-to-air outs ratio: 1.15 last season, 0.96 for career.... Induced 5 double plays in 51 opportunities (one per 10).... Allowed 9 doubles, 2 triples in 73⅓ innings.... Stranded 4 inherited runners, allowed 7 to score (36%).... Opposing base stealers: 10-for-10 (100%); 0 pickoffs, 1 balk.

Comments: Was Atlanta's first-round selection in the 1986 draft, and the fifth pick overall. Two pitchers were selected before him: Greg Swindell (2d, by the Indians) and Kevin Brown (4th, by the Rangers). For more on the first round of the '86 draft, see the Thomas Howard comments.... Started and pitched six innings in a combined no-hitter against the Padres on September 11. It was the longest outing of his career in only his third start. He, Mark Wohlers, and Alejandro Pena became the first pitchers in National League history to team-up to pitch a no-hitter. That's hard to believe, considering that it's happened six times in American League history, most recently by the Orioles earlier last season.... Incidentally, Mercker led the International League in starts (27) as well as strikeouts (144) in 1989.... Allowed only two extra-base hits to left-handed batters last season: a double by Andy Van Slyke and a home run by Will Clark. Van Slyke, with a homer in 1990, is the only other lefty swinger to take him deep.... Opponents have a career average of .244 at Atlanta Stadium, .225 on other grass fields, and .205 on artificial surfaces. But he has allowed fewer home runs at the Launching Pad (one every 55 at-bats) than he has on the road (one every 35 at-bats).... Drove in a run with a bases loaded walk against Jim Gott last season, one of only two RBIs in his career.

Mike Morgan — Throws Right

Los Angeles Dodgers	W-L	ERA	AB	H	HR	BB	SO	BA	SA	OBA
Season	14-10	2.78	871	197	12	61	140	.226	.307	.278
vs. Left-Handers			495	113	9	43	78	.228	.321	.290
vs. Right-Handers			376	84	3	18	62	.223	.287	.262
vs. Ground-Ballers			409	89	5	27	78	.218	.298	.265
vs. Fly-Ballers			462	108	7	34	62	.234	.314	.289
Home Games	6-5	3.32	440	100	7	32	71	.227	.305	.281
Road Games	8-5	2.23	431	97	5	29	69	.225	.309	.275
Grass Fields	11-6	2.97	634	141	8	43	97	.222	.290	.273
Artificial Turf	3-4	2.26	237	56	4	18	43	.236	.350	.290
April	2-2	1.42	113	20	3	6	12	.177	.265	.218
May	3-2	2.52	131	33	1	9	25	.252	.351	.300
June	4-1	2.91	164	35	1	7	24	.213	.262	.247
July	0-1	3.09	122	30	1	12	18	.246	.344	.319
August	1-3	3.60	155	36	3	16	23	.232	.316	.304
Sept./Oct.	4-1	2.84	186	43	3	11	38	.231	.306	.275
Leading Off Inn.			237	53	6	8	37	.224	.338	.249
Bases Empty			570	122	11	26	93	.214	.304	.250
Runners On			301	75	1	35	47	.249	.312	.327
Runners/Scor. Pos.			162	41	0	27	33	.253	.321	.356
Runners On/2 Out			135	33	0	22	22	.244	.333	.354
Scor. Pos./2 Out			84	21	0	19	20	.250	.345	.394
Late-Inning Pressure			104	25	1	8	12	.240	.317	.298
Leading Off			29	7	1	2	1	.241	.345	.290
Runners On			41	11	0	4	5	.268	.341	.340
Runners/Scor. Pos.			21	5	0	4	3	.238	.381	.346
First 9 Batters			283	58	1	14	60	.205	.247	.245
Second 9 Batters			264	63	4	23	41	.239	.337	.302
All Batters Thereafter			324	76	7	24	39	.235	.333	.287

Loves to face: Eric Davis (.158, 3-for-19)
Dale Murphy (.185, 5-for-27, 0 BB)
Robby Thompson (.118, 2-for-17)
Hates to face: Daryl Boston (.375, 6-for-16, 3 2B, 2 HR)
Brett Butler (.459, 17-for-37, 0 SO)
Steve Finley (.471, 8-for-17, 2 HR)

Miscellaneous statistics: Ground outs-to-air outs ratio: 2.17 last season, 3d highest in N.L.; 1.83 for career.... Induced 23 double plays in 140 opportunities (one per 6.1), 2d-best rate in N.L.... Allowed 22 doubles, 6 triples in 236⅓ innings.... Allowed 7 first-inning runs in 33 starts (1.91 ERA, 3d lowest in N.L.).... Batting support: 3.61 runs per start.... Opposing base stealers: 24-for-31 (77%); 3 pickoffs, 0 balks.

Comments: His 14–10 record broke a streak of 10 straight seasons without a winning record, which had equaled the third longest in major league history. George Brunet had a 13-year streak (1956–69) and Sid Hudson an 11-year streak (1941–54). Brunet posted a winning record only once during his 15-year career, and Hudson's 11-year streak ended his career after posting a 17–16 mark as a rookie in 1940. Their combined career earnings, including Brunet's 20 or so seasons in the Mexican League, are roughly what Morgan will earn in April.... Opponents hit only one home run in 283 at-bats during his first pass through the order, but averaged one every 53 ABs thereafter.... Hasn't allowed a first-inning home run in his last 38 starts, dating back to September 1990. Opponents batted .195 during the first inning last season, the 4th-lowest mark among N.L. pitchers.... Recorded a save in his only relief appearance of the season (July 7). He must have learned at the hand of the master, his ex-Dodgers teammate John Candelaria, who earned a save in his only relief appearance in five different seasons.... Came to the majors at age 19 straight from Valley H.S. in Las Vegas courtesy of Charles O. Finley, and walked eight batters without a strikeout in 12 innings that season. He walked an average of 4.21 batters per nine innings through 1985, but only 2.36 per nine since then.... Was the only pitcher in the league to hit two sacrifice flies last season.... Has only four hits in 49 career ABs with runners in scoring position.

Terry Mulholland — Throws Left

Philadelphia Phillies	W-L	ERA	AB	H	HR	BB	SO	BA	SA	OBA
Season	16-13	3.61	887	231	15	49	142	.260	.374	.299
vs. Left-Handers			158	40	6	6	19	.253	.411	.279
vs. Right-Handers			729	191	9	43	123	.262	.366	.304
vs. Ground-Ballers			409	108	4	20	65	.264	.357	.299
vs. Fly-Ballers			503	127	11	30	80	.252	.384	.295
Home Games	11-2	2.96	485	121	5	28	83	.249	.336	.293
Road Games	5-11	4.44	402	110	10	21	59	.274	.420	.308
Grass Fields	3-8	4.81	277	83	7	11	42	.300	.451	.325
Artificial Turf	13-5	3.12	610	148	8	38	100	.243	.339	.288
April	2-2	2.91	132	33	0	8	10	.250	.311	.293
May	4-1	3.35	166	40	5	8	23	.241	.373	.278
June	0-5	7.66	97	36	3	10	13	.371	.567	.423
July	3-2	2.25	149	37	2	5	33	.248	.369	.271
August	3-1	3.64	165	43	4	11	31	.261	.394	.307
Sept./Oct.	4-2	3.56	178	42	1	7	32	.236	.303	.267
Leading Off Inn.			230	58	2	9	34	.252	.365	.286
Bases Empty			534	129	6	26	89	.242	.346	.281
Runners On			353	102	9	23	53	.289	.416	.327
Runners/Scor. Pos.			190	57	7	16	24	.300	.484	.344
Runners On/2 Out			146	45	5	14	19	.308	.473	.369
Scor. Pos./2 Out			86	28	4	11	9	.326	.547	.402
Late-Inning Pressure			121	26	3	5	19	.215	.339	.258
Leading Off			32	6	0	2	6	.188	.250	.278
Runners On			41	12	2	1	3	.293	.512	.310
Runners/Scor. Pos.			17	7	2	1	0	.412	.941	.444
First 9 Batters			283	73	3	15	51	.258	.346	.297
Second 9 Batters			274	70	4	17	41	.255	.369	.298
All Batters Thereafter			330	88	8	17	50	.267	.403	.303

Loves to face: Will Clark (.071, 2-for-28, 1 2B, 1 HR, 0 BB)
Darrin Jackson (.063, 1-for-16)
Felix Jose (.125, 2-for-16)

Hates to face: Fred McGriff (.600, 6-for-10, 2 HR)
Ryne Sandberg (.343, 12-for-35, 4 HR)
Lonnie Smith (.538, 14-for-26, 0 BB)

Miscellaneous statistics: Ground outs-to-air outs ratio: 1.10 last season, 1.21 for career.... Induced 16 double plays in 162 opportunities (one per 10).... Allowed 42 doubles (tied for most in N.L.), 7 triples in 232 innings.... Allowed 18 first-inning runs in 34 starts (4.76 ERA).... Batting support: 3.74 runs per start.... Opposing base stealers: 6-for-11 (55%); 6 pickoffs, 0 balks.

Comments: Only Jack Morris won more games in his home ballpark last season than Mulholland, who shared the N.L. lead with Zane Smith. Mulholland also led the world in road losses.... Won more games last season than any other N.L. pitcher who started for his club on opening day.... Led the N.L. in complete games (7) and shutouts (3) after the All-Star break.... In 1990, he had no winning or losing streak of more than two games. But last season he had four separate winning streaks of at least three games, and one doozy of a losing streak, losing all five starts in June and posting the league's highest ERA for the month.... Ground out-to-air out ratio dropped as game progressed: 1.29 during his first pass through the order, 1.15 during his second pass, 0.92 thereafter.... Opponents have a career average of .285 on grass fields, .253 on artificial surfaces.... Opponents have hit at least 25 points higher in road games than they have in home games in each of his five seasons in the majors. Career breakdown: .238 at home, .292 on the road. That translates in wins and losses: 19–13 at home, 13–25 on the road.... Walked 35 batters in 54⅔ innings as a rookie in 1986 (5.76 per nine innings), but has an average of 2.10 per nine innings since returning to the majors in 1988.... The 1989 deal in which the Phillies acquired Mulholland, Dennis Cook, and Charlie Hayes from the Giants for Steve Bedrosian and Rick Parker is looking better and better for the Phillies.

Randy Myers — Throws Left

Cincinnati Reds	W-L	ERA	AB	H	HR	BB	SO	BA	SA	OBA
Season	6-13	3.55	480	116	8	80	108	.242	.342	.347
vs. Left-Handers			122	35	3	26	38	.287	.426	.407
vs. Right-Handers			358	81	5	54	70	.226	.313	.326
vs. Ground-Ballers			216	54	1	35	53	.250	.319	.352
vs. Fly-Ballers			264	62	7	47	55	.235	.360	.348
Home Games	3-5	3.75	260	63	5	44	57	.242	.358	.347
Road Games	3-8	3.30	220	53	3	36	51	.241	.323	.347
Grass Fields	1-4	3.44	132	34	2	17	27	.258	.348	.342
Artificial Turf	5-9	3.58	348	82	6	63	81	.236	.339	.349
April	0-1	2.84	26	8	0	5	7	.308	.346	.419
May	1-2	3.57	64	18	1	12	14	.281	.391	.395
June	3-2	1.69	75	12	0	11	23	.160	.213	.267
July	0-3	5.87	80	20	2	14	17	.250	.363	.347
August	1-4	3.34	119	32	3	22	20	.269	.412	.380
Sept./Oct.	1-1	3.45	116	26	2	16	27	.224	.310	.321
Leading Off Inn.			116	25	1	14	23	.216	.302	.300
Bases Empty			259	59	6	39	63	.228	.340	.329
Runners On			221	57	2	41	45	.258	.344	.368
Runners/Scor. Pos.			129	34	1	24	31	.264	.326	.369
Runners On/2 Out			92	19	1	16	16	.207	.283	.324
Scor. Pos./2 Out			63	13	1	11	12	.206	.254	.324
Late-Inning Pressure			159	43	1	29	34	.270	.352	.382
Leading Off			43	11	0	5	8	.256	.326	.333
Runners On			68	22	1	16	11	.324	.441	.448
Runners/Scor. Pos.			41	12	0	10	8	.293	.317	.426
First 9 Batters			294	69	1	55	75	.235	.299	.352
Second 9 Batters			101	27	5	13	20	.267	.446	.348
All Batters Thereafter			85	20	2	12	13	.235	.365	.330

Loves to face: Craig Biggio (.077, 1-for-13)
Eddie Murray (.067, 1-for-15, 2 BB)
Andy Van Slyke (.111, 3-for-27)

Hates to face: Andres Galarraga (.308, 4-for-13, 2 HR, 4 BB)
Junior Noboa (.800, 4-for-5, 1 SO)
Mike Sharperson (.273, 3-for-11, 1 2B, 2 3B, 4 BB)

Miscellaneous statistics: Ground outs-to-air outs ratio: 1.01 last season, 0.75 for career.... Induced 14 double plays in 141 opportunities (one per 10).... Allowed 18 doubles, 3 triples in 132 innings.... Allowed 12 first-inning runs in 12 starts (7.50 ERA).... Batting support: 3.33 runs per start.... Record of 2–6, 3.45 ERA as a starter; 4–7, 3.65 ERA in 46 relief appearances.... Stranded 27 inherited runners, allowed 8 to score (77%).... Opposing base stealers: 4-for-11 (36%, 3d-lowest rate in N.L.); 2 pickoffs, 1 balk.

Comments: Myers and Les Lancaster were the only pitchers in the majors to start at least 10 games and make at least 40 relief appearances. Four other Cincinnati pitchers have done that: Tom Hume (1979), Mario Soto (1980), Ted Power (1986), and Norm Charlton (1990).... Prior to last season, opposing left-handed batters had never batted higher than .181.... Struck out an average of 7.36 batters per nine innings, the lowest rate of his career. That's not surprising for a season in which he started 12 games after pitching exclusively as a reliever prior to 1991—compiling an average of 9.97 during that time. That's a perfect example of why it ain't kosher to compare the career strikeout rates of Sandy Koufax or Nolan Ryan to those of Myers, Rob Dibble, Tom Henke, or Bryan Harvey. Among the 50 pitchers with the highest strikeout rates in major league history—and here we're including anyone with 200 innings or more in order to prove a point—33 pitched more often in relief than as a starter. The four relievers just mentioned all rank among the top eight, as do Dick Radatz and Ryne Duren. Among 191 players who pitched since 1980, with at least 50 career starts and 50 relief appearances, 160 had higher strikeout rates in relief; 75 had rates at least one strikeout per nine innings higher as a reliever than as a starter.... Further evidence: Myers has a career rate of 26 strikeouts per 100 batters faced during his first pass through the batting order, but only 15 strikeouts per 100 batters faced thereafter.

Chris Nabholz   Throws Left

Montreal Expos	W-L	ERA	AB	H	HR	BB	SO	BA	SA	OBA
Season	8-7	3.63	566	134	5	57	99	.237	.336	.307
vs. Left-Handers			95	22	2	10	26	.232	.400	.305
vs. Right-Handers			471	112	3	47	73	.238	.323	.307
vs. Ground-Ballers			234	56	1	27	37	.239	.329	.321
vs. Fly-Ballers			332	78	4	30	62	.235	.340	.297
Home Games	3-5	3.36	271	59	3	29	51	.218	.336	.295
Road Games	5-2	3.89	295	75	2	28	48	.254	.336	.318
Grass Fields	1-2	6.56	92	27	2	11	13	.293	.413	.362
Artificial Turf	7-5	3.11	474	107	3	46	86	.226	.321	.296
April	0-3	4.56	94	23	2	12	11	.245	.394	.330
May	2-0	3.33	87	16	1	11	22	.184	.310	.283
June	0-1	4.64	86	25	0	8	13	.291	.372	.347
July	0-0	0.00	0	0	0	0	0	.000	.000	.000
August	0-3	4.78	122	31	0	10	15	.254	.344	.311
Sept./Oct.	6-0	2.15	177	39	2	16	38	.220	.294	.284
Leading Off Inn.			145	37	3	16	27	.255	.407	.329
Bases Empty			339	80	5	34	67	.236	.339	.306
Runners On			227	54	0	23	32	.238	.330	.309
Runners/Scor. Pos.			124	32	0	15	16	.258	.347	.338
Runners On/2 Out			91	15	0	12	8	.165	.231	.269
Scor. Pos./2 Out			54	9	0	9	3	.167	.222	.297
Late-Inning Pressure			17	4	0	7	1	.235	.294	.458
Leading Off			4	1	0	3	0	.250	.250	.571
Runners On			6	1	0	3	0	.167	.333	.444
Runners/Scor. Pos.			3	1	0	2	0	.333	.667	.600
First 9 Batters			195	40	2	19	44	.205	.292	.273
Second 9 Batters			198	48	0	16	36	.242	.318	.296
All Batters Thereafter			173	46	3	22	19	.266	.405	.355

Loves to face: Charlie Hayes (.143, 2-for-14)
Tom Pagnozzi (0-for-8)
Darryl Strawberry (0-for-6, 4 SO)

Hates to face: Felix Jose (.636, 7-for-11, 3 SO)
Randy Ready (.308, 4-for-13, 4 BB)
Chris Sabo (.714, 5-for-7, 3 2B, 1 HR)

Miscellaneous statistics: Ground outs-to-air outs ratio: 0.96 last season, 0.94 for career.... Induced 9 double plays in 100 opportunities (one per 11).... Allowed 35 doubles, 3 triples in 153⅔ innings.... Allowed 11 first-inning runs in 24 starts (3.75 ERA).... Batting support: 4.17 runs per start.... Opposing base stealers: 15-for-26 (58%); 8 pickoffs (3d most in N.L.), 1 balk.

Comments: Allowed an average of one home run every 30.7 innings, the best rate of any major league pitcher with as many innings as he pitched.... Hasn't allowed a first-inning home run in his last 27 starts, dating back to September 1990.... His innings were split among three batterymates, and his ERA varied greatly: 2.64 with Nelson Santovenia, 3.12 with Mike Fitzgerald, 4.74 with Gilberto Reyes.... Pitched 43⅓ innings to Fitzgerald without allowing a home run, the highest total by any N.L. battery that didn't allow one last season.... Led the major leagues with six victories during September, an especially encouraging sign for Nabholz, who spent 49 days on the disabled list with tendinitis (June 17–August 5).... Career record of 5–7 from April through August, but 9–2 on or after September 1.... Opponents have a career batting average of .199 at Olympic Stadium, .238 on the road.... We've already pointed out some of the impressive totals accumulated by Expos rookie pitchers last season (see the Jeff Fassero comment). Keep in mind that Nabholz didn't contribute to those totals; although he's only a couple months older than Brian Barnes, Nabholz pitched 70 innings for Montreal in 1990, exhausting his rookie eligibility.

Bob Ojeda   Throws Left

Los Angeles Dodgers	W-L	ERA	AB	H	HR	BB	SO	BA	SA	OBA
Season	12-9	3.18	705	181	15	70	120	.257	.376	.323
vs. Left-Handers			136	35	1	7	36	.257	.324	.301
vs. Right-Handers			569	146	14	63	84	.257	.388	.328
vs. Ground-Ballers			321	67	5	23	66	.209	.296	.259
vs. Fly-Ballers			384	114	10	47	54	.297	.443	.373
Home Games	6-4	3.01	368	95	6	34	67	.258	.356	.319
Road Games	6-5	3.38	337	86	9	36	53	.255	.398	.327
Grass Fields	8-6	3.30	478	127	12	43	80	.266	.395	.323
Artificial Turf	4-3	2.95	227	54	3	27	40	.238	.335	.322
April	1-3	5.32	92	31	3	5	10	.337	.467	.367
May	3-1	3.23	143	38	3	18	23	.266	.371	.345
June	2-1	1.19	109	22	0	7	17	.202	.266	.246
July	2-3	4.60	113	32	5	13	16	.283	.487	.364
August	1-0	3.30	105	24	1	15	21	.229	.324	.320
Sept./Oct.	3-1	2.33	143	34	3	12	33	.238	.357	.297
Leading Off Inn.			181	45	5	15	29	.249	.381	.310
Bases Empty			413	109	12	38	71	.264	.409	.327
Runners On			292	72	3	32	49	.247	.329	.316
Runners/Scor. Pos.			174	40	0	23	29	.230	.282	.306
Runners On/2 Out			120	22	2	13	22	.183	.292	.263
Scor. Pos./2 Out			83	15	0	11	15	.181	.241	.277
Late-Inning Pressure			30	10	0	7	5	.333	.400	.474
Leading Off			9	3	0	2	1	.333	.444	.455
Runners On			9	0	0	4	2	.000	.000	.357
Runners/Scor. Pos.			6	0	0	2	1	.000	.000	.250
First 9 Batters			251	61	2	21	49	.243	.331	.298
Second 9 Batters			239	67	6	25	35	.280	.414	.345
All Batters Thereafter			215	53	7	24	36	.247	.386	.327

Loves to face: Mike Fitzgerald (.050, 1-for-20, 3 BB)
Joe Oliver (.056, 1-for-18)
Todd Zeile (.067, 1-for-15)

Hates to face: Ken Caminiti (.636, 7-for-11, 1 HR)
Dale Murphy (.500, 13-for-26, 1 HR)
Ryne Sandberg (.458, 11-for-24, 3 HR)

Miscellaneous statistics: Ground outs-to-air outs ratio: 1.49 last season, 1.12 for career.... Induced 12 double plays in 160 opportunities (one per 13).... Allowed 31 doubles, 4 triples in 189⅓ innings.... Allowed 14 first-inning runs in 31 starts (3.48 ERA).... Batting support: 3.81 runs per start.... Opposing base stealers: 23-for-38 (61%); 6 pickoffs, 2 balks.

Comments: Posted 3.70 ERA in 99⅔ innings with Mike Scioscia catching, 2.48 in 83⅓ innings with former Met-mate Gary Carter calling the signals.... Sports quiz: Name the only other pitcher besides Ojeda to have pitched for the Red Sox, Mets, and Dodgers. Answer below.... Led the majors in ERA for the month of June.... Before last season, had held left-handed batters to .190 average in his first five years in N.L.... The only homer he allowed to a lefty last season was hit by Fred McGriff, Sept. 25.... One of four N.L. pitchers to face at least 100 batters during the first inning without allowing a home run: Frank Viola (132), Ojeda (129), Mike Morgan (123), and Tommy Greene (102).... Home runs allowed: in A.L., 33 with bases empty, 31 with runners on base; in N.L., 47 with bases empty, 20 with runners on base.... His only shutout of the last two years was sandwiched between his two shortest outings of 1991.... Has allowed more than 12 base runners per nine innings (generally the N.L. break-even point) in each of the last three years; his annual ERAs in those three years (3.47, 3.66, 3.18) are testimony to his ability to pitch with runners on base. Career breakdown: Opponents have hit .261 with bases empty, .245 with runners on base, .228 with runners on base and two outs.... Quiz answer: Don Aase.... His career winning percentage of .549 puts him in between Frank Viola (.545) and Dennis Martinez (.550).

Omar Olivares — Throws Right

St. Louis Cardinals	W-L	ERA	AB	H	HR	BB	SO	BA	SA	OBA
Season	11-7	3.71	609	148	13	61	91	.243	.356	.316
vs. Left-Handers			345	81	5	42	48	.235	.322	.321
vs. Right-Handers			264	67	8	19	43	.254	.402	.309
vs. Ground-Ballers			278	58	3	26	53	.209	.266	.279
vs. Fly-Ballers			331	90	10	35	38	.272	.432	.347
Home Games	7-5	3.33	356	88	7	31	51	.247	.357	.314
Road Games	4-2	4.24	253	60	6	30	40	.237	.356	.319
Grass Fields	1-1	5.68	140	36	5	17	22	.257	.414	.335
Artificial Turf	10-6	3.13	469	112	8	44	69	.239	.339	.310
April	0-0	5.14	26	6	0	3	5	.231	.346	.310
May	0-0	7.20	18	5	1	2	2	.278	.611	.333
June	1-1	5.30	129	34	3	17	10	.264	.380	.351
July	2-2	4.88	90	23	3	13	17	.256	.389	.350
August	4-2	2.13	156	38	2	10	22	.244	.321	.298
Sept./Oct.	4-2	2.87	190	42	4	16	35	.221	.332	.288
Leading Off Inn.			163	34	1	11	28	.209	.282	.259
Bases Empty			377	88	8	36	61	.233	.342	.307
Runners On			232	60	5	25	30	.259	.379	.331
Runners/Scor. Pos.			123	33	1	17	15	.268	.350	.352
Runners On/2 Out			103	27	1	12	15	.262	.369	.339
Scor. Pos./2 Out			63	18	0	9	11	.286	.365	.375
Late-Inning Pressure			51	10	1	9	9	.196	.314	.328
Leading Off			14	2	1	4	3	.143	.357	.333
Runners On			13	2	0	3	1	.154	.154	.313
Runners/Scor. Pos.			3	0	0	2	0	.000	.000	.400
First 9 Batters			215	54	4	19	39	.251	.377	.315
Second 9 Batters			201	42	4	18	25	.209	.299	.281
All Batters Thereafter			193	52	5	24	27	.269	.394	.353

Loves to face: Craig Biggio (0-for-7)
Tom Foley (.100, 1-for-10)
Tim Wallach (.063, 1-for-16)

Hates to face: Ron Gant (.800, 4-for-5, 1 2B, 2 HR)
Ryne Sandberg (.444, 4-for-9, 1 HR)
Larry Walker (.533, 8-for-15)

Miscellaneous statistics: Ground outs-to-air outs ratio: 1.34 last season, 1.31 for career.... Induced 12 double plays in 111 opportunities (one per 9.3).... Allowed 22 doubles, 4 triples in 167⅓ innings.... Allowed 14 first-inning runs in 24 starts (4.88 ERA).... Batting support: 4.21 runs per start.... Opposing base stealers: 10-for-21 (48%); 1 pickoff, 1 balk.

Comments: Think of the 10 N.L. players who batted .300 last season: Pendleton, Morris, Gwynn, McGee, Jose, Larkin, Bonilla, Clark, Sabo, and Calderon. There were 48 pitchers against whom these guys combined for 40 or more at-bats. Double-O was the only one to hold them to a collective batting average below .200. The top ten batted only .195 (8-for-41) against him.... Started 24 games, second most among N.L. rookies, and led that group in both wins and innings pitched.... Over the last 20 years, only two other Cardinals rookies have pitched as many innings in a season: Joe Magrane (170⅓ in 1987) and Ken Hill (196⅔ in 1989).... Cardinals rookies combined for a 16–15 record. Among N.L. clubs, only the Astros (23) and Cubs (22) had more victories from rookies.... Opponents have a career average of .285 in day games, .234 at night.... Shared the lead among N.L. pitchers by starting five double plays as a fielder. Among the three others who did it (Greg Maddux, Dennis Martinez, and Zane Smith), Olivares was the least likely: He pitched fewer innings and had a lower ground outs-to-air outs ratio: io than the other three.... Batted .226 (12-for-53) last season. Cardinals pitchers had the highest batting average (.163) of any staff in the league.... Other famous Double-Os: one-flap down Jeff(rey) Leonard, the Raiders' Jim Otto, the Celtics' Robert Parish, Popeye's Olive Oil, and pitcher Orval Overall, 106–71 with the Reds and Cubs in the first two decades of the century.

Al Osuna — Throws Left

Houston Astros	W-L	ERA	AB	H	HR	BB	SO	BA	SA	OBA
Season	7-6	3.42	293	59	5	46	68	.201	.304	.311
vs. Left-Handers			109	26	3	10	24	.239	.349	.298
vs. Right-Handers			184	33	2	36	44	.179	.277	.318
vs. Ground-Ballers			137	32	3	30	34	.234	.350	.371
vs. Fly-Ballers			156	27	2	16	34	.173	.263	.254
Home Games	4-3	4.35	150	29	4	23	32	.193	.340	.301
Road Games	3-3	2.45	143	30	1	23	36	.210	.266	.322
Grass Fields	2-0	2.61	73	14	1	10	19	.192	.260	.294
Artificial Turf	5-6	3.69	220	45	4	36	49	.205	.318	.317
April	1-0	1.00	33	7	0	3	3	.212	.242	.270
May	0-2	3.55	44	7	1	6	13	.159	.273	.260
June	3-0	2.63	53	14	0	9	8	.264	.340	.371
July	2-1	1.56	58	8	1	14	17	.138	.207	.315
August	1-2	3.60	54	13	0	7	11	.241	.315	.313
Sept./Oct.	0-1	7.71	51	10	3	7	16	.196	.431	.311
Leading Off Inn.			66	10	1	9	18	.152	.242	.253
Bases Empty			157	25	3	23	41	.159	.261	.267
Runners On			136	34	2	23	27	.250	.353	.359
Runners/Scor. Pos.			79	21	2	19	17	.266	.392	.394
Runners On/2 Out			58	8	1	11	16	.138	.207	.286
Scor. Pos./2 Out			38	7	1	11	10	.184	.289	.380
Late-Inning Pressure			183	36	3	31	39	.197	.301	.315
Leading Off			43	6	0	5	13	.140	.186	.229
Runners On			85	24	2	16	13	.282	.435	.394
Runners/Scor. Pos.			53	14	2	13	10	.264	.434	.389
First 9 Batters			284	54	3	43	67	.190	.268	.296
Second 9 Batters			9	5	2	3	1	.556	1.444	.692
All Batters Thereafter			0	0	0	0	0	—	—	—

Loves to face: Eddie Murray (0-for-7)
Paul O'Neill (0-for-5, 4 SO)
Mike Scioscia (0-for-4, 4 SO)

Hates to face: Will Clark (.400, 2-for-5, 1 HR)
Delino DeShields (3-for-3, 1 BB)
Tom Pagnozzi (1-for-1, 1 2B, 3 BB)

Miscellaneous statistics: Ground outs-to-air outs ratio: 0.86 last season, 0.93 for career.... Induced 5 double plays in 82 opportunities (one per 16).... Allowed 13 doubles, 1 triple in 81⅔ innings.... Saved 12 games in 28 opportunities (43%).... Stranded 33 inherited runners, allowed 20 to score (62%).... Opposing base stealers: 2-for-2 (100%); 0 pickoffs, 1 balk.

Comments: Led N.L. rookies with 12 saves, three fewer than Milwaukee's Doug Henry.... National League ERA leaders among rookies who pitched at least 80 innings: Chuck McElroy, Chi. (1.95); Jose Melendez, S.D. (3.27); Osuna (3.42); Kip Gross, Cin. (3.47); Darryl Kile, Hou. (3.69).... Osuna's ERA was as low as 1.97 on Aug. 22, but he allowed 17 earned runs in his 17⅔ innings the rest of the way.... Osuna and McElroy both made 71 appearances to rank second to Mike Stanton (74), the major league rookie leader. Only 19 pitchers in major league history have appeared in 70 games in their rookie seasons, starting with Hoyt Wilhelm in 1952. For 17 years, Wilhelm was the only rookie to do it; then Dan McGinn of Montreal did it in 1969, four rookies did it in the 1970s, and 10 more in the 1980s.... Faced 18 batters in bases-loaded situations and walked four of them; he tied teammate Dwayne Henry for the N.L. lead in forced-in runs (Henry had three walks and a hit batsman with the bases loaded). In the majors last season, there was an average of one walk for every 11.5 plate appearances (excluding intentional walks, it was one every 12.5); with the bases loaded, the major league average was one walk every 17.2 plate appearances. Houston led the N.L. with 13 bases-loaded walks; St. Louis and San Diego, with three apiece, had the fewest in the league.... Hadn't allowed a home run to a left-handed batter until those good buddies, Darryl Strawberry and Kal Daniels, got to him in the same game on September 12. Will Clark added one in October.

Alejandro Pena

Throws Right

Mets/Braves	W-L	ERA	AB	H	HR	BB	SO	BA	SA	OBA
Season	8-1	2.40	302	74	6	22	62	.245	.341	.293
vs. Left-Handers			150	29	3	13	35	.193	.280	.256
vs. Right-Handers			152	45	3	9	27	.296	.401	.329
vs. Ground-Ballers			126	27	0	11	27	.214	.254	.273
vs. Fly-Ballers			176	47	6	11	35	.267	.403	.307
Home Games	4-1	3.05	147	38	3	13	31	.259	.381	.313
Road Games	4-0	1.84	155	36	3	9	31	.232	.303	.273
Grass Fields	6-1	2.26	220	52	3	19	47	.236	.318	.293
Artificial Turf	2-0	2.78	82	22	3	3	15	.268	.402	.291
April	0-0	2.00	29	5	0	3	3	.172	.241	.242
May	1-0	4.22	43	12	1	5	6	.279	.442	.354
June	3-0	2.51	56	17	1	2	13	.304	.393	.317
July	2-0	2.45	52	14	1	7	13	.269	.365	.350
August	0-1	3.38	62	18	3	2	14	.290	.452	.313
Sept./Oct.	2-0	0.51	60	8	0	3	13	.133	.133	.175
Leading Off Inn.			69	9	1	3	12	.130	.174	.167
Bases Empty			176	43	3	12	29	.244	.313	.293
Runners On			126	31	3	10	33	.246	.381	.293
Runners/Scor. Pos.			70	19	3	8	20	.271	.471	.329
Runners On/2 Out			66	21	1	9	21	.318	.424	.400
Scor. Pos./2 Out			42	12	1	8	14	.286	.405	.400
Late-Inning Pressure			144	34	2	9	27	.236	.313	.276
Leading Off			31	4	0	1	3	.129	.129	.156
Runners On			64	15	2	5	16	.234	.375	.278
Runners/Scor. Pos.			39	10	2	4	13	.256	.487	.304
First 9 Batters			295	72	6	22	60	.244	.342	.293
Second 9 Batters			7	2	0	0	2	.286	.286	.286
All Batters Thereafter			0	0	0	0	0	—	—	—

Loves to face: Kevin Bass (.105, 2-for-19)
Gary Redus (.063, 1-for-16)
Darryl Strawberry (0-for-13)

Hates to face: Brett Butler (.391, 9-for-23, 1 HR)
Ken Caminiti (.500, 6-for-12, 1 HR)
Ryne Sandberg (.349, 15-for-43, 3 HR)

Miscellaneous statistics: Ground outs-to-air outs ratio: 0.72 last season, 0.99 for career.... Induced 6 double plays in 50 opportunities (one per 8.3).... Allowed 9 doubles, 1 triple in 82⅓ innings.... Saved 15 games in 18 opportunities (83%), 5th-highest rate in N.L.... Stranded 19 inherited runners, allowed 8 to score (70%).... Opposing base stealers: 8-for-12 (67%); 0 pickoffs, 2 balks.

Comments: Held left-handed batters to a much lower batting average than right-handers, the largest such disparity of his career. Left-handers, as you might expect, have a higher career average against him than do right-handers (.249 to .232).... Allowed one hit in 22 at-bats with runners on base in his last 13 appearances of regular season. He then held Pirates hitless in eight at-bats with runners on base in the Championship Series, but the first batter he faced in the World Series, Chili Davis, belted a two-run homer to end the streak.... Three saves vs. Pittsburgh tied N.L. Championship Series record shared by Dave Giusti (1971), Steve Bedrosian (1989), and Randy Myers (1990).... Pitched in Late-Inning Pressure Situations in only 21 of his 44 appearances with Mets, but in 13 of 15 games with Braves; had saves in 11 of those 15 games.... Opponents' on-base average leading off innings was the lowest in the majors last season (minimum: 50 BFP).... Won his first six decisions of the season, the longest winning streak of his career.... The last time the Braves made a midseason acquisition that had World Series ramifications was back in 1957, when on the June 15 trading deadline they traded Danny O'Connell, Ray Crone, and Bobby Thomson (yes, *that* Bobby Thomson, whom they had acquired from the Giants in 1954) to the Giants in exchange for Red Schoendienst. The Redhead went on to lead the league in hits, en route to Milwaukee's only World Championship.

Mark Portugal

Throws Right

Houston Astros	W-L	ERA	AB	H	HR	BB	SO	BA	SA	OBA
Season	10-12	4.49	637	163	19	59	120	.256	.400	.318
vs. Left-Handers			366	89	10	37	79	.243	.380	.313
vs. Right-Handers			271	74	9	22	41	.273	.428	.326
vs. Ground-Ballers			311	76	9	26	62	.244	.379	.305
vs. Fly-Ballers			326	87	10	33	58	.267	.420	.331
Home Games	4-5	3.06	290	71	3	24	58	.245	.321	.304
Road Games	6-7	5.76	347	92	16	35	62	.265	.467	.330
Grass Fields	4-6	7.02	237	73	10	31	41	.308	.519	.384
Artificial Turf	6-6	3.13	400	90	9	28	79	.225	.330	.277
April	2-1	5.82	66	19	3	3	13	.288	.485	.319
May	3-1	3.82	141	34	3	13	31	.241	.376	.305
June	1-2	3.25	126	29	1	8	27	.230	.286	.272
July	2-1	3.79	76	21	2	9	12	.276	.395	.353
August	2-1	5.04	96	22	4	9	21	.229	.417	.295
Sept./Oct.	0-6	5.88	132	38	6	17	16	.288	.485	.368
Leading Off Inn.			158	44	6	15	26	.278	.449	.341
Bases Empty			384	96	11	27	78	.250	.383	.301
Runners On			253	67	8	32	42	.265	.427	.342
Runners/Scor. Pos.			143	44	6	20	24	.308	.497	.379
Runners On/2 Out			103	26	2	8	18	.252	.388	.306
Scor. Pos./2 Out			62	16	2	5	15	.258	.435	.313
Late-Inning Pressure			47	17	1	7	7	.362	.468	.444
Leading Off			11	5	1	2	3	.455	.818	.538
Runners On			20	7	0	5	2	.350	.400	.480
Runners/Scor. Pos.			11	5	0	2	0	.455	.455	.538
First 9 Batters			240	66	6	20	45	.275	.396	.331
Second 9 Batters			202	49	7	23	44	.243	.421	.320
All Batters Thereafter			195	48	6	16	31	.246	.385	.300

Loves to face: Jose Uribe (.067, 1-for-15, 2 BB)
Larry Walker (0-for-8)
Matt Williams (.094, 3-for-32)

Hates to face: Jeff Blauser (.462, 6-for-13, 3 HR)
Ron Gant (.471, 8-for-17, 1 HR)
Jose Vizcaino (3-for-3, 2 2B)

Miscellaneous statistics: Ground outs-to-air outs ratio: 1.18 last season, 1.26 for career.... Induced 15 double plays in 129 opportunities (one per 8.6).... Allowed 29 doubles, 3 triples in 168⅓ innings.... Allowed 19 first-inning runs in 27 starts (6.08 ERA).... Batting support: 4.70 runs per start, 9th-highest average in N.L.... Opposing base stealers: 12-for-19 (63%); 1 pickoff, 1 balk.

Comments: Over the last two seasons, Portugal has allowed only seven home runs in 656 at-bats in the Astrodome (one every 94 at-bats), but a whopping 33 homers in 728 at-bats on the road (one every 22 at-bats).... Opponents have hit four grand-slam homers (including Fred McGriff's last season) in only 43 career at-bats.... Suffers from Dennis Martinez Syndrome (right-handed pitchers who are more troubled by right-handed batters than by left-handers) to an extreme degree: left-handed batters have a .239 career batting average; right-handers, .283.... Spent 26 days on the disabled list with a strained right hip (July 18–August 12). He was 8–5 (3.94 ERA) before his injury, but only 2–7 (5.52 ERA) afterward, losing his last six decisions. Before 1991, he had been 6–21 before the All-Star break, 23–9 after.... Had 120 strikeouts and averaged 6.42 whiffs per nine innings, but never struck out three batters in an inning last season.... As a batter, didn't strike out until his 49th plate appearance (Aug. 29), falling short of his stated goal of a season without a strikeout. Finished season with four strikeouts in 58 times up, lowest rate among major league pitchers (minimum: 50 plate appearances); Zane Smith finished second with eight strikeouts in 89 appearances. One of our favorite statistics of all-time: In 1946, Johnny Sain, a pitcher for the Boston Braves, had 104 plate appearances without a single strikeout. (In his career, Sain fanned only 20 times in 856 trips to the plate.)

Dennis Rasmussen — Throws Left

San Diego Padres	W-L	ERA	AB	H	HR	BB	SO	BA	SA	OBA
Season	6-13	3.74	572	155	12	49	75	.271	.385	.328
vs. Left-Handers			104	24	2	8	19	.231	.327	.286
vs. Right-Handers			468	131	10	41	56	.280	.397	.337
vs. Ground-Ballers			245	66	3	18	34	.269	.351	.321
vs. Fly-Ballers			327	89	9	31	41	.272	.410	.332
Home Games	4-5	3.88	230	62	4	18	30	.270	.365	.325
Road Games	2-8	3.65	342	93	8	31	45	.272	.398	.329
Grass Fields	5-10	4.03	427	118	9	36	50	.276	.384	.332
Artificial Turf	1-3	2.89	145	37	3	13	25	.255	.386	.314
April	0-0	—	0	0	0	0	0	—	—	—
May	1-0	0.64	50	11	0	2	11	.220	.260	.259
June	2-2	2.00	139	37	4	9	17	.266	.396	.315
July	0-6	4.95	140	37	2	20	14	.264	.336	.354
August	1-3	4.26	127	34	3	11	17	.268	.417	.321
Sept./Oct.	2-2	5.34	116	36	3	7	16	.310	.448	.344
Leading Off Inn.			139	39	3	13	14	.281	.403	.342
Bases Empty			323	89	6	27	43	.276	.387	.333
Runners On			249	66	6	22	32	.265	.382	.320
Runners/Scor. Pos.			120	31	3	14	16	.258	.392	.326
Runners On/2 Out			109	31	2	10	14	.284	.413	.345
Scor. Pos./2 Out			58	16	1	8	8	.276	.414	.364
Late-Inning Pressure			38	10	0	4	4	.263	.316	.333
Leading Off			10	2	0	2	1	.200	.200	.333
Runners On			12	4	0	2	1	.333	.500	.429
Runners/Scor. Pos.			4	2	0	1	1	.500	1.000	.600
First 9 Batters			196	63	5	17	31	.321	.434	.374
Second 9 Batters			186	42	3	11	22	.226	.333	.269
All Batters Thereafter			190	50	4	21	22	.263	.384	.336

Loves to face: Vince Coleman (.083, 1-for-12)
Spike Owen (.100, 3-for-30, 3 BB)
Luis Salazar (.087, 2-for-23)

Hates to face: Pedro Guerrero (.733, 11-for-15)
Lloyd McClendon (.478, 11-for-23, 2 HR)
Matt Williams (.600, 12-for-20, 3 HR)

Miscellaneous statistics: Ground outs-to-air outs ratio: 1.02 last season, 0.81 for career.... Induced 13 double plays in 127 opportunities (one per 10).... Allowed 17 doubles, 6 triples in 146⅔ innings.... Allowed 25 first-inning runs in 24 starts (7.23 ERA, 3d highest in N.L.).... Batting support: 3.50 runs per start, 8th-lowest average in N.L.... Opposing base stealers: 21-for-27 (78%); 4 pick-offs, 1 balk.

Comments: You won't see his picture on the Padres' calendar for "July"; last year, he went 0–6 in six July starts, becoming the only N.L. pitcher to lose six games in a calendar month last year.... His nine-game losing streak was the longest in the majors last season; he not only lost nine straight decisions, he dropped nine straight starts (June 26–Aug. 9).... Opened the season on the disabled list, but then allowed only one earned run in 30 innings over his first four starts.... The only pitcher to throw a complete-game shutout against the Cubs at Wrigley Field last season.... Opponents' batting average of .355 during the first inning was the third highest against any N.L. pitcher.... Left-handed batters have a higher career batting average than right-handers (.263 to .254).... His winning percentage has declined in each of the last five seasons, after posting a record of 18–6 (.750) for the Yankees in 1986. Yearly records since then: 13–8 (.619), 16–10 (.615), 10–10 (.500), 11–15 (.423), 6–13 (.316). Only eight other pitchers have ever had five consecutive declines in seasons of at least 15 decisions; two of them were top-notch guys who suffered small year-to-year declines and were still above .500 even after the fifth drop: Three Finger Brown (.813 to .656, 1906–11) and Ted Higuera (.652 to .524, 1985–90). But none of the eight has fallen as far as Rasmussen (.750 to .316) during the declining span.... Despite all of that, Ras's ERA was lower last year than it was in his 18–6 season (3.88).

Dave Righetti — Throws Left

San Francisco Giants	W-L	ERA	AB	H	HR	BB	SO	BA	SA	OBA
Season	2-7	3.39	267	64	4	28	51	.240	.330	.317
vs. Left-Handers			72	12	0	2	13	.167	.167	.197
vs. Right-Handers			195	52	4	26	38	.267	.390	.357
vs. Ground-Ballers			105	24	1	15	21	.229	.276	.333
vs. Fly-Ballers			162	40	3	13	30	.247	.364	.305
Home Games	1-4	4.14	136	32	2	11	32	.235	.346	.295
Road Games	1-3	2.60	131	32	2	17	19	.244	.313	.338
Grass Fields	2-7	4.18	213	55	4	21	40	.258	.366	.328
Artificial Turf	0-0	0.57	54	9	0	7	11	.167	.185	.274
April	2-0	3.24	31	7	1	3	7	.226	.355	.294
May	0-2	5.74	65	22	0	6	10	.338	.385	.403
June	0-1	3.07	49	11	0	8	6	.224	.286	.328
July	0-1	1.93	30	6	1	3	5	.200	.333	.265
August	0-1	1.32	46	4	1	2	13	.087	.152	.160
Sept./Oct.	0-2	4.50	46	14	1	6	10	.304	.457	.385
Leading Off Inn.			56	9	0	8	13	.161	.214	.277
Bases Empty			138	30	3	13	25	.217	.319	.294
Runners On			129	34	1	15	26	.264	.341	.340
Runners/Scor. Pos.			81	24	1	9	16	.296	.383	.366
Runners On/2 Out			58	15	1	9	12	.259	.362	.368
Scor. Pos./2 Out			40	12	1	6	9	.300	.425	.404
Late-Inning Pressure			199	48	3	23	37	.241	.322	.323
Leading Off			41	7	0	6	7	.171	.220	.292
Runners On			99	27	1	12	20	.273	.343	.345
Runners/Scor. Pos.			64	18	1	8	13	.281	.344	.351
First 9 Batters			260	60	4	28	50	.231	.323	.311
Second 9 Batters			7	4	0	0	1	.571	.571	.571
All Batters Thereafter			0	0	0	0	0	—	—	—

Loves to face: Ivan Calderon (.133, 2-for-15)
Jack Howell (0-for-10, 9 SO)
Don Slaught (0-for-14)

Hates to face: George Bell (.393, 11-for-28, 3 2B, 2 3B, 3 HR)
Alfredo Griffin (.474, 9-for-19)
Eddie Murray (.333, 14-for-42, 1 HR)

Miscellaneous statistics: Ground outs-to-air outs ratio: 1.14 last season, 1.04 for career.... Induced 5 double plays in 62 opportunities (one per 12).... Allowed 12 doubles, 0 triples in 71⅔ innings.... Saved 24 games in 31 opportunities (77%).... Stranded 27 inherited runners, allowed 5 to score (84%), 2d-highest rate in majors.... Opposing base stealers: 8-for-12 (67%); 4 pickoffs, 1 balk.

Comments: Opponents' batting average with runners in scoring position was his highest in any full season in the majors.... Averaged a career-low 6.40 strikeouts per nine innings.... His first two appearances of the year both came in save situations; he was not used again in such a situation until June, after 16 nonsave-situation appearances.... Has saved 247 games since becoming a full-time reliever in 1984; only Lee Smith (265) and Jeff Reardon (264) have more over that span.... Lowest career ERAs, active pitchers (minimum: 1000 IP): Orel Hershiser (2.77), Roger Clemens (2.85), Dwight Gooden (2.91), Jeff Reardon (3.03), Righetti (3.13).... Rags has never posted an ERA higher than 3.79 in any of 12 seasons in the majors. Among active pitchers, only Lee Smith shares that distinction. The last longer streak: Kent Tekulve, 14 years, 1975–88.... Held left-handed batters to their lowest average since his rookie year; he was the only major league pitcher who faced at least 50 left-handed batters and did not allow an extra-base hit to any of them. The last lefty to get an extra-base hit off him: Greg Brock, a game-winning three-run homer at Yankee Stadium, Aug. 25, 1990.... Has allowed only one homer in 137 batters faced with the bases full; George Bell hit it at Exhibition Stadium in 1986, as Rags blew a save opportunity for what would have been Doug Drabek's first big-league win; Righetti's reaction: He dropped to his knees on the mound, and after Don Denkinger tossed him a new ball, he angrily threw it over the right field fence.

Jose Rijo

Throws Right

Cincinnati Reds	W-L	ERA	AB	H	HR	BB	SO	BA	SA	OBA
Season	15-6	2.51	755	165	8	55	172	.219	.305	.272
vs. Left-Handers			437	110	5	38	93	.252	.352	.311
vs. Right-Handers			318	55	3	17	79	.173	.239	.215
vs. Ground-Ballers			341	79	0	21	83	.232	.296	.275
vs. Fly-Ballers			414	86	8	34	89	.208	.312	.269
Home Games	9-0	2.99	355	73	6	35	74	.206	.290	.275
Road Games	6-6	2.06	400	92	2	20	98	.230	.317	.268
Grass Fields	4-4	1.86	296	66	1	15	75	.223	.297	.260
Artificial Turf	11-2	2.91	459	99	7	40	97	.216	.309	.279
April	1-1	2.67	94	17	0	7	21	.181	.213	.240
May	3-1	3.08	147	39	4	11	33	.265	.388	.309
June	2-0	2.21	126	22	2	8	32	.175	.278	.222
July	1-0	2.77	49	12	0	1	7	.245	.347	.260
August	4-2	2.11	158	31	1	14	39	.196	.247	.264
Sept./Oct.	4-2	2.49	181	44	1	14	40	.243	.343	.301
Leading Off Inn.			195	37	2	11	47	.190	.277	.240
Bases Empty			483	97	7	29	115	.201	.304	.249
Runners On			272	68	1	26	57	.250	.305	.309
Runners/Scor. Pos.			159	34	0	18	44	.214	.277	.285
Runners On/2 Out			121	27	1	13	29	.223	.306	.304
Scor. Pos./2 Out			78	15	0	8	23	.192	.282	.276
Late-Inning Pressure			28	7	0	2	7	.250	.321	.300
Leading Off			8	1	0	1	4	.125	.125	.222
Runners On			6	3	0	1	0	.500	.667	.571
Runners/Scor. Pos.			2	1	0	0	0	.500	1.000	.500
First 9 Batters			244	51	2	19	57	.209	.295	.269
Second 9 Batters			250	52	2	16	56	.208	.280	.257
All Batters Thereafter			261	62	4	20	59	.238	.337	.289

Loves to face: Doug Dascenzo (0-for-12)
Tom Foley (0-for-11)
Jose Lind (.105, 2-for-19)
Hates to face: Bobby Bonilla (.400, 8-for-20, 3 HR)
Mark Grace (.462, 12-for-26, 1 HR)
John Kruk (.346, 9-for-26, 2 2B, 1 3B, 3 HR)

Miscellaneous statistics: Ground outs-to-air outs ratio: 1.06 last season, 1.14 for career.... Induced 15 double plays in 117 opportunities (one per 7.8).... Allowed 33 doubles, 4 triples in 204⅓ innings.... Allowed 18 first-inning runs in 30 starts (4.50 ERA).... Batting support: 5.10 runs per start, 5th-highest average in N.L.... Opposing base stealers: 16-for-19 (84%); 5 pickoffs, 4 balks (3d most in N.L.).

Comments: Rijo has made 97 starts in the National League; his ERA in four years with the Reds is 2.59 (including relief games). Among N.L. pitchers who have made 100 or more starts over the past 50 years, here are the 10 lowest ERAs: Mort Cooper, 2.64; John Tudor, 2.66; Tom Seaver, 2.73; Sandy Koufax, 2.76; Orel Hershiser, 2.77; Juan Marichal, 2.86; Andy Messersmith, 2.88; Max Lanier, 2.907; Dwight Gooden, 2.910; Harry Brecheen and Bob Gibson, 2.914. Rijo is on the verge of going to the head of the class.... Career breakdown: 19-30, 4.75 ERA in four years as A.L. youngster; 49-28, 2.59 ERA in four years as Cincinnati mainstay; his .636 winning percentage with Reds is third best in team history (minimum: 50 decisions), behind Don Gullett (.674) and Pedro Borbon (.653).... Opponents' on-base average and slugging percentage were both lowest among qualifying N.L. pitchers.... Allowed an average of one home run every 25.5 innings, the best rate of his career, and the second-best rate in the majors among ERA qualifiers.... Also achieved a career best with his rate of 2.42 walks per nine innings, more than a full walk lower than his career average.... Winning percentage of .714 last season followed a .636 percentage in 1990. Over the last 50 years, only two other Reds' pitchers have had consecutive seasons with winning percentages as high (minimum: 14 decisions): Don Gullett (1975-76) and Jim Maloney (1965-66).... Rijo and Eric Plunk are the only pitchers with at least two balks in each of the past six seasons. And Cindy Crawford can't speak Portugese, either.

Don Robinson

Throws Right

San Francisco Giants	W-L	ERA	AB	H	HR	BB	SO	BA	SA	OBA
Season	5-9	4.38	465	123	12	50	78	.265	.417	.334
vs. Left-Handers			251	70	5	39	46	.279	.422	.371
vs. Right-Handers			214	53	7	11	32	.248	.411	.286
vs. Ground-Ballers			257	61	4	26	45	.237	.362	.304
vs. Fly-Ballers			208	62	8	24	33	.298	.486	.370
Home Games	3-2	2.77	226	51	6	26	43	.226	.372	.304
Road Games	2-7	6.03	239	72	6	24	35	.301	.460	.362
Grass Fields	4-5	3.44	323	78	8	35	61	.241	.384	.316
Artificial Turf	1-4	6.69	142	45	4	15	17	.317	.493	.375
April	0-0	3.86	39	12	0	3	8	.308	.462	.357
May	1-4	5.97	112	32	6	13	18	.286	.518	.357
June	2-2	3.38	117	30	1	13	20	.256	.359	.336
July	2-1	2.89	66	13	1	8	13	.197	.288	.280
August	0-2	6.75	77	24	3	12	9	.312	.494	.400
Sept./Oct.	0-0	2.35	54	12	1	1	10	.222	.352	.228
Leading Off Inn.			115	28	5	9	18	.243	.452	.298
Bases Empty			274	67	9	25	47	.245	.427	.310
Runners On			191	56	3	25	31	.293	.403	.367
Runners/Scor. Pos.			115	42	3	21	19	.365	.539	.447
Runners On/2 Out			84	25	2	17	16	.298	.417	.416
Scor. Pos./2 Out			54	21	2	15	10	.389	.556	.522
Late-Inning Pressure			25	5	1	3	2	.200	.320	.276
Leading Off			8	2	1	0	0	.250	.625	.250
Runners On			8	3	0	0	1	.375	.375	.333
Runners/Scor. Pos.			5	1	0	0	1	.200	.200	.167
First 9 Batters			228	48	1	22	42	.211	.294	.280
Second 9 Batters			149	50	8	14	23	.336	.597	.388
All Batters Thereafter			88	25	3	14	13	.284	.432	.382

Loves to face: Bob Melvin (0-for-5)
Dave Parker (.100, 1-for-10, 5 SO)
Tony Pena (.077, 1-for-13)
Hates to face: Jack Clark (.220, 13-for-59, 3 2B, 7 HR)
Kirk Gibson (.429, 6-for-14, 1 HR)
Steve Sax (.321, 9-for-28)

Miscellaneous statistics: Ground outs-to-air outs ratio: 0.99 last season, 0.87 for career.... Induced 8 double plays in 82 opportunities (one per 10).... Allowed 25 doubles, 5 triples in 121⅓ innings.... Allowed 6 first-inning runs in 16 starts (3.38 ERA).... Batting support: 3.94 runs per start.... Record of 5-8, 5.21 ERA as a starter; 0-1, 2.45 ERA in 18 relief appearances.... Stranded 6 inherited runners, allowed 3 to score (67%).... Opposing base stealers: 10-for-15 (67%); 1 pickoff, 0 balks.

Comments: Pitched 14 years in N.L. before signing with Angels in January. He had been the senior pitcher in the senior circuit (debut: April 1978), an honor he now bequeathes to Dave Smith (debut: April 1980).... His final N.L. act was not very popular in La-la-land: On Sept. 28, with the Dodgers holding a two-game lead over Atlanta, the Giants took a 4-1 lead over L.A. into the bottom of the ninth. After one out, Dave Righetti, on for the save, walked three batters in a row for the first time since 1984; Robinson came on to retire Brett Butler and Lenny Harris for his first save since 1988.... Has been on the disabled list eight times in his major league career, but was the only pitcher to throw at least 100 innings for the Giants in each of the last four seasons. Too bad they were expecting 200.... Opponents batted .193 during the first inning of his starts, third lowest among N.L. pitchers last season. The bad news: He walked an average of 6.19 batters per nine innings during the opening frame, the second-highest rate in the league.... Has both started and relieved in all but two of his 14 seasons in the majors. Career breakdown: 79-73 (3.97 ERA) in 218 starts, 28-29 (3.18 ERA) in 295 relief games.... Robinson's career batting average is tops among active pitchers with at least 100 at-bats. The top five: Robinson (.227), Tim Leary (.221), Derek Lilliquist (.213), Charlie Hough (.208), Rick Aguilera (.203). When Robby signed with Angels it left all five of those guys up the stream without a paddle—in other words, in the DH league.

Bruce Ruffin
Throws Left

Philadelphia Phillies	W-L	ERA	AB	H	HR	BB	SO	BA	SA	OBA
Season	4-7	3.78	459	125	6	38	85	.272	.386	.327
vs. Left-Handers			111	28	1	6	22	.252	.333	.291
vs. Right-Handers			348	97	5	32	63	.279	.402	.338
vs. Ground-Ballers			219	53	3	15	44	.242	.347	.292
vs. Fly-Ballers			240	72	3	23	41	.300	.421	.357
Home Games	3-3	3.21	279	71	5	25	54	.254	.384	.313
Road Games	1-4	4.78	180	54	1	13	31	.300	.389	.349
Grass Fields	1-2	5.40	85	24	1	7	15	.282	.353	.344
Artificial Turf	3-5	3.45	374	101	5	31	70	.270	.393	.323
April	0-0	—	0	0	0	0	0	—	—	—
May	0-0	—	0	0	0	0	0	—	—	—
June	1-0	2.78	83	22	0	7	12	.265	.337	.319
July	2-3	2.84	152	39	2	9	30	.257	.349	.296
August	0-2	5.19	96	30	2	11	15	.313	.448	.376
Sept./Oct.	1-2	4.45	128	34	2	11	28	.266	.414	.329
Leading Off Inn.			114	35	0	8	26	.307	.404	.358
Bases Empty			247	72	3	18	42	.291	.409	.342
Runners On			212	53	3	20	43	.250	.358	.309
Runners/Scor. Pos.			116	28	2	14	24	.241	.362	.313
Runners On/2 Out			85	15	0	5	20	.176	.212	.222
Scor. Pos./2 Out			54	7	0	4	14	.130	.148	.190
Late-Inning Pressure			43	12	0	2	4	.279	.302	.326
Leading Off			12	3	0	1	1	.250	.250	.357
Runners On			13	6	0	1	1	.462	.538	.500
Runners/Scor. Pos.			5	2	0	0	0	.400	.400	.400
First 9 Batters			205	52	2	23	41	.254	.356	.330
Second 9 Batters			131	38	3	9	27	.290	.443	.331
All Batters Thereafter			123	35	1	6	17	.285	.374	.315

Loves to face: Junior Ortiz (.125, 1-for-8)
Tim Raines (.211, 4-for-19)
Steve Sax (.227, 5-for-22)
Hates to face: Tom Brunansky (.467, 7-for-15)
Glenn Davis (.400, 8-for-20, 2 HR)
Kevin McReynolds (.424, 14-for-33, 3 HR)

Miscellaneous statistics: Ground outs-to-air outs ratio: 1.13 last season, 1.92 for career.... Induced 12 double plays in 112 opportunities (one per 9.3).... Allowed 28 doubles, 3 triples in 119 innings.... Allowed 11 first-inning runs in 15 starts (6.91 ERA).... Batting support: 3.40 runs per start.... Record of 3–7, 3.72 ERA as a starter; 1–0, 3.94 ERA in 16 relief appearances.... Stranded 8 inherited runners, allowed 4 to score (67%).... Opposing base stealers: 7-for-11 (64%); 1 pickoff, 0 balks.

Comments: One of five pitchers who have posted losing records in each of the last five seasons. The others: Kevin Gross, Jamie Moyer, Dan Plesac, Pete Smith. The last pitcher with a losing record in six straight seasons was Mark Thurmond (1985–90), who hasn't been seen since.... Struck out an average of 6.43 batters per nine innings, the highest rate of his career.... Opponents collected seven hits in 13 at-bats with the bases loaded last season.... Lowest career batting averages among active players with at least 200 at-bats: Don Carman (.057), Mike Bielecki (.074), Terry Mulholland (.076), Ruffin (.080), Jim Deshaies (.080).... Struck out in eight consecutive plate appearances in July, the longest streak in the majors last season.... Did not allow more than one home run in any game last season. His average of one home run allowed every 19.8 innings was 10th best among N.L. pitchers with at least 100 innings.... Opponents' career breakdown: .290 by right-handers (one home run every 52 at-bats), .256 by left-handed batters (one home run every 105.5 at-bats).... Only two left-handed batters have homered against him in the last four years: Will Clark (1989) and Larry Walker (1991).... Has faced Darryl Strawberry 44 times (including 39 official at-bats) without ever being taken deep; no other pitcher has avoided Darryl's hammer in so many confrontations.

Curt Schilling
Throws Right

Houston Astros	W-L	ERA	AB	H	HR	BB	SO	BA	SA	OBA
Season	3-5	3.81	291	79	2	39	71	.271	.364	.356
vs. Left-Handers			149	38	1	27	40	.255	.342	.367
vs. Right-Handers			142	41	1	12	31	.289	.387	.344
vs. Ground-Ballers			126	34	1	19	33	.270	.365	.366
vs. Fly-Ballers			165	45	1	20	38	.273	.364	.349
Home Games	3-3	3.64	181	50	2	26	46	.276	.354	.365
Road Games	0-2	4.08	110	29	0	13	25	.264	.382	.341
Grass Fields	0-1	4.26	72	18	2	10	14	.250	.431	.341
Artificial Turf	3-4	3.65	219	61	0	29	57	.279	.342	.361
April	0-1	3.75	44	11	1	5	12	.250	.500	.327
May	1-2	5.11	55	20	0	7	15	.364	.418	.435
June	2-2	6.00	33	10	0	4	9	.303	.394	.378
July	0-0	0.00	0	0	0	0	0	.000	.000	.000
August	0-0	3.10	77	20	1	13	15	.260	.364	.363
Sept./Oct.	0-0	2.86	82	18	0	10	20	.220	.244	.304
Leading Off Inn.			61	21	0	10	10	.344	.393	.437
Bases Empty			133	36	2	15	26	.271	.368	.345
Runners On			158	43	0	24	45	.272	.361	.366
Runners/Scor. Pos.			104	28	0	17	32	.269	.365	.369
Runners On/2 Out			65	16	0	11	18	.246	.338	.355
Scor. Pos./2 Out			51	13	0	9	13	.255	.314	.367
Late-Inning Pressure			105	30	1	18	26	.286	.400	.390
Leading Off			21	7	0	6	4	.333	.381	.481
Runners On			59	16	0	9	16	.271	.373	.368
Runners/Scor. Pos.			37	11	0	8	10	.297	.405	.422
First 9 Batters			271	74	2	37	66	.273	.369	.359
Second 9 Batters			20	5	0	2	5	.250	.300	.318
All Batters Thereafter			0	0	0	0	0			

Loves to face: Todd Benzinger (0-for-5, 3 SO)
Scott Coolbaugh (0-for-5, 3 SO)
Hates to face: Ivan Calderon (3-for-3, 2 BB)
Juan Samuel (1-for-1, 3 BB)
Jeff Treadway (2-for-2, 1 2B, 1 3B)

Miscellaneous statistics: Ground outs-to-air outs ratio: 1.10 last season, 0.91 for career.... Induced 4 double plays in 83 opportunities (one per 21).... Allowed 15 doubles, 3 triples in 75⅔ innings.... Stranded 18 inherited runners, allowed 10 to score (64%).... Opposing base stealers: 3-for-7 (43%); 0 pickoffs, 1 balk.

Comments: Among N.L. pitchers who faced as many leadoff batters as Schilling, only Shawn Boskie and Danny Jackson allowed a higher on-base average leading off innings. Remember: A team is three times more likely to score in an inning when its leadoff batter reaches base than in an inning in which the first batter is retired.... Had five saves over the first four weeks of the season, but recorded only three more over the remaining five months. Led Houston in games finished, but ranked second in saves to Al Osuna.... Stranded 12 of the last 13 runners he inherited.... This 25-year-old has already been involved in trades for both Mike Boddicker and Glenn Davis.... Allowed only two home runs in 75⅔ innings, the 4th-lowest rate among N.L. pitchers (minimum: 50 innings). Neither of those homers was hit in the Astrodome.... Opponents have a career batting average of .260 during his first pass through the order, but are batting .329 in subsequent at-bats.... Made 108 starts and only seven relief appearances during his minor league career in the Baltimore organization, and started all four of his games in his debut season with the Orioles (1988), but over the last two seasons all 91 appearances have come in relief. Career breakdown: 0–4 (10.59 ERA) in five starts, 4–7 (3.30 ERA) in 95 relief appearances.... Born in Anchorage, Alaska, and works in Texas. Didn't Michelle Shocked already write that song?

John Smiley
Throws Left

Pittsburgh Pirates	W-L	ERA	AB	H	HR	BB	SO	BA	SA	OBA
Season	20-8	3.08	774	194	17	44	129	.251	.381	.292
vs. Left-Handers			153	30	3	5	30	.196	.320	.220
vs. Right-Handers			621	164	14	39	99	.264	.396	.309
vs. Ground-Ballers			307	70	5	17	59	.228	.332	.268
vs. Fly-Ballers			467	124	12	27	70	.266	.413	.308
Home Games	10-5	2.98	364	90	7	24	60	.247	.385	.293
Road Games	10-3	3.17	410	104	10	20	69	.254	.378	.291
Grass Fields	4-3	3.31	206	51	6	14	28	.248	.374	.302
Artificial Turf	16-5	2.99	568	143	11	30	101	.252	.384	.289
April	4-0	2.28	102	20	1	5	12	.196	.275	.234
May	3-1	3.67	103	31	0	6	18	.301	.398	.336
June	2-4	3.65	142	36	5	4	29	.254	.373	.279
July	3-2	3.62	121	31	3	13	24	.256	.364	.326
August	4-1	3.43	148	41	4	8	24	.277	.480	.314
Sept./Oct.	4-0	2.03	158	35	4	8	22	.222	.367	.263
Leading Off Inn.			204	51	2	12	34	.250	.358	.298
Bases Empty			491	120	9	29	88	.244	.363	.291
Runners On			283	74	8	15	41	.261	.413	.295
Runners/Scor. Pos.			153	40	2	11	22	.261	.373	.304
Runners On/2 Out			115	26	4	6	17	.226	.400	.264
Scor. Pos./2 Out			67	17	1	6	8	.254	.358	.315
Late-Inning Pressure			56	14	1	8	6	.250	.357	.344
Leading Off			18	5	1	2	1	.278	.500	.350
Runners On			19	4	0	1	2	.211	.316	.250
Runners/Scor. Pos.			7	2	0	0	1	.286	.286	.286
First 9 Batters			276	59	3	11	66	.214	.301	.244
Second 9 Batters			267	73	9	16	34	.273	.472	.318
All Batters Thereafter			231	62	5	17	29	.268	.342	.319

Loves to face: Howard Johnson (.103, 4-for-39)
Charlie O'Brien (0-for-8)
Gerald Young (.056, 1-for-18, 4 BB)
Hates to face: Andre Dawson (.447, 17-for-38, 4 HR, 0 BB)
Felix Jose (.444, 8-for-18)
Matt Williams (.429, 9-for-21, 4 HR)

Miscellaneous statistics: Ground outs-to-air outs ratio: 1.06 last season, 0.91 for career.... Induced 11 double plays in 127 opportunities (one per 12).... Allowed 38 doubles, 6 triples in 207⅔ innings.... Allowed 9 first-inning runs in 32 starts (1.97 ERA, 4th lowest in N.L.); only 7 of those runs were earned, the same amount of first-inning earned runs he allowed to Atlanta in two postseason starts.... Batting support: 4.63 runs per start.... Opposing base stealers: 18-for-31 (58%); 6 pick-offs, 1 balk.

Comments: Smiley became only the second player in history to win 20 games with as few as two complete games. Bob Welch did it in 1990.... Picked up a win in relief of Zane Smith on October 1, Smiley's 19th of the season; he then won number 20 on the last day of the season.... Rate of walks (1.91 per nine innings) was a career low.... Yearly batting averages by opposing left-handers since 1987: .195, .159, .243, .301, .196. Career breakdown: .214 by left-handers, .251 by right-handers.... Opponents have hit for a higher average in road games than at Three Rivers Stadium in each of his six seasons in the majors. So why does he have roughly the same career record on the road (29–20) as at home (31–22)?... Underwent the rudest postseason treatment for a 20-game winner since Don Newcombe (27–7 during the season) lost two games, allowing 11 runs in 4⅔ innings, in 1956 World Series.... Championship Series recap: 18 batters faced, eight runs allowed (seven earned) on eight hits (two singles, four doubles, two home runs), walked one, hit one, 0–2 record, 23.63 ERA. He lasted two innings in Game Three, and two-thirds of an inning in Game Seven. Only one other starter had ever failed to reach the third inning twice in a postseason series: Art Ditmar in the 1960 World Series; he lasted one-third of an inning in Game One and 1⅓ innings in Game Five, then got wrongly blamed for Mazeroski's homer in a decades-later TV commercial.

Bryn Smith
Throws Right

St. Louis Cardinals	W-L	ERA	AB	H	HR	BB	SO	BA	SA	OBA
Season	12-9	3.85	749	188	16	45	94	.251	.381	.297
vs. Left-Handers			441	120	7	29	41	.272	.401	.319
vs. Right-Handers			308	68	9	16	53	.221	.351	.266
vs. Ground-Ballers			293	75	2	18	34	.256	.352	.307
vs. Fly-Ballers			456	113	14	27	60	.248	.399	.291
Home Games	5-4	3.52	403	95	7	25	46	.236	.365	.283
Road Games	7-5	4.24	346	93	9	20	48	.269	.399	.314
Grass Fields	3-4	4.47	181	51	6	10	27	.282	.436	.330
Artificial Turf	9-5	3.65	568	137	10	35	67	.241	.363	.287
April	3-0	3.00	101	23	3	5	15	.228	.347	.271
May	1-3	5.63	149	44	3	8	20	.295	.423	.331
June	2-1	2.38	124	30	1	9	9	.242	.371	.291
July	3-3	3.52	141	34	3	7	18	.241	.355	.283
August	2-1	5.05	139	36	5	10	16	.259	.439	.316
Sept./Oct.	1-1	2.84	95	21	1	6	16	.221	.316	.272
Leading Off Inn.			196	55	6	7	15	.281	.439	.309
Bases Empty			473	116	6	20	56	.245	.345	.280
Runners On			276	72	10	25	38	.261	.442	.324
Runners/Scor. Pos.			164	41	5	19	33	.250	.415	.323
Runners On/2 Out			123	31	3	13	20	.252	.415	.328
Scor. Pos./2 Out			82	22	3	12	19	.268	.451	.368
Late-Inning Pressure			23	5	0	1	2	.217	.391	.250
Leading Off			7	2	0	0	0	.286	.429	.286
Runners On			8	1	0	0	1	.125	.375	.125
Runners/Scor. Pos.			3	1	0	0	1	.333	1.000	.333
First 9 Batters			259	61	6	12	37	.236	.344	.276
Second 9 Batters			256	68	6	14	35	.266	.406	.312
All Batters Thereafter			234	59	4	19	22	.252	.393	.304

Loves to face: Kevin Bass (.120, 3-for-25, 1 HR)
Delino DeShields (.167, 3-for-18)
Larry Walker (.071, 1-for-14)
Hates to face: Daryl Boston (.700, 7-for-10)
John Kruk (.340, 17-for-50, 2 HR)
Andy Van Slyke (.383, 18-for-47, 2 HR)

Miscellaneous statistics: Ground outs-to-air outs ratio: 1.08 last season, 1.57 for career.... Induced 11 double plays in 129 opportunities (one per 12).... Allowed 39 doubles, 5 triples in 198⅔ innings.... Allowed 16 first-inning runs in 31 starts (4.35 ERA).... Batting support: 4.68 runs per start, 10th-highest average in N.L.... Opposing base stealers: 19-for-27 (70%); 0 pickoffs, 1 balk.

Comments: Only three pitchers as old as Smith made 30 starts last season: Jack Morris, Dennis Martinez, and Frank Tanana. How old is he? Smith was once in a trade that involved *both* Rudy May and Don Stanhouse (1977); he turned 36 in August.... He's started 176 games over the last six years, but has only one shutout to his credit during that time. He pitched three complete games last season, after failing to pitch into the ninth inning in any of 25 starts in 1990.... For the seventh year in a row, allowed a higher batting average with runners on base than with the bases empty.... For five years in a row, 1986 to 1990, Smith didn't stray more than two games from the .500 mark: 10–8, 10–9, 12–10, 10–11, 9–8. Among pitchers with at least 15 decisions each year, only one pitcher in major league history had stayed similarly close to .500 for so long. That, of course, was Long Bob Ewing, Reds and Phillies, 1906–10. Smith took a 12–9 record into the final week of the season, but did not take his starting turn on the season's final weekend, ending his bid for Mediocrity Immortality. Or so you might think. But now Smith has a streak of six consecutive 15-decision seasons within *three* games of .500, tying yet another record shared by the more recent trio of Nolan Ryan (1975–80), Rick Waits (1976–81), and Milt Wilcox (1978–83). Can Smith make history? We'd put the chances at 50–50.

Dave Smith

Throws Right

Chicago Cubs	W-L	ERA	AB	H	HR	BB	SO	BA	SA	OBA
Season	0-6	6.00	129	39	6	19	16	.302	.535	.396
vs. Left-Handers			74	28	4	10	7	.378	.676	.459
vs. Right-Handers			55	11	2	9	9	.200	.345	.313
vs. Ground-Ballers			58	24	4	7	5	.414	.707	.485
vs. Fly-Ballers			71	15	2	12	11	.211	.394	.325
Home Games	0-3	5.60	66	18	4	7	9	.273	.485	.351
Road Games	0-3	6.46	63	21	2	12	7	.333	.587	.440
Grass Fields	0-4	5.88	102	31	5	13	13	.304	.559	.388
Artificial Turf	0-2	6.43	27	8	1	6	3	.296	.444	.424
April	0-2	9.53	23	10	2	5	4	.435	.783	.536
May	0-0	0.00	23	4	0	1	3	.174	.174	.208
June	0-2	4.50	45	12	1	6	4	.267	.489	.365
July	0-1	7.94	24	7	1	5	4	.292	.542	.414
August	0-0	0.00	0	0	0	0	0	.000	.000	.000
Sept./Oct.	0-1	16.88	14	6	2	2	1	.429	.857	.500
Leading Off Inn.			29	11	2	2	4	.379	.690	.419
Bases Empty			61	17	2	10	8	.279	.426	.380
Runners On			68	22	4	9	8	.324	.632	.410
Runners/Scor. Pos.			43	13	2	9	4	.302	.535	.423
Runners On/2 Out			30	11	1	7	3	.367	.667	.486
Scor. Pos./2 Out			23	9	1	7	1	.391	.696	.533
Late-Inning Pressure			101	31	4	15	12	.307	.495	.402
Leading Off			24	9	2	1	4	.375	.667	.400
Runners On			51	17	2	8	5	.333	.569	.433
Runners/Scor. Pos.			33	10	1	8	3	.303	.455	.439
First 9 Batters			129	39	6	19	16	.302	.535	.396
Second 9 Batters			0	0	0	0	0	—	—	—
All Batters Thereafter			0	0	0	0	0	—	—	—

Loves to face: Gary Carter (.059, 1-for-17)
Robby Thompson (.111, 2-for-18)
Jeff Treadway (0-for-10)

Hates to face: Tony Gwynn (.533, 8-for-15)
Orlando Merced (2-for-2, 2 HR, 2 BB)
Mike Sharperson (2-for-2, 1 2B, 1 3B, 1 BB)

Miscellaneous statistics: Ground outs-to-air outs ratio: 1.13 last season, 1.39 for career.... Induced 5 double plays in 33 opportunities (one per 6.6).... Allowed 4 doubles, 4 triples in 33 innings.... Saved 17 games in 24 opportunities (71%).... Stranded 12 inherited runners, allowed 9 to score (57%).... Opposing base stealers: 3-for-3 (100%); 0 pickoffs, 1 balk.

Comments: First pitcher in major league history to lose as many as six games while pitching fewer than 34 innings for the season. Honorable mention goes to Frank LaCorte, 1–8 in 37 innings for the 1977 Braves.... Smith's 0–6 mark matched the Cubs' franchise record for most losses in a winless season, set by Dick Drott in 1960. In the team's 116-year history, only one other pitcher was even 0–5 (Dan McGinn in 1972).... He allowed as many home runs in 33 innings last season as he had in the previous four seasons (235⅔ innings) combined. That's what going from the Astrodome to Wrigley Field will do for you. Before last year, he had never allowed a home run in 103 opponents' at-bats at Wrigley; last year, he yielded four in 66 at-bats there.... Before last season, he had held opponents to .190 career batting average with runners on base and two outs, and had never allowed even a .250 average in that category in any of 11 previous seasons in the majors.... Of his first 22 appearances with Chicago, 21 came during Late-Inning Pressure Situations. Jim Essian apparently lost some confidence in Smith, summoning him in LIPS in only seven of his last 13 appearances.... Walked 5.18 batters per nine innings, the highest rate of his career, and more than two walks above his career average. His strikeout rate last year (4.36 per nine innings) was nearly two strikeouts below his career rate. Also set unwanted career highs for opponents' batting average (.302) and baserunners per nine innings (16.1).

Lee Smith

Throws Right

St. Louis Cardinals	W-L	ERA	AB	H	HR	BB	SO	BA	SA	OBA
Season	6-3	2.34	281	70	5	13	67	.249	.352	.281
vs. Left-Handers			165	42	3	11	43	.255	.364	.301
vs. Right-Handers			116	28	2	2	24	.241	.336	.252
vs. Ground-Ballers			113	33	1	6	30	.292	.398	.325
vs. Fly-Ballers			168	37	4	7	37	.220	.321	.251
Home Games	6-1	1.38	171	39	1	7	39	.228	.269	.257
Road Games	0-2	3.95	110	31	4	6	28	.282	.482	.319
Grass Fields	0-0	2.25	46	12	0	3	12	.261	.348	.306
Artificial Turf	6-3	2.36	235	58	5	10	55	.247	.353	.276
April	2-0	1.38	45	6	0	2	14	.133	.156	.170
May	0-2	6.14	31	10	1	2	6	.323	.581	.364
June	1-0	1.72	58	13	0	3	16	.224	.293	.258
July	2-0	2.70	54	16	2	1	12	.296	.444	.309
August	1-1	1.50	49	13	1	3	8	.265	.347	.308
Sept./Oct.	0-0	2.31	44	12	1	2	11	.273	.364	.304
Leading Off Inn.			61	15	2	3	13	.246	.377	.281
Bases Empty			153	38	2	6	29	.248	.359	.277
Runners On			128	32	3	7	38	.250	.344	.287
Runners/Scor. Pos.			87	23	2	6	25	.264	.368	.309
Runners On/2 Out			66	17	2	3	20	.258	.394	.290
Scor. Pos./2 Out			51	15	2	3	14	.294	.471	.333
Late-Inning Pressure			245	62	5	11	58	.253	.355	.284
Leading Off			53	14	2	2	11	.264	.415	.291
Runners On			114	29	3	6	34	.254	.351	.289
Runners/Scor. Pos.			76	20	2	5	22	.263	.368	.305
First 9 Batters			280	70	5	13	67	.250	.354	.282
Second 9 Batters			1	0	0	0	0	.000	.000	.000
All Batters Thereafter			0	0	0	0	0	—	—	—

Loves to face: John Kruk (0-for-10)
Andy Van Slyke (.040, 1-for-25, 1 HR, 4 BB)
Herm Winningham (.077, 1-for-13, 1 2B, 7 SO)

Hates to face: Mariano Duncan (.500, 5-for-10, 2 3B)
Billy Hatcher (.667, 4-for-6)
Mike Scioscia (.438, 7-for-16, 1 HR)

Miscellaneous statistics: Ground outs-to-air outs ratio: 0.70 last season, 1.05 for career.... Induced 3 double plays in 51 opportunities (one per 17).... Allowed 8 doubles, 3 triples in 73 innings.... Saved 47 games in 53 opportunities (89%), highest rate in N.L.... Stranded 14 inherited runners, allowed 12 to score (54%), 3d-lowest rate in N.L.... Opposing base stealers: 10-for-12 (83%); 0 pickoffs, 0 balks.

Comments: Appeared in at least 60 games in each of the last 10 seasons, a major league record. Only two other pitchers in major league history have had streaks of even eight straight 60-game seasons: Pedro Borbon (1972–79) and Jeff Reardon (1982–89). Two others, Rollie Fingers and Kent Tekulve, had seven-year streaks.... Of his 67 appearances, 61 came in Late-Inning Pressure Situations, the highest percentage (91%) of any pitcher in the major leagues. Only one other pitcher made at least 90 percent of his appearances in LIPS—John Franco.... In his successful drive toward the N.L. record for saves, Smith entered a game in a nonsave situation only once after August 3.... Saves by month: April (8), May (4), June (8), July (7), August (10), September (8), October (2).... Faced a single batter in only one of his 67 appearances.... Smith, Jeff Reardon, and Rollie Fingers are the only pitchers who have at least 50 career saves for three different clubs.... Needs 36 strikeouts to become only the fifth pitcher to accumulate 1000 strikeouts in relief; the others: Hoyt Wilhelm, Goose Gossage, Rollie Fingers, and Lindy McDaniel.... Walked an average of only 1.60 batters per nine innings, the lowest rate of his career, and more than two walks lower than his previous career rate. Five of his 13 walks were intentional (and yes, they *do* count when determining walks per nine innings).

Zane Smith   Throws Left

Pittsburgh Pirates	W-L	ERA	AB	H	HR	BB	SO	BA	SA	OBA
Season	16-10	3.20	873	234	15	29	120	.268	.370	.292
vs. Left-Handers			146	39	1	5	32	.267	.315	.291
vs. Right-Handers			727	195	14	24	88	.268	.381	.292
vs. Ground-Ballers			375	91	3	11	55	.243	.309	.265
vs. Fly-Ballers			498	143	12	18	65	.287	.416	.312
Home Games	11-3	2.78	491	132	10	14	69	.269	.385	.291
Road Games	5-7	3.74	382	102	5	15	51	.267	.351	.293
Grass Fields	1-6	5.24	184	61	4	7	21	.332	.429	.352
Artificial Turf	15-4	2.70	689	173	11	22	99	.251	.354	.275
April	2-1	2.70	108	33	2	5	14	.306	.417	.333
May	5-1	1.87	160	33	0	3	27	.206	.256	.220
June	1-4	3.96	141	43	3	8	13	.305	.418	.344
July	2-2	5.92	103	32	2	5	14	.311	.485	.339
August	2-1	2.70	159	45	3	2	20	.283	.346	.290
Sept./Oct.	4-1	3.17	202	48	5	6	32	.238	.361	.263
Leading Off Inn.			231	70	6	2	36	.303	.429	.309
Bases Empty			554	142	8	14	81	.256	.350	.275
Runners On			319	92	7	15	39	.288	.404	.320
Runners/Scor. Pos.			182	55	4	11	20	.302	.434	.340
Runners On/2 Out			125	34	2	6	18	.272	.392	.316
Scor. Pos./2 Out			76	23	1	4	10	.303	.434	.354
Late-Inning Pressure			95	28	2	1	12	.295	.379	.302
Leading Off			26	10	0	1	6	.385	.385	.407
Runners On			32	10	0	0	2	.313	.344	.313
Runners/Scor. Pos.			12	5	0	0	0	.417	.417	.417
First 9 Batters			301	79	7	10	48	.262	.399	.284
Second 9 Batters			293	80	4	10	40	.273	.365	.298
All Batters Thereafter			279	75	4	9	32	.269	.344	.292

Loves to face: Tom Pagnozzi (.056, 1-for-18, 2 BB)
                   Darryl Strawberry (.159, 7-for-44, 1 HR)
                   Andy Van Slyke (.100, 2-for-20)

Hates to face: Barry Larkin (.429, 15-for-35, 3 HR)
                   Terry Pendleton (.458, 22-for-48, 1 HR)
                   Benito Santiago (.385, 10-for-26, 4 HR)

Miscellaneous statistics: Ground outs-to-air outs ratio: 2.51 last season, highest in N.L.; 2.08 for career.... Induced 27 double plays in 149 opportunities (one per 5.5), best rate in N.L. for second consecutive season.... Allowed 36 doubles, 4 triples in 228 innings.... Allowed 17 first-inning runs in 35 starts (4.11 ERA).... Batting support: 4.57 runs per start.... Opposing base stealers: 26-for-34 (76%); 0 pickoffs, 0 balks.

Comments: Top-10 hitters in the league batted .458 against Smith, their highest collective average vs. any pitcher (minimum: 40 at-bats).... Despite 28–19 record over last two seasons, his career mark still stands 11 games below .500 (67–78).... Walked only 1.14 batters per nine innings last season, lowest rate of his career; he had averaged 2.09 in 1990, 3.18 in 1989.... The last Pirates pitcher to have a walk rate as low as Smith's 1991 mark? Bill Swift, 1.09 walks per nine innings in 1932.... Smith walked only one of 98 batters faced during Late-Inning Pressure Situations.... Pitched the shortest nine-inning game in the majors last year, a 1–0 win over Houston's Pete Harnisch that lasted an hour and 45 minutes.... Allowed left-handed batters 39 hits in 146 at-bats last season; over two previous years combined, he had allowed that group only 38 hits in 253 at-bats. Of the 77 home runs he has allowed in his career, only five have been hit by lefties (with no more than one in any single season): Barry Bonds (twice), Darryl Strawberry, Will Clark, and Greg Brock.... Best strategy against him is still to put baserunners in motion and avoid potential double plays. He's not especially adept at holding runners, nor at pitching with runners in scoring position: Opponents have batted over .280 in those situations in five of last six years.... Led N.L. pitchers with 10 RBIs last season; Pirates pitchers as a group led N.L. in that department (26).

John Smoltz   Throws Right

Atlanta Braves	W-L	ERA	AB	H	HR	BB	SO	BA	SA	OBA
Season	14-13	3.80	849	206	16	77	148	.243	.360	.305
vs. Left-Handers			486	140	10	60	69	.288	.422	.363
vs. Right-Handers			363	66	6	17	79	.182	.278	.221
vs. Ground-Ballers			422	107	6	34	80	.254	.365	.309
vs. Fly-Ballers			427	99	10	43	68	.232	.356	.301
Home Games	9-7	4.10	512	138	12	32	81	.270	.406	.312
Road Games	5-6	3.36	337	68	4	45	67	.202	.291	.295
Grass Fields	10-11	4.24	647	165	14	53	105	.255	.394	.311
Artificial Turf	4-2	2.43	202	41	2	24	43	.203	.252	.285
April	0-3	3.64	110	28	2	9	15	.255	.364	.311
May	2-3	4.20	149	39	5	13	26	.262	.463	.321
June	0-4	6.55	134	41	3	18	27	.306	.425	.380
July	4-2	7.85	115	32	6	13	12	.278	.504	.354
August	4-1	1.41	158	28	0	10	37	.177	.228	.226
Sept./Oct.	4-0	1.57	183	38	0	14	31	.208	.251	.263
Leading Off Inn.			216	57	4	21	38	.264	.370	.329
Bases Empty			499	121	11	45	89	.242	.357	.306
Runners On			350	85	5	32	59	.243	.366	.303
Runners/Scor. Pos.			192	50	4	26	37	.260	.422	.341
Runners On/2 Out			140	34	2	11	17	.243	.386	.298
Scor. Pos./2 Out			96	26	2	10	12	.271	.458	.340
Late-Inning Pressure			61	12	0	1	10	.197	.230	.210
Leading Off			18	6	0	1	3	.333	.444	.368
Runners On			20	4	0	0	3	.200	.200	.200
Runners/Scor. Pos.			9	3	0	0	2	.333	.333	.333
First 9 Batters			295	61	2	24	66	.207	.278	.268
Second 9 Batters			286	74	6	24	51	.259	.378	.314
All Batters Thereafter			268	71	8	29	31	.265	.433	.334

Loves to face: Darren Daulton (0-for-19)
                   Andre Dawson (.050, 1-for-20)
                   Dwight Smith (0-for-14)

Hates to face: Brett Butler (.438, 14-for-32)
                   Eric Davis (.556, 10-for-18, 4 HR)
                   Tony Gwynn (.515, 17-for-33, 2 HR)

Miscellaneous statistics: Ground outs-to-air outs ratio: 1.06 last season, 0.85 for career.... Induced 18 double plays in 183 opportunities (one per 10).... Allowed 38 doubles, 7 triples in 229⅔ innings.... Allowed 16 first-inning runs in 36 starts (4.00 ERA).... Batting support: 4.42 runs per start.... Opposing base stealers: 14-for-27 (52%); 4 pickoffs, 2 balks.

Comments: Started Game Seven of both Championship Series and World Series, becoming only the fourth pitcher to start a decisive game of both series in the same year; Blue Moon Odom (1972), Pete Vuckovich (1982), and Bret Saberhagen (1985) have also done it.... Career rate of 7.93 hits allowed per nine innings is lowest in Braves' history (minimum: 600 innings). That's *Braves'* history (dating from 1876), not just Atlanta history.... Smoltz has pitched 111 games in the majors, all as a starter. Since 1900, only one other pitcher has started at least 100 games without ever appearing in relief: teammate Tom Glavine (139).... Career opponents' batting average breakdown: .263 by left-handed batters, .200 by right-handers; .244 in night games, .208 in day games.... Became more of a ground-ball pitcher as game went on: Ground out-to-air out ratio was 0.75 during his first pass through the order, 1.12 during second pass, 1.39 thereafter.... After posting league's highest ERA during July, his August ERA was second lowest in N.L., and his ERA from September 1 on was the best.... Led majors with 20 wild pitches.... Had 2–11 record before All-Star break, 12–2 after. No pitcher since 1918 had finished a season with more wins than losses after standing nine games below .500 at some point during the season. (In 1918, Scott Perry of the Philadelphia Athletics rebounded from 5–14 to 20–19.) This year, Dr. Llewallyn's psychology practice should be quite busy during the break, Georgia state license or no.

Rick Sutcliffe

Throws Right

Chicago Cubs	W-L	ERA	AB	H	HR	BB	SO	BA	SA	OBA
Season	6-5	4.10	364	96	4	45	52	.264	.379	.338
vs. Left-Handers			218	63	4	30	24	.289	.436	.366
vs. Right-Handers			146	33	0	15	28	.226	.295	.294
vs. Ground-Ballers			166	38	2	23	21	.229	.343	.321
vs. Fly-Ballers			198	58	2	22	31	.293	.409	.352
Home Games	3-1	3.18	206	47	3	18	37	.228	.335	.284
Road Games	3-4	5.40	158	49	1	27	15	.310	.437	.404
Grass Fields	3-3	4.30	251	66	3	27	41	.263	.382	.327
Artificial Turf	3-2	3.64	113	30	1	18	11	.265	.372	.361
April	1-2	4.32	63	17	1	6	3	.270	.397	.329
May	1-2	8.59	93	32	1	11	11	.344	.495	.406
June	0-0	0.00	0	0	0	0	0	.000	.000	.000
July	0-0	—	0	0	0	0	0	.000	.000	.000
August	2-0	1.75	126	28	1	17	25	.222	.270	.308
Sept./Oct.	2-1	3.27	82	19	1	11	13	.232	.402	.316
Leading Off Inn.			91	25	1	11	9	.275	.363	.353
Bases Empty			206	54	3	23	25	.262	.393	.336
Runners On			158	42	1	22	27	.266	.361	.340
Runners/Scor. Pos.			103	25	1	20	21	.243	.340	.344
Runners On/2 Out			69	19	1	12	17	.275	.406	.383
Scor. Pos./2 Out			50	13	1	11	15	.260	.420	.393
Late-Inning Pressure			12	3	0	2	1	.250	.333	.357
Leading Off			4	2	0	1	0	.500	.500	.600
Runners On			6	1	0	0	1	.167	.333	.167
Runners/Scor. Pos.			3	0	0	0	1	.000	.000	.000
First 9 Batters			140	45	3	19	14	.321	.479	.393
Second 9 Batters			137	29	0	10	29	.212	.270	.262
All Batters Thereafter			87	22	1	16	9	.253	.391	.362

Loves to face: Paul Molitor (.050, 1-for-20, 2 BB)
John Russell (.059, 1-for-17, 1 HR)

Hates to face: Von Hayes (.441, 26-for-59, 5 HR)
Lloyd Moseby (.467, 7-for-15, 1 2B, 3 3B, 2 HR, 6 BB)
Dave Winfield (.419, 13-for-31, 5 HR)

Miscellaneous statistics: Ground outs-to-air outs ratio: 1.34 last season, 0.99 for career.... Induced 12 double plays in 67 opportunities (one per 5.6).... Allowed 20 doubles, 5 triples in 96⅔ innings.... Allowed 14 first-inning runs in 18 starts (7.00 ERA).... Batting support: 4.22 runs per start.... Opposing base stealers: 21-for-23 (91%); 0 pickoffs, 2 balks.

Comments: Allowed an average of one home run every 24.2 innings, the best rate of his career and the best by a Cubs pitcher since 1986, when Steve Trout allowed only six HRs in 161 innings (minimum: 15 GS).... Among N.L. pitchers, only teammate Frank Castillo faced more right-handed batters without allowing a home run last season.... Split his time on the mound almost equally among four batterymates: Damon Berryhill (22⅓ innings), Joe Girardi (21), Hector Villanueva (32⅓), and Rick Wilkins (21).... Only two opposing base runners were caught stealing with Sutcliffe on the mound last season, but they were good ones: Brett Butler and Otis Nixon.... Posted the highest ERA in the majors during May.... Has pitched a total of 118 innings over the last two seasons, after accumulating more than 200 innings in six of the previous eight.... One of nine N.L. pitchers to make two visits to the disabled list last season. The others: Atlee Hammaker, Norm Charlton, Larry Andersen, Scott Garrelts, Danny Jackson, Scott Scudder, Bob Walk, and Ed Whitson. Sutcliffe opened the season on the D.L. before making his debut 10 days into the campaign, then spent another 58 inactive days from June 9 through August 5.... His four September starts were on rests of 10 days, five days, seven days, and seven days. Buyer beware.... Returns to the American League having defeated each of the 26 major league teams except for Cleveland.

Bob Tewksbury

Throws Right

St. Louis Cardinals	W-L	ERA	AB	H	HR	BB	SO	BA	SA	OBA
Season	11-12	3.25	733	206	13	38	75	.281	.413	.317
vs. Left-Handers			405	113	4	31	30	.279	.393	.327
vs. Right-Handers			328	93	9	7	45	.284	.439	.304
vs. Ground-Ballers			300	74	7	14	32	.247	.380	.287
vs. Fly-Ballers			433	132	6	24	43	.305	.436	.337
Home Games	6-3	3.24	350	93	5	18	34	.266	.400	.308
Road Games	5-9	3.26	383	113	8	20	41	.295	.426	.325
Grass Fields	3-5	2.47	214	61	5	9	24	.285	.407	.310
Artificial Turf	8-7	3.56	519	145	8	29	51	.279	.416	.320
April	2-1	3.24	91	21	1	7	17	.231	.308	.280
May	1-1	4.29	81	30	0	5	3	.370	.519	.411
June	3-2	1.66	160	37	2	8	18	.231	.306	.272
July	1-3	2.32	118	31	4	5	15	.263	.407	.296
August	1-2	5.90	118	40	1	6	8	.339	.542	.364
Sept./Oct.	3-3	3.24	165	47	5	7	14	.285	.436	.312
Leading Off Inn.			189	54	3	9	23	.286	.434	.325
Bases Empty			442	127	8	18	50	.287	.423	.320
Runners On			291	79	5	20	25	.271	.399	.313
Runners/Scor. Pos.			169	48	4	15	16	.284	.438	.328
Runners On/2 Out			121	28	3	8	16	.231	.339	.285
Scor. Pos./2 Out			83	21	3	6	9	.253	.373	.303
Late-Inning Pressure			49	10	0	7	7	.204	.286	.304
Leading Off			14	5	0	2	2	.357	.571	.438
Runners On			22	2	0	3	4	.091	.136	.200
Runners/Scor. Pos.			10	1	0	1	2	.100	.100	.182
First 9 Batters			241	73	2	13	29	.303	.419	.333
Second 9 Batters			242	58	5	10	21	.240	.360	.274
All Batters Thereafter			250	75	6	15	25	.300	.460	.342

Loves to face: Kevin Bass (0-for-8)
Joe Girardi (.100, 1-for-10)
Hal Morris (0-for-12)

Hates to face: Daryl Boston (.563, 9-for-16)
Ryne Sandberg (.412, 7-for-17, 2 HR)
Andy Van Slyke (.455, 10-for-22)

Miscellaneous statistics: Ground outs-to-air outs ratio: 1.17 last season, 1.40 for career.... Induced 19 double plays in 143 opportunities (one per 7.5).... Allowed 42 doubles (tied for most in N.L.), 8 triples (3d most in N.L.) in 191 innings.... Allowed 27 first-inning runs in 30 starts (6.00 ERA), with an N.L.-high batting average of .395.... Batting support: 4.03 runs per start.... Opposing base stealers: 10-for-20 (50%); 0 pickoffs, 0 balks.

Comments: Faced 93 batters without a strikeout (May 15–June 8), longest N.L. streak over the past 12 years.... Career rate of 1.89 walks per nine innings is 2d lowest among active pitchers (minimum: 500 IP), behind Bret Saberhagen (1.79).... Career strikeout rate (3.49 per nine) is 3d lowest among same group, behind Jeff Ballard (2.81) and Bill Swift (3.46).... Eighty-five percent of opposing batters put the ball in play last season, the highest average in the N.L. (minimum: 100 IP). In 1990, Tewksbury compiled the highest such mark in the N.L. (88.6%) since 1980, when Bill Lee had a slightly higher mark (88.7%). The highest in major league history: 89.9 percent, by Pedro Borbon in 1975.... Which brings us to the subject of the meaningless category of strikeout-to-walk ratios for pitchers. Statistics are meant to enlighten, not obscure. Many statistics combine various elements in a useful way. For example, a player might compile a high slugging average by hitting 45 doubles, or 25 home runs, or 30 of each. But in all of those cases, the high average is the mark of an accomplished hitter. But in the case of strikeouts-to-walks, the whole is worth far less than the parts. Tewksbury is a case in point; because his walk rate is so low, his SO/BB ratio is respectable. But so what? Don't we learn much more about him through the components (extremely low rates in both individual categories) than we do by boiling them together and making mush? This is a case of the apples tasting far better than the apple sauce.

Randy Tomlin

Throws Left

Pittsburgh Pirates	W-L	ERA	AB	H	HR	BB	SO	BA	SA	OBA
Season	8-7	2.98	669	170	9	54	104	.254	.354	.315
vs. Left-Handers			134	23	1	13	30	.172	.216	.261
vs. Right-Handers			535	147	8	41	74	.275	.389	.329
vs. Ground-Ballers			269	68	2	18	42	.253	.342	.302
vs. Fly-Ballers			400	102	7	36	62	.255	.363	.323
Home Games	5-4	2.83	349	86	4	25	64	.246	.335	.301
Road Games	3-3	3.16	320	84	5	29	40	.262	.375	.330
Grass Fields	2-1	2.15	187	42	5	15	22	.225	.348	.282
Artificial Turf	6-6	3.32	482	128	4	39	82	.266	.357	.327
April	2-0	2.70	72	16	3	5	5	.222	.361	.278
May	1-1	2.45	70	18	0	7	12	.257	.371	.333
June	0-2	3.38	89	20	0	9	18	.225	.303	.310
July	3-0	0.88	105	23	2	11	17	.219	.305	.293
August	2-1	3.77	161	40	3	11	26	.248	.379	.303
Sept./Oct.	0-3	3.92	172	53	1	11	26	.308	.378	.350
Leading Off Inn.			162	43	2	20	16	.265	.358	.350
Bases Empty			359	87	4	37	45	.242	.323	.318
Runners On			310	83	5	17	59	.268	.390	.310
Runners/Scor. Pos.			156	44	1	15	28	.282	.378	.349
Runners On/2 Out			117	33	3	6	23	.282	.419	.323
Scor. Pos./2 Out			69	21	1	6	12	.304	.406	.368
Late-Inning Pressure			48	13	2	3	8	.271	.458	.340
Leading Off			13	3	0	2	3	.231	.308	.375
Runners On			14	6	1	1	2	.429	.786	.500
Runners/Scor. Pos.			8	2	0	1	1	.250	.375	.333
First 9 Batters			238	57	5	23	44	.239	.353	.311
Second 9 Batters			217	44	0	16	32	.203	.258	.264
All Batters Thereafter			214	69	4	15	28	.322	.453	.371

Loves to face: Ken Caminiti (.077, 1-for-13)
Vince Coleman (.071, 1-for-14)
Charlie O'Brien (.125, 2-for-16)

Hates to face: Andre Dawson (.545, 6-for-11, 2 HR)
Charlie Hayes (.600, 6-for-10)
Ryne Sandberg (.667, 6-for-9, 1 HR)

Miscellaneous statistics: Ground outs-to-air outs ratio: 1.37 last season, 1.42 for career.... Induced 15 double plays in 162 opportunities (one per 11).... Allowed 28 doubles, 6 triples in 175 innings.... Allowed 14 first-inning runs in 27 starts (3.33 ERA).... Batting support: 5.15 runs per start, 4th-highest average in N.L.... Opposing base stealers: 17-for-29 (59%); 8 pickoffs (3d most in N.L.), 3 balks.

Comments: Led N.L. pitchers with a 0.60 ERA against the Reds, and a 0.53 ERA against the Astros. He was the only left-handed pitcher to shut out the Reds last season. But he saved his best for the Mets, against whom he had a 4–0 mark.... Had a streak of 23 consecutive scoreless innings in July, tying him for the 3d-longest streak in the league last season, and helped him compile the lowest ERA in the majors for the month.... Was 0–3 with six no-decisions over his last nine starts, after having posted an 8–4 record with a 2.35 ERA through mid-August. His inning of scoreless relief in the regular-season finale dropped his ERA back below 3.00 for the season.... Opponents' on-base percentage leading off innings was the 4th highest in the league.... Laid down 13 sacrifice bunts last season, matching Zane Smith for most on the Pirates' staff, which led the league with 48 sac bunts.... The only opposing left-hander to take him deep last season was Mark Grace.... Career batting average of .196 by opposing left-handed batters, .256 by right-handers.... Although a ground-ball pitcher, his career total of 252⅔ innings is 2d highest among active pitchers who have never been involved in a double play as a fielder. Tommy Greene, who has pitched 259 innings without a DP, has a career ratio of 0.84, well below Tomlin's.... Only five active pitchers have career ERAs below 3.00 as starters (minimum: 200 IP). They are Hershiser (2.73), Clemens (2.85), Gooden (2.92), Tomlin (2.92), and Tim Belcher (2.98).

Frank Viola

Throws Left

New York Mets	W-L	ERA	AB	H	HR	BB	SO	BA	SA	OBA
Season	13-15	3.97	905	259	25	54	132	.286	.423	.325
vs. Left-Handers			193	45	5	11	35	.233	.363	.273
vs. Right-Handers			712	214	20	43	97	.301	.440	.339
vs. Ground-Ballers			395	113	5	20	64	.286	.382	.321
vs. Fly-Ballers			510	146	20	34	68	.286	.455	.328
Home Games	8-8	4.26	486	142	13	28	65	.292	.426	.328
Road Games	5-7	3.64	419	117	12	26	67	.279	.420	.323
Grass Fields	10-12	3.84	665	184	17	38	93	.277	.406	.315
Artificial Turf	3-3	4.33	240	75	8	16	39	.313	.471	.355
April	3-0	0.86	116	28	1	5	17	.241	.293	.273
May	3-2	3.46	159	45	5	10	23	.283	.428	.324
June	2-3	4.15	172	49	4	14	22	.285	.407	.337
July	3-2	2.66	153	33	5	7	24	.216	.353	.255
August	1-5	8.33	130	48	6	10	25	.369	.585	.408
Sept./Oct.	1-3	4.60	175	56	4	8	21	.320	.463	.348
Leading Off Inn.			229	63	7	10	31	.275	.437	.305
Bases Empty			531	148	17	32	73	.279	.431	.320
Runners On			374	111	8	22	59	.297	.412	.333
Runners/Scor. Pos.			203	55	4	19	34	.271	.365	.329
Runners On/2 Out			164	43	5	15	24	.262	.402	.328
Scor. Pos./2 Out			98	23	3	14	15	.235	.367	.336
Late-Inning Pressure			102	31	4	7	8	.304	.451	.345
Leading Off			31	6	1	0	3	.194	.355	.194
Runners On			34	11	1	2	1	.324	.412	.351
Runners/Scor. Pos.			13	4	0	0	0	.308	.308	.286
First 9 Batters			289	66	5	18	59	.228	.325	.273
Second 9 Batters			293	87	10	16	43	.297	.461	.332
All Batters Thereafter			323	106	10	20	30	.328	.477	.366

Loves to face: Henry Cotto (.059, 1-for-17, 1 2B)
Pete Incaviglia (.154, 6-for-39, 1 HR, 21 SO)
Mickey Tettleton (0-for-14)

Hates to face: Julio Franco (.425, 17-for-40, 2 HR)
Lloyd Moseby (.360, 18-for-50, 4 HR)
Alan Trammell (.293, 17-for-58, 5 HR)

Miscellaneous statistics: Ground outs-to-air outs ratio: 1.14 last season, 0.90 for career.... Induced 15 double plays in 173 opportunities (one per 12).... Allowed 41 doubles (3d most in N.L.), 4 triples in 231⅓ innings.... Allowed 5 first-inning runs in 35 starts (1.03 ERA, lowest in N.L.).... Batting support: 3.40 runs per start, 4th-lowest average in N.L.... Opposing base stealers: 6-for-22 (27%, lowest rate in majors); 6 pickoffs, 1 balk.

Comments: Opponents had 122 first-inning at-bats without a home run. He hasn't allowed a first-inning homer in 46 starts since August 12, 1990.... ERA in home games was 3d highest among qualifying N.L. pitchers last season.... His April ERA was the lowest in the N.L, but his August ERA was the highest in the league.... Strikeout rate fell as game progressed: one every 5.3 plate appearances during his first pass through the order, one every 7.3 during his second pass, one every 11.7 thereafter.... Opponents batted only .228 during his first pass through the order, but hit .313 thereafter.... His seven-game losing streak was the longest by a Mets starter since Ed Lynch lost seven straight in 1984. The last Mets starter with a longer streak: Jerry Koosman, 9 in 1977.... Walked an average of 2.24 batters per nine innings during time with the Mets, the 2d-lowest rate in franchise history (minimum: 500 IP), behind Lynch (1.95).... Viola's the first pitcher to hurl 200 innings in nine consecutive seasons since the 1981 season snapped streaks of at least 10 years by Bert Blyleven, Steve Carlton, Phil Niekro, Gaylord Perry, and Don Sutton.... After his second major league season, Viola had a career record of 11–25 with a 5.38 ERA. Only three other pitchers in this century lost as many as 28 of their first 40 decisions but eventually won 150 or more games: Red Ruffing (273 career wins), Camilo Pascual (174 wins), and Jim Kaat (283). Pascual was 10–30 after 40 decisions; the others, including Viola, were all 12–28.

Bob Walk

Throws Right

Pittsburgh Pirates	W-L	ERA	AB	H	HR	BB	SO	BA	SA	OBA
Season	9-2	3.60	433	104	10	35	67	.240	.363	.302
vs. Left-Handers			244	63	5	21	30	.258	.385	.323
vs. Right-Handers			189	41	5	14	37	.217	.333	.274
vs. Ground-Ballers			195	43	1	20	30	.221	.303	.303
vs. Fly-Ballers			238	61	9	15	37	.256	.412	.301
Home Games	4-2	3.48	231	56	3	18	39	.242	.346	.301
Road Games	5-0	3.74	202	48	7	17	28	.238	.381	.303
Grass Fields	2-0	3.93	124	27	5	14	15	.218	.387	.307
Artificial Turf	7-2	3.46	309	77	5	21	52	.249	.353	.300
April	0-0	4.22	39	8	2	6	7	.205	.410	.311
May	1-0	2.13	46	11	2	6	8	.239	.370	.352
June	5-0	3.68	110	25	2	10	15	.227	.373	.298
July	1-2	2.63	99	21	2	6	17	.212	.333	.252
August	0-0	0.00	0	0	0	0	0	.000	.000	.000
Sept./Oct.	2-0	4.63	139	39	2	7	20	.281	.360	.320
Leading Off Inn.			108	23	2	10	20	.213	.324	.286
Bases Empty			263	55	5	25	41	.209	.316	.285
Runners On			170	49	5	10	26	.288	.435	.328
Runners/Scor. Pos.			101	28	3	8	13	.277	.426	.330
Runners On/2 Out			68	11	1	5	14	.162	.235	.219
Scor. Pos./2 Out			42	5	0	5	6	.119	.167	.213
Late-Inning Pressure			13	4	0	0	2	.308	.385	.308
Leading Off			4	2	0	0	1	.500	.750	.500
Runners On			5	1	0	0	1	.200	.200	.200
Runners/Scor. Pos.			4	1	0	0	0	.250	.250	.250
First 9 Batters			189	48	6	15	26	.254	.392	.316
Second 9 Batters			149	38	2	13	26	.255	.349	.321
All Batters Thereafter			95	18	2	7	15	.189	.326	.243

Loves to face: Jose Uribe (.120, 3-for-25)
Tim Wallach (.164, 9-for-55, 1 HR)
Matt Williams (0-for-9, 1 BB)

Hates to face: Ken Oberkfell (.422, 19-for-45)
Lonnie Smith (.647, 11-for-17, 3 HR)
Darryl Strawberry (.400, 8-for-20, 1 2B, 4 HR)

Miscellaneous statistics: Ground outs-to-air outs ratio: 1.19 last season, 1.25 for career.... Induced 7 double plays in 80 opportunities (one per 11).... Allowed 21 doubles, 1 triple in 115 innings.... Allowed 15 first-inning runs in 20 starts (6.30 ERA).... Batting support: 5.35 runs per start, 2d-highest average in N.L.... Opposing base stealers: 7-for-11 (64%); 1 pickoff, 2 balks.

Comments: Led the National League with five wins during June.... Has finished each of the last five seasons with at least two more wins than losses; among N.L. pitchers, only Dwight Gooden has a streak that long (eight years for Doc).... Funny, but those guys also rank first and second among N.L. pitchers in batting support over the past five years (minimum: 100 GS). Gooden got 5.20 runs per start; Walk received an average of 4.68 runs. In fact, each of the top 11 on that list had a winning record, compiling a .576 winning percentage (619–456).... Career record of 76–57 (3.97 ERA) in 208 starts, 6–4 (3.12 ERA) in 74 relief appearances.... Visited the disabled list twice last season for stints of 29 days (April 15–May 14) and 36 days (July 27–September 1).... He pitched to a decision in only nine of 20 starts last season, and in only 14 of his last 37 starts dating back to May 1990.... Over the last four seasons, he has allowed 17 home runs at Three Rivers Stadium, 31 on the road.... Although the three franchises for which Walk has pitched date back to the beginning of time, only one other pitcher has appeared in at least 25 games for the Pirates, Braves, and Phillies: Larry McWilliams.... We wonder if he read last year's *Analyst*, in which we wrote that his 370 career at-bats were 5th most among active batters who had never homered. In his second at-bat of the 1991 season, Walk homered against Danny Jackson.

Wally Whitehurst

Throws Right

New York Mets	W-L	ERA	AB	H	HR	BB	SO	BA	SA	OBA
Season	7-12	4.19	518	142	12	25	87	.274	.409	.311
vs. Left-Handers			270	80	7	15	46	.296	.452	.334
vs. Right-Handers			248	62	5	10	41	.250	.363	.285
vs. Ground-Ballers			248	65	3	11	42	.262	.375	.304
vs. Fly-Ballers			270	77	9	14	45	.285	.441	.317
Home Games	3-7	4.43	242	68	5	12	44	.281	.405	.319
Road Games	4-5	3.98	276	74	7	13	43	.268	.413	.304
Grass Fields	4-9	4.31	337	90	8	17	62	.267	.395	.307
Artificial Turf	3-3	3.97	181	52	4	8	25	.287	.436	.318
April	1-1	3.60	72	20	2	2	7	.278	.444	.297
May	2-1	3.18	64	14	1	4	15	.219	.313	.275
June	1-2	3.41	125	34	3	5	23	.272	.392	.300
July	1-3	4.94	89	22	3	6	16	.247	.404	.299
August	0-3	7.31	73	26	1	4	12	.356	.507	.385
Sept./Oct.	2-2	3.60	95	26	2	4	14	.274	.400	.314
Leading Off Inn.			135	36	4	3	16	.267	.422	.288
Bases Empty			318	83	6	13	48	.261	.374	.294
Runners On			200	59	6	12	39	.295	.465	.336
Runners/Scor. Pos.			113	30	2	9	30	.265	.389	.317
Runners On/2 Out			79	18	1	9	18	.228	.367	.307
Scor. Pos./2 Out			47	12	1	8	12	.255	.404	.364
Late-Inning Pressure			48	16	1	0	5	.333	.458	.333
Leading Off			15	4	0	0	2	.267	.333	.267
Runners On			15	4	0	0	1	.267	.533	.267
Runners/Scor. Pos.			6	2	0	0	1	.333	.333	.333
First 9 Batters			258	65	7	12	54	.252	.395	.293
Second 9 Batters			167	49	2	10	24	.293	.389	.331
All Batters Thereafter			93	28	3	3	9	.301	.484	.323

Loves to face: Andres Galarraga (0-for-9)
Mark Grace (.143, 2-for-14)
Tim Wallach (0-for-10)

Hates to face: Craig Biggio (.667, 6-for-9)
Barry Larkin (.500, 5-for-10, 1 HR)
Ryne Sandberg (.400, 4-for-10, 2 HR)

Miscellaneous statistics: Ground outs-to-air outs ratio: 2.37 last season, 2d highest in N.L.; 2.12 for career.... Induced 12 double plays in 92 opportunities (one per 7.7).... Allowed 24 doubles, 5 triples in 133⅓ innings.... Allowed 12 first-inning runs in 20 starts (4.95 ERA).... Batting support: 3.85 runs per start.... Record of 5–11, 4.53 ERA as a starter; 2–1, 2.77 ERA in 16 relief appearances.... Stranded 4 inherited runners, allowed 4 to score (50%).... Opposing base stealers: 9-for-17 (53%); 0 pickoffs, 4 balks (3d most in N.L.).

Comments: His six-game losing streak started only hours after the Mets traded Ron Darling, in effect giving Whitehurst a locked spot in the rotation. He was 5–4 with a 3.17 ERA at the time of Darling's departure, 2–8 with a 5.56 ERA thereafter. That six-game losing streak was the longest by a Mets starter since 1987, when Darling lost six in a row.... Record of 5–11 as a starter represented the lowest winning percentage by a Mets starter since Pete Falcone went 6–14 in 1979 (minimum: 15 decisions).... Among N.L. pitchers with at least 100 innings last season, only Zane Smith walked fewer batters per nine innings than Whitehurst. His career rate of 1.65 per nine innings places him neatly into a crevice between Christy Mathewson (1.59) and Grover Cleveland Alexander (1.65). Also in that nook: Kevin Tapani (1.64).... Walked the leadoff hitter only three times in 139 innings, but one of them was Astros rookie pitcher Darryl Kile, 0-for-his-career.... Started 20 games but never reached the ninth inning.... Strikeout rate fell as games progressed: one every 5.1 batters on his first pass through the order, one per 7.6 on his second pass, one per 10.9 thereafter.... Career record of 5–12 (4.75 ERA) in 21 starts, 3–1 (3.06 ERA) in 62 relief appearances.... Spent 15 days on the disabled list with a thigh bruise. You know, the kind of injury that keeps a hockey player out of a game for a shift or two.

Mitch Williams — Throws Left

Philadelphia Phillies	W-L	ERA	AB	H	HR	BB	SO	BA	SA	OBA
Season	12-5	2.34	308	56	4	62	84	.182	.266	.330
vs. Left-Handers			68	13	0	12	17	.191	.279	.353
vs. Right-Handers			240	43	4	50	67	.179	.262	.323
vs. Ground-Ballers			103	19	0	19	24	.184	.243	.317
vs. Fly-Ballers			206	37	4	43	60	.180	.277	.335
Home Games	9-2	2.11	168	32	0	34	50	.190	.244	.343
Road Games	3-3	2.61	140	24	4	28	34	.171	.293	.314
Grass Fields	1-2	3.65	85	15	4	15	19	.176	.341	.308
Artificial Turf	11-3	1.84	223	41	0	47	65	.184	.238	.338
April	0-2	2.57	46	7	1	12	12	.152	.304	.339
May	0-0	3.12	32	8	1	4	11	.250	.375	.351
June	1-1	3.75	45	12	1	10	12	.267	.400	.411
July	0-0	1.50	43	7	1	6	9	.163	.256	.294
August	8-1	1.21	73	10	0	16	22	.137	.164	.309
Sept./Oct.	3-1	2.79	69	12	0	14	18	.174	.217	.306
Leading Off Inn.			62	11	2	14	12	.177	.290	.354
Bases Empty			133	31	3	31	29	.233	.338	.393
Runners On			175	25	1	31	55	.143	.211	.280
Runners/Scor. Pos.			102	11	1	21	33	.108	.167	.269
Runners On/2 Out			81	11	0	13	23	.136	.198	.263
Scor. Pos./2 Out			53	7	0	9	18	.132	.170	.258
Late-Inning Pressure			246	44	3	56	70	.179	.260	.342
Leading Off			51	9	1	12	11	.176	.255	.354
Runners On			140	18	1	27	47	.129	.200	.280
Runners/Scor. Pos.			78	8	1	17	26	.103	.154	.275
First 9 Batters			304	56	4	61	82	.184	.270	.332
Second 9 Batters			4	0	0	1	2	.000	.000	.200
All Batters Thereafter			0	0	0	0	0	—	—	—

Loves to face: Mark Grace (0-for-9)
Rex Hudler (0-for-10)
Darryl Strawberry (0-for-10, 7 SO)
Hates to face: Kevin Bass (.500, 3-for-6, 1 2B, 2 HR)
Ozzie Smith (.417, 5-for-12, 3 2B)
Andy Van Slyke (.313, 5-for-16, 1 HR)

Miscellaneous statistics: Ground outs-to-air outs ratio: 0.60 last season, 0.67 for career.... Induced 3 double plays in 97 opportunities (one per 32).... Allowed 12 doubles, 1 triple in 88⅓ innings.... Saved 30 games in 39 opportunities (77%).... Stranded 18 inherited runners, allowed 6 to score (75%).... Opposing base stealers: 12-for-14 (86%); 1 pickoff, 1 balk.

Comments: He won eight games during August, the most ever by a relief pitcher in one calendar month. No other pitcher, starter or reliever, won more than six games in any month last season. Three of those wins resulted when Williams squandered a lead and subsequently became the pitcher of decision.... Ranked second in the majors with 11 wins after the All-Star break.... Opponents were hitless in 16 at-bats with the bases loaded, the best of any pitcher in the majors last season. Opponents have a career average of .160 with the bags full, but Williams has walked 20 of 135 batters faced in those situations.... Has hit 41 batters in 511 innings, the highest ratio among active pitchers.... Opponents' batting averages with runners on base and with runners in scoring position were the lowest single-season marks in the 17-year history of *The Player Analysis*.... His streak of 39 consecutive batters faced with runners in scoring position without allowing a hit was the longest in the N.L. last season (July 6–August 17).... He also had the N.L.'s longest streak of hitless batters faced in Late-Inning Pressure Situations (31, July 30–August 9).... Has allowed a career average of 6.46 hits per nine innings, the lowest rate among active pitchers (minimum: 500 IP). That's slightly lower than Nolan Ryan's career average (6.50); but Williams's walk rate (6.76 per nine innings) is not only the highest among active pitchers, it's the 2d highest of all-time, behind Tommy Byrne (6.85).

Trevor Wilson — Throws Left

San Francisco Giants	W-L	ERA	AB	H	HR	BB	SO	BA	SA	OBA
Season	13-11	3.56	740	173	13	77	139	.234	.343	.308
vs. Left-Handers			160	27	1	22	39	.169	.213	.270
vs. Right-Handers			580	146	12	55	100	.252	.379	.319
vs. Ground-Ballers			325	80	2	34	63	.246	.335	.319
vs. Fly-Ballers			415	93	11	43	76	.224	.349	.300
Home Games	8-4	2.71	426	91	7	43	78	.214	.317	.288
Road Games	5-7	4.81	314	82	6	34	61	.261	.379	.335
Grass Fields	11-7	3.23	563	126	10	58	101	.224	.330	.297
Artificial Turf	2-4	4.70	177	47	3	19	38	.266	.384	.343
April	0-2	6.92	50	13	1	11	12	.260	.340	.397
May	1-2	2.87	108	22	2	10	20	.204	.333	.271
June	3-2	3.23	143	38	3	15	19	.266	.399	.338
July	3-3	4.29	132	29	3	14	25	.220	.333	.302
August	2-0	2.63	150	36	2	12	35	.240	.360	.294
Sept./Oct.	4-2	3.64	157	35	2	15	28	.223	.293	.293
Leading Off Inn.			183	40	1	23	31	.219	.262	.309
Bases Empty			433	96	7	42	79	.222	.314	.294
Runners On			307	77	6	35	60	.251	.384	.329
Runners/Scor. Pos.			178	47	4	26	34	.264	.416	.358
Runners On/2 Out			128	26	2	20	25	.203	.313	.320
Scor. Pos./2 Out			81	20	2	18	14	.247	.395	.396
Late-Inning Pressure			61	16	2	8	9	.262	.377	.348
Leading Off			16	3	0	4	4	.188	.188	.350
Runners On			21	4	0	4	3	.190	.238	.320
Runners/Scor. Pos.			12	2	0	4	1	.167	.167	.375
First 9 Batters			298	68	4	39	56	.228	.312	.322
Second 9 Batters			229	63	7	21	46	.275	.454	.332
All Batters Thereafter			213	42	2	17	37	.197	.268	.263

Loves to face: Delino DeShields (0-for-13)
Terry Pendleton (.111, 2-for-18)
Darryl Strawberry (0-for-13)
Hates to face: Ivan Calderon (.429, 3-for-7, 2 HR)
Ken Caminiti (.333, 6-for-18, 2 2B, 3 HR)
Mariano Duncan (.400, 6-for-15)

Miscellaneous statistics: Ground outs-to-air outs ratio: 1.72 last season, 1.65 for career.... Induced 18 double plays in 151 opportunities (one per 8.4).... Allowed 32 doubles, 5 triples in 202 innings.... Allowed 24 first-inning runs in 29 starts (7.45 ERA, 2d highest in N.L.).... Batting support: 3.90 runs per start.... Record of 13–8, 3.47 ERA as a starter; 0–3, 4.30 ERA in 15 relief appearances.... Stranded 6 inherited runners, allowed 2 to score (75%).... Opposing base stealers: 8-for-20 (40%, 4th-lowest rate in N.L.); 6 pickoffs, 3 balks.

Comments: Shutout victory over Dodgers on final Saturday of season clinched division title for Atlanta.... Finished season without allowing an earned run in his last 26 innings against Los Angeles.... Posted a 2.85 ERA in 110⅔ innings with Kirt Manwaring behind the plate, and a 4.43 ERA in 91⅓ innings with either Steve Decker or Terry Kennedy.... His ERA in home games was 6th best among qualifying N.L. pitchers; his ERA in road games was 6th worst in the league, but it was only the 3d highest on the Giants staff—lower than either Bud Black (5.28) or John Burkett (4.90).... Opponents batted only .219 leading off innings last season, but his rate of walks to leadoff batters (one every nine batters faced) was 4th highest among N.L. pitchers.... Allowed only four extra-base hits to left-handed batters, none after a Mark Grace double on June 22.... Opposing left-handers have a career batting average of .188, compared to .241 by right-handers. Only two left-handed batters have ever homered against him: David Justice (1990) and Paul O'Neill (1991).... Opponents have a career average of .214 in his first pass through the order, .277 in his second pass, and .202 in subsequent at-bats.... Career record of 21–18 (3.69 ERA) in 54 starts, 2–5 (4.45 ERA) in 35 relief appearances.... As a batter, he reached base safely in eight consecutive plate appearances leading off innings. The only other Giants players with streaks that long over the past 10 years: Mike Aldrete (1988) and Will Clark (1989). None had a longer streak.

ROOKIES AND PROSPECTS SECTION

Is it possible to predict how a player will do in an upcoming season based on his past performance? The concept may seem foreign to baseball fans, but that's exactly how the country's horseplayers make their living—or try to. At least one baseball publication prints projected batting statistics for the upcoming season for every player in the majors—an inane endeavor that melts the peaks and valleys off each player's range of possibilities until three-quarters of them look like clones of Ken Caminiti. No one we know takes those predictions seriously, and for good reason— they simply have no reason to trust them. The better question is, can such a system be done well?

We once observed that baseball predictions provide cheap thrills, and that unlike stock market recommendations and weather forecasts, at least no one loses money or gets wet when they're wrong. But the proliferation of fantasy leagues has changed that. Our readers now want and deserve something better—a system that acknowledges the wide range of career paths that a player might subsequently take, but one that nevertheless identifies the most likely middle road. Toward that end, we spent much of last summer field-testing a series of forecasting routines against more than 100 years of baseball history. By matching the projections for hundreds of rookies from the past against their subsequent performances, we were able to fine-tune the process. The model that resulted proved surprisingly accurate—so accurate, in fact, that we felt these projections deserved a section of their own. From our own experience, we guarantee that those who don't play in fantasy leagues will find this information as fascinating as those who do will find it useful.

The Rookies and Prospects Section is unlike anything we've published before in that its *raison d'etre* is not fact but fantasy. On the other hand, the forecasts are based on an analysis of past players so comprehensive and fact-based that it would have been inconceivable even a year or two ago—as unlikely as, say, a Japanese League refugee tearing up the American League, or nearly 20 no-hitters over a two-year period.

Our forecasts here are limited to rookies—the players about whom we have the most to learn. (We could try to project Cecil Fielder's 1992 season, but would it really tell you anything you don't already know?) By modifying various characteristics of the forecasting model, accurate projections were possible not only for rookies who played throughout the season, but also for late-season arrivals—prospects recalled in September who played regularly during the final month. Specifically, this section will include rookies with at least 200 plate appearances for the season, and others who batted at least 50 times from September 1 on.

For each player, basic batting totals and a few pertinent breakdowns are shown. (For rookies with at least 250 plate appearances, this will duplicate a few lines also found in the Batters Section.) That information is followed by a listing of the five rookies since 1960 with the most comparable batting statistics.

(When fewer than five *recent* comparable rookies were found, players were listed without regard to when they played.) The projections follow, based on an analysis of the careers of not only the five statistical clones shown above them, but also those of dozens or perhaps hundreds more, regardless of when they played.

Projections are made for the upcoming season and for the players' career totals on both a best-guess and a best-case basis. The latter is a purposely optimistic forecast representing a statistical appraisal of the upper limits that the player might reasonably attain— not an absolute limit, but one that he stands roughly one chance in five of achieving. Beyond that, who knows?

How accurate can you expect the projections to be? Let's look at the rookie class of 1964 as an example. That season became one of our prime testing grounds because of its range of rookies, from busts like Derrell Griffith and Mike White to superstars like Dick Allen, Tony Conigliaro, and Tony Oliva. We projected the next-season performance for 33 rookies who batted at least 200 times. The ultimate forecasting model produced these results: At-bats were within 10 percent for half the players, within 30 percent for all but seven. Batting average predictions fell within 15 points of the actual figures for half, within 30 points for all but two. Home-run estimates came within three for 27 of the 33 players. Some highlights:

Dick Allen	AB	H	2B	3B	HR	RBI	BB	SO	BA	SA	OBA
Projected	621	198	36	11	28	111	77	114	.319	.548	.396
Actual	632	201	38	13	29	91	67	138	.318	.557	.382

Jesus Alou	AB	H	2B	3B	HR	RBI	BB	SO	BA	SA	OBA
Projected	376	95	15	4	3	36	13	34	.252	.338	.279
Actual	376	103	11	0	3	28	13	35	.274	.327	.305

Gates Brown	AB	H	2B	3B	HR	RBI	BB	SO	BA	SA	OBA
Projected	463	123	23	5	16	66	39	49	.265	.434	.323
Actual	426	116	22	6	15	54	31	53	.272	.458	.326

Dick Green	AB	H	2B	3B	HR	RBI	BB	SO	BA	SA	OBA
Projected	469	124	22	4	11	60	29	81	.264	.399	.307
Actual	435	115	14	5	11	37	27	87	.264	.395	.311

John Herrnstein	AB	H	2B	3B	HR	RBI	BB	SO	BA	SA	OBA
Projected	312	76	12	2	6	33	27	73	.243	.351	.305
Actual	303	71	12	4	6	25	22	67	.234	.360	.288

Hawk Taylor	AB	H	2B	3B	HR	RBI	BB	SO	BA	SA	OBA
Projected	211	50	8	2	3	23	9	46	.238	.330	.272
Actual	225	54	8	0	4	23	8	33	.240	.329	.272

A final issue: When should the optimistic forecast be given greater consideration? The best-case projections are especially pertinent for rookies who won starting jobs after the All-Star break. Consider the case of Hal Morris, who spent most of the first half of 1990 in the minors but started regularly for Cincinnati for the last three months of the season. Remember that the projections are based on an analysis of players with similar batting statistics in their own rookie seasons. Morris's forecast was therefore based on rookies who, among their other characteristics, had roughly 300 at-bats. Some, like Morris himself, might have played regularly for a half-season. But others (and most likely the majority of the group) were part-timers who pulled several hundred at-bats together over the course of six months. The prognosis for the former group is obviously much better, but the best-guess forecast is based primarily on the latter group. Compare the estimates below for Morris's 1991 season to his actual performance:

	AB	H	2B	3B	HR	RBI	BB	SO	BA	SA	OBA
Best Guess	458	126	23	7	9	59	33	53	.275	.420	.324
Optimistic	537	168	32	14	16	94	58	28	.313	.516	.382
1991 Actual	505	164	42	2	14	68	44	61	.324	.495	.375

Morris's actual performance ultimately approximated the optimistic estimate. So, for best results, give more weight to the optimistic scenario for players who are significantly more productive after the All-Star break than before it. That would include the prospects who batted at least 50 times in September and October, but less than 200 times for the season.

Did someone mention pitchers? They are included in this section as well, although without projections. (Believe us—if we develop a forecasting model as accurate for pitchers as the one for batters, you'll read about it here first.) Each season, there are a dozen or so pitchers who take regular turns in the rotation over the final month of the season but fail to pitch enough over the entire season to be included in our Pitcher Section. Often they become regular starters a year later; such was the case with Rich Delucia, Alex Fernandez, Chris Nabholz, and Randy Tomlin last season. They will appear in the Rookies and Prospects Section on a basis similar to those found in the Pitcher Section—basic statistics, significant breakdowns, and miscellaneous statistics.

Have fun!

Jeff Bagwell

Bats Right
Born May 27, 1968

Houston Astros	AB	H	2B	3B	HR	RBI	BB	SO	BA	SA	OBA
Season	554	163	26	4	15	82	75	116	.294	.437	.387
vs. Left-Handers	206	66	10	0	7	37	33	37	.320	.471	.417
vs. Right-Handers	348	97	16	4	8	45	42	79	.279	.417	.369
vs. Ground-Ballers	252	75	10	2	4	40	35	49	.298	.401	.394
vs. Fly-Ballers	305	88	16	2	11	42	41	67	.289	.462	.379

Most Comparable Rookie Seasons:

Bernie Allen	573	154	27	7	12	64	62	82	.269	.403	.341
Wally Joyner	593	172	27	3	22	100	57	58	.290	.457	.353
Mike A. Marshall	465	132	17	1	17	65	43	127	.284	.434	.346
Gary Matthews	540	162	22	10	12	58	58	83	.300	.444	.369
Rich Rollins	624	186	23	5	16	96	75	62	.298	.428	.375

Projections for 1992:

Best Guess	546	152	29	7	17	80	88	100	.278	.449	.379
Optimistic	592	177	37	10	26	106	122	64	.299	.526	.420

Projections for career:

Best Guess	4715	1309	221	39	132	661	705	940	.278	.425	.373
Optimistic	6599	1923	352	91	239	1063	1286	952	.291	.481	.408

Bret Barberie

Bats Left and Right
Born Aug. 16, 1967

Montreal Expos	AB	H	2B	3B	HR	RBI	BB	SO	BA	SA	OBA
Season	136	48	12	2	2	18	20	22	.353	.515	.435
vs. Left-Handers	37	10	3	0	1	5	6	5	.270	.432	.364
vs. Right-Handers	99	38	9	2	1	13	14	17	.384	.545	.462
vs. Ground-Ballers	68	28	6	2	1	5	9	12	.412	.603	.487
vs. Fly-Ballers	68	20	6	0	1	13	11	10	.294	.426	.386

Most Comparable Rookie Seasons:

W. Butch Davis	122	42	2	6	2	18	4	19	.344	.508	.366
Danny Litwhiler	142	49	2	2	5	17	3	13	.345	.493	.360
George Nicol	128	47	7	4	0	22	2	4	.367	.484	.378
John Stone	113	40	10	3	2	21	5	8	.354	.549	.383
Joe Sugden	139	46	13	2	2	23	14	2	.331	.496	.393

Projections for 1992:

Best Guess	498	129	24	6	9	56	117	57	.260	.387	.402
Optimistic	590	180	43	8	18	76	158	57	.305	.497	.453

Projections for career:

Best Guess	3488	981	190	32	82	543	974	522	.281	.425	.439
Optimistic	5160	1494	356	67	155	861	1903	564	.290	.475	.482

Juan Bell

Bats Left and Right
Born Mar. 29, 1968

Baltimore Orioles	AB	H	2B	3B	HR	RBI	BB	SO	BA	SA	OBA
Season	209	36	9	2	1	15	8	51	.172	.249	.201
vs. Left-Handers	48	5	1	0	0	0	0	16	.104	.125	.104
vs. Right-Handers	161	31	8	2	1	15	8	35	.193	.286	.228
vs. Ground-Ballers	77	9	3	1	0	3	2	16	.117	.182	.139
vs. Fly-Ballers	132	27	6	1	1	12	6	35	.205	.288	.236

Most Comparable Rookie Seasons:

Mark Belanger	184	32	5	0	1	10	12	46	.174	.217	.226
Frank Coggins	171	30	6	1	0	7	9	33	.175	.222	.218
Terry Humphrey	215	40	8	0	1	9	16	38	.186	.237	.244
Mike Miley	224	39	3	2	4	26	16	54	.174	.259	.230
Joe Rudi	181	32	5	1	1	12	12	32	.177	.232	.229

Projections for 1992:

Best Guess	53	9	1	0	0	3	1	18	.167	.204	.189
Optimistic	218	50	10	1	5	23	10	37	.231	.353	.267

Projections for career:

Best Guess	691	141	25	4	4	60	28	168	.204	.271	.236
Optimistic	1780	433	82	18	39	199	103	291	.243	.376	.286

Mike Bordick

Bats Right
Born Jul. 21, 1965

Oakland A's	AB	H	2B	3B	HR	RBI	BB	SO	BA	SA	OBA
Season	235	56	5	1	0	21	14	37	.238	.268	.289
vs. Left-Handers	58	13	1	0	0	6	4	6	.224	.241	.274
vs. Right-Handers	177	43	4	1	0	15	10	31	.243	.277	.293
vs. Ground-Ballers	111	29	3	1	0	8	4	13	.261	.306	.305
vs. Fly-Ballers	124	27	2	0	0	13	10	24	.218	.234	.274

Most Comparable Rookie Seasons:

Kent Anderson	223	51	6	1	0	17	17	42	.229	.265	.285
Jim Essian	199	49	7	0	0	21	23	28	.246	.281	.325
Bobby Pfeil	211	49	9	0	0	10	7	27	.232	.275	.258
Jimmy Rosario	192	43	6	1	0	13	33	35	.224	.266	.339
Rick Sweet	226	50	8	0	1	11	27	22	.221	.270	.306

Projections for 1992:

Best Guess	167	38	6	1	1	14	10	26	.230	.290	.273
Optimistic	332	91	17	6	5	39	30	32	.273	.405	.334

Projections for career:

Best Guess	809	193	24	5	5	70	50	133	.238	.297	.283
Optimistic	1734	457	69	18	30	196	142	197	.264	.376	.321

Andujar Cedeno

Bats Right
Born Aug. 21, 1969

Houston Astros	AB	H	2B	3B	HR	RBI	BB	SO	BA	SA	OBA
Season	251	61	13	2	9	36	9	74	.243	.418	.270
vs. Left-Handers	80	17	4	0	0	10	1	24	.213	.262	.220
vs. Right-Handers	171	44	9	2	9	26	8	50	.257	.491	.293
vs. Ground-Ballers	103	17	2	0	3	16	3	28	.165	.272	.193
vs. Fly-Ballers	148	44	11	2	6	20	6	46	.297	.520	.325

Most Comparable Rookie Seasons:

Tony Curry	245	64	14	2	6	34	16	53	.261	.408	.308
John Ellis	226	56	12	1	7	29	18	47	.248	.403	.304
Bill Freehan	300	73	12	2	9	36	39	56	.243	.387	.332
Jim Presley	251	57	12	1	10	36	6	63	.227	.402	.246
Nelson Simmons	251	60	11	0	10	33	26	41	.239	.402	.312

Projections for 1992:

Best Guess	282	69	12	2	7	36	11	82	.246	.382	.274
Optimistic	493	139	29	9	22	84	23	97	.283	.511	.316

Projections for career:

Best Guess	2605	656	108	16	69	326	92	698	.252	.385	.279
Optimistic	6022	1644	291	72	229	892	301	1301	.273	.459	.309

Wes Chamberlain

Bats Right
Born Apr. 13, 1966

Philadelphia Phillies	AB	H	2B	3B	HR	RBI	BB	SO	BA	SA	OBA
Season	383	92	16	3	13	50	31	73	.240	.399	.300
vs. Left-Handers	140	38	8	1	7	26	16	18	.271	.493	.350
vs. Right-Handers	243	54	8	2	6	24	15	55	.222	.346	.270
vs. Ground-Ballers	193	46	4	3	6	23	13	30	.238	.383	.290
vs. Fly-Ballers	190	46	12	0	7	27	18	43	.242	.416	.311

Most Comparable Rookie Seasons:

Paul Casanova	429	109	16	5	13	44	14	78	.254	.406	.279
Leo Gomez	391	91	17	2	16	45	40	82	.233	.409	.305
Jim L. Hickman	392	96	18	2	13	46	47	96	.245	.401	.327
Ramon Webster	360	92	15	4	11	51	32	44	.256	.411	.317
Mark Whiten	407	99	18	7	9	45	30	85	.243	.388	.296

Projections for 1992:

Best Guess	334	81	15	2	11	39	23	58	.243	.398	.294
Optimistic	522	142	29	7	24	78	55	68	.272	.491	.342

Projections for career:

Best Guess	1469	366	60	10	46	179	112	265	.249	.397	.303
Optimistic	3485	909	158	34	140	505	340	503	.261	.446	.328

Milt Cuyler
Bats Left and Right
Born Oct. 7, 1968

Detroit Tigers	AB	H	2B	3B	HR	RBI	BB	SO	BA	SA	OBA
Season	475	122	15	7	3	33	52	92	.257	.337	.335
vs. Left-Handers	122	33	6	1	0	8	13	19	.270	.336	.345
vs. Right-Handers	353	89	9	6	3	25	39	73	.252	.337	.332
vs. Ground-Ballers	229	53	6	3	1	26	26	44	.231	.297	.317
vs. Fly-Ballers	246	69	9	4	2	7	26	48	.280	.374	.353

Most Comparable Rookie Seasons:

	AB	H	2B	3B	HR	RBI	BB	SO	BA	SA	OBA
Mariano Duncan	562	137	24	6	6	39	38	113	.244	.340	.293
Mike Hershberger	427	112	14	2	4	46	37	36	.262	.333	.322
Willie Randolph	430	115	15	4	1	40	58	39	.267	.328	.356
Jerry Remy	569	147	17	5	1	46	45	55	.258	.311	.314
Wayne Tolleson	470	122	13	2	3	20	40	68	.260	.315	.319

Projections for 1992:

	AB	H	2B	3B	HR	RBI	BB	SO	BA	SA	OBA
Best Guess	502	133	22	6	7	53	62	90	.264	.370	.346
Optimistic	575	165	31	12	16	76	92	70	.287	.469	.387

Projections for career:

	AB	H	2B	3B	HR	RBI	BB	SO	BA	SA	OBA
Best Guess	3694	975	155	38	36	348	449	640	.264	.356	.345
Optimistic	5797	1616	272	86	126	716	908	760	.279	.421	.378

Steve Decker
Bats Right
Born Oct. 25, 1965

San Francisco Giants	AB	H	2B	3B	HR	RBI	BB	SO	BA	SA	OBA
Season	233	48	7	1	5	24	16	44	.206	.309	.262
vs. Left-Handers	86	19	2	1	3	13	2	11	.221	.372	.231
vs. Right-Handers	147	29	5	0	2	11	14	33	.197	.272	.279
vs. Ground-Ballers	101	18	2	0	1	8	9	17	.178	.228	.248
vs. Fly-Ballers	132	30	5	1	4	16	7	27	.227	.371	.273

Most Comparable Rookie Seasons:

	AB	H	2B	3B	HR	RBI	BB	SO	BA	SA	OBA
Steve Bowling	194	40	8	1	1	13	37	42	.206	.273	.335
Larry Burright	249	51	6	5	4	30	21	67	.205	.317	.268
Tommy Matchick	227	46	6	2	3	14	10	46	.203	.286	.237
Jim Northrup	219	45	12	3	2	16	12	50	.205	.315	.248
Duane Walker	239	52	10	0	5	22	27	58	.218	.322	.298

Projections for 1992:

	AB	H	2B	3B	HR	RBI	BB	SO	BA	SA	OBA
Best Guess	184	41	7	1	2	19	11	36	.222	.307	.267
Optimistic	365	97	19	5	14	49	29	40	.265	.461	.321

Projections for career:

	AB	H	2B	3B	HR	RBI	BB	SO	BA	SA	OBA
Best Guess	880	205	30	5	17	92	55	159	.233	.335	.279
Optimistic	1585	405	69	14	47	193	124	195	.255	.405	.311

Gary DiSarcina
Bats Right
Born Nov. 19, 1967

California Angels	AB	H	2B	3B	HR	RBI	BB	SO	BA	SA	OBA
Season	57	12	2	0	0	3	3	4	.211	.246	.274
vs. Left-Handers	18	4	1	0	0	1	0	1	.222	.278	.222
vs. Right-Handers	39	8	1	0	0	2	3	3	.205	.231	.295
vs. Ground-Ballers	15	4	1	0	0	0	0	2	.267	.333	.313
vs. Fly-Ballers	42	8	1	0	0	3	3	2	.190	.214	.261

Most Comparable Rookie Seasons:

	AB	H	2B	3B	HR	RBI	BB	SO	BA	SA	OBA
Gene Alley	51	11	1	0	0	0	2	12	.216	.235	.246
Max Alvis	51	11	2	0	0	3	2	13	.216	.255	.246
Jim Dwyer	57	11	1	1	0	0	1	5	.193	.246	.208
Chip Hale	67	14	3	0	0	4	1	6	.209	.254	.222
Luis Mercedes	54	11	2	0	0	2	4	9	.204	.241	.260

Projections for 1992:

	AB	H	2B	3B	HR	RBI	BB	SO	BA	SA	OBA
Best Guess	43	6	1	0	0	3	1	7	.133	.164	.163
Optimistic	209	57	8	2	6	28	14	17	.274	.421	.322

Projections for career:

	AB	H	2B	3B	HR	RBI	BB	SO	BA	SA	OBA
Best Guess	756	180	26	5	7	69	40	98	.238	.315	.278
Optimistic	3692	991	168	42	103	501	260	235	.268	.420	.318

Chris Donnels
Bats Left
Born Apr. 21, 1966

New York Mets	AB	H	2B	3B	HR	RBI	BB	SO	BA	SA	OBA
Season	89	20	2	0	0	5	14	19	.225	.247	.330
vs. Left-Handers	34	10	1	0	0	2	5	7	.294	.324	.385
vs. Right-Handers	55	10	1	0	0	3	9	12	.182	.200	.297
vs. Ground-Ballers	32	9	0	0	0	1	1	7	.281	.281	.303
vs. Fly-Ballers	57	11	2	0	0	4	13	12	.193	.228	.343

Most Comparable Rookie Seasons:

	AB	H	2B	3B	HR	RBI	BB	SO	BA	SA	OBA
R. Bobby Brown	78	17	3	1	0	3	4	18	.218	.282	.257
Garry Hancock	80	18	3	0	0	4	1	12	.225	.262	.236
Mickey Hatcher	84	19	2	0	1	5	2	12	.226	.286	.245
Jim McKnight	85	19	0	1	0	5	2	13	.224	.247	.243
Mike Woodard	82	20	1	0	0	9	5	3	.244	.256	.289

Projections for 1992:

	AB	H	2B	3B	HR	RBI	BB	SO	BA	SA	OBA
Best Guess	45	6	0	0	0	3	6	15	.133	.143	.232
Optimistic	214	56	10	3	3	24	47	30	.261	.376	.395

Projections for career:

	AB	H	2B	3B	HR	RBI	BB	SO	BA	SA	OBA
Best Guess	314	74	9	1	1	24	48	57	.237	.288	.340
Optimistic	1288	343	57	16	19	152	314	166	.266	.381	.411

Darrin Fletcher
Bats Left
Born Oct. 3, 1966

Philadelphia Phillies	AB	H	2B	3B	HR	RBI	BB	SO	BA	SA	OBA
Season	136	31	8	0	1	12	5	15	.228	.309	.255
vs. Left-Handers	22	6	2	0	0	4	0	6	.273	.364	.273
vs. Right-Handers	114	25	6	0	1	8	5	9	.219	.298	.252
vs. Ground-Ballers	68	16	3	0	0	3	2	7	.235	.279	.257
vs. Fly-Ballers	68	15	5	0	1	9	3	8	.221	.338	.254

Most Comparable Rookie Seasons:

	AB	H	2B	3B	HR	RBI	BB	SO	BA	SA	OBA
Steve Hammond	126	29	5	1	1	11	4	18	.230	.310	.255
Andy Kosco	158	35	5	0	2	13	7	31	.222	.291	.256
Dave Meier	147	35	8	1	0	13	6	9	.238	.306	.269
Andre Robertson	118	26	5	0	2	9	8	19	.220	.314	.271
Tracy Woodson	136	31	8	1	1	11	9	21	.228	.324	.277

Projections for 1992:

	AB	H	2B	3B	HR	RBI	BB	SO	BA	SA	OBA
Best Guess	107	21	3	0	0	8	3	15	.200	.238	.225
Optimistic	314	83	16	3	9	35	21	27	.263	.418	.310

Projections for career:

	AB	H	2B	3B	HR	RBI	BB	SO	BA	SA	OBA
Best Guess	1012	245	41	5	12	95	44	127	.242	.327	.275
Optimistic	2147	569	100	22	49	259	136	167	.265	.401	.310

Bernard Gilkey
Bats Right
Born Sep. 24, 1966

St. Louis Cardinals	AB	H	2B	3B	HR	RBI	BB	SO	BA	SA	OBA
Season	268	58	7	2	5	20	39	33	.216	.313	.316
vs. Left-Handers	137	26	5	0	2	9	20	15	.190	.270	.297
vs. Right-Handers	131	32	2	2	3	11	19	18	.244	.359	.336
vs. Ground-Ballers	135	27	5	1	2	11	16	16	.200	.296	.288
vs. Fly-Ballers	133	31	2	1	3	9	23	17	.233	.331	.344

Most Comparable Rookie Seasons:

	AB	H	2B	3B	HR	RBI	BB	SO	BA	SA	OBA
Jamie Allen	273	61	10	0	4	21	33	52	.223	.304	.308
Buddy Bradford	281	61	11	0	5	24	23	67	.217	.310	.277
Jimmie Coker	252	54	5	3	6	34	23	45	.214	.329	.281
Pete Stanicek	261	60	7	1	4	17	28	45	.230	.310	.306
Duane Walker	239	52	10	0	5	22	27	58	.218	.322	.298

Projections for 1992:

	AB	H	2B	3B	HR	RBI	BB	SO	BA	SA	OBA
Best Guess	230	54	9	2	3	24	29	27	.235	.331	.323
Optimistic	381	99	21	5	15	49	71	25	.259	.455	.377

Projections for career:

	AB	H	2B	3B	HR	RBI	BB	SO	BA	SA	OBA
Best Guess	993	237	38	9	16	91	143	109	.238	.342	.335
Optimistic	2491	655	115	31	69	287	468	168	.263	.417	.381

Leo Gomez

Bats Right
Born Mar. 2, 1967

Baltimore Orioles	AB	H	2B	3B	HR	RBI	BB	SO	BA	SA	OBA
Season	391	91	17	2	16	45	40	82	.233	.409	.302
vs. Left-Handers	114	25	4	0	6	16	13	20	.219	.412	.288
vs. Right-Handers	277	66	13	2	10	29	27	62	.238	.408	.308
vs. Ground-Ballers	175	42	10	1	7	23	16	35	.240	.429	.306
vs. Fly-Ballers	216	49	7	1	9	22	24	47	.227	.394	.300

Most Comparable Rookie Seasons:

	AB	H	2B	3B	HR	RBI	BB	SO	BA	SA	OBA
Tony Armas	363	87	8	2	13	53	20	99	.240	.380	.281
Byron Browne	419	102	15	7	16	51	40	143	.243	.427	.311
Paul Casanova	429	109	16	5	13	44	14	78	.254	.406	.279
Jim Pagliaroni	376	91	17	0	16	58	55	74	.242	.415	.340
Mike Young	401	101	17	2	17	52	58	110	.252	.431	.348

Projections for 1992:

	AB	H	2B	3B	HR	RBI	BB	SO	BA	SA	OBA
Best Guess	388	95	18	2	14	51	40	70	.246	.409	.318
Optimistic	522	143	29	6	27	83	82	68	.274	.506	.373

Projections for career:

	AB	H	2B	3B	HR	RBI	BB	SO	BA	SA	OBA
Best Guess	2026	495	80	10	70	242	238	395	.244	.398	.325
Optimistic	4004	1027	176	32	172	583	570	588	.257	.445	.350

Luis Gonzalez

Bats Left
Born Sep. 3, 1967

Houston Astros	AB	H	2B	3B	HR	RBI	BB	SO	BA	SA	OBA
Season	473	120	28	9	13	69	40	101	.254	.433	.320
vs. Left-Handers	122	21	7	1	1	13	12	31	.172	.270	.257
vs. Right-Handers	351	99	21	8	12	56	28	70	.282	.490	.342
vs. Ground-Ballers	212	55	14	3	7	28	13	44	.259	.453	.307
vs. Fly-Ballers	264	65	14	6	6	41	28	59	.246	.413	.329

Most Comparable Rookie Seasons:

	AB	H	2B	3B	HR	RBI	BB	SO	BA	SA	OBA
Greg Briley	394	105	22	4	13	52	39	82	.266	.442	.334
Chris Brown	432	117	20	3	16	61	38	78	.271	.442	.331
Garry Maddox	458	122	26	7	12	58	14	97	.266	.432	.289
Carmelo Martinez	488	122	28	2	13	66	68	82	.250	.395	.343
Lee May	438	116	29	2	12	57	19	80	.265	.422	.297

Projections for 1992:

	AB	H	2B	3B	HR	RBI	BB	SO	BA	SA	OBA
Best Guess	514	136	24	4	18	68	47	91	.265	.431	.328
Optimistic	572	166	31	8	27	93	70	72	.290	.516	.369

Projections for career:

	AB	H	2B	3B	HR	RBI	BB	SO	BA	SA	OBA
Best Guess	3570	918	160	29	104	459	320	700	.257	.405	.319
Optimistic	5801	1591	281	62	230	861	688	821	.274	.463	.352

Dave Howard

Bats Left and Right
Born Feb. 26, 1967

Kansas City Royals	AB	H	2B	3B	HR	RBI	BB	SO	BA	SA	OBA
Season	236	51	7	0	1	17	16	45	.216	.258	.267
vs. Left-Handers	80	18	2	0	1	10	6	12	.225	.287	.276
vs. Right-Handers	156	33	5	0	0	7	10	33	.212	.244	.262
vs. Ground-Ballers	99	23	5	0	0	8	6	18	.232	.283	.276
vs. Fly-Ballers	137	28	2	0	1	9	10	27	.204	.241	.260

Most Comparable Rookie Seasons:

	AB	H	2B	3B	HR	RBI	BB	SO	BA	SA	OBA
Ruben Amaro	264	61	9	1	0	16	21	32	.231	.273	.289
Kirt Manwaring	200	42	4	2	0	18	11	28	.210	.250	.252
Mike Phillips	283	62	6	1	2	20	14	37	.219	.269	.257
Juan Rios	196	44	5	1	1	5	7	19	.224	.276	.252
Doug Strange	196	42	4	1	1	14	17	36	.214	.260	.278

Projections for 1992:

	AB	H	2B	3B	HR	RBI	BB	SO	BA	SA	OBA
Best Guess	166	37	6	1	1	13	11	36	.222	.283	.273
Optimistic	344	88	17	5	7	40	34	37	.257	.402	.326

Projections for career:

	AB	H	2B	3B	HR	RBI	BB	SO	BA	SA	OBA
Best Guess	761	175	25	3	6	63	52	139	.231	.294	.281
Optimistic	2051	515	84	19	42	229	179	250	.251	.373	.312

Thomas Howard

Bats Left and Right
Born Dec. 11, 1964

San Diego Padres	AB	H	2B	3B	HR	RBI	BB	SO	BA	SA	OBA
Season	281	70	12	3	4	22	24	57	.249	.356	.309
vs. Left-Handers	28	8	0	1	1	2	5	5	.286	.464	.394
vs. Right-Handers	253	62	12	2	3	20	19	52	.245	.344	.299
vs. Ground-Ballers	135	38	4	2	1	13	13	21	.281	.363	.349
vs. Fly-Ballers	146	32	8	1	3	9	11	36	.219	.349	.272

Most Comparable Rookie Seasons:

	AB	H	2B	3B	HR	RBI	BB	SO	BA	SA	OBA
Bob Kearney	298	76	11	0	8	32	21	50	.255	.372	.305
Jim Leyritz	303	78	13	1	5	25	27	51	.257	.356	.319
Fred Manrique	298	77	13	3	4	29	19	69	.258	.362	.304
Johnny Oates	253	66	12	1	4	21	28	31	.261	.364	.336
Rich Reese	332	86	15	2	4	28	18	36	.259	.352	.298

Projections for 1992:

	AB	H	2B	3B	HR	RBI	BB	SO	BA	SA	OBA
Best Guess	290	70	11	2	5	31	24	60	.242	.346	.301
Optimistic	419	118	22	7	10	57	52	52	.283	.444	.363

Projections for career:

	AB	H	2B	3B	HR	RBI	BB	SO	BA	SA	OBA
Best Guess	1126	285	45	9	15	104	82	226	.253	.351	.305
Optimistic	1969	535	92	22	43	238	189	299	.272	.407	.337

Mike Huff

Bats Right
Born Aug. 11, 1963

Indians/White Sox	AB	H	2B	3B	HR	RBI	BB	SO	BA	SA	OBA
Season	243	61	10	2	3	25	37	48	.251	.346	.361
vs. Left-Handers	121	28	4	1	3	9	16	21	.231	.355	.333
vs. Right-Handers	122	33	6	1	0	16	21	27	.270	.336	.388
vs. Ground-Ballers	100	23	2	2	0	12	16	15	.230	.290	.358
vs. Fly-Ballers	143	38	8	0	3	13	21	33	.266	.385	.363

Most Comparable Rookie Seasons:

	AB	H	2B	3B	HR	RBI	BB	SO	BA	SA	OBA
Thomas Howard	281	70	12	3	4	22	24	57	.249	.356	.309
Bob Molinaro	286	75	5	5	6	27	19	12	.262	.378	.309
Bob Montgomery	205	49	11	2	2	24	16	43	.239	.341	.295
Joe Nolan	213	49	7	3	4	22	34	28	.230	.347	.337
Greg Pryor	222	58	11	0	2	15	11	18	.261	.338	.297

Projections for 1992:

	AB	H	2B	3B	HR	RBI	BB	SO	BA	SA	OBA
Best Guess	198	48	7	1	3	20	29	45	.240	.332	.338
Optimistic	400	114	19	7	10	57	101	53	.285	.441	.431

Projections for career:

	AB	H	2B	3B	HR	RBI	BB	SO	BA	SA	OBA
Best Guess	987	251	39	7	14	100	144	184	.254	.350	.350
Optimistic	2149	599	105	25	45	284	404	314	.279	.414	.394

Todd Hundley

Bats Left and Right
Born May 27, 1969

New York Mets	AB	H	2B	3B	HR	RBI	BB	SO	BA	SA	OBA
Season	60	8	0	1	1	7	6	14	.133	.217	.221
vs. Left-Handers	19	2	0	0	0	3	3	9	.105	.105	.250
vs. Right-Handers	41	6	0	1	1	4	3	5	.146	.268	.205
vs. Ground-Ballers	29	3	0	0	0	3	3	5	.103	.103	.182
vs. Fly-Ballers	31	5	0	1	1	4	3	9	.161	.323	.257

Most Comparable Rookie Seasons:

	AB	H	2B	3B	HR	RBI	BB	SO	BA	SA	OBA
Al Chambers	67	14	3	0	1	7	18	20	.209	.299	.378
Manny Lee	78	16	0	1	1	7	4	10	.205	.269	.245
Lee Mazzilli	77	15	2	0	2	7	14	10	.195	.299	.320
Larry Parrish	69	14	5	0	0	4	6	19	.203	.275	.268
Cap Peterson	74	15	1	1	1	8	3	20	.203	.284	.235

Projections for 1992:

	AB	H	2B	3B	HR	RBI	BB	SO	BA	SA	OBA
Best Guess	121	27	4	1	1	11	10	30	.222	.306	.281
Optimistic	342	92	19	7	11	50	41	53	.268	.460	.347

Projections for career:

	AB	H	2B	3B	HR	RBI	BB	SO	BA	SA	OBA
Best Guess	1700	413	66	10	25	179	161	408	.243	.338	.310
Optimistic	4114	1092	203	52	140	587	487	653	.265	.442	.344

Brian Hunter
Bats Right
Born Mar. 4, 1968

Atlanta Braves	AB	H	2B	3B	HR	RBI	BB	SO	BA	SA	OBA
Season	271	68	16	1	12	50	17	48	.251	.450	.296
vs. Left-Handers	121	33	4	0	6	22	6	17	.273	.455	.305
vs. Right-Handers	150	35	12	1	6	28	11	31	.233	.447	.288
vs. Ground-Ballers	100	25	5	1	4	18	4	16	.250	.440	.276
vs. Fly-Ballers	171	43	11	0	8	32	13	32	.251	.456	.306

Most Comparable Rookie Seasons:

Nick Esasky	302	80	10	5	12	46	27	99	.265	.450	.326
Darrell Evans	260	63	11	1	12	38	39	54	.242	.431	.342
Dave Henderson	324	82	17	1	14	48	36	67	.253	.441	.329
Tony Perez	281	73	14	4	12	47	21	67	.260	.466	.312
George Thomas	288	79	12	1	13	59	21	70	.274	.458	.325

Projections for 1992:

Best Guess	324	79	15	3	11	41	21	52	.244	.410	.291
Optimistic	484	133	27	8	24	82	44	58	.275	.508	.336

Projections for career:

Best Guess	2655	669	112	16	99	354	175	445	.252	.418	.299
Optimistic	6034	1665	302	64	277	1001	529	803	.276	.485	.335

Reggie Jefferson
Bats Left and Right
Born Sep. 25, 1968

Reds/Indians	AB	H	2B	3B	HR	RBI	BB	SO	BA	SA	OBA
Season	108	21	3	0	3	13	4	24	.194	.306	.221
vs. Left-Handers	25	4	1	0	0	3	0	7	.160	.200	.160
vs. Right-Handers	83	17	2	0	3	10	4	17	.205	.337	.239
vs. Ground-Ballers	68	15	3	0	2	9	1	11	.221	.353	.232
vs. Fly-Ballers	40	6	0	0	1	4	3	13	.150	.225	.205

Most Comparable Rookie Seasons:

George Hendrick	121	22	1	1	4	15	3	22	.182	.306	.203
Jim Hutto	92	17	2	0	3	12	5	20	.185	.304	.228
Tommie Reynolds	94	19	1	0	2	9	10	22	.202	.277	.280
Bob Robertson	96	20	4	1	1	9	8	30	.208	.302	.270
Dave Schneck	123	23	3	2	3	10	10	26	.187	.317	.249

Projections for 1992:

Best Guess	151	34	5	1	4	13	6	30	.225	.337	.254
Optimistic	351	93	17	5	17	51	20	45	.264	.484	.305

Projections for career:

Best Guess	1452	351	55	7	31	155	62	277	.241	.352	.274
Optimistic	3095	819	143	32	117	420	186	429	.265	.445	.308

Pat Kelly
Bats Right
Born Oct. 14, 1967

New York Yankees	AB	H	2B	3B	HR	RBI	BB	SO	BA	SA	OBA
Season	298	72	12	4	3	23	15	52	.242	.339	.287
vs. Left-Handers	99	26	5	0	1	7	4	13	.263	.343	.292
vs. Right-Handers	199	46	7	4	2	16	11	39	.231	.337	.285
vs. Ground-Ballers	138	35	5	2	2	9	6	22	.254	.362	.293
vs. Fly-Ballers	160	37	7	2	1	14	9	30	.231	.319	.283

Most Comparable Rookie Seasons:

Juan Bernhardt	305	74	9	2	7	30	5	26	.243	.354	.256
Len Gabrielson	310	74	13	2	5	24	20	45	.239	.342	.286
Tommie Reynolds	270	64	11	3	1	22	36	41	.237	.311	.328
Jerry White	278	68	11	1	2	21	27	31	.245	.313	.313
Walt Williams	275	66	16	3	3	15	17	20	.240	.353	.285

Projections for 1992:

Best Guess	258	62	10	2	4	25	12	46	.241	.338	.276
Optimistic	439	120	24	7	11	56	31	46	.272	.435	.322

Projections for career:

Best Guess	1627	409	67	14	21	158	83	264	.252	.348	.289
Optimistic	3562	968	166	43	78	413	246	393	.272	.408	.320

Chuck Knoblauch
Bats Right
Born Jul. 7, 1968

Minnesota Twins	AB	H	2B	3B	HR	RBI	BB	SO	BA	SA	OBA
Season	565	159	24	6	1	50	59	40	.281	.350	.351
vs. Left-Handers	148	38	8	1	0	6	14	10	.257	.324	.325
vs. Right-Handers	417	121	16	5	1	44	45	30	.290	.360	.360
vs. Ground-Ballers	239	69	9	3	0	22	28	13	.289	.351	.367
vs. Fly-Ballers	326	90	15	3	1	28	31	27	.276	.350	.339

Most Comparable Rookie Seasons:

Damaso Garcia	543	151	30	7	4	46	12	55	.278	.381	.295
Alfredo Griffin	624	179	22	10	2	31	40	59	.287	.364	.331
Dick Howser	611	171	29	6	3	45	92	38	.280	.362	.375
Kirby Puckett	557	165	12	5	0	31	16	69	.296	.336	.317
Steve Sax	638	180	23	7	4	47	49	53	.282	.359	.335

Projections for 1992:

Best Guess	540	145	23	7	6	57	64	33	.269	.371	.348
Optimistic	616	183	33	13	12	82	97	17	.297	.451	.394

Projections for career:

Best Guess	4075	1118	182	39	36	393	469	269	.274	.365	.350
Optimistic	5866	1683	305	85	99	751	820	248	.287	.418	.376

Ced Landrum
Bats Left
Born Sep. 3, 1963

Chicago Cubs	AB	H	2B	3B	HR	RBI	BB	SO	BA	SA	OBA
Season	86	20	2	1	0	6	10	18	.233	.279	.313
vs. Left-Handers	13	5	0	1	0	2	2	4	.385	.538	.467
vs. Right-Handers	73	15	2	0	0	4	8	14	.205	.233	.284
vs. Ground-Ballers	43	13	2	0	0	4	4	7	.302	.349	.362
vs. Fly-Ballers	43	7	0	1	0	2	6	11	.163	.209	.265

Most Comparable Rookie Seasons:

Tom Heintzelman	74	17	4	0	1	6	9	14	.230	.324	.314
Gonzalo Marquez	83	19	3	0	1	6	3	8	.229	.301	.257
Danny Monzon	76	17	1	1	0	4	11	9	.224	.263	.323
Paul Runge	87	19	3	0	1	5	18	18	.218	.287	.354
Guy Sularz	101	23	3	0	1	7	9	11	.228	.287	.292

Projections for 1992:

Best Guess	48	5	1	0	0	2	4	13	.102	.124	.180
Optimistic	214	54	9	1	4	24	35	30	.250	.357	.356

Projections for career:

Best Guess	323	75	11	2	2	28	37	63	.233	.291	.312
Optimistic	1113	296	50	12	23	132	198	164	.266	.396	.378

Ray Lankford
Bats Left
Born Jun. 5, 1967

St. Louis Cardinals	AB	H	2B	3B	HR	RBI	BB	SO	BA	SA	OBA
Season	566	142	23	15	9	69	41	114	.251	.392	.301
vs. Left-Handers	220	52	11	7	0	26	16	48	.236	.350	.290
vs. Right-Handers	346	90	12	8	9	43	25	66	.260	.419	.308
vs. Ground-Ballers	233	62	7	5	6	27	20	42	.266	.416	.325
vs. Fly-Ballers	333	80	16	10	3	42	21	72	.240	.375	.284

Most Comparable Rookie Seasons:

Von Hayes	527	132	25	3	14	82	42	63	.250	.389	.307
Carmelo Martinez	488	122	28	2	13	66	68	82	.250	.395	.343
Omar Moreno	492	118	19	9	7	34	38	102	.240	.358	.296
Robby Thompson	549	149	27	3	7	47	42	112	.271	.370	.324
Jake Wood	663	171	17	14	11	69	58	141	.258	.376	.319

Projections for 1992:

Best Guess	515	136	23	7	12	58	49	88	.265	.404	.331
Optimistic	580	172	31	8	20	79	69	47	.297	.483	.373

Projections for career:

Best Guess	3598	936	154	41	68	389	296	656	.260	.383	.318
Optimistic	5064	1416	238	84	112	709	550	544	.280	.426	.351

Scott Leius

Bats Right
Born Sep. 24, 1965

Minnesota Twins	AB	H	2B	3B	HR	RBI	BB	SO	BA	SA	OBA
Season	199	57	7	2	5	20	30	35	.286	.417	.378
vs. Left-Handers	128	39	5	2	3	13	28	17	.305	.445	.427
vs. Right-Handers	71	18	2	0	2	7	2	18	.254	.366	.274
vs. Ground-Ballers	97	28	4	2	5	12	9	18	.289	.526	.349
vs. Fly-Ballers	102	29	3	0	0	8	21	17	.284	.314	.403

Most Comparable Rookie Seasons:

Scott Bradley	220	66	8	3	5	28	13	7	.300	.432	.340
Ron Hassey	223	64	14	0	4	32	19	19	.287	.404	.344
Lynn Jones	213	63	8	0	4	26	17	22	.296	.390	.349
Mickey Klutts	197	53	14	0	4	21	13	41	.269	.401	.315
Ron Pruitt	219	63	10	2	2	32	28	22	.288	.379	.370

Projections for 1992:

Best Guess	320	82	15	3	7	39	46	45	.258	.386	.352
Optimistic	491	145	29	9	16	82	96	39	.295	.487	.411

Projections for career:

Best Guess	1231	327	51	10	19	136	166	185	.266	.370	.354
Optimistic	2838	799	136	38	76	367	507	303	.281	.437	.391

Darren Lewis

Bats Right
Born Aug. 28, 1967

San Francisco Giants	AB	H	2B	3B	HR	RBI	BB	SO	BA	SA	OBA
Season	222	55	5	3	1	15	36	30	.248	.311	.358
vs. Left-Handers	75	21	4	1	1	6	12	8	.280	.400	.386
vs. Right-Handers	147	34	1	2	0	9	24	22	.231	.265	.343
vs. Ground-Ballers	104	28	0	3	1	9	16	13	.269	.356	.367
vs. Fly-Ballers	118	27	5	0	0	6	20	17	.229	.271	.350

Most Comparable Rookie Seasons:

Steve Finley	217	54	5	2		25	15	30	.249	.318	.299
Tommy Herr	222	55	12	5	0	15	16	21	.248	.347	.299
Lee Lacy	243	63	7	3	0	12	19	37	.259	.313	.314
Freddie Patek	208	53	4	2	2	18	12	37	.255	.322	.297
Alan Wiggins	254	65	3	3	1	15	13	19	.256	.303	.293

Projections for 1992:

Best Guess	278	68	11	2	3	28	50	40	.244	.325	.360
Optimistic	460	126	26	8	10	62	117	31	.274	.429	.423

Projections for career:

Best Guess	1480	365	54	13	13	135	272	192	.246	.327	.365
Optimistic	2918	801	141	34	47	337	654	238	.274	.395	.408

Mark Lewis

Bats Right
Born Nov. 30, 1969

Cleveland Indians	AB	H	2B	3B	HR	RBI	BB	SO	BA	SA	OBA
Season	314	83	15	1	0	30	15	45	.264	.318	.293
vs. Left-Handers	87	24	3	0	0	7	5	12	.276	.310	.305
vs. Right-Handers	227	59	12	1	0	23	10	33	.260	.322	.289
vs. Ground-Ballers	142	31	5	1	0	9	5	15	.218	.268	.243
vs. Fly-Ballers	172	52	10	0	0	21	10	30	.302	.360	.333

Most Comparable Rookie Seasons:

Dave Concepcion	265	69	6	3	1	19	23	45	.260	.317	.321
Sam Khalifa	320	76	14	3	2	31	34	56	.237	.319	.312
Rance Mulliniks	271	73	13	2	3	21	23	36	.269	.365	.328
Dickie Thon	267	68	12	2	0	15	10	28	.255	.315	.283
Bobby Valentine	281	70	10	2	1	25	15	20	.249	.310	.288

Projections for 1992:

Best Guess	365	94	14	4	3	35	18	48	.259	.345	.294
Optimistic	510	145	27	9	9	62	39	42	.285	.426	.337

Projections for career:

Best Guess	2507	657	104	20	23	259	137	312	.262	.347	.301
Optimistic	5362	1498	267	65	102	665	396	462	.279	.411	.330

Scott Livingstone

Bats Left
Born Jul. 15, 1965

Detroit Tigers	AB	H	2B	3B	HR	RBI	BB	SO	BA	SA	OBA
Season	127	37	5	0	2	11	10	25	.291	.378	.341
vs. Left-Handers	12	5	1	0	1	1	2	1	.417	.750	.500
vs. Right-Handers	115	32	4	0	1	10	8	24	.278	.339	.323
vs. Ground-Ballers	64	23	5	0	0	6	4	11	.359	.438	.397
vs. Fly-Ballers	63	14	0	0	2	5	6	14	.222	.317	.286

Most Comparable Rookie Seasons:

Jose Herrera	126	36	5	0	2	12	3	14	.286	.373	.303
Domingo Ramos	127	36	4	0	2	10	7	12	.283	.362	.322
Mackey Sasser	123	35	10	1	1	17	6	9	.285	.407	.319
Mike Squires	150	42	9	2	0	19	16	21	.280	.367	.351
Pete Varney	107	29	5	1	2	8	6	28	.271	.393	.311

Projections for 1992:

Best Guess	201	48	7	2	3	22	15	41	.239	.337	.295
Optimistic	368	104	22	6	12	57	47	45	.284	.468	.365

Projections for career:

Best Guess	890	233	35	6	10	95	72	185	.262	.349	.319
Optimistic	2926	814	144	38	77	391	331	343	.278	.433	.353

Kenny Lofton

Bats Left
Born May 31, 1967

Houston Astros	AB	H	2B	3B	HR	RBI	BB	SO	BA	SA	OBA
Season	74	15	1	0	0	0	5	19	.203	.216	.253
vs. Left-Handers	20	5	0	0	0	0	2	8	.250	.250	.318
vs. Right-Handers	54	10	1	0	0	0	3	11	.185	.204	.228
vs. Ground-Ballers	28	6	0	0	0	0	1	5	.214	.214	.241
vs. Fly-Ballers	46	9	1	0	0	0	4	14	.196	.217	.260

Most Comparable Rookie Seasons:

Lou Camilli	81	16	2	0	0	0	8	10	.198	.222	.271
Gary Kolb	64	12	1	0	0	2	6	10	.188	.203	.258
Ronn Reynolds	66	13	1	0	0	2	8	12	.197	.212	.285
Ken Rudolph	76	15	3	0	0	7	6	20	.197	.237	.257
Carl Taylor	71	15	1	0	0	7	10	10	.211	.225	.310

Projections for 1992:

Best Guess	75	14	2	0	1	6	5	23	.184	.237	.235
Optimistic	221	60	12	3	4	29	22	36	.273	.409	.340

Projections for career:

Best Guess	347	79	11	2	2	25	23	82	.227	.289	.276
Optimistic	1530	403	70	16	28	179	154	242	.264	.386	.332

Chito Martinez

Bats Left
Born Dec. 19, 1965

Baltimore Orioles	AB	H	2B	3B	HR	RBI	BB	SO	BA	SA	OBA
Season	216	58	12	1	13	33	11	51	.269	.514	.303
vs. Left-Handers	29	6	1	0	1	1	2	10	.207	.345	.258
vs. Right-Handers	187	52	11	1	12	32	9	41	.278	.540	.310
vs. Ground-Ballers	95	27	5	0	4	12	2	22	.284	.463	.299
vs. Fly-Ballers	121	31	7	1	9	21	9	29	.256	.554	.305

Most Comparable Rookie Seasons:

Mike Diaz	209	56	9	0	12	36	19	43	.268	.483	.330
Kevin Maas	254	64	9	0	21	41	43	76	.252	.535	.361
Jim Morrison	240	66	14	0	14	35	15	48	.275	.508	.319
Bill Schroeder	210	54	6	0	14	25	8	54	.257	.486	.286
Mitch Webster	213	58	8	2	11	30	20	33	.272	.484	.336

Projections for 1992:

Best Guess	397	96	18	2	16	51	23	82	.242	.422	.284
Optimistic	531	152	35	8	36	104	37	81	.285	.582	.334

Projections for career:

Best Guess	802	197	33	4	33	109	41	180	.246	.420	.284
Optimistic	3236	849	158	28	147	551	213	590	.262	.465	.309

Tino Martinez
Bats Left
Born Dec. 7, 1967

Seattle Mariners	AB	H	2B	3B	HR	RBI	BB	SO	BA	SA	OBA
Season	112	23	2	0	4	9	11	24	.205	.330	.272
vs. Left-Handers	35	9	2	0	1	1	4	7	.257	.400	.333
vs. Right-Handers	77	14	0	0	3	8	7	17	.182	.299	.244
vs. Ground-Ballers	51	11	1	0	1	6	1	13	.216	.294	.222
vs. Fly-Ballers	61	12	1	0	3	3	10	11	.197	.361	.310

Most Comparable Rookie Seasons:

	AB	H	2B	3B	HR	RBI	BB	SO	BA	SA	OBA
Bob Christian	129	28	4	0	3	16	10	19	.217	.318	.275
Todd Cruz	118	24	7	0	2	15	3	19	.203	.314	.224
Darren Daulton	103	21	3	1	4	11	16	37	.204	.369	.312
Len G. Gabrielson	120	26	5	0	3	15	8	23	.217	.333	.267
Danny Goodwin	91	19	6	1	1	8	5	19	.209	.330	.251

Projections for 1992:

	AB	H	2B	3B	HR	RBI	BB	SO	BA	SA	OBA
Best Guess	138	33	5	1	3	12	15	23	.237	.346	.314
Optimistic	333	90	19	7	16	51	55	40	.271	.510	.375

Projections for career:

	AB	H	2B	3B	HR	RBI	BB	SO	BA	SA	OBA
Best Guess	991	238	38	4	21	95	116	162	.240	.350	.321
Optimistic	2923	781	133	33	104	388	491	362	.267	.442	.374

Brent Mayne
Bats Left
Born Apr. 19, 1968

Kansas City Royals	AB	H	2B	3B	HR	RBI	BB	SO	BA	SA	OBA
Season	231	58	8	0	3	31	23	42	.251	.325	.315
vs. Left-Handers	22	2	0	0	0	3	3	8	.091	.091	.179
vs. Right-Handers	209	56	8	0	3	28	20	34	.268	.349	.332
vs. Ground-Ballers	111	29	3	0	2	13	9	22	.261	.342	.314
vs. Fly-Ballers	120	29	5	0	1	18	14	20	.242	.308	.316

Most Comparable Rookie Seasons:

	AB	H	2B	3B	HR	RBI	BB	SO	BA	SA	OBA
Larry Brown	247	63	6	0	5	18	22	27	.255	.340	.317
Mike Heath	258	66	8	0	3	27	17	18	.256	.322	.303
Van Kelly	209	51	7	1	3	15	12	24	.244	.330	.286
Eddie Leon	213	51	6	0	3	19	19	37	.239	.310	.303
Gary Sutherland	231	57	12	1	1	19	17	22	.247	.320	.300

Projections for 1992:

	AB	H	2B	3B	HR	RBI	BB	SO	BA	SA	OBA
Best Guess	247	60	10	2	3	26	29	49	.244	.333	.324
Optimistic	439	121	25	7	11	61	73	47	.276	.442	.381

Projections for career:

	AB	H	2B	3B	HR	RBI	BB	SO	BA	SA	OBA
Best Guess	1870	472	75	11	22	197	226	355	.252	.339	.334
Optimistic	3817	1052	191	44	73	478	590	444	.276	.406	.374

Orlando Merced
Bats Left and Right
Born Nov. 2, 1966

Pittsburgh Pirates	AB	H	2B	3B	HR	RBI	BB	SO	BA	SA	OBA
Season	411	113	17	2	10	50	64	81	.275	.399	.373
vs. Left-Handers	53	11	3	1	0	6	3	10	.208	.302	.263
vs. Right-Handers	358	102	14	1	10	44	61	71	.285	.413	.388
vs. Ground-Ballers	181	50	8	0	3	15	27	36	.276	.370	.368
vs. Fly-Ballers	230	63	9	2	7	35	37	45	.274	.422	.377

Most Comparable Rookie Seasons:

	AB	H	2B	3B	HR	RBI	BB	SO	BA	SA	OBA
Jerry Adair	386	102	21	1	9	37	35	51	.264	.394	.327
Mike Fiore	339	93	14	1	12	35	84	63	.274	.428	.420
Brook Jacoby	439	116	19	3	7	40	32	73	.264	.369	.315
Felix Jose	426	113	16	1	11	52	24	81	.265	.385	.306
Leon Roberts	447	115	17	5	10	38	36	94	.257	.385	.314

Projections for 1992:

	AB	H	2B	3B	HR	RBI	BB	SO	BA	SA	OBA
Best Guess	469	120	21	4	11	54	67	88	.256	.388	.350
Optimistic	552	160	32	9	20	79	114	71	.289	.488	.413

Projections for career:

	AB	H	2B	3B	HR	RBI	BB	SO	BA	SA	OBA
Best Guess	2389	625	97	17	49	269	355	496	.262	.378	.358
Optimistic	4320	1212	213	49	140	587	843	621	.281	.450	.399

Luis Mercedes
Bats Right
Born Feb. 20, 1968

Baltimore Orioles	AB	H	2B	3B	HR	RBI	BB	SO	BA	SA	OBA
Season	54	11	2	0	0	2	4	9	.204	.241	.259
vs. Left-Handers	33	7	0	0	0	0	1	8	.212	.212	.235
vs. Right-Handers	21	4	2	0	0	2	3	1	.190	.286	.292
vs. Ground-Ballers	24	5	1	0	0	2	4	5	.208	.250	.321
vs. Fly-Ballers	30	6	1	0	0	0	0	4	.200	.233	.200

Most Comparable Rookie Seasons:

	AB	H	2B	3B	HR	RBI	BB	SO	BA	SA	OBA
Gene Alley	51	11	1	0	0	0	2	12	.216	.235	.246
Gary Disarcina	57	12	2	0	0	3	3	4	.211	.246	.251
Jim Dwyer	57	11	1	1	0	0	1	5	.193	.246	.208
Fran Mullins	62	12	4	0	0	3	9	8	.194	.258	.297
Dwayne Murphy	52	10	2	0	0	5	7	14	.192	.231	.289

Projections for 1992:

	AB	H	2B	3B	HR	RBI	BB	SO	BA	SA	OBA
Best Guess	55	7	1	0	0	4	3	12	.125	.159	.168
Optimistic	254	68	10	2	7	34	25	28	.268	.410	.335

Projections for career:

	AB	H	2B	3B	HR	RBI	BB	SO	BA	SA	OBA
Best Guess	676	165	24	3	8	66	53	116	.244	.325	.299
Optimistic	3930	1042	184	44	112	528	399	334	.265	.420	.334

Hensley Meulens
Bats Right
Born Jun. 23, 1967

New York Yankees	AB	H	2B	3B	HR	RBI	BB	SO	BA	SA	OBA
Season	288	64	8	1	6	29	18	97	.222	.319	.276
vs. Left-Handers	178	42	6	1	5	19	12	54	.236	.365	.297
vs. Right-Handers	110	22	2	0	1	10	6	43	.200	.245	.239
vs. Ground-Ballers	98	18	3	1	1	5	5	39	.184	.265	.231
vs. Fly-Ballers	190	46	5	0	5	24	13	58	.242	.347	.298

Most Comparable Rookie Seasons:

	AB	H	2B	3B	HR	RBI	BB	SO	BA	SA	OBA
Alan Ashby	254	57	10	1	5	32	30	42	.224	.331	.308
Buddy Bradford	281	61	11	0	5	24	23	67	.217	.310	.277
Rick Cerone	282	63	8	2	3	20	23	32	.223	.298	.283
Greg Gagne	293	66	15	3	2	23	20	57	.225	.317	.276
Greg Myers	250	59	7	1	5	22	22	33	.236	.332	.276

Projections for 1992:

	AB	H	2B	3B	HR	RBI	BB	SO	BA	SA	OBA
Best Guess	246	59	10	1	4	26	18	81	.239	.340	.292
Optimistic	414	110	23	6	14	54	42	76	.266	.449	.335

Projections for career:

	AB	H	2B	3B	HR	RBI	BB	SO	BA	SA	OBA
Best Guess	1549	372	61	8	30	164	115	496	.240	.347	.294
Optimistic	2945	780	133	31	84	355	290	563	.265	.417	.332

Mickey Morandini
Bats Left
Born Apr. 22, 1966

Philadelphia Phillies	AB	H	2B	3B	HR	RBI	BB	SO	BA	SA	OBA
Season	325	81	11	4	1	20	29	45	.249	.317	.313
vs. Left-Handers	65	12	0	0	0	3	3	11	.185	.185	.221
vs. Right-Handers	260	69	11	4	1	17	26	34	.265	.350	.334
vs. Ground-Ballers	166	39	4	2	1	11	14	20	.235	.301	.301
vs. Fly-Ballers	159	42	7	2	0	9	15	25	.264	.333	.326

Most Comparable Rookie Seasons:

	AB	H	2B	3B	HR	RBI	BB	SO	BA	SA	OBA
Juan Castillo	321	72	11	4	3	28	33	76	.224	.312	.298
Tim Corcoran	324	86	13	1	1	27	24	27	.265	.321	.317
Taylor Duncan	319	82	15	2	2	37	19	38	.257	.335	.300
H. Chico Ruiz	311	76	13	2	2	16	7	41	.244	.318	.262
Pete Stanicek	261	60	7	1	4	17	28	45	.230	.310	.306

Projections for 1992:

	AB	H	2B	3B	HR	RBI	BB	SO	BA	SA	OBA
Best Guess	247	56	8	2	2	21	21	35	.228	.294	.291
Optimistic	456	123	21	7	8	54	57	48	.269	.402	.352

Projections for career:

	AB	H	2B	3B	HR	RBI	BB	SO	BA	SA	OBA
Best Guess	1335	334	50	11	10	109	118	201	.250	.327	.312
Optimistic	2857	765	130	36	45	316	343	306	.268	.386	.347

Andy Mota

Bats Right
Born Mar. 4, 1966

Houston Astros	AB	H	2B	3B	HR	RBI	BB	SO	BA	SA	OBA
Season	90	17	2	0	1	6	1	17	.189	.244	.198
vs. Left-Handers	35	4	0	0	0	1	1	11	.114	.114	.139
vs. Right-Handers	55	13	2	0	1	5	0	6	.236	.327	.236
vs. Ground-Ballers	38	7	1	0	0	1	0	7	.184	.211	.184
vs. Fly-Ballers	52	10	1	0	1	5	1	10	.192	.269	.208

Most Comparable Rookie Seasons:

	AB	H	2B	3B	HR	RBI	BB	SO	BA	SA	OBA
Lorenzo Gray	78	14	3	0	1	4	8	16	.179	.256	.257
Ron Lolich	80	15	1	0	2	8	4	20	.188	.275	.227
John Mizerock	81	15	1	1	1	6	24	16	.185	.259	.373
Johnny Paredes	91	17	2	0	1	10	9	17	.187	.242	.261
Bill Plummer	102	19	4	0	2	9	4	20	.186	.284	.218

Projections for 1992:

	AB	H	2B	3B	HR	RBI	BB	SO	BA	SA	OBA
Best Guess	71	12	2	0	0	4	1	17	.171	.194	.179
Optimistic	205	54	10	2	4	23	3	25	.264	.394	.277

Projections for career:

	AB	H	2B	3B	HR	RBI	BB	SO	BA	SA	OBA
Best Guess	415	89	13	1	3	33	4	84	.215	.276	.224
Optimistic	1044	271	44	11	20	113	17	127	.260	.380	.273

Dean Palmer

Bats Right
Born Dec. 27, 1968

Texas Rangers	AB	H	2B	3B	HR	RBI	BB	SO	BA	SA	OBA
Season	268	50	9	2	15	37	32	98	.187	.403	.281
vs. Left-Handers	81	20	3	0	9	16	11	30	.247	.617	.337
vs. Right-Handers	187	30	6	2	6	21	21	68	.160	.310	.256
vs. Ground-Ballers	108	20	2	2	7	13	16	37	.185	.435	.302
vs. Fly-Ballers	160	30	7	0	8	24	16	61	.188	.381	.266

Most Comparable Rookie Seasons:

	AB	H	2B	3B	HR	RBI	BB	SO	BA	SA	OBA
Eric Anthony	239	46	8	0	10	29	29	78	.192	.351	.281
Joe Lahoud	218	41	5	0	9	21	40	43	.188	.335	.315
Lance Parrish	288	63	11	3	14	41	11	71	.219	.424	.249
Jim Presley	251	57	12	1	10	36	6	63	.227	.402	.246
Eric Soderholm	287	54	10	0	13	39	19	48	.188	.359	.240

Projections for 1992:

	AB	H	2B	3B	HR	RBI	BB	SO	BA	SA	OBA
Best Guess	156	38	8	1	6	20	21	53	.245	.432	.334
Optimistic	493	136	31	9	24	77	93	114	.276	.522	.392

Projections for career:

	AB	H	2B	3B	HR	RBI	BB	SO	BA	SA	OBA
Best Guess	2142	544	88	16	79	286	255	679	.254	.421	.335
Optimistic	5922	1603	291	81	221	883	735	1553	.271	.459	.352

Geronimo Pena

Bats Left and Right
Born Mar. 29, 1967

St. Louis Cardinals	AB	H	2B	3B	HR	RBI	BB	SO	BA	SA	OBA
Season	185	45	8	3	5	17	18	45	.243	.400	.322
vs. Left-Handers	93	28	7	1	4	13	6	24	.301	.527	.358
vs. Right-Handers	92	17	1	2	1	4	12	21	.185	.272	.286
vs. Ground-Ballers	78	17	3	2	1	7	8	21	.218	.346	.295
vs. Fly-Ballers	107	28	5	1	4	10	10	24	.262	.439	.341

Most Comparable Rookie Seasons:

	AB	H	2B	3B	HR	RBI	BB	SO	BA	SA	OBA
Doug DeCinces	167	42	6	3	4	23	13	32	.251	.395	.307
John Marzano	168	41	11	0	5	24	7	41	.244	.399	.275
Jim Nettles	168	42	5	1	6	24	19	24	.250	.399	.327
Merritt Ranew	218	51	6	8	4	24	14	43	.234	.390	.281
Carl Warwick	163	39	6	2	4	17	20	36	.239	.374	.324

Projections for 1992:

	AB	H	2B	3B	HR	RBI	BB	SO	BA	SA	OBA
Best Guess	249	57	10	2	6	29	22	59	.229	.357	.292
Optimistic	388	106	22	7	15	57	50	65	.273	.482	.357

Projections for career:

	AB	H	2B	3B	HR	RBI	BB	SO	BA	SA	OBA
Best Guess	1264	312	54	10	27	139	126	310	.247	.370	.316
Optimistic	3522	971	184	39	107	473	461	574	.276	.441	.361

Phil Plantier

Bats Left
Born Jan. 27, 1969

Boston Red Sox	AB	H	2B	3B	HR	RBI	BB	SO	BA	SA	OBA
Season	148	49	7	1	11	35	23	38	.331	.615	.420
vs. Left-Handers	25	8	1	0	3	13	3	11	.320	.720	.367
vs. Right-Handers	123	41	6	1	8	22	20	27	.333	.593	.431
vs. Ground-Ballers	65	22	4	0	5	15	9	15	.338	.631	.427
vs. Fly-Ballers	83	27	3	1	6	20	14	23	.325	.602	.414

Most Comparable Rookie Seasons:

	AB	H	2B	3B	HR	RBI	BB	SO	BA	SA	OBA
Bret Barberie	136	48	12	2	2	18	20	22	.353	.515	.437
Sam Horn	158	44	7	0	14	34	17	55	.278	.589	.350
Ron Jones	124	36	6	1	8	26	2	14	.290	.548	.303
Pedro Munoz	138	39	7	1	7	26	9	31	.283	.500	.328
Doug Rader	162	54	10	4	2	26	7	31	.333	.481	.362

Projections for 1992:

	AB	H	2B	3B	HR	RBI	BB	SO	BA	SA	OBA
Best Guess	353	95	18	4	9	46	65	76	.270	.417	.386
Optimistic	551	168	36	11	25	98	156	60	.304	.546	.459

Projections for career:

	AB	H	2B	3B	HR	RBI	BB	SO	BA	SA	OBA
Best Guess	2797	775	134	23	76	403	512	660	.277	.423	.390
Optimistic	7175	2069	403	114	278	1284	1989	1261	.288	.492	.444

Ivan Rodriguez

Bats Right
Born Nov. 30, 1971

Texas Rangers	AB	H	2B	3B	HR	RBI	BB	SO	BA	SA	OBA
Season	280	74	16	0	3	27	5	42	.264	.354	.276
vs. Left-Handers	71	17	6	0	1	9	2	9	.239	.366	.260
vs. Right-Handers	209	57	10	0	2	18	3	33	.273	.349	.282
vs. Ground-Ballers	129	36	10	0	1	14	1	14	.279	.380	.282
vs. Fly-Ballers	151	38	6	0	2	13	4	28	.252	.331	.271

Most Comparable Rookie Seasons:

	AB	H	2B	3B	HR	RBI	BB	SO	BA	SA	OBA
Oscar Gamble	275	72	12	4	1	19	27	37	.262	.345	.329
Jay Johnstone	254	67	12	4	3	17	11	36	.264	.378	.296
Mark Lewis	314	83	15	1	0	30	15	45	.264	.318	.299
Rance Mulliniks	271	73	13	2	3	21	23	36	.269	.365	.328
Tom O'Malley	291	80	12	4	2	27	33	39	.275	.364	.350

Projections for 1992:

	AB	H	2B	3B	HR	RBI	BB	SO	BA	SA	OBA
Best Guess	362	93	15	3	6	37	6	50	.256	.362	.269
Optimistic	526	152	29	9	13	71	13	48	.288	.450	.307

Projections for career:

	AB	H	2B	3B	HR	RBI	BB	SO	BA	SA	OBA
Best Guess	4436	1160	191	32	94	507	100	619	.262	.382	.279
Optimistic	6031	1715	295	68	205	873	189	596	.284	.458	.307

David Segui

Bats Left and Right
Born Jul. 19, 1966

Baltimore Orioles	AB	H	2B	3B	HR	RBI	BB	SO	BA	SA	OBA
Season	212	59	7	0	2	22	12	19	.278	.340	.316
vs. Left-Handers	98	33	4	0	1	12	4	8	.337	.408	.363
vs. Right-Handers	114	26	3	0	1	10	8	11	.228	.281	.276
vs. Ground-Ballers	101	25	1	0	1	14	7	11	.248	.287	.294
vs. Fly-Ballers	111	34	6	0	1	8	5	8	.306	.387	.336

Most Comparable Rookie Seasons:

	AB	H	2B	3B	HR	RBI	BB	SO	BA	SA	OBA
Mark Brouhard	186	51	6	3	2	20	7	41	.274	.371	.302
Doug Flynn	219	62	5	2	1	20	10	24	.283	.338	.316
Tom Pagnozzi	195	55	9	0	0	15	11	32	.282	.328	.322
Bob Sheldon	181	52	3	3	0	14	13	14	.287	.337	.336
Eddie Williams	201	55	8	0	3	10	18	31	.274	.358	.335

Projections for 1992:

	AB	H	2B	3B	HR	RBI	BB	SO	BA	SA	OBA
Best Guess	256	63	11	2	3	26	18	26	.246	.337	.297
Optimistic	368	99	22	6	9	50	40	23	.270	.430	.342

Projections for career:

	AB	H	2B	3B	HR	RBI	BB	SO	BA	SA	OBA
Best Guess	1283	332	56	8	14	134	98	124	.259	.348	.313
Optimistic	2654	732	136	31	50	338	250	185	.276	.406	.339

Craig Shipley
Bats Right
Born Jan. 7, 1963

San Diego Padres	AB	H	2B	3B	HR	RBI	BB	SO	BA	SA	OBA
Season	91	25	3	0	1	6	2	14	.275	.341	.298
vs. Left-Handers	44	14	2	0	1	2	2	8	.318	.432	.348
vs. Right-Handers	47	11	1	0	0	4	0	6	.234	.255	.250
vs. Ground-Ballers	43	13	1	0	0	1	0	5	.302	.326	.318
vs. Fly-Ballers	48	12	2	0	1	5	2	9	.250	.354	.280

Most Comparable Rookie Seasons:

	AB	H	2B	3B	HR	RBI	BB	SO	BA	SA	OBA
Ramon Aviles	101	28	6	0	2	9	10	9	.277	.396	.344
Glenn Brummer	87	24	7	0	0	9	10	11	.276	.356	.352
Dane Iorg	85	23	4	1	0	4	4	10	.271	.341	.305
Javier Ortiz	83	23	4	1	1	5	14	14	.277	.386	.383
Bernie Smith	76	21	3	1	1	6	11	12	.276	.382	.369

Projections for 1992:

	AB	H	2B	3B	HR	RBI	BB	SO	BA	SA	OBA
Best Guess	87	18	3	0	1	7	2	16	.207	.274	.224
Optimistic	226	62	13	3	6	33	7	20	.276	.431	.300

Projections for career:

	AB	H	2B	3B	HR	RBI	BB	SO	BA	SA	OBA
Best Guess	645	158	24	3	6	62	17	99	.245	.319	.265
Optimistic	1613	434	73	17	40	212	57	176	.269	.409	.295

Terry Shumpert
Bats Right
Born Aug. 16, 1966

Kansas City Royals	AB	H	2B	3B	HR	RBI	BB	SO	BA	SA	OBA
Season	369	80	16	4	5	34	30	75	.217	.322	.283
vs. Left-Handers	135	28	6	0	2	12	9	25	.207	.296	.277
vs. Right-Handers	234	52	10	4	3	22	21	50	.222	.338	.286
vs. Ground-Ballers	167	31	7	3	0	15	16	34	.186	.263	.262
vs. Fly-Ballers	202	49	9	1	5	19	14	41	.243	.371	.300

Most Comparable Rookie Seasons:

	AB	H	2B	3B	HR	RBI	BB	SO	BA	SA	OBA
Juan Castillo	321	72	11	4	3	28	33	76	.224	.312	.298
Roger Freed	348	77	12	1	6	37	44	86	.221	.313	.310
Paul Householder	417	88	11	5	9	34	30	77	.211	.326	.265
Phil Roof	369	77	14	3	7	44	37	95	.209	.320	.282
Mike Ryan	369	79	15	3	2	32	29	68	.214	.287	.273

Projections for 1992:

	AB	H	2B	3B	HR	RBI	BB	SO	BA	SA	OBA
Best Guess	265	60	10	2	4	24	19	52	.225	.324	.278
Optimistic	451	119	23	7	10	54	44	58	.264	.411	.331

Projections for career:

	AB	H	2B	3B	HR	RBI	BB	SO	BA	SA	OBA
Best Guess	1531	368	61	13	19	144	105	297	.241	.335	.290
Optimistic	3164	824	143	39	66	362	276	437	.260	.393	.321

Eddie Taubensee
Bats Left
Born Oct. 31, 1968

Cleveland Indians	AB	H	2B	3B	HR	RBI	BB	SO	BA	SA	OBA
Season	66	16	2	1	0	8	5	16	.242	.303	.288
vs. Left-Handers	10	4	0	0	0	0	1	2	.400	.400	.455
vs. Right-Handers	56	12	2	1	0	8	4	14	.214	.286	.258
vs. Ground-Ballers	25	3	1	0	0	5	1	4	.120	.160	.143
vs. Fly-Ballers	41	13	1	1	0	3	4	12	.317	.390	.378

Most Comparable Rookie Seasons:

	AB	H	2B	3B	HR	RBI	BB	SO	BA	SA	OBA
Bob Aspromonte	58	14	3	0	0	2	4	12	.241	.293	.291
Billy Bean	66	17	2	0	0	4	5	11	.258	.288	.311
Jim Gantner	69	17	1	0	0	7	6	11	.246	.261	.308
Ken Landreaux	76	19	5	1	0	5	5	15	.250	.342	.297
Mark Lemke	58	13	4	0	0	2	4	5	.224	.293	.275

Projections for 1992:

	AB	H	2B	3B	HR	RBI	BB	SO	BA	SA	OBA
Best Guess	144	32	5	1	2	14	9	30	.222	.308	.269
Optimistic	441	129	24	8	16	64	42	58	.291	.490	.354

Projections for career:

	AB	H	2B	3B	HR	RBI	BB	SO	BA	SA	OBA
Best Guess	1974	500	77	15	27	207	168	373	.253	.349	.313
Optimistic	4293	1207	212	54	139	613	460	513	.281	.453	.352

Jim Thome
Bats Left
Born Aug. 27, 1970

Cleveland Indians	AB	H	2B	3B	HR	RBI	BB	SO	BA	SA	OBA
Season	98	25	4	2	1	9	5	16	.255	.367	.298
vs. Left-Handers	20	1	0	0	0	0	0	5	.050	.050	.050
vs. Right-Handers	78	24	4	2	1	9	5	11	.308	.449	.357
vs. Ground-Ballers	46	18	3	2	1	8	3	6	.391	.609	.440
vs. Fly-Ballers	52	7	1	0	0	1	2	10	.135	.154	.167

Most Comparable Rookie Seasons:

	AB	H	2B	3B	HR	RBI	BB	SO	BA	SA	OBA
Ed Crosby	95	24	4	1	0	6	7	5	.253	.316	.305
Steve Garvey	93	25	5	0	1	6	6	17	.269	.355	.314
Mel Hall	80	21	3	2	0	4	5	17	.262	.350	.307
Thurman Munson	86	22	1	2	1	9	10	10	.256	.349	.335
Karl Rhodes	86	21	6	1	1	3	13	12	.244	.372	.345

Projections for 1992:

	AB	H	2B	3B	HR	RBI	BB	SO	BA	SA	OBA
Best Guess	225	51	10	2	5	23	13	36	.227	.349	.271
Optimistic	463	130	26	7	19	61	38	49	.280	.486	.336

Projections for career:

	AB	H	2B	3B	HR	RBI	BB	SO	BA	SA	OBA
Best Guess	2716	703	114	22	47	309	153	366	.259	.369	.300
Optimistic	5064	1441	253	63	165	705	405	445	.285	.458	.339

John Vanderwal
Bats Left
Born Apr. 29, 1966

Montreal Expos	AB	H	2B	3B	HR	RBI	BB	SO	BA	SA	OBA
Season	61	13	4	1	1	8	1	18	.213	.361	.222
vs. Left-Handers	16	1	0	0	0	1	0	8	.063	.063	.059
vs. Right-Handers	45	12	4	1	1	7	1	10	.267	.467	.283
vs. Ground-Ballers	32	7	3	0	0	4	0	10	.219	.313	.212
vs. Fly-Ballers	29	6	1	1	1	4	1	8	.207	.414	.233

Most Comparable Rookie Seasons:

	AB	H	2B	3B	HR	RBI	BB	SO	BA	SA	OBA
Mike Adams	66	14	2	0	3	6	17	18	.212	.379	.375
Rick Herrscher	50	11	3	0	1	6	5	11	.220	.340	.292
Kelvin Moore	67	15	1	1	2	6	3	23	.224	.358	.258
Charlie Shoemaker	52	11	2	2	0	3	0	9	.212	.327	.213
Ed Spiezio	73	16	5	1	2	10	5	11	.219	.397	.270

Projections for 1992:

	AB	H	2B	3B	HR	RBI	BB	SO	BA	SA	OBA
Best Guess	116	24	3	0	2	11	2	34	.210	.300	.222
Optimistic	240	63	11	2	10	34	5	48	.262	.445	.279

Projections for career:

	AB	H	2B	3B	HR	RBI	BB	SO	BA	SA	OBA
Best Guess	634	150	26	4	12	69	11	173	.237	.350	.252
Optimistic	1677	434	84	15	63	229	42	307	.259	.440	.278

Mo Vaughn
Bats Left
Born Dec. 15, 1967

Boston Red Sox	AB	H	2B	3B	HR	RBI	BB	SO	BA	SA	OBA
Season	219	57	12	0	4	32	26	43	.260	.370	.339
vs. Left-Handers	33	7	2	0	0	7	2	8	.212	.273	.257
vs. Right-Handers	186	50	10	0	4	25	24	35	.269	.387	.352
vs. Ground-Ballers	84	24	3	0	1	12	10	15	.286	.357	.371
vs. Fly-Ballers	135	33	9	0	3	20	16	28	.244	.378	.318

Most Comparable Rookie Seasons:

	AB	H	2B	3B	HR	RBI	BB	SO	BA	SA	OBA
John Doherty	223	57	14	1	3	15	8	13	.256	.368	.283
Leo Hernandez	203	50	6	1	6	26	12	19	.246	.374	.290
George Mitterwald	187	48	8	0	5	13	17	47	.257	.380	.320
German Rivera	227	59	12	2	2	17	21	30	.260	.357	.324
Ken Singleton	198	52	8	0	5	26	30	48	.263	.379	.361

Projections for 1992:

	AB	H	2B	3B	HR	RBI	BB	SO	BA	SA	OBA
Best Guess	247	60	9	2	4	28	32	47	.244	.343	.332
Optimistic	375	104	22	7	13	54	63	51	.279	.482	.384

Projections for career:

	AB	H	2B	3B	HR	RBI	BB	SO	BA	SA	OBA
Best Guess	1257	312	57	6	17	140	159	232	.249	.344	.334
Optimistic	3526	992	182	36	85	471	600	464	.281	.426	.387

Mark Whiten

Bats Left and Right
Born Nov. 25, 1966

Blue Jays/Indians	AB	H	2B	3B	HR	RBI	BB	SO	BA	SA	OBA
Season	407	99	18	7	9	45	30	85	.243	.388	.297
vs. Left-Handers	109	28	7	2	2	10	9	26	.257	.413	.311
vs. Right-Handers	298	71	11	5	7	35	21	59	.238	.379	.291
vs. Ground-Ballers	208	49	13	3	3	21	17	41	.236	.370	.293
vs. Fly-Ballers	199	50	5	4	6	24	13	44	.251	.407	.301

Most Comparable Rookie Seasons:

Jerry Adair	386	102	21	1	9	37	35	51	.264	.394	.327
Paul Casanova	429	109	16	5	13	44	14	78	.254	.406	.279
Jim L. Hickman	392	96	18	2	13	46	47	96	.245	.401	.327
Leon Roberts	447	115	17	5	10	38	36	94	.257	.385	.314
Rick Sofield	417	103	18	4	9	49	24	92	.247	.374	.289

Projections for 1992:

Best Guess	337	84	14	2	9	38	26	59	.250	.383	.305
Optimistic	528	149	29	7	20	76	60	69	.283	.479	.357

Projections for career:

Best Guess	1693	423	67	16	40	190	128	324	.250	.379	.304
Optimistic	4030	1075	186	45	149	562	410	619	.267	.446	.336

Rick Wilkins

Bats Left
Born Jul. 4, 1967

Chicago Cubs	AB	H	2B	3B	HR	RBI	BB	SO	BA	SA	OBA
Season	203	45	9	0	6	22	19	56	.222	.355	.307
vs. Left-Handers	38	9	1	0	1	5	3	14	.237	.342	.326
vs. Right-Handers	165	36	8	0	5	17	16	42	.218	.358	.303
vs. Ground-Ballers	90	19	4	0	3	11	11	21	.211	.356	.317
vs. Fly-Ballers	113	26	5	0	3	11	8	35	.230	.354	.298

Most Comparable Rookie Seasons:

Tony Bernazard	183	41	7	1	5	18	17	41	.224	.355	.291
Steve Buechele	219	48	6	3	6	21	14	38	.219	.356	.267
Vern Fuller	206	46	10	0	7	21	19	55	.223	.374	.290
Bobby Johnson	175	37	6	1	5	16	16	55	.211	.343	.279
Jim Maler	221	50	8	3	4	26	12	35	.226	.344	.267

Projections for 1992:

Best Guess	207	46	8	1	5	22	18	53	.222	.340	.287
Optimistic	371	96	20	5	15	49	47	62	.260	.461	.344

Projections for career:

Best Guess	839	195	33	4	17	87	78	218	.233	.342	.299
Optimistic	2777	724	137	25	86	348	335	551	.261	.421	.341

Bernie Williams

Bats Left and Right
Born Sep. 13, 1968

New York Yankees	AB	H	2B	3B	HR	RBI	BB	SO	BA	SA	OBA
Season	320	76	19	4	3	34	48	57	.237	.350	.336
vs. Left-Handers	104	21	6	0	2	13	17	11	.202	.317	.309
vs. Right-Handers	216	55	13	4	1	21	31	46	.255	.366	.349
vs. Ground-Ballers	155	38	9	2	0	12	22	31	.245	.329	.339
vs. Fly-Ballers	165	38	10	2	3	22	26	26	.230	.370	.333

Most Comparable Rookie Seasons:

Pat Kelly	298	72	12	4	3	23	15	52	.242	.339	.279
Jerry Morales	347	83	15	7	4	18	35	54	.239	.357	.310
Hosken Powell	381	94	20	2	3	31	45	31	.247	.333	.327
Dale Sveum	317	78	13	2	7	35	32	63	.246	.366	.316
Walt Williams	275	66	16	3	3	15	17	20	.240	.353	.285

Projections for 1992:

Best Guess	353	89	14	3	4	34	47	60	.252	.346	.341
Optimistic	481	134	25	8	11	61	90	56	.279	.434	.394

Projections for career:

Best Guess	2175	549	96	18	30	224	314	367	.252	.354	.348
Optimistic	4859	1315	238	60	107	588	968	594	.271	.410	.393

Scott Aldred
Born Jun. 12, 1968

Detroit Tigers	W-L	ERA	AB	H	HR	BB	SO	BA	SA	OBA
Season	2-4	5.18	218	58	9	30	35	.266	.427	.352
vs. Left-Handers			33	8	1	6	2	.242	.364	.359
vs. Right-Handers			185	50	8	24	33	.270	.438	.351
vs. Ground-Ballers			101	33	5	14	12	.327	.535	.405
vs. Fly-Ballers			117	25	4	16	23	.214	.333	.306
Home Games	1-3	7.02	131	39	7	17	23	.298	.489	.376
Road Games	1-1	2.63	87	19	2	13	12	.218	.333	.317
Grass Fields	2-3	5.51	188	51	9	23	33	.271	.441	.347
Artificial Turf	0-1	3.24	30	7	0	7	2	.233	.333	.378
First 9 Batters			81	23	3	11	15	.284	.457	.362
Second 9 Batters			75	19	2	11	14	.253	.333	.349
All Batters Thereafter			62	16	4	8	6	.258	.500	.343

Miscellaneous statistics: Ground outs-to-air outs ratio: 0.75 last season, 0.75 for career.... Induced 5 double plays in 49 opportunities (one per 10).... Allowed 6 doubles, 1 triple in 57⅓ innings.... Allowed 8 first-inning runs in 11 starts (6.97 ERA).... Batting support: 5.27 runs per start.... Opposing base stealers: 5-for-7 (71%); 2 pickoffs, 1 balk.

Wilson Alvarez
Born Mar. 24, 1970

Chicago White Sox	W-L	ERA	AB	H	HR	BB	SO	BA	SA	OBA
Season	3-2	3.51	204	47	9	29	32	.230	.407	.325
vs. Left-Handers			18	4	0	1	3	.222	.222	.263
vs. Right-Handers			186	43	9	28	29	.231	.425	.330
vs. Ground-Ballers			106	25	4	12	17	.236	.396	.314
vs. Fly-Ballers			98	22	5	17	15	.224	.418	.336
Home Games	1-1	2.79	69	14	3	8	8	.203	.362	.286
Road Games	2-1	3.89	135	33	6	21	24	.244	.430	.344
Grass Fields	2-1	4.05	142	30	7	21	23	.211	.408	.311
Artificial Turf	1-1	2.20	62	17	2	8	9	.274	.403	.357
First 9 Batters			77	13	1	10	13	.169	.273	.264
Second 9 Batters			75	17	7	13	13	.227	.533	.337
All Batters Thereafter			52	17	1	6	6	.327	.423	.397

Miscellaneous statistics: Ground outs-to-air outs ratio: 1.12 last season, 1.12 for career.... Induced 9 double plays in 42 opportunities (one per 4.7).... Allowed 7 doubles, 1 triple in 56⅓ innings.... Opposing base stealers: 0-for-4 (0%); 1 pickoff, 0 balks.

Andy Ashby
Born Jul. 11, 1967

Philadelphia Phillies	W-L	ERA	AB	H	HR	BB	SO	BA	SA	OBA
Season	1-5	6.00	160	41	5	19	26	.256	.431	.341
vs. Left-Handers			93	23	3	10	15	.247	.409	.317
vs. Right-Handers			67	18	2	9	11	.269	.463	.370
vs. Ground-Ballers			57	16	1	12	8	.281	.404	.403
vs. Fly-Ballers			103	25	4	7	18	.243	.447	.301
Home Games	0-3	6.49	103	29	3	10	18	.282	.466	.353
Road Games	1-2	5.17	57	12	2	9	8	.211	.368	.318
Grass Fields	1-0	1.29	23	3	1	5	2	.130	.261	.286
Artificial Turf	0-5	6.94	137	38	4	14	24	.277	.460	.350
First 9 Batters			65	14	0	6	14	.215	.308	.292
Second 9 Batters			60	19	3	7	10	.317	.567	.394
All Batters Thereafter			35	8	2	6	2	.229	.429	.333

Miscellaneous statistics: Ground outs-to-air outs ratio: 1.06 last season, 1.06 for career.... Induced 2 double plays in 28 opportunities (one per 14).... Allowed 9 doubles, 2 triples in 42 innings.... Opposing base stealers: 0-for-1 (0%); 0 pickoffs, 0 balks.

Ricky Bones
Born Apr. 7, 1969

San Diego Padres	W-L	ERA	AB	H	HR	BB	SO	BA	SA	OBA
Season	4-6	4.83	212	57	3	18	31	.269	.354	.321
vs. Left-Handers			116	31	2	11	13	.267	.345	.323
vs. Right-Handers			96	26	1	7	18	.271	.365	.317
vs. Ground-Ballers			114	28	0	10	18	.246	.316	.306
vs. Fly-Ballers			98	29	3	8	13	.296	.398	.336
Home Games	3-3	5.40	135	38	1	9	20	.281	.348	.322
Road Games	1-3	3.92	77	19	2	9	11	.247	.364	.318
Grass Fields	4-4	5.32	174	46	2	14	27	.264	.339	.316
Artificial Turf	0-2	2.70	38	11	1	4	4	.289	.421	.341
First 9 Batters			94	24	0	5	15	.255	.298	.293
Second 9 Batters			74	16	0	11	12	.216	.243	.310
All Batters Thereafter			44	17	3	2	4	.386	.659	.396

Miscellaneous statistics: Ground outs-to-air outs ratio: 1.36 last season, 1.36 for career.... Induced 4 double plays in 36 opportunities (one per 9.0).... Allowed 7 doubles, 1 triple in 54 innings.... Allowed 6 first-inning runs in 11 starts (4.91 ERA).... Batting support: 5.91 runs per start.... Opposing base stealers: 3-for-4 (75%); 0 pickoffs, 0 balks.

Ryan Bowen

Throws Right
Born Feb. 10, 1968

Houston Astros	W-L	ERA	AB	H	HR	BB	SO	BA	SA	OBA
Season	6-4	5.15	272	73	4	36	49	.268	.360	.353
vs. Left-Handers			160	46	2	22	30	.287	.381	.365
vs. Right-Handers			112	27	2	14	19	.241	.330	.336
vs. Ground-Ballers			136	35	0	16	28	.257	.287	.331
vs. Fly-Ballers			136	38	4	20	21	.279	.434	.375
Home Games	3-2	3.16	156	39	0	18	25	.250	.308	.326
Road Games	3-2	8.07	116	34	4	18	24	.293	.431	.388
Grass Fields	3-0	3.63	66	17	1	11	14	.258	.318	.363
Artificial Turf	3-4	5.63	206	56	3	25	35	.272	.374	.350
First 9 Batters			105	26	1	14	24	.248	.352	.336
Second 9 Batters			98	25	2	13	15	.255	.347	.342
All Batters Thereafter			69	22	1	9	10	.319	.391	.395

Miscellaneous statistics: Ground outs-to-air outs ratio: 1.20 last season, 1.20 for career.... Induced 5 double plays in 58 opportunities (one per 12).... Allowed 13 doubles, 0 triples in 71⅔ innings.... Allowed 13 first-inning runs in 13 starts (9.00 ERA).... Batting support: 4.46 runs per start.... Opposing base stealers: 12-for-13 (92%); 0 pickoffs, 1 balk.

Clifford Brantley

Throws Right
Born Apr. 12, 1968

Philadelphia Phillies	W-L	ERA	AB	H	HR	BB	SO	BA	SA	OBA
Season	2-2	3.41	114	26	0	19	25	.228	.281	.341
vs. Left-Handers			74	16	0	14	14	.216	.230	.337
vs. Right-Handers			40	10	0	5	11	.250	.375	.347
vs. Ground-Ballers			43	8	0	8	11	.186	.209	.315
vs. Fly-Ballers			71	18	0	11	14	.254	.324	.357
Home Games	1-1	3.60	71	18	0	12	13	.254	.310	.353
Road Games	1-1	3.09	43	8	0	7	12	.186	.233	.321
Grass Fields	1-0	2.45	28	6	0	3	5	.214	.286	.290
Artificial Turf	1-2	3.70	86	20	0	16	20	.233	.279	.355
First 9 Batters			42	8	0	9	10	.190	.238	.333
Second 9 Batters			43	10	0	5	10	.233	.279	.320
All Batters Thereafter			29	8	0	5	5	.276	.345	.382

Miscellaneous statistics: Ground outs-to-air outs ratio: 1.23 last season, 1.23 for career.... Induced 1 double plays in 28 opportunities (one per 28).... Allowed 4 doubles, 1 triple in 31⅔ innings.... Opposing base stealers: 6-for-8 (75%); 0 pickoffs, 0 balks.

Rheal Cormier

Throws Left
Born Apr. 23, 1967

St. Louis Cardinals	W-L	ERA	AB	H	HR	BB	SO	BA	SA	OBA
Season	4-5	4.12	267	74	5	8	38	.277	.401	.300
vs. Left-Handers			48	7	0	1	10	.146	.146	.163
vs. Right-Handers			219	67	5	7	28	.306	.457	.329
vs. Ground-Ballers			87	18	0	3	17	.207	.287	.233
vs. Fly-Ballers			180	56	5	5	21	.311	.456	.332
Home Games	4-2	4.08	160	47	1	3	18	.294	.406	.309
Road Games	0-3	4.18	107	27	4	5	20	.252	.393	.287
Grass Fields	0-3	4.18	107	27	4	5	20	.252	.393	.287
Artificial Turf	4-2	4.08	160	47	1	3	18	.294	.406	.309
First 9 Batters			90	19	2	3	16	.211	.344	.245
Second 9 Batters			84	19	1	4	13	.226	.310	.267
All Batters Thereafter			93	36	2	1	9	.387	.538	.385

Miscellaneous statistics: Ground outs-to-air outs ratio: 0.94 last season, 0.94 for career.... Induced 6 double plays in 46 opportunities (one per 7.7).... Allowed 16 doubles, 1 triple in 67⅔ innings.... Allowed 3 first-inning runs in 10 starts (0.90 ERA).... Batting support: 3.20 runs per start.... Opposing base stealers: 1-for-4 (25%); 0 pickoffs, 1 balk.

Bryan Hickerson

Throws Left
Born Oct. 13, 1963

San Francisco Giants	W-L	ERA	AB	H	HR	BB	SO	BA	SA	OBA
Season	2-2	3.60	193	53	3	17	43	.275	.378	.333
vs. Left-Handers			47	11	0	4	10	.234	.255	.294
vs. Right-Handers			146	42	3	13	33	.288	.418	.346
vs. Ground-Ballers			84	25	1	9	17	.298	.393	.366
vs. Fly-Ballers			109	28	2	8	26	.257	.367	.308
Home Games	1-1	3.74	82	19	1	5	23	.232	.341	.276
Road Games	1-1	3.49	111	34	2	12	20	.306	.405	.374
Grass Fields	1-2	3.38	134	36	2	12	31	.269	.388	.329
Artificial Turf	1-0	4.11	59	17	1	5	12	.288	.356	.344
First 9 Batters			104	30	1	10	27	.288	.385	.351
Second 9 Batters			66	16	1	5	14	.242	.333	.296
All Batters Thereafter			23	7	1	2	2	.304	.478	.360

Miscellaneous statistics: Ground outs-to-air outs ratio: 0.88 last season, 0.88 for career.... Induced 6 double plays in 39 opportunities (one per 6.5).... Allowed 11 doubles, 0 triples in 50 innings.... Opposing base stealers: 6-for-10 (60%); 1 pickoff, 0 balks.

Paul McClellan

Throws Right
Born Feb. 8, 1966

San Francisco Giants	W-L	ERA	AB	H	HR	BB	SO	BA	SA	OBA
Season	3-6	4.56	270	68	12	25	44	.252	.437	.316
vs. Left-Handers			143	39	7	16	19	.273	.462	.350
vs. Right-Handers			127	29	5	9	25	.228	.409	.277
vs. Ground-Ballers			126	31	3	11	20	.246	.357	.307
vs. Fly-Ballers			144	37	9	14	24	.257	.507	.325
Home Games	2-2	4.33	132	34	4	12	28	.258	.402	.317
Road Games	1-4	4.79	138	34	8	13	16	.246	.471	.316
Grass Fields	2-5	4.64	198	48	7	21	38	.242	.399	.317
Artificial Turf	1-1	4.34	72	20	5	4	6	.278	.542	.316
First 9 Batters			98	26	6	12	17	.265	.510	.345
Second 9 Batters			99	24	2	6	17	.242	.333	.290
All Batters Thereafter			73	18	4	7	10	.247	.479	.313

Miscellaneous statistics: Ground outs-to-air outs ratio: 1.00 last season, 1.00 for career.... Induced 6 double plays in 50 opportunities (one per 8.3).... Allowed 12 doubles, 1 triple in 71 innings.... Allowed 7 first-inning runs in 12 starts (3.75 ERA).... Batting support: 4.92 runs per start.... Opposing base stealers: 12-for-17 (71%); 0 pickoffs, 0 balks.

Mike Mussina

Throws Right
Born Dec. 8, 1968

Baltimore Orioles	W-L	ERA	AB	H	HR	BB	SO	BA	SA	OBA
Season	4-5	2.87	322	77	7	21	52	.239	.354	.286
vs. Left-Handers			182	39	3	14	29	.214	.302	.273
vs. Right-Handers			140	38	4	7	23	.271	.421	.304
vs. Ground-Ballers			151	39	1	11	20	.258	.331	.307
vs. Fly-Ballers			171	38	6	10	32	.222	.374	.268
Home Games	3-1	2.74	161	36	2	11	30	.224	.298	.276
Road Games	1-4	3.00	161	41	5	10	22	.255	.410	.297
Grass Fields	4-4	2.55	297	67	6	19	50	.226	.330	.273
Artificial Turf	0-1	7.11	25	10	1	2	2	.400	.640	.444
First 9 Batters			97	16	1	10	20	.165	.237	.243
Second 9 Batters			105	27	2	2	21	.257	.352	.269
All Batters Thereafter			120	34	4	9	11	.283	.450	.336

Miscellaneous statistics: Ground outs-to-air outs ratio: 0.77 last season, 0.77 for career.... Induced 9 double plays in 55 opportunities (one per 6.1).... Allowed 14 doubles, 1 triple in 87⅔ innings.... Allowed 2 first-inning runs in 12 starts (1.50 ERA).... Batting support: 4.17 runs per start.... Opposing base stealers: 4-for-8 (50%); 0 pickoffs, 1 balk.

Dave Otto

Throws Left
Born Nov. 12, 1964

Cleveland Indians	W-L	ERA	AB	H	HR	BB	SO	BA	SA	OBA
Season	2-8	4.23	382	108	7	27	47	.283	.395	.333
vs. Left-Handers			69	21	0	4	3	.304	.333	.347
vs. Right-Handers			313	87	7	23	44	.278	.409	.330
vs. Ground-Ballers			150	42	2	8	14	.280	.373	.321
vs. Fly-Ballers			232	66	5	19	33	.284	.409	.341
Home Games	1-6	4.12	226	63	5	11	31	.279	.398	.315
Road Games	1-2	4.39	156	45	2	16	16	.288	.391	.358
Grass Fields	1-8	4.45	350	98	7	25	45	.280	.400	.331
Artificial Turf	1-0	2.00	32	10	0	2	2	.313	.344	.361
First 9 Batters			136	40	1	12	17	.294	.382	.349
Second 9 Batters			122	32	3	6	14	.262	.377	.308
All Batters Thereafter			124	36	3	9	16	.290	.427	.341

Miscellaneous statistics: Gound outs-to-air outs ratio: 1.84 last season, 1.77 for career.... Grounded into 11 double plays in 84 opportunities (one per 7.6).... Allowed 14 doubles, 4 triples in 100 innings.... Allowed 8 first-inning runs in 14 starts (5.14 ERA).... Batting support: 3.50 runs per start.... Opposing base stealers: 4-for-8 (50%); 1 pickoff, 0 balks.

Arthur Rhodes

Throws Left
Born Oct. 24, 1969

Baltimore Orioles	W-L	ERA	AB	H	HR	BB	SO	BA	SA	OBA
Season	0-3	8.00	147	47	4	23	23	.320	.469	.405
vs. Left-Handers			13	2	0	3	3	.154	.154	.313
vs. Right-Handers			134	45	4	20	20	.336	.500	.414
vs. Ground-Ballers			78	27	4	14	16	.346	.577	.441
vs. Fly-Ballers			69	20	0	9	7	.290	.348	.363
Home Games	0-1	6.14	56	14	2	10	13	.250	.393	.358
Road Games	0-2	9.28	91	33	2	13	10	.363	.516	.434
Grass Fields	0-2	6.82	132	39	4	22	23	.295	.447	.391
Artificial Turf	0-1	21.00	15	8	0	1	0	.533	.667	.529
First 9 Batters			58	19	2	11	6	.328	.517	.423
Second 9 Batters			64	21	1	7	13	.328	.422	.389
All Batters Thereafter			25	7	1	5	4	.280	.480	.400

Miscellaneous statistics: Ground outs-to-air outs ratio: 0.84 last season, 0.84 for career.... Induced 2 double plays in 42 opportunities (one per 21).... Allowed 8 doubles, 1 triple in 36 innings.... Opposing base stealers: 7-for-9 (78%); 0 pickoffs, 0 balks.

Throws Left

Rosario Rodriguez

Born Jul. 8, 1969

Pittsburgh Pirates	W-L	ERA	AB	H	HR	BB	SO	BA	SA	OBA
Season	1-1	4.11	57	14	1	8	10	.246	.333	.348
vs. Left-Handers			20	5	0	1	4	.250	.250	.286
vs. Right-Handers			37	9	1	7	6	.243	.378	.378
vs. Ground-Ballers			23	4	1	4	7	.174	.348	.321
vs. Fly-Ballers			34	10	0	4	3	.294	.324	.368
Home Games	0-1	6.48	33	9	1	2	5	.273	.424	.333
Road Games	1-0	1.29	24	5	0	6	5	.208	.208	.367
Grass Fields	1-0	1.42	21	3	0	6	5	.143	.143	.333
Artificial Turf	0-1	6.00	36	11	1	2	5	.306	.444	.359
First 9 Batters			57	14	1	8	10	.246	.333	.348
Second 9 Batters			0	0	0	0	0	—	—	—
All Batters Thereafter			0	0	0	0	0	—	—	—

Miscellaneous statistics: Ground outs-to-air outs ratio: 1.19 last season, 1.09 for career.... Induced 1 double plays in 17 opportunities (one per 17).... Allowed 2 doubles, 0 triples in 15⅓ innings.... Stranded 6 inherited runners, allowed 0 to score (100%).... Opposing base stealers: 0-for-1 (0%); 0 pickoffs, 0 balks.

Throws Right

Mel Rojas

Born Dec. 10, 1966

Montreal Expos	W-L	ERA	AB	H	HR	BB	SO	BA	SA	OBA
Season	3-3	3.75	184	42	4	13	37	.228	.375	.280
vs. Left-Handers			89	22	2	9	15	.247	.449	.310
vs. Right-Handers			95	20	2	4	22	.211	.305	.250
vs. Ground-Ballers			75	18	2	5	16	.240	.400	.293
vs. Fly-Ballers			109	24	2	8	21	.220	.358	.271
Home Games	1-2	3.12	64	13	1	3	10	.203	.328	.250
Road Games	2-1	4.11	120	29	3	10	27	.242	.400	.295
Grass Fields	1-1	3.45	60	14	1	3	12	.233	.350	.262
Artificial Turf	2-2	3.90	124	28	3	10	25	.226	.387	.289
First 9 Batters			176	40	4	13	35	.227	.381	.283
Second 9 Batters			8	2	0	2	.250	.250	.222
All Batters Thereafter			0	0	0	0	0			

Miscellaneous statistics: Ground outs-to-air outs ratio: 0.83 last season, 0.83 for career.... Induced 1 double plays in 33 opportunities (one per 33).... Allowed 9 doubles, 3 triples in 48 innings.... Stranded 9 inherited runners, allowed 6 to score (60%).... Opposing base stealers: 5-for-6 (83%); 0 pickoffs, 0 balks.

Throws Left

Pete Schourek

Born May 10, 1969

New York Mets	W-L	ERA	AB	H	HR	BB	SO	BA	SA	OBA
Season	5-4	4.27	331	82	7	43	67	.248	.390	.334
vs. Left-Handers			110	29	2	13	18	.264	.391	.336
vs. Right-Handers			221	53	5	30	49	.240	.389	.333
vs. Ground-Ballers			167	39	2	24	39	.234	.329	.330
vs. Fly-Ballers			164	43	5	19	28	.262	.451	.339
Home Games	4-1	3.31	184	42	1	27	40	.228	.288	.327
Road Games	1-3	5.54	147	40	6	16	27	.272	.517	.343
Grass Fields	4-3	3.34	234	53	5	32	50	.226	.329	.322
Artificial Turf	1-1	6.66	97	29	2	11	17	.299	.536	.364
First 9 Batters			179	45	6	31	38	.251	.425	.363
Second 9 Batters			89	25	0	9	18	.281	.360	.343
All Batters Thereafter			63	12	1	3	11	.190	.333	.227

Miscellaneous statistics: Ground outs-to-air outs ratio: 0.52 last season, 0.52 for career.... Induced 1 double plays in 78 opportunities (one per 78).... Allowed 14 doubles, 6 triples in 86⅓ innings.... Stranded 9 inherited runners, allowed 9 to score (50%).... Opposing base stealers: 12-for-12 (100%); 0 pickoffs, 0 balks.

Throws Right

Anthony Young

Born Jan. 19, 1966

New York Mets	W-L	ERA	AB	H	HR	BB	SO	BA	SA	OBA
Season	2-5	3.10	187	48	4	12	20	.257	.374	.303
vs. Left-Handers			112	33	3	6	10	.295	.446	.328
vs. Right-Handers			75	15	1	6	10	.200	.267	.268
vs. Ground-Ballers			84	23	2	4	8	.274	.405	.303
vs. Fly-Ballers			103	25	2	8	12	.243	.350	.304
Home Games	1-3	3.77	114	34	3	5	15	.298	.439	.325
Road Games	1-2	2.18	73	14	1	7	5	.192	.274	.272
Grass Fields	2-4	3.32	168	44	4	11	19	.262	.387	.309
Artificial Turf	0-1	1.50	19	4	0	1	1	.211	.263	.250
First 9 Batters			82	18	0	5	11	.220	.232	.264
Second 9 Batters			65	14	2	4	8	.215	.385	.257
All Batters Thereafter			40	16	2	3	1	.400	.650	.455

Miscellaneous statistics: Ground outs-to-air outs ratio: 2.13 last season, 2.13 for career.... Induced 4 double plays in 37 opportunities (one per 9.3).... Allowed 8 doubles, 1 triple in 49⅓ innings.... Opposing base stealers: 3-for-4 (75%); 0 pickoffs, 0 balks.

BALLPARKS

The Ballparks section lists, for all 26 parks in use last season, a variety of statistics about the games played there over the past several years.

The effect of each ballpark on performance has become an almost obsessively discussed topic in the last decade. Even the simplest conversation about an off-season trade these days is likely to touch on such factors as the relative dimensions of the two parks involved, whether they have natural or artificial turf, the size of their foul territory, and how far they are above sea level. Without going into the sometimes sticky question of the reasons for such differences, we present here the facts of those differences, park by park.

For each stadium, a box contains the basic statistics for the games played there, as contrasted with that home team's games played on the road. The totals listed are the complete statistics *for both teams* in those games. Totals and percentage differences are listed for the 1991 season, and for the five-year period from 1987 through 1991. (The differences, in many cases, don't reflect the change between the actual raw totals printed, but rather between related per-game averages. For instance, we print the number of runs scored in home and road games, but compute the difference between the average number of runs *per game*.) Since the statistics represent performances by roughly the same set of players, the differences can be attributed to the peculiarities of the park. (The one case where this assumption does not hold is Toronto's Skydome, which opened during the 1989 season. Excluded from the home totals for 1989 are the following games that were played at Exhibition Stadium: three each against Kansas City, New York, Texas, Seattle, California, Minnesota, Cleveland, and Chicago; and two against Oakland. This may create a skew in the statistics; we are confident that this is not a major problem, and it will shrink in significance as the years progress. For comparative purposes, we have listed the 1986–90 statistics for the old Comiskey Park alongside the 1991 statistics for new Comiskey, though the new park is used alone in the stadium rankings.

Following the pages of ballpark data are tables that rank the stadiums according to their effects on various elements of play. To illustrate, let's say that you find that the Oakland Coliseum reduced scoring by 14.3 percent over the past five seasons. You won't have to look through twenty-five other boxes to see where this ranks; the table marked "Ranked by Effect on Runs" will show that it stands dead last, with a negative percentage more than twice that of the next-lowest American League park.

In addition to scoring, we've ranked the parks in seven other categories. The fields with artificial playing surfaces are marked with an asterisk, giving you a quick read on what kind of impact they have had on the category in question. While the effect on batting average is open to question, the effects on such categories as extra-base hit percentage, stolen-base percentage, and errors are unmistakable.

BALTIMORE ORIOLES · MEMORIAL STADIUM

	1991 SEASON			1987–1991		
	Home Games	Road Games	Pct. Diff.	Home Games	Road Games	Pct. Diff.
G	81	81	0.0	404	404	0.0
AB	5572	5658	−1.5	27579	27611	−0.1
1B	1004	1030	−1.0	4905	5072	−3.2
2B	259	291	−9.6	1241	1301	−4.5
3B	19	35	−44.9	96	173	−44.4
HR	152	165	−6.5	816	784	4.2
R	716	766	−6.5	3505	3686	−4.9
BA	.257	.269	−4.3	.256	.265	−3.6
SLG	.392	.420	−6.6	.397	.410	−3.3
XB%	.217	.240	−9.8	.214	.225	−4.9
E	116	85	36.5	556	526	5.7
SHO	7	7	0.0	45	39	15.4

CHICAGO WHITE SOX · COMISKEY PARK

	1991 SEASON			1986–1990		
	Home Games	Road Games	Pct. Diff.	Home Games	Road Games	Pct. Diff.
G	81	81	0.0	403	405	−0.5
AB	5480	5562	−1.5	27213	27432	−0.8
1B	995	968	4.3	5003	4887	3.2
2B	221	220	2.0	1175	1210	−2.1
3B	34	35	−1.4	243	160	53.1
HR	153	140	10.9	583	763	−23.0
R	715	724	−1.2	3494	3489	0.6
BA	.256	.245	4.5	.257	.256	0.6
SLG	.393	.373	5.3	.383	.395	−3.1
XB%	.204	.209	−2.2	.221	.219	0.9
E	114	125	−8.8	621	649	−3.8
SHO	10	10	0.0	35	48	−26.7

BOSTON RED SOX · FENWAY PARK

	1991 SEASON			1987–1991		
	Home Games	Road Games	Pct. Diff.	Home Games	Road Games	Pct. Diff.
G	81	81	0.0	404	406	−0.5
AB	5614	5393	4.1	27920	27553	1.3
1B	1016	952	2.5	5354	5109	3.4
2B	332	259	23.1	1625	1252	28.1
3B	26	33	−24.3	142	150	−6.6
HR	145	128	8.8	674	667	−0.3
R	752	691	8.8	3892	3592	8.9
BA	.271	.254	6.4	.279	.261	7.2
SLG	.416	.386	7.9	.420	.389	7.8
XB%	.261	.235	11.0	.248	.215	15.2
E	134	103	30.1	620	571	9.1
SHO	13	12	8.3	57	59	−2.9

CLEVELAND INDIANS · CLEVELAND STADIUM

	1991 SEASON			1987–1991		
	Home Games	Road Games	Pct. Diff.	Home Games	Road Games	Pct. Diff.
G	82	80	2.5	406	404	0.5
AB	5593	5500	1.7	27895	27505	1.4
1B	1143	1030	9.1	5401	5030	5.9
2B	250	265	−7.2	1238	1282	−4.8
3B	37	27	34.8	157	174	−11.0
HR	63	126	−50.8	634	722	−13.4
R	648	687	−8.0	3639	3519	2.9
BA	.267	.263	1.4	.266	.262	1.6
SLG	.359	.390	−8.0	.390	.400	−2.5
XB%	.201	.221	−9.1	.205	.224	−8.6
E	127	134	−7.5	631	615	2.1
SHO	15	11	33.0	58	49	17.8

CALIFORNIA ANGELS · ANAHEIM STADIUM

	1991 SEASON			1987–1991		
	Home Games	Road Games	Pct. Diff.	Home Games	Road Games	Pct. Diff.
G	81	81	0.0	405	405	0.0
AB	5394	5475	−1.5	27644	27678	−0.1
1B	927	1019	−7.7	5082	5164	−1.5
2B	216	279	−21.4	1079	1308	−17.4
3B	18	32	−42.9	120	168	−28.5
HR	133	123	9.8	758	652	16.4
R	594	708	−16.1	3393	3610	−6.0
BA	.240	.265	−9.6	.255	.263	−3.4
SLG	.361	.395	−8.8	.385	.394	−2.3
XB%	.202	.234	−13.8	.191	.222	−14.1
E	109	118	−7.6	592	626	−5.4
SHO	16	9	77.8	63	47	34.0

DETROIT TIGERS · TIGER STADIUM

	1991 SEASON			1987–1991		
	Home Games	Road Games	Pct. Diff.	Home Games	Road Games	Pct. Diff.
G	81	81	0.0	405	405	0.0
AB	5540	5603	−1.1	27245	27899	−2.3
1B	997	1001	0.7	4713	5160	−6.5
2B	234	282	−16.1	1117	1327	−13.8
3B	28	43	−34.1	135	175	−21.0
HR	198	159	25.9	901	746	23.7
R	839	772	8.7	3731	3809	−2.0
BA	.263	.265	−0.8	.252	.266	−5.1
SLG	.423	.416	1.6	.402	.406	−0.9
XB%	.208	.245	−15.1	.210	.225	−6.9
E	117	110	6.4	628	610	3.0
SHO	3	12	−75.0	43	42	2.4

KANSAS CITY ROYALS · ROYALS STADIUM

	1991 SEASON			1987–1991		
	Home Games	Road Games	Pct. Diff.	Home Games	Road Games	Pct. Diff.
G	81	81	0.0	404	404	0.0
AB	5694	5530	3.0	27621	27456	0.6
1B	1040	1042	-3.1	5119	5095	-0.1
2B	293	268	6.2	1435	1206	18.3
3B	58	25	125.3	259	148	74.0
HR	87	135	-37.4	461	683	-32.9
R	722	727	-0.7	3470	3478	-0.2
BA	.260	.266	-2.4	.263	.260	1.4
SLG	.377	.397	-4.9	.384	.389	-1.3
XB%	.252	.219	15.0	.249	.210	18.4
E	120	115	4.3	598	595	0.5
SHO	11	10	10.0	57	64	-10.9

NEW YORK YANKEES · YANKEE STADIUM

	1991 SEASON			1987–1991		
	Home Games	Road Games	Pct. Diff.	Home Games	Road Games	Pct. Diff.
G	81	81	0.0	404	404	0.0
AB	5516	5599	-1.5	27638	27721	-0.3
1B	1002	1022	-0.5	5112	5072	1.1
2B	266	278	-2.9	1265	1331	-4.7
3B	19	42	-54.1	107	164	-34.6
HR	166	133	26.7	798	752	6.4
R	736	715	2.9	3655	3704	-1.3
BA	.263	.263	0.0	.263	.264	-0.2
SLG	.409	.399	2.4	.404	.405	-0.4
XB%	.221	.238	-7.1	.212	.228	-7.1
E	113	130	-13.1	598	579	3.3
SHO	9	12	-25.0	45	48	-6.3

MILWAUKEE BREWERS · COUNTY STADIUM

	1991 SEASON			1987–1991		
	Home Games	Road Games	Pct. Diff.	Home Games	Road Games	Pct. Diff.
G	80	82	-2.4	404	406	-0.5
AB	5564	5670	-1.9	27785	27900	-0.4
1B	1061	1121	-3.5	5298	5308	0.2
2B	262	239	11.7	1234	1224	1.2
3B	33	42	-19.9	156	172	-8.9
HR	135	128	7.5	653	684	-4.1
R	796	747	9.2	3715	3683	1.4
BA	.268	.270	-0.7	.264	.265	-0.2
SLG	.400	.395	1.3	.390	.395	-1.1
XB%	.218	.200	8.5	.208	.208	-0.2
E	116	117	1.6	665	626	6.8
SHO	8	14	-41.4	46	46	0.5

OAKLAND A'S · OAKLAND—ALAMEDA COUNTY COLISEUM

	1991 SEASON			1987–1991		
	Home Games	Road Games	Pct. Diff.	Home Games	Road Games	Pct. Diff.
G	81	81	0.0	405	405	0.0
AB	5399	5492	-1.7	27010	27795	-2.8
1B	903	994	-7.6	4758	4955	-1.2
2B	240	259	-5.7	1072	1311	-15.9
3B	25	32	-20.5	118	166	-26.8
HR	143	171	-14.9	657	821	-17.6
R	708	828	-14.5	3297	3845	-14.3
BA	.243	.265	-8.4	.245	.261	-6.3
SLG	.376	.417	-9.9	.366	.409	-10.5
XB%	.227	.226	0.2	.200	.230	-12.9
E	112	117	-4.3	601	618	-2.8
SHO	14	10	40.0	65	44	47.7

MINNESOTA TWINS · METRODOME

	1991 SEASON			1987–1991		
	Home Games	Road Games	Pct. Diff.	Home Games	Road Games	Pct. Diff.
G	81	81	0.0	405	405	0.0
AB	5585	5462	2.3	27782	27366	1.5
1B	1087	977	8.8	5210	5050	1.6
2B	288	255	10.5	1479	1279	13.9
3B	47	26	76.8	193	132	44.0
HR	137	142	-5.6	733	739	-2.3
R	746	682	9.4	3805	3519	8.1
BA	.279	.256	8.9	.274	.263	4.2
SLG	.421	.391	7.8	.420	.400	5.0
XB%	.236	.223	5.5	.243	.218	11.2
E	116	109	6.4	544	583	-6.7
SHO	8	12	-33.3	36	57	-36.8

SEATTLE MARINERS · KINGDOME

	1991 SEASON			1987–1991		
	Home Games	Road Games	Pct. Diff.	Home Games	Road Games	Pct. Diff.
G	81	81	0.0	405	404	0.2
AB	5539	5441	1.8	27577	27174	1.5
1B	958	980	-4.0	4847	5005	-4.6
2B	267	259	1.3	1347	1247	6.4
3B	35	26	32.2	166	147	11.3
HR	138	124	9.3	778	611	25.5
R	693	683	1.5	3653	3434	6.1
BA	.252	.255	-1.1	.259	.258	0.3
SLG	.388	.381	1.9	.404	.382	5.8
XB%	.240	.225	6.4	.238	.218	9.2
E	91	122	-25.4	572	597	-4.4
SHO	12	11	9.1	51	57	-10.7

TEXAS RANGERS · ARLINGTON STADIUM

	1991 SEASON				1987–1991		
	Home Games	Road Games	Pct. Diff.		Home Games	Road Games	Pct. Diff.
G	81	81	0.0		406	403	0.7
AB	5591	5781	−3.3		27540	27443	0.4
1B	1009	1060	−1.6		5000	4804	3.7
2B	276	290	−1.6		1217	1292	−6.1
3B	38	24	63.7		167	144	15.6
HR	156	172	−6.2		746	680	9.3
R	804	839	−4.2		3806	3662	3.2
BA	.265	.267	−1.1		.259	.252	2.7
SLG	.411	.415	−1.0		.396	.384	3.2
XB%	.237	.229	3.9		.217	.230	−5.8
E	132	118	11.9		644	613	4.3
SHO	12	7	71.4		39	44	−12.0

TORONTO BLUE JAYS · SKYDOME

	1991 SEASON				1989–1991		
	Home Games	Road Games	Pct. Diff.		Home Games	Road Games	Pct. Diff.
G	81	81	0.0		217	243	−10.7
AB	5522	5437	1.6		14849	16581	−10.4
1B	967	913	4.3		2597	2964	−2.2
2B	276	236	15.1		713	772	3.1
3B	36	31	14.3		113	108	16.8
HR	147	107	35.3		406	369	22.9
R	703	603	16.6		1840	2049	0.6
BA	.258	.237	9.1		.258	.254	1.5
SLG	.401	.351	14.4		.403	.380	6.0
XB%	.244	.226	7.8		.241	.229	5.4
E	110	124	−11.3		280	370	−15.3
SHO	12	13	−7.7		28	32	−2.0

ATLANTA BRAVES · ATLANTA–FULTON COUNTY STADIUM

	1991 Season			1987–1991		
	Home Games	Road Games	Pct. Diff.	Home Games	Road Games	Pct. Diff.
G	81	81	0.0	401	405	−1.0
AB	5510	5375	2.5	27723	27077	2.4
1B	1009	882	11.6	5201	4727	7.5
2B	254	236	5.0	1276	1194	4.4
3B	31	40	−24.4	137	150	−10.8
HR	156	103	47.7	709	601	15.2
R	786	607	29.5	3765	3267	16.4
BA	.263	.235	12.2	.264	.246	7.2
SLG	.405	.351	15.5	.397	.368	7.8
XB%	.220	.238	−7.6	.214	.221	−3.5
E	175	113	54.9	747	630	19.8
SHO	6	10	−40.0	39	53	−25.7

HOUSTON ASTROS · ASTRODOME

	1991 Season			1987–1991		
	Home Games	Road Games	Pct. Diff.	Home Games	Road Games	Pct. Diff.
G	81	81	0.0	406	404	0.5
AB	5500	5458	0.8	27473	27392	0.3
1B	958	965	−1.5	4886	4805	1.4
2B	262	226	15.0	1192	1149	3.4
3B	47	26	79.4	190	172	10.1
HR	71	137	−48.6	425	691	−38.7
R	632	690	−8.4	3062	3379	−9.8
BA	.243	.248	−1.9	.244	.249	−2.1
SLG	.347	.374	−7.4	.347	.379	−8.4
XB%	.244	.207	17.8	.220	.216	2.2
E	126	138	−8.7	621	672	−8.0
SHO	16	13	23.1	68	55	23.0

CHICAGO CUBS · WRIGLEY FIELD

	1991 Season			1987–1991		
	Home Games	Road Games	Pct. Diff.	Home Games	Road Games	Pct. Diff.
G	83	77	7.8	407	401	1.5
AB	5760	5261	9.5	28283	27341	3.4
1B	1040	940	1.1	5426	4905	6.9
2B	250	228	0.2	1232	1258	−5.3
3B	36	40	−17.8	203	192	2.2
HR	168	108	42.1	774	585	27.9
R	782	647	12.1	3795	3298	13.4
BA	.259	.250	3.7	.270	.254	6.4
SLG	.403	.370	8.8	.410	.378	8.4
XB%	.216	.222	−2.8	.209	.228	−8.3
E	142	96	37.2	754	585	27.0
SHO	3	5	−44.3	39	42	−8.5

LOS ANGELES DODGERS · DODGER STADIUM

	1991 Season			1987–1991		
	Home Games	Road Games	Pct. Diff.	Home Games	Road Games	Pct. Diff.
G	81	81	0.0	405	403	0.5
AB	5425	5432	−0.1	27246	27374	−0.5
1B	1046	978	7.1	5145	4813	7.4
2B	172	221	−22.1	950	1255	−23.9
3B	17	40	−57.4	100	155	−35.2
HR	103	101	2.1	508	584	−12.6
R	622	608	2.3	2992	3223	−7.6
BA	.247	.247	0.0	.246	.249	−1.1
SLG	.342	.358	−4.5	.344	.370	−6.9
XB%	.153	.211	−27.4	.169	.227	−25.2
E	128	116	10.3	694	650	6.2
SHO	10	12	−16.7	71	65	8.7

CINCINNATI REDS · RIVERFRONT STADIUM

	1991 Season			1987–1991		
	Home Games	Road Games	Pct. Diff.	Home Games	Road Games	Pct. Diff.
G	81	81	0.0	404	405	−0.2
AB	5462	5459	0.1	27427	27437	−0.0
1B	956	1001	−4.5	4796	4876	−1.6
2B	264	217	21.6	1349	1200	12.5
3B	32	30	6.6	145	166	−12.6
HR	181	110	64.5	791	607	30.4
R	749	631	18.7	3526	3239	9.1
BA	.262	.249	5.5	.258	.250	3.4
SLG	.422	.360	17.2	.404	.372	8.8
XB%	.236	.198	19.5	.238	.219	8.5
E	100	133	−24.8	551	648	−14.8
SHO	7	13	−46.2	39	65	−39.9

MONTREAL EXPOS · OLYMPIC STADIUM

	1991 Season			1987–1991		
	Home Games	Road Games	Pct. Diff.	Home Games	Road Games	Pct. Diff.
G	68	93	−26.9	392	418	−6.2
AB	4535	6222	−27.1	26634	28216	−5.6
1B	764	1092	−4.0	4609	5002	−2.4
2B	201	289	−4.6	1278	1207	12.2
3B	33	48	−5.7	197	193	8.1
HR	68	138	−32.4	538	623	−8.5
R	449	785	−21.8	3099	3338	−1.0
BA	.235	.252	−6.7	.249	.249	−0.1
SLG	.339	.380	−10.9	.372	.372	0.1
XB%	.234	.236	−0.6	.242	.219	10.9
E	110	154	−2.3	650	682	1.6
SHO	10	14	−2.3	47	66	−24.1

NEW YORK METS · SHEA STADIUM

	1991 Season			1987–1991		
	Home Games	Road Games	Pct. Diff.	Home Games	Road Games	Pct. Diff.
G	82	79	3.8	405	402	0.7
AB	5556	5269	5.4	27185	27397	−0.8
1B	1028	909	7.2	4743	4778	−0.0
2B	236	240	−6.7	1152	1296	−10.4
3B	41	29	34.1	148	162	−7.9
HR	112	113	−6.0	641	694	−6.9
R	680	606	8.1	3238	3470	−7.4
BA	.255	.245	4.1	.246	.253	−2.8
SLG	.373	.366	1.9	.370	.388	−4.7
XB%	.212	.228	−7.0	.215	.234	−8.0
E	137	122	8.2	664	652	1.1
SHO	11	9	17.8	58	45	27.9

ST. LOUIS CARDINALS · BUSCH STADIUM

	1991 Season			1987–1991		
	Home Games	Road Games	Pct. Diff.	Home Games	Road Games	Pct. Diff.
G	84	78	7.7	410	402	2.0
AB	5547	5183	7.0	27704	27056	2.4
1B	992	974	−4.8	5028	5025	−2.3
2B	250	240	−2.7	1367	1242	7.5
3B	60	35	60.2	267	180	44.9
HR	73	109	−37.4	396	499	−22.5
R	638	661	−10.4	3308	3230	0.4
BA	.248	.262	−5.4	.255	.257	−0.8
SLG	.354	.385	−8.0	.366	.371	−1.3
XB%	.238	.220	8.1	.245	.221	11.2
E	116	126	−14.5	596	635	−8.0
SHO	10	9	3.2	50	65	−24.6

PHILADELPHIA PHILLIES · VETERANS STADIUM

	1991 Season			1987–1991		
	Home Games	Road Games	Pct. Diff.	Home Games	Road Games	Pct. Diff.
G	83	79	5.1	407	404	0.7
AB	5659	5342	5.9	27576	27174	1.5
1B	982	896	3.5	4753	4885	−4.1
2B	273	236	9.2	1360	1182	13.4
3B	30	39	−27.4	187	159	15.9
HR	114	108	−0.4	640	619	1.9
R	675	634	1.3	3496	3334	4.1
BA	.247	.239	3.3	.252	.252	−0.1
SLG	.366	.359	2.1	.384	.375	2.3
XB%	.236	.235	0.4	.246	.215	14.0
E	107	141	−27.8	546	663	−18.3
SHO	12	11	3.8	59	42	39.4

SAN DIEGO PADRES · SAN DIEGO/JACK MURPHY STADIUM

	1991 Season			1987–1991		
	Home Games	Road Games	Pct. Diff.	Home Games	Road Games	Pct. Diff.
G	81	81	0.0	405	404	0.2
AB	5448	5459	−0.2	27124	27483	−1.3
1B	982	996	−1.2	4810	5114	−4.7
2B	191	209	−8.4	1038	1194	−11.9
3B	27	41	−34.0	170	166	3.8
HR	137	123	11.6	695	582	21.0
R	635	647	−1.9	3226	3278	−1.8
BA	.245	.251	−2.1	.247	.257	−3.6
SLG	.366	.372	−1.6	.375	.376	−0.2
XB%	.182	.201	−9.5	.201	.210	−4.4
E	131	128	2.3	671	699	−4.2
SHO	12	11	9.1	59	47	25.2

PITTSBURGH PIRATES · THREE RIVERS STADIUM

	1991 Season			1987–1991		
	Home Games	Road Games	Pct. Diff.	Home Games	Road Games	Pct. Diff.
G	84	78	7.7	408	402	1.5
AB	5572	5399	3.2	27409	27306	0.4
1B	1001	1023	−5.2	4711	4928	−4.8
2B	253	242	1.3	1304	1250	3.9
3B	48	34	36.8	206	207	−0.9
HR	116	127	−11.5	606	639	−5.5
R	696	704	−8.2	3346	3457	−4.6
BA	.254	.264	−3.6	.249	.257	−3.2
SLG	.380	.392	−3.2	.378	.388	−2.7
XB%	.231	.212	8.8	.243	.228	6.4
E	107	119	−16.5	631	635	−2.1
SHO	10	7	32.7	48	44	7.5

SAN FRANCISCO GIANTS · CANDLESTICK PARK

	1991 Season			1987–1991		
	Home Games	Road Games	Pct. Diff.	Home Games	Road Games	Pct. Diff.
G	81	81	0.0	405	405	0.0
AB	5392	5506	−2.1	27205	27736	−1.9
1B	915	1017	−8.1	4770	5020	−3.1
2B	213	235	−7.4	1145	1216	−4.0
3B	39	39	2.1	157	205	−21.9
HR	131	153	−12.6	696	695	2.1
R	611	735	−16.9	3241	3581	−9.5
BA	.241	.262	−8.2	.249	.257	−3.3
SLG	.368	.402	−8.7	.379	.391	−3.0
XB%	.216	.212	1.7	.214	.221	−2.8
E	125	118	5.9	649	623	4.2
SHO	15	8	87.5	57	45	26.7

RANKED BY EFFECT ON RUNS

	1991 SEASON			1987–1991		
	Home Games	Road Games	Pct. Diff.	Home Games	Road Games	Pct. Diff.
Atlanta Stadium	786	607	29.5	3765	3267	16.4
Wrigley Field	782	647	12.1	3795	3298	13.4
*Riverfront Stadium	749	631	18.7	3526	3239	9.1
Fenway Park	752	691	8.8	3892	3592	8.9
*Metrodome	746	682	9.4	3805	3519	8.1
*Kingdome	693	683	1.5	3653	3434	6.1
*Veterans Stadium	675	634	1.3	3496	3334	4.1
Arlington Stadium	804	839	−4.2	3806	3662	3.2
Cleveland Stadium	648	687	−8.0	3639	3519	2.9
County Stadium	796	747	9.2	3715	3683	1.4
*Skydome	703	603	16.6	1840	2049	0.6
*Busch Stadium	638	661	−10.4	3308	3230	0.4
*Royals Stadium	722	727	−0.7	3470	3478	−0.2
*Olympic Stadium	449	785	−21.8	3099	3338	−1.0
Comiskey Park (New)	715	724	−1.2	715	724	−1.2
Yankee Stadium	736	715	2.9	3655	3704	−1.3
San Diego Stadium	635	647	−1.9	3226	3278	−1.8
Tiger Stadium	839	772	8.7	3731	3809	−2.0
*Three Rivers Stadium	696	704	−8.2	3346	3457	−4.6
Memorial Stadium	716	766	−6.5	3505	3686	−4.9
Anaheim Stadium	594	708	−16.1	3393	3610	−6.0
Shea Stadium	680	606	8.1	3238	3470	−7.4
Dodger Stadium	622	608	2.3	2992	3223	−7.6
Candlestick Park	611	735	−16.9	3241	3581	−9.5
*Astrodome	632	690	−8.4	3062	3379	−9.8
Oakland Coliseum	708	828	−14.5	3297	3845	−14.3

RANKED BY EFFECT ON HOME RUNS

	1991 SEASON			1987–1991		
	Home Games	Road Games	Pct. Diff.	Home Games	Road Games	Pct. Diff.
*Riverfront Stadium	181	110	64.5	791	607	30.4
Wrigley Field	168	108	42.1	774	585	27.9
*Kingdome	138	124	9.3	778	611	25.5
Tiger Stadium	198	159	25.9	901	746	23.7
*Skydome	147	107	35.3	406	369	22.9
San Diego Stadium	137	123	11.6	695	582	21.0
Anaheim Stadium	133	123	9.8	758	652	16.4
Atlanta Stadium	156	103	47.7	709	601	15.2
Comiskey Park (New)	153	140	10.9	153	140	10.9
Arlington Stadium	156	172	−6.2	746	680	9.3
Yankee Stadium	166	133	26.7	798	752	6.4
Memorial Stadium	152	165	−6.5	816	784	4.2
Candlestick Park	131	153	−12.6	696	695	2.1
*Veterans Stadium	114	108	−0.4	640	619	1.9
Fenway Park	145	128	8.8	674	667	−0.3
*Metrodome	137	142	−5.6	733	739	−2.3
County Stadium	135	128	7.5	653	684	−4.1
*Three Rivers Stadium	116	127	−11.5	606	639	−5.5
Shea Stadium	112	113	−6.0	641	694	−6.9
*Olympic Stadium	68	138	−32.4	538	623	−8.5
Dodger Stadium	103	101	2.1	508	584	−12.6
Cleveland Stadium	63	126	−50.8	634	722	−13.4
Oakland Coliseum	143	171	−14.9	657	821	−17.6
*Busch Stadium	73	109	−37.4	396	499	−22.5
*Royals Stadium	87	135	−37.4	461	683	−32.9
*Astrodome	71	137	−48.6	425	691	−38.7

RANKED BY EFFECT ON BATTING AVERAGE

	1991 SEASON			1987–1991		
	Home Games	Road Games	Pct. Diff.	Home Games	Road Games	Pct. Diff.
Atlanta Stadium	.263	.235	12.2	.264	.246	7.2
Fenway Park	.271	.254	6.4	.279	.261	7.2
Wrigley Field	.259	.250	3.7	.270	.254	6.4
Comiskey Park (New)	.256	.245	4.5	.256	.245	4.5
*Metrodome	.279	.256	8.9	.274	.263	4.2
*Riverfront Stadium	.262	.249	5.5	.258	.250	3.4
Arlington Stadium	.265	.267	−1.1	.259	.252	2.7
Cleveland Stadium	.267	.263	1.4	.266	.262	1.6
*Skydome	.258	.237	9.1	.258	.254	1.5
*Royals Stadium	.260	.266	−2.4	.263	.260	1.4
*Kingdome	.252	.255	−1.1	.259	.258	0.3
*Veterans Stadium	.247	.239	3.3	.252	.252	−0.1
*Olympic Stadium	.235	.252	−6.7	.249	.249	−0.1
Yankee Stadium	.263	.263	−0.0	.263	.264	−0.2
County Stadium	.268	.270	−0.7	.264	.265	−0.2
*Busch Stadium	.248	.262	−5.4	.255	.257	−0.8
Dodger Stadium	.247	.247	−0.0	.246	.249	−1.1
*Astrodome	.243	.248	−1.9	.244	.249	−2.1
Shea Stadium	.255	.245	4.1	.246	.253	−2.8
*Three Rivers Stadium	.254	.264	−3.6	.249	.257	−3.2
Candlestick Park	.241	.262	−8.2	.249	.257	−3.3
Anaheim Stadium	.240	.265	−9.6	.255	.263	−3.4
Memorial Stadium	.257	.269	−4.3	.256	.265	−3.6
San Diego Stadium	.245	.251	−2.1	.247	.257	−3.6
Tiger Stadium	.263	.265	−0.8	.252	.266	−5.1
Oakland Coliseum	.243	.265	−8.4	.245	.261	−6.3

RANKED BY EFFECT ON SLUGGING PERCENTAGE

	1991 SEASON			1987–1991		
	Home Games	Road Games	Pct. Diff.	Home Games	Road Games	Pct. Diff.
*Riverfront Stadium	.422	.360	17.2	.404	.372	8.8
Wrigley Field	.403	.370	8.8	.410	.378	8.4
Fenway Park	.416	.386	7.9	.420	.389	7.8
Atlanta Stadium	.405	.351	15.5	.397	.368	7.8
*Skydome	.401	.351	14.4	.403	.380	6.0
*Kingdome	.388	.381	1.9	.404	.382	5.8
Comiskey Park (New)	.393	.373	5.3	.393	.373	5.3
*Metrodome	.421	.391	7.8	.420	.400	5.0
Arlington Stadium	.411	.415	−1.0	.396	.384	3.2
*Veterans Stadium	.366	.359	2.1	.384	.375	2.3
*Olympic Stadium	.339	.380	−10.9	.372	.372	0.1
San Diego Stadium	.366	.372	−1.6	.375	.376	−0.2
Yankee Stadium	.409	.399	2.4	.404	.405	−0.4
Tiger Stadium	.423	.416	1.6	.402	.406	−0.9
County Stadium	.400	.395	1.3	.390	.395	−1.1
*Royals Stadium	.377	.397	−4.9	.384	.389	−1.3
*Busch Stadium	.354	.385	−8.0	.366	.371	−1.3
Anaheim Stadium	.361	.395	−8.8	.385	.394	−2.3
Cleveland Stadium	.359	.390	−8.0	.390	.400	−2.5
*Three Rivers Stadium	.380	.392	−3.2	.378	.388	−2.7
Candlestick Park	.368	.402	−8.7	.379	.391	−3.0
Memorial Stadium	.392	.420	−6.6	.397	.410	−3.3
Shea Stadium	.373	.366	1.9	.370	.388	−4.7
Dodger Stadium	.342	.358	−4.5	.344	.370	−6.9
*Astrodome	.347	.374	−7.4	.347	.379	−8.4
Oakland Coliseum	.376	.417	−9.9	.366	.409	−10.5

RANKED BY EFFECT ON EXTRA–BASE HIT PERCENTAGE

	1991 SEASON			1987–1991		
	Home Games	Road Games	Pct. Diff.	Home Games	Road Games	Pct. Diff.
*Royals Stadium	.252	.219	15.0	.249	.210	18.4
Fenway Park	.261	.235	11.0	.248	.215	15.2
*Veterans Stadium	.236	.235	0.4	.246	.215	14.0
*Metrodome	.236	.223	5.5	.243	.218	11.2
*Busch Stadium	.238	.220	8.1	.245	.221	11.2
*Olympic Stadium	.234	.236	−0.6	.242	.219	10.9
*Kingdome	.240	.225	6.4	.238	.218	9.2
*Riverfront Stadium	.236	.198	19.5	.238	.219	8.5
*Three Rivers Stadium	.231	.212	8.8	.243	.228	6.4
*Skydome	.244	.226	7.8	.241	.229	5.4
*Astrodome	.244	.207	17.8	.220	.216	2.2
County Stadium	.218	.200	8.5	.208	.208	−0.2
Comiskey Park (New)	.204	.209	−2.2	.204	.209	−2.2
Candlestick Park	.216	.212	1.7	.214	.221	−2.8
Atlanta Stadium	.220	.238	−7.6	.214	.221	−3.5
San Diego Stadium	.182	.201	−9.5	.201	.210	−4.4
Memorial Stadium	.217	.240	−9.8	.214	.225	−4.9
Arlington Stadium	.237	.229	3.9	.217	.230	−5.8
Tiger Stadium	.208	.245	−15.1	.210	.225	−6.9
Yankee Stadium	.221	.238	−7.1	.212	.228	−7.1
Shea Stadium	.212	.228	−7.0	.215	.234	−8.0
Wrigley Field	.216	.222	−2.8	.209	.228	−8.3
Cleveland Stadium	.201	.221	−9.1	.205	.224	−8.6
Oakland Coliseum	.227	.226	0.2	.200	.230	−12.9
Anaheim Stadium	.202	.234	−13.8	.191	.222	−14.1
Dodger Stadium	.153	.211	−27.4	.169	.227	−25.2

RANKED BY EFFECT ON STRIKEOUT PERCENTAGE

	1991 SEASON			1987–1991		
	Home Games	Road Games	Pct. Diff.	Home Games	Road Games	Pct. Diff.
San Diego Stadium	.167	.161	3.8	.160	.148	8.5
*Astrodome	.173	.159	8.5	.163	.152	7.3
Oakland Coliseum	.153	.147	4.2	.158	.148	6.9
Tiger Stadium	.151	.152	−1.0	.149	.141	6.1
Memorial Stadium	.152	.143	6.4	.143	.135	5.7
County Stadium	.137	.126	8.9	.143	.136	4.9
Shea Stadium	.152	.149	2.0	.166	.159	4.5
*Metrodome	.132	.131	0.9	.140	.136	3.0
*Olympic Stadium	.169	.158	6.8	.163	.159	2.7
Arlington Stadium	.167	.152	10.4	.167	.163	2.3
Candlestick Park	.155	.152	1.8	.156	.154	1.7
Anaheim Stadium	.159	.157	1.3	.151	.149	1.5
*Veterans Stadium	.163	.160	1.3	.152	.152	0.1
*Three Rivers Stadium	.153	.142	7.4	.144	.145	−0.1
*Kingdome	.151	.140	7.7	.144	.145	−0.3
Dodger Stadium	.167	.157	6.9	.161	.162	−0.6
Wrigley Field	.145	.148	−2.2	.149	.150	−0.8
Yankee Stadium	.140	.151	−6.8	.144	.147	−1.6
Fenway Park	.144	.150	−4.1	.144	.147	−2.1
*Skydome	.163	.165	−1.1	.151	.155	−2.8
Comiskey Park (New)	.141	.148	−4.9	.141	.148	−4.9
Cleveland Stadium	.136	.149	−8.9	.138	.146	−5.8
*Riverfront Stadium	.155	.172	−9.8	.152	.162	−5.9
*Bush Stadium	.132	.148	−11.0	.134	.145	−7.3
Atlanta Stadium	.144	.163	−11.8	.141	.155	−8.9
*Royals Stadium	.149	.166	−9.9	.145	.165	−12.0

RANKED BY EFFECT ON STOLEN BASE PERCENTAGE

	1991 SEASON			1987–1991		
	Home Games	Road Games	Pct. Diff.	Home Games	Road Games	Pct. Diff.
*Metrodome	.744	.595	25.0	.710	.647	9.6
*Astrodome	.707	.644	9.8	.772	.712	8.4
*Busch Stadium	.661	.593	11.5	.728	.683	6.6
*Veterans Stadium	.756	.758	−0.2	.729	.695	5.0
*Kingdome	.691	.658	5.1	.685	.658	4.0
*Riverfront Stadium	.701	.689	1.7	.714	.690	3.5
*Royals Stadium	.658	.601	9.4	.699	.680	2.9
Memorial Stadium	.649	.667	−2.7	.682	.665	2.5
*Olympic Stadium	.681	.663	2.7	.725	.714	1.5
San Diego Stadium	.627	.612	2.4	.668	.662	0.9
*Skydome	.721	.709	1.7	.685	.678	0.9
Tiger Stadium	.691	.613	12.6	.670	.668	0.3
Oakland Coliseum	.674	.692	−2.6	.683	.689	−0.9
County Stadium	.630	.681	−7.6	.692	.704	−1.7
Cleveland Stadium	.596	.680	−12.4	.661	.672	−1.7
Yankee Stadium	.744	.732	1.6	.686	.704	−2.6
Atlanta Stadium	.698	.701	−0.5	.665	.687	−3.2
Comiskey Park (New)	.610	.633	−3.6	.610	.633	−3.6
*Three Rivers Stadium	.641	.738	−13.2	.681	.708	−3.9
Candlestick Park	.582	.643	−9.5	.622	.650	−4.4
Shea Stadium	.665	.667	−0.2	.712	.758	−6.1
Fenway Park	.629	.629	0.0	.631	.672	−6.1
Wrigley Field	.667	.677	−1.5	.661	.706	−6.3
Dodger Stadium	.660	.699	−5.6	.644	.688	−6.4
Anaheim Stadium	.541	.630	−14.2	.609	.652	−6.6
Arlington Stadium	.624	.701	−11.0	.679	.733	−7.4

RANKED BY EFFECT ON ERRORS

	1991 SEASON			1987–1991		
	Home Games	Road Games	Pct. Diff.	Home Games	Road Games	Pct. Diff.
Wrigley Field	142	96	37.2	754	585	27.0
Atlanta Stadium	175	113	54.9	747	630	19.8
Fenway Park	134	103	30.1	620	571	9.1
County Stadium	116	117	1.6	665	626	6.8
Dodger Stadium	128	116	10.3	694	650	6.2
Memorial Stadium	116	85	36.5	556	526	5.7
Arlington Stadium	132	118	11.9	644	613	4.3
Candlestick Park	125	118	5.9	649	623	4.2
Yankee Stadium	113	130	−13.1	598	579	3.3
Tiger Stadium	117	110	6.4	628	610	3.0
Cleveland Stadium	127	134	−7.5	631	615	2.1
*Olympic Stadium	110	154	−2.3	650	682	1.6
Shea Stadium	137	122	8.2	664	652	1.1
*Royals Stadium	120	115	4.3	598	595	0.5
*Three Rivers Stadium	107	119	−16.5	631	635	−2.1
Oakland Coliseum	112	117	−4.3	601	618	−2.8
San Diego Stadium	131	128	2.3	671	699	−4.2
*Kingdome	91	122	−25.4	572	597	−4.4
Anaheim Stadium	109	118	−7.6	592	626	−5.4
*Metrodome	116	109	6.4	544	583	−6.7
*Busch Stadium	116	126	−14.5	596	635	−8.0
*Astrodome	126	138	−8.7	621	672	−8.0
Comiskey Park (New)	114	125	−8.8	114	125	−8.8
*Riverfront Stadium	100	133	−24.8	551	648	−14.8
*Skydome	110	124	−11.3	280	370	−15.3
*Veterans Stadium	107	141	−27.8	546	663	−18.3